West's Business and Personal Law

Teacher's Wraparound Edition

West's Business and Personal Law

Teacher's Wraparound Edition

Donald L. Carper
Professor of Business Law
Department of Organizational Behavior and Environment
School of Business Administration
California State University, Sacramento

Roger LeRoy Miller
Department of Legal Studies
Clemson University

Donna Parker Murray
Cluster Coordinator
Business and Management Center
Business Magnet High School
Dallas, Texas

West Publishing Company
Minneapolis/St. Paul   New York   San Francisco   Los Angeles

Preface to the Teacher's Wraparound Edition

West has been the world's leading legal publisher for over 120 years. Today, with *West's Business and Personal Law* you can bring this tradition of excellence and wealth of resources into your business and personal law classroom.

West's Business and Personal Law is an exciting new program written, designed, and produced for today's high school business and personal law course. With the most comprehensive package of resources, support materials, and media ever produced for business and personal law, this program offers you unlimited flexibility.

Certainly, because you are teaching business and personal law, we do not have to convince you of the increasing importance of the law in our society. Additionally, as you know, the law is important both for your students today and in their future lives.

The United States is perhaps the most law-oriented country in the world, boasting the highest ratio of lawyers to population anywhere. Additionally, the laws that affect individuals in their everyday lives and in their jobs are expanding and changing more than ever before. Knowledge of the law is clearly not just for someone who knows he or she is going to become a lawyer or going to go into business; rather, learning about the law is a part of learning about life itself in our complicated society. Our goal in preparing *West's Business and Personal Law* has been to transmit to your students our excitement about the way a knowledge and understanding of the law can help everyone at home, at work, and at play.

Today, studying the law consists of much more than memorizing statutes and uniform codes and we reflect this grander scale in the pages that follow. The law today involves all of society's contemporary concerns:

• Ethics
• Globalization
• Multicultural Diversity
• Preventative Law

Throughout all of the chapters in this comprehensive text, you will find references to the above concerns. Additionally, you and your students will find chapters that are directly relevant to their lives. These chapters cover such issues as minors and the law and family law. Special sections called Legal Perspectives also offer your students an opportunity to find out about emerging modern law in the area of sports, entertainment, copyrights, patents, and entrepreneurship.

In the next paragraphs we briefly describe the entire *West's Business and Personal Law* package, including:

- The Student Edition
- The Teacher's Wraparound Edition
- The Teacher's Resource Binder
- Multimedia Components, including videos, videodiscs, and software

◆ THE MAJOR FEATURES OF *WEST'S BUSINESS AND PERSONAL LAW*

When you glance through the Student Edition for *West's Business and Personal Law*, you will find several features that have been included to build and broaden your students' understanding of important business and personal law concepts. All of these features are designed to make the teaching and learning experience more meaningful. These features are also made teacher friendly in this Wraparound Edition, which includes distinct teaching suggestions for each and every feature found in the student book.

LEGAL FOCUS

Throughout each chapter are several *Legal Focus* features. There are two basic types of Legal Focus features found in each chapter—*Legal Focus Problems* and *Legal Focus Examples*. These features help to sharpen student understanding and pique student interest. The *Legal Focus* features help the students to see the legal concepts in a real-world setting, therefore promoting greater understanding. Each *Legal Focus* feature is supported in this Wraparound Edition with distinct teaching notes.

LAW IN ACTION

Every chapter includes *Law in Action* features. Each of these features presents important and high interest information relating to the concepts discussed in the chapter. There are four types of Law in Action features:

Law in Your Life—These features relate business and personal law concepts directly to the students' lives and discuss such important topics as small claims courts, indorsing checks, and landlord-tenant relations.

International Perspectives—These exciting and timely features discuss such diverse topics as resolving international business disputes and marriage in other cultures.

Law and the Businessperson—This feature, specifically designed to help your students consider the legal issues that are faced by business people, discusses such wide-ranging topics as shoplifting, worker safety, and partnership buyouts.

Legal Issue—This important feature discusses some of the foundations and landmarks of our legal system as well as some contemporary issues. Legal

Issues topics include school desegregation and judicial review.

CASES

Because the study of cases is so important to understanding business and personal law, West has taken extraordinary steps to ensure that your students understand the importance of cases and their role in our legal system. From the thorough discussion of how to read cases and case citations found in Chapter 1 through the Table of Cases in the Resource Center at the back of the student text, cases are thoroughly interwoven throughout *West's Business and Personal Law*. As you might expect, cases are used as examples and cited in chapters throughout the book. Additionally, cases receive distinct treatment in each of the following:

A Case in Point—Each chapter (except Chapter 6, Ethics and Social Responsibility) includes one *A Case in Point* feature. Each of these features summarizes a vital case (complete with full case citation) relating to an important aspect of the chapter. The *A Case in Point* feature details the facts of the case, the issue involved, the decision of the court and the reasons for the court's decision.

Applying the Law . . . You Be the Judge—Students have an opportunity to examine cases from a judge's perspective in the *Applying the Law . . . You Be the Judge* feature found in each chapter's end-of-chapter review material. This feature gives students an opportunity to demonstrate their mastery of chapter concepts by applying those concepts to summarized case problems. Each of these case problems includes a full case citation and is reinforced by thorough answers, which are included in this Teacher's Wraparound Edition.

Handbook of Selected Court Cases—This useful classroom supplement includes a summary as well as excerpted language of the court for more than 50 significant court cases, all of which are mentioned in the text. Each of the *A Case in Point* cases are included in the *Handbook of Selected Court Cases*. The *Handbook of Selected Court Cases* is just one more way in which *West's Business and Personal Law* allows you to bring the resources of America's premier legal publisher into your business and personal law classroom.

WRAPAROUND EDITION SUPPORT

As stated earlier, each of these Student Edition features is supported in the Teacher's Wraparound Edition with distinct teaching suggestions including pre-reading tips, discussion starter questions, analyze and apply activities, enrichment activities and answers for all content related questions found in the student text.

CHAPTER ENDING MATERIALS

Each chapter ends with two or three pages of important review materials:

Chapter Summary—An extensive chapter summary designed to be the ideal review tool for your students.

Using Legal Language—This vocabulary activity reinforces students' understanding of key terms from each chapter.

Checking for Comprehension—These questions can be used by you or can be assigned to your students.

Applying Legal Concepts—These activity and project suggestions allow your students to demonstrate their mastery of course concepts in an observable way.

Applying the Law . . . You Be the Judge—Case problems with citations for your students to complete.

Answers—This Teacher's Wraparound Edition includes complete answers for all content questions in the student text chapter review materials.

◆ THE RESOURCE CENTER

Found at the end of both the student text and this Teacher's Wraparound Edition, the *West's Business and Personal Law* Resource Center is filled with a wealth of important, interesting and useful resources.

LEGAL SOURCE DOCUMENTS

No modern text on business and personal law would be complete without a serious sampling of legal source documents. Included in the Resource Center for *West's Business and Personal Law* are the following:

- Declaration of Independence
- U.S. Constitution (fully annotated to enable your students to understand this cornerstone of our American legal system)
- Uniform Commercial Code (excerpts)
- Sherman Antitrust Act of 1890 (excerpts)
- Federal Trade Commission Act of 1914 (excerpts)
- Title VII of the Civil Rights Act of 1964 (excerpts)
- Americans with Disabilities Act of 1990 (excerpts)
- Civil Rights Act of 1991 (excerpts)

SPANISH EQUIVALENTS FOR IMPORTANT LEGAL TERMS IN ENGLISH

This helpful resource for both students and teachers provides the Spanish language equivalents for hundreds of important legal terms in English.

CAREERS IN LAW

This informative student resource discusses a wide variety of careers in law including attorney-at-law, court reporter, law office manager, police officer, video technician and more. Educational requirements as well as specific duties and tasks are discussed for each career.

GLOSSARY AND INDEX

A complete glossary featuring all of the key terms presented in this text, as well as an Index, can also be found at the end of the student edition and this Teacher's Wraparound Edition.

 # ABOUT THE TEACHER'S WRAPAROUND EDITION

The Teacher's Wraparound Edition of *West's Business and Personal Law* is structured to be the ideal teaching tool for today's business and personal law classroom. Here a wealth of teaching information is provided at your fingertips. *West's Business and Personal Law* Teacher's Wraparound Edition includes complete chapter introductory material featuring mastery objectives, prereading activity suggestions, and a resource and assignment guide.

A variety of interesting teaching strategies including discussions starter questions, enrichment suggestions, extension activities, reteaching activities, critical thinking activities, and collaborative learning activities are provided for each chapter. Additionally you will find distinct teaching strategies for each special feature found in the student edition, answers for all content questions found in the student edition, and answers for photo caption questions.

The Teacher's Wraparound Edition also includes the following special features:

Legal Background—Each Legal Background feature provides you, the teacher, with additional information relating to chapter concepts.

Multicultural Perspectives—This special feature includes both research assignment suggestions as well as important quotes and information designed to help you present course material in a manner that fosters an appreciation of our multicultural society.

State Law—These short features highlight important or interesting state laws found throughout our country.

Ethical Concerns—Because ethical concerns have become an increasingly important part of the legal, and regulatory environment, *Ethical Concerns* features have been included for each chapter. These features provide teaching suggestions and discussion starters designed to prompt an examination of the ethical concerns related to chapter content.

Suggested Additional Resources—A listing of Suggested Additional Resources is also included for each unit of the student text.

Additionally, this Teacher's Wraparound Edition acts as your guide for using the many exciting supplemental components that complete the *West's Business and Personal Law* instructional program.

THE TEACHER'S RESOURCE BINDER

The *West's Business and Personal Law* Teacher's Resource Binder includes the following:

Test Bank—For your convenience, the following reproducible tests are available: a pretest, a test for each chapter, an exam for half of the text and one final exam.

Worksheets—A reviewing legal concepts worksheet and an enrichment activity worksheet are included for each chapter.

Transparency Acetates—The Teacher's Resource Binder contains a complete package of transparency acetates for overhead projection in the classroom. Included in this package are key actual business forms.

Mock Trial—Complete instructions and materials for staging a mock trial in your classroom are also included. This mock trial package makes use of a *Drama of the Law* videocassette to be discussed later in this Preface.

Handbook on Critical Thinking and Writing—The *Handbook on Critical Thinking and Writing in Business Law*, written by text author Roger LeRoy Miller, provides an overview of techniques used in critical thinking. The *Handbook* is closely tied to some of the examples given in the chapters of *West's Business and Personal Law* and additionally offers twelve steps to effective writing.

Media Guide—A complete Media Guide for the wealth of media supplements is included in the Teacher's Resource Binder. This includes the Videodisc Instructor's Manual as well as the Instructor's Manual for the *Drama of the Law* video series. This Media Guide features bar codes and frame numbers for the Videodisc as well as teaching suggestions and scripts for the *Drama of the Law*.

 ## VIDEOCASSETTES

No business and personal law text would be complete without supplemental visual materials. *West's Business and Personal Law* offers an unmatched media package.

An extensive videocassette library is now available for adopters of *West's Business and Personal Law*. These instructional videos can help you in the teaching of business and personal law in a variety of areas including ethics and social responsibility, employment law, and others.

THE DRAMA OF THE LAW VIDEO SERIES

West is proud to announce a videocassette series entitled *The Drama of the Law*. This is the first law teleseries that uses humor and wit to teach important legal concepts to today's business and personal law students. The scripts were written by John J. Osborne, Jr., author of *The Paper Chase* and

The Associates. (Most of these videos are also available on the West's Business Law and Legal Environment Videodisc, which is discussed later in this Preface).

These videos are accompanied by a unique *Instructor's Manual* for *The Drama of the Law* Video Series found in the Media Guide section of the *Teacher's Resource Binder.* For each video there is a complete shooting script of the video in which certain portions of the dialogue have been underlined and numbered. In the pages that follow each script there is a section entitled Teaching Points of Law. This section includes a lead-in question for your students, numbered points showing the legal implications of the underlined text in the video script and an answer to the lead-in questions.

WEST'S BUSINESS LAW AND LEGAL ENVIRONMENT VIDEODISC

Technology has provided instructors of business law with yet another way to present teaching materials: the videodisc. We have made available for this edition of *West's Business and Personal Law,* a complete videodisc that provides you with the latest method for presenting important topics to your students. The *West's Business Law and Legal Environment Videodisc* includes the following:

- the videos from the *Drama of the Law* video series
- excerpts from sample trials, ethics videos and other videos,
- hundreds of still frame exhibits.

THE LECTURE BUILDER SOFTWARE

Those who use the *West's Business Law and Legal Environment Videodisc* will find that the LECTURE BUILDER Software can allow for complete customization of each separate lecture. This software works with any Macintosh system and any IBM or compatible using the Windows operating system environment. The LECTURE BUILDER permits the instructor to pick and choose the order of the still frames and the motion videos from any part of the videodisc. Also the motion videos can be edited by the instructor in any fashion desired. The LECTURE BUILDER also has a fully automated mode with programmable time segments.

WESTEST

This computerized testing software, available on DOS, DOS Windows, and Macintosh, includes a complete test bank for *West's Business and Personal Law.* WESTEST allows you to create, edit, store, and print tests. The system is menu driven with a desktop format and offers the options of using keystrokes or mouse, accelerator keys, and function keys. You can randomly generate or selectively choose questions, add new questions, or edit existing questions.

CLASSROOM MANAGEMENT SYSTEM

West's Classroom Management System enables instructors to keep track of student performance using a convenient spreadsheet format. This program, available for DOS, DOS Windows, or Macintosh allows for easy entry of student information and assignment data. The instructor has the ability to customize grading parameters by changing grading criteria or determining assignment weighting. As information is entered, the screen is immediately updated to show student and assignment information including the mean, median, standard deviation, missing assignments, low score, high score, or total points possible. The user can choose which of this information is available on screen. After class information has been entered, the instructor can generate several reports based on this information. These reports include student performance summaries, assignment reports, and overall class reports. All of these reports include a graphical representation of the data in the form of a "box plot."

INTERACTIVE SOFTWARE— CONTRACTS AND SALES

The use of computers in many areas of learning has increased dramatically in recent years., To accompany *West's Business and Personal Law*, we have developed two unique, interactive programs—Interactive Software Contracts and Interactive Software Sales—for the teaching/learning of contracts and sales. These programs use HyperText and allow for flexibility in learning the subject matter based on each user's level of understanding.

Over 120 years worth of experience as the world's premier legal publisher has been applied to the production of *West's Business and Personal Law*, to produce not only the right book but also the right package for today's business and personal law classroom. We believe that you will find the *West's Business and Personal Law* program to be unmatched in quality and scope.

West's Business Law and Legal Environment Videodisc Operating Instructions

GETTING STARTING WITH YOUR VIDEODISC:

Once you have placed the disc in the videodisc player, press "play" on the remote control. It takes approximately thirty seconds to access the first screen on the videodisc.

USING THE REMOTE CONTROL:

Display lets you see the frame and chapter numbers displayed on the monitor as you operate the videodisc player. To hide the chapter and frame display, press the "Display" button again.

Chapter/Frame provides direct access to any specific chapter or frame on the videodisc. Pressing the "chapter/frame" button will display either the word "Chapter" or "Frame" in the upper left-hand corner of your monitor. The remote alternates between chapter and frame each time you press this button.

If you wish to go directly to a specific chapter, for example chapter one, press the "Chapter/Frame" button on the remote control until the word "Chapter" is flashing in the upper right corner of the screen. Next, enter the number "1" on the remote control. When the number appears in left hand corner, press "Search" and the player will bring you the first screen in Chapter 1. Follow the same procedure for each chapter you wish to access.

If you wish to go directly to a specific frame, press the "Chapter/Frame" button until the word "Frame" is flashing in the upper right hand corner of the screen. Next, enter the desired frame number on the remote control and press the "Search" button. (Note, to hide the frame display, press "Clear".)

Step/Still advances the videodisc frame by frame either forward or backward. You will need to use this button when advancing through a series of still frame images. Hitting this button will also freeze a frame of rolling video.

Scan allows you to fast forward through the disc either forward or backward.

Play must be pressed to begin any motion segment on the videodisc. Note: A play icon will appear on the bottom corner of your screen for each motion segment as a reminder to press "play".

Clear cancels all programming functions on the remote control. For example, if you have entered a frame number incorrectly, press the clear button and enter your frame number again.

Pause will stop a video segment. A blank blue screen will appear on the disc and you must hit pause again to resume play. To freeze a frame of rolling video, see step/still above.

Cues for Using the *West's Business Law* and *Legal Environment* Videodisc can be found throughout this *Teacher's Wraparound Edition*. In addition, a complete directory of still frames and motion segments for the Videodisc can be found in the *Media Guide* that is included in your *Teacher's Resource Binder*.

Supreme Court Chief Justices and Associate Justices Since 1789

Each justice is listed along with a notation of the president who nominated him or her and the home state of the justice. (** indicates chief justices)

**John Jay, 1789–1795
George Washington
New York

John Rutledge, 1789–1791
George Washington
South Carolina

William Cushing, 1789–1810
George Washington
Massachusetts

James Wilson, 1789–1798
George Washington
Pennsylvania

John Blair, 1789–1796
George Washington
Virginia

Robert H. Harrison, 1789–1790
George Washington
Maryland

James Iredell, 1790–1799
George Washington
North Carolina

Thomas Johnson, 1791–1793
George Washington
Maryland

William Paterson, 1793–1806
George Washington
New Jersey

**John Rutledge, 1795[a]
George Washington
South Carolina

Samuel Chase, 1796–1811
George Washington
Maryland

**Oliver Ellsworth, 1796–1799
George Washington
Connecticut

Bushrod Washington, 1798–1829
John Adams
Virginia

Alfred Moore, 1799–1804
John Adams
North Carolina

**John Marshall, 1801–1835
John Adams
Virginia

William Johnson, 1804–1834
Thomas Jefferson
South Carolina

Henry Brockholst Livingston, 1806–1823
Thomas Jefferson
New York

Thomas Todd, 1807–1826
Thomas Jefferson
Kentucky

Joseph Story, 1811–1845
James Madison
Massachusetts

Gabriel Duval, 1812–1835
James Madison
Maryland

---

[a] John Rutledge served as Chief Justice from August, 1795, until he was rejected in December of the same year.

Smith Thompson, 1823–1843
James Monroe
New York

Robert Trimble, 1826–1828
John Quincy Adams
Kentucky

John McLean, 1829–1861
Andrew Jackson
Ohio

Henry Baldwin, 1830–1844
Andrew Jackson
Pennsylvania

James M. Wayne, 1835–1867
Andrew Jackson
Georgia

**Roger B. Taney, 1836–1864
Andrew Jackson
Maryland

Philip P. Barbour, 1836–1841
Andrew Jackson
Virginia

John Catron, 1837–1865
Andrew Jackson
Tennessee

John McKinley, 1837–1852
Martin Van Buren
Alabama

Peter V. Daniel, 1841–1860
Martin Van Buren
Virginia

Samuel Nelson, 1845–1872
John Tyler
New York

Levi Woodbury, 1845–1851
James K. Polk
New Hampshire

Robert C. Grier, 1846–1870
James K. Polk
Pennsylvania

**Benjamin R. Curtis,
1851–1857**
Millard Fillmore
Massachusetts

John A. Campbell, 1853–1861
Franklin Pierce
Alabama

Nathan Clifford, 1858–1881
James Buchanan
Maine

Noah H. Swayne, 1862–1881
Abraham Lincoln
Ohio

Samuel F. Miller, 1862–1890
Abraham Lincoln
Iowa

David Davis, 1862–1877
Abraham Lincoln
Illinois

Stephen J. Field, 1863–1897
Abraham Lincoln
California

**Salmon P. Chase, 1864–1873
Abraham Lincoln
Ohio

William Strong, 1870–1880
Ulysses S. Grant
Pennsylvania

Joseph P. Bradley, 1870–1892
Ulysses S. Grant
New Jersey

Ward Hunt, 1872–1882
Ulysses S. Grant
New York

****Morrison R. Waite,
1874–1888**
Ulysses S. Grant
Ohio

John M. Harlan, 1877–1911
Rutherford B. Hayes
Kentucky

William B. Woods, 1880–1887
Rutherford B. Hayes
Georgia

Stanley Matthews, 1881–1889
James A. Garfield
Ohio

Horace Gray, 1881–1902
Chester A. Arthur
Massachusetts

Samuel Blatchford, 1881–1893
Chester A. Arthur
New York

Lucius Q.C. Lamar, 1888–1893
Grover Cleveland
Mississippi

****Melville W. Fuller,
1888–1910**
Grover Cleveland
Illinois

David J. Brewer, 1889–1910
Benjamin Harrison
Kansas

Henry B. Brown, 1890–1906
Benjamin Harrison
Michigan

George Shiras, Jr., 1892–1903
Benjamin Harrison
Pennsylvania

Howell E. Jackson, 1893–1895
Benjamin Harrison
Tennessee

Edward D. White, 1894–1910
Grover Cleveland
Louisiana

**Rufus W. Peckham,
1895–1909**
Grover Cleveland
New York

Joseph McKenna, 1898–1925
William McKinley
California

Oliver W. Holmes, 1902–1932
Theodore Roosevelt
Massachusetts

William R. Day, 1903–1922
Theodore Roosevelt
Ohio

**William H. Moody,
1906–1910**
Theodore Roosevelt
Massachusetts

Horace H. Lurton, 1909–1914
William H. Taft
Tennessee

**Charles E. Hughes,
1910–1916**
William H. Taft
New York

****Edward D. White,
1910–1921**
William H. Taft
Louisiana

**William Van Devanter,
1911–1937**
William H. Taft
Wyoming

Joseph R. Lamar, 1911–1916
William H. Taft
Georgia

Mahlon Pitney, 1912–1922
William H. Taft
New Jersey

**James C. McReynolds,
1914–1941**
Woodrow Wilson
Tennessee

John H. Clarke, 1916–1922
Woodrow Wilson
Ohio

Louis D. Brandeis, 1916–1939
Woodrow Wilson
Massachusetts

**William H. Taft, 1921–1930
Warren G. Harding
Connecticut

**George Sutherland,
1922–1938**
Warren G. Harding
Utah

Pierce Butler, 1922–1939
Warren G. Harding
Minnesota

**Edward T. Sanford,
1923–1930**
Warren G. Harding
Tennessee

Harlan F. Stone, 1925–1941
Calvin Coolidge
New York

**★★Charles E. Hughes,
1930–1941**
Herbert C. Hoover
New York

Owen J. Roberts, 1930–1945
Herbert C. Hoover
Pennsylvania

**Benjamin N. Cardozo,
1932–1938**
Herbert C. Hoover
New York

Hugo L. Black, 1937–1971
Franklin D. Roosevelt
Alabama

Stanley R. Reed, 1938–1957
Franklin D. Roosevelt
Kentucky

Felix Frankfurter, 1939–1962
Franklin D. Roosevelt
Massachusetts

**William O. Douglas,
1939–1975**
Franklin D. Roosevelt
Connecticut

Frank Murphy, 1940–1949
Franklin D. Roosevelt
Michigan

**★★Harlan F. Stone,
1941–1946**
Franklin D. Roosevelt
New York

James F. Byrnes, 1941–1942
Franklin D. Roosevelt
South Carolina

**Robert H. Jackson,
1941–1954**
Franklin D. Roosevelt
New York

**Wiley B. Rutledge,
1943–1949**
Franklin D. Roosevelt
Iowa

Harold H. Burton, 1945–1958
Harry S Truman
Ohio

**★★Frederick M. Vinson,
1946–1953**
Harry S Truman
Kentucky

Tom C. Clark, 1949–1967
Harry S Truman
Texas

Sherman Minton, 1949–1956
Harry S Truman
Indiana

★★Earl Warren, 1953–1969
Dwight D. Eisenhower
California

John M. Harlan, 1955–1971
Dwight D. Eisenhower
New York

**William J. Brennan, Jr.,
1956–1990**
Dwight D. Eisenhower
Indiana

**Charles E. Whittaker,
1957–1962**
Dwight D. Eisenhower
Missouri

Potter Stewart, 1958–1981
Dwight D. Eisenhower
Ohio

Byron R. White, 1962–
John F. Kennedy
Colorado

**Arthur J. Goldberg,
1962–1965**
John F. Kennedy
Illinois

Abe Fortas, 1965–1969
Lyndon B. Johnson
Tennessee

**Thurgood Marshall,
1967–1991**
Lyndon B. Johnson
New York

**★★Warren E. Burger,
1969–1986**
Richard M. Nixon
Minnesota

Harry A. Blackmun, 1970–
Richard M. Nixon
Minnesota

**Lewis F. Powell, Jr.,
1972–1987**
Richard M. Nixon
Virginia

**★★William H. Rehnquist,
1972–**
Richard M. Nixon
Arizona

John Paul Stevens, 1975–
Gerald R. Ford
Illinois

Sandra Day O'Connor, 1981–
Ronald W. Reagan
Arizona

Antonin Scalia, 1986–
Ronald W. Reagan
Virginia

Anthony M. Kennedy, 1988–
Ronald W. Reagan
California

David H. Souter, 1990–
George H. W. Bush
Maine

Clarence Thomas, 1991–
George H. W. Bush
Mississippi

West's Business
and Personal Law

West's Business and Personal Law

Donald L. Carper
Professor of Business Law
Department of Organizational Behavior and Environment
School of Business Administration
California State University, Sacramento

Roger LeRoy Miller
Department of Legal Studies
Clemson University

Donna Parker Murray
Cluster Coordinator
Business and Management Center
Business Magnet High School
Dallas, Texas

West Publishing Company
Minneapolis/St. Paul   New York   San Francisco   Los Angeles

◆ West's Commitment to the Environment ◆

In 1906, West Publishing Company began recycling materials left over from the production of books. This began a tradition of efficient and responsible use of resources. Today, up to 95 percent of our legal books and 70 percent of our college and school texts are printed on recycled, acid-free stock. West also recycles nearly 22 million pounds of scrap paper annually—the equivalent of 181,717 trees. Since the 1960s, West has devised ways to capture and recycle waste inks, solvents, oils, and vapors created in the printing process. We also recycle plastics of all kinds, wood, glass, corrugated cardboard, and batteries, and have eliminated the use of styrofoam book packaging. We at West are proud of the longevity and the scope of our commitment to the environment.

Production, Prepress, Printing and Binding by West Publishing Company.

Composition: American Composition & Graphics, Inc.
Copyediting: Beverly Peavler, Naples Editing Service
Artwork: Miyake Illustration

COPYRIGHT ©1994   By WEST PUBLISHING COMPANY
610 Opperman Drive
P.O. Box 64526
St. Paul, MN 55164-0526

00 99 98 97 96 95 94 93   8 7 6 5 4 3 2 1 0

Library of Congress Cataloging-in-Publication Data

Carper, Donald L.
    West's business and personal law/Don L. Carper, Roger LeRoy Miller, Donna Parker Murray.
       p.   cm.

    Includes index.
    ISBN 0-314-01391-1 (hard : alk. paper)
    1. Commercial law—United States. 2. Contracts—United States. 3. Business law—United States.   I. Miller, Roger LeRoy, 1942–   .   II. West Publishing Company.   III. Title.
KF889.3.C39   1993
346.73'07—dc20
[347.3067]
Student Edition: 0-314-01391-1
Teacher's Wraparound Edition: 0-314-01952-9

92-45780
∞   CIP

Contents in Brief

UNIT SIX
PERSONAL LAW 614

THE RESOURCE CENTER A-1

Contents

◆ UNIT FOUR
AGENCY AND EMPLOYEE LAW 466

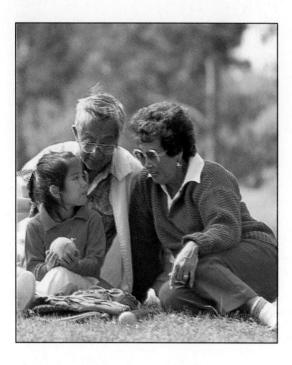

DEDICATION

To my wife, Patricia, for her courage
and special sacrifice in this effort, and
my son, Scott, who started high school
when the writing on this text began and
graduated at its publication.

Donald L. Carper

To my children Shawn and Sabine.
Thanks for taking school seriously.

Roger LeRoy Miller

To my husband, Eric, and my parents,
Robert and Carol.

Donna Parker Murray

UNIT 1

Suggested Additional Resources

The American Arbitration Association - Write to: Public Relations Director, American Arbitration Association, 140 West 51st Street, New York, NY 10020.

American Jurisprudence, 2d ed. Rochester, NY: Lawyer's Co-operative Publishing Co., 1973.

Aristotle, *The Nicomachean Ethics.* New York: Oxford University Press, 1925.

Black's Law Dictionary, 6th ed. St. Paul, MN: West Publishing Co., 1990.

Bowen, Catherine Drinker. *Miracle at Philadelphia: The Story of the Constitutional Convention, May to September, 1787.* Boston: Little, Brown, 1966.

Frankena, William K. *Ethics.* Englewood Cliffs, NJ: Prentice-Hall, 1963.

The Guide to American Law. St. Paul, MN: West Publishing Co., 1983. - Annual updates are available.

Stevens Jr., Otis H. and Scheb II, John M. *American Constitutional Law.* St. Paul, MN: West Publishing Co., 1993.

United States Government Manual. Washington, D.C.: U.S. Government Printing Office - Lists all federal departments and administrative agencies with information about their activities and personnel.

UNIT 1

Understanding the Law and Our Legal System

Americans today find themselves increasingly subject to law and its influence. It is a major part of our society. Most business activities are controlled by legal rules. These rules govern all parts of business; raising money, hiring and firing people, selling and advertising, repairing or replacing defective products, and so on. As you will learn, business law includes laws relating to contracts, sales, the formation of businesses, government regulation of business, insurance, employment, and more.

In your personal life, the law also influences your behavior, often defining what you can and cannot do. The law also regulates marriage, insurance, employment, gifts, inheritances, driving a motor vehicle, owning a home, and renting an apartment. Knowledge of the law will help you in your professional career and personal life.

In Unit One, we lay a foundation for topics to be discussed later in this book. We discuss many of the laws and procedures affecting the law, as well as discussing our legal system.

Mastery Objectives

By the end of this chapter, students should be able to:

- Narrate a brief history of the American legal system
- Identify sources of American law
- Contrast the adversary system and inquisitorial system

- Distinguish civil law versus criminal law
- Compare federal law versus state law
- Classify substantive and procedural law
- Describe actions at law and actions in equity
- Tell when the Uniform Commercial Code applies

Prereading Activity

Write the word *Law* on the board. Ask students to relate orally something they know about law. Write key words from students' input. Categorize the concepts students bring out under titles such as: federal, state, municipal, common law, statutory, administrative, criminal, civil, and other topics that fit your list.

LEGAL BACKGROUND

In this chapter, we define several foundational legal terms and ideas. The chapter is broad, but concepts such as the nature of the adversary system and equity courts provide good opportunities for discussion. We also provide some down-to-earth insights into why the study of law is important to your students.

The key to life-long learning is one's ability to seek knowledge independently. We open the law library door slightly with a discussion of how to find and read law cases. We also introduce learning law from actual cases with a recent New York homeowner's problems with ghosts.

Chapter
1

Introduction to the Law

Activity Sheets
Reviewing Legal Concepts 1 *TRB*
Enrichment Activity 1 *TRB*

Student Activity Workbook
Chapter 1 Activities

Tests
Chapter 1 Test *TRB*
Chapter 1 WESTEST Computerized Testing

Handbook of Selected Court Cases
Stambousky v. *Ackley*
Brown v. *Board of Education of Topeka*

**West's Business Law and Legal
Environment Videodisc**
Still Frames and Motion Segments as shown

Enrichment

Allow a student volunteer to lead the class through a brainstorming session on laws that affect their daily lives. The discussion leader should list on the board all of the applicable laws mentioned by the students. Some sample laws include: food purity laws that regulate the types of food that you can buy and sell and consume, food labelling laws, hazardous materials or toxic materials laws that regulate what types of insulation builders may use, etc.

Critical Thinking Activity

Ask students to write down on paper a list of laws that affect them as minors. Then ask them to write why they think each law was made. Were they made to restrict or to protect the minors? How?

Collaborative Learning Activity

Ask students to break into groups of three or four to make a list of laws/rules that your school enforces. Then ask them to share their thoughts with the rest of the class on how these "laws" help students.

Vocabulary Activity

Before the students read the section that begins with the title "What Do We Mean By Law?" ask student volunteers to define the word *law* in their own words. Then allow students to read the definition found on the next page to see how their definitions compare with the one provided in the text.

"Our nation is founded on the principle that observance of the law is the eternal safeguard of liberty and defiance of the law is the surest road to tyranny."
John F. Kennedy, 1917–1963
Thirty-fifth president of the United States, 1961–1963

When John F. Kennedy spoke the words written above, he did not know that the ultimate defiance of the law—murder—would cut short his career as this nation's thirty-fifth president. No one questions what the law against taking another's life means or why it exists. No one disagrees with Kennedy that observance of the law is indeed a necessary aspect of individual liberty in this or in any other nation. We are a society of laws and, for the most part, law-abiding individuals.

Laws affect you virtually every day of your life. Your state has a law that requires that you go to school until age sixteen. Your state has a law that you must pass a test in order to get a driver's license and must be at least a certain minimum age, often sixteen, to get that license. There also exist many laws that deal with what happens when you, as a person not legally considered an adult, buy a major appliance or automobile. These laws affect you personally whenever you make such purchases.

The fact is, you cannot escape the law, because it applies to virtually everything that you do today and will do tomorrow. And if you are thinking about a career in the world of business, the study of law is not only helpful, it is essential.

In a sense, your decision to learn more about business and personal law is very practical. For example, you cannot help but be better off if you know how much the law requires an employer to pay you for part-time work. Certainly, if you damage a videotape that you rent, you will be better off if you know what your true legal rights and responsibilities are. If you are on the job working for a big or a little company, you will need to know your rights as a worker if you get injured. These are some of the practical aspects of business and personal law.

We have used the word *law* in the last few paragraphs, but we have not yet really defined it. In the next several sections, we define *law* and describe where American law comes from and how it can be classified. Then we introduce business law and describe how to use court cases and read court opinions.

◆ WHAT DO WE MEAN BY *LAW*?

When somebody tells you about a specific law that requires you to have a valid driver's license in order to legally drive on public streets, you know what that person is talking about. Specific laws are, for the most part, easy to understand. They are printed in a set of books, and you can look them up at any time. But business and personal law does not just involve specific laws that your city council or your state lawmakers pass. The study of law includes much more, because not all law is made by city councils and state lawmakers. Some of it comes from custom, some of it comes from decisions made by judges, and some of it comes from the United States Constitution, as well as from various state constitutions. Here is a general definition of what law is:

◆ **law** Enforceable rules that govern how individuals deal with each other and how each individual interacts with society as a whole.

Law consists of enforceable rules that govern how individuals deal with each other and how each individual interacts with society as a whole.

The law, then, provides a set of established rules. One rule requires you to stop at red lights. Another rule requires you to pay for the food on supermarket shelves that you want to buy. Yet another rule—one governing the relationship between each individual and society as a whole—prohibits you from taking another person's life.

Clearly, the thousands and thousands of rules that govern our lives and form the law must be enforceable to have any meaning. That means there has to be a system that resolves conflicts between individuals. For the most part, that system is our court system. But it also involves lawyers, police personnel, and prisons.

◆ FROM WHERE DID AMERICAN LAW COME?

Law in America has a long history dating back to the English legal system. Today, the law in America is constantly changing as new rules and new interpretations of past rules are made by the courts and the *legislatures*—the law-making bodies in our cities, states, and federal government.

We begin our examination of the sources of American law by looking back toward English law. The American colonists brought with them the legal system that had developed in England over a period of hundreds of years. Some of the earliest courts in the English system started almost a thousand years ago.

EARLY ENGLISH COURTS OF LAW

◆ **common law** The body of judge-made law. The common law system originally developed under the English court system.

For centuries, business disputes and disputes between individuals had been settled according to local customs throughout England. Many of these customs differed in different regions of that country. All of this was to change beginning in 1066 when William the Conqueror conquered England. He established a *king's court* to develop a uniform set of customs, or rules, for the whole country. All of those rules taken together became common to the entire English countryside. Not surprisingly, we now refer to this body of law as **common law**, because it was meant to be common everywhere in the country.

State Law

As of early 1992, the Texas State Constitution had been amended 339 times, far above the national average of 113 times. However, the champion amenders are Alabama, with 538 amendments, and California, with 480 amendments. This is in sharp contrast to the state constitutions of Illinois and Montana, both of which have been recently revised, Illinois in 1991 and Montana in 1992. Illinois has only 7 amendments and Montana only 16 amendments.

Today we think of common law, whether it be from England or from America, as mainly law derived from decisions made by judges who presided over conflicts that ended up in court. For example, there is a whole body of common law concerned with the extent to which one neighbor can create a nuisance to an adjoining neighbor by, say, playing music too loudly or letting dogs run wild in the neighborhood. Throughout many centuries in England and in America, judges ruled on conflicts involving one neighbor accusing another of creating a nuisance. The decisions in these cases formed a body of rules about nuisances.

Back in England from the eleventh and twelfth centuries on, parts of many important decisions made by judges were put in Year Books. Other judges would often look into these Year Books to see if a particular type of conflict had been ruled on before. A judge faced with a person suing a neighbor because of barking dogs could see if another judge had already made a rule for such conflicts, for example. In this way, English judges maintained the same rules for all of England.

SOURCES OF AMERICAN LAW

As you know, Americans had a revolution and succeeded in becoming independent from England. Nonetheless, Americans kept many of the English legal traditions and rules after the Revolution. Specifically, we continued the tradition of a common law legal system. The only state that has not followed that tradition is Louisiana, because of its French heritage. Its legal traditions follow those of France. In any event, as a common law country, the United States follows the decisions of judges throughout the land. In addition, our law is based on three other elements:

1. **Constitutions. A constitution** in America is a written document that spells out the powers and limits of a government. In the United States, we have fifty-one constitutions—the U.S. Constitution and the fifty state constitutions. The U.S. Constitution is, of course, the supreme law of the land. That means that if a state law conflicts with the U.S. Constitution, the state law is not valid.
2. **Statutes.** As mentioned before, city councils, state legislatures, and Congress make laws all the time. These are called **statutes**. Much of what used to be common law—say, with respect to dealings between buyers and sellers of cars—has been incorporated into statute law in this country. When you go buy a car, many of the rules governing that purchase are spelled out in statutes passed by your state legislature.
3. **Administrative law.** Every city has agencies that control some part of how businesses and individuals can act. For example, most cities have a municipal pollution control office. The people who work in that office establish rules about how things can be done. For example, most city pollution-control agencies regulate the burning of lawn clippings and leaves. In many cities, people are not allowed to burn anything. They have to take such debris to a municipal dumping site. At the state and federal levels, there are also pollution-control agencies

◆ **constitution** A written document that spells out the powers and limits of a government.

◆ **statute** A law originated by the U.S. Congress or a state legislative body, passed by that body and usually signed by the executive official, the president or governor.

◆ **administrative law** The branch of public law concerned with the powers and actions of administrative agencies. It consists of the rules, regulations, orders, and decisions of the agencies.

Critical Thinking Activity

Our common law heritage places a high value on continuity. Orally discuss reasons why continuity is important in our legal system.

Enrichment

Ask a student to define the doctrine of *stare decisis*. Then start a class discussion on recent cases in which the precedent was overturned. For example, a minor child divorcing his parents was such a case in Florida in 1992.

Reteaching Activity

Write the following question on the board: "How are precedents used in our legal system?" Have each student write a one- or two-sentence answer to this question; then have students share their work with a partner. Each pair of students should then write a one- or two-sentence answer based on their own responses. Allow volunteers to share their answers with the class.

Vocabulary Activity

Allow a student volunteer to explain the meaning of the sentence: "The common law is not chiselled in stone, however."

Automobile safety standards are created and enforced as part of administrative law.

♦ **precedent** A court decision that provides an example or authority for deciding later cases involving identical or similar facts. To serve as precedents, cases must have been decided in the same state and in the same or a higher court.

♦ ***stare decisis*** ("to stand on decided cases") The practice of deciding new cases with reference to former decisions, or precedents.

that generate numerous rules about how much smoke factories can emit and how much of what pollutants factories can put in oceans, rivers, and lakes. Collectively, these organizations are called administrative agencies. The rules that they generate make up the body of **administrative law**. Administrative law is defined as the regulations, orders, rules, and decisions of administrative agencies.

CONTINUITY AND THE COMMON LAW

If every judge made any decision he or she wanted to, no matter what other judges had decided in the past, our legal system would be very confusing. Suppose you agreed to pay a mechanic to fix your car, had the job done, made the payment, and then found out that the mechanic did not quite do what was promised and what you paid for. If the mechanic refused to "make good" the promised repair job, you might decide to sue. Your lawyer could look up previous cases and find out how judges had ruled. In this way, he or she could predict what might happen if you actually went to court. That is because our common law heritage is one that places a high value on continuity—keeping things the same.

Court decisions become **precedents** for later cases. A case used as precedent is a prior case with facts the same as or similar to facts in a new case under consideration. Judges are in principle bound by precedent unless they find good reason to change it. There is a name for this practice of deciding new cases by considering former decisions. It is called the doctrine of ***stare decisis***, which means "to stand on decided cases." *Stare decisis* is a cornerstone of the English and American judicial systems, for it requires that judges at least attempt to follow precedent.

Why *Stare Decisis* Is Important   The doctrine of *stare decisis* is important to the American legal system for many reasons. One is that it makes our legal system and the courts more efficient. Judges and their assistants can use the opinions of similar cases as guidelines, rather than starting from scratch. Additionally, the doctrine of *stare decisis* gives more stability to our legal system. Perhaps most importantly, when judges follow the doctrine of *stare decisis*, their biases for or against a particular person or business have less of a chance to enter into their opinions.

When Precedent Is Overturned   The common law is not chiseled in stone, however. Precedents are overturned. When that happens, a great deal of publicity usually surrounds the decision. A court may overturn a precedent because it believes that the reasoning used in previous court decisions is no longer valid, given changes in society or technology.

Many court decisions with respect to very sensitive issues such as prayer in school are overturned. A state court may rule that, for example, one minute of silent prayer at the beginning of every school day is legal. The highest court of the land, the United States Supreme Court, may disagree—and it did. It decided that schools cannot impose one minute of silent prayer, because that would go against the First Amendment to the

Ethical Concern

LEGAL BACKGROUND

◆ Law in Action

LEGAL ISSUE: SCHOOL DESEGREGATION

Whenever an important precedent is overruled, a major change in the lives of everyone in the United States can occur. One case that caused such a change was called *Brown v. Board of Education of Topeka*.[1] It was brought by the parents of Linda Carol Brown against the Board of Education of Topeka, Kansas. Mr. and Mrs. Brown wanted Linda to attend an all-white school only a few blocks away from their house. Instead, she was forced to go to an all-black school that was twenty-one blocks away. In deciding in favor of the Browns, the U.S. Supreme Court overthrew a precedent that had existed for fifty-eight years. That precedent allowed for "separate but equal" edu-

cational facilities, and it was used to justify segregation in many areas of American life. The Supreme Court said:

> Does segregation of children in public schools solely on the basis of race, even though the physical facilities and other tangible [physical] factors may be equal, deprive children of the minority groups of equal educational opportunities? We believe that it does. . . . [Segregation generates in children] a feeling of inferiority as to their status in the community that may affect their hearts and minds in a way unlikely ever to be undone. . . . In the field of education the doctrine of "separate but equal" has no place. Separate educational facilities are inherently unequal.

After the Supreme Court overturned precedent with respect to segregated education facilities, other segregated aspects of our society increasingly became integrated.

1. 347 U.S. 483, 74 S.Ct. 686, 98 L.Ed. 873 (1954).
(These references refer to where to find this court opinion in legal reference books. We explain in the A Case in Point feature on pages 25–26 what these references mean.)

U.S. Constitution, which implies a separation of "church and state." To take another example, for many years the courts ruled that state laws prohibiting women from engaging in numerous occupations, such as operating heavy machinery, were constitutional. Gradually, some courts started to disagree. They would strike down local and state laws that prohibited women from entering certain occupations. They did this in spite of the fact that numerous other court decisions had upheld these laws in the past. What we saw in these cases was a gradually emerging set of new precedents. These new precedents labeled laws prohibiting women from certain jobs as illegal forms of discrimination against women.

One of the most far-reaching examples of overturning precedent involved the segregation that existed for many years in our school systems as discussed in the Law in Action feature above.

SOME MORE THOUGHTS ON STATUTORY LAW

A hundred years ago, most of the law in this country was common law. Increasingly, though, law in the United States is based on statutes passed by

Lead a class discussion about why more law in this country today is statutory law compared to 100 years ago, when most of the law was common law.

Allow a student volunteer to define the word *adversary* for the class. Explain to the class that one definition of *adversary* is "enemy." How does this definition relate to our system of justice?

Legal Focus Problem

Read aloud the Legal Focus Problem found here to the class. Allow student volunteers to suggest possible answers to this problem.

---

local, state, and federal legislatures. Passing law is, of course, the job of legislatures such as the U.S. Congress. Typically, for a statute to become law, the president or governor has to approve it. Much of the burden of the courts today is to interpret and clarify statutes passed by legislatures.

◆ LEGAL FOCUS – PROBLEM

A federal law enacted by the Congress makes it a crime to transport stolen "motor vehicles" across state lines. In other words, if you steal a car and drive it around town, you have committed a *state* crime. But if you steal a car and drive to another state, you have violated a *federal* criminal law. The federal law defined the term *motor vehicle* as "an automobile, automobile truck, automobile wagon, motorcycle, or any other self-propelled vehicle not designed for running on rails." An interesting question arose when a plane was stolen and transported from one state to another. Does the federal statute apply to this situation?

The United States Supreme Court held that the airplane was not a motor vehicle for purposes of the federal statute against transporting stolen motor vehicles from state to state.[2] The Court held that "in everyday speech 'vehicle' called up the picture of a thing moving on land." So, in effect, the U.S. Supreme Court's interpretation of the federal statute meant that it was not a federal crime to move a stolen plane from state to state. That does not mean that the thief got away with stealing the airplane. Rather, it meant that he was prosecuted under state law instead of federal law.

◆ WE HAVE AN ADVERSARY SYSTEM OF JUSTICE

◆ adversary system
A legal system in which parties to a legal action are opponents and are responsible for bringing the facts and law related to their case before the court.

Whenever you take one side of an argument and someone else takes the other side, the two of you become adversaries. You decide to make your point by supporting your argument the best you can. The other person does the same, but in favor of his or her argument.

The U.S. legal system also pits one adversary against the other. In this **adversary system**, parties to legal actions are opponents. Those who sue are called the **plaintiffs**, and those who are sued are called the **defendants**. In cases involving murder, theft, and the like, the accused is, of course, the defendant and the plaintiff's role is taken by the state, which represents the people. The judge is a neutral and generally passive participant in this courtroom process. This simple concept is important.

◆ plaintiff The person who brings an action in court against another person.

In our adversary system of law, the opponents are those who are responsible for producing the evidence. There is relatively unrestricted argument

◆ defendant The person against whom an action in court is brought.

2. *McBoyle v. United States*, 283 U.S. 25, 51 S.Ct. 340, 75 L.Ed. 816 (1931).

In an adversary system, each attorney will present the facts and argue the law in the light most favorable to their client's interests. A judge oversees the process, making rulings on the admissibility of evidence and appropriateness of the attorney's conduct.

by each side in its own favor and against the opponent. The judge normally acts as a referee, similar to a referee at a high school football or basketball game. She or he determines whether the rules of how the trial should proceed are properly followed by each of the opposing parties. Once each party has presented its case, either the judge or the **jury**—those people who sit in judgment on the case—makes a decision based on the facts that the parties have presented in court.

A system that contrasts with ours is the so-called **inquisitorial system**. This is a system in which judges take a much more active role. They make many inquiries of the plaintiff and the defendant, and they do not depend on the parties to provide all of the relevant information. In the inquisitorial system, judges investigate, question witnesses, and seek their own evidence. Inquisitorial systems exist in Germany, Argentina, France, and many other countries.

Many believe that our adversary system of law has helped produce one of the fairest legal systems the world has ever known. It is not a perfect approach, however. It places a great premium on advocacy skills—skills of persuasion—even if the truth occasionally suffers. Guilty defendants may be found innocent because their attorneys are so persuasive. Conversely, an innocent defendant may be found guilty because the plaintiff's attorneys

♦ **jury**   A group of persons chosen to decide questions of fact in legal actions.

♦ **inquisitorial system**   A legal system that allows the judge to investigate, question witnesses, and seek out evidence.

Vocabulary Activity

Before reading this material on criminal versus civil law, ask a student volunteer to define *criminal law* and *civil law* to the class.

Extension Activity

Tell students to find newspaper articles relating to criminal and civil cases. Have them copy or cut out the articles, paraphrase the cases, and tell whether they are civil or criminal cases.

Legal Focus Example

Allow a student volunteer to read aloud this Legal Focus Example to the class. Remind students that they can use the legal focus features as review tools when studying for tests.

10

were able to argue effectively, even though the defendant actually did nothing wrong. Our adversary system requires good attorneys, and they cost money. Many complain that our system is too expensive. Some people who have valid reasons to sue decide that they cannot go to court because they cannot afford an attorney.

◆ **THE TYPES OF LAW THAT YOU WILL LEARN ABOUT**

There are many different types of law in this country. In the rest of this book, you will learn at least a little bit about virtually all of them. We have already mentioned some types of law, but to make the distinctions more clear-cut, we will classify the types of law here. There is no single best way to classify law, but the following classifications should help you understand who ends up being the plaintiff and who ends up being the defendant when a particular case goes to court.

CRIMINAL VERSUS CIVIL LAW

At the beginning of this chapter, we talked about the assassination of President John F. Kennedy. The assassin violated criminal law when he took the president's life. **Criminal law**, which we discuss more extensively in Chapter 4, involves a wrong committed against society, or the public. If someone you know is caught stealing a portable CD player, the owner of the CD player does not bring charges for the commission of the crime of stealing. Rather, somebody in your state government, on behalf of the state (and its people), will press charges for theft. This is because theft is considered a wrong against society in general. That is why murder and theft are considered crimes against the state. In almost every criminal case, the government tries to impose a penalty on a guilty person. Penalties involve money fines, imprisonment, and the death penalty in certain states.

Civil law is defined as dealing with duties that exist between persons or between persons and their government. If you are involved in a car accident because you did not stop for a stop sign, you have violated the duty to be reasonably careful when driving, and you have harmed somebody. That person will sue you under civil law. In any civil case, the party suing tries to make the other party perform a duty or pay for the damages caused by the failure of that duty. In the auto accident example, the party suing you would want you to pay for any damages to the car and any medical expenses, among other things.

It is possible, even common, that one act can involve both criminal law and civil law. If a wrongdoer injures the public, the public prosecutor can pursue criminal charges. The victim of the crime can also pursue a civil action to compensate him or her for any harm suffered. Exhibit 1-1 contrasts criminal with civil law.

◆ **criminal law** Law related to wrongs committed against the public, punishable by fines, imprisonment, or both.

◆ **civil law** Law related to the duties that exist generally between persons or between persons and the government, except the duty not to commit crimes.

State Law

As is pointed out here, the United States Constitution is the supreme law of the land, and no law in violation of the United States Constitution is valid. This does not mean, however, that some laws in violation of the U.S. Constitution are not still on the books in some states. For example, in Texas there are several provisions in the Texas Constitution that are in violation of the U.S. Constitution. An exam-ple of one such violation is that according to the Texas Constitution, property ownership is mandatory as a qualification for the right to vote in local bond elections, despite the fact that, under the U.S. Constitution, property ownership is not permitted as a qualification for the right to vote. It is important to remember that while these laws may still be on the books, they are not valid or enforced.

	Civil	Criminal
Nature	Rights and duties of individuals to each other	Wrongs against society
Person bringing court action	Person Injured	Government—either federal, state, or local prosecutor
Usual result sought	Money for injuries or performance of a duty	Imprisonment, fines, or both

EXHIBIT 1-1
THE CONTRASTS BETWEEN CRIMINAL AND CIVIL LAW

 LEGAL FOCUS – EXAMPLE

Suppose you had an agreement to buy your friend's used car. You gave your friend $1,500 and expect delivery tomorrow. In the meantime, your friend finds someone else who is willing to pay more. The next day, instead of your friend's used car, you get your $1,500 back. If you decide to sue your friend because he has broken an agreement with you, you are the plaintiff and your friend is the defendant. You are now engaged in a civil lawsuit.

STATE VERSUS FEDERAL LAW

Most of the law that you, as an individual or as a future business person, depend on is state law. **State law** consists of your state constitution, all of the laws passed by your state legislature, the rules and regulations created by state agencies, and the decisions of state courts.

Federal law, as you might imagine, involves only that law generated in Washington, D.C., and by agencies of the federal government. It consists of the U.S. Constitution, all laws passed by the U.S. Congress, treaties, presidential orders, and rules and regulations created by federal administrative agencies such as the Environmental Protection Agency, as well as all decisions of the federal courts throughout the United States. Remember that the supreme law of the land is the United States Constitution. No law in violation of the U.S. Constitution is valid.

For just about every federal agency that exists, there is an equivalent state agency. That means that many of the rules, regulations, and laws pertaining to particular subjects at the federal level also exist at the state level. Consider laws regulating the emission of pollution from automobiles, for example. The United States Congress has passed a series of laws requiring

◆ **state law** Law consisting of state constitutions, statutes originated by the state legislatures, regulations created by state agencies, and decisions of state courts.

◆ **federal law** Law consisting of the U.S. Constitution, statutes originated by Congress, treaties and presidential orders, regulations created by federal administrative agencies, and decisions of the federal courts.

reductions in the amount of emissions allowable from new automobile engine exhaust systems. At the same time, individual states have also passed laws and regulations on the same subject matter. In particular, California has usually had pollution standards for new automobiles that were stricter than the federal government's. The federal courts have ruled that states can require compliance with pollution emission standards that are stricter than those of the federal government. And many states, including California, go one step further. They require that all car owners have their vehicles tested every year to assure continuing compliance with either the federal or state pollution emission limitations. No federal law requires such annual testing. So at least in the case of automobile emission requirements, states can enforce laws stricter than those found on the books of the U.S. Congress.

PROCEDURAL VERSUS SUBSTANTIVE LAW

Have you ever completed a homework assignment that you thought you had done quite well only to receive a poor grade because you had not followed your teacher's instructions exactly? If so, then you have experienced the difference between *form* and *substance*. You might have gotten the gist—the substance—of the assignment perfectly right. But because you did not follow the exact procedure—the form—for presenting your answer, you were penalized.

◆ **procedural law**
Legal rules for processing civil and criminal cases through the court system.

In the law, the same division between form and substance exists. It is the difference between procedural and substantive law. **Procedural law** consists of all the legal rules for processing both civil and criminal cases through the court system. One procedural law involves the right to a trial by jury, as outlined in the Bill of Rights. A more modern procedural law gives those accused of a crime the right to an attorney, even if they do not have enough money to pay for one. **Substantive law**, in contrast, defines duties, establishes rights, and prohibits wrongs. The law against taking another person's life is part of substantive law. The law protecting you from discrimination in housing, schooling, and the like is part of substantive law.

◆ **substantive law**
Law that defines duties, establishes rights, and prohibits wrongs.

One good example of procedural law involves the time limitation on suing people. Let's say that you got in an auto accident and your car was damaged. If you waited ten years to sue the person who ran into you, under most circumstances, you would no longer be able to sue. You would have violated a basic procedural law that requires that lawsuits be brought within a specific time period. Such procedural laws are called **statutes of limitations**. In many states, a lawsuit to recover for damaged property in an automobile accident has to be filed within one year.

◆ **statute of limitations** Statute that requires anyone claiming a legal right against another to begin proceedings to enforce that right within a specific period of time.

There are many reasons behind statutes of limitations. The most obvious has to do with fairness. Would it be fair to bring suit against someone ten years after an alleged wrong was committed? Another reason has to do with people's memories. After all, people cannot remember things forever. Witnesses to an automobile accident cannot be expected to recall what they saw ten years, or even two years, after the fact. Procedural laws, such as statutes of limitations, usually have a good reason to exist.

Collaborative Learning Activity

Ask a student to define the difference between substantive law and procedural law. Have the students work with a partner to compose a list of procedural laws and a list of substantive laws.

Reteaching Activity

Ask a few students to take turns reading aloud the section on courts of law and courts of equity.

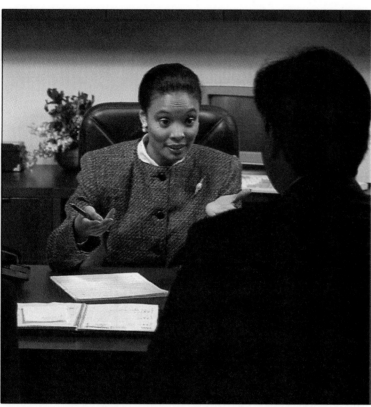

Procedural issues are argued by the attorney before a judge rather than before a jury. The judge will decide procedural issues because they are questions of law. Failure to follow proper procedures can cause an otherwise winning case to be lost.

IT'S A MATTER OF EQUITY—OR IS IT?

When people talk about an *equitable* solution to a problem, they mean a *fair* solution. To examine these solutions, we return to England. In the king's courts hundreds of years ago, sometimes a judge found that he or she could not be very fair. The law was clear-cut on certain issues. Often, because of certain aspects of the law, even if it was obvious that somebody had been wronged, the person who had committed the wrong could not be made to pay any penalty.

Courts of Law Suppose you were an English subject of those times. You agreed to work for somebody on his farm, but at the last minute you got a better job in the city and did not show up. If the farmer took you to court, the king's court was only allowed to award the farmer (1) money, (2) items of value, or (3) land. The court could not force you to work for the farmer, even if the farmer was unable to find anybody else at the time.

Reteaching Activity

Ask your students to list types of equity awarded in court.

A maxim is a proposition or general statement. Some common maxims relating to actions in equity are as follows:

1. Whoever seeks equity must do equity. (Anyone who wishes to be treated fairly must treat others fairly.)
2. When there is equal equity, the law must prevail. (The law will determine the outcome of a controversy in which the merits of both sides are equal.)
3. One seeking the aid of an equity court must come to the court with clean hands. (Plaintiffs must have acted fairly and honestly.)
4. Equity will not suffer a right to exist without a remedy. (Equitable relief will be awarded when there is a right to relief and there is no adequate remedy at law.)
5. Equity regards substance rather than form. (Equity is more concerned with fairness and justice than with legal technicalities.)
6. Equity aids the vigilant, not those who rest on their rights. (Equity will not help those who neglect their rights for an unreasonable period of time.)

EXHIBIT 1-2
EQUITABLE PRINCIPLES AND MAXIMS

◆ **remedy** Relief given to a wronged party, by law or by contract, to enforce a right or prevent or compensate for the violation of a right.

The three **remedies**—the relief given to the wronged party—just mentioned were called *remedies at law*. The courts that could decide remedies at law became known as *courts of law*. Basically, if you wanted any remedy other than money, these courts of law were helpless. That did not seem fair or equitable.

Courts of Equity   Those people who did not think they could get an adequate remedy in a court of law started petitioning the king to help them out. The king often referred such citizens to his advisor, called the *chancellor*. People said that the chancellor was the "keeper of the king's conscience." The chancellor would often decide on a remedy other than money that seemed fair.

A whole new body of law started to develop around the remedies on which the chancellor decided. New formal courts were established that were called either the chancellor's courts or the chancellory courts. These courts became known as courts of **equity** (fairness). The courts heard what were called *actions in equity* and granted what were called *remedies in equity*.

◆ **equity** A branch of law supplying special rules and procedures when legal rules are inadequate to promote justice and fairness.

So two distinct court systems developed in England. The equity courts were there to provide fairness and justice whenever the courts of law could not. When people sued, they had to specify whether they were bringing an "action at law" or an "action in equity." Their decision determined which court system they used.

Enrichment

Ask a student volunteer to read aloud Exhibit 1-2 to the class. As the volunteer reads each of the maxims on this list, discuss with the students how these maxims might apply to the example of an equitable dispute that occurs when a friend did not honor an agreement to sell you his used car.

	Equity	Law

Subject matter	Family law
	Probate
	Trusts
	Remedy at law is
	  inadequate
		Everything that is not
		  a matter in equity

Nature of trial	No jury	Jury
Remedies	Specific perfomance Injunctions Rescission Restitiution Reformation	Money damages

EXHIBIT 1-3
CONTRAST BETWEEN A MATTER IN EQUITY AND A MATTER AT LAW

In the United States today, there is really almost no distinction between courts of law and courts of equity in most states. In other words, almost every court can hear actions in equity and actions in law. You and your attorney do not have to worry about specifying one. The distinctions do still exist, though, when issues of procedure arise. Matters in equity often have procedural requirements different from those for matters at law. For example, matters in equity are usually heard by a judge rather than by a jury. The judge decides what is fair. If you sue because your friend did not honor an agreement to sell you his used car, you probably will have a judge hear your case.

A whole set of old-world sayings have become part of the procedure relating to most actions in equity. Some of these are given in Exhibit 1-2.

Examples of Equitable Disputes   Consider some other disputes that are typically heard as equitable matters. One of the most common involves the family. A child custody battle does not involve remedies at law but rather remedies in equity—with whom, in fact, should the child live? Adoption proceedings are clearly of an equitable nature. Anytime someone who is not an adult is involved in a problem, usually equitable matters are at issue. Even when a juvenile is accused of a crime, it is considered a matter in equity. Therefore, the minor does not have a right to a jury trial as an adult does. You will read more about this important topic in Chapter 26. When someone dies and leaves property (an estate), the administration of that property is a matter in equity and is typically heard by a special court. You will read more about such problems in Chapter 32.

1. Common law is law derived from decisions made by judges who preside over conflicts that end up in court.
2. Judges are in principle bound by precedent unless they find good reason to change precedent.
3. Society and/or the public are the plaintiffs in criminal law cases because the offenses are

considered to be committed against them. Somebody in the government acts on behalf of the government (and its people).
4. If any law violates that of the U.S. Constitution, it is not valid.
5. Procedural law consists of all the legal rules for processing both civil and criminal cases through the court system.

Critical Thinking Activity

Lead a class discussion about the reason business cannot be regulated simply by handshakes and supposed understandings of what business customs are.

16   Understanding the Law and Our Legal System

 LEGAL FOCUS ~ EXAMPLE

If your neighbor has kept you up with his barking dogs night after night, this is a matter in equity. You may get a court to issue an order to your neighbor to keep his dogs in the garage from the hours of 10 P.M. to 7 A.M.

In any event, with today's typical court procedure, the plaintiff will request at the same time both legal and equitable remedies in the same action. If you sue your neighbor because his barking dogs are keeping you awake, you may ask the court to cause him to keep them in the garage and also to pay you the amount of money it cost you to hire a lawyer to bring the lawsuit. Virtually any court can grant both legal and equitable remedies. Exhibit 1-3 summarizes the differences between matters in equity and matters at law.

Now that we have looked at the different types of law in general, we will consider the law that governs the behavior of businessmen and businesswomen. Many of you, in one way or another, will be in the business world, either as an employee working for a businessperson or as the manager or owner of a business.

◆ CHECKING YOUR PROGRESS

1. How is common law developed?
2. Are judges required to follow the doctrine of *stare decisis*?
3. Who is considered to be the plaintiff in criminal law cases? Who actually participates in the legal proceedings to represent society?
4. Explain the statement, "the supreme law of the land is the United States Constitution."
5. What type of law guides a civil lawsuit through the court system?

◆ MODERN AMERICAN BUSINESS LAW

Business is the backbone of a growing, vibrant nation. Business cannot be regulated simply by handshakes and supposed understandings of what business customs are. Rather, our complicated business world is regulated by a large body of law called commercial, or business, law. Business law includes virtually all the topics in the book that you are now reading, such as the way agreements must be formed to be legal and binding, the way individual businesspersons can get together to form partnerships in business, and the way giant companies can raise money in order to make huge investments.

Much of business law in the past was common law based on the customs developed through hundreds of years in England. Within each state in the United States, a whole body of separate commercial law developed as state common law. In principle, then, it is possible that there exists a different legal rule for the same business transaction in every state. To avoid having fifty different rules for the same activity, sets of commercial law codes have been developed.

THE DEVELOPMENT OF UNIFORM LAW CODES

It is hard enough to do business on a national level without having to worry about a multitude of different laws for every transaction. Consequently, over a hundred years ago, the U.S. legal community started to try to make commercial laws uniform throughout the states. To do so, a group called the National Conference of Commissioners on Uniform State Laws began meeting in the late 1800s. Its goal was, and continues to be today, to draft model codes. A **code** is a collection of statutes or rules on a particular subject. The way that two people join together to run a business as partners is an example.

It is possible to have fifty different rules about how such partnerships should be formed. It is also possible to come up with a uniform code that all states enact. That is in fact what happened when the Uniform Partnership Act was developed by the National Conference of Commissioners on Uniform State Laws. This group has developed similar model codes in other areas of the law, such as how big businesses (called corporations in most circumstances) must act and how credit should be offered to consumers. One of the most important uniform codes for those of you who will have any dealings in the business world is the **Uniform Commercial Code**, usually called the **UCC**.

THE UNIFORM COMMERCIAL CODE (UCC)

Buying and selling are the principle activities of most businesses. If you go into the fresh fruit business, you will be buying fruit from wholesalers and farmers and selling it to retail customers. What happens when you order lettuce and some of it rots after the trucking company chosen by the lettuce farmer has to make a detour because of bad road conditions? Questions such as this one have to be answered by commercial law.

In order that the answers to such questions be the same no matter what state you did business in, the Uniform Commercial Code was created. The UCC takes all of the common business practices and puts them into one uniform set of rules. The UCC encourages more business transactions by

◆ **code** A collection of statutes or rules on a particular subject.

◆ **Uniform Commercial Code (UCC)** A uniform law enacted in part by all fifty states to create certainty in the area of commercial contracts and to make the law consistent with common business practices.

Teaching Note

Excerpts from the Uniform Commercial Code can be found in the Resource Center at the back of this book. You might have students turn to this section and skim these excerpts to get a feeling for how such codes are worded.

Collaborative Learning Activity

Obtain a copy of the Uniform Commercial Code, or use the excerpts found in the Resource Center at the back of this text. Divide students into groups of two or four, and have each group interpret a law to the class orally.

Read

Before reading this feature, you might want to go around the room asking each student why he or she chose to enroll in your law course. What was he or she hoping to gain from the course? Then allow a student volunteer to read aloud to the class this *Law in Action* feature.

Discuss

Use the following questions to stimulate a class discussion: What do you think of Marcus Tullius Cicero's claim that no one could be a truly educated person without studying law? Is this still true today? Why is it nonetheless important that we study law? Do you think most people find the law interesting? Why do you think lawyers and law cases seem to be the subject of so much popular entertainment (i.e., television shows, movies, books)?

Collaborative Learning Activity

Divide the class into groups of three or four students, and have each group create a list of five things about the law that they hope to learn in this course. For each item on their list, they should also have one or two reasons why this item is important. Allow the groups to share their lists with the rest of the class.

Discussion Starter

Make the statement: "Ignorance of the law is no excuse for breaking it." Ask students to interpret this statement. Do they think this is fair? Unfair? Why? What would our society be like if every person who claimed he or she did not know the proper law was released?

Collaborative Learning Activity

Read aloud the questions found in the numbered list on this page. Ask students to guess the answers and write them down on their own sheets of paper. Then divide the class into groups of three or four to find the correct answers throughout the book.

 Law in Action

LAW IN YOUR LIFE: WHY STUDY LAW?

Most students do not question the need to learn English, for how else can we communicate? Few students question the need to learn basic arithmetic and mathematics. But what about the study of law? By now you have discovered that the law is all around you. It affects virtually every aspect of your life today and will affect your life tomorrow. Just as a practical matter, then, knowledge of the law is useful and important.

Marcus Tullius Cicero, consul and statesman of ancient Rome (106–43 B.C.), believed that no one could be a truly educated person without studying law. However, while U.S. students study government and history, little attention is given in schools to the study of our legal system or rules. Recently, the director of the California State Bar Foundation, Robert Oliver, said: "There is a real need for access to basic legal facts to help people make informed decisions about their lives and avoid possible difficulties." The lack of attention to the law in schools is a mystery to many because of the importance of law all our lives. Perhaps the neglect is unintentional, occurring because of competition for time and resources in the schools.

For most of you, the legal system has been something in the background. As you near graduation from high school, the legal system will grow more prominent, moving from the background to become something affecting your everyday life. In the chapters that follow, we will discuss legal rules dealing with crime, motor vehicle accidents, agreements to buy things, families, business, death, work, apartments, insurance, and much more. You may be able to get by in life without knowing these rules, but if you

do know the law and the interests it protects, you will be much better off.

The law is often exciting, interesting, and clearly relevant to your life, but not always. A problem involving a breach, or violation, of an agreement may only seem interesting to the people involved in the conflict. However, even these conflicts may teach us rules or an approach to a problem from which we can profit.

Why study law? Because you learn how conduct between people is regulated, and you learn your rights and your duties. If you are unconvinced, consider the following situations. The solutions to these everyday problems are found in chapters in this book.

1. You buy a stereo marked for sale "as is," and one week later it breaks. Can you return it for a refund? The legal rules necessary to answer this question are found in Chapter 15.

2. You apply for a job delivering flowers by truck. The employer refuses to hire you, claiming it is because you are seventeen and too young for the job. Is the employer correct? The legal rules necessary to answer this question are found in the Chapter 22 Legal Perspective.

3. You pay $100 to put a $750 racing bicycle on layaway at a store. When you return to purchase the bicycle, you find a sign on the front door of the store declaring "Sorry—we have closed because of bankruptcy." Will you get your $100 back? The legal rules necessary to answer this question are found in Chapter 19.

Have the students look at the title for this section: "How to Use Court Cases." Ask them who needs to know how to use court cases. Allow student volunteers to answer the question; then point out that along with lawyers and judges, many other people, such as paralegals, legal clerks, legal writers, historians, and business law students, need to know how to use court cases.

Have a student volunteer research libraries in your community to find where students can go to locate printed court decisions. Allow the student to report his or her findings to the class.

assuring businesspersons that their agreements will be enforced as long as they are in accordance with the UCC's guidelines. All states (except Louisiana) and the District of Columbia, as well as the Virgin Islands, have adopted the entire Uniform Commercial Code. (Louisiana, because of its French-law tradition, has not adopted all of the Uniform Commercial Code.)

In Chapters 14 and 15, you will read more about how the Uniform Commercial Code dictates the rules regarding sales of goods in our economy.

◆ HOW TO USE COURT CASES

Every time we have made a reference to a judge or a court, we have implicitly been talking about a court case. Because we are a common law country, court cases have a special importance. They often provide precedents for a new case. Any judge, lawyer, or concerned citizen can examine written court cases to find out what the common law is with respect to any particular conflict or dispute. Perhaps as important, court cases are about actual legal problems of real people and businesses. Each case is an individual drama in which the parties seek justice, help, and power. When you read about a real court case, you can see firsthand the legal problems of people in businesses and how the law can be used to resolve those problems.

Each chapter in this book presents to you one case as a real-life illustration of how our courts interpret and apply the law. Throughout the book, other court decisions are referred to in footnotes. You have already been introduced to a footnote about the Supreme Court case involving racial discrimination in education, *Brown v. Board of Education of Topeka*. Additionally, some of the problems at the end of each chapter are based on actual legal disputes. You need to know, then, how court cases are referred to. You need to know the shorthand that is used to identify these court cases. When is a case from the U.S. Supreme Court, and when is it from a state court? What year was the case decided? Where can you find it if you decide to do research on that case?

FEDERAL COURT DECISIONS

Within the federal courts, numerous decisions are published. When they involve actual trials where parties offer evidence, the decisions in those federal trial courts are published in West's *Federal Supplement*. It is abbreviated as F.Supp. If one of the parties at a federal trial does not agree with the decision, that party can appeal the decision to a higher court within the federal system. These courts are called the federal circuit courts of appeal, and their decisions are reported in West's *Federal Reporter*, abbreviated as

Teaching Note

One handy source for finding court cases is *West's Business and Personal Law Handbook of Selected Court Cases.* This handbook includes the actual language of the court, with excerpts from more than 60 significant court cases, all of which are mentioned in *West's Business and Personal Law*. This is a useful and interesting resource for both you and your students.

either F. or F.2d. The "2d" refers to the second series of this reporting system. Opinions handed down by the United States Supreme Court are officially reported in the *United States Reports*, abbreviated as simply U.S. The *United States Reports* are published by the federal government. They include reports of the Supreme Court dating back to the August term of 1791. United States Supreme Court decisions can also be found in West's *Supreme Court Reporter*, abbreviated S.Ct., and the *Lawyer's Edition of the Supreme Court Reports*, abbreviated L.Ed. and L.Ed.2d. Later in this section, in Exhibit 1-4, you will see some sample citations for federal court decisions, as well as other court decisions.

STATE COURT DECISIONS

While very few state trial courts publish their decisions, all state courts of appeals do so. The official reports from these courts appear in volumes called *Reports*, which are numbered consecutively. Some states have decided to save money by letting West Publishing Company publish the decisions of their state courts of appeals. In any event, all state courts of appeals' decisions are printed in West Publishing Company's *Regional Reporters*, which form part of the National Reporter System. Most lawyers and libraries subscribe to West's National Reporter System because it is distributed quickly and widely. The National Reporter System divides the states into the following geographical areas: *Atlantic* (A. or A.2d), *South Eastern* (S.E. or S.E.2d), *South Western* (S.W. or S.W.2d), *North Western* (N.W. or N.W.2d), *North Eastern* (N.E. or N.E.2d), *Southern* (So. or So.2d), and *Pacific* (P. or P.2d). The "2d" after any of the abbreviations in the National Reporter System refers to the second series for that particular reporter.

When decisions from courts of appeals have been published, there is a special way to refer to them. Typically, the following is done:

1. Give the name of the case, such as *Jones v. Adams*.
2. Then give the volume, name, and page of the state's official reporter if it exists.
3. Then give the volume, regional name, and page number of the West's National Reporter.
4. In some cases, the volume, name, and page number of the case from another selected reporter is also given.

◆ **citation**
Information identifying legal research materials. For example, the citation for a court case gives the reporter's volume number, name, and page number.

All of this information makes up a **citation**. A citation gives full, abbreviated details that allow you to find a particular court decision.

In all the cases presented in your text, we provide the citation, the name of the court hearing the case, and the year of the court's decision. Some states, such as those with more than one court of appeals (California, Illinois, and New York, for example) have more than one reporter. Sample citations are listed and explained in Exhibit 1-4.

Extension Activity

Write sample case citations on the board or an overhead transparency. Ask students to read the citations aloud and tell what the abbreviations mean.

VIDEODISC NOTE
Much of the material that is conveyed in the exhibits of *West's Business and Personal Law* is also conveyed in the still frames on the **West Business Law and Legal Environment Videodisc**. For more information and directions for use, please see the Index and Description of Contents for the **West Business Law and Legal Environment Videodisc** that is found in your *Teacher's Resource Binder*.

State Courts[a]

398 MASS. 254, 496 N.E.2d 827 (1986)

N.E. is the abbreviation for West's publication of state court decisions rendered in the northeastern region of the National Reporter System. *2d* indicates that this case was included in the second series of those reports.

Mass. is an abbreviation for *Massachusetts Reports*, Massachusetts' official reports of the decisions of its highest court, the supreme judicial court, which is comparable to other state's supreme courts.

The numbers 398 and 496 refer to reporter's volumes. The numbers 254 and 827 refer to the first pages in those volumes on which this case can be found.

59 Cal. 2d 428, 380 P.2d 644, 30 Cal. Rptr. 4 (1963)

Cal. Rptr. is the abbreviation for West's unofficial reports—titled *California Reporter*—of the decisions of California courts.

Cal. is an abbreviation for the *California Reports*. This is the official state publication for the decisions of the highest California court, the Supreme Court.

828 S.W.2d 56 (Tex.App.–San Antonio 1991)

Tex.App.–San Antonio is an abbreviation denoting Texas' court of appeals. Including the abbreviation with the citation to West's regional reporter makes it clear that this case was decided in Texas at the appellate level in the San Antonio court district.

There is no parallel citation to a state reporter, because Texas discontinued its publication of the decisions of its courts in the 1950s.

a. The case names have been deleted from these citations to emphasize the publications. It should be kept in mind, however, that the name of a case is as important as the specific page numbers in the volumes in which it is found. If a citation is incorrect, the correct citation may be found in a publication's index of case names. The date of a case is also important, both to provide a check on error in citations and because a recent case is likely to have more value as an authority than earlier cases.

EXHIBIT 1-4
SAMPLE COURT CITATIONS

Vocabulary Activity

Allow students to work with partners to write down the definitions of the vocabulary terms in the section titled, "How to Read Court Case Opinions." Also have the students interpret the sample court citations found in the exhibits. Let them know that they will need to know these vocabulary terms and abbreviations in order to look up law cases for future reference in the law library.

Extension Activity

Diagram on the board the relationship of the parties in the trial court process *(plaintiff* v. *defendant)* and the parties to an appeal in an appellate court.

Federal Courts

477 U.S. 131, 106 S.Ct. 2440, 91 L.Ed.2d 110 (1986).

S.Ct. is an abbreviation for the *Supreme Court Reporter,* part of the West Publishing Company's National Reporter System, *L.Ed* is an abbreviation for Lawyers Edition *U.S. Supreme Court Reports.* Both of these publications are private unofficial reports of U.S. Supreme Court decisions.

U.S. is an abbreviation for the *United States Reports.* This is the official federal publication for the decisions of the highest United States court, the Supreme Court.

792 F.2d 1423 (9th Cir. 1986)

9th Cir. is an abbreviation denoting that this case was decided in the United States Court of Appeals for the Ninth Circuit.

F. is an abbreviation for *Federal Reporter,* a part of the West Publishing Company's National Reporter System. This publication reports cases from the United States Court of Appeal.

352 F.Supp. 1105 (S.D.N.Y. 1972)

S.D.N.Y. is an abbreviation indicating that the United States District Court for the Southern District of New York decided this case.

F.Supp. is an abbreviation for *Federal Supplement,* a part of the West Publishing National Reporter System. This publication reports cases from the United States district courts.

Exhibit 1-4
Sample Court Citations (Continued)

◆ How to Read Court Case Opinions

The cases that you will read in this text have been condensed and often reworded from the full text given by the court itself. Sometimes you may have to review an actual court case for a research project or even for an actual legal situation in which you have become involved. The following sections will help you to read and understand what has become known as

◆ **case law** Rules of law announced in court decisions.

case law, or the law that is contained in court opinions.

Case Titles

In the title of a case, such as *Adams v. Jones,* the *v.* stands for *versus,* which means "against." In the trial court, Adams was the plaintiff—the person who filed the suit. Jones was the defendant. But suppose the case is ap-

Lead an oral discussion about the differences in unanimous, majority, concurring, and dissenting opinions. Ask students to tell why each is important.

Ask volunteers to conduct research about each of the Supreme Court justices and write a two- to three-page biography about their legal careers. If typewriters or computers are available, have students key and print the reports.

Take a field trip to the closest law library. Show your students how to use the law library. While there, assign each of them a case to review. Have them turn in a written report on the case and the court's decision.

pealed. On the one hand, the appellate court will sometimes place the name of the party appealing the decision first, so that the case might be called *Jones v. Adams*, if Jones was the party who appealed the case. On the other hand, some appellate courts retain the trial court order of names. It is therefore often impossible to distinguish the plaintiff from the defendant in the title of a reported appellate court decision. You must carefully read the facts of each case to determine the identity of each party. Otherwise, the discussion by the appellate court will be difficult to understand.

TERMINOLOGY

The following terms and phrases are frequently encountered in court opinions and legal publications. Because it is important to understand what is meant by these terms and phrases, we define and discuss them here.

Decisions and Opinions   Most decisions reached by appellate courts are explained in written **opinions**. The opinion contains the court's reasons for its decision, the rules of law that apply, and the judgment. There are four possible types of written opinions for a case decided by an appellate court. When all judges or justices unanimously agree on an opinion, the opinion is written for the entire court and can be deemed a **unanimous opinion**. When there is not a unanimous opinion, a **majority opinion** is written, outlining the views of the majority of the judges or justices deciding the case. Often, a judge or justice who feels strongly about making or emphasizing a point that was not made or emphasized in the unanimous or majority opinion will write a **concurring opinion**. That means the judge or justice agrees (concurs) with the judgment given in the unanimous or majority opinion, but for different reasons. In other than unanimous opinions, a **dissenting opinion** is usually written by a judge or justice who does not agree with the majority. The dissenting opinion is important because it may form the basis of the arguments used years later in overruling the precedential majority opinion.

Judges and Justices   The terms **judge** and **justice** are usually synonymous and represent two designations given to judges in various courts. All members of the United States Supreme Court, for example, are referred to as justices. *Justice* is the formal title usually given to judges of appellate courts, although this is not always the case. In New York, a justice is a trial judge of the trial court (which is called the Supreme Court), and a member of the court of appeals (the state's highest court) is called a judge. The term *justice* is commonly abbreviated to J., and *justices* to JJ. A United States Supreme Court case might refer to Justice Kennedy as Kennedy, J., or to Chief Justice Rehnquist as Rehnquist, C.J.

Appellants and Appellees   The **appellant** is the party who appeals a case to another court or jurisdiction from the court or jurisdiction in which the case was originally brought. (A jurisdiction is an area over which a particular court has authority.) Sometimes, an appellant who ap-

◆ **opinion** The written decision of the court, containing the reason for the decision, the rules of law that apply, and the judgment.

◆ **unanimous opinion** A written court decision on which the judges deciding the case unanimously agree.

◆ **majority opinion** A written court decision outlining the views of the majority of the judges deciding the case.

◆ **concurring opinion** A written opinion of a judge who agrees with the unanimous or majority opinion but feels strongly about making or emphasizing a point that was not made or emphasized in that opinion.

◆ **dissenting opinion** A written opinion of a judge who does not agree with the majority opinion.

◆ **judge or justice** The person who presides over the court.

◆ **appellant** A party who appeals a case to another court.

1. A person must understand the abbreviations that identify which court heard the case, what year it was decided, and in which publication the description can be found.

2. The *United States Reports* (U.S.), West's *Supreme Court Reporter* (S.Ct.), and the *Lawyer's Edition of the Supreme Court Reports* (L.Ed. and L.Ed.2d.) include reports of opinions handed down by the United States Supreme Court.

3. West's *National Report System* divides the states into the Atlantic, South Eastern, South Western, North Eastern, Southern, and Pacific geographical areas.

4. In the trial court the name of the plaintiff is listed first and the defendant second. Although some appellate courts keep the same order, others sometimes place the name of the party appealing the decision first, which could reverse the order.

5. The opinion contains the court's reasons for its decision, the rules of law that apply, and the judgment.

◆ **petitioner** Often used interchangeably with *appellant*. Also refers to a party who initiates a proceeding in equity.

◆ **appellee** A party against whom an appeal is taken.

◆ **respondent** Often used interchangeably with *appellee*. Sometimes refers to a party who responds in a matter in equity.

peals from a judgment is referred to as the **petitioner** (which is also the term used to refer to a party who initiates a proceeding in equity). The **appellee** is the party against whom the appeal is taken. Sometimes, an appellee is referred to as the **respondent**.

Abbreviations   In court opinions, as well as in other areas of this text, certain terms appearing in the names of firms or organizations will often be abbreviated. The terms *Company*, *Incorporated*, and *Limited*, for example, will frequently appear in their abbreviated forms as *Co.*, *Inc.*, and *Ltd.*, respectively, and *Brothers* is commonly abbreviated to *Bros.* Certain organizations or legislative acts are also frequently referred to by their initials or acronyms. In all such cases, to prevent confusion, we will give the complete name of the organization or act upon first mentioning it in a given section of the text.

A SAMPLE COURT CASE

Knowing how to find and read a court opinion is an important step in legal research. A further step involves "briefing" the case to help understand it. Legal researchers routinely brief cases by summarizing and reducing the opinions to their most important elements.

There is one case at the end of each chapter in this text except Chapter 6. Each case has been analyzed and briefed by the authors. The essentials of each case are presented in a format consisting of four sections: *Facts*, *Issue*, *Decision*, and *Reason*. This format is illustrated in the sample court case below. Notes in the margins explain the different kinds of information that can be found in each section.

◆ CHECKING YOUR PROGRESS

1. How can someone who examines written court cases tell which court handled the case?

2. What publications carry opinions handed down by the United States Supreme Court?

3. What are the geographical regions in West's National Reporter System?

4. Why is it not always possible to distinguish the plaintiff from the defendant in a citation of an appellate case?

5. List the general information that is included in an appellate court opinion.

◆ A CASE IN POINT ◆

STAMBOVSKY v. ACKLEY
New York, Appellate Division, Second Department, 1991.
169 A.D.2d 254
572 N.Y.S.2d 672

⎱ 1
⎱ 2
⎱ 3
⎱ 4

FACTS   Jeffrey Stambovsky, the plaintiff, was horrified to discover that the house he contracted to buy was widely believed to be possessed by ghosts. These ghosts had reportedly been seen by the defendant seller and members of her family on numerous occasions over the nine years prior to selling the house. The defendant had reported the presence of ghosts in both a national publication, *Readers' Digest*, and the local press. The plaintiff buyer, a resident of New York City, did not know about the "reputation" of the house in Nyack Village where the house was located. Plaintiff brought this lawsuit to rescind (get out) of the contract, to buy the house, and to have his down payment of $33,000 returned to him. The New York trial court dismissed the plaintiff's lawsuit before the trial, holding that the doctrine of *caveat emptor* (let the buyer beware) applied to real estate transactions and Stambovsky was expected to investigate any facts important to him in a sale. Stambovsky appealed. On appeal, Stambovsky argued that the seller, Ackley, knew about the ghosts, and had a responsibility to tell him the house was haunted.   ⎱ 5

ISSUE   Does New York law require that a seller of a house report to a potential buyer that a house is haunted as an exception to the common law doctrine of *caveat emptor*?   ⎱ 6

DECISION   The appellate court reversed the trial court and held the plaintiff had a right to pursue his lawsuit and have a trial.   ⎱ 7

REASON   While the court agreed with the defendant that the plaintiff did not have a cause of action at common law, they held that equitable doctrines applied when a seller fails to tell a buyer critical facts regarding the subject matter of a contract. Rescission of a contract is an equitable remedy available when a contract is not "fair and open." "The unusual facts of this case clearly warrant a grant of equitable relief to Stambovsky." The defendant also argued that the existence or non-existence of ghosts is not a material fact because the existence of ghosts has never been proved. The court responded with some humor, "From the perspective of a person in the position of plaintiff herein, a very practical problem arises with respect to the discovery of a paranormal phenomenon: "Who you gonna' call?" as the title song to the movie 'Ghostbusters' asks." The court applying yet another equitable doctrine, called *estoppel*, held that a "defendant seller [who had] deliberately fostered the public belief that her home was possessed" should not be able to now deny it because it is to her legal advantage. Furthermore, although the existence of   ⎱ 8

Teaching A Case In Point

Read
Before reading this *A Case in Point* feature, ask the students the following questions: How many of you have ever heard that a house was "haunted"? Do you think the law counts for haunted houses? What do you think would happen if the buyer of a home sued because his/her new home was haunted? Then read aloud this *A Case in Point* feature to the class.

Discuss
Use the following questions to stimulate a class discussion: What was the result of this suit? Did the court assert that the house truly was haunted? Why then did the court reverse the trial court decision? Do you feel that this decision was fair? Why or why not?

Teaching Note

This case is included in the *West's Business and Personal Law Handbook of Selected Court Cases.*

◆ A CASE IN POINT (CONTINUED) ◆

ghosts may not be a fact, the reputation of the house as haunted certainly is a fact. "The impact of the reputation thus created goes to the very essence of the bargain between the parties, greatly impairing both the value of the property and its potential for resale." The court, recognizing it was creating new law, justified its holding, "where fairness and common sense dictate that an exception should be created, the evolution of the law should not be stifled by rigid application of a legal maxim [caveat emptor]." — 8

1. The name of the case is *Stambovsky v. Ackley*. Stambovsky is the plaintiff; and Ackley and another defendant, Ellis Realty, not included in the title are the defendants.
2. The court deciding the case was the New York Appellate Division, an intermediate level court in the New York state court system.
3. This citation is from the New York state reporter and indicates that this case can be found in Volume 169 of the Appellate Division, Second Series, on page 254.
4. This citation is a parallel citation to a West's regional reporter and indicates this case can also be found in Volume 572 of the New York Supplement, Second Series, on page 672.
5. The *Facts* section identifies the plaintiff and the defendant, describes the events leading up to this lawsuit, the allegations made by the plaintiff, the defendant's response to these allegations, and (since this case is an appellate court decision) the trial court's decision and the party appealing that decision. The appealing party's contention on appeal is also included here.
6. The *Issue* section presents the central issue (or issues) to be decided by the court. In this case, the appellate court face with an issue raised by the plaintiff (Stambovsky) on appeal. Cases often involve more that one issue.
7. The *Decision* section, as the term itself indicates, contains the court's decision on the issue or issues before the court. The decision reflects the opinion of the majority of the judges or justices hearing the case. Decisions by appellate courts are frequently phrased in reference to the lower court's decision. That is, the appellate court may "affirm" the lower court's ruling or "reverse" it. In this particular case, the decision by the appellate court reversed part of the judgement of the lower court.
8. The *Reason* section indicates what relevant laws and judicial principles were applied in forming the particular conclusion arrived at in the case at bar. ("before the court"). In this case, the common law doctrine of caveat emptor was changed by the courts application of equitable doctrines.

In order to help students review what they have learned in Chapter 1, you might wish to:
1. Have a student volunteer, or volunteers, read aloud the Chapter Summary.
2. Allow the students to work with partners to complete the *Using Legal Language* activity.
3. Assign the *Checking for Comprehension* exercise as homework.

4. Allow the students to work in small groups to complete the *Applying Legal Concepts* activities.
5. As a class, complete the *Applying the Law* activities. (Please note that you may have to help students with vocabulary so that they adequately understand all the *Applying the Law* material.)

In order to check student mastery of chapter concepts, you may wish to use the Chapter 1 test that is found in your *Teacher's Resource Binder* or use WESTEST computerized testing for Chapter 1.

CHAPTER REVIEW 1

 ## SUMMARY

FROM WHERE DID AMERICAN LAW COME?

1. *Common law*—Common law originated in England with the creation of the king's courts. It consists of past judicial decisions and reasoning. U.S. common law is based on English common law traditions. The common law applies the doctrine of *stare decisis*—the rule of precedent.
2. *Constitutional law*—Constitutional law is law as expressed by federal and state constitutions. The U.S. Constitution is the supreme law of the land.
3. *Statutory law*—Statutory laws are created by federal, state, and local governing bodies.
4. *Administrative law*—Regulations, orders, rules, and decisions of administrative agencies make up administrative law.

WE HAVE AN ADVERSARY SYSTEM OF JUSTICE

1. *Adversary system*—In the adversary system, parties to legal actions are opponents. Opponents are responsible for presenting all facts and legal theories to support their positions. The judge is a neutral participant.
2. *Inquisitorial system*—The inquisitorial system allows judges to investigate, question witnesses, and seek out evidence independent of the parties to a lawsuit.

THE TYPES OF LAW THAT YOU WILL LEARN ABOUT

Criminal versus Civil Law

1. *Criminal law*—Criminal law is concerned with wrongs against society. Society, represented by the government, seeks to impose a penalty.

2. *Civil law*—Civil law concerns the duties that exist between persons or between persons and the government. The injured party tries to make the other party perform a duty or pay damages.

State versus Federal Law

1. *State law*—State law consists of state constitutions, statutes originated by the state legislatures, regulations created by state agencies, and decisions of state courts.
2. *Federal law*—Federal law consists of the U.S. Constitution, statutes originated by Congress, treaties and presidential orders, rules and regulations created by federal administrative agencies, and decisions of federal courts.

Procedural versus Substantive Law

1. *Procedural law*—Legal rules for processing civil and criminal cases through the court system.
2. *Substantive law*—Law that defines duties, establishes rights, and prohibits wrongs.

Actions at Law versus Actions in Equity

1. *Actions at law*—Historically, an action at law took place in a king's court. Basically, the only remedy available was money.
2. *Actions in equity*—Historically, an action in equity took place in a chancellor's court when a remedy other than money was sought.
3. Today, in the United States, there is little distinction between courts of law and courts of equity in most states. However, some procedural differences exist between matters at law and matters in equity. Equitable matters include family law and estates.

Modern American Business Law

Laws governing the business world are referred to as commercial law, or business law. The most important source of commercial law in

---

1–D, 2–B, 3–G, 4–I, 5–C, 6–F, 7–H, 8–A, 9–E, 10–J

Checking for Comprehension (Answers)

1. Constitutions, statutes, and governmental administrative agencies serve as the basis for law in the United States.
2. *Stare decisis* is a Latin phrase meaning "to stand on decided cases." In the king's courts of medieval England, it became customary for judges to refer to past decisions (precedents) in deciding cases involving similar issues. Over time, because of the application of the doctrine of *stare decisis* to issues that came before the courts, a body of jurisprudence was formed that came to be known as the "common law"— because it was common to the entire English realm. Common law was applied in the American colonies prior to the War of Independence and was adopted by the American states following the Revolution. Common law continues to be applied today in all cases except those falling under specific state or federal

statutory law. The doctrine of *stare decisis* is fundamental to the development of our legal tradition because without the acceptance and application of this doctrine, the evolution of any objective legal concepts—i.e., a legal "tradition" would have been impossible.

3. Since the common law has been adopted in most jurisdictions by state statutes, and since legislatures have given common law the same force and effect as statutes, judges should technically have the same authority to overrule common law or statutory law. Most courts and legislatures, however, do not take such a view. Courts do not always treat common law with the same deference as statutory law because common law is judge-made law, and therefore the courts feel that it can be changed by judges, whereas statutory law, having been created by the legislature, should only be interpreted, not changed.

4. The major difference between the adversary and inquisitorial systems of law is the role the judges play. In the adversary system judges are neutral and generally passive participants in the courtroom process. Judges take a more active role in the inquisitorial system, in which they investigate, question witnesses, and seek their own evidence.

5. Civil law deals with conflicts between two individuals. In criminal law one of the parties is society as a whole. Court action is brought by the injured person in a civil case and by a government representative

in a criminal case. The results sought are usually performance or money in civil cases; fines or imprisonment may be the end result of a criminal action.

6. Substantive law can exist alone; however, procedural law must be considered if any substantive law is brought to court.

7. A code is a collection of statutes or rules on a particular subject. Sets of commercial law codes have been developed to avoid different rules (i.e., rules in each state) for the same activity.

8. The Uniform Commercial Code encourages more business transactions by assuring businesspeople that their agreements will be enforced as long as they are in accordance with the UCC's guidelines. Louisiana is the only state that has not adopted the entire UCC. Louisiana law is based on French, rather than English, tradition.

9. This would be a civil proceeding because the store owner has a duty to customers to provide a safe place for them to shop. Joe was injured because of the negligence of the store

the United States is the Uniform Commercial Code (UCC). The UCC has been adopted by all the states (although only in part by Louisiana).

◆ USING LEGAL LANGUAGE

Directions: Match each term with the statement that best defines that term.

1. administrative law
2. adversary system
3. appellant
4. case law
5. citation
6. dissenting opinion
7. equity
8. precedent
9. private law
10. procedural law

A. rules of law announced in court decisions

B. a legal system in which parties to legal actions are opponents and are responsible for bringing the facts and law related to their case before the court

C. a branch of law supplying special rules and procedures when legal rules are inadequate to promote justice and fairness

D. law relating to the rights and duties of private persons and groups in relation to each other

E. a party who appeals a case to another court

F. the written opinion of a judge who does not agree with the majority opinion

G. a court decision that provides an example or authority for deciding later cases involving identical or similar facts

H. the branch of public law concerned with the powers and actions of administrative agencies

I. information identifying legal research materials

J. legal rules for processing civil and criminal cases through the court

◆ CHECKING FOR COMPREHENSION

1. In addition to common law, what three sources serve as the basis for law in the United States?

2. In the chapter we state that the doctrine of *stare decisis* "became a cornerstone of the English and American judicial systems." What does *stare decisis* mean, and why has this doctrine been so funda-

mental to the development of our legal tradition?

3. Should judges have the same authority to overrule statutory law as they have to overrule common law? Explain.

4. What is the major difference between the adversary and the inquisitorial systems of law?

Applying the Law . . . You Be the Judge (Answers)

1. The court agreed with Ms. Flagiello that the doctrine of charitable immunity be overturned. The common law rule had been created to encourage charitable hospitals to serve patients who otherwise were unable to get hospital care. Since the origin of the rule, charitable hospitals have grown into large institutions, serving both paying and nonpaying patients. The court noted that the nature of these hospitals and the services they provide had changed fundamentally since the rule's creation. The court held that all hospitals should be expected to treat patients with care, and carelessness should not be excused because it occurred at a charitable hospital. "[W]hen a rule [is] conceived in error or when the times and circumstances have so changed as to render it an instrument of injustice," the policy of case law can be changed by the court.

2. When not protected by a constitutional provision, rights may be abolished by statute. The statute was constitutional even though it destroyed a cause of action that existed under common law, as no one has a vested right to the continuation of a common law rule unless the common law rule is guaranteed by a constitution. The cause of action for alienation of affections was not protected by any constitution and therefore could be abolished by the legislature. Thus, the court decided in Pressnell's favor.

3. Sandoval won. Gabel argued that her lawsuit was based on the attorney-client contract, and that a four-year statute of limitations for written contract actions should apply. However, the court held that the lawsuit was a malpractice action, and it was dismissed because it was filed after the two-year statute of limitations period for malpractice actions in Texas. This case is ironic, as Gabel's claim was based on Sandoval's own initial failure to observe a statute of limitations.

5. Describe two differences between civil law and criminal law.

6. Can procedural law and substantive law exist independently? Explain.

7. What is a code and why were uniform codes developed?

8. How does the Uniform Commercial Code (UCC) encourage more business transactions? Has it been adopted by all states? Why?

9. Joe Caldor entered a hardware store to purchase an item. While he was there, a mounted display shelf holding gallon cans of paint fell on him. He suffered numerous injuries as a result and could not work for three months. He sued the owner of the hardware store for damages. Explain why this is a civil, and not a criminal, proceeding.

10. Assume that you want to read the entire court opinion in the case of *U.S.* v. *Sun and Sand Imports, Ltd.*, 725 F.2d 184 (2d Cir. 1984). The case deals with the transportation, via interstate commerce, of flammable sleepwear for children in violation of the Flammable Fabrics Act. Explain specifically where you would find the court's opinion.

◆ APPLYING LEGAL CONCEPTS

1. Diagram the relationship of the parties in the U.S. legal adversary system and list the role each plays.

2. Outline the sources of American law. List at least two relevant points about each type of law.

◆ APPLYING THE LAW . . . YOU BE THE JUDGE

1. Mary Flagiello was a paying patient at the Pennsylvania Hospital, a non-profit charitable hospital. She was seriously injured through the carelessness of two hospital employees. Under Pennsylvania law, Ms. Flagiello clearly would have had a successful lawsuit against the hospital had it been a usual profit making hospital. However, because the hospital was non-profit, her lawsuit was dismissed under a well-established common law doctrine, called charitable immunity. This doctrine held that because charitable hospitals serve a great public need, they should not be held responsible for the carelessness of the hospital staff. Ms. Flagiello argued that the Pennsylvania supreme court had the right and the responsibility to allow her lawsuit. She argued that charitable immunity did not make sense in 20th century America. Did the court find for Ms. Flagiello, or was the court bound by precedent? [*Flagiello v. The Pennsylvania Hospital*, 417 Pa. 486, 208 A.2d 193 (1965)]

2. Consuelo Gabel sued her attorney, Ruben Sandoval, claiming that he had failed to file a civil rights lawsuit on time, causing her to lose her right to sue. An action against an attorney for failure to act in a careful fashion is called a malpractice lawsuit. Gabel, however, waited more than two years to file her malpractice suit against Sandoval. Sandoval claimed the lawsuit should be dismissed against him because Gabel waited too long to make her claim. What was the result? [*Gabel v. Sandoval*, 648 S.W.2d 398 (1983)]

Prereading Activity

Read aloud the preamble to the United States Constitution and Article III, Section 1 (see the Resource Center). Ask students to tell in their own words what these passages mean. Discuss the need for federal judicial powers.

Mastery Objectives

By the end of this chapter, students should be able to:
- Tell the Constitutional principles for government
- Explain the judicial review process
- Define federalism
- Identify the qualifications and terms of appointment for justices of the United States Supreme Court
- Delineate freedoms of speech and religion

Chapter
2
Law and Individual Rights

Chapter 2
Resources and Assignment Guide

Tests
Chapter 2 Test *TRB*
Chapter 2 WESTEST Computerized Testing

Activity Sheets
Reviewing Legal Concepts 2 *TRB*
Enrichment Activity 2 *TRB*

Handbook of Selected Court Cases
Lee v. *Weisman*
Hazelwood School District v. *Kuhlmeier*

Student Activity Workbook
Chapter 2 Activities

**West's Business Law and Legal
Environment Videodisc**
Still Frames and Motion Segments as shown

*"The American constitution is the most wonderful work ever struck off at a
given time by the brain and purpose of man."*
William Gladstone, 1809–1898
British prime minister, four times between 1868 and 1894

Imagine a country in which police officers could stop you, throw you in jail, and conveniently lose track of you. Your frantic parents and friends would find no trace of you and would think you had been kidnapped. You might languish in a jail cell for months before you were brought before a judge and accused of some crime, which might simply be speaking out negatively against the current government.

Such a scenario does not happen in the United States because our Constitution protects individual rights. Because of rights spelled out in the Constitution, you cannot be thrown in jail without being charged with a crime. You cannot be prevented from speaking your mind, from practicing the religion of your choice, or from requesting that your government correct a wrong that you might think it has committed.

This nation has a long tradition of protecting the rights of individuals. It also has a long tradition of a sense of fair play. These traditions are embodied in the supreme law of the land—the U.S. Constitution, including its twenty-seven amendments. The U.S. Constitution is an important part of the American legal system for you, as an individual, for it gives you many ways to question both the law and the conduct of your government officials. While our legal system recognizes the right of government to create laws to protect and regulate conduct, it also recognizes the right of individuals to be free from government control in certain situations.

There are often conflicts between the desire of governmental officials to regulate our behavior for the good of the country and each individual's desire to do what she or he wishes. No one questions the government's right to make a law against people screaming "fire" in a crowded movie theater. If someone did that, many people might get hurt during the stampede out of the building. But what about a law that puts restrictions on advertising? How much can the government regulate commercial speech, such as advertising? After all, the First Amendment to the U.S. Constitution guarantees freedom of speech.

Much of what you will read about in this chapter has to do with the First Amendment and the other amendments that are part of the **Bill of Rights**. The Bill of Rights is our major source of protection for individual rights. The Bill of Rights also affects how businesspeople can conduct their businesses. The regulation of advertising is just one aspect of this area.

◆ **Bill of Rights**
The first ten amendments to the Constitution; protects the individual from various types of interference by the federal government.

Multicultural Perspectives

Have students peruse periodicals to discover applications of law in other countries that differ from those of the United States, especially cases in which persons are placed in jail for political reasons. Discuss some of the cases in class.

Teaching Note

The complete text of the Bill of Rights is included in the Constitution, which is found in the Resource Center at the back of this book. You might wish to have a student volunteer read the Bill of Rights to the class at this point.

31

Critical Thinking Activity

Have your students write an essay on why the U.S. Constitution seems to remain applicable to our lifestyle even though it was written in 1787. A class discussion may evolve from these essays.

Ethical Concern

Prompt a discussion on the First Amendment guarantees of freedom of speech versus the censoring of music, books, and videos.

Extension Activity

Call on students to read aloud the amendments to the U.S. Constitution. (See the Resource Center.) Discuss the rights and/or restrictions detailed in each amendment.

32

In this chapter, you will see that the Constitution not only sets forth the powers of government, but also places limits on those powers. Legal cases that involve the United States Constitution are interesting and extremely important. They often reflect an attempt by the courts to balance governmental power with the rights of the individual.

◆ THE UNITED STATES CONSTITUTION

You have seen the word *constitution* a number of times. A constitution, formally defined, is a declaration of fundamental principles by which a nation is governed. As you saw in Chapter 1, the United States Constitution is the supreme law of the land. No state may pass a law that conflicts with the Constitution, nor may the United States Congress. In the U.S. Constitution, you will find the powers of each of the three branches of government—executive, legislative, and judicial. Moreover, the Constitution also limits the powers of these branches of government. By limiting the power of government, the Constitution provides legal protection for your rights as an individual. Among constitutions throughout the world, the United States Constitution is unique. It is the world's oldest written single-document constitution that is still being used.

The Preamble to the Constitution includes the following words: "We the People of the United States . . . do ordain and establish this constitution for the United States of America." It is the people who have formed the government in the United States. The people are the only source of governmental power in this country. Such power is not generated by kings, queens, or some outside force. You can read the full Constitution, including its amendments, in the Resource Center. There you will also see our notes about what the Constitution means. Here, we will look more closely at two important aspects of the Constitution: the way it limits governmental power and its underlying assumptions about people's natural rights.

LIMITING GOVERNMENT

For the most part, the limits on government are found in the Bill of Rights, the first ten amendments to the Constitution. The Bill of Rights puts limits on the behavior of politicians, public officials, police officers, and bureaucrats.

But not everybody agrees on the meaning of the words in the Constitution. Therefore, some group of individuals must decide the meaning of those words. That group is our judiciary, or court system. When you as an individual believe that your constitutional rights have been violated, you can go to our court system. You can, for example, challenge a public official because you believe she or he violated the Constitution. It is the courts

Legal Focus Case Problem

Have a student volunteer read aloud this Legal Focus Case Problem. Remind students that they can use the Legal Focus features as review tools when studying for tests.

Discussion Starter

Read aloud the second paragraph of the Declaration of Independence: "We hold these truths to be self-evident, that all Men are created equal . . . the Pursuit of Happiness. . . ." Have students discuss situations that occur today that do not comply with this right.

Teaching with the Videodisc

The still frames listed below from the **West's Business Law and Legal Environment Videodisc** can be used with this chapter. To access this material, use the bar codes or the frame numbers included in the Videodisc Instructor's Manual found in the *TRB*.

Powers Granted by the Constitution: National Government
Powers Granted by the Constitution: National and State Governments
Powers Granted by the Constitution: State Governments
National Powers Denied by the Constitution
National and State Powers Denied by the Constitution
State Powers Denied by the Constitution

Law and Individual Rights   33

that have the power to determine whether or not an action of government is constitutional.

LEGAL FOCUS - CASE PROBLEM

In 1952, the United Steel Workers Union threatened a national strike to stop production at the nation's steel mills. At that time, the country was involved in the Korean War. President Harry S Truman believed that the steelworkers' strike would impair his ability to conduct the war efficiently. He ordered the secretary of commerce to seize and operate our country's steel mills. There seems to be nothing in the Constitution that directly gives any president the power to take over private manufacturing businesses in the United States. Therefore, was the seizure order within the president's power? That is what the Supreme Court had to decide.[1] The Supreme Court held "that this seizure order cannot stand." It listed the following reasons:

1. Every president's power must derive from either an act of Congress or the Constitution. The Supreme Court found nothing in either of these to give the president the power to take over the steel mills.
2. Just before the seizure, Congress had refused to pass a law authorizing presidential seizure whenever there was a labor dispute.
3. The order was not a legitimate exercise of the president's military power as commander in chief of the armed forces. Labor disputes should be handled by the nation's lawmakers, if anybody.

So there you have it. The United States Supreme Court can say no even to the president of the United States. As we discuss further on page 35, the United States Supreme Court can also tell the United States Congress, any state legislature, and federal and state administrative agencies that a law it has passed or an action it has taken is unconstitutional. The United States Constitution is the supreme law of the land.

CONSTITUTIONAL LAW AND NATURAL RIGHTS

The second paragraph of the Declaration of Independence begins with this sentence: "We hold these Truths to be self-evident, that all Men are created equal, that they are endowed by their Creator with certain inalienable Rights, that among these are Life, Liberty, and the Pursuit of Happiness. . . ."

Our nation's founders were referring to inalienable—or natural—rights. **Natural rights** are *inherent*, meaning that they cannot be taken away from a person and are beyond the power of government to grant or deny. The natural rights to life, liberty, and the pursuit of happiness are based on **natural law**.

◆ **natural rights**
Rights that are beyond the power of government to grant or deny.

◆ **natural law**
Basic moral law that is consistent with nature, applies to all persons, does not change, and lasts for all time.

---

1. *Youngstown Sheet and Tube Co. v. Sawyer*, 343 U.S. 579, 72 S.Ct. 863, 96 L.Ed. 1153, (1952).

Reteaching Activity

Have students make a list of natural rights and a list of constitutional rights. Then give an oral quiz with examples of actions having legal ramifications, and ask students to identify whether a natural or constitutional law was broken because of an action. For example, someone robbed you at gunpoint, someone stole your unlocked car, someone burned a cross in your yard, someone did not pay his or her taxes, your neighbor asked you to turn down your music.

Legal Focus
Case Example

Read the Legal Focus example to the class. Students might be encouraged to discuss with their parents the *United States* v. *Nixon* ruling and the Watergate scandal and ask: Did the outcome of the *United States* v. *Nixon* strengthen their confidence in our system of government? Why or why not?

Extension Activity

Have a volunteer or a group of volunteers research the life and works of John Locke. What were the most important ideas developed by Locke? How can the influence of Locke's ideas be seen in the Declaration of Independence and the U.S. Constitution? Ask the volunteer or volunteers to prepare written or oral presentations of their findings.

Enrichment

Ask volunteers to do research about the Watergate coverup. Have them write a report about the activities leading up to surrender of the tapes.

Natural law can be traced back to ancient Greece. The Greek philosopher Aristotle (384–322 B.C.) believed that natural law has the same force everywhere and does not depend on individual situations, cultures, or history. A law prohibiting murder, for example, does not reflect the values accepted by a particular society at a particular time. Rather, it is based on a universally accepted moral feeling that murder is wrong. To murder someone is thus a violation of natural law.

Much of U.S. **constitutional law** is based on natural law as presented by John Locke, an important English political philosopher who wrote in the late 1600s. He argued that no one is born with an obligation to obey government rulers—that all individuals are born free, equal, and independent. He was probably the one who first stated that everyone has the natural right to life, liberty, and property. (The writers of the Declaration of Independence changed that to life, liberty, and happiness.) Natural rights put limits on what government can do. You can see many of these limits in the Bill of Rights.

Much of constitutional law involves restricting the power of government authority. Our Constitution includes the *principle of limited government*, which means that government can only do what the people allow it to do. The idea of limited government is often called the *rule of law*. Government officers, themselves, are never above the law. Government, which refers to the *individuals* who form it, must always obey the laws found in the Constitution. In other words, no person is above the law, including the president of the United States. When a president violates the law, he must pay the consequences. Whether the president of the United States had the right to refuse to give information to a federal trial court arose as an issue during the so-called Watergate scandal.

◆ **constitutional law** A fundamental law that spells out the general organization, powers, and limits of a government.

◀ LEGAL FOCUS – CASE EXAMPLE

In 1973, evidence came to light that President Richard M. Nixon had been involved in covering up a criminal activity that had occurred during his reelection campaign in 1972. When one part of the government wanted Nixon's documents, he refused. The United States Supreme Court, in one of its most famous constitutional cases, *United States v. Nixon,*[2] ruled against the president. He was forced to surrender information in the form of tape recordings that had been made by concealed microphones in various White House offices and in the executive office building. On the tape for June 23, 1972, Nixon was heard approving a plan to use the Central Intelligence Agency to block the FBI investigation.

2.   418 U.S. 683, 94 S.Ct. 3090, 41 L.Ed.2d 1039 (1974); *certiorari* denied 431 U.S. 933, 97 S.Ct. 2641, 53 L.Ed.2d 250 (1977); rehearing denied 433 U.S. 916, 97 S.Ct. 2992, 53 L.Ed.2d 1103 (1977).

Lead a discussion about the importance of judicial review. Where would the power to interpret laws possibly lie if the judiciary did not have the power?

 JUDICIAL REVIEW

The power of **judicial review** refers to the courts' ability to decide whether an act of a legislature does or does not violate the Constitution. At the national level, if the U.S. Supreme Court believes that a federal or state law violates the U.S. Constitution, that law is declared *unconstitutional.* Such a law no longer has any validity or legitimacy—it is as if it did not exist.

Suppose, for example, that your state passes a law that specifically allows state police officers to monitor telephone conversations (wiretapping) without formally obtaining permission from a judge. The U.S. Supreme Court might strike down that law as unconstitutional because it violates the Fourth Amendment to the Constitution. What if you had been convicted of a crime based on evidence obtained through the illegal wiretapping of your phone lines? Your conviction would probably be overturned because of the unconstitutional nature of the law that allowed tapping your phone.

The Constitution does not *explicitly* state that the principle of judicial review should be put into practice. Most constitutional scholars do believe, however, that the framers *meant* that the federal courts should have that power. In the 1803 case of *Marbury v. Madison*, judicial review became part of the United States' system of government. The Supreme Court ruled for the first time that part of an act passed by the Congress was unconstitutional. Chief Justice John Marshall declared that it is "the province and duty of the Judiciary department to say what the law is."

◆ **judicial review**
The power of the federal courts to determine whether a particular law violates the Constitution.

Ask these questions to help the students discuss the opinion of Constitutional scholars that the Framers meant the federal courts to have the power of judicial review: How would you defend or attack this opinion? If the Framers intended the federal courts to have that power, why didn't they include an explicit statement of that power in the Constitution? Why is this an important power for the courts?

Extension Activity

Have students look up information about each of the Framers of the Constitution. Have them write a one- to two-page biography about each. Discuss whether each would have wanted judicial review power as a major principle of the Constitution.

◆ **FEDERALISM**

When you enter the business world, you may look to the U.S. Constitution for what you can and cannot do. More likely, though, the nuts-and-bolts restrictions on your business will be found in the laws of your state, county, and municipality.

Clearly, there are many layers of laws in the United States: some from the federal government (the Constitution and laws passed by Congress), some from the state government (the state constitution and the state congress), and some from your city (the rules and regulations passed by your city council and various agencies). If you live in Texas, you are governed by the laws of Texas and of the national government. That is because you live under a federal system of government, or **federalism**. The national, or federal, government coexists with various state governments.

During the framing of our Constitution, the states feared too much centralized control. The Constitution therefore allows for numerous states' rights. Under our federal system of government, some powers belong to the federal government, while the others belong to the fifty states. The result is that there are over 80,000 governmental units in the United States

◆ **federalism** A system in which two or more levels of government direct the affairs of the same people in the same location.

Read

Ask the students to read this *Law in Action* feature to themselves. Then have volunteers review the specifics of the *Marbury* v. *Madison* case so that all students understand the situation clearly.

Discuss

Encourage the students to discuss the feature by asking: How do you imagine Chief Justice Marshall must have felt when this case came before the Supreme Court? What problems might either decision have created for Marshall and the Supreme Court? Do you imagine that this dilemma affected the decision that Marshall helped to make?

Review

Use these questions to help the students review the *Law in Action* feature. What decision did the Supreme Court make regarding Jefferson and Madison's refusal to deliver the commission intended for Marbury? What other more far-reaching decision did Marshall express for the Supreme Court?

Extension Activity

Have a few students write a report on Thomas Jefferson and John Adams. Explain to them that both men worked together in forming the Declaration of Independence, then later in life both became presidents of the United States. Refer to how they worked against each other on the issue of the national government, yet worked together on something as important as the Declaration of Independence.

Law in Action

LEGAL ISSUE: *MARBURY V. MADISON* (1803)

John Adams was president of the United States from 1797 to 1801. He supported the idea of a strong national government. In 1800, he lost his bid for reelection, and Thomas Jefferson won. Adams thought that after Jefferson became president his supporters would weaken the power of the national government by giving the states more rights. He also feared that Jefferson's supporters would be anti-business. So during the final hours of his presidency, he worked feverishly to "pack" the judiciary with loyal supporters who favored a strong national government. He made what have become known as "midnight appointments" just before Jefferson took office.

All the judicial appointments had to be certified and delivered. The task of delivery fell on Adams's secretary of state, John Marshall. Out of the fifty-nine midnight appointments, Marshall delivered only forty-two. He assumed that the remaining seventeen would be sent out by Jefferson's new secretary of state, James Madison. The new administration refused to cooperate in packing the judiciary, however. Jefferson would not deliver the remaining commissions.

William Marbury, along with three others to whom the commissions had not been delivered, decided to sue. The suit was brought directly to the Supreme Court. The plaintiffs sought a *writ of mandamus*, an order issued by a court to force a government official to do something. The Supreme Court was authorized to issue such writs by the Judiciary Act of 1789.

Coincidentally, John Marshall had stepped down as Adams's secretary of state only to become chief justice of the Supreme Court. He was now in a position to decide the case

for which he was in part responsible.[3]

Marshall was faced with a dilemma: If he ordered the appointments delivered, the new secretary of state could simply refuse. The Court had no way to force action, because it had no police force. Also, Congress was controlled by the Jeffersonian Republicans. It might impeach Marshall for such an action.[4] But if Marshall simply allowed Secretary of State Madison to do as he wished, the Court's power would be severely eroded.

Marshall stated for the unanimous Court that Jefferson and Madison had acted incorrectly in refusing to deliver Marbury's commission. Marshall also stated, however, that the Supreme Court did not have the authority to hear this particular case, because the section of the law that gave it such authority was unconstitutional.

The Judiciary Act of 1789 specified that the Supreme Court could issue writs of mandamus as part of its authority. Marshall didn't agree and pointed out that Article III of the Constitution, which spells out the Supreme Court's authority, does not mention writs of mandamus. In other words, Congress did not have the right to expand the Court's jurisdiction, so this section of the Judiciary Act of 1789 was unconstitutional and hence void.

With this decision, the power of the Supreme Court was enlarged. The decision stated: "A law repugnant [offensive] to the Constitution is void."

---

3. Today, any justice who has been involved in the issue before the Court would probably disqualify himself or herself because of a conflict of interest.
4. In fact, in 1805, Congress did impeach Supreme Court Justice Samuel Chase, a Federalist, though he was not convicted.

We have a federal system of government. Around the world, however, there are other systems of government, such as a unitary system and a confederal system. The confederal system, or confederation, is a league of independent states. A unitary system is a centralized system in which state and/or local governments exercise only those powers given by the central government. In France a modified form of the unitary system is in effect. Ask several students to learn more about the French system of government. Then ask those students to share their findings with the class.

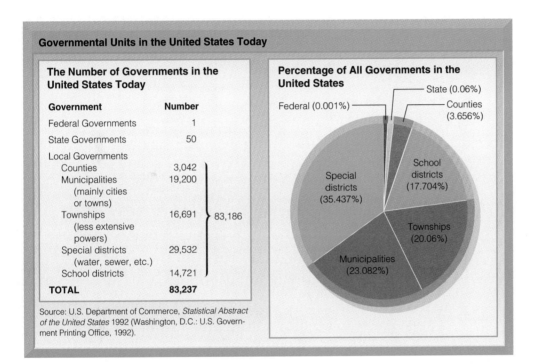

Governmental Units in the United States Today

The Number of Governments in the United States Today

Government	Number	
Federal Governments	1	
State Governments	50	
Local Governments		
Counties	3,042	
Municipalities (mainly cities or towns)	19,200	
Townships (less extensive powers)	16,691	83,186
Special districts (water, sewer, etc.)	29,532	
School districts	14,721	
TOTAL	**83,237**	

Source: U.S. Department of Commerce, *Statistical Abstract of the United States* 1992 (Washington, D.C.: U.S. Government Printing Office, 1992).

Percentage of All Governments in the United States

- Federal (0.001%)
- State (0.06%)
- Counties (3.656%)
- Special districts (35.437%)
- School districts (17.704%)
- Townships (20.06%)
- Municipalities (23.082%)

EXHIBIT 2-1
GOVERNMENTAL UNITS IN THE UNITED STATES TODAY

today, as can be seen in Exhibit 2-1. These more than 80,000 separate governments are run by over half a million elected and appointed government officials.

Our federal system divides authority between the national and state governments through our written constitution. All levels of government have the power to pass laws that directly influence the people. The federal government's laws are supreme. But the federal government cannot overrule state and local laws unless they conflict with a federal law.

Exhibit 2-2 lists the powers granted by the Constitution to the federal government and to the state government. In the center of that diagram, you can see the powers that are *concurrent*, which means they are granted to both federal and state governments.

Whenever there is a conflict between a state and the federal government, it is usually the United States Supreme Court that settles the conflict. The question of whether or not a conflict in law exists is a difficult and important one. One important area in which federal and state law sometimes conflict is the regulation of business and commercial activities. Beginning on page 54 in this chapter, you will see how the Court has decided such questions.

Assign a group of students to research the United States Supreme Court justices—how they are appointed, how long their term is, what their duties are, etc.

Have students look up information about each of the current U.S. Supreme Court justices. Have them outline the work experiences of the justice, then report orally to the class.

---

38   Understanding the Law and Our Legal System

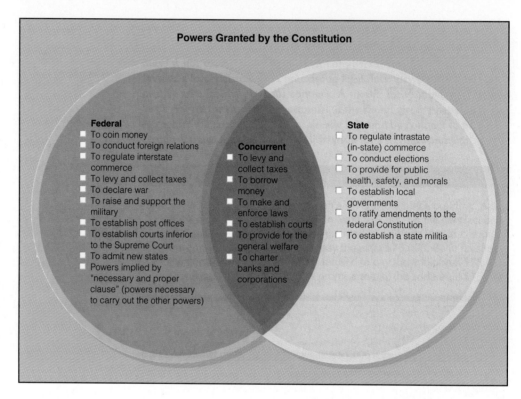

Powers Granted by the Constitution

Federal
- To coin money
- To conduct foreign relations
- To regulate interstate commerce
- To levy and collect taxes
- To declare war
- To raise and support the military
- To establish post offices
- To establish courts inferior to the Supreme Court
- To admit new states
- Powers implied by "necessary and proper clause" (powers necessary to carry out the other powers)

Concurrent
- To levy and collect taxes
- To borrow money
- To make and enforce laws
- To establish courts
- To provide for the general welfare
- To charter banks and corporations

State
- To regulate intrastate (in-state) commerce
- To conduct elections
- To provide for public health, safety, and morals
- To establish local governments
- To ratify amendments to the federal Constitution
- To establish a state militia

EXHIBIT 2-2
POWERS GRANTED BY THE CONSTITUTION

◆ THE MAKEUP OF THE UNITED STATES SUPREME COURT

When you hear that the Supreme Court has made a decision about some important case, you are hearing about the actions of individuals. These individuals—nine of them—are the justices of the United States Supreme Court. The justices are so important that when one of them retires or leaves office, the decision about that person's replacement makes national news.

The Constitution created the Supreme Court. In Article III, Section 1, we read that "The judicial Power of the United States, shall be vested in one supreme Court and in such inferior Courts as the Congress may from time to time ordain and establish."

The Constitution goes on to indicate that all federal judges, including the justices of the Supreme Court, "shall hold their Offices during good Behavior." In other words, the judges hold office until voluntary retire-

Ethical Concern

Ask students to study Exhibit 2-3, the Profile of Supreme Court Justices. Ask them why they think there are more men, more Caucasians, more collegeeducated, and more Protestant justices. Do they foresee a change in this pattern? What has happened lately to change this pattern?

Critical Thinking Activity

Ask a student to lead a discussion about the following: The Constitution says nothing about the qualifications of Supreme Court justices. Look at the Profile of Supreme Court Justices (Exhibit 2-3) in the text. How many had legal experience before being appointed to the Court? Why do you think most judges have experience in the legal field?

Enrichment

Help the students discuss and respond to Exhibit 2-3, Profile of Supreme Court Justices, to 1993: What portrait of the "typical justice" emerges from this exhibit? In what respects is that typical justice different from you? From the general population? What do you consider the significance of those differences?

Profile of Supreme Court Justices to 1993

	Number of Justices (106 = Total)
Occupational Position before Appointment	
Private legal practice	25
State judgeship	21
Federal judgeship	26
U.S. attorney general	7
Deputy or assistant U.S. attorney general	2
U.S. solicitor general	2
U.S. senator	6
U.S. representative	2
State governor	3
Federal executive post	9
Other	3
Religious Background	
Protestant	83
Roman Catholic	10
Jewish	5
Unitarian	7
No religious affiliation	1
Age on Appointment	
Under 40	5
41–50	31
51–60	56
61–70	14
Political Party Affiliation	
Federalist (to 1835)	13
Democratic-Republican (to 1828)	7
Whig (to 1861)	1
Democrat	42
Republican	42
Independent	1
Educational Background	
College graduate	90
Not college graduate	16
Sex	
Male	105
Female	1
Race	
Caucasian	104
Other	2

EXHIBIT 2-3
PROFILE OF THE SUPREME COURT JUSTICES TO 1993

ment or death, unless the judge is disqualified because of some wrongful behavior. Nothing is said about the qualifications of Supreme Court justices, only that the president shall appoint them with the advice and consent of the Senate.

Nonetheless, all have shared certain characteristics. The makeup of the federal judiciary is far from typical of the American public. Exhibit 2-3 summarizes the backgrounds of all of the 106 Supreme Court justices that have served up to 1993.

As you can see in the exhibit, most of the justices were in private legal practice or held state or federal judgeships at the time of their appointment. Among the justices in federal executive posts at the time of appointment were some who held the high offices of secretary of state, comptroller of the treasury, secretary of the navy, postmaster general, secretary of the interior, chairman of the Securities and Exchange Commission, and secretary of labor. In the "other" category in the table are two justices who were professors of law (including William Howard Taft, a former president) and one justice who was a North Carolina state employee responsible for organizing and revising the state's statutes.

Note also that the great majority of justices have had a college education. By and large, those who did not attend college or receive a degree lived in the late eighteenth and early nineteenth centuries, when college education was much less common than it is today. In recent years, degrees from such schools as Yale, Harvard, Columbia, and other prestigious institutions have been typical. It is interesting that many of the earlier college-educated justices did not hold their degrees in law. In fact, it was not until 1957 that all the members serving on the Court were graduates of law schools.

Out of 106 judges, the majority have been male. Indeed, until 1981, *all* have been male. Then Sandra Day O'Connor was appointed by the president and confirmed by the Senate.

◆ CHECKING YOUR PROGRESS

1. What part of the Constitution, by limiting governmental control, provides a major source of protection of individual rights and affects how business people can conduct business?

2. What are the three branches of government and what document describes the powers of each?

3. If people think their constitutional rights have been violated, what can they do?

4. Explain the Constitutional principle of limited government.

5. What is the effect on a federal or state law if the U.S. Supreme Court believes that it violates the U.S. Constitution?

6. Why are some powers granted by the Constitution concurrent? Give an example.

Checking Your Progress (Answers)

1. The Bill of Rights is a major source of protection for both individuals and businesses.

2. The three branches of government are the executive, legislative, and judicial. The U.S. Constitution describes the powers of each branch.

3. If people think their constitutional rights have been violated, they can go to the courts to have the judiciary decide whether the Constitution has been followed.

4. The Constitutional principle of limited government means that government can only do what the people allow it to do. The rule of law is that government officers are never above the law.

5. If the U.S. Supreme Court believes that a federal or state law violates the U.S. Constitution, that law is declared unconstitutional and is no longer valid—it is as if it did not exist.

6. Some constitutional powers are concurrent because both federal and state laws are necessary for society to function. For example, both levels of government need money to function, so both can levy and collect taxes; both can borrow money; both can make and enforce laws; both can provide for the general welfare; etc.

Read

Introduce this feature about Sandra Day O'Connor by reading the first paragraph of the feature aloud to the class. Explain to students that O'Connor will always be a very important historical figure, if for no other reason than her position as the first woman on the Supreme Court. Have a volunteer read the rest of this feature aloud to the class.

Discuss

Stimulate a class discussion of this material by asking the following questions: Do you think there is additional pressure on O'Connor because she is the only woman on the Supreme Court? Now that the Supreme Court is composed of eight men and one woman, does it fairly represent the population of the United States?

Extend

To further the students' understanding of the make up of the current Court, ask them to choose one of the eight remaining justices and write a profile of that man. The profile should be similar to this profile of Sandra Day O'Connor.

Review

Use the following questions to review the content of this feature. From what university did O'Connor receive her law degree? What experiences with discrimination has O'Connor had?

◆ **Law in Action**

LAW IN YOUR LIFE: SANDRA DAY O'CONNOR (1930–   )

Many children pretend, and some even expect, that they will grow up to be the president of the United States of America. If you are a female, however, history has not given you much encouragement for such dreams. Until 1981, history told the same story with respect to the United States Supreme Court. Then President Reagan picked Sandra Day O'Connor. She was unanimously confirmed by the Senate on September 21.

Sandra Day O'Connor was born in El Paso, Texas, and raised on her grandfather's 162,000-acre Lazy B Ranch near Duncan, Arizona. She graduated with a bachelor's degree in economics from Stanford University in 1950. Two years later, she earned a law degree from Stanford University Law School. While at Stanford, she served as editor of the *Stanford Law Review*, an academic journal published by law students. She was also a member of the Order of the Coif, a prestigious academic honorary society.

Despite her record and honors, she had some difficulty in finding employment where she could use her legal training. This was common for women professionals in the early 1950s. After serving briefly as deputy county attorney for San Mateo County, California, from 1952 to 1953, she accompanied her husband to Germany during his military service. In Germany, she worked as a civilian attorney for the army. She later worked part-time as a lawyer while raising her three sons. In 1965, she became an assistant attorney general for the state of Arizona.

In 1969, she was appointed to fill a vacancy in the Arizona Senate and retained the seat in the next year's election. She was chosen senate majority leader as a Republican in 1972—the first woman majority leader in the state's history. Active in Republican politics, O'Connor also co-chaired the Arizona Committee to Re-Elect the President (President Nixon) in 1972. In 1974, she was elected to the Superior Court for Maricopa County, which includes Phoenix. Five years later, she was appointed to the Arizona Court of Appeals. On August 19, 1981, President Reagan nominated her as an associate justice.

Justice O'Connor's well-thought-out, carefully reasoned opinions have earned her the respect of her fellow justices as well as of the nation. She has clearly shown that the discrimination against women in the federal judicial system was a mistake.

LEGAL BACKGROUND

Even though the courts and the Bill of Rights stand guard over the rights and liberties of Americans, it is important to remember that the ultimate responsibility to protect these rights lies with us, the American people. Each generation must learn anew to uphold its rights by voting, expressing opinions to elected representatives, and bringing cases to the attention of the courts when constitutional rights are threatened. Judge Learned Hand, an often-quoted United States Circuit Court judge, made the point this way: "I often wonder whether we do not rest our hopes too much upon Constitutions, upon laws and upon courts. These are false hopes; believe me, these are false hopes. Liberty lies in the hearts of men and women; when it dies there, no Constitution, no law, no court can ever do much to help it."

Reteaching Activity

Ask students to write a paragraph or two on the following questions: What is the Bill of Rights? Who were the Federalists and the AntiFederalists? What were the Anti-Federalists afraid of?

Critical Thinking Activity

Ask students to write an essay on what they think America would be like if there were no Bill of Rights.

 THE BILL OF RIGHTS

After the final draft of the Constitution was approved on September 17, 1787, it faced the long road to ratification, formal approval by the states. One group, called the Federalists, was in favor of ratification. Another group, called the Anti-Federalists, opposed it. The Federalists favored a strong central government. The Anti-Federalists contended that the Constitution was a document written by aristocrats that would lead the nation to aristocratic tyranny. They argued that the Constitution would create an overly powerful central government that would limit personal freedom.

The Anti-Federalists' strongest argument was that the Constitution lacked a bill of rights. They warned that without a bill of rights, a strong national government might take away the political rights won during the American Revolution. They demanded that the new Constitution clearly guarantee personal freedoms.

Consequently, in order for the Constitution to be ratified in several important states, the Federalists had to provide assurances that amendments would be passed to protect individual liberties against violations by the national government. At the state ratifying conventions, protection of many specific rights was recommended. More than two hundred state recommendations had to be sifted through. The job went to James Madison, who came up with sixteen. When Congress considered them in 1789, it eliminated four. Ten were passed and form what we now call the Bill of Rights. Interestingly, in 1992, 203 years later, one of the two that did not

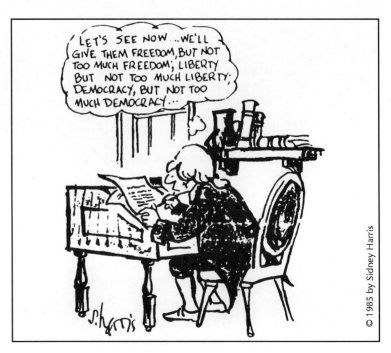

© 1985 by Sidney Harris

VIDEODISC NOTE
Much of the material that is conveyed in the exhibits of *West's Business and Personal Law* is also conveyed in the still frames on the **West Business Law and Legal Environment Videodisc**. For more information and directions for use, please see the Index and Description of Contents for the **West Business Law and Legal Environment Videodisc** that is found in your *Teacher's Resource Binder*.

The Bill of Rights

First Amendment	Guarantees freedom of religion, speech, press, assembly, and petition.
Second Amendment	Guarantees the right to keep and bear arms, because a state requires a well-equipped citizen army for its own security.
Third Amendment	Prohibits the lodging of soldiers in peacetime without the dweller's consent.
Fourth Amendment	Prohibits unreasonable searches and seizures of persons or property.
Fifth Amendment	Prohibits derivation of life, liberty, or property without due process of law, and fair payment when private property is taken for public use, such as in eminent domain; prohibits compulsory self-incrimination and double jeopardy (trial for the same crime twice).
Sixth Amendment	Guarantees the accused in a criminal case the right to a speedy and public trial by an impartial jury and with counsel; allows the accused to cross-examine witnesses against him or her and to solicit testimony from witnesses in his or her favor.
Seventh Amendment	Guarantees a trial by jury for the accused in a civil case involving $20 or more.
Eight Amendment	Prohibits excessive bail and fines, as well as cruel and unusual punishments.
Ninth Amendment	Establishes that the people have rights in addition to those specified in the Constitution.
Tenth Amendment	Establishes that those powers neither delegated to the national government nor denied to the states are reserved for the states.

EXHIBIT 2-4
THE BILL OF RIGHTS

pass was finally ratified by the necessary number of states and became the Twenty-Seventh Amendment. Look at Exhibit 2-4. There you see a brief explanation of the first ten amendments to the Constitution, ratified on December 15, 1791.

The Bill of Rights provides constitutional guarantees of freedom of expression and belief, of individual security, and of equal and fair treatment before the law. The Ninth Amendment states that the rights guaranteed in

LEGAL BACKGROUND

Equal in importance to the due process clause of the Fourteenth Amendment is its final clause declaring that "no State shall . . . deny to any person within its jurisdiction the equal protection of the law." Known as the equal protection clause, it means that states must treat all their citizens in an equal manner and may not draw *unreasonable* distinctions between different classes of people. The equal protection clause has been at the heart of many civil rights disputes.

◆ **reserved powers**
Powers reserved by the states, spelled out in the Tenth Amendment to the U.S. Constitution.

the Constitution are not the only rights that people have. The Tenth Amendment spells out the **reserved powers** of the states.

Reserved powers are not given to the national government, nor can they be taken away from the states by the national government. Reserved powers include each state's right to regulate commerce within its borders and to provide for a state militia. In essence, states have authority over all of their internal affairs and over the health, safety, and welfare of their people. When you go to a public school that was created by your state government, that is an example of a state exercising its reserved powers. If you decide to get married or divorced, the laws regulating those actions are part of the reserved powers of the state. If you are not allowed to legally drive an automobile before the age of sixteen in your state, that is another example of the reserved powers of the state.

APPLYING THE BILL OF RIGHTS TO THE STATES

For many years, the Bill of Rights wasn't applied to state or local government. The Founders believed that states, being closer to the people, would be less likely to violate their own citizens' liberties. The Founders did not realize that some state governments would, at times, actually violate individual liberties more often than the national government.

States, however, cannot deny basic civil rights. One reason is that state constitutions usually contain their own bills of rights with which state governments must comply. Another reason is a clause in the Fourteenth Amendment to the Constitution known as the **due process clause**. The due process clause has been interpreted by the courts to restrict the power of individual states to interfere with individual rights.

◆ **due process clause** Part of the Fourteenth Amendment to the U.S. Constitution; limits the government's power to deprive any person of life, liberty, or property without due process of law.

No state shall make or enforce any law which shall abridge the privileges or immunities of citizens of the United States; nor shall any state deprive any person of life, liberty, or property, without due process of law, nor deny to any person within its jurisdiction the equal protection of the laws. (Emphasis added)

Due process is concerned with certain fundamental rights recognized by the legal system. That system and its officers are also responsible for ensuring that certain procedures—which are essentially "rules of fair play"—are followed in making decisions, in determining guilt or innocence, and in punishing those who have been found guilty. Thus, "due process" is about fairness by government in the treatment of individuals. Laws which violate fundamental freedoms and laws which do not allow fair procedures, such as allowing a person an opportunity to be heard, violate the due process clause.

The Supreme Court has interpreted the due process clause to mean that no state may deny any person any right that is "basic or essential to the American concept of ordered liberty." In a long series of cases, starting in 1925, the Supreme Court gradually began to say that states could not abridge, or lessen, a right that the national government could not abridge. They used the Fourteenth Amendment's due process clause as justification. Especially during the 1960s, the Supreme Court broadened its interpreta-

Critical Thinking Activity

Lead a discussion about U.S. Supreme Court Justice Hugo Black's remark, "Freedom to speak and write about public questions is as important to the life of our government as is the heart of the human body. . . . If that heart be weakened, the result is debilitation; if it be stilled, the result is death."

tions to limit state action in most areas in which federal action is banned. For all practical purposes, the Bill of Rights guarantees rights against infringement by both state and national governments.

The importance of the Fourteenth Amendment in securing the constitutional rights and liberties of American citizens is further discussed in "Law in Action—*Gideon v. Wainwright*" in Chapter 4.

In this chapter, we discuss two of the individual freedoms protected in the Bill of Rights—freedom of speech and freedom of religion. You will read about more constitutional rights in later chapters, especially Chapters 4 and 26.

Critical Thinking Activity

Write on the board the following quote from Oliver Wendell Holmes, Jr.: "We need to protect not free thought for those who agree with us, but freedom for the thought that we hate." Ask students to write a short essay on what they feel this means.

◆ FIRST AMENDMENT FREEDOMS

The Bill of Rights protects individuals *against* abuses of power by the federal government. Consequently, the Bill of Rights begins with the words "Congress shall make no law. . . ." According to Justice Hugo Black, who served on the United States Supreme Court from 1937 to 1971, the Bill of Rights is "a collection of 'Thou Shalt Nots' directed at the government."

One of the major freedoms guaranteed to us is the freedom of speech. But this freedom is only one of those guaranteed by the First Amendment. According to the First Amendment, Congress shall not make any law that:

1. Establishes a religion.
2. Prohibits the free exercise of religion.
3. Restricts free speech.
4. Restricts the press.
5. Restricts peaceable assembly.
6. Restricts the right of people to petition (formally ask) government to correct its mistakes.

These freedoms of religion, speech, press, assembly, and petition have been applied to the states through the due process clause of the Fourteenth Amendment. Justice Hugo Black remarked in 1941 that "Freedom to speak and write about public questions is as important to the life of our government as is the heart to the human body. . . . If that heart be weakened, the result is debilitation; if it be stilled, the result is death."

FREEDOM OF SPEECH

How many times have you heard someone say, "I can say what I want. It's a free country"? This common expression reveals the philosophy underlying our notion of what democracy in America means. In many nondemocratic countries throughout the world, individuals do not have the right to free speech. We take that right for granted. The First Amendment to the

Vocabulary Activity

Ask students to define the terms *pure speech, speech plus*, and *symbolic speech*. Ask volunteers to identify specific examples of each.

Extension Activity

Ask a volunteer to find out what forms of symbolic speech are not protected under the First Amendment. Have them share their findings with the class.

Legal Focus Case Example

Read to the class the Legal Focus Case Example found here. Remind students that they can use the Legal Focus features as review tools when studying for tests.

Enrichment

Ask a group of interested students to research the *Hazelwood School District* v. *Cathy Kuhlmeier* case to find out what exactly the controversy was about. Have these students report their findings to the class and discuss why they think the decision was against the students. Do they think this was fair? Unfair? Why or why not?

Teaching Note

This case is included in the *West's Business and Personal Law Handbook of Selected Court Cases.*

U.S. Constitution is designed especially to protect ideas that may be unpopular or different.

Defining Free Speech   Not everybody has the same idea of free speech. First of all, it does not apply just to the spoken word but also to broader forms of communication, such as writing, communication over the airwaves on radio and TV, printing, and even actions. Each form of speech has a different degree of protection under the rulings of the U.S. Supreme Court. The Court has distinguished three general categories of speech that are protected by the First Amendment.

Pure speech is the peaceful expression of thought and opinion before a willing audience. This is the neighborly chat or the candidate's campaign speech. This type of speech is generally protected under the First Amendment.

Speech plus is verbal expression combined with some sort of action, such as marching or demonstrating. Because *speech plus* involves actions, it may be subject to government restrictions that do not apply to pure speech. The Supreme Court has ruled that while *speech plus* is protected by the First Amendment, it cannot obstruct traffic, block sidewalks, or endanger public safety.

Symbolic speech involves nonverbal expressions using symbols. Picketing in a labor dispute or wearing a black armband in protest are fairly common examples. As another example, during the Vietnam War in the late 1960s and early 1970s, protesters often used such symbolic "speech" as burning their draft cards to express their opposition to the war. (Draft cards were notices sent to males by the federal government confirming that they were available to be called for military service.) The Supreme Court has given symbolic speech substantial protection. It has ruled, however, that some forms of symbolic speech are not protected under the First Amendment.

◆ LEGAL FOCUS – CASE EXAMPLE

Three students working on a student newspaper, the *Spectrum,* sued the school district, arguing that their First Amendment right to freedom of expression had been violated. After a *bench trial*—heard only in front of the judge—the U.S. District Court of the Eastern District of Missouri held that the students' First Amendment rights had not been violated. The court argued that school officials may restrain students' speech when this seems "reasonable" and when it is related directly to a school activity.

The case went all the way to the U.S. Supreme Court, which ruled against the students, in *Hazelwood School District v. Cathy Kuhlmeier.*[5] Justice Byron White, writing for the majority, said that "school officials may impose reasonable restrictions on the speech of students. . . ."

---

5.   484 U.S. 260, 108 S.Ct. 562, 98 L.Ed.2d 592 (1988).

Ask your students to collect from newspapers, magazines, and television news recent news items involving freedom of speech. Give them a week or two to collect these news items, and then have a class discussion about them.

Let interested students research the details of the 2 Live Crew trials in 1990. Encourage them to present their findings in an original "rap" (or in a more conventional oral report).

Discussion Starter

Encourage the students to discuss fighting words: What specific phrases or sentences might be considered fighting words? To what extent does the definition of fighting words depend on the circumstances in which they are uttered?

Freedom of speech includes more than political speeches and rallies, it can include performances for musical groups. Attempts to ban 2 Live Crew performances were held to be a violation of the performer's freedom of speech.

Limits on Freedom of Speech   No rights are absolute, and therefore freedom of speech is not absolute, as you just saw in the example about student publications. Constitutional protection has never been given to certain classes of speech. Among the most obvious are obscenities, words that purposely and wrongfully harm the reputation of another, and words that either threaten or inspire immediate violence.

The U.S. Supreme Court, at the beginning of World War II, made the following remarks on this issue. This quotation is from a Supreme Court case, *Chaplinsky v. New Hampshire*, decided in 1942:

> *There are certain well-defined and narrowing limited classes of speech, the prevention and punishment of which have never been thought to raise any Constitutional problem. These include the lewd and obscene, the profane, the libelous [something that wrongfully harms the reputation of another], and the insulting or "fighting" words—those which by their very utterance inflict injury or tend to incite an immediate breach of the peace. It has been well observed that such utterances are no essential part of any exposition of ideas, and are of such slight social value as a step to truth that any benefit that may be derived from them is clearly outweighed by the social interest in order and morality.*[6]

6. *Chaplinsky v. New Hampshire*, 315 U.S. 568, 62 S.Ct. 766, 86 L.Ed. 1031 (1942).

Extension Activity

Allow a volunteer or group of volunteers to research the *Bigelow* v. *Virginia* case from 1975. How does this case relate to government restrictions on commercial speech? Volunteers should be allowed to present their findings to the class in the form of an oral report.

Legal Focus Problem

Read aloud this Legal Focus Problem dealing with free speech. Allow student volunteers to suggest possible answers to this problem. Have the volunteers explain the reasons for their answers.

Enrichment

Invite a local attorney to come to your classroom to discuss the laws concerning freedom of speech, religion, etc. Perhaps he/she can share some of his/her cases with the class.

In other words, for "compelling" reasons, governments may and do constitutionally restrict certain forms of speech.

Can anybody yell anything he or she wants at any time and still be protected by the First Amendment? This is a question that has faced the Supreme Court, and the answer is no.

◆ LEGAL FOCUS – PROBLEM

John Smith became bored with the movie he was watching at the Grand Palace Theater. He felt that most of the other customers were as bored as he was, in spite of the fact that the theater was very crowded with apparently interested viewers. He decided to leave the theater, but just before he reached the exit, he had an idea. He ran partway down the aisle shouting: "Fire! Fire! Fire!" and then turned around and ran out of the theater. Was John Smith's speech and behavior protected by the First Amendment?

Although this situation is completely made up, United States Supreme Court Justice Oliver Wendell Holmes used it as an example when he defined the limits of free speech. Free speech must be balanced with the needs of society to protect itself from unreasonable conduct. Holmes said in 1917:

> *The character of every act depends upon the circumstances in which it is done. The most stringent protection of free speech would not protect a man in* falsely shouting *fire in a theater and causing panic. . . . The question in every case is whether the words used are used in such circumstances and are of such a nature as to create a* clear and present danger *that they will bring about the substantive evils that Congress [and every state] has a right to prevent.*[7]

Regulation of Time and Place of Speech   Governments do have the right even under the First Amendment to regulate the time and place and often the manner of public speech. You cannot just start using a megaphone to scream your ideas to everyone around you at two in the morning in a quiet suburb. But the government is not allowed to favor the speech of one group over that of another. If two groups want to conduct a rally at the same place at the same time, the police authorities clearly have to refuse one group. But the group refused also has to be given the right to hold the rally at a later time or at a different place.

Commercial Speech   Numerous freedom-of-speech cases have to do with the distinction between commercial and noncommercial speech. As stated earlier in this chapter, advertising is a type of commercial speech. Commercial speech is given less constitutional protection than private or

---

7. *Schenck v. U.S.,* 249 U.S. 47, 39 S.Ct. 247, 63 L.Ed. 470 (1919).

Multicultural Perspectives MC

Ask a group of students to research the religious problems occurring in the Middle East that pertain to different religious sects. Have students share their findings with the class.

Extension Activity

Have a student volunteer or group of volunteers research the subject of religion in the former Soviet Union. How was religion treated during the Communist regime in the Soviet Union? What religious practices were illegal? What religious practices, if any, were allowed? How has the situation changed? Have the students present their findings to the class in the form of an oral report. Encourage the students to incorporate visual aids and original source documents into their presentation.

political speech. The U.S. Supreme Court has allowed numerous restrictions on such speech, so long as there is a valid public purpose in restricting it and the restriction is no more than necessary to accomplish this purpose. If the government wants to restrict false advertising, the U.S. Supreme Court will not allow it to restrict *all* advertising. For example, after overwhelming evidence came to light about the negative effects of smoking on health, the government sought to restrict advertising of cigarettes. It succeeded in passing legislation in 1970 to prohibit all cigarette advertising on radio and television. But it did not restrict advertising of this product everywhere, and cigarette advertisements still appear on billboards and in magazines.

FREEDOM OF RELIGION

Think for a moment about several problems regarding the practice of religion that can face students and administrators at public schools. Joan, a sophomore at Blue High School, wants permission to leave school during class hours to attend religious classes at her church. Should she be allowed to leave? At Oak High School, in a neighboring state, administrators have set aside thirty seconds during homeroom period to allow students to engage in silent prayer. Is this legal? Understanding the Constitution and how it has been interpreted by the Supreme Court can help you answer the questions just posed.

The First Amendment states that the Congress "shall make no law respecting an establishment of religion, or prohibiting the free exercise thereof." Thus, the First Amendment guarantees the freedom of religion in two ways. The first part of this quote has been called the **establishment clause**. Congress cannot establish a state religion. In contrast, some coun-

◆ **establishment clause** Part of the First Amendment to the U.S. Constitution; prohibits the government from establishing a state religion.

Freedom to worship the religion of one's choice is a basic fundamental right guaranteed to U.S. residents under the First Amendment to the Constitution.

Encourage the students to discuss their responses to the relationship between the establishment clause, the government, and religion in general: Do you think it is appropriate? Do you find it offensive? Do you think that some individuals or groups find it offensive?

Have the students brainstorm a list of ways in which religion is a part of public life. Have a volunteer list each of these examples on the board. Ask the students whether they believe any of these examples represents a breach of the separation of church and state.

---

50   Understanding the Law and Our Legal System

Unusual religious practices are protected forms of religious worship, as long as they do not jeopardize health, safety, or the morals of the community. The Supreme Court upheld a state law that forbids the use of poisonous snakes in religious rites.

♦ **free exercise clause** Part of the First Amendment to the U.S. Constitution; prohibits the government from interfering in people's free exercise of their religious beliefs.

tries do have state religions, such as Islam in Iran. The second way in which the First Amendment guarantees freedom of religion involves the so-called **free exercise clause**. This clause prohibits government from interfering in the free exercise, or practice, of religious beliefs. In short, government actions are supposed to be neutral toward religion. Government is not supposed to be for or against any one religion in any way.

Separation of Church and State The establishment clause is often called the separation of church and state clause. Here, the word *state* simply means any type of government institution. In the United States, this separation has never meant that the government cannot support religion in general. Indeed, religion is a part of public life. Most government officials take an oath of office in the name of God. Our coins and paper currency carry the motto "In God We Trust." Religious representatives serve with each branch of the armed forces. Recently, presidential candidates have invoked the saying "God bless this country," or other such sayings, at the ends of their acceptance speeches.

Furthermore, certain laws can have an impact on religion. Many cities and some states in the past have had laws requiring many businesses to be

Read

Ask a volunteer to read aloud to the class the title of this *Law in Action* feature. Then ask the class: Do you think that local governments should be allowed to sponsor Christmas displays? Why or why not? Then have the students read this *Law in Action* feature.

Discuss

Ask the students to recall or discuss any publicly-sponsored holiday displays (Christmas or Hanukkah) in their communities. Where were the displays? What was included in them? Did they engender any controversy? If so, what were the issues, and how were they resolved? If not, why not?

Review

Ask the students these review questions: What was the outcome of the *Lynch* v. *Donnelly* case? What type of organization is the ACLU?

 Law in Action

LEGAL ISSUE: GOVERNMENT-SPONSORED CHRISTMAS DISPLAYS

Retailers in America know the importance of Christmas. Some major retailers obtain 40 percent of their annual sales revenues during the Christmas season. Retailers and consumers are not the only ones to get caught up in the spirit of the season. Cities spend tax dollars to decorate streets and government offices. Most of these decorations are not religious and apparently offend few individuals. Candy canes and pictures of Santa Claus abound.

What about obviously religious scenes? Does any government in the United States have the legal right to use public funds to display religious symbols on government (public) property? This issue relates to the establishment clause of the First Amendment to the United States Constitution: "Congress shall make no law respecting an establishment of religion."

A major test of whether a city or county may spend public funds on religious scenes during the Christmas season occurred in 1984. The city of Pawtucket, Rhode Island, included a crèche in a larger, nonreligious Christmas display, which included reindeer, candy-striped poles, and a Christmas tree. A crèche is a model representing Mary, Joseph, and others around the crib of Jesus in the stable at Bethlehem. The entire display was in a private park in a shopping district, rather than on government property. It was the city's official display, however, and had been both erected and maintained by city employees. In *Lynch v. Donnelly,*[8] the Supreme Court held that the crèche could

be included as long as it was just one part of a holiday display. The presence of the crèche was deemed constitutional; it did not violate the establishment clause.

What about the simultaneous display by local governments of objects that are symbols from different religions? One organization that has had a say in such cases is the American Civil Liberties Union (ACLU)—a nationwide organization whose purpose is to support the personal freedoms of individuals. The ACLU is a membership organization that often brings suits to protect what the organization believes to be violations of civil liberties. Because the organization often challenges popular positions and protects unpopular causes, it is controversial.

The ACLU sued Allegheny County, where Pittsburgh, Pennsylvania, is located. In the lawsuit, the ACLU claimed that two displays erected in Pittsburgh were "frankly religious displays." The first was a crèche displayed by Allegheny County, which annually erected a crèche in the county courthouse. The second, first used in 1982, was a menorah (a religious symbol used in the eight-day celebration of Chanukah in the Jewish religion), which was displayed near the annual Christmas tree on the steps of the city–county building. While the county displayed nonreligious holiday symbols in the courthouse, they were not displayed alongside the crèche, as they were in the *Lynch* case. Therefore, the Court held that displaying the crèche was unconstitutional.[9]

---

8. 465 U.S. 668, 104 S.Ct. 1355, 79 L.Ed.2d 604 (1984).

9. *County of Allegheny v. American Civil Liberties Union,* 492 U.S. 573, 109 S.Ct. 3086, 106 L.Ed.2d 472 (1989).

Ethical Concern

Have your students read about the two cases from this *Law in Action* feature about government-sponsored Christmas displays. Generate a class discussion on these issues. Do they agree with these decisions? Have they seen an "obvious religious scene" displayed on government grounds anywhere in their local area?

Critical Thinking Activity

Have the students write short essays explaining why they think government-sponsored holiday displays can become such important issues. Have students exchange their essays to proofread and correct any mistakes. Allow student volunteers to share their essays with the class.

 Law in Action (Continued)

The menorah, however, did not violate the First Amendment's prohibition against the establishment of religion, because it was situated close to the forty-five-foot-high Christmas tree. By allowing the menorah to be positioned near the Christmas tree, the city of Pittsburgh had hoped to calm any fears that it was "endorsing" any one religion.

During oral arguments, Justice Scalia asked the attorney representing the ACLU, "How can you possibly be endorsing either Christianity or Judaism when you have symbols of both?" The attorney answered, "You are endorsing Judeo-Christian symbols with an appalling lack of consideration for those who don't adhere to the Judeo-Christian tradition." Justice Scalia asked the

attorney representing the city of Pittsburgh what the city did for Muslims. The attorney answered "Nothing" and noted that a Muslim witness in the case had testified that the Muslim faith does not use outward symbols. Justice Scalia continued his queries with the general question: "[M]ustn't the city do something for every religion in order to avoid appearing to endorse one religion over another?" Justice Stevens wondered, Where do you draw the line? Should a religion with only three or four adherents also be represented?

Supreme Court justices clearly do not have an easy job. In addition to their other duties, they periodically have to function, as Justice Kennedy said, as "a national theology board."

closed on Sunday. These Sunday closing laws were upheld by the Supreme Court for many years because the government felt it had a legitimate interest in providing a day with limited work activities. The U.S. Supreme Court has argued that in modern times, having a day off is simply good for promoting the health and welfare of workers. It has nothing to do with forcing them to go to church. Other Sunday laws prohibit the formation or performance of agreements that would otherwise be legal if they were entered into on any other day. For example, such a law may prohibit the sale or purchase of alcoholic beverages.

The Supreme Court has also held that the establishment clause of the First Amendment does not prohibit a city from including religious symbols in its annual Christmas display. Doing so in a purely neutral manner is not always easy, though, as you will find out in the following feature.

Free Exercise of Religion Do individuals have the right to act any way they want to on the basis of their religious beliefs? Not entirely. There is an important distinction between belief and practice. We cannot be compelled by the government to accept or reject any religious belief, but our right to practice our beliefs does have some limitations. Through the years, the Supreme Court has followed the general principle that people are free

Multicultural **Perspectives**

Allow a student volunteer or group of volunteers to research the practice of polygamy among other cultures. Volunteers should present their findings to the class in the form of an oral report.

Enrichment

Assign teams of students to visit local businesses to find out company policies about accommodating employees' religious beliefs. Have the teams report their findings to the class.

Legal Focus Case Problem

to believe and worship as they wish so long as their conduct violates no laws that validly protect the health, safety, or morals of the community.

> ### ◆ LEGAL FOCUS ~ CASE EXAMPLE
>
> The Mormon church has traditionally been important in Utah. Prior to Utah's admittance into the union in 1896, polygamy, the practice of having more than one wife at a time, was encouraged by the teachings of the religion. Many Mormons had more than one wife. Part of the agreement to allow Utah to be admitted to the union, however, was for Utah to stop allowing polygamy, a practice prohibited by federal law. Some Mormons argued that such a prohibition violated the First Amendment to the Constitution. When one man named Reynolds was convicted of polygamy, he appealed the case. He argued that the law violated his constitutional right to the free exercise of his religious beliefs. The case went all the way to the United States Supreme Court. The Court ruled against Reynolds because polygamy was a crime, and crimes are not protected by the First Amendment.[10]

More recently, members of religious groups that use illegal drugs as part of their religious ceremonies have been convicted of various crimes relating to the use of those drugs. Whenever these individuals have appealed to the courts, they have lost. Again, it is because the Constitution does not protect criminal behavior, even if it is part of a religious ceremony.

Religious Freedom and the Business World The Sabbath, or holy day, falls on different days for different religions. Most of us are aware that the Sabbath for Christians is on Sunday, for Jews on Saturday, and for Muslims on Friday. To what extent does a business have to accommodate, or take into account, the religious practices of its different employees?

The federal government, through its administrative regulations, requires that private employers must "reasonably accommodate" the religious practices of their employees. There is an exception. If such accommodation would cause undo hardship on the employer's business, then it is not required. The Civil Rights Act of 1964 is the basis of such regulation, because it prohibits discrimination by most private employers on the basis of race, religion, or ethnic origin.

> ### ◆ LEGAL FOCUS ~ CASE PROBLEM
>
> William Frazee applied to Kelly Services for temporary work. Kelly offered him a temporary retail position that required him to work on Sunday. Frazee refused the job. He responded that, as a Christian, he

---

10. *Reynolds v. United States*, 98 U.S. 145, 25 L.Ed. 244 (1878).

Vocabulary Activity

Ask the students to define *commerce* in their own words and then to check the definitions given in a dictionary. How do these definitions relate to the word as it is used in the phrase *commerce clause?*

Discussion Starter

Begin a discussion by asking your students the pros and cons of government regulating commerce. Who do these regulations protect?

Extension Activity

Ask several students to research the regulations concerning banks. How did deregulation affect the failures of so many savings and loans? Have students share their information with the class. Ask the class if they think regulation is wise.

could not work on "the Lord's day." Frazee then applied to the Illinois Department of Employment Security for unemployment benefits, claiming he had good cause for his refusal to work on Sunday. His application was denied. Frazee claimed that the denial of unemployment benefits violated his First Amendment right to the free exercise of his religion. He was, however, not a member of any particular church. The reviewing body for the employment security department denied his claim, stating that "[w]hen a refusal of work is based on religious convictions, the refusal must be based upon some tenets or dogma accepted by the individual of some church, sect, or denomination, and such a refusal based solely on an individual's personal belief is personal and noncompelling and does not render the work unsuitable." Frazee took his case to court, and it finally got to the United States Supreme Court. Was Frazee eligible for state unemployment benefits?

Yes. The Supreme Court held that the denial of unemployment benefits to Frazee violated the free exercise clause of the First Amendment. The Court stated that the First Amendment protection "rested on the fact that each of the claimants had a sincere belief that religion required him or her to refrain from the work in question. Never did we suggest that unless a claimant belongs to a sect that forbids what his job requires, his belief, however sincere, must be deemed a purely personal preference rather than a religious belief."[11]

◆ BUSINESS, THE CONSTITUTION, AND THE COMMERCE CLAUSE

The focus of this chapter has been law and individual liberties, but the U.S. Constitution is also important in our study of business law. The Constitution expressly grants the federal government the power to regulate commerce—commercial dealings—among the states. Article I, Section 8, of the United States Constitution grants Congress the power "[t]o regulate Commerce with foreign Nations, and among the several States, and with the Indian Tribes." This is known as the **commerce clause**.

What does "to regulate commerce" mean? The power to regulate commerce means the federal government can regulate most business activities in the United States. This power was provided to the federal government to allow for uniform rules governing the movement of goods through the states.

◆ **commerce clause**
Part of Article I, Section 8, of the U.S. Constitution; gives the federal government the right to regulate commerce.

11. *Frazee v. Illinois Department of Employment Security*, 489 U.S. 829, 109 S.Ct. 1514, 103 L.Ed.2d 914 (1989).

Read

Before the students read this *Law in Action* feature, explain to them that it concerns a very famous case from 1803 that was decided by the Supreme Court under the leadership of Chief Justice John Marshall. Remind students that Marshall was Chief Justice when the court handed down its equally famous *Marbury* v. *Madison* decision. Then allow the students to read this *Law in Action*.

Discuss

Use the following questions to stimulate discussion of this *Law in Action* feature: How did the decision in the *Gibbons* v. *Ogden* case help to define *commerce* as it is used in the Constitution? How did this decision strengthen the powers of Congress?

Extend

Have students work in small groups to learn more about monopolies. What examples of monopolies can they find? Under what circumstances are monopolies legal today? What major monopolies have been broken up? By whom? Why?

Extension Activity

Assign each student a federal agency that regulates commerce to research. Have students report their findings to the class.

Law and Individual Rights   55

◆ Law in Action

LEGAL ISSUE: IS STEAMBOAT TRAVEL INTERSTATE COMMERCE?

The framers of the Constitution did not define the word *commerce*. Therefore, it was up to the courts to decide what constituted interstate commerce—and thus what could be regulated by the federal government. Did commerce include travel by steamboat between two states? This was the issue before the courts in the famous case of *Gibbons v. Ogden*.

In 1803, Robert Fulton, the inventor of the steamboat, and Robert Livingston, the American minister to France, obtained the exclusive right, called a *monopoly*, to use steamboats on the waters of New York State. They obtained this monopoly from the New York State legislature. Using their monopoly rights, they licensed Aaron Ogden to operate steamboats between New York and New Jersey. Thomas Gibbons also wanted to operate steamboats between New York and New Jersey, and he did so. But New York did not give him permission. Therefore, Ogden sued Gibbons in the New York State courts, and Ogden won.

Gibbons appealed to the U.S. Supreme Court.

The Supreme Court and Chief Justice Marshall looked at the commerce clause and decided to define *commerce* as all business dealings, including steamboat travel. The Court ruled against the monopoly that Ogden had obtained through license from Fulton and Livingston. Gibbons had to be allowed to compete.

Marshall used this opportunity not only to expand the definition of *commerce* but also to increase the power of the national government to regulate commerce. Marshall said: "What is this power? It is the power . . . to prescribe [set down] the rule by which commerce is to be governed. This power, like all others vested in Congress, is complete in itself." In other words, Marshall said that the power of the national government to regulate commerce had only those limitations specifically found in the Constitution and no others.

 State Law

In Florida, and other states, there is a three-day cooling-off period for all door-to-door sales in the state—which means you may cancel within three days any door-to-door sale in which a salesperson has come to your home.

Since the *Gibbons v. Ogden* decision in 1824, the national government has used the commerce clause to increase its authority over virtually all areas of economic activity. Few economic activities (even those completely *within* a particular state) are outside the regulatory power of the national government. When you buy meat in the supermarket, it is graded according to federal government specifications, which are overseen by the U.S. Department of Agriculture. When you ride in a car, many of the safety features of that car have been required by an agency of the federal government. When a door-to-door salesperson sells you something, many of the rules governing that sale come from the Federal Trade Commission. And when tragedy hits your family and a death occurs, the information you are given about the cost of preparing and burying the body is now regulated by the federal government.

WHAT POWER TO REGULATE COMMERCE DO STATE GOVERNMENTS HAVE?

Each state has an interest in regulating local activities. As part of its inherent sovereignty—its power to govern—each state possesses **police powers**. Police powers are the rights and powers of each state to protect and promote the health, safety, and welfare of its citizens.

◆ **police powers**
The inherent rights and powers of the states to protect and promote the public health, safety, and general welfare of their citizens.

◀ LEGAL FOCUS ~ PROBLEM

Suppose Georgia passes a law requiring the use of contoured rear-fender mudguards on trucks and trailers operating on its highways. The statute makes the use of straight mudguards illegal. In thirty-five other states, however, straight mudguards are legal. In fact, in the neighboring state of Florida, straight mudguards are required. There is some evidence suggesting that contoured mudguards may be a little safer than straight mudguards. Does the Georgia statute conflict with the federal government's interest in interstate commerce?

Truckers traveling through Georgia would have a problem. What would be legal in Georgia would be illegal in other states, including Florida, and vice versa. Clearly, the Georgia law would therefore affect interstate commerce, as truckers carry goods from state to state. Georgia's purpose in passing the statute would probably be safety. But would the possibility of a small increase in safety justify requiring truckers to either avoid Georgia or change their mudguards when they passed through? The Georgia statute would conflict with the U.S. Constitution and would thus not be enforceable.

◆ CHECKING YOUR PROGRESS

1. What did the Anti-Federalists want to do to the Constitution to limit the power of a central government?
2. What does "due process" mean to an individual?
3. Why did the U.S. Supreme Court allow governmental restrictions on the advertising of cigarettes?
4. Do individuals have the right to act any way they want to on the basis of their religious beliefs?

Teaching A Case In Point

Read

Before the students read about this case, explain to them that it deals with a freedom of religion suit. Students might want to go back and reread or skim the section on freedom of religion in this chapter in preparation for reading about this case. Allow a student volunteer to read this feature to the class.

Discuss

Use the following questions to stimulate class discussion of this feature: Do you feel that prayers should be allowed in public schools? Why or why not? What types of prayers, if any, would you allow? In what circumstances, if any, would you allow prayer in public schools?

Collaborative Learning

Divide the class into small groups, and ask each group to write a newspaper editorial or persuasive speech designed to defend or oppose the following proposition: "School-sponsored prayer in public schools should not be allowed because it violates the United States Constitution." Allow a volunteer from each group to present to the class the finished product of the group.

Review

Use the following questions to review the content of this case: What is at issue in the *Lee* v. *Weisman* case? What decision was reached by the district court in this case? What decision was reached by the United States court of appeal in this case? What decision was reached by the Supreme Court in this case?

◆ A CASE IN POINT ◆

ROBERT E. LEE v. DANIEL WEISMAN

United States Supreme Court, 1992.
___U.S.___
112 S.Ct. 2649
120 L.Ed.2d 467

A student in a Providence, Rhode Island, middle school brought a lawsuit through her father to prevent the inclusion of prayer in public school graduation ceremonies. Her claim was that the practice of allowing prayer in graduation exercises constituted an establishment of religion by the government-run schools.

FACTS Robert Lee, the principal of Nathan Bishop Middle School, invited Rabbi Leslie Gutterman to deliver prayers at the public school graduation ceremony. When invited, the rabbi was told that the prayers at the ceremony should be not tied to any particular religious group (such prayer is called nonsectarian prayer). Daniel Weisman, the father of a student, Deborah Weisman, brought an action to prohibit school officials from including prayer in the ceremony. He was unsuccessful, and the ceremony took place with the Weismans in attendance. Weisman then brought a lawsuit to permanently halt prayers at future ceremonies, including Deborah's high school graduation. The district court found that including prayers in public high school graduation exercises violated the establishment clause of the First Amendment. A United States court of appeal affirmed the district court. The United States Supreme Court agreed to review the decision of the lower courts.

ISSUE Does including a nonsectarian prayer in a state public high school graduation ceremony constitute the establishment of a religion by government in violation of the First Amendment of the United States Constitution?

DECISION Yes. The United States Supreme Court by a five-to-four margin agreed with the lower courts. The Court held that prayer, even if it is nonsectarian, violates the United States Constitution when it is part of a public high school graduation ceremony.

REASON Justice Kennedy wrote the majority opinion of the court, and he acknowledged the difficulty of deciding cases involving religious activities in public settings. The Court made several observations about this public ceremony and its participants. First, high school graduations are important public ceremonies. Second, even if attendance is voluntary, as it was for the Providence school's graduation ceremony, students and their families wish to attend. Third, if prayers are offered, students are expected to observe the prayers in some respectful way. Any student who does not wish to participate in the prayer lacks a reasonable alternative. The student can either participate, perhaps against conscience, or risk disapproval from his or her classmates. Because school officials direct the activity, and even control the content of the prayer, they create a dilemma for the student. "One timeless lesson [of the First Amendment] is that if citizens are subject to state-sponsored religious exercises, the state [denies] its own duty to guard and respect [the] . . . conscience and belief which is the mark of a free people."

Teaching Note

This case is included in the *West's Business and Personal Law Handbook of Selected Court Cases.*

Reviewing Chapter 2

In order to help students review what they have learned in Chapter 2, you might wish to:

1. Have a student volunteer, or volunteers, read aloud the Chapter Summary.
2. Allow the students to work with partners to complete the *Using Legal Language* activity.
3. Assign the *Checking for Comprehension* exercise as homework.
4. Allow the students to work in small groups to complete the *Applying Legal Concepts* activities.
5. As a class, complete the *Applying the Law* activities.

Assessment Strategies

In order to check student mastery of chapter concepts, you may wish to use the Chapter 2 test that is found in your *Teacher's Resource Binder* or use WESTEST computerized testing for Chapter 2.

◆ A CASE IN POINT (CONTINUED) ◆

DISSENT Justice Scalia wrote a dissent that was joined by three other justices. The dissent argued that "[t]he history and tradition of our Nation are replete with public ceremonies featuring the prayers of thanksgiving." Justice Scalia argued that the participation required of a dissenting student was not significant. The student was required to do no more than stand or be silent, that which is required during the Pledge of Allegiance. He argued that the government cannot demand that a citizen agree with the Pledge of Allegiance, any more than it can demand agreement with the prayer, yet silent observation can be and is expected. Justice Scalia also felt that, in spite of the majority opinion, prayer could still be given at graduation ceremonies if school officials made it clear that observation of the prayer did not imply agreement with it.

CHAPTER REVIEW

◆ SUMMARY

THE UNITED STATES CONSTITUTION

The United States Constitution is the declaration of fundamental principles by which our nation is governed. It is the supreme law of the land.

1. The Constitution creates and defines the powers of the three branches of government: the executive, legislative, and judicial.
2. The Constitution limits the power of each branch of the government.
3. The Constitution says that the the government cannot intrude on the fundamental liberties and rights of the people.
4. Each of the fifty states has its own written constitution.

JUDICIAL REVIEW

Judicial review is the process by which the judicial branch determines whether a law is contrary to the Constitution. The doctrine of judicial review was first stated by the Supreme Court in *Marbury v. Madison* in 1803.

FEDERALISM

Federalism is a political arrangement in which two or more levels of government direct the affairs of the same people in the same location. In the United States, the two main levels of government are the federal government and the state government. If a state law interferes or conflicts with federal law, the federal law rules.

THE MAKEUP OF THE UNITED STATES SUPREME COURT

The court consists of nine justices appointed by the president and confirmed by the United States Senate. They serve on the court until voluntary retirement, death, or removal for misbehavior.

THE BILL OF RIGHTS

The first ten amendments to the U.S. Constitution make up the Bill of Rights. The Bill of Rights is applied to state and local governments through the Fourteenth Amendment's due process clause.

1. Yes. Both state and federal courts have the power to declare acts of the legislative and executive branches of government unconstitutional and thus void, if such acts are not in accordance with the Constitution. The doctrine of judicial review was first enunciated by the United States Supreme Court in Chief Justice John Marshall's *Marbury* v. *Madison* opinion.

2. If there is a conflict between federal and state law, the federal government's laws prevail. Some legal powers are concurrent; they are granted to both federal and state governments.

3. The Tenth Amendment spells out the reserved powers of the states. These powers are not given to the national government, nor can they be taken away from the states by the federal government.

4. Pure speech is the peaceful expression of thought and opinion and is generally protected under the First Amendment; speech plus is verbal expression combined with some sort of action and may be subject to governmental restrictions; symbolic speech involves nonverbal expressions using symbols and may or may not be protected under the First Amendment.

5. Yes, free speech must be balanced with the needs of society. Governments have the right to regulate the time and place and manner of public speech. Additionally, a distinction is made between commercial and noncommercial speech. Advertising is given less constitutional protection than private or political speech.

6. The two ways the First Amendment guarantees the freedom of religion are through (1) the establishment clause, under which Congress is prohibited from establishing a state religion and (2) the free exercise clause, which prohibits government from interfering in the free exercise of religious beliefs.

7. The power to regulate most business activities was given to the federal government to allow for uniform rules to be applied to the movement of goods throughout the states.

FIRST AMENDMENT FREEDOMS

The First Amendment guarantees many personal freedoms. Of great importance are the freedoms of speech and religion.

1. *Freedom of speech*—All persons in the United States have the right to freedom of speech, press, assembly, and petition.

2. *Freedom of religion*—The government may neither establish any religion nor prohibit the free exercise of religious practices.

BUSINESS, THE CONSTITUTION, AND THE COMMERCE CLAUSE

A provision of the Constitution called the commerce clause gives Congress the right to regulate commerce among the states. On the basis of this constitutional power, as interpreted by the U.S. Supreme Court, business in the United States has been subject to the jurisdiction of the federal courts and to regulation by the federal government.

◆ USING LEGAL LANGUAGE

Directions: Match each term with the statement that best defines that term.

1. bench trial
2. Bill of Rights
3. Constitution
4. federalism
5. judicial review
6. natural law
7. police powers
8. pure speech
9. supremacy doctrine
10. symbolic speech

A. The _____ consists of the first ten amendments to the federal Constitution.

B. The First Amendment protects _____, which is the peaceful expression of thought and opinion before a willing audience.

C. _____ is basic moral law which is consistent with nature, applies to all persons, and does not change.

D. Under _____ two or more levels of government direct the affairs of the same people in the same location.

E. The inherent right and power of the state to protect or promote the public health, safety, or general welfare of their citizens are called _____.

F. The first amendment protects _____, which involves nonverbal expressions using symbols.

G. The _____ is a written declaration of fundamental principles by which a nation is governed.

H. The power of the federal courts to determine whether a particular law violates the Constitution is found in _____.

I. The _____ is the rule that any state law that conflicts with federal law is invalid.

J. A _____ occurs when a case is heard only in front of a judge.

8. Federalism is a political arrangement in which two or more levels of government (federal and state) direct the affairs of the same people in the same location. If there is a conflict between federal law and state law, the federal law controls.
9. If an employee's right to the free exercise of his or her religion conflicts with the demands of an employer, the employer must "reasonably accommodate" the employee's religious needs. If the employer fires Tollens without first attempting a reasonable accommodation of her religious needs, very likely a court would hold that the firm violated Title VII of the Civil Rights Act of 1964. What constitutes "reasonable accommodation" usually varies depending on the specific circumstances of each case. Here, the employer should consider the reasonableness of its demands and consider alternative efforts that might be undertaken to meet its deadlines. For example, the employer might arrange for Tollens to work longer than eight hours a day during the rest of the week to compensate for her not working on Saturday. Or perhaps it would be in the firm's best interest to hire additional, temporary employees until its backlog of orders is filled.

Applying the Law . . . You Be the Judge (Answers)

1. The United States Supreme Court did not agree with Taxpayers. The Court upheld the ordinance because it furthered a substantial interest of the city of Los Angeles (to improve its appearance) that is basically unrelated to the suppression of free expression. Further, the ordinance curtailed no more speech than was necessary to accomplish its purpose. If the ordinance had banned the only forum available for the public expression of ideas, the result would have been different. In this case, however, the Court reasoned that the citizens of Los Angeles had numerous alternative forums for free public speech. The Court thus held that the city's interest in passing the ordinance outweighed the slight curtailment of free speech imposed by the ordinance.

 ## CHECKING FOR COMPREHENSION

1. Judicial review allows the courts to decide whether actions of the legislative and executive branches are constitutional. Is this a correct statement? Explain.

2. All levels of government have the power to pass laws. If there is a conflict, which level prevails? Can the federal and state government have the same legal powers?

3. What is the effect of the Tenth Amendment?

4. Describe the three general categories of free speech as distinguished by the U.S. Supreme Court and tell how they are protected by the First Amendment.

5. Does the federal government have the right to restrict free speech?

6. In what two ways does the First Amendment guarantee the freedom of religion?

7. Why does the Constitution expressly grant the federal government the power to regulate commerce among the states?

8. Explain Federalism in the United States.

9. A business has a backlog of orders, and to meet its deadlines management decided to run the firm seven days a week, eight hours a day. One of the employees, Marjorie Tollens, refuses to work on Saturday on religious grounds. Her refusal to work means that the firm may not meet its production deadlines and may therefore suffer a loss of future business. Tollens is fired by the firm, and she is replaced by an employee who is willing to work seven days a week. Tollens claims that her employer, in terminating her employment, violated her constitutional right to freely exercise her religion. Do you agree? Why or why not?

APPLYING LEGAL CONCEPTS

1. Using Table 2-2, "Profile of Supreme Court Justices to 1992," create bar graphs illustrating various sections of the table.

2. Debate the following issues: (1) Nine is/is not an appropriate number of justices to serve on the Supreme Court; (2) the President should appoint Supreme Court Justices/Supreme Court Justices should be elected; (3) Supreme Court Justices should serve until voluntary retirement/should serve only a specified number of years.

APPLYING THE LAW . . . YOU BE THE JUDGE

1. A Los Angeles city ordinance prohibits the posting of signs on public property (such as lamp posts, utility posts, hydrants, traffic signs, and so on). During a campaign in which Roland Vincent was running for City Council, his supporters wanted to post signs on the cross-arms supporting utility poles. The group campaigning for Vincent (called "Taxpayers") challenged the city ordinance prohibiting signs on such property, claiming that the ordinance was unconstitutional because it violated the freedom of speech guaranteed by the First Amendment. Do you agree with Taxpayers? [*Los Angeles City Council v. Taxpayers for Vincent*, 466 U.S. 789, 104 S.Ct. 2118, 80 L.Ed.2d 772 (1984)]

2. Thomas worked in the nonmilitary operations of a large firm. When the production

2. The United States Supreme Court held that religious beliefs and practices do not have to be acceptable, logical, or comprehensible to others for them to merit the protection of the First Amendment guarantee to the free exercise of religion. Right or wrong, Thomas's religious convictions were honestly and openly held, and the Court concluded that his transfer to the war-materials plant, where he was directly involved in the manufacture of weapons, effectively placed him in the position of having to choose between his job and his religious principles. Thomas's departure from the company was thus a result of a decision made by the employer, and Thomas should be entitled to unemployment compensation.

3. The United States Supreme Court concluded that the ordinance was unconstitutional on its face because it reached too far into the realm of protected (noncommercial) speech. The Court emphasized that commercial speech could be forbidden and regulated in situations in which noncommercial speech

of nonmilitary goods was discontinued by the company, Thomas was transferred to a plant producing war materials. Thomas left his job, claiming that it violated his religious principles to participate in the manufacture of materials to be used in destroying life. In effect, he argued, the transfer to the war-materials plant forced him to quit his job. He was denied unemployment compensation by the state, which maintained that Thomas had not been effectively "discharged" by the employer but had voluntarily terminated his employment. Does the state's denial of unemployment compensation to Thomas violate the free exercise clause of the First Amendment? [*Thomas v. Review Board of the Indiana Employment Security Division*, 450 U.S. 707, 101 S.Ct. 1425, 67 L.Ed.2d 624 (1981)]

3. The city of San Diego enacted an ordinance that imposed substantial prohibitions on the erection of outdoor advertising displays within the city. The purpose of the ordinance was "to eliminate hazards to pedestrians and motorists brought about by distracting sign displays" and "to preserve and improve the appearance of the City." The ordinance permitted on-site commercial advertising (defined as a sign advertising goods or services available on the property where the sign was located) but forbade other commercial advertising and noncommercial advertising using fixed-structure signs. The ordinance did provide for exceptions, such as temporary political campaign signs. Companies that were engaged in the outdoor-advertising business brought suit in state court to enjoin enforcement of the ordinance. In evaluating the constitutionality of the ordinance, the question before the court was whether San Diego's interests in the safety and appearance of its city could justify the restrictions placed on commercial and noncommercial freedom of speech. How did the court decide? [*Metromedia, Inc. v. City of San Diego*, 453 U.S. 490, 101 S.Ct. 2882, 69 L.Ed.2d 800 (1981)]

could not, but San Diego's ordinance effectively inverted this position. Although San Diego's goals—traffic safety and the city's appearance—were substantial government interests, and the city went no further than necessary in seeking to accomplish its ends, the ordinance provided a broad exception for on-site commercial advertisements with no similar exception for noncommercial speech. The Court stated that although the city could distinguish between the relative value of categories of commercial speech, the city does not have the same range of choice to evaluate or distinguish among various noncommercial interests. With respect to noncommercial speech, the city may not choose the appropriate subjects for public discourse: "To allow a government the choice of permissible subjects for public debate would be to allow that government control over the search for political truth." Finally, the Court reasoned that because some commercial messages could be conveyed on billboards throughout the commercial and industrial zones, the city must allow billboards conveying other noncommercial messages in those zones.

Prereading Activity

Ask students if they know anyone who has ever been to court. Ask students if they have watched a trial on television. Lead a discussion about court procedures students have seen or what they have experienced within the court system.

Mastery Objectives

By the end of this chapter, students will be able to:
- Differentiate the various connotations of the term *court*
- Distinguish between the types of jurisdiction
- Describe the federal court system
- Explain the adversary system of justice
- Demonstrate how to use small claims court
- List the steps to follow a case through court

Chapter 3

Courts and the Legal System

Resources and Assignment Guide

Activity Sheets
Reviewing Legal Concepts 3 *TRB*
Enrichment Activity 3 *TRB*

Student Activity Workbook
Chapter 3 Activities

Tests
Chapter 3 Test *TRB*
Chapter 3 WESTEST Computerized Testing

Handbook of Selected Court Cases
Donnelly v. *Yellow Freight System, Inc.*
Reuther v. *Fowler & Williams, Inc.*

West's Business Law and Legal Environment Videodisc
Still Frames and Motion Segments as shown

Ethical Concern

Have students prepare a short report citing several modern-day occurrences that reflect "a government of *men*, and not of *laws*." (Modern day means in this century.) To get them started, point out what happened in Nazi Germany before World War II started, when thousands of innocent people lost their businesses and homes for no reason.

Critical Thinking Activity

What forms people's beliefs—parents, tradition, religion, peers, etc.? Why does perception of what is fair differ among diverse groups?

Legal Focus Example

Have a student volunteer read aloud to the class this humorous Legal Focus Example. Be sure that the students understand that even though this Legal Focus Example is of a humorous nature, it also illustrates the need for unbiased and fair judges and judgments.

"A government of laws, and not of men."
John Adams (1735–1826)
Second President of the United States (1797–1801)

You are walking or driving home from school one day and a police officer pulls you over. The officer tells you that she suspects that you have committed a crime. She does not tell you what crime nor why you are under suspicion. Instead, she puts you in her patrol car and takes you to the local jail, where you are booked and put into a cell. Your parents are not notified, nor are any of your friends. You stay there for several days. Finally, you are let out with no explanation, not even an apology.

The scenario just described is a frightening possibility. But it is one that rarely if ever happens in modern-day America. Why not? Because this is a nation, as President John Adams once said, that has a government of laws rather than of men and women. What he was saying in the quote that started this chapter is that no individuals can decide on their own what is right and what is wrong. Our rules of conduct are now governed by the laws that are created by the lawmakers whom we elect. Those laws are applied by our court system. Our court system also applies many of the rules and customs handed down from the common law in England, which you learned about in Chapter 1.

The United States has a rich blend of cultures. It is particularly important that we be governed by laws so that everyone, no matter what that person's cultural background, is treated fairly. Indeed, the more diverse a nation, the more important the rule of law to fairly resolve disputes.

◆ LEGAL FOCUS – EXAMPLE

The traffic court judge found himself facing two attorneys, both of whom he knew very well. "Gentlemen," he said, "I could not be very objective in either of your cases, so I'm going to let you judge each other's cases." Both lawyers agreed. The first climbed to the bench. "You are charged with driving 40 in a 25-mile-an-hour zone. How do you plead?" he asked. "Guilty," responded attorney number two. "I fine you $25," said number one. Then they exchanged places. "You are charged with driving 40 in a 25-mile-an-hour zone," said number two. "What is your plea?" "Guilty," said number one. "Then I fine you $100," said number two. "Hey! That's unfair," said the first. "I only fined you $25." "Yes," was the reply, "but there is too much speeding going on. This is the second case we've had like that today."

The story is amusing, but the treatment of the second driver is indeed inconsistent and unfair. It shows what may happen when a biased judge

Teaching Note

The Legal Perspective that follows this chapter is integral to course content and should not be skipped. Further, some items in the end of the chapter review section relate to this Legal Perspective.

Divide the class into groups of four, and encourage each group to define and discuss the word *bias*. Why is neutrality needed in our system to eliminate bias? Have students give examples of bias that they have seen. Which laws protect them from such bias?

Teaching with the Videodisc

The still frames listed below from the **West's Business Law and Legal Environment Videodisc** can be used with this chapter. To access this material, use the bar codes or the frame numbers included in the Videodisc Instructor's Manual found in the *TRB*.

The Organization of the Federal Court System
Federal and State Jurisdiction
Stare Decisis in the Dual Court System
A Typical State Court System
A Typical Lawsuit
Stages in Civil Procedure

The videodisc also has the following motion segment:

Pendent Jurisdiction

Extension Activity

Allow a volunteer or a group of volunteers to research the court or courts that are nearest your school. What is the name of this court(s)? Over what subject matters and geographic areas does this court have jurisdiction? What kinds of legal cases could not be heard in your local court?

Vocabulary Activity

Call on individual students to explain the different connotations of the word *court*.

◆ **bias** A prior opinion or belief; a prejudice. A biased person may be unable to make a fair decision.

◆ **court** A place provided by government where people may go to resolve legal disputes. There are different types of courts for different types of disputes.

◆ **lawsuit**, or **litigation** Civil court proceeding brought to enforce a right between persons.

decides the case. A judge has a **bias** when he or she has a personal interest in the outcome of a case. Bias also exists if a judge reaches a conclusion about a case before hearing it.

Our system strives to provide both reasonable consistency and *neutrality*, the elimination of bias. The rule of law is served by an independent neutral forum (a place) and a neutral decision maker (a judge and jury). In the United States, this forum is our court system. A **court** is a place where facts are determined and rules applied. The purpose of a court is to ensure that decisions about important issues are consistent and fair and are not made on the basis of individual emotions.

In the world of business, disputes arise all the time between buyers and sellers and between employers and employees. In your own personal life, you may be involved in a legal dispute, particularly if you drive a car. Statistics show that your chances of being in an auto accident at least once in your life are almost 100 percent. If somebody hits you while you are going through an intersection and bangs up your car, putting you out of work for six weeks, you may end up suing. If you do, you will be involved in what is called **litigation**. Talking about litigation is another way of talking about a **lawsuit**, which can be defined as an action pending between two private parties within our court system. In the case of your suing the driver of the car that hit your car, you would probably be involved in a lawsuit in your state court system.

Every state's court system has certain characteristics. That means that there are fifty different types of state court systems. In addition, the federal government has its own court system, and so does our nation's capital, the District of Columbia. You will be reading about the common features of the state court systems in this chapter, as well as about the federal court system. At the end of the chapter is a Legal Perspective that follows a typical case through a typical state court system. While obviously there are courts that hear criminal cases, the focus of this chapter is noncriminal, or civil, disputes.

◆ WHAT IS A COURT?

A court is both a place and a system. It is a place where people may go to resolve disputes in a peaceful and logical way. In this sense, the word *court* describes a location ("I'll see you in court!"); all participants, including the attorneys, the clerks, the witnesses, the parties, and the public ("Court is in session"); and the judge or justice ("If the court please, may I be heard at this time?").

Courts are also part of a system. There are different courts for different types of legal disputes. Some courts determine the facts of individual disputes. Other courts review decisions of lower courts for correctness, consistency, and fairness.

Select students to research and report to the class on the following topic: "Why are so many legal terms derived from Latin words?"

Read to the class the Legal Focus Problem found here. Allow student volunteers to suggest possible answers to this problem.

Ask the students to define the following terms on paper: *jurisdiction, long-arm statute, subject-matter jurisdiction, general jurisdiction, limited jurisdiction, small claims court,* and *venue.* Have them write an example of the kind of case in which each term would apply.

Vocabulary Activity

Ask students to explain why the "long-arm" statute is so named.

JURISDICTION

To understand the courts, we must first understand the notion of jurisdiction. In Latin, *juris* means "law," and *diction* means "to speak." Thus, "the power to speak the law" is the precise meaning of the term **jurisdiction**. The term is used many ways, but always in relation to right and power. Questions of jurisdiction are about political boundaries, persons and property, and the type and amount of a dispute.

Jurisdiction describes the geographical area (usually a political boundary, such as a state) within which a court has the right and power to decide cases. For example, the Texas Supreme Court may be said to have jurisdiction to hear a particular case in Texas. Before any court can hear a case, it must also have jurisdiction over the person being sued. And if someone brings a suit over property, a court must have jurisdiction over that property.

♦ **jurisdiction** The power of a court to hear and decide a specific case.

JURISDICTION OVER PERSONS

Many questions arise about which courts have jurisdiction over which people.

LEGAL FOCUS – PROBLEM

Maya Wolfe, a citizen of Florida, was walking near a busy street in Tallahassee, Florida. A large crate flew off a passing truck—a drive-it-yourself rental driven by Jorge Centosa—and hit her. Maya suffered extensive injuries. Jorge left his name and address. Now the question for Maya is, can she bring her suit in a Florida state court?

The answer depends on whether Jorge can be served with a *summons*—an order informing him that a lawsuit has been filed against him. The summons has to be served within the boundaries of the state of Florida for a state court to have the power and right to hear the case. If Jorge is a resident of Florida or lives elsewhere but does extensive business within the state of Florida, then personal jurisdiction by Florida state courts is normally possible.

What if Jorge had given Maya an address in the neighboring state of Georgia? Can Maya still sue Jorge in Florida, or does she have to go to Georgia? The answer is not always clear. Normally, a court's power is limited to the geographic boundaries of the state in which it is located. Fortunately for Maya, though, a court can often obtain jurisdiction over a nonresident who is being sued through what is called a **long-arm statute**. Nonresidents are people who do not live in the state in which a suit is being filed. In this example, a nonresident is anybody who does not live in Florida. A long-arm statute is a state law that gives a court the power to

♦ **long-arm statute** State law that authorizes a court to hear cases brought against nonresidents in certain circumstances.

Critical Thinking Activity

Ask students to write a paragraph explaining why municipal courts are courts of limited jurisdiction.

Ethical Concern

Point out to your students that many times a change of venue is requested because of the media's pre-trial publicity of a case. Start a discussion by asking the question: Do you think the media should have stricter rules on covering upcoming court cases? Why or why not?

hear cases involving nonresidents who are being sued, in some circumstances. In most states, long-arm statutes allow a state resident to sue a nonresident who has been involved in an automobile accident. In our particular problem, if Jorge lives in Georgia, Maya may still sue him in Florida because of Florida's long-arm statute. Jorge will normally be given notice of the lawsuit by mail.

SUBJECT-MATTER JURISDICTION

There are literally thousands of county, state, and federal courts in the United States. Certainly, common sense tells you that if you wanted to dispute a traffic ticket, you would not go to the United States Supreme Court. And common sense tells you that if you thought that you had been discriminated against and that your constitutional rights had been violated, you would not go to the local traffic court with your problem. Each court has jurisdiction over certain matters. **Subject-matter jurisdiction** determines which types of cases a court can hear.

A court of **general jurisdiction** can decide almost any type of case but normally does not get involved in very specific types of disputes, such as traffic violations. Courts of **limited jurisdiction**, in contrast, can only hear subject matters that are very well defined. A traffic court only hears traffic violations, for example, and some courts only hear cases involving family disputes—divorces and child custody.

Normally, the law that creates a court specifies its subject-matter jurisdiction. Sometimes a court's subject-matter jurisdiction may be limited by law to a specified amount of money. So-called **small claims courts** in each state can only hear disputes involving relatively limited amounts of money, such as anything up to $3,000. (You'll read more about these courts later in this chapter.)

VENUE

For courts in each category, there are several possible physical locations. In other words, there is not just one state court; rather, there are many scattered throughout each state. If you bring a lawsuit against someone, you have to decide which court is in the right geographic location for your situation. The term **venue** is used to define the proper place within a judicial district to bring your lawsuit. Typically, a court trying a suit should be close to where the incident leading to the suit occurred or close to where the parties involved in the suit live. Normally, this means that the court should be in the same county. In the problem described earlier, Maya would not try to bring her lawsuit in a state court in Miami when the accident occurred in Tallahassee, Florida.

Certain famous cases receive tremendous pre-trial publicity. If the suit is going to go to a jury trial, the parties involved may ask for a *change of venue* in order to ensure that an impartial jury can be found. Normally, requests for a change in venue occur in serious criminal cases.

♦ **subject-matter jurisdiction** The type of cases a court is authorized to hear. The difference between courts of general jurisdiction and courts of special, or limited, jurisdiction lies in the different subject matter of cases heard.

♦ **general jurisdiction** Court that is authorized to hear and decide virtually any type of case.

♦ **limited jurisdiction** Court that is limited in the types of cases it can hear and decide.

♦ **small claims court** State court of limited jurisdiction created to consider matters involving a small sum of money damages.

♦ **venue** The proper place within a judicial district to bring a lawsuit.

Critical Thinking Activity

Lead a class discussion by asking students why they think a change of venue was requested in the Rodney King case. Did the change of venue cause additional problems? Why?

Legal Focus
Case Example

Read this Legal Focus Case Example to the class. Then allow class members to share what they remember regarding the Rodney King case and its aftermath. As an extension assignment, you might allow volunteers to look up what has happened since 1992 to Rodney King or the police officers accused of assaulting him, or what has happened to the Los Angeles neighborhoods that were destroyed in the resulting riots.

◀ **LEGAL FOCUS - CASE EXAMPLE**

One of the most famous cases involving a change of venue in the 1990s occurred in Los Angeles, California, in the spring of 1992. An African-American motorist named Rodney King was chased in his car, stopped, and beaten by four Los Angeles police officers. The officers were accused of using excessive force. The beating was taped by a bystander, who provided the video to television stations nationwide, and the videotape was replayed thousands of times across the nation. The publicity surrounding the beating caused the attorneys for the police officers to request a change of venue from Los Angeles. The attorneys argued that the officers could not get a fair trial. The request was granted. The trial was transferred to Simi Valley, some 40 miles away. There, the Simi Valley jurors entered a "not guilty" verdict. The verdict was followed by several days of rioting in South Central Los Angeles—the most extensive and expensive inner-city rioting in the history of the United States. Critics of the jury verdict argued that the change of venue to a community that contained very few minorities was improper, particularly given that the jury did not reflect the cultural and ethnic makeup of the community in which the alleged excessive force by the four white police officers occurred.

The force used by police officers to arrest a suspect, Rodney King, led to several police officers being arrested later for excessive use of force. Because of the extensive pre-trial publicity, the defendants requested and were granted a change of venue.

67

State Law

One type of trial court found in the state of Texas is the Municipal Court. These courts deal mainly with traffic violations and are frequently referred to as traffic courts. In 1991 Texas Municipal Courts were kept very busy. The 849 Municipal Courts handled an incredible 6,024,681 cases, of which more than 5 million—88 percent—were traffic violations.

 # THE STATE COURT SYSTEM

The typical state court system consists of both trial and appellate courts. Consider the typical state court system shown in Exhibit 3-1. It has three main levels: (1) trial courts of general or limited jurisdiction, (2) intermediate appellate courts, and (3) the highest court (usually the supreme court).

TRIAL COURTS

trial court The court where the facts of a dispute are heard and decided.

If you are ever involved in a lawsuit that goes to trial, you normally will have the suit heard in a **trial court**. A trial court has several purposes. The first purpose is to determine the facts of the dispute: "What happened between the competing parties?" To determine the facts, the trial court will hear **evidence**, information presented at the trial by the parties and accepted by the court. Examples of evidence are testimony of witnesses, photographs, documents, handwriting samples, dented fenders, and the like. The parties to a lawsuit decide what evidence they wish to produce. The trial court then determines what rules of law apply to the facts. Finally, the trial court must apply those rules to the proven facts to decide who wins and what they win. Trial courts have **original jurisdiction**—the right to hear a case first to decide it.

evidence Information presented at the trial by the parties and accepted by the court. Examples of evidence include testimony of witnesses, photographs, documents, handwriting samples, dented fenders, and the like.

State trial courts have either general or limited jurisdiction. Trial courts with general subject-matter jurisdiction are called *county*, *district*, *superior*, or *circuit* courts.[1] The jurisdiction of these courts is often determined by the size of the county in which the court sits. Many important cases involving businesses begin in these general trial courts.

original jurisdiction The power of a court to take a case, try it, and decide it.

Trial courts that have limited subject-matter jurisdiction are called *inferior courts* or *minor judiciary* courts. We already mentioned the small claims court when we discussed limited-jurisdiction courts. It is an example of an inferior trial court. Most local municipal courts—the ones that hear traffic violations in particular—are inferior trial courts of limited jurisdiction.

APPELLATE COURTS

appellate court Court that reviews the actions of trial courts.

After a trial has been held, a decision is made either by the judge, if it is a trial without a jury, or by the jury. The party that loses the trial may not agree with the decision. That party may request a review of the trial. This review is handled by another court, called an **appellate court**. Appellate courts review decisions by lower courts. Appellate courts are sometimes called reviewing courts for this reason. Appellate courts do not hear new evidence or make new determinations of facts. Rather, they focus on whether the law was correctly stated or applied to the facts by the trial court. Appellate courts may approve of what the trial court did and let the

---

1. The name in Ohio is Court of Common Pleas; the name in New York is Supreme Court.

State Supreme Court

Highest state court. Some states call it the court of appeals, supreme judicial court, or supreme court of appeals.

Intermediate Appellate Courts

Only twenty-three states have intermediate appellate courts.

Probate Court*

This court handles wills, adminstration of estates, and guardianship of minors and others. Some states call it surrogate court or orphans' court.

Superior Court

Highest state trial court with general jurisdiction. Some states call it circuit court, district court, court of common pleas, or (in New York) supreme court.

Domestic Relations Court*

Some states call it family court or juvenile court.

Municipal Court*

In some states, municipal justices or magistrates hear less important cases.

County Court*

This court has limited jurisdiction in civil and criminal cases. Some states call it common pleas court or district court.

Justice of the Peace Court

Lowest state court. Limited jurisdiction in civil and criminal cases. Some states call it police magistrate court. This court does not exist in all states.

*Courts of limited jurisdiction, such as probate, domestic relations, municipal, or county courts, may be separate courts or may be part of a trial court of general jurisdiction.

EXHIBIT 3-1
A TYPICAL STATE COURT SYSTEM

Enrichment

Bring in a few newspapers to your classroom, and ask your students to read the section that reports on crimes and wrongdoings. Ask your students to identify the court in which each case will be tried.

VIDEODISC NOTE
Much of the material that is conveyed in the exhibits of *West's Business and Personal Law* is also conveyed in the still frames on the **West Business Law and Legal Environment Videodisc**. For more information and directions for use, please see the Index and Description of Contents for the **West Business Law and Legal Environment Videodisc** that is found in your *Teacher's Resource Binder*.

Ask students to write a paragraph or two on the differences among trial courts, appellate courts, and the Supreme Court.

Ask a student to lead a class discussion about why there is at least one federal district court in every state and territory.

Checking Your Progress (Answers)

1. The purpose of a court is to ensure that decisions about important issues are consistent and fair and not made on the basis of indivdual whim.
2. A court is a place where facts in disputes are presented and a judge and jury apply rules to decide important issues in a fair and consistent manner.
3. Jurisdiction can be based on (a) political boundaries, (b) persons and property, or (c) type and amount of the dispute.
4. A change of venue might be necessary if the issue cannot be solved fairly because of pretrial publicity or the inability to find an impartial jury.
5. The three purposes of a trial court are (a) to determine the facts of a dispute, (b) to determine rules of law, and (c) to apply those rules.

trial court's decision stand. Alternatively, they may tell the trial court to retry the case or do something else that it was not going to do.

Not everybody who loses a case at the trial court level will appeal. One of the reasons is that appealing a case is expensive and time consuming. The appeal may drag on for years. Indeed, most trial decisions are either not appealed or stand up when they are appealed.

Every state has at least one appellate, or review, court. The subject-matter jurisdiction of these courts is usually limited to hearing appeals. About half the states have two levels of appellate courts. The most common name for the first-level, or intermediate-level, appellate court is the *court of appeals*. The second-level appellate court is the state's highest court and is usually called the *supreme court*.[2] If the state has but one level of appellate court, it is usually also called the *supreme court*. The decisions of each state's highest court on all questions of state law are final. Only when an issue of federal law exists can the United States Supreme Court overrule the state's highest court.

◆ CHECKING YOUR PROGRESS

1. What is the purpose of a court?
2. What is a court?
3. List three questions of jurisdiction.
4. Why might a change of venue be necessary?
5. What are the three purposes of a trial court?

◆ THE FEDERAL COURT SYSTEM

Just as there is a state government—with a legislature, a chief executive (the governor), and a court system—there is a federal government, which includes the federal court system. The federal court system is in many ways similar to a state court system. It has three levels consisting of trial courts, courts of appeal, and one supreme court. Look at Exhibit 3-2 to see the organization of our federal court system. All federal judges and justices, including the nine justices of the United States Supreme Court, are appointed by the president, with the advice and consent of the Senate. The U.S. Constitution says that federal judges "shall hold their offices during good Behavior," meaning the appointments are for life.

---

2. In New York, it is called the Court of Appeals.

Highest State Courts	Supreme Court of the United States	
Special Court Regional Rail Reorganization	Courts of Appeal for the United States and the District of Columbia	Courts of Appeal for the Federal Circuit
U.S. Court of Military Appeals*		U.S. Claims Court
		Court of International Trade
	U.S. Bankruptcy Court	District Courts of the United States
Departments, Agencies, and Officers	U.S. Tax Court	Courts of the Territories and Insular Possessions

*Highest court in the military system.

EXHIBIT 3-2
THE ORGANIZATION OF THE FEDERAL COURT SYSTEM

JURISDICTION OF THE FEDERAL COURTS

State courts have specific jurisdictions, and so do the federal courts. If you have a traffic accident with your neighbor involving a minor fender bender, normally you cannot go to federal court with your problem if you want to bring a lawsuit. The jurisdiction of the federal courts is established by the U.S. Constitution and the Congress. The Constitution established

VIDEODISC NOTE
Much of the material that is conveyed in the exhibits of *West's Business and Personal Law* is also conveyed in the still frames on the **West Business Law and Legal Environment Videodisc**. For more information and directions for use, please see the Index and Description of Contents for the **West Business Law and Legal Environment Videodisc** that is found in your *Teacher's Resource Binder*.

Read

Before the students begin reading this *Law in Action* feature, let them share their own knowledge about—and perhaps experiences with—small claims court. Ask: What is the purpose of small claims court? Whom are small claims courts intended to serve? Have you or any of your family members ever been to small claims court? If so, why, and with what results? Based on what you now know, do you anticipate that you will ever use a small claims court? Why or why not? After a short discussion, have the students read the feature independently.

Discuss

Use questions such as these to guide students in using the *Law in Action* feature: Why might each of the examples at the beginning of this feature lead you to a small claims court? What other examples can you think of? Why are these courts called small claims courts? How do the procedural rules in a small claims court differ from those of traditional trial courts? Why is checking with the clerk of a small claims court an essential first step? How will sitting in on several small claims proceedings help you? What does it mean that "the small claims court does not act as a collection agency"? Why is it important to understand this fact

before you file suit? If you were preparing to go to small claims court, would you consult with a friend who was a lawyer? Do you think you would pay for a consultation with a lawyer? Why or why not? How could inaccuracies in your presentation prejudice your case? What does it mean to settle the case out of court? Why is it important to have written evidence of any attempts to settle out of court?

Ask your students to think of a time when they feel that they have been treated unfairly by a business. Have your students write a sample demand letter to this business.

Law in Action

LAW IN YOUR LIFE: SMALL CLAIMS COURTS

- The sole on one of your brand new sneakers separates from the rest of the shoe. The store you bought them from refuses to repair or replace them.
- A company repairs your car and guarantees its work for ninety days. Three weeks later, it refuses to honor the guarantee.
- A dry cleaner ruins your expensive jacket after you have worn it only once.

If you ever felt helpless in situations like these, there are ways you can get help. Local government consumer protection and licensing agencies, the Better Business Bureau, and negotiation and persistence might help you resolve your problem. You should also send a formal demand letter to the offending party. (See Exhibit 3-3.) This document should be no more than two double-spaced, typewritten pages and should clearly summarize the facts, as well as your demand of the other party. If your attempts to resolve your problem do not succeed, you can use the local small claims court.

WHAT ARE SMALL CLAIMS COURTS?

In legal terms, a small claims court is a state court of limited jurisdiction created to consider matters involving a small sum of money damages. A street definition may be more helpful—the people's court. Small claims court is where an average citizen without legal training can seek to resolve legal disputes in a speedy, informal, and uncomplicated manner.

Your address
Date

Addressee
Company Name
Street Address
City, State Zip Code

Dear Sir or Madam,

I am writing this letter to inform you of my dissatisfaction with [name of product with serial number or the service performed], which I purchased [the date and location of purchase].

My complaint concerns [the reason(s) for your complaint]. I believe that in all fairness you should [the specific action you desire for satisfaction] in order to resolve this problem.

I sincerely look forward to your reply and a speedy resolution to my complaint. I will allow two weeks before referring this complaint to the appropriate consumer agency.

Yours truly,

Your Name

Enclosure (include copies, not originals, of all related records)

EXHIBIT 3-3
DEMAND LETTER

THE PURPOSE OF THE SMALL CLAIMS COURT

The purpose of the small claims court is the same as that of any other trial court—to determine facts and apply the law to the case—although the way the court operates is very different. Small claims courts exist to help "the little person" get his or her "day in court." However, because businesses usually have a large number of small claims, they are the most frequent users of small claims courts.

Ask a student to call your local small claims court to find out the maximum amount of damages that a person can sue for in small claims court in your state, and how much the court costs are.

Let the students work in small groups to discuss what they have learned about small claims court. Who uses this court? How do those people use the court? What kind of results are usually achieved? Then have the group members work together to write a short story or a skit about people involved in a small claims suit.

Extension Activity

Ask a student from a law school in your area to come to talk to the class about how to prepare for an action in small claims court. To prepare for the session, have the class members collaborate on a "wrong" that could happen to a young person, e.g., an auto accident, or a claim against a local store or mail-order company.

 Law in Action (Continued)

HOW DOES A SMALL CLAIMS COURT WORK?

The small claims court may be a separate court or a subdivision of another court, depending on state law. Because each state creates its own small claims courts, exactly how the courts operate varies from state to state. The maximum amount of damages recoverable ranges from $250 to more than $5,000, depending on the state. The common maximum range is $1,500–2,500. Many states have recently increased the dollar limits for these courts.[3]

The procedural rules in a small claims court differ from those of traditional trial courts. There are fewer legal documents. Often, the only formal document required of the person bringing suit is a simple preprinted form with boxes for the person to check. Checked boxes will indicate the type of lawsuit and what the person hopes to recover. In a usual trial court, there are formal rules of evidence, but in small claims courts, evidence rules are relaxed. There is no jury in small claims court. In the interests of economy and simplicity, most states do not permit attorneys to represent parties in small claims court.

During the trial, each party tells his or her version of the dispute, calling on witnesses for support or for added facts. Each party also presents any supporting documents or other physical evidence. The judge may ask questions. Then, without any elaborate ar-

gument or research, he or she decides the case. Sometimes, the judge rules immediately after the trial, but often the judge informs the parties of the decision later, by mail.

HOW CAN YOU USE A SMALL CLAIMS COURT?

To use a small claims court, first ask the clerk of the small claims court in your area whether the court can handle your kind of case. For example, some large cities have special courts to handle problems between renters and landlords. Check with the clerk to see if your state has a small claims advisory group. Some states (and some local law schools) provide people with help in preparing small claims actions.

Make sure that the court has jurisdiction over the person or business you wish to sue. Usually, this person must live, work, or do business in the court's territory. If you're trying to sue an out-of-town person or firm, you may run into problems. You probably should go to the state government, usually the secretary of state, to find out where to send the summons, which tells the person or business about the suit. Also, remember that the small claims court does not act as a collection agency. If you file a suit against someone with no money or a firm that no longer is in business, you'll have a very difficult time collecting even if you win.

PREPARING FOR TRIAL

How should you prepare for the small claims trial? Obviously, if you know a lawyer, seek advice from him or her. In any event, be ready to show the judge any receipts, canceled checks, written estimates,

(continued on page 74)

---

3. For example, current maximum recoveries are indicated in this sample of states: California, $5,000 for the first two claims in a year and $2,500 for any additional claims; Texas, $1,000 in counties with populations below 400,000 and $2,500 in counties with populations above 400,000; Illinois, $2,500; Indiana, $3,000; Massachusetts and North Carolina, $1,500.

Extension Activity

Take your students to visit your local small claims court to view a few cases. You should be able to see more than one case. Contact the judge to find out which day would be best in order to see several cases.

Ethical Concern

Ask your students to imagine that they had taken a small business owner to small claims court for $1,000 in damages due to a faulty automobile repair. The defendant was negligent. Judgment was made in your favor; however, the small business went bankrupt. Can you collect? Start a class discussion around this situation. Is it fair? Was it worth going to court for? What can you do?

◆ Law in Action (Continued)

contracts, and other documents that provide proof about payments, costs, and so on. Set the entire affair down in the order in which it happened, with supporting evidence so you can show the judge. Make sure that your dates are accurate. Inaccurate information can hurt your case. It is important to hand the judge a copy of the demand letter you sent earlier. It will not only present your version of the story but will also show your reasonable approach to the situation.

If you are disputing something such as a household or auto repair job, you may have to get a third party—someone in the same trade—to testify as an "expert." It is often difficult to get people to testify against others in their own profession. The expert may, however, be willing to give a written statement. Many small claims courts consider such statements acceptable evidence. Bring any physical evidence of your claim into court. If, for example, your neighborhood dry cleaner shrank a wool sweater of yours, be sure to show it to the judge.

When you are at the courthouse filing your complaint, observe a few small claims court cases. Seeing other cases will give you an idea of what to expect when your day in court arrives. Write a list of your evidence and witnesses. Practice your intended presentation of the case. Reading your presentation is not very effective, so rehearse it. Think about the case the defendant will make. Think about the evidence and reasoning you will need to counter the other party's probable case.

WHAT HAPPENS IN COURT?

The judge will let you present your case in simple language without the help of a lawyer. In fact, as mentioned, in most states neither party may have a lawyer present.

You may receive the judge's decision immediately or by notice within a few weeks. In some states, either party can appeal if he or she loses, but in many states only the person being sued can appeal. If you think about appealing, remember to consider the costs of the action in time, grief, and money. Is the benefit worth those costs?

If your opponent tries to settle the case out of court, make sure the terms of the settlement are written. You should sign all written documents and file them with the court. The judge can use the settlement agreement as the judgment of the court. It is best to have your opponent appear with you before the judge to present the settlement terms. If you win or if you settle out of court, you should be able to get your opponent to pay for the court costs, which may be as high as $85 or more.

YOU HAVE TO WATCH OUT

Complications can arise in small claims court proceedings. In many states, the person being sued can transfer a case to a regular civil court. In most civil courts, your efforts are useless unless you have an attorney. If the case is transferred to the civil court, you must pay the expense of an attorney or drop the suit.

Also, winning in small claims court does not mean you will get paid. For example, the judgment may order your opponent to pay you $100 on a $150 claim (which, of course, is still $100 more than you started with). But no matter what that party is ordered to pay you, the small claims court does not act as a collection agency. The judgment merely gives you the legal right to make your claim. You may be able to get a document that allows you to take property, bank accounts, or wages of the party you sued if

Courts and the Legal System · 75

 Law in Action (Continued)

you can show that the party is not paying you. This document is, however, ineffective if the party has no money or property.

You should also realize that you probably will have to make several trips to the courthouse. Some small claims courts have evening sessions and some do not. People bringing suit spend between ten and thirty hours on court-related activities, such as filing papers, preparing the case, and so on. Going to court—even small claims court—takes time and energy.

To be a truly rational decision maker, you must weigh the potential benefits of going to court against the potential costs. If the potential gain to you means less than the value you place on saving your time and energies, it may be best to forget the whole matter. If, however, you believe that your case is just and you have lost a significant sum of money, "take it to court."

A SUMMARY OF HOW TO HANDLE YOUR CASE

1. Identify your opponent properly.
2. Send a demand letter.
3. Find the correct court.
4. File a claim.
5. Notify the defendant.
6. Assemble the evidence and witnesses.
7. Rehearse your presentation to the court.
8. Continue to try and settle out of court.
9. Present your case.
10. Stand up when you make your first address to the judge.
11. Do not read your statement; rather, present it conversationally.
12. Be brief.
13. Do not interrupt your opponent or any of the witnesses.
14. Bring the necessary physical materials, such as a diagram, a faded rug, a battered bicycle tire, or the like.
15. Remember that a judgment in your favor does not guarantee payment of the claim.

the Supreme Court and authorized Congress to establish other "inferior," or lower-level, federal courts. Among the inferior courts created by Congress are an intermediate appellate court called the United States Courts of Appeal, and a trial court of general jurisdiction, the United States District Courts.

The jurisdiction of a federal court includes any federal constitutional issue or issues relating to federal law—law passed by the United States Congress. Federal court jurisdiction also extends to federal treaties, lawsuits in which the United States government is a party, and lawsuits between citizens of different states. When citizens of different states are involved in a lawsuit and the controversy exceeds $50,000, a **diversity of citizenship** case exists. Under most circumstances, when there is diversity of citizenship and the amount in controversy exceeds $50,000, the parties can try the case in either state court or federal court. In other words, these courts have **concurrent jurisdiction**.

◆ **diversity of citizenship** A basis for federal court jurisdiction over a lawsuit when the parties are citizens of different states and the amount in controversy exceeds $50,000.

◆ **concurrent jurisdiction** Jurisdiction that exists when more than one court has the power to hear a case.

VIDEODISC NOTE
Much of the material that is conveyed in the exhibits of *West's Business and Personal Law* is also conveyed in the still frames on the **West Business Law and Legal Environment Videodisc**. For more information and directions for use, please see the Index and Description of Contents for the **West Business Law and Legal Environment Videodisc** that is found in your *Teacher's Resource Binder*.

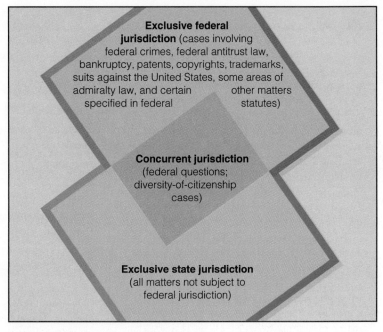

EXHIBIT 3-4
EXCLUSIVE AND CONCURRENT JURISDICTION

◇ LEGAL FOCUS ~ PROBLEM

Molly, who lives permanently in California, is driving in Texas. Hank, who has lived all his life in Texas, runs into Molly. She is out of work for a year and a half because of her injuries, and her brand new luxury car is demolished. She claims damages well in excess of $50,000. Because the amount of damages exceeds $50,000 and because Molly and Hank are residents of different states, she can sue in federal court. Can Molly, though, if she wants to, file the case in a Texas state court instead?

The answer is yes. Because state and federal courts have concurrent jurisdiction in cases involving diversity of citizenship when damages exceed $50,000, the person suing can decide to which court she will bring the case.

Most cases involve **exclusive jurisdiction**—they can only be tried in one court system. If you own a big business that cannot pay its bills anymore, you may decide to declare bankruptcy, which is a constitutional right that will release you from your duty to pay all of your business's

♦ **exclusive jurisdiction**
Jurisdiction that exists when a case can only be heard in a particular court.

Ask the students to identify the federal district court or courts in your state.

Guide the students in discussing Exhibit 3-5, noting especially its relevance to your own area.

debts. You cannot go to state court to file your bankruptcy case. You have to go to federal court, because the federal court system has exclusive jurisdiction over bankruptcy. Conversely, if you are involved in a divorce, you cannot take your divorce case to federal court. States have exclusive jurisdiction over domestic matters in almost all situations. Exhibit 3-4 illustrates the concepts of concurrent and exclusive jurisdiction.

THE FEDERAL TRIAL COURT LEVEL—THE UNITED STATES DISTRICT COURTS

In the state court system, the trial courts have original and general jurisdiction. At the federal level, the United States district courts are the equivalent. Every state and territory within the United States has at least one federal district court. Some states have more than one judicial district because they are so big. As population has changed, the exact number of federal district courts within each state has also changed.

EXHIBIT 3-5
U.S. COURTS OF APPEALS AND U.S. DISTRICT COURTS

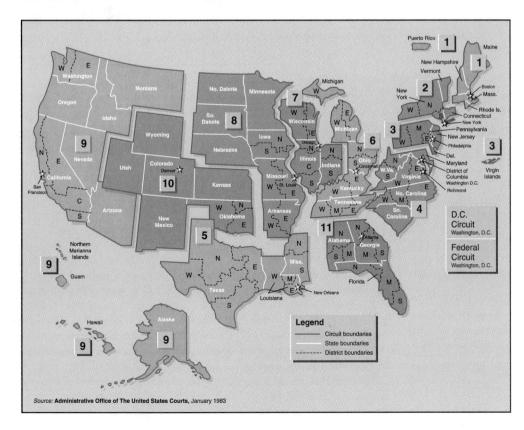

Legend
— Circuit boundaries
— State boundaries
----- District boundaries

Source: **Administrative Office of The United States Courts,** January 1983

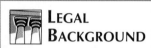

LEGAL BACKGROUND

Federal jurisdiction (except for the jurisdiction of the Supreme Court), the number of federal courts, and the number of federal judges are set by Congress. The Judicial Improvements Act of 1990 included Congress' most recent change in the number of federal judges. The Act contained other provisions as well, illustrating the variety of law that sometimes appears in a single bill.

The Judicial Improvements Act of 1990 included provisions aimed at reducing expense and delay in the judicial system, created 85 new judgeships, and addressed needs for other changes in the system and in other laws. The Act contains eight titles. Titles I through IV deal directly with federal court reform. Title V amends the anti-trust laws. Titles VI, VII, and VIII amend various provisions of the copyright laws as they apply to computer software, visual artists, and architectural work.

Read

Introduce this *Law in Action* feature by stimulating a class discussion on "funny" names. Ask the students whether they believe a funny name creates a hardship for a child. Would the name "Prune" create hardships? If so, what type of hardships? Do you feel that the government should step in to prevent parents from giving their children unusual and/or funny names? Why or why not? Then have a volunteer read aloud this *Law in Action* feature.

Discuss

Stimulate a class discussion of this *Law in Action* feature by asking the following questions: How old is the law that allows public officials in France to overrule family choices of names? According to French officials what purpose does this law serve? Does the law actually serve this purpose? Do you feel it is appropriate for the law to protect children from the whims of their parents when it comes to names? Why or why not?

 Law in Action

INTERNATIONAL PERSPECTIVES: WHAT DO YOU MEAN I CAN'T CALL HER PRUNE

Among those questions posed since the beginning of civilized thought is—what is the appropriate reach of the law? After all, any rule of law will define a duty that a person thereafter will owe society. All legal rules necessarily limit individual freedom. In the United States, the balance between individual freedom and societal needs is an everyday concern. Each new law is measured, in part, by its effect on individual liberty. In other cultures, lawmakers pay far less attention to the effect of a rule of law on individual freedoms.

For example, if you have lived your entire life in the United States, you do not expect to have to get approval from the government to name your child.

Not every country agrees that naming a child is the sole responsibility of the parent. In France, a law dating from the days of Napoleon (1803) limits the naming of children to the names of religious and historical figures. Local public officials can legally overrule family choices. A family can appeal to the courts but is usually unsuccessful.

In a recent case, a French beekeeper named his daughter Prune, which in French means plum. A local prosecuting attorney informed the family that the name was ridiculous and illegal. He renamed the child Mae Kim, her middle names.

If being ridiculous was illegal in the United States, a lot of names would be challenged. Probably the most well-known example is that of James Hogg, governor of Texas from 1891 to 1895. He named his daughter Ima Hogg.[1]

1. E. S. Browning, "In France the Name You Give Your Child May Not Last Long." *Wall Street Journal.*

In most federal matters, U.S. district courts have original jurisdiction. This means that federal district courts are where the bulk of all federal cases begin. The remainder are more specialized and therefore start in specialized, limited-jurisdiction federal courts, such as the United States Tax Court and the United States Bankruptcy Court.

THE FIRST LEVEL OF REVIEW—THE UNITED STATES COURTS OF APPEALS

◆ **judicial circuit**
The geographical limits of the jurisdiction of a federal circuit court of appeals.

Congress has established geographical divisions called **judicial circuits**, shown in Exhibit 3-5. In each circuit, there is a U.S. court of appeals. Each of the states, along with the District of Columbia and the U.S. territories, is assigned to one of these circuits. There are twelve geographical judicial circuits. In addition, there is a thirteenth circuit called the federal circuit.

The courts of appeals normally hear cases appealed from the federal district courts. The decisions of the courts of appeals are final in most cases, but an appeal to the U.S. Supreme Court is possible. Some of the federal agencies, such as the Federal Trade Commission, issue rulings that can be appealed directly to one of the U.S. courts of appeals.

LEGAL BACKGROUND

Use of the word *circuit* as in *judicial circuits* can be traced historially to the period when a single judge rode the circuit to hold trials systematically in each county within the designated territory. In geographic locations with small populations, this method of dispensing justice eliminates the expense of providing every small village with its own judiciary.

THE FINAL REVIEWING COURT—THE UNITED STATES SUPREME COURT

The U.S. Supreme Court consists of nine justices. (The term *justice* is traditionally used in the highest appellate courts, instead of *judge*.) The Supreme Court has original, or trial, jurisdiction in rare instances—for example, in legal disputes between two or more states. It most often acts, however, as the court of final appeal. It can decide to review any case decided by any of the federal courts of appeals. It also has appellate authority over some cases decided in the state courts—for example, decisions involving constitutional issues such as free speech. Thousands of cases are submitted for review to the U.S. Supreme Court. The Court, however, chooses only a small percentage to review each year.

◆ THE RIGHT TO A JURY TRIAL

Virtually every courtroom drama, whether in a book of fiction, a television series, or a popular feature movie, involves a lawyer speaking to a **jury**, asking its members to believe her case. Most trials, in fact, do take place in front of juries. It is the jury that is responsible for determining the facts of a case.

   The judge usually does not take an active role in the presentation of the case. Rather, the lawyer, acting as the client's advocate, presents the facts to convince the jury of the truth of that version. Judges usually are responsible for making sure that the proper law has been applied. In some cases, however, trials are held in front of a judge only. These are called **bench trials**.

   The United States Constitution guarantees the right to trial by jury in the Seventh Amendment, which states that "where the value in controversy shall exceed $20, the right of trial by jury shall be preserved." The various states have similar guarantees in their own constitutions. Most states, though, require a higher minimum dollar amount. Iowa, for example, requires that the value in controversy exceed $1,000 in civil cases.

   Criminal cases are quite another matter. The Sixth Amendment to the U.S. Constitution states the following:

> *In all criminal prosecutions, the accused shall enjoy the right to a speedy and public trial, by an impartial jury of the State and district wherein the crime shall have been committed, ...*

The Fourteenth Amendment has been interpreted to require a jury trial in virtually any serious matter in state courts. In any event, defendants in criminal cases may waive their right to a jury trial. That means that they simply indicate that they are willing to have their case tried before a judge only. It is then the judge who makes the necessary findings of the facts and imposes a sentence without the aid of a jury.

◆ **jury** A group of citizens chosen to hear and decide questions of fact in legal actions.

◆ **bench trial** Trial held before a judge, with no jury.

Critical Thinking Activity

Have students discuss in a one-page written essay the advantages and disadvantages of having nine judges appointed to the U.S. Supreme Court.

Discussion Starter

Encourage the students to discuss the differences between a bench trial and a jury trial. Ask: What would probably motivate a defendant to choose a bench trial? A jury trial?

Enrichment

Assign teams of students the task of researching how your state, county, and city prepare their lists of prospective jurors. Have each team prepare a written report and/or an oral report and present its findings to the class.

Extension Activity

Contact a judge to schedule a good time to take your class to see a trial by jury.

LEGAL BACKGROUND

Nearly a century ago, the Supreme Court issued its definitive decision regarding the jury's duty to apply the law unquestioningly to the facts of the case. Consequently, jurors are told that they must apply the law as explained by the judge to those facts regardless of their own views of the law's morality or fairness.

Some have challenged the idea that jurors should blindly apply the law to resolve a particular legal dispute. A number of grass roots organizations, whose members span the political spectrum, have sprung up to press for the formal recognition by the federal and state governments of the right of a jury to not only find the facts of the case but also to define the law that should be applied to those facts. In short, the jury would decide whether the law was just or fair before applying it to the case.

Those opposed to the idea, including judges and lawyers, argue that this would allow juries to act as unelected representatives, essentially making the law. Since jurors cannot be punished for their verdicts, there would be few legal constraints on the breadth of their decisions.

80

Enrichment

Ask a judge to come to your classroom and talk about his or her duties, about juries, and about how cases are tried. Have students prepare questions for the speaker in advance.

Legal Focus Problem

Divide the class into small groups to read and discuss the Legal Focus Problem found here, dealing with jury selection. Each group should choose a leader to explain his/her group's response to the question posed by this Legal Focus.

JURY SELECTION

If you were being sued or accused of a crime, you certainly would want the people judging you—normally the jury—not to bring any personal emotions and prejudices to the trial. Consequently, each state has come up with a jury-selection procedure that attempts to place on each jury unbiased, impartial individuals.

The names of potential jurors are usually selected from voter registration lists, home ownership lists, and sometimes driver's license lists in a particular location. The judge, prosecutor, and defense attorneys examine prospective jurors to ensure that their judgment will be impartial in a process called ***voir dire***, a French phrase meaning "to speak the truth." Usually *voir dire* consists of questions asked orally to individual prospective jurors. The questions are meant to determine whether each person could render a fair judgment.

♦ ***voir dire*** The questioning of prospective jurors to expose possible bias.

 LEGAL FOCUS - PROBLEM

You were driving along minding your own business when some car darted out of a side street and forced you off the road. You are now involved in a civil trial and have hired an attorney. Your attorney, Sooky Lee, is conducting voir dire. Sooky asks each prospective juror, "Have you ever been sued for causing an automobile accident?" One person says yes. Does the "yes" answer indicate that this person might be a biased juror who could not give you an impartial hearing of the facts? What should your attorney, Sooky Lee, do?

The answer is not straightforward. A potential juror's experience or knowledge of a situation may or may not show bias. After all, everyone has a set of beliefs and opinions based on his or her culture, education, family background, income level, and experience. The relevant question is whether a potential juror's experience makes that person unable to be fair in a particular case. Whenever the bias is obvious, a judge may excuse the prospective juror for cause. In the situation just described, the prospective juror who had been sued for causing an automobile accident might in fact not be as impartial as someone without this experience. Here, the judge might, and often will, excuse that prospective juror for cause.

♦ **challenge for cause** Challenge to a prospective juror based on possible bias in the dispute before the court.

There are no limits to the number of **challenges for cause**. Once there was a Brinks Warehouse robbery trial in Boston, Massachusetts. Over 1,000 prospective jurors were excused for cause. The reason was that extensive newspaper accounts had caused many of the prospective jurors to have strong opinions about the defendant's guilt.

♦ **peremptory challenge** Challenge to a prospective juror without cause; limited in number by statute.

Each attorney can also issue a **peremptory challenge**, a challenge without cause. Peremptory challenges allow attorneys to eliminate prospective jurors for any reason, except on the basis of race. However, only a few prospective jurors can be excused in this way—six, for exam-

Discussion Starter

Prompt a discussion with your students about the importance of jury duty. Remind them that serving as a juror is helping the United States legal process. Why must a juror be fair and impartial? Why would someone who has been burglarized probably not be a good juror for a burglary case?

Legal Focus Problem

Ask a student volunteer to read aloud this Legal Focus Problem. Remind students that they can use the Legal Focus features as review tools when studying for tests.

Critical Thinking Activity

Have a student lead a discussion about why the government had to deem it illegal for an employer to penalize or discriminate against an employee serving as a juror.

ple, in civil actions, and generally only a few more in criminal actions. Reasons need not be stated for a peremptory challenge.

EXEMPTIONS FROM JURY DUTY

In some jurisdictions, there are certain individuals who are automatically exempt, or disqualified, from jury duty. For example, in federal courts, noncitizens, minors, persons unable to read, write, and understand English, convicted criminals, and people who have lived in the state for less than a year are automatically disqualified. Many states have adopted similar exemptions. Certain individuals may be temporarily excused from jury service for good reasons. Whenever a person's absence from a job or family would cause an unreasonable hardship, there is normally a good reason for an exemption.

◀ LEGAL FOCUS ~ PROBLEM

Assume you have completed high school and college and you are now working on your first job. You have been on the job for a year and a half and have a good chance of promotion. In the mail, you receive a request to appear for jury duty. You inform your employer that you have to go downtown during the following week. When you do, you are selected to sit on a jury in a trial that ends up lasting two weeks. Can your employer fire you and hire someone in your place?

The answer is normally no. It is illegal for an employer to penalize or discriminate against any employee simply because that employee is serving or has served on a jury. Firing the employee is also illegal. Discriminating against such an employee by deducting part of his or her wages or making the employee use paid vacation days while serving on a jury is also illegal.

Individuals who serve on juries are paid $30 per day in the federal court system and somewhat less in the state courts. Certain jurisdictions provide jurors with reimbursement of transportation expenses.

◆ CHECKING YOUR PROGRESS

1. What document establishes the limits of federal jurisdiction?
2. What are the three levels of the federal court system?
3. What federal courts have original and general jurisdiction?
4. What is the responsibility of a jury?
5. Explain the process of voir dire.

? Ethical Concern

Ask students if they think attorneys should use private companies to research potential juror lists. Tell them to write a paragraph supporting their opinion.

Checking Your Progress (Answers)

1. The United States Constitution sets the limits of federal jurisdiction.
2. The three levels of federal courts are (a) U.S. District Court, (b) U.S. Court of Appeals, and (c) U.S. Supreme Court.
3. The United States District Court.
4. A jury determines the facts of the case.
5. *Voir dire* is the process of questioning prospective jurors to expose possible biases.

Teaching A Case In Point

Read

Before the students read this case, ask a student volunteer to define *exclusive jurisdiction* and *concurrent jurisdiction*. In order to understand this case, it is important that students have an understanding of these terms. After a brief discussion of the meaning of these terms, allow a student volunteer to read the case aloud to the class.

Discuss

Use the following questions to stimulate a discussion of this case: Why did Donnelly sue Yellow Freight Systems? Where did she originally file suit? On what grounds did Yellow Freight Systems appeal the verdict? What was the decision of the United States Court of Appeals?

Teaching Note

This case is included in the *West's Business and Personal Law Handbook of Selected Court Cases.*

Analyze and Apply

Have students work with partners to rewrite in their own words the following statement from the court decision: "Whether enacted by state government or federal government, the same policy issues underlie employment discrimination laws. Thus from a theoretical viewpoint, state courts are as amenable to Title VII claims as federal courts."

◆ A CASE IN POINT ◆

DONNELLY v. YELLOW FREIGHT SYSTEM, INC.

United States Court of Appeals, Seventh Circuit, 1989.
874 F.2d 402.

In this case, the court considered whether federal courts have exclusive jurisdiction over employment discrimination claims brought under the Civil Rights Act of 1964. If the federal courts have exclusive jurisdiction, then the plaintiff's suit was filed too late because she filed it in a state court. If the state courts have concurrent jurisdiction, the plaintiff can still have her day in court.

FACTS In March of 1985, Colleen Donnelly filed charges with the Equal Employment Opportunity Commission (EEOC) stating that Yellow Freight System, Inc., had discriminated against her. She charged they failed to offer her employment as a dockworker because of her sex. On March 15, Donnelly received a "Notice of Right to Sue within Ninety Days" from the EEOC. This is a procedure required by federal law for claims under the Civil Rights Act of 1964. If a party fails to sue within this ninety-day period, he or she loses the right to sue. Donnelly filed suit against Yellow Freight within the ninety-day period in an Illinois state court. She claimed that Yellow Freight had violated the Illinois Human Rights Act, which also prohibits employment discrimination. Later, after the ninety-day period had passed, she decided to take the suit to a federal district court. Donnelly also changed her claim to state a violation of the federal Civil Rights Act. The district

court found that Donnelly had been discriminated against. Yellow Freight appealed the decision. Yellow Freight argued that the trial court was wrong to allow Donnelly to file her claim in a federal court after the ninety-day period had expired.

ISSUE Did filing in a state court claiming a violation of state discrimination law satisfy the ninety-day filing requirement for a federal civil rights claim? The answer depends on whether the federal courts exercise *exclusive* or *concurrent* jurisdiction over claims under the 1964 Civil Rights Act. If state and federal courts have *concurrent* jurisdiction over these claims, then Donnelly met the ninety-day requirement. If federal courts have *exclusive* jurisdiction, she did not file in time.

DECISION Claims alleging violations of the Civil Rights Act of 1964 may be brought in either a state or a federal court. Concurrent jurisdiction exists.

REASON The court listed the reasons why *concurrent* jurisdiction exists. First, state courts may assume jurisdiction over a federal cause of action unless Congress says in the federal statute that federal courts have *exclusive* jurisdiction. Sharing jurisdiction is part of the history of our federal system. Second, the Civil Rights Act of 1964 was not intended to be the only law prohibiting employment discrimination. On the contrary, Congress intended to encourage states to pass discrimination laws. "Whether enacted by state government or federal government, the same policy issues underlie employment discrimination laws. Thus from a theoretical viewpoint, state courts are as amenable to Title VII claims as federal courts."

In order to help students review what they have learned in Chapter 3, you might wish to:
1. Have a student volunteer, or volunteers, read aloud the Chapter Summary.
2. Allow the students to work with partners to complete the *Using Legal Language* activity.
3. Assign the *Checking for Comprehension* exercise as homework.

4. Allow the students to work in small groups to complete the *Applying Legal Concepts* activities.
5. As a class, complete the *Applying the Law* activities.

In order to check student mastery of chapter concepts, you may wish to use the Chapter 3 Test that is found in your *Teacher's Resource Binder* or use WESTEST computerized testing for Chapter 3.

Courts and the Legal System　　　　　　83

CHAPTER 3 REVIEW

 ## SUMMARY

FUNCTION OF COURTS

1. The rule of law involves applying existing rules (laws) to deciding disputes.

2. The purpose of a court is to provide a neutral place and unbiased parties so that the rule of law can be applied fairly and impartially.

TYPES OF JURISDICTION

1. *Jurisdiction over persons or property*—Territorial boundaries within which a court has authority over the defendant or the defendant's property.

2. *Jurisdiction over subject matter*—Authority of a court to hear a particular type of case.

   a. Limited jurisdiction—Exists when a court is limited to specific subject matter, such as traffic violations or divorce.

   b. General jurisdiction—Exists when a court can hear any kind of case.

3. *Original jurisdiction*—Exists with courts that have authority to hear a case for the first time (trial courts).

4. *Appellate jurisdiction*—Exists with courts of appeal and review.

5. *Concurrent jurisdiction*—Exists when two different courts have authority to hear the same case.

6. *Exclusive jurisdiction*—Exists when only a state court or only a federal court has authority to hear a case.

TYPES OF COURTS

1. *Trial courts*—Courts of original jurisdiction, where an action begins.

   a. State—Courts of general jurisdiction

can hear any case. Courts of limited jurisdiction include divorce courts, probate courts, traffic courts, and small claims courts. Small claims courts provide access to the courts for matters involving small sums. Procedures in small claims courts are relaxed, and attorneys are generally not allowed.

   b. Federal—The federal district court is the equivalent of the state trial court. Federal courts of limited jurisdiction include the U.S. Tax Court, the U.S. Bankruptcy Court, and the U.S. Claims Court.

2. *First-level appellate courts*—Courts of appeal and review, generally without original jurisdiction. Many states have first-level appellate courts. In the federal court system, the U.S. circuit courts of appeals are the first-level appellate courts.

3. *Supreme court*—The highest court.

   a. Each state has a supreme court, although it may be called by some other name. Any further appeal goes to the U.S. Supreme Court, but this is only possible if a federal question is involved.

   b. The U.S. Supreme Court is the highest court in the federal court system. Its decisions on the Constitution and federal law are final.

4. *Jury*—Parties generally have a right to a jury trial.

   a. If a party waives the right to a jury trial, a judge will decide the facts.

   b. A jury trial is a constitutional right in

Using Legal Language (Answers)

Student answers may vary but should show an understanding of the legal definition of each word.

Checking for Comprehension (Answers)

1. A judge is considered biased if he or she has a personal interest in the outcome of a case or has reached a conclusion about a case before it is heard.
2. The purpose of a court is to ensure that decisions about important issues are consistent and fair and not made on the bias of an individual.
3. Each state court hears cases regarding matters within its jurisdiction. The federal courts hear cases involving the federal Constitution and statutory laws involving the United States, and lawsuits between different states. The District of Columbia courts hear cases within the D.C. jurisdiction of the city.
4. The difference lies in the subject matter, which is usually defined in law. A court with limited or special jurisdiction hears only cases about a specific subject matter; a court of general jurisdiction can decide virtually any type of case.
5. A case should be tried close to the place where the incident leading to the suit occurred, or where the parties live.
6. Sometimes it is impossible to provide a free trial if there is too much publicity before the trial.
7. United States District Courts are the trial courts of

84

original and general jurisdiction. The U.S. Courts of Appeals hear appeals from district courts within their respective circuits. The U.S. Supreme Court reviews cases decided by any of the federal courts of appeals. The Supreme Court may hear original cases in disputes between two or more states.
8. States usually do not permit attorneys to represent parties in small claims proceedings in order to keep the proceedings simple and to keep the cost down.

9. The cases heard on the television program *People's Court* are settled technically by arbitration, not by trial. The types of disputes seen on the television show are selected because they are somehow more interesting than most disputes heard and resolved in small claims court. Student answers will vary as to the pros and cons.
10. Student answers will vary. The minimum dollar limitation was set to ensure that a jury was not seated to try insignificant cases for minimal amounts of money.

any criminal matter where a serious penalty is the punishment.

 c. The jury is a group of persons selected from a panel of randomly chosen local citizens.

 d. Jurors are selected after questioning

(*voir dire*) to determine bias. Jurors may be excused as a result of challenges for cause or peremptory challenges (challenges without cause). The number of peremptory challenges allowed is limited.

USING LEGAL LANGUAGE

Directions: Write at least one sentence to explain the meaning of each term as it applies to law.

1.	trial	
2.	appellate	
3.	complaint	
4.	court	
5.	defendant	
6.	demurrer	
7.	deposition	
8.	discovery	
9.	evidence	
10.	garnishment	
11.	judgment	

12.	jurisdiction
13.	jury
14.	litigation
15.	motion
16.	plaintiff
17.	pleading
18.	summons
19.	venue
20.	verdict
21.	voir dire

CHECKING FOR COMPREHENSION

1. In what circumstances would a judge be considered biased?

2. What is the purpose of a court?

3. What is the jurisdiction of each of the 52 court systems in the United States?

4. What is the difference between a court of limited (special) jurisdiction and a court of general jurisdiction?

5. Where is the usual proper venue in a lawsuit?

6. Why is venue sometimes changed?

7. Describe the three-tier model of the federal court system.

8. Why do states usually not permit attorneys to represent parties in small claim proceedings?

9. What are the differences between the television program *People's Court* and a real small claims proceeding? The success of popular television programs such as *People's Court* is not without controversy. What are the pros and cons of these types of programs?

10. The federal Constitution provides that any party to civil lawsuit has a right to a trial by jury in federal cases at law, "where the value in controversy shall exceed $20." The federal Constitution had its 200th anniversary in 1987. What was the reason for providing a minimum dollar limitation? Is that purpose still served? Discuss the implications of providing rights tied to dollar amounts in laws.

APPLYING LEGAL CONCEPTS

1. Design a chart showing the federal court system. Design a chart showing the court system in your state.

2. Illustrate the layout of a court showing the location of the judge, jury, plaintiff, and defendant. Write a description of the responsibilities of each.

 APPLYING THE LAW . . . YOU BE THE JUDGE

1. Ramirez, a hotel employee, was struck by the descending gate of a service elevator while she was performing her normal duties. She suffered back injuries. She sued Otis Elevator, the company that manufactured and serviced the freight elevator, alleging Otis defectively designed and manufactured the elevator. Seven months later, Ramirez requested documents about repair, inspection, or maintenance work performed on the elevator before the accident. Otis objected because Ramirez had not alleged negligent repair or maintenance. Ramirez amended her pleadings to include claims of negligence. In response to Ramirez's discovery requests, Otis produced repair and maintenance records. However, records for the twelve months before the accident were not available because an employee had accidentally deleted them from the computer. Ramirez moved for sanctions against Otis because Otis had destroyed the pre-accident records during the suit's pendency. She requested a new trial. The District court entered judgment on jury verdict against her, and she appealed. Will she win appeal? [*Ramirez v. Otis Elevator*, 837 S.W.2d 405 (1992)]

2. The plaintiff in Luker v. Luker attempted to stretch the reach of the long-arm statute beyond due process limits. The plaintiff, a Texas resident, was injured in an automobile accident in Louisiana while riding in a car driven by her sister-in-law, a Louisiana resident. She later sued her sister-in-law in Texas to recover for the injuries she sustained and effected service on her under the statute. When the sister-in-law appeared, she challenged personal jurisdiction and the trial court sustained her plea. The plaintiff appealed, relying on the fact that her sister-in-law had once lived in Texas, had purchased and financed an automobile there, and currently possessed only a Texas driver's license. What will the court decide? [*Luker v. Luker*, 776 S.W.2d 624 (1989)]

Applying the Law . . . You Be the Judge (Answers)

1. No. The Court of Appeal held that (1) refusal to strike the elevator company's pleading was within the trial court's discretion; and (2) evidence discovered during trial did not entitle the plaintiff to a new trial.
2. Affirming the dismissal, the appellate court held that these contacts were too few to satisfy the requirements of due process.

Before students read this *Legal Perspective* dealing with civil court procedure, you might want to remind them of what they have already learned about our common law system: i.e., we have an adversary system of justice in which each adversary is entitled to present his or her version of the facts through an advocate. An attorney is each adversary's advocate.

Teaching Note

Definitions for boldface terms that appear in *Legal Perspectives* can be found at the end of each *Legal Perspective*. As students read through the *Legal Perspective*, they should refer to these definitions to ensure that they understand the concepts presented.

LEGAL BACKGROUND

This is the first *Legal Perspective* in the book. A Legal Perspective *(LP)* is a mini-chapter focusing on an important area of law related to the chapter it follows. This LP is about civil procedure. The question posed and answered is: What are the procedural requirements to begin, continue, and complete a civil lawsuit? Exhibits in the LP illustrate important concepts, including one exhibit that illustrates the chronology of a civil case from filing of the action to appeal.

LEGAL PERSPECTIVE

FOLLOWING A CASE THROUGH THE COURT SYSTEM

◆ COURT PROCEDURE

A large body of law called procedural law establishes the rules and standards involving disputes in courts. The rules are complex, and they vary. Federal rules of procedure differ from procedural rules for state courts. Procedural rules differ in criminal and civil cases as well. Criminal procedure is the subject of a Legal Perspective in Chapter 4. Here, we consider civil procedure.

◆ THE PLEADINGS

Kevin Anderson was driving his car at the intersection of Main Street and Rodeo Drive in Los Angeles, California. When his attention strayed, Kevin ran a red light and struck Lisa Martinez's car. Martinez suffered injuries to her face, her left arm, and both legs. She had medical and hospital expenses as well as lost wages for four months during which she was unable to work.

Lisa Martinez decides to sue Kevin Anderson for the injuries she suffered in the collision. She consults an attorney at law, or lawyer. Lisa's attorney should investigate to satisfy herself or himself that Lisa has a **cause of action**—that is, a legal right or adequate legal basis for suing. If Lisa pursues the lawsuit, then both she and Kevin will have to file pleadings with the court. **Pleadings** are formal written statements to a court made by each side to a dispute.

Lisa's attorney begins the lawsuit by filing a pleading called a **complaint** with the county clerk. The complaint contains the following statements: (1) facts necessary for the court to take jurisdiction, (2) facts necessary to show the plaintiff's right to sue, and (3) what the plaintiff seeks (usually a request for money for injuries and damages). Lisa Martinez, the person suing, is the **plaintiff**. Kevin Anderson, the person being sued, is the **defendant**. We include an example of a complaint in Exhibit LP3-1.

After the complaint has been filed, the clerk issues a **summons**. The summons informs the defendant, Anderson, that he has a prescribed time (for example, thirty days) to respond to the complaint. Martinez's attorney will arrange with a **process server** (the county sheriff or a private party) to deliver a copy of the summons and complaint personally to the defendant, Kevin Anderson. Proper delivery of legal documents is called **service of process**.

If Kevin cannot be found, or if he evades delivery of the documents, he may nonetheless be "constructively served." This type of service of process uses a combination of notification by mail and publication of a summons in a local newspaper. Serving a copy of the summons and complaint (or publication of summons) gives Kevin notice that he is sued. It also gives the court jurisdiction (or power) over his person and so allows the court to decide the controversy.

CHOICES AVAILABLE AFTER RECEIPT OF THE SUMMONS AND COMPLAINT

After a copy of the summons and complaint has been served to the defendant, he must respond to the complaint. Anderson should

Assign each student a partner with whom to work on using in a sentence each of the boldface legal terms in this Legal Perspective section. Allow volunteers to share their sentences with the class.

VIDEODISC NOTE
Much of the material that is conveyed in the exhibits of *West's Business and Personal Law* is also conveyed in the still frames on the **West Business Law and Legal Environment Videodisc**. For more information and directions for use, please see the Index and Description of Contents for the **West Business Law and Legal Environment Videodisc** that is found in your *Teacher's Resource Binder.*

IN THE LOS ANGELES SUPERIOR COURT
FOR THE LOS ANGELES JUDICIAL DISTRICT

CIVIL NO. 8-1026

Lisa Martinez
_____
Plaintiff

COMPLAINT

Kevin Anderson
_____
Defendant

Comes now the plaintiff and for her cause of action against the defendant alleges and states as follows:

1. This action is between plaintiff, a California resident living at 1434 Palm Drive, Anaheim California, and defendant, a California resident living at 6950 Garrison Avenue, Los Angeles, California.

2. On September 10, 1994, plaintiff, Lisa Martinez, was exercising good driving habits and reasonable care in driving her car through the intersection of Rodeo Drive and Wilshire Boulevard when defendant, Kevin Anderson, negligently drove his vehicle through a red light at the intersection and collided with plaintiff's vehicle.

3. As a result of the collision, plaintiff suffered severe physical injury that prevented her from working and property damage to her car. The costs she incurred included $20,000 in medical bills, $11,000 in lost wages, $5,000 for automobile repairs, and $75,000 for pain and suffering.

WHEREFORE, plaintiff demands judgment against the defendant for the sum of $111,000 plus interest at the maximum legal rate and the costs of this action.

By _____
Roger Harrington
Attorney for the Plaintiff
800 Orange Avenue
Anaheim, CA 91426

EXHIBIT LP3-1
SAMPLE COMPLAINT

Collaborative Learning Activity

Divide the class into groups of four. Ask each group to illustrate a civil court case with a poster, drawing, collage, or other creative means.

Legal Focus Problem

Read aloud the Legal Focus Problem found here. Allow student volunteers to suggest possible answers to the question posed at the end of this problem.

LEGAL PERSPECTIVE (CONTINUED)

hire an attorney to represent his interests. If he does not respond to the complaint, the court may enter a **default judgment** against him. The plaintiff will win the case if the defendant does nothing.

The usual pleading in response to a complaint is an **answer**. An answer responds to the charges and demands made in the plaintiff's complaint. In the answer, Anderson may deny all Martinez's statements, or he may admit any statements in the complaint that he believes are true and deny the rest. The attorney usually prepares the answer and files it with the county clerk.

Anderson might also state his own claim that Martinez was negligent (legally careless) and thus owes him money for damage to his car. This is called a **counterclaim**. If Anderson files a counterclaim, Martinez will reply. A **reply** is an answer to a counterclaim.

Instead of an answer, an attorney can file another type of pleading in response to a complaint. The attorney can make a motion to dismiss the complaint. A **motion** is any formal request to a court for some action. A **motion to dismiss** (also called a **demurrer** in some states) is used when the complaint, even if true, is legally insufficient to require an answer. The motion to dismiss says in effect that even if all of the plaintiff's claims are true, the defendant breached, or violated, no legal duty. It is called a "so what" motion.

LEGAL FOCUS ~ PROBLEM

Suppose that in a complaint, plaintiff Allen Cantwell says that Wally, the defendant, "wrongfully, viciously, and wantonly stuck out his tongue" at Allen, "causing great and severe mental anguish." Has Allen stated a cause of action in his complaint?

No. Even if the defendant admits the plaintiff's allegations, there should be no legal recovery for the plaintiff. Simply sticking out one's tongue is normally legal. The defendant should file a motion to dismiss.

When a judge grants a motion to dismiss, the case is dismissed. A trial is a waste of time for both the defendant and the court if there is no legal basis for action. The losing party has the right to appeal the dismissal, however. Any verdict that ends a trial creates a right to an appeal.

However the defendants respond to the complaint, they must serve their pleading in response on the plaintiff. Most states allow the defendant to serve the responsive pleading by mailing it to the plaintiff's attorney.

DISMISSALS AND JUDGMENT BEFORE TRIAL

Few lawsuits actually come to trial. Usually, the matter is resolved through a voluntary settlement between the parties outside of court. But there are also many procedural ways to dispose of a case without a trial. Many of them involve pretrial motions. For instance, if there is no possible defense to the claim, the plaintiff may seek a judgment before the trial (**motion for summary judgment**). If no real case is presented in the pleadings by the plaintiff, the defendant may ask the judge to dismiss the case based on the pleadings (**motion for judgment on the pleadings**). If either one of these motions is granted, the case is dismissed before trial. As with the demurrer, the plaintiff could appeal the court's granting of the motion.

88

Enrichment

Ask the students if they, or someone they know, has ever been asked to give a deposition in a civil case. Allow the students to share with the class their recollections of this event.

Legal Focus Example

Allow a student volunteer to read aloud to the class this Legal Focus Example. Remind students that they can use the Legal Focus features as review tools when studying for tests.

 ### PROCEEDINGS BEFORE THE TRIAL

Once a civil lawsuit has begun, a year or more may pass before the trial takes place. In some states or counties, shortages of judges create crowded court schedules (called *calendars* or *dockets*). This, in turn, can cause delays as long as five years before a trial begins. In rural and less populous areas, the trial may occur as soon as the attorneys are prepared.

DISCOVERY

After filing the pleadings, the parties have broad outlines of what they must prove at trial to win the lawsuit. Both plaintiff and defense attorneys need to prepare their cases properly and prepare to counter the case of the opponent. To do this, they gather information from the opposing party and from other witnesses in a process called **discovery**. Discovery (1) educates each party about the facts surrounding the lawsuit, (2) promotes voluntary settlement of the dispute by revealing strengths and weaknesses in the case of each party, and (3) eliminates surprises that might otherwise arise at the trial and might lead to an unfair trial and verdict.

Depositions and Interrogatories Discovery can involve the use of depositions. In a **deposition**, an opposing party or any witness gives sworn testimony under oath. An authorized court official, usually a court reporter, records the testimony. Judges are not present, and depositions are not taken in courtrooms. Depositions are often taken at the office of one of the attorneys.

Attorneys from both sides ask questions of witnesses giving depositions. The answers are written, sworn to, and signed. These answers help the attorneys prepare their cases.

They can also be used in court to *impeach* a party or a witness. In this case, to impeach means to show that the witness is not truthful. A witness is impeached if he or she makes major changes in his or her testimony at the trial. Depositions can also be used as testimony if a witness cannot be present at the trial.

 ### LEGAL FOCUS ~ EXAMPLE

Kevin Anderson may want to take the deposition of Lisa Martinez's physician to question him or her about the extent and nature of Lisa's injuries. Lisa will want to take Kevin's deposition to find out exactly what caused the accident. Both parties may wish to take depositions from witnesses to the accident.

Interrogatories are a series of written questions for which written answers are prepared and then signed under oath. The main difference between interrogatories and depositions is that interrogatories are sent only to the parties (the plaintiff and the defendant), not to witnesses. The parties can prepare their answers to the questions with their attorneys helping them in the wording of the answers.

In addition to depositions and interrogatories, a party can get documents and the like from others to inspect and examine during discovery. A party can also gain "entry upon land" to inspect it. Anderson, for example, can get permission to inspect and duplicate Martinez's medical records and repair bills.

(continued on page 90)

Extension Activity

Ask students to search recent newspapers for articles containing the legal terms in this Legal Perspective. Read some of the articles to your class, and have them define the terms orally.

LEGAL PERSPECTIVE (CONTINUED)

Compliance with Discovery Requests

If a party refuses to cooperate with discovery requests, a judge may order the party to do so. A party's refusal to cooperate can be judged contempt of court. **Contempt of court** is willful refusal to obey a legitimate order of a court, and it is punishable by a fine, imprisonment, or both.

THE PRETRIAL CONFERENCE

Either party or the court can request a pretrial hearing or conference. A **pretrial hearing** usually takes place after the discovery process is over. The conference consists of an informal discussion between the judge and the opposing attorneys. The purpose of the hearing is to identify the matters that are in dispute and to plan the course of the trial. At the pretrial hearing, the judge may encourage the parties to settle without a trial (an out-of-court settlement).

◆ AT THE TRIAL

At the beginning of the trial, both attorneys may make **opening statements** outlining the facts they intend to prove during the trial. After the opening statements, the plaintiff's attorney presents the plaintiff's case. This involves calling witnesses and introducing into evidence documents, photographs, or whatever bears on the issues.

Evidence is everything that the finder of fact—that is, the jury or, when there is no jury, the judge—may use in deciding the true facts. For example, the oral testimony of a witness presented under oath is evidence. In contrast, remarks of the attorneys are not. Attorneys are hired after the events in question have taken place and are thus not competent to testify as witnesses.

Evidence is only admitted if it is the kind of evidence that a jury may consider. There are many rules concerning what evidence is and is not admissible. For example, to be admitted, evidence must be **relevant** (related to the fact in dispute). Attorneys for either party may object to the introduction of evidence they believe is not admissible. The judge rules on all objections made by attorneys on offered evidence, because the admissibility of evidence is a question of law. If the judge agrees with the objection, it is **sustained**. If the judge disagrees with the objection, it is **overruled**.

The plaintiff's lawyer has the **burden of proof**. That is, he or she must prove that the acts referred to in the complaint took place. In the usual civil case, the burden is met by proving the case by a **preponderance of the evidence**. In other words, the lawyer shows that it is more probable than not that the plaintiff is right.

Martinez's attorney will call the first witness for the plaintiff and examine, or question, the witness. This questioning is **direct examination**. After Martinez's attorney finishes, the witness is subject to **cross-examination** by Anderson's attorney. When both attorneys finish with the first witness, Martinez's attorney calls the next plaintiff's witness. Each witness is subject to cross-examination by both attorneys.

After the plaintiff's case has been presented, the defendant's attorney may make a **motion for a directed verdict**. If the plaintiff did not present sufficient believable evidence to support his or her legal claim, the motion is granted. Motions for directed verdicts at this stage of trial are usually unsuccessful.

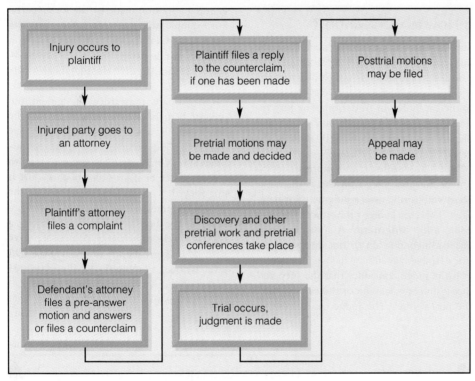

EXHIBIT LP3-2
A TYPICAL LAWSUIT

The defendant's case is next. The defense attorney has the right to call and examine his or her witnesses, and the plaintiff has the right to cross-examine. At the end of the defendant's case, either attorney can move for a directed verdict. These motions are seldom granted, however. A judge will grant a directed verdict against a party only when convinced that the party did not produce any reliable evidence supporting his or her position in the lawsuit.

After both sides have finished producing their witnesses, each attorney presents a **closing argument**. The plaintiff's lawyer is first. In the closing arguments, the two opposing attorneys will urge the court to return a verdict that favors their respective clients.

Next, in a jury trial, the judge instructs the jury in the law applying to the case. The jury retires to the jury room to deliberate a verdict. In the Martinez–Anderson case, a jury will decide whether the plaintiff or the defendant wins. If the jury decides in favor of the plaintiff, it must also decide how much money damages to award to the plaintiff.

(continued on page 92)

LEGAL PERSPECTIVE (CONTINUED)

HOW IS A CASE ENDED?

Suppose that in our auto accident case, the jury was convinced that Martinez should be paid for her injuries. It concluded that the accident resulted from the careless operation of the car by Kevin Anderson. The jury returned a verdict in the plaintiff's favor and decided on an award of $100,000. Is the verdict the voice of the court?

No. The **verdict** is the expressed opinion of the jury. Based on the verdict, the court will usually issue a judgment for damages. The concluding pronouncement of a court is its **judgment**. A judgment may order someone to do or not do something (for example, pay money damages).

If the judge concludes that the jury verdict is unreasonable, he or she can overturn the jury verdict. The judge can do this by granting a motion made by the losing party. For example, the court can grant a **motion for a new trial** (to order a new trial) or a **motion for a judgment notwithstanding a verdict** (to give the judgment to the other party).

Once a party is awarded a judgment, the judicial branch of government has usually completed its work. The losing party may appeal the judgment of the court. Sometimes a party may return to court to modify a court order or if an order of the court is not obeyed.

Most disputes are settled out of court because of the time and expense of trying a lawsuit. Of the cases that go to trial, about 97 percent are permanently resolved at the trial level without an appeal. An illustration of trial procedures is found in Exhibit LP3-2.

TERMS TO REMEMBER

♦ **cause of action**   Legal basis for a lawsuit.

♦ **pleading**   Formal written statement or form presented to a court by each side in a dispute.

♦ **complaint**   The pleading used to begin a lawsuit. It contains (1) facts necessary for the court to take jurisdiction, (2) facts necessary to show the plaintiff's right to a remedy, and (3) remedy the plaintiff seeks (usually a request for money for injuries and damages).

♦ **plaintiff**   The person who brings a lawsuit.

♦ **defendant**   The person sued in a lawsuit.

♦ **summons**   Document served on a defendant with a complaint. It tells the defendant that he or she should respond to the complaint or risk losing the lawsuit.

♦ **process server**   Person who delivers a copy of the summons and complaint personally to the defendant.

♦ **service of process**   Proper delivery of legal documents.

♦ **default judgment**   Judgment entered against a defendant who fails to respond to a complaint.

♦ **answer**   Defendant's response to a complaint.

- **counterclaim** Claim against the plaintiff by a defendant in a lawsuit; in effect, the counterclaim sues the plaintiff.

- **reply** Plaintiff's answer to a counterclaim.

- **motion** Formal request to a court for an action.

- **motion to dismiss**, or **demurrer** Pleading in which a defendant claims that the plaintiff has failed to state a legal basis on which to sue. It is sometimes called a "so what" motion.

- **motion for summary judgment** Request for a judgment based on the argument that no issues of fact exist in the dispute.

- **motion for judgment on the pleadings** Request for a judgment based on the argument that the pleadings fail to state a cause of action.

- **discovery** The gathering of information from the opposing party or from witnesses before a trial.

- **deposition** The taking of sworn testimony of witnesses before trial; a form of discovery.

- **interrogatories** Series of written questions for parties or witnesses, who prepare written answers and then sign under oath; a form of discovery.

- **contempt of court** Willful refusal to obey a legitimate order of a court; punishable by a fine and/or imprisonment.

- **pretrial hearing** Informal discussion between a judge and the opposing attorneys before a trial. The purpose is to plan the course of the trial and encourage settlement.

- **opening statements** Statements made by the parties' attorneys at a trial before presentation of evidence. The purpose is to inform the court of what evidence they intend to offer and what they believe it will prove.

- **relevant evidence** Evidence likely to prove the facts in dispute.

- **sustained** A ruling by which the judge agrees with an objection to offered evidence.

- **overruled** A ruling by which the judge disagrees with an objection to offered evidence.

- **burden of proof** The requirement a party must meet to win the case.

- **preponderance of the evidence** Greater part of the evidence; the burden of proof in the usual civil case. Proving one's case by the preponderance of the evidence involves proving that the facts one is arguing are more probable than not.

- **direct examination** In a trial, the first questioning of a witness by the side that called that witness.

- **cross-examination** The questioning of an opposing witness during the trial.

- **motion for a directed verdict** Argument to a judge by a defendant that the plaintiff did not present sufficient believable evidence in a trial to support the plaintiff's legal claim; asks the judge to rule in the defendant's favor.

- **closing arguments** Arguments at the end of a trial by the opposing attorneys.

- **verdict** The expressed opinion of the jury.

- **judgment** The concluding pronouncement of the court.

- **motion for a new trial** Request to a judge for a new trial.

- **motion for judgment notwithstanding a verdict** Request to a judge to reverse the jury verdict; argues that there is no reasonable way the jury should have reached the verdict, given the evidence presented at trial.

LEGAL BACKGROUND

This chapter may be the only formal study of criminal law most of your students ever have. Television, movies, and experiences may provide the rest of what they learn about criminal law. Crimes are public wrongs committed against the community as a whole. In order to be convicted of a crime, the defendant must commit a legally prohibited act and possess the required state of mind. Crimes are defined by legislatures (such as Congress or a state legislature) into three categories: felonies, misdemeanors, and violations.

Crimes are public wrongs and should be distinguished from private wrongs called torts, which are discussed in the next chapter. In a criminal case, the government is the plaintiff, and the defendant can be sentenced to jail or ordered to pay a fine. In a tort case, a private person is the plaintiff, and a defendant can be ordered to pay the plaintiff damages.

Our focus in this chapter is on crimes against property committed by and against businesses, as well as the defenses to these crimes.

94

Prereading Activity

Group students into pairs, and instruct each pair to list as many differences between civil law and criminal law as they can in five minutes. At the end of five minutes, call on students to share the differences they listed.

Mastery Objectives

By the end of this chapter, students will be able to:
- Define criminal law
- Establish criminal liability
- Explain defenses against criminal liability
- Classify crimes
- Describe crimes affecting business
- Explain how bail is used in the legal process

Chapter

4

Criminal Law

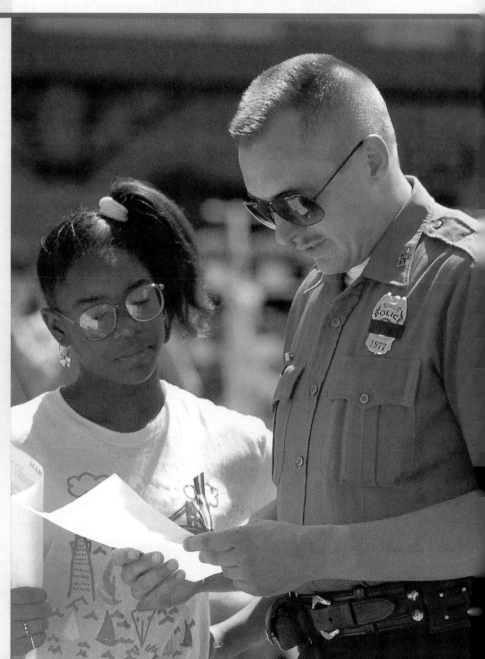

Activity Sheets
Reviewing Legal Concepts 4 *TRB*
Enrichment Activity 4 *TRB*

Student Activity Workbook
Chapter 4 Activities

Tests
Chapter 4 Test *TRB*
Chapter 4 WESTEST Computerized Testing

Handbook of Selected Court Cases
State v. *Bernardy*
Becker v. *Texas*

**West's Business Law and Legal
Environment Videodisc**
Still Frames and Motion Segments as shown

"Nobody ever commits a crime without doing something stupid."
Oscar Wilde, 1854–1900
English novelist writing in "The Picture of Dorian Gray"

There is a reason that so many television news stories and dramatic series are involved with crime. The fact is that crime permeates the American landscape. Murders, rapes, robberies, assaults, pickpocketing, and the like occur every day. Crime is on the rise and has been for some time in this country. But even in the past, when crime was not so rampant, certain criminals became famous. Billy the Kid, Al Capone, and others have been the stuff of which legends, books, and movies have been made. When important criminals are caught, attorneys who defend them also make the news. Indeed, no other area of law arouses so much interest as criminal law. In spite of this high interest, far more legal problems relate to private matters. Most attorneys never even handle a criminal case during their entire career.

Criminal matters are not the focus of your text, but they are important and worthy of your study. In the discussion of criminal law that follows, you will find out what type of behavior is criminal as well as the definitions of certain crimes, particularly business-related crimes. In the Legal Perspective feature on criminal procedure, you will see the important rights that exist for persons accused of crimes.

◆ WHAT IS A CRIME?

In Chapter 1 we defined a crime as a wrong against society. To find out which actions are crimes, you have to look in the law books that report the laws passed by state or federal legislatures. Remember that crimes are not the same thing as the wrongful acts that one private party commits against another, as when someone runs his or her car into another person's car. In Chapter 5 we will be looking at the law relating to noncriminal lawsuits.

◆ THE CLASSIFICATION OF CRIMES

There are different ways of classifying crimes. Usually crimes are classified depending on their degree of seriousness, ranging from the most serious, called felonies, to misdemeanors and petty offenses.

FELONIES VERSUS MISDEMEANORS

Felonies are serious crimes punishable by death or imprisonment in a federal or state penitentiary for more than a year. Examples of felonies are murder, rape, and kidnapping. **Misdemeanors** are less serious crimes.

◆ **felony** A serious crime punishable by death or imprisonment in a federal or state penitentiary for more than a year. Murder, rape, robbery, burglary, selling illegal drugs, and kidnapping are felonies.

◆ **misdemeanor** A crime punishable by a fine or by confinement for up to a year. Disorderly conduct, shoplifting, and trespass are common misdemeanors.

**Critical Thinking
Activity**

Ask the students to name some crimes. Have a student volunteer list students' examples on the board. Then instruct the students to explain how each of the crimes listed on the board is harmful to society. Annotations

**Critical Thinking
Activity**

Assign a one-page essay in which students give their opinions about the legal premise that crimes are considered to be wrongs against society.

**Teaching with
the Videodisc**

The still frames listed below from the **West's Business Law and Legal Environment Videodisc** can be used with this chapter. To access this material, use the bar codes or the frame numbers included in the Videodisc Instructor's Manual found in the *TRB*.

*Essentials of Criminal
  Liability*
*Criminal Liability
  Defenses*
*Steps in the Criminal
  Process*

**Motion Segments
on Videodisc**

*Freedom and Fairness:
  Judges Instructions –
  Burden of Proof*
*Freedom and Fairness:
  Role of Judge and Jury*
*Freedom and Fairness:
  Comparison of Civil and
  Criminal Law*

Ask students to make a chart of the three classifications of crimes. Have them cite examples of each crime and the punishment that goes with the crime.

Collaborative Learning Activity

Assign a group of students to visit your police department or municipal offices and inquire about petty offenses such as traffic violations. Tell them to find out the amount of the fine for each offense. Have them make a chart of the offenses and the accompanying fines to display in the class.

Have the students work in groups to write shorts skits in which there is apparent criminal activity but no one will be held criminally responsible. Allow the groups to share their skits with the class. You might wish to remind the groups that their skits should be appropriate for your classroom.

Teaching Note

The Legal Perspective that follows this chapter is integral to course content and should not be skipped. Further, some items in the end of the chapter review section relate to this Legal Perspective.

They are punishable by a fine or by imprisonment in a county jail for up to a year. Notice the distinction between a felony and a misdemeanor. People convicted of misdemeanors do *not* go to federal or state penitentiaries, but rather to local jail facilities. Some examples of misdemeanors are minor shoplifting and disorderly conduct.

PETTY OFFENSES

◆ **petty offense**, or **infraction** A minor offense against the state. Traffic offenses and violations of building codes are examples.

Numerous types of improper activity are classified as **petty offenses**, or **infractions**. These are the most minor of crimes. They are also the ones that you are most likely to commit in your lifetime, because most traffic violations are considered petty offenses. Petty offenses typically are punished by a fine, or a brief jail sentence, or both. Those petty offenses that can only carry fines as their punishment are not classified as true crimes.

◆ WHO CAN BE LEGALLY RESPONSIBLE FOR COMMITTING A CRIME?

The fact that someone does something that appears to be a criminal activity does not necessarily mean that person can be convicted of a crime. Two elements must exist at the same time for a person to be convicted: (1) the person must have the *intent*, or *specified state of mind*, to commit the criminal action and (2) the action must actually occur. Even when both of these elements of a crime exist, there may be defenses to the criminal conduct. We discuss these defenses later in the chapter.

Can very young children be found responsible for committing a crime? See the discussion on pages 99–100.

Ethical Concern

Have the students look at the Legal Focus Problem on this page. In this case Ronald is not guilty of a crime, but is his behavior ethical? Explain to students that ethical behavior and ethics will be explored further in Chapter 6.

Criminal Law 97

THE CRIMINAL ACT

Every criminal law prohibits certain behavior. For something to be a crime, an act normally has to occur. That is to say, a person must *do* something (a guilty act) in order to commit a crime.

 LEGAL FOCUS – PROBLEM

Ronald Shocker has been planning to murder his rich father to inherit his money. For over nine months, he has been developing and refining an elaborate scheme to commit the murder. He has not yet done anything. Is he nonetheless guilty of a crime?

The answer is normally no. Mere thoughts do not constitute criminal activity. Thus, Ronald has not committed a crime yet. The guilty act requirement is based on the notion that a person should be punished only for the *harm* done to society. Merely thinking about killing somebody or robbing a bank may be morally wrong, but the thoughts themselves do not create any harm to society. It is only when these thoughts are translated into action that the harm actually occurs.

Now, it is true that sometimes not doing something constitutes a crime. If, for example, the law commands a person to do something and that person chooses not to do it, a crime may have been committed. For example, the law states that if you earn over a certain amount of money each year, you must file an income tax return. If you fail to file a tax return, in most cases that constitutes a crime. Consider another example. The law in all states says that if you have a serious automobile accident, you must report that accident to the police. If you do not, you will have committed a crime.

INTENT TO COMMIT A CRIME

"It is deliberate purpose that constitutes . . . criminal guilt."
Aristotle, 384–322 B.C.
Greek philosopher

Committing a crime also requires a wrongful mental state. This is called **criminal intent**. A person with criminal intent knowingly and purposely intends to commit a criminal act. The necessary mental state varies depending on the crime involved. Murder, for example, is the act of taking a life, and the mental state is the intent to take a life. For **theft**, the guilty act is the taking of another person's property. The mental state therefore involves both the knowledge that the property belongs to another and the intent to keep it from its rightful owner. Without the mental state required by law for a particular crime, there is generally no crime.

It is important that you do not confuse *intent* with *motive*. You can intend to do something without having any particular motive. Your **motive** is the reason behind your intent. Motive is not an element in determining

♦ **criminal intent**
A wrongful mental state in which a person knowingly and purposely intends to commit a criminal act.

♦ **theft** The guilty act of taking another person's property.

♦ **motive** The reason for a criminal act.

Extension Activity

Allow student volunteers to research famous or notorious crimes. Students should prepare an oral report in which they briefly describe the nature of the crime, the outcome of the investigation, and trial of the criminal. For each crime, students should also explain the criminal intent. Allow students time to present their reports to the class.

97

It has been said that the substantive criminal law's use of such concepts as criminal intent and the reasonable man creates a legal reality in which the American criminal is seen as an outlaw-by-choice, one who freely and rationally chooses to break the social compact. This legal vision of the criminal is in accord with the dominant American social ethics of free will and equality. Others, however, point out that the social reality of the American criminal is actually one of outlaw-by-force-of-circumstance rather than outlaw-by-choice. By ignoring the way in which such social conditions as wide-spread mental illness, unemployment, poverty, and racial intolerance contribute to crime, the legal system exculpates our political and economic systems from any complicity in the causes of crime.

Legal Focus Problem

Ask a student volunteer to read aloud to the class this first Legal Focus Problem. Remind students that in the last Legal Focus, Ronald Shocker was not guilty of a crime. Then allow student volunteers to share their responses to the question posed at the end of this Legal Focus.

98

Legal Focus Problem

Divide the class into small groups to read and discuss the Legal Focus Problem found at the bottom of this page. Each group should choose a leader to explain his or her group's response to the question posed at the end of this Legal Focus.

whether a crime has been committed. Having a good motive behind your intent does not justify criminal behavior. Robin Hood may have been robbing the rich to give to the poor—his motive—but he still satisfied the two necessary elements for having committed the crime of theft. Suppose Carl steals Marsha's bicycle. His motive for doing this might be to sell the bicycle to raise money to help victims of a tornado. He still committed a crime.

The only reason a motive is interesting is that it satisfies our curiosity as to why a person behaved the way she or he did. In murder mysteries, the police are always trying to discover somebody's motive for murdering someone else in order to justify placing that person under suspicion.

CRIMINAL RESPONSIBILITY FOR THE ACTS OF ANOTHER

Criminals often try to get others involved in their illegal activities. Sometimes the act of attempting to get others involved creates in itself a crime.

> **◀ LEGAL FOCUS – PROBLEM**
>
> Ronald Shocker, from this chapter's first legal focus problem, decides to translate his plans to murder his rich father into action. He asks and encourages his friend, Jarold Becker, to help him in the murder. So far, though, no true action has occurred—Ronald's father is still alive. There has not even been an attempt on his life. Nonetheless, has a crime occurred?

◆ **criminal solicitation** An act requesting or encouraging another to commit a crime.

The answer is yes. Ronald acted when he requested someone else to help commit a crime. Even if his friend Jarold said no, Ronald is guilty of **criminal solicitation**, an act requesting or encouraging another to commit a crime.

The next obvious question is, what about Jarold? If Jarold says no, he is clearly not guilty of a crime. But what if Jarold says yes? He agrees to help Ronald in exchange for some payment. Has Jarold now committed a crime? The answer is no, because agreeing to commit a crime without actually acting in some way is not criminal. Remember, wrongful intent might be here, but no guilty act has occurred.

> **◀ LEGAL FOCUS – PROBLEM**
>
> Jarold has decided to work with Ronald in eliminating Ronald's rich father. To further the plan, Jarold purchases a gun and some ammunition. He begins following Ronald's father. Additionally, Ronald and Jarold go to a practice range each day to improve their ability to fire a gun. Has Ronald committed another crime? Has Jarold committed a crime?

Ethical Concern

Ask your students to write a paragraph or two on the crime of conspiracy. Ask them to state their opinions on whether they feel someone who conspired, yet did not pull the trigger, should be guilty of murder.

The answer is yes. Both Ronald and Jarold are guilty of the crime of **conspiracy**. A criminal conspiracy exists when two or more persons have joined to do an illegal act. Once an act of preparation, such as purchasing a gun, has been performed, then the agreement to commit a crime has become a criminal conspiracy.

What happens if one or both of these individuals actually kills Ronald's father? They are both guilty of murder, even if only one "pulled the trigger." Anybody who conspired with the person who committed the crime is guilty of the committed crime.

◆ **conspiracy** A plan by two or more persons to commit an illegal act. The conspiracy is complete once an act in furtherance of the crime is performed.

◆ DEFENSES TO BEING HELD CRIMINALLY RESPONSIBLE

Even when an individual has intent and commits a criminal act, sometimes the law recognizes several **defenses** that free that individual of being criminally responsible for his or her acts. For example, if a person is very young, that may be a defense. The burden of proving a defense rests on the person who is accused of the crime.

Note that a defense is not the same thing as an **alibi**. An alibi is a statement that the person accused was someplace else at the time of the crime and therefore was physically unable to commit it. In any event, the defenses that you'll read about below do not involve alibis. The accused person is not saying that he or she did not commit the act or acts in question. Instead, the accused person seeks to show that the acts were not criminal because of one or more of the following defenses.

◆ **defense** The counter-argument made by a defendant as to why he or she should not be held responsible in a legal proceeding.

◆ **alibi** A declaration that the accused was someplace else at the time of the crime.

BEING TOO YOUNG—INFANCY

Age is often an important element in determining the defense for a crime. A person who has not reached the legal age of adulthood may be able to use the defense of **infancy**. Under the common law, children up to age seven were considered incapable of committing a crime. The belief was that young children lacked the moral sense to understand the right and wrong of what they were doing. Children between the ages of seven and fourteen were presumed to be incapable of committing a crime. This presumption, however, could be disproved by showing that the child understood the wrongful nature of the act.

In most states, once a person has attained the age of eighteen, that person can be held criminally responsible for his or her actions. Under certain circumstances, adult criminal responsibility may begin as young as fourteen years of age. You will read about juvenile justice in Chapter 26. Look at Exhibit 4-1. There you see how the common law reflects the responsibility of "infants."

◆ **infancy** The state or period before the legal age of adulthood.

Vocabulary Activity

Have a student volunteer compare the word *defense,* as defined here, with the word *excuse.* Is a defense to a crime the same thing as an excuse for the crime? Why or why not?

Critical Thinking Activity

Ask your students to hand in a paper describing the differences between an alibi and a defense. This can be a short paragraph.

Discussion Starter

Ask your students to study Exhibit 4-1. Tell them to note the difference between the words *absolute* and *presumption* and the words *incompetence* and *competence*. Start a discussion on these meanings, and ask them to talk about known cases involving minors being tried as adults.

Enrichment

As the students have learned, many courts do not accept intoxication as a valid defense in a crime. Furthermore, in many cases intoxication may be a crime in itself, such as public intoxication, which is a crime in many communities. A very important related crime is driving while intoxicated. This may be a good opportunity to discuss this subject with your class. Perhaps you might invite a representative from local law enforcement to speak to your class about the dangers of driving while intoxicated.

100

Ethical Concern

Start a discussion on the defense of intoxication; involuntary vs. voluntary. Are there any obvious loopholes to this defense? How can you prove you were involuntarily intoxicated? Point out to your students that most intoxicated people drink voluntarily, and it would be very difficult to prove otherwise.

Enrichment

Ask several students to research cases in which the defendant used insanity as a defense. Ask them to share their information with the class.

Age 0–7	Absolute presumption of incompetence.
Age 7–14	Presumption of incompetence, but government may oppose.
Age 14 +	Presumption of competence, but infant may oppose.

EXHIBIT 4-1
RESPONSIBILITY OF INFANTS FOR CRIMINAL ACTS UNDER COMMON LAW

INTOXICATION

♦ **intoxication**
The state of being under the influence of either drugs or alcohol.

When a person takes alcoholic beverages or drugs, that person, no matter who she or he is, becomes more or less intoxicated. The term **intoxication** refers to the state of being under the influence of either drugs or alcohol. When a person has taken lots of drugs or alcohol, that person may in fact be incapable of having the necessary state of mind for performing a particular crime. In other words, criminal intent may be lacking if the intoxication was severe enough.

Many courts do not accept intoxication as a valid defense to a crime. After all, in most cases, the person accused of a crime who raises the defense of intoxication voluntarily became intoxicated—nobody forced him or her to take the drugs or alcohol. If, though, someone is *involuntarily* intoxicated—if that person didn't know that what he or she was drinking had illegal drugs in it, for example—then the courts are more apt to accept intoxication as a valid defense to a crime. Indeed, whenever a person could not have understood his or her acts because of involuntary intoxication, this usually forms a complete defense to the criminal activity that ensued.

INSANITY

♦ **insanity** The state in which mental illness or disease makes a person incapable of forming criminal intent.

♦ **M'Naghten test** A legal test for criminal insanity. It holds that a defendant is not responsible if, at the time of the offense, he or she did not understand the nature and quality of the act or did not know that the act was wrong.

Insanity is a legal term that applies to any person who is sufficiently mentally disturbed to be treated in a special way under the law. Obviously, a person suffering from mental illness is probably not capable of the wrongful state of mind that is required for committing a crime. Thus, insanity can be a defense to a criminal charge. The courts have had much difficulty in deciding on an appropriate definition for legal insanity, however. One definition of insanity is the following:

A person is not responsible for criminal conduct if at the time of such conduct as a result of mental disease or defect, he lacks substantial capacity either to appreciate the wrongfulness of his conduct or to conform his conduct to the requirements of the law.

The definition above comes from a model code of criminal law that some states have followed. Other states use what has been known as the *M'Naghten test*. According to the **M'Naghten test**, a criminal defendant is not responsible if, at the time of the offense, he or she did not understand

Ask a volunteer to research the defense of "temporary insanity." What is it? When is it usable? How has it been abused? When the student shares this information with the class, stimulate a class discussion on the topic.

Ask your students to refer to the photograph and the caption below the photograph. Ask them if anyone knows what the legal tests for insanity are. If not, ask a volunteer to find out and share the information with the rest of the class.

Read this Legal Focus Example to the class. Ask the class if they can think of any examples of mistakes that could also fit here. Allow volunteers to share their examples with the class.

Criminal Law 101

One of the most famous insanity defenses involved John Hinkley, who wounded President Ronald Reagan. Hinkley said he was attempting to get actress Jodi Foster's attention.

the nature and quality of the act or did not know that the act was wrong. Yet another definition uses the "irresistible-impulse" definition of insanity. Under this definition, the person with an irresistible impulse may know an act is wrong but cannot keep from doing it.

Most commonly, the insanity defense is used in murder trials. The lawyers for the person accused of murder attempt to show that, at least at the time that the client committed the murderous act, the client did not know what he or she was doing because he or she was insane.

MISTAKE

You might have heard the saying that "ignorance of the law is no excuse." This saying has some truth to it, because ignorance of the law and even a mistaken idea of what the law is do not ordinarily constitute valid defenses to criminal responsibility. If you are pulled over by an officer who says that you were speeding, the fact that you did not know that the speed limit was twenty-five miles an hour does not give you any defense. All citizens are presumed to know most basic criminal laws. And in fact, the defense of mistake rarely is believable when crimes are committed.

◆ LEGAL FOCUS - EXAMPLE

Oliver Wheaton mistakenly drives off in Julie Tyson's car because he thinks it is his. There is no theft, because theft requires knowledge that the property belongs to another. Notice here that Wheaton does not claim that he does not know that theft of someone else's car is against the law. Rather, he thinks he is driving his own car.

At ski resorts, at the base of the mountain and on top, there are often hundreds of pairs of skis. Sometimes someone puts on someone

Legal Focus Problem

Read to the class the Legal Focus Problem found here. Allow student volunteers to suggest possible answers to the question posed at the end of this Legal Focus Problem.

Ethical Concern

Start a short discussion on what are referred to as victimless crimes. Ask your students to take a stand on whether they feel that someone committing a so-called victimless crime should or should not be considered a criminal, since all parties involved did so with consent. Ask each side to elect a chairperson to debate the issue. Be sure students remember the definition of crime. How is society affected by so-called victimless crimes?

---

102   Understanding the Law and Our Legal System

else's skis and the bindings, by a stroke of coincidence, happen to fit perfectly. That person has made a mistake and cannot be charged with a crime.

CONSENT

♦ **consent**
Voluntary agreement to a proposition or act of another.

What if a victim of a crime consents to that crime or even encourages it? **Consent** usually cannot be used as a defense to a crime. The law is written so that it forbids crimes even with the victims' consent. Suppose that you have terminal cancer and are suffering greatly. You ask your close friend to put you out of your misery. He does so. Even if you tape-record your consent with sixteen people present, your friend still will be guilty of a crime.

When a person willingly sells drugs to a person willingly buying drugs, consent clearly is involved on both sides. But both individuals are normally guilty of criminal activity nonetheless. Prostitution also involves two consenting adults, and yet prostitution is still a crime in most states. Indeed, in every state, there is a list of *victimless* crimes for which consent does not offer a valid defense.

When, then, does consent offer a defense? Consent can be used as a defense when it cancels the harm that the law was designed to prevent. If someone loaned you her car, clearly your possession of the car cannot be viewed as the crime or theft.

DURESS

♦ **duress** A wrongful threat causing another person to perform an act that he or she would not otherwise perform.

Duress is defined as a wrongful threat that causes one person to perform an act that she or he would not otherwise have performed. Typically, a person acting under duress cannot have the mental state necessary to commit a crime. The wrongful threat must be a threat of serious bodily harm or death against the victim or a member of his or her immediate family. Moreover, the person who committed the crime under duress must not have gotten involved through his or her own fault.

> ### ◀ LEGAL FOCUS ~ PROBLEM
>
> One night you are walking down the street after a movie. A thug grabs you and holds a gun to your throat. He forces you to walk with him to a jewelry store. With the gun still to your throat, he gives you a hammer and makes you break the glass window case and give him a diamond necklace that was on display. He then runs away. You have just committed an illegal act. Are you guilty of a crime?

The answer is no. You engaged in the illegal act only under extreme duress—the threat of losing your life if you did not do what the thug told you to do. What, though, would have happened if the thug had given you

Allow a student volunteer to read aloud to the class this Legal Focus Problem. Remind students that they can use the Legal Focus features as review tools when studying for tests.

Ask students to develop a chart listing the defenses of a crime. Have them incorporate the definition of each defense, examples of it, and the exceptions to it.

Criminal Law   103

a knife and told you to kill the manager of a fast-food store who was standing outside? Duress could not be used as a defense. Taking another's life, even when your own is threatened through duress, is not legally justified.

JUSTIFIABLE USE OF FORCE

Probably the most well-known defense to criminal liability is self-defense. **Self-defense** is the right to protect oneself from the criminal conduct of others. The use of force is justified to defend one's self, house, and property and to prevent a crime. But a person can only use the amount of force necessary under the circumstances.

◆ **self-defense** The right to protect oneself from the criminal conduct of others.

  LEGAL FOCUS - PROBLEM

Sean Holland and his girlfriend, Michelle Snow, were listening to records at Michelle's house. Suddenly there was a banging on Michelle's unlocked door, and it was flung open. Butch stood at the door, carving knife in one hand and beer bottle in the other. Sean's first thought was to run out the back door, but Michelle grabbed her father's pistol from a desk and aimed it at Butch. Butch lunged toward Michelle. Afraid for her life, Michelle pulled the trigger and killed Butch with one well-aimed shot. Does Michelle have a defense against a homicide charge?

In most circumstances, Michelle does have a defense against a homicide charge. Butch caused Michelle to have a genuine and reasonable fear of immediate great bodily harm. A person facing the possibility of great bodily harm can normally use deadly force to protect herself. **Deadly force** is that force likely to result in death or serious bodily harm. Deadly force can be used to defend oneself if all of the following conditions are met:

◆ **deadly force** Force likely to result in death or serious bodily harm.

1. There is a reasonable belief that death or serious bodily harm will otherwise immediately result.
2. The attacker is using unlawful force. (In contrast, an example of *lawful* force is that exerted by a police officer.)
3. The victim did not begin or cause the attack.

In our legal focus problem, Michelle's behavior in defending her house and herself seems justified.

If a criminal's behavior is not life threatening, the victim may use non-deadly force in defense. The amount of force allowed is the amount necessary to protect the victim's life, person, or property only, and no more.

ENTRAPMENT

Let's say you are walking down the street by your school minding your own business and someone comes up to talk to you. That person is nice, is well dressed, and seems sincere. He suggests that you help him do some-

Stimulate a class discussion by asking the following questions: Why do you think statutes of limitations exist? Do you feel it would be wrong to prosecute someone for a minor theft ten years after the theft? Do you feel it is wrong that those guilty of certain crimes should escape prosecution merely because of a statute of limitations? Explain your answers.

Checking Your Progress (Answers)

1. Crimes are considered offenses against society; the plaintiff is always the government. In a civil suit the injury is private, and the victim is the plaintiff. Persons convicted of crimes may be punished. Civil suits focus on compensating the victim. Statutes are the source of criminal law. Common law is usually the rule applied in civil suits.
2. Felonies are serious crimes, punishable by death or imprisonment in a federal or state penitentiary for more than a year. Misdemeanors are less serious than felonies, punishable by fines or confinement in a local jail for up to a year. Petty offenses (infractions) are minor crimes, punishable by short jail sentences, fines, or both.
3. There must be a guilty act and wrongful intent.

4. Defenses to criminal liability include: infancy—not having reached legal age of adulthood; intoxication—incapable of having the necessary state of mind; insanity—not capable of the wrongful state of mind required to commit a crime; duress—under the threat of serious bodily harm or death; self-defense—the right to protect oneself; entrapment—encouraged by a government official to commit a crime; or statute of limitations—limit on time in which the state can prosecute a crime.

Ethical Concern

Start a class discussion by asking your students if they think there should be a statute of limitations on rape or kidnaping. Why or why not? Why is there not a statute of limitations for murder, while there is for rape and for kidnaping?

thing illegal. You refuse. The person continues to pester you day after day after day. Finally, just to get him off your back, you agree to participate in the illegal activity, but only once. Once you engage in that activity, the person who got you to do it turns around and arrests you because he is an undercover officer.

♦ **entrapment** A defense that can be offered when a police officer or other government agent has suggested commission of a crime and has induced, or encouraged, an individual to commit it.

What that police officer has just done is **entrapment**, defined as suggesting to another that he or she commit a crime while encouraging that person to do so. The defense of entrapment is designed to prevent police and other government personnel from encouraging crime. The defense of entrapment requires that both the suggestion and the inducement come from the government agent. The defense is not, however, intended to prevent the police from setting up traps for life-long criminals. The crucial issue is whether the person who committed the crime intended to commit the crime. If the answer is yes, entrapment does not exist. If, however, the crime is committed because of the suggestion and encouragement of the government agent, entrapment exists.

STATUTE OF LIMITATIONS

Let's say that you shoplifted a couple of notebooks when you were in the third grade. Now you are getting ready to go to college, and the shop owner finally decides to prosecute you because he knew all along that you had taken the notebooks. In almost all circumstances, he would not be able to do anything. Under virtually all circumstances, you could not be held responsible for that crime even if you admitted to it. You are protected by what is known as a *statute of limitations*. Such a law places a limit on the time period during which the state can prosecute a crime. If the state does not prosecute within this time period, the opportunity is lost forever. Time limits vary from state to state for different crimes.

The reasons behind statutes of limitations are many. One is that they limit the time that people have to live under the threat of criminal prosecution. Another reason involves the fact that delaying a prosecution for many years makes it virtually impossible to discover the truth. Witnesses die or disappear, people forget, and evidence is destroyed. One crime, though, has no statute of limitations—murder.

◆ CHECKING YOUR PROGRESS

1. In what ways are crimes different from other wrongful acts?
2. What are the differences in the three classifications of crimes?
3. What two elements must be present in a crime?
4. List and explain three defenses to criminal liability.

Critical Thinking Activity

Ask students to respond to the questions: Do you agree with all of the defenses of criminal liability described? If not, with which do you disagree, and why? Have them write their response using no more than two pages.

Extension Activity

Start a bulletin board by asking your students to bring in recent newspaper and magazine articles on various crimes. Ask each student who brings in an article to highlight the legal terms that you have discussed in class that are found in the article.

Enrichment

Ask your students to come up with a list of procedures that businesses can implement to prevent forgery. For example, retailers can document each gift certificate issued to make sure that when someone comes in to use one, there is a way to prove that that particular certificate has actually been issued and paid for. Have them do this as a homework assignment. Ask students to share their ideas with the class the next day.

Legal Focus Problem

Read aloud the Legal Focus Problem found here. Allow student volunteers to suggest possible answers to the question posed at the end of this Legal Focus Problem.

Criminal Law   105

CRIMES THAT AFFECT BUSINESS

When we go into the world of business, we are more likely to encounter certain kinds of crimes than others. Shoplifting is a crime that obviously affects businesses. Employees can also steal money by manipulating the "books." In this section, we look at these business-related crimes and many others.

FORGERY

The dishonest making or altering of any writing that changes the legal rights and liabilities of another is **forgery**. Forgery usually involves signing someone else's name in order to illegally receive a benefit from that act.

> ### ◀ LEGAL FOCUS ~ PROBLEM
>
> Edward Pollock signed Matt Bennett's name to the back of a check made out to Matt Bennett. Then Edward went to a bank and cashed the check, saying that he was Matt Bennett. He even produced a printed business card that showed he was Matt Bennett. Has Edward committed the crime of forgery?

♦ **forgery** The false or unauthorized signing of a document, or the false making of a document, with the intent to defraud.

The answer is certainly yes. Pollock does not have authorization from Bennett to sign Bennett's name on the back of a check made out to Bennett.

Forgery can also involve falsifying public records. Suppose you break into your school's main computer through the phone system, and then change your grades in your favor (or the grades of some of your friends). You have committed forgery. If you alter your driver's license to show that you are twenty-one so that you can get into bars and nightclubs, you have committed forgery. If you use a sophisticated color printer to create counterfeit money, you have committed forgery. Indeed, the advent of sophisticated laser printing systems has made it possible for individuals to engage in much forgery. Now it is relatively easy for criminals to cheat businesses out of millions of dollars a year by forging retail gift certificates, discount coupons, and the like.

BURGLARY

Originally, **burglary** was defined as breaking and entering into the dwelling of another at night with the intent to commit a felony—usually stealing something. The law's purpose was clearly to protect an individual's home and its occupants against intruders. Today, most state laws define burglary without any reference to the time of day that the breaking and entering of someone's house occurs. Other states do not require that the building entered be someone's house. Still other states do not even require that the entry into the building be forced.

♦ **burglary** Unlawful entry into a building with the intent to commit a felony.

Legal Focus Problem

Allow a student volunteer to read aloud this Legal Focus Problem. Remind students that they can use the Legal Focus features as review tools when studying for tests.

Collaborative Learning Activity

Have a student go to the administrative offices of your school district to find out how many robberies have occurred in your school district during the last 12 months. Then have the student work with other students to design a graph showing the changes in frequency over the 12-month period. Draw this on paper or design a spreadsheet to create a graph.

Reteaching Activity

Ask your students to work with partners to develop charts showing the differences among the different kinds of theft: larceny—petty and grand; robbery; burglary; and shoplifting.

Extension Activity

Ask a volunteer to find out what the dollar amount is in your state that distinguishes petty larceny from grand larceny.

106

ROBBERY

◆ LEGAL FOCUS ‑ PROBLEM

Shelia Carstairs was broke. All she needed was $25, enough to pay for her bus fare home. She tried for a few hours to get people to help her, but without success. Frustrated, she found an empty glass bottle and looked around for the oldest, most helpless person she could find. Minnie Sternbaum was that person. She faced Minnie, waving the bottle, and said, "Give me your purse or I will beat you within an inch of your life." Minnie obeyed. Shelia ran away, thinking to herself, "I'm glad she gave in—I never would have hit her." What crime has Shelia committed?

◆ **robbery** The forceful and unlawful taking of personal property from another.

◆ **assault (criminal)** The wrongful threatened use of immediate force against another.

◆ **battery (criminal)** Unlawful harmful or offensive physical contact by one person against another.

Robbery is the forceful and unlawful taking of personal property from another. The use of force or intimidation is an important element in robbery. Even though a bottle is not a typical weapon, Shelia's threatening use made it so. Shelia's theft of Minnie's purse is the crime of robbery.

Robbery is not the only crime Shelia committed. The wrongful threatened use of immediate force against Minnie is the crime of **assault**. But because Minnie was not actually touched or hit, Shelia did not commit the crime of **battery**.

Shelia's lack of intent to hit Minnie is not a defense to either robbery or assault. She intended to steal the purse, and she threatened to use force to accomplish the theft. Obviously, the more typical robbery involves the taking of property from a business or individual by threatened use of a gun or knife.

LARCENY

◆ **larceny** The wrongful taking of another's personal property.

If you have ever had the displeasure of discovering that someone picked your pocket or handbag, you probably said, "I've been robbed." Actually, though, a crime of robbery involves the use of force or fear. What you experienced was not robbery but rather larceny. Any person who wrongfully takes and carries away another's personal property is guilty of the crime of **larceny**. Larceny requires the intent to permanently deprive the owner of his or her property.

Often, there is a question as to what "property" is. What if you tap into your school's main computer during the night in order to use it, for free, for a business that you are running on the side? You have not physically stolen anything, because computer time is not something you can actually see or feel. Nonetheless, most courts consider stealing computer time as larceny. Stealing the use of telephone wires by the device known as a blue box is also covered by laws against larceny. If you ever hook up a cable TV system to your own television without paying, that too is usually considered larceny.

Read

As an introduction to this feature, let the students discuss their own ideas about lawyers and criminal cases. Ask: Are all accused persons defended by lawyers? Is it their right to be defended by a lawyer? Under what circumstances might a defendant appear without a lawyer? What is a lawyer expected to do for a defendant in a criminal case? Why? After this introductory discussion, ask volunteers to read the *Law in Action* feature aloud to the rest of the class.

Discuss

Encourage a class discussion of this *Law in Action* feature by posing questions such as these: Is there a difference between the right to have a lawyer and the right to be provided with a lawyer? What is the *due process clause* of the Fourteenth Amendment? How did Gideon feel that he had been denied his due process rights? What is the ACLU? Who is it intended to serve? How effective do you believe it has been? Analyze and apply. Let the students work in groups to find out more about the lawyers who are appointed to represent criminal defendants who cannot afford to hire their own lawyers. The members of each group may decide whether to learn about public defenders or about private practice lawyers doing *pro bono* work. The students can gather their information by reading reference works, biographies and other non-fiction books, or magazine articles, and/or by interviewing lawyers. Then lead a class discussion in which the members of all of the groups share and compare their findings.

Collaborative Learning Activity

Divide your class into groups of three or four. Ask them what is to prevent someone from claiming that he or she unknowingly wrote a bad check. Then have each group devise a list of several clues that would suggest that the person did, in fact, write the bad check knowingly.

Criminal Law   107

 Law in Action

LEGAL ISSUE: *GIDEON V. WAINWRIGHT* (1963)

The Sixth Amendment to the U.S. Constitution provides that "in all criminal prosecutions, the accused shall enjoy the right . . . to have the assistance of counsel for his defense." By the passage of the Fourteenth Amendment in 1868, following the Civil War, this and other rights and privileges contained in the Bill of Rights were to be secured for all U.S. citizens, and no state could "deprive any person of life, liberty, or property, without due process of law." Nearly a century passed, however, before the right to counsel was made available to accused persons in state criminal proceedings.

In 1963, the landmark decision in *Gideon v. Wainwright* secured the right to counsel for criminal defendants in state cases with serious criminal penalties. The case began in 1962 when Clarence Earl Gideon sent a *petition* (a formal plea) to the United States Supreme Court to review his conviction. He had been convicted of breaking into a pool hall and stealing money in Panama City, Florida. In his petition, Gideon claimed that he could not afford to pay a lawyer to file the petition for him. He also claimed that his conviction and sentencing to a five-year term in prison violated the due process clause of the Fourteenth Amendment to the Constitution. Gideon stated that he had asked for the assistance of a lawyer at the time of his trial and the court had refused. He claimed that "to try a poor man for a felony without giving him a lawyer was to deprive him of due process of law."

Gideon was successful—with the help of the American Civil Liberties Union and its appointed lawyer, Abe Fortas. (Abe Fortas later became a Supreme Court justice.) The Court decided in Gideon's favor, stating that persons accused of felonies who can show they are unable to afford a lawyer must be given one at the government's expense. Represented by an attorney appointed by the Court, Gideon was retried and found to be innocent of the charges. A biography of Clarence Earl Gideon and a discussion of the significance of this case are presented in *Gideon's Trumpet*, by Anthony Lewis (New York: Vintage Books, 1964).

States normally distinguish between *grand* larceny and *petty* larceny, depending on the value of the property stolen. Grand larceny is a felony, and petty larceny is a misdemeanor. One common example of petty larceny is **shoplifting**—the taking of property from a store without paying for it. If, however, the value of the goods stolen is high enough, shoplifting can become a felony.

◆ **shoplifting**
Taking property from a retail store without paying for it; a type of larceny, usually a misdemeanor.

OBTAINING GOODS BY FALSE PRETENSES

At some point in your life, you will probably have a checking account. Toward the end of your pay period, you might actually run out of money in the account. What if, nonetheless, you go food shopping and write a check that you know will be "bounced" by your bank because you have insufficient funds in your checking account? Have you committed a

Legal Focus Problem

Divide the class into small groups to read and discuss the Legal Focus Problem found here. Each group should choose a leader to explain his or her group's response to the questions posed at the end of this Legal Focus. Additionally, each group should discuss the ethical issues relating to receiving stolen goods. Is it equally wrong to receive stolen goods as it is to steal? Why or why not? What does the act of paying for stolen goods do to our society? Whom does it hurt? Whom does it help?

Extension Activity

Explain to your students that many businesses "bond" employees who handle large sums of money. Ask your students to interview a local business owner to find out what procedures he or she uses to prevent embezzlement and shoplifting. Ask students to share their findings with the class.

---

crime? The answer is normally yes. You have committed the crime of obtaining goods by false pretenses. Individuals commit this crime frequently, creating a serious problem for businesses.

RECEIVING STOLEN GOODS

No one doubts that it is a crime to receive stolen goods. The person who receives stolen goods may be responsible for committing this crime even without knowing the goods were stolen. Most state laws say that, if the person *should* have known that the goods were stolen, the person can be assumed to have had the intent to deprive the owner of the goods.

◆ LEGAL FOCUS ~ PROBLEM

Sam purchased a used car radio and CD player from Jasper at the Greater Tuna Flea Market. The price was reasonable but not cheap. Sam installed the unit and proudly showed it off to some friends at school. Donna noticed how similar the unit was to one that had been stolen from her mother's car. Upon inspection, she saw that the serial number was the same as the one on her mother's stereo. Is Sam guilty of a crime? Who gets to keep the radio and CD player?

Sam appears innocent of any wrongdoing. He does not seem to have known or suspected that Jasper was selling stolen goods. However, Donna's mother has a right to get back the radio and CD player. If Sam can find Jasper, he can sue Jasper for selling him goods illegally. The lesson is clear: Be sure of people from whom you buy goods. Are they honest? Do they own or have a right to sell the goods? If not, you can lose your money and may be subject to criminal charges. If someone you don't know offers you a brand new "boom box" for only $25, and you know that it is worth several hundred dollars, you cannot claim ignorance about the boom box being stolen property.

EMBEZZLEMENT

◆ **embezzlement**
The fraudulent taking of another person's property or money by a person who was entrusted with it; often involves an employee who steals money from an employer.

When a person entrusted with another person's property or money fraudulently keeps it, **embezzlement** occurs. (*Fraudulently* means by use of dishonesty.) Typically, embezzlement involves an employee who steals money from an employer. Employees such as officers or accountants can "jimmy" accounting records to cover up the fact that they have kept company money for their own benefit. Banks and other businesses are especially concerned about embezzlement.

An intent to return the embezzled property is not a defense to this crime. Often, though, an owner will *not* seek prosecution of an embezzler who does return what has been taken. The owner usually will not take the time to make a complaint, give depositions, and appear in court. The

Critical Thinking Activity

Have a student lead a class discussion regarding the Legal Focus, addressing why Shelly is guilty of arson, fraud, solicitation, and conspiracy.

Critical Thinking Activity

Electronic mail, or E-mail, is a way of corresponding via computer rather than physically sending something through the U.S. mail system. If the computer is used to defraud the public, should it be considered mail fraud? Have students write and defend their opinions.

Legal Focus Problem

Allow a student volunteer to read the second Legal Focus Problem aloud to the class. Remind students that they can use the Legal Focus features as review tools when studying for tests.

Extension Activity

Contact your local Better Business Bureau, and ask them if they can send you any information on how to detect a fraudulent business. Also ask a representative there what kinds of businesses have recently been reported as fraudulent.

owner may also wish to avoid bad publicity. Publicity about a bank embezzlement does not give customers confidence about the safety of their money at the bank.

ARSON

The willful and malicious (spiteful or hateful) burning of a building owned by another is **arson**. At common law, arson applied only to burning another person's house. The law was designed to protect human life. Today, arson statutes apply to other kinds of buildings (including your own house) and, in some states, personal property. Arson also includes destroying buildings using explosives.

◆ **arson** The willful and malicious burning of a building owned by another.

  LEGAL FOCUS - PROBLEM

Shelly Allison owns an apartment building that is falling apart. The building is well insured. She hires Ralph Gothmeyer to set fire to it, and Ralph torches the building. Ralph is the one who did the actual illegal act, so does that mean Shelly is innocent of any crime?

Ralph, of course, is guilty of arson. Shelly is also guilty of arson. In addition, if she makes an insurance claim, she is guilty of defrauding her insurance company. Criminal fraud occurs when a person knowingly misrepresents important facts to another. If the insurance fraud is proven, the insurer need not pay the claim. Shelly is also guilty of solicitation and of conspiracy. (Shelly is in deep trouble.)

Firefighters may investigate a suspicious fire for evidence of arson.

MAIL FRAUD

  LEGAL FOCUS - PROBLEM

David Johnson advertises that he has a sure cure for cancer. He has sent out advertisements through the U.S. mail claiming that for $45 he will send the customer "the secret cancer cure the government is hiding from the people." Johnson knows his claimed cure will not work. Has Johnson committed any crimes?

It is a federal crime to use the mails to defraud, or cheat, the public, so Johnson can be prosecuted for fraudulent use of the mails. Illegal use of the mails involves: (1) mailing or causing someone else to mail a writing to carry out a scheme to defraud and (2) an organized scheme to take customers' money by false pretenses. Mail fraud is complete when the victim relies on and is harmed by the deception.

Read

Introduce this *Law in Action* feature by asking the class the following questions: What is bail? What is a bail bond? Who needs a bail bond? Who provides a bail bond?

Discuss

Use the following questions to discuss and review this *Law in Action* feature: When the accused is granted a bail bond, who is assuming a financial risk? What happens when the accused appears at trial? What happens if the accused does not show up at trial? Is bail always granted? Why or why not? Does the refusal to grant bail indicate anything about the defendant's guilt or innocence?

Extend

You might allow a student volunteer to research bail bonds in your community by contacting local bail bond providers and asking them what the accused would have to pay a bail bondsman to provide a bond if his or her bail was $5,000, $10,000, and $20,000. Allow the student volunteer to report his or her findings to the class.

Vocabulary Activity

Discuss why illegal acts committed by an individual or corporation in business are called "white-collar crimes."

Law in Action

LAW IN YOUR LIFE: HOW CAN YOU MAKE BAIL?

It has been said that "justice delayed is justice denied." This can be true in a criminal case when a suspect is arrested and not allowed to obtain a release before trial by posting bail. If you drive around any large city, you will see business signs saying "Bail Bonds" close to the criminal courts. And you can hear phrases such as "Carl had to make bail," "Bruno jumped bail," and "Susan the bounty hunter" on television and in the movies. How do bail and the bail bond business relate to criminal law?

Bail is a sum of money or property given to the court by an accused in exchange for his or her release from jail before trial. If the accused appears at the trial, the bail money is returned. If a suspect cannot afford bail, he or she must remain in jail until the trial or until he or she is able to purchase a **bail bond**. A bail bond is a promise by another to pay the bail if the defendant fails to appear at the trial.

There are persons in the business of issuing bail bonds. Such a person will issue a bail bond if he or she believes the accused will show up at the trial. The person issuing that bond assumes a risk. If the accused ap-

pears at trial, the bond is returned, and the accused pays the issuer a fee—usually 10 percent of the bail amount. If the accused does not show up at the trial, he or she has "skipped" bail, and the bail bond issuer must pay the court the bail amount. Skip tracers or bounty hunters will seek the accused to return him or her to custody. The bond issuer can then get back the bail money from the court.

If the court feels there is little risk that a defendant will not appear at trial, it may release the defendant on his or her own recognizance—that is, his or her promise to appear. After all, the suspect may be acquitted (declared not guilty) in the trial. Factors such as how serious the crime is, how likely it is that the accused is guilty, and whether the accused has ties to the community all contribute to decisions about bail.

◆ **bail** A sum of money or property given to the court by an accused in exchange for his or her release from jail before trial.

◆ **bail bond** A promise by another to pay the bail if the defendant fails to appear at trial.

◆ WHITE-COLLAR CRIMES

◆ **white-collar crime** Nonviolent illegal act committed by an individual or corporation in business.

Murderers, thieves, and drug dealers are not the only criminals who make the headlines. Sometimes, well-respected community leaders who are prominent in the world of business find themselves in jail. Typically, they have committed what are known as **white-collar crimes**. Such crimes involve illegal acts committed by individuals or corporations in a business setting. The term *white-collar* refers to people in business management, who always used to wear white shirts (and ties), in contrast to manufacturing workers, who used to wear blue shirts and are called blue-collar workers.

Multicultural Perspectives

Ask a few interested students to hand in reports on the judicial systems of England, Japan, and Mexico and how these judicial systems differ from ours in dealing with crimes.

The acts involved in white-collar crime usually involve using nonviolent means to obtain a personal or business advantage. Typically, such crime is committed in the course of a legitimate occupation. There is no way to know the true cost of white-collar crimes, but the estimates are certainly in the billions of dollars per year.

In the following four sections, you will read about important white-collar crimes concerning computers, bribery, corporate crimes, and criminal violations of a federal law against racketeering.

COMPUTER CRIME

The term **computer crime** describes many types of criminal conduct. It includes any act directed against computers or computer parts, as well as crimes using computers as instruments of criminal conduct. Existing laws are frequently inadequate in dealing with the various types of computer crimes. As mentioned earlier, larceny statutes were originally passed to prohibit the taking and carrying away of property belonging to another. But computer crimes frequently do not require a physical "taking and carrying away" of another's property. Some states have expanded their definition of property so that computer crimes are covered by larceny statutes. Computer crime law is in an early stage of development.

Computer crime is difficult to detect. Some victimized companies, and even the government, have discovered multimillion-dollar thefts only after a considerable amount of time has gone by. Even after computer crime is detected, tracing the criminal can be difficult. The identity of the wrongdoer is "hidden" by the anonymous computer system. It is also often true that no one with enough knowledge to discover the crime is supervising the wrongdoer's activities.

♦ **computer crime**
An act directed against computers or computer parts or a crime using computers as instruments of criminal conduct.

Why is computer crime often considered a separate crime from larceny? What are the challenges to law enforcement in bringing persons engaged in computer crime to justice?

Extension Activity

Ask for volunteers to visit local businesses to find out what systems are used to secure computer information. Have the volunteers work together to plan which businesses to visit and by whom. Have them develop a brief questionnaire from which to solicit information during their visits.

Extension Activity

Take a field trip to your local jail. If possible, have an officer or guard take your students on a tour of the grounds and facilities.

Caption Answer

Computer crime is often considered a separate crime from larceny, because larceny statutes were originally passed to prohibit the taking and carrying away of property, while computer crimes frequently do not require a physical "taking and carrying away." Computer crime presents challenges to law enforcement because it is difficult to detect; tracing the criminal can be difficult, as he or she is often hidden by an anonymous computer system; and the criminal often has knowledge that is superior to those who supervise his or her legitimate business activities.

Ask a student volunteer to read aloud this Legal Focus Example dealing with computer crimes. Ask students to volunteer any other examples of computer crimes with which they are familiar.

Computer crimes are considered wrongs against society rather than just wrongs against another party. How is society harmed by computer crimes? What price does society pay for computer crimes?

Enrichment

You might want to allow the students to watch the movie *War Games* or the movie *Sneakers* or any other movies about computer crime. Discuss the ramifications of the crime depicted on the victims, on the criminals, and on society.

112

112   Understanding the Law and Our Legal System

 LEGAL FOCUS - EXAMPLE

In the movie *War Games*, a teenage genius accessed a military computer system and almost set off World War III. In 1983, in real life, a group of Milwaukee teenagers (the "414 gang") broke into computer systems across the United States. In 1989, Robert Morris, Jr., a Cornell University student, was accused of paralyzing a computer research network involving six thousand computers. Allegedly, Morris unleashed a "virus" that copied itself repeatedly and used up much of the computers' memory. The activities of these and other so-called computer "hackers" have brought the alarming vulnerability of computer systems to the attention of those who rely on these systems.

To control computer crime, protective measures have been undertaken by federal and state governments as well as by business firms. The Counterfeit Access Device and Computer Fraud and Abuse Act was passed in 1984. It makes it a federal crime to use a computer without authorization. Several states have also passed legislation specifically addressing the problem of computer crime. In Idaho, for example, using computer information without authorization is a misdemeanor, and illegally changing information is a felony. South Dakota has made it illegal to disclose passwords. All unauthorized computer use is a felony in Hawaii. Other states have revised their laws, or are doing so, to cover various types of computer crimes.

One of the major problems faced in controlling computer crime is that it cannot be prosecuted if it is not reported. Many computer crimes go unreported because business firms are reluctant to broadcast the vulnerability of their systems. Companies hurt by the crime do not want it known. They are afraid that their customers will doubt the accuracy and security of computer-generated material—a very legitimate fear.

Businesses look to prevention rather than enforcement. They increase their security measures to prevent unauthorized persons from using their computer systems. Many corporations and government agencies use costly passwords, scrambling devices, and dial-back services that require ID numbers.

BRIBERY

♦ **bribery** The offering, requesting, or receiving of anything of value with the aim of influencing a public official.

Bribery is the offering, requesting, or receiving of anything of value with the aim of influencing a public official. The wrongful behavior is the promise or exchange of value to get public officials to use their offices for a private purpose. It is also unlawful to bribe a foreign official.

Sometimes payments between people in private business to control access to information is called commercial bribery. Examples of commercial

Legal Focus Example

Read this Legal Focus Example to the class. Ask the class if they can think of any examples that could also fit here. Allow volunteers to share their examples with the class.

State Law

Ask a few interested students to research the new stalking laws that some states, such as Florida, have recently added to their statutes.

Legal Focus Problem

Read the Legal Focus Problem found here to the class. Allow student volunteers to suggest possible answers to the question posed at the end of this Legal Focus Problem.

bribes include payments to get private information, to cover up an inferior product, or to secure new business. The theft of business secrets sometimes involves commercial bribes. For example, a person in one firm may offer an employee in a competing firm a payoff for trade secrets.

◆ LEGAL FOCUS – EXAMPLE

Why isn't lobbying illegal? To lobby is to try to influence or persuade a legislator to favor a cause or vote a certain way. The act of persuading or trying to convince the public official is legal. Indeed, the First Amendment guarantee of freedom of speech is the basis of the legality of most lobbying activities. Each citizen and organization is free to try to persuade legislators to vote in a certain way. If, however, the persuasion is combined with money or other value given in exchange for the vote, it is bribery.

CORPORATE CRIME

Corporations are businesses and not real people. (See Chapter 24 for a discussion of corporations.) The law considers a corporation an "artificial" person. As an artificial person, a corporation is held criminally responsible for an act if the penalty for the act is a fine and if intent is not an element of the crime. A corporation is held to lack the ability to form the criminal intent necessary for many crimes. Officers of corporations can, however, be held responsible for their criminal behavior. For example, a corporation cannot be responsible for committing perjury—the crime of lying under oath. The officer who committed the perjury is, however, personally responsible.

A corporation cannot be convicted of a crime that is punished by imprisonment or by the death penalty. If a criminal statute allows a fine in addition to or in place of these penalties, however, a corporation can be convicted of the crime.

◆ LEGAL FOCUS – PROBLEM

A statute requires that adequate safety equipment be installed on all factory machines. Acme Corporation fails to meet the requirement. A worker dies as a result. Can the corporation be found responsible for the crime?

If the statute provides for a fine, the corporation can be found responsible for a criminal homicide. Corporate officers who could have prevented the wrong might also be prosecuted. In the 1990s, some corporate officers have actually been sentenced to serve jail time because they failed to prevent serious safety violations in their corporations' factories.

Allow student volunteers to research RICO prosecutions that have occurred in your state in recent years. Each student should prepare an oral report that includes a description of the alleged RICO offenses and the outcome of the trial and present this report to the class.

Teaching A Case In Point

Read
Before the students read this case, explain to them that it deals with the use of force to protect another. Then allow a student volunteer to read this case aloud to the class.

Discuss
Stimulate a class discussion of this case by asking the following questions: Why did the trial court jury convict Bernardy of assault? How did the court of appeals rule on Bernardy's appeal? What was the result of the trial court's decision? Was the trial court's jury at fault for their decision? Why or why not?

114

Teaching Note

This case is included in the *West's Business and Personal Law Handbook of Selected Court Cases.*

CRIMINAL VIOLATIONS OF FEDERAL RACKETEERING LAW

When the word *racketeering* is mentioned, scenes of the Mafia out of the *Godfather* movies, or *Goodfellows*, or *Bugsy* are conjured up. In 1970, in an attempt to fight organized crime (the Mafia), Congress passed the Organized Crime Control Act of 1970. It included the Racketeer Influenced and Corrupt Organizations Act, otherwise known as RICO. The purpose of the act was to curb the apparently increasing entry of organized crime into the legitimate business world. The act prohibits the purchase of legitimate business interests with illegally obtained funds.

Most criminal RICO offenses have little, if anything, to do with normal business activities. These offenses involve gambling, arson, and extortion. However, securities fraud (involving the sale of stocks and bonds) and mail fraud are also criminal RICO violations. In addition, RICO has become an effective tool in attacking white-collar crimes. Under criminal provisions of RICO, any individual found guilty of a violation is subject to a fine of up to $25,000 per violation or imprisonment for up to twenty years—or both.

◆ A CASE IN POINT ◆

STATE v. BERNARDY
Washington Court of Appeals, 1980.
25 Wash.App. 146,
605 P.2d 791.

The use of force to protect another person from harm was considered by the court to be justifiable in this case.

FACTS   The defendant, Bernardy, came to the defense of his friend Harrison in a fight with Wilson. Wilson started the fight, and after Harrison had knocked Wilson down, Bernardy (who was wearing tennis shoes) kicked Wilson several times in the head. Bernardy stated that he did so because he believed an onlooker, Gowens, would join forces with Wilson against Harrison. Bernardy maintained that his use of force was justifiable because he was protecting an-

other (Harrison) from injury. The trial court judge instructed the jury that state law did not allow the use of force to protect another from reasonably certain harm. Bernardy was convicted for assault.

ISSUE   Is the use of force to protect another person from harm justified?

DECISION   Yes. The trial court's ruling was reversed by the court of appeals, and the case was sent back to the lower court for retrial.

REASON   The court held that an individual "who acts in the defense of another, reasonably believing him to be the innocent party and in danger of imminent injury, is justified in using force to protect that person. . . . The jury could have found the existence of the privilege if it had been properly instructed."

1. Although both robbery and larceny involve the taking of another's property, robbery uses force or fear, but larceny does not.
2. Yes. Shoplifting could be grand larceny if the item stolen is valued at or above the amount the state has set for determining the theft to be grand larceny.
3. No. The true owner of goods does not lose title when they are stolen. Therefore, the owner is entitled to the return of his or her property.
4. Factors such as how serious the crime, how likely the guilt of the accused, and the lack of a defendant's ties to the community all contribute to the amount of bail.
5. Lobbying is legal unless the persuasion is combined with giving something of value in exchange for the vote, which is bribery.
6. The Racketeer Influenced and Corrupt Organizations Act covers organized crimes such as gambling, arson, and extortion in addition to white-collar crimes such as securities and mail fraud.

 ## CHECKING YOUR PROGRESS

1. What is the difference between robbery and larceny?
2. Could shoplifting be grand larceny?
3. If you unknowingly buy goods that have been stolen, can you keep them even if the owner discovers you have them?
4. What factors are considered in the amount of bail a court sets?
5. Is it illegal to try to convince a public official to vote a certain way?
6. What types of crime are covered by RICO?

CHAPTER 4 REVIEW

 ## SUMMARY

DEFINITION

Criminal law is concerned with acts against society. Criminal law attempts to discourage these acts by punishing wrongdoers.

CLASSIFICATION OF CRIMES

Crimes are classified by degree of seriousness.

1. *Felonies*—Serious crimes punishable by death or by imprisonment in a federal or state penitentiary for more than a year.
2. *Misdemeanors*—Crimes punishable by a fine or by imprisonment for up to a year. Misdemeanors are sometimes defined as offenses for which offenders are imprisoned in a local jail instead of a penitentiary.
3. *Petty offenses*—Minor offenses (such as traffic violations) that are often not classified as crimes.

CRIMINAL LIABILITY

1. Two elements are necessary to establish criminal liability: (a) The performance of a prohibited act; (b) The intent to commit a prohibited act.

2. The act of requesting assistance to commit a crime is criminal solicitation.
3. An agreement to commit a crime is a criminal conspiracy after either party performs some act of preparation to commit the crime.
4. A co-conspirator is guilty of a crime committed by the other conspirator.

DEFENSES TO CRIMINAL LIABILITY

Infancy, Intoxication, Insanity, Mistake, Consent, Duress, Justifiable use of force, Entrapment, Statute of limitations.

CRIMES AFFECTING BUSINESS

Forgery, Burglary, Robbery, Larceny, Obtaining goods by false pretenses, Receiving stolen goods, Embezzlement, Arson, Mail fraud.

WHITE-COLLAR CRIME

Computer crime, Bribery, Corporate crime, Criminal RICO violations.

1–B, 2–E, 3–F, 4–J, 5–H,
6–I, 7–C, 8–A, 9–G, 10–D

1. a–The theft of Jerry's wallet is larceny, stealing property in any manner; b–Shoplifting, taking property from a store without paying for it, is a form of larceny.
2. Bribery, receiving stolen property, and conspiracy involve more than one person.
3. Since James provided the opportunity and incentive for Laura to commit the crime and assisted her in committing it, it is doubtful that she would have committed the crime

without James's inducements. Laura's defense of entrapment might be upheld by the court.
4. a–Sarah has committed the crime of larceny when she wrongfully takes the property of another; b–Sarah has committed robbery when she forcibly takes the personal property of another; c–Sarah has committed burglary by breaking and entering a dwelling with intent to commit a felony.

---

116   Understanding the Law and Our Legal System

 USING LEGAL LANGUAGE

Directions: Match each term with the statement that best defines that term.

1. alibi
2. arraignment
3. burglary
4. crime
5. duress
6. embezzlement
7. forgery
8. Miranda warnings
9. misdemeanor
10. motive

A. warnings police must give persons detained or arrested as criminal suspects

B. declaration that the accused was someplace else at the time of a crime

C. false or unauthorized signing of a document, or the false making of a document, with intent to defraud

D. the reason for a criminal act

E. hearing at which an accused is brought before a court to hear the charges against him or her and to enter a plea to the charges

F. unlawful entry into a building with the intent to commit a felony

G. a crime punishable by a fine or by confinement for up to a year

H. a wrongful threat inducing another person to perform an act that he or she would not otherwise perform

I. the fraudulent taking of another person's property or money by a person who was entrusted with it

J. a wrong against society, defined in a statute, and punishable by society

 CHECKING FOR COMPREHENSION

1. Determine from the facts below what type of crime (larceny, burglary, embezzlement, arson, etc.) is committed in each case.
   (a) Jerry is walking through an amusement park when his wallet, with $2,000 in it, is "picked" from his pocket.
   (b) Harry walks into a camera shop. Without force and without the owner noticing, Harry walks out of the store with a camera.

2. Of the following crimes, which one (or ones) involves illegal activity on the part of more than one person?

Bribery, Forgery, Embezzlement, Larceny, Receiving stolen property, Conspiracy.

3. James, an undercover police officer, stops Laura on a busy street. James offers to sell Laura an expensive wristwatch for a fraction of its value. After some questioning by Laura, James admits that the watch is stolen property, although he says he was not the thief. Laura pays for and receives the wristwatch and is immediately arrested by James for receiving stolen property. At trial, Laura contends entrapment. What is the result of the trial?

1. Stahl is correct. In order for Stahl to have committed the crime of embezzlement, the money would have to have been entrusted to his care. The court could find no evidence that the money had been so entrusted to Stahl by the store owner. The facts of the case showed that only the owner could handle the money. Stahl did not have the keys to the drop-box, did not have permission to remove the money for any purpose, and had to pry the box open to get the money. Note, however, that although Stahl had not committed the crime of embezzlement, he had committed the crime of larceny.

2. A Utah trial court found Seekford to be guilty of theft because it concluded that Seekford harbored an intent to steal the car at the time it was rented in the state of Utah. Therefore, the court held that an element of the offense was committed in Utah and Utah thus had jurisdiction.

3. No. The court ruled that Khoury was guilty of grand larceny. In order for larceny to exist, the property (1) must be taken with the intent to deprive the owner permanently of his or her property, and (2) asportation (carrying away) must occur. The asportation element requires that the goods be severed from the possession or custody of the owner and placed in the possession of the thief. The court found that Khoury's removal of the property from the shelves constituted asportation and that Khoury had removed the goods from the shelves to his cart with the intention of permanently depriving the store of possession.

4. Identify the three crimes in the following situations, stating the differences among them. Although the situations are similar, they represent three different crimes. (a) While passing Joanne's house one night, Sarah sees a portable television set left unattended on Joanne's lawn. Sarah takes the television set, carries it home, and tells everyone she owns it. (b) While passing Joanne's house one night, Sarah sees Joanne outside with a portable television set. Holding Joanne at gunpoint, Sarah forces her to give up the set. Then Sarah runs away with it. (c) While passing Joanne's house one night, Sarah sees a portable television set in a window. Sarah breaks the front-door lock, enters, and leaves with the set.

 ## APPLYING LEGAL CONCEPTS

1. Look through the newspaper for several days. Cut out articles about crimes. Tape them to a poster or notebook page with headings for different categories of crimes such as felonies, misdemeanors, petty offenses. Make a separate poster or page for articles about crimes affecting business.

2. Research crime statistics in your city or state for the past year. Develop a bar graph showing the number of felonies and the number of misdemeanors for each month. During which month were the most felonies committed, the most misdemeanors?

 ## APPLYING THE LAW . . . YOU BE THE JUDGE

1. Joe Stahl worked the late shift at a store. The store owner had instructed him that, whenever a certain amount of money accumulated in the cash register, Stahl was to insert all but $50 into a drop-box. The drop-box was always kept locked, and only the owner had a key to it. One night Stahl disappeared, as did the lock-box. When Stahl was convicted of embezzling funds he had taken from the drop-box, he appealed, asserting that he could not have committed the crime of embezzlement since the funds in the drop-box had never been entrusted to him by his employer. Is Stahl correct? [*State v. Stahl*, 93 N.M. 62, 596 P.2d 275 (1979)]

2. Seekford rented a car in Utah and drove with some friends to Texas. After they arrived in Texas, Seekford assured his friends that he would return the rented car. The car was never returned to the rental agency; however, it was found abandoned several months later in Texas. The state of Utah brought suit against Seekford, who was convicted of larceny. Seekford appealed, alleging that since the criminal act had taken place in Texas, the state of Utah did not have jurisdiction. Under Utah state law, a person is subject to prosecution in Utah for an offense committed either within or outside the state. What element of the offense could have been committed in Utah? [*State v. Seekford*, 638 P.2d 525 (Utah 1981)]

3. Khoury went to a department store, spent some time shopping, and eventually filled a large, empty chandelier box with approximately $900 worth of tools. When he went to the check-out counter, the cashier indicated she wanted to look inside the box before accepting Khoury's payment for the chandelier. Khoury then pushed the cart back into the store and left the premises. Khoury was convicted of grand larceny by the trial court. On appeal, Khoury said that, since he hadn't actually removed any goods from the store, he had not committed larceny. Is Khoury correct? [*People v. Khoury*, 108 Cal.App.3d Supp. 1, 166 Cal.Rptr. 705 (1980)]

Discussion Starter

Prereading Activity

Introduce this Legal Perspective on criminal law procedure by reminding students that in the last Legal Perspective, they learned about general court procedures. In this Legal Perspective they will be learning about procedures that are specific to criminal law. Then have student volunteers take turns reading this Legal Perspective aloud to the class.

LEGAL BACKGROUND

Just as there are procedures in a civil action, there are procedures in a criminal action. This LP is a compliment to the Chapter 2 discussion on the Bill of Rights. Whereas most civil procedures are determined by custom and convenience, criminal procedures are often based on Constitutional rights flowing from the Bill of Rights. We illustrate these rights with a discussion of the Miranda warnings and the exclusionary rule for evidence illegally obtained.

Discussion Starter

As the students consider constitutional safeguards to guarantee the rights of individuals against the state, you may want to raise these discussion questions: What concerns have been raised in recent years regarding too much interest in the rights of defendants and too little interest in the rights of victims? What arguments are presented in favor of protecting victims' rights? In favor of protecting defendants' rights? Can both be protected? Why or why not? Which do you believe should take precedence? Why?

LEGAL PERSPECTIVE

CRIMINAL LAW PROCEDURE

"It is better that ten guilty persons escape than that one innocent suffer."
William Blackstone, 1723–1780
English jurist and educator

Our criminal justice system presumes that it is far worse to punish an innocent person than to let a guilty person go free. Criminal law presumes a person is innocent until proved guilty, and the state must prove guilt beyond a reasonable doubt. Criminal law procedures exist to protect the rights of the individual and to preserve this presumption of innocence.

 ### CONSTITUTIONAL SAFEGUARDS

Criminal law brings the power of the state to bear against an individual. To counterbalance the power of the state, the Constitution provides specific safeguards for those accused of crimes. The Supreme Court has ruled that most of these safeguards apply in state as well as federal courts. The due process clause of the Fourteenth Amendment is the source of these rights in state prosecutions. The safeguards include:

1. Fourth Amendment protection from unreasonable searches and seizures. This safeguard is meant to protect people from interference and intrusion by government officials. To conduct a search, government officials must usually have a **warrant**—permission to search—granted by a judge.

2. Fourth Amendment requirement that no warrants for a search or an arrest can be issued without probable cause.

Probable cause is a strong likelihood that a person has committed or is about to commit a crime.

3. Fifth Amendment requirement that no one can be deprived of "life, liberty, or property without due process of law."

4. Fifth Amendment prohibition against double jeopardy. This safeguard protects people from being tried twice for the same criminal offense.

5. Fifth Amendment privilege against self-incrimination. This safeguard protects a defendant from being forced to testify against himself or herself.

6. Sixth Amendment guarantees of a speedy trial, a trial by jury, a public trial, the right to confront witnesses, and the right to a lawyer at various stages in some proceedings.

7. Eighth Amendment prohibition against excessive bails and fines and cruel and unusual punishment.

The U.S. Supreme Court has been active in defining these rights.

CRIMINAL PROCESS

A criminal prosecution differs significantly from a civil case. These differences reflect the desire to safeguard the rights of the individual from the greater power and resources of government.

Investigation During an investigation, there are limits on police conduct. For example, the Fourteenth Amendment to the U.S. Constitution prohibits unreasonable searches by the federal government. The due process clause of the Fourteenth Amendment similarly restricts state officials, including the police. If police officers conduct an unreasonable search and seizure, the evidence produced generally cannot be used to convict the accused. This rule, created to prevent illegal police conduct, is the **exclusionary rule**.

Police officers usually must get approval to search (called a search warrant) from a judge before they can conduct a search. To get a search warrant, they must convince the judge that probable cause exists that they will find evidence damaging to the person subject to the warrant. Probable cause exists if the police officers have specific information showing that it is likely they will find incriminating evidence. A search is also justified without a warrant when the time delay or circumstances involved in getting a warrant are unreasonable. Examples of appropriate searches without warrants include searches of suspects that take place as part of lawful arrests and searches consented to by the suspects.

Some rules about searches in specific situations are as follows:

1. Plain-view searches—If a police officer sees contraband (illegal items) or a dangerous weapon in a car in plain view, he or she can seize it. The officer may then also search the immediately surrounding area.

2. Stop and frisk—If an officer has a reasonable suspicion that a serious criminal activity has taken place, he or she may stop and question the suspect and "frisk" the suspect for a weapon.

3. Hot pursuit—An officer may pursue a fleeing suspect into a private building without a search warrant.

4. Emergency—Under emergency situations, it may not be possible to get a search warrant. An example is a break-in to rescue the victim of a crime, seen through a window to be in need of help.

5. Open field—An officer may search an open field suspected to contain contraband if there is no reasonable expectation of privacy in the area. Observations from airplanes or helicopters generally do not require a search warrant.

6. Abandoned property—An officer may search an abandoned automobile or house or personal property discarded by a suspect.

Interrogation Before interrogation, or questioning, a suspect may have the constitutional right to **Miranda warnings**. Police officers must inform anyone they arrest as a suspect in a criminal activity (1) that the person has the right to remain silent, (2) that anything the person says can and will be used against the person in a court of law, (3) that the person has a right to have a lawyer present before questioning, and (4) that the state must provide a lawyer for any person who cannot afford one. If the arresting officer does not inform the suspect of all these rights, then incriminating statements made by the suspect, such as a confession, cannot be used against him or her.

Arrest An **arrest** occurs when a person is taken into custody to be charged with a crime. There must be probable cause to believe that the accused has committed a crime. Again, probable cause is a strong likelihood (not just a chance) that the person has committed or is about to commit a crime. Arrests, however, may sometimes be

(continued on page 120)

119

One of the most famous cases of an accused pleading *nolo contendere* occurred in 1973, when then-Vice President Spiro Agnew pleaded "no contest" to tax evasion and promptly resigned. You might ask a student volunteer to research the Agnew trial. Find what periodicals of the day said regarding his no contest plea. What was the effect of that plea? What penalties did Agnew suffer? Allow the volunteer to report his or her findings to the class.

Work with the students to arrange for a local public defender to visit the class. Ask the public defender to speak briefly about his or her work, then allow time for the students to ask questions (you may want to help the students plan interesting and appropriate questions for the speaker).

Guide the students in considering and discussing the arguments for and against plea bargaining: Which do you find more convincing? What alternatives to plea bargaining do you believe should be considered?

LEGAL PERSPECTIVE (CONTINUED)

made without a warrant—for example, if there is no time to get one. In this case, the action of the arresting officer is still judged by the probable cause standard.

Booking After arrest, the suspect is subject to booking. The police term *booking* refers to searching, fingerprinting, and photographing the person who has been arrested.

Accusation Individuals must be formally charged with the commission of specific crimes before they are brought to trial. This formal charge is an **accusation**. The name of the accusation depends on how it is used. An accusation made by the district attorney is an *information*. An accusation made by a grand jury[1] is an *indictment*. In misdemeanor cases, an accusation is a *complaint*. If sufficient evidence exists to justify bringing the individual to trial, an accusation is issued.

Arraignment An **arraignment** brings the accused before the court to hear the charges against him or her and to enter a plea. An accused can plead *guilty* (I did it), *not guilty* (I did not do it), or *nolo contendere*. The plea of *nolo contendere* means the defendant will not contest the criminal charge. The plea is not an admission of guilt but is an acceptance of the criminal penalty. For most purposes, this plea is the same as a guilty plea. The defendant is not, however, admitting responsibility. (An admission of responsibility can be used against a person later in a civil lawsuit brought by the victim.) In some states, the defendant can plead

---

1. A grand jury is a group of citizens appointed to a panel to hear preliminary evidence of crimes and determine if accusations should be issued. The panel serves for a certain period of time. Grand juries also often investigate complaints of governmental wrongdoing or inefficiency.

not guilty by reason of insanity (if I did it, I lacked the mental capacity to be responsible). At the arraignment, the release of the defendant and the amount of bail are also considered. (Bail is discussed in The Law in Action feature in Chapter 4.)

Plea bargain Often, following arraignment, the district attorney decides whether to **plea bargain** with the defendant. Plea bargaining offers the defendant a chance to plead guilty to a lesser related crime—for example, larceny instead of robbery. In exchange for the guilty plea, the state drops the more serious charge. Prosecutors consider the time, expense, and uncertainty of the criminal trial when deciding whether to offer a plea bargain. If the defendant accepts the bargain, it is because the lesser sentence is attractive compared with the chance of conviction for the more serious crime.

Immunity At times, a prosecutor may wish to get information from a person accused of a crime. Accused persons are understandably reluctant to give information that will be used against them. The Fifth Amendment to the Constitution grants everyone the privilege against self-incrimination ("taking the Fifth"). This constitutional privilege protects the defendant from being compelled to testify against himself or herself in a criminal case. If the state wishes to get information from a person accused of a crime, it can grant immunity from prosecution—that is, it can promise not to prosecute. Once immunity is given, the person can no longer refuse to testify on Fifth Amendment grounds. Often, granting immunity from prosecution for a serious crime is part of plea bargaining. The state uses the

Discussion Starter

Help the students examine both the advantages and disadvantages of determinate sentencing. Then ask: Do you think the current trend toward determinate sentencing is healthy? Why or why not?

testimony to prosecute accomplices for serious crimes carrying heavy penalties.

Pretrial The U.S. Constitution requires a speedy trial for all criminal actions unless the defendant waives, or gives up, this right. Usually, *speedy* means within sixty days.

A defendant in a criminal case may waive the right to a speedy trial. The defendant's attorney may wish more time to investigate the case or deal with work schedule conflicts. (Television lawyers don't have these conflicts, even though they participate in major trials every week, but real lawyers do.) Sometimes, delay is useful when a crime has aroused public opinion. Although the defendant is presumed innocent, he or she may be the object of public anger and hostility. After delay, emotions usually cool, and the chance of receiving a fair, unemotional trial is improved.

Recall that discovery is the process of obtaining information from the opposing party or other witnesses. Discovery is limited in a criminal case, because the defendant has a privilege against self-incrimination. Although the defendant cannot be forced to testify against himself or herself, however, the prosecutor does not have the same privilege. In other words, the district attorney must allow the defendant's attorney to examine the state's evidence against the defendant, including names of witnesses against the defendant. The Sixth Amendment to the U.S. Constitution gives the accused the right "in all criminal prosecutions, to be confronted with the witnesses against him." Furthermore, physical evidence (such as weapons, clothing, and stolen goods) may be seized and held by the district attorney before the trial, and the defendant or the defendant's attorney has the right to inspect this evidence before trial. It may seem that the defendant has an advantage over the prosecution. This apparent advantage is an illusion, however. Few criminal defendants have the money to match the state's resources in investigating a criminal case.

Trial The prosecutor (the state) has the *burden of proof* at the trial. The reasonable doubt test is used to judge guilt. The prosecution must show the guilt of the defendant, based on all the evidence, beyond a reasonable doubt. A reasonable doubt is a doubt that would cause a reasonable person to hesitate before acting in a matter important to him or her. Returning a verdict of "not guilty" is not the same as saying the defendant is innocent. A "not guilty" verdict means that guilt was not proved beyond all reasonable doubt.

Courts have complex rules about the types of evidence—such as testimony of witnesses, fingerprints, and cloth fibers—that may be presented, especially in jury trials. These rules are designed to ensure that evidence in trials is relevant and reliable and does not cause prejudice against the defendant. The defense attorney will cross-examine witnesses to try to show that the prosecution's evidence is not believable or reliable (trustworthy). The state may also cross-examine witnesses presented by the defendant.

Sentencing Most states have **determinate sentencing** laws. These laws provide set penalties for defendants convicted of crimes. A few states have **indeterminate sentencing** laws, which provide a range of prison terms; the term to be served by an individual defendant is decided by a state board.

(continued on page 122)

Vocabulary Activity

Divide your class into two teams. Have each team line up in single file across from the other team. Orally define a term described in this Legal Perspective, and allow one member from each team to try to answer with the proper term. The first team whose member answers correctly scores one point; the answering team member then will go to the end of his or her line. The member of the other team who didn't answer correctly must sit down. The team with the most students standing at the end of the class is the winning team.

LEGAL PERSPECTIVE (CONTINUED)

A first offender may be given probation. **Probation** suspends the offender's sentence, so he or she does not have to serve time in prison. However, the defendant must meet the conditions of probation (which include not committing any more criminal acts). If the conditions are not met, the offender may be sent to prison to serve the suspended term.

Parole is the conditional release from prison of a convict who has not yet served his or her full term. If the parolee meets the conditions of parole, he or she completes the term outside of jail. If, however, the person violates parole, he or she can be sent back to prison to complete the original prison sentence. As a condition of parole or probation, convicted felons waive their right not to be searched without a search warrant. Searches can take place at any time and any place.

VICTIMS' RIGHTS

Since the early 1980s, there has been an explosion of new federal and state legislation to support victims' rights in the criminal justice system. Among the new laws are the following:

1. Laws that require notice to victims and/or their families before a defendant is sentenced. Often, victims may present testimony or other statements at sentencing hearings.

2. Laws requiring notice when a convicted felon has a parole hearing.

3. Laws that require some types of earnings of the convicted felon to be placed in a victims' reimbursement fund.

4. Laws that allow victims to submit claims to have their losses paid by the state.

◆ TERMS TO REMEMBER

◆ **warrant** A written authorization from a judge to arrest an accused.

◆ **probable cause** Strong likelihood that a person has committed or is about to commit a crime.

◆ **exclusionary rule** Rule that excludes evidence obtained as a result of unreasonable search and seizure from being used to convict the accused.

◆ **Miranda warnings** Warnings police must give persons detained or arrested as criminal suspects.

◆ **arrest** Official taking of a person into custody to charge him or her with a crime.

◆ **accusation** Formal charge accusing a person of the commission of a specific crime; made before a trial.

◆ **arraignment** Hearing at which an accused is brought before a court to hear the

charges against him or her and to enter a plea to the charges.

◆ **plea bargain** Agreement between prosecution and defendant providing that the defendant will plead guilty to a lesser crime.

◆ **determinate sentencing** Sentencing that provides set penalties for specific types of crimes.

◆ **indeterminate sentencing** Sentencing that provides a wide range of prison terms for a specific type of crime; the term to be served is decided by a state board.

◆ **probation** A sentence under which a convicted defendant may avoid prison by meeting certain conditions over a stated period of time.

◆ **parole** The release from prison of a convict who has not yet served his or her full term. The release requires that the parolee meet certain conditions to remain out of prison.

Mastery Objectives

By the end of this chapter students will be able to:
- Describe intentional torts against persons
- Describe intentional torts against property
- Explain negligence and strict liability
- Apply common defenses to torts
- Differentiate between intentional torts and unintentional torts

Tort Law

Chapter 5

Prereading Activity

Prepare a poster or draw on the board a table with the following headings for blank columns. As the class progresses through the chapter, have students list various kinds of torts as each is studied.

Headings:

chart 1
Intentional Torts
Against Persons   *Against Property*
chart 2
Unintentional Torts
Negligence   *Strict Liability*
chart 3
Defenses to Torts
chart 4
Differences
Intentional Torts Unintentional Torts

Discussion Starter

Provide students with a few examples of torts, and have them draw from their own experiences and imagination a list of supposed torts. Have a discussion on whether or not these are torts.

Chapter 5
Resources and Assignment Guide

Activity Sheets
Reviewing Legal Concepts 5 *TRB*
Enrichment Activity 5 *TRB*

Student Activity Workbook
Chapter 5 Activities

Tests
Chapter 5 Test *TRB*
Chapter 5 WESTEST Computerized Testing

Handbook of Selected Court Cases
Johnson v. *K-mart Enterprises, Inc.*
Bray v. *Kate, Inc.*

West's Business Law and Legal Environment Videodisc
Still Frames and Motion Segments as shown

"There is no wrong without a remedy."
Legal maxim

Lots of things can go wrong in your life. You could be walking in a supermarket aisle when a stock clerk runs into you with a heavy box, causing you serious injury. You could be calmly riding in your car when another driver fails to yield to a red light and runs into you, smashing your car and you, too. You could be well on your way to financial success and independence when a jealous co-worker untruthfully reports to the press that you have been stealing money from your employer, causing you to be fired.

Clearly, in each of these situations, you will have been wronged. And you will probably want to sue. If and when you do, you will be engaged in a civil law action in which you contend that someone else has committed a **tort**. The word *tort* comes from Latin, and it means "to twist." An easy way to think of a tort is to think of twisting your ankle in a hole left in the floor of a restaurant by a lazy worker. A tort is a civil wrong or injury for which a court will provide a remedy to compensate you for the wrong. In the last chapter, you learned about criminal law. Criminal law is distinct from civil law, of which torts are just a part. This is a good place to make that distinction even more clear.

◆ **tort** A wrongful act for which a court may award damages.

◆ THE DIFFERENCE BETWEEN CIVIL LAW AND CRIMINAL LAW

To understand torts, it is helpful to contrast tort law with criminal law. The law of crimes is about harm to the public. A criminal act is seen as so objectionable that it is considered to be a wrong against the *state*—that is, against society. Therefore, the state—our government—prosecutes a person assumed of committing a criminal act. Even though there is an identifiable individual victim, the law considers the public to be the real victim of the crime.

The person suffering a direct injury does have rights, however. A person who is injured by the wrongful conduct of another is the victim of a tort. The tort may or may not also be a crime. The tort action, however, is a *civil* action by which one person brings a private suit against another. Exhibit 5-1 summarizes the difference between civil and criminal law.

◆ THE BASIS OF TORT LAW

In this chapter's opening quote, two things were mentioned—wrongs and remedies. The wrongs we refer to here are torts, or as they are sometimes

VIDEODISC NOTE
Much of the material that is conveyed in the exhibits of *West's Business and Personal Law* is also conveyed in the still frames on the **West Business Law and Legal Environment Videodisc**. For more information and directions for use, please see the Index and Description of Contents for the **West Business Law and Legal Environment Videodisc** that is found in your *Teacher's Resource Binder.*

Extension Activity

For a homework assignment have students write a one-page essay describing an example of a wrong that contains both a criminal and a civil offense. Have them not only distinguish between the two, but also explain why the tort affected the individual and why the crime affected society.

Differences between Civil and Criminal Law

1. Crimes are considered offenses against society. Although a person is the subject of the criminal act, the law presumes society in general is the victim. Thus, crimes are prosecuted by public officials, not by individual victims. The plaintiff is always the government, federal or state.

2. Persons convicted of crimes may be punished for their wrongs against society. Lawsuits for civil wrongs focus on compensating the individual victim, not punishing the wrongdoer.

3. Statutes are the source of criminal law. Both definitions of crimes and criminal punishment are provided in statutes. Civil wrongs are mostly defined in the common law.

EXHIBIT 5-1
DIFFERENCES BETWEEN CIVIL AND CRIMINAL LAW

Legal Focus Problem

Allow a student volunteer to read aloud this Legal Focus Problem. Have him or her suggest possible answers for the question posed at the end of this Legal Focus feature.

Collaborative Learning Activity

Divide your students into groups of four and have them consider the possible legal remedies that Joe could seek.

called, *tortious acts*. Tort law recognizes that some acts are wrong because the acts cause injuries to others. It also recognizes that the injured person or persons should have the right to a remedy, or some type of compensation.

◀ LEGAL FOCUS ─ PROBLEM

Joe is walking down the street minding his own business on a warm summer day. For some unknown reason, Fred attacks him. In the struggle, Joe falls and breaks his leg. A passing police officer restrains and arrests Fred. For what wrongful acts is Fred responsible?

Fred has clearly committed a criminal act by attacking Joe. But Joe can also bring a tort lawsuit against Fred to recover compensation for the injuries that he suffered in the fall. Those injuries can be translated into what are called **damages**. Damages are defined as the money sought as a remedy.
The remaining sections in this chapter describe the wrongs and remedies associated with several general areas of tort law: intentional torts against persons, intentional torts against property, unintentional torts, and strict liability, which we will define later.

◆ **damages** Money sought as a remedy for a wrong, such as a tortious act (tort).

◆ INTENTIONAL TORTS AGAINST PERSONS

If you are playing around with one of your friends, and you push that person, you clearly intended to carry out that action. This intent is the basis of

Ask your students to think of a time when they were horsing around with someone and one of them got hurt. Could this be considered a tort? What could have happened? Students need to realize that even playful behavior can result in a lawsuit.

Divide the class into groups of four. Assign each group a different intentional tort. Have the students create an example of their assigned tort. Have each group present its information to the class.

Legal Focus Problem

Read the Legal Focus Problem found here to the class. Allow student volunteers to suggest possible answers to the question posed at the end of this Legal Focus feature.

♦ **intentional tort**
A wrongful act knowingly committed.

♦ **tortfeasor** A person who commits a tort.

an **intentional tort**. The one committing the tort must intend to commit the wrongful act. This person is called a **tortfeasor**. An act is considered wrongful if its consequences interfere with the interests of another in a way not permitted by law. If, when you playfully push your friend, you cause a serious injury, it does not matter what your *motive* was. In other words, an evil or harmful motive is not required for you to commit an intentional tort. Indeed, you may even have a good motive for what turns out to be a tort. You might have given your friend a shove because you thought that person needed to be cheered up. But if, because of your actions, your friend is seriously injured, you have nonetheless committed an intentional tort.

Now, how does the law decide what someone's intent was? The law assumes that individuals intend the *normal* consequences of their actions. Thus, when you give your friend a strong push—even if it is done as a joke and without an evil motive—it is clearly an intentional tort if injury results. This is so because someone who is forcefully pushed can ordinarily be expected to fall. In contrast, a light pat on the shoulder is normally not an intentional tort.

Intentional torts may be committed against persons or against property. Intentional torts against persons include assault and battery, infliction of mental distress, false imprisonment, defamation, invasion of privacy, and fraud.

ASSAULT AND BATTERY

> #### ◀ LEGAL FOCUS ~ PROBLEM
>
> Kelly Townsend was standing in line behind Rudy Teng to buy tickets to the latest Steven Segal action movie. Kelly overheard Rudy make a negative remark about Kelly's high school. Kelly yelled at Rudy, "I should hit you for that remark." Before Rudy could respond, Kelly said: "Actually there is no 'ought to' about it—I am going to rearrange your face." Kelly then hit Rudy in the face. Did Kelly commit any torts?

♦ **assault (civil)**
An intentional, unexcused act that creates in another a reasonable apprehension or fear of an immediate harmful or offensive contact.

The answer is certainly yes. Kelly committed two torts, *assault* and *battery*. Any intentional, unexcused act that creates a reasonable apprehension of immediate harmful or offensive contact is an **assault**. Apprehension is concern about the contact. It is not the same as fear. If a reasonable person would wish to avoid the contact, then apprehension exists, even if the person is unafraid. In the example above, Kelly's first statement was not an assault. Kelly did not say he was going to hit Rudy; he said he should. There was no immediate threat. The second statement was an assault, whether or not Rudy was afraid. The threat was immediate.

The *completion* of the threat, if it results in harm to the person who was threatened, is a **battery**. A battery is defined as harmful or offensive physical contact that is intentional and unexcused. When Kelly actually hit Rudy, a battery resulted.

◆ **battery (civil)**
Harmful or offensive physical contact that is intentional and unexcused.

◆ LEGAL FOCUS – PROBLEM

Raney sneaks up behind Susan while she is having a conversation with one of her girlfriends. As Susan turns around to walk away, her face almost touches Raney's. Raney cannot control himself and gives her a quick kiss on the cheek. Susan barely knows Raney and does not like what he just did. Has Raney committed a tort?

The answer again is yes. Battery does not require contact that is harmful. If the contact is merely offensive, such as this unwelcome kiss, then the tort of battery has nonetheless been committed. Contact to any part of the body or anything attached to it is a battery. For example, the harmful or offensive touching of a hat or other item of clothing, a purse, a chair, or an automobile can be a battery. Of course, a person needs to be either wearing, holding, or sitting on the property. The offensiveness of the conduct is determined by the *reasonable-person standard*. The reasonable-person standard is an objective test of how a reasonable person would have acted under the same circumstances. (The section "Breach of the Duty of Care" later in the chapter discusses this standard.)

In a civil action, if the plaintiff proves there was an offensive contact, the plaintiff has a right to compensation. There is no need to show that the defendant acted out of anger or ill will. The underlying motive does not matter. Damages from a battery can be compensated for emotional harm as well as for physical harm. In the law, as stated before, the term *damages* relates to the compensation that may be recovered by a person who has suffered some type of loss or sustained some type of injury.

Several legal defenses can be raised by a defendant who is sued for assault or battery.

1. **Consent.** When a person consents to the act that damages him or her, there is generally no liability for the damage done. If you tell your best friend to hit you in the arm because you want to see what it feels like, you have consented to the harmful contact. Normally, you could not then sue your friend for the tort of battery.

2. **Self-defense.** An individual who is defending his or her life or physical well-being can claim self-defense. A person has a right to use whatever force is reasonably necessary to prevent harmful contact. A key word here is *reasonably*. If you are in a crowd of people at a rock concert and are worried about getting pushed, it would not be considered reasonable for you to spray the crowd around you with twelve-gauge shotgun pellets to prevent them from making physical contact.

Teaching with the Videodisc

The still frames listed below from the **West's Business Law and Legal Environment Videodisc** can be used with this chapter. To access this material, use the bar codes or the frame numbers included in the Videodisc Instructor's Manual found in the *TRB*.

*Crimes Affecting Business
White Collar Crimes*

Teaching with the Videodisc

At this time you may wish to show the students the motion segment entitled, "Negligence and Assumption of Risk" from the **West's Business Law and Legal Environment Videodisc.** This fictional dramatization is a part of *West's Business Law's Drama of the Law Series.* Each of these dramatizations was written by award-winning writer John J. Osborne, Jr. (originator and author of *The Paper Chase*). Each of these was created by Osborne and West to bring points of law to life.

In the segment titled, "Negligence and Assumption of Risk," one of the characters, Maria, through a calamitous turn of events, both assumes a risk for an accident that befalls her and also suffers the tort of battery.

Each of the legal implications included in this motion segment is discussed in the Drama of the Law *Instructor's Manual* which is included in your *Teacher's Resource Binder.*

While your students may not have been presented with the concepts of negligence and assumption of risk yet, viewing this motion segment now may help to give them a better understanding of civil law and its intricacies. To access this motion segment, you can use the bar code provided here or punch in the frame number below.

Search Frame 4712

128

Legal Focus Problem

Allow a student volunteer to read aloud this Legal Focus Problem. Have the student suggest a possible answer to the question posed at the end of this Legal Focus feature.

 State Law

Assign a group of students the task of researching to determine if your state has a statute that gives stores a right to hold a person suspected of shoplifting. Have them report the specifics of the law, such as the length of time a person can be detained.

3. **Defense of others.** An individual can act in a reasonable manner to protect others who are in danger. If you are at the mall one day and see the class bully beating up a young child, you can use reasonable force to protect the child. The bully will normally not win if he sues you for the tort of battery afterward.

4. **Defense of property.** Reasonable force may be used to remove intruders from one's home. Force that is likely to cause death or great bodily injury, however, cannot normally be used just to protect property.

INFLICTION OF MENTAL DISTRESS

◀ LEGAL FOCUS – PROBLEM

Vera Babbitt, a notorious prankster, telephoned Michelle Cooperberg. She told Michelle that her husband had just been terribly injured in a horrible accident. "He is near death at the Our Lady of Hope Hospital." Twenty minutes later, Vera phoned Michelle again and told her it was just a joke. Has Vera committed a tort?

◆ **infliction of mental distress** Extreme and outrageous intentional behavior that causes severe emotional distress to another.

Yes. The name of the tort is **infliction of mental distress**. The tort describes extreme and outrageous intentional behavior that results in severe emotional distress to another. Vera's phone call was not funny. As a result of Vera's conduct, Michelle suffered intense mental pain and anxiety. Vera's behavior amounts to extreme and outrageous conduct. Society does not accept this type of conduct as being right. Vera normally will be responsible to Michelle for the damages caused by her behavior. It is difficult to prove the existence of mental suffering, though. Because of this difficulty, a few states require that the mental disturbance be demonstrated by some physical illness.

FALSE IMPRISONMENT

◆ **false imprisonment** The intentional confinement or restraint of another person's movements without justification.

Intentional confinement or restraint of another person's activities without justification is **false imprisonment**. The person can be confined by physical barriers, physical restraint, or threats of physical force. A person locked inside of a closet is confined by a physical barrier. A person physically held against his will by two large men is confined by physical constraint. A person standing untouched next to a tool shed in the country is considered confined as well, if a gang of drug dealers tells that person that if he moves anywhere within the next five hours he will be shot.

Businesses are often sued for false imprisonment when store employees stop persons suspected of shoplifting. There are exceptions, however, which are discussed in this chapter's Law in Action feature.

Extension Activity

Have a team of students visit stores in your community to find out what procedures are followed to detain a shoplifter and what the store policies are regarding employees and shoplifters. Have them compare the procedures for large chain stores and individually owned stores. Additionally, they should find out if policies have changed in the last five years. Results can be reported to the class orally or in written form.

Read

Before the students read this feature on shoplifting, point out to students that each year shoplifting costs American businesses millions of dollars and that just as businesses need to prevent shoplifting, so too must they protect themselves from lawsuits that might arise from their efforts to eliminate the shoplifting. Then allow a student volunteer to read aloud this *Law in Action* feature.

Discuss

Many of your students may currently work in retail or may have previously held jobs in the retail industry. Ask those students to discuss with the class any measures their employers took to eliminate shoplifting. Did store personnel receive any special type of training in how to approach and handle suspected shoplifters? Were any shoplifters ever apprehended at the store? What was the result?

Enrichment

You might ask a representative from a local retailer to speak to your class about the problem of shoplifting and how he or she deals with this problem (you may want to work with students to prepare appropriate questions for the speaker).

Critical Thinking Activity

Divide the class into small groups, and have each group discuss the reasons apprehension of shoplifters has become dangerous in recent years.

Law in Action

LAW AND THE BUSINESSPERSON: SHOPLIFTING

The business of retailing—selling goods to the public—is huge in the United States. It is a business that employs millions of people. Particularly during the end-of-the-year holidays, many retail stores hire high school and college students. If you have not done so already, someday you may work as a store clerk. Later on, you may even own a business that sells retail to the public.

One of the most serious problems facing retail businesses is shoplifting. An important question is, to what extent can a businessperson detain, or hold, a suspected shoplifter without being successfully sued for false imprisonment or some other charge? The answer depends on the state in which the action occurs. Many states have statutes creating a **shopkeeper's privilege**. These statutes give merchants the right to detain a suspected shoplifter in certain situations. A typical statute gives a merchant the right to detain a suspect for a reasonable time if the merchant has probable cause to believe the suspect has shoplifted. Probable cause exists when there is reasonable cause to believe a person has taken an item and does not intend to pay for it.

Many stores wait until a suspect has passed the payment counter without paying for an item before stopping him or her. The suspect cannot then say that he or she intended to pay for the item. The suspect can be held only in a *reasonable* manner and for a *reasonable* length of time.

In other words, suspected shoplifters can be confronted, accused, and temporarily detained if reasonable procedures are used. Again, the key word here is *reasonable*. If a businessperson keeps a suspected shoplifter in a locked storeroom for six hours because the manager is busy and has not called the police, this is not reasonable.

Suppose you work in a store and it is your job to question a suspected shoplifter. When you do, you must choose your words carefully. You cannot be nasty. (In one case, for example, the words "a big fat woman like you" served as the basis for a tort action.) You cannot accuse the person outright of shoplifting. You cannot make everyone else around that person aware that you are accusing him or her of shoplifting.

If you think someone has shoplifted, act on your suspicion before the suspect leaves the store. Many states will allow detention only if the suspected shoplifter is still in the store. An employee who must handle shoplifters should be properly trained on how to apprehend a suspect.

In recent years, the apprehension of shoplifters has become dangerous. Store employees have been physically beaten and sometimes shot by suspected shoplifters when the latter were confronted. The wise action is to notify the store manager or security personnel rather than to act yourself. A store clerk should not risk harm from physical violence.

◆ TERMS TO REMEMBER ◆

◆ **shopkeeper's privilege** Privilege, established by statute, by which a seller of goods may detain a suspected shoplifter in certain situations.

Pair your students with partners to define the two types of defamation: *slander* and *libel*. Ask them to make a chart showing the differences between them and the defenses for both of them. Also have them cite some examples illustrating when both slander and libel have been committed and when they haven't.

Legal Focus Example

Read this Legal Focus Example to the class. Ask the class if they can think of any examples that could also fit here. Allow volunteers to share their examples with the class.

---

130   Understanding the Law and Our Legal System

DEFAMATION

◆ **defamation** Any unprivileged communication that is published or spoken and that causes injury to another's good name, reputation, or character.

◆ **slander** Oral defamation.

◆ **libel** Written defamation.

Defamation of character involves wrongfully hurting a person's good reputation. To defame is to make false, harmful statements about others. The law imposes a general duty on all persons to refrain from making false, harmful statements about others. There are two ways of committing defamation. One is by writing false and harmful statements about others, and the other is by orally making such statements. Oral defamation is called **slander**. Written defamation is called **libel**. (An easy way to remember the distinction is to think that **s**aying something bad is **s**lander. Being **l**iterary when you do so is **l**ibel.)

◆ LEGAL FOCUS – EXAMPLE

Nelda yells at Marta, calling her a thief in front of several witnesses. Later, Nelda prints a flyer claiming Marta is a thief. Nelda passes the flyer out to everyone in the neighborhood. If the statement is untrue, the yelling is slander, and the use of the flyers is libel.

In the world of business, overly aggressive competitors sometimes make false and damaging statements about a competing product. This is also considered defamation and has a special name—*disparagement of goods*, where disparagement means casting a bad light on, or belittling, something.

The Publication Requirement   The basis of the tort of defamation is the publication of a statement or statements that hold an individual up to contempt, ridicule, or hatred. *Publication* here means that the defamatory statements are made to or within the hearing of someone other than the person being defamed.

◆ LEGAL FOCUS – PROBLEM

Thompson writes Andrews a private letter accusing him of embezzling funds. Peters calls Gordon dishonest and incompetent when no one else is around. Is either communication a defamation?

The letter is not libel, and the conversation is not slander. Neither Thompson nor Peters communicated the message to a third party. What if a third party overhears defamatory statements by chance? The courts usually hold this to be a publication. Anyone who republishes, or repeats, defamatory statements is liable even if that person reveals the source of the statement. Some radio stations delay the broadcast of live programs, such as talk shows, for several seconds to avoid this kind of liability.

Ethical Concern

Read aloud the fourth type of false statement that is virtually always considered a tort of defamation: "A statement that an unmarried woman is unchaste." Why is this considered a defamation when the same statement about an unmarried man would not be? What does this say about our society?

Enrichment

Point out to your students the fact that public figures are related to matters of public interest; therefore, it is more difficult for them to claim defamation than it is for a private individual. Cite some examples with movie stars and public officials in which this applies. Ask your students to write a paragraph or two on whether they think this is fair or unfair. Have each student share his or her paragraph with the class.

The common law defines four types of false statements that are virtually always considered torts of defamation.

1. A statement that another has a loathsome communicable disease.
2. A statement that another has committed wrongs while engaging in a profession or trade. If someone falsely tells his friends that the bookkeeper at the local record store forges checks every month, that would automatically be considered a tort of defamation against the bookkeeper.
3. A statement that another has committed or has been imprisoned for a serious crime.
4. A statement that an unmarried woman is unchaste.

Defenses against Defamation Truth is an *absolute* defense against a defamation charge. In other words, if you are accused of slander or libel but can show that what you said or wrote is without any doubt true, then the truth of your statement serves as an absolute defense against a charge of slander or libel. Suppose, for example, that you write in a local newspaper that the principal of your school has been divorced three times. You cannot be convicted of defamation by the principal if in fact he or she has actually been divorced three times.

There is another defense against defamation which involves the legal concept of **privilege**. A legal privilege is a right to do something. For example, attorneys and judges have the privilege of making statements about people involved in a trial without fear of being sued for defamation. Members of Congress, while on the floor of Congress, have the privilege to say just about anything about their fellow members of Congress without worrying about a lawsuit for defamation. Indeed, we say that members of Congress have an *absolute* privilege. That means that even if a member of Congress knows that a statement he or she makes about another member is untrue, no successful defamation lawsuit can be brought by the injured party.

In general, false and defamatory statements made in the press about public figures are privileged if they are made without **actual malice**. To make a statement with actual malice, a person must either know the statement is false or make the statement with reckless disregard for the truth. A person who makes a statement with reckless disregard for the truth just does not care whether the statement is true or false.

When discussing defenses to defamation charges, we have to make the distinction between private individuals and public figures. Public figures include public officers and employees who exercise substantial government power. Persons in the public limelight are also considered public figures. Statements made about public figures are usually related to matters of public interest. Also, public figures—unlike private individuals—generally have some access to publicity, which allows them to answer abusive falsehoods. For these reasons, public figures have a greater burden of proof in defamation cases than do private individuals.

◆ **privilege** A legal right to do (or not do) something.

◆ **actual malice** Intent to harm someone. Ill will.

Carol Burnett is shown as a witness testifying in her defamation lawsuit against the National Enquirer.

Have students peruse recent newspapers and magazines for statements that could be libelous about individuals. Have them bring the article (or a copy) to class. Discuss whether the person is a "public figure" or "private individual." Decide whether the person could sue for damages or whether there could be a defense against defamation.

Legal Focus Problem

Allow a student volunteer to read aloud this Legal Focus Problem. Ask the students whether they consider you a "public figure."

Critical Thinking Activity

Have students write a paragraph telling why they think a school board member or school superintendent would be considered a public figure, but a teacher would not.

Ethical Concern

Begin a class discussion on defamation by describing a scenario that occurs when an untrue rumor is spread about someone in school. Is everyone who speaks the rumor guilty of slander? What if someone who spread the rumor truly believed it to be true? Is this slander?

Extension Activity

Allow a group of student volunteers to work together in researching how technology has led to new and more exotic ways to invade the privacy of others. Students might look at eavesdropping on cellular phone calls and/or phone calls made from portable telephones, computer hacking, etc. Student volunteers should report their findings to the class in the form of an oral report.

To recover damages, a public figure must prove that a defamatory statement was made with actual malice. On occasion, tabloid newspapers, such as *The National Enquirer*, have been sued by movie stars for libel. These movie stars, who are obviously public figures, have occasionally won when they have proved to a jury that the newspaper knew the statements that it published were false. In other words, the movie stars have won their libel lawsuits when they have proved actual malice on the part of the newspapers.

◆ LEGAL FOCUS ~ PROBLEM

Teachers and coaches are important to high school students and on most campuses are very well known. But are they public figures for the purposes of the law of defamation?

While few states have considered the issue, a 1979 California case held that a teacher who was criticized in a magazine for her classroom textbook choices was not a public figure. School board members and school superintendents are, however, held to be public figures.

INVASION OF PRIVACY

Americans cherish their privacy. While the Constitution does not explicitly guarantee the right to privacy, most Americans are pretty sure that they have the right to lead a private life without prying public eyes observing their every move. At common law, the tort of **invasion of privacy** has existed for many years. Four acts qualify as invasion of privacy.

1. **The use of a person's name or picture for business purposes without permission.** You cannot, for example, reproduce a photograph of Madonna and sell Madonna T-shirts without permission from her. (Don't ask; she won't give it.)
2. **Intrusion upon an individual's affairs or seclusion.** Of course, there is no hard-and-fast definition of what *intrusion* means and when it constitutes invasion of privacy. If you hang around in front of someone's house a couple of times so you can talk to that person, that probably would not be considered invasion of privacy. But if you do the same thing day after day for several weeks, that probably would be.
3. **Publication of information that places a person in a false light.** This could be a story crediting to someone ideas that he or she does not hold (such as racist views) or actions that he or she did not take (such as failing to help someone in need). Publishing such a story might also be defamation.
4. **Public disclosure of private facts about an individual that an ordinary person would find objectionable.** The disclosure is not wrongful if it is about a public figure or if the release of the information serves a public interest.

◆ **invasion of privacy** Publishing or otherwise making known or using information relating to the private life and affairs of a person without that person's permission or approval.

Discussion Starter

Have your students read aloud the section on fraud. Stimulate a class discussion based on the question: If Fred bought the car because he liked the model, regardless of its mileage, is this still considered fraud? Point out to your students that in order for fraud to exist the buyer must have *relied* on the false statement. Have a class discussion on this fact.

Discussion Starter

Ask a student volunteer to read aloud the definition of *puffery*. Then ask the students to recall examples of when a salesperson used puffery with them. Make sure that your students understand the difference between fraud and puffery.

Legal Focus Problem

Allow a student volunteer to read aloud this Legal Focus Problem. Ask the student to answer the question posed at the end of this Legal Focus Problem. As a followup ask: How common are statements such as these?

Tort Law   133

FRAUD (MISREPRESENTATION OR DECEIT)

Fraud begins with a false or an incorrect statement. An innocent mistake is not usually fraud. Fraud exists when a misrepresentation is made by a person who knows the facts to be false and intends to mislead another. The tort of fraud consists of the following elements.

1. **A misrepresentation of facts by one who knows the truth.** For example, Max tells Fred his Ford Mustang has 45,000 miles on the odometer. Max has tampered with the odometer and knows that 75,000 is a more accurate figure. A misrepresentation may also be made with reckless disregard for the truth.

2. **Intent to coax another to rely on the misrepresentation.** Max tells Fred about the mileage to get Fred to purchase "this low-mileage car for a bargain price."

3. **Justifiable reliance by the misled party.** When you rely on someone's statements, you are usually justified in doing so if the other person holds himself or herself out as knowing the truth. Fred has reason to rely on Max's statement that his Ford Mustang's odometer reading is only 45,000 miles. There is no easy way that Fred could be aware that the mileage has been tampered with by Max.

4. **Damages suffered as a result of reliance.** Fred buys the car. If Fred had known the true mileage on the car, he might not have bought it. Even if he had decided to purchase it, he clearly would not have paid as much.

5. **The misrepresentation causes an injury.** The injury is usually a loss of money or the purchase of something worth much less than the purchase price. Fred's car, which has travelled 30,000 more miles than he was told, is worth significantly less in the marketplace than he believed it would be.

Fraud requires more than seller's talk. Seller's talk, often called **puffery**, expresses a seller's high opinion of what he or she sells. Fraud exists only when a person represents as a material, or important, fact something he or she knows is untrue.

◆ **fraud** A misrepresentation of a material fact made knowingly with the intent to deceive another, who is then deceived to his or her detriment, or harm.

◆ **puffery** Seller's talk. Claims about the quality of goods, usually exaggerated. Not considered fraud.

◆ LEGAL FOCUS - PROBLEM

Kitterage, a small-town accountant, was talking to River City Products about employing him as an accountant. Kitterage said, "I am the best accountant in town." Then he said, "Employ me and you will never be sorry." He also tried to sell the company a used computer, saying, "This computer will never be outdated." Can any of these statements be considered misrepresentations of facts?

No. All of these statements are seller's talk. Kitterage is giving River City an opinion of services and a product he wishes to sell. None of these statements, even if untrue, is fraud. If, however, Kitterage said that the computer had never needed repairs, when in fact it had been repaired several times, that is a misrepresentation of a material fact.

Normally, the tort of fraud requires reliance on a *statement of fact*. Sometimes, however, reliance on a *statement of opinion* may involve the tort of fraud. For example, what if a lawyer knowingly misstates an opinion about the law? A court may hold that a person had a right to rely on this opinion. In these limited situations, when the individual stating the opinion has a superior knowledge of the subject matter, the statement of opinion may be the basis of fraud.

◆ CHECKING YOUR PROGRESS

1. A tort occurs when someone is injured by the wrongful conduct of another. Is the resulting court action a civil or a criminal action?

2. If a person follows through on a threat to harm someone else, what tort has he or she committed?

3. Must a person have been locked behind closed doors to be able to sue for false imprisonment?

4. What is an absolute defense against a defamation charge?

◆ INTENTIONAL TORTS AGAINST PROPERTY

We have already talked a little about property. Most of us think of property as those things that we own, such as cars, stereos, clothes, and books. Property also includes houses and land. Today, the definition of *property* has expanded to include the rights to television series and movies, computer programs, computer time, and so on.

Wrongs against property include (1) trespass to land and (2) trespass to personal property and conversion. The wrong is committed against the legal possessor of the land or personal property. The law distinguishes real property from personal property (these are discussed in Chapters 28 and 29). *Real property* is land and things "permanently" attached to the land, such as buildings. Personal property consists of all other property and is basically movable. A house and lot are real property. The furniture inside is personal property. Money and securities are also personal property.

TRESPASS TO LAND

◆ **trespass to land**
Wrongful entry onto the real property of another.

Any time an uninvited person goes onto land owned by another, the person commits the tort called **trespass to land**. A person can also commit the tort of trespass to land by remaining on the land after permission to be there has been taken away or by being responsible for something else en-

Read aloud this Legal Focus Example to the class, then ask the students how many of them feel that they have been guilty of trespassing on at least one occasion. Ask the students which of the types of trespassing listed in this Legal Focus they were guilty of. (Note

that most of your students will have walked and/or driven on someone else's land at some time.) Remind the students that this Legal Focus feature will be particularly helpful when studying for tests.

Call to the students' attention the photo of the No Trespassing Sign on this page. Remind the students that before a person can be a trespasser, the person must be made to know that he or she is a trespasser. The owner of the property should make it clear that others are not allowed on the property. Then ask the students what is one exception to that rule? (Any person who enters property to commit an illegal act is a trespasser even without posted signs.)

Discussion Starter

Do you consider trespassing a serious tort? Why or why not?

Tort Law   135

---

tering the land (for example, by throwing something onto the property). Actual harm to the land is not essential. The tort protects the right of an owner to exclusive possession of the land. If no harm is done, though, the landowner usually can collect only **nominal damages** (such as $1).

LEGAL FOCUS ~ EXAMPLE

Common types of trespass to land include the following:

- Walking or driving on someone's land.
- Shooting a gun over someone's land.
- Throwing rocks at or spraying water on a building that belongs to someone else.
- Building a dam across a river that causes water to back up on someone else's land.
- Placing part of a building on an adjoining landowner's property.

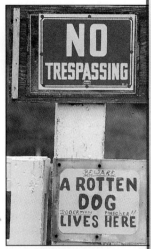

How do "private property" or "no trespassing" signs assist property owners?

Trespass Criteria, Rights, and Duties Before a person can be a trespasser, the person must be made to know he or she is a trespasser. The owner of the property should make it clear that others are not allowed on the property. "Posted" trespass signs clearly tell people they are trespassers if they come onto the property. In contrast, a guest in your home is not a trespasser—unless he or she has been asked to leave and refuses. Any person who enters property to commit an illegal act (such as a thief entering a lumberyard at night to steal lumber) is a trespasser, even without posted signs.

Many states hold that the landowner has a duty, or responsibility, toward any person on the property, even a trespasser, to act reasonably. For example, a landowner may have a duty to post a notice that the property is patrolled by guard dogs. The landowner can, however, remove trespassers from the premises using reasonable force without being liable for assault and battery.

Defenses against Trespass to Land If going onto the property of another is warranted, or justified, a complete defense to trespass exists. An example occurs when a trespasser enters land to assist someone in danger. Furthermore, if the person claiming to be the owner did not actually have the right to possess the land in question, he or she does not have the right to sue for trespass.

◆ **nominal damages** A small money award granted to a plaintiff who suffered no actual loss.

TRESPASS TO PERSONAL PROPERTY AND CONVERSION

A person who harms or interferes with the personal property of another commits the tort of **trespass to personal property**. Another word for personal property is *personalty*. Therefore, this is sometimes known as the tort of trespass to personalty. Trespass to personal property involves damaging the personal property of another or interfering with the owner's right to use, possess, or enjoy the property.

◆ **trespass to personal property** A brief, temporary, intentional interference with the personal property of another.

Read

Introduce this *Law in Action* feature by asking students the following questions: What lengths do you think businesspeople should be allowed in protecting their property? Should they be able to hold burglars against their will until the police arrive? Should they be allowed to use violence—i.e., pushing, shoving, hitting—in order to hold burglars against their will? Should they be allowed to use deadly force?

After the students have discussed these questions, allow a student volunteer to read aloud this *Law in Action* feature.

Discuss

Why was the landowner in the *Katko* v. *Briney* case held responsible for damages when Prentice Rasheed was not? What were the differences in these two cases? Do you agree with the court decision in each of these cases? Why or why not?

Critical Thinking Activity

During the riots in Los Angeles in 1992, shopkeepers were carrying guns while guarding their stores against looters. Were the looters trespassers? Were the shopkeepers justified in using deadly force to protect their property? Have students write their thoughts on paper, then discuss them in class.

Analyze and Apply

Divide the class into two groups, and stage a class debate on the following topic: "Business owners should be allowed to use deadly force in protecting their property from criminals."

Legal Focus Example

Read this Legal Focus Example to the class. Ask the class if they can think of any examples that could also fit here. Allow volunteers to share their examples with the class.

Law in Action

LAW AND THE BUSINESSPERSON: HOW FAR CAN YOU GO TO PROTECT YOUR BUSINESS PROPERTY?

Many business owners have invested their life savings in starting their small companies. They, and others, need to know how far they can go in protecting their businesses. While the answer may seem clear to the businessperson, it isn't always that clear to the courts. The law of trespass and protection of property against trespassers never is cut and dried. The usual means of protecting property against trespassers, such as hiring security forces and installing alarm systems, are accepted, but some other methods are not.

In *Katko v. Briney*,[1] for example, a landowner had prepared a "mantrap" to protect an old, abandoned farmhouse from thieves. A spring gun was set so it would fire when anyone entered the vacant house. A petty thief lost most of his leg when the gun fired at him as he entered the building. The landowner was held responsible for damages as punishment—despite the "no trespassing" signs on the property and the thief's illegal presence. In general, courts will hold that a landowner cannot do mechanically what he cannot do in person. Deadly force cannot be used without sufficient justification.

Rare exceptions to this principle have been made. For example, in 1986, a Dade County, Florida, grand jury refused to indict a shopkeeper for a death resulting from a trap. The shopkeeper, Prentice Rasheed, had constructed an electrified wire grid to deter potential burglars. Rasheed's store was located in an area of Miami noted for its high crime rate. It had been burglarized seven times and, according to Rasheed, had received little police protection. Indeed, he said he had "begged" the city to provide protection. Rasheed testified that he had created the grid only to "shock"—not to kill—potential intruders. He was "deeply sorry" that death had resulted from his device.[2]

Shopkeepers are not the only people who are afraid of crime. Many others worry about crime as well. Should you have a loaded gun in your house or store? That is not a simple question to answer. Statistics show, though, that keeping a loaded gun in the house is dangerous. A loaded firearm in a house is forty-three times more likely to kill the owner or a member of the owner's family than an intruder.

2. *The Miami Herald*, February 10, 1987, p. 2.

1. 183 N.W. 2d 657 (Iowa 1971).

LEGAL FOCUS ~ EXAMPLE

Marla takes Phillip's watch as a practical joke. She hides it so Phillip cannot find it for several days. Marla has committed a trespass to personal property.

Reteaching Activity

Ask your students to make a list of all the intentional torts mentioned in this chapter. Have them define and give an example of each of them.

Discussion Starter

Ask your students if they were aware that they could be guilty of a tort even if they *mistakenly* hurt someone. Stimulate a class discussion by defining *negligence* and ask them if they agree with the criteria.

Legal Focus Example

Allow a student volunteer to read aloud this Legal Focus Example to the class. Ask the students which of two possible torts is the more serious. Why?

If there is a good reason for the interference with personal property, then a complete defense exists. Most states, for example, allow automobile repair shops to hold a customer's car when the customer refuses to pay for completed repairs.

If somebody takes your textbook for a few minutes and then gives it back, the value of that textbook to you really has not been reduced very much. But if somebody takes your textbook for days on end, preventing you from studying for an important exam, then the value of that personal property has been greatly reduced. Now the tort of **conversion** has occurred. Conversion is defined as an unauthorized *taking* of the personal property of another and a wrongful exercise of rights of ownership. Conversion is the civil counterpart of the crime of theft. A store clerk who steals merchandise from the store commits the crime of theft and also the tort of conversion. When conversion occurs, the lesser offense of trespass to personal property also occurs. If the taking of the property was unlawful, there is trespass; keeping the property is conversion.

Good intentions are not a defense against conversion. In fact, conversion can be an entirely innocent act. Someone who buys stolen goods, for example, is guilty of conversion even if that person is unaware that the goods were stolen. If the true owner sues the buyer, the buyer must pay the owner the full value of the property. The buyer, of course, has a right to sue the thief for the loss (assuming the thief can be found).

♦ **conversion** The unauthorized *taking* of the personal property of another and the wrongful exercise of the rights of ownership.

◆ UNINTENTIONAL TORTS (NEGLIGENCE)

"I didn't mean to hurt you." Sometimes people do not mean to hurt other people, but those other people get hurt anyway. Certainly, if you are driving carefully, you never intend to hurt anybody. Nonetheless, you might cause an auto accident unintentionally. You still could be guilty of a tort even though what you did was unintentional. This tort is usually called **negligence**. It occurs when someone causes an injury to another by failing to act carefully. Many of the actions discussed in the section on intentional torts against persons would be torts of negligence if they were done carelessly *but without intent*.

♦ **negligence** The failure to exercise the standard of care that a reasonable person would exercise in similar circumstances.

 LEGAL FOCUS ~ EXAMPLE

If Hector intentionally shoves Judy, who falls and breaks an arm as a result, Hector has committed an intentional tort. If, however, Hector carelessly bumps into Judy, and she falls and breaks an arm as a result, Hector's action constitutes negligence. In either situation, Hector has committed a tort.

Reteaching Activity

Go over this list of four questions we can ask to decide if a particular act constitutes negligence with the class. Be sure that students understand these four questions, and explain to them that each of these questions, will be discussed in the next four sections of text.

Critical Thinking Activity

Doctors, engineers, and accountants have a higher obligation than other citizens to behave reasonably in their conduct toward others. Ask students why this is expected.

Enrichment

Secure copies of the physician's Hippocratic Oath and the Codes of Ethics for lawyers and other professionals. Assign small groups of students to analyze each element of the various oaths to see if it sets a higher standard of care than that expected of ordinary citizens.

Caption Answer

Professionals such as doctors, dentists, psychiatrists, architects, engineers, accountants, lawyers, and so on are expected to have a special level of knowledge and ability consistent with their profession and have a higher standard of care.

To decide if a particular act constitutes negligence, we can ask four questions.

1.   Did the defendant owe a duty of care to the plaintiff?
2.   Did the defendant breach that duty?
3.   Did the plaintiff suffer an injury as a result of the defendant's breach of the duty of care?
4.   Did the defendant's breach cause the plaintiff's injury?

Each of these four elements is discussed below.

THE DUTY OF CARE

In a society in which people must live among other people, some actions can be tolerated and some cannot; some actions are reasonable and some are not. **Duty of care** is the requirement that we behave reasonably in our conduct toward others. People are free to act as they please so long as their actions do not invade the well-being of others. If a person's action harms the well-being of others, though, that person has breached a duty of care.

People with knowledge, skill, or intelligence superior to that of an ordinary person must act in a manner consistent with their capabilities. That means such individuals have a higher standard of care. Their duty is that which is reasonable given their capabilities. That means that professionals (doctors, dentists, psychiatrists, architects, engineers, accountants, lawyers, and so on) must have a special level of knowledge and ability consistent with their profession.

BREACH OF THE DUTY OF CARE

Tort law measures duty by the **reasonable-person standard**. To determine whether a duty of care has been breached, the courts ask how a rea-

◆ **duty of care**
The requirement that each of us behave reasonably in our conduct toward others.

◆ **reasonable-person standard**
The standard of fair behavior that a reasonably careful and thoughtful person would observe. The test to meet to avoid responsibility for negligence.

Any professional is assumed to have special knowledge and ability. How does this affect a professional's standard of care?

Enrichment

Allow a student volunteer to research Aristotle and his contributions to our society. The student should report his or her findings in a brief oral report to the class.

Reteaching Activity

Repeat the following sentence from the text to the students, "There is no negligence if there is no injury." Be sure that students understand that negligence in this case refers to the legal definition of *negligence*. While one may be guilty of not using due care, if there is no injury to another party he or she will not be found negligent in a lawsuit.

Legal Focus Example

Allow a student volunteer to read aloud this Legal Focus Example. Remind students that one is only liable if harm or injury results.

sonable person would have acted in the same circumstances. The reasonable-person standard is an attempt to be objective. It does not necessarily describe how a particular person would act. Rather, it is society's judgment on how people should act. The so-called reasonable person is careful, conscientious, even-tempered, and honest. The reasonable-person test is also frequently used by the courts in other areas of law.

Failure to be reasonable may be seen in an act (setting fire to a building) or an omission (neglecting to put out a fire). It may be an intentional act, a careless act, or a carefully performed but dangerous act that results in injury. Courts consider the nature of the act (whether it is outrageous or commonplace), how the act is performed (cautiously versus carelessly), and the nature of the injury (serious or slight) to determine whether a duty of care has been breached.

THE INJURY REQUIREMENT AND DAMAGES

"It makes no difference whether a good man has defrauded a bad man or a bad man defrauded a good man . . . the law can look only to the amount of damage done."
Aristotle (384–322 B.C.)
Greek philosopher

There is no negligence if there is no injury. To recover damages (receive compensation), a person must have suffered some loss, harm, wrong, or invasion of a protected interest. Essentially, the purpose of tort law is to compensate people for legally recognized injuries resulting from wrongful acts. If no harm or injury results from a given negligent action, there is nothing to compensate—and no tort.

◇ LEGAL FOCUS – EXAMPLE

If you carelessly bump into someone, who stumbles and falls as a result, you are liable in tort for the person's injuries. If the person is unharmed, however, there is no suit for damages, because no injury was suffered.

CAUSATION

Another element necessary to a tort is causation. In other words, if a person fails in a duty of care and someone suffers injury, the wrongful activity must have caused the harm in order for a tort to have been committed.

Causation in Fact and Proximate Cause   In deciding whether there is causation, the court must address two questions:

1. Is there **causation in fact**? That is, did the injury happen because of the defendant's act, or would the injury have occurred anyway? If an

◆ **causation in fact**
An act or omission without which an injury would not have occurred.

People in business have to be insured against the possibility of an adverse judgment in tort litigation. The costs of litigation, the amounts of the judgments, and consequently the insurance premiums have increased considerably in the past two decades. The number of multimillion dollar verdicts in tort cases has risen from 7 in 1970 to more than 600 in 1991. Today, 20 percent of the cost of a $45 stepladder goes to insurance.

Businesses are not the only entities being sued. So too are federal, state, and local governments. When a disabled weather buoy off Massachusetts failed to send a storm warning, several fishermen lost their lives. The federal government had to pay their families $1.2 million. When a speeder in California hit a light pole, an injured passenger argued that the pole should have broken on impact. The state was ordered to pay a $400,000 settlement.

140

Legal Focus Problem

Divide the class into small groups to read and discuss the Legal Focus Problem found here. Each group should choose a leader to explain his or her group's response to each of the questions posed at the end of this Legal Focus. Have the groups review their answers after they have read the next paragraph dealing with *foreseeability*.

Legal Focus Example

Read aloud the Legal Focus Example found here. Ask the students to compare and contrast this Legal Focus Example with the Legal Focus Problem found above.

◆ **proximate cause**
Substantial cause of an injury. An act that could have been foreseen to cause the injury.

injury would not have occurred without the defendant's act, then there is causation in fact. Causation in fact can usually be determined by the *but for* test. "But for" the wrongful act, the injury would not have happened.

2. Was the act the **proximate cause** of the injury? That is, was it the primary or insuing cause? How far should a defendant's liability extend for a wrongful act that was an important factor in causing injury? As a matter of public policy, the courts have created a limitation on liability for careless conduct. The court will ask whether the connection between an act and an injury is strong enough to justify imposing liability—that is, whether the act was the proximate cause of the injury.

◆ LEGAL FOCUS ~ PROBLEM

Acker carelessly leaves a campfire burning. The fire not only burns the forest but also sets off an explosion in a nearby chemical plant. Chemicals from the plant spill into a river, killing all the fish for a hundred miles downstream. The economy of a downstream tourist resort is ruined. Is Acker liable to the resort owners? To the tourists whose vacations were ruined?

These are questions of proximate cause. Proximate cause is not a question of fact but one of law and policy.

The *foreseeability* test has been used as a measure of proximate cause for most of this century. The harm caused by the careless act must be foreseeable. Otherwise, proximate cause is lacking, and the defendant is not responsible. In our example, the person who carelessly left the campfire burning could easily have predicted that harm to the trees would take place. However, harm to the tourist resort because of fish being killed as a result of the exploding chemical does not appear foreseeable. This is not a chain of events against which a reasonable person would usually guard. If a reasonable person could not have foreseen the consequences of the harm done or the victim of the harm, proximate cause does not exist. Of course, a court must determine whether something is or is not foreseeable, and it is difficult to predict how the court will decide.

Intervening Forces   An intervening force—something that happens between a wrongful act and an injury to another—may break the connection between the act and the injury. If so, it cancels the wrongful act.

◆ LEGAL FOCUS ~ EXAMPLE

Keeping a can of gasoline in the trunk of one's car creates a foreseeable risk of creating an explosion and fire and is thus a negligent act. If lightning strikes the car, exploding the gas tank and the can as well as injuring passing pedestrians, the lightning cancels

Allow a student volunteer to read aloud this first Legal Focus Problem. Discuss with the students the answer to the question posed at the end of this Legal Focus Problem. Ask your students if they agree with this doctrine. Remind students that they can use the Legal Focus features as review tools when studying for tests.

Write the words *res ipsa loquitur* on the board. Ask your students to define the term and to list on paper several examples.

Allow a student volunteer to read aloud this Legal Focus Problem. Discuss with the class the answer to the question posed at the end of this Legal Focus Problem. It might be interesting to note how many students catch the pun that is hidden in this Legal Focus Problem illustrating the doctrine of "The Facts Speak for Themselves."

the original negligence as a cause of the damage, because it was not foreseeable.

Critical Thinking Activity

Ask students to analyze why the doctrine of *res ipsa loquitur* has been applied to train derailments and falling elevators? Have them write the analysis in one-page reports.

In negligence cases, the negligent party will often try to show that something intervened after his or her action. This person will argue that the second act was the proximate cause of injury.

An action to avoid injury from another's careless act is not an intervening act. Suppose a person is hurt as he leaps from a vehicle in an attempt to escape injury from the negligent act of another driver, for example. The original wrongdoer is liable even if the injury results from the escape attempt. The same is true when a third person tries to rescue someone endangered by a negligent act.

◆ LEGAL FOCUS – PROBLEM

Ludlam commits an act that endangers Schwaller. Yokem sees that Schwaller is in danger and attempts a rescue. The rescue is successful, but Yokem is injured. Is Ludlam responsible for the injury to Yokem?

Ludlam is responsible for injuries to Yokem and any injuries Schwaller may sustain under the "danger invites rescue" doctrine. Rescuers can injure themselves, or the person rescued, or even a stranger, but the original wrongdoer is still liable.

Res Ipsa Loquitur   Generally, in lawsuits involving negligence, the plaintiff has to prove that the defendant was negligent. In certain situations, however, the courts infer that negligence has occurred. In this type of case, the defendant must prove that he or she was *not* negligent.

The inference of a defendant's negligence is known as the doctrine of **res ipsa loquitur**, "the facts speak for themselves." This doctrine applies only when the event that created the injury is one that ordinarily does not occur without negligence. *Res ipsa loquitur* has been applied to train derailments, wheels falling off moving vehicles, falling elevators, and bricks or window panes falling from a defendant's premises. For the doctrine to apply, the event must be caused by something only the defendant controls.

◆ **res ipsa loquitur** "The facts speak for themselves." A legal principle that applies when the event creating an injury is one that ordinarily does not occur without negligence.

◆ LEGAL FOCUS – PROBLEM

Richard Caute, while walking down the sidewalk on First Avenue in New York, is hit on the head by a fax machine. Miraculously, Richard does not die, but he is severely injured. It is proven that the fax machine belonged in the Acme Bookkeeping office on the third floor of the office building next to the sidewalk where Richard was hit. Richard is, however, unable to find any proof of how the fax machine

Discussion Starter

Define the *assumption of risk* defense to your class. Start a list on the board of all the possible situations that may be considered risky, and therefore, a defense to negligence.

Reteaching Activity

With the class, go over the definitions found here for *contributory* and *comparative negligence*. Make sure that students understand the similarities and the differences between these two important terms.

Extension Activity

Ask a volunteer to find out which type of negligence is used in your state—comparative or contributory. Ask this student to share his or her findings with the class.

Extension Activity

Have your students come up with an idea for a bulletin board illustrating the forms of negligence. Have them put up the bulletin board.

Collaborative Learning Activity

Divide your class into groups of four. Instruct each group to write a report explaining the differences among intentional torts, unintentional torts, and strict liability.

happened to fall out of the building. Is this an appropriate situation to apply the doctrine of *res ipsa loquitur*?

This is a classic situation for the doctrine "the facts speak for themselves." The fax machine was under the control of Acme's office staff. A fax machine would not ordinarily fall out of a window unless some office worker was careless.

DEFENSES TO NEGLIGENCE

The basic defenses in negligence cases are (1) assumption of risk and (2) contributory and comparative negligence.

Assumption of Risk   A person who voluntarily puts himself or herself in a risky situation, knowing the risk involved, normally is not allowed to recover damages. This is the defense of **assumption of risk**. A driver entering a stock car race knows there is a risk of being killed or injured in a crash. The driver assumes, or takes on, the risk of injury.

As suggested, this defense requires (1) knowledge of the risk and (2) voluntary assumption of the risk. The risk can be assumed by agreement, or assumption of risk can be implied by a person's knowledge of the risk and that person's later conduct. The person assumes only the risk normally associated with the activity. In our example, the driver assumes the risk of being injured in the race. The driver does not assume the risk that the racetrack will give way during the race because of a construction defect.

Contributory and Comparative Negligence   People are expected to exercise reasonable care in looking out for themselves. In some states, negligence suits are prevented because an injured person was not careful. This is the defense of **contributory negligence**. Here, both parties were negligent, and their combined negligence caused the injury. In states recognizing the contributory negligence defense, it can be a complete defense to a negligence action.

For example, assume you were in an auto accident at a four-way stop sign. You and the other driver both ran your respective stops. You suffered no injury, but the other driver did. Your combined negligence caused that injury. In some states, though, the other driver could not recover anything, because you could use as your defense contributory negligence.

Most states no longer allow contributory negligence to bar a cause of action completely. Instead, they allow a reduced recovery based on the doctrine of **comparative negligence**. Comparative negligence allows both the plaintiff's and the defendant's negligence to be considered. Liability for damages is based on proportionate responsibility. A majority of jurisdictions have adopted a "pure" form of comparative negligence. It allows the plaintiff to recover damages, even if the extent of his or her fault is greater than that of the defendant. If the plaintiff was 80 percent at fault and the defendant 20 percent at fault, for example, the plaintiff may recov-

---

◆ **assumption of risk**   A doctrine under which a plaintiff who voluntarily puts himself or herself in a risky situation, knowing the risk involved, is not allowed to recover. The defense of assumption of risk requires (1) knowledge of the risk and (2) voluntary assumption of the risk.

◆ **contributory negligence**   A concept whereby a complaining party's own negligence contributed to his or her harm. Usually a complete defense to a negligence action.

◆ **comparative negligence**   A concept whereby liability for injury is shared by all persons whose carelessness led to the injury. Liability is shared on the basis of proportionate fault.

Teaching with the Videodisc

At this time you may wish to re-show the students the motion segment titled, "Negligence and Assumption of Risk" from the **West's Business Law and Legal Environment Videodisc.** This fictional dramatization is a part of *West's Business Law's Drama of the Law Series.* Each of these dramatizations was written by award winning writer John J. Osborne, Jr. (originator and author of *The Paper Chase*). Each of these was created by Osborne and West to bring points of law to life for your students.

In the segment entitled, "Negligence and Assumption of Risk," one of the characters, Maria, through a calamitous turn of events, both assumes a risk for an accident that befalls her and also suffers the tort of battery at the hands of another character, Vinnie.

Each of the legal implications included in this motion segment is discussed in the Drama of the Law Instructor's Manual which is included in your *Teacher's Resource Binder.*

To access this motion segment, you can use the bar code provided here or punch in the frame number below.

Search Frame 4712

er 20 percent of his or her damages. In contrast, some states' comparative negligence statutes have a "50 percent" rule. The plaintiff recovers nothing if he or she was more than 50 percent at fault.

◆ STRICT LIABILITY

Some actions are just inherently so risky that no matter how careful you are when you do them, the law holds you strictly responsible for any accidents that occur. This category of torts is called **strict liability**, or liability without fault.

Intentional torts and torts of negligence involve acts that depart from a reasonable standard of care and cause injuries. In contrast, under the doctrine of strict liability, liability for injury is imposed for reasons other than fault. Strict liability for damages caused by abnormally dangerous or exceptional activities is an example of this doctrine. Strict liability is applied in such cases because of the extreme risk of the activity.

There are other applications of the strict liability principle. Persons who keep dangerous animals, for example, are strictly liable for any harm inflicted by the animals. Generally, courts consider the circumstances surrounding an activity—such as when and where it is occurring—in deciding that strict liability should be applied.

An important application of strict liability is in the area of product liability. Liability for defective products is a matter of social policy. It is based on two factors: (1) The manufacturing company can better bear the cost of injury because it can spread the cost throughout society by increasing prices of goods and services. (2) The manufacturing company is making a profit from its activities and should bear the cost of injury as an operating expense. Product liability is discussed in greater detail in Chapter 15.

◆ **strict liability**
Liability regardless of fault. Usually, strict liability involves damages caused by abnormally dangerous activities.

◆ CHECKING YOUR PROGRESS

1. If one of your friends goes into your house before you arrive home from school, has he or she committed a tort?

2. Describe the two questions that must be answered to determine if the element of causation is present.

3. Why would a negligent party in a lawsuit want to show that something intervened after his or her action?

4. What is the effect of the *res ipsa loquitur* doctrine in a lawsuit?

5. Describe two defenses in negligence cases.

Reteaching Activity

Have each student make a list of all of the torts mentioned in this chapter. Have them define and give an example of each tort.

Checking Your Progress (Answers)

1. If the friend was uninvited, he or she is trespassing, which is a tort.
2. Did the injury happen because of the defendant's act (causation of fact)? Was the harm caused by the defendant's careless act foreseeable (proximate cause)?
3. If an intervening force breaks the connection between a wrongful act and injury to another, it cancels the wrongful act.
4. The burden of proof shifts to the defendant to prove that he or she was not negligent if the *res ipsa loquitur* doctrine is applied in a case.
5. Two defenses in negligence cases are (1) assumption of risk, in which a plaintiff voluntarily puts himself or herself in a risky situation and (2) contributory and comparative negligence, in which a defendant contributes in part to the injury.

143

Teaching A Case In Point

Read

Introduce this *A Case In Point* by explaining to students that this particular case involves a defendant with whom the students may be familiar, i.e., K-mart Enterprises, Inc. Explain to the students that this case involves a suit brought about as a result of a suspected shoplifting in K-mart. You might allow the students to discuss what they know of the security measures of the K-mart stores. Then have a student volunteer read aloud this *A Case In Point* to the class.

Discuss

Use the following questions to stimulate a class discussion of this *A Case In Point*. Why did Johnson sue K-mart? Was Johnson guilty of shoplifting? How do you think Johnson felt when she was stopped by the security officer? How do you think the security officer's accusation would make you feel? Do you feel Johnson was right in suing K-mart? Would you have filed a law suit? Do you agree or disagree with the court's decision? Explain your answer.

Teaching Note

This case is included in the *West's Business and Personal Law Handbook of Selected Court Cases.*

◆ A CASE IN POINT ◆

JOHNSON v. K-MART ENTERPRISES, INC.
Court of Appeals of Wisconsin, 1980.
98 Wis.2d 533, 297 N.W.2d 74.

This case provides a good example of a court's trying to balance the storeowner's right to protect against shoplifting, on the one hand, against a customer's right to be free from false accusation, on the other. The Wisconsin shopkeeper's statute provides some extra weight on the storeowner's side of the scale.

FACTS Johnson entered the defendant's store carrying her small child in an infant seat. When she tried to leave the store, she was stopped in a public place by a security officer, who said that another employee had reported seeing her steal the infant seat. To show ownership, Johnson pointed to cat hair, food crumbs, and stains on the seat. After a twenty-minute delay, the security officer apologized to Johnson and permitted her to leave. The trial court dismissed her action for false imprisonment, and Johnson appealed.

ISSUE Did the defendant have probable cause to detain Johnson, and was the twenty-minute detention of Johnson reasonable

in these circumstances?

DECISION Yes, to both. The appellate court upheld the trial court's finding that the defendant acted reasonably and with probable cause.

REASON The court first addressed the issue of probable cause. Under a Wisconsin statute, it is the shopkeeper's privilege to detain a shopper if the merchant has probable cause for believing the shopper stole the merchant's goods. The court held as a matter of law that the merchant, through its security guard, had probable cause to believe the plaintiff had shoplifted because another employee reported that she had seen the theft. The court then turned to Johnson's complaint that her detention was accomplished in an unreasonable manner because she was detained in a public place for an unreasonable period of time. The court balanced the customer's liberty interest against the merchant's need for protection against shoplifting, a need protected by the Wisconsin statute. The court held the twenty-minute detention was reasonable. The court found that the defendant had only stopped the plaintiff, asked her to return to the store, informed her that she was suspected of shoplifting, produced the incriminating witness, apologized to her, and finally released her—none of which was unreasonable. Also, Johnson never asked to go to a more private place.

In order to help students review what they have learned in Chapter 5, you might wish to:
1. Have a student volunteer, or volunteers, read aloud the Chapter Summary.
2. Allow the students to work with partners to complete the *Using Legal Language* activity.
3. Assign the *Checking for Comprehension* exercise as homework.

4. Allow the students to work in small groups to complete the *Applying Legal Concepts* activities.
5. As a class, complete the *Applying the Law* activities. (Please note that you may have to help students with vocabulary so that they adequately understand all of the *Applying the Law* material.)

In order to check student mastery of chapter concepts, you may wish to use the Chapter 5 test that is found in your *Teacher's Resource Binder* or use WESTEST computerized testing for Chapter 5.

Using Legal Language (Answers)

1–C, 2–D, 3–F, 4–A, 5–I, 6–H, 7–J, 8–E, 9–G, 10–B

Tort Law   145

CHAPTER 5 REVIEW

 ## SUMMARY

INTENTIONAL TORTS AGAINST PERSONS

1. *Assault and battery*—An intentional act that creates in another a reasonable fear of immediate harmful or offensive contact is an assault. Assault resulting in physical contact is called battery.

2. *Infliction of mental distress*—Extreme and outrageous intentional behavior that results in severe emotional distress to another.

3. *False imprisonment*—Intentional confinement or restraint of another person's movements without justification.

4. *Defamation (libel and slander)*—A false statement of fact, not made under privilege, which is communicated to a third person and which causes damage to a person's reputation or a product's reputation. For public figures, actual malice must be proved. Libel is written defamation, and slander is oral defamation.

5. *Invasion of privacy*—Publishing or using information relating to the private life and affairs of a person without that person's permission or approval.

6. *Fraud*—A false statement made by one party with the intention of misleading another. The other person justifiably relies on the statement and is harmed as a result.

INTENTIONAL TORTS AGAINST PROPERTY

1. *Trespass to land*—Invasion of another's real property without consent or privilege. Specific rights and duties apply once a person is established as a trespasser.

2. *Trespass to personal property and conversion*—Unlawfully damaging or interfering with the owner's right to use, possess, or enjoy his or her personal property constitutes trespass to personal property. When personal property of the owner is wrongfully taken and placed in the use of the trespasser, conversion occurs.

UNINTENTIONAL TORTS

Negligence—The careless performance of a legally required duty or the failure to perform a legally required act. It must be proved that a legal duty exists, that the defendant breached that duty, and that the breach caused damage or injury.

Strict liability—A person is held liable, regardless of care exercised, for damages or injuries caused by his or her product or activity. This includes liability for defective products (product liability) and liability for abnormally dangerous activities.

USING LEGAL LANGUAGE

Directions: Match each term with the statement that best defines that term.

1. battery
2. conversion
3. defamation
4. fraud
5. invasion of privacy

A. _____ exists when a misrepresentation is made by a person who knows the facts to be false and intends to mislead another.

B. A person who commits a tort by intending to commit a wrongful act is called a _____.

1. Yes. The law assumes people are responsible for their actions if they are intentional and wrongfully interfere with the interests of others. It does not matter what the motive was; a tort is committed if the actions harm someone.

2. Legal defenses for someone who is sued for assault or battery, or both are: consent, self-defense, defense of others, or defense of property.

3. Slander is making false or harmful statements about others; writing the statements is libel. Libel is easier to prove because there is a permanent record.

4. Torts of negligence place blame for not exercising reasonable care, but fault is not a factor in strict liability.

5. There is no question that Ruth's actions breached the duty of reasonable care necessary to park a car on the hill. Furthermore, there is little doubt that Jim has been injured by a roof falling on him and not through his own negligence. Therefore, Jim's major task will be to connect Ruth's breach of duty to his injury. The issue of foreseeability becomes a test of proximate cause, the connection needed for Jim's recovery for damages. In other words, Jim must show that the chain of events was a foreseeable result of Ruth's carelessness.

Applying the Law...
You Be the Judge (Answers)

1. The court did not agree with either of the defendants' arguments. The court pointed out that the defendants' first argument—that conversion had not occurred—was erroneous. Conversion does not require appropriation of another's property to one's own use but may consist of retaining complete control over the property in exclusion of the owner's right. Obviously, the defendants had retained complete control over Rouse's car by retaining his keys. As to the second argument, again the court disagreed with the defendants that conversion of the keys did not amount to conversion of the automobile itself. To support this point, the court discussed a case in which it was held that a defendant's refusal to deliver to the plaintiff warehouse tickets that would have enabled the plaintiff to gain possession of cotton amounted to a conversion of the cotton. The defendants also argued that Rouse could have called his wife, who had

---

6. malice
7. negligence
8. puffery
9. shopkeeper's privilege
10. tortfeasor

C. The completion of a threat creates a _____ if it is offensive physical contact and results in harm to another person.

D. _____ is the unauthorized taking of the personal property of another and the wrongful exercise of the rights of ownership.

E. Salespeople engage in _____ when the legally exaggerate claims about the goods.

F. Unprivileged communication that is either spoken or published is _____ if it results in injury to a person's character.

G. The law, _____, gives a seller of goods the right to detain a suspected shoplifter.

H. Defamatory statements that are made in the press are privileged if they are made without actual _____.

I. _____ occurs when someone publishes information relating to the private life of a person without that person's permission.

J. Someone may be guilty of _____ if he or she fails to exercise the standard of care that a reasonable person would exercise in similar circumstances.

◆ CHECKING FOR COMPREHENSION

1. Has a person committed an intentional tort if he or she did not intend to harm anyone else? Explain.

2. If someone is sued for assault or battery, what are some legal defenses?

3. Describe two torts that involve defamation of character. Which way is easier to prove? Why?

4. How do torts of negligence and torts of strict liability differ?

5. Ruth carelessly parks her car on a steep hill, leaving the car in neutral and failing to engage the parking brake. The car rolls down the hill, knocking down an electric line. The sparks from the broken line ignite a grass fire. The fire spreads until it reaches a barn one mile away. The barn houses dynamite, and the burning barn explodes, causing part of the roof to fall on and injure a passing motorist, Jim. Can Jim recover from Ruth? Why or why not?

◆ APPLYING LEGAL CONCEPTS

1. Scan recent newspapers and magazines for statements about individuals that could be libelous. Write a narrative of the news story. Write a two-page paper discussing

another set of keys at home, and thereby could have moved his automobile. The court found no case requiring plaintiffs to exhaust all possible means of regaining possession of property being withheld from them without legal excuse, after demanding its return.

2. Yes. The court held that an occupier of the premises has a duty to use ordinary care to keep its premises in a reasonably safe condition and to warn customers of any foreseeable hazards. What constitutes a foreseeable hazard depends on whether a reasonably pru-

dent person would conclude that harm could likely result from the conditions. Here the manager knew of the storm conditions, knew that water accumulated rapidly on the floor, and knew or should have known that the water created a hazard. The court found that the manager's failure to remove the water constituted negligence, and the store was held liable for Hawkins's injuries.

3. The court pointed out that historically landowners had no duty to warn or take action to prevent harm to invitees when the

risks involved were outside the landowner's premises. In this case, however, the court felt it appropriate to depart from this traditional rule and held the theater owner liable for negligence. In the eyes of the court, the theater "owed the Mostert family an affirmative duty to exercise reasonable or ordinary care for their safety which includes an obligation to advise them of off-premises dangers that might reasonably be foreseeable." First, the court noted that the theater was apparently aware of the severe thunderstorm and the fact that officials had demanded that citizens stay off the streets to avoid injury. Second, the injury suffered occurred within minutes after leaving the theater and was closely related to the defendant's conduct. Third, the defendant suffered the greatest possible injury—death. Fourth, despite the theater's knowledge of the existence and threatening nature of the storm outside, and theatergoers' unawareness of the conditions, the theater issued no warning to its invitees. Fifth, a rule that business managers have a duty to invitees regarding dangers off their premises may reduce injuries in the future. And finally, the extent of the burden of the defendant in this case would have been minimal—merely issuing a warning to the theatergoers concerning the weather conditions outside.

whether the person is a "public figure" or "private individual." Tell whether the individual could sue for damages. If there could be a defense against defamation, explain the legal principle that applies.

◆ APPLYING THE LAW . . . YOU BE THE JUDGE

1. The plaintiff, Rouse, was negotiating a new car purchase with the defendant's salespersons. Rouse gave the salespersons the keys to the car he then owned, which was to be traded for the new automobile. When Rouse decided not to purchase a new car, the sales representatives said they had lost the keys. Rouse summoned the police, and when they arrived the salespersons produced the missing keys and stated that they "just wanted to see him cry a while." Rouse sued for damages for the conversion of his property. The defendants argued first that there was no conversion, and, second, if there was a conversion, it was a conversion of the keys to the automobile, not of the automobile itself. Discuss the merits of the defendants' claims and whether the court will agree with either of their arguments. [*Russell-Vaughn Ford, Inc. v. Rouse*, 281 Ala. 567, 206 So.2d 371 (1968)]

2. HEB Grocery Company has retail grocery stores scattered throughout Texas. Hawkins went to shop for groceries at one of the HEB stores. A heavy rainstorm and north wind had caused water to be tracked into the store by customers and to be blown through the door each time the door opened. As Hawkins entered through the automatically opening door, she slipped and fell in the approximately one-half inch of rain water that had accumulated on the floor. The manager knew of the weather conditions and had employees mop the floor on numerous occa-

sions. There was no sign posted that warned customers of the water hazard. Can Hawkins recover from HEB for injuries sustained when she slipped on the water-covered floor? Explain. [*H.E.B. Grocery Co. v. Hawkins*, 594 S.W.2d 187 (Tex.Civ.App. 1980)]

3. One night in August of 1985, Gerrit and Kay Mostert and their daughter went to a movie theater, American's Frontier Six Theaters (AMC), in Cheyenne, Wyoming. While they were in the theater, the National Weather Service warned the community that a severe thunderstorm was imminent and that flash floods and tornadoes could occur. Civil authorities demanded that citizens stay indoors in safe areas to avoid injury or death. Although the theater managers were aware of the dangerous weather conditions and the warning, they did not inform departing theater patrons of the perilous situation. Shortly after driving away from the theater parking lot, the Mosterts encountered a flooded area, and, during their attempt to escape, the daughter drowned. The Mosterts brought an action against the theater owners, CBL & Associates, claiming that the theater was negligent for its failure to warn those leaving the theater of the danger. Discuss whether the theater had a duty to inform the Mosterts and others leaving the theater of the hazardous weather conditions. [*Mostert v. CBL & Associates*, 741 P.2d 1090 (Wyo. 1987)]

Have the students look at the cartoon found on this page. Ask a student volunteer to explain the source of humor in this cartoon. How does this cartoon help to explain the term "alternative dispute resolution"? To what are these means of dispute resolution an alternative?

Prereading Activity

Introduce this Legal Perspective by asking the students the following questions: How many of you have heard the term *arbitration?* How was this term used? (Many of your students may be familiar with *arbitration* as it is employed in major league baseball, where many players and teams use arbitration to settle salary disputes.) Point out to students that arbitration is just one means of alternative dispute resolution, then allow student volunteers to take turns reading aloud this Legal Perspective.

LEGAL PERSPECTIVE

ALTERNATIVE DISPUTE RESOLUTION

"Lawsuits consume time and money, and rest and friends."

George Herbert, 1593–1633
English poet

Americans like to sue. At least, that's what it looks like if you examine the number of lawsuits filed in this country. The percentage of total national income devoted to tort costs is higher in the United States than anywhere else on earth. It is five times more than in Canada, France, West Germany, Britain, and Japan. The number of multi-million-dollar verdicts in tort cases rose from only 7 in 1970 to an estimated 500 in 1994. And while tort costs in other nations are stable, costs are rising in the United States. Not surprisingly, if you are in business, you have to be insured against the possibility of tort litigation.

Suing and being sued are expensive activities. Lawyers charge anywhere from $75 to $400 an hour for their time. If you sue or are sued, you end up spending a lot of your own time preparing for the lawsuit and making a court appearance.

As an alternative to costly legal battles in the normal court system, many businesses and individuals have turned to what is known as **alternative dispute resolution** techniques, or **ADR**. This is a broad term that describes several methods of resolving disputes through means other than the courts. The most common ADR methods are negotiation, mediation, arbitration, use of an ombudsman, private judging, expert fact finding, mini-trials, and summary jury trials.

"I had a terrible nightmare last night. I dreamt everyone settled out of court."

Reprinted Courtesy of A General Media Company © 1987.

NEGOTIATION

Negotiation is communication for the purpose of persuasion. It is a dispute resolution method used by everybody—we all negotiate, with parents, siblings, friends, and teachers.

Indeed, it is important to remember to try to negotiate disputes. Frequently, people sue one another without attempting to resolve their differences privately. Everyone should make several attempts to resolve most of their problems through mutual agreement. There is an old saying in the law: "A bad agreement is better than a good lawsuit." People can always live with what they have voluntarily agreed to. Living with a court-imposed solution is not always easy.

Although we all negotiate, most people can substantially improve their negotiation

Reteaching Activity

Have the students work in groups to create a chart explaining the similarities and differences among negotiation, mediation, and arbitration. Each group should choose a leader who will be asked to share his or her group's chart with the rest of the class.

 LEGAL BACKGROUND

This Legal Perspective introduces a new area of discussion focussing on the recent trend in the law to look at all options available to injured parties when seeking to redress legal insult. Crowded court dockets have forced the courts and lawyers to consider alternatives to resolving disputes through trial courts. Several options are discussed in this LP but arbitration is given the most emphasis here. Remember to remind students that in most cases arbitrator awards or agreements reached through other means are enforceable, even though they are not judgments of the court. These alternatives to litigation would be illusions were it not for the willingness of the courts to uphold finality.

skills by observing a few rules. Improving your negotiation skills and the importance of compromise in lawsuits are the subjects of the Legal Perspective in Chapter 13.

 ## MEDIATION

Mediation is an assisted negotiation in which a neutral third party assists disputing parties in voluntarily resolving their dispute. A mediator helps parties in conflict to resolve their dispute by agreement. The mediator has no power to impose a resolution to a dispute. A successful mediator does not take sides in the dispute. Mediation has been used in labor disputes for many years, but its use in commercial and other types of disputes is recent. Mediation is the subject of the Legal Perspective in Chapter 27.

 ## ARBITRATION

A more formal method of ADR is **arbitration**. In an arbitration, the dispute is formally submitted to a neutral third person (not a court judge). This person, the arbitrator, decides the dispute. The arbitrator's decision is legally binding. The arbitrator, who is selected by the parties, becomes a private judge. Virtually any commercial matter can be submitted to arbitration. Arbitration is also encouraged on the international level.

WHEN DO PARTIES DECIDE TO ARBITRATE?

Parties to a contract may agree that if a dispute arises about the contract, they will submit it to arbitration rather than use the courts. This agreement may be spelled out in an "arbitration clause" in the contract.

Parties who do not have a contract to arbitrate may agree to arbitrate any time after a dispute arises.

WHY DO PARTIES AGREE TO ARBITRATE?

Parties agree to arbitrate for several reasons: (1) Arbitration proceedings are private, and the courts are public. Sometimes parties want to handle their disputes in private. (2) Arbitrations are usually speedier. Rather than wait for a courtroom, the parties can schedule an arbitration to take place within a short time. (3) Arbitrations are usually less expensive.

WHO CAN BE AN ARBITRATOR?

In terms of legal qualifications, arbitrators must have contractual capacity (discussed in Chapter 9), must be impartial, and must be voluntarily selected by the parties. Arbitrators are usually chosen because they are experts in disputes similar to the one being arbitrated. For example, in a complex case involving the value of a work of art, the parties might select an arbitrator who is an expert in the value of artworks. Parties may agree to use any number of arbitrators. It is common to have one arbitrator in a small dispute and three arbitrators when dollar damages are high. Many arbitrators are lawyers.

WHAT PROCEDURES ARE USED IN AN ARBITRATION?

The parties in an arbitration can create their own procedural rules. State and federal statutes often provide for the procedures to be used when the parties have not done so. Third-party associations such as the **American Arbitration Association (AAA)** also provide procedural rules and

(continued on page 150)

Vocabulary Activity

Have a student volunteer look up the word *ombudsman* in a dictionary and compare the dictionary definition of *ombudsman* with the definition found in this Legal Perspective.

LEGAL PERSPECTIVE (CONTINUED)

administrative assistance for parties seeking arbitration. Standard AAA procedural rules can be incorporated in contracts by the parties. Procedural rules involving the arbitration hearing—for example, rules of evidence—are more relaxed than rules in a court.

HOW DO ARBITRATORS REACH A DECISION?

An arbitrator acts as finder of both law and fact, as judge and as jury. Cases usually proceed as they would in a court, with the plaintiff first and the defendant second. The arbitrator provides a final resolution of the dispute, called an award, usually within thirty days after hearing the case.

WHAT IF YOU LOSE IN ARBITRATION?

All the states and the federal government have statutes that allow the courts to enforce an arbitrator's award, if that is necessary. A losing party may appeal an arbitrator's decision to a court. However, except in cases of bias or gross error, courts seldom overturn arbitration awards. For example, an error of law made by an arbitrator *is not* grounds to overturn an arbitration award. Parties who have agreed to arbitrate disputes can be made to do so even if they change their minds about arbitration.

ARBITRATION SERVICES

Services to conduct arbitrations are provided by both government agencies and private organizations. The major source of arbitration services is the American Arbitration Association (AAA). Most of the largest law firms in the nation are members of this association. The AAA settles more than 60,000 disputes a year in its numerous offices around the country. Settlements usually are made quickly. At times, they are made in informal settings, such as a conference room or even a hotel room. Cases brought before the AAA are heard by an expert or a panel of experts in the subject matter area of the dispute. Usually, about half of these experts are lawyers. To cover its costs, the nonprofit organization charges a fee, paid by the party filing the claim. In addition, each party to the dispute pays for the arbitrators and the costs of the hearing room.

ARBITRATION VARIATIONS

The term *arbitration* usually means that a third party (or parties) makes a final binding decision for the disputants. There are, however, variations of the process. Variations include *nonbinding arbitration*, *court-annexed arbitration*, and *issue arbitration*. In nonbinding arbitration, the parties are not bound by the arbitrator's decision. Court-annexed arbitration is usually nonbinding. It is part of a mandatory process parties must participate in before a trial in some states. For example, the Hawaii court system has adopted a program of mandatory, nonbinding arbitration for disputes involving less than $150,000. Recently, Colorado enacted a statute requiring all civil actions involving damages of less than $50,000 to be arbitrated, as part of a pilot project involving eight judicial districts in the state. In issue arbitration, part of a dispute is submitted to arbitration. Only the part submitted is decided by the arbitrator.

◆ OMBUDSMAN

An **ombudsman** is a third party usually selected by *one* of the parties in an attempt to help resolve a dispute. The ombudsman is actively involved in determining the facts and suggesting possible resolutions. The

150

Reteaching Activity

Have the students work with partners to write a two- to three-paragraph explanation of why alternative dispute resolution is an attractive option for many businesses.

ombudsman will investigate, propose and advocate solutions, and often make public his or her independent findings and recommendations. In some organizations, the ombudsman is a permanent employee who processes and regularly resolves disputes within the group. An ombudsman, like a mediator, has no authority to impose a solution. Both the mediator and the ombudsman start as neutral parties. The ombudsman, unlike the mediator, is not expected to remain neutral, however.

 PRIVATE JUDGING

Private judging is also called rent-a-judge. It began in 1976 in California. Under a California statute, litigants can bypass the formal court system and have their case heard before retired judges. Cases can be "tried before a referee selected and paid by the litigants and empowered by the statute to enter decisions having the finality of trial court judgments." In California, and in the dozen or so other states with similar statutes, jurors can be selected from the public jury rolls to participate in such trials. Verdicts can be appealed to a state appellate court.

Private judging offers clear advantages. It provides more flexibility and privacy than a normal trial. With private judging, parties can immediately schedule the trial and still have access to usual trial procedures. They can appeal adverse rulings through the appellate courts.

Private judging is also the most controversial ADR process, however. The costs of a private judging trial are paid solely by the parties. Therefore, it allows wealthy disputants to bypass the trial calendar. In fact, the rent-a-judge system has been called "Cadillac justice." In contrast, people who cannot afford it have to wait their turn in the public courts.

Private courts are also criticized because it is feared they may lure away judges from the public courts. Judges are paid more by private clients. Furthermore, hearings in private courts are not open to the public or press. Wealthy corporations and other parties can shield their activities from the public eye.

 EXPERT FACT FINDING

Neutral **expert fact finding** is a nonbinding process in which an appointed expert investigates or hears facts on selected issues. At the conclusion, he or she makes findings of fact. These findings may assist in negotiations or may even be admissible in a more formal process. The recommendations often result in a negotiated settlement of the dispute. Fact finding may be part of a negotiation, a mediation, or an arbitration.

MINI-TRIAL

A **mini-trial** is a voluntary process through which parties, usually large business organizations, agree to an informal trial-like proceeding. The sides agree to the procedural rules, exchange information, and select a neutral advisor. The focal point of the process is to present the facts of the case to a special private jury. The jury is composed of high-ranking company officials with authority to settle the dispute. As jurors, the officials learn about the dispute by hearing both sides. The now well-informed managers often can negotiate a settlement and avoid an actual court trial.

(continued on page 152)

Reteaching Activity

Work through the Checklist for Deciding Whether to Sue with the students. Read each of the points in this checklist aloud to the class and then stimulate a class discussion of this checklist by asking the following questions: Do you think that most people who sue make their decision based on questions and advice such as is found in this checklist? Why or why not? What are the possible results from suing without thinking about these points in advance? Is this checklist applicable only in business law situations? Why or why not?

LEGAL PERSPECTIVE (CONTINUED)

 ## SUMMARY JURY TRIAL

A **summary jury trial** is similar to a mini-trial. Such trials have been used extensively in federal district courts. Before trial, parties present their cases to a private mock jury. The mock jury is composed of lay citizens chosen (and employed) to mirror what an actual jury would be expected to do. The presentations are brief, and no witnesses are called. The jury is asked to return its verdict quickly. After the verdict, the attorneys question the jurors about their decision. The process is nonbinding and is used to assist in a settlement. The lawyers gain insight about the probable result of an actual trial and the reaction of real jurors to their cases. If a settlement is not reached, both sides have the right to a full trial later.

 ## CHECKLIST FOR DECIDING WHETHER TO SUE

Although litigation is often necessary, it is not always necessary. A decision to sue or to defend a suit should be carefully thought out because of the direct and indirect costs involved. In making this decision, consider the following checklist:

1. Are you prepared to pay for going to court?
2. Is there a way for you to settle your grievance without going to court? You may be better off settling now for a smaller figure.
3. Can you use some form of alternative dispute resolution? Before you say no, investigate these alternatives—they are usually cheaper and quicker than the standard judicial process.
4. Make your decision based on the advice of a competent legal professional.

 ## TERMS TO REMEMBER

◆ **alternative dispute resolution (ADR)** Methods of resolving disputes through means other than the courts.

◆ **negotiation** Communication for the purpose of persuasion.

◆ **mediation** The use of a neutral third party to assist disputing parties in voluntarily resolving their dispute.

◆ **arbitration** A method of resolving disputes in which the parties to a dispute select a neutral third person to hear and decide the dispute. The arbitrator's decision is binding.

◆ **ombudsman** A neutral third party who investigates and encourages resolutions of disputes.

◆ **private judging** A method of alternative dispute resolution that uses legally trained arbitrators who follow court procedures in hearing a case. Normal rights of court appeal are usually available.

◆ **expert fact finding** A nonbinding process in which an appointed third-party expert investigates or hears facts on selected issues.

◆ **mini-trial** An informal, nonbinding, trial-like proceeding voluntarily engaged in by disputing parties, usually large business organizations.

◆ **summary jury trial** A nonbinding process in which parties present their cases to a private mock jury, which advises the parties as to the probable verdict in an actual trial.

Mastery of Objectives

By the end of this chapter, students will be able to:

- Describe business ethics
- Explain the nature of ethical issues
- Categorize ethical standards
- Differentiate duty-based and utilitarian ethics
- Distinguish between law and ethics
- Analyze corporate ethical responsibility to consumers, employees, and society

Prereading Activity

On cards (or the board), write situations like the following examples. Ask students if each situation is unethical or illegal. Examples: (1) A local lumberyard doubles the price of lumber after a tornado destroys many homes in the area. (2) A student takes home a reference book that is not supposed to be removed from the library. (3) An employer releases five employees in order to make higher profits. (4) You have not studied enough for a test, so you stay home from school that day. (5) You have information that a competing company is depending on a one-day sale to earn enough money to stay in business, and you advertise lower prices than your competitor even though you must take lower profits or even losses on some items. (6) You are applying for a job and tell the interviewer you type 85 words a minute, even though you only did so once on a one-minute timing and usually type 50 words a minute.

Teaching with Images

Have the students look at the photograph of the man standing in front of the maze that appears here. Ask each of the students to write a one-paragraph explanation of how this photo relates to the subject of ethics and social responsibility. Allow student volunteers to share their essays with the class.

Ethics and Social Responsibility

Chapter 6

153

Enrichment

Have the students look at the definition of ethics supplied here: "Standards of fair and honest conduct applied to social behavior." Then have the students interview at least four people each. The students should ask each of these people what the word *ethics* means to them. Students should then compare these definitions with the definition in the text. Allow student volunteers to share some of the results of their interviews with the rest of the class and engage the class in discussion regarding the similarities and differences among the definitions.

Collaborative Learning Activity

Divide the class into groups of three. Direct each group to compose a definition of ethics and give at least three examples of unethical behavior. Orally discuss each group's definition. Ask students what factors influenced their definitions and examples.

154

"Of what avail are empty laws if we lack principle?"
Horace (Quintas Horatius Flaccus), 65–8 B.C.
Roman poet and satirist

Most of you reading this text know the difference between right and wrong—at least for obvious actions. You know it is wrong to murder and steal. You know it is wrong to hurt other people (except perhaps in times of war if you are a soldier). But when you someday go into the world of business, your notions of right and wrong may not be well enough defined to help you make correct decisions. To make such decisions, you have to develop a strong sense of ethics.

Ethics are standards of fair and honest conduct for social behavior. Ethical standards are not created by courts or legislatures. The customs, religious beliefs, and other values of a community or a nation determine what is ethical. The circumstances surrounding a particular action may also determine whether the action is ethical.

Can ethics be taught in school? There are many who believe that they cannot be. These people believe that ethical values come from parents, friends, churches, and other institutions that teach what is acceptable in their communities.

It is unlikely that any one educational experience can create either an ethical or an unethical person. Each of us is the product of a series of experiences. These experiences, good and bad, establish for us what is right and wrong. Although neither this course in business and personal law nor this single chapter can teach a person to be ethical, studying about ethics can at a minimum help you identify the nature of ethics, especially in a business setting. Perhaps just as important, studying ethics can provide you with useful theories and tools for personal ethical decision making. In this chapter, you'll learn about ethical standards and about the responsibilities that corporations have to society.

◆ **ethics** Standards of fair and honest conduct applied to social behavior.

◆ BUSINESS ETHICS

◆ **business ethics** Ethical principles used in business decisions, such as good faith, honesty, and reasonableness.

Business ethics are ethical principles used in business decisions. *Good faith*, *honesty*, *reasonableness*, and similar terms used in law are ethical terms. They express community opinion as to right and wrong behavior. Business people must make complicated decisions with ethical elements. And, as with other decisions, they must sometimes make trade-offs—that is, to get one desired goal, they must trade off, or sacrifice, some other desired goal. People beginning a career in business need to recognize the ethical questions in business decisions and the trade-offs required by those decisions.

Divide the class into six groups and assign each group one of the five following religions: Buddhism, Taoism, Hinduism, Islam, Judaism, Christianity. Ask each group to research that religion and report back to the class. Each group should discuss how the religion was founded, any sacred texts, major divisions within the religion, where the religion is practiced, and a short (no more than one paragraph) discussion of the religion's main beliefs. Allow each group to present its findings to the class in the form of an oral presentation.

Legal Focus Problem

Divide the class into small groups to read and discuss the Legal Focus Problem found here. Each group should choose a leader to explain his or her group's response to each of the questions posed in this Legal Focus.

◆ WHERE ETHICAL STANDARDS COME FROM

Ethical standards do not simply exist, as gravity does. The scientific and technological achievements of the modern world do not give guidance in establishing ethical standards of behavior. Ethical standards are by nature subjective—that is, subject to individual views. As mentioned, the standards are based on religious and other community values concerning what is good, fair, right, or just. Still, each of us has to decide what to believe and how to translate these personal beliefs into action.

Where can we turn for guidance in making decisions about ethics? Many resources are available, because the inquiry into the nature of "the good" is an age-old pursuit. Broadly speaking, ethical reasoning related to business has been characterized by two basic approaches. One approach defines ethical behavior as a set of duties. The other determines whether an action is ethical by its consequences. We examine each of these approaches here.

DUTY-BASED ETHICS

 LEGAL FOCUS – PROBLEM

Is it wrong to cheat on an examination, if no one will ever know you cheated and cheating will help you get into a good college? What if you intend to devote yourself after college to the service of others? Is it wrong to lie to your parents if the lie harms no one but helps keep family relations pleasant?

These questions weigh the end, or consequences, of an action against the means used to attain the end. If you believe that you have an ethical duty not to cheat or lie, these acts can never be justified by the consequences—even if the consequences are charitable or desirable. This view characterizes **duty-based ethics**. In the American culture, the dominant duty-based ethical standards come from religious sources.

Religious Duty-Based Ethics   The tradition represented by the Jewish and Christian religions is rooted in the belief that certain absolute truths have been revealed through the prophets, the Bible, and religious institutions. The "Thou shalt nots" of the Ten Commandments and Christ's instruction to help and care for others ("Love thy neighbor as thyself") are examples. These teachings establish for those who believe in them an absolute ethical duty to act according to them. In this tradition, it is not the consequences of an act that determine if the act is ethical. The nature of the act itself determines whether it is ethical.

◆ **duty-based ethics**
Ethical theory holding that proper behavior is measured by the performance of duties based on a set of deeply held values. Religious principles are an example of duty-based ethics.

LEGAL BACKGROUND

The study of ethics goes beyond the law to ask questions about fairness; a person's or business's actions may be legal, but they are not necessarily fair. Ethics is based on moral principles and values. It asks questions about ideals and the quality of relationships.

The first concept examined in this chapter is the nature of business ethics and the question of where ethical standards come from. Two forms of ethical reasoning are explored, enabling students to discuss ethical conduct as it relates to social issues. The relationship between law and ethics is explored, and the concept of business social responsibility is introduced.

This chapter will not make the student more ethical, but we believe it will give you a framework by which to discuss right and wrong in reference to people and business problems as they occur throughout the text.

Legal Focus Example

Ask a student volunteer to read aloud this first Legal Focus Example. Remind students that they can use the Legal Focus features as review tools when studying for tests.

Enrichment

Ask a student volunteer to research the life and philosophy of Immanuel Kant and present his or her findings to the class in the form of a short oral report.

Legal Focus Example

Read this Legal Focus Example to the class. Ask the class if they can think of any other examples of Kant's principles in action. Allow students to share their examples with the class.

Discussion Starter

Ask a student to describe Kant's central premise on ethics. Stimulate a discussion on ethics by asking students what would happen if every student in the school were 30 minutes tardy to school every day. Ask students for more examples.

     Understanding the Law and Our Legal System

 LEGAL FOCUS ~ EXAMPLE

Leah decides to rob the rich to help the poor, like Robin Hood. If Leah does steal, she is acting unethically by duty-based standards, despite her humane motive. Leah is "sinning" because stealing violates the Seventh Commandment ("Thou shalt not steal").

Of course, there are numerous other religion-based ethical principles throughout the world. They include, but are not limited to, Buddhism, Hinduism, Islam (the Moslem religion), and Taoism. Each has its own set of ethical standards.

Religious ethical standards are absolute. When an act is prohibited by religious teachings, it is unethical. It should not be done, regardless of the consequences. Telling a lie for the sake of gaining a promotion is unethical—even if no one is harmed by the lie and the liar's future seems more promising.

Kant and Duty-Based Ethics A duty-based approach to ethics is also characteristic of the philosophy of Immanuel Kant (1724–1804). The philosopher Kant identified some general guiding principles of moral behavior.

Kant believed in the fundamental worth of human beings. He believed that each person is endowed with moral integrity and the capacity to reason and conduct his or her affairs rationally. He believed the thoughts and actions of all individuals should be respected. When human beings are treated merely as means to some end, they are being treated like objects and are being denied their basic humanity.

Another central premise in Kantian ethics is that individuals should evaluate their actions by considering what would happen if everyone in society performed these actions.

 LEGAL FOCUS ~ EXAMPLE

You are considering whether to cheat on an examination. If you agree with Kant's principles, you will decide not to cheat. If everyone cheated, an examination would be meaningless. Similarly, you would not cut in line to purchase a ticket for a rock concert. If everyone cut in line, the line would disappear, and chaos would result.

Problems with Duty-Based Ethics There are several problems with duty-based ethics. For example, people can disagree about what duties exist. Different religions, although they agree on many things, differ fundamentally on others; and Kant gives us no specific guidance here. Furthermore, how do we deal with conflicting duties? Because of problems

Discussion Starter

Read the following Discussion Starter to the class: "Your school club decides to sell nachos as a fund-raising activity. School policy does not allow groups to sell food in the cafeteria during lunch periods. Your group decides to set up a table outside the entrance to the cafeteria. What are the ethical implications of this activity? Does this involve duty-based or utilitarianism ethics?"

Legal Focus Problem

Read to the class the Legal Focus Problem found here. Allow student volunteers to suggest possible answers to this problem.

Reteaching Activity

Read to the students the following quote from the student text: "Ethical decision making may involve fulfilling, not just one ethical responsibility but several. When one ethical duty conflicts with another, we have to decide which duty is the most important and act accordingly." Ask for a student volunteer to explain how this concept relates to the photograph that was used at the beginning of this chapter. Does the image of the man before the maze make more sense to your students now?

Enrichment

Have a student volunteer research the life of Jeremy Bentham and report his or her findings to the class in the form of a brief oral report.

---

such as these, applying duty-based ethics may be difficult. This is true in the business world as well as in personal life.

◆ LEGAL FOCUS ~ PROBLEM

A business executive negotiating with another firm's representatives feels it is necessary to "stretch the truth" or "hold back" information to get the best deal for his employer. Is this a violation of the religious teaching that one should not lie? Is it a violation of Kant's principle of acting as we would have others act?

It is probably unethical in both religious and Kantian terms. Consider, however, that the executive also owes an ethical duty to his employer to make decisions that are profitable for the firm. And suppose the executive knows that, unless the deal is made, his employer will have to lay off several long-time employees. These employees depend on the firm for food on their table. In this case, is "stretching the truth" consistent with the religious ethical duty to be compassionate toward others? Is it consistent with the Kantian directive to act only as we would have others act?

As this example shows, ethical decision making may involve fulfilling not just one ethical responsibility but several. When one ethical duty conflicts with another, we have to decide which duty is the most important and act accordingly. The executive might conclude that the ethical duty to be fully honest is more important than the duty owed the business. This decision might involve a personal cost, such as the loss of a salary raise, which could also affect the executive's family. Alternatively, the executive might decide that the ethical duty owed to the business and its employees is the more important one. You can see that often ethical decisions are not clear-cut. Decisions may involve choices, not between good and bad alternatives, but between good and less good alternatives.

UTILITARIANISM

"Thou shalt act so as to generate the greatest good for the greatest number." This is a paraphrase of the major assumption of utilitarian theory. **Utilitarianism** is a philosophical theory developed by Jeremy Bentham (1748–1832). In contrast to duty-based ethical systems, utilitarianism is outcome oriented. It focuses on the consequences of an action. It does not focus on the nature of the action itself or on any set of established moral values or religious beliefs.

Right and Wrong in Utilitarianism Under utilitarian ethics, an action is right when, among the people it affects, it produces the greatest amount of good for the greatest number. When an action affects the majority adversely, it is wrong. Applying the utilitarian theory requires us to do the following things: (1) Determine the alternative actions available in a given

◆ **utilitarianism**
Ethical theory, proposed by Jeremy Bentham, that focuses on the consequences of an action. Acting ethically means generating the greatest good for the greatest number of people.

Legal Focus Problem

Divide the class into small groups to read and discuss the Legal Focus Problem found here. Each group should choose a leader to explain his or her group's response to the question posed in this Legal Focus.

Ethical Concern

Ask your students to imagine that a friend of theirs has just asked them if they could copy an assignment from them: What are some of the possible negative results that could occur from this situation? Is it unethical? If you agree to this, is this an unethical act done by both parties? How? How could you handle this situation tactfully?

◆ **cost–benefit analysis** A way to reach a decision in which the costs of a given action are compared with the benefits of the action.

situation. (2) Determine who will be affected by these actions. (3) Predict the negative and positive effects of each alternative action on these individuals. (This is called a **cost–benefit analysis**.) (4) Choose the alternative that will produce the greatest good for the greatest number of people.

Problems with Utilitarianism Utilitarianism also suffers from some problems. One important problem is the need to predict what effects an action will have. An accurate prediction of the overall welfare, happiness, or other good that a given decision will produce requires a knowledge of what the decision's actual consequences, both negative and positive, will be. Rarely, if ever, can all the possibilities associated with a decision be accurately predicted. This is especially true with decisions that affect millions of people.

Another problem is that the cost–benefit method requires the decision maker to assign values to expected good and bad outcomes. But it isn't easy to do this.

Yet another problem with utilitarianism is that it usually involves winners and losers. It is often impossible to satisfy everyone with a policy action based on utility.

◆ LEGAL FOCUS – PROBLEM

Johnson owns many manufacturing plants. One of the plants is much older than the others. Equipment at the old plant is outdated and inefficient. The costs of production at the plant are twice the costs in any of Johnson's other plants. What should Johnson do about the plant? (He cannot raise the price of the product to make up for these higher costs, because that would make the product too high-priced compared with competing products.)

In a utilitarian analysis of the problem, the costs of closing the plant, including the financial burden of laid-off employees, are weighed against the benefits of closing the plant. Benefits include the future financial security of the firm and the fact that the employees at the other plants retain their jobs. If Johnson decides the issue from a utilitarian perspective, he may close the plant. Closing the plant will yield the greatest benefit for the largest number of people. The winners are those helped by the decision. The losers are the workers at the old plant, who lose their jobs.

Utilitarianism is criticized by some because it seems to reduce human beings to plus and minus signs on a worksheet. Utilitarian reasoning has been used to "justify" human costs that many find unacceptable.

There are other theories of ethical responsibility besides the ones we have just discussed. Each of them involves making difficult choices. In the business world, ethical choices often involve managers choosing between what they believe is right and what they know will increase the profits of their companies.

As your students begin to study ethics and the law, you may wish to pass on to them this quote regarding morality from Martin Luther King, Jr.: "Midnight is the hour when men desperately seek to obey the Eleventh Commandment, 'Thou shalt not get caught.'

According to the ethic of midnight, the cardinal sin is to be caught and the cardinal virtue is to get by. . . . This mentality has brought a tragic breakdown of moral standards, and the midnight of moral degeneration deepens."

Ethics and Social Responsibility   159

◆ ETHICS AND THE LAW

In all societies, ethics and the law go hand in hand. Law can never operate in a vacuum. It cannot be a series of rules imposed on society. The law must reflect a society's customs and values. It must enforce principles of behavior that society thinks right and just. Law is thus an expression of the social forces at work in the society of which it is a part.

LAW AS AN EXPRESSION OF SOCIAL FORCES

Law both affects and is affected by the society in which it functions. Some scholars focus on how the law affects society. These scholars emphasize the law's role as a guiding force. They examine how important historical legal cases (such as those prohibiting segregation and discrimination) affect social and political movements (for civil rights and equal opportunity, for example). Supporters of this view consider the law itself an active force bringing about social changes. Other scholars focus on the law as a force in society that preserves the status quo. They believe the law does not bring about social changes. Instead, the law changes over time in response to social changes.

LEGAL FOCUS ~ EXAMPLE

When business was just getting its start in the United States, the watchword was "Let the buyer beware" (sometimes stated as **caveat emptor**). Today, the tables have turned. The watchword is now "Let the seller beware" (also stated as **caveat venditor**). In other words, the consumer once was responsible for watching out for the seller; now the reverse is true. The switch happened because of changing social forces. In the past, buyers and sellers had more equal bargaining power. Particularly in rural settings, buyers knew the sellers and even the manufacturers of goods. Today, most of America lives in big cities. Manufacturers of goods can be located thousands of miles away. It just seems more appropriate that consumers should not have to worry so much about everything that they buy. Rather, our consumer protection laws now make the seller and the manufacturer of goods much more responsible for any problems that arise out of consumers' use of those goods.

◆ *caveat emptor*
"Let the buyer beware."

◆ *caveat venditor*
"Let the seller beware."

THE LIMITS OF LAW

Many ethical decisions are made for us—by our laws. That is because, as we have seen, law reflects many of a society's ethical values. Nonetheless, simply obeying the law does not fulfill all ethical obligations. In the interest of preserving personal freedom, as well as for practical reasons, the law does not—and cannot—make all ethical requirements into legal requirements. No law says that it is *illegal* to lie to one's family, for example,

Legal Focus Example

Allow a student volunteer to read aloud this Legal Focus Example. Remind students that they can use the Legal Focus features as review tools when studying for tests.

 Ethical Concern

Ask your students if they think it is ethical or unethical to hold back the fact that a city is plagued with a deadly disease. The hospital administrator claims that she has it under control. Should she keep it from the public to contain possible mass hysteria? Stimulate a discussion around this topic.

Critical Thinking Activity

Write on the board: "'Laws that do not embody public opinion can never be enforced.' Elbert Hubbard." Ask students if they agree or disagree and why.

Checking Your Progress (Answers)

1. Ethical standards are subjective because they are subject to individual views.
2. The main duty-based ethical standards in the American culture come from religious sources. Religious teachings vary; thus duties may not be the same. Also, duties may conflict, causing additional problems.
3. To apply the utilitarian theory of ethics, first, determine alternate actions available in a situation; second, determine who will be affected by the actions; third, assess the negative and positive effects of each alternative action on the individuals; and fourth, choose the action that will produce the maximum societal utility.
4. Society and law affect each other. However, business law tends to respond to social forces.
5. No. Simply obeying the law does not fulfill all ethical obligations because the law does not make all ethical requirements legal requirements.

---

though it may be *unethical* to do so. Similarly, though it may be convenient for businesspersons to satisfy themselves by merely obeying the law, this approach is not always ethical. Consider the following hypothetical dilemma.

◆ LEGAL FOCUS - PROBLEM

The U.S. government discovers that a child's toy is dangerous and has caused the death of some children. This finding leads to a government ban on the sale of this toy. The manufacturer is, however, left with many unsold toys. Although banned in the United States, the toy can legally be exported to nations without consumer protection laws. Is it ethical to export the toy to these nations?

Duty-based ethical analysis would suggest that selling a product that is likely to cause harm to others is wrong. The fact that the purchasers are residents of another country does not change the duty. What about utilitarian analysis, which compares the benefits and burdens of the decision? By any accounting, the loss of a child's life should lead to a high negative cost for a decision to sell the product. In this view, too, the decision is legal but unethical.

◆ CHECKING YOUR PROGRESS

1. Why are ethical standards considered to be subjective?
2. From what source are most American duty-based ethics derived? What problems arise from duty-based ethics?
3. List the steps in applying the utilitarian theory of ethics.
4. Is law affected by society or does society affect law?
5. If someone is obeying the law, is he or she fulfilling all ethical obligations? Explain.

◆ ETHICS IN BUSINESS DECISION MAKING

Ethical decision making is never simple. Even in our private lives, ethical issues sometimes arise for which there are no "right" answers. We usually weigh the consequences of all possible responses to the issue and choose the response that has the least negative results. In the business context, such ethical dilemmas arise frequently. Not just one but several groups of

Teaching with the Videodisc

At this time, you may wish to show the students the motion segment titled *Mistake* from the **West Business Law and Legal Environment Videodisc**. This fictional dramatization is part of *West's Business Law's Drama of the Law Series*. Each of these dramatizations was written by award-winning writer John J. Osborne, Jr. (originator and author of *The Paper Chase*). Each of these was created by

Osborne and West to bring points of law to life for your students.

In this segment, Mr. Melnick shows up at a supermarket ready to take advantage of an unbelievable price advertised for peppers. Explain to the students that they will see this video again when you discuss sales. However, at this time, the students should look at the actions of Vinnie, Mr. Melnick, and Oscar from an ethical perspective.

To access this motion segment, you can use the bar code provided here or punch in the frame number below the bar code.

Search Frame 26751

people—shareholders, employees, consumers, and others—might be affected by business decisions. In such situations, businesspersons must make trade-offs. They must sacrifice one desired goal to get another.

◆ LEGAL FOCUS ~ EXAMPLE

A pharmaceutical company has developed a new medication that is very effective in the treatment of high blood pressure. The only problem is that the company estimates that one person in a million using the product may have a violent allergic reaction to the medication and may even die. Thus, a decision to sell the product may lead to higher profits, allow many consumers to enjoy the product's benefits, and save many lives. A decision *not* to sell the product will protect a few individuals from the harmful side effects, but may cost many lives. The trade-off is: Sell the drug and expose a few individuals to possible harm while allowing all other consumers to enjoy the benefits of the new product. Or don't sell the drug and avoid any harmful side effects, but prevent consumers from receiving any of the drug's benefits.

The best decisions in business are those that are good for business profits and are also legal and ethical. Exhibit 6-1 illustrates the relationships among these areas. To achieve the best decision, it is often necessary to make trade-offs like the one in the previous example.

EXHIBIT 6-1
ETHICAL DECISION MAKING

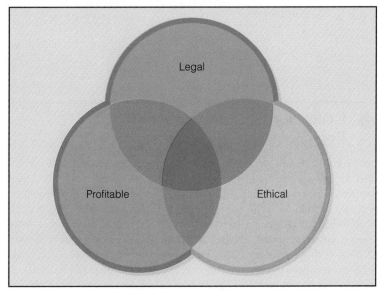

Legal Focus Example

Ask a student volunteer to read aloud this Legal Focus Example. Ask the class what decision they would make if they were the chief executive officer of this pharmaceutical company. Students should explain why they made the decision they did. What are the probable results of that decision? Note: If there is strong disagreement among your students over the proper response in this situation, you may wish to stage a class debate built around this Legal Focus Example.

Read

Before the students read this *Law in Action* feature, you might ask for a student volunteer to recall what the class learned in Chapter 2 regarding freedom of religion in this country. After the student volunteer has refreshed the memories of the class, allow another student volunteer to read aloud this *Law in Action* feature.

Discuss

Stimulate a class discussion of this *Law in Action* feature by asking the following questions: How far do you believe an employer should be forced to go in order to accommodate an employee's religious requirements?

Should it matter if the employee is a believer in a religion with a lot of practitioners in the community? What type of proof do you believe an employer should ask for from an employee who claims that a work-related practice interferes with his or her religion?

 Law in Action

LAW IN YOUR LIFE: ETHICS AND THE FIRST AMENDMENT FREE EXERCISE CLAUSE

The First Amendment to the Constitution states that "Congress shall make no law respecting an establishment of religion, or prohibiting the free exercise thereof." This so-called free exercise clause has led to some ethical difficulties in work situations.

As discussed in Chapter 2, an employer must *reasonably accommodate* an employee's religious requirements. The ethical issue raised by this requirement can be understood through an example. Suppose none of your employees want to work on Saturdays. You require them to anyway—except the ones who claim working would violate their religious beliefs. To exempt some employees, but not others, from a job requirement might not seem fair. If employees believe they are being treated unequally by their employer, job morale may suffer. Less work may get done, and the employer may make less money. How far must an employ-

er go in accommodating the religious beliefs of employees? What is "reasonable" accommodation? It is not always clear to the courts and is generally decided case by case.

A related question is this: Should a person who voluntarily leaves a job for religious reasons have a right to state unemployment benefits? Normally, state laws say that only employees who have been fired or laid off can qualify for unemployment compensation. Employees who quit their jobs cannot get such benefits. But if an employee cannot perform required job duties without going against his or her religious convictions, isn't that employee effectively "forced" to quit? In recent cases, the United States Supreme Court has held that when employees are effectively forced to leave their employment because of religious conflict, they are to be treated as if they had been fired. They are entitled to state unemployment compensation.

◆ CORPORATE SOCIAL RESPONSIBILITY

The business world consists of many different types of firms. While the vast majority are owned by single individuals, the most important, called corporations, are not. They are owned by the people, sometimes numbering in the millions, who have bought shares of stock and thus become shareholders. The firms that you hear most about in the news—IBM, Apple, General Motors, Exxon, and others—are corporations. Corporations consist of the shareholders and the people who run the corporations.

Because corporations are so big and account for the majority of manufacturing in the United States, some people believe that they have a special

Point out to students that corporations often try to improve their name recognition among potential consumers by producing advertisements and television commercials that trumpet their corporate social responsibility. Ask students if they can think of any examples of such advertisements. You might want students to copy or clip examples from current magazines and share them with the class. Ask the students their opinions on such advertising. Does advertising such as this make the students more or less apt to purchase products from this corporation? Why or why not?

responsibility to society. Therefore, the issue of corporate social responsibility is frequently discussed inside and outside corporations. We can define **corporate social responsibility** as the duty of corporations to act in a manner consistent with what is best for society. But society consists of many groups. Within the corporation, the groups are shareholders, employees, and consumers. Some argue that the corporations' primary and only duty is to make shareholders as happy as possible by making the highest profits. But there are other duties, and we will examine them here.

> ◆ **corporate social responsibility** The duty of corporations to act in a manner consistent with what is best for society.

DUTY TO SHAREHOLDERS

What is the corporation's responsibility to its shareholders, the corporation's owners? The people who run corporations are regarded as caretakers of the shareholders' funds. These people have a duty to act in the shareholders' interest—and this means that the primary goal of corporations should be to make profits as high as possible. The Nobel-prize-winning economist Milton Friedman effectively phrases this view:

> *In a free enterprise, private property system, a corporate executive is an employee of the owners of the business [shareholders]. He has a direct responsibility to his employers. That responsibility is to conduct the business in accordance with their desires, which generally will be to make as much money as possible while conforming to the basic rules of society, both those embodied in law and those embodied in ethical custom.*[1]

DUTY TO CONSUMERS

Others contend that the corporation has an ethical duty to look beyond profit to the welfare of consumers. Therefore, if a corporation produces a type of baby food that babies like and mothers buy but that may not be healthful for babies because of a high chemical or sugar content, the corporation should not market the baby food.

Can the corporation willfully ignore the well-being of the consumer? As mentioned above, an underlying ethic of modern-day corporations is to make profits. Can this goal be met if the welfare of consumers is ignored? Many observers of corporations do not believe that any of them can willfully ignore the welfare of consumers and still survive. After all, corporations are in competition with each other. If one corporation consistently makes a product that is lower in quality and higher in price than another corporation's, the first one will lose business to the second. Consumers may take time to figure out which is the better product, but they won't be fooled forever. Similarly, any corporation that knowingly sells consumers dangerous products, when it could easily have avoided the danger, will find that it makes lower profits than it could have by protecting consumers. Consequently, it may be that competition forces corporations to worry about consumers all the time, so that those who run corporations undertake this ethical duty without being told.

Extension Activity

Have a few volunteers research the catastrophe in the early 1980s that the makers of Tylenol encountered when cyanide was found in some Tylenol products. What was the outcome of this tragedy? What new procedures resulted from this incident?

Caption Answer

Duty to consumers is met by the use of the tamper-proof medicine bottle.

Duty to what group is met by the use of the tamper proof seals on food and medication?

1. Milton Friedman, "Does Business Have Social Responsibility?" *Bank Administration*, April 1971, pp. 13–14.

◆ LEGAL FOCUS – EXAMPLE

Eli Lilly had an arthritis drug, Oraflex, approved for sale in the United States without informing the Food and Drug Administration of thirty-two overseas deaths associated with the use of this drug. The dangers of Oraflex only became apparent to the American public when an eighty-one-year-old woman died as a result of taking the drug and a $6 million verdict was rendered against Lilly.

In the example above, the Eli Lilly Corporation may or may not have acted unethically. Supporters of the company argue that every drug has potential side effects. Indeed, some people die from taking aspirins. That does not mean that aspirins should be banned. Rather, both the good and the bad effects of drugs have to be examined.

DUTY TO EMPLOYEES

One of the primary concerns of every employer is controlling the workplace environment. Business success requires qualified, competent, and loyal employees. In turn, employees want interesting work for a fair wage in a safe work environment.

There are several major statutes that regulate the workplace and establish minimum legal duties for employers. Many of these legal duties are discussed in Chapters 21 and 22. Whether employers owe more to their employees than the law requires is a recurring question. Do employers have the responsibility to retrain workers before their skills become obsolete? What duties does an employer owe to employees at an outdated physical plant that will be closed? The answers to these and many other questions are part of the daily debate in every newspaper in the country.

DUTY TO SOCIETY

Many believe that the corporation's primary duty is to society. Because so much of the wealth and power of this country is controlled by corporations, they have a responsibility to use that wealth and power in socially beneficial ways. From this perspective, corporations are caretakers of society. They are charged with a host of ethical duties. They should promote human rights, strive for equal treatment of minorities in the workplace, and generally not make profits by engaging in activities that society has deemed unethical. They should also share some of their wealth with society in the form of charity.

Many corporations are responsive to social needs, and they routinely donate to hospitals, medical research, the arts, universities, and programs that benefit society.

Enrichment

Many professional organizations have written codes of ethics. Have volunteers research the codes of ethics of legal professional organizations, advertising professional organizations, accounting professional organizations, and teacher professional organizations. Place examples of codes on a bulletin board in the classroom.

Ethics and Social Responsibility 165

Many corporations sponsor sporting events for persons who are physically or mentally challenged. What benefits do corporate shareholders realize from such activities?

Legal Focus Example

Go over the Legal Focus Example at the bottom of this page with the students; then divide the class into small groups and assign each group a local corporation. The group should research that corporation's practices to determine in what ways that corporation is responsive to social needs. Allow each group to report its findings to the class.

Caption Answer

Student answers may vary but should reflect an understanding that both corporate shareholders and the community at large are generally enriched by examples of corporate social responsibility such as depicted here.

◆ LEGAL FOCUS – EXAMPLE

Corporations over the last fifty years have engaged in numerous activities that benefit all of society. Here are just a few examples: B. Dalton Bookseller put up $3 million to launch a massive drive against functional illiteracy. The Bank of America created a $10 million revolving-loan program. The money is loaned to community development groups at a 3 percent interest rate. The Coca-Cola Company established the National Hispanic Business Agenda, a major program to expand ties with the Hispanic community. Levi Strauss & Company, as one of its many philanthropic projects, established its AIDS Initiatives program to fund public education concerning AIDS and patient care for the victims of that disease.

Instruct students to write letters to major corporations inquiring about benefits, working conditions, and average salaries for various kinds of jobs within the companies. They should also inquire about any corporate programs or policies for working with the community. Students should direct their letters to the corporations' public relations or human resources departments.

Checking Your Progress (Answers)

1. All business decisions must be legal but may not necessarily be ethical. Sometimes businesspeople must sacrifice one desired goal to get another.
2. Corporations are responsible for their actions to shareholders, employees, consumers, and in some cases, society in general.
3. One way corporations can promote human rights is to strive for equal treatment of all employees. Other ways include contributing money and volunteer time and resources to programs that benefit society.

Reteaching Activity

Divide your class into groups and have students use their own words to define and discuss all of the terms found in this chapter.

In order to help students review what they have learned in Chapter 6, you might wish to:
1. Have a student volunteer, or volunteers, read aloud the Chapter Summary.
2. Allow the students to work with partners to complete the *Using Legal Language* activity.
3. Assign the *Checking for Comprehension* exercise as homework.

4. Allow the students to work in small groups to complete the *Applying Legal Concepts* activities.
5. As a class, complete the *Applying the Law* activities. (Please note that you may have to help students with vocabulary so that they adequately understand all of the *Applying the Law* material.)

THE CORPORATE BALANCING ACT

It is impossible for corporations to be all things to all people at all times. The persons who run corporations have to make numerous trade-offs in determining corporate goals. They do have an ethical duty to shareholders, because they control the shareholders' wealth. Furthermore, by law, corporations have an ethical duty not to market defective or unreasonably dangerous products. Similarly, corporations have a duty to provide safe working conditions for their employees—and this also is written into law. But there is no law that says which of these duties should come first. There is no law suggesting how much weight each duty should be given beyond the minimum prescribed by law.

The trade-offs are more complicated when we realize that these duties overlap. For example, if a corporation is to run smoothly and productively, it must recruit qualified employees. To attract qualified employees, it must offer a competitive salary, a good benefits package, and desirable working conditions. Ideally, if the corporation is well managed by the qualified personnel, profits will increase, and both shareholders and employees will benefit. But this ideal result is not a certainty. What is certain is that the expenses involved in offering these things to employees will reduce shareholder profits in the short run. Similarly, charitable activities that receive wide publicity may benefit shareholders in the long term (because the public image of the corporation may attract consumers). Also, such activities may better the quality of life for everyone. Such long-run possible benefits are difficult to calculate, however. In sum, ethical decision making in the corporate context is not easy.

◆ CHECKING YOUR PROGRESS

1. Must all business decisions be legal? be ethical?
2. To what groups are corporations responsible for their actions?
3. In what ways can corporations meet their ethical duties to society?

Assessment Strategies

In order to check student mastery of chapter concepts, you may wish to use the Chapter 6 test that is found in your *Teacher's Resource Binder* or use WESTEST computerized testing for Chapter 6.

Using Legal Language (Answers)

1–D, 2–F, 3–C, 4–G, 5–J, 6–A, 7–H, 8–E, 9–I, 10–B

Checking for Comprehension (Answers)

1. Kant believed that each person is endowed with moral integrity and the capacity to reason and conduct his or her affairs rationally, and that individuals should evaluate their actions by considering what would happen if everyone in society performed these actions. Religious ethics, on the other hand, are based on teachings by which people who believe in them must abide. In religious ethics it is not the consequences but the nature of the act itself that determines whether it is ethical.

2. Businesspeople must make many decisions. Sometimes they must trade off, or sacrifice, a desired goal in order to get another desired goal.

3. Utilitarianism is outcome-oriented; it focuses on the consequences of actions rather than on preestablished moral values or religious beliefs as in duty-based ethics.

4. No. Some ethical obligations are based on personal morals and beliefs. Law is based on established obligations to society.

5. Ethical conduct can and usually does produce greater profits in the long run by creating customer confidence in the producer. To protect the business from outside costs, such as litigation, ethical goals must be considered and implemented. The group that makes a company's ethical decisions should consist of persons who can rationally determine the ethical value of a decision and balance it against the cost of that decision to the company.

6. Student answers will vary. The conservation of natural resources and other environmental considerations are ethical concerns today and will be tomorrow. The dilemma facing many corporations today is that if they concern themselves with environmental consid-

CHAPTER 6 REVIEW

 ## SUMMARY

Ethics—Standards of fair and honest conduct applied to social behavior. Ethical conduct has to do with what is just and fair.

Business ethics—Ethical principles used in business decisions, such as good faith, honesty, and reasonableness.

Ethical standards—Standards based on religious or other community values concerning what is good, fair, right, or just.

1. *Duty-based ethics*—System that defines ethical behavior as a set of duties.

   a. *Religious duty-based ethics*—Duty-based ethics based on the Jewish and Christian religious traditions, incorporating sources such as the prophets, the Bible, and religious institutions.

   b. *Kant's duty-based ethics*—Ethical theory proposed by Immanuel Kant. Each person should be treated with respect and not used as a means to an end. Individuals should evaluate their actions by considering what would happen if everyone in society performed these actions.

2. *Utilitarianism*—Ethical theory, proposed by Jeremy Bentham, that focuses on the consequences of an action. Acting ethically means generating the greatest good for the greatest number of people.

Ethics and the Law—Ethics and law go hand in hand but are not always the same. Not all societal values are made the subject of law.

Ethics in Business Decision Making—The businessperson must consider three questions in making a decision: Is the decision a good business decision in terms of profitability? Is it legal? Is it ethical? The best decision has three yes answers.

Corporate Social Responsibility—Corporations are seen as having duties to shareholders, employees, consumers, and society at large. They must balance the sometimes conflicting interests of these various groups.

 ## USING LEGAL LANGUAGE

Directions: Match each term with the statement that best defines that term.

1. business ethics
2. *caveat emptor*
3. *caveat venditor*
4. corporate social responsibility
5. duty-based ethics
6. ethics
7. Kant's duty-based ethics
8. positive law
9. tradeoff
10. utilitarianism

A. standards of fair and honest conduct applied to social behavior

B. ethical theory proposed by Jeremy Bentham that focuses on the consequences of an action

C. assumes the seller has the most risks in a sales transaction

D. ethical principles such as good faith, honesty, and reasonableness, used in business decisions

E. clear statement of which actions are allowed and which are prohibited erations that lead to higher costs, they will be at a competitive disadvantage. Thus, most business firms rely on the government to regulate all business firms in order to protect the environment.

7. Student responses will vary. In support of Friedman's position, one could argue that business firms exist to make profits—that is why they are created. For the most part, the reason people invest in corporate enterprises is because they hope to make a good return on their investment. Corporate directors and officers clearly have a primary duty to the shareholder-owners of the corporation to run the business profitably—as long as their profit-making activities do not violate the law or widely supported public policy. One could argue against Friedman's position by stating that, given the power of corporations, they have an ethical duty to promote social goals in the society of which they are a part. In addition, ethical social actions can be profitable for a corporation because they improve the public image of the firm; hence, more people will want to invest in the firm or purchase the firm's products.

8. Student responses will vary. Many managers believe that ethical corporate behavior improves the public image and goodwill of the firm and therefore leads to increased profits. Increased profits can also result from greater job satisfaction among employees, including managers, who work for ethically responsible firms. Some believe that socially responsible firms tend to attract committed and responsible personnel,

whose efficient management of the firm also results in higher profits.

9. A company's ethical responsibility to its workers is to provide them with a fair wage and decent working conditions. Shareholders expect corporate management to maximize profitability so as to maximize the market value of the corporation. Often there is a conflict between such profit maximization and providing fair wages and decent working conditions. Corporations can exercise their ethical responsibilities to their workers only to

the extent that competitive forces allow them to do so.

10. If utilitarian ethics are considered, it would be ethical to continue to manufacture the product because the product would provide the greatest good for the greatest number of people. However, Kantian ethics might deem the continued manufacturing of the product unethical because to do so would be treating the users who sustained injuries merely as a means to an end and thus denying their basic humanity. Religious duty-

---

F. assumes the buyer has the most risks in a sales transaction

G. the concept that corporations can and should act ethically and be accountable to society for their actions

H. ethical theory holding that proper behavior is measured by the performance of du-

ties based on a set of deeply held values

I. something that is given up to get something else

J. ethical theory under which individual's should evaluate their actions by considering what would happen if everyone in society performed the same actions

◆ CHECKING FOR COMPREHENSION

1. Compare religious ethics and Kantian ethics.

2. What is meant by the statement that business people must sometimes make tradeoffs?

3. How is the philosophical theory of utilitarianism different from duty-based moral theory?

4. Does obeying the law fulfill all ethical obligations? Explain.

5. Should corporations have social or ethical goals in addition to profit-making goals? Explain.

6. Should the conservation of natural resources and other environmental considerations be ethical concerns of businesses? Explain.

7. Economist Milton Friedman once wrote, "There is one and only one social responsibility of business . . . to increase its profits." What arguments could you raise in defense of this position? Against it?

8. Many managers believe that corporations can best maximize profits by engaging in ethical corporate behavior. Discuss what reasons they might give for drawing this conclusion.

9. What is a company's ethical responsibility to its workers? How can a company balance its ethical responsibilities to its employees and its responsibilities to its shareholders?

10. A corporate executive must decide whether to continue manufacturing a very popular product that has injured some users in the past several years. The corporation has complied with all government requirements to warn consumers that the product may be dangerous if it is not used as intended. So far, the company has escaped liability for these injuries. Assume that continuing the manufacture of the product is legal. Is it ethical?

◆ APPLYING LEGAL CONCEPTS

1. Assume that your principal decides that one school program must be eliminated next year. Possible programs to eliminate are football, honor society, the computer lab, or an advanced placement class that some students need for college. Design a survey to ask fellow students to select which of the four possible programs they

think should be eliminated. Report the results to your class and discuss the ethical implications of students' decisions.

2. Create a bar graph showing how many students at each grade level decided to eliminate each alternative.

based ethics would most likely consider continued manufacture of the product unethical because the possibility of knowingly allowing someone to be injured would be contrary to most religious beliefs.

Applying the Law . . .
You Be the Judge (Answers)

1. The appellate court agreed with Novosel that discharge from one's employment solely on the basis of one's political views "violates a clear mandate of public policy" to protect the constitutional rights of employees to voice their political opinions freely. Quoting from another case, the court stated that "the special status of corporations has placed them in a position to control vast amounts of economic power that may, if not regulated, dominate not only the economy but also the very heart of our democracy, the electoral process."
2. The court ruled that the right of privacy for blood donors entitles them to have their identities kept confidential. The donation of blood by others would be discouraged if a donor would run the risk of such publicity. This would be harmful to the general welfare and therefore was to be avoided. Consequently, the blood bank has no legal or ethical duty to furnish the names.
3. Honda should not be held responsible, according to the Supreme Court of Washington, which affirmed the trial court's decision to grant Honda's motion for summary judgment. The court cited Comment j to Section 402A of the Restatement (Second) of Torts, which states, "Where a warning is given, the seller may reasonably assume that it will be read and heeded; and a product bearing such a warning, which is safe for use if it is followed, is not in defective condition, nor is it unreasonably dangerous." The court acknowledged that Honda had not warned consumers of "every conceivable danger" that could occur to children riding its mini trail bikes on public streets; nonetheless, its warning did indicate that the bikes were intended for off-road use only and that helmets should be worn. The parents repeatedly warned their children of the precise danger they encountered, and the boys, who were apparently normal children almost nine years old, undoubtedly knew that riding the bikes on public roads and ignoring stop signs could cause them injury. The court concluded that "Honda satisfied its duty to warn under the law of negligence and strict liability."

◆ APPLYING THE LAW . . . YOU BE THE JUDGE

1. John Novosel was an employee of Nationwide Insurance Co. for almost fifteen years. He was never reprimanded or disciplined and rose steadily through company ranks. Toward the end of his employment, a memo circulated throughout the company requesting employees to assist Nationwide's lobbying in the Pennsylvania House of Representatives. Specifically, employees were asked to collect signatures for a petition urging changes in Pennsylvania's no-fault laws that apply to automobile insurance. Novosel refused. Privately, he told others he did not agree with the company's position. Within a few weeks, he was fired. He filed suit. Pennsylvania law prohibits an employment discharge that "abridges a significant and recognized public policy." Novosel argued that "a significant and recognized public policy" can be derived from the important political freedoms expressed in the Pennsylvania constitution and the First Amendment of the United States Constitution. The trial court dismissed the suit, and Novosel appealed. Should an employer's power to hire and fire be used to dictate an employee's political activities? What if an employee is a prominent, outspoken member of an organization that contemporary society considers offensive (e.g., the Ku Klux Klan)? [*Novosel v. Nationwide Insurance Co.*, 721 F.2d 894 (3d Cir. 1983)]

2. Rasmussen, after being hit by an automobile, was taken to a hospital where he was given a number of blood transfusions. It was later determined that he had AIDS. To find out the names and addresses of all the blood donors, he filed a petition for a court order against the blood bank that had furnished the blood to the hospital. He wanted to know if any of them had AIDS so that he could prove that he had contracted the disease from one of the transfusions he received. Does the blood bank have an ethical or a legal duty to furnish the names of donors? [*Rasmussen v. South Florida Blood Service, Inc.*, (Fla) 500 So.2d 533 (1987)]

3. Two eight-year old boys, Bratz and Baughn, were injured while riding a mini-trail bike manufactured by Honda Motor Co. Bratz, who was driving the bike while Baughn rode as a passenger behind him, ran three stop signs without stopping before colliding with a truck. Bratz wore a helmet, but it flew off on impact because it was unfastened. Baughn was not wearing a helmet. The owner's manual for the mini-bike stated in bold print that the bike was intended for off-the-road use only and urged users to "Always Wear a Helmet." A prominent label on the bike itself also warned that the bike was for off-the-road use only and that it should not be used on public streets or highways. In addition, Bratz's father had repeatedly told the boy not to ride the mini-bike in the street. The parents of the injured boys filed suit against Honda, alleging that the mini-trail bike was unreasonably dangerous. Honda claimed it had sufficiently warned consumers of potential dangers that could result if the bike was not used as directed. Should Honda be held responsible for the boys' injuries? Why or why not? [*Baughn v. Honda Motor Co.*, 107 Wash.2d 127, 727 P.2d 655 (1986)]

Prereading Activity

You may want to introduce this Legal Perspective on international law by reading to the students the following quote from President Harry S Truman: "When Kansas and Colorado have a quarrel over the water in the Arkansas River they don't call out the National Guard in each state and go to war over it. They bring a suit in the Supreme Court of the United States and abide by the decision. There isn't a reason in the world why we can't do that internationally." Point out to students that although Truman's sentiments seemed reasonable enough, the fact is that international law and solving international disputes is much more complicated than that.

LEGAL BACKGROUND

International law is very much like ethics because, in most cases, parties or countries decide on their own what they will and will not do because there is no standard enforcement mechanism. Many American citizens have realized, to their detriment, when dealing with a foreign country, that they are "not in Kansas anymore," and the ruby slippers don't work. And yet countries and individuals trade on a daily basis, relying on custom, treaties, and good will. The introduction of the Foreign Corrupt Practices Act in the LP provides a basis for discussing how appropriate it is for the U.S. Congress to tell American companies how to behave in another country.

LEGAL PERSPECTIVE

INTERNATIONAL LAW

Since ancient times, independent peoples and nations have traded their goods with one another. Thus, international business transactions are not unique to the modern world. What is new is that business is becoming increasingly *multinational* in character. A multinational business is one with property, ownership, or both in several countries. It is not uncommon, for example, for a U.S. corporation to have manufacturing plants in a foreign country. Many foreign corporations have operations within the United States.

Transacting business on an international level is different from transacting business within the boundaries of one nation. Buyers and sellers in the international marketplace face far greater risks than those who do business in only one country. The laws, customs, and ethical standards governing international transactions are more complex and uncertain. For example, the Uniform Commercial Code governs many disputes between U.S. buyers and sellers of goods. What if a U.S. buyer fails to carry out a contract agreement formed with a British seller? What law governs the dispute—British or American?

unwritten laws observed by otherwise independent nations and governing the acts of individuals as well as states. The key difference between national law and international law is that national law can be enforced by government authorities. No single government can enforce international law. By definition, a *nation* is a sovereign entity. This means there is no higher authority to which that nation must submit. If a nation violates an international law, the most that other countries or international organizations can do (if persuasive tactics fail) is resort to coercive actions—actions using force or threats. Coercive actions include cutting off diplomatic relations with the violating nation; setting up boycotts, by which other nations refuse to have dealings with the violating nation; and the last resort, war.

International law attempts to reconcile the national and international needs of each nation. Each nation wishes to control its own affairs but also wishes to benefit from trade and harmonious relations with other nations. Although no sovereign nation can be compelled to obey a law of another nation, nations can and do voluntarily agree to be governed in certain respects by international law. They do so to aid international trade and commerce and civilized discussion.

 ### WHAT IS INTERNATIONAL LAW?

National law is the law of a particular nation. The legal system of each country reflects its own unique cultural, historical, economic, and political background. When disputes arise that cannot be settled within a nation, international law comes into play. **International law** is a body of written and

SOURCES OF INTERNATIONAL LAW

One important source of international law is customs that have evolved among nations in their relations with one another. An international custom is a general practice accepted as law.

Critical Thinking Activity

Have the students work with partners to write a one-paragraph explanation of the following entry from the student text: "The key difference between national law and international law is that national law can be enforced by government authorities. No single government can enforce international law." Allow volunteers to share their paragraphs with the rest of the class.

Enrichment

Allow a group of volunteers to research and report to the class on the United Nations. Their report should discuss the structure of the United Nations, membership of the United Nations, and recent activities of the United Nations. Explain to students that they will also be asked to explain the importance of the General Assembly of the United Nations, as well as the United Nations International Court of Justice.

Legal Focus Example

Ask a student volunteer to read aloud this Legal Focus Example. Ask the students whether they feel the buyer should have to pay damages even if the procedures and laws applied in the Swedish court are *not* consistent with U.S. law and policy.

Foreign companies doing business in the U.S. can sue or be sued in our courts.

Treaties and other explicit agreements between or among foreign nations provide another important source of international law. A *treaty* is an agreement or contract between two or more nations that is approved formally by the supreme power of each nation. Bilateral agreements are agreements between two nations to govern their commercial exchanges or other relations with one another. Multilateral agreements are those formed by several nations.

International organizations and conferences also contribute to international law. These organizations adopt resolutions, declarations, and other types of standards that often require a particular behavior of nations. The General Assembly of the United Nations, for example, has adopted many resolutions and declarations that include principles of international law. Disputes about these resolutions and declarations may be brought before the United Nations International Court of Justice. The Court has power to settle legal disputes only when nations voluntarily submit to its jurisdiction.

◆ LEGAL PRINCIPLES AND DOCTRINES

Several legal principles and doctrines have evolved in the courts of nations to resolve conflicts with foreign elements. The three important legal principles discussed below are based primarily on courtesy and respect. They are applied in the interests of maintaining harmonious relations among nations.

THE PRINCIPLE OF COMITY

Under the principle of **comity,** one nation will defer, or submit, to the laws and judicial decrees of another country voluntarily. The nation that defers will do so only when those laws and judicial decrees are consistent with its own law and public policy. This practice is based primarily on courtesy and respect.

 LEGAL FOCUS - EXAMPLE

A Swedish seller and an American buyer have formed a contract. The buyer does not perform as promised in the contract. The seller sues the buyer in a Swedish court, which awards damages. The buyer's assets (including money) are in the United States, so the judgment cannot be enforced unless it is enforced by a U.S. court of law. If the procedures and laws applied in the Swedish court are consistent with U.S. law and policy, the United States court will enforce the Swedish judgment.

THE ACT OF STATE DOCTRINE

The **act of state doctrine** provides that the courts of one country will not question the

(continued on page 172)

Legal Focus Example

Read aloud this Legal Focus Example. Have a student volunteer explain how the act of state doctrine may prevent Flaherty's recovery in a U.S. court of law.

Extension Activity

Have volunteers research the passage of the Foreign Corrupt Practices Act of 1977. Have the students use periodicals such as news magazines and newspapers to detail some of the business scandals that led to the introduction and passage of this act.

LEGAL PERSPECTIVE (CONTINUED)

public acts of a recognized foreign government within the foreign government's own territory. This doctrine rests on the theory that the judicial branch should not conduct international relations. To question the acts of foreign governments interferes with duties of the executive branch of government.

The act of state doctrine has important consequences for individuals and firms doing business with and investing in other countries. For example, this doctrine is frequently employed in cases involving **expropriation**. Expropriation occurs when a government seizes a privately owned business or privately owned goods for a proper public purpose and awards just compensation.

 LEGAL FOCUS ~ EXAMPLE

Tim Flaherty, an American businessperson, owns a mine in Brazil. The government of Brazil seizes the mine for public use. Brazil claims that the profits Tim has realized from the mine in preceding years constitute just compensation. Tim disagrees. The act of state doctrine may prevent Tim's recovery in a U.S. court of law.

THE DOCTRINE OF SOVEREIGN IMMUNITY

When certain conditions are satisfied, the doctrine of **sovereign immunity** immunizes foreign nations from the jurisdiction of U.S. courts. This means that a person cannot sue a foreign country in a U.S. court. Together with the act of state doctrine, the doctrine of sovereign immunity means that firms or individuals that own property in foreign countries get little legal protection

from U.S. courts against government actions taking place in these countries.

U.S. companies can generally, however, get access to the courts in the foreign country. The political stability of the country and courts is a risk to be considered before doing business in a foreign country. A major reason why foreign companies invest heavily in the United States is because of the relative political stability of the United States and the fair treatment they can expect in U.S. courts.

◆ ETHICS BECOMES LAW IN INTERNATIONAL BUSINESS: THE FOREIGN CORRUPT PRACTICES ACT OF 1977

In addition to affecting the welfare of shareholders and consumers, corporate decisions may also involve global issues. In recent years, corporate managers have had to weigh global ethical considerations when making company decisions. How corporations meet such ethical challenges is, according to some, one factor among many that can be used to measure a firm's corporate social responsibility.

For example, bribery of foreign government officials has been part of international business transactions for centuries. Not until 1977, however, was the bribery of foreign officials raised as an ethical issue. In the 1970s, the U.S. press, and government officials as well, uncovered several business scandals involving large *side payments* (secret payments to officials) by American corporations. For example, Lockheed Aircraft paid foreign representatives for securing advantageous international trade contracts. Because enough groups concluded that this type of behavior was unethical, Congress prohibited it by passing the Foreign Corrupt Practices Act (FCPA) in 1977.[1] The previous trade-off—looking the other way when U.S. corporate managers bribed foreign government officials to get more profitable foreign contracts—was no longer considered acceptable.

American corporations wishing to do business abroad, particularly in less developed countries and in the Middle East, have probably always engaged in some sort of side-payment system to win contracts. In America, most construction contracts are private. In many foreign countries, however, the majority of major construction and manufacturing contracts are decided on by government officials. In these countries, extensive government regulation controls trade and industry. Side payments to government officials in return for favorable business contracts are common in these countries. Indeed, in many countries, side

payments are not considered unethical, as they are in the United States. U.S. corporations doing business in less-developed countries were largely following the saying, "When in Rome, do as the Romans do."

The FCPA prohibits bribes—defined as giving anything of value—to foreign government officials if the purpose of the payment is to get or keep business for the U.S. company. Any violation of the act can result in fines of up to $1 million. The act also provides for imprisonment of officers or directors of convicted companies for up to five years. Those officers and directors can also be fined up to $10,000, and the fine cannot be paid by the company.

The passage of the FCPA has created a dilemma for U.S. business firms seeking to do business abroad. An employee of a U.S. corporation has a responsibility to do what is in the best interest of the corporation's shareholders. Often, that necessitates some sort of side payment to a foreign official or officials to get a profitable contract abroad. Such offers of side payments now violate the FCPA.

---

1. 15 U.S.C. Sections 78 *et seq.* [*et seq.* means "and the following sections"]

TERMS TO REMEMBER

◆ **national law**   The law of a particular nation.

◆ **international law**   The body of written and unwritten laws governing relations between independent nations.

◆ **comity**   The voluntary deference by one nation to the laws of another nation.

◆ **act of state doctrine**   Doctrine that provides that the courts of one country will not

question the public acts of a recognized foreign government within the foreign government's own territory.

◆ **expropriation**   Government seizure of a privately owned business or privately owned goods for a proper public purpose and with just compensation.

◆ **sovereign immunity**   Immunity of a nation from the jurisdiction of another nation's courts.

Suggested Additional Resources

Calamari, John D., and Perillo, Joseph M. *Calamari and Perillo's Hornbook of Contracts,* 3d ed. St. Paul, MN: West Publishing Co., 1987.

The Guide to American Law. St. Paul, MN: West Publishing Co., 1983. Annual updates are available.

Jentz, Miller, Cross. *West's Business Law: Alternate Edition,* 5th ed. St. Paul, MN: West Publishing Co., 1993.

Kionka, Edward J. *Kionka's Torts in a Nutshell,* 2d ed. St. Paul, MN: West Publishing Co., 1992.

Restatement of the Law, Contracts, 2d ed. St. Paul, MN: American Law Institute Publishers, 1981.

Weaver, Jefferson H. *The Compact Guide to Contract Law: A Civilized Approach to the Law.* St. Paul, MN: West Publishing Co., 1990.

Weaver, Jefferson H. *The Compact Guide to Tort Law: A Civilized Approach to the Law.* St. Paul, MN: West Publishing Co., 1991.

White, James J., and Sommers, Robert S. *White and Sommers's Hornbook on the Uniform Commercial Code,* 3d ed. St. Paul, MN: West Publishing Co., 1988.

UNIT 2

The Law of Contracts

Contract law deals with the making and keeping of promises. The law encourages people to form contracts for lawful purposes. Modern life is brimming with contractual relationships. The daily activities of ordinary consumers involve rights and obligations or duties based on contract law. You enter into contracts and acquire rights and obligations when you borrow money, buy a stereo, purchase a hamburger, put gas in a car, get your lunch at the school cafeteria, go to a movie, get a job, and on and on. Contract law is designed to provide stability and predictability—certainty—for both buyers and sellers in the marketplace.

Why do we study contract law? Contract law is the framework for all business law. It is the law that most affects our daily lives. In the following chapters, you will learn that contract law is the basis for much of the law in more specialized areas. You will also learn that statutes, such as the Uniform Commercial Code, provide legal rules that parties can often change by express terms in their contracts.

Prereading Activity

First, ask the students if they have ever formed a contract with another person. Tell them the definition of a contract: "an agreement between two or more parties that creates an obligation to do or not do something." Then ask them to write examples of contracts they might enter into as students or consumers. Read the examples aloud before completing this chapter, but do not discuss them.

Mastery Objectives

By the end of this chapter, students will be able to:
- List contract requirements
- Describe seven ways in which contracts are formed
- Explain contract performance
- Determine contract enforceability

Chapter 7

Introduction to Contracts

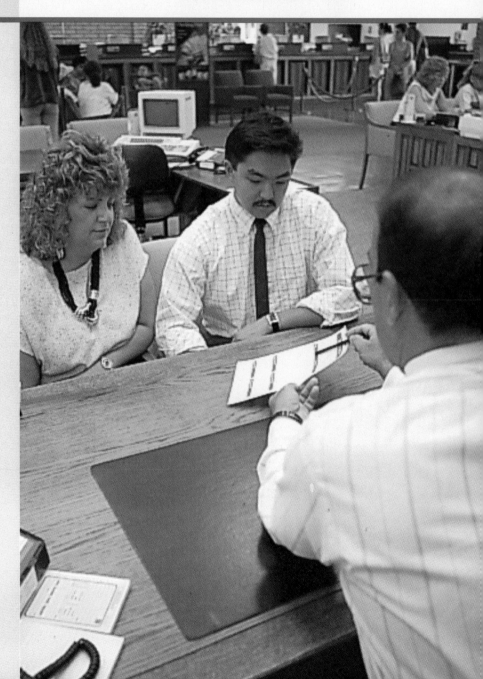

Chapter 7 Resources and Assignment Guide	Tests

Chapter 7
Resources and Assignment Guide

Activity Sheets
Reviewing Legal Concepts 7 *TRB*
Enrichment Activity 7 *TRB*

Student Activity Workbook
Chapter 7 Activities

Tests
Chapter 7 Test *TRB*
Chapter 7 WESTEST Computerized Testing

Handbook of Selected Court Cases
Moore v. *Kuehn*
Seawell v. *Continental Casualty Company*

West's Business Law and Legal Environment Videodisc
Still Frames and Motion Segments as shown

Contract law reflects our social values, interests, and expectations at a given point in time. How many people in our society make promises or commitments that are legally binding? What excuses will our society accept for breaking such promises? What promises are contrary to public policy and therefore legally void, or invalid? If a promise goes against the interests of society, will the courts enforce it? If a child or an insane person makes a promise, should it be enforced? Resolving such questions is what contract law is about.

◆ THE FUNCTION OF CONTRACTS

◀ LEGAL FOCUS – PROBLEM

Rosalie invited an acquaintance, Jonathan, to her high school prom. Jonathan accepted the offer and, eager to please Rosalie, spent lavishly preparing for the evening. He got a haircut and he purchased a new jacket, new shoes, and flowers. On the evening of the dance, Jonathan arrived at Rosalie's house and found out that she had left for the evening. Jonathan is considering suing Rosalie for breach of contract to recover his expenses. Does he have a lawsuit?

Contract law allows parties to make enforceable promises. If you think about it, you will realize that many promises people make do not create legal obligations. Sometimes the promises create *moral* rather than *legal* obligations. A moral obligation defines what you should do. Failure to perform a moral obligation, such as an agreement to give a friend a ride, does not usually create a legal liability. Sometimes, promises create both a moral and a legal obligation (as when a friend promises to pay you for gas expenses to drive her to a neighboring city). Agreements to go on dates are not contracts; they are social arrangements. Although Rosalie may have breached a moral obligation, she is not required to pay Jonathan's expenses because she did not keep the date.

Most people keep promises because of a sense of duty. Furthermore, keeping a promise is usually in the self-interest of each party. Often the **promisor** (the person making the promise) and the **promisee** (the person to whom the promise is made) are not aware of the rules of contract law. They may rely on the *good faith*—the honesty and thoughtfulness—of the other person. In business situations, however, parties should follow the rules of contract law carefully to avoid potential problems.

Contract law is an essential part of the market economy. Contract law allows businesspersons to plan and act without needing to rely only on the good faith of other persons—persons they may not even know. Duty and good faith are usually enough. However, when price changes or other

◆ **promisor** A person who makes a promise.

◆ **promisee** A person to whom a promise is made.

Legal Focus Problem

Read to the class the Legal Focus Problem found here. Allow student volunteers to suggest possible answers to the question posed at the end of this problem.

? Ethical Concern

Guide the students in looking at the Legal Focus Problem from an ethical perspective rather than a legal one. Ask: "Were Rosalie's actions unethical? Why or why not? What would you do if you were in Jonathan's shoes?"

Critical Thinking Activity

Ask students why duty and good faith are not enough to ensure that parties will fulfill their promises. (A discussion of ethics will reinforce Chapter 6.)

Reteaching Activity

Have the students role play several different oral contract situations and allow their classmates to point out, in each situation, who is the promisor and who is the promisee.

Vocabulary Activity

Allow student volunteers to define the term *good faith* in their own words. Explain to students that *good faith* is a very common legal term used in discussing contracts.

business problems make it costly to obey a promise, then duty and good faith may not be enough. Contract law is then useful to assure that the parties keep their promises and is necessary to allow an innocent party some form of legal remedy. Indeed, in business, questions and disputes concerning contracts arise daily.

The features of contract law vary from state to state. Much of contract law is based on common law. The Uniform Commercial Code does, however, modify many important rules of contract law.

◆ THE UNIFORM COMMERCIAL CODE

In the twentieth century, there has been a movement to create various "uniform" acts or codes to make state laws more consistent across the United States. The most significant uniform code is the Uniform Commercial Code (UCC), which has been adopted, at least in part, by all fifty states. When adopted by a state, the UCC becomes the statutory law of that state. Common law rules still provide the answers to most contract questions. However, statutory law, particularly the UCC, changes the common law in certain contract situations.

At this point in our study of contracts, the most important thing to know about the UCC is when the UCC applies in a contract situation. Article 2 (Sales) is the most important part of the UCC for our contracts discussion. Article 2 applies, in general, when the purpose of a contract is a sale of goods. A **sale** is a transfer of ownership for a price. **Goods** are a type of movable personal property, such as tables, chairs, hairbrushes, and automobiles. We will discuss common law rules, and some of the changes that have been made in these rules, here in the contracts unit. We will discuss sales law separately in Chapters 14 and 15. A discussion of personal property appears in Chapter 28.

◆ **sale** A transfer of ownership for a price.

◆ **goods** Items of tangible, movable personal property.

◆ THE BASIC REQUIREMENTS OF A CONTRACT

The following list describes the requirements of a contract. We will explain each requirement more fully in the chapter mentioned with that requirement.

1. **Agreement**. An agreement includes an *offer* and an *acceptance*. One party must offer to enter into a legal agreement, and another party must accept the terms of the offer (Chapter 8).

2. **Consideration**. Any promises made by parties require legally sufficient and bargained-for *consideration*—something of value received or promised to convince a person to make a deal (Chapter 9).

1. No, failure to perform a
moral obligation does not
usually create a legal
liability.
2. The person to whom the
promise is made is the
promisee.
3. Statutory law such as the
Uniform Commercial Code
changes the common law in
certain contract situations.

3. **Contractual capacity**. Both parties entering into the contract must have contractual *capacity*. That is, the law must recognize them as having characteristics qualifying them as competent parties (Chapter 9).

4. **Legality**. The contract's purpose must be to accomplish some goal that is *legal* and not against society's interests (Chapter 10).

5. **Genuineness of assent**. The apparent consent of both parties must be *genuine* (Chapter 10).

6. **Form**. The contract must be in the *form* the law requires. As an example, some contracts must be in writing to be enforceable (Chapter 11).

The first three items in this list are formally known as the *elements of a contract*. The last three are possible *defenses to the formation or the enforcement of a contract*.

◆ DEFINITION OF A CONTRACT

A **contract** is an agreement that can be enforced in a court. It is normally formed by two or more parties exchanging promises. A **promise** is a declaration that something either will or will not happen in the future. If the contractual promise is not performed, the party who made it is liable to the person to whom the promise was made. The nonperforming party may be required to pay money damages for failure to perform. In a few situations, the party will be required to perform the promised act.

◆ **contract** A legally enforceable agreement to do or not do a specified thing.

◆ **promise** A declaration that something either will or will not happen in the future.

◆ CHECKING YOUR PROGRESS

1. If an agreement creates a moral rather than a legal obligation, has a contract been formed?

2. A promisor is the person making a promise. What is the person to whom the promise is made called?

3. What law supersedes common law in contract disputes?

◆ TYPES OF CONTRACTS

There are many types of contracts. The best method of explaining each is to compare one type of contract with another.

BILATERAL VERSUS UNILATERAL CONTRACTS

◆ **offeror** A person who makes an offer.

◆ **offeree** A person to whom an offer is made.

◆ **bilateral contract** A contract that includes a promise in exchange for a promise.

Every contract requires at least two parties. The **offeror** is the party who makes the offer. The **offeree** is the party to whom the offeror makes the offer. The offeror always promises to do or not to do something. The offeror is thus also a *promisor*. The acceptance of an offer by the offeree *binds* the offeror—that is, places the offeror under an obligation—and creates the contract.

Whether the contract is *unilateral* or *bilateral* depends on what the offeree must do to accept the offer and thus form a contract. If, to accept, the offeree must make a promise to perform, the contract is a *bilateral contract*. *Bi* means "two," as in *bicycle*, which has two wheels. A **bilateral contract** is two promises, a "promise for a promise." No performance, such as the payment of money or the delivery of goods, is necessary for a contract to be formed. The contract's existence begins at the moment when promises are exchanged.

◀ **LEGAL FOCUS ─ PROBLEM**

Don Lee calls Philip Hamid on the telephone. "Philip, I will pay you $2,000 if you promise to paint my house. You should begin painting it next week." Don continues, describing the color, type of paint, and other particulars of the job. Philip responds, "I promise." Is this an example of a bilateral contract?

Home purchases are almost always bilateral contracts. Why?

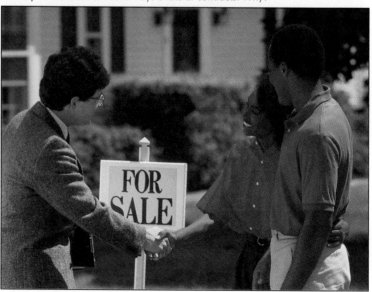

Read this Legal Focus Example to the class. Ask the class if they can think of any other examples that might also fit here. Allow volunteers to share their alternate examples with the class.

Ask your students if a contract exists when they put 50¢ into a vending machine for a soda. What type of contract is this? If the soda is not delivered, are they entitled to the lost money?

Legal Focus Problem

Ask a student volunteer to read this Legal Focus Problem aloud to the class. Remind students that they can use the Legal Focus features as review tools when studying for tests.

This is a bilateral contract, because Don makes a promise and requests and receives a promise in return. The contract is formed when Philip responds, though performance will not begin for a week.

If an offer is phrased so the offeree can only accept by performance, the contract is a *unilateral contract*. *Uni* means "one," as in *unicycle*, which has one wheel. A **unilateral contract** is a "promise for an act."

◆ **unilateral contract** A contract that includes a promise in exchange for an act.

> ### ◆ LEGAL FOCUS ~ EXAMPLE
>
> Joe says to Celia, "If you walk across the Brooklyn Bridge, I'll give you $25." This is a classic example of a unilateral contract. Joe has promised to pay Celia only if she walks the entire span of the bridge. Only after Celia's complete crossing has she accepted Joe's offer to pay $25. If she chooses not to walk the bridge, there are no legal consequences.

With a bilateral contract, a binding agreement is created before either party has to perform (do what they promised). A bilateral contract is easy to create. The parties need only exchange promises. However, once the contract is created, each party has legal responsibilities to the other.

When a person makes an offer for a unilateral contract, no contract exists until the person to whom the offer was made decides to perform. If that person decides not to perform (accept the offer), there are no legal consequences. Also, the offer can usually be withdrawn (it is revocable—capable of being taken back, or canceled) anytime until performance.

> ### ◆ LEGAL FOCUS ~ PROBLEM
>
> Roberta offered to buy Ed's sailboat, moored in San Francisco, if it was delivered to Roberta's dock in Newport Beach. Newport Beach is about 300 nautical miles south of San Francisco. Ed rigged the boat and set sail. Shortly before he arrived at Newport Beach, Ed received a radio message from Roberta: "So sorry, Ed, I have changed my mind." Is there a contract?

Roberta's offer is for a unilateral contract. The offeree, Ed, can only accept it by performing the requested act—delivering the sailboat at Newport Beach. Can Roberta revoke, or cancel, her offer after Ed has begun but has not yet completed performance?

Because Roberta's offer is for a unilateral contract, and because only Ed's delivery of the sailboat at her dock is an acceptance, Roberta's revocation would ordinarily terminate, or end, the offer. However, the modern-day view is that once the offeree has made a substantial beginning of performance, he or she has a reasonable time to complete performance. Ed has made a substantial beginning of performance by sailing almost 300

Critical Thinking Activity

Ask students their opinions on why unilateral contract acceptance has changed to the modern-day view that once there is a substantial beginning of performance, the promisee has a reasonable time to complete performance.

Ask a student volunteer to look up the word *revoke* in the dictionary and then explain how this word relates to *revocation* and *irrevocable*. Make sure that students understand these terms, as they will occur often in our discussion of contracts.

Divide the class into small groups to read and discuss the Legal Focus Problem found here. Each group should choose a leader to explain the group's response to the question posed at the end of this problem. Read aloud to the class the steps necessary for an implied-in-fact contract, found below; then have the groups work to show where this Legal Focus meets each of these three steps.

Reteaching Activity

Pair students with partners, and have them make lists of types of implied contracts and types of express contracts.

182   The Law of Contracts

miles. Therefore, under the modern-day view, Roberta's offer is irrevocable; it cannot be canceled. Even though Ed has not yet arrived at Newport Beach, Roberta may not revoke her offer. Instead, she must allow a reasonable time for Ed to deliver the boat and bind her to the contract.

EXPRESS VERSUS IMPLIED CONTRACTS

♦ **express contract**
A contract whose terms are stated in oral and/or written form (rather than being implied from the circumstances).

An **express contract** is an agreement in which the terms are fully and explicitly stated in words. The words may be oral or written. A signed lease for an apartment or a house is an express *written contract*. If a classmate calls you on the phone and agrees to buy your old skateboard for $50, an express *oral contract* is created.

In contrast, a contract implied from the conduct of the parties is an **implied-in-fact contract**. A contract of this kind may also be called simply an *implied contract*. Here, the *conduct* of the parties, rather than their words, creates and defines the terms of the contract.

♦ **implied-in-fact contract**   A contract implied from the conduct of the parties (not an express contract).

◇ LEGAL FOCUS – PROBLEM

Last summer, Isaiah created his own small business running errands for senior citizens. The good news was that he earned plenty of money. The bad news was that the time to pay taxes eventually came. Isaiah needed a tax accountant to complete his income tax return. A look through the Yellow Pages found a tax accountant at an office in his neighborhood. A phone call got him an appointment. He went to the office and explained his problem. Debra, the accountant, gave Isaiah a pamphlet with her fee schedule. The next day he returned, with all the necessary information and documents, such as canceled checks and W-2 forms. Isaiah gave them to the secretary. He said nothing except "cold out there, isn't it" and walked out the door. Is there a contract?

Isaiah has entered into an implied-in-fact contract. The contract is implied by each party's conduct. Debra expects payment for completing Isaiah's tax return. By bringing in the records needed to do the work, Isaiah has implied an intent to pay Debra the usual and reasonable fees for her services.

Steps Necessary for an Implied-in-Fact Contract   The following three steps establish an implied-in-fact contract in a lawsuit:

1. The plaintiff furnished some service or property.
2. The plaintiff expects payment for that service or property. The defendant knew or should have known that payment was expected.
3. The defendant had a reasonable opportunity to refuse the services or property but did not.

Orally, give examples of several contracts, and ask your students to identify whether each is bilateral or unilateral, express or implied, or quasi. Some examples of contracts are: your aunt offers to pay you $10,000 if you go to college; you offer $500 for a friend's car and he accepts; you are injured on a ski slope and are treated by a fellow skier, who turns out to be a physician.

Discuss the meanings of the terms *objective* and *subjective;* then ask students to write a one-page paper in which they apply the definitions to the objective theory of contracts.

Students' answers may vary but should reflect an understanding of express contracts, implied-in-fact contracts, and quasi-contracts.

Objective Theory of Contracts   The intent to enter into a contract is necessary to form any type of contract. Intent is decided by the **objective theory of contracts.** It is not determined by a party's personal, or subjective, intentions or beliefs. A party's intent to enter into a contract is judged by outward, objective facts. We can see this in our tax-preparation example. The question is, what would a reasonable offeree in Debra's position believe was meant by Isaiah's language or action? Isaiah's actions—returning with all the information necessary for Debra to do the tax work—would appear to a reasonable person as an offer to contract.

In brief, courts need evidence that a contract exists. They usually rely only on objective factors (facts, conduct, and circumstances) when passing judgment on a contract dispute.

♦ **objective theory of contracts**   Theory by which the intent to contract is judged by what a reasonably objective party would believe was meant by a person's language and conduct.

Describe three sets of circumstances involving emergency techniques that would provide an example of an express contract, an implied in-fact-contract, and a quasi-contract?

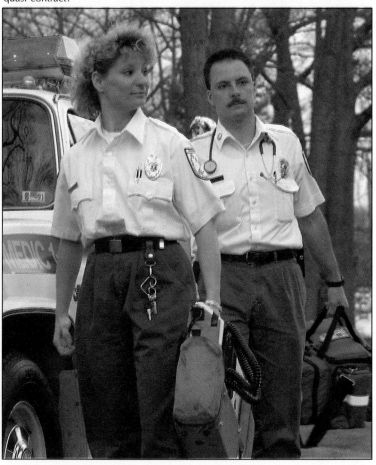

Legal Focus Problem

Read to the class the first Legal Focus Problem found here. Allow student volunteers to suggest possible answers to this problem.

Enrichment

Ask your students to write down five possible quasi contracts.

Legal Focus Problem

Have a student volunteer read the second Legal Focus Problem aloud to the class. Allow student volunteers to suggest possible answers to the question posed at the end of this problem.

Discussion Starter

Ask your students if a quasi contract is created when you are injured on a ski slope and a fellow skier doctors your broken leg, but the skier is not a doctor. Point out to your students that the person must be licensed in order to receive payment for medical services.

State Law

Have volunteers research which states recognize contracts under seal, obtain samples of contracts and seals, and then report their findings to the class.

QUASI CONTRACTS

 LEGAL FOCUS ~ PROBLEM

A vacationing doctor, Vanesa Dwight, was driving down the highway when she saw Carl Emerson lying on the side of the road, unconscious and very ill. She gave substantial medical aid that saved Carl's life. Because Carl was unconscious, he could not request the medical aid. He was not even aware that the aid had been given. Carl was grateful but refused to pay Vanesa's bill for services when it arrived. "I never told her to help me, so it's hard luck for her." Will Vanesa be paid?

Carl has a point. A true contract does not exist. He never made an offer. He couldn't; he was unconscious. However, Carl received a valuable benefit under circumstances in which the law will *imply in law* a *quasi contract*.

Quasi is a Latin term meaning "approximately" or "as if." Thus, the law will treat a quasi contract "as if" it were a contract. A **quasi contract** is an obligation created by law, not by mutual agreement of the parties. It is not a true contract. Quasi contracts arise to prevent *unjust enrichment*. Unjust enrichment occurs when people profit or are enriched unfairly at the expense of others. The law provides that the recovery should be the reasonable value of the benefit. Thus, Carl will have to pay the doctor for the reasonable value of the medical services he received.

◆ **quasi contract**
An obligation created by law. Not a true contract. The purpose is to prevent one party from being unjustly enriched at the expense of another.

LEGAL FOCUS ~ PROBLEM

Shauna took her car to the local car wash. She asked to have it washed and to have the gas tank filled. While it was being washed, Shauna went to get a haircut at the nearby shopping center. In the meantime, one of the workers at the carwash mistook Shauna's car for another he was to wax. Two hours later, when Shauna returned, she was presented with a bill for a full tank of gas, a wash, and a wax. Must she pay for the wax?

◆ **formal contract**
A contract that by law requires a special form or method of creation (formation) to be enforceable.

Clearly, Shauna received a benefit. But she received this benefit because of a mistake by the carwash employee. The benefit was not *unjustly* received under these circumstances. People cannot normally be forced to pay for benefits "thrust" upon them. The cost of the wax is on the carwash.

◆ **contract under seal** A formal contract with a special seal attached.

FORMAL VERSUS INFORMAL CONTRACTS

Formal contracts require a special form or method of creation to be enforceable. An example of a formal contract is a **contract under seal**, which is a contract with a special seal attached. About ten states recognize a contract under seal. These states allow enforcement of the contract under seal though it may lack an important element required in most contracts,

◆ **recognizance**
An acknowledgment by a person in court of a duty to pay a certain sum if a certain event occurs.

Law in Action

Read

Before the students read this *Law in Action* feature, have them look at the title: "Legal Issue: Is an Agreement to Form a Contract a Contract?" Ask students whether or not they believe an agreement to form a contract is a contract. Then have a student volunteer read this *Law in Action* feature aloud to the rest of the class.

Discuss

Stimulate a class discussion of this *Law in Action* feature by asking the following questions: What was Sewell's original claim against W. R. Grace and Co.? At what point was there an agreement to form a contract? What did Sewell do following this agreement to form a contract? At what point did Sewell claim the contract had been breached? Why did the trial court hold that there was no contract? Did Sewell have any legal claim against Grace for the damages caused by the contaminated fertilizer?

Law in Action

LEGAL ISSUE: IS AN AGREEMENT TO FORM A CONTRACT A CONTRACT?

Sometimes parties agree to form a contract at some point in the future. Even if one of the parties assumes that this "agreement to agree" is itself a contract, it is not. A promise to form a future contract is not a contract. Consider, for example, the North Carolina case of *Seawell v. Continental Casualty Company*.

In 1984 Richard Seawell, a farmer, used a fertilizer manufactured by W. R. Grace & Company on his tobacco crop. Grace discovered that some of the fertilizer contained a contaminating chemical. Grace and the company that insured Grace, Continental Casualty Company, began investigating the problem. They settled some claims made against Grace by farmers who used the fertilizer.

Seawell and several other farmers in his area elected a committee to meet with representatives of Grace and Continental Casualty. At the meeting, Grace and Continental agreed to pay the farmers for damaged tobacco according to a certain formula. A decision as to specific damages was to be made at future meetings between the insurance adjusters (persons who settle claims for insurance companies) and the individual farmers. The farmers were assured that they

would not suffer any losses resulting from the use of Grace fertilizer.

After the meeting, an insurance adjuster came to Seawell's farm. He estimated the amount of production and sampled some of Seawell's tobacco. He did not agree at this visit on any specific damage figure to pay Seawell. Seawell harvested his tobacco and sold his crop. He then filed suit against Grace and the insurance company for not settling his claim. He claimed they had breached their "contract."

Did a contract exist? Are all the elements to a contract present? Seawell thought so, and other people in similar situations might agree with him. The trial court held, however, that because no specific damage amounts were determined for each farmer at the meeting, there was no contract. The offer made by Grace and the insurance company was too indefinite in its terms to become a contract. The court concluded that, at best, it was an "agreement to agree." The intention to settle in the future with each farmer on an individual basis was not a contract. Although Seawell did not have a contract, he still had legal claims against Grace for the damages caused by using the contaminated fertilizer.

consideration. (The doctrine of consideration is discussed in Chapter 9.) Another type of formal contract is a recognizance. A **recognizance** is an acknowledgment by a person in court of a duty to pay a certain sum if a certain event occurs. A bail bond in a criminal matter is an example of a recognizance bond. (See the discussion of bail bonds in Chapter 4.)

Informal contracts (also called *simple contracts*) include all other contracts. For most contracts, no special form is required, except that certain types of contracts must be in writing (discussed in Chapter 11).

◆ **informal contract**
A contract that does not require any special form to be valid. Most contracts are informal contracts.

Have your students compare on paper the differences between a void and a voidable contract.

Pair each student with a partner, and ask the pairs to use their own words in defining all of the terms found in this chapter that describe contracts. Have your students also give an example of each term.

Ask your students to work together to make a bulletin board depicting the different types of contracts.

Checking Your Progress (Answers)

1. A unilateral contract exchanges a promise for an act.
2. Yes, an offer can be revoked in a unilateral contract as long as the offeree has not acted, because a contract has not been formed.
3. A party's intent to enter into a contract is judged by outward, objective facts.
4. No, a contract to *form* a future contract is not a contract.
5. A contract is considered executory if the one or both sides have not performed.
6. Yes, a voidable contract is valid; however, one party has the right to revoke or accept the contract without legal penalty.

♦ **executed contract** A contract that has been fully performed by all parties.

♦ **executory contract** A contract that has not been completely performed.

♦ **valid contract** An agreement which includes all the necessary elements to be an enforceable contract.

♦ **void contract** An agreement that cannot be enforced. Not really a contract at all.

♦ **voidable contract** A contract giving one party the right to cancel the contract without legal penalty.

♦ **unenforceable contract** A valid contract that cannot be enforced because of some legal defense.

EXECUTED VERSUS EXECUTORY CONTRACTS

Contracts are also classified according to whether they have been performed. A contract fully performed by all parties is an **executed contract**. A contract that neither party has performed is an **executory contract**. If one party has fully performed but the other has not, the contract is executed on the one side and executory on the other. The contract is considered executory.

VALID, VOID, VOIDABLE, AND UNENFORCEABLE CONTRACTS

A **valid contract** has all the necessary elements of an enforceable contract. Those elements consist of an offer and an acceptance, supported by legally sufficient consideration, for a legal purpose, made by parties who have the legal capacity to enter into the contract. Each element is discussed in detail in the following chapters.

A **void contract** is really not a contract at all. The terms *void* and *contract* are contradictory. A void contract produces no legal obligations for any of the parties. A contract can be void because the purpose of the contract is illegal (for example, most gambling contracts are void for this reason).

A **voidable contract** is a *valid* contract that gives one party the right to revoke or accept rights under the contract without legal penalty. The party can choose to avoid any duty to perform or can choose to *ratify* (make valid) the contract. If the party avoids the contract, both parties are released. If the contract is ratified, both parties must fully perform their legal obligations. Most contracts made by minors are voidable by the minor (see the Legal Perspective feature in Chapter 9). Contracts entered into by fraud are voidable by the misled party. Contracts involving mutual mistake, duress, or undue influence are also voidable (see Chapter 10).

An **unenforceable contract** is a contract that cannot be enforced because of certain legal defenses against it. It is an otherwise valid contract made unenforceable by some statute or law. For example, certain contracts must be in writing to be enforceable, except in certain exceptional circumstances (see Chapter 11).

◆ CHECKING YOUR PROGRESS

1. A bilateral contract involves a promise for a promise. What are the two elements of a unilateral contract?

2. Can an offer be revoked legally in a unilateral contract?

3. How is a party's intent to enter into a contract determined?

4. If another party accepts your offer to form a contract in the future, has a contract been formed?

5. What is the term used to describe a contract in which one or both parties have not performed?

6. Is a voidable contract a valid contract?

Read

You might introduce this *A Case In Point* feature by explaining to students that the case here, *Moore* v. *Kuehn,* illustrates the court's use of the objective theory of contracts. (Remind students that the objective theory of contracts is the theory by which the intent to contract is judged by what a reasonably objective party would believe was meant by a person's language and conduct.) Then ask a student volunteer to read this *A Case In Point* feature to the class.

Discuss

Use the following questions to stimulate a class discussion on this feature: At what point did Moore make an offer to Kuehn? In what form was this offer? What prompted Moore to begin and subsequently complete the repairs suggested in the proposal? Why did the Kuehns claim that no contract was ever formed? What was the court's decision? What reasons did the court give for its decision?

◆ A CASE IN POINT ◆

MOORE v. KUEHN
Missouri Court of Appeals, 1980.
602 S.W.2d 713.

This case illustrates a court's use of the objective theory of contract. The court reviews the conduct of the parties and the circumstances surrounding the transaction to determine whether an express or an implied-in-fact contract existed.

FACTS James and Margaret Kuehn asked George Moore to submit an estimate in writing for work needed to repair a damaged building. Moore submitted a proposal for $7,600, but the Kuehns did not sign it. They informed Moore that they wanted more time to look over the proposal before agreeing to it. James Kuehn, however, told Moore that the roof needed fixing and to "get on it." Moore began and subsequently completed the repairs suggested in the proposal, without objection by the Kuehns. The Kuehns never signed the proposal. When Moore asked for payment, the Kuehns paid Moore only $5,500. Moore sued for the balance—the amount specified in the proposal minus the amount paid—plus payment for some additional work and related court costs. He was awarded $2,531.

The Kuehns appealed, claiming no contract was ever formed.

ISSUE Did a contract exist between Moore and the Kuehns?

DECISION Yes. The appellate court affirmed the judgment of the trial court. It held that under the circumstances, an implied-in-fact contract existed.

REASON The court based its judgment on the objective theory of contract formation. Under this theory, when one party argues that there was no intent to form a contract, the court looks at statements, the conduct of the parties, and all the surrounding circumstances. In this case, the court said that it is clear law that a written offer may be accepted orally. Since Moore's written proposal was the only offer Kuehn could have accepted when he told Moore to "get on it," the terms of the offer controlled (defined the contract), and a contract was established. Further, the Kuehns' silent consent and acceptance of Moore's completion of the other repair work in the proposal was an implied acceptance of the contract as it related to those terms. Since the Kuehns benefitted from Moore's performance, their refusal to sign the proposal did not overcome their implied acceptance of the contract. In fact, they never questioned any of the work and even helped Moore at one point.

Teaching Note

This case is included in the *West's Business and Personal Law Handbook of Selected Court Cases.*

In order to help students review what they have learned in Chapter 7, you might wish to:
1. Have a student volunteer, or volunteers, read aloud the Chapter Summary.
2. Allow the students to work with partners to complete the *Using Legal Language* activity.
3. Assign the *Checking for Comprehension* exercise as homework.
4. Allow the students to work in small groups to complete the *Applying Legal Concepts* activities.
5. As a class, complete the *Applying the Law* activities. (Please note that you may have to help students with vocabulary so that they adequately understand all of the *Applying the Law* material.)

Assessment Strategies

In order to check student mastery of chapter concepts, you may wish to use the Chapter 7 test that is found in your *Teacher's Resource Binder* or use WESTEST computerized testing for Chapter 7.

Using Legal Language (Answers)

1–C, 2–I, 3–G, 4–B, 5–H, 6–J, 7–D, 8–A, 9–F, 10–E

188

Checking for Comprehension (Answers)

1. The basic elements of a contract are agreement, consideration, contractual capacity, legality, genuineness of assent, and form.
2. An express contract is an agreement in which the terms are fully and explicitly stated in oral or written words. An implied contract, however, is formed by the conduct of the parties, rather than their words.
3. A party's intention to enter into a contract is judged by outward, objective facts.
4. No, the agreement is too indefinite to become a contract.
5. No. If one party has fully performed but the other has not—the contract is executed on the one side and executory on the other—the contract is considered executory.
6. One of the parties to a voidable contract may choose not to perform a valid contract, thus making it unenforceable. Statute or law

---

188   The Law of Contracts

CHAPTER 7 REVIEW

 ## SUMMARY

UNIFORM COMMERCIAL CODE

The Uniform Commercial Code has been adopted in part by all fifty states. Article 2 of the code, Sales, modifies rules for contracts involving the sale of goods.

CONTRACT REQUIREMENTS

1. Agreement.
2. Consideration.
3. Contractual capacity.
4. Legality.
5. Genuineness of assent.
6. Form.

CONTRACT FORMATION

1. *Bilateral*—A promise for a promise.
2. *Unilateral*—A promise for an act (acceptance is the completed performance of the act).
3. *Express*—Formed by words (oral, written, or a combination).
4. *Implied in fact*—Formed by the conduct of the parties.

5. *Quasi contract*—Imposed by law to prevent unjust enrichment.
6. *Formal*—Requires a special form for creation.
7. *Informal*—Requires no special form for creation.

CONTRACT PERFORMANCE

1. *Executed*—A fully performed contract.
2. *Executory*—A contract not fully performed.

CONTRACT ENFORCEABILITY

1. *Valid*—A contract that has the necessary contractual elements: offer and acceptance, consideration, parties with legal capacity, and a legal purpose.
2. *Void*—No contract exists, or the contract imposes no legal obligations.
3. *Voidable*—One party has the option of either avoiding or enforcing the contractual obligation.
4. *Unenforceable*—A contract exists, but it cannot be enforced because of a legal defense.

USING LEGAL LANGUAGE

Directions: Match each term with the statement that best defines that term.

1. bilateral contract
2. contract
3. contract under seal
4. executory contract
5. express contract
6. formal contract
7. offeree
8. promisor
9. unilateral contract

A. A _____ is the party to a contract who makes a promise to do something.
B. If a contract has not been fully performed, it is called a (an) _____.
C. Parties enter a _____ if the contract includes a promise in exchange for a promise.
D. There are two parties to a contract, the _____ is the person to whom the offer is made.

7. This is a unilateral offer. To be accepted,
Jennifer's offer requires more than Gordon's
promise to perform; it requires his actual performance. Until Gordon completes the mowing of Jennifer's yard, no contract has been
formed. Important legal points: (1) Since no
contract was formed, Gordon may legally
decide not to mow the lawn. (2) At any time
prior to Gordon's performance, Jennifer can
withdraw her offer. (3) If Gordon had already

started mowing the lawn prior to a withdrawal by Jennifer, courts would differ as to
legal results. Some courts would view the
offer as now irrevocable; others would rule
that such performance was equivalent to a
promise, resulting in a bilateral contract.
Another court might allow Jennifer to withdraw her offer but would reward Gordon the
reasonable value of his partial performance
under the theory of quasi contract. Some
courts would consider the offer revocable

because the requested act
was not completely per-
formed.
8. In the modern view, most
courts would hold that there
was a unilateral contract
formed between McElfresh
and Big Burger, and that Big
Burger could not revoke
once McElfresh started to
perform. Since the terms of
the agreement were fully
and explicitly stated in the
banner, McElfresh and Big
Burger created an express
contract. The contract was
executory until McElfresh
fully performed. The con-
tract could also be classified
as valid, enforceable, and
informal.

Applying the Law . . .
You Be the Judge
(Answers)

1. Engelcke claimed that the
contract was express and
that there was no breach on
Engelcke's part because
Eaton had not delivered a
completed design in accordance with the agreement.
The court ruled the contract
was an implied-in-fact contract and allowed Eaton to
sue for the reasonable value
of his services. There was
mutual agreement for Eaton
to design the game and for
Eaton to perform the service
for Engelcke. Since the
essential terms (price, and
time and manner of performance) were not expressed
in word, either orally or in
writing, the contract was
implied-in-fact.
2. The hospital might recover under contract theory on
the grounds that the law will
imply a contract (a quasi
contract) in this situation.
The court reasoned that a
person who supplies ser-
vices to another without the
other's knowledge or con-

---

10.   void contract

E.   An agreement that cannot be enforced is a
      _____ and is not really a contract at all.

F.   Parties enter a _____ if the contract in-
      cludes a promise for an act.

G.   An example of a formal contract is a
      _____ which is a contract with a special
      seal attached.

H.   A contract that is oral and/or in written
      form is an _____, it is not implied from
      the circumstances.

I.   A _____ is a legally enforceable agree-
      ment to do or not do a specified thing.

J.   A _____ requires a special form or
      method of creation to be enforceable.

◆ CHECKING FOR COMPREHENSION

1.   List the basic elements of a contract.

2.   Explain the difference between express
      and implied contracts.

3.   How is a party's intent to form a contract
      judged?

4.   If two parties agree to meet later this year
      to look over a used car, then exchange an
      undetermined amount of money for the
      car, have they formed a contract by mak-
      ing this agreement?

5.   Can a contract be both executed and ex-
      ecutory at the same time?

6.   Explain the difference between voidable
      and unenforceable contracts.

7.   Jennifer says to her neighbor, Gordon, "If
      you mow my lawn, I'll pay you $25."
      Gordon orally accepts her offer. Is there a

contract? Is it a bilateral or unilateral contract? What is the legal importance of the
distinction?

8.   High-Flying Advertising, Inc. contracted
      with Big Burger Restaurants to fly a ban-
      ner above the Connecticut beaches. The
      banner offered $5,000 to any person who
      could swim from the Connecticut beaches
      to Long Island across Long Island Sound
      in less than a day. McElfresh saw the
      streamer and accepted the challenge. He
      started his marathon swim that same day at
      10 a.m. After he had been swimming for
      four hours and was about halfway across
      the Sound, McElfresh saw another plane
      pulling a banner that read: "Big Burger re-
      vokes." Is there a contract between McEl-
      fresh and Big Burger? If there is a contract,
      what type(s) of contract is (are) formed?

◆ APPLYING LEGAL CONCEPTS

1.   Write each of the following types of con-
      tracts on separate 4 × 6 cards: bilateral
      contract, unilateral contract, express con-
      tract, implied contract, quasi contract, for-
      mal contract, informal contract, executed

contract, executory contract, valid contract, void contract, voidable contract, and
unenforceable contract. On the back of
each card, write an explanation of the
contract named on that card. Work with a

sent is entitled to recover restitution if the services are normally the type that are charged for, if the services were necessary to prevent impending suffering or bodily harm, if it is likely that the person would have consented to them and agreed to pay for them if the person had known about them, and if it is not possible for the person to give actual consent. The rationale for such a rule is quite clear. In an emergency situation, such as exists when a person is in need of medical attention but is unconscious and unable to promise to pay for it, the attention can be provided, and the person rendering the service can be assured of payment. 3. Even though the calendar was mailed in the same envelope, the contract did not make any specific reference to it. The school calendar, therefore, was not a part of the contract. Thus, the district was not obligated to treat as holidays any days which were so specified in the calendar. The days in question are regular school days, requiring teachers and students to attend.

4. Yes and yes. The court ruled that "A contract's essential requirements are: competent parties, valid subject matter, legal consideration, mutuality of obligation, and mutuality of agreement." To be binding, the terms must be "reasonably certain and definite." The contract must be supported by consideration. In addition, the parties must mutually agree to the contract's essential terms and conditions to make the contact binding. Mutual consent is gathered from the language employed by the parties or manifested in their words or actions. In this situation, the school's promise to evaluate the applications according to academic standards is stated in a "definitive manner" in its bulletin. Steinberg accepted this in good faith and paid his $15 application fee, which served as valid consideration. When the school accepted this money, it bound itself to honor the obligations stated in its bulletin. Therefore, its failure to use the stated academic criteria in evaluating applications constituted a breach of its contractual obligation to Steinberg.

partner. Using the cards, one partner read the definition of the term aloud, the other partner tell what type of contract is being described.

2. Working in groups of three or four, read the definition of a contract from the cards prepared in activity 1. Call on someone in the group to give an example of the type of contract being described. Pass the cards to another student to read a definition and call on another to give an example. Continue until all cards have been used.

◆ APPLYING THE LAW . . . YOU BE THE JUDGE

1. Engelcke Manufacturing, Inc., planned to design and manufacture Whizball, an electronic game. Engelcke asked Eaton to design the electronic schematic for it. Engelcke told Eaton he would pay him the reasonable value of his services after the project's completion. No written contract was signed. The specific amount and terms were also not discussed. Eaton had produced a plan that represented 90 percent of the finished design when Engelcke terminated his employment. Eaton sued Engelcke for breach of an implied-in-fact contract. Engelcke claimed that they had an express contract. Why did Engelcke claim an express contract rather than an implied-in-fact contract? [*Eaton v. Engelcke Manufacturing, Inc.*, 37 Wash.App. 677, 681 P.2d 1312 (1984)]

2. Sosa Crisan, an eighty-seven-year-old widow, collapsed while shopping at a local grocery store. The Detroit police took her to the Detroit city hospital. She was admitted, and she remained there fourteen days. Then she was transferred to another hospital, where she died some eleven months later. Crisan had never regained consciousness after her collapse at the grocery store. After she died, Detroit hospital sued her estate to recover the expenses of both the ambulance that took her to the hospital and the expenses of her hospital stay. Is there a contract between Sosa Crisan and the hospital? If so, how much can the Detroit hospital recover? [*In re Estate of Crisan*, 362 Mich. 569, 107 N.W.2d 907 (1961)]

3. Ferguson-Florissant School District mailed a teaching contract to Adamick. Enclosed in the envelope was a copy of the school calendar. Teachers were later required to attend school on dates the calendar showed as holidays. Adamick sued the school district to prevent it from holding classes on those three days. The District argued that the calendar could be changed by the District. Was the school calendar a part of the contract between Adamick and the District? Will the teachers and students be required to attend class? [*Adamick v. Ferguson-Florissant School District* (Mo.App.) 483 S.W.2d 629 (1972)]

4. Steinberg applied to the Chicago Medical School and paid an application fee of $15. The school, a private educational institution, rejected his application. Steinberg sued the school, claiming that it did not evaluate his application according to the academic entrance criteria printed in the school's bulletin. He argued that the school based its decision primarily on non-academic consideration, such as the applicant's family relationship to the school's faculty and members of its board of trustees, and the ability of the applicant or his family to donate large sums of money to the school. Steinberg said the school breached the contract it had created when it accepted his application fee by evaluating his application according to the unpublished non-academic criteria. Was there a contract? Did the school breach? [*Steinberg v. Chicago Medical School*, 41 Ill.App.3d 804, 354 N.E.2d 586 (1976)]

Mastery Objectives

By the end of this chapter, students will be able to:
- Describe offer requirements of a contract
- Explain how contract offers can be terminated
- Illustrate an offer, counteroffer, acceptance
- Explain what constitutes acceptance of a contract
- Identify exceptions to contract offer/acceptance rules

Prereading Activity

Webbing activity: Write the word *contract* on the board. Around it write words from the chapter (such as *offer, acceptance, revocation, agreement, intention,* etc.). Ask students to think about what the words mean to them. Call on students to tell what each word means to them. Explain briefly how each word relates to a contract.

Teaching with Images

Ask students to volunteer responses to the following question: What does this photo of a child with a lemonade stand have to do with offer and acceptance? Allow the students to share their responses.

 LEGAL BACKGROUND

This chapter explains the nature of agreement, which forms the basis of a contract. Through a discussion of offer and acceptance, the chapter helps students begin to understand when and how promises become legally binding. The text also discusses nonoffer situations. The chapter basically diagrams the genesis of a legal obligation from conception to birth. It provides, perhaps for the first time in the text, enough detail to understand the technical requirements of the law. For example, an attempt to create a contract in one way may be a contract, and an attempt to create it somewhat differently may not be a contract. Precision becomes important; form as well as substance is significant.

Offer and Acceptance

Chapter 8

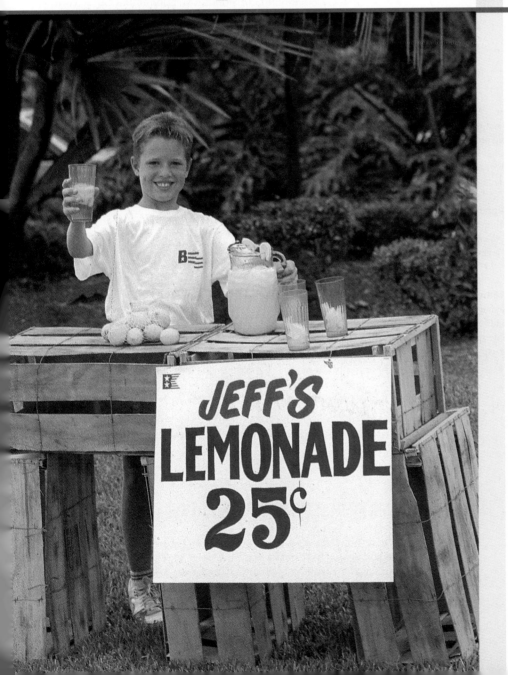

JEFF'S LEMONADE 25¢

Critical Thinking Activity

Guide the students in reading the material under Requirements of the Offer. Make sure that the students understand these three requirements; then ask student volunteers to recall recent business transactions in which they took part that met all three of these requirements.

Reteaching Activity

Have your students write down and explain the three elements that are necessary in order for an offer to be effective.

Legal Focus Problem

Read to the class the Legal Focus Problem found here. Allow student volunteers to suggest possible answers to the problem. Ask the students if they have ever expressed sentiments similar to those expressed by June.

Chapter 8
Resources and Assignment Guide

Activity Sheets
Reviewing Legal Concepts 8 *TRB*
Enrichment Activity 8 *TRB*

Student Activity Workbook
Chapter 8 Activities

Tests
Chapter 8 Test *TRB*
Chapter 8 WESTEST Computerized Testing

Handbook of Selected Court Cases
Peterson v. *Pilgrim Village*
Glover v. *Jewish War Veterans of the United States*

West's Business Law and Legal Environment Videodisc
Still Frames and Motion Segments as shown

"A lean agreement is better than a fat judgment."
Proverb

As we stated in Chapter 7, a valid and enforceable contract meets six requirements: agreement, consideration, contractual capacity, legality, genuineness of assent, and proper form. The nature of agreement is examined in this chapter. The remaining elements are examined in the next three chapters.

AGREEMENT

◆ **offer** A promise to do or not do something proposed as an exchange for a specified act or promise of another.

◆ **acceptance** An act or promise given in response to an offer and showing a desire to contract.

◆ **agreement** An understanding of two or more minds. An enforceable agreement is a contract.

Ordinarily, agreement is shown by an offer and an acceptance. An **offer** is a promise to do or not do something in the future proposed as an exchange for a specified act or promise of another. An **acceptance** is an act or promise given in response to an offer showing a desire to contract. **Agreement** exists when an offer made by one party is accepted by the other. When questions arise as to whether an agreement has been made, the law of contracts generally follows the objective theory of contracts, as discussed in Chapter 7. The objective theory holds that the words and conduct of an offeror mean whatever a reasonable person in the offeree's position would think they mean.

REQUIREMENTS OF THE OFFER

As discussed in Chapter 7, the parties to a contract are the *offeror* and the *offeree*. Three elements are necessary for an offer to be effective:

1. There must be a *serious, objective intention* by the offeror.
2. The terms of the offer must be reasonably *definite*.
3. The offer must be *communicated* to the offeree.

Once an effective offer is made, the offeree has the power to accept it. If the offeree accepts, a contract results, as long as the other essential elements are present.

INTENT

 LEGAL FOCUS ~ PROBLEM

Adam and three classmates ride to school each day in June's new automobile. The car has a market value of $8,000. One cold morning, just after everyone got into the car, June's car would not start. She yelled in anger, "I'll sell this car to anyone for $20!" Adam dropped the $20 in her lap. Does Adam, the offeree, have a contract with June and a right to the car? Did June, the offeror, intend to create a contract?

One of the elements necessary in order for an offer to be effective is that the offer must be *communicated* to the offeree. Ask students to list ways in which oral and written communication takes place in business today. Encourage them to include technological methods such as fax and computer transmission via modem.

Divide the class into small groups to read and discuss the Legal Focus Case Problem found here. Have each group diagram this Legal Focus Case Problem, pointing out where it does, and does not, meet the three requirements of the offer.

Have students work with partners to list and explain the elements of intention.

Legal Focus Problem

Read to the class the Legal Focus Problem found here. Allow the student volunteers to suggest possible answers to the question posed at the end of this problem.

Teaching with the Videodisc

The still frames listed below from the **West's Business Law and Legal Environment Videodisc** can be used with this chapter. To access this material, use the bar codes or the frame numbers included in the Videodisc Instructor's Manual found in the *TRB*.

Agreement
Agreement: Offer
Agreement: Acceptance
Timing Rules on Offer
  and Acceptance

The first requirement of an effective offer is a serious, objective intention to contract on the part of the offeror. The offeror's intent is not decided by his or her undisclosed *personal* intentions. Intent is determined by what a reasonable person in the offeree's position would think was meant by the offeror's words and actions. Offers obviously made in anger, in excitement, or as a joke do not meet the objective intent test. Since these offers are not effective, an offeree's acceptance does not create an agreement.

In our example, a reasonable person would be aware of June's frustration. The obvious difference in value between the car's market price and the $20 mentioned in June's offer would show the offeree that her offer was not serious. Since the offer lacked objective intent, Adam did not create a contract when he tried to accept.

The following examples explain common situations in which there is no offer because there was no intent to contract.

1. **Expressions of Opinion**.

LEGAL FOCUS ~ CASE PROBLEM

Hawkins took his son to McGee, a doctor. Hawkins asked McGee to operate on the son's hand. McGee stated that the boy would be in the hospital three or four days and that the hand would *probably* heal a few days later. McGee performed the surgery, but the son's hand did not heal for a month. Hawkins sued McGee, claiming that the doctor had made an offer that included terms guaranteeing that the hand would heal in a few days. Did Hawkins win the lawsuit?[1]

An expression of opinion is not an offer. It does not show an intention to enter a binding agreement. In this case, the court held that McGee did not make an offer to heal the son's hand in three or four days. The doctor merely expressed an opinion as to when the hand would heal.

2. **Statements of Intention**.

LEGAL FOCUS ~ PROBLEM

Joanne said, "I *plan* to sell my five shares of stock in Novation, Inc., for $150 each." John replied, "I'll buy them" and held out $750—$150 for each share of her stock. Is there a contract?

No. Joanne merely expressed her intention to enter into a contract in the future. She did not say she wanted a contract now. Even though John tried to accept, no contract was formed. A reasonable person

1. *Hawkins v. McGee*, 84 N.H. 114, 146 A. 641 (1929).

Have your students bring in an ad from the local newspaper that expresses an offer. Ask them to highlight the part of the ad that they believe expresses the offer.

Legal Focus Problem

Read to the class the Legal Focus Problem found here regarding Tartop & Company. Remind students that they can use the Legal Focus features as review tools when studying for tests.

Read to the class this Legal Focus Example regarding a classified advertisement. Ask the class if they can think of any other examples that could also fit here. Allow students to share their examples with the class.

would conclude that Joanne was only *thinking about* selling her stock, not promising to sell.

3. **Preliminary Negotiations**. A request or invitation to negotiate is not an offer. Such language only expresses a willingness to discuss the chance of entering into a contract. Examples are statements such as "Will you sell Forest Acres?" or "I wouldn't sell my car for less than $1,000." A reasonable person in the offeree's position knows that these statements do not show an intent to contract. Similarly, when the government needs construction work done, contractors are invited to submit bids. The *invitation* to submit bids is not an offer. The contractor does not bind the government by submitting a bid. The bids that the contractors submit are *offers*. The government can bind the contractor by accepting the bid.

4. **Advertisements, Catalogs, and Circulars**. In general, mail-order catalogs, price lists, and circular letters meant for the public are treated not as offers to contract but as invitations to negotiate.

◀ LEGAL FOCUS ~ PROBLEM

Tartop & Company advertised a used paving machine. The ad, which was mailed to hundreds of firms, read: "Used paving machine. Builds curbs and finishes cement work all in one process. Price $11,250." General Paving, Inc., called Tartop and said, "We accept your offer." Is a contract formed?

No. A reasonable person would conclude that Tartop was not promising to sell the paving machine. Instead, Tartop was seeking offers to buy it. A seller never has an unlimited supply of goods. If advertisements were offers, then everyone who "accepted" after the seller's supply was gone could claim a contract right.

◀ LEGAL FOCUS ~ EXAMPLE

You put an ad in the classified section of your local newspaper offering to sell your guitar for $75. Seven people call and "accept" your "offer" before you can remove the ad from the newspaper. If the ad were truly an offer, you would be bound by seven contracts to sell your guitar. But since *initial* advertisements are treated as *invitations* to make offers rather than offers, you have seven offers to choose from. You can accept the best one without assuming any liability for the six you reject.

Collaborative Learning Activity

Divide the class into three or four small groups. Have each group create and act out at least three offer situations. In these offer situations one should meet the three requirements of an offer and two should be somehow lacking one of these three requirements. As each group acts out its offer situations, have student volunteers describe how each offer situation does or does not meet the requirements.

Enrichment

Have a group of students research auction procedures. Have them role play the parts of an auctioneer and customers and conduct a mock auction, auctioning articles in the classroom.

Reteaching Activity

Have your students read the section in this chapter titled Definiteness. Have them write an explanation of what it means. Have students cite examples with the definitions.

Caption Answer

Students should understand that generally speaking, it is the purchaser or customer who makes the offer at a garage sale.

Businesses often use price lists and catalogs to sell their products. These lists, like advertisements, are invitations to negotiate or trade. A seller's price list is not an offer to sell at that price. The list merely invites the buyer to offer to buy at that price. In fact, the seller usually prints "prices subject to change" on the price list. There are exceptional occasions, however, when an advertisement or a price quotation contains such definite terms that it can be interpreted as an offer. This chapter's Law in Action feature is an example of such a situation.

5. **Other Nonoffer Situations**. An agreement to agree or form a contract in the future is not an offer because too many terms are indefinite. Another nonoffer situation is an auction. Although the auctioneer appears to be "offering" goods for sale on behalf of a seller, the bidder is the one who makes the offer. The auctioneer accepts the bid and completes the contract by knocking the hammer. A bidder can take back an offer while the auctioneer calls "going once, going twice, third and last call." If the bid is not withdrawn and the hammer falls, the contract is formed.

DEFINITENESS

The second requirement for an effective offer is that the terms must be reasonably definite so a court can determine if the parties have performed the contract. The *terms* of a contract are the promises, conditions, and descriptions it includes. Among the important terms in a contract are the contract's subject matter (its main topic), the parties to the contract, the price to be exchanged for the subject matter, and the time for performance. All these must be identified reasonably definitely.

Who makes the offer at a garage sale? Is it the seller or the customer?

Read

You might want to prepare students to read this *Law in Action* feature by asking them to find and copy and/or clip advertisements from a local newspaper that include specific prices for specific products. Have the students bring these to class. Allow the students to share some of their advertisements, then have a student volunteer read this *Law in Action* feature aloud to the class.

Discuss

Stimulate a class discussion of this feature by asking the following questions: In this case, who was the *offeror?* Who was *offeree?* Why did Lefkowitz sue the Great Minneapolis Surplus Store, Inc.? On what grounds did the store appeal the decision of the trial court? What was the decision of the appellate court? What reasons did the appellate court give for this decision?

Enrichment

Have students again share with the class the advertisements they have copied and/or clipped. As each student shares his or her advertisement, allow the other students to explain whether or not this ad is similar to the ad run by the Great Minneapolis Surplus Store and, therefore, constitutes an offer.

Extension Activity

Ask volunteers to investigate Federal Trade Commission rules that prohibit deceptive advertising and summarize their findings in a one-page written report.

◆ Law in Action

LEGAL ISSUE: WHEN IS AN AD AN OFFER?

Although most advertisements are treated as invitations to negotiate, an advertisement can be an offer under unusual circumstances. If an ad makes a promise definite enough, then it can be an offer. That was the situation in *Lefkowitz v. Great Minneapolis Surplus Store, Inc.,*[2] a case brought before the Supreme Court of Minnesota in 1957. A lawsuit was filed after a merchant refused to sell to a customer a fur stole for $1, as promised in a newspaper advertisement.

The customer, Lefkowitz, read the following ad on April 13, 1956, in a Minneapolis newspaper:

> "Saturday 9 A.M.
> 2 Brand New Pastel
> Mink 3-Skin Scarfs
> Selling for $89.50
> Out they go
> Saturday. Each . . . $1.00
> 1 Black Lapin Stole
> Beautiful,
> worth $139.50 . . . $1.00
> First Come
> First Served"

Lefkowitz was the first customer to appear at the counter on the Saturday morning of the sale. He was told that because of a "house rule," the offer was intended only for women. As a man, he could not make the purchase.

2.   251 Minn. 188, 86 N.W.2d 689 (1957).

Lefkowitz sued the store for breach of contract and won. The store appealed the decision, contending that no contract existed because no offer had been made. The store argued that the advertisement was solely an invitation to customers to offer to buy goods on the advertised terms. When a customer made an offer, it could be accepted or rejected by the store.

The appellate court held for Lefkowitz. "[W]here the offer is clear, definite, and explicit, and leaves nothing open for negotiation, it constitutes an offer, acceptance of which will complete the contract. . . . We are of the view on the facts before us that the offer by the defendant of the sale of the Lapin fur was clear, definite, and explicit, and left nothing open for negotiation." The plaintiff appeared at the seller's place of business first, as requested by the advertisement. He offered the purchase price of the article and was entitled to performance on the part of the store. As to the "house rule," the court concluded that the store did "not have the right, after acceptance, to impose new or arbitrary conditions not contained in the published offer."

The advertisement in this case was held sufficiently definite to create an offer. The quantity was specified (one fur stole), as was the price ($1), the value ($139.50), and the person who could accept (first come, first served). (*Note:* Today the store could have been charged with violating Federal Trade Commission rules that prohibit deceptive advertising.)

◆ LEGAL FOCUS ~ PROBLEM

Lea Wadman took her car to Mark Podorkowski's Auto Repair. She told Mark she wanted him to repair her leaking radiator. She was willing to pay $125 and needed the car by the next day. Mark told Lea he would repair the car as stated in her offer. Lea signed a work invoice that restated the contract terms, then told Mark she would see him the next day. What are the important terms of this contract?

The subject matter of the contract is the repair of Lea's car radiator. The parties are Lea and Mark. The price to repair the radiator is $125. The time for performance is by the next day. The contract appears very clear and specific. Some vagueness does exist, however. How is the $125 to be paid—in cash, by check, through trade of property, or by credit card? Without a further understanding between the parties, the court would require payment in cash. At what time tomorrow should performance be complete—noon, 5 P.M., before midnight, or some other time? The court would no doubt hold that the end of the usual work day (probably 5 P.M.) is the appropriate time. Though the contract is not totally clear as to terms, the offer is sufficiently definite to be considered a contract.

Offers often invite an acceptance that makes the contract definite.

◆ LEGAL FOCUS ~ EXAMPLE

Marcus Business Machines contacts your school and offers to sell "from one to ten MacCool copying machines for $1,600 each; state number desired in acceptance." The school agrees to buy two copiers. Since quantity is specified in the acceptance, the contract is enforceable because the terms are definite.

Definiteness of terms is an area in which the UCC changes the law for contracts involving a sale of goods. Sales contracts need not be as definite as other contracts. The Uniform Commercial Code contains several "gap-filling" provisions. When it is clear that parties intended to create a contract, but some terms are not specified, the courts will fill in gaps with "reasonable" terms. For instance, if the place of delivery is left out of a contract, the place of delivery is the seller's place. If the price is omitted, the price is a reasonable market price. The term *reasonable* appears again and again in the UCC.

COMMUNICATION

A third requirement for an effective offer is communication of the offer to the offeree.

Ask a student volunteer to read this Legal Focus Problem aloud to the class. Allow a volunteer to answer the question posed at the end of this case problem. Ask the volunteer whether he or she feels that Glover was rightfully, ethically owed the reward.

Guide the students in regarding the Legal Focus Problem at the top of this page. Did Mrs. Glover do the right thing by giving information to the police that led to the arrest and conviction of the murderers of Maurice L. Bernstein? Are her actions more or less com-

mendable in light of the fact that she did not know there was a reward? Does she deserve the reward regardless of whether or not she knew that a reward existed? If you were a member of the Jewish War Veterans, what action would you recommend? Why?

Teaching Note

This case *(Glover v. Jewish War Veterans of the United States)* is included in the *West's Business and Personal Law Handbook of Selected Court Cases.*

Caption Answer

Usually, advertisements are invitations to negotiate or trade and do not constitute an offer.

Vocabulary Activity

Have students compare the use of the word *revocation* here to the use of *revocable* and *irrevocable* in Chapter 7 when dealing with contracts. Make sure that students understand the similarities and differences that exist between these two contexts.

198

---

198   The Law of Contracts

Do advertisements qualify as a communication of an offer?

◇ LEGAL FOCUS ~ CASE PROBLEM

The Jewish War Veterans of the United States placed an ad in a newspaper offering a reward of $500 "to the person or persons furnishing information resulting in the apprehension and conviction of the persons guilty of the murder of Maurice L. Bernstein." Mrs. Glover gave police information that led to the arrest and conviction of the murderers. She, however, did not know that a reward had been offered. She did not learn of the reward until several days after she had given her information. Does a contract between Mrs. Glover and the Jewish War Veterans exist?[3]

No contract exists. Mrs. Glover's act was not an acceptance, because her act was not in response to the offer. To accept an offer and create a contract, the offeree must know of the existence of the offer.

A few states would allow Mrs. Glover to recover the reward, not on contract principles but as a matter of public policy. These states believe it unfair to deny someone a reward because of their lack of knowledge of an offer. Many rewards offered by government do not require people to know about the reward to be able to collect it.

◆ TERMINATION OF THE OFFER

The communication of an effective offer to an offeree gives the offeree power to create a binding, legal obligation—a contract. This power of acceptance, however, does not continue forever. It can be terminated by action of the parties or by operation of law.

TERMINATION BY ACTION OF THE PARTIES

An offer may be terminated by the action of the parties in any of three ways: revocation of the offer, rejection of the offer by the offeree, or counteroffer by the offeree.

◆ **revocation** The withdrawal of an offer by the offeror.

Revocation of the Offer **Revocation** is the withdrawal of the offer by the offeror. Except under certain limited circumstances, the offeror usually can revoke the offer. *This is true even if he or she promised to keep the offer open.* The revocation is effective only if it is communicated to the offeree before the offeree accepts the offer. The offeror can revoke the offer by expressly taking it back (such as by saying "I withdraw my previous offer of October 17"). The offeror can also revoke the offer through certain behavior.

---

3. *Glover v. Jewish War Veterans of the United States, Post No. 58*, 68 A.2d 233 (1949).

Multicultural

Perspectives

The intricacies of offer and acceptance may be even more important in those lands where bartering is still a mainstay of the economy. Have students research the use of bartering in other lands and present to the class a short oral report on the bartering patterns of a specific land. If possible, this report should include information on what constitutes offer and acceptance in barter situations.

 LEGAL FOCUS ~ PROBLEM

Serafine offers to sell her trail bike to Gary. Before Gary accepts the offer, he learns from a friend that Serafine has sold it to JaMon. Can Gary still accept the offer?

No. Serafine's sale of the bike to JaMon is inconsistent with the continued existence of her offer to Gary. Thus, the offer to Gary is revoked. An offer is revoked when the offeror acts in a way that is inconsistent with the offer and the offeree learns of it. Even though Gary learned of the sale through a third party, it effectively revokes Serafine's offer to sell the bike to him.

Most states hold that a revocation is effective when the offeree or the offeree's agent actually receives it. (An *agent* of the offeree is someone the offeree has given the power to act on the offeree's behalf—for example, a purchasing clerk in a business.) Therefore, a letter of revocation mailed on April 1 and delivered at the offeree's residence or place of business on April 3 becomes effective on April 3.

An offer made to the public can be revoked in the same way it was originally made.

 LEGAL FOCUS ~ EXAMPLE

A department store offers a $10,000 reward to anyone giving information leading to the apprehension of the persons who burglarized the store. The offer is published in three local papers and four papers in neighboring communities. To revoke the offer, the store can publish the revocation in all seven papers for the same number of days it published the offer. The revocation is then available to the general public, even if some particular offeree is unaware of it.

Although most offers are revocable, some can be made irrevocable—that is, they cannot be revoked. Certain offers made by merchants under the UCC may be irrevocable. These offers, called **firm offers**, are offers for the sale of goods made in writing and signed by the merchant. Firm offers are binding for the time stated, up to three months.

Another form of irrevocable offer is an **option contract**, often used in the negotiation of real estate sales. An enforceable option is really part of two separate, related contracts. One contract is an agreement that gives the offeree a fixed time to accept the offer in the second contract. During this period, the offeror does not have the legal right to revoke. The offeree pays the offeror something of value to create the option contract.

◆ **firm offer** An offer for the sale of goods made in writing and signed by a merchant. The UCC provides that a firm offer is binding for the time stated, up to three months.

◆ **option contract** An agreement whose subject matter is the right to buy or sell something at a certain price at a certain time.

199

Legal Focus Example

Read this first Legal Focus Example to the class. Ask the class if they can think of any other examples of option contracts that could also fit here. Allow volunteers to share their examples with the class.

Legal Focus Example

Allow a student volunteer to read this Legal Focus Example aloud to the class. Ask the student to describe each of the ways that Healthy Soup Company can reject the offer.

Ethical Concern

Have your students read the Legal Focus Example about Carrie's baseball card collection. Ask them to discuss the ethics of Jamie getting his $10 back. Explain that the $10 was the consideration to the contract to keep the offer exclusively open to Jamie.

 LEGAL FOCUS ~ EXAMPLE

Carrie offers to sell Jamie her baseball card collection for $350. Jamie tells Carrie that he really wants to buy the collection but that it will take him some time to earn the money. Carrie tells Jamie, "I'll sell it to Don, then." Jamie replies, "I will pay you $10 right now if you promise to keep the offer open for two weeks." Carrie agrees and takes Jamie's $10.

This is an example of an option contract. The option contract keeps the offer open for the two weeks. Carrie cannot revoke for that period. In that two-week time, Jamie can decide whether he wishes to buy the baseball card collection for the $350. The purchase of the baseball card collection will still not occur if Jamie decides he doesn't want it or he cannot raise the $350 to buy it.

If Jamie decides not to buy the collection, does he get his $10 back? No. He paid that sum and received what he bargained for, the absolute right to purchase the collection during the agreed period.

Carrie could return the money, but it does not make sense for her to do so. For example, what if the value of the cards increased to $1,000 in the two-week period? Jamie could buy the cards for $350 and make a fast profit, and Carrie would be out of luck.

Rejection of the Offer by the Offeree   An offer may be rejected by the offeree. The offer is then terminated. Any later attempt by the offeree to accept is a new offer. A new offer gives the original offeror (now the offeree) the power of acceptance.

A rejection is ordinarily accomplished by words or conduct that show an intent to say no to the offer. As with revocation, rejection of an offer is effective only when it is actually received by the offeror or the offeror's agent.

 LEGAL FOCUS ~ EXAMPLE

Growgood Farms mails a letter to Healthy Soup Company offering to sell carrots at 10 cents a pound. Healthy Soup Company can reject the offer by writing or telephoning Healthy Farms and expressly rejecting the offer. Or Healthy can offer to buy the carrots at 8 cents per pound (a counteroffer); by doing this, it rejects the original offer.

Merely asking about the offer is not a rejection. Suppose a friend offers to buy your stereo for $50 and you respond, "Is this your best offer?" or "Will you pay me $75 for it?" A reasonable conclusion is that you did not reject the offer but merely inquired about it. You can still accept and bind your friend to the $50 purchase price.

Counteroffer by the Offeree

 LEGAL FOCUS ~ PROBLEM

Burke offers to sell his home to Lang for $170,000. Lang responds, "Your price is too high. I'll pay $165,000." Is Lang's response a counteroffer?

A **counteroffer** is a rejection of the original offer together with a new offer. Lang's response is a counteroffer; it terminates Burke's offer to sell at $170,000 and creates a new offer by Lang to purchase the house at $165,000. This situation reflects a common law rule called the **mirror-image rule**. The rule requires that the offeree's acceptance match the offeror's offer exactly—a mirror of the offer. If the acceptance contains any material change or addition to the terms of the original offer, it is a counteroffer, and not an acceptance. The original offeror can accept the terms of the counteroffer and create a valid contract.

The mirror-image rule has caused many problems in commercial transactions. This is particularly true in contracts involving the sale of goods. In such contracts, the seller and buyer often use different standardized purchase forms. Seldom do the terms of these purchase forms match each other exactly. This fact is generally not noticed until difficulties occur. To deal with the problems, the UCC modified the mirror-image rule for sale-of-goods transactions. The UCC allows a contract to be formed if the offeree shows an intent to create a contract, though the attempt would be a counteroffer at common law. The differences in terms are resolved according to rules in the UCC.

◆ **counteroffer** A rejection of the original offer together with a new offer.

◆ **mirror-image rule** Rule requiring that an offeree's attempted acceptance match the terms of an offer exactly in order for a contract to be formed. If it does not match the offer exactly, it is considered an implied rejection and a counteroffer.

TERMINATION BY OPERATION OF THE LAW

The offeree's power to create a binding contract is terminated by the operation of the law if any of the following conditions occur.

1. **Lapse of time**. An offer ends automatically by law when the time stated in the offer passes. For example, suppose Jane offers to sell her boat to Jonah if he accepts within twenty days. Jonah must accept within the twenty-day period or the offer will lapse, or end. The time stated in an offer normally begins to run when the offer is actually received by the offeree. If no time for acceptance is stated in the offer, the offer ends after a *reasonable* time. What is a reasonable period? It depends on the subject matter of the contract, business and market conditions, and other important circumstances. An offer to sell fresh fruit will end sooner than an offer to sell farm equipment. Fresh fruit is

Divide the class into groups of two or three, and have them write a summary of the different ways to terminate an offer.

Divide the class into four groups. Have each group write up its own Legal Focus Example for these four conditions under which termination by operation of the law can occur.

Extension Activity

Have a volunteer find out what the legal maximum interest rates are in your state.

Caption Answer

An offer automatically ends if the specific subject matter of the offer (in this case the house) is destroyed before the offer is accepted.

perishable and subject to greater fluctuations in market value than farm equipment.

2. **Destruction of the subject matter**. An offer automatically ends if the *specific* subject matter of the offer is destroyed before the offer is accepted. For example, if Lisa Bekins offers to sell her cow to Christopher Yatsen, but the cow dies before Christopher can accept, the offer is automatically terminated.

3. **Death or incompetence of the offeror or offeree**. An offeree's power of acceptance ends when the offeror or offeree dies. An offer also ends if either party loses the legal capacity to create the proposed contract. For example, a party who has been injured in an automobile accident and is in a coma has lost the legal capacity to form a contract.

4. **Illegality of the proposed contract**. A statute or court decision that makes an offer illegal automatically terminates the offer. If Sue offers to lend Jack $20,000 at 15 percent annually, and a statute prohibiting loans at interest rates greater than 14 percent is passed before Jack can accept, the offer is automatically terminated.

If a buyer made an offer to purchase a house, what is the effect on the offer if a fire destroys the house?

1. An agreement exists and is complete when an offer is made by one party and is accepted by the other.
2. The language in a request to negotiate only expresses a willingness to discuss the chance of entering into a contract.
3. No. If the exact manner of payment is not specifically stated in a contract, the court would require payment in cash.
4. The offeror must communicate the revocation to the offeree before the offeree accepts the offer.
5. The common law mirror-image rule requires that the offeree's acceptance match the offeror's offer exactly. Since businesses often use standardized purchase forms that do not match, the UCC allows a contract to be formed if the offeree shows an intent to create a contract.

 # CHECKING YOUR PROGRESS

1. When is an agreement complete?
2. Why is a request to negotiate not an offer?
3. When two parties form a contract for payment for work done, such as repairs to equipment, must the manner of payment be specifically stated?
4. What must an offeror do if he or she wants to revoke the offer?
5. What problem is created by the mirror-image rule, and how is it solved in the UCC?

◆ ACCEPTANCE

Acceptance is a voluntary act by the offeree that shows assent, or agreement, to the terms of an offer. Acceptance may be expressed through either words or conduct. Acceptance must be unequivocal, or absolute, and must be communicated to the offeror.

WHO CAN ACCEPT?

 LEGAL FOCUS – PROBLEM

Jean makes an offer to Paul. Paul is not interested, but Paul's friend José, accepts the offer. Is a contract formed?

No. Only the offeree can accept the offer. A third person cannot substitute for the offeree and accept the offer. After all, the identity of the offeree is as much a part of the offer as any other term.

UNEQUIVOCAL ACCEPTANCE

To exercise the power of acceptance, the offeree must accept unequivocally—that is, absolutely. This is the mirror-image rule discussed before. If the acceptance gives new conditions or materially changes the original offer, the acceptance is a counteroffer rejecting the original offer. An acceptance may, however, be a "grumbling acceptance" expressing some dissatisfaction with the contract. For example, "I accept the offer, but I wish I could have gotten a better price" is an effective acceptance. So, too, is "I accept, but can you shave the price?" On the other hand, the statement "I accept the offer, but only if I can pay on ninety days' credit" is a counteroffer, not an acceptance.

Legal Focus Problem

Read to the class the Legal Focus Problem found here. Allow student volunteers to suggest possible answers to the problem.

SILENCE AS ACCEPTANCE

Ordinarily, silence is not acceptance, even if the offeror states, "By your silence and inaction you will be deemed to have accepted this offer." This general rule applies because an offeree should not have the responsibility of doing something actively to reject an offer.

Sometimes, though, the offeree does have a duty to speak. Silence is acceptance when an offeree takes a benefit offered when he or she had a reasonable opportunity to reject it. The offeree must know the benefit was offered with the expectation of payment.

 LEGAL FOCUS ~ PROBLEM

Jewel Jameson watched while a stranger mowed her lawn. The stranger wore a T-shirt that identified him as an employee of Lawnsharp Mowing Service. Jewel had not asked the stranger to mow the lawn. It turned out that he had come to the wrong address. Is Jewel liable for the reasonable value of the lawn-mowing job? Did she have a duty to speak?

The answer to both questions is yes. Here, Jewel's silence is an acceptance, and an implied-in-fact contract is created. Jewel must pay a reasonable amount for the stranger's work. This rule normally applies only when the offeree has received a beneficial good or service.

Sometimes the terms of a prior contract require a person to notify a seller that he or she does not wish to buy certain goods. In this case, a failure to act is acceptance. Many record, tape, and book clubs use contracts, agreed to by offerees, requiring offerees to notify the company when they do not want a product.

Silence can also be acceptance when the offeree has had prior dealings with the offeror. In business situations, sellers and buyers often have routine contracts where they buy and sell goods to one another over time. Certain ways of behaving can become part of a contract because of these prior dealings.

 LEGAL FOCUS ~ EXAMPLE

Huggy Bear Grocery Store routinely gets shipments of strawberries from Farm Fresh, a wholesale produce supplier, at the beginning of each strawberry season. The arrangement has existed for over ten years. Huggy Bear always notifies Farm Fresh before the season if they do not wish any strawberries to be shipped. Huggy Bear's failure to notify Farm Fresh before shipment (Huggy Bear's silence) would create a contract for a usual shipment of strawberries.

COMMUNICATION OF ACCEPTANCE

Must the offeree notify the offeror of acceptance? The answer depends on the nature of the contract. In a unilateral contract, the full performance of some act is acceptance. Acceptance is usually obvious, and notification is unnecessary. Exceptions do exist, such as when the offeror requests notice of acceptance. Also, if the offeror has no adequate means of finding out that the requested act has been performed, notice must be given.

In a bilateral contract, *communication*, or notification of acceptance, is necessary. The contract is formed when the promise is made (rather than when the act is performed). The offeree must use reasonable efforts to communicate the acceptance to the offeror. Communication of acceptance is not necessary, however, if the offer does not require it. Furthermore, if the offer can be accepted by silence (an exceptional situation), no communication is necessary.

MANNER AND TIMELINESS OF ACCEPTANCE

An acceptance must be timely. That is, it must be given before the offer is terminated or revoked. Problems arise when the parties are not dealing face to face but are using the mail, telephone, fax, or other means of long-distance communication. In such cases, the offeree may use an authorized manner of communication—that is, a manner of communication approved by the offeror. The general legal rule is that a manner of communication is authorized if it is the same one the offeror used or one that is quicker.

Acceptance takes effect, and the contract is formed, at the time the communication is sent by authorized manner. This principle is often called the **mailbox rule**. Under this rule, if the authorized manner of communication is by mail, acceptance is valid when the communication is put in a mailbox—not when it is received by the offeror. The mailbox rule tries to prevent the confusion that occurs when an offeror sends a letter of revocation, but the offeree sends a letter of acceptance before receiving the revocation. Remember, a letter of revocation is not effective until it is *received* by the offeree.

◆ **mailbox rule**
Rule providing that an acceptance is effective when it is sent by an authorized manner (for example, placed in a mailbox).

◆ LEGAL FOCUS - PROBLEM

On Saturday, Arthur mailed Jane an offer to sell her his car for $1,000. On Monday, Arthur changed his mind. Not having heard from Jane, he sent her a letter revoking his offer. On Wednesday, before she had received Arthur's letter of revocation, Jane mailed a letter of acceptance to Arthur. Later, Jane demanded that Arthur sell his car to her as promised, but Arthur claimed that no contract existed because he had revoked his offer prior to Jane's acceptance. Is Arthur correct?

Checking Your Progress (Answers)

1. No. Only the offeree can accept the offer.
2. No. The offeree must accept unequivocally.
3. Communication of acceptance is required in a bilateral contract, but it is generally not required in a unilateral contract.
4. If an offer is made by mail, an acceptance of that offer is effective when sent if it is returned by mail or some faster means.

Extension Activity

Have each student bring a contract to class. It may be formal or informal. Ask them to highlight the offer and the acceptance. Make a display of the contracts so that all of the students may see them.

Collaborative Learning Activity

Divide your class into groups of three or four. Have each group study a topic in this chapter and then summarize it orally for the class. Each group may select a chairperson to do the speaking. Use the following as topics: Intention, Definiteness, Communication, Termination by Action of the Parties, Termination by Operation of the Law, Acceptance, and Communication of Acceptance.

No. For a revocation to be effective, it must be received by the offeree before he or she has accepted the offer. Jane sent her acceptance by an authorized means (the same means used by Arthur) before she received or was aware of the attempted revocation of the offer. Because of the mailbox rule, the acceptance was good when sent.

When an offeror specifies how acceptance should be made (for example, by first-class mail or telegram), the contract is not formed unless the offeree uses that means of acceptance.

There are three basic exceptions to the rule that a contract is formed when acceptance is sent by authorized means:

1. If an acceptance is improperly sent, it is generally not effective until received by the offeror. Examples include a letter incorrectly addressed or sent without the proper postage.
2. The offeror can specifically require that an acceptance be received by the offeror by a certain time. For example, John says in an offer to sell his car for $500 to Paula, that Paula's acceptance must be received by John, at his home, before April 8.
3. Sometimes, an offeree sends a rejection first, then later changes his or her mind and sends an acceptance. This chain of events could cause confusion. In such cases, the law cancels the mailbox rule. The first communication to be received by the offeror determines whether a contract is formed. If the rejection comes first, there is no contract.

◆ CHECKING YOUR PROGRESS

1. Can a contract be formed if the original offeree declines, but someone else decides to accept the offer?
2. Is a contract fulfilled if an offeree accepts part of the offer and rejects the rest?
3. Is communication of acceptance required in a unilateral contract? in a bilateral contract?
4. Explain the mailbox rule.

Read

Introduce this *A Case In Point* feature by explaining to students that this deals with the enforceability of a contract that calls for the plaintiff (Petersen) to receive a salary plus a share of the profits. Make sure that all of your students understand the meanings of the terms *salary* and *profits* before you continue.

Then allow a student volunteer to read this case aloud to the class.

Discuss

Stimulate a class discussion of this case by asking the following questions: Why did Petersen sue Pilgrim Village? What was the decision of the court? What reasons did the court give for its decision?

Offer and Acceptance 207

◆ A CASE IN POINT ◆

PETERSEN v. PILGRIM VILLAGE
Supreme Court of Wisconsin, 1950.
256 Wis. 621,
42 N.W.2d 273.

Is a contract that provides for a salary plus "a share of the profits" too unclear to enforce? This case tells the plight of a plaintiff, Victor Petersen, who worked first as a construction supervisor and then as a manager for the defendant company.

FACTS Pilgrim Village employed Petersen under a contract providing a stated salary. Petersen claimed that Pilgrim had told him when he began working that he would share in the profits of the corporation. He claimed that Pilgrim repeatedly promised him he would be paid these profits. Petersen

and Pilgrim, however, never came to any definite agreement as to an appropriate percentage of the profits. When Petersen left Pilgrim's employ, Pilgrim refused to pay Petersen any share of the profits.

ISSUE Did Pilgrim have a contractual duty to pay Petersen a percentage of the profits?

DECISION No. Pilgrim had no contractual duty to pay Petersen any percentage of the company's profits because no contract about profits was ever formed.

REASON Pilgrim's offer was too indefinite for a court to decide its terms with any reasonable degree of certainty. The court held, "An offer must be so definite in its terms, or require such definite terms in the acceptance, that the promises and performances to be rendered by each party are reasonably certain."

CHAPTER REVIEW
8

 ## SUMMARY

OFFER—REQUIREMENTS

1. *Intent*—There must be a serious, objective intention by the offeror to contract. Nonoffer situations include (a) expressions of opinion, (b) statements of intention, (c) preliminary negotiations, and (d) generally, advertisements, catalogs, and circulars.

2. *Definiteness*—The terms of the offer must be sufficiently definite to allow enforcement by a court.

3. *Communication*—The offer must be communicated to the offeree.

OFFER—TERMINATION

1. *By action of the parties*

   a. Revocation—Except in certain circumstances, the offer can be revoked by the offeror at any time before acceptance without liability. Revocation must be communicated to the offeree or the offeree's agent. Some offers,

In order to help students review what they have learned in Chapter 8, you might wish to:

1. Have a student volunteer, or volunteers, read aloud the Chapter Summary.
2. Allow the students to work with partners to complete the *Using Legal Language* activity.
3. Assign the *Checking for Comprehension* exercise as homework.
4. Allow the students to work in small groups to complete the *Applying Legal Concepts* activities.
5. As a class, complete the *Applying the Law* activities. (Please note that you may have to help students with vocabulary so that they adequately understand all of the *Applying the Law* material.)

Assessment Strategies

In order to check student mastery of chapter concepts, you may wish to use the Chapter 8 test that is found in your *Teacher's Resource Binder* or use WESTEST computerized testing for Chapter 8.

---

208   The Law of Contracts

such as the merchant's firm offer and option contracts, are irrevocable.

  b. Rejection—The offeree can reject the offer by words or actions that show a clear intent not to accept the offer or consider it further.

  c. Counteroffer—A rejection of the original offer and the making of a new offer.

2. *By operation of law*

  a. Lapse of time—The offer terminates at the end of the time specified in the offer or, if no time is stated in the offer, at the end of a reasonable time.

  b. Destruction of the specific subject matter of the offer—Automatically terminates the offer.

  c. Death or incompetence—Terminates the offer.

  d. Illegality—Supervening illegality terminates the offer.

ACCEPTANCE

1. Can be made only by the offeree.

2. Must be unequivocal. Under the common law, if new terms or conditions are added to an acceptance, it is a counteroffer (according to the mirror-image rule).

3. Acceptance of a bilateral offer can be communicated to the offeror by any authorized means of communication and is effective when sent. Unless the manner of communication is expressly specified by the offeror, the same manner used by the offeror or a faster one is authorized.

4. Acceptance of a unilateral offer is effective upon full performance of the requested act. Generally, no communication is necessary.

◆ USING LEGAL LANGUAGE

Directions: Match each term with the statement that best defines that term.

1. acceptance
2. agreement
3. communication
4. counteroffer
5. firm offer
6. mailbox rule
7. mirror-image rule
8. offer
9. option contract
10. revocation

A. the withdrawal of an offer by the offeror

B. requirement that an offeree's acceptance match the terms of an offer

C. a requirement that involves transmitting the offer to the offeree

D. an understanding of two or more minds

E. an agreement whose subject matter is the right to buy or sell something at a certain price at a certain time

F. a rejection of the original offer which is also a new offer

G. provides that if an offer is made by mail, an acceptance is effective when it is sent

H. an act or promise given in response to an offer showing a desire to contract

I. an offer for the sale of goods made in writing and signed by a merchant

J. a promise to do or not do something proposed as an exchange for a specified act or promise of another

1. First, there must be a serious, objective intention by the offeror. Second, the terms of the offer must be certain or definite. Third, the offer must be communicated to the offeree. All three elements must be present in an effective offer.
2. An expression of opinion is not an offer because it does not show an intention to enter into a binding agreement.

3. Too many terms are indefinite in an agreement to form a contract in the future.
4. A serious, objective intention to contract must be communicated to the offeree by the offeror. Also, the terms of the offer must be reasonably definite.
5. Generally items advertised for sale in a catalog are invitations to negotiate rather than offers to contract.

6. An offer will terminate if it is revoked by the offeror before being accepted by the offeree, is rejected by the offeree, or the offeree makes a counteroffer.
7. Lapse of time, destruction of the subject matter, death or incompetence of one of the parties, or illegality are conditions that would cause a contract to be terminated by operation of the law.
8. Yes. Exceptions to the rules of acceptance are (1) an improperly sent acceptance, (2) specific conditions by the offeror, and (3) a rejection sent by the offeree prior to sending an acceptance.
9. An invitation to submit bids is considered an invitation to parties to make offers. New Futures Construction Company is the offeror, and the city of Haven is the offeree.
10. No. Jason's offer was a public offer, and he revoked the offer in the same way that it had been originally communicated. Nothing further was required for an effective revocation.

 ## CHECKING FOR COMPREHENSION

1. What are the three elements of an offer? Can an offer be effective if one of the three elements is missing?

2. Is the expression of an opinion an offer? Why or why not?

3. Why is an agreement to form a contract in the future not considered to be an offer which forms a contract?

4. What are the requirements of an effective contract offer?

5. Is a picture of a stereo, along with the shipping price, in a mail-order catalog an effective offer to initiate a contract?

6. What actions by contract parties would cause an offer to be terminated?

7. What are the four conditions that could cause a contract to be terminated by law?

8. Are there any exceptions to the rule that a contract is formed when acceptance is sent by authorized means?

9. The city of Haven plans to construct a new City Hall. Invitations to submit bids (proposed charges for the work) on the construction project are sent to several local contractors. New Futures Construction Company responds with the lowest bid. In this situation who is the offeror and who is the offeree?

10. On June 1, Jason placed an ad in a local newspaper offering a reward of $100 to anyone who found his wallet. When his wallet had not been returned by June 15, Jason purchased another wallet. Jason also took steps to get duplicates of his driver's license, credit cards, and other items he had lost. He placed another ad in the same newspaper revoking his offer. The second ad was the same size as the original. On June 20, Frank, who had seen the first ad but not the second, returned Jason's wallet and requested the $100. Jason did not accept the wallet and refused to pay Frank, claiming he had revoked his offer. Frank sued Jason for the money. Will Jason have to pay the reward?

APPLYING LEGAL CONCEPTS

1. Design an outline or a flow chart showing the steps in forming a contract from offer through acceptance.

2. Acquire a sample contract from a local business such as a retail store, an apartment complex, or a service business, such as an automobile repair shop. Analyze the contract to see if it meets the requirements described in the chapter. Underline the sections about elements pertaining to offer and acceptance.

APPLYING THE LAW . . . YOU BE THE JUDGE

1. The Olivers were planning to sell off some of their ranch land and mentioned this fact to Southworth, a neighbor. Southworth expressed interest in purchasing the property and later notified the Olivers that he had the money available to buy it. The Olivers told Southworth they would let him know shortly about the details concerning the sale. The Olivers later sent a letter to Southworth—and (unknown to Southworth) to several other neighbors—giving information about the sale, including the price, the location of the property, and the amount of acreage involved.

Applying the Law . . . You Be the Judge (Answers)

1. In determining whether a writing is an offer or simply an invitation to negotiate, the courts will ask the following question: Would a reasonable person in the position of the offeree believe that an offer had

(continued on next page)

been made? In this case, the Olivers' letter was a follow-up to earlier conversations between them and Southworth. Southworth had told the Olivers he wanted to buy the land and was awaiting the information contained in the letter. Given these circumstances and the fact that the letter contained specific information pertaining to the terms of the sale, the court concluded that a reasonable person in Southworth's position would have concluded that the Olivers' letter was an offer to sell Southworth the land. Southworth's contract, which was proper acceptance of the offer, thus created a valid, enforceable contract.

2. The precise issue is whether a newspaper advertisement constitutes an offer that can be accepted to form a contract or whether such an advertisement is merely an invitation to make an offer. Most jurisdictions that have dealt with the issue have considered an advertisement to be a mere invitation to make an offer, unless the circumstances indicate otherwise. The court held "that in the absence of special circumstances, a newspaper advertisement, which contains an erroneous purchase price through no fault of the defendant advertiser and which contains no other terms, is not an offer which can be accepted so as to form a contract." Since the advertisement is only an invitation to make the offer, "there is no meeting of the minds nor the required mutual assent by the two parties" to form a contract.

3. Wilkins is correct. When no time limit is stated for an offer, it lapses after a reasonable time. The fact that the offeror had not withdrawn the offer did not matter. Since there was a one-year delay, the court declared as a matter of law that a reasonable time had expired and that the offer had lapsed.

4. The trial court held for Anderson, and on appeal the judgment was affirmed. The court held that an implied-in-fact contract was created. "An implied contract is as valid and enforceable as if it were express or written."

Although Higgins's intention was not expressly made, her actions clearly evidenced an intent to contract for the repairs. The court noted that Higgins had requested that Anderson tow the vehicle to its garage, authorized Anderson to disassemble the engine, and allowed the vehicle to remain in the Anderson's garage for 22 days. The court held that these actions by Higgins gave Anderson reason to believe that Higgins had consented to the repairs. Higgins was therefore held liable.

When Southworth received the letter, he sent a letter to the Olivers "accepting" their offer. The Olivers stated that the information letter had not been intended as an "offer." It merely was a starting point for negotiations. Southworth brought suit against the Olivers to enforce the "contract." Did a contract exist? [*Southworth v. Oliver*, 284 Or. 361, 587 P.2d 994 (1978)]

2. On July 31, 1966, Lee Calan Imports, Inc. (Calan), advertised a 1964 Volvo Station Wagon for sale in the Chicago *Sun Times*. Calan had instructed the newspaper to advertise the price of the automobile at $1,795. Through an error of the newspaper, however, and without fault on the part of Calan, the newspaper inserted a price of $1,095 for the automobile in the advertisement. Christopher O'Brien visited Calan's car lot, examined the automobile, and stated that he wished to purchase it for $1,095. One of Calan's sales agents at first agreed, but then refused to sell the car for the erroneous price listed in the advertisement. O'Brien sued Calan for breach of contract, claiming that the ad was an offer which had been accepted by O'Brien. O'Brien died before the trial, and his administrator (O'Keefe) continued the suit. Discuss whether a contract exists. [*O'Keefe v. Lee Calan Imports, Inc.*, 128 Ill.App.2d 410, 262 N.E.2d 758 (1970)]

3. After Wilkins and Butler had an automobile accident, Wilkins offered to settle the matter for $4,500. There was no reply from Butler. One year later Butler stated she ac-

cepted the offer. Wilkins claimed that the offer had lapsed and could not be accepted. Butler claimed that she could accept the offer because it had never been withdrawn. Who is correct? [*Wilkins v. Butler*, 187 Ga.App. 84, 369 S.E.2d 267 (1988)]

4. Anderson Chevrolet/Olds, Inc., leased a truck to Higgins. The lease agreement provided that the "lessee shall pay for all maintenance and repairs to keep the vehicle in good working order and condition." A little over a year later, Higgins had the truck towed by Anderson to Anderson's garage, as it had stopped running. After inspecting the vehicle, Anderson determined that it would be necessary to disassemble the engine to ascertain the damage and repairs needed. Anderson did so and informed Higgins of the needed repairs and estimated costs. Higgins sent some employees to confirm the damage. Twenty-two days later, without hearing from Higgins, Anderson made the repairs and sent Higgins a bill for $1,407 (approximately equal to the estimate). Higgins sent employees to pick up the truck, but Anderson would not release the truck without payment. When Higgins refused, Anderson filed suit. Higgins claimed that there was no contract for the truck repairs. Discuss whether Anderson had a contract to repair the truck even though Higgins never expressly accepted Anderson's offer of repair. [*Anderson Chevrolet/Olds., Inc. v. Higgins*, 57 N.C.App. 650, 292 S.E.2d 159 (1982)]

Mastery Objectives

By the end of this chapter, students will be able to:

- Explain legal sufficiency of consideration
- Establish when to ask about adequacy of consideration
- Describe how claims can be settled
- Tell when promissory estoppel applies
- Determine who has contractual capacity
- Outline minors' responsibilities in contract law

Prereading Activity

Before students enter the room, write on the board: "You can't get something for nothing." Ask students what the statement means and what it has to do with contracts. Explain the concept of consideration.

Consideration and Capacity

Chapter

9

LEGAL BACKGROUND

Your students should now understand that not every promise is binding. Continuing the discussion of when a promise is binding, this chapter focuses on consideration and capacity.

In the first half of the chapter, the requirement of consideration is explained. For centuries, it has been said that no informal promise is enforceable without consideration. Since the beginning of the common law tradition in England, good reasons for enforcing promises have developed. The concept of consideration along with exception to its requirement is discussed here in some detail. We have also attempted to illustrate the areas where questions of consideration are raised.

The second half of this chapter discusses the effect of lack of capacity on the validity of a contract. The validity of contracts created by incompetent persons and persons under the influence of alcohol is discussed.

211

Vocabulary Activity

Ask student volunteers to use the word *gratuitous* in a sentence and then explain the meaning of the word *gratuitous* in the phrase, *gratuitous promise*.

Extension Activity

Have students ask parents or teachers about any contracts they have made. Have them list the consideration each party gave to form the contract. For example, automobile—promise to pay. Follow up by writing the lists in two columns on the chalkboard and discussing whether each is actually consideration.

Legal Focus Problem

Read to the class the Legal Focus Problem found here. Allow student volunteers to suggest possible answers to the question posed at the end of this problem. Then explain to students that in this example, the consideration is the act of painting the garage.

Legal Focus Problem

Read this second Legal Focus Problem to the class. Allow student volunteers to suggest possible answers to the question at the end of this problem. Why does consideration not exist in this instance?

212   The Law of Contracts

"When a man keeps hollering, 'It's the principle of the thing,' he's talking about the money."
Frank Hubbard, 1868–1930
American humorist

In our legal system, there are promises the courts will enforce and promises the courts will not enforce. The law does not provide a remedy for every promise broken. Under the common law, the primary basis for the enforcement of promises is *consideration*. This requirement distinguishes between gratuitous promises and bargained-for promises. When people make **gratuitous promises**, they expect nothing in return. In contrast, the process of bargaining is the process by which contracts are negotiated. Thus, we can say that consideration distinguishes contracts from gifts.

♦ **gratuitous promise** A promise given without expectation of receiving something in return.

◆ CONSIDERATION AND ITS REQUIREMENTS

♦ **consideration** Value given in return for a promise. Consideration consists of two parts: (1) something of *legal value* must be given in exchange for the promise, and (2) it must be part of a *bargained-for* exchange.

Consideration is value given in return for a promise. Consideration consists of two parts: (1) Something of *legal value* is given in exchange for a promise. (2) This occurs as part of a *bargained-for* exchange. The "something of legal value" may be a return promise. It may also be (1) an act (other than a promise); (2) a forbearance (which involves *not* doing something); or (3) the creation, modification, or termination of a legal relation.

 LEGAL FOCUS – PROBLEM

Jerry says to Max, "If you paint the garage green, I will pay you $100." Max paints the garage green. Can Max legally require Jerry to pay the $100? Does consideration exist?

The answer to both questions is yes. The act of painting the garage is the consideration that creates a contractual obligation. Jerry must pay Max the $100.

 LEGAL FOCUS – PROBLEM

If Jerry says to Max, "In consideration of the fact that you are not as wealthy as my other friends, I will pay you $500." Can Max legally require Jerry to pay him the $500? Does consideration exist?

Vocabulary Activity

Explain *detriment*. Discuss how it applies in the phrase *legal detriment*.

Reteaching Activity

Have a volunteer define *forbearance* in his or her own words and give an example of it.

Legal Focus Problem

Have a student volunteer read this Legal Focus Problem aloud to the class. Remind students that they can use the Legal Focus features as review tools when studying for tests. Be sure students understand that in this instance the consideration is the used lawn mower, not the $50.

Ethical Concern

Have your students imagine that Jim, a friend, offered to sell his car to you for $300 plus 35 percent interest. You accepted. The next day you found out that the bank only charges 12 percent interest. Since value is determined by the parties, is this considered a valid contract? Stimulate a class discussion on this scenario. At the end of the discussion, make sure your students realize that there is a legal maximum interest rate.

Teaching with the Videodisc

The still frames listed below from the **West's Business Law and Legal Environment Videodisc** can be used with this chapter. To access this material, use the bar codes or the frame numbers included in the Videodisc Instructor's Manual found in the *TRB*.

Consideration:
   Bilateral/Unilateral
Two Elements in
   Consideration
Legal Sufficiency
Possible Exceptions to
   Preexisting Duty Rule
Promises Enforceable
   without Consideration
Minor's Right to Disaffirm
Mental Incompetency
   and Validity
Intoxication and Validity

Consideration and Capacity 213

No. Jerry's promise is not enforceable, because Max did not pay anything (give consideration) for the $500 promised. Jerry simply gave his motive for an intended *gift* to Max. Use of the word *consideration* does not, alone, mean that consideration was given.

LEGAL SUFFICIENCY

To create a binding contract, consideration must be legally sufficient. To be legally sufficient, consideration for a promise must generally be a **legal detriment** to the promisee. That means the promisee must incur some cost in exchange for the promise. This need not be an actual dollar cost. The promisee can incur a legal detriment in two ways: (1) by doing or promising to do something there was no prior legal duty to do or (2) by forbearance. **Forbearance** is refraining from, or promising to refrain from, doing something one would otherwise have had a legal right to do.

◆ **legal detriment**
Legal cost; for example, doing something one is not already required to do or refraining from doing something one has a right to do.

◆ **forbearance**
Refraining from, or promising to refrain from, doing something one has a legal right to do.

SUFFICIENCY AND ADEQUACY OF CONSIDERATION

We have said that consideration must be legally sufficient. Consideration is thought to be legally sufficient if the exchange provides anything of any value. (The courts often use the phrase "consideration need only be more than a mere peppercorn.") In contrast, adequacy refers to "how much" consideration is given, or the fairness of the bargain. Usually, adequacy of consideration is not an issue if consideration is legally sufficient. Parties are generally free to contract as they wish, including being free to enter bad bargains. If people could sue merely because they entered an unwise contract, the courts would be overloaded with frivolous suits (lawsuits without merit.)

◆ LEGAL FOCUS ~ PROBLEM

Eric offered to sell Francis his used lawnmower for $50. Francis agreed and paid Eric the money. The next day Francis found out that Eric had paid only $5 for the mower last year. He also found similar used mowers available for less than $25. Is the consideration for the contract from Eric sufficient? Adequate?

Certainly. Value is determined by bargaining parties. What a willing buyer will pay a willing seller determines the selling price. The possibility that Francis got a bad bargain does not make the consideration either insufficient or inadequate.

In extreme cases, a court of law may look to the adequacy of the consideration. A low payment may suggest fraud (lying), duress (unlawful pressure causing someone to do something), or undue influence (taking advantage of a special relationship).

PREEXISTING DUTY

A promise to do what one is already required to do (a preexisting legal duty) is not usually legally sufficient consideration. The promise does not involve a legal detriment. A preexisting legal duty may be imposed by law or may arise from a previous contract. A sheriff, for example, cannot collect a reward for capture of a criminal, if the sheriff already has a legal duty to capture the criminal. If a party already is bound by contract to perform a certain act, that act cannot be consideration for a second contract.

LEGAL FOCUS ~ PROBLEM

Beau, Inc., began construction on a seven-story office building. After three months, Beau demanded an extra $75,000 on the contract or "I'll quit the job." The owner of the land had no one else to complete the construction. He agreed to pay the extra $75,000. Beau finished the construction but the owner refused to pay the additional $75,000. Can Beau enforce the owner's promise to pay the additional $75,000?

If the homeowner promised these firefighters $1,000 if they put the fire out, and they did, would the promise to pay the money be enforceable?

No. The agreement to pay the additional $75,000 is not enforceable. It is not supported by legally sufficient consideration. Beau was already required to complete the office building for the lesser sum. Beau did nothing (incurred no legal detriment) in exchange for the owner's promise to pay the additional $75,000.

Unforeseen Difficulties   The rule regarding preexisting duty is meant to prevent blackmail and the so-called hold-up game. But what if an honest contractor who has contracted with a landowner to build a house runs into major unforeseen difficulties? In such cases, the courts will sometimes allow exceptions to the preexisting duty rule.

Rescission and New Contract   The law recognizes that two parties can agree to rescind a contract that has not yet been performed. **Rescission** is the unmaking of a contract; it returns both parties to the positions they occupied before the contract was made. The parties in essence agree to revoke the contract. A rescission is supported by mutual consideration, because each party gives up the legal right to the other party's performance. When rescission and the making of a new contract take place at the same time, the courts frequently are given a choice (as in the earlier Beau, Inc., example) of applying the preexisting duty rule or allowing rescission and the new contract to stand.

◆ **rescission** The unmaking of a contract.

PAST CONSIDERATION

Promises made to reward a person for actions or events that took place before the promise to reward are unenforceable. These promises lack consideration, because the element of bargained-for exchange is missing. In short, you can bargain for something in the present or the future, but you cannot bargain for something that has already happened. **Past consideration** is not consideration.

◆ **past consideration** Promise to reward a person for actions or events that took place before the promise to reward.

◆ LEGAL FOCUS – PROBLEM

Elsie, a real estate agent, does her friend Judy a favor by selling Judy's house and not charging any commission. Later, Judy says to Elsie, "In return for your generous act, I will pay you $3,000." If Judy does not pay Elsie, can Elsie collect the $3,000?

Most of us would want Judy to do what she promised. However, Judy is stating her intention to give Elsie a gift, and the law will not make someone give a gift if she changes her mind. Judy's promise is given for past consideration and is unenforceable. In contrast, if the promise had been made before the sale, consideration would exist, and the promise would be enforceable.

Reteaching Activity

Ask a volunteer to define the term *past consideration* for the class. Help students to understand that a contract for *past* consideration is not valid; it must be present or future consideration.

Collaborative Learning Activity

Write different scenarios on 4 x 6 cards. Distribute the cards to groups of three to four students. Ask them to decide which of the scenarios have legally sufficient consideration to be contracts and to establish why or why not. Then have each group present its findings to the class. Examples: (1) Your teacher promises to assign an A to your test if you answer all questions correctly. (2) Your teacher promises to mark you present each day you attend class. (3) You promise to pay for your textbook if you borrow it from your school and you lose it. (4) Your friend says that you can borrow his car Saturday night if you wash it and fill the gas tank Friday.

Legal Focus Problem

Ask a student volunteer to read this Legal Focus Problem aloud to the class. Remind students that they can use the Legal Focus features as review tools when studying for tests.

Read to the class the Legal
Focus Problem found here.
Allow student volunteers to
suggest possible answers to
the question posed at the
end of this problem. You
might want to walk through
the Legal Focus with the students to make sure they
understand that it deals with
a problem with considera-
tion in which promises are
exchanged but performance
by the parties is uncertain.

Have a student volunteer look up the word
illusory and share the dictionary definition
with the class. How does this definition relate
to the phrase *illusory promise*?

 ## PROBLEMS CONCERNING CONSIDERATION

Problems concerning consideration usually fall into one of the following
categories:

1. Situations in which promises are exchanged but performance by the
   parties is uncertain.
2. Settlement of claims.
3. Certain promises enforceable without consideration (under the doctrine of *promissory estoppel*).

The courts' solutions to these types of problems offer insight into how the
law views the complex concept of consideration.

UNCERTAIN PERFORMANCE—ILLUSORY VERSUS NONILLUSORY PROMISES

If the terms of the contract express such uncertainty of performance that
the promisor has not actually promised to do anything, the promise is said
to be *illusory*—without consideration and unenforceable.

 ### LEGAL FOCUS ~ PROBLEM

Millie, a high school government teacher, says to her students: "All of
you have worked hard, and if you continue to perform at this high
level, I will pay for a pizza party for the class at the end of the year—
if I think it is warranted." The students continue to work hard, and
class grades are high, but no party is given. Can the students enforce
the promise?

This is an *illusory promise*, or no promise at all, because performance depends solely on the decision of the teacher. There is no bargained-for consideration. The statement declares merely that the teacher may or may not
do something in the future. The teacher is not obligated (incurs no detriment) now or in the future.

Three types of business contracts are generally held as enforceable even
though there is some certainty as to the amount of performance legally
required.

◆ **requirements
contract** A contract
in which the buyer
agrees to purchase from
the seller, and the seller
agrees to sell to the
buyer, all of some good
the buyer requires.

Requirements Contracts   A contract in which the buyer agrees to purchase from the seller, and the seller agrees to sell to the buyer, all of some
good the buyer needs, or requires, is a **requirements contract**. Requirements contracts are common in the business world and are normally
enforceable.

Critical Thinking Activity

Have your students demonstrate their understanding of the differences among requirements contracts, output contracts, and option-to-cancel clauses by writing two or three paragraphs explaining these types of contracts.

Legal Focus Example

Ask a student volunteer to read the second Legal Focus Example aloud to the class. Have the volunteer explain what part of this contract is the consideration.

Legal Focus Example

Read the third Legal Focus Example to the class. Ask the class if they can think of any other examples that could also fit here. Allow volunteers to share their examples with the class.

Consideration and Capacity 217

◆ LEGAL FOCUS ~ EXAMPLE

Wannabe Manufacturing uses coal to operate and heat its plant. Wannabe agrees to purchase from Black Rock Coal Company all the coal that Wannabe will require to heat and to run the plant for one year at a set price per ton.

Because the agreement is based on the established need of the buyer and because the contract requires the buyer to purchase the goods to fill those needs from the seller, the contract is enforceable. If, however, the buyer promises to purchase only if the buyer *wishes* or *desires* to do so, or if the buyer reserves the right to buy the goods from someone other than the seller, the promise is illusory (without consideration), and the promise is unenforceable by either party.

There is a *good-faith limitation* on *requirements* contracts. The quantity allowed under such contracts is what is required during a *normal and usual* year.

Output Contracts   An **output contract** is a contract in which the seller agrees to sell to the buyer, and the buyer agrees to purchase from the seller, all of something the seller produces.

◆ LEGAL FOCUS ~ EXAMPLE

U.S. Steel agrees to sell to Bowing Aircraft all the I-beams it produces during the month of March at an agreed-upon price per beam. This contract is a binding nonillusory output contract.

◆ **output contract**
A contract in which the seller agrees to sell to the buyer, and the buyer agrees to purchase from the seller, all of something the seller produces.

There is also a *good-faith limitation* on *output* contracts. The quantity allowed under such contracts is the amount of output during a *normal* year. The quantity sold must be consistent with normal or prior output.

Option-to-Cancel Clauses   A contract created to last over time may allow one or both parties to cancel before the stated period has passed.

◆ LEGAL FOCUS ~ EXAMPLE

Max and Linda negotiated and signed a three-year lease in which the tenant Linda reserved the right to cancel, with notice, at any time after one year's occupancy. The uncertainty of performance is that the contract may or may not last for the entire three-year period.

The contract is enforceable because Linda, the person who cancels the contract, is giving up her right to enforce the contract for the agreed period.

Checking Your Progress (Answers)

1. Consideration for a contract can be (1) a return promise, (2) an act (other than a promise), (3) a forbearance, or (4) the creation, modification, or termination of a legal relation.

2. Legal detriment can exist (1) by doing or promising to do something there was no prior legal duty to do or (2) by forbearance.

3. No. Adequacy of consideration is not an issue.

4. No. A promise to do what one is already required to do is not usually legally sufficient consideration.

Contracts for the services of professional athletes often provide clauses for either cancellation or renewal after a stated time.

◆ CHECKING YOUR PROGRESS

1. Describe three kinds of consideration for a contract.

2. What are two ways that legal detriment can exist?

3. Is the value of the consideration an issue in determining the legality of a contract?

4. Is preexisting duty consideration?

Legal Focus Problem

Read to the class the first Legal Focus Problem found here. Allow student volunteers to suggest possible answers to this problem.

Legal Focus Problem

Have a student volunteer read the second Legal Focus Problem aloud to the class. Ask student volunteers to explain how the situation in this problem is different from the one in the previous Legal Focus Problem found above.

 ## SETTLEMENT OF CLAIMS

In the business world, contracting parties often wish to renegotiate the terms of existing contracts. If both parties change their performance in some way, then mutual detriment, consideration, exists. But what if one party agrees to accept less than the agreed performance from the other party? Can that party change his or her mind and claim the original performance? The person trying to enforce the original performance is claiming that his or her promise to accept less than the agreed performance was not supported by consideration from the performing party.

 ### LEGAL FOCUS - PROBLEM

Sean owed a friend, James, $2,000 for an unpaid debt. The amount owed was undisputed. One day, James saw Sean on the street, and asked him for the money. Sean replied, "I don't have $2,000, but I'll pay you $1,500. Take it or leave it." James agreed to take the lesser amount. Can James sue Sean for the remaining $500 of the debt?

Yes, because Sean paid no *consideration* for James's agreement (promise) to take less. Sean had a preexisting duty to pay $2,000. Sean suffered no detriment (that is, offered no new consideration) for the new promise to accept less, so the promise is not enforceable.

When the amount of the debt is in *dispute*, an agreement by the person owed the money to take less is supported by consideration.

 ### LEGAL FOCUS - PROBLEM

In the example involving Sean and James, assume that the amount of debt was disputed. Sean genuinely believed he only owed $1,500, but James claimed Sean owed $2,000. Sean offered to pay $1,750 in return for a release from the amount claimed by James. James agreed and accepted the $1,750. Can James sue and collect from Sean the remaining $250, the difference between what he was paid and the amount he believed to be the true debt?

No, Sean paid consideration for James's promise to release him from the debt. When a good faith dispute—an honest disagreement—about the

Divide the class into small groups to read and discuss the first Legal Focus Problem found here. Each group should choose a leader to explain its response to the question posed at the end of this problem.

Ask the students to think about the following: If you write "paid in full" on the check you write to make the last payment on your car and the credit company cashes it, can the credit company collect more money if they discover that they had calculated the interest wrong, but you disagree? Discuss the legal and the ethical implications.

Legal Focus Problem

Read to the class the second Legal Focus Problem found here. Allow student volunteers to suggest possible answers to the question posed at the end of this problem. You might want to point out to students the advice in the following paragraph: "It is important that people know the extent of their injuries or damages before signing a release in such situations."

amount owed exists, each party has a right to a legal action to determine the amount owed. Giving up that right is a legal detriment that constitutes consideration.

Such debt settlement disputes are unfortunately common. One example occurs when a debt is in dispute and the debtor sends, and the creditor cashes, a check marked "payment in full." If no good faith dispute exists about the amount owed, cashing the check will not release a party from paying the rest of the debt in most states.

◆ LEGAL FOCUS ~ PROBLEM

Both Sean and James agreed that Sean owed James $2,000. Sean sent James a check for $1,500. On the back of the check, Sean wrote: "Cashing this check acknowledges payment in full of (Sean's) debt to (James)." James cashed the check. Can James collect the additional $500?

Since there is no good faith dispute as to the amount owed, James can cash the check and still sue to collect the additional $500 in most states.

If there is a good faith dispute, however, cashing the check can create an enforceable settlement agreement. Assume the facts described in the preceding example, except Sean and James had an honest disagreement—good faith dispute—about the amount owed. Cashing the $1,500 check would then imply a promise to accept the lesser amount. The promise is supported by consideration because of the dispute over the amount owed. Even if James scratches off "payment in full," cashing the check represents an enforceable settlement of a disputed claim under common law. Note that it is important that the creditor (the person who receives the payment) has *notice* that the payment is intended as full settlement of the debt.

Many state statutes allow for parties to negotiate and release claims without consideration if a written **release** is given. A release is one or both parties' giving up of their legal claims against the other party. The release bars further recovery beyond the terms stated in the release. The release must be in writing and must clearly state that it releases the claims.

◆ **release**
Relinquishing of a claim or right.

◆ LEGAL FOCUS ~ PROBLEM

Linda was in an automobile accident caused by Paul's negligence. Paul offers to give Linda $500 if she will release him from further liability resulting from the accident. Linda believes this amount adequate, so she agrees to and signs a release. Later, Linda learns that the damage to her car is $900. Can Linda collect the balance from Paul?

Read

Before the students read this *Law in Action* feature, ask a student volunteer to explain the meaning of the terms *debtor* and *creditor*. If his or her definitions are inaccurate, refer the students to a dictionary, and have a volunteer read the dictionary definitions to the class. Point out to students that this *Law in Action*

feature deals with one aspect of the *debtor/creditor* relationship. Then have a student volunteer read this *Law in Action* feature aloud to the class.

Discuss

What must exist between the *debtor* and the *creditor* in order for a debtor to satisfy a debt by paying a lesser sum? What is the best

proof of such a *bona fide* dispute? How does the adage "A bird in the hand is worth two in the bush" relate to this discussion of discharging a debt by payment of a lesser sum?

 Law in Action

LAW IN YOUR LIFE: "YES, BUT WILL YOU TAKE A LITTLE LESS?"

Understanding whether agreements to settle claims or discharge debts are enforceable is important in business. Debtors sometimes offer to pay less than what they owe, and creditors often accept these offers.

If you are the debtor, to satisfy a debt by paying a lesser sum, you must have a bona fide dispute with the creditor about the amount owed. A *bona fide dispute* exists if parties disagree in good faith about the amount owed. The best proof of such a disagreement is often prior written correspondence about the dispute. If the dispute is genuine, you may offer a check for the amount that you believe is owed. On the back of the check, state that the payment is a complete payment for the debt. The adage "a bird in the hand is worth two in the bush" leads many creditors to cash such checks. At that point, your obligation is usually completely discharged.

Suppose you are the creditor. If a check is offered to you in discharge of an obligation, you must decide whether to accept it or not. If the amount of the debt is *not* in dispute, then in most states you can cash the

check, no matter what is written on the back of it, and still sue for the difference. A word of caution is in order, however. The courts may not agree that the obligation is not in dispute. The other party, acting as a "reasonable" person, has to know the amount owed in order for the amount to be undisputed. If he or she has a good-faith claim, as described above, the amount is, in fact, in dispute; and your cashing the check will be an agreement that the obligation is discharged.

CHECKLIST FOR DISCHARGING A DEBT BY PAYMENT OF A LESSER SUM

1. If the debtor writes on the back of his or her check that the check is in complete payment for the debt obligation, and the check is cashed, the debtor's obligation is normally discharged, if the amount owed is in bona fide dispute.

2. In the majority of cases, if the debt amount is not disputed, the creditor can cash the check and still sue to collect the difference.

No. Linda signed a written release of claims against Paul. Because this is a written release no consideration is required. However, in this example consideration does exist. Linda is giving up her right to sue for damages, should they be more than $500. It is important that people know the extent of their injuries or damages before signing a release in such situations. A few states still require consideration in order to enforce a release.

Divide the class into small groups, and have each group complete the following sentences:

1. There must be a promise. In other words . . .
2. The *promisee* must justifiably rely on the promise. In other words . . .
3. The reliance must be of a substantial and definite character. In other words . . .
4. The enforcement of the promise must serve the interests of justice. In other words . . .

Each group should choose a leader to share its sentences with the rest of the class.

PROMISSORY ESTOPPEL

◆ **promissory estoppel** A doctrine allowing enforcement of a promise otherwise unsupported by consideration. The doctrine applies when a person makes an important promise upon which another reasonably relies to his or her detriment.

Sometimes individuals rely on promises even though they are not supported by consideration. In a few situations, courts enforce promises not supported by consideration. The doctrine of **promissory estoppel** (also called *detrimental reliance*) provides that a person who has reasonably relied on the promise of another can hope to get some help from the courts. The doctrine of promissory estoppel requires four elements:

1. There must be a promise.
2. The promisee must justifiably rely on the promise.
3. The reliance must be of a substantial and definite character.
4. The enforcement of the promise must serve the interests of justice.

◆ LEGAL FOCUS - PROBLEM

Uncle Fred tells his niece, Sue, "I'll pay you $150 a week so you won't have to work anymore." Sue quits her job, but her uncle refuses to pay. Can Sue enforce the promise?

Under the doctrine of promissory estoppel, Sue may be able to enforce the promise. She will need to show that Uncle Fred knew she intended to quit. She will also need to show that her reliance on his promise was reasonable under the circumstances.

We, the authors, advise you not to trust such promises. Sue should have convinced her uncle to bargain for something, to change the promise to make a gift into a contract.

◆ CAPACITY TO CONTRACT

"Liberty of contract is not an absolute concept. It is relative to many conditions of time and place and circumstance."
Benjamin Cardozo, 1870–1938
Associate justice of the United States Supreme Court, 1932–1938

Courts generally want contracts to be enforceable. However, as Justice Cardozo said in the quotation just given, liberty of contract is not absolute. Not all people can make legally binding contracts. One requirement is that a person must have **contractual capacity**, the legal right to contract.

◆ **contractual capacity** The legal right to contract.

Courts generally presume that contractual capacity exists. In some situations, however, it does not. A person determined by a court to be mentally incompetent, for example, cannot form a legally binding contract with another party. In other situations, a party may have the capacity to enter a valid contract but also have the right to avoid liability under it. For example, minors usually are not legally bound by contracts. In most situations, a

Read to the class the Legal Focus Problem found here. You might want to explain to the class that in this Legal Focus Problem, the names Lucy and Zehmer are last names and that both of the participants in this particular problem were men. Allow a student volunteer to suggest a possible answer to the question posed at the end of this problem, and ask the same volunteer to read the paragraph that follows. Stimulate a class discussion regarding this Legal Focus Problem by asking the following questions: Do you believe Zehmer did not understand the legal consequences of entering into the contract? Why or why not? Why do you believe Zehmer later tried to void the contract? Do you think the alcohol impaired his judgment such that he made a bad business decision? How is making a bad business decision different than not understanding the legal consequences of an agreement? What point does this Legal Focus Problem make regarding mixing alcohol and important decisions?

minor can avoid a contract any time before reaching adulthood. Issues of contractual capacity are discussed in this section and in this chapter's Legal Perspective.

INTOXICATED PERSONS

A contract made with an intoxicated person may be either voidable or valid. If the person was drunk enough to lack mental capacity, the transaction is voidable by the intoxicated person. This is true even if the person became intoxicated voluntarily. For the contract to be voidable, the person's reason and judgment must have been weakened sufficiently that he or she did not understand the legal consequences of entering into the contract. If the person was intoxicated but understood these legal consequences, the contract is enforceable. The fact that a contract is foolish or that it favors one party does not by itself make the contract voidable.

It may be difficult to prove that a party was drunk enough to be able to avoid legal duties. Many courts look at the objective signs of sobriety rather than measuring the intoxicated party's mental state.

◆ LEGAL FOCUS – CASE PROBLEM

For eight years or so, Lucy had been anxious to buy Zehmer's farm. Zehmer had always told Lucy that he was not interested in selling. One night, Lucy stopped in to visit with the Zehmers at a restaurant they operated. Lucy said to Zehmer, "I bet you wouldn't take $50,000 for that place." Zehmer replied, "Yes, I would, too; you wouldn't give fifty." Throughout the evening the conversation returned to the sale of the farm. At the same time, the parties were drinking whiskey. Eventually, Lucy convinced Zehmer to write up an agreement for sale of the farm. Zehmer wrote the agreement on the back of a restaurant check and asked his wife to sign it. She did. When Lucy subsequently tried to enforce the agreement, Zehmer argued that he was "high as a Georgia pine" at the time and that the offer had been made in jest: "two doggoned drunks bluffing to see who could talk the biggest and say the most." Lucy said that although he felt the drinks, he was not intoxicated and, from the way Zehmer handled the transaction, did not think Zehmer was either. Can the Lucy–Zehmer agreement be avoided on the basis of mental incapacity resulting from intoxication?

No. The agreement to sell the farm was binding, and the Zehmers could not rescind the contract. The opinion of the court was that the evidence given about the nature of the conversation, the appearance and completeness of the agreement, and the signing all tended to show that a serious business transaction and not a casual jest was intended. "The record

1. There must be a bona
fide dispute with the creditor about the amount owed.
2. Yes. Many state statutes
allow for parties to release
and compromise claims
without proof of consideration.
3. No. A person who has
reasonably relied on the
promise of another may
legally enforce the promise.
4. If the court determines a
person is mentally incompetent, any contract entered
into afterward is void.

is convincing that Zehmer was not intoxicated to the extent of being unable to comprehend the nature and consequences of the . . . [agreement]."[2]

MENTALLY INCOMPETENT PERSONS

Contracts made by mentally incompetent persons may be either void,
voidable, or valid. If a person is adjudged—that is, determined by a
court—to be mentally incompetent, a guardian is appointed. After appointment, only the guardian can enter a binding legal contract for the
mentally incompetent person. Thereafter, contracts made by the mentally
incompetent person are void.

A person who has not been subject to court proceedings may contract.
If the person understands the nature and effect of entering into a certain
contract, even though the person lacks capacity to engage in other activities, the contract is valid. The person is considered mentally competent for
contractual purposes.

The contract is voidable, however, if the mentally incompetent person
lacks the mental capacity to comprehend the contract's subject matter, nature, and consequences. The person determined mentally incompetent can
avoid the contract, but the other party cannot. Modern courts do not require that a person be completely irrational to avoid contracts on the
grounds of mental incompetency. A contract is voidable if, by reason of a
mental illness or defect, an individual was unable to act reasonably regarding
the transaction and the other party had reason to know of the condition.

A voidable contract may be either avoided or ratified. A ratification is an
acceptance of the contract after the party becomes competent to contract.
A ratification can occur after the person becomes mentally competent or
after a guardian is appointed who ratifies the contract. Mentally incompetent persons are liable (in quasi contract) for the reasonable value of necessaries they receive (such as food or clothing.)

◆ CHECKING YOUR PROGRESS

1. What condition must exist if paying a lesser sum is to release the
   debtor from further obligation?

2. Can a party ever be released from a contract if consideration is
   not given?

3. Is consideration necessary under the doctrine of promissory
   estoppel?

4. If a person is adjudged mentally incompetent, is a contract he or
   she makes void or voidable?

2. *Lucy v. Zehmer*, Supreme Court of Appeals of Virginia, 196 Va. 493, 84 S.E.2d
516 (1954).

Teaching A Case In Point

Introduce this *A Case In Point* feature by having the students look at the *litigants* involved in *Lanfier* v. *Lanfier*. What can the students infer from this case citation? (Students should infer from the names of the litigants that this suit involves family members suing one another.) After the students have discussed this, have a student volunteer read aloud this

A Case In Point feature regarding *consideration*.

Discuss

Use the following questions to stimulate a class discussion of this *A Case In Point* feature: Who was the *plaintiff* in this case? Who were the *defendants?* What was the *plaintiff* trying to secure through this suit? How did the trial court rule in this case? How did the appellate court rule in this case? What reasons did the appellate court give for its decision?

◆ A CASE IN POINT ◆

LANFIER v. LANFIER

Supreme Court of Iowa, 1939.
227 Iowa 258,
288 N.W. 104.

August Schultz promised to transfer real estate to his grandchild if the plaintiff's mother would name the child after him. The only problem was, she already had named the child after the grandfather. After the grandfather died, could the grandchild enforce the promise? Was the consideration sufficient to require enforcement of the promise?

FACTS This suit concerned title to certain real property. The plaintiff was a minor bringing suit through his father. The defendants were the heirs of August Schultz and the administrators of his estate. An oral contract was allegedly made between Schultz and the plaintiff (through the plaintiff's mother). In this contract, Schultz agreed to give the plaintiff certain real estate if the plaintiff's mother would name the plaintiff (his grandson) after him. He also agreed to reserve to the plaintiff's parents a life estate (good for their lifetimes only) in that real estate. The plaintiff's parents accepted the proposal, since they had already named the

plaintiff after Schultz. Schultz never arranged for the title of the property to pass to the plaintiff. He did, however, deliver possession of the real estate to the plaintiff's parents. The plaintiff requested that the court determine him to be the absolute owner of the real estate. The trial court agreed and awarded the property to the plaintiff based on the alleged oral contract. The heirs of Schultz and the administrators of his estate appealed.

ISSUE Was the contract between Schultz and the plaintiff's mother supported by consideration?

DECISION No. The plaintiff did not get title to the property. The court found that the consideration was insufficient to support the contract.

REASON The court determined that the consideration in this contract created no detriment to the promisee. The plaintiff was named after his grandfather several months before the oral contract was made. The court stated that "past or moral consideration is not sufficient to support an executory contract." The plaintiff argued that his love and affection constituted sufficient consideration to support the contract, but the court held that such a promise created "at most bare moral obligations."

Teaching Note

This case is included in the *West's Business and Personal Law Handbook of Selected Court Cases.*

In order to help students review what they have learned in Chapter 9, you might wish to:

1. Have a student volunteer, or volunteers, read aloud the Chapter Summary.
2. Allow the students to work with partners to complete the *Using Legal Language* activity.
3. Assign the *Checking for Comprehension* exercise as homework.
4. Allow the students to work in small groups to complete the *Applying Legal Concepts* activities.
5. As a class, complete the *Applying the Law* activities. (Please note that you may have to help students with vocabulary so that they adequately understand all of the *Applying the Law* material.)

In order to check student mastery of chapter concepts, you may wish to use the Chapter 9 test that is found in your *Teacher's Resource Binder* or use WESTEST computerized testing for Chapter 9.

CHAPTER REVIEW

SUMMARY

CONSIDERATION

Consideration consists of:

1. something of *legal value* given in exchange for a promise;
2. which occurs as part of a *bargained-for* exchange.

Legal Sufficiency of Consideration

To be legally sufficient, consideration must generally be a legal detriment to the promisee. Legal detriment is doing or promising to do something that one had no prior legal duty to do or refraining from or promising to refrain from doing something one had a right to do.

Adequacy of Consideration

Adequacy of consideration relates to "how much" consideration is given and whether a fair bargain was reached. If the consideration is legally sufficient, courts will only ask about adequacy of consideration when fraud, undue influence, or duress is involved.

Problems Concerning Consideration

1. *Uncertain performance*—If the promisor has not actually promised to do anything, the promise is said to be *illusory*—without consideration and unenforceable. Requirements, output, and contracts where parties have an option to cancel are usually held to be sufficiently definite to be enforceable.
2. *Settlement of claims*—One party to an existing contract may perform or agree to perform less than that originally promised in exchange for a promise from the other party to accept that lesser performance. The promise to accept the lesser performance may or may not be enforceable depending on whether consideration exists.
   a. If both parties agree to change their performances in some way, the prom-

ises are supported by consideration.
   b. If no disagreement exists between the parties on the performance owed, a promise to accept less is not enforceable. The promise is not supported by consideration.
   c. If a good faith disagreement exists on the performance owed, the parties can agree to settle the claim. Consideration exists to support the agreement.
   d. Release—A written agreement in which one party agrees to accept the amount stated in the document and give up any rights to further recovery. Many states do not require consideration; however, some do.
3. *Promissory Estoppel*—Promissory estoppel is an equitable doctrine by which courts sometimes enforce promises not supported by consideration. The doctrine is applied when:
   a. There is a promise.
   b. The promisee justifiably relies on the promise.
   c. The reliance is of a substantial and definite nature.
   d. Injustice can be avoided only by enforcing the promise.

CAPACITY TO CONTRACT

Minors

A minor is a person who has not yet reached the age of majority. In most states the age of majority is eighteen for contract purposes. Contracts with minors are voidable at the option of the minor.

Intoxicated Persons

1. A contract entered into by an intoxicated person is voidable by the intoxicated per-

Consideration and Capacity   227

son if the person was drunk enough to lack mental capacity, even if the intoxication was voluntary.

2. A contract with an intoxicated person is enforceable if, despite being intoxicated, the person understood the legal consequences of entering into the contract.

Mentally Incompetent Persons

1. A contract made by a person determined by a court to be mentally incompetent is void.

2. A contract made by a mentally incompetent person not adjudged by a court to be mentally incompetent may be voidable at the option of the mentally incompetent person or may be valid if the person understands the nature and effect of entering into the contract.

 # USING LEGAL LANGUAGE

Directions: Match each term with the statement that best defines that term.

1. consideration
2. contractual capacity
3. disaffirm
4. forbearance
5. legal detriment
6. minor
7. past consideration
8. promissory estoppel
9. release
10. rescission

A. The doctrine of _____ allows enforcement of a promise otherwise unsupported by consideration.

B. A person exercises _____ when he or she refrains from, or promises to refrain from, doing something that he or she has a legal right to do.

C. To be legally sufficient, consideration for a promise must generally be a _____ to the promisee.

D. Value given in return for a promise is _____. It consists of two parts: something of legal value given in exchange for the promise and a part of a bargained-for exchange.

E. Promises made to reward a person for actions or events that took place before the promise to reward are considered to be _____.

F. Many state statutes allow for parties to _____ and compromise claims without proof of consideration.

G. For a party to enter into a contract, he or she must have the legal right to contract which is called _____.

H. When someone legally avoids or sets aside a contractual duty, they _____ the contract.

I. In most situations a _____ can avoid a contract any time before reaching adulthood.

1. Yes. In the absence of fraud, undue influence, or duress, adequacy of consideration is not a question.
2. If two parties agree to rescind a contract—unmake the contract—both parties return to the position they were in before the contract was made.
3. To discharge a debt by payment of a lesser sum, first, the amount owed must be a bona fide dispute; and the parties must agree to accept the lesser amount as satisfaction for the debt.
4. Ratification can occur after the person is mentally competent or after a guardian is appointed who ratifies the contract.
5. Void means the contract is not enforceable; voidable means one or both of the parties may disaffirm or ratify; ratify means the contracts can be enforced.
6. John was correct in contending that no legally binding contract had been formed. He had offered to pay Lewis for doing something Lewis already had a preexisting legal duty to do; therefore, Lewis did not incur a legal detriment.
7. Legally, promises made to reward a person for actions or events that took place before the promise to reward are unenforceable. Students' views about the ethics of this situation may vary.
8. a–Since Kessler had not been adjudicated by the court as insane, the contract is voidable by the guardian. The guardian's disaffirmance is proper, and in

most states Kessler would have to return the full purchase price. b–If the contract was made after Kessler had been adjudicated insane, the contract would be void.

Applying the Law . . .
You Be the Judge (Answers)

1. Yes. Stating that the adequacy of consideration must be determined at the time a contract is agreed on, and not from the hindsight of how parties fare under it, the court explained that insurance has a value to the insured even if events on which the payment of benefits is conditioned do not occur. Regarding the cost of the insurance to Citibank, the court explained that it was not the court's function to review the amount of consideration to decide whether either party made a bad bargain, unless the amount was "so grossly inadequate as to shock the conscience of the court." The court said that it

---

J. _____ is the unmaking of a contract; returning both parties to the positions occupied before the contract.

CHECKING FOR COMPREHENSION

1. Has a legal contract been formed if your uncle offers to sell you his 1990 model automobile for $10, and you pay him the ten dollars?

2. Explain what occurs if a contract is rescinded.

3. What factors must be present to discharge a debt by payment of a lesser sum?

4. Can a contract made by a person who is mentally incompetent be ratified? If so, when?

5. Explain the difference between a contract being void, voidable, or ratified.

6. Ben hired Lewis to drive his racing car in a race. John, a friend of Lewis, promised to pay Lewis $3,000 if he won the race. Lewis won the race, but John refused to pay the $3,000. John contended that no legally binding contract had been formed since he had received no consideration from Lewis for his promise to pay the $3,000. Lewis sued John for breach of contract, arguing that winning the race was the consideration given in exchange for John's promise to pay the $3,000. What rule of law discussed in this chapter supports John's claim?

7. Darrell, a recent college graduate, is on his way home for the Christmas holidays. He gets caught in a snowstorm and is taken in by an elderly couple who provide him with food and shelter. After the snowplows have cleared the road, Darrell proceeds home. Darrell's father, Bruce, is most appreciative of the elderly couple's action and in a letter promises to pay them $500. The elderly couple, in need of money, accept Bruce's offer. Because of a dispute between Darrell and his father, Bruce refuses to pay the elderly couple the promised $500. Discuss whether the elderly couple can legally hold Bruce to his promise to pay for the services they rendered to Darrell.

8. Al has been the owner of a car dealership for a number of years. One day, Al sold one of his most expensive cars to Kessler. At the time of the sale, Al thought Kessler acted in a peculiar manner, but he gave the matter no further thought until four months later, when Kessler's court-appointed guardian appeared at his office, tendered back the car, and demanded Kessler's money back. The guardian informed Al that Kessler had been adjudged insane two months previously by a proper court.

(A) Discuss the rights of the parties.

(B) If Kessler had been adjudicated insane at the time of the contract, what would be the legal effect of the contract?

APPLYING LEGAL CONCEPTS

1. Think about something you would like to do that would require a contract. Write an agreement on paper, including the terms and places for signature. (Tell who the parties would be.) Read the contract aloud to the class. Discuss if there is sufficient consideration and if the parties have legal capacity.

2. Key the contract developed in activity 1 on the computer or typewriter.

could not say that its conscience was shocked by the exchange of two months of $100,000 of common carrier travel insurance coverage in return for the Finemans' payment of 83¢.

2. Generally, any contract entered into by a minor is voidable at the option of the minor. An exception to this rule is made, however, when the contract is for necessaries, such as food, clothing, or shelter. The question before the court in this case was whether the apartment leased by Sheridan and Wilwerding was a necessary. Because the tenants voluntarily lived away from home, with the understanding that they could return home at any time, the court ruled that they were not in need of shelter and thus the contract was not essential to their needs. Since the rental of the apartment was not a necessary, the court upheld the minor's right to void the contract, either during their minority or within a reasonable time after reaching their majority. Webster could not claim that the lease contract had been breached because by the minors' avoidance of the contract, the parties stood as if no contract had ever been formed.

3. Yes. Contracts of a minor are voidable at any time during minority or within a reasonable time after reaching the age of majority. What will be deemed a reasonable period of time by the courts depends on the facts of a particular case. Generally, however, it should be a sufficient amount of time to allow the minor, upon reaching the age of majority, to determine whether he or she will affirm or disaffirm the contractual obligation. In this case, the court held that since the contract was for the sale of personal property that was constantly depreciating in value, the minor had waited too long before attempting to disaffirm the contract. In this instance, ten months was deemed an unreasonable period of time. The fact that Smith made ten monthly payments after reaching the age of majority was strong evidence that Smith had ratified the contract, and the court so held.

4. Yes. The purpose of the radio station's offer to pay a listener $25,000 was to increase its listening audience. It purchased conduct, namely listening, by its promise. The station was therefore bound by contract to pay the money to Jennings when he detected that there was not a three-song sequence.

◆ APPLYING THE LAW . . . YOU BE THE JUDGE

1. Ellen and Gabriel Fineman held Master-Cards issued by Citibank. Holders of these cards paid an annual $15 fee. A retail installment credit agreement, contained the following statement: "We can change this Agreement including the *finance charge* and the *annual percentage rate* at any time." The agreement did provide for thirty days' notice of any such changes, and the cardholder had a right to reject the changes in writing and return the credit card. Two months before the expiration of the Finemans' cards, Citibank notified them that it was increasing its annual fee to $20. Citibank notified them it was also providing its cardholders with extra services and benefits, such as "$100,000 common carrier travel insurance." The Finemans did not object in writing, nor did they return the cards. Citibank added 83 cents to the Finemans' next bill, the prorated portion of the increase for the two months remaining on their cards. The Finemans filed suit (a class-action lawsuit on behalf of all cardholders) to recover the increased charges. Among other claims, the Finemans said there was no consideration for the modification. They argued the travel insurance was not adequate consideration for the modification since they never received any benefits from the insurance and its cost to Citibank was negligible. Was there adequate and legally sufficient consideration for Citibank's modification of the annual credit card fee? [*Fineman v. Citicorp USA, Inc.*, 137 Ill.App.3d 1035, 485 N.E.2d 591, 92 Ill.Dec. 780 (1985)]

2. In 1982, Webster Street Partnership, Ltd. (Webster), entered into a lease agreement with Matthew Sheridan and Pat Wilwerding. Webster was aware that both Sheridan and Wilwerding were minors. Both tenants were living away from home, apparently with the understanding that they could re-turn home at any time. Sheridan and Wilwerding paid the first month's rent but then did not pay the rent for the next month and vacated the apartment. Webster sued them for breach of contract. They claimed that the lease agreement was voidable since they were minors. Who will win, and why? [*Webster Street Partnership, Ltd. v. Sheridan*, 220 Neb. 9, 368 N.W.2d 439 (1985)]

3. Smith purchased a car on credit from Bobby Floars Toyota, Inc., a month before his eighteenth birthday. Smith made regular monthly payments for eleven months, but then returned the car to the dealer and made no further payments on it. The dealer sold the car and sued Smith to recover the difference between the selling price and money Smith still owed to the dealer. Smith refused to pay arguing that he was a minor at the time of the purchase and had disaffirmed the contract after he had reached the age of majority. Will the car dealer succeed in its claim that the ten monthly payments made after Smith turned eighteen are ratification of the purchase contract? [*Bobby Floars Toyota, Inc., v. Smith*, 48 N.C.App. 580, 269 S.E.2d 320 (1980)]

4. Radio Station KSCS is a country music radio station. On one of its programs it announced that it would pay $25,000 to any listener who detected that it did not play three consecutive songs. While Jennings was listening to the radio he heard a program in which two songs were followed by a commercial. When he claimed the $25,000, the station refused to pay. Radio Station KSCS claimed there was no consideration for its promise to pay that amount. Is there sufficient consideration to create a contractual agreement? [*Jennings v. Radio Station KSCS*, (Tex.App.) 708 S.W.2d 60 (1986)]

Introduce this Legal Perspective by having a student read aloud the Legal Perspective title, "Minors and Contract Law." Explain to students that *minors* have different rights when entering into contracts than do adults (those who have reached the age of majority). Ask students to explain why they think these differences exist. Then allow student volunteers to take turns reading this Legal Perspective aloud to the class.

For the purposes of contracts, 18 is the age of majority in most states.

LEGAL BACKGROUND

The issue of capacity of contracts as it relates to minors is so timely for high school students that we separated its treatment from the discussion of capacity in the chapter. Minority or infancy is, however, one subtopic of capacity. The general rule is that minors can avoid contracts if they wish. The contracts are voidable at the minor's option. Many students find it difficult to believe that minors can avoid contracts, and other students are surprised that minors have any contract rights at all.

There are some practical insights into this area that should be helpful. Since 18 rather than 21 became the standard age of adulthood, very little ligation has arisen from this area. The fact of the matter is that minors usually perform their promises just as adults because they believe it to be right or because they are concerned about their actions becoming part of their credit rating. Also, most merchants will not contract with minors on important affairs without a parental cosign, in which case the parents are liable.

LEGAL PERSPECTIVE

MINORS AND CONTRACT LAW

At common law, a minor was a male under the age of twenty-one or a female under the age of eighteen. Today in most states the age of majority—the age at which one is legally an adult—is eighteen years for contract purposes. Many states treat a person as an adult earlier if the person is married.

With a few exceptions, contracts with a minor are voidable by the minor. The minor has two choices. The minor can accept, or ratify, the contract, making it enforceable. Or the minor can renounce, or disaffirm, the contract and avoid the contract obligations. An adult who contracts with a minor cannot avoid contractual du-

ties. Unless the minor decides to avoid the contract, the adult party is bound by it.

◆ DISAFFIRMANCE

A minor can enter into any contract an adult can, provided the contract is not one prohibited by law for minors (for example, the sale of alcoholic beverages). The difference is that a minor can usually disaffirm the contract.

DISAFFIRMANCE IN GENERAL

A minor can avoid a contract by demonstrating an intention to disaffirm, to not be

What effect does turning 18 have on a teenagers legal and practical ability to contract?

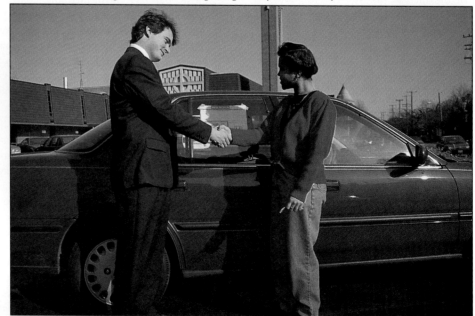

Discussion Starter

In most states the age of majority for contract purposes is 18. Ask students to discuss whether they agree or disagree that 18 should be the age of majority. List on the board the reasons students give. Also list pros and cons for students and for adults contracting with students.

Legal Focus Problem

Read to the class the Legal Focus Problem found here. Allow student volunteers to suggest possible answers to the question posed at the end of this problem.

Extension Activity

Have a student volunteer research your state's contract laws regarding minors. Does your state place the *duty of restitution* on minors?

Ethical Concern

If a state does not place the duty of restitution on minors, they may avoid a contract even if they have damaged the goods for which they contracted. Ask students if they think Jim Garrison, the minor who returned a damaged computer to Radio Shack, should be held responsible for the damages. Should his parents be held responsible?

Legal Focus Example

Have a student volunteer read this Legal Focus Example to the class. Ask the class if they can think of any other examples that could also fit here. Have volunteers share their examples with the class.

bound by it. The technical definition of **disaffirmance** is the legal avoidance, or setting aside, of a contractual duty. Words or conduct may express this intent.

Disaffirmance can take place any time during minority or for a reasonable time after the minor comes of age. In some states, in a contract for the sale of land by a minor, the minor cannot disaffirm the contract until after reaching majority.

Disaffirmance must be timely. Suppose Clarke wishes to disaffirm a contract she made as a minor but fails to disaffirm until two years after she has reached the age of majority. A court will probably hold that the contract has been ratified (see the discussion of ratification below).

DUTY OF RESTORATION

When a contract has been performed, minors cannot disaffirm it without returning the goods they have received. In most states, the minor must only return the goods (or other consideration), providing the goods remain in the minor's possession or control. This is the *duty of restoration*.

> ### LEGAL FOCUS - PROBLEM
>
> Jim Garrison, a seventeen-year-old, purchases a computer from Radio Shack. While transporting the computer to his home, Garrison negligently drops it, breaking the plastic casement. The next day he returns the computer to Radio Shack and disaffirms the contract. Does Radio Shack have to accept the broken computer and return the payment?

In most states, Jim's return fulfills his duty, even though the computer is now damaged.

This rule protects minors from reckless commitments because it discourages adults from dealing with them.

On the other hand, a few states place an additional duty on the minor—*the duty of restitution*. These states believe that the interests of those who deal with minors are also legitimate. The theory is that the adult should be returned to the position he or she held before entering the contract. Under this theory, in the example just given, Garrison would be required to return the computer and pay Radio Shack for the damage.

If a minor disaffirms a contract, he or she must disaffirm the *entire* contract. The minor cannot decide to keep part of the goods and return the remainder, for example. When a minor disaffirms, the minor can usually recover all property that he or she has transferred to an adult as consideration. However, if goods have been transferred to a good-faith purchaser—someone who purchases for value and is unaware of contract defenses—the minor loses the right to a return of the goods. The minor still has a right to a return of the value of the goods, however.

> ### LEGAL FOCUS - EXAMPLE
>
> Carla, a minor, sells her coin collection to Freda, a coin collector. A few days later, Freda sells the coin collection to Maxwell. Maxwell pays a fair price and was unaware that Freda had bought the coin collection from a minor. If Carla wished to avoid the contract, she no longer would be able to get the coin collection back because it had been sold to a good-faith purchaser.

(continued on page 232)

Ask a student volunteer to read this list of the ways in which different states deal with *a minor's misrepresentation of age*. Then stimulate a class discussion about this subject by asking the following questions: Which of the four ways listed here do you feel is the best way to deal with a minor's misrepresentation of age? Which of these is the most fair to the minor? Which of these is the most fair to the other party in the contract? Do any of these methods involve an element of punishment? Do you feel that an element of punishment should be involved?

Critical Thinking Activity

Ask students to write a short essay telling whether they think a minor who misrepresents his or her age when entering into a contract should be held responsible for fulfilling the contract or be allowed to avoid the contract. Should he or she be sued for damages?

LEGAL PERSPECTIVE (CONTINUED)

The Effect of a Minor's Misrepresentation of Age Suppose a minor tells a seller she is twenty-one years old when she or he is really seventeen. The misrepresentation of an important fact to encourage another to enter into a contract is ordinarily fraud. There is, however, considerable disagreement among the states as to how to treat a misrepresentation of age by a minor.

1. The majority view that is a minor can disaffirm the contract even though she or he has misrepresented her or his age. Moreover, the minor is not even liable for the tort of fraud for such a misrepresentation in some jurisdictions. These courts recognize that the tort suit is an indirect enforcement of the minor's contract.

2. Other jurisdictions will bind the minor to a contract when the minor has misrepresented his or her age. Several states have passed statutes for precisely this purpose. In these states, lying about age is enough to prohibit disaffirmance. Other statutes prohibit disaffirmance by a minor engaged in business as an adult.

3. Some courts refuse to allow minors who misrepresent their ages to disaffirm fully performed contracts unless they can return the consideration received. The combination of the minors' misrepresentation and their unjust enrichment has persuaded several courts to prevent minors from claiming contractual incapacity.

4. Some courts allow a misrepresenting minor to disaffirm the contract, but they hold the minor liable for damages in tort. Here, the defrauded party may sue the minor for misrepresentation or fraud.

Emancipation Emancipation is the release of a minor by his or her parents. It involves completely surrendering the right to the minor's control, care, custody, and earnings. It is a cancellation of parental obligations. Several states permit minors to petition for emancipation themselves. In these states, a grant of emancipation may also remove a minor's lack of capacity to contract, but generally emancipation does not affect a minor's contractual capacity.

LIABILITY FOR NECESSARIES, INSURANCE, AND LOANS

A minor who contracts for necessaries, such as food, clothing, and shelter, can still disaffirm the contract. The minor is, however, liable for the reasonable value of the goods. The legal duty to pay a reasonable value does not arise from the contract. It is imposed by law under a theory of quasi contract. One theory is that the minor should not be unjustly enriched. Thus, the minor is responsible for purchases that fulfill basic needs. Another theory is that unless minors can be held liable for the reasonable value of the goods, sellers will not contract with them. Minors might then be denied the opportunity to purchase necessary goods.

Traditionally, insurance has not been considered a necessary, so minors can usually disaffirm insurance contracts. Some jurisdictions, however, prohibit the right to disaffirm such contracts—for example, when minors contract for life insurance on their own lives.

Loans are seldom considered to be necessaries, even if the minor spends the borrowed money on necessaries. However, if a lender makes a loan to a minor for the express purpose of allowing the minor to pur-

Collaborative Learning Activity

Divide the class into groups. Each group should create and act out an example of one facet of contract law relating to minors. These facets might include disaffirmance, duty of restoration, a minor's misrepresentation of age, liability for necessaries, ratification, and minors and sales personnel. Allow each group to present its example to the class. You may wish to remind students that their presentation should be appropriate for your classroom.

Vocabulary Activity

Ask students if they have ever heard the term *ratification* before. In what context was this term used? (Many students may be familiar with the term *ratification* from history and/or government classes where the *ratification* of the United States Constitution was discussed.) Have students compare that use of the term *ratification* with the legal use shown here.

Reteaching Activity

Have students list the three ways a minor can ratify a contract.

Extension Activity

Have groups of two or three students inquire at local businesseses to find out if the businesses will contract with minors; for example, purchase of goods such as a diamond ring at a jewelry store, a compact disc player at an electronics store, a suit at a department store, a loan at the bank, a membership in a health club, a membership in a video club or store, car insurance, or health insurance for athletes. Instruct each group to outline its findings, then report to the class.

chase necessaries, and the lender personally makes sure that is how the money is spent, the minor is obligated to repay the loan.

RATIFICATION

A contract **ratification** is the act of accepting and giving legal force to an obligation that previously could be avoided. A minor, on reaching the age of majority, can ratify a contract. The three methods of ratification are express ratification, conduct, and failure to disaffirm the contract within a reasonable period of time.

Express ratification occurs when the minor, on reaching majority, states orally or in writing that he or she intends to be bound by the contract. After reaching majority, the minor can also demonstrate an intent to ratify the contract by conduct (by enjoying the benefits of the contract, for example). This is particularly true if the adult party to the contract has performed his or her part of the bargain. A minor's failure to disaffirm a contract within a reasonable time after reaching majority may also be ratification. If the contract is still executory (if it has not yet been performed or has been only partially performed), failure to disaffirm the contract does not necessarily imply ratification.

MINORS AND THE SALESPERSON

Sales personnel, particularly those who are paid on a commission basis, are often eager to make contracts. Sometimes these salespersons must deal with a minor who lacks the capacity to contract. It is important for them to remember that a contract signed with a minor (unless it is for necessaries) is voidable. The minor may exercise the option to disaffirm the contract, even though the adult who entered into the contract with the minor cannot avoid his or her contractual duties.

A salesperson selling consumer durables, such as console televisions or automobiles, must be careful of contracting with a minor. The salesperson should heed the adage "When in doubt, check." The salesperson should know the legal age of majority in his or her state. Proof of legal age should be required of a customer when there is any doubt concerning his or her age.

CHECKLIST FOR THE SALESPERSON

1. Determine the legal age of majority in the state.
2. When in doubt about the age of a customer, require proof of legal age.
3. If proof is not provided, require that a parent or guardian sign the contract.

 TERMS TO REMEMBER

◆ **disaffirmance** Legal avoidance, or setting aside, of a contractual duty.

◆ **ratification** Accepting and giving legal force to an obligation that could have been avoided.

Mastery Objectives

By the end of this chapter, students will be able to:
- Describe contracts contrary to statute
- Determine if a contract is contrary to public policy
- Explain the effect of illegality on contracts
- Identify mistakes in contract formation
- List the four elements of fraud in contract misrepresentation
- Distinguish between undue influence and duress

Prereading Activity

Ask students if they know the terms *loan shark, usury,* and *gambling.* Then ask them what the terms have in common.

LEGAL BACKGROUND

To this point in the unit, your students have studied how a contract comes into existence. This chapter changes course somewhat and raises issues about the circumstances under which an apparent contract was made.

The first half of the chapter discusses circumstances under which an agreement that appears to be valid can be void because the subject matter is illegal. Illegality for purposes of contract law is a very broad concept that ranges from violations of criminal laws to violations of public policy. In the second half of the chapter, issues are raised regarding the state of mind of contracting parties. Did the parties really agree to a contract, or do circumstances exist under which a person can avoid an apparent obligation? Mistake, fraudulent misrepresentation, duress, and undue influence are discussed as examples of circumstances where genuine assent may be lacking.

234

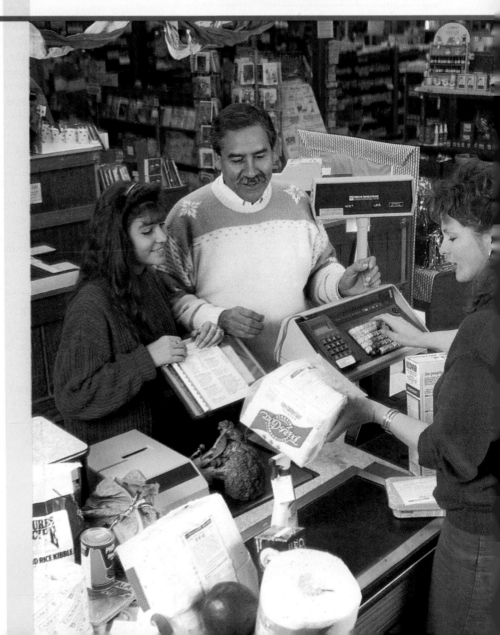

Chapter

10

Legality and Genuineness of Assent

"Law is a pledge that the citizens of a state will do justice to one another."
Aristotle, 384–322 B.C.
Greek philosopher

Courts generally hope to enforce a contract. If parties create an agreement, the courts believe they should help in its enforcement. However, there are situations where a contract cannot or should not be enforced. Can you imagine the courts hearing and helping two criminals who are fighting over a share of money from a robbery? As you would expect, the courts would not assist people in enforcing such a contract because it is illegal. However, it is not always clear what exactly is an illegal contract, and how the courts should handle the variety of situations relating to illegal agreements. Contracts may also be unenforceable if genuine assent is lacking. Genuine assent may be absent for several reasons, one of which is fraud. A party who lies to another party about an important fact related to a contract has committed fraud. If fraud exists, genuine assent does not, and no true agreement is present.

As Aristotle stated, the law seeks to ensure that "the citizens of a state will do justice to one another." If the law were to enforce illegal contracts or contracts where genuine assent is not present, injustice would result. In this chapter, we examine problems of justice in contract enforcement relating to legality of contracts and genuine assent.

◆ CONTRACTS CONTRARY TO STATUTE

A contract to do something illegal is void from the start and not enforceable. A contract calling for a tort or an action counter to public policy is also illegal and unenforceable. A contract, or a clause in a contract, may be illegal even if no specific statute prohibits the action expected by the contract. This section discusses several statutory areas that can affect the legality of contracts: usury laws, gambling laws, Sabbath laws, and licensing statutes.

USURY LAWS

Every state has laws setting maximum rates of interest chargeable on loans. Someone lending money at an interest rate above the lawful maximum is guilty of **usury**. The maximum allowable rate of interest varies from state to state. The maximum rate for commercial or business lenders often varies even within one state based on the nature of the business. For example, banks, credit unions, and pawn brokers are often allowed to charge different maximum rates. The maximum rate a private lender may charge is usually what most people understand as the usury rate. A private lender in-

◆ **usury** Charging an illegal interest rate.

Have students research the maximum rate of interest, the legal rate of interest, and the judgment rate of interest in your state. Students should create a line graph plotting each amount.

Usury is one of the subjects at the heart of William Shakespeare's *The Merchant of Venice.* Have a student volunteer or group of student volunteers read *The Merchant of Venice* and then discuss with the class what the play says about usury, justice, and prejudice. You might encourage one of the students to enliven the presentation by performing Portia's soliloquy, which begins, "The quality of mercy is not strained. . . ."

Instruct students to write a one-page essay answering the question: "Do you think it is a good idea to allow lenders to charge higher interest rates to some borrowers?"

State Law

Have students research the maximum rates of interest allowable on loans in your state and at least four other states. Have them design a bar graph showing the maximums for the various states.

VIDEODISC NOTE
Much of the material that is conveyed in the exhibits of *West's Business and Personal Law* is also conveyed in the still frames on the **West Business Law and Legal Environment Videodisc.** For more information and directions for use, please see the Index and Description of Contents for the **West Business Law and Legal Environment Videodisc** that is found in your *Teacher's Resource Binder.*

◆ **legal rate of interest** A rate fixed by statute to be used when contracting parties forget to fix a rate of interest in a loan.

◆ **judgment rate of interest** A rate of interest fixed by statute added to an unpaid money judgment until it is paid.

cludes your parents, other family, friends, acquaintances, and even the neighborhood loan shark.

The maximum rate for usury purposes is different from the legal or the judgment rate of interest. The **legal rate of interest** is a rate fixed by statute when contracting parties forget to fix a rate of interest in a loan. Statutes also provide for a **judgment rate of interest** that determines the interest added to a court-awarded money judgment until it is paid. The maximum rate for private lenders, the legal rate of interest, and the judgment rate are provided for five representative states in Exhibit 10-1.

Exceptions   Usury statutes set a maximum allowable rate of interest, but many exceptions exist for business transactions. For example, many states exempt all corporate loans from the usury laws. In addition, most states have special statutes allowing much higher interest rates on small loans which are often higher risk and less profitable to the lender. If the statutes

EXHIBIT 10-1
SAMPLE STATE INTEREST RATES

State	Maximum Rate[1]	Legal Rate	Judgment Rate
California	10%[2]	7%	10%
Florida	18%	12%	12%
New York	16%	9%	9%
Ohio	8%	10%	10%
Texas	10%[3]	6%	18%
West Virginia	8%	6%	10%

[1] Rate *usually* only applies to private (non-business) lenders. Also, federal law may preempt state usury laws for certain commercial lenders.
[2] A higher interest tied to the federal discount rate may be allowed.
[3] Applies to oral contracts; higher, variable rate allowed for written contracts.

Critical Thinking Activity

Many companies such as banks charter their credit card divisions in another state rather than the state in which their main office is located. Lead a discussion by asking students why they think they do so.

Legal Focus Problem

Read to the class the Legal Focus Problem found here. Allow student volunteers to suggest possible answers to the question at the end of this problem.

State Law

From 1984 to 1992, 32 states (including Texas, Florida, New York, Michigan, and California) as well as the District of Columbia, had taken in a total of almost $100 billion in state lottery revenues. In 1992, the estimate was almost $22 billion in lottery revenues. If your state has a lottery, you might ask students to research lottery revenues for your state in the previous year. If your state does not have a lottery, you might ask students to research any lottery proposals that have come before the state legislature, or before voters, in the last five to ten years. Why did these measures fail?

---

did not allow higher rates on small loans, many borrowers could not get loans at the normal lawful maximum interest rate. Many might be forced to borrow from "loan sharks" who use illegal methods to enforce repayment of loans.

Installment Loans   Many states have special statutes regulating interest on installment loans, especially retail and motor-vehicle installment sales. **Installment loans** require payment of a debt over time, usually with monthly payments. Rates allowed on installment contracts vary greatly from state to state.

Sales agreements often give the purchaser a chance to pay charges through a revolving charge account. With a charge account, a purchaser can make many credit purchases (by using a credit card at a department store, for example). After receiving the bill, the purchaser can either pay it in full or pay a minimum monthly amount. For the privilege of paying the balance later, the purchaser pays monthly interest on the balance. Many courts have concluded that revolving charge accounts are not really "loans of money" but instead are a type of higher price for goods. These revolving charge accounts are not controlled by usury laws.

Effects of Usury   Even if a loan is usurious, many states allow the lender to recover the loan amount along with interest at the legal maximum. Essentially, the lender is denied recovery of the excess interest. In other states, the lender can recover the principal but not the interest. In a few states, the usurious loan is considered void. In a void transaction, the lender cannot recover either the principal or the interest.

EAB Best Rates

CREDIT PRODUCTS	Interest Rate %	Annual Percentage Rate (APR)
30 Yr. Fixed Mortgage	8.00	8.2
15 Yr. Fixed Mortgage	7.50	7.9
3 Yr. Adj. Mortgage	6.750	7.9
Home Adv. Credit Line	6.00	6.0
Home Advantage Loan	9.95	
New Auto Loan	8.75	
Overdraft Account	15.50	
Secured Loan	9.75	

Are most bank loans subject to state usury laws?

◆ **installment loan**
A loan that requires payment of a debt over time, usually with monthly payments.

GAMBLING LAWS

In general, bets and games of chance are illegal. All states have statutes that regulate gambling. **Gambling** is any scheme that involves distribution of property by chance among persons who have paid something of value for the chance to receive the property. A few states allow gambling. Several states have also legalized state-operated lotteries.

Sometimes it is difficult to distinguish a gambling contract from the risk sharing inherent in most contracts.

◆ **gambling** Any scheme that involves distribution of property by chance among persons who have paid something of value for the opportunity to receive the property.

◆ LEGAL FOCUS – PROBLEM

Isaacson takes out a life insurance policy on Donohue. Isaacson names himself as the beneficiary (the person to be paid) under the policy. Is this a legal contract or a gambling agreement?

At first glance, the life insurance policy contract appears legal. However, Isaacson is simply gambling on how long Donohue will live. To prevent this type of contract, only someone with an **insurable interest** is allowed

◆ **insurable interest**
A real economic risk related to rights in property or a person's well-being.

Reteaching Activity

Ask a volunteer to define the term *insurable interest* for your class. Then have each student make a list of situations in which he or she has an insurable interest.

Critical Thinking Activity

Point out to students that, as they learned in Chapter 2, there is a constitutionally implied separation of church and state. Ask students to consider this separation of church and state and then write a one-paragraph discussion of Sabbath laws and whether or not they feel these laws violate the spirit of the Constitution.

to recover on an insurance contract. An insurable interest exists when a person has a real economic risk related to the property or person insured. If your watch is stolen or damaged, for example, you suffer a real loss. If someone else's watch is stolen or broken, you may feel bad, but you suffer no direct economic loss. Thus, you have an insurable interest in your watch, but not in the other person's. Isaacson cannot collect on an insurance policy on Donohue's life (or home or auto) because Isaacson does not have an insurable interest in Donohue or his property. If Isaacson was a part owner of Donohue's automobile, however, he could legally collect on an insurance policy on the auto because he has a property interest.

SABBATH LAWS

Statutes called Sabbath, or Sunday, laws prohibit the formation or performance of certain contracts on a Sunday. A contract created on Sunday is legal unless a statute prohibits it. Many states, however, have some type of Sunday statute.

In some states, all contracts entered into on a Sunday are illegal. Several states have laws that forbid the carrying on of "all secular labor and business on The Lord's Day." Statutes in other states prohibit only the sale of merchandise, particularly alcoholic beverages, on a Sunday. These laws are called **blue laws**.

◆ **blue laws** Laws restricting business activities on Sunday.

Exceptions to Sunday laws permit the making of contracts for necessities (such as food) and works of charity. A fully performed contract entered into on a Sunday cannot be rescinded (canceled). How actively Sunday laws are enforced varies from state to state and even among communities within a particular state. Many states do not enforce their Sunday laws, and some states have held such laws to be unconstitutional.

LICENSING STATUTES

All states require licensing of certain professionals before they may practice their profession. Doctors, lawyers, real estate brokers, architects, electricians, teachers, and stockbrokers are examples of the professionals who must be licensed. Some licenses require extensive schooling and examinations. These licenses represent to the public that the license holder has a special skill. Other licenses require only that the applicant be of good moral character.

Some contracts with unlicensed persons are enforceable, and some are not. The essential factor is the type of licensing statute. Some statutes expressly provide that the lack of a license in certain occupations bars the enforcement of work-related contracts. Where this is not the case, one must look to the purpose for licensing a particular occupation. If the purpose is to protect the public from unauthorized practitioners, a contract with an unlicensed individual is illegal and unenforceable. On the other hand, if the purpose is simply to raise revenues, the contract is enforceable.

Legal Focus
Case Problem

Divide the class into small groups to read and discuss the Legal Focus Problem found here. Each group should choose a leader to explain its response to the question posed at the end of this problem.

 Ethical Concern

Guide your students in discussing the Legal Focus case on this page. Stimulate a class discussion about the fairness of this decision. What are the laws that prevented the realtor from collecting the commission? Why do you think such laws exist?

Caption Answer

Generally, a combination of education, professional experience, and test completion is required to secure an architect's license. Since architects are licensed to protect the public from unauthorized practitioners, a contract with an unlicensed individual is illegal and unenforceable.

What requirements do you think an architect must meet to be licensed? If a person contracts to perform architect services, but is not licensed, is the contract enforceable?

◆ LEGAL FOCUS – CASE PROBLEM

Paris was a real estate broker licensed in the state of Georgia. Paris contacted Cooper, a Florida resident who was interested in purchasing some Gulf County, Florida, acreage. Paris visited the property in Florida, helped prepare Cooper's written offer of purchase, worked with Cooper's attorney on the sales contract, and attended the closing of the sale in Panama City, Florida. As a result of this sale, Paris received a $315,070 commission. Can Cooper recover the commission on the basis that the contract is unenforceable because Paris was not licensed to conduct real estate transactions in Florida?

Ethical Concern

Guide your students in discussing the Legal Focus on this page by asking them if a contract to encourage marriage is legal. Why is a contract that discourages it illegal? Ask your students what is meant by a contract that encourages marriage. Is a wedding a marriage contract? Is it an engagement?

Vocabulary Activity

Divide the class into groups of three or four to discuss the meaning of *good will* as it relates to business. Write a page describing what is included in good will and how the dollar value of good will can be determined. Allow one person from each group to present the group's conclusions to the class.

Extension Activity

Have two or three volunteers find out what would happen in your state if an engagement to marry was broken. Would the man be able to get the engagement ring back, or would the woman be allowed to keep it? Does it make a difference whether he or she broke the engagement?

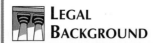

LEGAL BACKGROUND

Contracts in restraint of trade are contracts or combinations that tend, or are designed, to eliminate or stifle competition, create a monopoly, artificially maintain prices, or otherwise hamper or obstruct the course of trade as it would be carried on if it were left to the control of natural economic forces.

Yes. An agent must have a real estate license to represent a client in a real estate transaction and expect to collect a fee. Such licenses are granted by each state to protect the citizens of that state. A license in Georgia does not authorize the agent to practice in Florida. Paris, the agent, could not collect the commission, and if the commission had been paid, the client could sue for its return.[1]

CONTRACTS CONTRARY TO PUBLIC POLICY

Although contracts involve private parties, the courts may refuse to enforce some contracts because of the negative impact of the contracts on society. These contracts are *contrary to public policy*. Examples of contracts contrary to public policy include contracts to commit an immoral act and contracts forbidding marriage.

 LEGAL FOCUS ~ EXAMPLE

Everett offers Ted $500 if he will leave town and not marry Everett's daughter Michelle. Ted accepts, but the resulting contract is not enforceable. It is void. If Ted marries Everett's daughter, Everett cannot sue him for breach of contract. Contracts that limit the ability of someone to marry are considered to be in violation of public policy.

Other contracts contrary to public policy include contracts in restraint of trade, unconscionable contracts, and exculpatory clauses.

CONTRACTS IN RESTRAINT OF TRADE

A contract in restraint of trade is any contract that interferes with or inhibits free trade. Such contracts often violate one or more federal or state statutes. Contracts in restraint of trade are usually held to be against the public interest, because the public interest favors free competition.

There are two major exceptions. They involve situations in which an agreement called a *covenant not to compete* is part of an otherwise enforceable contract for the sale of a business or employment contract. To be legal, such agreements can be no more extensive in time, scope, and distance than necessary to protect the interests of the contracting parties.

A promise by a person selling a store not to open a new store close to the old store is an example of a covenant not to compete. This promise allows the seller to sell, and the purchaser to buy, the "good will" and reputation of a business.

---

1. *Cooper v. Paris*, 413 So.2d 772 (Fla.App., 1st Dist. 1982).

Legal Focus Example

Extension Activity

Teaching Note

Excerpts from the Sherman Antitrust Act are included in the Resource Center at the back of this book.

Read this Legal Focus Example to the class. Ask the class if they can think of any other examples that could also fit here. Allow volunteers to share their examples with the class.

Often contracts in restraint of trade are in violation of the Sherman Antitrust Act. You might ask a volunteer to research the Sherman Antitrust Act and report to the class on the nature of the act, the political and business climate in which the act was passed, and enforcement of the act. You might refer the student to history texts as a resource for his or her research.

◆ LEGAL FOCUS ~ EXAMPLE

A well-known merchant sells her store. A month later, the merchant opens a competing business a block away. Many of the merchant's old customers will go to the merchant's new store. Because of the new store, any amount the buyer paid for the good name and reputation of the old business is a waste of money. This "good will" may have been sold to the new merchant at a significant price.

When a contract to sell a business includes a promise by the seller not to compete with the new buyer, the promise is enforceable to the extent that it is reasonable as to time, scope, and distance. A covenant not to compete that is not part of the sale of a business is void because it unreasonably restrains trade and so is contrary to public policy.

Agreements not to compete can also be part of employment contracts. It is common for middle-level and upper-level managers to agree not to work for competitors or start new businesses for a specified time after leaving employment. The restriction on competition must be reasonable. The restriction should not be any greater than necessary to protect a legitimate business interest.

◆ LEGAL FOCUS ~ CASE PROBLEM

In 1982, Thomas Rector and four other employees of Paramount Termite Control Company signed a noncompetition agreement with Paramount as part of their employment contract. The employees agreed that for two years after leaving Paramount's employment, they would not "solicit business from any customer of PARAMOUNT where the purpose thereof is to provide . . . the services of pest control . . . with which customer the Employee established contact while in the employ of PARAMOUNT at any time during the two (2) years next preceding the termination of the Employment Agreement." The agreement covered the areas the employees serviced as Paramount employees. Later, the employees resigned from Paramount and began working for a Paramount competitor that solicited business in counties prohibited by the noncompetition agreement. Paramount sought to enforce the promise. Did Paramount succeed?

Yes. The Supreme Court of Virginia held that the restriction on competition was reasonable in time (two-year period) and reasonable in the geographic area covered. The court applied three criteria: (1) From the standpoint of the employer, was the restraint reasonable—no greater than necessary to protect a legitimate business interest of the employer? (2) From the standpoint of the employee, was the restraint reasonable—not unduly harsh and oppressive in limiting the employee's ability to earn a

Legal Focus Case Problem

Read aloud to the class this Legal Focus Problem dealing with Paramount Termite Control. Allow a student volunteer to suggest a possible answer to the question posed at the end of this problem.

Ethical Concern

Guide the students in reading the Legal Focus Problem regarding Thomas Rector and Paramount Termite Control Company, by asking the following questions: Do you believe that Paramount Termite Control Company acted ethically in requiring its employees to sign a noncompetition agreement as a part of their employment contract? Why or why not? Did Thomas Rector and the other employees behave in an ethical manner when they resigned from Paramount and began working for a Paramount competitor in counties prohibited by the noncompetition agreement? Why or why not?

Ask the students if they have ever heard the phrase "in good conscience." In what context have they heard that phrase? What does that phrase mean? How does the phrase "in good conscience" relate to the phrase "unconscionable contract or clause" as defined here?

Legal Focus Problem

Read this Legal Focus Problem to the class. Remind students that they can use the Legal Focus features as review tools when studying for tests.

---

242   The Law of Contracts

living? (3) Was the restraint reasonable as sound public policy? The court concluded that the restraint was no greater than reasonably necessary to protect Paramount's legitimate business interest. The five employees "had frequent contacts with Paramount's customers" and "were familiar with Paramount's methods of estimating the cost of its work, its specifications for doing the work, and its techniques of pest control." The court also found the geographic restriction reasonable, as it only applied to those counties in which the employees had previously worked and not all counties within the state. Finally, given sufficient competition in the area, the court held the restrictions did not unreasonably restrain trade or violate public policy. The agreements were valid.[2]

UNCONSCIONABLE CONTRACTS AND EXCULPATORY CLAUSES

Ordinarily, a court does not look at the fairness of a contract. The court does not second-guess the bargain or the adequacy of consideration. The court assumes that people are intelligent, and it will not bail them out because they have made an unwise or foolish bargain. Sometimes, however, bargains are so burdensome that the courts relieve innocent parties of part or all of their duties. Such a bargain is an **unconscionable contract or clause**. (A clause is a section of a contract.)

◆ **unconscionable contract or clause**
A contract or clause that is grossly unfair because of its terms or circumstances or both.

An unconscionable contract is one that shocks the conscience—that is terribly unfair. A contract can be unconscionable if a party is unable to understand the contract terms. A lack of understanding can arise because of small print, difficult language ("legalese"), lack of opportunity to read the contract, lack of opportunity to ask questions about the contract's meaning, and other factors. Courts generally focus on language that deprives one party of the benefits of the agreement or leaves that party without remedy for nonperformance by the other.

◆ **exculpatory clause** A contract provision that releases a party from liability for his or her wrongful acts.

Closely related to unconscionable contracts are **exculpatory clauses**. Exculpatory clauses release a party from liability in the event of monetary or physical injury, *even if the released party was at fault*. Often, these clauses are held unconscionable, and the courts will not enforce them. For example, exculpatory clauses that forgive the harm caused by a negligent employer to an employee are normally unenforceable.

◆ LEGAL FOCUS ～ PROBLEM

Madison Manufacturing Company hires a laborer and has her sign a contract stating: "Said employee hereby agrees with employer, in consideration of such employment, that she will take upon herself all risks incident to her position and will never hold the company liable for any injury or damage she may sustain, in her person or

2. *Paramount Termite Control Co. v. Rector*, 238 Va. 171, 380 S.E.2d 922, (Virginia 1989).

Ethical Concern

Stimulate a class discussion on the following scenario: Maria Gonzalez signs a contract to buy an automobile from an automobile dealership. She does not understand English very well; therefore, the salesperson tells her that her payments will be $150 per month for three years. When her nephew looks at the contract he finds that the contract states she will pay $150 per month for *six* years. Is this unconscionable? Does Maria have a right to sue the dealership?

otherwise, by accidents or injuries in the factory, or which may result from defective machinery or carelessness or misconduct of herself or any other employee in service of the employer." Is this enforceable?

This contract clause attempts to eliminate Madison's liability for injuries to an employee. Such a clause would probably be held contrary to public policy. Also, exculpatory clauses involving public utilities, such as a railroad or an electric company, are usually unenforceable. A railroad, for example, cannot use an exculpatory clause to avoid liability for the negligent maintenance of its trains.

When one party has vastly superior bargaining power, a contract between that party and another may also be deemed unconscionable. Such situations usually involve an adhesion contract. An **adhesion contract** is a contract drafted by a dominant party and then presented to the other party—the adhering party—on a "take it or leave it" basis. Unconscionable clauses, those that "shock the conscience" of a court, are more likely to be found in adhesion contracts than contracts where the parties truly bargained over terms.

◆ **adhesion contract** A standard "form" contract drafted by a dominant party and then presented to the other party—the adhering party—on a "take it or leave it" basis.

◀ LEGAL FOCUS – PROBLEM

A welfare recipient with a fourth-grade education agrees to purchase a refrigerator for $2,000. He signs a two-year installment contract with a high but legal interest rate. The same type of refrigerator usually sells for $400 on the market. Is it possible that this contract is unconscionable?

Some courts have held this type of contract to be unconscionable, even though courts generally do not inquire into the adequacy of the consideration. Both the Uniform Commercial Code and the Uniform Consumer Credit Code (UCCC) (which deals with consumer loan contracts) allow courts to set aside unconscionable contracts.

The fact that the terms of a contract favor one party over another is not enough in itself to make the contract unconscionable. Unless the unfairness is considered outrageous, courts will not set aside the contract. The philosophy is that persons are bound by their agreements, even if an agreement turns out to be a bad bargain.

◆ EFFECT OF ILLEGALITY

An illegal contract is usually void. The contract is treated as if it never existed. For most illegal contracts, both parties are treated as being equally at

Legal Focus Problem

Divide the class into small groups to read and discuss this Legal Focus Problem. Each group should discuss whether or not this contract is unconscionable. Did the seller of the refrigerator behave ethically or unethically, in the group's opinion? Each group should choose a leader to explain its responses to the class.

Critical Thinking Activity

Ask the students to write short essays discussing the relationship between *unconscionable contracts* and *caveat emptor.* Allow volunteers to share their essays with the class.

Read

You might want to introduce this *Law in Action* feature by reminding the students of the relationship of *unconscionability* to *caveat emptor*. (See Critical Thinking Activity, previous page.) Then allow a student volunteer to read this *Law in Action* feature aloud to the class.

Discuss

Stimulate a class discussion of this *Law in Action* feature by asking the following questions: Does the UCC define *unconscionability?* Why not? How does *unconscionability* relate *to ethics?* Is the *doctrine of unconscionability* used to assure that all contracts are ethical? Do you feel that it should be? Why or why not?

244   The Law of Contracts

Law in Action

LEGAL ISSUE: UNCONSCIONABILITY—WHERE ETHICS MEETS THE LAW

he doctrine of unconscionability is a good example of how the law tries to encourage ethical behavior. This doctrine holds that some contracts are so unfair to one party as to be unenforceable, even though the party agreed to the contract's terms.

The Uniform Commercial Code provides that a court may consider the fairness of any sales contract. If a contract or contract clause is unconscionable, the court may refuse to enforce the contract. Alternatively, the court may enforce the other parts of the contract, but not the unconscionable clause, or limit the application of the clause to avoid an unconscionable result.

The UCC does not define the term *unconscionability*. The drafters of the UCC did, however, add explanatory comments to guide in the code's interpretation. The comments suggest a basic test for unconscionability. Is the clause so one-sided under the circumstances existing at the time of the making of the contract as to be unconscionable?

Unconscionable actions, like unethical actions, cannot be precisely defined. Information about the particular facts and specific circumstances surrounding the contract is essential. For example, a contract with a person who cannot read well might be seen as unfair and unenforceable. The same contract with a major business firm would be upheld.

The doctrine of unconscionability could be used to assure that all contracts are ethical. However, the courts have not used it in this way. Only extremely one-sided contracts that "shock the conscience" are found unconscionable. Courts are reluctant to hold a contract or contractual clause unconscionable in all but the most extreme situations. If a contract is determined to be unconscionable and unenforceable, a trade-off is made. A person is excused from an unfair agreement, but at the expense of the court's interfering with contract enforcement.

The performance of contract promises is one of the cornerstones of society. It is not disposed of lightly by the courts. On the contrary, the courts will try to save contracts rather than hold them unenforceable.

fault, and the courts do not aid either party in enforcement. If the contract is executory (not yet completed), neither party can enforce it. If one party has performed, the other party cannot recover either the contracted performance or anything else of value.

Sometimes one party to an illegal contract is unjustly enriched at the expense of the other. This does not unduly concern the law—with a few exceptions (to be discussed shortly). The major reason for this hands-off attitude is the belief that it is improper to allow a plaintiff who has broken the law to receive the aid of the courts. Another reason is the hoped-for deterrent effect of this general rule. A plaintiff suffering a loss because of an illegal bargain is discouraged from making illegal bargains in the future.

EXCEPTIONS TO THE GENERAL RULE

There are some exceptions to the general rule that parties to an illegal bargain cannot sue for breach or reimbursement.

Justifiable Ignorance of the Facts   If one party is relatively innocent (the party does not appreciate that the contract is illegal), that party can often recover payments in a partially executed contract. The courts do not enforce the contract but allow the parties to return to their original positions.

It is also possible sometimes for an innocent party who has fully performed to enforce the contract against the guilty party.

◆ LEGAL FOCUS – PROBLEM

Debbie contracts with Tucker to purchase ten crates of goods that are illegal to sell or buy. Tucker hires a trucking firm (which is unaware of the scheme) to deliver the shipment to Debbie. Tucker pays the firm the normal fee of $500. Is the contract between Tucker and the trucking firm illegal?

The law holds that the shipment, use, and sale of the goods is illegal. The trucking firm, however, being an innocent party, can legally collect the $500 from Tucker.

Members of Protected Classes   When a statute protects a certain class of people, a member of that class can enforce an illegal contract though the other party cannot.

◆ LEGAL FOCUS – EXAMPLE

Many states have statutes that prohibit certain employees (such as flight attendants) from working more than a specified number of hours per month. An employee who works more than the maximum can recover for those extra hours of service. The employer could not, however, require that the employees work more than the maximum hours even if they agreed.

A client of an unlicensed person who is required to have a professional license can usually seek restitution, or return of payments. Often a court will assist these clients even if they knew the person was unlicensed.

Withdrawal from an Illegal Agreement   If the illegal part of a bargain has not yet been performed, a party often can withdraw from the bargain and recover the consideration they provided.

Legal Focus Problem

Read to the class the Legal Focus Problem found here. Allow student volunteers to suggest possible answers to the question at the end of this problem.

Reteaching Activity

Have students list the three exceptions to the rule that prohibits parties of an illegal agreement from suing for breach of contract.

Legal Focus Example

Read this Legal Focus Example to the class. Ask the class if they can think of any other examples that could also fit here. Allow volunteers to share their examples with the class.

Read to the class the Legal Focus Problem found here. Allow student volunteers to suggest possible answers to the question posed at the end of this problem.

Checking Your Progress (Answers)

1. The legal rate of interest is a rate fixed by statute when contracting parties forget to fix a rate of interest on a loan, but a judgment rate of interest is interest added to a money judgment established by the court.
2. No. Many courts conclude that revolving charge accounts are not really loans of money; therefore, usury laws would not apply.
3. If the purpose of the licensing of that profession is to protect the public, the contract is illegal and unenforceable. However, if the purpose is to raise revenues, the contract is enforceable.
4. A contract can be unconscionable if a party is unable to understand the terms because of small print, difficult language, or lack of opportunity to read the contract or ask questions.

5. An exculpatory clause releases a party from liability in the event of monetary or physical injury. Therefore, the clause is often unenforceable.
6. No. An adhesion contract is drafted by a dominant party and presented to the other party to accept or not accept.
7. Courts usually will not aid either party in enforcing an illegal contract and treat the contract as if it never existed.

Teaching with the Videodisc

At this time, you may wish to show the students the motion segment titled *Mistake* from the **West Business Law and Legal Environment Videodisc.** This fictional dramatization is part of *West's Business Law's Drama of the Law Series.* Each of these dramatizations was written by award-winning writer John J. Osborne, Jr. (originator and author of *The Paper Chase*). Each of these was created by

 LEGAL FOCUS ~ PROBLEM

Martha and Andy decide to wager (illegally) on the outcome of a boxing match. Each deposits money with a stakeholder, who agrees to pay the winner of the bet. At this point, each party has performed part of the agreement. The illegal part of the agreement does not occur, however, until the money is paid to the winner. Before the fight, Martha decides the bet was a bad idea. She asks the stakeholder to return her money. Does she have a legal right to a return of the money?

Yes. Before the boxing match, either party can withdraw from the agreement by giving notice of retraction to the stakeholder.

Contract Illegal through Fraud, Duress, or Undue Influence
Sometimes, illegal contracts involve two blameworthy people, but one party is more at fault than the other. When a party has been induced to enter into an illegal bargain by fraud, duress, or undue influence from the other party to the agreement, the victimized party may be able to recover some value of his or her performance from the more corrupt party.

◆ CHECKING YOUR PROGRESS

1. What is the difference between the legal rate of interest and the judgment rate of interest?
2. Is a revolving charge account at a department store controlled by usury laws?
3. Is a contract with an unlicensed professional enforceable if the profession requires a person to have a license to practice?
4. What factors can cause a contract to be judged unconscionable?
5. How does an exculpatory clause affect a contract?
6. Do both parties have equal input into an adhesion contract?
7. How are illegal contracts treated by the court?

◆ GENUINENESS OF ASSENT

♦ **genuine assent**
A true objective "meeting of the minds."

An otherwise valid contract may be unenforceable if the parties have not genuinely assented to the terms. **Genuine assent** exists if there is a true, objective "meeting of the minds" between the contracting parties. Genuine assent is lacking if there is mistake, fraudulent misrepresentation, undue influence, or duress. If the law enforced contracts lacking true assent, injustice would result. In this section, we examine problems related to genuineness of assent.

Osborne and West to bring points of law to life for your students.

In this segment, Mr. Melnick shows up at a supermarket ready to take advantage of an unbelievable price advertised for peppers. This segment illustrates how easily mistakes can be made and their legal consequences. Note: You may have already shown this motion segment as a part of your discussion of Chapter 6, Ethics and Social Responsibility.

Each of the legal implications included in this motion segment is discussed in the *Drama of the Law Instructor's Manual,* which is included in your *Teacher's Resource Binder.* To access this motion segment, you can use the bar code provided here or punch in the frame number below. Note: This *Drama of the Law* video is also available on videotape for nonvideodisc users.

Search Frame 26751

MISTAKES

If both parties are mistaken about an important contract fact, an agreement lacks mutual assent, and no contract exists. It is important to distinguish between mistakes as to fact and mistakes as to judgment of value or quality. Only mistakes of fact have legal significance. In contract formation, mistakes can be of two types—unilateral and bilateral, or mutual.

BILATERAL MISTAKES

A **bilateral mistake** is made by both parties. (You might want to recall the way that the words *bilateral* and *unilateral* were used in Chapter 7.) When both parties are wrong about the same material fact, either party can rescind the contract. The mistake must be about a *material fact*—one that is important and central to the contract. If the mutual mistake concerns instead the value or quality of the object of the contract, the contract can be enforced by either party. The theory behind this rule is that both parties assume certain risks when they enter a contract. Without this rule, any party who believed he or she did not get a fair bargain could argue bilateral mistake.

◆ **bilateral mistake**
A mistake made by both parties to a contract about the same material fact.

LEGAL FOCUS ~ PROBLEM

Jane Collins contracts to purchase one of two skateboards owned by Mike Mattens. Jane thinks she has purchased a red one, a premier skateboard. Mike thinks Jane has purchased the blue one, his less valuable skateboard. Does a contract exist?

No. Jane and Mike have made a genuine mutual mistake of fact. Jane believes the contract subject matter is the red skateboard, while Mike believes it is the blue one. Nothing is more material than the subject matter of the contract. Since both parties are mistaken about the subject matter, no contract exists.

LEGAL FOCUS ~ PROBLEM

Suppose instead Jane contracts to buy the blue skateboard believing it to be worth $100 when it really is worth only $25. Can Jane escape the contract because of her mistake?

No. Jane's mistake is one of value or quality, not fact. A mistake of this nature does not normally affect the enforceability of the contract.

Legal Focus Problem

Ask a student volunteer to read this first Legal Focus Problem aloud to the class. Have the volunteer explain how this problem illustrates a *bilateral mistake.* Then allow the student volunteer to answer the question posed at the end of this Legal Focus Problem.

Enrichment

Have students read both of the Legal Focus Problems on this page. Stimulate a discussion on the supposition that Mike told Jane that the skateboard was two years old, but later she found out it was four years old. Is this a bilateral mistake, fraud, puffing, or just his own mistake? Is the fact that the skateboard is four years old a material fact?

Legal Focus Problem

Have a student volunteer read aloud to the class this second Legal Focus Problem dealing with Jane and the purchase of a skateboard. Ask the volunteer to explain how this mistake is different from the mistake above; then allow the volunteer to answer the question posed at the end of this problem.

UNILATERAL MISTAKES

♦ **unilateral mistake** A mistake by one party to a contract about some material fact.

A **unilateral mistake** is a mistake by one party about some material fact. A unilateral mistake does not usually allow the mistaken party to get out of the contract. The contract is enforceable.

 LEGAL FOCUS ~ EXAMPLE

Ellen intends to sell her stereo for $550. She learns Howard is interested in buying a used stereo, so she writes him a letter offering it to him. She types in a price of $450 by mistake. Howard immediately writes back, accepting Ellen's offer. In this case, there is a contract to sell the stereo for $450. Although Ellen intended to sell her stereo for $550, she made a unilateral mistake. She must sell at the $450 price in her letter.

There are two exceptions to this rule. The contract may not be enforceable (1) if the other party to the contract knows or should know a mistake was made or (2) if the error was due to a mathematical mistake in addition, subtraction, division, or multiplication and was done accidentally and without gross negligence.

LEGAL FOCUS ~ PROBLEM

Odell Construction Company made a bid (an offer in a construction contract) to install the plumbing in an apartment building. Herbert Odell, the president, added up his costs, but his secretary forgot to give him the figures for the pipe fittings. Because of the omission, Odell's bid was $6,500 below that of the other bidders. The prime contractor, Sunspan, Inc., accepted Odell's bid. Is Odell bound by the contract at the mistaken price?

Probably. If Sunspan was unaware of Odell's mistake and could not reasonably have been aware of it, the contract is enforceable. Odell is required to install the plumbing at the bid price. However, if it could be shown that Sunspan knew of the error, or if Odell's bid was so much lower than the others that Sunspan should have known the bid was a mistake, the contract can be rescinded, or cancelled. Sunspan is not allowed to accept an offer knowing it is a mistake. The law of contracts protects only *reasonable* expectations.

Ethical Concern

Fraudulent misrepresentation is another area where law and ethics directly intersect. To explore the ethical issues in this section, you might divide the class into groups and have each group discuss one of the Legal Focus features in this section. They should examine the Legal Focus feature from a duty-based–ethics point of view and from a utilitarian-ethics point of view. Each group should choose a leader to share its reactions with the class.

◆ FRAUDULENT MISREPRESENTATION

"You can fool some of the people all of the time, and all of the people some of the time, but you cannot fool all of the people all of the time."
Abraham Lincoln, 1809–1865
Sixteenth president of the United States, 1861–1865

As discussed earlier, fraud is a tort. In addition, if fraud exists in regard to a contract, the victim of the lie has agreed to a contract much different from the one he or she intended. The presence of fraud thus affects the genuineness of the innocent party's consent to the contract. A contract induced by fraud is not voluntary and does not involve true "mutual assent."

Can you think of some fraudulent activities that might occur at a carnival midway?

Caption Answer

Student answers may vary but should reflect an understanding of the definition of *fraudulent activities*.

249

Have students list and define the four elements of fraud.

Legal Focus
Case Problem

Read this Legal Focus Problem aloud to the class. Allow student volunteers to suggest possible answers to this problem. Note that the case discussed in this Legal Focus Problem, *Vokes* v. *Arthur Murray, Inc.*, is also excerpted in the *West's Business and Personal Law Handbook of Selected Court Cases.* You might wish to copy this case from the *Handbook* and distribute these copies to your students.

Teaching Note

This case *(Vokes v. Arthur Murray, Inc.)* is included in the *West's Business and Personal Law Handbook of Selected Court Cases.*

Start two lists on the board, one on statements of opinion and one on misrepresentation of facts. Ask students to volunteer examples for each list.

An innocent party to a contract induced by fraud can usually avoid the contract, since his or her consent was not voluntary. The innocent party usually has two choices. The first option is to rescind the contract and seek restoration of his or her position before the contract. The second option is to enforce the contract and seek damages for injuries caused by the fraud.

Typically, there are four elements of fraud:

1. A misrepresentation of a material fact occurs.
2. There is an intent to deceive.
3. The innocent party justifiably relies on the misrepresentation.
4. The innocent party is injured.

MISREPRESENTATION OF A MATERIAL FACT

The first element of fraud is a misrepresentation of a material fact. A misrepresentation can be express when it takes the form of words or actions. For example, the statement "This painting is a Picasso" is an express misrepresentation of fact if the portrait was painted by another artist.

A statement of opinion is generally not subject to a claim of fraud. For example, claims such as "This computer will never break down" and "This car will last for years and years" are statements of opinion. You should recognize opinions as such and not rely on them. A fact is objective and can be verified. You can debate an opinion. Therefore, a seller can "huff and puff his or her goods" without being liable for fraud. In certain situations, particularly when a naive purchaser relies on a so-called expert's opinion, the innocent party may be entitled to rescission.

◀ LEGAL FOCUS – CASE PROBLEM

Audrey Vokes was a fifty-one-year-old widow. While she was attending a dance party at Davenport's School of Dancing, an instructor sold her a specially priced dance course—eight half-hour dance lessons for $14.50. Later, over a sixteen-month period, she bought a total of fourteen dance courses. This amounted to 2,302 hours of dancing lessons at a price of $31,090.45. The staff selling the lessons continually assured her that she was very talented, was progressing in her lessons, and had great dance potential and that they were "developing her into a beautiful dancer." Eventually, Vokes sued to rescind her contract for the unused dance lessons. She contended that she had not progressed in her dancing ability, had no "dance aptitude," and had difficulty even "hearing the musical beat." Could Vokes's contract be rescinded because the salespersons misrepresented her dancing ability?

Yes. The court allowed Vokes to avoid the contract. The court held that the contract had been procured by false representations of her talents and abilities. "A statement of a party having . . . superior knowledge may be

Legal Focus Problem

Allow a student volunteer to read this first Legal Focus Problem aloud to the class. Remind students that they can use the Legal Focus features as review tools when studying for tests.

Discussion Starter

Guide the students in discussing the Legal Focus Problem found here on material fact and misrepresentation by asking if this case would constitute fraud if Cummings wanted to buy the horse as a domestic animal. Would the blind eye still be considered a material fact? Have students formulate other changes in the story that may turn the decision around.

regarded as a statement of fact although it would be considered as opinion if the parties were dealing on equal terms."[3]

Misrepresentation by Conduct   Misrepresentations can be made not only by words and writings but also by conduct. For example, misrepresentation by conduct occurs if a seller, by his or her actions, prevents a buyer from learning a material fact to the contract.

 LEGAL FOCUS – PROBLEM

Cummings contracts to purchase a racehorse from Garner. The horse is blind in one eye. When Garner shows the horse, he skillfully conceals this fact by turning the horse's head so Cummings cannot see the defect. Is this concealment fraud?

Yes, this knowing concealment constitutes fraud. Another example of misrepresentation by conduct is the false denial of knowledge or information concerning facts that are material to the contract when such knowledge or information is requested. It is important for a purchaser to ask many questions.

Misrepresentation of Law   A misrepresentation of law does not *ordinarily* allow a party to rescind a contract.

 LEGAL FOCUS – PROBLEM

Debbie has a parcel of property that she is trying to sell to Barry. Barry asks Debbie if he can build a structure more than three stories tall on the property. Debbie doesn't know anything about building laws, but she tells Barry, "You can build a condominium fifty stories high if you want." Barry buys the land and later discovers that Debbie's statement was false. Can Barry avoid the contract?

Barry cannot avoid the contract, because people (including Barry) are assumed to know state and local laws. Some courts, however, would reach an opposite result if the seller specifically knew the statement about the law was untrue—for example, if Debbie knew that a zoning ordinance restricted structures to one story. In addition, an exception may exist if the misrepresenting party is a professional with expertise in the law—for example, if Debbie is a lawyer, real estate agent, or property developer.

Misrepresentation by Silence   Ordinarily, neither party to a contract has a duty to volunteer facts. A contract normally is not set aside because important information is not volunteered.

Enrichment

Ask the students if they have ever heard the phrase, "Ignorance is no excuse for the law." What does this phrase mean? How does this phrase relate to *misrepresentation of law?*

Legal Focus Problem

Read to the class the second Legal Focus Problem found here. Allow student volunteers to suggest possible answers to the questions posed at the end of this problem.

3.   *Vokes v. Arthur Murray, Inc.,* District Court of Appeal of Florida, Second District, 212 So.2d 906 (1968).

LEGAL FOCUS ~ EXAMPLE

Suppose you are selling a car that has been in an accident but has been repaired. You probably do not have to volunteer this information to a potential buyer. However, if the purchaser asks whether the car has had extensive body work, and you lie, you have committed a fraudulent misrepresentation.

If a *serious* defect or *serious* potential problem is known to the seller, he or she has a duty to speak if the defect is not reasonably discoverable by the buyer. For example, if a city fails to tell bidders about subsoil conditions that will cause great expense in constructing a sewer, the city is guilty of fraud. Finally, parties in a fiduciary relationship (a relationship of trust, such as that between partners, between doctor and patient, and between attorney and client) have a duty to disclose material facts.

INTENT TO DECEIVE

The second element of fraud is knowledge by the misrepresenting party that the facts represented are false. This "guilty knowledge" is an *intent to deceive*. If all elements of fraud exist except intent to deceive, most courts will allow an action for negligent misrepresentation. Negligent misrepresentation allows the innocent party to rescind the contract but does not allow a suit for damages.

RELIANCE ON THE MISREPRESENTATION

The third element of fraud is justifiable reliance by the deceived party on the misrepresentation of fact. The reliance on the deception must be reasonable under the circumstances and must be an important factor (although not necessarily the sole factor) in convincing the party to contract. Reliance is never justified if the innocent party knows the true facts or relies on obviously extravagant statements.

 LEGAL FOCUS ~ PROBLEM

A used-car dealer tells Bart, "This old Cadillac gets great gasoline mileage. I took it on a trip last week and got over fifty miles to the gallon." Bart knows about cars and knows the statement to be an exaggeration. He still decides to buy the old car. If Bart changes his mind, does he have an action for fraud when it turns out the car only gets 12 miles per gallon?

No. Bart did not actually rely on the statement, because he knew better. There is no fraud.

INJURY TO THE INNOCENT PARTY

The final element of fraud is injury to the innocent party. For a person to recover damages caused by fraud, proof of an injury is required. The measure of damages is ordinarily equal to what the value of the property would have been if it had been delivered as represented, less what it is actually worth. In effect, this gives the innocent party the benefit of the bargain.

 LEGAL FOCUS ~ EXAMPLE

> Fred pays $50 for a novel believing it to be autographed by the author. Fred thinks he has made a good deal, because the usual price for a novel autographed by this author is $150. In truth, the signature was a fraud placed on the book by the seller, Shirley. The normal selling price of the novel was $20. Fred's damages are not $30, but $130, the difference between the value of the property as represented and its actual worth.

In addition, in fraud actions, courts may award **punitive damages**, which are also referred to as **exemplary damages**. Punitive damages are based on the public policy consideration of punishing the defendant or setting an example for similar wrongdoers. These damages are granted to a plaintiff over and above the compensation for the loss.

In an action to rescind a contract, many courts do not require proof of injury. Since rescission returns the parties to their positions before the contract, a showing of injury is considered unnecessary.

♦ **punitive**, or **exemplary damages**
Damages to punish the defendant or set an example for similar wrongdoers.

◆ UNDUE INFLUENCE

Undue influence occurs when one party greatly influences another party, overcoming the party's free will. Such influence can exist in a close relationship. Minors and elderly people are often under the influence of guardians, for example. If a guardian gets a young or elderly ward to enter into a contract that benefits the guardian, undue influence may have been exerted. Undue influence can arise from several confidential or fiduciary relationships: attorney–client, doctor–patient, guardian–ward, parent–child, husband–wife, and trustee–beneficiary. The essential feature of undue influence is that one party takes advantage of the other. A contract created under excessive or undue influence lacks genuine assent and is voidable.

♦ **undue influence**
A situation in which one party greatly influences another party, overcoming the party's free will.

LEGAL FOCUS ~ EXAMPLE

> When Mabel Taylor reached her eightieth birthday, she was no longer able to drive her car. Her nephew, Ray, convinced her she should sell

him the car for $50. Ray told Mabel that if she did not agree, then he would no longer visit her. The actual value of the car was $7,000. This agreement is not enforceable because Ray is taking advantage of his special relationship with Mabel.

◆ DURESS

Assent to the terms of a contract is not genuine if one of the parties is forced into the agreement. Recognizing this, the courts allow that party to rescind the contract. Forcing a party into a contract under the fear created by threats is legally defined as **duress**.

◆ **duress (civil)**
Threat of or actual physical harm that deprives a person of the freedom of will to choose and decide.

 LEGAL FOCUS ~ EXAMPLE

Sharkside Loan Company threatens to harm you or your family unless you agree to borrow money from them at a very high interest rate. Sharkside is guilty of exerting duress.

In addition, using blackmail to induce consent to a contract is duress. The victim of the duress can choose to carry out the contract or to avoid the entire transaction.

Economic need is generally not a basis for a finding of duress, even when one party charges a very high price for an item the other party needs. If the party charging the price also creates the need, however, economic duress may be found.

 LEGAL FOCUS ~ PROBLEM

The Internal Revenue Service assessed a large tax and penalty against Sam Thompson. Thompson retained Earl Eyman to represent him to reduce the tax and penalty. The last day before the deadline for filing a reply with the IRS, Eyman refused to represent Thompson. He said he would reconsider if Thompson signed an agreement to pay a much higher fee than originally agreed for his services. Is the agreement enforceable?

The agreement is not enforceable. Although Eyman threatened only to withdraw his services, something he could do, he delayed his withdrawal until the last day. It would have been impossible for Thompson at that late date to get adequate representation elsewhere. Because Thompson was forced into signing the contract or losing his right to challenge the IRS assessment, the contract is voidable.

1. A mutual mistake about a material fact would cause a contract to be void.
2. If one party to a contract knows or should know a mistake was made, or if there was an accidental mathematical error made without gross negligence, a contract is enforceable.
3. An innocent party to a contract induced by fraud may rescind the contract and go back to the position he or she was in before the contract or sue for money damages for the loss of the bargain.
4. Misrepresentation can occur if one of the parties offers incorrect facts or neglects to tell all the facts he or she is legally required to tell.
5. Punitive damages are awarded to punish the defendant or to set an example for similar wrongdoers.
6. Undue influence occurs when one party greatly *influences* another party. Duress arises if one party *forces* another into a contract under the fear of threats.

◆ CHECKING YOUR PROGRESS

1. What type of mistake would legally cause a contract to be void?
2. What are two exceptions to the rule that a contract is enforceable if there is a unilateral mistake?
3. What options does an innocent party to a contract induced by fraud have?
4. In what ways can misrepresentation occur in contract formation?
5. Why are punitive damages sometimes awarded in contract fraud?
6. Explain the difference between undue influence and duress.

◆ A CASE IN POINT ◆

BENNETT v. U.S. CYCLING FEDERATION

Court of Appeal of California, 1987.
193 Cal.App.3d 1485,
239 Cal.Rptr. 55.

A sponsor of a cycling race claimed that an exculpatory clause released it from liability for an injury received by one of the cyclists during the race. Was the sponsor correct?

FACTS On June 10, 1984, Albert Bennett, the plaintiff, entered an amateur bicycle race. The event was conducted by the defendant, the United States Cycling Federation. Bennett had signed a document provided by the defendant that stated in part: "In consideration of the acceptance of my application for entry in the above event, I hereby waive, release, and discharge any and all claims for . . . damage which I may have, or which may hereafter accrue to me,

as a result of my participation in said event." The release also included a clause by which Bennett was to assume risks associated with bicycle racing. While participating in the scheduled racing event, Bennett collided with an automobile driven by James Ketchum. Bennett stated that, during the race, the vehicle was allowed onto the track by an agent of the defendant. The agent knew, or should have known, of the hazard it presented to the cyclists. The defendant, claiming that it had no liability because of the release signed by Bennett, moved for summary judgment. The motion was granted by the trial court. Bennett appealed.

ISSUE Did Bennett's release excuse the defendant from liability for Bennett's injuries?

DECISION Not necessarily. The court ruled that the summary judgment was improper and sent the case back for trial. The court thought it unclear whether Bennett

---

Read
Before the students read this *A Case In Point* feature, remind them of the definition of *exculpatory clause* that is found in the text. ("An *exculpatory clause* is a contract provision that releases a party from liability for his or her wrongful acts.") Allow a student volunteer to read this *A Case In Point* feature aloud to the class.

◆ A CASE IN POINT (CONTINUED) ◆

had assumed the risk of an automobile being on the race course.

REASON To be effective, a written release forgiving an individual from future negligence or misconduct must be clear, unambiguous, and explicit in expressing the intent of the signing parties. The court, citing the Restatement (Second) of Torts, said, "it must also appear that [the agreement's] terms were intended by both parties to apply to the particular conduct of the defendant which has caused the harm. Again, where the agreement is drawn by the defendant and the plaintiff passively accepts it, its terms will ordinarily be construed strictly against the defendant."

The court concluded that a signer of "the bicycle release at issue here must be held to have waived any hazards relating to bicycle racing that are obvious or that might rea-

sonably have been foreseen." The court agreed with the plaintiff that foreseeable hazards included "collisions with other riders, negligently maintained equipment, bicycles which were unfit for racing but nevertheless passed by organizers, [and] bad road surfaces." It was doubtful, however, that the plaintiff or any participant would have appreciated the risk of colliding with a car traveling on the closed race course. The court concluded, "we recognize that, conceivably, the circumstances of a bicycle race might be such that a participant should reasonably anticipate the risk of moving vehicles on the course. We hold there is an issue of material fact on that point." The summary judgment in the defendant's favor cannot stand. (Note that the reversal in this case does not mean the plaintiff wins the case. It means the case goes to trial so a jury can decide whether the bicyclist assumed the risk of injury from an automobile on the track.)

CHAPTER REVIEW

10

◆ SUMMARY

LEGALITY

Contracts Contrary to Statute

1. *Usury laws*—A lender who makes a loan at an interest rate above the maximum rate of interest allowed by statute is guilty of usury.

2. *Gambling laws*—Gambling contracts inconsistent with state statutes are illegal and void.

3. *Sabbath laws* (Sunday laws)—Sabbath laws prohibit the formation or the performance of certain contracts on Sunday.

4. *Licensing statutes*—Contracts entered into by persons who do not have a license, when one is required by statute, are not enforceable *unless* the underlying purpose of the statute is to raise revenues (and not to protect the public from unauthorized practitioners).

In order to help students review what they have learned in Chapter 10, you might wish to:

1. Have a student volunteer, or volunteers, read the Chapter Summary aloud to the class.
2. Allow the students to work with partners to complete the *Using Legal Language* activity.
3. Assign the *Checking for Comprehension* exercise as homework.

4. Allow the students to work in small groups to complete the *Applying Legal Concepts* activities.
5. As a class, complete the *Applying the Law* activities. (Please note that you may have to help students with vocabulary so that they adequately understand all of the *Applying the Law* material.)

In order to check student mastery of chapter concepts, you may wish to use the Chapter 10 test that is found in your *Teacher's Resource Binder* or use WESTEST computerized testing for Chapter 10.

Contracts Contrary to Public Policy

1. *Contracts in restraint of trade*—Contracts whose purpose is to reduce or restrain free competition are illegal unless the restraint is reasonable. An exception is a *covenant not to compete*. An agreement of this kind is usually enforced by the courts if the terms are reasonable as to time, scope, and distance and if the covenant is part of a contract for the sale of a business or an employment contract.

2. *Unconscionable contracts and exculpatory clauses*—A contract or contract clause that is unconscionable is illegal and cannot be enforced.

Effect of Illegality

1. In general, an illegal contract is void. The courts will aid neither party when both parties are considered to be equally at fault.

2. Exceptions
   a. Recovery may be allowed when one party to the contract is relatively innocent.
   b. Recovery may be allowed when one party to the contract is a member of a group of persons protected by statute.
   c. Recovery may be allowed when one party was induced to enter into an illegal bargain through fraud, duress, or undue influence.

GENUINENESS OF ASSENT

Mistakes

1. *Bilateral mistakes*—When both parties are mistaken about a material fact, such as identity, either party can avoid the contract. If they are mistaken about value or quality, either party can enforce the contract.

2. *Unilateral mistakes*—Generally, the mistaken party is bound by the contract *unless* the other party knows or should have known of the mistake or (in some states) the mistake is an inadvertent mathematical error.

Misrepresentation

1. *Fraudulent misrepresentation*—When fraud occurs, usually the innocent party can enforce or avoid the contract. The elements of fraud are:
   a. A misrepresentation of a material fact must occur.
   b. There must be an intent to deceive.
   c. The innocent party must justifiably rely on the misrepresentation.
   d. For damages to be awarded, the innocent party must be injured.

2. *Other misrepresentation*—Intent to deceive need not be shown. Usually, the innocent party can rescind the contract but cannot seek damages.

Undue influence—Arises from special relationships, such as fiduciary or confidential relationships, when one party's free will is overcome by the other party. Usually, the resulting contract is voidable.

Duress—Defined as forcing a party to enter a contract under the fear created by a threat—for example, the threat of violence or economic pressure. The contract is generally voidable, and the party forced to enter the contract can rescind the contract.

◆ USING LEGAL LANGUAGE

Directions: Match each term with the statement that best defines that term.

1. adhesion contract
2. bilateral mistake

A. a contract provision that releases a party from liability for his or her wrongful acts.

1. In some states a lender of a valid transaction can recover the loan principal and interest at the legal maximum; in others the lender can recover only the principal if the loan is usurious, and in some states the lender can recover nothing.
2. Contracts could be illegal because of statutes covering usury, gambling, Sunday transactions, or licensing of professionals.
3. If enforcement of a contract would have a negative impact on society, the court may refuse to enforce it.

4. An illegal contract is usually void; exceptions include justifiable ignorance of the facts in contracts made with members of protected classes.
5. A contract is voidable if a material fact is misrepresented, there is an intent to deceive, the innocent party relies on the representation, and the innocent party is injured.
6. Contracts in restraint of trade, unless part of a sale of a business or employment contract, are deemed illegal and will not be enforced by a court of law.

1. The court held that Lanci was entitled to void the settlement agreement. Lanci's mistake as to the amount of the policy limits was known or should have been known by Metropolitan. Quoting from Section 153 of the Restatement of Contracts, the court stated that "[w]here a mistake of one party at the time a contract was made as to a basic assumption on which he made the contract has a material

---

3. duress
4. exculpatory clause
5. fraud
6. genuine assent
7. judgment rate of interest
8. legal rate of interest
9. undue influence
10. usury

B. occurs when one party greatly influences another party, overcoming the party's free will
C. a knowing false representation of material fact, made with intent to deceive another who contracts to their injury in reliance on the lie
D. a true, objective "meeting of the minds"
E. a standard form contract drafted by a dominant party and then presented to the other party on a "take it or leave it" basis
F. a rate of interest fixed by statute added to an unpaid money judgment until it is paid
G. both parties to a contract are wrong about the same material fact
H. charging an illegal interest rate
I. any threat of or actual physical harm that deprives a person of the freedom of will to choose and decide
J. a rate fixed by statute when contracting parties forget to fix a rate of interest in a loan

◆ CHECKING FOR COMPREHENSION

1. What are the possible recovery options if a loan is found to be usurious?
2. What types of statutes could cause a contract to be illegal?
3. Can public policy cause a contract to be illegal? Explain.
4. What is the effect of illegality on a contract?
5. What are the four elements of fraud that would cause a contract to be voidable?
6. Joseph, who owns the only pizza parlor in Middletown, learns that Giovanni is about to open a competing pizza parlor in the same small town. The new restaurant is planned just a few blocks from Joseph's restaurant. Joseph offers Giovanni $10,000 in return for Giovanni's promise not to open a pizza parlor in the Middletown area. Giovanni accepts the $10,000 but goes ahead with his plans, anyway. When Giovanni opens his restaurant, Joseph sues to enjoin Giovanni's continued operation of his restaurant or to recover the $10,000. The court denies recovery. On what basis?

◆ APPLYING LEGAL CONCEPTS

1. Read the local newspaper, magazines, and/or watch television commercials for one week. Look for instances (at least three) of misrepresentation in the advertising. Write a report describing each advertisement, establish the misrepresentation, discuss any ethical factors that may be present.

effect on the agreed exchange of performances . . . , the contract is voidable by him if he does not bear the risk of the mistake . . . , and . . . the other party had reason to know of the mistake or his fault caused the mistake."

2. No. The court reasoned the credit card system did not make loans to the customers of Sears, and therefore the usury law did not apply. The practical effect of the credit card charges was that a person buying on such credit cards paid a higher price for goods and services than a person purchasing with cash.

3. The court first held that the transaction was a conditional sale and not a lease. Therefore, the UCC provisions dealing with unconscionable sales contracts were applicable. The court then looked at the Connecticut Unfair Trade Practice Act allegation. The court held that the act was to be liberally construed and that protection must be given to "the unthinking, the unsuspecting and the credulous as well as the sophisticated." Clearly, Murphy did not have equal bargaining power with McNamara. She was disadvantaged because of her economic circumstance and thus had to purchase on credit. No attempt was made to advise her of the true purchase price, and the "unscrupulous collection practices" amounted to a violation of the CUTPA. In addition, the court held that the provisions of the contract were unconscionable under Section 2-302 of the UCC. That section permits a court, as matter of law, to find any contract or clause therein to be unconscionable and to refuse to enforce the contract or any remainder of the contract to be performed. The court held that "an excessive price charged a consumer with unequal bargaining power" can constitute an unconscionable contract. Here, the court held that Murphy had paid McNamara 80 percent of the retail price. Therefore, Murphy should be allowed to keep the set, and McNamara's claim should be restricted to the difference between the set's reasonable value and the amount Murphy had paid.

2. Acquire loan agreements for a car loan from a bank, a credit union, and a car dealer's finance company. Assume you are buying a $15,000 car. Calculate the total amount to be repaid, at the company's current interest rate, for a two-year, a three-year, and a four-year loan. Figure the amount you would have to pay if you were charged the legal rate of interest for your state.

◆ APPLYING THE LAW . . . YOU BE THE JUDGE

1. Steven Lanci was involved in an automobile accident with an uninsured motorist. Lanci was insured with Metropolitan Insurance Co., although he did not have a copy of the insurance policy. Lanci and Metropolitan entered settlement negotiations, during which Lanci told Metropolitan that he did not have a copy of his policy. Ultimately, Lanci agreed to settle all claims for $15,000, noting in a letter to Metropolitan that $15,000 was the "sum you have represented to be the . . . policy limits applicable to this claim." After signing a release, Lanci learned that the policy limits were actually $250,000, and he refused to accept the settlement proceeds. When Metropolitan sued to enforce the settlement agreement, Lanci argued that the release was signed as the result of a mistake and was void. Should the court enforce the contract or void it? [*Lanci v. Metropolitan Insurance Co.*, 388 Pa.Super. 1, 564 A.2d 972 (1989)]

2. Sears, Roebuck and Co. issued credit cards to people so they could buy on credit and be billed once a month for their purchases. If they paid the balance shown on the monthly statement within 30 days, no service charge was added. If they did not pay in full, a service charge of 1.5 percent a month on the balance, but no less than 50 cents, was added. Overbeck charged purchases on a Sears credit card and paid the monthly service charges. Later, he sued Sears claiming that the 18 percent rate was usurious because the maximum legal rate was 6 percent. His suit was to recover the excess interest on behalf of himself and all other credit card holders. Will the court decide the interest rate is usurious? [*Overbeck v. Sears, Roebuck and Co.*, 169 Ind.App. 501, 349 N.E.2d 286 (1976)]

3. Carolyn Murphy is a welfare recipient with four minor children. Brian McNamara is in the business of renting and selling television and stereo sets. After seeing McNamara's advertisement for "rent to own" televisions, Murphy signed a lease agreement with McNamara for a twenty-five inch Philco color TV at $16 per week. The lease payments were to run for seventy-eight weeks, after which she would become the owner. At no time did McNamara tell Murphy that the total lease payments amounted to $1,268, including delivery charge. The retail sale price of the set was $499. Murphy had paid about $436 when she read a newspaper article criticizing the lease plan. When she learned that she was required to pay $1,268, Murphy stopped making payments. McNamara's employees attempted to take possession and made threats through telephone and written communications. Murphy filed suit, alleging that the contract violated the Connecticut Unfair Trade Practices Act and state usury laws and that the contract terms were unconscionable under Section 2-302 of the Uniform Commercial Code. Discuss her allegations, particularly her claim that the contract is unconscionable under the UCC. [*Murphy v. McNamara*, 36 Conn.Supp. 183, 416 A.2d 170 (1979)]

Mastery Objectives

- Define the Statute of Frauds
- Determine what types of contracts must be in writing
- Assess the sufficiency of written agreements
- Detail steps to consider in forming oral contracts
- Explain the parol evidence rule
- Tell how courts interpret ambiguous contracts

LEGAL BACKGROUND

A contract that is otherwise valid may be unenforceable if it is not in proper form—certain types of contracts are required by the Statute of Frauds to be in writing. If a contract is required by law to be in writing and it is not, it may be unenforceable. These contracts are not void or even voidable, they just cannot be enforced.

No less important is the parol evidence rule, which holds that often when a contract is in writing, oral testimony about the agreement is not even allowed.

In this chapter we discuss when contracts must be in writing and the effect of a written contract on a party's rights. We also discuss exceptions to the parol evidence rule and the Statute of Frauds.

We close this chapter with a discussion of the rules of interpretation used by courts when a dispute exists as to the meaning of an agreement .

Chapter

11 Writing and Form

Activity Sheets
Reviewing Legal Concepts 11 *TRB*
Enrichment Activity 11 *TRB*

Student Activity Workbook
Chapter 11 Activities

Tests
Chapter 11 Test *TRB*
Chapter 11 WESTEST Computerized Testing

Handbook of Selected Court Cases
Chesapeake Financial Corp. v. *Laird*
Pando v. *Fernandez*

**West's Business Law and Legal
Environment Videodisc**
Still Frames and Motion Segments as shown

> *"A verbal contract isn't worth the paper it's written on."*
> **Samuel Goldwyn, 1882–1974**
> **Movie producer**

We have seen that generally the parties to a contract can create their contract in any way they want. There is an exception to this general rule, however. An otherwise valid contract may not be enforceable if it is not in the proper form. For example, some types of contracts are required to be in writing. If no written evidence of the contract exists, it may not be enforceable. In this chapter, we examine the kinds of contracts that must be in writing. We then consider some rules relating to the way contract terms are interpreted and proven in court.

◆ THE STATUTE OF FRAUDS— REQUIREMENT OF A WRITING

The **Statute of Frauds** is the name given to a law requiring that certain contracts be proved by a signed writing. The name came from an English statute passed in 1677 to prevent perjury—lying in court—about the existence of contracts. Today, most states have laws modeled after the English act.

The Statute of Frauds requires that parties suing to enforce certain types of contracts prove their existence and terms with signed writings. The types of contracts affected were believed to be important or complex. Under the Statute of Frauds, the following types of contracts require some form of writing:

1. Contracts involving interests in land.
2. Contracts that cannot be performed within one year from the date of creation.
3. Promises to pay the debt or perform the duty of another.
4. Promises made in return for a promise of marriage.
5. Contracts for the sale of goods priced at $500 or more.

CONTRACTS INVOLVING INTERESTS IN LAND

Under the Statute of Frauds, a contract involving an interest in land must be in writing. The contract may involve the sale of land or other matters, such as leases, that affect an interest in land.

Sale of Land   Land includes real property and all physical objects permanently attached to the land (such as buildings, plants, trees, and the soil). A contract to sell land must be in writing to be enforceable. Something less than a formal written contract can sometimes satisfy this requirement. The courts may accept a written memorandum—something in writing that proves the existence of the contract.

◆ **Statute of Frauds**
Statute under which certain types of contracts must be proved by a signed writing to be enforced in court.

Have a student volunteer read this first Legal Focus Problem to the class. Ask the volunteer to answer the question posed at the end of the passage and explain which of the five types of contracts under the Statute of Frauds is involved in this problem.

Ask a student volunteer to read this second Legal Focus Problem aloud to the class. Allow student volunteers to suggest possible answers to the question posed at the end of this problem.

Read to the class the first Legal Focus Problem found on page 263. Allow student volunteers to answer the question posed at the end of this problem.

Enrichment

Have students list the three criteria that might be present in order for a land contract to exist without a signed writing. Have students make up a scenario that would qualify as an example.

Extension Activity

Have a student volunteer obtain a sample mortgage contract. The student may be able to obtain this sample mortgage contract from a local bank or savings and loan. Allow the volunteer to exhibit and explain this mortgage contract to the class.

---

262   The Law of Contracts

 LEGAL FOCUS ~ PROBLEM

Carol contracts orally to sell Seaside Shelter to Arnold. A few days after the agreement, Carol decides not to sell. Can Arnold enforce the contract?

Arnold cannot enforce the contract and neither can Carol. The Statute of Frauds is a *defense* to the enforcement of an oral contract to transfer land.

An exception exists in some states for a buyer who has possession of the land. There are usually three requirements in such cases:

1. The buyer has possession of the land (has moved onto the property).
2. The buyer made permanent improvements to the land (for example, remodeled a house).
3. The buyer paid part of the purchase price.

Other Interests   The Statute of Frauds also requires written contracts to transfer other interests in land, such as real estate mortgages and leases.

♦ **mortgage** A written instrument giving a creditor an interest in the debtor's property as security for a debt.

A real estate **mortgage** transfers an interest in land so that the interest can act as security for the repayment of a loan. If a buyer must borrow money from a bank to purchase real property, the bank will require some sort of security—a way to get its money back if the buyer does not repay the loan. The mortgage provides this security by giving the bank conditional title to the property. That means the bank has the right to sell the property if the borrower does not live up to the loan agreement. When the borrower pays off the debt, the property belongs wholly to that person once again. To be enforceable, a mortgage must be shown by a writing.

♦ **lease** A transfer by a landlord of the right to occupy or use land for a certain time to a tenant.

A **lease** is a transfer of the right to occupy or use land for a certain time. Because leases are important legal documents, they should be and usually are in writing. Many states do not require written proof of a lease of one year or less. However, any lease lasting more than one year must normally be in writing.

THE ONE-YEAR RULE

Contracts that cannot be performed within one year from the date of formation must be in writing to be enforceable. This rule shows the concern that a witness's memory is not to be trusted for longer than a year. If the contract, by its terms, makes performance within the year *possible* (even if not probable), the contract need not be in writing.

 LEGAL FOCUS ~ PROBLEM

Jamal is set to graduate from college. An employer orally contracts with Jamal to employ him for two years at $2,000 per month. Is this contract required to be in writing?

Ethical Concern

Stimulate a class discussion on the legality and morality of marrying someone for the promise of money. Why is it legal to marry for a promise of money but not legal to accept money for the promise *not* to marry?

Legal Focus Problem

Allow a student volunteer to read this Legal Focus Problem aloud to the class. Make sure that students understand that in this problem Yakov could *possibly* complete performance within a one-year period; therefore, no writing is required.

Ethical Concern

The Statute of Frauds was instituted to prevent harm to innocent parties by requiring written evidence of certain agreements. If a contract is oral when it is required to be in writing, it will not usually be enforced. The statute has been criticized because it can be used as a technical defense by a party breaching an oral contract. Some scholars have suggested that the statute has caused more fraud than it has prevented. Because the statute limits the kinds of contracts that will be enforced and because it can be used as a technical defense, it renders some commercial transactions more cumbersome. Should it be abandoned?

Many nations have repealed similar statutes. Britain has repealed theirs, except for the land and suretyship provisions, and the United States has agreed (in the United Nations Convention for the International Sale of Goods) that the Statute of Frauds would not apply to contracts between U.S. firms and firms in other nations. Nevertheless, it is the law for those doing business within U.S. borders. The retention of this statute in this country suggests that we are willing to accept the tradeoff that it represents.

Yes. The terms of the contract exceed one year. To enforce this contract, the parties must have written evidence; the oral agreement is not enough.

The one-year period begins to run the day after the contract is made.

LEGAL FOCUS ~ PROBLEM

Jamal's date of graduation is June 1. On graduation day, Acme Corporation orally contracts with Jamal to employ him for one year starting immediately. Is this contract required to be in writing?

No. The period begins to run on June 2, the day after the contract is made. Since performance begins on June 1, the contract will be completed within a year. The Statute of Frauds does not apply.

LEGAL FOCUS ~ PROBLEM

Michael hires Yakov to build Michael's house for $100,000. They do not put their agreement in writing. Because Yakov is working on the project in his spare time, no date is set for completion of the project. Yakov does, however, predict that it will take somewhere between nine months and eighteen months to complete the construction. In fact, it takes Yakov thirteen months to complete the project. If Michael refuses to pay Yakov, can Yakov enforce the oral agreement?

Yes. No writing is required, because the contract can be performed within a year. The test is whether performance is possible within a year. Even if performance is not *likely* to be completed within one year, if it is *possible*, the contract does not require written proof. It was possible for Yakov to complete performance, even though he did not. Exhibit 11-1 illustrates the one-year rule.

Although the law did not require Michael and Yakov to put their contract in writing, they should have done so. Memories fade, and it is difficult to prove what parties agreed to. It is smart to put important and complicated contracts in writing even if the law does not require it.

PROMISES TO PAY THE DEBT OR PERFORM THE DUTY OF ANOTHER

A promise made by one person to pay a debt or perform a duty of another must be in writing. This is a secondary promise. A parent who agrees to pay a child's loan if the child fails to pay makes a secondary promise. The promise must be in writing and signed to be enforceable. This secondary promise is a *cosign*. This term suggests the requirement of a writing.

Much of the material that is conveyed in the exhibits of *West's Business and Personal Law* is also conveyed in the still frames on the **West Business Law and Legal Environment Videodisc**. For more information and directions for use, please see the Index and Description of Contents for the **West Business Law and Legal Environment Videodisc** that is found in your *Teacher's Resource Binder*.

Legal Focus Problem

Divide the class into small groups to read and discuss the first Legal Focus Problem found here. Have each group diagrams both the *original oral contract* and the *secondary promise*. Their diagrams should show which of these is an *enforceable oral contract* and which is not *enforceable*.

Enrichment

You might explain to students that it is reasonably common for parents to cosign loans for their children even though the children have reached the age of majority. Encourage students to discuss mortgages, leases, and cosigns with their parents.

Legal Focus Problem

Read to the class the Legal Focus Problem that begins on the bottom of this page. Allow student volunteers to suggest possible answers to the questions posed at the end of this problem. Have a student volunteer also explain the main purpose of Carlton's promise.

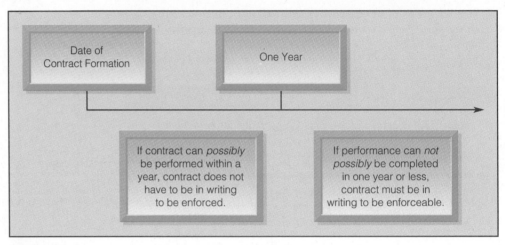

EXHIBIT 11-1
CONTRACTS IMPOSSIBLE TO PERFORM WITHIN ONE YEAR

LEGAL FOCUS ~ PROBLEM

Kenneth calls Joanne's Floral Boutique and asks Joanne to send his mother a dozen roses for Mother's Day. He tells Joanne to send him the bill. The florist phones Kenneth's father, Maxwell, and asks him to pay the bill if Kenneth does not. Maxwell agrees. The florist delivers the flowers. If Joanne's Floral Boutique is not paid, can it enforce the promise of either Kenneth or Maxwell?

Kenneth's promise to pay for the flowers is an oral contract supported by legally sufficient consideration (Joanne's sending the roses) and is enforceable. However, Maxwell's promise is a secondary one. He promised to pay if his son did not. As his promise is not in writing, it is not enforceable because of the Statute of Frauds.

The "Main Purpose" Rule   A writing is not required when the main reason for making a secondary promise is to secure a personal benefit. When the party intends to secure a personal benefit, he or she is really answering for his or her own debt.

LEGAL FOCUS ~ PROBLEM

Carlton Banacek has ordered a specially designed racing bike from John Hokanjian, a famous bicycle builder. Carlton learns that John owes money to Flash Company, which supplies him with the

Extension Activity

Have students research periodicals for information about disputes over prenuptial agreements; then have them report on them orally to the class. Each report should include the parties, the allegations, and the outcome. Most publicity will involve highly visible celebrities. Point out that prenuptial agreements will be discussed in Chapter 27.

materials he needs to build bikes. Because John has not been making payments on his debt, Flash is threatening to take back materials it has sold John on credit. John cannot complete Carlton's bike without these materials. Carlton orally promises Flash that he will guarantee John's debt if Flash promises to not take back the supplies. Is Carlton's oral promise enforceable? Was the main purpose of Carlton's promise to protect his own interests?

The answer to both questions is yes. The main purpose of Carlton's promise is to allow John to keep the materials he needs to finish Carlton's bike. The promise is enforceable even though it is not in writing.

Promises Made in Return for a Promise of Marriage

Any promise to pay money or to give property in exchange for a promise to marry must be in writing. This rule applies to *prenuptial agreements* (agreements made before marriage). Prenuptial agreements define each partner's ownership rights in the other partner's property. For example, one partner may wish to limit the property an expected spouse would get if the marriage ended in divorce. The prenuptial arrangements made in consideration of marriage must be in writing to be enforceable.

Contracts for the Sale of Goods Priced at $500 or More

The UCC requires a signed writing or memorandum for the sale of goods priced at $500 or more.

◆ Legal Focus ~ problem

Pauline telephoned Breaker City and ordered a forty-five-inch rear-projection television. The price for the set was $2,250. Breaker agreed and scheduled delivery so that Pauline would have the set in time to watch the national bowling tournament. The day before the scheduled delivery, Pauline called Breaker City and told the store not to send the set. Does Breaker City have an enforceable contract with Pauline?

No. The agreement is for a sale of goods, since a television set is tangible personal property, and the contract price exceeded $500. Breaker City cannot enforce the promise without a writing or memorandum signed by Pauline.

There are several exceptions to the Statute of Frauds as it applies to the sale of goods. This chapter's Law in Action illustrates one such exception.

Is a credit card slip a writing?

Legal Focus Problem

Read to the class the Legal Focus Problem found here. Allow student volunteers to suggest possible answers to the question posed at the end of this problem. As a followup, you might have a student volunteer contact a local retailer that sells televisions and/or large appliances and obtain a blank copy of their agreement for a *Sale of Goods*. Allow the student volunteer to exhibit and explain the agreement form to the class.

Caption Answer

A signed and completed credit card slip is a *writing*.

Teaching with the Videodisc

The still frames listed below from the **West's Business Law and Legal Environment Videodisc** can be used with this chapter. To access this material, use the bar codes or the frame numbers included in the Videodisc Instructor's Manual found in the *TRB*.

Contracts Covered by the Statute of Frauds
Statute of Frauds Requirements
Contracts Impossible to Perform in One Year
Computation of Time under the One Year Provision
Collateral Promises
Parol Evidence Rule

◆ CHECKING YOUR PROGRESS

1. What is considered "land" in a contract or the sale of land?
2. Explain the one-year rule as it applies to contracts.
3. What is the term used when a person promises to pay the debt of another person? Must the promise be in writing?
4. According to the UCC, must a contract for the sale of goods be in writing?

◆ THE STATUTE OF FRAUDS— SUFFICIENCY OF THE WRITING

The Statute of Frauds does not require a complete written contract signed by both parties. The statute can also be satisfied with a far less extensive writing, a *memorandum*.

The memorandum can consist of any confirmation, invoice, sales slip, check, or telegram. Such items, singly or in combination, may be writings sufficient to satisfy the Statute of Frauds. Requirements for the memorandum are (1) It must be signed by the party against whom enforcement is sought, and (2) It must contain at least the essential terms of the contract.

It is not required that both parties sign the memorandum. The essential signature is the signature of the person against whom enforcement is sought (the person being sued).

◆ LEGAL FOCUS - PROBLEM

Eric and Shelly orally agreed that Shelly would lease Eric's house for three years for $600 a month rent. Shelly found an old standard-form lease, filled out the terms, signed it, and gave it to Eric, saying, "Please sign this lease, Eric." Eric responded by telling Shelly he had changed his mind and now would like $750 a month rent. Can Shelly enforce Eric's oral promise to lease the property for three years at $600 a month? Does the lease she signed satisfy the Statute of Frauds?

Shelly cannot enforce Eric's promise. A lease for a three-year term must be in writing to be enforceable. Although Shelly prepared the lease, Eric did not sign it, and Eric is the party against whom enforcement is sought. In other words, for a party to enforce a contract, the writing must be signed by the other party. Thus, it is possible for a contract to be enforceable by one party, but not by the other.

Read

Introduce this *Law in Action* feature by reading the title, "Law and the Businessperson: The Problem with Oral Contracts," and then ask students if any of them can recall how Samuel Goldwyn summed up the problem with oral contracts. ("A verbal contract isn't worth the paper it's written on.") Then allow a student volunteer to read this *Law in Action* feature aloud to the class.

Analyze and Apply

Go over the four items in the checklist for oral contracts that is included in this *Law in Action* feature. Then have students write a Legal Focus Example for each of the four items on the checklist. Have volunteers share their examples with the class.

Extension Activity

Have a few volunteers research some new technology in communications that makes doing business faster. Some examples include the facsimile, electronic mailboxes, video phones, and cellular phones.

Law in Action

LAW AND THE BUSINESSPERSON: THE PROBLEM WITH ORAL CONTRACTS

Most business contracts should be in writing, even contracts not covered by the Statute of Frauds. However, oral contracts are frequently made over the telephone, particularly between parties who do business regularly. How can this situation be handled?

Any time an oral contract is made, each party should send a memorandum of the oral agreement to the other party. The memorandum, or confirmation, accomplishes two purposes: (1) it shows the party's clear intention to form a contract, and (2) it provides the party's belief as to the contract terms. If the party receiving the memorandum disagrees with the stated terms or intent, the disagreement can be discussed before performance begins.

What about the sale of goods between merchants? There is a special rule for sales contracts under the UCC. A written confirmation received by one merchant can satisfy the Statute of Frauds requirement of a writing for both parties. Normally, a memorandum only binds the party who signs it. The merchant receiving the confirmation can, however, object to it in writing within ten days of its receipt. The merchant receiving

the confirmation should review it carefully to determine if it is consistent with the oral contract. If the writing changes the agreement, the merchant can object in writing (the Statute of Frauds still applies), and the parties can resolve differences without liability. If the merchant does not object, the written confirmation is evidence of the terms of the oral contract. Because this is a UCC rule, it does not apply to contracts for services or interests in real property.

CHECKLIST FOR ORAL CONTRACTS

1. When possible, use written contracts.
2. If you enter into an oral contract over the telephone, send a written confirmation outlining your understanding of the oral contract.
3. If you receive a written memorandum, or confirmation from the other party, read it carefully to make sure that its terms agree with what you believed the agreement to be.
4. If you have any objections, put them in writing and send them to the other party within ten days.

The signature can be anywhere on the writing. It need not be at the end. And a signature can be initials or even a mark rather than a full name. The law does not require a witness. However, without a witness, it is hard to prove, for example, who created a mark and whether the mark was intended as a signature.

A memorandum giving evidence of an oral contract must also contain the essential terms of the contract. Usually, to be sufficient under the Statute of Frauds, the writing must name the parties, subject matter, consideration,

Read to the class the Legal Focus Problem found here. Allow student volunteers to suggest possible answers to the question posed at the end of this problem. Then have a student volunteer read the paragraph that immediately follows this Legal Focus Problem. Make sure that students understand that as the text states, "The moral is clear: if an oral promise that is important to you is made in negotiations, make sure it is part of the written contract. If it is not, you probably cannot enforce the promise."

Reteaching Activity

Have a volunteer use his or her own words to explain the parol evidence rule to the class.

LEGAL BACKGROUND

Parol is another word for "oral" or "verbal." Black's *Law Dictionary* explains the *parol evidence rule* thusly: "Under this rule, when parties put their agreement in writing, all previous oral agreements merge in the writing, and a contract as written cannot be modified or changed by *parol evidence,* in the absence of a plea of mistake or fraud in the preparation of the writing."

268

Multicultural

Perspectives

The form required to prove a contract's existence is often related to the stage of development of that country's legal system. In many countries throughout the world, people still deal informally with their neighbors. Typical of these dealings is the custom of barter, or trade, of the Tswana tribe in Botswana, Africa. In this system of bartering, when the goods are exchanged, the contract is complete, but even in a barter transaction, the possibility exists that one performance will take place in the future.

For example, assume that one person promises to deliver a goat at a later time in exchange for a number of pots and pans. The neighbor accepts the promise of the goat for the wares, and both parties seek wit-

and quantity. Contracts for the sale of land, in some states, also require a clear statement of the location of the property and the price to be paid.

As we stated earlier, to be careful, everyone should put contracts involving important or complicated matters in writing, even if the law does not require that the contracts be in writing. Furthermore, the contract should be complete and should be signed by all the parties, even if the law would be satisfied by a less formal writing. Then, if problems arise concerning performance of the contract, the written agreement detailing the promised performance by each party can be proved in court.

◆ THE PAROL EVIDENCE RULE

♦ **parol evidence rule** A rule of evidence that says a written contract can be proved only by itself; evidence of prior negotiations or agreements that contradict or vary the terms of the contract will not be allowed.

Another rule related to written contracts is the **parol evidence rule**. This is a rule of evidence that focuses on how a written contract is to be interpreted. The parol evidence rule states that a contract can be proved only by itself. That is, the only proof of what the contract says is the actual written contract. This rule stops a party from introducing any evidence of prior negotiations or agreements that contradict or vary the terms of the written contract. The written contract is ordinarily assumed to be the complete agreement.

◆ LEGAL FOCUS – PROBLEM

Mike and Carl spend several hours negotiating the painting of Carl's house. At one point in the negotiation, Mike tells Carl he will stain the redwood deck as part of the project. Carl and Mike finally agree on terms and put them in a writing, which both of them sign. The signed contract is complete but does not provide for anything other than painting the house. After the job is done, Carl complains that Mike failed to paint the redwood deck and has breached the contract. Mike argues that painting the redwood deck did not end up as part of the written agreement. Can Carl produce evidence of Mike's discussion about the redwood deck?

No. This example illustrates the purpose of the parol evidence rule. Parties very often negotiate about different terms, countering back and forth. When they finally create the written contract, it should state the terms upon which the parties finally agree. To allow parties to bring up offers and counteroffers that did not become part of the written contract would reduce the value of the written contract. The moral is clear: If an oral promise that is important to you is made in negotiations, make sure it is part of the written contract. If it is not, you probably cannot enforce the promise.

Because of the rigidity of the parol evidence rule, courts allow several exceptions:

nesses to the transaction. The deal will then be struck in the presence of the witnesses, with each witness aware that he or she may be called upon to testify to the tribal chief at a later date if the goat is not delivered.

The most common time limit for delivery is one year. If at the end of one year the debt is not paid, the seller of the pots will demand payment by the buyer's relatives. The seller of the pots and pans will provide

the witnesses to support his claim to the goat.

As the value of the credit sale grows, the importance of the witnesses also grows. If the value of the sale is large enough, the head man of the clan, or even the tribal chief, will be asked to act as a witness. When someone this important is involved, certain rituals are prescribed to complete the transaction.

1. Evidence of a *later* change in a written contract can be introduced into court. Note that an oral change may not be enforceable if it is covered by the Statute of Frauds (for example, a later agreement to increase the price of goods sold to more than $500).
2. Oral evidence can be introduced to show that the contract was voidable or void (for example, induced by mistake, fraud, or misrepresentation). If deception led one of the parties to agree to the terms of a written contract, oral evidence showing fraud is allowed. Courts allow such evidence to discourage bad faith.
3. When the terms of a written contract are unclear, evidence is allowed to show the meaning of the terms.
4. When the written contract is incomplete and lacks one or more essential terms, the courts allow evidence to "fill in the gaps."
5. Evidence to show an *obvious* or *gross* clerical (or typographical) error is allowed.

◆ LEGAL FOCUS ~ PROBLEM

Sharon agrees to lease 1,000 square feet of office space at the monthly rate of $3 per square foot from Stone Enterprises. The signed written lease provides for a monthly lease payment of $30 rather than the $3,000 agreed to by the parties. Is oral evidence admissible to show the mistake in the written contract?

Yes. An obvious or gross clerical error exists. Since the error is obvious, Stone Enterprises is allowed to present evidence to correct the mistake.

Important in the determination of whether evidence is allowable is whether the written contract was intended to be a complete statement of the agreement. If it was, it is an *integrated* contract—a contract with all terms included. Evidence to contradict an integrated contract is not allowed. If the contract is only partially integrated, evidence of consistent additional terms is allowed to add to the written agreement.

If a term is included as part of the written contract can you enforce it?

◆ INTERPRETATION OF CONTRACTS

Common law rules of contract interpretation have evolved over time. Their purpose is to provide the courts with guidelines for determining the meaning of and giving effect to contracts.

THE PLAIN MEANING RULE

When a contract is clear and certain, or *unambiguous*, a court will enforce it according to its plain terms. There is no need for the court to interpret the

Collaborative Learning Activity

Have students work together to collect items they can use to create a bulletin board displaying written versus oral contracts.

Checking Your Progress (Answers)

1. A memorandum can consist of any form as long as it is a written confirmation.
2. A memorandum must include the name of the parties, the subject matter, consideration, and quantity.
3. To ensure that an oral contract is enforced, a person should send a written confirmation outlining his or her understanding of the oral contract, read carefully a written memorandum or confirmation received from the other party, and write and send any objections to the other party within ten days.
4. Under the parol evidence rule, the only proof of what the contract says is the actual written contract. No other proof is necessary to enforce it.
5. Additional evidence can be introduced to show a later change in a written contract, to show that the contract was void or voidable, to clarify ambiguous terms, to fill in missing terms, or to correct obvious clerical errors.
6. The court interprets the language of unclear terms to try to accomplish the purpose of the parties.

language of the contract. The meaning of the contract terms must be determined from *the face of the contract*—from the written document alone. This is sometimes referred to as the *plain meaning rule*. Under this rule, if a contract's words are clear and unambiguous, a court cannot consider other evidence.

INTERPRETATION OF AMBIGUOUS TERMS

When a written contract contains *ambiguous*, or unclear, terms, a court will interpret the language to try to accomplish the purpose of the parties. The primary purpose of rules of interpretation is to determine the parties' intent from the language used in their agreement. A court will not make or remake a contract. It will not interpret the contract according to what the parties *claim* they meant when they made it. The following rules are used by the courts in interpreting ambiguous contract terms:

1. As much as possible, a reasonable, lawful, and effective meaning will be given to all of a contract's terms.
2. A contract is interpreted as a whole contract; individual, specific clauses are considered subject to the contract's general intent. All writings that are part of the same transaction are interpreted together.
3. Terms that were clearly negotiated separately by the parties are given greater consideration than standardized terms.
4. A word is given its ordinary, commonly accepted meaning. A technical term is given its technical meaning.
5. Specific and exact wording is given greater attention than general language.
6. Handwritten terms prevail over typewritten. Typewritten terms prevail over printed ones.
7. A contract should be drafted in clear and unambiguous language. A party who uses ambiguous language is responsible for the ambiguities she or he wrote. Thus, where the language has more than one meaning, it is interpreted against the party who drafted the contract.

◆ CHECKING YOUR PROGRESS

1. What form must a memorandum take to satisfy the Statute of Frauds?
2. Under the Statute of Frauds, what must be included in a memorandum showing an oral contract?
3. What should a person do to ensure an oral contract is enforced?
4. How does the parol evidence rule affect interpretation and enforcement of contracts?
5. In what situations can additional evidence be introduced to enforce contracts?
6. What does the court do if a written contract contains ambiguous terms?

Read

Before the students read this *A Case In Point* feature, you might wish to remind them that under the Statute of Frauds the following types of contracts require some form of writing:

1. Contracts involving interests in land
2. Contracts that cannot be performed within one year from the date of creation
3. Promises to pay the debt or perform the duty of another
4. Promises made in return for a promise of marriage
5. Contracts for the sales of goods priced at $500 or more

Explain to the students that the case *Chesapeake Financial Corporation* v. *Laird* is an example of how the Statute of Frauds one-year rule is applied. Then allow a student volunteer to read this *A Case In Point* feature aloud to the class.

Discuss

Why did Donald Laird and Joseph Martin sue Chesapeake Financial Corporation? What was the trial court's decision in that case? What was Chesapeake Financial Corporation's reaction to the trial court's decision? What was the decision of the Supreme Court of Maryland? What reasons did the Supreme Court of Maryland give for its decision?

◆ A CASE IN POINT ◆

CHESAPEAKE FINANCIAL CORP. v. LAIRD

Supreme Court of Maryland, 1981.
289 Md. 594,
425 A.2d 1348.

The following case is an example of how the Statute of Frauds one-year rule is applied. Note that the parties did not anticipate performance within one year. Even so, the oral contract was enforceable, because performance was *possible* within one year.

FACTS Donald Laird and Joseph Martin, land developers, orally contracted with Chesapeake Financial Corporation to develop some real estate together. According to the agreement, Chesapeake was to provide the financing for the venture. Chesapeake later refused to provide the necessary funding. Laird and Martin sued for damages as a result of Chesapeake's alleged misrepresentation. Chesapeake asserted the Statute of Frauds as a defense. Chesapeake claimed that the oral contract was unenforceable because the parties had not anticipated completing the project within one year's time. Under the Maryland Statute of Frauds, "any agreement that is not to be performed within the space of one year from the making

thereof" is required to be in writing. The trial court held for Laird and Martin and awarded damages. Chesapeake appealed.

ISSUE The issue was whether the contract was capable of performance within one year. If the answer is yes, the contract falls outside the Statute of Frauds and is enforceable. If the answer is no, it falls under the Statute of Frauds requirement that such contracts be in writing, and Chesapeake could avoid the obligations of the contract.

DECISION The Supreme Court of Maryland held that the contract terms could have been performed within one year. Thus, the oral contract was enforceable. The Supreme Court affirmed the court's decision.

REASON Although the parties expected that the project would take at least two years to complete, it would not have been *impossible* to perform the contract within one year. The court stated that it had historically "interpreted 'literally and very narrowly' the words of the statute [regarding the one-year rule]. . . . [Chesapeake has] not clearly demonstrated that, under the terms of the alleged oral contract, as contrasted with the expectations of the parties, it could not be performed within one year."

Teaching Note

This case is included in the *West's Business and Personal Law Handbook of Selected Court Cases.*

Assessment Strategies

In order to help students review what they have learned in Chapter 11, you might wish to:

1. Have a student volunteer, or volunteers, read the Chapter Summary aloud to the class.

2. Allow the students to work with partners to complete the *Using Legal Language* activity.

3. Assign the *Checking for Comprehension* exercise as homework.

4. Allow the students to work in small groups to complete the *Applying Legal Concepts* activities.

5. As a class, complete the *Applying the Law* activities. (Please note that you may have to help students with vocabulary so that they adequately understand all of the *Applying the Law* material.)

In order to check student mastery of chapter concepts, you may wish to use the Chapter 11 test that is found in your *Teacher's Resource Binder* or use WESTEST computerized testing for Chapter 11.

CHAPTER 11 REVIEW

◆ SUMMARY

CONTRACTS REQUIRED TO BE IN WRITING BY THE STATUTE OF FRAUDS

Contracts Involving Interests in Land

1. *Application*—Applies to any contract for an interest in land, such as a sale or a lease.

2. *Exceptions*—

   a. Some states will enforce a contract for the sale of land if a person has moved onto the property, made permanent improvements, and paid part of the purchase price.

   b. Many states allow oral leases of a year or less to be enforceable.

Contracts That Cannot Be Performed within One Year

1. *Application*—Applies only to contracts that cannot possibly be performed fully within one year from the date of the contract's formation.

2. *Exceptions*—None.

Promises to Pay the Debt or Perform the Duty of Another

1. *Application*—Applies to secondary promises—promises to pay the debt or perform the duty of another person.

2. *Exception*—Main-purpose rule, whereby a person makes a secondary promise mainly to secure a personal benefit.

Promises Made in Return for a Promise of Marriage

1. *Application*—Applies to promises to pay money or give property in exchange for a promise to marry (includes prenuptial agreements).

2. *Exceptions*—None.

Contracts for the Sale of Goods Priced at $500 or More

1. *Application*—Applies only to the sale of goods priced at $500 or more.

2. *Exceptions*—Several; for example, under the UCC, a written confirmation of an oral agreement between merchants that is received by one merchant can satisfy the requirement for both merchants.

SUFFICIENCY OF THE WRITING

A written memorandum may constitute an enforceable contract under the Statute of Frauds. It must be signed by the party against whom enforcement is sought and must contain the essential terms of the contract.

PAROL EVIDENCE RULE

Stops a party from introducing at trial any evidence of prior negotiations or agreements that contradict or vary the terms of the written contract. The written contract is assumed to be the complete embodiment of the parties' agreement. There are exceptions to this rule.

INTERPRETATION OF CONTRACTS

Unambiguous Terms

When the terms of a contract are unambiguous, a court will enforce the contract according to its plain terms, the meaning of which must be determined from the written document alone.

Ambiguous Terms

When the terms of a contract are ambiguous, courts will follow certain rules of interpretation.

Using Legal Language (Answers)

1–H, 2–F, 3–E, 4–B, 5–G, 6–I, 7–C, 8–D, 9–J, 10–A

Checking for Comprehension (Answers)

1. The original statute was passed to prevent perjury about the existence of contracts.
2. A real estate mortgage is a transfer of an interest in land as security for the repayment of a loan to *buy* property; a lease is a transfer of the right to *occupy* property. Mortgages must be in writing, but a lease may not have to be in writing unless it is for more than one year.
3. Student answers will vary but should discuss the difficulty in proving what was agreed to or even that a contract exists.
4. Yes, a written memorandum can only be enforced against a party who has signed it.
5. To interpret ambiguous contract terms, the court (1) applies a lawful, reasonable, effective meaning, (2) interprets the contract as a whole, (3) gives greater consideration to terms clearly negotiated by the parties, (4) gives commonly accepted meaning to words, (5) gives greater attention to specific and exact wording, (6) considers handwritten terms over typewritten or printed terms, and (7) interprets against the party who drafted the contract with ambiguous words.
6. No. Only oral contracts that are impossible to perform within one year fall under the Statute of Frauds. However unlikely it may be that Francis will die within a year, the possibility does exist. Therefore, the contract does not fall under the the Statute of Frauds and is enforceable.

 ## USING LEGAL LANGUAGE

Directions: Match each term with the statement that best defines that term.

1. ambiguous term
2. lease
3. memorandum
4. mortgage
5. parol evidence rule
6. plain meaning rule
7. prenuptial agreement
8. real property
9. secondary promise
10. Statute of Frauds

A. The _____ is the name given to laws requiring that certain contracts be proven by a signed writing.

B. A creditor acquires an interest in the debtor's property as security for the debt with a written instrument called a _____.

C. A _____ defines each partner's ownership rights in the other partner's property prior to being married.

D. Contracts involving _____, which is land and everything attached to it, must be in writing.

E. A _____ showing the oral contract must contain the essential terms of the contract.

F. With a _____ a landlord transfers the right to occupy or use land for a certain time to a tenant.

G. The _____ is a rule of evidence requiring that a contract be proved only by itself.

H. When the term of a written contract is unclear, it is an _____, and evidence is admissible to show the meaning of the term.

I. Sometime referred to as the _____, the meaning of the terms of a contract must be determined from the face of the contract—from the written document alone.

J. A co-sign is a _____ and must be in writing.

CHECKING FOR COMPREHENSION

1. Why was the statute of frauds created?
2. What is the difference between a real estate mortgage and a lease? Must mortgages or lease contracts be in writing?
3. Why is it important to put important and complicated contracts in writing even if the law does not require it?
4. Does the Statute of Frauds require that a written memorandum be signed by both parties if it is to be enforced against both?
5. What rules do courts use to interpret contracts with ambiguous terms?
6. On January 1, 1993, Dominic, in exchange for consideration, orally promised to pay Francis $300 a month for as long as Francis lived. Payments were to be made on the first day of every month. Dominic made the payments regularly for nine

Writing and Form 273

1. Yes. The court held that the parties could fully perform their oral contract within one year from the date of its formation. The agreement had been that Fernandez was to furnish the funds and Pando was to purchase the ticket, select the numbers, return it to Pando, and pray. The winning numbers were scheduled to be drawn within days, and at that point the obligations of the parties became fixed, including Fernandez's obligation to share her prize with Pando. The fact that payment was to take place over a ten-year period did not affect this obligation. Fernandez should have notified the state Lottery Division to divide future payments equally between herself and Pando.

2. Yes. The written contract called for the payment of a specified amount for doing specified work. There was no statement in the written contract that the obligation to pay was conditional upon the state of California providing funding. Proof of such a condition would contradict the obligation imposed by the written contract. Parol evidence was, therefore, not admissible to prove the existence of an oral condition that would contradict the contract.

3. Yes. The court of appeals affirmed the trial court's judgment. The court explained that detrimental action and justifiable reliance on an oral promise may be sufficient to override application of the Statute of Frauds and compel enforcement of the promise. Quoting Section 139(1) of the Restatement of Contracts, the court held that "[t]he absence of a written contract cannot defeat a claim for relief when injustice to a promisee who has reasonably and justifiably relied on a promise can be prevented only by recognizing a right of recovery against the promisor." In other words, the court held that the plaintiffs were entitled to relief under the theory of promissory estoppel.

---

274   The Law of Contracts

months and then quit. Francis claimed that Dominic had breached the oral contract and sued Dominic for damages. Dominic argued that the contract was unenforceable because, under the Statute of Frauds, contracts that cannot be performed within one year must be in writing. Will Dominic succeed in this defense?

APPLYING LEGAL CONCEPTS

1. Write a memorandum for an oral contract in which you agree to purchase a television set from another student in your class. Key the memorandum on a typewriter or computer. Give a copy to the other party (student). Has a contract been formed?

2. Design a poster illustrating the types of contracts that fall under the Statute of Frauds.

APPLYING THE LAW . . . YOU BE THE JUDGE

1. Fernandez orally promised Pando that if Pando helped her win the New York state lottery, she would share the proceeds equally with him. Pando agreed to purchase the tickets in Fernandez's name. He would select the lottery numbers, and pray for the divine intervention of a saint to help them win. Fernandez won $2.8 million in the lottery, which was to be paid over a ten-year period. When Fernandez failed to share the winnings equally, Pando sued for breach of her contractual obligation. Fernandez countered that their contract was unenforceable under the Statute of Frauds, since the contract could not be performed within one year. Could the contract be performed within one year? [*Pando by Pando v. Fernandez*, 127 Misc.2d 224, 485 N.Y.S.2d 162 (1984)]

2. Rincones agreed to pay Windberg to write a portion of a book. A contract was written which specified the compensation to be paid. Windberg refused to pay the amount, claiming that the duty to pay was conditional upon receiving funding from the state of California. He did not receive the funding so he claimed there was no duty to pay. Will the court require Windberg to pay Rincones the amount they agreed? [*Rincones v. Windberg*, (Tex.App.) 705 S.W.2d 846 (1986)]

3. The plaintiffs, the Nicols, Hoerrs, Turners, and Andersons, purchased subdivision lots from Ken Nelson. The lots bordered an undeveloped tract and offered scenic views of an adjacent lake. When Nelson and his partners took steps to develop the previously undeveloped tract, the plaintiffs sued. The trial court found that the plaintiffs had purchased their lots only after receiving oral assurances from Nelson that (1) the tract would remain undeveloped open space, (2) the property was owned by a company that had no plans to build on the land, (3) he held an option to purchase the property if it became available, and (4) he would not develop the land if it came under his ownership. Concluding that the plaintiffs had reasonably relied on Nelson's oral promise, the trial court enjoined Nelson's development of the property. Nelson appealed, arguing that the Statute of Frauds, which requires that contracts involving interests in real property be in writing, barred enforcement of his oral promise. Will the appellate court affirm the trial court's judgment? [*Nicol v. Nelson*, 776 P.2d 1144 (Colo.App. 1989)]

Prereading Activity

Write the following column headings on the board: RIGHTS, DUTIES. Call on students to tell a right or a duty they have (to or from their home, school, city, state, nation, etc.). Have a student list appropriate examples on the board in the correct column. Explain that contracts involve rights and duties and that both can be assigned/delegated to someone else. Chapter 12 describes the legal application of contracts to the third party.

Mastery Objectives

By the end of this chapter, students will be able to:
- Distinguish between assignments and delegations
- Describe rights that can be assigned
- Describe duties that can be delegated
- Identify third party beneficiaries' rights
- Relate ways to discharge a contract

Third Party Rights and Discharge

Chapter

12

LEGAL BACKGROUND

This chapter combines a discussion of who besides the contracting parties can enforce a contract, with a discussion of when a performance under a contract is sufficient or can be excused.

Parties who contracted with one another, those in privity, generally are the only ones with standing to enforce the contract. There are two important exceptions: assignment of rights and delegation of duties, and third party intended beneficiaries. Under an assignment of rights or a delegation of duties, one of the parties transfers his or her rights or obligations to a third party, giving the third party the rights or obligations of the transferring party. If a contract was created in part to confer a benefit upon a third party, that third party can often enforce the contract.

When contracting parties do what they promised to do, their duties are discharged, and the contract is successfully completed. Proper performance is the most common form of discharge. But what is proper performance? This chapter discusses some common issues about the question of performance.

You might want to explain to students that *Black's Law Dictionary* explains *privity of contract* as "that connection or relationship that exists between two or more contracting parties. It is essential to the maintenance of an action on any contract that there subsists a privity between the plaintiff and defendant in respect of the matter sued on."

Legal Focus Problem

Allow a student volunteer to read this Legal Focus Problem aloud to the class. Ask the students to identify the parties who are in privity of contract in this example. Then ask the students to answer the question posed at the end of this problem.

Vocabulary Activity

Discuss *beneficiary*, as in "third party beneficiary." What is the root of the word? Ask students how they have heard the term used.

276

Chapter 12
Resources and Assignment Guide

Activity Sheets
Reviewing Legal Concepts 12 *TRB*
Enrichment Activity 12 *TRB*

Student Activity Workbook
Chapter 12 Activities

Tests
Chapter 12 Test *TRB*
Chapter 12 WESTEST Computerized Testing

Handbook of Selected Court Cases
Warren v. *Denison*
H. R. Moch Co. v. *Rensselaer Water Co.*

West's Business Law and Legal Environment Videodisc
Still Frames and Motion Segments as shown

"[In the case of] a promise made for the benefit of another, he for whose benefit it is made may bring an action for its breach."
Lawrence v. Fox, 1859

I f a contract is valid and legally enforceable, attention turns to the rights and duties of the parties. A relationship is created between parties to a contract called **privity of contract**. Parties in privity of contract have rights and duties because of the contract. Usually, third parties—parties not in privity—have no rights.

* **privity of contract** A relationship created between parties to a contract.

LEGAL FOCUS - PROBLEM

I offer to sell you my watch for $100, and you accept. Later, I refuse to deliver the watch to you, though you are ready to give me the $100. You decide to overlook my action, which is a breach of the contract. However, your close friend, Ann, is unhappy and files a lawsuit against me. Can she receive a judgment?

The answer is no, because she was not a party to the contract. You, as a party, have rights under the contract and could sue. Ann is not the proper party to sue. That is, she lacks *standing to sue*.

You are probably convinced by now that for every rule of contract law, there is an exception. Exceptions exist because law is a human institution, created for human ends. When justice is not served by a rule of law, exceptions to the rule must be, and are, made. There are two exceptions to the rule requiring privity of contract.

The first exception is that parties to a contract can transfer their contract rights, or duties, or both to others. A contract right is the performance the person bargained to receive—for example, the right to a payment of money. A contract duty is the performance the person bargained to give—for example, the duty to mow someone's lawn. Legally, these transfers are called **assignments of rights** or **delegations of duties**.

The second exception to the privity of contract rule is the **third party beneficiary contract**. Here, the third party has rights created by the original contract. The law of assignments, delegations, and third party beneficiary contracts is discussed in the first half of this chapter.

At some point, parties to the contract must know when their duties are completed. How do you know when a contract is finished? The second part of this chapter deals with the **discharge** of a contract. Discharge is normally accomplished after both parties have performed the acts promised in the contract.

* **assignment of rights** The act of transferring to another all or part of one's rights arising under a contract.

* **delegation of duties** The act of transferring to another all or part of one's duties arising under a contract.

* **third party beneficiary contract** A contract created at least in part to benefit a third party. The third party has rights to enforce the contract.

* **discharge** The termination of one's contract obligation.

The still frames listed below from the **West's Business Law and Legal Environment Videodisc** can be used with this chapter. To access this material, use the bar codes or the frame numbers included in the Videodisc Instructor's Manual found in the *TRB*.

Third Party Beneficiary Contract Relationships
Assignment Relationships
Assignment of Rights
Delegation Relationships
Delegation Duties

ASSIGNMENTS AND DELEGATIONS

Assignment and delegation occur *after* the original contract is made, when one of the original contracting parties transfers to another party (the third party) a right or duty in the contract. As mentioned, contract *rights* can be transferred by *assignment*, and contract *duties* can be transferred by *delegation*.

ASSIGNMENTS

In a bilateral contract, the parties have corresponding rights and duties. One party has a *right* to require the other to perform some task. This party is the *obligee*—the one owed a right. The other party has a *duty* to perform the task. This is the *obligor*—the one who owes a duty. The transfer of a right to a third person is an *assignment*. When rights under a contract are assigned, the rights of the *assignor*—the party making the assignment—usually end. The third party—the *assignee*, the party receiving the assignment—has a right to demand performance from the other original party to the contract, the obligor.

LEGAL FOCUS ~ PROBLEM

Alice Ackerman entered into a contract with Brenda Barlow. Ackerman agreed to haul some trash to the county dump for Barlow for $50. Ackerman hauled the trash, but Barlow has not yet paid Ackerman. Ackerman assigns to Carl Cramer the right to receive the $50 to settle an old debt Ackerman owes Cramer. Here, Ackerman is the assignor, the person making an assignment. Cramer is the assignee, the person receiving an assignment. Barlow is the obligor, the person who owes a duty—in this case, the duty to pay $50. Can Cramer compel Barlow to pay him the $50?

Yes. Ackerman has assigned to Cramer her rights under the original contract with Barlow. The assignee takes the assignor's original rights, the money owed by Barlow. Cramer can enforce payment in a court of law if Barlow does not pay him the $50. This transaction is illustrated in Exhibit 12-1.

The rights an assignee receives are subject to any defenses that the obligor has against the assignor–obligee. For example, if Ackerman had not hauled the trash to the dump, Barlow would have had a defense to paying Ackerman the $50. If Ackerman had transferred her right to Cramer, Barlow would have had the same defense against any claim by Cramer. Barlow would not have been required to pay either Ackerman or Cramer, because the assignor–obligee of the promise to haul trash (Ackerman) would have breached the contract.

As the students have learned, *assignment of rights* is the transferring to another all or part of one's rights arising under a contract. Have a student volunteer compare and contrast this use of the word *assignment* and a more familiar use, as in *homework assignments*.

Legal Focus Problem

Read this Legal Focus Problem aloud to the class. Make sure the students understand that under the original contract, Ackerman and Barlow were in privity of contract and that Ackerman assigned her rights under the contract to a third party, Cramer. Then allow a student volunteer to suggest a possible answer to the question posed at the end of this problem.

Reteaching Activity

As you work through this section, have students make a list of all the possible cases in which rights may not be legally assigned. Students should use their lists as a review tool when studying for the chapter test.

Legal Focus Problem

Ask a student volunteer to read this Legal Focus Problem aloud to the class. Have the student answer the question posed at the end of this problem. To reinforce what the students learned regarding the parol evidence rule in the last chapter, you might build on this Legal Focus by asking the following question: Suppose Bill and April agreed in their oral negotiations that the contract could not be assigned by April, but that this provision was left out of the written contract. If April assigns to Carly, can Carly then require Bill to build the house for her?

278

VIDEODISC NOTE
Much of the material that is conveyed in the exhibits of *West's Business and Personal Law* is also conveyed in the still frames on the **West Business Law and Legal Environment Videodisc**. For more information and directions for use, please see the Index and Description of Contents for the **West Business Law and Legal Environment Videodisc** that is found in your *Teacher's Resource Binder*.

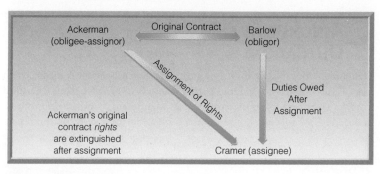

EXHIBIT 12-1
ASSIGNMENT RELATIONSHIPS

Rights That Cannot Be Assigned   Most rights can be assigned, except in special circumstances. The following is a list of some of these special circumstances.

1.   A statute expressly prohibits assignment of a particular right.

> ### ◄ LEGAL FOCUS – EXAMPLE
>
> Mary is a new employee of Computer Future, Inc. Computer Future is an employer under workers' compensation statutes in the state. (Workers' compensation is an insurance plan that pays workers for lost days of work for job-related injuries.) Mary is a covered employee, and she has a high-risk job. In need of a loan, Mary borrows money from Stark. Before Stark will agree to loan Mary the money, he requires that Mary assign to him all workers' compensation benefits that she might get if she is ever injured on the job. If Mary is injured, Stark cannot collect her benefits. *Future* workers' compensation benefits are rights that state statutes will not allow to be assigned.

2.   If a contract stipulates that the rights cannot be assigned, then *ordinarily* they cannot be assigned.

> ### ◄ LEGAL FOCUS – PROBLEM
>
> Bill and April enter into a contract that provides that Bill will build a house for April. The contract includes this statement: "This contract cannot be assigned by April. Any assignment renders this contract void, and all rights under the contract end." April assigns her rights to Carly. Can Carly require Bill to build the house for her?

No. The contract clearly provides that no assignment can be made. Carly cannot enforce the contract against Bill because the attempted assignment violates the agreement. There are a few situations in which the courts will not allow a party to ban an assignment of a right in a contract. For example, a contract cannot generally prohibit assigning the right to receive money. This prohibition would be against public policy, because public policy favors the free flow of money in our economy.

3. When a contract is *personal* in nature, the rights under the contract cannot be assigned unless all that remains is a money payment.

◆ LEGAL FOCUS – PROBLEM

Natalie Bartels agrees to tutor Marla Acett's children. Acett assigns to Melinda Cameer her right to Bartels's services. Can Cameer require Bartels to tutor her children?

Cameer cannot require Bartels to perform. Cameer's children may be more difficult to tutor than Acett's. If Acett could assign her rights to Bartels's services to Cameer, it would change Bartels's obligation. Because personal services are unique, rights to receive personal services cannot be assigned.

4. A right cannot be assigned if an assignment will materially increase or alter the duties of the obligor—that is, increase or alter those duties in an important way.

◆ LEGAL FOCUS – PROBLEM

Aman owns a hotel. She purchases an insurance policy on the hotel with Northwest Insurance. The policy insures against fire, theft, floods, and vandalism. Aman attempts to assign the insurance policy to Ceres, who owns another hotel. Is the assignment effective?

No. It substantially alters Northwest Insurance's duty of performance. Insurance companies evaluate the particular risk of each insurance policy they issue and tailor their policies to fit that risk. If the policy is assigned to a third party, the insurance risk is materially altered. Therefore, the assignment does not give Ceres any rights against Northwest Insurance.

Notice of Assignment After a valid assignment of rights, the third party should notify the obligor (Barlow in Exhibit 12-1) of the assignment. The law does not require this notice, and the assignment is effective even without notice. However, two major problems arise when notice of the assignment is not given:

Enrichment

Have your students read the first Legal Focus Problem on this page referring to Ackerman assigning her rights to Cramer. What actions could have prevented Cramer from losing his rights to collect? Have your students cite many things that an assigner can do to protect himself or herself.

Legal Focus Problem

Read this second Legal Focus Problem aloud to the class. Make sure that the students understand that although Cramer, the assignee, cannot collect from Barlow, Cramer can collect from Ackerman.

---

1. If the assignor assigns the same right to two different persons, which one has the right to the performance? Notification may be needed to make this determination. The majority rule is that the first person given the assignment has the right. However, some states follow a different rule: The first assignee who gives notice to the obligor has the right.

> ### ◀ LEGAL FOCUS - PROBLEM
>
> Barlow owes Ackerman $1,000. On May 1, Ackerman assigns her right to receive the $1,000 to Cramer. No notice of the assignment is given to Barlow. On June 1, for past services Ackerman assigns the same monetary claim to Dorman. Dorman immediately notifies Barlow of the assignment. Who has a right to the $1,000?

The answer depends on the state where the events happened. In the majority of states, Cramer has priority, because Cramer's assignment was first in time. In some states, though, Dorman has priority, because Dorman gave notice to Barlow first.

2. Until the obligor has notice of assignment, the obligor can discharge his or her obligation by performance to the assignor. Once the obligor receives proper notice, he or she must provide performance to the assignee.

> ### ◀ LEGAL FOCUS - PROBLEM
>
> Barlow owes Ackerman $1,000 on a contractual obligation. Ackerman assigns this monetary claim to Cramer. No notice of assignment is given to Barlow. Barlow pays Ackerman the $1,000. Can the assignee, Cramer, collect from Barlow?

No. Although the assignment was valid, Barlow's payment to Ackerman was a discharge of the debt. Cramer's failure to notify Barlow of the assignment caused Cramer to lose the right to collect from Barlow. If Cramer had given Barlow notice of the assignment, Barlow would have had to pay Cramer to discharge the debt. Cramer does, however, have rights against Ackerman.

DELEGATIONS

Parties can also transfer duties. Duties are not assigned, they are delegated. Normally, a delegation of duties does not release the party making the delegation (the *delegator*) from any obligations. If the party to whom the duty has been delegated (the *delegatee*) fails to perform, the delegator—who is the original obligor—must perform. No special form is required to dele-

VIDEODISC NOTE
Much of the material that is conveyed in the
exhibits of *West's Business and Personal Law*
is also conveyed in the still frames on the
**West Business Law and Legal Environment
Videodisc**. For more information and direc-
tions for use, please see the Index and
Description of Contents for the **West Business
Law and Legal Environment Videodisc** that is
found in your *Teacher's Resource Binder*.

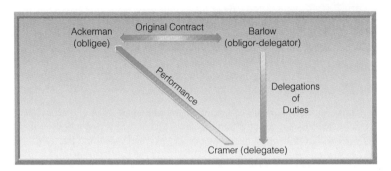

EXHIBIT 12-2
DELEGATION RELATIONSHIPS

gate duties. As long as the delegator expresses an intention to make the
delegation, it is effective. Delegation relationships are illustrated in Exhibit
12-2.

Duties That Cannot Be Delegated With a few exceptions, any duty
can be delegated. Delegation is not allowed in the following situations:

1. When performance depends on the *personal* skills or talents of the
    obligor.

◆ LEGAL FOCUS – PROBLEM

Amos hires Barbara to teach him how to sell corporation stock.
Barbara, an experienced businessperson known for her expertise in
corporate stock sales, decides to delegate her duties to a third party,
Carstairs. Is the delegation effective?

No. Barbara contracted to render a service founded on Barbara's *expertise or special skill*. The delegation changes Amos's rights under the
contract. Therefore, Carstairs cannot perform Barbara's duties.

2. When a special trust has been placed in the obligor.

◆ LEGAL FOCUS – EXAMPLE

Paul hires Sherry to deliver some goods to another city. He selects
Sherry because, as he tells her, this delivery is of *special* importance
and she has proven very reliable in the past. Although the task is
routine, the circumstances suggest special trust and reliance in Sherry
and the duty cannot be delegated.

Discussion Starter

Stimulate a class discussion on the situation found in the second Legal Focus Problem about Bartless delegating his duties to Cumber. Have students demonstrate their understanding of delegating duties through the discussion.

Legal Focus Problem

Read through this second Legal Focus Problem with the class. Make sure that the class understands that Cumber is the *delegatee*, that Bartlett is *obligor*, and that Ambon is the *obligee*. Then ask a student volunteer to suggest a possible answer for the question posed at the end of this problem.

3. When performance by a third party will vary from that expected by the obligee (to whom performance is owed) under the contract.

4. When the contract expressly prohibits delegation.

◆ LEGAL FOCUS ~ PROBLEM

Bart contracts with Albert to pick up and deliver construction machinery to Albert's property. Bart delegates this duty to Carly, who is in the business of delivering heavy machinery. Is the delegation effective?

Yes. The performance is of a *routine*, not a *personal*, nature and there is no express reservation prohibiting delegation. It does not change Albert's rights under the contract.

Effect of a Delegation If a delegation of duties is enforceable, the obligee must accept performance from the delegatee. The obligee can only refuse performance if the duty is one that cannot be delegated. At the same time, as noted earlier, a valid delegation of duties does not relieve the delegator of obligations under the contract. If the contract is not performed, the delegator is still liable to the obligee.

Liability of the Delegatee to the Obligee Can the person who promises to perform a task for another be held responsible to the person with the right to the performance if the person who promises does not perform? Or in other words, if the delegatee does not perform, can the obligee hold the delegatee liable? If the delegatee promised the performance to directly benefit the obligee, there is an "assumption of duty" by the delegatee. Breach of this duty makes the delegatee liable to the obligee.

◆ LEGAL FOCUS ~ PROBLEM

Bartlett contracts to build Ambon a house according to Ambon's blueprint. Bartlett becomes seriously ill and subcontracts with Cumber to build the house for Ambon. Here Bartlett is the obligor–delegator, Cumber is the delegatee and Ambon is the obligee. Cumber fails to build the house. Can Ambon hold Cumber responsible for her promise to Bartlett to build Ambon's house?

Since the delegatee, Cumber, contracted with Bartlett (the obligor) to build the house for the benefit of Ambon (the obligee), Ambon can sue Bartlett, or Cumber, or both.

Most states also hold that when a contract provides for "assignment of all rights," the transfer also is an "assumption of duties." The courts hold that the probable intent of the parties when using such general words is to create both an assignment of rights and an assumption of duties.

1. The relationship between parties to a contract is called privity of contract.
2. Parties to a contract may assign their contract rights and/or delegate their contract duties.
3. If the assignment would materially increase or alter the duties of the obligor, a right cannot be assigned.

4. The original obligor must perform if the delegatee does not.
5. Yes. If a contract is for service of a personal nature, delegation of duties may be prohibited.

Legal Focus Example

Read through this Legal Focus Example with the class. Make sure that students understand that although the contract is between Jones and Standard Life, Johann is the intended beneficiary of the contract and, therefore, can enforce the promise made by the life insurance company.

◆ CHECKING YOUR PROGRESS

1. What is the term for the relationship created between contract parties giving them rights and duties?

2. Can parties to a contract transfer to another their contract rights or their contract duties?

3. Can contract rights be assigned if the obligor must alter his or her duty to perform?

4. If a delegatee fails to perform the actions specific in a contract, who is responsible for doing so?

5. Can a contract specifically prohibit delegation?

◆ THIRD PARTY BENEFICIARIES

We said at the beginning of the chapter that to have contractual rights, a person normally must be a party to the contract. An exception exists when the original contracting parties intend that the contract performance directly benefit a third person. The third person becomes a beneficiary of the contract and has legal rights. Beneficiaries can sue to enforce a promise that was made purposely for their benefit. Not all persons who benefit from contracts are given the right to enforce beneficial promises, however. The courts distinguish between intended beneficiaries (who can sue to enforce the promise) and incidental beneficiaries (who cannot).

INTENDED BENEFICIARIES

An **intended beneficiary** is one for whose benefit a contract was made. This beneficiary can sue the promisor directly for breach of the contract. In determining whether a third party beneficiary is an intended beneficiary, the courts generally use the reasonable person test. Would a reasonable person in the position of the third party beneficiary believe that the promisee intended to give him or her the right to bring suit to enforce the contract?

◆ **beneficiary** A person who receives benefits from a contract.

◆ **intended beneficiary** A third party beneficiary for whose benefit a contract is formed. Intended beneficiaries can sue the promisor to enforce the contract.

◀ LEGAL FOCUS – EXAMPLE

A very common intended beneficiary contract is a life insurance contract. In a typical contract, Jones (the promisee) pays premiums to Standard Life, a life insurance company. Standard Life (the promisor) promises to pay a certain amount of money on Jones's death to anyone Jones designates as a beneficiary. The designated beneficiary, Johann, is an intended beneficiary under the life insurance policy. Johann can enforce the promise made by the insurance company to pay her on Jones's death.

Collaborative Learning Activity

Divide the class into small groups, and have each group read through the two examples of *incidental beneficiaries* found here. Then have the group write two more original examples of contracts in which third parties are incidental beneficiaries.

Critical Thinking Activity

Have students write two or three paragraphs on the differences among a delegatee, an intended beneficiary, and an incidental beneficiary.

Critical Thinking Activity

Read to the class the following quote found on U.S. currency. "This note is legal tender for all debts, public and private." Then have the students relate this quote to the definition of *tender* found here.

The presence of one or more of the following factors indicates an intended benefit to a third party.

1. Performance is to be rendered directly to the third party.
2. The third party has a right to control the details of performance.
3. The third party is expressly named in the contract.

Incidental Beneficiaries

◆ **incidental beneficiary** A party who benefits from a contract but whose benefit was not the reason the contract was formed.

The benefit that an **incidental beneficiary** receives from a contract between two parties is unintentional. Therefore, an incidental beneficiary cannot enforce a contract to which he or she is not a party. The following are examples involving incidental beneficiaries. In each situation, the third party has no rights in and cannot enforce the contract.

1. Jules contracts with Vivian to build a cottage on Vivian's land. Jules's plans specify that Super Insulation Company's insulation materials must be used in constructing the house. Super Insulation Company is an incidental beneficiary. It cannot enforce the contract or require that Jules purchase its insulation materials.
2. Ed contracts with Mario to build a recreational center on Mario's land. Once the center is constructed, it will increase the property values in the neighborhood. If Ed refuses to build the center, Fred, a neighboring property owner, cannot enforce the contract.

◆ Ways to Discharge a Contract

◆ **performance** The fulfillment of one's obligation under a contract.

As noted earlier, parties to contracts need to know when their duties are finished, or discharged. The most common way to discharge one's contractual duties is by **performance**—by doing what one promised to do in the contract. There are, however, many other ways a contract can be discharged. These can generally be classified as discharge by agreement or by operation of law.

Discharge by Performance

◆ **tender** An unconditional offer to perform by a person who is ready, willing, and able to do so.

The contract ends when both parties perform. Performance can also be accomplished by tender. **Tender** is an unconditional offer to perform by a person who is ready, willing, and able to do so. A buyer who offers to pay for goods has tendered payment and can demand delivery of the goods. The party making the tender has done everything possible to carry out the terms of the contract. If the other party then refuses to perform, the tendering party can sue for breach of contract.

It is important to distinguish among three types of performance: (1) complete (or strict), (2) substantial, and (3) inferior. A contract may also specify that performance must meet the personal satisfaction of either the contracting party or a third party. Such a provision will also affect the degree of performance required under the contract.

Critical Thinking Activity

Have students write a paragraph on the differences between strict and substantial performance.

Legal Focus Problem

Ask a student volunteer to read aloud this Legal Focus Problem. Have the volunteer answer the question posed at the end of this problem by reading the first paragraph at the top of the next page. Reinforce student understanding of the concept of incidental beneficiaries. Ask the students whether or not the Ace Brand Co. could have sued Euron Construction Co. for failing to use their plasterboard products in fulfilling the duties of this contract. (Students should understand that Ace Brand was an incidental beneficiary and, therefore, cannot enforce this contract.)

Caption Answer

For the first question, students' answers may vary. The repair shop's performance would be judged by the reasonable person standard.

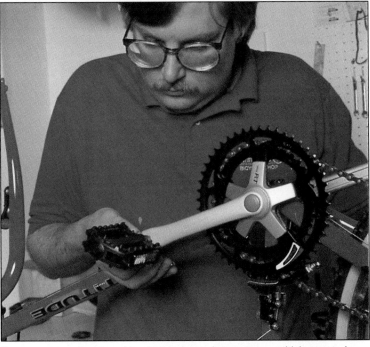

If you contract to have your bicycle tuned up, what services would the repair shop perform? How would the repair shop's performance be judged?

Complete (or Strict) Performance versus Substantial Performance
In most contracts, the parties fully discharge their obligations by performing their duties in a way consistent with the terms of the contract. This is called complete, or strict, performance.

Sometimes a party fulfills most (but not all) of the duties or completes the duties in a way that is contrary to the terms of the contract. Does the failure of one party to give complete performance discharge the other party's duty to perform?

◆ LEGAL FOCUS ~ PROBLEM

Erin and Ben contract with Euron Construction Company to build their house. The contract specifies that Ace Brand plasterboard be used for the walls. The builder cannot get Ace Brand and installs Diamond Brand instead. All other features of the house conform to the contract. Does this change discharge the buyers from paying for the house upon completion?

Legal Focus Problem

Divide the class into small groups to read and discuss the Legal Focus Problem dealing with substantial performance, found here. Each group should choose a leader to explain its response to the question posed at the end of this problem.

LEGAL BACKGROUND

Black's Law Dictionary explains that substantial performance "exists where there has been no willful departure from the terms of the contract, and no omission in a central points, and the contract has been honestly and faithfully performed in its material and substantial particulars, and the only variance from the strict and literal performance consists of technical or unimportant omissions or defects."

Courts usually answer this question by evaluating whether the term in dispute (here, the requirement to use Ace Brand) was an important and clear expectation of the parties. If the use of Ace Brand plasterboard was required and important, a court may hold the use of Ace Brand to be essential. Using Diamond Brand plasterboard—even if Diamond Brand is equivalent in quality to Ace Brand—would in that case mean that the builder was not entitled to payment. Complete, or strict, performance of the contract would be required. If, however, the court decides that the disputed term was a guideline—for instance, that Ace Brand was a guideline to specify the type and quality of plasterboard to be used—then the court may hold that only substantial (not complete) performance is required.

For the sake of justice and fairness, the courts often hold that a party's obligation to perform is discharged as long as the other party has given **substantial performance**. To qualify as substantial, the performance must be close to the performance promised in the contract. It must also create substantially the same benefits as promised in the contract. If one party's performance is substantial, the other party's duty to perform remains (although damages could be assessed against the party who did not perform completely).

◆ **substantial performance**
Performance whereby a party to a contract honestly performs most, but not all, elements of the contract.

◀ LEGAL FOCUS ~ PROBLEM

Aaron purchased a new Plymouth Voyager from Quantum Leap Motors. He discovered after arriving home that the dealer had forgotten to include some touch-up paint that had been provided for in the sales agreement. The cost of the touch-up paint is $7. Has Quantum Leap substantially performed?

Clearly, the breach is minor, and Aaron cannot avoid the contract on this basis. He does have a right to the touch-up paint or the $7. The Case in Point at the end of the chapter gives an example of the application of the rule of substantial performance.

Another way to talk about complete versus substantial performance is in terms of whether a problem with performance is *material*, or major. If it is, there is a material breach of contract, and the contract can be avoided by the other party. If it is not—that is, if performance is substantial—the contract may go forward, even though there has been a *minor* breach. We discuss this further later in this chapter.

Performance to the Satisfaction of Another Contracts often provide that a completed work must personally satisfy one of the parties (or sometimes a third person). If a person is not satisfied with the completed work, can that person refuse to perform?

When the subject matter of the contract is personal, a party may provide that performance must be to his or her personal satisfaction. For example, contracts for portraits, works of art, medical or dental work, and tailoring

Ethical Concern

Third Party Rights and Discharge   287

are considered personal. A party's dissatisfaction with the performance must be in good faith (honest).

◆ LEGAL FOCUS – PROBLEM

Scott Lee hired Alvin Artiste to paint Scott's portrait to his satisfaction. When the portrait was completed, he took one look at it and said, "That is the ugliest thing I have ever seen." He refused to pay for the portrait. Several local art appraisers consider it to be a superior painting that is representative of Scott's appearance. Can Scott refuse the portrait and not pay Alvin?

Yes, as long as Scott has expressed his opinion in good faith. This is the type of personal contract in which requiring performance to one's satisfaction is permissible. As long as Scott is truly not satisfied, it is not important that others believe the performance is satisfactory.

Contracts that involve mechanical fitness, utility, or marketability need only be performed to the satisfaction of a reasonable person. For example, construction contracts or manufacturing contracts are usually *not* considered personal, so the party's personal satisfaction is irrelevant. As long as the performance will satisfy a reasonable person, the contract is fulfilled.

◆ LEGAL FOCUS – PROBLEM

Marsh's Autobody agrees to repair the damage to Bokovich's automobile after his right front door is hit in a parking lot collision. Marsh's completes the repair, repaints the door, and it appears fine. Bokovich says he is not satisfied—stating, "I just don't like it"—and refuses to pay for the repair. What will result?

Most courts would require Bokovich to pay for the repair if a reasonable person would be satisfied with the repair.

Sometimes contracts require performance to the satisfaction of a third party—for example, "to the satisfaction of Robert Ames, the supervising engineer." Again if the third person, Robert Ames, is unsatisfied, most courts would require the performance to be accepted if it would satisfy a reasonable person unless the subject matter of the contract is personal.

Inferior Performance (Material Breach of Contract) A **breach of contract** is the failure to perform a contractual duty. When the breach is material, the innocent party is excused from the performance of contractual duties. The party also has a right to sue for damages caused by the breach.

If the breach is *minor* (not material), the innocent party's duty to perform may be suspended until the breach is fixed, or *cured*. Once the minor

◆ **breach of contract** Failure to perform part or all of the required duties under a contract.

Legal Focus Problem

Allow a student volunteer to read this second Legal Focus Problem aloud to the class. Have the volunteer answer the question posed at the end of this problem. Ask the students how this Legal Focus Problem differs from the one above.

Have your students discuss
the differences between
substantial performance and
inferior performance. Make
sure that students under-
stand that the main difference is whether it is a
"material" breach or not.

Have students work with partners to make a
chart for all the types of performances discussed in this chapter. Instruct students to
have headings for the following: type of performance, terms of performance, and an
example of the performance.

Legal Focus Problem

Guide the students in reading through this Legal Focus
Problem dealing with Shasta
Manufacturing Co. and its
arrangement to manufacture
and sell personal computers
to New Age, Inc. Allow student volunteers to suggest
possible answers to the
question posed at the end of
this problem. Then have a
student read the answer to
this problem in the para-
graph immediately below
this Legal Focus feature.

Enrichment

Have the students look at
the Legal Focus Problem on
this page again. Ask them
why Shasta said it would
not deliver the 100,000
computers at the agreed-
upon contract price. Ask:
"Can you understand why
Shasta was not willing to
lose $500,000 and the con-
tract?" Then explain to students that even though they
may sympathize with
Shasta, Shasta's act is an
anticipatory breach of the
contract that allows New
Age the option of proceeding immediately to pursue
remedies even though the
actual contract delivery date
has yet to arrive.

---

breach is cured, the innocent party must resume performance of the contractual obligations. The nonbreaching party may sue for damages but may
not avoid the contract. Only a material breach discharges the nonbreaching party from the contract. This policy requires contracts to be performed
when only minor problems occur but allows them to be terminated when
major problems arise.

Anticipatory Breach   Sometimes one party may refuse to perform his
or her contractual obligations before the actual time for performance.

◄ LEGAL FOCUS ~ PROBLEM

Shasta Manufacturing Company contracted to manufacture and sell
100,000 personal computers to New Age, Inc. New Age is a
computer retailer with 500 outlet stores. Delivery was set eight
months from the date of the contract. The contract price was based
on the seller's present cost of inventory parts purchased from others.
One month later, three inventory suppliers raised their prices to
Shasta. Based on these new prices, Shasta estimated it would lose
$500,000 in the contract with New Age. Shasta immediately wrote a
letter to New Age. In the letter Shasta said it would not deliver the
100,000 computers at the agreed-upon contract price. Did Shasta
breach the contract, though the time for performance was seven
months in the future?

◆ **anticipatory
breach** Some act by
one party to a contract
that tells the other party
that the first party will
not perform when it
comes time to do so.

Yes. Shasta's act is called **anticipatory breach** or *anticipatory repudiation.*
(*Repudiation* means rejection.) When anticipatory breach occurs, it is treated as a material breach of contract. The nonbreaching party may sue immediately. There are two reasons for treating an anticipatory breach as an
immediate material breach:

1. The nonbreaching party should not be required to remain ready and
   willing to perform when the other party has already repudiated the
   contract.
2. The nonbreaching party should have the opportunity to seek a similar
   contract elsewhere.

Until the nonbreaching party treats a repudiation as a breach, the
breaching party can change its mind. It does so by notifying the innocent
party of its intent to perform. Thus, in the problem, as long as New Age
did not treat Shasta's letter as a breach, Shasta could change its mind and
notify New Age that it would deliver the computers after all.

DISCHARGE BY AGREEMENT

Any contract can be discharged by the agreement of the parties. This can
happen in several ways: by rescission, by novation, by substituted agreement, and by accord and satisfaction.

Divide the class into small groups. Tell each group to reread the Legal Focus Problem on the preceding page that deals with Shasta Manufacturing Co. and New Age, Inc. Explain that just as Shasta Manufacturing Co. needs to get out of its contract with New Age due to rising costs, so too New Age, due to money problems, needs to get out of its contract with Shasta Manufacturing Co. Have each group work together to draw up a written contract for *mutual rescission* of the previous Shasta Manufacturing Co./New Age, Inc. contract. Each group should choose a leader to share its mutual rescission contract with the class.

Discharge by Mutual Rescission **Mutual rescission** occurs when parties cancel the contract and return themselves to the positions they occupied before the contract's formation. For *mutual rescission* to take place, the parties must make another agreement that also satisfies the legal requirements for a contract—there must be an *offer*, an *acceptance*, and *consideration*. Each party's giving up the right to performance satisfies the requirement for consideration.

Discharge by Novation A **novation** substitutes a new party for one of the original parties to the contract. Essentially, the original parties and another party all get together and agree to the substitution. The requirements of a novation are as follows:

1. The existence of a previous valid obligation.
2. Agreement by all the parties to a new contract.
3. Agreement to end the old obligation by discharging the original party.
4. Formation of a new, valid contract.

    A novation differs from a delegation in two ways. First, a novation involves all of the parties in the agreement. A delegation agreement requires just two parties. Second, the original obligor is no longer liable under the contract. In a delegation, the original obligor remains liable.

◄ LEGAL FOCUS – EXAMPLE

Sloan's Office Mart contracts to sell its office-equipment business to Logan Enterprises. Logan later decides that expansion is not a good idea now. However, Logan knows that another party, the MBI Corporation, is interested in purchasing Sloan's business. If all three parties gather and agree that MBI will purchase the business and Logan will be released from responsibility, it is a novation.

    The novation discharges the original contract between Sloan's and Logan and replaces it with the new contract between Sloan's and MBI Corporation. Logan prefers the novation because it discharges all the contract liabilities stemming from its contract with Sloan's.

Discharge by Substituted Agreement A *compromise*, or settlement agreement, that arises out of an honest dispute over the obligations in an existing contract is legally valid. The agreement is substituted as a new contract. The new contract may expressly or impliedly revoke and discharge the obligations in any prior contract.

Discharge by Accord and Satisfaction An **accord** is an agreement to perform an act to satisfy an existing contractual duty. A **satisfaction** is the performance of the accord agreement. For a contract to be discharged by

◆ mutual rescission An enforceable agreement to cancel a contract and return the parties to the positions they occupied before the contract's formation.

◆ novation The substitution, by agreement, of a new contract for an old one, with the rights under the old one being terminated. A new party is substituted for an original party.

◆ accord An agreement to perform an act to satisfy an existing contractual duty.

◆ satisfaction The performance of an accord agreement.

Legal Focus Example

Read this Legal Focus Example to the class. Ask the class if they can think of any other examples that could also fit here. Have volunteers share their examples with the class.

Read this Legal Focus
Example aloud to the class.
Then write the following
names and terms on the
board:

Bill
Martha
$4,000
Martha's automobile

Then ask the students the
following questions: In this
Legal Focus Example, who
is the obligor? Who is the
obligee? What is required
for Martha to satisfy the
judgment? What is required
from Martha as a satisfaction of the accord?

Caption Answer

Student answers may vary
but should reflect an understanding of what is meant
by "negotiated substitutions
to performance."

Name some examples of negotiated substitutions to performance.

accord and satisfaction, the parties must agree to accept a performance different from the performance originally promised. An accord and its satisfaction, or performance, discharge the original contractual obligation. Until
satisfaction, the parties do not give up the rights they had before the accord.

◆ LEGAL FOCUS – EXAMPLE

Bill gets a judgment against Martha for $4,000. Later, both parties
agree that the judgment can be satisfied (paid) by Martha's
transferring her automobile to Bill. This agreement to accept the auto
instead of $4,000 in cash is the accord. If Martha transfers her
automobile to Bill, the accord agreement is fully satisfied, and the
$4,000 debt is discharged. If Martha refuses to transfer her car, the
accord is breached. Since an original obligation is merely suspended
in an accord, Bill can bring an action to enforce the judgment for
$4,000 in cash.

DISCHARGE BY OPERATION OF LAW

Under some circumstances, contractual duties may be discharged by operation of law. These circumstances include the running of a statute of limitations, bankruptcy, and the impossibility or impracticability of performance.

Statutes of Limitations   A statute of limitations limits the time during
which a party can sue. For example, the limitations period for bringing

suits for breach of an oral contract is usually two or three years and for written contracts, four to five years. After the applicable limitations period has passed, neither party can bring suit to enforce a contract.

Bankruptcy   A discharge in bankruptcy will ordinarily stop enforcement of most of a debtor's contracts by the creditors. As we will discuss in Chapter 19, a proceeding in bankruptcy attempts to distribute the property owned by the debtor to creditors in a fair fashion. Any party who has contracted with a person who is in a bankruptcy proceeding would be considered a creditor. After the debtor's property has been distributed in the bankruptcy and the proceeding is concluded, the debtor is discharged from most of his or her obligations, including contracts.

Discharge by Impossibility of Performance   Sometimes contract performance is objectively impossible. In that case, the doctrine of **impossibility of performance** may discharge the contract. Here, *objective impossibility* ("It can't be done") must be distinguished from *subjective impossibility* ("I simply can't do it"). If you had a contract duty to pay money, and you could not pay it on time because the bank was closed, that would be an example of subjective impossibility. In effect, you would be saying, "It is impossible for *me* to perform," not "It is impossible for *anyone* to perform." Personal excuses do not discharge a contract, and the non-performing party is normally held in breach of contract.

> ◆ **impossibility of performance**   A doctrine by which a party to a contract is relieved of his or her duty to perform because performance becomes impossible.

   Three situations generally qualify as objective impossibility of performance.

1.   One party to a personal contract dies or becomes disabled (incapacitated) prior to performance.

◆ LEGAL FOCUS ~ EXAMPLE

Fred, a famous dancer, contracts with Ethereal Dancing Guild to play a leading role in its new ballet. Before the ballet can be performed, however, Fred becomes ill and dies. His personal performance was essential to the completion of the contract. His death discharges the contract.

2.   The specific subject matter of the contract is destroyed.

◆ LEGAL FOCUS ~ EXAMPLE

A-1 Farm Equipment agrees to sell Bill Gudgel the green tractor on its lot. A-1 promises to have it ready for Gudgel to pick up on Saturday. On Friday night, a truck veers off the nearby highway and smashes into the tractor, destroying it beyond repair. Because the contract was for this specific tractor, A-1's performance is impossible because of the accident.

Legal Focus Example

Read this first Legal Focus Example to the class. Ask the class if they can think of any other examples that could also fit here. Allow volunteers to share their examples with the class.

Legal Focus Example

Read aloud to the class this second Legal Focus Example dealing with the agreement between A-1 Farm Equipment and Bill Gudgel. Point out to the class that in this example, the tractor was destroyed beyond repair. Stimulate a discussion by asking the following questions: What if the tractor had not been destroyed beyond repair? Do you think that Gudgel would have accepted the tractor for the same consideration after it had been repaired? Would you?

Read

Remind students that our laws often reflect our society's ethical perspective. The doctrine of impossibility of performance is an example of such a law. Then have the students read the *Law in Action* feature.

Analyze and Apply

Have the students write a one-page anecdote that demonstrates the doctrine of impossibility of performance. Explain to the students that their anecdotes should begin with an explanation of the original contract, the intervening event that led to impossibility of performance, and the results for both parties of the contract. Allow student volunteers to share their anecdotes with the class.

Legal Focus Example

Read this Legal Focus Example aloud to the class. Ask the class if they can think of any other examples that could also fit here. Allow volunteers to share their examples.

◆ Law in Action

LAW AND THE BUSINESSPERSON: IMPOSSIBILITY OF PERFORMANCE

he doctrine of impossibility of performance raises ethical issues. Is it fair to hold a party liable for breach of contract, when performance of the contract is impossible? If the answer is no, a trade-off is being made. The importance of honoring contractual obligations is being balanced against the fairness of requiring an impossible performance.

Before the late nineteenth century, courts seldom recognized impossibility as a defense. But as society's ethics change with the passage of time, the law also changes to reflect society's new views of ethical behavior. Today, courts are more willing to discharge a contract when its performance is impossible. Holding a party responsible when that party is not at fault no longer coincides with society's notions of fairness.

The classic case of impossibility of performance was *Taylor v. Caldwell.*[1] In *Taylor,* the plaintiff contracted with the defendant to rent the defendant's music hall for a series of concerts. Before the first concert, but after the contract had been made, the music hall was destroyed by fire. The court held that the defendant was discharged from performing, because performance was impossible.

The doctrine of impossibility applies when parties could not have reasonably predicted the event that makes the performance impossible. Excuse from performance also requires that the party claiming the defense has acted ethically. Thus, a party cannot arrange events to make performance impossible. Assume, for example, that Blake sells a used car to Erin on Friday, with delivery of the car to take place on Monday. If Blake negligently (or purposely) crashes the car to avoid delivering it, his performance is not excused. If, however, the car is stolen and completely demolished in an accident, performance is excused.

---

1. 122 Eng.Rep. 309, K.B. 1863.

---

3. A change in law makes performance illegal.

◆ LEGAL FOCUS – EXAMPLE

Mike agrees to construct an apartment building for Sheila. The county changes the zoning laws so that they prohibit the construction of residential rental property in that area. The change in law makes the contract impossible to perform.

Commercial Impracticability   In recent years, some courts have recognized a doctrine called *commercial impracticability.* The doctrine applies in situations where performance turns out to be dramatically more difficult or more expensive than expected. In one case, for example, the California

Read to the class the Legal Focus Problem found here. Allow student volunteers to suggest a possible answer to the question posed at the end of this problem. As an extension assignment, you might wish to have a student volunteer research the nationalization of the Suez Canal by Egypt and report his or her findings to the class. When did this event occur? Why did Egypt take these steps?

Discuss the doctrine of commercial impracticability. Ask students if they think commercial impracticability should only apply when there is extreme risk or unpredictable risks, or large dollar amounts. Discuss the policy of retail stores refunding or not refunding money if the price of an item goes down. Also discuss the policy of reducing prices to meet competitors' advertised prices.

Supreme Court discharged a contract because a party would have had to pay ten times more than the original estimate to excavate a certain amount of gravel.

The doctrine is applied in extreme situations where the added burden of performing was not within the reasonable expectations of the parties at the time the contract was made. All contracts create risk. If you agree to buy a TV for $250, and the next week it goes on sale for $200, you have assumed that risk. Commercial impracticability only protects against more extreme and less predictable risks.

◆ LEGAL FOCUS – CASE PROBLEM

A carrier of goods was to deliver wheat from the west coast of the United States to a port in Iran. The Suez Canal, the usual route, was to be used for shipment. Before delivery, the Suez Canal was taken over by Egypt and closed. The carrier was forced to travel around Africa and the Cape of Good Hope. The added expense was approximately $42,000 more than the contract price of $306,000. The original journey of 10,000 miles was extended by an additional 3,000 miles. Did the doctrine of commercial impracticability allow the carrier to consider the performance impossible?[2]

The court held that performance was not to be excused on the grounds of commercial impracticability. The court reasoned that the closing of the Suez Canal was foreseeable. The carrier had assumed this risk and was required to perform.

Temporary Impossibility   If an event makes it temporarily impossible to perform an act required under a contract, performance is suspended until the impossibility ceases. Then, ordinarily, the parties must perform as originally planned. If the lapse of time and change in circumstances have made performance a great deal more difficult, however, the contract may be discharged.

◆ LEGAL FOCUS – CASE EXAMPLE

Gene Autry, an actor in westerns, was drafted into the army in 1942. Being drafted rendered his long-term service contract temporarily impossible to perform. The contract was suspended until the end of the war. When the actor was released from the army, the value of the dollar had decreased so much that performance of the contract would have been a substantial burden to him. Therefore, the contract was discharged.[3]

Legal Focus Case Example

Read this Legal Focus Case Example to the class. Ask the class if they can think of any other examples of temporary impossibility that could also fit here. Allow volunteers to share their examples with the class.

Reteaching Activity

Divide the class into groups of four. Assign each member in the group one of the following topics to review: (1) Assignments and Delegations, (2) Third Party Beneficiaries, (3) Discharges of Contracts, and (4) Impossibility of Performance. Instruct students to outline the sections assigned to them and then summarize them to the other group members.

2. *Transatlantic Financing Corp. v. United States*, 363 F.2d 312 (D.C. Cir. 1966).
3. *Autry v. Republic Pictures*, 30 Cal.2d 144, 180 P.2d 888 (1947).

Teaching A Case In Point

Read

Remind the students that as they learned in this chapter, sometimes a party fulfills most (but not all) of the duties, or completes the duties in a way that is contrary to the terms of a contract, and that this is termed *substantial performance*. Explain to the students that the *A Case In Point* feature they are about to read deals with *substantial performance*. Then have a student volunteer read aloud the *A Case In Point* feature.

Discuss

Use the following questions to stimulate a class discussion of this *A Case In Point* feature. What were the terms of the original contract between the Warrens and Denison? Why did the Warrens refuse to pay the $48,400 still owed to Denison? What decision did the trial court reach in this case? What decision did the appellate court reach in this case? What reasons did the appellate court give for its decision?

Teaching Note

This case is included in the *West's Business and Personal Law Handbook of Selected Court Cases.*

Checking Your Progress (Answers)

1. The courts ask whether a reasonable person in the position of the third party beneficiary would believe that the promisee intended to confer upon him or her the right to bring suit to enforce the contract. (The *reasonable person* test)
2. The most common way to discharge a contract is by performance.
3. When there is a material breach of contract, the innocent party is excused from the performance of contractual duties.
4. For mutual rescission to take place, the parties must make another agreement (agreeing to rescind) that also satisfies the legal requirements for a contract.
5. The original parties to a contract and another party must agree to the substitution of one party, thus creating a discharge by novation.

◆ CHECKING YOUR PROGRESS

1. What do the courts use to determine whether a third party is an intended or incidental beneficiary?
2. What is the most common way to discharge a contract?
3. What is the effect of a material breach of contract?
4. What must occur for mutual rescission of a contract to take place?
5. Who is involved in a discharge by novation?
6. Impossibility of performance discharges a contract. Give an example of objective impossibility.
7. How is performance affected if an event makes it temporarily impossible to perform an act required under a contract?

◆ A CASE IN POINT ◆

WARREN v. DENISON
Court of Appeals of Texas, 1978.
563 S.W.2d 299.

In this case, substantial performance by a contractor is at issue.

FACTS Denison was a building contractor hired by the Warrens to construct a house on their property. A written contract provided that the Warrens would pay Denison $73,400 for the work. Further writings gave Denison the right to foreclose on (sell or take possession of) the house if the Warrens refused to make payments. After the Warrens took possession of the house, they noted several flaws in the construction of the home. Based on these flaws, the Warrens refused to pay $48,400 still owed to Denison. Denison began foreclosure proceedings, and the Warrens responded by suing Denison. The Warrens com-plained that Denison had breached the contract by his poor workmanship. The trial court ruled for Denison, and the Warrens appealed.

ISSUE Had Denison, despite his poor workmanship, discharged his duty under the contract?

DECISION Yes. The judgment for Denison was affirmed.

REASON The court noted that "literal performance of each and every particular of such [construction] contracts is virtually impossible. Rather than require perfect performance . . . substantial performance is regarded as full performance in allowing the builder to recover on the contract. . . . A job can be substantially performed with some breaches of workmanlike construction preventing perfect performance." The Warrens were ordered to pay the $48,400 still owed to Denison, minus $2,161.50—the amount necessary to repair Denison's "construction flaws."

Reviewing Chapter 12

In order to help students review what they have learned in Chapter 12, you might wish to:

1. Have a student volunteer, or volunteers, read the Chapter Summary aloud to the class.
2. Allow the students to work with partners to complete the *Using Legal Language* activity.
3. Assign the *Checking for Comprehension* exercise as homework.

4. Allow the students to work in small groups to complete the *Applying Legal Concepts* activities.
5. As a class, complete the *Applying the Law* activities. (Please note that you may have to help students with vocabulary so that they adequately understand all of the *Applying the Law* material.)

Assessment Strategies

In order to check student mastery of chapter concepts, you may wish to use the Chapter 12 test that is found in your *Teacher's Resource Binder* or use WESTEST computerized testing for Chapter 12.

CHAPTER 12 REVIEW

SUMMARY

THIRD PARTY CONTRACT RIGHTS

Assignment

1. An assignment is the transfer of rights under a contract to a third party. The assignee (the person to whom the rights are assigned) has a right to demand performance from the other original party to the contract (the obligor).

2. Generally, all rights can be assigned, except in the following circumstances:

   a. When assignment is expressly prohibited by statute.

   b. When the contract itself states that the rights cannot be assigned.

   c. When a contract calls for the performance of personal services.

   d. When the assignment will materially increase or alter the duties of the obligor.

3. Notice of the assignment should be given by the assignee to the obligor.

   a. If the assignor assigns the same right to two different persons, generally the first assignment in time is the first in right. In a minority of states, the first assignee to give notice take priority.

   b. Until the obligor is notified of the assignment, an obligor can tender performance to the assignor.

Delegation

1. A delegation is the transfer of duties under a contract to a third party. The delegatee (the third party) assumes the obligation of performing the contractual duties previously held by the delegator (the one making the delegation).

2. As a general rule, any duty can be delegated, except in the following circumstances:

   a. When performance depends on the personal skills or talents of the obligor.

   b. When a special trust has been placed in the obligor.

   c. When performance by a third party will vary materially from that expected by the obligee under the contract.

   d. When the contract expressly prohibits delegation.

3. A valid delegation of duties does not relieve the delegator of obligations under the contract. If the delegatee fails to perform, the delegator is still liable to the obligee.

Third Party Beneficiary Contract

A third party beneficiary contract is made for the purpose of benefiting a third party.

1. *Intended beneficiary*—One for whose benefit a contract is created. When the promisor fails to perform as promised, the third party can sue the promisor directly.

2. *Incidental beneficiary*—A third party who indirectly (incidentally) benefits from a contract but for whose benefit the contract was not specifically intended. Incidental beneficiaries have no rights to the benefits received and cannot sue the promisor to have them enforced.

WAYS TO DISCHARGE A CONTRACT

1. *Performance*—Complete or substantial performance discharges the contract.

2. *Breach*—Material nonperformance discharges the nonbreaching party's performance.

3. *Mutual rescission*—An enforceable agreement to restore parties to their positions before the contract was made.

1–F, 2–H, 3–D, 4–B, 5–J,
6–I, 7–E, 8–A, 9–C, 10–G

1. Student answers will vary. They may give examples of statutes that expressly prohibit assignment of a particular right; specific mention in the contract that rights cannot be assigned; contracts for personal action; or rights that would materially alter the obligor's duties.

---

4. *Novation*—By valid contract, a new party is substituted for an original party, thereby ending the old contract.

5. *Accord and satisfaction*—An agreement whereby the original contract can be discharged by performance different from that originally agreed upon.

6. *Objective impossibility of performance* owing to one of the following:

a. The death or incapacity of a person whose performance is essential to the completion of the contract.

b. The destruction of the specific subject matter of the contract prior to transfer.

c. A change in the law that makes the performance called for by the contract illegal.

d. The commercial impracticability of performance.

 ## USING LEGAL LANGUAGE

Directions: Match each term with the statement that best defines that term.

1. accord and satisfaction
2. anticipatory breach
3. assignment of rights
4. breach of contract
5. delegation of duties
6. intended beneficiary
7. novation
8. privity of contract
9. rescission
10. tender

A. a relationship created between parties to a contract

B. failure, without legal excuse, of a promisor to perform the obligations of a contract

C. a remedy which allows a party to cancel a contract and return the parties to the positions they occupied before the contract's formation

D. the act of transferring to another all or part of one's rights arising under a contract

E. the substitution by a new agreement with a new party for one of the original parties to a prior agreement

F. an agreement to perform an act to satisfy an existing contractual duty and the performance of the agreement

G. an unconditional offer to perform by a person who is ready, willing, and able to do so

H. some act by one party to a contract that tells the other party they will not perform when it becomes time to do so

I. a third party beneficiary for whose benefit a contract is formed

J. the act of transferring to another all or part of one's duties arising under a contract

2. First, the obligor may not know to whom he or she owes the duty to perform; and second, the obligor may not even know there is an assignment and complete the contract by performance to the original contract party, thus ending the obligation.
3. No, if the contract is not performed, the original party is still liable to the obligee.
4. A beneficiary in a life insurance contract is an intended beneficiary; a reasonable person would believe that the promisee intended to confer upon him or her the right to enforce the contract.
5. If the court decides that performance is substantial and terms of the contract are guidelines, the contract could be discharged. If, however, there is a material breach, the court may decide the contract is not yet discharged.
6. Yes, any contract can be discharged by the agreement of the parties.

7. A novation involves all of the parties of an agreement; a delegation involves only the obligee and delegatee. The original obligor is no longer liable in a novation, but he or she is in a delegation.
8. As a general rule, any rights created by a contract can be assigned. However, there are some exceptions, such as when the contract expressly and specifically prohibits or limits the right of assignment. Authorities differ on how a case like Terry's should be decided. Some courts would enforce the prohibition completely, holding that Terry's assignment to Richard is completely ineffective without the landlord's consent. Others would permit the assignment to be effective, with the landlord's remedy limited to Terry's breach and normal contract remedies.
9. a–The agreement is a novation. Bert's agreement with Cartwright to pay off Doug's debt for $1,100 (as compared to the $1,000 owed) is a valid contract, and a novation exists when a new, valid contract expressly or impliedly discharges a prior contract by the substitute party. b–The contract between Bert and Cartwright does not have to be in writing because Bert's obligation is primary. One of the requirements for a guaranty contract to fall under the State of Frauds (requiring a writing) is that by the terms of the contract, the guarantor's obligation to the creditor must be secondary.

◆ CHECKING FOR COMPREHENSION

1. Write an example of special circumstances in which an individual's contract rights cannot be assigned.

2. What problems could arise if notice of assignment is not given to the obligor?

3. When obligors delegate their duties, are they released from the contract?

4. Is a beneficiary in a life insurance contract an intended beneficiary or an incidental beneficiary? Why?

5. Does failure of complete performance discharge the other parties' performance? Explain.

6. Can the parties to a contract agree to discharge a contract at any time?

7. What is the difference between a novation and a delegation?

8. Terry is a college student. She signs a one-year lease agreement for September 1 through August 31. The agreement specifies that the lease cannot be assigned without the landlord's consent. Terry decides not to go to summer school and assigns the balance of the lease (three months) to a close friend, Richard. The landlord objects to the assignment and denies Richard access to the apartment. Terry claims that Richard is financially sound and should be allowed the full rights and privileges of an assignee. Discuss fully whether the landlord or Terry is correct.

9. Doug owes creditor Cartwright $1,000, which is due and payable on June 1. Doug has a car accident, misses several months of work, and consequently does not have the money on June 1. Doug's father, Bert, offers to pay Cartwright $1,100 in four equal installments if Cartwright will discharge Doug from any further liability on the debt. Cartwright accepts. Discuss the following: (a) Is the transaction a novation, or is it an accord and satisfaction? Explain. (b) Does the contract between Bert and Cartwright have to be in writing to be enforceable? (Review the Statute of Frauds.) Explain.

10. Millie contracted to sell Frank 1,000 bushels of corn to be grown on Millie's farm. Owing to drought conditions during the growing season, Millie's yield was much less than anticipated, and she could only deliver 250 bushels to Frank. Frank accepted the lesser amount but sued Millie for breach of contract. Can Millie defend successfully on the basis of objective impossibility of performance? Explain.

◆ APPLYING THE LAW . . . YOU BE THE JUDGE

1. Rensselaer Water Co. was under contract to the city of Rensselaer, New York, to provide water to the city, including water at fire hydrants. A warehouse owned by H. R. Moch Co. was totally destroyed by a fire which could not be extinguished because of inadequate water pressure at the fire hydrants. Moch brought suit against Rensselaer Water Co. for damages, claiming that Moch was a third party beneficiary to the city's contract with the water company. Will Moch be able to recover damages from the water company on the basis that the water company breached its contract with the city? Explain. [*H. R. Moch Co. v. Rensselaer Water Co.*, 247 N.Y. 160, 159 N.E. 896 (1928)]

2. Clement was seriously injured in a car accident with King. When Clement sued

10. Yes. When the subject matter of a contract is destroyed, the contract becomes objectively impossible to perform. Millie was objectively incapable of delivering the full 1,000 bushels of corn to Frank because her farm had not produced 1,000 bushels. Because of the objective impossibility of performing the contract, Millie's duties to Frank were discharged; she could not be held to have breached the contract.

Applying the Law . . . You Be the Judge (Answers)

1. No. The court ruled that Moch was not an intended third party beneficiary to the contract between the water company and the city. Moch was an incidental beneficiary only. The contract between the water company and the city established the water company's duty to the city and not to its individual inhabitants. The court gave numerous examples indicating how overwhelming the risk would be for contractors with a city if all individuals residing within the city had a cause of action as intended third party beneficiaries. 2. No. A legal malpractice claim is not assignable. A client's claim for malpractice arises from a personal relationship with an attorney. Since the duty breached is a personal duty, the claim arising from the alleged negligence of the attorney cannot be assigned. Had King obtained a money judgment against Prestwich, this claim could have been assigned to Clement.

3. Yes. The question was whether Owens was a mere incidental beneficiary, in which case he could have no claim for breach of contract, or whether he was an intended third party beneficiary. The court held that "an intention to benefit a third party may be gleaned from the contract as a whole and the party need not be named specifically as a beneficiary." The policy statement indicated an intent on the part of the contracting parties to benefit federal prisoners, including Owens.

4. Yes. Despite the contract provisions, the court allowed Parker to recover his money under the impossibility-of-performance doctrine. The court held that Parker never contemplated waiving the right to invoke the doctrine of impossibility of performance: "Although neither party to a contract should be relieved from performance on the ground that good business judgment was lacking, a court will not place upon language a ridiculous construction. We conclude that plaintiff did not waive his right to assert the doctrine of impossibility."

King, King retained Prestwich as her attorney. Due to the alleged negligence of Prestwich, Clement was able to obtain a $21,000 judgment on her claim against King. Clement received from King an attempted written assignment of King's malpractice claim against Prestwich to settle the judgment against her. Can King assign her cause of action against Prestwich to Clement? [*Clement v. Prestwich*, 114 Ill.App.3d 479, 448 N.E.2d 1039, 70 Ill.Dec. 161 (1983)]

3. Owens, a federal prisoner, was transferred from federal prison to the Nassau County Jail pursuant to a contract between the U.S. Bureau of Prisons and the county. The contract included a policy statement that required the receiving prison to provide for the safekeeping and protection of transferred federal prisoners. While in the Nassau County Jail, Owens was beaten severely by prison officials and suffered lacerations, bruises, and a lasting impairment that caused blackouts. Can Owens, as a third party beneficiary, sue the county for breach of its agreement with the U.S. Bureau of Prisons? [*Owens v. Haas*, 601 F.2d 1242 (2d Cir. 1979)]

4. In November 1959, Parker went to the Arthur Murray Dance Studio to redeem a certificate entitling him to three free dance lessons. At the time, Parker was a thirty-seven-year-old, college-educated bachelor who lived alone in a one-room attic apartment. During the free lessons, the instructor told Parker that he had exceptional potential to become an accomplished dancer and generally encouraged him to take more lessons. Parker signed a contract for seventy-five hours of lessons at a cost of $1,000. At the bottom of the contract, "NON-CANCELABLE NEGOTIABLE CONTRACT" was printed in boldface type. Parker attended lessons regularly and was further encouraged by the instructors despite his lack of progress. Contract extensions and new contracts for additional instructional hours were executed. Each contract and each extension contained the same boldface words given above. Some of the agreements contained the statement, "I UNDERSTAND THAT NO REFUNDS WILL BE MADE UNDER THE TERMS OF THIS CONTRACT," which was also printed in boldface type. On September 24, 1961, Parker was seriously injured in an automobile collision. The accident rendered him incapable of continuing his dance lessons. By that time, he had contracted for a total of 2,734 hours of lessons for which he had paid $24,812.80. Despite Parker's repeated written demands, the Arthur Murray Dance Studio refused to return any of Parker's money. Can Parker recover his money under the impossibility of performance doctrine? [*Parker v. Arthur Murray, Inc.*, 10 Ill.App.3d 1000, 295 N.E.2d 487 (1973)]

Introducing the Legal Perspective

Introduce this feature by asking students the names of popular types of entertainment that they have enjoyed in the last two weeks. Student responses may include movies, television shows, concerts, radio broadcasts, compact disc recordings, cassette recordings, etc. Remind the students that just as entertainment is designed to be a diversion, it is also big business.

Extension Activity

To underscore the amounts of money involved in the modern entertainment industry, have a student volunteer research and report to the class on the ten top-grossing motion pictures of all time. The student's report should include the name of each motion picture and the reported grosses for it.

LEGAL BACKGROUND

The combination of art, talent, and money provides the background for the topic of entertainment law. This LP provides some insight into the complicated problem of breach and damages involving entertainment contracts.

LEGAL PERSPECTIVE

ENTERTAINMENT LAW

Entertainment law is a type of commercial law, which deals with the buying and selling of goods and services. Entertainment law involves contracts, copyrights, trademarks, and general business practices in the entertainment community. These issues are primarily addressed within one of five major branches of the entertainment industry: movies, television, live theater, music, and print publishing. Each branch has a somewhat different method of doing business and paying entertainers.

The field of entertainment law has grown recently because of several industry trends. Modern technology has provided larger audiences for various forms of entertainment. This has lead to major investments of cash by bankers and businesspersons. Also, individuals in the entertainment industry have become more advanced in protecting their rights. They demand and expect very precise contractual obligations. Finally, many artistic products are now distributed internationally. This requires observing foreign laws and business practices.

An important aspect of the entertainment business is contracts. Modern entertainment contracts are complicated, because the problems they address are complicated. One important type of entertainment contract involves how profits are shared in the movie industry. Often, movie studios agree to pay movie stars a percentage of the profits a motion picture makes. Some very well-known stars receive a percentage of the *gross receipts* from the movies in which they appear. Gross receipts include all money received from the exhibition of a film. A star who receives a percentage of gross receipts receives part of every dollar that is spent by moviegoers. Income comes not only from theater tickets but from video rentals, video sales, foreign distributions, and television sales. Since it is not unusual these days for a major motion picture to have gross receipts of more than a hundred million dollars, you can see that even 1 percent of the gross profits (a million dollars) is a significant sum of money.

Anyone who has ever heard an Academy Award speech knows that besides movie stars and directors, many other people are involved in the production of a film. These include writers, producers, editors, and production coordinators. These individuals often have contacts giving them a percentage of *net profits*. Net profits are gross receipts minus the expenses of making and distributing the movie.

The calculation of net profits is a controversial topic. According to many major movie studios, very few pictures make a profit. These studios say that the one or two big blockbuster movies each year make up for the dozens of flops a movie studio produces. However, some critics of Hollywood financial practices say that studios actually turn a healthy profit on most films but use accounting methods to make costs seem higher, so that a film seems to be losing money. This practice allows the studios to avoid paying out any net profit percentages.

Although big stars draw moviegoers into the theaters, writers also have a great deal of influence over the success of a film. However, writers rarely receive the lucrative per-

(continued on page 300)

Enrichment

Allow a student volunteer or group of student volunteers to research the earnings of entertainment superstars such as Oprah Winfrey, John Lennon, Bill Cosby, Garth Brooks, etc. Students should report their findings to the class. Included in the reports should be information about specific terms dealing with such details as outside production deals, profit percentages, etc.

Extension Activity

In order to look at another side of entertainment law, you might have a student volunteer research the lawsuit filed by Valerie Harper against NBC Television. The dispute turned on whether Harper quit or was fired from the TV show *Valerie*. Harper won the suit and was awarded $1.8 million and a percentage of gross profits from the series. Allow the student to present his or her findings to the class in the form of an oral report.

LEGAL PERSPECTIVE (CONTINUED)

centage of gross profits given to big-name movie stars and directors. One famous contract dispute involved writer Art Buchwald, Paramount Pictures, and actor Eddie Murphy. Buchwald sold Paramount the outline of a story called "King for a Day," about an African prince visiting the United States in search of a bride. Paramount agreed by contract to compensate Buchwald if it used the story in a film. Later, Paramount executives told Buchwald they had no use for his story. A few years later, Paramount made a movie with the same premise called *Coming to America*, starring Murphy, without paying Buchwald anything.

Buchwald sued, contending that Paramount stole his idea when it made *Coming to America*. The trial court agreed and awarded Buchwald damages for breach of contract. The contract that Buchwald had signed provided that he was to receive a percentage of the film's net profits. Paramount claimed that despite a reported gross income of $125 million, the film had suffered a net loss of $18 million. To arrive at this figure, Paramount had deducted costs including $42.3 million in distribution fees, $36.2 million in distribution costs, $8 million in overhead expenses, and gross profit payments of $10 million to Eddie Murphy. Of course, Buchwald's attorneys disputed all of these "costs" and called them excessive. Eventually, in March 1992, the trial court judge awarded Buchwald $150,000 and his partner Alain Berheim $750,000. The decision was appealed.

This case has taught a few lessons—lessons that apparently some, but not all, entertainment insiders already knew. The first is that an artist should never agree to take as

payment a share of net profit; it is just too uncertain. Moviemakers argue that their lesson is not to accept any material they haven't asked for. They claim that is how Paramount got Buchwald's script.

Considering the time required for pretrial motions, trial, and appeals, a high-stakes dispute like the one just described could last several years. Because of this, entertainment lawyers have developed explicit contract language dealing with how accounting figures should be derived. Some contracts even call for auditing of production company expenses by independent accounting firms.

In addition to multimillion-dollar disputes, an entertainment law case often involves a clash of big egos. The typical entertainment contract joins an artist with a promoter. Promoters rely on artists to produce a high-quality product, and artists rely on promoters to encourage others to view that product. Therefore, a painter gets upset when an art gallery leaves her masterpiece in the back room. And the producer of a Broadway musical loses patience when the leading singer misses rehearsals. Attorneys mediate these conflicts in an attempt to reach a settlement. If all else fails, the case goes to trial.

Attorneys have sought to avoid such conflicts in a variety of ways. For example, they can include a clause in the artist/promoter contract requiring the promoter to use "best efforts" in promoting the artist's work. The contract may also call for a minimum advertising budget or specific promotional activities. From an entertainment standpoint, we all benefit from agreements that bring great artists and great promoters together.

Mastery Objectives

By the end of this chapter, students will be able to:

- Describe five broad categories of damages
- Explain effects of rescission and restitution on contract parties
- Tell when specific performance is a contract remedy

- Explain reformation
- Delineate quasi-contract recovery
- Explain the consequences of waiver of breach
- Summarize contract provisions limiting remedies

Chapter

Breach and Remedies

13

 LEGAL BACKGROUND

This is the final chapter in the contracts unit. Students conclude their study of contracts by examining the remedies available in breach of contract cases. A remedy is the means employed to enforce a right or to redress an injury. The usual legal remedy is money damages. We discuss the different types of damages and some common ways they are determined. Additional equitable remedies available in some contract breach cases are rescission, restitution, specific performance, and reformation. We have not emphasized the difference between legal and equitable remedies in the chapter, but generally a legal remedy is almost always available, whereas the equitable remedy is only available when the legal remedy is inadequate.

301

Enrichment

You might wish to point out to students that Solon, whose quote opened this chapter, is often referred to as one of the Seven Sages. Many sayings throughout history have been variously attributed to the figures known as the Seven Sages. The Seven Sages are generally considered to be Thales, Solon, Periander, Cleobulus, Chilon, Bias, and Pittacus.

Vocabulary Activity

Tell a student to look up the word *breach* in the dictionary and read the definitions aloud. Discuss the application to legal situations.

Legal Focus Problem

Ask a student volunteer to read this Legal Focus Problem aloud to the class. Have the student answer the question posed at the end of this problem. Follow up this problem by asking: "Why doesn't Edwin sue Marinot and recover $3,000 in damages, rather than $2,500?"

302

Chapter 13
Resources and Assignment Guide

Activity Sheets
Reviewing Legal Concepts 13 *TRB*
Enrichment Activity 13 *TRB*

Student Activity Workbook
Chapter 13 Activities

Tests
Chapter 13 Test *TRB*
Chapter 13 WESTEST Computerized Testing

Handbook of Selected Court Cases
Cox v. *Bishop*
Mohrlang v. *Draper*

West's Business Law and Legal Environment Videodisc
Still Frames and Motion Segments as shown

---

302   The Law of Contracts

> *"Men keep their engagements when it is to the advantage of both not to break them."*
> **Solon, sixth century B.C.**
> **Athenian legal reformer**

Normally, the reason a person enters into a contract with another is to receive benefits. And normally, as the Greek lawgiver Solon said centuries ago, a contract is not broken as long as "it is to the advantage of both" parties not to break it. However, if the advantage ends, breach of contract may result. As we have seen, a **breach of contract** happens when a party does not perform part or all of the duties required under a contract. Once a party fails to perform or performs inadequately, the other party—the nonbreaching party—can choose one or more of several remedies.

A **remedy** is the relief provided an innocent party when the other party has breached the contract. It is the means available to enforce a right or to compensate an injury. Not every remedy is available for every contract breach. The most common remedies available to a nonbreaching party are damages, rescission and restitution, specific performance, and reformation. This chapter describes each of these remedies as well as recovery based on quasi contract and limitations on remedies.

◆ **breach of contract** Failure to perform part or all of the required duties under a contract.

◆ **remedy** Relief given to an innocent party when the other party has breached a contract. The most common contract remedies are damages, rescission and restitution, specific performance, and reformation.

◆ **damages** Money sought as a remedy for a breach of contract or for a tortious act.

◆ **general damages** Compensation to the injured party for the actual loss of the bargain caused by the breach of contract.

 ## DAMAGES

A breach of contract gives the nonbreaching party the right to sue for money damages. **Damages** are intended to compensate, or pay, the nonbreaching party for the loss of the bargain. Often, courts say that innocent parties should be put in the position they would have been in had the contract been fully performed.

TYPES OF DAMAGES

There are basically four kinds of damages: general, consequential, punitive, and nominal.

General Damages   **General damages** compensate the injured party for the actual loss of the bargain caused by the breach of contract. They replace only the loss actually caused by the wrong or injury. The amount of general damages is the difference between the value of the promised performance and the value of the actual performance. This amount is then reduced by any loss that the injured party has avoided.

 LEGAL FOCUS ~ PROBLEM

Edwin Souter contracted with Marinot Industries to perform certain services exclusively for Marinot during August. Payment for services

As the students have learned, general damages compensate the injured party for the actual loss of the bargain caused by the breach of contract. You might wish to point out to students that the Chinese philosopher Confucius spoke to the issue of injury and justice when he said, "Recompense injury with justice, and recompense kindness with kindness."

Breach and Remedies   303

was to be $3,000. Marinot canceled the contract and is in breach. Edwin found another job during August that paid $500. What are Edwin's damages?

Edwin can sue Marinot for breach and recover $2,500 as general damages ($3,000 loss − $500 actual wages paid by the other job). Edwin can also recover from Marinot the amount he spent to find the other job. Expenses or costs caused directly by the breach of contract—such as those Edwin spent to find another job—are a type of general damages called *incidental damages*.

The measurement of general damages varies by type of contract. Certain types of contracts deserve special mention—contracts for the sale of goods and construction contracts.

1. **Sale of Goods.** In a contract for the sale of goods, the usual measure of general damages is an amount equal to the difference between the contract price and the market price.

◆ LEGAL FOCUS – PROBLEM

MediQuick Laboratories contracts with Cal Computer Industries to purchase ten model X-15 computer terminals for $8,000 each. Cal Computer fails to deliver the ten terminals. The current market price of the terminals is $9,000. What is MediQuick's measure of damages?

MediQuick's measure of damages is $10,000 (10 × $1,000, which is the difference between $9,000, the market price, and $8,000, the contract price). If the buyer breaches and the seller has not yet produced the goods, general damages are normally the lost profits on the sale (not the difference between the contract price and the market price).

2. **Construction Contracts.** The measure of damages in construction contracts often varies depending on which party breaches and when the breach occurs. Exhibit 13-1 explains the measurement of these damages.

Consequential (Special) Damages **Consequential damages** are indirect but foreseeable damages resulting from a party's breach of contract. They differ from general damages in that they are caused by special circumstances beyond the contract itself.

◆ **consequential damages** Indirect but foreseeable damages resulting from a party's breach of contract.

◆ LEGAL FOCUS – PROBLEM

Gilmore, the owner of a small town newspaper, contracts to have a specific part shipped to her. She needs the part desperately to repair

---

The still frames listed below
from the **West's Business
Law and Legal Environment
Videodisc** can be used with
this chapter. To access this
material, use the bar codes
or the frame numbers
included in the Videodisc
Instructor's Manual found
in the *TRB*.

*Remedies for Breach of
   Contract*
*Injured Party's Damages for
   Breach of Contract*

The following are motion
segments which are also on
the videodisc:

*Damages and Mitigation of
   Damages*
*Costs of Litigation for
   Breach of Contract*
*Factors to Consider in
   Business Litigation*

304

Legal Focus Case Problem

Divide the class into small groups to read and discuss the Legal Focus Problem found here. Each group should choose a leader to explain its response to the question posed at the end of this Legal Focus. Additionally, each group should also discuss the following: Did the court apply correctly, or misapply the rule announced in the case? Many argue that it misapplied the rule—notice was given (Hadley insisted that he told Baxendale that the mill was out of operation), and any reasonable person would know that profits were being lost. Those who argue that it was applied correctly will follow the court's reasoning.

---

304   The Law of Contracts

Party in Breach	Time of Breach	Measurement of Damages
Owner	Before contruction begins	Profits (contract price less cost of materials and labor)
Owner	After construction begins	Profits plus costs incurred up to time of breach
Owner	After construction is completed	Contract price
Contractor	Before construction is completed	Generally, all costs incurred by owner to complete construction

EXHIBIT 13-1
MEASUREMENT OF DAMAGES—BREACH OF CONSTRUCTION CONTRACTS

her printing press. In her discussion with the shipper, Gilmore tells him she must receive the part by Monday or she won't be able to print her paper and will lose $750. Can Gilmore recover the $750 in lost profits if the shipper is late?

Yes. When the party who breached the contract knows (or has reason to know) of special circumstances that will cause the innocent party to suffer an additional loss, the party is liable for that loss. A similar example occurs when a refrigeration company fails to provide a part for a refrigeration system used to keep a butcher's meat cold. The refrigeration company can be held liable for meat spoilage if it does not repair the refrigeration system on time.

Consequential damages can also be recovered in situations involving the sale of goods. Assume that a seller fails to deliver ordered goods, knowing that a buyer is planning to resell those goods immediately. Consequential damages may be awarded for the loss of profits from the planned resale. Again, the knowledge of the special circumstances is a requirement for recovery of consequential damages.

> ◆ **LEGAL FOCUS – CASE PROBLEM**

The leading case on "consequential" circumstances is *Hadley v. Baxendale,*[1] decided in 1854. This case involved a broken crankshaft

---

1.   9 Exch 341, 156 Eng. Rep. 145 (1854).

used in a mill operation. In the mid-1800s, it was common for large mills, such as the one the plaintiffs operated, to have more than one crankshaft in case the main one broke. Most people knew that flour mills had these spares. When the Hadleys' crankshaft broke, the mill had to shut down, because the Hadleys had no spare. The Hadleys took the shaft to Baxendale, who was to ship the crankshaft to another city, where a duplicate shaft was to be made. Baxendale promised to deliver the shaft the following day. He did not deliver it for several days, and so the reopening of the mill was delayed. The owners sued Baxendale to recover the profits they lost while the mill was closed. Did the Hadleys recover their lost profits?

No. The court held that Baxendale was unaware that the Hadleys did not have a backup crankshaft. Because of his lack of knowledge, he was not liable for special circumstances. "Where two parties have made a contract which one of them has broken, the damages which the other party ought to receive in respect of such breach of contract should be such as may fairly and reasonably be considered either arising naturally, i.e., according to the usual course of things, from such breach of contract itself, or such as may reasonably be supposed to have been in the contemplation of both parties, at the time they made the contract, as the probable result of the breach of it."

It is possible for an injured party to receive both general and consequential damages. How general and consequential damages are measured is illustrated in Exhibit 13-2.

EXHIBIT 13-2
INJURED PARTY'S DAMAGES FOR BREACH OF CONTRACT

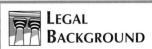

Have a student volunteer look up the word *nominal* in a dictionary and explain the dictionary definition to the class. The student should also relate how this definition of the word *nominal* relates to the phrase *nominal damages* discussed here.

Ask a volunteer to define the term *mitigating damages* for the class.

Legal Focus Example

Read the Legal Focus Example to the class. Ask the class if they can think of any other examples of cases in which nominal damages would be due that could also fit here. Allow volunteers to share their examples with the class.

Critical Thinking Activity

Have students write a paragraph or two analyzing the differences between punitive damages and nominal damages.

◆ **punitive**, or **exemplary**, **damages** Damages that punish the defendant or set an example for similar wrongdoers.

◆ **nominal damages** A small money award (often one dollar) granted to a plaintiff who suffered a wrong but no actual loss.

◆ **mitigation of damages** Rule requiring the injured party to try to reduce (mitigate) the damages suffered as a result of a breach of contract.

Punitive Damages Punitive, or **exemplary**, **damages** are generally not recoverable in a breach of contract action. Punitive damages are designed to punish and make an example of a guilty party in order to deter similar conduct in the future. Such damages have no legitimate place in contract law, since they are, in essence, penalties. A breach of contract is not unlawful in a criminal or societal sense. A contract is simply a civil relationship between the parties. The law may compensate one party for the loss of the bargain—no more and no less.

In a few situations, a person's actions are both a breach of contract and a tort. For example, the parties can establish by contract a certain reasonable standard or duty of care. Failure to live up to that standard is a breach of contract, and the act itself may also constitute negligence, a tort.

An intentional tort (such as fraud) may also be a breach of contract. In that case, it is possible for the innocent party to recover punitive damages for the tort in addition to compensatory and consequential damages for breach of contract.

Nominal Damages **Nominal damages** are awarded to an innocent party who has suffered a wrong but no actual damage—that is, no financial loss. Nominal-damage awards are small, such as a dollar, but they do establish that the defendant acted wrongfully.

◀ LEGAL FOCUS - EXAMPLE

Parrott contracts to buy potatoes at 50 cents a pound from Lentz. Lentz breaches the contract and does not deliver the potatoes. Meanwhile, the price of potatoes falls. Parrott can buy them in the open market at half the price he contracted for with Lentz. If Parrott sues Lentz, what will his damages be? Parrott is clearly better off because of Lentz's breach. Thus, in a breach of contract suit, Parrott will recover only nominal damages.

Most lawsuits for nominal damages are brought as a matter of principle. The theory is that a breach occurred and some damages should be imposed even though there was no actual loss. Since courts are paid for by the taxpayers, however, many judges believe Parrott is wasting our money if he sues.

MITIGATION OF DAMAGES

When a breach of contract occurs, the injured party is generally expected to try to reduce, or *mitigate*, the damages suffered. This is the **mitigation of damages** doctrine. What the injured party is expected to do in such a case depends on the situation.

LEGAL FOCUS ~ EXAMPLE

Suppose a tenant leaves the premises before the lease term has expired. Many states require that a landlord try to find a new tenant. If a new creditworthy tenant becomes available, the landlord must ordinarily lease the premises to this tenant. Any new lease would mitigate the damages recoverable from the former tenant. The former tenant is liable for the difference between the amount of the rent under the original lease and the rent received from the new tenant. If the landlord does not try to find a new tenant, many courts will reduce the damages the landlord can receive.

In the majority of states, wrongfully fired employees are expected to mitigate damages suffered by their employers' actions by finding new jobs. The damages awarded are their salaries less the incomes received in similar jobs obtained by reasonable means. An employee is not, however, required to take a job that is not of the same type and rank.

LIQUIDATED DAMAGES VERSUS PENALTIES

A **liquidated damages** provision in a contract states that a certain amount of damages will be paid if there is a future breach of contract. (*Liquidated* means determined, settled, or fixed.)

♦ **liquidated damages** Damages of a certain amount, specified in a contract, to be paid if there is a future default or breach of contract.

LEGAL FOCUS ~ PROBLEM

Barbara and Walter Kennedy entered into a contract with Gollust Construction, Inc. for Gollust to remodel a house for the Kennedys. In the contract there was a provision requiring Gollust to pay $100 for every day the company was late in completing the job. Would this provision in the contract be enforceable?

Probably. Liquidated damages provisions are enforceable unless they are found to be penalties. A **penalty** is an amount specified in a contract to be paid upon default or breach of contract; but it differs from a liquidated damages provision because it is *designed to penalize* the breaching party. Liquidated damages provisions are enforceable; penalty clauses are not.

To determine whether a particular provision is an enforceable liquidated damages provision or a penalty, the court must answer two questions. First, were the damages that might occur by breach difficult to estimate when the contract was created? Second, was the amount set as damages a reasonable estimate of those potential damages, and not excessive? If both answers are yes, the provision is enforced. In construction contracts, liquidated damages provisions are common. It is often legally difficult to estimate the amount of damages that might be caused by a delay in completing construction.

♦ **penalty** An amount specified in a contract to be paid upon default or breach of contract, that is *designed to penalize* the breaching party. Penalty clauses are not enforceable.

Legal Focus Example

Have a student volunteer read to the class this Legal Focus Example dealing with mitigation of damages. Make sure that students understand that in this case, the former tenant breached the contract and that the landlord is the injured party. Nonetheless, the landlord is expected to mitigate the damages by attempting to find new tenants.

Legal Focus Problem

Read aloud to the class this Legal Focus Problem dealing with liquidated damages versus penalties. Note to the students that in this Legal Focus Problem, the answer to the question posed at the end of the problem is neither "yes" nor "no" but, instead, "probably." Point out that in this case, different courts might answer the question differently, but make sure that students understand that in determining whether a particular provision is liquidated damages or a penalty, the court must answer the two questions listed in the student text:
1. Were the damages that might occur by breach difficult to estimate when the contract was created?
2. Was the amount set as damages a reasonable estimate of those potential damages and not excessive?

◆ RESCISSION AND RESTITUTION

◆ **rescission** An equitable remedy to undo, or cancel, a contract.

◆ **restitution** An equitable remedy to require each party to a contract to return goods, property, or money previously transferred to him or her.

Rescission is an action to undo, or cancel, a contract. A rescission returns innocent parties to their positions before the contract was made. In mutual rescission, discussed in Chapter 12, both parties agree to undo the contract. Rescission as a remedy is unilateral—that is, only one party wants to cancel the contract. When fraud, mistake, duress, or failure of consideration is present, rescission is an available remedy. The rescinding party must give prompt notice to the breaching party.

To rescind a contract, both parties must make **restitution** to each other by returning goods, property, or money previously transferred. If the goods or property have been consumed, restitution must be an equivalent amount of money.

◆ SPECIFIC PERFORMANCE

◆ **specific performance** An equitable remedy that calls for the performance of the act promised in the contract.

The remedy of **specific performance** calls for the performance of the act promised in the contract. This remedy is attractive since it provides the exact bargain promised in the contract. It also avoids some of the problems that exist in a suit for money damages. First, the nonbreaching party need not worry about collecting the judgment. Second, the nonbreaching party need not look around for another contract. Third, the actual performance may be more valuable than the money damages.

Although the equitable remedy of specific performance is often preferable to other remedies, it is not granted unless a money damage remedy is inadequate.

If the seller refuses to deliver this baseball card, would a lawsuit for specific performance be appropriate?

◀ LEGAL FOCUS – EXAMPLE

Contracts for the sale of goods rarely qualify for specific performance. Money damages ordinarily are adequate in such situations, because similar or identical goods can be bought or sold in the market. If the goods are unique, however, a court of equity will decree specific performance. For example, paintings, sculptures, and rare books and coins are so unique that money damages will not enable a buyer to obtain substantially identical substitutes in the market.

Specific performance is also available as a remedy in contracts relating to sales of land or interests in land. This type of contract is discussed in this chapter's Law in Action.

Courts normally refuse to grant specific performance of personal-service contracts. Sometimes damages are adequate if substantially identical service is available from other persons (for example, if you hire someone else to

Ethical Concern

Have your students discuss orally the definition of specific performance and the pros and cons of it. What if you sued someone for specific performance to paint your home, and they did an inferior job? What types of things would be best to sue for specific performance?

mow your lawn). Even for individually tailored personal-service contracts, courts are hesitant to order specific performance. To do so would be to support involuntary servitude—forced service—and public policy strongly discourages involuntary servitude. Also, courts do not want to monitor personal-service contracts.

 LEGAL FOCUS - PROBLEM

You contract with a brain surgeon to perform brain surgery on you. The surgeon refuses to perform. Will the court compel the surgeon to perform?

No. The court would not compel (and you really would not want) the surgeon to provide services under these circumstances. There is no way the court can assure a high-quality performance in such a situation. Similarly, courts often refuse to order specific performance of construction contracts, because courts are not set up to operate as construction supervisors or engineers.

REFORMATION

Reformation is a remedy used when the parties have not done a good job of describing their agreement in writing. Reformation allows a court to rewrite the contract to reflect the parties' true intentions. It is used most often when either fraud or mutual mistake (for example, a clerical error) occurs.

◆ **reformation** An equitable remedy whereby the court rewrites a contract to reflect the parties' true intentions.

 LEGAL FOCUS - EXAMPLE

Keshkek contracts to buy a certain piece of equipment from Shelley. The written contract refers to a piece of equipment other than the one both intended. A mutual mistake has occurred. Accordingly, a court could reform the contract so the writing conforms to Keshkek's and Shelley's original intention as to which piece of equipment is being sold.

Two other examples deserve mention. The first involves two parties who have made a binding oral contract. They also agree to put the oral contract in writing, but when they do, they make an error in stating the terms. Universally, the courts allow into evidence the correct terms of the oral contract. In this way, they reform the written contract.

The second is about written agreements (covenants) not to compete (see Chapter 10). If the agreement is for a valid and legitimate purpose (such as

Read

You might introduce this *Law in Action* feature by explaining to students that disputes involving contracts for the sale of real estate such as the case of *Mohrlang* v. *Draper* are discussed in this feature. In such cases, remedies at law are often inadequate to provide relief to a buyer when the seller refuses to go through with the promised conveyance of land. Then allow a student volunteer to read this Legal Focus feature aloud to the class.

Discuss

Stimulate a class discussion regarding this *Law in Action* feature by asking the following questions: Why was the land that Mohrlang agreed to purchase from Draper so desirable to Mohrlang? What was the intervening event

that caused Draper to breach the contract? Why did Mohrlang sue for specific performance? In this case, what was *specific performance?* What did the court decide? What reasons did the court give for its decision?

Teaching Note

This case is included in the *West's Business and Personal Law Handbook of Selected Court Cases.*

---

310   The Law of Contracts

◆ Law in Action

LAW AND THE BUSINESSPERSON: SPECIFIC PERFORMANCE, OR THIS LAND IS MY LAND

eal estate is unique. Each parcel of land is different from another. Because of this, a remedy of monetary compensation or the substitution of other property for breach of a contract for the sale of land is inadequate. The courts grant the remedy of specific performance instead. This is true even when performance may cause the seller to spend substantially more than anticipated.

Consider, for example, the case of *Mohrlang v. Draper.*[2] The plaintiff, Mohrlang, agreed to purchase a tract of land from Draper for $14,875. Mohrlang planned to build a solar home. The land was desirable because of its southern exposure. However, a buried gas line on the property prevented any construction on the lot. Draper had promised in the sales contract to have the gas line removed at his expense so Mohrlang could begin construction.

Shortly after the contract signing, Draper called the gas company for an estimate on moving the gas line. To his surprise—and shock—he learned it would cost $10,000 to relocate the gas line. Because of this, he refused to transfer the title to Mohrlang as promised in the contract. In the meantime, Mohrlang had hired an architect to draw up

plans for the home. Mohrlang sued for specific performance. Draper argued that the appropriate remedy was monetary damages because of the expense he would incur if required to perform. Mohrlang argued that because no other available lot had the unique characteristics or the southern exposure, specific performance should be allowed.

The Supreme Court of Nebraska agreed with Mohrlang and compelled Draper to go through with the sale. The court reasoned that Draper *could* have gotten the estimate of the cost of relocating the gas line before signing the contract. In the words of the court, "The inescapable inference is that complete information about relocating the gas line was available when Draper entered the contract to sell his lot. . . . It was Draper's neglect which increased his burden, not an unforeseeable circumstance."

When a seller contracts to sell an interest in land, any burdens voluntarily assumed should be thoroughly explored. Courts presume that individuals will look after their own interests when making contracts. If they don't, a court will not excuse them from promises to other parties with whom they have contracted.

2.   219 Neb. 630, 365 N.W.2d 443 (1985).

the sale of a business), but the area or time restraints are unreasonable, some courts may reform the restraints by making them reasonable. Other courts, however, throw the entire restrictive covenant out as illegal.

1. A breach of contract occurs when a party does not perform part or all of the required duties under a contract.
2. Punitive damages are penalties rather than compensation for actual loss. Since a contract is a relationship between parties, the law may compensate one party only for the loss of bargain.

3. Liquidated damage clauses are not enforceable when they are designed to penalize the breaching party. Penalty clauses in contracts are not enforceable.
4. If a contract is rescinded, an innocent party is returned to his or her position before the contract.
5. Specific performance is an appealing remedy for an injured party because it provides

the exact bargain promised in the contract and it avoids some of the problems in a suit for money damages.
6. Reformation allows a court to rewrite a contract to reflect the parties' true intentions if they have not done a good job of describing their agreement in writing.

◆ CHECKING YOUR PROGRESS

1. When does a breach of contract occur?
2. Why are punitive damages generally not recoverable in a breach of contract action?
3. When are liquidated damage clauses not enforceable?
4. What is the effect upon an innocent party if a contract is rescinded?
5. Why is specific performance an appealing remedy for an injured party?
6. What is reformation and when is this remedy used?

◆ RECOVERY BASED ON QUASI CONTRACT

As stated in Chapter 7, a quasi contract is not a true contract but an equitable theory imposing a duty on a party to prevent unjust enrichment. A quasi contract is an equitable basis for relief.

Quasi-contract recovery is useful when one party has partially performed under an unenforceable contract. It allows the party to recover the reasonable value of the partial performance. For quasi-contractual recovery to occur, the party seeking recovery must show the following:

1. A benefit was conferred on the other party.
2. The party seeking recovery conferred the benefit with the expectation of being paid.
3. The party seeking recovery did not act as a volunteer in conferring the benefit.
4. Retaining the benefit without paying would result in unjust enrichment of the party receiving the benefit.

◄ LEGAL FOCUS ~ PROBLEM

Ericson contracts to build two oil platforms for Petro Industries. The platforms are to be built over a period of three years, but the parties fail to make a written contract. Because the contract calls for a three-year performance, enforcement of the contract will be barred by the Statute of Frauds (see Chapter 11). What if Ericson completed one platform, and then Petro Industries informed him that it would not pay him? Would Ericson have any rights under the contract?

Enrichment

Make sure that students understand that a *quasi contract* is not a contract at all, but rather a court-imposed remedy to prevent injustice. The classic example of quasi contract use occurs when emergency services are rendered to a person who is unable to make a contract. In such a case, courts will require payment out of fairness to prevent unjust enrichment.

Legal Focus Problem

Allow a student volunteer to read this Legal Focus Example aloud to the class. Remind students that they can use the Legal Focus features as review tools when studying for tests.

Ask your students to list some reasons why someone may decide to waive his or her right to sue for a breach of contract.

Legal Focus Example

Ask a student volunteer to read aloud this Legal Focus Example dealing with a waiver of breach. Make sure that students understand that in this instance even though the buyer waived the seller's breach and accepted delivery of the coal despite the five-day delay, the seller still remains liable for any damages to the coal buyer caused by the delay.

Extension Activity

Have students bring in news articles regarding judgments in recent breach of contract lawsuits. Guide the students in examining the judgments. What part of each judgment is *compensatory damages?* What part of each judgment is *consequential damages?* Does the amount of damages seem fair based on the facts of the case?

312 The Law of Contracts

Although Ericson cannot enforce the contract, he can sue in quasi contract. A benefit has been conferred on Petro Industries, since one oil platform has been built. Ericson built the platform (conferred the benefit) expecting to be paid. He did not volunteer to build the platform; he built it under an unenforceable oral contract. Finally, allowing Petro Industries to retain the platform would enrich the company unjustly. Ericson can recover the reasonable value of the oil platform. The reasonable value is ordinarily equal to the fair market value.

◆ WAIVER OF BREACH

♦ **waiver** An intentional, knowing relinquishment of a legal right.

Under certain circumstances, a nonbreaching party may be willing to accept less than an agreed performance. People don't always wish to sue for breach. This giving up of the right to require full performance is a **waiver**. Businesspersons often waive breaches of contract by the other party to get whatever benefit is possible out of the contract. Also, even though a breach is accepted, the breaching party is still responsible for any damages caused by the breach.

◆ LEGAL FOCUS – EXAMPLE

A seller contracts with a buyer to deliver to the buyer 10,000 tons of coal on or before November 1. The contract calls for the buyer to make payment by November 10 for coal delivered. Because of a coal miners' strike, coal is unavailable. The seller breaches the contract by not delivering until November 5. The buyer may want to waive the seller's breach, accept delivery of the coal, and pay as contracted. The seller remains liable for any damages to the coal buyer caused by the five-day delay in shipping the coal.

Ordinarily, the waiver by a contracting party does not operate to waive future breaches of contract. However, a *pattern of conduct* that waives several successive breaches operates as a continuing waiver. To change this result, the nonbreaching party should give notice to the breaching party that full performance will be required in the future.

◆ PROVISIONS LIMITING REMEDIES

A contract's language may state that no damages can be recovered for certain types of breaches or that damages are limited to a maximum amount. A contract may also provide that the only remedy for breach is replacement, repair, or refund of the purchase price. Provisions stating that no damages can be recovered are called *exculpatory clauses* (see Chapter 10).

Ethical Concern

Stimulate a class discussion about the ethics of the following scenario: Joan buys a suit at a clearance sale from a local department store. When she gets home she finds that the suit has a stain on the sleeve, so she goes back to the store to return it. The store manager tells Joan that she will not get a refund for the stained suit because of the sign on the front of the rack. Joan did not see the sign before, but it is obvious to her now. The sign reads, "FINAL PURCHASES—NO RETURNS." What kind of clause was this sign? Is it legal? Was Joan treated fairly?

Provisions that affect the availability of certain remedies are called *limitation-of-liability clauses*.

THE REQUIREMENT OF MUTUAL ASSENT

Language limiting remedies is not always enforced by the court. These clauses may be considered to be against the public interest. Courts are concerned about whether each party was aware of the limitation. Did each party knowingly consent to it? Was the provision in fine print or on the back of a lengthy contract? If either party was unaware of the provision, it is not a part of the contract and cannot be enforced.

 LEGAL FOCUS – EXAMPLE

Motorists often park their cars in lots and receive small ticket stubs that say the operators of the lot are not liable for damages to cars parked in the lot. If a reasonable person would notice this exculpatory clause, it is enforceable. If the clause is inconspicuous and a

Are exclusionary clauses always enforceable?

Reteaching Activity

Ask a volunteer to define the term *exculpatory clauses* for the class.

Legal Focus Example

Read to the class the Legal Focus Example that begins on this page. Make sure that the students understand that in this instance, the exculpatory clause is not in question. What is in question is whether each of the parties was fully aware of the exculpatory clause's existence.

Caption Answer

Exclusionary clauses are not always enforced by the court. Both parties must be aware of the provision for it to be considered part of the contract and, therefore, enforced.

313

reasonable person would not notice it, the clause is not enforced. The motorist can then sue for damages caused to the car while in the parking lot. (Similarly, posted signs can exclude liability if they are clear and conspicuous.)

TYPE OF BREACH COVERED

Another concern with clauses that limit liability is what type of breach is excluded. For example, a provision excluding liability for fraudulent or intentional injury is not enforceable. Also, a clause excluding liability for illegal acts or violations of law will not be enforced.

Clauses excluding liability for negligence are enforceable in some cases. When an exculpatory clause for negligence is contained in a contract made between parties who have approximately equal bargaining positions, the clause usually will be enforced.

LEGAL FOCUS – PROBLEM

Delta Airlines buys six DC-9s from Douglas Aircraft. In the contract for sale, a clause excludes liability for errors in design and construction of the aircraft. Is the clause enforceable?

Yes. The clause should be upheld because both parties are large corporations with similar bargaining power. The equality of bargaining power assures that the exculpatory clause was not dictated by one of the parties and forced on the other.

◆ CHECKING YOUR PROGRESS

1. Does a waiver of breach of contract end a contract?
2. Must each party to a contract be aware of language limiting remedies in the contract to have court enforcement?

Read

Introduce this *A Case In Point* feature by explaining that this case deals with rescission and restitution. Remind the students that rescission is essentially an action to cancel a contract—to return the contracting parties to the position they were in before the transaction. Further remind the students that, generally, to rescind, the parties must make restitution by returning goods, property, or money conveyed to one another. This *A Case In Point* feature deals with a case in which the goods could not be returned. Ask a student volunteer to read this *A Case In Point* feature aloud to the class.

Discuss

Stimulate a class discussion of this feature by asking the following questions: What did the Bishops receive from Cox and Company? What did Cox and Company receive from the Bishops? Why did the Bishops seek to rescind this contract? How did the trial court rule in this case? What arguments did Cox give for the appeal of this case? What decision was reached by the court of appeals of Arkansas? What reasons were given for the court's judgment?

◆ A CASE IN POINT ◆

COX v. BISHOP
Court of Appeals of Arkansas, 1989.
28 Ark.App. 210,
772 S.W.2d 358.

Circumstances under which rescission and restitution may be ordered are illustrated in this case.

FACTS Jimmy and Brenda Bishop contracted with Dave Cox & Company to install a swimming pool in the Bishops' yard. They paid $13,500 for the pool and installation. Six months after the pool was installed, the Bishops discovered that it had risen six inches from the hole in which it had been put, exposing a sharp edge on which several children were hurt. The pool developed other problems, including leaks, cracks, and bulges. Alleging that the pool was unsafe, the Bishops filed suit for rescission of the contract. The trial court concluded that Cox had undertaken to install the pool properly, but "this was just a 'botched' job. There is a material breach of contract." The court ordered rescission of the contract and restitution of the Bishops' $13,500. Cox appealed, arguing that rescission was improper because the evidence did not support the court's conclusion. He also argued that because the Bishops had not returned to him what they received under the contract (the pool), rescission should not be granted.

ISSUE Did the evidence of the pool's improper installation support rescission of the contract and, though the pool was not returned, restitution of the Bishops' payment?

DECISION Yes. The trial court's judgment was affirmed.

REASON The appellate court noted "where there is a material breach of contract, substantial nonperformance, and entire or substantial failure of consideration, the injured party is entitled to rescission of the contract and restitution and recovery back of money paid." The court explained that "restitution is not to be granted in every case for breach of contract, but only where the breach is a 'vital' one, or if it represents a substantial 'failure of consideration.' This requirement of a substantial breach is a summary expression of the policy of fairness between the parties." Citing the problems with the pool and estimates that repair would cost as much as $20,000, the court affirmed the trial court's conclusions. The appellate court also pointed out that rescission was not improper "merely because circumstances . . . render it difficult to restore the parties exactly to their original situations." The court added that, in fact, the Bishops had sought to return the pool. They had asked the trial court to order it removed and the hole filled, but the request had been denied. The court emphasized that Cox had not objected to the denial.

Teaching Note

This case is included in the *West's Business and Personal Law Handbook of Selected Court Cases.*

In order to help students review what they have learned in Chapter 13, you might wish to:

1. Have a student volunteer, or volunteers, read the Chapter Summary aloud.
2. Allow the students to work with partners to complete the *Using Legal Language* activity.
3. Assign the *Checking for Comprehension* exercise as homework.
4. Allow the students to work in small groups to complete the *Applying Legal Concepts* activities.
5. As a class, complete the *Applying the Law* activities. (Please note that you may have to help students with vocabulary so that they adequately understand all of the *Applying the Law* material.)

In order to check student mastery of chapter concepts, you may wish to use the Chapter 13 test that is found in your *Teacher's Resource Binder* or use WESTEST computerized testing for Chapter 13.

CHAPTER REVIEW

 ## SUMMARY

COMMON REMEDIES AVAILABLE TO NONBREACHING PARTIES

Damages

A legal remedy designed to compensate the nonbreaching party for the loss of the bargain. By awarding money damages, the court tries to place the parties in the position they would have been in had the contract been fully performed. The nonbreaching party frequently has a duty to *mitigate* (lessen or reduce) the damages resulting from the contract breach.

1. *General damages*—Damages that compensate for injuries proved to be caused directly by the loss of the bargain resulting from the breach of contract.

2. *Consequential damages*—Damages resulting from special circumstances beyond the contract itself. They flow only from the consequences of a breach. For a party to recover consequential damages, the damages must be the foreseeable result of a breach of contract and known to the breaching party.

3. *Punitive damages*—Damages awarded to punish the breaching party. Not awarded in a breach of contract action unless a tort is involved.

4. *Nominal damages*—Damages small in amount (such as one dollar) awarded when a breach has occurred but no actual damages have been suffered. Awarded only to establish that the defendant acted wrongfully.

5. *Liquidated damages*—Damages that may be specified in a contract as the amount to be paid to the nonbreaching party in the event that the contract is breached. Liquidated damages clauses are enforced if the damages were difficult to estimate at the time the contract was formed and if the amount specified is reasonable. If found to be a penalty, the clause is not enforced.

Rescission and Restitution

1. *Rescission*—An action to cancel the contract and return the parties to the positions they occupied prior to the transaction. Available when fraud, mistake, duress, or failure of consideration is present.

2. *Restitution*—When a contract is rescinded, both parties must make restitution to each other by returning goods, property, or money previously conveyed.

Specific Performance

A remedy calling for the performance of the act promised in the contract. Only available in special situations—such as contracts for the sale of unique goods, including land, and where monetary damages would be an inadequate remedy. Specific performance is not available as a remedy in breached contracts for personal services.

Reformation

A remedy allowing a contract to be "reformed," or rewritten, to reflect the parties' true intentions. Available when an agreement is imperfectly expressed in writing.

Recovery Based on Quasi Contract

A theory imposed by the courts to obtain justice and prevent unjust enrichment in a situation where no enforceable contract exists.

WAIVER OF BREACH

When a nonbreaching party agrees to accept less than the promised performance in a contract, it is a waiver.

PROVISIONS LIMITING REMEDIES

1. *Exculpatory clause*—A clause stating that no damages (or only a limited amount of damages) can be recovered in the event the contract is breached.

2. *Limitation-of-liability clauses*—Provisions that affect the availability of certain remedies.

3. Clauses which limit remedies are not always enforced by the courts. The courts consider the clause in light of the public interest. Among the concerns are fairness, consent, equal bargaining power of the parties, and actual notice of the clause.

◆ USING LEGAL LANGUAGE

Directions: Match each term with the statement that best defines that term.

1. compensatory damages
2. consequential damages
3. liquidated damages
4. mitigation of damages
5. nominal damages
6. penalty
7. reformation
8. remedy
9. restitution
10. specific performance

A. In breached contracts for the sale of goods, the usual measure of _____ is an amount equal to the difference between the contract price and the market price.

B. An innocent party is entitled to a _____ when the other party has breached a contract.

C. When a breach of contract occurs, the injured party is generally expected to try to reduce the damages suffered, which is called _____.

D. The equitable remedy of _____ calls for the performance of the act promised in the contract.

E. An agreement for _____ assures that a certain amount of damages will be paid if there is a future default or breach of contract.

F. The equitable remedy of _____ requires a wrongdoer to return goods, property, or money previously transferred to him or her.

G. Indirect but foreseeable damages are _____ resulting from a party's breach of contract.

H. _____ is an equitable remedy where the court rewrites a contract to reflect the parties' true intentions.

I. A small monetary award, called _____, is often granted to a plaintiff when no actual damage was suffered.

J. A _____ is an agreed amount to be paid upon default or breach of contract, that is designed to punish the breaching party.

he or she relinquishes the legal right to claim failure of full performance. Hanford's acceptance of six late payments not only constitutes a waiver but also constitutes a pattern of conduct of waiver, and thus the waiver extends to the thirteenth and future payments—until such time as Hanford gives notice to Fulbright that full compliance with the contract will be required in the future. Hanford cannot hold Fulbright for breach upon the late thirteenth payment but can notify Fulbright that any further tender of late payments will constitute a breach.

8. Sweet, Inc., is unquestionably in breach of contract, which entitles Ben to monetary damages. Each claim for damages should be discussed separately. First, Ben is entitled to compensatory damages—those damages that Sweet could reasonably have foreseen would result from the breach. Generally, in the sale of goods, the measure of damages is the difference between the contract price and the market price at the time the buyer learned of the breach, plus any incidental expenses incurred. Thus Ben is entitled to all expenses he has incurred because of the breach, plus the difference between the market price at the time Ben learned of the breach and the contract price. Second, because Sweet was well aware of the use and need for the sugar, Sweet is also responsible for any damages flowing from the breach in light of this special circumstance. These damages, called consequential damages, will include the lost profits from this year's

318

Christmas sale orders. Third, whether the consequential damages will flow to loss of future sales is highly questionable. It is much easier for Ben to show the loss of this year's Christmas sales than the loss of future sales. Fourth, punitive damages are rarely awarded for breach-of-contract actions; they are basically reserved for certain torts in which society deems that the tortfeasor (wrongdoer) should be punished for his or her civil wrong. Ben is incorrect in claiming punitive damages based on Sweet's failure to perform.

Student charts should illustrate the following:
a—Yes, Eric can collect damages in the amount of $18 to cover the amount overpaid. The damages would be compensatory.
b—Yes, Jim can collect damages. He can collect $90 for the three days that Amy was late in finishing the paint job. The damages would be liquidated damages.

 ## CHECKING FOR COMPREHENSION

1. What are the most common remedies available to a nonbreaching party?

2. What is the difference between compensatory damages and consequential damages?

3. In what circumstances could punitive damages be recovered by a party in a breach of contract?

4. Give an example of a situation in which courts would apply the remedy of specific performance of an act promised in a contract and give an example of a situation in which courts would not apply the remedy.

5. Can an injured party recover anything if a quasi contract exists rather than a true contract? Explain.

6. To have the court enforce a contract, is mutual assent a necessary contract requirement if language limiting remedies is written in the contract? Explain.

7. Fulbright purchases an automobile from Hanford Motors. He pays $1,000 down and agrees to pay the balance in thirty-six monthly payments of $200 each. The terms of the agreement call for Fulbright to make each payment on or before the first of each month. During the next six months, Fulbright's payments are not made until the fifth of each month. Hanford accepts and cashes the payment check each time. When Fulbright tenders the thirteenth payment on the fifth of the next month, Hanford, claiming that Fulbright is in breach of contract, refuses to accept the check. He demands the entire balance owed. Fulbright claims that Hanford cannot hold her in breach. Discuss the result in detail.

8. Ben owns and operates a famous candy store. He makes most of the candy sold in the store, and business is particularly heavy during the Christmas season. Ben contracts with Sweet, Inc., to purchase 10,000 pounds of sugar, to be delivered on or before November 15. Ben informs Sweet that this particular order is to be used for the Christmas season business. Because of production problems the sugar is not tendered to Ben until December 10, at which time Ben refuses the order because it is so late. Ben has been unable to purchase the quantity of sugar needed to meet the Christmas orders and has had to turn down numerous regular customers, some of whom indicated they would purchase candy elsewhere in the future. The sugar Ben was able to purchase cost him 10 cents per pound above Sweet's price. Ben sues Sweet for breach of contract, claiming as damages the higher price paid for the sugar from others, lost profits from this year's lost Christmas sales, future lost profits from customers who indicated they would discontinue doing business with him, and punitive damages for failure to meet the contracted-for delivery date. Sweet claims Ben is limited to compensatory damages only. Discuss who is correct.

 ## APPLYING LEGAL CONCEPTS

Calculate the damages in the following examples. Specify if the damages are compensatory, consequential, punitive, nominal, or liquidated. Create a chart to illustrate. Add two examples of your own.

a. Eric contracts with Emily to buy twelve dozen homemade cookies at

1. No. Although the term *penalty* was used throughout the provision in question, the trial court found that the provision was, in fact, a liquidated damages clause, and this finding was upheld on appeal. The court held that the provision was similar to those in other employment contracts negotiated between school boards and teachers' organizations and that the amount of damages in those contracts was similar to that in Dewerff's contract. The court ruled that the requirements of a valid liquidated damages clause—that the sum be reasonable and the actual damages be difficult to ascertain—were met by the provision in Dewerff's contract, and it was thus enforceable.

2. Yes. Stodola's defense is valid. An exculpatory clause is to be given the scope intended the parties. Stodola declared in the contract that he assumed "no liability" for damage to the building. This clearly included liability based on any theory. Therefore, the clause covered and excluded liability based on negligence, even though nothing was expressly said about "negligence."

3. The $6,600 that Kerr sought as damages for lost profits on the cargo shipment are consequential damages. The question as to whether Kerr could recover these damages is one of foreseeability. Unless it was foreseeable to RCA that its failure to send the telegram would result in lost business profits to Kerr, RCA will not be liable for such damages. The Court of Appeals of New York held that since the words were in code, RCA was not bound to know that the message was related to a business transaction or that failure to send the message would result in lost business profits. In other words, the consequential damages that Kerr claimed were not reasonably foreseeable by RCA. Here compensatory damages, which are almost always awarded in contract cases, would be equal to the price of the telegram—which, of course, would amount to only a few dollars.

$3 per dozen and pays her $36. Emily delivers six dozen cookies, but is unable to complete the contract because her oven breaks. Can Eric collect damages? How much? Which kind of damages would it be?

b. Jim contracts with Amy from Art On The Move to draw a scene and paint his van. They agree in the contract that the paint job will cost $1,500 and Amy will pay $30 a day to Jim if the paint job is not finished in 10 days. Amy finishes the paint job three days late. Can Jim collect damages? How much? What kind of damages would it be?

◆ APPLYING THE LAW . . . YOU BE THE JUDGE

1. Dewerff was a teacher and basketball coach for Unified School District No. 315. The employment contract included a clause that read, in part: "Penalty for breaking contracts: . . . In all cases where a teacher under contract fails to honor the full term of his or her contract, a lump sum of $400 is to be collected if the contract is broken before August 1." Dewerff resigned on June 28, 1978, and he was told that the school would accept his resignation upon his payment of the $400 stipulated in the contract. When Dewerff refused to make the $400 payment, the school district sued for $400 as "liquidated damages" on the basis of the contract clause. Dewerff argued that the contract provision was a "penalty" clause and unenforceable in this situation. Is Dewerff correct? [*Unified School District No. 315, Thomas County v. Dewerff*, 6 Kan.App.2d 77, 626 P.2d 1206 (1981)]

2. Otis Elevator contracted with Don Stodola's Well Drilling Company to do the drilling work necessary to install an elevator in a high school building. The contract stated that Don Stodola assumed "no liability" for damage to the building. Because of alleged negligence of Don Stodola, the building cracked where the elevator was installed. When Otis Elevator sued Don Stodola, he raised the defense that the exculpatory clause barred any suit against him. Otis claimed that the clause could not bar liability for negligence because the clause did not expressly refer to negligence. Is Stodola's defense valid? [*Otis Elevator Co. v. Don Stodola's Well Drilling Co., Inc.* (Minn.App.) 372 N.W.2d 77 (1985)]

3. Kerr Steamship Co. delivered to RCA a twenty–nine-word, coded message to be sent to Kerr's agent in Manila. The message included instructions on loading cargo onto one of Kerr's vessels. Kerr's profits on the carriage of the cargo were to be about $6,600. RCA mislaid the coded message, and it was never sent. Kerr sued RCA for the $6,600 in profits that it lost because RCA never sent the message. Can Kerr recover? Explain. [*Kerr Steamship Co. v. Radio Corp. of America*, 245 N.Y. 284, 157 N.E. 140 (1927)]

Have the students look at the listed steps for the PUDGE method of negotiation. Which step(s) in this method of negotiation require effort on the part of the negotiator? Which step(s) require emotional control? Ask the students to think about their own strengths and weaknesses and to decide for themselves which of the five PUDGE steps would be most difficult for them.

Prereading Activity

You might introduce this Legal Perspective by discussing what the students already know about negotiation: What is *negotiation?* How do we use negotiation in our daily lives? What is required of each party in a negotiation? After the students have discussed negotiation, explain to them that in this feature they will learn more about negotiation as it relates to business law. Have student volunteers read this Legal Perspective aloud to the class.

LEGAL PERSPECTIVE

NEGOTIATION

Earlier in the book, in Chapter 5's Legal Perspective, we discussed alternatives to lawsuits. We said then that lawsuits are time-consuming, expensive, and emotionally draining. We told you that many businesses use ways other than lawsuits to settle disputes. These methods go by the general name of alternative dispute resolution, or ADR. One ADR method we discussed briefly was negotiation. It is time to discuss negotiation in more detail.

NEGOTIATION AND BREACH OF CONTRACT

Your first action after learning that someone has breached a contract should seldom, if ever, be filing a lawsuit. Instead, you should thoughtfully and carefully consider a strategy to negotiate a resolution to the problem. Just talking with the person about the problem may allow a reasonable solution that eliminates the need for a lawsuit.

Depending on the circumstances, you may or may not require the assistance of an attorney. Often, when a dispute is referred to a lawyer, negotiation is thought to have failed. However, negotiation usually continues even after a lawsuit has been filed, as part of the lawsuit strategy. And considering negotiation as an early strategy may encourage the lawyer to settle the matter *before* filing a lawsuit. Since more than 95 percent of all lawsuits are eventually settled by negotiation or dropped, it makes sense to negotiate early before spending money and time on a lawsuit.

HOW TO NEGOTIATE

Negotiation is defined as communication for the purpose of persuasion. It is something that we all do. You negotiate with your parents, brothers and sisters, friends, and teachers. Teenagers, for example, often negotiate with their parents for the keys to the car. The negotiation may go like this: Pat walks into the house and sees a parent. A conversation begins immediately. "Can I use the car on Saturday for a date?" The response is "No." Does the conversation stop after that? In most families, the conversation continues. The next exchange might be: "Why can't I use the car?" "Because I said so."

At this point, neither party is negotiating with the other. Neither is attempting to persuade. They are talking at, not with, each other. Attempts at persuasion are, however, likely to follow. The attempt might be as feeble as "Don't worry, I'll take good care of the car." It might be somewhat stronger, such as: "If I can borrow the car, I will mow the lawn."

If the point of negotiation is to persuade, then careful consideration of how best to present your views and get acceptable results makes sense. Most of us don't prepare, however. We don't think about how to negotiate; we just do it. In most cases, we do not do it very well.

It is possible you believe you are already a skilled negotiator, and you may be right. Negotiation, like most skills, can be improved, however. Skilled athletes do not stop trying to improve when they reach a certain level. They usually just work harder.

Enrichment

Instruct students to use the PUDGE method of negotiation to write a script for getting a raise on the job.

Collaborative Learning Activity

Have the students work with partners to create a practical situation in which negotiation might be used. Students should then discuss the situation and make a list of steps one would take to prepare to negotiate in that situation.

Reteaching Activity

Have each student write a one- to three-sentence explanation of *supportable arguments*. What are *supportable arguments?* Why are they important? Allow volunteers to share their work with the class.

Michael Jordan practices, and he practices constantly.

In this short discussion, we will consider a few techniques of successful negotiation, whether for legal disputes or everyday matters. Using even a few techniques can improve the ability of most people to negotiate. We suggest for your consideration our own PUDGE method of negotiation.

1. **P**repare.
2. **U**se supportable arguments.
3. **D**on't get personal.
4. **G**ive as well as take.
5. **E**stablish a relationship.

PREPARE

Preparation is essential to a successful negotiation. Preparation includes thinking about what you really want, how to approach the negotiation, and what alternatives are available. Assume you wish to purchase an automobile. Many of us decide we want a car, see one that looks attractive, and buy it (assuming we have the money). It is, however, a mistake to buy a car the day we decide we want to buy one.

When you are in this situation, take time to sit down with some paper and a pencil. Think about what you want. Then consider how you can get it. Begin by thinking about why you want a car. Needs such as transportation, recreational needs, image, and job can be considered. What cars interest you and why? Think about more than how the car looks. Is the car reliable? What is its resale value? Is it economical? Is it safe? These are among the concerns you should have. Find out about the value and market price of cars that interest you. After a general search for the right car, you need to re-

search any particular car that interests you. If it is a used car, have it inspected by an independent mechanic. Even determining when to buy a car is important. New cars in particular can be bought for thousands less at certain times of the year. Even on certain days of the month, you can get a better deal. All this preparation should be done before you actually negotiate anything with the seller of the car.

How do you prepare? Read books and magazine articles and talk to knowledgeable people. Just thinking about an approach and strategy will help you negotiate. Remember our example about borrowing the car for the weekend date? Pat just walked in and asked. Had Pat considered a strategy beforehand, a better time and way of asking might have been chosen.

USE SUPPORTABLE ARGUMENTS

When we begin to negotiate, we often begin by offering the worst reasons for someone to agree with us. We spend time arguing about opinions or feelings rather than facts.

Assume Max is selling his car, and his asking price is $2,000. Carly wants to buy the car. She obviously wants to pay as little as possible, but she does want the car. She decides to offer $1,000. She tells Max, "$1,000 is the amount *I want to pay* for the car." Max is offended by the low offer and rejects it.

Carly did not give Max any reason to accept the $1,000 offer. The reason given with the offer (that $1,000 is the amount she wants to pay) is not a reason likely to convince a party to accept.

Carly could instead offer a reason for Max to accept. The reason should be a

(continued on page 322)

Legal Focus Example

Have a student volunteer read this Legal Focus Example aloud to the class. Point out to the students that in this Legal Focus Example, Carly manages to keep the negotiation process alive by avoiding personal attacks.

LEGAL PERSPECTIVE (CONTINUED)

statement of fact honestly given that can be independently verified. It should not simply state a personal belief. What are some examples of supportable arguments? Carly might look through newspaper want ads for similar cars and find that the price for this type of car averages $1,000. She might also find that a used car price list places the value of this car at $1,000. Any independent outside source that establishes that the offer is reasonable provides a better reason for Max to accept than Carly's personal feelings.

Communication to persuade means convincing someone that it makes sense to reach an agreement with you. People seldom reach agreements to make you feel better or satisfy your personal beliefs. They instead look for some neutral facts or standards that suggest an agreement makes sense.

DON'T GET PERSONAL

Remember that when you negotiate, you are negotiating with a person, not a thing. People have feelings. They can be insulted. They can, of course, also insult you. If you hope to negotiate successfully with someone, be careful of that person's feelings. If someone insults you, change the nature of the discussion and move away from personal attacks.

A successful negotiator tries to reach an agreement, not win, and not insult or humiliate the other party. For example, making a take-it-or-leave-it offer is seldom a good idea. An offer of that type devalues the other person. It says the offeror is the only one who can establish the terms of the agreement. Furthermore, insults or negative comments seldom lead to agreement. Instead, insults lead to other insults. You

might win the battle of the insults, but you won't get a lasting agreement. Good negotiators listen to the other party. They do not interrupt, and they do not attack beliefs. They become active listeners who try to find out the basis for the other person's beliefs. The successful negotiator tries to create solutions without attacking another's feelings directly.

If the other party is emotional, it may seem that no agreement is possible. However, a thoughtful person who does not respond to anger can often turn a negotiation around. Allowing the other party to vent his or her anger without responding in the same way creates an opportunity for agreement.

◆ LEGAL FOCUS ~ EXAMPLE

Carly makes the $1,000 offer to Max for the car. He responds, "Your offer is insulting. Only a stupid person who knows nothing about cars would make it." Carly could respond, "You think I'm stupid! Well, you make a turkey seem smart." If that is how she responds, though, the negotiation is finished. Instead, Carly could say, "I am sorry you feel that way. I did not intend to insult you. Let me tell you why I believe my offer of $1,000 makes sense." We do not know if an agreement will be reached, but chances for agreement are saved by Carly's better choice of response.

GIVE AS WELL AS TAKE

Not all negotiations create win–win situations. A win–win situation occurs when both parties gain from a negotiation. However, many situations do allow for mutual

Collaborative Learning Activity

Divide the class into small groups. Have each group look again at the *Cox* v. *Bishop* case that was used in the *A Case In Point* feature at the end of this chapter. Have each group write an explanation of how this case could have been resolved through negotiation. Each group should select a leader to present its work to the class.

benefit. A negotiator should try to achieve a fair and good agreement that considers the needs of the other party. This is difficult because it is not the responsibility of a negotiator to protect the other party. It is, however, a responsibility not to take advantage of the other party. Most successful negotiators gain reputations as people who are tough to deal with, but honest and fair. Negotiators who are only tough are not in the same class as the ones who can be trusted.

We offer one general example of the benefits of reaching a fair agreement. In many agreements, the relationship is not ended when the deal is struck. Parties may still need to cooperate at a later time. In the example of Max and Carly, let us imagine two different agreements. In the first agreement, Max, desperate to sell the car, accepts Carly's low offer, though he feels insulted. He unhappily sells the car. In the second agreement, they dicker back and forth and finally agree on a fair price based on mutual needs and objective criteria. Later, Max, while looking through his garage, finds some additional parts for the car. If our second negotiation is the one that took place, Max might just give them to Carly. He surely won't after the first negotiation. Another possibility is that Carly later needs some information about the car's repair history. If she didn't get it at the time of the sale, after which agreement would Max be more likely to cooperate?

ESTABLISH A RELATIONSHIP

As we live our lives, we take many paths. One way of travel is to make people angry along the way. If we wish to walk that same path again, we will meet a hostile environment. Another way to walk a path is to treat people with care, respect, and honesty. That path is available for another pleasant walk. In every negotiation, there is an opportunity to establish or improve a relationship. Negotiating with that in mind is important.

Our discussion of negotiation occurs in a chapter about contract breach. Lawsuits can often protect and establish rights in these situations. They are often necessary, and even vital. However, they also usually damage or terminate relationships. In contrast, by negotiating, we can many times reach an accommodation that can preserve a customer, a supplier, or a friend. The trick is knowing when protection is necessary and when a friend is worth keeping.

CONCLUSION

The most important thing you can do before a negotiation is prepare. If you prepare, the other points we have made will no doubt occur to you. Using PUDGE will improve your negotiation skills. Remember, though, that there is nothing that works every time. Don't judge success by one good or bad experience. Also remember that being a good negotiator requires practice and experience.

 TERMS TO REMEMBER

♦ **negotiation** Communication for the purpose of persuasion.

Teaching Note

Excerpts from the Uniform Commercial Code can be found in the Resource center at the back of this book. You might have students turn to this section and skim these excerpts to get a feeling for how such codes are worded.

Suggested Additional Resources

Aaron, Richards. *Bankruptcy Law Fundamentals.* New York: Clark-Boardman Publishing Co., 1989.

Epstein, David G. *Epstein's Debtor-Creditor Law in a Nutshell,* 4d ed. St. Paul, MN: West Publishing Co., 1991.

The Guide to American Law. St. Paul, MN: West Publishing Co, 1983. Annual updates are available.

Hensen, Ray D. *Hensen's Hornbook on Secured Transactions Under the UCC,* 2d ed. St. Paul, MN: West Publishing Co., 1979.

Jentz, Miller, Cross. *West's Business Law: Alternate Edition,* 5d ed. St. Paul, MN: West Publishing Co., 1993.

Office of Consumer Affairs, write to: 1009 Premier Building, 1725 "I" St., N.W., Washington, D.C. 20201.

UNIT 3

Commercial and Consumer Law

Almost all activities that involve the sale of goods are covered by the Uniform Commercial Code, or UCC. The UCC has one purpose: To encourage business activities. It does so by making the law governing the purchase and sale of goods clear and simple. The UCC also provides a consistent law for most of the fifty states. Consider the following:

1. A transaction might involve a contract for the sale of goods. Article 2 of the UCC examines all the parts of this transaction.
2. A check might be used to pay for the goods. Article 3 on commercial paper covers this part of the transaction.
3. The seller may keep an interest in the goods until paid any balance owed. Article 9, secured transactions, covers this part of the transaction.

This unit deals with the legal issues that ordinarily arise in commercial transactions. It also discusses related statutes created to protect consumers, and introduces creditor and debtor rights and the unique American right to bankruptcy.

Mastery Objectives

By the end of this chapter, students will be able to:

- Describe "goods" under the Uniform Commercial Code
- Ascertain who holds title to goods at any given time
- Explain a merchant's obligation in a sales contract

- Characterize offer and acceptance in a sale
- List UCC requirements under the Statute of Frauds
- Delineate exceptions to the UCC Statute of Frauds
- Determine buyer/seller risk of loss

LEGAL BACKGROUND

Because of the nearly daily purchase of goods that we all make, studying the law relating to sales of goods is relevant not only to a study of business but also to our daily lives. This chapter introduces this topic and reviews some topics that were introduced in the contracts chapters.

The Uniform Commercial Code is probably the most important piece of commercial legislation in the history of the United States. Article 2 governs the law of the sale of goods. Because of its nearly uniform applicability, students may be confused about whether the UCC is a state or federal law. As a general rule the UCC favors the formation of contracts, and fewer formalities are required. It is important to note that different rules often apply to those who are UCC "merchants."

In this chapter we provide a brief discussion of UCC concepts of title, risk of loss, and insurable interest. The inclusion of the definitions of common delivery terms should also be useful to the students.

Chapter

14

Sales

Activity Sheets
Reviewing Legal Concepts 14 *TRB*
Enrichment Activity 14 *TRB*

Student Activity Workbook
Chapter 14 Activities

Tests
Chapter 14 Test *TRB*
Chapter 14 WESTEST Computerized Testing

Handbook of Selected Court Cases
Pestana v. *Karinol Corp.*
Landshire Food Service v. *Coghill*

West's Business Law and Legal Environment Videodisc
Still Frames and Motion Segments as shown

> *"Everyone lives by selling something."*
> **Robert Lewis Stevenson, 1850–1894**
> **Scottish novelist**

When we study sales contracts, we move away from common law principles to statutory law. As noted in the unit introduction, the statutory law governing sales transactions is the Uniform Commercial Code. The purpose of the UCC is to encourage commerce—the buying and selling of goods. It does so by making the laws governing the purchase and sale of goods more clear, simple, and consistent.

In this chapter, we describe the basics of the sales contract as set forth in the UCC. We then discuss the passage of title to goods, the risk of loss, and insurable interest.

◆ THE SALE OF GOODS

A sales contract is governed by the common law principles applicable to all contracts. The rules of offer, acceptance, consideration, capacity, and legality apply to all sales contracts. However, the UCC changes some of these common law rules for contracts for the sale of goods. The law of sales is found in Article 2 of the UCC, commonly called the Sales Act.

In determining what rules govern a contract, it is always a good idea to note the subject matter of the contract and the kind of parties involved. If the subject matter is goods, the UCC governs and changes some common law rules. If the subject matter is real estate or services, only common law principles apply. The relationship between general contract law and the law governing sales of goods is illustrated in Exhibit 14-1. Most sales rules apply to all sellers and buyers of goods. In some situations, rules only apply if one or both of the sellers are merchants.

At this point, we need to answer several basic questions about what we have been discussing: What is a sale? What are goods? Who is a merchant?

WHAT IS A SALE?

A **sale** is "the passing of title from the seller to the buyer for a price." **Title** is the formal right of ownership of property. The price is usually money, but it can also be other goods or services.

WHAT ARE GOODS?

To be *goods*, property must be *tangible*, and it must be *movable*. **Tangible property** has physical existence—it can be touched or seen. In contrast, **intangible property**—such as corporate stocks, patents, and ordinary contract rights—has conceptual existence. Its value is what it represents. A *movable* item is something that can be carried from place to place. Real estate or land is thus excluded from sales law.

◆ **sale** The passing of title to property from the seller to the buyer for a price.

◆ **title** The formal right of ownership of property.

◆ **tangible property** Property that has physical existence and can be distinguished by the senses of touch and sight. A car is tangible property.

◆ **intangible property** Property right created by law whose value is not in its physical existence. Ownership in a business or of a contract is an intangible property.

Prereading Activity

Tell students to list on a sheet of paper five "sales" in which they were the buying or selling party. Then ask them to write at what point they stopped being the owner if they were the seller or they became the owner if they were the buyer. Explain that the concepts of *title* and *risk of loss* as applied to sales are discussed in this chapter.

Enrichment

The first sentence of this chapter points out, "When we study sales contracts, we move away from common law principles to statutory law." Remind students that statutory law is an area of law dealing with statutes and that statutes are laws originated by the U.S. Congress or a state legislative body, passed by that body, and usually signed by the executive official, i.e., the president or governor.

Reteaching Activity

In order to make sure students fully understand the definitions of tangible and intangible property, have a student volunteer go to the chalkboard and write two headings. One heading should be "TANGIBLE PROPERTY" and the other heading should be "INTANGIBLE PROPERTY." Then have student volunteers call out examples of each of these types of property and have the student volunteer write each of the examples in the appropriate category.

Have students look through the yellow pages of the telephone book to find examples of merchants selling goods, real estate, and services. Write headings at the top of three columns: "GOODS," "REAL ESTATE," "SERVICES." Categorize companies listed in the yellow pages by writing the company name and what is being sold. Tell students to write "UCC" after those that would probably be covered by the UCC.

Have the students look at the list of items that are specifically identified as goods in the UCC. Remind students that these items were specifically identified as goods to avoid confusion. Then have students write a brief explanation (two to three sentences) for each of these items, explaining how confusion might have existed had these items not been specifically identified as goods. Allow volunteers to share their explanations with the class.

VIDEODISC NOTE
Much of the material that is conveyed in the exhibits of *West's Business and Personal Law* is also conveyed in the still frames on the **West Business Law and Legal Environment Videodisc**. For more information and directions for use, please see the Index and Description of Contents for the **West Business Law and Legal Environment Videodisc** that is found in your *Teacher's Resource Binder*.

328

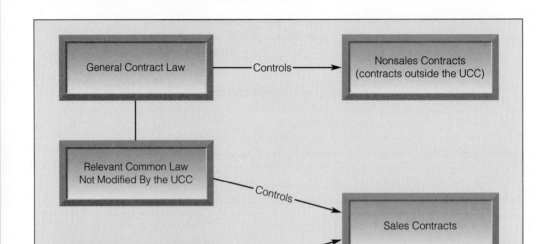

EXHIBIT 14-1
LAW GOVERNING CONTRACTS

To avoid confusion, some items are specifically identified as goods in the UCC.

1. A contract for the sale of minerals (including oil and gas) is a contract for the sale of goods if the seller is to remove the minerals from the land. However, if the buyer is to remove the minerals from the land, it is a contract for the sale of real estate.

2. A contract for the sale of growing crops or timber is always a contract for the sale of goods. If John purchases three tons of unharvested tomatoes, John has purchased goods.

3. A contract for specifically manufactured goods is a contract for the sale of goods, not services. If John hires Carlos to build him a special racing bike, John is buying a good.

4. The sale of food or drink by a restaurant is a sale of goods and not of services. Buying a hamburger and a side of french fries from your favorite fast food outlet is buying goods.

WHO IS A MERCHANT?

Sometimes, the UCC provides that special business standards should be imposed on merchants, because merchants are expected to have a high degree of business experience. The same higher standards do not apply to the casual or inexperienced ("consumer") seller or buyer.

Discussion Starter

Stimulate a class discussion by asking students if they would be considered merchants if they had a yearly garage sale? Monthly? Weekly? What is the difference between a casual seller and a merchant?

Legal Focus Example

Read this Legal Focus Example to the class. Ask the class if they can think of any other examples that could also fit here. Allow volunteers to share their examples.

Reteaching Activity

In order to be sure that your students can understand how the UCC changes the general law of contracts, you might want them to refresh their memory of *offer* and *acceptance* by having them reread the Chapter 8 Summary.

Sales   329

A **merchant** is a person who *deals in goods* of the kind involved in the sales contract. Persons are also merchants if they hold themselves out as having knowledge and skill unique to the practices or goods involved in the transaction. Merchants include retailers, wholesalers, and manufacturers of the goods being sold. They may also include banks and universities. A merchant for one type of good is not necessarily a merchant for another type.

♦ **merchant** A businessperson who regularly *deals in goods* of the kind involved in the sales contract.

 LEGAL FOCUS – EXAMPLE

A sporting-equipment retailer is a merchant when selling tennis equipment but not when selling stereo equipment. A private party who holds a once-a-year garage sale is not a merchant. That same person is a merchant if he or she holds a garage sale every weekend.

In summary, a person is a merchant when he or she either regularly deals in or is very knowledgeable about the goods being sold.

 ## THE SALES CONTRACT

We have said that the UCC changes the general law of contracts in some ways. The following sections summarize these changes.

THE OFFER

In general contract law, a contract is formed when an offer is accepted. In sales transactions, however, it is often difficult to determine exactly when a contract is created. The UCC states that a contract can exist even if the moment it was created cannot be determined.

Open Terms   The common law of contracts requires that an offer be definite. If the offer is definite, the parties (and the courts) can determine its essential terms when it is accepted. A sales contract is not too indefinite even if one or more terms are left open as long as (1) the parties intended to form a contract and (2) there is a reasonable basis for the court to grant an appropriate remedy. The UCC allows parties to provide for the following *open terms* in a contract, among others.

Open Price Term   If the parties have not agreed on a price, the court will determine a reasonable price at the time for delivery. If the price is not agreed to through the fault of one party, the other party can either treat the contract as canceled or fix a reasonable price.

Open Payment Term   When parties do not specify how payment is to be made, payment is due at the time when and the place where the buyer is to receive the goods. The buyer can make payment using any commercially normal means—for example, a check or credit card. If the seller demands payment in cash, the buyer must be given a reasonable time to get it.

Have students write a paragraph or two on the firm offer rule and its exception.

Legal Focus Example

Read to the class this Legal Focus Example dealing with the concept of the *firm offer*. Ask the class if they can think of any other examples of firm offers that could also fit here. Allow volunteers to share their examples with the class.

Teaching with the Videodisc

The still frames listed below from the **West's Business Law and Legal Environment Videodisc** can be used with this chapter. To access this material, use the bar codes or the frame numbers included in the Videodisc Instructor's Manual found in the *TRB*.

Law of Sales
Law Governing Contracts
Contract Law Compared with Law of Sales
Battle of the Forms
Article 2 Statute of Frauds
UCC Article 2 Delivery Terms
When Title Passes in Absence of Agreement
Passage of Risk of Loss in Absence of Breach
Voidable Title
Void Title
Entrusting of Goods to a Merchant
Seller's Remedies for Buyer's Breach
Buyer's Remedies for Seller's Breach
Tender of Performance by Seller
Performance by the Buyer

Open Delivery Term   When the method of delivery is not specified, delivery is at the seller's place of business. If the seller does not have a place of business, delivery is at the seller's residence. When goods are located someplace else and both parties know it, delivery is made there. If the time for shipment or delivery is not agreed on, then delivery is within a "reasonable time."

Two facts should be kept in mind about open terms. First, the more terms left open, the less likely a court will be to find that the parties intended a contract. Second, if the *quantity* term—how many or how much of something is being sold—is not agreed to, the courts generally have no basis for determining a remedy. The sales contract will fail unless the contract is an output or a requirements contract.

In an **output contract**, the seller agrees to sell and the buyer agrees to buy all of what the seller produces. In a **requirements contract**, the buyer agrees to purchase and the seller agrees to sell all the buyer needs, or requires. Because both output and requirements contracts are common in the business world, the UCC specifically provides for their enforcement.

Merchant's Firm Offer   A special rule called the **firm offer** rule applies only to merchants. Under common law contract principles, an offer can be revoked, or withdrawn, at any time before acceptance. The major exception is an option contract. As discussed in Chapter 8, under an option contract, a price is paid to the offeror for his or her promise to keep the offer open for a stated period.

The UCC adds the firm offer exception. A offer made by a merchant made in writing cannot be revoked for the stated period or a reasonable time not exceeding three months. The offer must, however, be both *written* and *signed* by the merchant.

◀ LEGAL FOCUS – EXAMPLE

Ben Ford cannot make up his mind about buying some new Ezeview binoculars "on sale until November 16th" for $55 at Raus Department Store. Ryan Razzsett, the store manager, gives Ben a signed note stating, "Raus Department Store will sell to Ben Ford, Ezeview binoculars for $55 until December 1st." Because the offer is in writing and signed by the merchant, Ben has the right to buy the binoculars for $55 for the two weeks.

ACCEPTANCE

Acceptance of an offer to buy or sell goods generally may be made in any reasonable manner and by any reasonable means.

◆ **output contract**
A contract in which the seller agrees to sell to the buyer, and the buyer agrees to purchase from the seller, all of something the seller produces.

◆ **requirements contracts**   A contract in which the buyer agrees to purchase from the seller, and the seller agrees to sell to the buyer, all of some good the buyer requires.

◆ **firm offer**   An offer for the sale of goods made in writing and signed by a merchant. The UCC provides that a firm offer is binding for the time stated, up to three months.

LEGAL BACKGROUND

Under the common law, unauthorized means of acceptance are effective as long as acceptance is received by any specified deadline. (Replying by letter to an offer asking for a reply by fax within five days is effective, for instance, as long as it is received within five days.) When an offeror does not specify a means of acceptance, the UCC provides that it can be made by any means of communication reasonable under the circumstances. (For example, replying by overnight delivery service to an offer asking for a reply within five days would be considered effective.)

◆ LEGAL FOCUS ~ EXAMPLE

An offer states, "Answer by telephone within five days." If the offeree sends a letter, and it is received within five days, a valid contract is formed.

Under the common law, if Alder makes an offer to Beale, and Beale accepts but adds a slight change, there is no contract. As explained in Chapter 8, the so-called mirror-image rule, by which the acceptance must mirror the offer, makes Beale's action a rejection of, and a counteroffer to, Alder's offer.

Under the UCC, if the offeree's response indicates a *definite* acceptance of the offer, a contract is formed. This is true even if the acceptance includes terms in addition to or different from those in the original offer. The UCC, however, provides that the offeree's communication is not an acceptance if the changed terms are made subject to, or conditional upon, the offeror's agreement.

LEGAL FOCUS ~ PROBLEM

Phillips offers to sell Hunt 650 pounds of turkey thighs at a specified price and with specified delivery terms. Hunt responds, "I accept your offer for 650 pounds of turkey thighs, *as evidenced by a city scale weight certificate*, at the price and delivery terms stated in your offer." Is a contract formed?

Yes. A contract is created, even though the acceptance adds the words "as evidenced by a city scale weight certificate." If, however, Hunt says, "I accept your offer for 650 pounds of turkey thighs *on the condition* that the weight be evidenced by a city weight certificate," there is no contract. It is a counteroffer, which, of course, Phillips could accept.

If a contract is formed even though the acceptance varies from the offer, the question becomes, what are the terms of the contract? Do the terms of the offer govern, or the terms of the acceptance? The UCC answers this question. In doing so, it attempts to solve the so-called *battle of the forms* between business buyers and sellers.

◆ LEGAL FOCUS ~ EXAMPLE

The battle of the forms describes a common business situation. The buyer phones the seller and places an order. Immediately after placing the order, the buyer confirms it by sending a purchase order to the seller. (Exhibit 14-2 is an example of a purchase order. The front of the form is the actual order for particular goods. The back contains

Reteaching Activity

You might want to remind students that in Chapter 9 consideration was defined as "value given in return for a promise." Consideration consists of two parts: (1) something of legal value must be given in exchange for the promise and (2) it must be part of a bargain for exchange.

Legal Focus Problem

Allow a student volunteer to read the first Legal Focus Problem aloud to the class. Make sure that students understand that there is no consideration for Louise's promise to pay more for the goods. Then ask a student volunteer to suggest a possible answer to the question posed at the end of this problem.

Legal Focus Problem

Read the second Legal Focus Problem to the class. Ask a student volunteer to compare the situation in this problem to the situation in the Legal Focus Problem above. In which Legal Focus Problem does Louise not act in good faith? In which Legal Focus Problem does Jim not act in good faith?

Ethical Concern

Tell students to write two or three paragraphs explaining how the UCC forces parties to be ethical through the concept of *good faith* and telling whether they think the law should force contract parties to act ethically.

standard contract clauses and terms governing the sale.) The seller completes a form called a confirmation of order and sends a copy to the buyer. Often, these forms have different terms. Often, they cross in the mail. Usually, the products arrive as ordered, on schedule, and the buyer pays. However, what if a problem occurs and the forms sent by the parties differ? We have the battle of the forms. If one of the parties argues that there is no contract because of the differences, that party is wrong. The UCC provides a method of sorting out whether the offeror or offeree's terms prevail in such situations.

CONSIDERATION

The rules of consideration that apply to the making of a contract are not changed by the UCC. However, the UCC replaces the common law rule that contract changes, or modifications, require new consideration. The UCC states that "an agreement *modifying a contract* needs no consideration to be binding."

Contract modifications must be requested in good faith. Modifications forced on another party are not enforceable.

◀ LEGAL FOCUS ~ PROBLEM

Jim agrees to manufacture and sell certain goods to Louise for a stated price. Later, a sudden change in the market makes it difficult for Jim to sell the items to Louise at the agreed price without a loss. Jim tells Louise of his situation, and Louise agrees to pay more for the goods. Later, Louise reconsiders and refuses to pay more than the original price. Will the courts enforce Louise's agreement to pay more for the goods?

Under the UCC, Louise's promise to modify the contract is enforceable. It needs no consideration to be binding. Louise is bound by the modified contract. In this example, a shift in the market is a *good faith* reason for contract modification. **Good faith** in the UCC means honesty in fact and the observance of reasonable commercial standards of fair dealing in the trade.

◆ **good faith**
Honesty in fact and the observance of reasonable commercial standards of fair dealing in the trade.

◀ LEGAL FOCUS ~ PROBLEM

Assume that in the situation involving Jim and Louise, there has been no change in the market. However, Jim knows that Louise desperately needs the goods immediately. He refuses to deliver unless Louise agrees to pay more money. If Louise promises to pay the additional money, is the promise enforceable?

EXHIBIT 14-2

AN EXAMPLE OF A PURCHASE ORDER (FRONT)

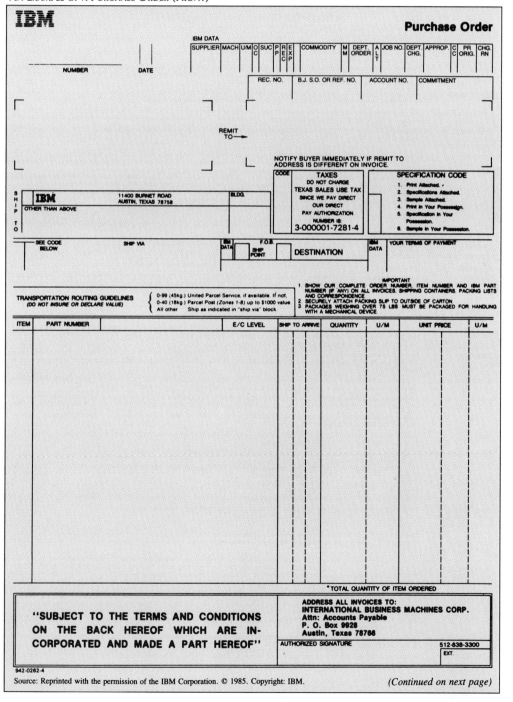

Source: Reprinted with the permission of the IBM Corporation. © 1985. Copyright: IBM.

(Continued on next page)

Enrichment

Guide the students in examining the sample purchase order that begins on this page and continues on the next page. Point out that the front of the form will contain the actual order for particular goods while the back of the form lists standard contract clauses and terms governing the sale. You might also point out to students that there is a large notice in the bottom left-hand corner of the front of the form that reads "Subject to the terms and conditions on the back hereof which are incorporated and made a part hereof." Explain to students that this notice appears on the front of the form next to the signature and verifies that the signee is agreeing to the terms and conditions enumerated on the back of the form.

Collaborative Learning Activity

Divide the class into groups of three. Assign each group a portion of the STANDARD TERMS AND CONDITIONS of the IBM Purchase Order in Exhibit 14-2 to analyze. Then have each group explain its section to the class.

Extension Activity

Have students acquire sample purchase order forms from local businesses. Individual students can orally describe the terms of the purchase orders to the class. Groups of students can compare the terms of a number of samples and write their findings in a report.

EXHIBIT 14-2 (CONTINUED)
AN EXAMPLE OF A PURCHASE ORDER (BACK)

STANDARD TERMS AND CONDITIONS

IBM EXPRESSLY LIMITS ACCEPTANCE TO THE TERMS SET FORTH ON THE FACE AND REVERSE SIDE OF THIS PURCHASE ORDER AND ANY ATTACHMENTS HERETO:

PURCHASE ORDER CONSTITUTES COMPLETE AGREEMENT   This Purchase order, including the terms and conditions on the face and reverse side hereof and any attachments hereto, contains the complete and final agreement between International Business Machines Corporation (IBM) and Seller. Reference to Seller's bids or proposals, if noted on this order, shall not affect terms and conditions hereof, unless specifically provided to the contrary herein, and no other agreement or quotation in any way modifying any of said terms and conditions will be binding upon IBM unless made in writing and signed by IBM's authorized representative.

ADVERTISING   Seller shall not, without first obtaining the written consent of IBM, in any manner advertise, publish or otherwise disclose the fact that Seller has furnished, or contracted to furnish to IBM, the material and/or services ordered hereunder.

APPLICABLE LAW   The agreement arising pursuant to this order shall be governed by the laws of the State of New York. No rights, remedies and warranties available to IBM under this contract or by operation of law are waived or modified unless expressly waived or modified by IBM in writing.

CASH DISCOUNT OR NET PAYMENT PERIOD   Calculations will be from the date an acceptable invoice is received by IBM. Any other arrangements agreed upon must appear on this order and on the invoice.

CONFIDENTIAL INFORMATION   Seller shall not disclose to any person outside of its employ, or use for any purpose other than to fulfill its obligations under this order, any information received from IBM pursuant to this order, which has been disclosed to Seller by IBM in confidence, except such information which is otherwise publicly available or is publicly disclosed by IBM subsequent to Seller's receipt of such information or is rightfully received by Seller from a third party. Upon termination of this order, Seller shall return to IBM upon request all drawings, blueprints, descriptions or other material received from IBM and all materials containing said confidential information. Also, Seller shall not disclose to IBM any information which Seller deems to be confidential, and it is understood that any information received by IBM, including all manuals, drawings and documents will not be of a confidential nature or restrict, in any manner, the use of such information by IBM. Seller agrees that any legend or other notice on any information supplied by Seller, which is inconsistent with the provisions of this article, does not create any obligation on the part of IBM.

GIFTS   Seller shall not make or offer gifts or gratuities of any type to IBM employees or members of their families. Such gifts or offerings may be construed as Seller's attempt to improperly influence our relationship.

IBM PARTS   All parts and components bailed by IBM to Seller for incorporation in work being performed for IBM shall be used solely for such purposes.

OFF-SPECIFICATION   Seller shall obtain from IBM written approval of all off-specification work.

PACKAGES   Packages must bear IBM's order number and show gross, tare and net weights and/or quantity.

PATENTS   Seller will settle or defend, at Seller's expense (and pay any damages, costs or fines resulting from), all proceedings or claims against IBM, its subsidiaries and affiliates and their respective customers, for infringement, or alleged infringement, by the goods furnished under this order, or any part or use thereof of patents (including utility models and registered designs) now or hereafter granted in the United States or in any country where Seller, its subsidiaries or affiliates, heretofore has furnished similar goods. Seller will, at IBM's request, identify the countries in which Seller, its subsidiaries or affiliates, heretofore has furnished similar goods.

PRICE   If price is not stated on this order, Seller shall invoice at lowest prevailing market price.

QUALITY   Material is subject to IBM's inspection and approval within a reasonable time after delivery. If specifications are not met, material may be returned at Seller's expense and risk for all damages incidental to the rejection. Payment shall not constitute an acceptance of the material nor impair IBM's right to inspect or any of its remedies.

SHIPMENT   Shipment must be made within the time stated on this order, failing which IBM reserves the right to purchase elsewhere and charges Seller with any loss incurred, unless delay in making shipment is due to unforeseeable causes beyond the control and without the fault or negligence of Seller.

SUBCONTRACTS   Seller shall not subcontract or delegate its obligations under this order without the written consent of IBM. Purchases of parts and materials normally purchased by Seller or required by this order shall not be construed as subcontracts or delegations.

(NON-U.S. LOCATIONS ONLY)   Seller further agrees that during the process of bidding or production of goods and services hereunder, it will not re-export or divert to others any IBM specification, drawing or other data, or any product of such data.

TAXES   Unless otherwise directed, Seller shall pay all sales and use taxes imposed by law upon or on account of this order. Where appropriate, IBM will reimburse Seller for this expense.

TOOLS   IBM owned tools held by Seller are to be used only for making parts for IBM. Tools of any kind held by Seller for making IBM's parts must be repaired and renewed by Seller at Seller's expense.

TRANSPORTATION   Routing—As indicated in transportation routing guidelines on face of this order.
F.O.B.—Unless otherwise specified, ship collect, F.O.B. origin.
Prepaid Transportation (when specified)—Charges must be supported by a paid freight bill or equivalent.
Cartage   ) No charge allowed
Premium Transportation   ) unless authorized
Insurance   ) by IBM.
Consolidation—Unless otherwise instructed, consolidate all daily shipments to one destination on one bill of lading.

COMPLIANCE WITH LAWS AND REGULATIONS   Seller shall at all times comply with all applicable Federal, State and local laws, rules and regulations.

EQUAL EMPLOYMENT OPPORTUNITY   There are incorporated in this order the provisions of Executive Order 11246 (as amended) of the President of the United States on Equal Employment Opportunity and the rules and regulations issued pursuant thereto with which the Seller represents that he will comply, unless exempt.

EMPLOYMENT AND PROCUREMENT PROGRAMS   There are incorporated in this order the following provisions as they apply to performing work under Government procurement contracts: Utilization of Small Business Concerns (if in excess of $10,000) (Federal Procurement Regulation (FPR) 1-1.710-3(a)); Small Business Subcontracting Program (if in excess of $500,000) (FPR 1-1.710-3 (b)); Utilization of Labor Surplus Area Concerns (if in excess of $10,000) (FPR 1-1.805-3(a)); Labor Surplus Area Subcontracting Program (if in excess of $500,000) (FPR 1-1.805-3 (b)); Utilization of Minority Enterprises (if in excess of $10,000) (FPR 1-1.1310-2 (a)); Minority Business Enterprises Subcontracting Program (if in excess of $50,000) (FPR 1-1.1310-2(b)); Affirmative Action for Handicapped Workers (if $2,500 or more) (41 CFR 60-741.4); Affirmative Action for Disabled Veterans and Veterans of the Vietnam Era (if $10,000 or more) (41 CFR 60-250.4); Utilization of Small Business Concerns and Small Business Concerns Owned and Controlled by Socially and Economically Disadvantaged Individuals (if in excess of $10,000) (44 Fed. Reg. 23610 (April 20, 1979)); Small Business and Small Disadvantaged Business Subcontracting Plan (if in excess of $500,000) (44 Fed. Reg. 23610 (April 20, 1979)).

WAGES AND HOURS   Seller warrants that in the performance of this order Seller has complied with all of the provisions of the Fair Labor Standards Act of 1938 of the United States as amended.

WORKERS' COMPENSATION, EMPLOYERS' LIABILITY INSURANCE   If Seller does not have Workers' Compensation or Employer's Liability Insurance, Seller shall indemnify IBM against all damages sustained by IBM resulting from Seller's failure to have such insurance.

No. This modification lacks a legitimate commercial reason. It is ineffective, because Jim is violating his duty of good faith.

STATUTE OF FRAUDS

The UCC includes a Statute of Frauds provision that applies to contracts for the sale of goods. If the price of goods in a sales contract is $500 or more, there must be a writing to enforce the contract. The parties can satisfy the Statute of Frauds by a written memorandum of an oral agreement. Any writing must be signed by the party against whom enforcement is sought. (See the discussion of the Statute of Frauds in Chapter 11.)

Sufficiency of the Writing   The UCC has relaxed the requirements necessary to satisfy the Statute of Frauds. A writing or a memorandum is sufficient if it shows that the parties intended to form a contract. It must, however, be signed by the party (or someone authorized to act for the party) against whom enforcement is sought. The contract is not enforceable for more goods than the quantity shown in the writing. All other terms can be proved in court by oral testimony.

Written Confirmation between Merchants   The UCC provides a special rule for merchants. Merchants can satisfy the writing requirement

EXHIBIT 14-3
INFORMAL SALES CONTRACT

7-19-93

Dear Brandon:

Bargaining with you is no fun; you drive a hard bargain. This letter confirms our agreement that I will sell to you my blue mountain bike, my weight set with bench, the Blaster stereo set with speakers and the trampoline for $650. If I didn't need the money for college, you never would get my things for that price. Have fun with my stuff and good luck on your senior year at ole Bella Vista High.

Your friend the graduating kid,

Scott
Scott

Legal Focus Problem

Allow a student volunteer to read the first Legal Focus Problem aloud to the class. Have the students suggest a possible answer to the question posed at the end of this problem. Remind students that if the merchant who receives a written confirmation does not object in writing within ten days after receipt, the writing will be enforceable against him or her, even though he or she has not signed anything.

Collaborative Learning Activity

Divide the class into groups of three, and have them write down two examples of situations for each of the three exceptions to the UCC Statute of Frauds.

Legal Focus Problem

Guide the students in reading the second Legal Focus Problem, and explain to students that in this case, even though there was no written contract, Womach will probably not be allowed to claim the Statute of Frauds as a defense because the draperies are specially manufactured goods for a particular buyer and are probably not suitable for resale to others in the ordinary course of the seller's business, and because Carla had not only substantially started to manufacture the goods; she had finished the manufacturing of the goods.

336

when one merchant sends a signed written confirmation to the other merchant. The writing must state the terms of the agreement. The merchant receiving the confirmation can object to it in writing within ten days. If the receiving merchant does not object, the contract is enforceable, though he or she has not signed anything.

◆ LEGAL FOCUS ~ PROBLEM

Alfonso is a merchant buyer in Cleveland. He telephones and orders $4,000 worth of goods from Goldstein, a New York City merchant seller. Two days later, Goldstein sends a written confirmation detailing the terms of the oral contract. Alfonso receives the confirmation letter. He opens it and puts it in a pile of papers to be read later. If later, Alfonso does not want the contract enforced, can he use the Statute of Frauds as a defense? He has not signed anything.

Alfonso must give Goldstein a written notice of objection to the contents of the confirmation within ten days of receipt. If he leaves the confirmation in the pile to gather dust, it will satisfy the UCC's merchant exception.

Exceptions   Besides the merchant exception, there are three other exceptions to the UCC Statute of Frauds.

1. An oral contract for specially manufactured goods is enforceable without a writing. The seller must have substantially begun manufacture of the goods, and they cannot be suitable for resale to others.

◆ LEGAL FOCUS ~ PROBLEM

Womach orders custom-made draperies for her new boutique from Carla's Curtains. The price is $1,000, and the contract is oral. The merchant seller, Carla, finishes the draperies and tenders delivery to Womach. Womach refuses to pay for them, though the job has been completed on time. Womach claims she is not liable because the contract is oral. Can Womach claim the Statute of Frauds as a defense?

Probably not. If the unique style of the draperies makes it improbable that the seller can find another buyer, Womach is liable to the seller. Carla made a substantial beginning in manufacturing the special draperies before Womach's repudiation. (Indeed, she finished the job.) Of course, the court must still be convinced that an oral contract existed.

2. The party against whom enforcement of a contract is sought admits in pleadings (written answers), testimony, or other court proceedings

Guide the class in looking at these three
exceptions to the UCC Statute of Frauds. Do
you feel that each of these three exceptions is
fair to both parties? Why or why not? Are
there any other exceptions to the UCC Statute
of Frauds that you believe should be made?
Please explain.

Divide the class into small groups to read and
discuss the first Legal Focus Problem found
here. Each group should choose a leader to
explain its response to the question posed at
the end of this problem.

Guide the students in discussing *usage of trade*. Point
out that in interpreting a
commercial agreement,
courts will often look to
usage of trade or the common practices and methods
followed in a particular
place, vocation, or trade.
Stimulate a class discussion
regarding usage of trade by
asking the following questions: Do you feel that usage
of trade should be considered in interpreting com-
mercial agreements? How
does this hinder merchants
who are new to a particular
business?

Sales 337

that a contract for sale was made. Enforceability is limited to the quantity of goods admitted.

 LEGAL FOCUS - PROBLEM

Lane and Sugg negotiate an agreement over the telephone. During the
negotiations, Lane requests a delivery price for 500 gallons of
gasoline and a separate price for 700 gallons of gasoline. Sugg replies
that the price would be the same, $1.10 per gallon. Lane orally orders
500 gallons. Sugg honestly believes that Lane ordered 700 gallons
and tenders that amount. Lane refuses the shipment of 700 gallons,
and Sugg sues for breach. Lane's answer and testimony admit an oral
contract was made, but only for 500 gallons. Is the contract
enforceable? If so, for what quantity?

Since Lane admits the existence of the oral contract, Lane cannot
plead the Statute of Frauds as a defense. However, the contract is enforceable only to the extent of the quantity admitted (500 gallons).

3. Payment is made and accepted or goods have been received and accepted. This is a "partial performance" exception. The oral contract is
enforced to the extent of actual performance.

These exceptions and other ways in which sales law differs from general
contract law are summarized in Exhibit 14-4.

COURSE OF DEALING, USAGE OF TRADE, AND COURSE OF PERFORMANCE

In interpreting a commercial agreement, the court will look to typical
commercial practices and to the circumstances surrounding the particular
contract and the parties. These practices and circumstances are called
course of dealing, usage of trade, and course of performance. **Course of
dealing** includes the actions and communications that took place between
the parties before the agreement in question was made. **Usage of trade** is
a practice or method of dealing followed regularly in a particular place, vocation, or trade. **Course of performance** is the conduct that has occurred under the terms of a particular agreement.

Legal Focus Problem

Read to the class the second
Legal Focus Problem found
here. Have student volun-
teers suggest possible
answers to the question
posed at the end of this
problem.

**Critical Thinking
Activity**

Tell a student to write on
the board: *Usage of trade*.
Ask another student to dictate the definition: *a practice or method of dealing
followed regularly in a particular place, vocation, or
trade*. Ask students to think
of examples of usage of
trade; call on individuals to
give examples as a student
lists them on the board.

◆ **course of dealing**
Prior conduct between
contracting parties that
establishes a common
basis for their
understanding.

◆ **usage of trade**
A common business
practice in a place,
vocation, or trade.

◆ **course of
performance** The
way the parties conduct
themselves toward each
other after the contract
is created.

 LEGAL FOCUS - PROBLEM

Janson's Lumber Company contracts with Barrymore to sell
Barrymore a specified number of "2-by-4s." The lumber in fact does
not measure 2 inches by 4 inches but rather 1⅞ inches by 3¾ inches.
If Barrymore objects to the lumber delivered, can usage of trade and
course of prior dealings show that the lumber complied with the
contract?

Vocabulary Activity

Divide students into groups of four to study and define the vocabulary terms: *open terms, open price term, open payment term, open delivery term, firm offer, good faith, Statute of Frauds, course of dealing, usage of trade,* and *course of performance.*

Ethical Concern

Define the term *unconscionable* to your students. Then ask them to write an essay on their thoughts about the unconscionable clause. Should consumers just be required to be better-informed, or is this clause really necessary nowadays?

---

338   Commercial and Consumer Law

	Contract Law	**Sales Law**
Contract Terms	Contract must contain all material terms.	Open terms acceptable, if parties intended to form a contract, but contract is not enforceable beyond quantity term.
Acceptance	Mirror-image rule applies. If additional terms are added in acceptance, a counter-offer is created.	Additional terms will not negate acceptance unless acceptance is made expressly conditional on assent to the additional terms.
Contract Modification	Requires consideration.	Does not require consideration.
Irrevocable Offers	Option contracts (with consideration).	Merchant's firm offers (without consideration).
Statute of Frauds Requirements	All material terms must be included in the writing.	Writing required only if sale of goods of $500 or more but not enforceable beyond quantity specified. *Exceptions:* 1. Contracts for specially manufactured goods. 2. Contracts admitted to under oath by party against whom enforcement is sought. 3. Contracts will be enforced to the extent goods are delivered or paid for. 4. Confirmatory memorandum (between merchants): Contract is enforceable if merchant fails to object in writing to confirming memorandum within 10 days.

EXHIBIT 14-4
MAJOR DIFFERENCES BETWEEN CONTRACT LAW AND SALES LAW

Yes. Janson's can prove that 2-by-4s are never exactly 2 inches by 4 inches by applying usage of trade or course of dealing, or both. Janson's can show that in previous transactions, Barrymore took 1⅝-inch-by-3¾-inch lumber without objection. In addition, Janson's can show that in the trade, 2-by-4s are commonly 1⅝ inches by 3¾ inches.

UNCONSCIONABILITY

The UCC allows the court to evaluate a contract or any clause in a contract for unconscionability. An **unconscionable contract** is one that is so

◆ **unconscionable contract** A contract that is so unfair and one-sided that it would be unreasonable to enforce it.

unfair and one-sided that it is unreasonable to enforce it. If the court determines that a contract was unconscionable *at the time it was made*, the court can (1) refuse to enforce the contract, (2) enforce the remainder of the contract without the unconscionable clause, or (3) limit the application of any unconscionable clauses to avoid an unconscionable result.

◆ CHECKING YOUR PROGRESS

1. What legal principles apply in the sale of goods, of real estate, of services?
2. What is the legal definition of a sale?
3. Explain intangible property and give three examples.
4. Why does the UCC impose higher business standards on merchants than on consumers?
5. Under the UCC, what will the court do if parties to a contract have not agreed on a price?
6. How is acceptance to an offer to buy or sell goods made?
7. How does the "mirror-image rule" of offer-to-acceptance differ under the UCC from common law?

◆ TITLE, RISK OF LOSS, AND INSURABLE INTEREST

After a sales contract has been made, when does the buyer become the new owner of the goods? If the goods are damaged before the buyer takes delivery, who suffers the loss? What is sufficient delivery? Parties can agree on the answers to these and other questions in the sales contract. If they don't, the UCC provides the answers.

TITLE

Before an interest in goods passes from the seller to the buyer, the goods must exist and be identified to the contract. This second condition means the goods must be identified so they are distinguished from all other similar goods. **Identification**, then, is a designation of goods as the subject matter of the sales contract.

♦ **identification**
Designation of goods as the subject matter of sales contract.

◀ LEGAL FOCUS ~ EXAMPLE

Usually, identification is simply a matter of specific designation. For example, you contract to purchase a fleet of five cars. The contract lists the serial numbers for the cars. Another example is the purchase of all the wheat in a specific bin at a stated price per bushel.

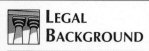
Before the UCC, title was a central concept in sales law. The party who had title bore the risk of a loss of goods (and could thus buy insurance against it). It was often difficult to determine when title passed from seller to buyer, however, and thus which party had title at the time of loss. The UCC divorced the question of title from the question of the rights and obligations of buyers, sellers, and others (subsequent purchasers, creditors). Title remains relevant under the UCC in some situations, and the UCC has rules for locating title. In most situations, however, the UCC replaces the concept of title with three other concepts—identification, risk of loss, and insurable interest. Generally, the UCC attempts to place a loss on the party who breaches a contract, the party who has physical control of the goods, or the party who was most likely to have thought of obtaining insurance. Of course, the rules do not apply if a different party caused the loss or if the parties allocated the risk in their contract. The last point is most important; parties can agree on who will bear the risk of loss.

340

Legal Focus Example

Read this Legal Focus Example aloud to the class. To make sure the students understand this example, use the following explanation. Wanamaker, Inc. purchases 500 pounds of coffee beans from Bean, Inc. The beans are stored at a commercial warehouse. At the time that Wanamaker, Inc. pays for the beans, Beans, Inc. gives Wanamaker, Inc. the warehouse receipt for the 500 pounds of coffee beans. At the time when Wanamaker, Inc. receives the warehouse receipt, title for the coffee beans has passed from Beans, Inc. to Wanamaker, Inc.

Legal Focus Problem

Read to the class the Legal Focus Problem found here. Allow student volunteers to suggest possible answers to the questions posed in the problem.

Once the goods have been identified, the buyer can get insurance on the goods and recover from third parties who damage the goods.

Passage of Title   Once goods exist and are identified, title can pass. Unless an agreement states otherwise, title passes to the buyer at the time and the place the seller performs the *physical* delivery of the goods. The delivery arrangements determine when this happens.

Shipment and Destination Contracts   A contract that requires or authorizes the seller to ship goods by carrier (such as a trucking company) is a **shipment contract**. Here, the seller is required only to deliver the goods into the hands of a carrier. Title passes to the buyer at the time and place of shipment. Delivery contracts are generally assumed to be shipment contracts if nothing to the contrary is stated in the contracts.

In a **destination contract**, the seller must deliver the goods to a particular destination. Usually, the destination is the buyer's city. Title passes to the buyer when the goods are tendered at the agreed destination.

Delivery without Movement of the Goods   Often, documents of title are used to transfer ownership of goods. A **document of title** is a writing that represents ownership of goods. Documents of title include bills of lading and warehouse receipts. A **bill of lading** is a receipt for goods signed by a carrier, such as a trucker. It serves as a contract for the transportation of the goods. A **warehouse receipt** is a receipt issued by a warehouser for goods stored in his or her warehouse. When a document of title is required, title passes to the buyer when and where the document is delivered.

♦ **shipment contract**   A sales contract by which the seller is responsible for delivering the goods to a carrier.

♦ **destination contract**   A term in a sales contract where the seller is responsible for delivering the goods to a specific destination.

♦ **document of title**   A paper, such as a bill of lading or warehouse receipt, exchanged in the regular course of business to show the right to possession of goods.

♦ **bill of lading**   A receipt for goods signed by a carrier such as a trucker that serves as a contract for the transportation of goods.

♦ **warehouse receipt**   A receipt issued by a warehouser for goods stored in the warehouse.

◆ LEGAL FOCUS – EXAMPLE

If goods are stored in a warehouse, title passes to the buyer upon delivery of the warehouse receipt to the buyer. The goods never move. The buyer can leave the goods at the warehouse, and title is unaffected.

If documents of title are not used and delivery is made without moving the goods, title to identified goods passes when and where the sales contract is made. If the goods have not been identified, title will pass when identification is made.

◆ LEGAL FOCUS – PROBLEM

Rogers sells lumber to Kimble. Kimble agrees to pick up the lumber at the yard. When does title pass if the lumber was identified before the contract was signed? When does title pass if the lumber was not identified?

Teaching with the Videodisc

At this time you may wish to show the students the motion segment titled *Risk of Loss* from the **West Business Law and Legal Environment Videodisc.** This fictional dramatization is a part of *West's Business Law's Drama of the Law Series.* Each of these dramatizations was written by award-winning writer John J. Osborne, Jr. (originator and author the *The Paper Chase*). Each of these was created by Osborne and West to bring points of law to life for your students.

The segment titled *Risk of Loss* illustrates, in a real-world setting, the passage of risk of loss in a breached sales contract.

Each of the legal implications included in this motion segment is discussed in the *Drama of the Law Instructor's Manual*, which is included in your *Teacher's Resource Binder.*

To access this motion segment, you can use the bar code provided here or punch in the frame number below.

Search Frame 16447

If the lumber was identified (segregated, marked, or in any other way distinguished from all other lumber), title passes to Kimble at contract signing. If the lumber is still in storage bins at the mill, however, title passes to Kimble when the lumber to be sold under this contract is identified.

RISK OF LOSS

If goods are destroyed or damaged after the contract is made but before performance is completed, who suffers the loss? Risk of loss is not solely based on ownership. For example, the parties can make an agreement that controls when risk of loss passes from the seller to the buyer. Specific terms in the contract can also help in determining when risk of loss passes to the buyer. These terms are listed in Exhibit 14-5.

Delivery with Movement of the Goods—Carrier Cases   If there is no express agreement as to when risk passes, the following rules apply in carrier cases—that is, when goods are shipped.

Shipment Contracts   In a shipment contract, risk of loss passes to the buyer when the goods are properly delivered to the carrier.

EXHIBIT 14-5
CONTRACT TERMS—DEFINITIONS

Term	Definition
F.O.B.	(free on board)—Indicates that the selling price of goods includes transportation costs (and that the seller carries risk of loss) to the specific F.O.B. place named in the contract. The place can be either the place of shipment (for example, seller's city or place of business) or at place of destination (for example, buyer's city or place of business).
F.A.S.	(free alongside vessel)—Requires that the seller at his or her own expense and "risk" deliver the goods alongside the vessel before risk passes to the buyer.
C.I.F. or C.&F.	(cost, insurance, and freight, or just cost and freight)— Requires, among other things, that the seller "put the goods in possession of a carrier" before risk passes to the buyer. (These are basically pricing terms and remain shipment contracts, not destination contracts.)
Delivery ex-ship	(delivery from the carrying vessel)—Means that risk of loss does not pass to the buyer until the goods leave the ship or are otherwise properly unloaded.

Extension Activity

Have volunteers use the phone book to locate wholesalers and/or trucking companies in your area. Have them call and ask for a sample bill of lading to be mailed to the school for the class to study. Analyze each form to see where the seller and buyer would be indicated and where the goods would be listed. Discuss when title would transfer and who is responsible while the goods are being transported.

VIDEODISC NOTE
Much of the material that is conveyed in the exhibits of *West's Business and Personal Law* is also conveyed in the still frames on the **West Business Law and Legal Environment Videodisc.** For more information and directions for use, please see the Index and Description of Contents for the **West Business Law and Legal Environment Videodisc** that is found in your *Teacher's Resource Binder.*

Legal Focus Problem

Read to the class the Legal Focus Problem found here. Allow student volunteers to suggest possible answers to this problem.

Reteaching Activity

Assign each student a partner to work with in defining and giving examples (on paper) for all of the risk of loss rules found in this section.

Caption Answer

Risk of loss is not solely based on ownership, and specific shipping terms can determine when risk of loss passes to the buyer.

Collaborative Learning Activity

Divide the class into small groups. Have each group reread Exhibit 14-5 and the Legal Focus Problem at the top of this page. Then assign each group one of the four contract terms listed in Exhibit 14-5, and have each group write a Legal Focus Problem dealing with its contract term. Each group should choose a leader to share its Legal Focus Problem with the class. Allow student volunteers from the other groups to answer the question posed at the end of each Legal Focus Problem.

◆ LEGAL FOCUS ~ PROBLEM

A seller in Houston, Texas, sells 500 cases of grapefruit to a buyer in New York. The goods are sent F.O.B. Houston. F.O.B. means "free on board." F.O.B. Houston means the goods are to be sent free of charge to the seller. The buyer pays the transportation charges from Houston. When does risk of loss pass?

Risk passes to the buyer when the goods are properly placed in the carrier's possession in Houston. If the goods are damaged in transit, the loss is the buyer's (though the buyer has legal rights against the carrier, subject to limitations).

Destination Contracts In a destination contract, the seller must deliver the goods to a particular destination. The risk of loss passes to the buyer when the goods are tendered to the buyer at that destination. If the contract in the preceding example had been F.O.B. New York, the risk of loss during transit would have been the seller's.

Delivery without Movement of the Goods Frequently, the buyer is to pick up the goods from the seller. If the seller is a merchant, risk of loss passes to the buyer when he or she takes possession of the goods. If the seller is not a merchant, risk of loss passes to the buyer upon tender of de-

What effect do shipping terms have on risk of loss?

You might explain the differences between *sale-on-approval* and *sale-or-return* contracts by explaining that a sale-on-approval is a "trial sale" and the risk stays on the seller until the buyer accepts the goods or keeps them beyond the trial period. A "sale-or-return" gives the buyer the option of keeping or returning the goods. Risk of loss shifts when the buyer takes possession. If the goods are returned, the risk shifts back to the seller when the goods are delivered.

Read to the class the Legal Focus Example found at the bottom of this page. Ask the class if they can think of any other examples that could also fit here. Allow volunteers to share their examples.

Invite a local merchant to your classroom to speak to your students about sales, returns, and risk of loss. Have your students make a list of questions to ask the merchant before he or she visits.

livery. A tender of delivery occurs when the seller makes conforming goods available to the buyer (with any necessary notice).

Sale-on-Approval and Sale-or-Return Contracts A **sale on approval** is not a sale until the buyer accepts (approves) the offer. A **sale or return** is a sale that can be canceled by the buyer without liability. Specific rules apply to the passage of risk in these sales.

Sale on Approval When a seller allows a buyer to take the goods on a trial basis before the buyer decides to buy, a sale on approval occurs. Title and risk of loss from causes beyond the buyer's control stay with the seller until the buyer accepts (approves) the goods. The buyer can accept expressly (by saying "I accept"), or by doing something inconsistent with the trial purpose, or by keeping the goods after the end of the trial period. If the buyer decides not to buy the goods, he or she should notify the seller within the trial period.

Sale or Return With a sale or return contract, the seller allows a buyer to return all or a portion of the goods. If a buyer wishes to keep any portion of the goods, those goods are sold to him or her. When the buyer receives possession at the time of sale, the title and risk of loss pass to the buyer. Both remain with the buyer until the goods are returned to the seller. If the buyer fails to return the goods within the agreed time, the sale is completed. The return of the goods is at the buyer's risk and expense.

Under a contract of sale or return, the buyer has title immediately, whereas under a contract for sale on approval, the buyer does not have title until the sale is approved. It is often difficult to determine from a particular transaction which exists—a contract for sale on approval or a contract for sale or return. The UCC states that (unless otherwise agreed) if the goods are for the buyer to use, the transaction is a sale on approval. If the goods are for the buyer to resell, the transaction is a sale or return.

Consignment In a **consignment**, the owner of goods (the *consignor*) delivers them to another (the *consignee*) to sell. A consignment is a type of sale or return. If the consignee sells the goods, she or he must pay the consignor for them. If the goods are not sold, they are returned to the consignor.

Risk of Loss If the Sales Contract Is Breached A breach of the contract by either party may affect the risk of loss. Generally, the party in breach bears the risk of loss.

One type of breach involves nonconforming goods. Risk of loss does not pass to the buyer if the goods do not conform to the contract.

◆ **sale on approval** A conditional sale of goods that becomes absolute when the buyer decides to buy or use the goods in a way consistent with intent to buy the goods.

◆ **sale or return** A conditional sale in which the buyer can return all or a portion of the goods.

◆ **consignment** A transaction in which the owner of goods delivers them to another who has the authority to sell them.

◇ LEGAL FOCUS ~ EXAMPLE

A buyer orders blue widgets from a seller, F.O.B. the seller's plant. The seller ships black widgets, giving the buyer the right to reject. The widgets are damaged in transit. The risk of loss falls on the seller. The

Have a student volunteer
read this Legal Focus Problem aloud to the class. Have
the student suggest a possible answer to the question
posed at the end of this
problem. Remind students
that they can use the Legal
Focus features as review
tools when studying for
tests.

A buyer and seller can have an insurable
interest in identical goods at the same time.
Discuss whether both can recover from an
insurance company if the goods are damaged
or destroyed.

risk would have been on the buyer if blue widgets had been shipped.

INSURABLE INTEREST

Buyers and sellers often buy insurance to protect themselves against damage, loss, or destruction of goods. A party purchasing insurance must have
an **insurable interest** in the insured item to obtain a valid policy. Insurance laws—not the UCC—determine insurable interest. The UCC is
helpful, however, because it contains certain rules regarding the buyer's
and seller's insurable interest in goods.

◆ **insurable interest**
A real economic risk
related to rights in
property or a person's
well-being. A person
with an insurance
interest can purchase
insurance coverage.

Buyer's Insurable Interest   Buyers have an insurable interest in *identified* goods. The moment the goods are identified in the contract by the
seller, the buyer has a "special" property interest that allows him or her to
obtain necessary insurance coverage.

◄ LEGAL FOCUS – PROBLEM

In March, a farmer sells a cotton crop he hopes to harvest in October.
After the crop is planted, the buyer insures it against hail damage. In
September, a hailstorm ruins the crop. When the buyer files a claim
under her insurance policy, the insurer refuses to pay the claim,
asserting that the buyer has no insurable interest in the crop. Is the
insurer correct?

No, the insurer is not correct. The buyer had an insurable interest in the
crop when it was planted, since she had a contract to buy it.

Seller's Insurable Interest   A seller has an insurable interest in goods as
long as he or she keeps title to the goods. Even after title passes to a buyer,
however, a seller who has a "security interest" in the goods (a right to secure payment) still has an insurable interest and can insure the goods.

Both a buyer and a seller can thus have an insurable interest in identical
goods at the same time. One must, however, have an actual loss to recover
from an insurance company.

SALES BY NONOWNERS

Problems occur when persons attempt to sell goods they do not own or
goods they have acquired by questionable means. The UCC covers the
rights of two parties who lay claim to the same goods, sold with problems
of title.

Void Title   A buyer may unknowingly purchase goods from a seller who
is not the owner of the goods. If the seller is a thief, the seller's title is
void—legally, no title exists. The true owner can reclaim the goods from
the buyer.

Legal Focus Example

Guide the students in looking at this Legal Focus Example. To make sure the students understand this example, ask the following questions: What does it mean when it says "Jim has void title to those goods"? Why is this true? Who has legitimate title to the goods while they are in Jim's possession? Who has legitimate title to the goods after Jim has sold the goods to Sandra?

Ethical Concern

Have students read the Legal Focus Example on this page. Stimulate a class discussion about whether the buyer in good faith is being treated fairly when the real owner of the goods claims them. What are the rights of the unsuspecting buyer?

Sales   345

 LEGAL FOCUS – EXAMPLE

If Jim steals goods owned by Margaret, Jim has void title to those goods. If Jim sells the goods to Sandra, Margaret can reclaim them from Sandra. It does not matter that Sandra acted in good faith and honestly did not know that the goods were stolen. Sandra can, however, sue Jim for breach of contract because he sold goods he did not own. (This is discussed further in Chapter 15.)

Voidable Title   One who has goods obtained by fraud in his or her possession has *voidable title* to those goods. Also, a person's title to goods is voidable if the person paid for the goods with a check without sufficient funds in the bank or if the goods were purchased from a minor.

A seller with voidable title has the power to transfer a good title to a **good faith purchaser** for value. A good faith purchaser is one who buys without knowledge of any defect in the seller's title. The real owner cannot recover goods from a good faith purchaser for value. In contrast, if the buyer of the goods is not a good faith purchaser for value, then the actual owner of the goods can reclaim them from the buyer (or from the seller, if the goods are still in the seller's possession).

The following Law in Action feature is about the sale of an automobile that had been fraudulently purchased by the seller. Note the importance of the "good faith purchaser" rule in the court's determination of whether the buyer received valid title to the Rolls Royce.

The Entrustment Rule   Entrusting goods to a merchant *who deals in goods of that kind* gives the merchant the power to transfer the title to those goods to a buyer in the ordinary course of business. *Entrusting* means both delivering goods to a merchant and leaving purchased goods with a merchant for later delivery or pickup. A "buyer in the ordinary course" is a person who buys in good faith from a person who deals in goods of that kind.

◆ **good faith purchaser** A purchaser of goods who buys without knowledge of any circumstance that would cause her or him to have a reasonable doubt about the seller's title to the goods being sold.

Legal Focus Problem

Read to the class the Legal Focus Problem found here. Allow student volunteers to suggest possible answers to the question posed at the end of this problem. You might stimulate a class discussion regarding the entrustment rule by asking the following questions: Do you believe that it is fair to Jan that Kim gets good title against Jan's claim of ownership while Jan can merely sue the jeweler for breach of contract in the tort of conversion? Would it matter if the watch was a family heirloom?

 LEGAL FOCUS – PROBLEM

Jan leaves her watch with a jeweler to be repaired. The jeweler sells both new and used watches. The jeweler sells Jan's watch to Kim, a customer, who does not know that the jeweler did not have the right to sell the watch. Does Kim have good title despite the fact that the watch belongs to Jan and not the jeweler?

Yes. Kim gets *good title* against Jan's claim of ownership. Jan had entrusted the goods to the jeweler, who sold them in the ordinary course of business. Jan can sue the jeweler for breach of contract and the tort of conversion.

Read

Introduce this *Law in Action* feature by asking students the following questions: What would you think if you heard that someone was selling a Rolls Royce automobile for less than fair market value? If you could afford it, would you be interested in buying the car? Why or why not? What if the seller acted suspiciously? Would you change your mind about purchasing the car? Why or why not? Then have a student volunteer read this *Law in Action* feature aloud to the class.

Discuss

Stimulate a class discussion of this *Law in Action* feature by asking the following questions: How did Hyken find out about the Rolls Royce that was for sale? What was the asking price of the car? Was this price high or low? What type of identification did Coghill provide? How did Coghill explain the fact that the newspaper ad described a 1980 Rolls Royce when the car was a 1979 model? How did Hyken pay Coghill for the automobile? Why did the St. Louis County police take possession of the automobile from Hyken? Who really had title to the

Rolls Royce? What did Hyken have to prove to be acknowledged as a good faith purchaser? What was the decision of the Missouri Court of Appeals in the *Landshire Food Service, Inc.* v. *Coghill* case? What reasons did the court give for this decision? Do you feel that Hyken should have been suspicious about the seller's rights in the vehicle? Why or why not? Do you feel that the court decision was fair?

◆ Law in Action

LAW IN YOUR LIFE: GROUNDS FOR SUSPICION

In early September of 1984, Barry Hyken saw an ad in a St. Louis newspaper for the sale of a 1980 Rolls Royce Corniche for $62,000. Hyken was a businessperson and the owner of Landshire Food Service, Inc. As a hobby, he collected and traded expensive imported cars. Hyken called a friend and dealer of imported automobiles and asked whether $62,000 was a good price for a 1980 Rolls Royce Corniche. The friend thought the asking price was on the low side of fair market value. He told Hyken that he "could not go wrong" if he bought the car for that amount.

Hyken arranged a meeting with the seller at a hotel near the St. Louis Airport. The seller represented himself as J. A. Coghill. When Hyken requested identification, the seller produced a New Hampshire driver's license with a New Hampshire address and an air-carrier crew card with an Illinois address. Hyken did not question the difference between the addresses or Coghill's "explanation" of the difference—that he was moving from Illinois to the St. Louis area. When Hyken asked Coghill why the newspaper ad read "1980 Rolls Royce," when the car was a 1979 model, Coghill said it was a newspaper misprint.

Hyken agreed to purchase the auto. The parties met at Hyken's office to complete the sale. Coghill produced an Illinois certificate of title that was signed by J. A. Coghill as seller and dated August 25, 1984. It showed the transferee as Executive Jet Leasing. Coghill explained that this assignment was an attempted transfer to his company, which he had not completed on the advice of his accountants. Coghill crossed out Executive Jet Leasing and wrote in "Landshire

If you buy a stolen car can you get title?

Foods and B. J. Hyken" as the transferees, without correcting the date. Coghill also signed an affidavit (statement under oath) stating that the first transferee had been inserted by mistake. Hyken then gave Coghill a cashier's check for $58,500 and a check from Landshire Foods for $3,500. On September 17, Hyken registered the title and paid the sales tax.

Two weeks later, the St. Louis County Police took possession of the vehicle at the request of Illinois authorities and placed it in a police garage. It turned out that the seller was not J. A. Coghill. Mr. Coghill was an Illinois resident who had sold his 1979 Rolls Royce Corniche in August of 1984 to a person who claimed to be Daniel Bellman. Bellman had given Coghill a cashier's check for $94,500 and requested that the transferee on the Illinois certificate of title be listed as his business firm, Executive Jet Leasing. When Coghill learned from his bank that the cashier's check was forged, he reported the vehicle as stolen.

When goods are obtained by fraud, the person obtaining the goods has voidable title.

Ethical Concern

Ask a volunteer to define a *good faith purchase*. Stimulate a class discussion on the outcome of this case. Why was Hyken not considered a good faith purchaser? Help students realize that they must be cautious when buying goods from others.

 Law in Action (Continued)

If the fraudulently obtained goods are then sold to a good-faith purchaser, the buyer can claim valid title against the original owner. Thus, if Hyken could prove he was a good faith purchaser, he would have valid title to the vehicle. To be a good faith purchaser, Hyken would have had to have purchased the auto without knowing of any circumstances that would make a person of ordinary care ask about the seller's title to the goods. Were the irregularities attending the sale of the Rolls Royce sufficient to have caused a "person of ordinary prudence" to be suspicious about the seller's rights in the vehicle?

The Missouri Court of Appeals[1] held that, under these circumstances, a reason-

able person would have been suspicious. The contradictory addresses given by the seller, the vehicle's low price, and the existence of a prior transferee on the title (indicating a prior assignment) should have, according to the court, made a reasonable person investigate whether the seller had good title. Since Hyken did not investigate, he was not a good faith purchaser in the eyes of the law. "A buyer will not be protected," the court stated, "where he is put on notice of the irregularities in a seller's title either by defects in the face of the certificate or by other circumstances. The requisite notice 'may be imparted to a prospective purchaser by actual or constructive notice of facts which would place a reasonably prudent person upon inquiry as to the title of the car he is about to purchase.'"

1. *Landshire Food Service, Inc. v. Coghill,* 709 S.W.2d 509 (Mo.App. 1986).

◆ CHECKING YOUR PROGRESS

1. How is the UCC application of consideration different from the common law application?

2. How can parties to contracts for sale of goods satisfy the Statute of Frauds?

3. If no specific agreement exists, when does title of the goods pass to the buyer?

4. Describe the consignment procedure and tell who has title during the consignment.

Checking Your Progress (Answers)

1. Modifications require new consideration under common law but do not under the UCC.
2. Parties to contracts for sale of goods can satisfy the Statute of Frauds by written memorandum of an oral agreement or by writing an agreement if the sales contract is $500 or more.
3. Title passes to the buyer at the time and the place where the seller performs the physical delivery of the goods, based on the delivery arrangements.
4. A consignment is a type of sale or return in which the owner of goods delivers them to another to sell. Title to the goods is held by the consignee while he or she has posession of them.

Teaching A Case In Point

Read

Introduce this feature by explaining to the students that it deals with the effect of shipping terms on the risk of loss. Then have a student volunteer read this *A Case In Point* feature aloud to the class.

Discuss

Use the following questions to stimulate a class discussion about this *A Case In Point* feature: Who is the defendant in this case? Who is the plaintiff? What delivery terms were contained in the contract? What happened to the watches that were shipped by Karinol? What was the decision of the trial court in this case? What was the decision of the appellate court? What reasons did the court give for its decision?

◆ A CASE IN POINT ◆

PESTANA v. KARINOL CORP.

District Court of Appeal of Florida, Third District, 1979.
367 So.2d 1096.

In this case, the court reviewed the effect of shipping terms on risk of loss. Under the UCC, the F.O.B. point determines whether a contract is a shipment contract or a destination contract. That determination is critical in shifting risk of loss from the seller to the buyer if the goods are lost or damaged in transit. Consider in reading the case whether either insurance or a different F.O.B. point might have better protected the buyer.

FACTS The defendant, Karinol Corporation, contracted to ship watches to the plaintiff, Pestana, in Chetumal, Mexico. The contract contained no delivery terms, such as F.O.B., and no specific terms for allocation of loss while the goods were in transit. The plaintiff–buyer, Pestana, had made a deposit. The watches were shipped by Karinol, but they were lost in transit. Pestana sought a refund for the deposit, claiming that the risk of loss was the seller's.

Karinol claimed that Pestana suffered the risk of loss and owed the balance of the purchase price. The trial court held for the defendant, Karinol Corporation, and ruled that the buyer, Pestana, was liable for the loss.

ISSUE Who should bear the risk of loss when no provision concerning risk allocation or delivery terms is included in the sales contract?

DECISION The buyer. The appellate court upheld the trial court's decision.

REASON After discussing risk of loss under both shipment and destination contracts, the court held that when the contract has "(a) no explicit provisions allocating the risk of loss while the goods are in the possession of the carrier and (b) no delivery terms such as F.O.B. place of destination, . . . [s]uch a contract, without more, constitutes a shipment contract wherein the risk of loss passes to the buyer when the seller duly delivers the goods to the carrier. . . ." Thus, "where the risk of loss falls on the buyer at the time the goods are lost or destroyed, the buyer is liable to the seller for the purchase price of the goods sold."

In order to help students review what they have learned in Chapter 14, you might wish to:
1. Have a student volunteer, or volunteers, read the Chapter Summary aloud.
2. Allow the students to work with partners to complete the *Using Legal Language* activity.
3. Assign the *Checking for Comprehension* exercise as homework.

4. Allow the students to work in small groups to complete the *Applying Legal Concepts* activities.
5. As a class, complete the *Applying the Law* activities. (Please note that you may have to help students with vocabulary so that they adequately understand all of the *Applying the Law* material.)

Sales   349

CHAPTER 14   REVIEW

SUMMARY

FORMATION OF SALES CONTRACTS

What Are Goods?

1. Tangible movable property.
2. Minerals, if they are to be removed from the property by the seller. (If to be removed by the buyer, minerals are real property.)
3. Growing crops and timber.
4. Property that is specially manufactured.
5. Food, even when prepared (as in a restaurant).

What Is a Merchant?

1. A person who regularly deals in goods of the type being sold.
2. A person with special knowledge about the goods being sold.

Offer and Acceptance

1. A contract can exist even if the moment of its creation cannot be determined.
2. Not all terms have to be included for a contract to result; for example, particulars of performance can be left open.
3. A signed written offer by a *merchant* is called a firm offer, and is binding for the time stated.
4. Not all terms have to be included for a contract to result.
5. Variations in terms between the offer and the acceptance may not be a rejection but may be an acceptance.
6. Acceptance may be made by any reasonable means.

Consideration

A modification of a contract for the sale of goods made in good faith does not require consideration.

Requirements under the Statute of Frauds

1. All contracts for the sale of goods priced at $500 or more must be in writing.
2. Exceptions to the requirement include:
   a. A written confirmation of an oral contract *between merchants* is not objected to in writing by the receiver within ten days.
   b. The oral contract is for specially manufactured goods, and the seller has substantially started to manufacture the goods.

Course of Dealing, Usage of Trade, and Course of Performance

1. Course of dealing includes previous actions and communications between the contracting parties.
2. Usage of trade is any business practice or method of dealing followed so regularly in a place, vocation, or trade as to justify an expectation that it will be observed in the transaction in question.
3. Course of performance is conduct that occurs under the terms of a particular agreement.

Unconscionability

An unconscionable contract is one that is so unfair and one-sided that it would be unreasonable to enforce it.

TITLE, RISK OF LOSS, AND INSURABLE INTEREST

Shipment Contracts

In absence of agreement, title and risk pass upon seller's delivery of conforming goods to the carrier.

1–E, 2–A, 3–I, 4–G, 5–C,
6–J, 7–D, 8–H, 9–F, 10–B

Checking for Comprehension (Answers)

1. All sales contracts are governed by the rules of offer, acceptance, consideration, capacity, and legality.
2. Student answers will vary. They should describe a situation in which the person has knowledge and skill unique to the practices or goods involved in the transaction. They could also describe a situation in which the person regularly deals in, or is very knowledgeable about, the goods being sold.
3. The court will determine: a "reasonable price at the time for delivery" if the price is omitted; that payment is due at the time and place when the buyer is to receive the goods if the parties do not specify how payment is to be made; and that delivery is at the seller's place of business if method of delivery is not specified.
4. Exceptions to the UCC Statute of Frauds include the following: (1) when a merchant receives a signed written confirmation from another merchant, he or she can object to it in writing within ten days; (2) an oral contract for specially manufactured goods is enforceable if the seller has sub-

350

stantially begun manufacture of the goods and they cannot be suitable for resale to others; (3) the party against whom enforcement of a contract is sought admits in pleadings, testimony, or other court proceedings that a contract for sale was made; or (4) payment is made and accepted or goods have been received and accepted.
5. The risk of loss passes to the buyer when the goods are properly delivered to the carrier in a shipment contract but passes to the buyer when the goods are delivered to the buyer in a destination contract.
6. In a sale on approval, title to goods transfers to the buyer when he or she accepts or approves the goods, does something inconsistent with the *trial* purpose, or keeps the goods after the trial period ends.
7. If the seller of goods stole them, the true owner retains title rather than the buyer or the seller because the seller's title is void. If the seller obtained the goods by fraud, he or she

---

Destination Contracts

In absence of agreement, title and risk pass upon seller's tender of delivery of conforming goods to the buyer at the point of destination.

Goods That Are to Be Delivered without Physical Movement

1. In absence of agreement, if the goods are not represented by a document of title:

   a. Title passes upon the physical delivery of the goods.

   b. Risk generally passes to the buyer upon the buyer's receipt of the goods.

Sale-on-Approval Contracts

Title and risk of loss from causes beyond the buyer's control remain with the seller until the buyer approves (accepts) the goods.

Sale-or-Return Contracts

When the buyer receives possession of the goods, title and risk of loss pass to the buyer. The buyer can return both to the seller upon return of the goods.

Passage of Risk of Loss in a Breached Sales Contract

Generally, the party in breach bears the risk of loss.

Insurable Interest

1. Buyers have an insurable interest in goods the moment the goods are identified to the contract by the seller.

2. Sellers have an insurable interest in goods as long as they have (1) title to the goods or (2) a security interest in the goods.

Sales by Nonowners

1. Between the owner and a good-faith purchaser:

   a. Void title—Title cannot be transferred to anyone, including a good faith purchaser.

   b. Voidable title—Title is transferred to a good faith purchaser.

   c. Goods that are entrusted to a merchant—Title is transferred to a good faith purchaser.

◆ USING LEGAL LANGUAGE

Directions: Match each term with the statement that best defines that term.

1. document of title
2. firm offer
3. good faith purchaser
4. insurable interest
5. intangible property
6. sale
7. sale on approval
8. shipment contract
9. unconscionable
10. usage of trade

A. an offer for sale of goods made in writing and signed by a merchant

B. a common business practice in a place, vocation, or trade

C. a property right created by law, its value is not in its physical existence

D. a conditional sale that becomes absolute when the buyer decides to buy or use the goods in a way consistent with intent to buy the goods

E. bills of lading, warehouse receipts, and other papers exchanged in the regular course of business that show the right to possession of goods

F. a contract that is so unfair and one-sided that it would be unreasonable to enforce it.

has voidable title, but title transfers to a good-faith purchaser who buys without knowledge of any defect in the seller's title.

8. Under the Statute of Frauds, any contract for the sale of goods priced at $500 or more must be in writing to be enforceable. An exception to this rule is made when the contract has been partially performed. An oral agreement will be enforceable to the extent that payment has been made and accepted or to the extent that goods have been received

and accepted. Since Vernon accepted Fresher Food's down payment of $125, their contract will be enforceable to this amount. That means that Vernon is obligated to deliver to Fresher Foods 100 bushels of corn (which, at $1.25 per bushel, totals $125).

9. Yes. Under the UCC, a merchant offeror, who in a signed writing gives assurance that an offer will remain open, creates an irrevocable offer (without payment of consideration) for the time period stated in the assur-

ance, up to a three-month period. Jennings, as a merchant, was obliged to hold the offer (which had been made in a signed writing— the letter) open until October 9. Wheeler's acceptance of the offer prior to October 9 created a valid contract, which Jennings breached when he sold the Thunderbird to a third party.

10. The answer depends on whether Jennings properly revoked his offer prior to Wheeler's acceptance. If Jennings had sold the car to a third party prior to October 9 and had notified Wheeler that he was revoking his offer to sell the Thunderbird to Wheeler, the revocation would be valid because Jennings was not a merchant. As a nonmerchant, Jennings would be allowed to revoke his offer at any time prior to October 9 and prior to acceptance. If Jennings failed to notify Wheeler of his revocation, as seems to be the situation here, Jennings would be bound in contract to sell the Thunderbird to Wheeler upon Wheeler's acceptance of the offer.

G. a real economic risk related to rights in property or a person's well being

H. a term in a sales contract where the seller is responsible for delivering the goods to a carrier

I. a purchaser of goods who buys without knowledge of any circumstances that cause her or him to have a reasonable doubt about the seller's title to the goods being sold

J. the passing of title to property from the seller to the buyer for a price

◆ CHECKING FOR COMPREHENSION

1. What legal principles govern all sales contracts?

2. Describe a situation in which an individual party in a sales contract would be held to the same high standard as a merchant.

3. A contract is enforceable under the UCC even if some terms are open. How are each of the following open terms handled by the court: open price, open payment, open delivery?

4. Describe four exceptions to the UCC Statute of Frauds.

5. Who is responsible for damaged or destroyed goods in a shipment contract, a destination contract?

6. When does title to goods transfer to the buyer in a sale on approval?

7. Who holds title to goods if a buyer purchases goods from a seller who is not the owner and who lacks the right to sell?

8. Fresher Foods, Inc. *orally* agreed to purchase from Dale Vernon, a farmer, 1,000 bushels of corn for $1.25 per bushel. Fresher Foods paid $125 down and agreed to pay the remainder of the purchase price upon delivery, which was

scheduled for one week later. When Fresher Foods tendered the balance of $1,125 on the scheduled day of delivery and requested the corn, Vernon refused to deliver it. Fresher Foods sued Vernon for damages, claiming Vernon had breached their oral contract. Can Fresher Foods recover, and, if so, to what extent?

9. On September 1, Jennings, a used-car dealer, wrote a letter to Wheeler in which he stated: "I have a 1955 Thunderbird convertible in mint condition which I will sell you for $13,500 at any time before October 9. [signed] Peter Jennings." By September 15, having heard nothing from Wheeler, Jennings sold the Thunderbird to another party. On September 29, Wheeler accepted Jennings's offer and tendered the $13,500. When Jennings told Wheeler he had sold the car to another party, Wheeler claimed Jennings had breached their contract. Is Jennings in breach? Explain.

10. If, in problem 9, Jennings had been a student instead of a used-car dealer, would the answer to the question be different? In what way?

Applying the Law . . . You Be the Judge (Answers)

1. The court held that the oral contract (including the guaranty as part thereof) was a sale of goods and fell under the UCC 2-201, which provides that a contract for the sale of goods for the price of $500 or more is not enforceable unless there is a writing sufficient to indi-

cate that a sale has been made or an exception is applicable. The primary contention of Cudahy is that Holloway is a merchant, and UCC 2-201(2) provides that the Statute of Frauds is not a defense between merchants if one sends the other a written confirmation and the one receiving the confirmation does not object in writing within ten days of receipt of the confirmation. A merchant is defined by the UCC as "a person who deals in goods of the kind or otherwise by occupation holds himself out as having knowledge or skill peculiar to the practices or goods involved in the transaction." The court held that Holloway, as a real estate broker, was not a merchant in the purchase or use of cheese. In fact, the court stated, "the nature of [Holloway's] occupation precluded her dealing in goods at all." Thus, the "between merchants" exception to the Statute of Frauds is not applicable, and Holloway's Statute of Frauds defense was upheld.

2. Yes. Crump is fully responsible for the cost of repairs brought on by the lightning. Under UCC 2-509(3), the risk of loss passed to Crump upon his receipt of the antenna. The fact that title remained with Lair is unimportant with respect to the risk of damage to the antenna. In rejecting the concept that title controls which party bears the risk of loss, the

code generally places the risk of loss upon the party in possession and control of the goods. Here, Crump enjoys the benefit of ownership in that he has both use and possession of the antenna. The policy behind this result is that Crump is in a better position to control the use of the antenna and to insure against damage to it. In fact, most homeowners have insurance policies to cover just such damage.

3. Honeycutt did not succeed in his defense, and Lane was able to recover. This case is

governed by UCC 2-403, which allows good-faith purchasers to retain possession when they have purchased from persons with voidable titles. Garrett had a voidable title since he purchased the boat and trailer with a check that bounced. Honeycutt, however, was not a good-faith purchaser. He paid $2,500 for items valued at more than $6,000, and he accepted a document that was not an official certificate of title. This "was sufficient to support the court's finding that defendant was not a good-faith purchaser."

 ## APPLYING LEGAL CONCEPTS

In a workgroup of three or four students, design a purchase order for a fictitious company. Determine the company name and products sold. Write the terms and conditions. Key the purchase order on a typewriter or computer and print a copy for each student. Compare the purchase orders designed by each group.

 ## APPLYING THE LAW . . . YOU BE THE JUDGE

1. Peggy Holloway was a real estate broker who guaranteed payment for shipment of over $11,000 worth of mozzarella cheese sold by Cudahy Foods Co. to Pizza Pride in Jamestown, North Carolina. The entire arrangement was made orally. Cudahy mailed to Holloway an invoice for the order, and Holloway did not object in writing to the invoice within ten days of receipt. Later, when Cudahy demanded payment from Holloway, Holloway denied ever guaranteeing payment for the cheese and raised the Statute of Frauds as an affirmative defense. Cudahy claims that the Statute of Frauds cannot be used as a defense as both Cudahy and Holloway are merchants, and Holloway failed to object within ten days to Cudahy's invoice. Discuss Cudahy's argument. [*Cudahy Foods Co. v. Holloway*, 286 S.E.2d 606 (N.C.App. 1982)]

2. Crump, a television fanatic, purchased a television antenna and antenna tower from Lair Distributing Co., with a ten-year conditional sales contract that obligated him to make monthly payments. The contract provided that Lair Co. would retain title until Crump had completed all payments. The contract stated, among other things, that Crump was not to move or tamper with the antenna during the ten-year payment period. About a year

later, lightning struck and destroyed Crump's antenna. At Crump's request, Lair Co. performed extensive repairs on it. Crump refused to pay for the repairs, claiming that risk of loss or damage resulting from the lightning should be borne by Lair. Was Lair successful in suing for the cost of its repairs? [*Lair Distributing Co. v. Crump*, 48 Ala.App. 72, 261 So.2d 904 (1972)]

3. Fred Lane was the owner of Lane's Outboard and was engaged in the business of selling boats, motors, and trailers. He sold a new boat, motor and trailer to a person who called himself John Willis. Willis took possession of the goods and paid for them with a check for $6,285. The check was later dishonored. About six months later, Jimmy Honeycutt bought the boat, motor, and trailer for $2,500 from a man identified as "Garrett," who was renting a summer beach house to the Honeycutts that year. Honeycutt had known Garrett for several years. Lane sought to recover the boat, motor, and trailer from Honeycutt. Honeycutt's sole defense was that he was a good faith purchaser and therefore Lane should not be able to recover from him. Discuss whether Lane will succeed in his defense. [*Lane v. Honeycutt*, 14 N.C.App. 436, 188 S.E.2d 604 (1972)]

Mastery Objectives

By the end of this chapter, students will be able to:
- List types of warranties
- Explain how warranties are created
- Describe possible defenses to warranties
- Identify product liability

Prereading Activity

Ask students about purchases they have made in which the salesperson talked to them about the product. Did the salesperson make any promises about what the product would do? Did the product actually work the way the salesperson said? Ask the students what they did if the product did not work as the salesperson said it would. What responsibilities and what rights do a salesperson and a purchaser have in sales transactions?

Sales Warranties and Product Liability

Chapter

15

LEGAL BACKGROUND

Because of the complexity of many sales performance issues, we have chosen to cover what we believe to be the most important topic—warranties. A warranty under the UCC is an express or implied promise about the goods. In every case, a plaintiff seeking recovery for breach of warranty must prove that a warranty was made, that any disclaimer is inoperative, and that the warranty has been breached.

This chapter also combines the warranty discussion with tort issues to address the very important topic of product liability. Product liability is the general term used for suits brought by buyers against retailers and manufacturers for defective products and injuries resulting from the defects. These suits may be brought on several theories, including: breach of warranties provided in the UCC, negligence, and strict liability. Over the past 25 years, few areas of law have undergone the development that product liability has, and the differences in laws among the states can be considerable. Actually these differences in part explain why we discuss multiple theories for similar harm to product users.

353

Guide the students in discussing the three conditions for an express warranty under the UCC that are shown here. For each numbered point have the students suggest possible examples.

Extension Activity

Have the students look through newspapers and magazines for advertisements that include express warranties, and have them copy or clip the ads. Students should circle or underline the advertising copy that includes the express warranty in each example and explain how each is an express warranty under the UCC. Allow student volunteers to share their clippings and explanations with the class.

Enrichment

Have your students demonstrate their understanding of the difference between express warranties and statements of opinions by having them write a list of examples of both express warranties and statements of opinions.

354

Chapter 15
Resources and Assignment Guide

Activity Sheets
Reviewing Legal Concepts 15 *TRB*
Enrichment Activity 15 *TRB*

Student Activity Workbook
Chapter 15 Activities

Tests
Chapter 15 Test *TRB*
Chapter 15 WESTEST Computerized Testing

Handbook of Selected Court Cases
Roth v. *Ray-Stel's Hair Stylists, Inc.*
McKinney v. *Revlon, Inc.*

West's Business Law and Legal Environment Videodisc
Still Frames and Motion Segments as shown

---

354   Commercial and Consumer Law

"I'll warrant him heart-whole."
William Shakespeare, 1564–1616
English dramatist and poet

Warranty is an age-old concept. In sales law, a warranty is a promise by the selling party that the buyer can rely on certain facts. Just as Shakespeare warranted his friend "heart-whole" in the play *As You Like It*, so sellers warrant to buyers that their goods are as represented.

In years past, the doctrine of **caveat emptor**—let the buyer beware—was the rule in most sales contracts. In recent years, caveat emptor has been replaced by an expansion of consumer rights. The Uniform Commercial Code provides for numerous product warranties in sales contracts. Product warranties are the subject matter of the first part of this chapter. In the latter part of the chapter, we discuss liability for physical harm and property damage caused by a product or its use.

◆ **caveat emptor**
"Let the buyer beware"; a doctrine under which the buyer took the risk as to the quality of goods purchased.

◆ EXPRESS WARRANTIES

A seller can create an **express warranty** by making statements about the quality, condition, description, or performance potential of the goods. Under the UCC, express warranties are created by a seller in the following ways:

◆ **express warranty**
A statement, part of a sales contract, in which the seller assures the quality, condition, description, or performance potential of the goods.

1. The goods conform to any statement or promise of fact that the seller makes to the buyer about the goods. Such statements or promises are usually made during the bargaining process. The statement "These drill bits will *easily* penetrate stainless steel without becoming dull" is an express warranty.

2. The goods conform to a description of the goods. A label that reads "Crate contains one 150-horsepower diesel engine" and a contract that calls for the delivery of a "beige cashmere coat" create express warranties. The goods must conform to the descriptions.

3. The goods conform to any sample or model. If a salesperson demonstrates a food processor and then sells you one in a box, when you open the box you should find a product that conforms to the sample.

An express warranty can exist even if the seller did not intend one. The UCC does not require that the seller "use formal words such as 'warrant' or 'guarantee' or that he has a specific intention to make a warranty." It is necessary only that a reasonable buyer would believe that a particular representation (such as those just described) was part of the bargain.

STATEMENTS OF OPINION

Sellers' statements about the value or worth of goods do not create express warranties. Neither do recommendations or other opinions about the goods.

Call on volunteers to come before the class. Hand each volunteer a common item from the classroom, such as a textbook, a stapler, etc. Then have each volunteer make a sales pitch for that item. Instruct the volunteers to include both puffing and express warranties in their sales pitches. Have class members identify those parts of the sales pitch that include an express warranty. Have class members identify those parts of the sales pitch that are merely puffing.

◀ LEGAL FOCUS - PROBLEM

Billie, the seller claims, "This is the best used car to come along in years. It has four new tires and a 350-horsepower engine just rebuilt this year." Are the statements made by Billie express warranties?

Billie made several statements of fact that can create warranties: The automobile has an engine; it is a 350-horsepower engine; it was rebuilt this year; there are four tires on the automobile; and the tires are new. However, the seller's *opinion* that the vehicle is "the best used car to come along in years" is puffing and creates no warranty. *Puffing* is a word used to describe normal sellers' exaggerations about goods for sale. Similarly, statements about the value of goods, such as "it's worth a fortune" or "anywhere else you'd pay $10,000 for it," do not usually create warranties.

An exception does exist; the opinion of an expert can create a warranty.

◀ LEGAL FOCUS - PROBLEM

Stevens is an art dealer and an expert in seventeenth-century paintings. He states to Boller, a purchaser, that in his opinion a particular painting is a Rembrandt. Boller buys the painting. Did Stevens create an express warranty?

Yes. Stevens, as an expert, warrants the accuracy of his opinion.

It is not always easy to distinguish puffing from an express warranty. Whether the buyer's reliance on the seller's statement is reasonable is often the controlling factor. For example, a salesperson's statement that a ladder "will never break" and "will last a lifetime" is so improbable that no reasonable buyer should rely on it. The how and where of the statement is also important in determining the reasonableness of the buyer's reliance. For example, it is generally more reasonable for a buyer to rely on a statement made in a written advertisement than on a salesperson's oral statement.

◆ IMPLIED WARRANTIES

An **implied warranty** is one that the law implies from the nature or circumstances of the transaction. Warranties of title, merchantability, and fitness for a particular purpose are among the warranties in this category.

WARRANTIES OF TITLE

A **warranty of title** arises automatically in most sales contracts. Two warranties of title are discussed here.

Legal Focus Problem

Allow a student volunteer to read aloud this Legal Focus Problem. Ask the volunteer which of Billie's statements are express warranties. Which are puffing?

Critical Thinking Activity

Tell students to write down examples of "puffing" as they watch TV commercials over a week's time. Have them list at least ten examples, telling the product and the statement made about the product. Additionally, have them tell if the statement was verbal or visual.

Legal Focus Problem

Ask a student volunteer to read this Legal Focus Problem aloud to the class. Ask the student to answer the question posed at the end of this problem. Remind students that they can use the Legal Focus features as review tools when studying for tests.

♦ **implied warranty**
A warranty that the law implies through either the situation of the parties or the nature of the transaction.

♦ **warranty of title**
An implied assurance that the seller owns or has the right to sell goods.

Good Title   In a sales transaction, the seller impliedly promises (warrants) that he or she owns the goods sold and that any transfer of title is rightful.

◀ LEGAL FOCUS ～ PROBLEM

Stan steals goods from Lloyd and sells them to Cordelia. Cordelia does not know they are stolen. If Lloyd discovers that Cordelia has the goods, Lloyd has the right to reclaim them from her. Does Cordelia have any rights?

Under the UCC, Cordelia can sue Stan for breach of warranty of title. A thief cannot transfer good title even to an innocent purchaser because the thief lacks title to the stolen goods. When Stan sold Cordelia the goods, Stan *impliedly* warranted that title was valid. Since this was untrue, Stan breached the warranty of title. Stan is liable to Cordelia for damages.

No Liens   A second warranty of title can protect buyers from others, such as creditors, who claim rights against the goods. Here, the seller warrants that the goods are free of any claims by others. Such claims are described by many names, including encumbrances, security interests, debts, claims, charges, liabilities, and liens. (This is discussed further in Chapter 19.) If a creditor legally repossesses the goods from a buyer who had no actual knowledge of the security interest, the buyer can recover from the seller for breach of warranty.

◀ LEGAL FOCUS ～ PROBLEM

Harvey buys a used color television set from Suarez for cash. A month later, Roper repossesses the set from Harvey. Roper proves that she has a valid security interest in the television set, since Suarez has missed five payments. Harvey demands his money back from Suarez. Will he succeed?

The law supports Harvey. The seller of goods impliedly warrants that goods are delivered free from any security interest of which the buyer was unaware.

Disclaimer of Title Warranty   Warranties of title can usually be disclaimed, or denied. A disclaimer requires clear and specific language to be effective. A seller can modify as well as disclaim a warranty.

Read this first Legal Focus Example to the class. Explain to the class that in this example, Acme Manufacturing is only transferring such rights, title, and interest as it has in the goods. Make sure students understand that this does not mean that Acme owns the goods but that Acme probably has at least some title to those goods. Remind students that they can use the Legal Focus features as review tools when studying for tests.

Explain to the class that to say a product is *merchantable* is to say that it is fit for the market. Ask the students to provide examples of merchantable products. One possible example you might suggest to the students is meat. For the meat a butcher sells to be merchantable, it must be of reasonable quality and must not be tainted. Allow student volunteers to share their examples with the class.

Legal Focus Problem

Ask a student volunteer to read this Legal Focus Problem aloud to the class. Stimulate a class discussion of this problem by asking the following questions: What is the general purpose for which one uses an axe? What happened when Sue Joplin tried to use the axe she purchased at Gershwin's Hardware Store for this purpose?

Legal Focus Example

Read aloud to the class this second Legal Focus Example, which details non-merchantable goods. Ask the class if they can think of any other examples of non-merchantable goods that could also fit here. Allow volunteers to share their examples with the class.

Sales Warranties and Product Liability · 357

 LEGAL FOCUS ~ EXAMPLE

An example of a modified warranty of title is this: "Acme Manufacturing, the seller, asserts that it is transferring only such rights, title, and interest as it has in the goods named in this contract." This warranty does not promise that Acme owns the goods. The warranty modifies the usual implied warranty of title and warrants less than actual title.

Warranty disclaimers are discussed further later in this chapter.

IMPLIED WARRANTY OF MERCHANTABILITY

 LEGAL FOCUS ~ PROBLEM

Sue Joplin buys an axe at Gershwin's Hardware Store. No express warranties are made. The first time Joplin chops wood with the axe, the handle breaks, and she is injured. She immediately notifies Gershwin. An examination of the axe shows that the wood in the handle is rotten. The condition could not have been noticed by either Gershwin or Joplin. Joplin notifies Gershwin that she holds him responsible for the medical bills. Does Joplin have a case?

Gershwin is responsible, because a merchant seller of goods warrants that the goods sold are fit for normal use. This axe was obviously not fit for normal use.

An **implied warranty of merchantability** arises automatically in every sale of goods made by a merchant seller. A retailer of ski equipment thus makes an implied warranty of merchantability on all skis sold. In contrast, a neighbor selling skis at a garage sale does not.

As noted earlier, goods that are *merchantable* are those that are "reasonably fit for the ordinary purposes for which such goods are used." They must be of at least average, fair, or medium-grade quality. Goods must also be adequately packaged and labeled. Furthermore, they must conform to any promises or statements of fact made on the container or label. Finally, merchantability requires that a product be safe.

♦ **implied warranty of merchantability**
An implied promise by a merchant seller that goods are reasonably fit for the general purpose for which they are sold. This warranty exists in every sale by a merchant unless specifically disclaimed.

 LEGAL FOCUS ~ EXAMPLE

Nonmerchantable goods are light bulbs that explode when switched on, pajamas that burst into flames at slight contact with a stove burner, high heels on shoes that break off under normal use, and shotgun shells that explode prematurely.

Read aloud this sentence from the student text to the class: "It is not necessary that a merchant know that goods are unmerchantable or unsafe to be held responsible." Stimulate a class discussion about this topic by asking the following questions: What type of burden does this place on merchants? Do you feel that it is fair to place this burden on merchants? Do you think that most merchants are able to determine if a good is unmerchantable or unsafe? Why or why not?

Legal Focus Example

Read this Legal Focus Example aloud to the class. Make sure that the students understand that in this example, the bright blue paint is merchantable. It is of high quality, and it is suitable for the purpose of painting interior walls; however, in this case, it is not fit for the particular purpose of matching the color of your bedroom walls, which are a light shade somewhere between coral and peach. Ask the class if they can think of any other examples of products that are unfit for a particular purpose. Allow volunteers to share their examples with the class.

Legal Focus Problem

Ask a student volunteer to read aloud this Legal Focus Problem. Have the volunteer suggest a possible answer to the question posed at the end of this problem. Then guide the students in looking through this Legal Focus Problem to see exactly when each of the three conditions for an implied warranty of fitness for a particular purpose is met in this problem.

Critical Thinking Activity

Have your students define *implied warranty of fitness for a particular purpose*. Then ask them to write a paragraph or two on the contrast between it and an implied warranty of merchantability. Ask them to list examples with the explanations.

---

358   Commercial and Consumer Law

It is not necessary that a merchant know that goods are unmerchantable or unsafe to be held responsible. In an action for breach of implied warranty, it is necessary only to show that an implied warranty existed, that the warranty was broken, and that the breach of warranty was the cause of the damage sustained.

The serving of food or drink, whether eaten at a restaurant or taken out, is a sale of goods subject to the warranty of merchantability. "Merchantable" food is food fit to eat. The courts assume that consumers should expect to find an occasional bone in fish fillets, cherry pits in cherry pie, a nutshell in a package of shelled nuts, and so on. Such substances are natural parts of the food. A breach in a food case involves substances that consumers should not reasonably expect to find in the food.

IMPLIED WARRANTY OF FITNESS FOR A PARTICULAR PURPOSE

> ### ◀ LEGAL FOCUS ‑ EXAMPLE
>
> You need a gallon of paint to match the color of your bedroom walls, a light shade somewhere between coral and peach. You take a wall chip sample to your local hardware store and request a gallon of paint that color. Instead, you are given a gallon of bright blue paint. The salesperson has not breached any warranty of implied merchantability—the bright blue paint may be of high quality and suitable for interior walls. The clerk has, however, breached an implied warranty of fitness for a particular purpose.

◆ **implied warranty of fitness for a particular purpose**
A warranty that arises when a buyer, having stated the intended use of the goods to be purchased, relies on the expertise of the seller of the goods.

The **implied warranty of fitness for a particular purpose** is another important implied warranty. It arises under the following conditions. First, the seller knows how the buyer intends to use the goods sold. Second, the buyer relies on the seller's skill, and the seller knows it. Third, the seller recommends the goods as suitable. Unlike an implied warranty for merchantability, this warranty can arise in any sales transaction. The seller need not be a merchant.

As suggested in the example just described, a "particular purpose of the buyer" differs from the "ordinary purpose for which goods are used" (merchantability). Goods can be merchantable but unfit for a buyer's particular purpose.

> ### ◀ LEGAL FOCUS ‑ PROBLEM
>
> Bloomberg buys a shortwave radio from Radio Shop. She tells the salesperson that she wants a set strong enough to pick up Radio Luxembourg, which is 8,000 miles away. Radio Shop sells Bloomberg a Model X set. The set works, but it does not pick up Radio Luxembourg. Bloomberg wants her money back. Will she succeed?

Have the students work with partners to explain the three conditions under which the implied warranty of fitness for a particular purpose can arise. Student answers should list (1) the seller knows how the buyer intends to use the goods sold; (2) the buyer relies on the seller's skill, and the seller is aware of this; and (3) the seller recommends the goods as suitable.

Caption Answer

In this case, the seller would be aware of how the buyer intends to use the goods, and if the buyer then relies on the seller's skills and the seller is aware of it, an implied warranty of fitness for a particular purpose would arise.

If a novice hiker asks and is given advice about hiking gear, does an implied warranty of fitness for particular purpose arise?

Radio Shop breached the implied warranty of fitness for the buyer's particular purpose. Bloomberg should recover. The salesperson knew specifically that Bloomberg wanted a set that would pick up Radio Luxembourg. Bloomberg relied on the salesperson to furnish a radio to serve that purpose. Since the recommended model did not perform, the warranty was breached.

OTHER IMPLIED WARRANTIES

The UCC recognizes that implied warranties can arise (or be excluded or modified) from course of dealing, course of performance, or usage of trade. When both contracting parties know of a well-recognized trade custom, for example, the courts assume they intended that custom to apply to their contract.

◆ LEGAL FOCUS – EXAMPLE

It is an industry-wide custom to lubricate a new car before it is delivered. The dealer fails to lubricate Garcia's new car before delivering it. The dealer can be held liable to Garcia for resulting damages, under breach of implied warranty.

LEGAL BACKGROUND

As the student text points out, "The UCC recognizes that implied warranties can arise from course of dealing, course of performance, or usage of trade." These terms were introduced and defined in Chapter 14. In this chapter, the following definitions were given: *course of dealing*—prior conduct between contracting parties that establishes a common basis for their understanding; *course of performance*—the way the parties conduct themselves toward each other after the contract is created; *usage of trade*—a common business practice in a place, vocation, or trade.

Legal Focus Example

Read this Legal Focus Example aloud to the class. Ask the class if they can think of any other examples of usage of trade that could also fit here. Allow volunteers to share their examples with the class.

1. A seller creates an express warranty by making statements about the quality, condition, description, or performance potential of the goods.

2. No. Recommendation or other opinions about the goods are not warranties. However, if the salesman is an expert and the products are unique, the "expert's" opinion may create a warranty.

3. Breach of warranty requires that an implied warranty existed, that the warranty was broken, and that the breach of warranty was the cause of the damage sustained.

4. If express and implied warranties are not consistent, usually the express warranties will prevail. Implied warranties are routinely present; however, a seller's action in presenting an express warranty increases the buyer's reliance on the claim.

Legal Focus Example

Read aloud to the class this Legal Focus Example of overlapping warranties. Remind the students that they can use the Legal Focus features as review tools when studying for tests.

Discussion Starter

Read aloud to the class this sentence from the bottom of this page: "To exclude express warranties, the seller can refrain from making any promise of fact about the goods, or describing the goods, or using a sample model." Stimulate a class discussion about this by asking the following questions: What does this mean for the seller who wishes to exclude express warranties? What type of sales pitch can he or she use? How does this hinder the seller of inferior merchandise? How does this benefit buyers?

---

360   Commercial and Consumer Law

 OVERLAPPING WARRANTIES

Sometimes, more than one warranty exists in a single transaction. An implied warranty of merchantability, an implied warranty of fitness for a particular purpose, or both can exist in addition to an express warranty.

 LEGAL FOCUS - EXAMPLE

A sales contract for a new car states that "this car engine is warranted to be free from defects for 12,000 miles or twelve months, whichever occurs first." There is an express warranty against all defects and an implied warranty that the car is fit for normal use.

Express and implied warranties are considered *cumulative* if they are consistent with one another. That is, the warranties are both (or all) effective. If they are not consistent, then usually express warranties take precedence over implied warranties (except an implied warranty of fitness for a particular purpose).

 CHECKING YOUR PROGRESS

1. How is an express warranty created?

2. If a salesman recommends his products by saying they are "the best on the market," has he created an express warranty?

3. What are the conditions for a breach of implied warranty?

4. Although express and implied warranties are construed as cumulative if they are consistent with one another, which will prevail if they are not consistent? Why?

 WARRANTY DISCLAIMERS

◆ **disclaimer** A denial of a warranty that might otherwise exist.

A warranty **disclaimer** is a denial that a warranty exists. A qualification or limitation to a warranty reduces the warranty coverage. Since each warranty is created in a special way, each can be disclaimed or qualified by the seller in a specific manner.

EXPRESS WARRANTIES

To exclude express warranties, the seller can refrain from making any promise of fact about the goods, or describing the goods, or using a sample model. Remember that any of these can create an express warranty.

Extension Activity

Ask students to acquire sales contracts from local retailers and read the contracts to locate disclaimers. Have them report to the class by reading the disclaimers aloud. Discuss with the students the ethics of the disclaimers.

Enrichment

Ask the students to think of some examples of products that may be sold *as is*. Examples might include used goods, or display models of such products as televisions, stereos, large appliances, etc. Remind the students that although the use of the term *as is* limits the seller's responsibility as to the quality of the goods, the seller is, normally, still responsible for the safety of the goods.

Legal Focus Example

Read this Legal Focus Example to the class. Remind the students that they can use the Legal Focus features as review tools when studying for tests.

Legal Focus Problem

Ask a student volunteer to read this Legal Focus Problem aloud to the class. Ask the student to suggest a possible answer to the question posed at the end of this Legal Focus Problem. As a followup, ask the student whether he feels that Forbes's behavior was ethical. Why or why not?

Sales Warranties and Product Liability   361

The UCC also allows express warranties to be disclaimed or limited by specific and clear language. A written disclaimer made in clear and conspicuous language and brought to the buyer's attention can exclude all oral express warranties that are not part of the written sales contract. This protects the seller if a buyer falsely claims that oral warranties were made. It also ensures that only representations by properly authorized individuals are included in the bargain.

Note that a buyer must be made aware of warranty disclaimers or modifications at the time the sales contract is made.

IMPLIED WARRANTIES

The use of the simple terms *as is* and *with all faults* can disclaim the implied warranties of merchantability and fitness. These broad disclaimers must be clearly marked or brought to the attention of the purchaser. Although *as is* and *with all faults* are very effective in limiting the seller's responsibility as to the quality of goods, the seller is normally still responsible for the safety of the product sold.

The implied warranty of fitness for a particular purpose can also be disclaimed by written conspicuous language specially disclaiming the warranty.

◆ LEGAL FOCUS – EXAMPLE

An implied warranty of fitness for a particular purpose can be disclaimed by a clear statement that "no implied warranty for particular purpose exists in this contract." However, instead, the usual disclaimer reads, "There are no warranties that extend beyond the description on the face hereof."

A merchantability disclaimer (other than *as is* or *with all faults*) must be more specific; it must mention *merchantability*. It need not be written; but if it is, the writing must be conspicuous.

◆ LEGAL FOCUS – PROBLEM

Forbes, a merchant, sells Maves a lawnmower. At the time of the sale, Forbes orally tells Maves that he does not warrant the merchantability of the mower. He explains that it is last year's model. The mower is defective and does not work. Maves sues Forbes for breach of implied warranty of merchantability. Will he be successful?

No. Forbes's oral disclaimer mentioning the word *merchantability* is a proper disclaimer. Obviously, though, a written disclaimer makes more sense, because it is easier to prove the disclaimer was made. Exhibit 15-1 provides an example of a typical warranty with a partial or limited disclaimer.

The UCC requirement that warranty disclaimers be conspicuous is based on the ethical premise that sellers should not take advantage of consumers who do not read the "fine print" on a standard contract form. If a seller fails to meet the UCC requirements, warranties will not be effectively disclaimed.

The ethical significance of this rule is best illustrated by the situation that existed before the UCC was widely adopted. Car buyers, for example, often signed standard purchase agreements, drafted by a manufacturer, without knowing what all the fine print meant. In one case, a party was injured as a result of an apparent defect in the steering wheel mechanism. The dealer and the manufacturer denied liability, asserting that the contract, which warranted that the dealer would repair defects at no charge, disclaimed warranty liability for injuries. The Supreme Court of New Jersey expressed outrage that the manufacturer had used its grossly disproportionate bargaining power and the unfair surprise of fine print to relieve itself of liability and to impose on the buyer the danger of injury that is posed by a defectively made car. The court held that the disclaimer was unconscionable and allowed recovery from the dealer and manufacturer.

By obligating merchants to meet specific requirements when disclaiming warranties, the UCC has

made dealing fairly with buyers a legal, as well as an ethical, obligation. Today if a warranty disclaimer unfairly surprises a buyer, chances are the disclaimer was not sufficiently conspicuous, and the unfairness of the bargain will not have to be so great as to shock the court's conscience before a remedy will be granted.

Have your students read Exhibit 15-1, the Example of a Warranty with a Limited Disclaimer. Ask your students to write down what the warranty actually does cover and what it is disclaiming.

Limited Warranty

Brown Inc. warrants this Brown Appliance to be free of defects in material and workmanship for a period of one year from the date of original purchase.

If the appliance exhibits such a defect, Brown Inc. will, at its option, repair or replace it, provided the consumer:

1. Returns the appliance postpaid and insured to

   Service Department, Brown Inc.,
   351 Main Street,
   Rivercity, Texas 74145

   or one of its authorized service centers.

2. Submits proof of date of original purchase.

This warranty does not cover finishes, nor does it cover damage resulting from accident, misuse, dirt, water, tampering, unreasonable use, servicing performed or attempted by unauthorized service agencies or units that have been modified or used for commercial purposes.

ALL IMPLIED WARRANTIES, INCLUDING ANY IMPLIED WARRANTY OF MERCHANTABILITY OR FITNESS FOR ANY PARTICULAR PURPOSE, ARE LIMITED IN DURATION TO ONE YEAR FROM DATE OF ORIGINAL PURCHASE. IN NO EVENT WILL BRAUN INC. BE RESPONSIBLE FOR CONSEQUENTIAL DAMAGES RESULTING FROM THE USE OF THIS PRODUCT.

Some states do not allow the exclusion or limitation of incidental or consequential damages, so the above limitation may not apply to you.

This warranty gives you specific legal rights, and you may have other legal rights which vary from state to state.

EXHIBIT 15-1
EXAMPLE OF A WARRANTY WITH A LIMITED DISCLAIMER

WARRANTY DISCLAIMERS AND UNCONSCIONABILITY

Courts are authorized by the UCC to review warranty disclaimers. A court can refuse to enforce the contract or delete a clause if it is unconscionable (see Chapter 10). A buyer's lack of bargaining position, the existence of "take-it-or-leave-it" choices, and a buyer's failure to understand or know of a warranty disclaimer are among the factors relevant to the issue of unconscionability. For example, a warranty disclaimer in small print hidden in the back of a long contract would be unconscionable. An unconscionable warranty disclaimer or limitation is ineffective.

Have students research (in the library or via computer database) the Federal Trade Commission and write a one- to two-page report describing the responsibilities of the commission.

Have your students demonstrate their knowledge of the difference between a full warranty and a limited warranty by writing a paragraph or two on the differences between them. Make sure they have included the term *disclaimer* in their writings.

Extension Activity

Have students research the Magnuson-Moss Warranty Act, then report to the class orally. The presentation should include the specifics of the act and when it was approved. The students should then lead a discussion about its effect on buyers and sellers.

Enrichment

Collect warranties from consumer goods (small appliances, etc.). Give one to each student to look for the items required under the Magnuson-Moss Warranty Act.

Reteaching Activity

Have the students work with partners to answer the following questions: Under the Magnuson-Moss Warranty Act, what does a "full warranty" require? What happens if a warranty fails to meet the requirements of a "full warranty"?

MAGNUSON–MOSS WARRANTY ACT

The **Magnuson–Moss Warranty Act** was designed to prevent deception in warranties by making them easier to understand. The act is enforced by the Federal Trade Commission (FTC). An injured consumer can also enforce the act. The act modifies UCC warranty rules when consumer sales transactions are involved.

The Magnuson–Moss Act does not require a written warranty to be given when consumer goods are sold. However, if a seller makes an express written warranty involving consumer goods costing more than $10, the act controls how the warranty is to be given. Any warranty under the act must be labeled as "full" or "limited." In addition, if the cost of the goods is more than $15, the warrantor (the person making the warranty) must make certain disclosures in language that is easy to understand. The disclosures must state the names and addresses of the warrantors and must identify the product warranted, the procedures for enforcement of the warranty, and any limitations on warranty remedies. It must also state that the buyer has legal rights.

A *full warranty* may not cover every problem that might arise with a consumer product, but it does give the buyer rights if the product is defective. A full warranty requires free repair or replacement of any defective part. If the product cannot be repaired within a reasonable time, the consumer has the choice of either a refund or a replacement without charge. The warranty does not cover unreasonable use or damage caused by the consumer.

A written consumer warranty that does not meet all the requirements of a full warranty is a *limited warranty*. The seller must state clearly that only a limited warranty is given.

Under the Magnuson–Moss Warranty Act, a seller making an express warranty in a sales contract cannot disclaim or modify either the implied warranty of merchantability or the implied warranty of fitness for a particular purpose. Sellers, however, can impose a time limit on the duration of an implied warranty. The time limit must correspond to the duration of the express warranty. It must also be reasonable, conscionable, and stated in clear and conspicuous language on the face of the warranty.

◆ **Magnuson–Moss Warranty Act** A federal law designed to prevent deception in warranties by making them easier to understand. The act is enforced by the Federal Trade Commission (FTC).

PRODUCT LIABILITY

Manufacturers and sellers of goods can be held liable to consumers, users, and bystanders for physical harm or property damage that is caused by goods. This liability is called **product liability**.

◆ **product liability** Responsibility for injury or damage caused by a defective product.

Read

You might introduce this *Law in Action* feature by asking the students the following question: In discussing cars, what is a *lemon?* Do you know anyone who has ever purchased a car that he or she described as a lemon? Why did this person describe this car as a lemon? Did he or she complain to the dealer about the car? Why or why not? If this person did complain to the dealer, what was the dealer's response? After the students have discussed what they know about lemons, have a student volunteer read this *Law in Action* feature aloud to the class.

Discuss

Use the following questions to stimulate a class discussion of this feature: How is *lemon* defined in this feature? How does a poorly manufactured car fit this description? In which cases can a consumer rescind the purchase of a car? What are the two prevalent views on what type of defect gives consumers a right under a lemon law? Which of these views do you feel is the most fair? Why? How do lemon laws benefit consumers?

Extend

Tell students to write to their legislators asking for information about your state's lemon law. Have students write to a neighboring state if your state does not have a lemon law. Encourage them to use a typewriter or computer to key the letter and envelope. Have the students discuss with the class how the law affects automobile buyers in your state.

---

364   Commercial and Consumer Law

Law in Action

LAW IN YOUR LIFE: LEMON LAWS

Beginning in 1963, when Chrysler Corporation initiated a five-year/50,000-mile "power train warranty," the auto industry discovered that warranties attracted consumers. That first Chrysler warranty increased its new car sales by 40 percent. For consumers, however, the warranty was not a cure-all for the problems arising from automobile purchases. Dealers and manufacturers often did not live up to their express or implied warranties. Unsatisfactory warranty service became the most frequent and significant complaint of consumers buying new cars.

The Magnuson-Moss Warranty Act aided consumers to some extent. However, much of the act applies only to full, or comprehensive, warranties. Since most automobile dealers and manufacturers offer limit warranties, the act rarely applies to auto sales contracts.

To help consumers who have had the bad luck of purchasing a "lemon," the majority of states now have "lemon laws." A lemon is loosely defined as a purchase that leaves a sour taste in your mouth—that makes you wish you hadn't bought it. Lemon laws generally allow a purchaser to rescind a contract involving the purchase of a new automobile under certain conditions. If a vehicle needs servicing four or more times for the same problem, or if the vehicle cannot be used for thirty business days within the first year, the consumer can rescind. Businesses often can require a complaining customer to go through informal settlement procedures before suing in court. (See the Legal Perspective in Chapter 5).

Lemon Laws help protect purchasers.

So far, the states are divided on what type of defect gives consumers a right under the law. Half of the states with lemon laws follow Connecticut's lead and require that the defect *substantially* impair the use and the value of the vehicle. The other half follow the California statute, requiring that the defect impair the use, value, or safety of the vehicle in any way.

Lemon laws greatly benefit consumers. They represent a growing recognition of the need to balance the bargaining scales between the individual consumer and the "giant" corporation. Currently, all states except Arkansas, South Carolina, and South Dakota have lemon laws covering the sale of new automobiles.

◆ **LEGAL FOCUS ~ EXAMPLE**

Joseph purchases a new sweater which unravels after having been worn twice. In this situation, Joseph will be concerned with quality, and his rights are based solely on contract and sales law. Product liability is concerned about a different kind of harm. For example, what if the sweater caused Joseph a rash because it had been treated with a dangerous chemical. The harm to Joseph will be to his physical well-being, and thus is a product liability type of harm.

Legal theories of product liability include the contract theory of warranty and tort theories of negligence and strict liability.

PRODUCT LIABILITY BASED ON WARRANTY

An important part of product liability law is the breach of warranty theory. If a person suffers physical injury or injury to other property because of substandard goods, he can seek recovery based on breach of warranty. The general rule is that *consumers, purchasers, and even users of goods* can recover *from any seller* for losses resulting from breach of implied and express warranties. In other words, most parties who are injured by goods can sue any seller of the goods, including the manufacturer, on warranty theory.

This extensive right to recover is an exception to the usual requirement that a party be in *privity* of contract (direct contract relationship) with another to sue on a contract theory.

◆ **LEGAL FOCUS ~ PROBLEM**

I purchase a ham from retailer Bill. I invite Janet to my house for dinner. I prepare the ham properly. Janet, my guest, becomes severely ill because the ham is spoiled. Can Janet sue Bill for breach of the implied warranty of merchantability?

Legal Focus Problem

Ask a volunteer to read this Legal Focus Problem aloud to the class. Make sure that students understand that Janet can sue Bill even though Janet was not the purchaser of the ham and therefore not in privity of the contract.

Yes. However, some discussion is necessary. Since warranty is based on the sales contract, the common law would allow only the purchaser of the ham to sue the retailer, and the warranty would extend only to the purchaser.

The UCC has addressed the problem of *privity* by eliminating the requirement of *privity* for certain types of injuries and for certain beneficiaries. However, there has been a sharp disagreement among the states as to how extensive warranty liability should be. To satisfy the different views of the states, the drafters of the UCC provided three alternatives in the UCC. Each of the alternatives allows an injured third person to sue even though they did not purchase the goods. However, the alternatives range from one which allows only the purchaser, family, and guests in the home of the

Ethical Concern

Ethical questions abound in the area of product liability. For instance, lawsuits have been brought against manufacturers even when it is the consumers who are at fault. Should consumers recover damages for harm caused by their own carelessness or product misuse or for accidents for which no one is at fault?

In one case, a young boy fell through a toilet seat and drowned in the water. His parents sued the toilet seat manufacturer for failing to place on the lid a sticker to warn parents to take protective measures such as buying a lock for the toilet lid or installing self-closing hinges on the bathroom door. The manufacturer agreed to pay $90,000. Many persons might question the ethics of requiring a manufacturer to warn of an obvious danger.

Reteaching Activity

Have the students work with partners to study the differences between product liability based on negligence and product liability based on strict liability. Have each pair make a list of examples of each.

Extension Activity

Have a few volunteers research the *Exxon-Valdez* oil spill tragedy that occurred in 1990. Have them share their findings with the class. Then stimulate a discussion of the crisis, and ask students if this was a case of strict liability or negligence.

purchaser to sue, to the most commonly adopted provision which allows a lawsuit by anyone who might be reasonably expected to be injured by the goods.

PRODUCT LIABILITY BASED ON NEGLIGENCE

In Chapter 5, we defined *negligence* as a failure to use the degree of care that a reasonable, prudent person would have used under the circumstances. If a seller does not exercise reasonable care and an injury results, he or she is liable for negligence.

A manufacturer must exercise due care to make a product safe. This due care must be exercised in all aspects of manufacturing the product. It includes product design and selection of the materials to make the product. It includes appropriate production, assembly, and testing of the product. It includes placing adequate warnings on the label to inform the user of potential dangers of which he or she might not be aware. And it extends to the inspection and testing of any purchased products used in the final product sold by the manufacturer.

The failure to exercise due care is negligence. A manufacturer is liable to any person who is injured by a negligently made (defective) product. The manufacturer is liable for harm regardless of whether a sale or a contract to sell was involved.

PRODUCT LIABILITY BASED ON STRICT LIABILITY

The doctrine of strict liability was introduced in Chapter 5. Under the strict liability doctrine, persons are responsible for their acts regardless of their intentions or their exercise of reasonable care. For example, a company that uses dynamite to blast for a road is strictly liable for any damage caused. Liability exists even if the company takes reasonable precautions to prevent such damages. The blasting company is responsible for all personal injuries resulting from the dynamite blast.

The doctrine of strict liability applies to manufacturers, wholesalers, and retailers (also processors, assemblers, packagers, bottlers, and distributors). A seller of any product that is in a defective condition and is unreasonably dangerous to the user or to the user's property is subject to liability for physical harm caused to the user or the property. The following conditions must also exist:

1. The seller is in the business of selling such products.
2. The product is expected to and does reach the user without substantial change in the condition in which it is sold.

The seller is liable even if all possible care has been taken in the preparation and sale of the product. Liability is imposed as a matter of public policy. It does not depend on a contract relationship or on proof of negligence. The seller's liability to an injured party is virtually unlimited. The courts extend the manufacturer's liability to bystanders as well as to users and consumers.

Multicultural Perspectives

Multinational corporations must consider the ethical values of Americans as well as the values of citizens of other countries in which they do business. This is especially true in the area of product liability. If there is a conflict, which value should prevail? For example, should companies sell products in other countries that they would not and/or could not sell in the United States because these products were unsafe or unmerchantable? Recently, the United Nations drafted a code of conduct for multinational corporations that would impose specific ethical requirements on firms involved in foreign business operations. Among other things, firms would be required to consider the health and safety of consumers and the environment of the host country, to respect human rights and fundamental freedoms, and to disclose whether their products have been banned in other countries.

Requirements of Strict Product Liability   The six basic requirements of strict product liability are as follows:

1. The defendant must sell the product in a defective condition.
2. The defendant must normally be in the business of selling that product.
3. The product must be unreasonably dangerous to the user or consumer because of its defective condition.
4. The plaintiff must suffer physical harm to self or property by use or consumption of the product.
5. The defective condition must be the proximate cause of the injury or damage.
6. The goods must not have been substantially changed from the time they were sold to the time the injury was sustained.

Thus, under this theory, in any action against a manufacturer or seller, the plaintiff need not show how the product became defective. The plaintiff must, however, show that at the time of the injury, the condition of the product was essentially the same as it was when it left the hands of the defendant manufacturer or seller.

If a defective toy causes harm to a child, who might be held responsible?

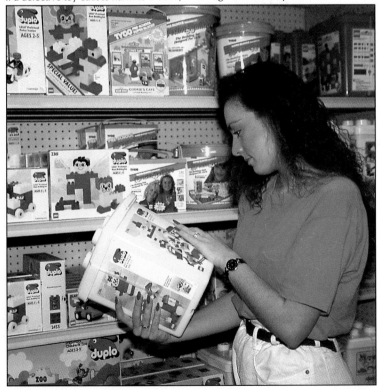

Have a student volunteer read the first Legal Focus Problem aloud to the class. Have the volunteer suggest a possible answer to the question posed at the end of this problem.

Critical Thinking Activity

Lead a class discussion about the cost of warranties to the consumer. Consumers are more aware of their rights and are suing manufacturers more frequently and for very large judgments. This cost is passed on to the consumers in the form of higher prices. Discuss whether the increased cost is "worth it." Discuss positive effects of increased product liability lawsuits.

Legal Focus Problem

Have a student volunteer read aloud the second Legal Focus Problem. Ask the volunteer to suggest a possible answer to the question posed at the end of this problem.

368

Reteaching Activity

Divide your class into groups of three or four, and have the groups define terms found in this chapter.

1. No, implied warranty disclaimers do not have to be in writing, but if they are, they must be conspicuous.
2. A full warranty does not cover unreasonable use or damage caused by the consumer.
3. Consumers, users, and bystanders who suffer physical harm or property damage benefit from product liability because they can hold manufacturers and sellers liable.

---

368   Commercial and Consumer Law

Strict Liability to Bystanders   All courts extend the strict liability of manufacturers and other sellers to injured bystanders.

 LEGAL FOCUS – PROBLEM

The motor of a car exploded, producing a cloud of steam. The steam caused a series of multiple collisions, since it prevented other drivers from seeing well. Is the automobile manufacturer liable for injuries caused by the explosion of the car's motor?

Yes, since the defective car motor caused the harm to the innocent third parties.

Defenses to Strict Liability   Frequently, a person is injured by a product because he or she did not use it carefully. If *product misuse* by a claimant can be proved, it may be a defense to reduce the claimant's recovery or stop it altogether.

 LEGAL FOCUS – PROBLEM

Burt is told by his mother to chip out a small hole in the family's cement patio. He goes to the family tool chest. Instead of selecting a heavy-duty chisel, he picks out a Phillips screwdriver. With hammer and screwdriver, he begins to chip out the cement. After fifteen minutes, the screwdriver shatters, and a sliver of metal lodges in Burt's eye. Does the manufacturer of the screwdriver have a defense to a strict liability claim for the harm to Burt's eye?

Screwdrivers are designed to screw and unscrew screws. They are not designed to chip cement. This misuse should be a defense for the manufacturer and seller of the screwdriver.

Assumption of risk can also be a defense in an action based on strict liability in tort. To establish this defense, the defendant must show that:

1. The plaintiff voluntarily participated in the risk and was aware of the potential danger.
2. The plaintiff knew and appreciated the risk created by the defect.
3. The plaintiff's decision to undertake the known risk was unreasonable.

In principle, negligence on the part of the plaintiff is not a defense in a strict product liability case. However, a growing number of states are holding that negligent or intentional actions of plaintiffs can reduce their claims for damages. This "comparing" of the plaintiff's conduct to the defendant's strict liability results in a doctrine looking very much like *comparative negligence*.

4. To be held responsible for damages under strict product liability, (1) the defendant must sell the product in defective condition; (2) the defendant must normally be in the business of selling the product; (3) the product must be unreasonably dangerous to the user because of its defective condition; (4) the plaintiff must suffer physical harm to self or property by use of the product; (5) the defective condition must be the proximate cause of the injury or damage; and (6) the goods must not have been substantially changed from the time the product was sold to the time the injury was sustained.

5. Yes, liability for personal injury caused by defective goods extends to lessees. Some courts hold that a leasing agreement creates an implied warranty for the duration of the lease.

◆ CHECKING YOUR PROGRESS

1. Must implied warranty disclaimers be in writing?
2. What is not covered under a full warranty?
3. What parties benefit from product liability? Why?
4. What are the basic requirements for a seller to be held responsible for damages under strict product liability?
5. Does strict product liability apply if a consumer leases a product rather than purchase it?

◆ A CASE IN POINT ◆

ROTH v. RAY-STEL'S HAIR STYLISTS, INC.

Massachusetts Appeals Court, 1984.
18 Mass.App. 975,
470 N.E.2d 137.

In this case, a warranty on the label of a hair-bleaching product was breached when a user suffered damages after using this product.

FACTS On March 13, 1980, Judith Roth went to her hairdresser to have her hair bleached. She had been using Ray-Stel's Hair Stylists, Inc., for the past seven years. The hair stylist used a new bleaching product, manufactured by Roux Laboratories, Inc., on Mrs. Roth's hair. Ray-Stel's had used other Roux products with excellent results. This product, however, caused loss of and damage to Mrs. Roth's hair. She was embarrassed for the next several months while her normal hair grew back. The product's label had guaranteed it would not cause damage to a user's hair. Roth sued Ray-Stel's Hair Stylists and Roux Laboratories, alleging negligence and breach of express and implied warranties resulting in personal injuries to her.

The trial court found liability on the part of Roux on the basis of negligence and breach of express warranty. It assessed damages of $5,000. The jury found no liability on the part of Ray-Stel's Hair Stylists. Roux appealed the judgment.

ISSUE Did the product's performance breach an express warranty?

DECISION Yes. The appellate court affirmed the trial court's ruling.

REASON When a product's label says that the product will (or will not) perform in a certain way, and it fails to (or does) do so, it violates an express warranty. As a result, the manufacturer is liable for the damage caused by the unfulfilled promise. According to the court, "the jury had before them all of the required elements for a claim of breach of express warranty."

369

Reviewing Chapter 15

Assessment Strategies

In order to help students review what they have learned in Chapter 15, you might wish to:

1. Have a student volunteer, or volunteers, read the Chapter Summary aloud.
2. Allow the students to work with partners to complete the *Using Legal Language* activity.
3. Assign the *Checking for Comprehension* exercise as homework.
4. Allow the students to work in small groups to complete the *Applying Legal Concepts* activities.
5. As a class, complete the *Applying the Law* activities. (Please note that you may have to help students with vocabulary so that they adequately understand all of the *Applying the Law* material.)

In order to check student mastery of chapter concepts, you may wish to use the Chapter 15 test that is found in your *Teacher's Resource Binder* or use WESTEST computerized testing for Chapter 15.

CHAPTER REVIEW

SUMMARY

WARRANTIES

Express Warranty—Created as part of a sale or bargain by statement or promise of fact, by a description of the goods, or by a sample of model shown.

Possible Defenses

1. Statement made is one of opinion, rather than fact, including normal puffing by the seller.
2. The warranty is excluded or limited by the contract.

Implied Warranties—Including warranties of title, merchantability, and particular purpose.

Warranty of Title—Created at the time of the sale. The seller warrants that he or she has the right to pass good and rightful title, and that the goods are free from unstated liens.

Possible Defense—Exclusion or modification only by specific language.

Warranty of Merchantability—Created when the seller is a merchant who deals in goods of the kind sold. Warranty that goods are "reasonably fit for the ordinary purposes for which such goods are used."

Possible Defenses

1. Specified disclaimer—can be oral or in writing but must mention merchantability and, if in writing, must be conspicuous.
2. Sales stated *as is* or *with all faults*.

Warranty of Fitness for a Particular Purpose—Created at time of sale when the buyer's purpose or use is expressly or impliedly known by the seller, and the buyer must purchase in reliance on the seller's selection: warranty that the goods are fit for the purpose that was told to the seller by the buyer.

Possible Defense

Specific disclaimer—must be in writing and must be conspicuous.

Magnuson–Moss Warranty Act—A federal statute which applies when express written warranties are made on consumer goods priced at more than $10. The act does not require warranties but, *if* warranties are made, the warranties must be labeled either as:

1. Full warranty—This warranty must provide for free repair or replacement of defective parts; refund or replacement for goods if they cannot be repaired in a reasonable time.
2. Limited warranty—The warranty must be so identified when less than a full warranty is being offered.
3. If a written warranty is provided under the act, then the implied warranty of merchantability and the implied warranty of fitness for a particular purpose cannot be disclaimed.

PRODUCT LIABILITY

Liability Based on Warranty

Express and implied warranties give manufacturers and sellers responsibility for harm caused to purchasers, users, and bystanders.

Liability Based on Negligence

1. Due care must be used by the manufacturer in designing the product, selecting materials, using the appropriate production process, assembling and testing the product, and placing adequate warnings on the label or product.
2. A manufacturer is liable for failure to exercise due care to any person who sustains an injury caused by a negligently made (defective) product.

Liability Based on Strict Product Liability

1. The defendant must sell the product in a defective condition.

2. The defendant must normally be engaged in the business of selling that product.

3. The product must be unreasonably dangerous to the user or consumer because of its defective condition.

4. The plaintiff must incur physical harm to self or property by use or consumption of the product. (Courts will also extend strict liability to include injured bystanders.)

5. The defective condition must be the cause of the injury or damage.

6. The goods must not have been substantially changed from the time they were sold to the time the injury was sustained.

Possible Defenses to Negligence and Strict Liability

1. Misuse of the product by the user or consumer in a way unforeseeable by the manufacturer.

2. Assumption of risk on the part of the user or consumer.

3. Negligence on the part of the user/consumer is usually not a defense. However, some states hold that a plaintiff's wrongful actions can reduce the amount of a damage claim.

 ## USING LEGAL LANGUAGE

Directions: Match each term with the statement that best describes that term.

1. caveat emptor
2. disclaimer
3. express warranty
4. implied warranty of fitness for a particular purpose
5. implied warranty of merchantability
6. implied warranty
7. lemon law
8. Magnuson-Moss Warranty Act
9. product liability
10. warranty of title

A. A statement concerning the quality, condition, description, or performance potential of goods is a _____ when it is part of a sales contract.

B. A _____ is a qualification or limitation to a warranty which might otherwise exist.

C. An implied assurance that the seller owns or has the right to sell goods is _____.

D. Let the buyer beware, _____, assumes the buyer takes the risk as to quality of goods in a sale.

E. A federal law called _____ is designed to prevent deception in warranties by making them easier to understand.

F. An implied promise by a merchant seller that goods are reasonably fit for the general purpose for which they are sold is _____.

G. A state statute called _____ is designed to assist a buyer of seriously defective goods to get a replacement or full refund.

H. _____ refers to the legal responsibility of manufacturers and sellers to compensate buyer, users, and even bystanders, for

1. Both express and implied warranties are promises that the buyer can rely on the fact that the goods are as represented. The difference between them is that an express warranty is created by the seller when he or she makes statements about the goods, whereas an implied warranty is created by law.
2. Implied warranty of merchantability arises every time a *merchant* sells goods that must be reasonably fit for the ordinary purpose for which such goods are used. Implied warranty of fitness for a particular purpose arises in any transaction in which the buyer relies on the *seller's* recommendation of goods as suitable, when the seller knows how the buyer intends to use the goods sold.
3. The UCC extends the common law privity (contract relationship between plaintiff and defendant) to certain beneficiaries for certain types of injuries as a result of breaches of implied or express warranties.
4. Students should write examples of assumption of risk, product misuse, or comparative fault.
5. *Caveat emptor*, let the buyer beware, was the rule in most sales contracts. Expansion of consumer rights has changed the emphasis in sales contracts. The UCC provides more protection for consumers. Student answers as to why

will vary, but reference to ethical business practices and concern for protection of individuals, who bargain in good faith, should be included in their responses.
6. The court held that Evanston's Poultry Farm had breached the implied warranties of merchantability and fitness for a particular purpose. Even if a defect is extremely difficult to discover, the seller is not relieved of warranty liability for goods provided to the buyer unless the implied warranties are properly

disclaimed. Since the chickens were sold in an inferior condition and Evanston's had not disclaimed any warranties, Evanston's was liable to Corinna for the defect.
7. Yes. To disclaim the implied warranty of fitness for a particular purpose, the disclaimer must be in writing and be conspicuous. Although the implied warranty of merchantability can be disclaimed orally, if the disclaimer is in writing, it must be conspicuously written. This means that the disclaimer

---

damages or injuries suffered because of defect in goods purchased.

I.   A warranty that arises when the buyer relies on the expertise of the seller of goods having stated the intended use of the goods is called _____.

J.   An _____ is a warranty that the law implies either through the situation, parties or the nature of the transaction.

◆ CHECKING FOR COMPREHENSION

1.   Explain how express and implied warranties are the same and how they are different.

2.   Describe two types of implied warranties.

3.   How does the Uniform Commercial Code change the common law theory of privity?

4.   Describe two defenses to strict liability.

5.   Define the doctrine of *caveat emptor*. How has the doctrine changed in recent years? Why?

6.   Corinna purchased 1,000 baby chickens from Evanston's Poultry Farm with the intention of starting a chicken business. After the chickens were delivered, Corinna discovered that they were afflicted with avian leukosis, a type of cancer. Corinna sued Evanston's Poultry for breach of the implied warranties of merchantability and fitness for a particular purpose. Evanston's Poultry claimed that the cancerous disease that afflicted the chickens was impossible to discover in baby chicks. Therefore, it should not be held liable for the defect. What will the court decide?

7.   Treng Nyguen purchased a CD player from Fisher Appliances. The sales contract included a provision explicitly disclaiming all express or implied warranties, including the implied warranty of merchantability. The disclaimer was printed in the same size and color type as the rest of the contract. The player turned out to be a "lemon" and never functioned properly. Nyguen sought a refund of the purchase price, claiming Fisher had breached the implied warranty of merchantability. Can Nyguen recover his money, even with the warranty disclaimer in the contract? Explain.

8.   Appleton was driving on an interstate highway when one of his tires blew out. The blow-out caused Appleton to lose control of his car, which collided with another vehicle and injured its driver. Appleton had not been driving negligently. Later it was discovered that a defect in the tire had caused the blowout. Appleton sued Good-Rubber Tires, Inc., the manufacturer of the tire, for damages caused by the accident. Will Appleton succeed in his suit? Explain.

◆ APPLYING LEGAL CONCEPTS

1.   (A) Find four magazine advertisements that give express warranties about the product being advertised. Clip, photo-

copy, or sketch the ad (including the text of the warranty). Attach a sheet of paper on which you explain what kind of war-must—either by different color or type size or some other technique—stand out from the context in which it is printed so as to readily alert the reader of the document of the disclaimer. In this case, the disclaimer was printed in the same size and color of type as the rest of the contract and was not conspicuous. If this was the only warranty disclaimer, it is not effective and Nyguen can recover.

8. In most states a person who suffers injury due to a defective product may sue the manufacturer directly for damages under the doctrine of strict liability. The manufacturer of a defective product is held to a standard of strict liability for damages resulting from that product when it is foreseeable that a defect in the product could result in injury to its user. In this case, it was foreseeable that the defective tire could result in injury due to an accident such as Appleton's. If Appleton can convince the court that the defective tire was the direct cause of the accident, that the tire was defective when he purchased it, and that the condition of the tire at the time of the accident was substantially the same as it had been when it left the manufacturer, the manufacturer will be liable under the doctrine of strict liability for damages caused by the accident.

ranty is given.

(B) Find two magazine advertisements that have a warranty disclaimer or qualification or limitation printed within the ad. Clip, photocopy, or sketch the ad (including all text). Attach a sheet of paper on which you tell whether the disclaimer or qualification or limitation are enforceable. Explain why.

◆ APPLYING THE LAW . . . YOU BE THE JUDGE

1. Robinson purchased a truck from Branch Moving and Storage Co. "as is" without inspecting it. Branch diligently and repeatedly advised Robinson of the risk he was taking by purchasing the unit without inspection. When the truck required several repairs because of defects in it, Robinson sued Branch for breach of warranty. At trial, Robinson won. Branch appealed. What was the result? [*Robinson v. Branch Moving and Storage Co.*, 28 N.C.App. 244, 221 S.E.2d 81 (1976)]

2. A disclaimer of the implied warranty of fitness must be in writing and must be conspicuous. If the implied warranty of merchantability is to be excluded by a writing, that writing must also be conspicuous. The following paragraph appeared in a sales contract. The page contained other type of larger and smaller sizes and boldface print, but no other words on the page were printed in italics.

   The equipment covered hereby is sold subject only to the applicable manufacturer's standard printed warranty, if any, in effect at the date hereof, receipt of a copy of which is hereby acknowledged, and no other warranties, express or implied, including without limitation, the implied warranties of *merchantability and fitness for a particular purpose* shall apply.

   Is this an effective disclaimer of the implied warranties according to UCC 2-316? [*Dorman v. International Harvester Co.*, 46 Cal.App.3d 11, 120 Cal.Rptr. 516 (1975)]

3. Ford Motor Co. manufactured and distributed the Ford Cortina, which had only a cardboard shield separating the fuel tank from the passenger compartment. Nanda suffered severe disabling burns when the gas tank in his car exploded upon being struck in the rear by another car. In a strict liability action by Nanda against Ford Motor Co., Nanda argued that the absence of a fire wall or metal shield between the fuel tank and the passenger compartment constituted an unreasonably dangerous defect in the product and that his injuries were caused by this defect. What was the result? [*Nanda v. Ford Motor Co.*, 509 F.2d 213 (7th Cir. 1974)]

1. The appellate court noted that under the UCC an implied warranty can be excluded or modified, even orally. It was clear that Robinson purchased the used truck "as is." He therefore could not raise an implied warranty claim against his seller.

2. No. Italics are not sufficient to make a disclaimer conspicuous. Large, bold print is required. The court therefore held that this disclaimer was not effective.

3. Nanda recovered from Ford Motor Co. for his injuries resulting from the unreasonably dangerous defect in design. Ford Motor Co. was held strictly liable for Nanda's injuries because (1) the company is normally engaged in the business of manufacturing and selling products; (2) the product was unreasonably dangerous when it left Ford; (3) the car had not been substantially changed since it was sold; and (4) the defective condition was the proximate cause of Nanda's physical injuries.

By the end of this chapter, students will be able to:
- Identify sources of consumer protection
- Interpret labeling and packaging laws
- Describe statutes that protect consumers in sales transactions

- Tell how regulations protect consumers' health
- List the purposes of the Consumer Product Safety Commission
- Delineate ways consumers' credit rights are protected

Prereading Activity

Lead a discussion about government regulations that students have studied in civics, government, or other courses. Discuss consumers' need for protection from unfair practices and unsafe products.

LEGAL BACKGROUND

Consumer transactions take a variety of forms, but broadly include those that involve an exchange of value for the purpose of acquiring goods, services, or land for family or personal use. It was traditionally assumed that in disputes involving consumers, the freedom to contract carried with it the obligation to live by the deal made. Therefore, the watchword in most transactions was *caveat emptor*—let the buyer beware. Over time that attitude has changed considerably, as goods no longer are manufactured by your neighbor, but by someone perhaps thousands of miles away.

Consumer protection includes restrictions on advertising, sales tactics, credit practices, and consumer safety. Because of the differences in state law, in this chapter we focus on federal legislation.

Chapter
16

Consumer Protection

<table>
<tr><td>

**Chapter 16
Resources and Assignment Guide**

Activity Sheets
Reviewing Legal Concepts 16 *TRB*
Enrichment Activity 16 *TRB*

Student Activity Workbook
Chapter 16 Activities

Tests
Chapter 16 Test *TRB*

</td><td>

Chapter 16 WESTEST Computerized Testing

Handbook of Selected Court Cases
Thompson Medical Co. v. *Federal Trade
    Commission*
Warner-Lambert Co. v. *Federal Trade
    Commission*

**West's Business Law and Legal
Environment Videodisc**
Still Frames and Motion Segments as shown

</td></tr>
</table>

Critical Thinking Activity

Call on volunteers to answer the following questions: What do you think of when you hear the term *consumer protection?* From whom do consumers need to be protected? Why? Are there costs involved in consumer protection? Who pays those costs?

Discussion Starter

Have your students read the quote that begins Chapter 16. Ask them to discuss the meaning of this quote and how it relates to our economy.

Extension Activity

You might wish to ask a representative from your local Better Business Bureau to speak to your class concerning the bureau's consumer protection activities. Encourage students to prepare questions in advance for your speaker.

---

*"Given the imbalance of knowledge and resources between a business
enterprise and each of its customers, economically it is more rational, and
imposes far less cost on society, to require a manufacturer to confirm his
affirmative product claims rather than impose a burden upon each
individual consumer to test, investigate, or experiment for himself."*
**FTC Commissioner Kirkpatrick
Case of In re Pfizer, Inc., 1972**

Consumer protection law consists of all statutes, agency rules, and common law judicial rulings that protect the interest of consumers. The period following the 1960s has been called "the age of the consumer" because so much legislation was passed to protect the consumer against the unfair practices and unsafe products of sellers. Today, both state and federal legislation regulate how businesses may advertise, engage in mail-order transactions, package and label their products, and so on. Also, numerous local, state, and federal agencies exist to help the consumer in settling grievances with sellers and producers. This chapter discusses the various sources of consumer protection and then describes consumer protection law in several areas: advertising, labeling and packaging, sales, health, product safety, and credit transactions.

◆ **consumer
protection law** All statutes, agency rules, and common law judicial rulings that protect the interests of consumers.

◆ SOURCES OF CONSUMER PROTECTION

Sources of consumer protection exist at all levels of government. Several federal laws—such as the Consumer Credit Protection Act and the Magnuson-Moss Warranty Act—were passed to establish duties for sellers and the rights of consumers. Exhibit 16-1 lists most of the federal consumer protection statutes. Federal administrative agencies, such as the Federal Trade Commission (FTC), provide another important source of consumer protection. Nearly every federal agency has an office of consumer affairs.

At the state level, the Uniform Commercial Code includes consumer protection provisions, and many states have passed additional consumer protection statutes. Most states have one or more consumer protection agencies.

Numerous private organizations, such as the Better Business Bureau, also exist to aid consumers. Finally, consumers can use the courts to obtain remedies for their grievances. Free legal services, mediation and arbitration programs, and small claims courts are sometimes available to help consumers resolve legal questions.

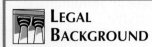
The Pure Food and Drug Act of 1906 was the first federal law enacted by Congress prohibiting the interstate transportation and sale of adulterated food, pursuant to Congress's power under the commerce clause.

The Pure Food and Drug Act and the Meat Inspection Act of 1906 were both inspired by public outcry over adulterated and poisonous foods and drugs. This outcry was inflamed by articles from "muckraking journalists" and by Upton Sinclair's *The Jungle* (1906). *The Jungle* and its impact on these statutes is discussed in the *Law in Action* feature in this chapter.

Samuel Hopkins Adams was the journalist responsible for exposing the dangers of patent medicines, in several sensational articles published in *Colliers*. As Adams pointed out, patent medicines contained mostly alcohol, drugs, and "undiluted fraud." Dr. Harvey H. Wiley was instrumental in the passage of the Pure Food and Drug Act of 1906, which was subsequently amended in 1912, 1913, and 1919.

Enrichment

With the class, go over this exhibit detailing federal consumer protection statutes. Have interested volunteers research the statute or agency rule of their choice. Students should present their findings in the form of short written reports similar to the legal brief on the Pure Food and Drug Act found on this page.

376   Commercial and Consumer Law

Statute or Agency Rule	Purpose
Advertising	
Federal Trade Commission Act (1914/1938)	Prohibits deceptive and unfair trade practices.
Public Health Cigarette Smoking Act (1970)	Prohibits radio and TV cigarette advertising.
FTC Rules of Negative Options (1973)	Federal Trade Commission rules regulating advertising of book and record clubs.
Smokeless Tobacco Act (1986)	Prohibits radio and TV advertising of smokeless tobacco products; requires special labeling to warn consumers of potential health hazards associated with smokeless tobacco.
Credit	
Consumer Credit Protection Act (Truth-in-Lending Act) (1968)	Offers comprehensive protection covering all phases of credit transactions.
Fair Credit Reporting Act (1970)	Protects consumers' credit reputations.
Equal Credit Opportunity Act (1974)	Prohibits discrimination in the extending of credit.
Fair Credit Billing Act (1970)	Protects consumers in credit-card billing errors and other disputes.
Fair Debt Collection Practices Act (1977)	Prohibits debt collector's abuses.
Counterfeit Access Device and Computer Fraud and Abuse Act (1984)	Prohibits the production, use, and sale of counterfeit credit cards or other access devices used to obtain money, goods, services, or other things of value.
Fair Credit and Charge Card Disclosure Act (1988)	Requires fuller disclosure of terms and conditions in credit-card and charge-card applications and solicitations.
Home Equity Loan Consumer Protection Act (1988)	Prohibits lenders from changing the terms of a loan after the contract has been signed; requires fuller disclosure in home equity loans of interest-rate formulas and repayment terms.
Health and Safety	
Pure Food and Drug Act (1906)	Prohibits adulteration and mislabeling of food and drugs sold in interstate commerce.
Meat Inspection Act (1906)	Provides for inspection of meat.
Federal Food, Drug and Cosmetic Act (1938)	Protects consumers from unsafe food products and from unsafe and/or ineffective drugs (superceded Pure Food and Drug Act of 1906)
Flammable Fabrics Act (1953)	Prohibits the sale of highly flammable clothing.
Poultry Products Inspection Act (1957)	Provides for inspection of poultry.
Child Protection and Toy Safety Act (1966)	Requires child-proof devices and special labeling.
National Traffic and Motor Vehicle Safety Act (1966)	Requires manufacturers to inform new car dealers of any safety defects found after manufacture and sale of auto.
Wholesome Meat Act (1967)	Updated Meat Inspection Act of 1906 to provide for stricter standards for slaughtering plants of red-meat animals.

EXHIBIT 16-1
FEDERAL CONSUMER PROTECTION STATUTES

State Law

As the student text makes clear, most states have one or more consumer protection agencies. Have a student volunteer, or group of volunteers, research the consumer protection agencies in your state. The vol- unteers should prepare a report discussing the name of each agency, its function, etc. Allow the volunteers to present their report to the class.

Statute or Agency Rule	Purpose
Health and Safety (cont'd)	
Consumer Product Safety Act (1972)	Established the Consumer Product Safety Commission to regulate all potentially hazardous consumer products.
Department of Transportation Rule on Passive Restraints in Automobiles (1984)	Requires automatic restraint systems in all new cars sold after September 1, 1990.
Toy Safety Act (1984)	Allows the Consumer Product Safety Commission to quickly recall toys and other articles intended for use by children that present a substantial risk of injury.
Drug-Price Competition and Patent-Term Restoration Act (Generic Drug Act) (1984)	Speeds up and simplifies Food and Drug Administration approval of generic versions of drugs on which patents have expired.
Labeling and Packaging	
Wool Products Labeling Act (1939)	Requires accurate labeling of wool products.
Fur Products Labeling Act (1951)	Prohibits misbranding of fur products.
Textile Fiber Products Identification Act (1958)	Prohibits false labeling and advertising of all textile products not covered under Wool and Fur Products Labeling Acts.
Hazardous Substances Labeling Act (1960)	Requires warning labels on all items containing dangerous chemicals.
Cigarette Labeling and Advertising Act (1965)	Requires labels warning of possible health hazards.
Child Protection and Toy Safety Act (1966)	Requires child-proof devices and special labeling.
Fair Packaging and Labeling Act (1966)	Requires that accurate names, quantities, and weights be given on product labels.
Smokeless Tobacco Act (1986)	Requires labels disclosing possible health hazards of smokeless tobacco; prohibits radio and TV advertising of smokeless tobacco products.
Sales and Warranties	
Interstate Land Sales Full Disclosure Act (1968)	Requires disclosure in interstate land sales.
Odometer Act (1972)	Protects consumers against odometer fraud in used-car sales.
FTC Door-to-Door Sales Rule (1973)	Federal Trade Commission rule regulating door-to-door sales contracts.
Real Estate Settlement Procedures Act (1974)	Requires disclosure of home-buying costs.
Magnuson-Moss Warranty Act (1975)	Provides rules governing content of warranties.
FTC Vocational and Correspondence School Rule (1980)	Federal Trade Commission rule regulating contracts with these types of schools.
FTC Used-Car Rule (1981)	Federal Trade Commission rule requiring dealers in used-car sales to disclose specified types of information in "Buyer's Guide" affixed to auto.
FTC Funeral Home Rule (1984)	Federal Trade Commission rule requiring disclosure by funeral homes regarding prices and services.

Reteaching Activity

You might want students to recall what they learned in the last chapter regarding the Magnuson-Moss Warranty Act of 1975. If the students' memories are unclear, you might have them reread the Chapter 15 Summary.

Teaching with the Videodisc

The still frames listed below from the **West's Business Law and Legal Environment Videodisc** can be used with this chapter. To access this material, use the bar codes or the frame numbers included in the Videodisc Instructor's Manual found in the *TRB*.

Consumer Protection Statutes and Regulations– Advertising

Consumer Protection Statues and Regulations– Inspection and Certification

Consumer Protection Statutes and Regulations– Labeling

Consumer Protection Statutes and Regulations– Sales and Warranties

For a week, have your students collect advertisements found in your local newspaper that contain possible misleading statements or half-truths. Have them create a large poster of all the ads collected, and instruct all students to read each ad to see if it is in fact deceptive. Instruct them to read any fine print at the bottom of these ads too.

Ask a student volunteer to read this Legal Focus Case Example to the class. Stimulate a class discussion about this example by asking the following questions: What claim did the makers of Campbell soup make about their soups? What facts did they offer in support of this claim? What important fact regarding heart disease did they not mention in their advertisements? What action did the FTC take? Do you believe that the FTC's actions were justified? Do you believe that the FTC should have also levied fines? Why or why not?

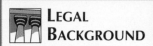

LEGAL BACKGROUND

The Federal Trade Commission, which is mentioned here, is the most important federal consumer protection agency. It was created in 1914 in response to a growing realization that consumers needed protection from dishonest or careless manufacturers. The FTC's activities are divided among three bureaus—the Bureau of Consumer Protection, the Bureau of Competition, and the Bureau of Economics. Through the Bureau of Consumer Protection, the FTC can stop any "unfair or deceptive act or practices" that treat consumers unfairly in their purchasing decisions.

378

 ## ADVERTISING

In the area of advertising, consumer protection law focuses on deceptive advertising. **Deceptive advertising** misleads consumers, either by making claims that are not true or by failing to give important facts.

Common law protection against deceptive advertising is based on fraud and requires proof that the advertiser intended to misrepresent facts about the product. Statutory law and administrative regulations, in contrast, focus on whether the advertising is likely to mislead, regardless of the advertiser's intent.

Numerous government agencies, both federal and state, exist to protect consumers from deceptive advertising. At the federal level, the most important agency regulating advertising is the Federal Trade Commission (FTC). The FTC has the power to determine what is a deceptive practice under the Federal Trade Commission Act.

◆ **deceptive advertising**
Advertising that misleads consumers by making unjustified or misleading claims.

DEFINING DECEPTIVE ADVERTISING

According to the FTC, an advertisement is deceptive if it is capable of being interpreted in more than one way and one of those interpretations is false or misleading. False or deceptive advertising comes in many forms. The deception may concern a product's quality, effects, price, origin, or availability. It may be a false statement or claim about a competitor's product. A failure to include important information about the product can be deceptive. Some advertisements contain "half-truths." A half-truth is information that is true but incomplete, leading consumers to a false conclusion.

 ### LEGAL FOCUS – CASE EXAMPLE

The makers of Campbell's soups advertised that "most" Campbell's soups were low in fat and cholesterol and thus were helpful in fighting heart disease. What the ad did not say was that Campbell's soups were high in sodium content. High-sodium diets may increase the risk of heart disease. The FTC concluded that Campbell's claims were deceptive and ordered that references to effectiveness in fighting heart disease be stopped.

Other ads contain claims not supported by adequate scientific evidence. These may or may not be considered deceptive. When the claim is incapable of measurement, as in, "At Avis, we try harder," there is no problem of deception.

An ad may be deceptive though it is literally true. An ad for "Teak Tables," for example, may be for tables manufactured by a firm named "Teak." The advertiser could claim the ad was truthful. Nonetheless, the ad is probably deceptive, because most consumers would believe that the

Have a few volunteers research new laws restricting the use of the word *light* on certain foods. Have these students share their information with the class.

Have students bring in a newspaper ad that contains half-truths or a form of deceptive advertising. Ask your students to highlight the deception in yellow and highlight the puffing in pink. Display these ads in your classroom for students to view.

Divide the class into small groups. Have each group read and discuss the four situations listed in the text in which bait-and-switch advertising occurs. Each group should then create and act out for the class a scenario based on one of these situations. Afterward, the group should be prepared to discuss with the class just how this situation qualifies as bait and switch.

ad referred to teak wood. The test for whether an ad is deceptive is *whether a reasonable consumer would be deceived by the ad.*

BAIT-AND-SWITCH ADVERTISING

The Federal Trade Commission has specific rules about some types of deceptive advertising. An important rule is contained in the FTC "Guides on Bait Advertising." Here, a low price on a particular product is the "bait" to lure the consumer into the store. The salesperson is instructed to "switch" the consumer to a different, more expensive item. The advertised item may be unavailable, or the salesperson may discourage the consumer from buying it. According to the FTC guidelines, **bait-and-switch advertising** occurs in any of the following situations:

1. The seller refuses to show the advertised item.
2. The seller fails to have adequate quantities of the item available.
3. The seller fails to promise to deliver the advertised item within a reasonable time.
4. The seller discourages employees from selling the item.

◆ LEGAL FOCUS - EXAMPLE

Goggle View Eyeglasses advertised eyeglasses from $37.50 complete, including the lenses, frames, and case. When customers came to the store, they were told the advertised glasses were inferior and were shown another model costing $65. Although it was possible to buy the $37.50 glasses, the customer had to deal with a furious sales pitch for the more expensive glasses. This is bait-and-switch advertising.

◆ **bait-and-switch advertising**
Advertising a product at a very attractive price (the "bait") and then informing the consumer, once he or she is in the door, that the advertised product is either not available or is of poor quality. The customer is then urged to purchase ("switched to") a more expensive item.

Discussion Starter

Stimulate a class discussion on bait-and-switch advertising by asking your students to share experiences they have had with bait-and-switch advertising.

Legal Focus Example

Read this Legal Focus Example to the class. Ask the class if they can think of any other examples of bait-and-switch advertising that could also fit here. Allow volunteers to share their examples with the class.

Some states have laws which require car dealerships to specify the number of cars available at special sale prices.

---

380   Commercial and Consumer Law

FTC ACTIONS AGAINST DECEPTIVE ADVERTISING

As mentioned, the FTC has the power to determine what is deceptive advertising. The FTC receives complaints of violations from many sources. Competitors of alleged violators, consumers, consumer organizations, trade associations, Better Business Bureaus, government organizations, and state and local officials are among those who complain. If complaints are widespread, the FTC investigates the problem.

If the FTC believes that an advertisement is unfair or deceptive after the investigation, it may hold a hearing. The hearing is similar to a trial. At the hearing, the accused company may present its defense.

If the FTC proves that an advertisement is unfair or deceptive, it may issue a *cease-and-desist order*. This order requires that the challenged advertising be stopped. The FTC may also require **counteradvertising**, or corrective advertising. In counteradvertising, a company must provide advertising that corrects earlier misinformation.

♦ **counteradvertising**
New advertising undertaken because of an FTC order to correct earlier false claims made about a product.

 LEGAL FOCUS ~ CASE EXAMPLE

Warner-Lambert Co., which sold the mouthwash Listerine, advertised that the product prevented colds and sore throats or lessened their severity. Because Listerine did and does not help prevent or treat colds, Warner-Lambert was ordered by the FTC to stop advertising that it did. The company was also ordered to include in the next 10 million dollars of its advertising the statement that "Listerine will not help prevent colds or sore throats or lessen their severity."[1]

FTC orders can be appealed in a court, but courts give great weight to an FTC ruling. The courts believe that the FTC, dealing continually with such cases, is a better judge than the courts of when a practice is deceptive.

◆ LABELING AND PACKAGING

Several labeling and packaging laws require manufacturers to give consumers accurate information or warnings about their products. In general, labels must be accurate. That means that they must use words as they are ordinarily understood by consumers. A box of cereal should not be labeled "giant" if that word exaggerates the amount of cereal in the box, for example. In addition, labels often must specify the raw materials used in the product. For example, a label may specify the percentage of cotton, nylon, or other fibers used in a shirt.

---

1. *Warner-Lambert Co. v. FTC,* 562 F.2d 749 (D.C. Cir. 1977).

The Fair Packaging and Labeling Act requires that consumer goods have labels that identify the product, often according to certain standard definitions. For example, before a product can be called peanut butter, it must contain at least 90 percent peanut ingredients. Otherwise, it is peanut spread. The name of the manufacturer and the name of the packer or distributor and its place of business must be included on the label. For food products, labels must state the net quantity of the contents and the quantity of each serving if the number of servings is stated.

The act also regulates the words used to describe packages, the terms associated with savings claims, disclosure of information for ingredients in nonfood products, and the standards for the partial filling of packages. Ingredients must be listed by common or usual names. The ingredients are to be listed in descending order according to their weight as part of the product. The Federal Trade Commission and the Department of Health and Human Services enforce this law.

Legal Focus Example

Ask a student volunteer to read this Legal Focus Example aloud to the class. Ask the students if they are familiar with this type of information, especially in regard to new car sales and/or car leases. How is this information presented in print advertisements? How is it presented in television commercials? How is it presented in radio commercials? Have the students compare the techniques advertisers use for presenting this "fine print" information.

◆ SALES

In the area of sales, consumer protection has several focal points. Many of the statutes protecting consumers in sales transactions focus on the disclosure of certain information in sales transactions. These statutes provide rules governing home or door-to-door sales, mail-order transactions, referral sales, and unsolicited merchandise—merchandise sent to someone who did not order it.

Several statutes govern the content of credit information contained in written and oral messages. If, for example, certain credit terms are used in an advertisement, other credit information must also be given.

◆ LEGAL FOCUS - EXAMPLE

Prolific Pontiac Sales states in a newspaper advertisement that individuals have thirty-six months to pay for a new automobile. The firm must also include the cash price of the automobile, the down payment, the finance charge, the amount of each periodic payment, and the annual percentage rate of interest.

The Postal Reorganization Act of 1970 governs the sending of *unsolicited products* through the mails. The law provides that such merchandise sent by U.S. mail may be retained, used, discarded, or disposed of in any manner thought appropriate by the recipient. The recipient has no obligation to the sender. Also, mailing unordered merchandise (except free samples) is an unfair trade practice and is not permitted. Mailings by charitable agencies and mailings made by mistake are exceptions.

LEGAL FOCUS ~ PROBLEM

Media Marketing sent Maria Mexasi a copy of the book *Southwestern Folk Remedies for a Modern Age* through the mail. Maria had not ordered the book, but she read the book and thoroughly enjoyed it. A few weeks later, Media sent Maria a bill for $27.50. Must Maria pay?

Maria owes nothing to Media, and she can keep the book. She should, however, respond by indicating to the company what she intends to do. Maria might also want to notify the U.S. Postal Service. The use of the mails in this way by Media is illegal. Some states extend similar protection to consumers who receive unsolicited goods sent by means other than the U.S. mail.

DOOR-TO-DOOR SALES

Door-to-door sales are governed by special statutes because of the nature of the door-to-door sales transactions. If a door-to-door salesperson enters a house, he or she usually has a captive audience. Repeat purchases are not as likely as they are in stores, so the seller has less incentive to treat the purchaser fairly. The seller is also unlikely to present alternative products and their prices.

♦ **cooling-off statute** FTC regulation that gives consumers three days to cancel any door-to-door sale.

A Federal Trade Commission regulation requires that door-to-door sellers give consumers three days to cancel any sale. This is called a **cooling-off statute**. It gives consumers time to change their minds. The FTC rule also requires that the notification be given in Spanish if the oral negotiations were in that language. Many states have their own cooling-off laws that permit the buyers of goods sold door-to-door to cancel their contracts. Consumers can take advantage of either the FTC rule or their own state statute, depending on which gives them the most protection.

Many individuals are aware of cooling-off statutes, but some believe these statutes apply to most, or even all, contracts. That is simply not true. Cooling-off statutes are the exception. They exist only in limited circumstances, such as door-to-door sales.

MAIL-ORDER SALES

At the top of the list of consumer complaints are problems stemming from product sales by telephone or mail. Consumers buying from mail-order houses typically have had less protection than when they purchase in stores. Many mail-order houses are outside the buyer's state, and it is costly to solve grievances in such situations.

Federal statutes make it illegal to use the mails to defraud individuals. Several states have also passed statutes governing mail-order sales practices. Insurance companies that solicit through the mails are among the industries regulated. State statutes are similar to the federal statutes governing mail fraud.

1. Common law protection for deceptive advertising is based on fraud and requires proof of intent to misrepresent facts; however, statutory and administrative law focus on whether the advertising is likely to mislead, regardless of intent.

2. Counteradvertising is an ad in which a company corrects earlier misinformation.

3. In addition to identifying the product, the name of the manufacturer and the packer or distributor and its place of business must be included on a label. Food product labels must also include net quantity of the contents.

4. If a recipient receives unsolicited merchandise in the mail, he or she has no obligation to the sender.

5. The Federal Trade Commission regulation that requires door-to-door sellers to give consumers three days to cancel any sale, thus giving them time to change their minds, is a "cooling-off statute."

◆ CHECKING YOUR PROGRESS

1. How does common law differ from statutory and administrative regulations pertaining to deceptive advertising?

2. What is *counter advertising*?

3. Under the Fair Packaging and Labeling Act, what information must be included on a label that identifies a product?

4. What is the recipient's obligation if he or she receives unsolicited merchandise in the mail?

5. Describe the "cooling-off statute" that applies to door-to-door sales.

◆ HEALTH PROTECTION

As discussed in the Law in Action feature in this chapter, in 1906 Congress passed the Pure Food and Drug Act. This law was the first step in protecting consumers against adulteration and misbranding of food and drug products. (To adulterate something is to make it impure.) This act, and later amendments, established standards for foods, specified safe levels of potentially dangerous food additives, and created classifications of foods and food advertising.

Under the Food and Drug Act, drugs must be proved to be effective, as well as safe, before they can be sold. Food additives that are carcinogenic (cancer-causing) to humans or animals are forbidden. Food and drug laws make manufacturers responsible for ensuring that the food they offer for sale will not cause injury to the health of purchasers. The Food and Drug Administration supervises and enforces most statutes related to health issues.

Also in 1906, Congress passed the Meat Inspection Act. This law instituted inspection requirements for all meat and poultry sold for human consumption. The Department of Agriculture is responsible for meat and poultry inspection, although regulations allow some businesses to inspect their own products.

Federal statutes also protect individuals from other harmful products. Public concern over the dangers of cigarette smoking has led to consumer warnings. These warnings must be placed on cigarette and little cigar packages and on containers of smokeless tobacco. Major-brand cigarette producers are required to rotate four warning labels on a quarterly basis. Smaller companies may use all four warnings at the same time at random. Each warning begins, "Surgeon General's Warning" and then states one of the following:

1. Smoking Causes Lung Cancer, Heart Disease, Emphysema, and May Complicate Pregnancy.

2. Quitting Smoking Now Greatly Reduces Serious Risks to Your Health.

Example of a federal meat inspection logo.

Almost every person knows someone who has been injured while using a product. Divide your class into groups of three to five students. Have each member of each group describe an incident in which someone was injured while using a product. These events could include slipping in a bathtub, puncturing a finger on a sewing machine, or receiving a cut from a rough piece of metal on a car. Emphasize that the injury must be the result of using a specific product. Each group should then choose the injury its members feel was most clearly the result of an unsafe product and compose a letter addressed to the Consumer Product Safety Commission describing the event. Read and post these letters in your classroom.

LEGAL BACKGROUND

The Consumer Product Safety Commission sets and enforces standards for toys with small parts and sharp points and edges, and checks for levels of lead in paints. It also carries out public information campaigns to inform consumers of which toys are safe for children of different ages. It investigates consumer complaints and reports of toy-related injuries and deaths. When a dangerous toy is found on the market, the CPSC issues a press release to alert retailers and consumers. Such press releases often lead to product recalls by manufacturers and stores to avoid possible lawsuits. For example, in 1990, the F. J. Strauss Company voluntarily recalled roughly 3,600 "Music Maker" toys because of excessive levels of lead and too many small parts that could be swallowed.

Did cigarette manufacturers voluntarily decide to provide health warnings on their cigarette packages?

3. Smoking by Pregnant Women May Result in Fetal Injury, Premature Birth, and Low Birth Weight.
4. Cigarette Smoke Contains Carbon Monoxide.

The Smokeless Tobacco Act of 1986 requires producers, packagers, and importers of smokeless tobacco (chewing tobacco) to label their products conspicuously with one of three warnings: (1) This product may cause mouth cancer. (2) This product may cause gum disease and tooth loss. (3) This product is not a safe alternative to cigarettes.

◆ CONSUMER PRODUCT SAFETY

Consumer product safety legislation began in 1953 with the Flammable Fabrics Act. The act prohibits the sale of highly flammable clothing or materials. Over the next several years, Congress passed legislation regulating specific classes of products or product design or composition. These laws were not focused on the overall safety of consumer products. Then, in 1972, Congress passed a law meant to protect consumers from unreasonable risk of injury from hazardous products. This was the Consumer Product Safety Act of 1972. The act created the Consumer Product Safety Commission (CPSC). The purpose of the CPSC was:

1. To protect the public against unreasonable risk of injury associated with consumer products.
2. To assist consumers in evaluating the comparative safety of consumer products.
3. To develop uniform safety standards for consumer products and to minimize conflicting state and local regulations.
4. To promote research and investigation into the causes and prevention of product-related deaths, illnesses, and injuries.

The CPSC is authorized to set standards for consumer products. The CPSC can ban the manufacture and sale of any product that may be hazardous to consumers. The CPSC can also require manufacturers to report information about any products proved to be hazardous.

The CPSC has authority to administer other product safety acts, not just the Consumer Product Safety Act. These include the Child Protection and Toy Safety Act of 1966, the Hazardous Substances Labeling Act of 1960, and the Flammable Fabrics Act.

◆ CREDIT PROTECTION

Because of the extensive use of credit by American consumers, credit protection has become an important area of consumer protection. An impor-

Law in Action

Read
Introduce this *Law in Action* feature by asking your students the following questions: Why do consumers trust the food products they now buy to be prepared in sanitary conditions? Do you think we could trust these products to be pure if the government did not regulate the food industry? Is our trust in our food suppliers always justified? Why or why not? Then have a student volunteer read this

Law in Action feature aloud to the class.

Discuss
Stimulate a class discussion of this feature by asking the following questions: How many of you had heard of Upton Sinclair prior to reading this feature? What did you think of the excerpt from *The Jungle* that is included here? Why do you think the Food and Drug Act and the Meat Inspection Act had been stalled for a long period of time prior to publication of *The Jungle*?

Extend
Have a student volunteer research the publication of Ralph Nader's book *Unsafe at Any Speed*. How can the publication of this book and its resulting furor be compared to the publication of *The Jungle*? What effect on consumer product safety laws did both books have? How were the situations different? Allow the student volunteer to present his or her findings to the class in the form of an oral report.

Consumer Protection · 385

 Law in Action

LEGAL ISSUE: THE FOOD AND DRUG ACT OF 1906

The Pure Food and Drug Act of 1906 is a legislative landmark in the area of consumer health protection. It marked the beginning of federal regulation of food and drugs in the United States. What caused the congressional action was the public outrage generated by a novel. The novel, published in 1905, was Upton Sinclair's *The Jungle*. It was an exposé of the Chicago meatpacking industry. The story was so revolting that no one who read it could remain unaffected. President Theodore Roosevelt demanded an immediate investigation of the Chicago meatpacking houses supposedly after reading the following paragraph:

> There was never the least attention paid to what was cut up for sausages; there would come all the way back from Europe old sausage that had been rejected, and that was mouldy and white—it would be dosed with borax and glycerine, and dumped into the hoppers, and made over again for home consumption. There would be meat that had tumbled out on the floor, in the dirt and sawdust, where the workers had tramped and spit uncounted billions of con-

sumption germs. . . . It was too dark in these storage places to see well, but a man could run his hand over these piles of meat and sweep off handfuls of the dried dung of rats. These rats were nuisances, and the packers would put poisoned bread out for them; they would die, and then rats, bread, and meat would go into the hoppers together. This is no fairy story and no joke; . . . there were things that went into the sausage in comparison with which a poisoned rat was a tidbit.[2]

President Roosevelt wrote to Sinclair and promised to have the novelist's charges fully investigated. Sinclair wrote back, advising the president to make sure that the investigators did their work "under cover." He felt "official" visitors would not get the full truth. The investigation was ordered, and the labor commissioner confirmed Sinclair's observations. Both the long-stalled Food and Drug Act and the Meat Inspection Act were passed immediately.

2. Upton Sinclair, *The Jungle* (New York: Penguin Edition, 1985), p. 163.

tant federal statute regulating credit is the Truth-in-Lending Act, passed by Congress in 1968. Others include the Fair Credit Reporting Act and the Fair Debt Collection Practices Act. In addition, the Uniform Consumer Credit Code seeks to make state laws governing credit consistent.

TRUTH IN LENDING

The Truth-in-Lending Act (TILA) is a disclosure law administered by the Federal Reserve Board. It requires sellers and lenders to disclose credit terms or loan terms so individuals can shop around for the best financing arrangements. TILA requirements apply only to persons who lend money or sell on credit or arrange for the extension of credit in the ordinary

The Truth in Lending Act requires that the terms and transactions involving consumer credit be fully explained to the prospective debtors. This act sets forth three basic rules:
1. A creditor cannot advertise a deal that ordinarily is not available to anyone except a preferred borrower.
2. Advertisements must contain either all of the terms of a credit transaction or none of them.
3. If the credit is to be repaid in more than four payments, the agreement must indicate, in clear and conspicuous print, that "the cost of credit is included in the price quoted for the goods and services."

Caption Answer

One protection limits the liability of a cardholder to $50 per card for unauthorized charges made before the creditor is notified that the card has been lost. Another protection prohibits a credit card company from billing a consumer for any unauthorized charges if the credit card was not issued properly by the credit card company.

Extension Activity

Invite a local credit bureau representative to come to your classroom and discuss the importance of good credit and how credit bureaus operate.

---

386   Commercial and Consumer Law

course of their business. Sales or loans made between two consumers are not covered by the act. Transactions covered by the act include retail and installment sales and installment loans, car loans, home-improvement loans, and certain real estate loans. The TILA requires that all credit terms be fully disclosed.

Equal Credit Opportunity   The TILA prohibits discrimination by lenders on the basis of race, religion, national origin, color, sex, marital status, or age. The act also prohibits discrimination based on whether an individual is receiving certain types of income, such as public assistance benefits. Creditors are prohibited from requesting any information from a credit applicant that could be used to discriminate.

Credit-Card Rules   The TILA also covers credit cardholders. One provision limits the liability of a cardholder to $50 per card for unauthorized charges *made before the creditor is notified that the card has been lost.* There is no liability if the company is notified before any unauthorized use. Another provision prohibits a credit-card company from billing a consumer for any unauthorized charges if the credit card was not issued properly by the credit-card company.

The act covers billing disputes related to credit-card purchases. When a debtor thinks that an error has occurred in billing or wishes to withhold payment for a faulty product purchased by credit card, the act identifies the appropriate steps for both the consumer and the credit-card company. Credit-card companies are required to provide their customers with information about the customers' rights. See Exhibit 16-2 for a bank's statement disclosing these rights, called a disclosure statement.

FAIR CREDIT REPORTING ACT

Credit information is used by businesses to determine whether to grant or deny credit. Businesses also make employment and insurance decisions based on credit information. To get credit information, businesses often turn to credit bureaus. The Fair Credit Reporting Act (FCRA) of 1970 helps consumers learn about the information kept by credit bureaus about them.

The FCRA regulates all credit bureaus, investigative reporting companies, detective and collection agencies, and computerized information-reporting companies. Under the act, consumers have the right to be notified when such companies are preparing reports about them and to have access to the information contained in the reports. Consumers can then determine and correct any important misinformation about their credit histories that is being given out. (The credit bureau is allowed to charge a consumer a reasonable fee for a copy of the report, such as $10 to $20.)

Upon request and proper identification, a consumer is entitled to know the nature and substance of information about him or her that is contained in an agency's file. The consumer can also learn who has received consumer credit reports. A report cannot be prepared on an individual consumer unless that person is notified and given the right to request information on the nature and scope of the investigation.

What are some of the legal protections available to the credit card holder?

Explain to the students that credit card fraud is a growing problem in our economy. There are many ways in which credit card fraud may take place. The most obvious is when a person's card is lost or stolen and used by another person. A similar problem takes place when someone orders merchandise over the phone using a credit card number he or she has found or stolen. A problem that used to be common but that has been decreasing in recent years is credit card forgery. The use of magnetic tape codes and laser-printed holograms has reduced but not eliminated this problem. Have your students examine the issue of credit card fraud, and then ask them to write a short explanation of how all consumers pay the cost of credit card fraud even when their own cards are never fraudulently used.

DISCLOSURE STATEMENT

Your **VISA** account enables you to make purchases (including purchases of wire transfer money orders) and obtain loans from us from time to time and allows you the choice of paying the balance in full or in monthly instalments. In addition to repaying the amount of any cash advance and purchase added to your **VISA** account, you may also be responsible for paying us a **FINANCE CHARGE.**

FINANCE CHARGE on Purchases. If you pay the new balance on your previous statement in full by the due date shown on that statement, there is no **FINANCE CHARGE.** If you don't pay the new balance on your previous statement in full by the due date, you will have to pay a **FINANCE CHARGE.** We will multiply your average daily balance which includes the unpaid previous balance and any new purchases, not previously billed, by the monthly periodic rate of **1½%.** This corresponds to an **ANNUAL PERCENTAGE RATE of 18%.**

FINANCE CHARGE on Cash Advances. There is no free period for cash advances; you'll pay a **FINANCE CHARGE** on cash advances from the day each advance is posted to your account until the day it's paid off. We'll multiply your average daily balance of unpaid cash advances by the monthly periodic rate of **1%.** This corresponds to an **ANNUAL PERCENTAGE RATE OF 12%.**

The total amount of **FINANCE CHARGE** to be paid will be the sum of the **FINANCE CHARGE** on purchases and the **FINANCE CHARGE** on cash advances.

Your Average Daily Balance. Here's how we figure the average daily balance of unpaid purchases and the average daily balance of unpaid cash advances:

1.   We start with the new balance from your previous statement, if not paid in full within 25 days after the statement closing date, and add all purchases posted in the current billing period as of the day posted.
2.   All cash advances made will be included in the average daily balance from the day posted to your account whether the new balance from the previous statement was paid in full or not.
3.   Any credits to your account during the billing period will be deducted as of the first day of the period and payments will be deducted as of the day received.
4.   Payments and credits are applied as far as they will go in this order:
     Payments: (a) to unpaid cash advances shown on a previous statement and **FINANCE CHARGE** on them; (b) to unpaid balance of purchases shown on a previous statement and **FINANCE CHARGE** on them; (c) to new cash advances and **FINANCE CHARGE** on them; (d) to new purchases.
     Credits are applied to any unpaid balance of purchases and **FINANCE CHARGE** on them.
5.   After deducting payments and credits from unpaid balances, we figure your daily balance of purchases and your daily balance of cash advances during the billing period. We add your daily balances of purchases and of cash advances and divide each sum by the number of days in the billing period. The result is your average daily balances of purchases and cash advances to be multiplied by the monthly periodic rates to determine the **FINANCE CHARGE** due for the period.

Payment Schedule. You can pay for all your purchases and cash advances in full at any time, or you can pay in monthly instalments. If you do not pay the entire balance within 25 days after the statement closing date, you must pay monthly instalments. If you pay in instalments, each payment must be at least **1/36th** of your new balance, but not less than **$5.** If your new balance is **$5** or less, you must pay it in full.

Collection Costs. You agree to pay all collection costs, including reasonable attorney's fees.

NOTICE: "See accompanying statement for important information regarding your rights to dispute billing errors".

EXHIBIT 16-2
BANK DISCLOSURE STATEMENT

FAIR DEBT COLLECTION PRACTICES ACT

In 1977, Congress passed the Fair Debt Collection Practices Act. The purpose of the act is to regulate the practices of collection agencies when they collect consumer debts. The act prohibits the following debt collection practices:

1.   Contacting the consumer at his or her place of employment if the employer objects.
2.   Contacting the consumer at an inconvenient time (such as 2 A.M.) or at any time if the consumer is represented by an attorney. Generally the debt collector must call between 8 A.M. and 9 P.M.
3.   Contacting third parties other than parents, spouses, or financial advisers about the payment of a debt unless authorized to do so by a court of law.
4.   Using harassment and intimidation, such as abusive language, or using false or misleading information, such as posing as a police officer. Of course, the collector may tell the debtor that the creditor will sue if the debtor does not pay.
5.   Communicating with the consumer after receipt of a notice that the consumer is refusing to pay the debt. The collection agency can, however, advise the consumer of further action it expects to take.

   The enforcement of this act is primarily the responsibility of the Federal Trade Commission. The act provides for damages and penalties that can be recovered for violation, including attorney's fees.

Divide the class into small groups. Ask each group to look at the practices that are prohibited by the Fair Debt Collection Practices Act. Have each group collaborate on writing an essay in support of the Fair Debt Collection Practices Act. In their essays, students should discuss the trade-off between legitimate rights of creditors and the human rights or personal rights of debtors. Each group should choose a leader to present its essay to the class.

LEGAL BACKGROUND

Under the Fair Credit Reporting Act, any report by an agency relating to a consumer's creditworthiness, credit standing, character, general reputation, personal characteristics, or mode of living is within the purview of the law. Statutory provisions cover information used or expected for use in the evaluation of the consumer for one of four purposes:
1. Credit or insurance for personal, family, or household use
2. Employment
3. Licenses to operate particular businesses or practice a profession
4. Any other legitimate business use
Many states have enacted statutes comparable to the Fair Credit Reporting Act.

Reteaching Activity

Have students work with partners to outline this chapter and study the terms and laws found in each section.

Checking Your Progress (Answers)

1. The purpose of the CPSC is (1) to protect the public against unreasonable risk of injury associated with consumer products, (2) to assist consumers in evaluating the comparative safety of consumer products, (3) to develop uniform safety standards for consumer products and to minimize conflicting state and local regulations, and (4) to promote research and investigation into the causes and prevention of product-related deaths, illnesses, and injuries.

2. The Truth-in-Lending Act (TILA) is a disclosure law. It requires people who sell on credit or lend money in the ordinary course of their business to disclose credit terms or loan terms to consumers. The act also prohibits discrimination by lenders and limits the liability of a credit cardholder.

3. TILA establishes limits of a cardholder's liability for unauthorized charges, protects consumers from unauthorized charges if the credit card was not issued properly, and covers billing disputes related to credit card purchases.

UNIFORM CONSUMER CREDIT CODE

The National Conference of Commissioners on Uniform State Laws has drafted the Uniform Consumer Credit Code (UCCC). The UCCC is an attempt to make a comprehensive body of rules about the most important aspects of consumer credit. Its purpose is similar to that of the Uniform Commercial Code. Some essential points of the UCCC are as follows:

1. It places statutory ceilings on interest rates and other charges.
2. It requires disclosure similar to that required by the truth-in-lending law.
3. It limits debt collection against take-home wages to a certain amount and prohibits the firing of an employee solely because of a single garnishment proceeding.
4. It allows for cancellation of a contract solicited by a seller in the consumer–debtor's home within three business days of the solicitation.
5. It provides criminal as well as civil penalties for violations.

The UCCC has only been adopted by a few states. Among those states that have adopted the UCCC, some have adopted only portions of it.

◆ CHECKING YOUR PROGRESS

1. What is the purpose of the Consumer Product Safety Commission?
2. What type of law is the Truth-in-Lending Act? What are the requirements of the Act?
3. What is the effect of the Truth-in-Lending Act on credit card holders?

Read

Introduce this *A Case In Point* feature by explaining to the class that it deals with utterly deceptive advertising for an over-the-counter pain killer. Remind the students that according to the FTC, an advertisement is deceptive if it is capable of being interpreted in more than one way and if one of those interpretations is false or misleading. Then have a student volunteer read this *A Case In Point* feature aloud to the class.

Discuss

Stimulate a class discussion of this *A Case In Point* feature by asking the following questions: What product was being advertised in this case? What claims were being made regarding that product? How could these claims be interpreted? What steps did the FTC take regarding this advertising? How did the court decide in this case? What reasons did the court give for its decision?

◆ A CASE IN POINT ◆

THOMPSON MEDICAL CO. v. FEDERAL TRADE COMMISSION

United States Court of Appeals, District of Columbia Circuit, 1986. 791 F.2d 189.

In this case, the court considers whether an advertisement for an over-the-counter pain-killer is deceptive.

FACTS This case concerned a complaint brought by the Federal Trade Commission against Thompson Medical Company. The complaint alleged that Thompson's advertising for "Aspercreme"—a topical analgesic (a painkiller applied directly to a part of the body) sold over the counter in drug stores—was false and misleading. According to Thompson's advertising, Aspercreme was supposed to help arthritis victims and others seeking relief from minor aches and pains. It was meant to be rubbed on the area where an analgesic effect was desired. Thompson's advertising strongly suggested that Aspercreme and aspirin were related. In one television advertisement, for example, Aspercreme was described as follows: "When you suffer from arthritis, imagine putting the strong relief of aspirin right where you hurt. Aspercreme is an odorless rub which concentrates the relief of aspirin. When you take regular aspirin, it goes throughout your body. . . . But, in seconds, Aspercreme starts concentrating all the tem-porary relief of two aspirin directly at the point of minor arthritis pain."

The FTC ordered Thompson to refrain from advertising Aspercreme as an effective painkiller until studies were conducted that proved its effectiveness. It also ordered Thompson to disclose in all advertising and labeling that Aspercreme does not contain aspirin. Thompson appealed the FTC decision, claiming that the FTC ruling was the same as ordering it to stop selling Aspercreme. The order would lead to the destruction of its business.

ISSUE Were the FTC's conclusions regarding Thompson's advertising of Aspercreme correct?

DECISION Yes. The appellate court affirmed the FTC order that Thompson stop deceptively advertising its product, Aspercreme.

REASON The court found that the FTC's conclusions were consistent with the technical evidence and concluded that Thompson had engaged in deceptive advertising about Aspercreme. "We cannot find fault," said the court, "in the Commission's conclusions or in the remedial measures it imposed. . . . If and when Thompson comes up with evidence that Aspercreme is effective, it will be free to again make efficacy [effectiveness] claims in its advertising. Until that time, it should not say what it cannot prove. The FTC's requirement of aspirin-content disclaimers also is entirely appropriate."

Teaching Note

This case is included in the *West's Business and Personal Law Handbook of Selected Court Cases*.

In order to help students review what they have learned in Chapter 16, you might wish to:
1. Have a student volunteer, or volunteers, read the Chapter Summary aloud.
2. Allow the students to work with partners to complete the *Using Legal Language* activity.
3. Assign the *Checking for Comprehension* exercise as homework.
4. Allow the students to work in small groups to complete the *Applying Legal Concepts* activities.
5. As a class, complete the *Applying the Law* activities. (Please note that you may have to help students with vocabulary so that they adequately understand all of the *Applying the Law* material.)

In order to check student mastery of chapter concepts, you may wish to use the Chapter 16 test that is found in your *Teacher's Resource Binder* or use WESTEST computerized testing for Chapter 16.

CHAPTER REVIEW

 ## SUMMARY

ADVERTISING

1. *Deceptive advertising*—Advertising that is false or may be misleading to consumers is prohibited by the FTC.
2. *Bait-and-switch advertising*—Advertising a lower priced product when the intention is not to sell the advertised product but to lure the consumer into buying a higher priced product is prohibited by the FTC.
3. *FTC actions against deceptive advertising:*
   a. Cease-and-desist orders—Requiring the advertiser to stop the challenged advertising.
   b. Counteradvertising—Requiring the advertiser to advertise to correct the earlier misinformation.

LABELING AND PACKAGING

Manufacturers must comply with the labeling or packaging requirements for their specific products. In general, all labels must be accurate and not misleading.

SALES

1. *Credit terms*—If certain credit terms about a product are advertised, other relevant credit and sale terms must also be included.
2. *Unsolicited merchandise sent by U.S. mail*—Such merchandise may be kept, used, discarded, or disposed of in any manner by the recipient without obligation.
3. *Door-to-door sales*—The FTC requires all door-to-door sellers to give consumers three days to cancel any sale.
4. *Mail-order sales*—Federal statutes regulate sales through the mails and prohibit the use of the mails to defraud individuals.

HEALTH PROTECTION

Health-protection laws govern the processing and distribution of meat and poultry, poisonous substances, and drugs and cosmetics. For some products (such as cigarettes), explicit warnings about health hazards are required.

CONSUMER PRODUCT SAFETY

The Consumer Product Safety Act of 1972 protects consumers from risk of injury from hazardous products. The Consumer Product Safety Commission can remove products that are deemed likely to be hazardous from the market and to ban the manufacture and sale of such products.

CREDIT PROTECTION

1. *Truth-in-Lending Act*—A disclosure law which requires sellers and lenders to disclose credit and loan terms. The Truth-in-Lending Act provides for:
   a. Equal credit opportunity prohibits discriminating on the basis of race, religion, marital status, sex, etc.
   b. Credit-card rules allow credit-card users to withhold payment if they purchased a faulty product by credit card or when there has been an error in billing until the dispute is resolved.
2. *Fair Credit Reporting Act*—A law that entitles consumers to be informed of a credit investigation, to request a copy of the credit report, and to correct information in their credit files.
3. *Fair Debt Collection Practices Act*—Prohibits debt collectors from using unfair debt colletion practices.
4. *Uniform Consumer Credit Code*—A comprehensive body of rules governing the

1. The period following the 1960s has been called "the age of the consumer" because much federal and state legislation was passed at that time to protect the consumer against the unfair practices and unsafe products of sellers.
2. The FTC receives complaints about deceptive advertising from businesses, consumers, consumer organizations, trade associations, Better Business Bureaus, government organizations, and state and local officials. If complaints are widespread, the FTC investigates the problem.
3. Students should use the chart in Exhibit 16-1 and write a description of two statutes.
4. Consumers can take advantage of either the FTC rule or their own state statute, depending on which gives the consumer the most protection.
5. Upton Sinclair's exposé of the meat-packing industry in his book *The Jungle* caused a federal investigation, which resulted in the passage of the Pure Food and Drug Act and the Meat Inspection Act of 1906.
6. The CPSC has authority to administer the Consumer Product Safety Act, the Child Protection and Toy Safety Act, the Federal Hazardous Substance Act, and the Flammable Fabrics Act.

---

most important aspects of consumer credit; adopted by only a few states.

USING LEGAL LANGUAGE

Directions: Match each term with the statement that best defines that term.

1. bait-and-switch advertising
2. cease-and-desist order
3. Consumer Product Safety Act
4. cooling-off statute
5. counter advertising
6. deceptive advertising
7. equal credit opportunity
8. Fair Credit Reporting Act
9. Truth-in-Lending Act
10. Uniform Consumer Credit Code

A. _____ misleads consumers, either by unjustified or misleading claims or omitting important facts concerning a product's performance or a service.

B. Advertising a product at a very attractive price, then informing the consumer once he or she is in the door that the advertised product is either not available or is of poor quality, then urging the customer to purchase a more expensive item, is known as _____.

C. _____ is undertaken because of an FTC order to correct earlier false claims made about a product.

D. The FTC Commission has a _____ that gives consumers three days to cancel any door-to-door sale.

E. The _____ is a disclosure law that requires sellers and lenders to disclose credit terms or loan terms so that individuals can shop around for the best financing arrangements.

F. Consumers are protected from risk of injury from hazardous products under the _____ of 1972.

G. The Truth in Lending Act creates _____ by prohibiting discrimination by lenders on the basis of race, religion, national origin, color, sex, marital status, and age.

H. A comprehensive body of rules governing the most important aspects of consumer credit can be found in the _____, although it is only adopted by a minority of states.

I. The _____ of 1970 assists consumers in learning about the information kept by credit bureaus about consumers.

J. If the FTC proves that an advertisement is unfair or deceptive, it may issue a _____ which requires that the challenged advertising be stopped.

7. The National Conference of Commissioners on Uniform State Laws has drafted the UCC to create a comprehensive body of rules about the most important aspects of consumer credit.

8. The Truth-in-Lending Act (TILA) deals specifically with lost, stolen, and unauthorized use of credit cards. For credit cards solicited by the cardholder and then lost or stolen, the act limits the liability of the cardholder to $50 for unauthorized charges made prior to the time the creditor is notified. There is no liability for any unauthorized charges made after the date of notice. In the case of the Midtown Department Store credit card stolen on May 31, the $500 charge made on June 1, which is prior to Alderman's notice, causes Alderman to be liable for the $50 limit. For the June 3 charge of $200 made after the notification, Alderman has no liability. TILA also deals with unsolicited credit cards. Unless a credit card-holder accepts an unsolicited card (such as by using it), the cardholder is not liable for any unauthorized charges. Moreover, the act prohibits the issuance of unsolicited credit cards. No notice by the credit card-holder of an unsolicited, unaccepted card is required to absolve the cardholder from liability for unauthorized charges. Therefore, Alderman owes $50 to the Midtown Department Store and nothing to High-Flying Airlines.

9. Yes. A Federal Trade Commission (FTC) regulation makes it a violation for door-to-door sellers to fail to give consumers three days to cancel any sale. In addition, a number of state statutes require this three-day "cooling-off" period to protect consumers from unscrupulous door-to-door sellers. Since the Petersons should be able to rescind the contract within the three-day period, Renowned Books was obligated to agree to cancel the contract. Its failure to allow rescission was in violation of the FTC regulation and of most state statutes.

CHECKING FOR COMPREHENSION

1. Why has the period following the 1960s been called "the age of the consumer?"

2. From whom does the FTC receive complaints about deceptive advertising? What does the FTC do about the complaints?

3. Describe two Federal Consumer Protection Statutes that protect students from deceptive labeling and packaging.

4. When both federal and state laws apply to door-to-door sales, which law must consumers follow to protect their rights?

5. What was a major factor in the passage of the Pure Food and Drug Act and the Meat Inspection Act of 1906?

6. What acts are administered by the Consumer Product Safety Commission?

7. Why has the Uniform Consumer Credit Code been drafted?

8. Alderman receives two new credit cards on May 1. One was solicited from Midtown Department Store and the other was unsolicited from High-Flying Airlines. During the month of May Alderman makes numerous credit-card purchases from Midtown Store. She does not use the High-Flying Airlines card. On May 31 a burglar breaks into Alderman's home and, along with other items, steals both credit cards. Alderman notifies the Midtown Department Store of the theft on June 2, but she fails to notify High-Flying Airlines. Using the Midtown credit card, the burglar makes a $500 purchase on June 1 and a $200 purchase on June 3. The burglar then charges a vacation flight on the High-Flying Airlines card for $1,000 on June 5. Alderman receives the bills for these charges and refuses to pay. Discuss Alderman's liability in these situations.

9. On June 28, a sales representative for Renowned Books called on the Petersons at their home. After a very persuasive sales pitch on the part of the sales agent, the Petersons agreed in writing to purchase a twenty-volume set of historical encyclopedias from Renowned Books for a total of $299. An initial down payment of $35 was required, with the remainder of the price to be paid in monthly payments over a one-year period. Two days later the Petersons, having second thoughts, contacted the book company and stated they had decided to rescind the contract. Renowned Books said this would be impossible. Has Renowned Books violated any consumer law by not allowing the Petersons to rescind their contract?

◆ APPLYING LEGAL CONCEPTS

1. Four families purchased toys from a well-known toy manufacturer. In each family a child was injured while playing with the toys. A jury awarded total damages to the four families in the total amount of $2,000,000. Determine the amount awarded to each family based on the following percentages: Adams family—15 percent; Benavides family—20 percent; Ijawa family—30 percent; and the remaining percentage to the Pilon family.

2. Design a bar graph to display the amount each family received from the toy manufacturer. Design a pie chart to show the percentage each family received.

1. Collections Accounts Terminal was held by the court to have violated the Fair Debt Collections Practices Act (FDCPA) of 1977. Under that act, "A debt collector may not engage in any conduct the natural consequences of which is to harass, oppress or abuse any person in connection with the collection of a debt." In this case, the court held that the tone of the collecting agency's letter was "one of intimidation, and was intended as such in order to effect a collection." Such intimidation was considered an abuse of the debtor and thus a violation of the general standard imposed by the FDCPA. Further, the act specifically bars any collection agency or creditor from contacting third persons in connection with a debt (with certain limited exceptions). In view of this legal prohibition, the threat by the collection agency to contact Rutyna's neighbors and employer concerning her debt constituted a false representation of the actions that the creditor could legally take. Section 1692e of the FDCPA prohibits a debt collector from using any "false, deceptive, or misleading representation or means in connection with the collection of any debt." Collection Accounts Terminal, both by its intimidating letter and by its false representation of what it would do if the debt were not paid, had clearly violated the FDCPA.

2. Martin is liable to American Express for the full $5,300 charged on his credit card. Martin voluntarily permitted McBride to use his credit card and thereby authorized its use. His attempts to limit the amount were ineffective as long as McBride retained the credit card with "apparent authority" to use it. Under the Truth-in-Lending Act (TILA), the liability of a cardholder is only $50 in cases of unauthorized use. Since McBride's use of the card was authorized, the $50 limit does not apply. Martin's credit card was not stolen or obtained by fraud or duress. If the agreement between Martin and McBride limited McBride's use to $500, then Martin has recourse against McBride for unauthorized use, but he cannot invoke TILA as a defense against American Express.

3. No. No liability arises in connection with a credit card unless it is a valid contract between the cardholder and the issuer. Since Ordoyne had neither signed nor approved the application in any way, he was not bound by any contract. Therefore, he was not liable for the charges to the account.

APPLYING THE LAW . . . YOU BE THE JUDGE

1. Josephine Rutyna was a sixty-year-old widow who, in late 1976 and early 1977, had incurred a debt for medical treatment of her high blood pressure and epilepsy. She assumed that the cost of the services had been paid by either Medicare or her private insurance company. In July of 1978, however, she was contacted by an agent of Collection Accounts Terminal, Inc. They stated that Rutyna still owed a debt of $56 for those services. She denied that she owed the debt. The following month she received a letter from the collection agency threatening to contact her neighbors and employer concerning the debt if the $56 was not paid immediately. Discuss fully whether the collection agency's letter violates any consumer protection law. [*Rutyna v. Collection Accounts Terminal, Inc.*, 478 F.Supp. 980 (N.D.Ill. 1979)]

2. Robert Martin loaned a business associate, E. L. McBride, his American Express credit card. He told McBride he could charge up to $500 on the card. Approximately two months later, Martin received an American Express statement that showed a balance due of approximately $5,300. Martin refused to pay the amount, claiming that he had not signed any of the credit invoices. He claimed his liability for the unauthorized charges was only $50 under the Truth-in-Lending Act. To what extent was Martin liable for payment to American Express on the $5,300? [*Martin v. American Express, Inc.*, 361 So.2d 597 (Ala.Civ.App. 1978)]

3. The First National Bank sued Ordoyne on an overdue credit card account. He proved that his wife had obtained the card by forging his name to the application and that he had not approved the issuance or the use of the credit card. He refused to pay. Was he liable for the charges to the account? [*First National Bank of Commerce v. Ordoyne*, (La.App.) 528 So.2d 1068 (1988)]

LEGAL BACKGROUND

Commercial paper plays an essential role in our economic system because it helps facilitate financial transactions in every sector of the economy. Understanding the basic nature of commercial paper is not particularly difficult. However, understanding the what and why of a negotiable instrument is one of the more challenging topics in the text.

Commercial paper may be either negotiable or nonnegotiable. The transfer of negotiable paper is governed by the UCC. The transfer of nonnegotiable paper is governed by the contracts law of assignment.

The primary purpose of commercial paper is to act as a convenient alternative for cash; therefore, its transfer must be easily accomplished and relatively risk free. A secondary purpose is to provide financing for business by the use of promissory notes and trade acceptances.

This chapter explains the different types of commercial paper, the requirements for negotiability, and the ways in which the instruments can be transferred.

394

Prereading Activity

Acquire samples of checks, drafts, promissory notes, and certificates of deposit. Pass copies around the classroom for students to view. Call on students to describe the attributes of the document in their hands. Discuss the advantages/disadvantages of having a piece of paper substitute for money.

Mastery Objectives

By the end of this chapter, students will be able to:
- Describe the functions of commercial paper
- Recognize types of commercial paper
- Explain ways to classify commercial paper
- Identify negotiable instruments
- Tell how negotiable instruments are transferred
- Demonstrate how to write indorsements

Chapter 17

Commercial Paper: Introduction, Negotiability, and Transferability

"Convenience is the basis of mercantile law."
Lord Mansfield, 1705–1793
British jurist

The vast number of commercial transactions that take place daily in business could not take place without commercial paper. **Commercial paper** includes any written promise or order to pay a sum of money, including checks, drafts, promissory notes, and certificates of deposit. Although accepting commercial paper is riskier than accepting money, it is less risky than other contract rights.

In the opening quotation, Lord Mansfield stresses the importance of convenience in mercantile law, or sales by merchants. The law of commercial paper grew out of commercial necessity. As early as the thirteenth century, merchants in foreign trade used commercial paper to finance and conduct their affairs. Problems in transportation and in the safekeeping of gold or coins prompted this practice. Today, the law of commercial paper in the United States is found in Articles 3 and 4 of the Uniform Commercial Code.

This chapter explains several basic concepts. First it describes the functions of commercial paper and how commercial paper is classified. Then it discusses the important concepts of negotiability and transferability.

◆ **commercial paper** Signed writing that contains an unconditional promise or order to pay an exact sum of money, either when demanded or at an exact future time. Includes drafts, checks, promissory notes, and certificates of deposit.

◆ THE FUNCTIONS OF COMMERCIAL PAPER

Commercial paper works in two ways: as a substitute for money and as a credit device. For convenience and safety, people often use commercial paper—a check—instead of money when paying for goods and services. The other major forms of commercial paper—drafts, promissory notes, and certificates of deposit—can be used in similar ways, to be held or exchanged instead of money for convenience and safety.

Commercial paper also represents an extension of credit. For example, a buyer who gives a seller a promissory note is promising to pay the debt at a later time. The terms of the note may provide that it is payable within sixty days. The seller has essentially extended sixty days' credit to the buyer. Even a check is an extension of credit until it is paid by the bank upon which it is drawn.

For commercial paper to be a substitute for money or a credit device, or both, it is essential that it be easily transferable. It is also important that there be little danger of its being uncollectible. These characteristics—ease of transfer and low risk—are the characteristics of *negotiable* commercial paper. The rules described in the following pages exist to accomplish these characteristics.

Divide the class into small groups. Each group should create and act out a situation in which a buyer uses a draft (check) to purchase a good or a service from a seller. As the students act out their role-play situation, other members of the small group should identify the draft, the drawer, the drawee, and the payee in this situation.

Legal Focus Example

Have a volunteer read this Legal Focus Example aloud to the class. Have the class work through this example, identifying the draft, the drawer, the drawee, and the payee. Make sure that students understand that in this case, the time draft used is an example of a trade acceptance in which the seller is both the drawer and the payee.

Enrichment

Ask students: What kinds of goods and services are typically paid by check? Which goods and services are typically only paid by cash? Record their responses on the board.

396   Commercial and Consumer Law

 TYPES OF COMMERCIAL PAPER

The UCC specifies four types of commercial paper: drafts, checks, promissory notes, and certificates of deposit (CDs). These are sometimes called *instruments*. A note or a CD has two original parties: the maker and the payee. A draft or a check has three original parties—the drawer, the drawee, and the payee. Sometimes, two of the parties to a draft can be the same person. Once an instrument is issued, additional parties can become involved. Let's examine these instruments and parties in greater detail.

DRAFTS

- **draft** Any instrument drawn on another (drawee) that orders the drawee to pay a certain sum of money.

- **drawer** A person who creates a draft (including a check).

- **drawee** The person who is ordered to pay money to another (the payee).

- **payee** The person to whom a negotiable instrument is payable.

A **draft** (also known as a bill of exchange) is an unconditional written order to pay a sum of money. The party creating it (the **drawer**) orders another party (the **drawee**) to pay the money, usually to a third party (the **payee**). The drawee is usually obligated to the drawer either by agreement or through a debtor–creditor relationship. Without an obligation, the drawee would not honor the order.

There are two types of drafts. A *time draft* is payable at a definite future time. A *sight* (or demand) *draft* is payable on demand, when the holder presents it for payment. A draft can be both a time and a sight draft; such a draft is payable at a stated time after demand.

LEGAL FOCUS ~ EXAMPLE

Jackson River Fabrics sells $50,000 worth of fabric to Comfort Creations, Inc., each fall. The usual terms require payment in ninety days. This year, Jackson River needs cash. It draws a time draft ordering Comfort Creations to pay $50,000 to the order of Jackson River Fabrics in ninety days. Jackson River presents the paper to Comfort Creations. Comfort Creations accepts by signing the face of the paper and returns it to Jackson River Fabrics. Comfort Creations' acceptance creates an enforceable promise to pay the instrument when it comes due in ninety days.

- **trade acceptance** A draft drawn by and payable to the seller of goods by the purchaser of the goods.

The time draft used in the above example is called a **trade acceptance**. The seller is both the drawer and the payee on this type of draft. The draft orders the buyer to pay a specified sum of money to the seller, usually at a stated time in the future. Jackson River can sell the draft in the commercial money market more easily than it can assign the $50,000 account receivable. An account receivable is an accounting term for money owed a business. Trade acceptances are standard credit instruments in sales transactions.

Enrichment

Guide the students in looking at Exhibit 17-1. Have student volunteers identify the drawer, drawee, and payee in this exhibit.

Vocabulary Activity

Explain to the students that the dictionary defines *promissory* as containing or conveying a promise or assurance. Have a volunteer relate this dictionary definition of *promissory* to the term *promissory note,* as used here.

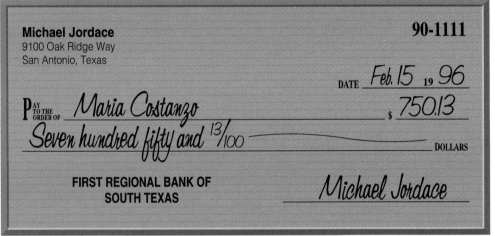

EXHIBIT 17-1
A TYPICAL CHECK

Teaching with the Videodisc

The still frames listed below from the **West's Business Law and Legal Environment Videodisc** can be used with this chapter. To access this material, use the bar codes or the frame numbers included in the Videodisc Instructor's Manual found in the *TRB.*

Order to Pay: Draft
Sample Draft
Sample Check
A Certified Check
A Cashier's Check
Promissory Note or
    Certificate of Deposit
Sample Note
Indorser–Indorsee
Eight Requirements for
    Negotiable Instruments
Holder
Indorsement
Conditional Indorsement
Qualified Indorsement
Restrictive Indorsements
Trust Indorsement
Trust Indorsement–Agent

CHECKS

A **check** is a type of draft that is drawn on a bank and payable on demand. See Exhibit 17-1 for a typical check. With certain types of checks, the bank is both the drawer and the drawee. For example, cashier's checks are drawn by the bank on itself and are payable on demand when issued. When traveler's checks are drawn on a bank, they are checks. However, they require the purchaser's signature before becoming payable. Technically, most traveler's checks are not checks but drafts. This is because the drawee is usually not a bank—for example, American Express is not a bank. Checks, including cashier's and traveler's checks, will be discussed in Chapter 18.

◆ **check** A draft drawn on a bank (the drawee) and payable to the payee on demand.

PROMISSORY NOTES

A **promissory note**, or *note,* is a written promise between two parties. One party is the **maker**, the person who promises to pay. The other party is the *payee,* the one to whom the promise is made. A promissory note can be made payable at a definite time or on demand. It can name a specific payee or merely be payable to bearer—that is, to whoever holds it. A sample note is shown in Exhibit 17-2.

Notes are used in a variety of credit transactions and often carry the name of the transaction. In a real estate transaction, for example, a promissory note secured by a mortgage on the property is a *mortgage note.* A note secured by personal property (such as an automobile) is a *collateral note.* Collateral is property pledged as security for the satisfaction of a debt. The

◆ **promissory note** An unconditional written promise to pay a sum of money to another by a certain time.

◆ **maker** A person who creates and is obligated under a promissory note or a certificate of deposit.

Extension Activity

Have a student volunteer research certificates of deposit that are currently available from local banks. Student research should include the current interest rate being paid, the extent of penalties for early withdrawal, etc. Have the student present his or her findings to the class in the form of a brief oral report. Encourage the student to create and use visual aids in his or her report.

Collaborative Learning Activity

Divide your students into four groups. Instruct each group to draw a poster-size copy of one of the following: draft, check, note, or CD. Display the posters for the class.

EXHIBIT 17-2
A TYPICAL PROMISSORY NOTE

property can be taken by the lender if the debt is not paid. A note payable in installments is an *installment note*. For example, paying for a television set over a twelve-month period may involve an installment note.

CERTIFICATES OF DEPOSIT

◆ **certificate of deposit (CD)** An instrument created by a bank acknowledging the receipt of money with a promise to repay it.

A **certificate of deposit (CD)** is an acknowledgment by a bank of the receipt of money and a promise to repay it. Certificates of deposit in small denominations are often sold by savings and loan associations, savings banks, and commercial banks. They are called small CDs and involve amounts up to $100,000. Certificates of deposit for amounts more than $100,000 are called large CDs.

◆ OTHER WAYS OF CLASSIFYING COMMERCIAL PAPER

We have seen that commercial paper can be classified as either a *demand instrument* or a *time instrument*. A demand instrument is payable on demand. All checks are demand instruments because, by definition, they must be payable on demand. Therefore, checking accounts are called *demand deposits*. Time instruments are payable at a future date.

In addition, commercial paper involving the payment of money can be classified as either an *order* to pay or a *promise* to pay. Checks and drafts are

Before introducing the concept of negotiable instruments to the class, remind the students that *instruments* in this case refers to commercial paper. As they learned, the UCC specifies four types of commercial paper: drafts, checks, promissory notes, and certificates of deposit. These are sometimes called instruments.

Divide the class into small groups. Have each group read and discuss the six criteria listed here that an instrument must meet in order to be considered negotiable. Then have the students work together to identify how Exhibit 17-1 and Exhibit 17-3 meet each of these criteria. Each group should choose a leader to present its work to the class.

orders to pay; certificates of deposit and promissory notes are promises to pay.

Finally, all commercial paper is either *negotiable* or *nonnegotiable*. This serves as another means of classification. Both its form and its content determine whether commercial paper is a **negotiable instrument**, as you will see in the next section. When an instrument is negotiable, its transfer from one person to another is governed by Article 3 of the UCC. Transfers of nonnegotiable instruments are governed by rules of assignment of contract rights (discussed in Chapter 12).

◆ **negotiable instruments**
Commercial paper that meets the requirements under the UCC for negotiability.

◆ WHAT IS A NEGOTIABLE INSTRUMENT?

Before an instrument is considered negotiable, it must meet certain criteria specified in the UCC. In brief, the instrument must be:

1. In written form.
2. Signed by the maker or drawer.
3. An unconditional promise or order to pay.
4. A sum certain in money.
5. Payable on demand or at a definite time.
6. Payable to order or to bearer.

An instrument lacking some criteria of negotiability still has value. However, because a nonnegotiable instrument is more risky when time for collection comes, parties consider it less desirable. Many are unwilling to accept nonnegotiable instruments as substitutes for cash or instruments of credit. Next, we examine the attributes of negotiability in greater detail.

WRITTEN FORM

Negotiable instruments must be in written form. That is because negotiable instruments must possess the certainty that only formal, written proof can give. A writing may be in ink, type, computer print, or some other lasting form.

There are certain practical limitations concerning the writing:

1. The writing must be on material that lends itself to *permanence*. Instruments carved in blocks of ice or recorded on other impermanent surfaces would not qualify as negotiable instruments.

◆ LEGAL FOCUS ~ EXAMPLE

Suppose Suzanne writes in the sand, "I promise to pay $500 to the order of Jack." This is not a negotiable instrument. Although it is in writing, it lacks permanence.

Legal Focus Example

Ask a student volunteer to read this Legal Focus Example aloud to the class. Then ask the volunteer to change the example so that Suzanne creates a negotiable instrument. Have him or her share this new example with the class.

Critical Thinking Activity

Write on the board: "I promise to pay Mary Goodstudent $500, signed [your name]." Ask a student to lead a discussion about whether the illustration is a negotiable instrument.

Legal Focus Example

Ask the students to read the first Legal Focus Example found at the top of this page. As a followup question, ask the students why it is important that the writing be portable. How would it affect trade if negotiable instruments were not portable?

Legal Focus Example

Read the second Legal Focus Example aloud to the class. Point out to students that in most cases where a mark (the X in this case) is allowed, the mark must by witnessed. This helps decrease uncertainty.

Reteaching Activity

To be certain of students' understanding of the term *unconditional promise,* ask a volunteer to define the term for the class.

2. The writing must be *portable*—able to be moved easily. If an instrument is not movable, it obviously is not freely transferable.

> ### ◀ LEGAL FOCUS - EXAMPLE
>
> Charles writes on the side of a cow, "I promise to pay Paul $500." Technically, this meets the requirements of a negotiable instrument, but since a cow cannot easily be transferred in the ordinary course of business, the "instrument" is nonnegotiable.

SIGNED BY THE MAKER OR DRAWER

For an instrument to be negotiable, it must be signed by (1) the maker, if it is a note or a certificate of deposit, or (2) the drawer, if it is a draft or a check. The UCC considers any mark intended as a signature to be valid. A rubber stamp bearing a person's signature is permitted and frequently used in business.

The location of the signature on the document is not important, though the usual place is the lower right-hand corner. A *handwritten* statement on the body of the instrument, such as, "I, Louise Ackerman, promise to pay John Grant," is sufficient to act as Louise's signature.

There are virtually no limitations on how a signature can be made. An unusual signature does, however, decrease an instrument's marketability, because it creates uncertainty.

> ### ◀ LEGAL FOCUS - EXAMPLE
>
> Martie Raye broke his hand in a climbing accident. When asked to sign a promissory note to pay for his medical care, he scrawled an "X." This signature is sufficient for negotiability under the UCC.

UNCONDITIONAL PROMISE OR ORDER TO PAY

The terms of a promise or order must be included in the writing on the face of a negotiable instrument. Terms include, for example, who is to be paid, where payment is to be made, and when payment should be made. These terms must not be conditioned upon some other event or agreement and must not state that the instrument is to be paid only out of a particular fund.

Promise or Order   For an instrument to be negotiable, it must contain an express, or stated, order or promise to pay. A mere acknowledgment of the debt is not sufficient under the UCC. A traditional I.O.U., for example, is only an admission of debt. It is not a negotiable instrument. If words such as "to be paid on demand" or "due on demand" are added, however, the promise requirement is satisfied.

Have a student volunteer read aloud to the class the first Legal Focus Problem found at the top of this page. Have the volunteer suggest an answer for the question posed at the end of this problem.

Have the students read to themselves the second Legal Focus Problem found here. Then have each student rewrite the instrument so that it includes a promise to pay. Allow volunteers to share their rewritten instruments with the class.

Reteaching Activity

Have the students look again at Exhibit 17-1. Allow a volunteer to point out the unconditional promise or order to pay that is included on this negotiable instrument.

Legal Focus Problem

Commercial Paper: Introduction, Negotiability, and Transferability   401

◆ LEGAL FOCUS ~ PROBLEM

Barney, the buyer, executes a promissory note using the words, "I promise to pay $1,000 to the bearer of this note." Does this language satisfy the requirement of a promise?

Yes. The statement "I promise to pay" is a definite promise for the purposes of negotiability.

◆ LEGAL FOCUS ~ PROBLEM

Consider this instrument. Is there a promise to pay?

To Rocky Bogordon

I acknowledge that I owe you forty dollars. I will pay you soon.

Isaac

Isaac Ruseau
8/23/96

No. There is no promise to pay; instead Isaac just admits the debt. This is an I.O.U.; it cannot be a negotiable instrument.

An order to pay is associated with three-party instruments, such as trade acceptances, checks, and drafts. An order directs a third party to pay the instrument as drawn. In a typical check, the word "pay" (to the order of a payee) is a command to the drawee bank to pay the check when presented. Thus, it is an order. The order is mandatory even if it is courteous (as in "Please pay"), as long as it is definite. An order stating, "I wish you would pay," is not definite and not sufficient.

Unconditionality of Promise or Order

◆ LEGAL FOCUS ~ PROBLEM

Andrew promised in a note to pay Frances $10,000 if the ship *The Royal Rapper* reached the port of Stockton, California. Is the note negotiable, or does the requirement that the ship reach port destroy negotiability?

The note is not negotiable. An instrument's usefulness is reduced if the instrument is burdened by conditional promises. A buyer would run the risk that the condition would not occur. No one could safely buy the note

Have a student volunteer read aloud to the class the Legal Focus Problem found at the bottom of this page. Allow the volunteer to suggest an answer to the question posed at the end of this problem. Make sure students understand that this note is not negotiable because negotiable instruments require an unconditional promise or order to pay. Ask the volunteer to explain what conditions exist in this Legal Focus Problem.

without first investigating whether the ship had arrived or was likely to arrive—an expensive and time-consuming undertaking. To avoid such problems, the UCC provides that only unconditional promises or orders are negotiable.

The definition of *unconditional* does not prevent certain common business notations on negotiable instruments. Many instruments state the terms of the underlying agreement as a matter of standard business practice. For example, the words "as per contract" or "This debt arises from the sale of goods X and Y" do not render an instrument nonnegotiable. Also, a mere reference to another agreement does not affect negotiability.

◀ LEGAL FOCUS ~ EXAMPLE

A reference on a note or a check to another agreement is often included to make a record or to give information. These notes sometimes refer to separate agreements. References to such agreements do not ordinarily destroy the negotiability of the instrument. For example, a statement that an instrument's payment is secured by collateral (for example, a 1993 Saturn automobile) does not make the instrument nonnegotiable. Rather, this statement increases the marketability of the instrument.

The UCC provides that government entities can issue negotiable instruments even if payment is to come only from a particular fund or source. For most other issuers, such a statement would make the instrument nonnegotiable.

SUM CERTAIN IN MONEY

Payment for negotiable commercial paper must be wholly in money. An instrument that provides for payment in diamonds, or in 1,000 hours of services, is not payable in money and is nonnegotiable. The Code defines money as "a medium of exchange authorized or adopted by a domestic or foreign government as a part of its currency."

◀ LEGAL FOCUS ~ PROBLEM

A maker of a note promises "to pay on demand $1,000 and fifty liters of cola." Is the note negotiable?

No, because the instrument is not payable *entirely* in money.

Sum certain means that the amount can be determined from the instrument without reference to any outside source. A demand note payable with 12 percent interest meets the requirement of sum certain. Its amount

Invite an officer from a local bank to come to your class to discuss common problems that occur in relation to checks and other negotiable instruments that are presented to the bank. Encourage students to prepare questions in advance for your speaker.

Allow a student volunteer to read this Legal Focus Example aloud to the class. Remind students that they can use the Legal Focus features as review tools when studying for tests.

Legal Focus Problem

Have a student volunteer read this Legal Focus Problem aloud to the class. Ask the volunteer to suggest a possible answer to the question posed at the end of this problem.

Enrichment

Have the students refer back to Exhibit 17-1 and Exhibit 17-2. Ask volunteers to explain how each of these negotiable instruments meets the definite time requirement.

can be determined at the time it is payable. When an instrument is payable at a rate fixed by state law, the instrument is negotiable—if it meets other criteria. However, a mortgage note tied to a variable rate of interest, such as one that changes with market conditions, is not negotiable.

PAYABLE ON DEMAND OR AT A DEFINITE TIME

The UCC requires that a negotiable instrument "be payable on demand or at a definite time."

Payable on Demand   If the instrument says nothing about when payment is due, it is payable on demand. Also, instruments that contain the words "Payable at sight" or "Payable upon presentment" are payable on demand. A check, by definition, is payable on demand.

Payable at a Definite Time   To be negotiable, an instrument other than a demand instrument must be payable at a definite time specified on the instrument. The maker or drawee need not pay until the specified time. Time is definite if the instrument is payable at a fixed time or on demand after a stated date. In contrast, if the instrument is only payable after an act or event that is uncertain as to time of occurrence, the instrument is not negotiable.

◆ LEGAL FOCUS - EXAMPLE

An instrument is dated June 1, 1994, and it states, "One year after the death of my grandfather, Henry Adams, I promise to pay to the order of James Harmon $500. [Signed] Jacqueline Wells." The instrument is not negotiable, because the date of the grandfather's death is uncertain. This is true even though the event is bound to occur—and even if it has already occurred.

When an instrument is payable "on or before" a stated date, it is clearly payable at a definite time. Although the maker has the option of paying before the stated maturity date, this uncertainty does not violate the definite-time requirement.

◆ LEGAL FOCUS - PROBLEM

Levine gives Hirsch an instrument dated May 1, 1994. The instrument indicates on its face that it is payable on or before May 1, 1995. Is it negotiable?

Yes, it satisfies the requirement. In contrast, an undated instrument made payable "one month after date" is nonnegotiable. In this situation,

Ask a student volunteer to read aloud the first Legal Focus Example found here. Remind the class that these are examples of an order instrument, which is a negotiable instrument that is payable to a specific payee (in this case Rocky Reed) or to any person the payee, by indorsement, designates.

Read the second Legal Focus Example aloud to the class, and then refer the students to Exhibit 17-1. Ask the students whether this is an order instrument or a bearer instrument. What would have to be changed in order for this to be a bearer instrument?

Critical Thinking Activity

Ask the students if they can give an example of an order instrument. (Students should understand that most checks are made out in such a way as to be order instruments.)

404

because the instrument is undated, there is no way to determine the maturity date from the face of the instrument.

PAYABLE TO ORDER OR TO BEARER

As we stated earlier, for a negotiable instrument to serve as a substitute for money, freedom to transfer is essential. To assure a proper transfer, the instrument must be "Payable to order or to bearer." These words are often called the magic words of negotiability. They indicate that at the time of issuance, it is expected that future unknown persons—not just the immediate party—will eventually be the owners. If an instrument is payable neither to order nor to bearer, the instrument is nonnegotiable.

◆ **order instrument**
A negotiable instrument that is payable to a specific payee or to any person the payee by indorsement designates.

Order Instruments The purpose of **order instruments**, or order paper, is to allow the maker or drawer to create an instrument for a specific person. That person can then transfer the instrument to anyone he or she wishes. In making an order instrument, the maker or drawer is agreeing to pay either the person named or whomever that person designates.

◀ LEGAL FOCUS ～ EXAMPLE

An instrument states, "Payable to the order of Rocky Reed" or "Pay to Rocky Reed or order." The maker or drawer states that a payment will be made to Reed or to anyone Reed designates. Both wordings create a negotiable instrument. In contrast, if an instrument states, "Payable to Rocky Reed" or "Pay to Rocky Reed only," the instrument is not negotiable. By using this wording, the maker or drawer indicates that only Reed will be paid.

◆ **bearer instrument** An instrument that does not designate a specific payee and is payable to anyone who has possession. Examples include an instrument made out to cash or to bearer.

Bearer Instruments A **bearer instrument** is one that does not designate a specific payee. The term **bearer** refers to a person who has possession of an instrument payable to bearer or indorsed in blank (blank indorsements are discussed shortly). The maker or drawer of a bearer instrument agrees to pay anyone who presents the instrument for payment.

◀ LEGAL FOCUS ～ EXAMPLE

Any instrument containing the following terms is a bearer instrument:
- "Payable to the order of bearer."
- "Payable to Rocky Reed or bearer."
- "Payable to bearer."
- "Pay cash."
- "Pay to the order of cash."

◆ **bearer** A person in possession of an instrument payable to bearer or indorsed in blank.

FACTORS NOT AFFECTING NEGOTIABILITY

Certain ambiguities and omissions do not affect the negotiability of an instrument. The UCC provides rules for clearing up ambiguous terms. A few of these rules follow:

1. An instrument that is undated is usually negotiable. A typical example is an undated check.
2. Postdating or antedating an instrument does not affect negotiability. If you write a check on December 1 but date it December 12, you have postdated it. If you write a check on December 1 but date it November 25, you have antedated it.
3. Handwritten terms control over typewritten and over printed terms. For example, if your check is printed, "Pay to the order of," and in handwriting you insert in the blank, "Jerry Adams or bearer," the check is a bearer instrument, not an order instrument.
4. Words "five hundred" outweigh figures "500" unless the words are ambiguous. This is important when the numerical amount and the written amount on a check differ.

◆ CHECKING YOUR PROGRESS

1. Explain the responsibilities of each party associated with a draft.
2. What is the difference between a time draft and a sight draft?
3. Why is a check considered a draft?
4. List two physical limitations concerning the writing of negotiable instruments.
5. Is an instrument payable for an amount of money, with interest, negotiable?
6. What are the "magic words" of negotiability?

◆ TRANSFER OF NEGOTIABLE INSTRUMENTS

Once issued, a negotiable instrument can be transferred by *negotiation* or *assignment*.

TRANSFER BY ASSIGNMENT

As you learned in Chapter 12, an assignment is a transfer of rights under a contract. According to UCC Article 3, if a transfer of negotiable paper does not meet the requirements of a negotiation, it is an assignment. The transferee is then an *assignee* rather than a *holder*. Since Article 3 only ap-

Have students work with partners and explain to each other the differences between a holder and an assignee.

Legal Focus Example

Ask a student volunteer to read this Legal Focus Example aloud to the class. Have a student look at Exhibit 17-1 and explain how Mario Costanzo could transfer this instrument to Bart Richmond; then have students explain who the indorser and who the indorsee are in this revised example.

Divide the class into groups of four. Give each group a blank check (or facsimile). Tell one student to write the check to another student in the group or to the bearer. Then have the payee transfer the check to the third student. Have the student write the name of the drawer, payee, assignee, or holder.

---

plies to negotiable instruments, an instrument that lacks any characteristic of a negotiable instrument can also be transferred as a contract right. Under general contract principles, any transfer by assignment to an assignee gives the assignee only the assignor's rights. Furthermore, any defenses good against an assignor are good against an assignee.

TRANSFER BY NEGOTIATION

Transfer by negotiation is the method used to retain the special nature of a negotiable instrument. **Negotiation** transfers the instrument in such a way that the transferee becomes a holder. A **holder** is any person in the possession of an instrument drawn, issued, or indorsed to him or her or to his or her order or to bearer or in blank. A holder receives at least as many rights in the instrument as the person who transferred it and may receive even more rights. A holder who receives greater rights is known as a *holder in due course*. The definition and requirements of a *holder in due course* are discussed in Chapter 18.

There are two methods of negotiating an instrument so the receiver becomes a holder. The method used depends on whether the instrument is order paper or bearer paper. An indorsement is necessary to transfer an order instrument. The UCC does not require an indorsement to transfer bearer paper by negotiation. Many transferees of bearer paper may still require indorsement for identification purposes, however.

INDORSEMENTS

An **indorsement** is a signature, with or without additional words or statements. It is most often written on the back of the instrument. A person who transfers an instrument by signing (indorsing) it and delivering it to another person is the **indorser**. The person to whom the instrument is transferred is the **indorsee**.

◆ **negotiation** The transferring of a negotiable instrument to another in such a way that the transferee becomes a holder.

◆ **holder** A person in possession of a negotiable instrument who is either the payee, a bearer, or one to whom the instrument is properly indorsed.

◆ **indorsement** A signature placed on an instrument for the purpose of transferring one's ownership in the instrument.

◆ **indorser** A person, either the payee or the holder of an instrument, who signs her or his name on the back of the instrument.

◆ **indorsee** The one to whom a negotiable instrument is transferred by indorsement.

◆ **blank indorsement** An indorsement made by the mere writing of the indorser's name on the back of the instrument.

◆ LEGAL FOCUS – EXAMPLE

Martha receives a graduation check for $100. She can transfer the check to her mother (or to anyone) by signing it on the back. Martha is an indorser. If Martha indorses the check, "Pay to Mary Grimes," Mary Grimes is the indorsee.

One purpose of an indorsement is to bring about the negotiation of order paper. Essentially, indorsement relates to the right of the holder to negotiate the paper and how the negotiation must be done. We will examine four categories of indorsements: blank, special, qualified, and restrictive.

Blank Indorsements A **blank indorsement** specifies no particular indorsee and can consist of a mere signature. For example, a check payable

Remind the students that negotiable instruments are often used because they are safer than cash. How does the use of a blank indorsement negate that safety? Have the students explain their answers.

Ask a student volunteer to read the first Legal Focus Example aloud to the class. Remind the students that they can use the Legal Focus features as review tools when studying for tests.

Legal Focus Example

Read aloud the Legal Focus Example regarding Arthur Rabe's indorsement of the check. Make sure students understand that by writing "Pay to Ted Sheppard" above Arthur's blank indorsement, Ted converted Arthur's blank indorsement into a special indorsement. Then have students look at the previous Legal Focus Example regarding Jennifer Hill. Suppose Jennifer wanted to indorse this check to a particular party, such as Michele Smith. Have a student volunteer explain what Jennifer should have written above her indorsement.

EXHIBIT 17-3
A BLANK INDORSEMENT

Jennifer Hill

"to the order of Jennifer Hill" can be indorsed in blank simply by having Hill's signature written on the back of the check. Exhibit 17-3 shows a blank indorsement.

An instrument payable to order and indorsed in blank becomes a bearer instrument. It can then be negotiated further by delivery alone. In other words, a blank indorsement converts an order instrument to a bearer instrument, which anybody can cash.

◆ LEGAL FOCUS – EXAMPLE

Jennifer Hill indorses in blank a check payable to her order and then loses it on the street. Reed finds it and sells it to Hollander for value without indorsing it. This is a negotiation, because Reed has delivered a bearer instrument. (It was an order instrument before it was indorsed.)

Special Indorsements A **special indorsement** specifies the person to whom the indorser intends to make the instrument payable. That is, it names the indorsee. No special words of negotiation are needed. Words such as "Pay to the order of Jones" or "Pay to Jones" followed by the signature of the indorser work. When an instrument is indorsed in this way, it is order paper. Recall, however, that if words such as "Pay to Jones" are used on the front of an instrument, it is nonnegotiable.

To avoid the risk of loss from theft, you can convert a blank indorsement to a special indorsement. This changes bearer paper back to order paper. The UCC allows a holder to "convert a blank indorsement into a special indorsement by writing above the signature of the 'indorser in blank' any contract consistent with the character of the indorsement."

◆ **special indorsement** An indorsement that specifies to whom or to whose order the instrument is payable.

◆ LEGAL FOCUS – EXAMPLE

A check is made payable to Arthur Rabe. Rabe indorses by blank indorsement on the back of the check. He hands the check to Ted

Read

Introduce this *Law in Action* feature by reminding students that commercial paper is used for its convenience and its safety. Explain to students that there are steps they can take to make sure that the commercial paper they use retains this safety feature. Then have a student volunteer read this *Law in Action* feature aloud to the class.

Extend

Have the students work in small groups to design posters explaining the importance of properly indorsing negotiable instruments. Students should be encouraged to have fun with their poster ideas and be allowed to focus on the indorsing of checks rather than trying to deal with other negotiable instruments.

Law in Action

LAW IN YOUR LIFE: INDORSING CHECKS

As a consumer or a businessperson, you will be writing and receiving checks. There are pitfalls involved in both activities.

The danger in signing a blank check is clear. Anyone can fill in an unauthorized amount and cash the check. You will have to honor the check for the unauthorized amount to any later holder in due course. (This matter is discussed in the next chapter.) You will have rights against the person who completed the check in an unauthorized way. However, that person may not have the money to repay you.

Just as a check signed in blank is dangerous, so is a negotiable instrument with a blank indorsement. It, too, is transferred as

easily as cash. When you make a bank deposit, you should indorse the back of the check in blank only in the presence of a teller. If you choose to sign it ahead of time, make sure you insert the words "For deposit only" before you sign your name. An instrument signed in blank can be negotiated by the finder, and the loss will be yours.

CHECKLIST FOR SIGNING NEGOTIABLE INSTRUMENTS

1. Never sign a blank check.
2. Never indorse in blank a negotiable instrument unless a bank teller is giving you a receipt for your deposit.

Sheppard (a negotiation). Ted, not wishing to cash the check immediately, wants to avoid any risk should he lose the check. He therefore writes, "Pay to Ted Sheppard," above Arthur's blank indorsement. (See Exhibit 17-4.) Ted has converted Arthur's blank indorsement into a special indorsement. Further negotiation now requires Ted Sheppard's indorsement plus delivery.

Qualified Indorsements Generally, an indorser, *merely by indorsing*, impliedly promises to pay the instrument if the drawer or maker does not

EXHIBIT 17-4
A SPECIAL INDORSEMENT

Pay to Ted Sheppard

Arthur Rabe

Legal Focus Example

Read aloud the first Legal Focus Example found here, which deals with the qualified indorsement. Make sure the students understand that by putting "without recourse" on the indorsement, the insurance agent is protecting himself or herself if the check is not paid.

Legal Focus Example

Have a student volunteer read the second Legal Focus Example aloud to the class. Make sure that students understand that Bridgett's indorsement is a special indorsement because it is made out specifically to Holly Hughes and that it is a qualified indorsement because she has added "without recourse" to her indorsement. Remind students that they can use the Legal Focus features as review tools when studying for tests.

Reteaching Activity

Have your students list and define the different types of indorsements.

Commercial Paper: Introduction, Negotiability, and Transferability   409

pay. A **qualified indorsement** is used by an indorser to disclaim or limit this contract liability. For this indorsement, the notation "without recourse" is common. A sample is shown in Exhibit 17-5.

A qualified indorsement is often used by persons acting as representatives.

◆ **qualified indorsement** An indorsement to disclaim or limit the indorser's contract liability. "Without recourse" is a qualified indorsement.

◀ LEGAL FOCUS ~ EXAMPLE

Insurance agents sometimes get checks payable to them but really intended as payment to the insurance company. An agent must indorse such payments through to the company. He or she should not be expected to make good on checks that are not paid (dishonored). The "without recourse" indorsement excuses the agent, unless he or she has breached a warranty.

Most blank and special indorsements are *unqualified indorsements*. They guarantee payment of the instrument in addition to transferring title to it. The qualified indorser is not guaranteeing such payment. The qualified indorsement still transfers good title to the indorsee, however; and the instrument can be negotiated further.

◀ LEGAL FOCUS ~ EXAMPLE

A check is made payable to the order of Bridgett Cage. Bridgett needs to negotiate the check to Holly Hughes, but she does not want to be liable if it is not paid. Bridgett indorses the check, "Pay to Holly Hughes, without recourse. [Signed] Bridgett Cage." Bridgett's indorsement is both special (made to the order of Holly Hughes) and qualified. For Holly to negotiate the check, Holly must indorse and deliver the check to the transferee.

EXHIBIT 17-5
A QUALIFIED INDORSEMENT

Without recourse
Marisa Cortes

409

1. An indorsement is necessary to transfer an order instrument.

2. The notation "without recourse" is common in a qualified indorsement. The notation allows the indorser to disclaim or limit the contract liability to pay the instrument if the drawer or maker does not pay.

3. The notations "pay any bank or banker" or "for deposit only" on an instrument ensure that only a bank can acquire rights of a holder.

EXHIBIT 17-6
RESTRICTIVE INDORSEMENT

♦ **restrictive
indorsement** An
indorsement that places
conditions on the
further transfer of the
instrument. "For
deposit only" is a
restrictive indorsement.

Restrictive Indorsements   The **restrictive indorsement** requires indorsees to comply with certain instructions regarding the funds involved. Restrictive indorsements come in many forms. One common type is an *indorsement for deposit.* This type of indorsement makes the indorsee (almost always a bank) a collecting agent of the indorser. (See Exhibit 17-6 for an illustration. The check here is payable and issued to Geraldine Sellers.) In particular, a "For deposit only" or "Pay any bank or banker" indorsement locks the instrument into the bank collection process. Only a bank can acquire the rights of a holder following such indorsements. A bank's liability for payment of an instrument with a restrictive indorsement is discussed in Chapter 18.

◆ CHECKING YOUR PROGRESS

1.   What key element is necessary to transfer an order instrument?

2.   In what type of indorsement is the notation "without recourse" used? What is the effect of the notation on the indorser?

3.   Write two notations that can be used to restrict the handling of the funds involved in a check only to the bank collection process.

Read
You might introduce this *A Case In Point* feature by having the students once again look at Exhibit 17-1. Point out that in this exhibit both the words and the numerical amount are equal ($750.13). What happens when there is a discrepancy between these two amounts? Explain to students that this case deals with just such an occurrence.

◆ A CASE IN POINT ◆

YATES v. COMMERCIAL BANK & TRUST COMPANY
District Court of Appeal of Florida, Third District, 1983.
432 So.2d 725.

In this case, the numerical amount and the written amount on a check were different. When the bank paid the numerical amount (which was more than the written amount), the plaintiff brought suit for the difference.

FACTS While acting as the personal representative of Marion Cahill's estate, Emmett McDonald wrote a check to himself drawn on the estate checking account at Commercial Bank & Trust Company. McDonald then disappeared with the funds. The payee and amount on the check read as follows: "Pay to the order of *Emmett E. McDonald $10075.00 Ten hundred seventy-five* Dollars." The bank paid McDonald $10,075.00 and debited Marion Cahill's estate for that amount. McDonald's successor

as personal representative of Cahill's estate, William Yates, brought suit against the bank. He claimed that the bank should have paid the amount written in words on the check. The suit was to recover $9,000—the difference between $10,075.00 and $1,075.00. The complaint was dismissed by the trial court, and Yates appealed.

ISSUE Should the bank be held liable to Yates for the $9,000?

DECISION Yes. The appellate court ordered the bank to replace the $9,000 taken from the estate's account.

REASON The court stated that under the UCC, words will control figures unless the words are ambiguous, in which case figures will control. The court thus concluded that "[u]nder this provision of the UCC, it was clearly improper for the bank to have paid the larger sum stated in numbers, rather than the smaller one unambiguously stated by McDonald's words. It is, therefore, *prima facie* [on the face of it] liable to the estate for the excess."

Discussion Starter
Stimulate a class discussion about this *A Case In Point* feature by asking the following questions: Why did the bank pay McDonald $10,075, debiting Marion Cahill's estate for that amount? Why did William Yates, as a representative of Cahill's estate, bring suit against the bank? What amount was written in words on the check? What was the difference between the amount written in words and the amount written in numerals on the check? What decision did the trial court reach in the case? What decision did the appellate court reach in the case? What reasons did the appellate court give for its decision?

CHAPTER REVIEW

17

 ## SUMMARY

FUNCTIONS OF COMMERCIAL PAPER

1. A substitute for money.
2. A credit device.

TYPES OF COMMERCIAL PAPER

1. *Draft*—An unconditional written order by a drawer to a drawee to pay money, usually to a third party (the payee). Drafts include:

In order to help students review what they have learned in Chapter 17, you might wish to:

1. Have a student volunteer, or volunteers, read aloud the Chapter Summary.
2. Allow the students to work with partners to complete the *Using Legal Language* activity.
3. Assign the *Checking for Comprehension* exercise as homework.
4. Allow the students to work in small groups to complete the *Applying Legal Concepts* activities.
5. As a class, complete the *Applying the Law* activities. (Please note that you may have to help students with vocabulary so that they adequately understand all of the *Applying the Law* material.)

Assessment Strategies

In order to check student mastery of chapter concepts, you may wish to use the Chapter 17 test that is found in your *Teacher's Resource Binder* or use WESTEST computerized testing for Chapter 17.

Using Legal Language (Answers)

1–H, 2–A, 3–E, 4–D, 5–J, 6–F, 7–B, 8–G, 9–C, 10–I

1. Commercial paper is used as a substitute for money, especially when paying for goods and services, and as a credit device when promising to pay a debt at a later time.
2. The UCC specifies that a negotiable instrument must be (1) in written form, (2) signed by the maker or drawer, (3) an unconditional promise or order to pay, (4) a sum certain in money, (5) payable on demand or at a definite time, and (6) payable to order or bearer.
3. Yes. Although an instrument lacking any UCC criteria for negotiability is a nonnegotiable instrument, the rules of assignment of contract rights do apply. Nevertheless, there is less risk to a negotiable instrument.
4. A promise to pay is made when one party promises to pay another party, as in a promissory note. Three parties are involved when

---

    a. Time and sight drafts: A time draft is payable at a definite future time; a sight, or demand, draft is payable on sight (when the holder presents it for payment).

    b. Trade acceptances: A trade acceptance is a time draft on which the seller is both the drawer and the payee. The draft orders the buyer to pay a specified sum of money, usually at a specified future time.

2. *Check*—A draft drawn on a bank and payable on demand. A bank may draw a check on itself (cashier's check).

3. *Promissory note*—An unconditional written promise to pay a sum of money to another by a certain time.

4. *Certificate of deposit (CD)*—An instrument created by a bank acknowledging the receipt of money with a promise to repay it.

OTHER WAYS OF CLASSIFYING COMMERCIAL PAPER

1. *Demand instruments and time instruments*—A demand instrument is payable on demand (when the holder presents it to the maker or drawee). Time instruments are payable at a future date.

2. *Orders to pay and promises to pay*—A commercial instrument may be classified as either an order to pay or a promise to pay. A check or a draft is an *order* to pay. A CD or a promissory note is a *promise* to pay.

3. *Negotiable and nonnegotiable instruments*—Transfers of negotiable instruments are governed by Article 3 of the UCC. Transfers of nonnegotiable instruments are governed by rules of assignment of contract rights.

REQUIREMENTS FOR NEGOTIABLE INSTRUMENTS

1. Must be in writing.
2. Must be signed by the maker or drawer.
3. Must be an unconditional promise or order.
4. Must be to pay a sum certain in money.
5. Must be payable on demand or at a definite time.
6. Must be payable to order or to bearer.

TYPES OF INDORSEMENTS

1. Blank (e.g., "Jennifer Hill").
2. Special (e.g., "Pay to Ted Sheppard, Arthur Rabe").
3. Qualified (e.g., "Without recourse, Brad Cage").
4. Restrictive (e.g., "For deposit only, Carol Sellers").

USING LEGAL LANGUAGE

Directions: Match each term with the statement that best defines that term.

1. certificate of deposit
2. draft
3. drawee
4. holder
5. indorsement
6. maker
7. negotiation
8. order instrument
9. promissory note

A. any instrument drawn on another (drawee) that orders the drawee to pay a certain sum of money

B. the transferring of a negotiable instrument to another in such a way that the transferee becomes a holder

C. an unconditional written promise to pay a sum of money to another by a certain time

D. a person in possession of a negotiable in-one party directs a third party to pay the instrument as drawn, such as a bank check.

5. A blank indorsement specifies no particular indorsee and can consist of a mere signature. Any one holder can collect on the instrument. A special indorsement specifies the person to whom the indorser intends to make the instrument payable. Only the person specified can collect. A qualified indorsement is used by an indorser to disclaim or limit the liability to pay the instrument if the drawer or maker does not pay. A restrictive indorsement requires indorsees to comply with certain instructions regarding the funds involved.

6. Since the instrument involved here is a check—which is a specialized form of draft—it is a three-party instrument. The three parties to the check are Barnes, the drawer; First Bank & Trust Co. of Colusa, the drawee; and the law firm of Bowers & Wolfe, the payee. Neither Bowers nor Wolfe is a payee to the instrument individually. The payee is the partnership. Wolfe, who signed the back of the instrument, is an indorser. The client, Donnelly, is not a party to this instrument, since his name does not appear on it. Wolfe is acting as agent for both her client and her law firm.

7. For an instrument to be negotiable, it must meet the following requirements:
a. be in writing
b. be signed by the maker or drawer
c. contain an unconditional promise or order
d. be a sum certain payable in money
e. be payable on demand or at a definite time
f. be payable to bearer or order.
The instrument in this case meets all the requirements; therefore, it is negotiable.

8. The note is nonnegotiable for the following reasons:
a. The note is not signed by the maker, Jeff Nolan.
b. The maker did not make a definite promise to pay but merely acknowledged that a debt was owed to Stephanie Craig.
c. Payment of the note is conditioned on the sale of Nolan's horse, Swiftfoot, and payment is to come from a particular fund—the proceeds of that sale.
d. The note is not payable at a definite time, as the note is undated; therefore, the end of the six-month period is uncertain.
e. The note is payable only to Stephanie Craig, not to her order or to bearer.
Any of these five factors would render the note nonnegotiable.

10. qualified indorsement

strument who is either the payee, a bearer, or to whom the instrument is properly indorsed

E. the person who is ordered to pay money to another (the payee)

F. a person who creates and is obligated under a promissory note or a certificate of deposit

G. a negotiable instrument that is payable to a specific payee or to any person the payee by indorsement designates

H. an instrument created by a bank acknowledging the receipt of money with a promise to repay it

I. an indorsement on a negotiable instrument to disclaim or limit his or her contract liability

J. a signature placed on an instrument for the purpose of transferring one's ownership in the instrument

◆ CHECKING FOR COMPREHENSION

1. Describe the two functions of commercial paper.

2. What criteria must be met for an instrument to be considered negotiable under the Uniform Commercial Code?

3. Can commercial paper be considered valid if it lacks any of the criteria for negotiability specified in the Uniform Commercial Code?

4. Explain the difference between a promise to pay and an order to pay in regard to negotiable instruments.

5. What is the effect of each of the four categories of indorsements?

6. A partnership called Bowers & Wolfe is a law firm. Wolfe won a case for her client, Donnelly, against Phillip Barnes. When Wolfe collected the judgment from Barnes, Barnes wrote out a check that read: "Pay to the order of Bowers & Wolfe $50,000 [signed] Phillip Barnes."

On the top of the check was printed "First Bank & Trust Company of Colusa." When Wolfe deposited the check in the account (called a trust account) that she had set up for her client, she signed the back of the check, "J. Wolfe." How are each of these parties designated in commercial paper law?

7. The following note is written by Muriel Evans on the back of an envelope: "I, Muriel Evans, promise to pay Karen Marvin or bearer $100 on demand." Discuss fully if this constitutes a negotiable instrument.

8. The following instrument was written on a sheet of paper by Jeff Nolan: "I, the undersigned, do hereby acknowledge that I owe Stephanie Craig one thousand dollars, with interest, payable out of the proceeds of the sale of my horse, Swiftfoot, next month. Payment is to be made on or

1. Roberts was correct in contending that Duxbury was not the holder. The paper was order paper and required Baines's indorsement in order to negotiate the paper so as to make Duxbury the holder. However, the transaction was effective to transfer or assign to Duxbury whatever rights were held by Baines. Therefore, as an assignee, Duxbury could sue Roberts.
2. The concept of negotiation is set forth in UCC 3-202, which describes it as "the transfer of an instrument in such form that the transferee becomes a holder." In this case, Marine Midland's receipt of checks that were issued to Dynamics is not, strictly speaking, a negotiation. Receipt of the checks by Marine Midland completed the issuance of the checks, and an instrument cannot be negotiated until it is issued. Issuance involves delivery to the payee or to an agent of the payee. Here Marine Midland Bank was acting as Dynamics's agent. Marine Midland's transfer of the checks to other parties, however, would be a negotiation. Negotiation of order paper involves delivery and any necessary indorsement. Clearly Marine Midland can deliver the instruments to other parties, and Marine Midland's indorsement will be valid because it is made by or on behalf of Dynamics. Also, the use of a rubber stamp in the indorsement process is effective for

negotiation as long as it is made by an authorized representative who intends it to serve as a signature.
3. The court stated that for an instrument to be negotiable it must contain "an unconditional promise or order to pay a certain sum in money. Negotiability is determined from the face, the four-corners, of the instrument without reference to extrinsic facts. The conditional or unconditional character of the promise or order is to be determined by what is expressed in the instrument itself." Addi-

tionally, the court noted that "a promise or order, otherwise unconditional, is not made conditional by the fact that the instrument is subject to implied or constructive conditions. There is nothing on the face of the draft before us that states payment of the draft is conditioned upon the delivery of proper title to the automobile." Since the draft just referred to a document involved in the transaction but did not condition payment on it, the draft was negotiable, and Holsonback was liable to First State to pay the draft.

---

before six months from date." Discuss specifically why this instrument is nonnegotiable.

APPLYING LEGAL CONCEPTS

1. Design a promissory note using a typewriter or a computer. Fill in the appropriate information with fictitious dates, names, and amounts.

2. Design a check using a typewriter or computer including places for all required elements of a negotiable instrument. Print the check. Fill in the appropriate information with fictitious names.

APPLYING THE LAW . . . YOU BE THE JUDGE

1. Roberts issued a promissory note payable to the order of Baines. Baines did not indorse the note when he gave it to Duxbury. However, Baines did give him a separate paper in which he stated that the note was being transferred to Duxbury. When Duxbury attempted to collect from Roberts, Roberts refused to pay claiming that he was not liable because Duxbury was not the holder of the paper. Is Duxbury the holder of the note? [*Duxbury v. Roberts*, 388 Mass. 385, 446 N.E.2d 401 (1983)]

2. Dynamics Corp. and Marine Midland Bank had a long-standing agreement under which Marine Midland received checks payable to Dynamics and indorsed and deposited them into Dynamics' account. Dynamics never saw the checks. They were made out to the order of Dynamics and delivered directly to Marine Midland. Marine Midland stamped the backs of the checks with Dynamics' name and insignia and transferred them. Within the meaning of the UCC, is the act of sending checks to Marine Midland Bank a

negotiation? If Marine Midland transfers the checks to other parties, is this a negotiation? [*Marine Midland Bank-New York v. Graybar Electric Co., Inc.*, 41 N.Y.2d 703, 395 N.Y.S.2d 403, 363 N.E.2d 1139 (1977)]

3. Higgins, a used-car dealer, sold a 1977 Corvette to Holsonback. Holsonback paid for the car with a draft drawn on the First State Bank of Albertville. On the draft were the following words: "EN-CLOSED—TITLE ON 77 CHEV. VETT. FREE OF ALL LIENS AND EN-CUMBRANCE." The bank paid Higgins. First State presented the draft to Holsonback for payment, but Holsonback refused to pay, claiming that Higgins was in breach of contract. When First State filed suit against Holsonback on his draft, Holsonback contended that the draft was nonnegotiable because the draft's reference to the title rendered the draft conditional. Discuss Holsonback's contention. [*Holsonback v. First State Bank of Albertville*, 394 So.2d 381 (Ala.Civ.App. 1980)]

Commercial Paper: Holder in Due Course, Defenses, and Checks

Chapter

415

Have the students look at the definition of *holder* that appears here: "One who possesses a negotiable instrument drawn, issued, or indorsed to him or her or to his or her order or to bearer or in blank." Allow student volunteers to give examples of a *holder*. One example is a person who is in possession of a check made out to him or her and otherwise possessing all of the characteristics of a negotiable instrument.

Reteaching Activity

Remind students that the student text points out that a person seeking payment prefers to have the rights of a holder in due course. Explain that a *holder* is barred from recovery if the defendant proves any defense against payment (real or personal). A *holder in due course* is barred only if the defendant proves a real defense.

416

Activity Sheets
Reviewing Legal Concepts 18 *TRB*
Enrichment Activity 18 *TRB*

Student Activity Workbook
Chapter 18 Activities

Tests
Chapter 18 Test *TRB*

Chapter 18 WESTEST Computerized Testing
Handbook of Selected Court Cases
Thomas v. *Marine Midland Tinkers National Bank*
American State Bank of Pierre v. *Northwest South Dakota Production Credit Association*

West's Business Law and Legal Environment Videodisc
Still Frames and Motion Segments as shown

---

416   Commercial and Consumer Law

"However gradual may be the growth of confidence, that of credit requires still more time to arrive at maturity."
Benjamin Disraeli, 1804–1881
Prime Minister of Great Britain, 1878–1880

As we explained in Chapter 17, commercial paper is used to extend credit as well as to act as a substitute for money. A note promising to pay another creates a debtor (the one promising) and a creditor (the one to be paid). The willingness of people to readily accept commercial paper and become creditors is based in part on the UCC protections they receive.

Disputes concerning commercial paper are often about payment on the instrument. A person seeking payment prefers to have the rights of a **holder in due course (HDC)**. A holder in due course is one who takes a negotiable instrument free of all claims and most defenses of other parties. The holder in due course has the right to collect payment on that instrument. This right takes priority over the claims of other parties.

In the first part of this chapter, we define holder in due course status. Next, after briefly discussing the liability associated with negotiable instruments, we describe defenses to prevent liability. Defenses fall into two general categories—**real** (or universal) **defenses** and **personal defenses**. Real defenses allow a party to avoid payment to *all holders* of a negotiable instrument, including an HDC. Personal defenses allow a party to avoid payment only to an *ordinary holder* of a negotiable instrument. In the final part of the chapter, we discuss checks and the bank–customer relationship.

◆ **holder in due course (HDC)** Any holder who acquires a negotiable instrument for value, in good faith, and without notice that the instrument is overdue, that it has been dishonored, or that any defense or claim to it exists on the part of any person.

◆ **real defense** Defense that can be used to avoid payment to all holders of a negotiable instrument (including an HDC).

◆ **personal defense** Defense that can be used to avoid payment to an ordinary holder of a negotiable instrument but not to an HDC.

◆ HOLDER AND HOLDER IN DUE COURSE (HDC)

According to the UCC, a *holder* is one who possesses a negotiable instrument "drawn, issued, or indorsed to him or his order or to bearer or in blank." The holder, by the terms of the instrument, is legally entitled to payment.

The holder has the status of an assignee of a contract right. That means a transferee of a negotiable instrument who is merely a holder (as opposed to a holder in due course) gets only those rights that the transferor had in the instrument. If there is a defense to the instrument, an ordinary holder cannot collect payment.

As suggested earlier, a holder in due course (HDC) is a special-status transferee of a negotiable instrument. The HDC acquires a higher level of immunity to payment defenses and to claims of ownership by other parties. The HDC status is beneficial because it increases the likelihood that the holder will be paid. How does one achieve this beneficial status?

The still frames listed below from the **West's Business Law and Legal Environment Videodisc** can be used with this chapter. To access this material, use the bar codes or the frame numbers included in the Videodisc Instructor's Manual found in the *TRB*.

Holder in Due Course
Taking without Notice

Rights of Transferee
Rights of Holders in Due Course under FTC Rule
Holder through a Holder in Due Course
Defenses against Holders and Holders in Due Course
Liability of Transfer
Signature Liability–Agent
Signature Liability–Primary and Secondary

Time for Proper Presentment
Presenter's Warranties
Tranferor's Warranties
A Certified Check
A Cashier's Check
Bank Collections
How a Check Is Cleared

Legal Focus Problem

Have a student volunteer read this Legal Focus Problem aloud to the class. Stimulate a class discussion of this Legal Focus Problem by asking the following questions: Has Larson given consideration to Niebuhr? Has Larson given value to Niebuhr? Why or why not? Why does Morrison not honor the $500 note? Why can't Larson collect from Morrison?

Critical Thinking Activity

Ask the students to compare the concept of *value* in commercial law with that of *consideration* in contract law. Not all consideration is value. The extraordinary protection conferred on a holder in due course is given only when an individual has parted with something that has real economic worth. Although a promise to do something is valid consideration in contract law, it is not value for purposes of determining holder-in-due-course status unless it is a formal promise such as another negotiable instrument given in exchange. Have the students write examples of value that can be given in exchange for a negotiable instrument. Allow students to share their examples with the class.

◆ REQUIREMENTS FOR HDC STATUS

The underlying requirement of "due course" status is that a person must be a holder of the instrument. That is, only a holder can be an HDC. The holder must also have taken the instrument (1) for value, (2) in good faith, and (3) without notice that it is overdue, that it has been dishonored, or that any person has a defense against it or a claim to it.

TAKING FOR VALUE

An HDC must have given *value* for the instrument. That means he or she gave something in return. A person who receives an instrument as a gift or who inherits it does not give value. In these situations, the person is an ordinary holder.

Value in the law of negotiable instruments may seem similar to consideration in the law of contracts, but there is an important difference. An *executory promise* (a promise to do something in the future) is valid consideration in a contract. It is not, however, value with regard to HDC status. A holder takes the instrument for value only to the extent that the agreed-upon consideration has been performed. Therefore, if the holder plans to pay for the instrument later, the holder has not yet given value. In that case, the holder is not yet a holder in due course.

◆ LEGAL FOCUS ～ PROBLEM

Marcia Morrison draws a $500 note payable to Reinhold Niebuhr in payment for goods. Niebuhr negotiates the note to Judy Larson, who promises to pay Niebuhr for it in thirty days. During the next month, Larson learns that Niebuhr breached the contract by delivering defective goods to Morrison. Morrison now will not honor the $500 note. Niebuhr has left town. What can Larson do?

Larson could hold Morrison liable on the note if Larson were a holder in due course, but she cannot collect from Morrison if she is only a holder. Since Larson did not give value before she learned of Morrison's defense, she is a mere holder. Morrison's defense—that Niebuhr breached the contract—is valid not only against Niebuhr but also against Larson. Suppose Larson had paid Niebuhr for the note at the time of transfer. Then, the agreed-upon consideration would have been performed, and Larson would be a holder in due course. As an HDC, she could hold Morrison liable on the note, though Morrison had a valid breach-of-contract defense against Niebuhr.

According to the UCC, there are three ways in which a holder can give value for an instrument:

Guide the students in reading the list of three ways in which a holder can give value for an instrument. Have the students look at the third criterion. Make sure students understand that a holder gives value by giving another negotiable instrument.

Have a student read this Legal Focus Example aloud to the class. Stimulate a class discussion of this example by asking the following questions: What is a promissory note? (If students are unclear as to the meaning of the term *promissory note,* refer them to the

Chapter 17 Summary to refresh their memories.) When should payment be made on a promissory note that is due on May 15? At what point does a promissory note due on May 15 become overdue?

LEGAL BACKGROUND

Because of the good-faith requirement, one must ask whether the purchaser, when acquiring the instrument, honestly believed that the instrument was not defective. If a person purchases a $10,000 note for $100 from a stranger on a street corner, the issue of good faith can be raised on the grounds of the suspicious circumstances *as well as* the grossly inadequate consideration. Note the UCC does not provide clear guidelines to determine good faith, so each situation must be examined separately.

1. A holder gives value to the extent that the agreed-upon consideration is paid or a security interest or lien acquired.
2. A holder gives value by taking an instrument in payment of or as security for previous debt.
3. A holder gives value by giving a negotiable instrument or an irrevocable commitment as payment.

TAKING IN GOOD FAITH

The second requirement for HDC status is that the holder take the instrument in *good faith.* To meet this requirement, the purchaser–holder must have acted honestly in the process of acquiring the instrument. *Good faith* is defined by the UCC as "honesty in fact in the conduct or transaction concerned." The good faith requirement applies only to the holder. It is not important whether the transferor acted in good faith.

TAKING WITHOUT NOTICE

The third requirement for HDC status involves *notice.* A person is not an HDC if he or she acquires an instrument knowing, or having reason to know, that it is defective in any of the following ways:

1. It is overdue.
2. It has been dishonored.
3. There is a defense against the instrument.
4. There is another claim to the instrument.

If a person has notice of any of these conditions, he or she is assumed to know or have reason to know about it. The UCC spells out what constitutes notice. Let's consider what constitutes notice that an instrument is overdue.

Overdue Instruments   All negotiable paper is either payable at a definite time (*time instrument*) or payable on demand (*demand instrument*). What is considered notice that an instrument is overdue depends on whether time or demand paper is transferred.

Time Instruments   A holder of a time instrument who takes the paper the day after its expressed due date has notice that it is overdue. Nonpayment by the due date informs any purchaser of the possibility that the primary party has a defense to payment.

◀ LEGAL FOCUS ~ EXAMPLE

A promissory note due on May 15 must be acquired before midnight on May 15. If it is purchased on May 16, the purchaser will be an ordinary holder, not an HDC.

Have your students make a list of and explain the requirements for a holder in due course.

Ask a student volunteer to read this Legal Focus Problem aloud to the class. Make sure the students understand that Barry and Sheila acquired the check by fraud. Joseph, however, in acquiring the check from Barry and Sheila, meets all the requirements as a holder in due course. He took the instrument for value in good faith and without notice that any person has a defense against it or a claim to it.

Sometimes instruments read, "Payable in thirty days." A note dated December 1 and payable in thirty days is due by midnight on December 31. If the payment date falls on a Sunday or holiday, the instrument is payable on the next business day.

Demand Instruments   A purchaser has notice that a demand instrument is overdue in two situations: if he or she takes the instrument either (1) knowing that a demand was made or (2) after an unreasonable length of time has passed since the instrument's creation. "A reasonable time for a check drawn and payable within the states and territories of the United States and the District of Columbia is *presumed* to be thirty days" (emphasis added).

◆ HOLDER THROUGH AN HDC

There is one way an ordinary holder can be treated as if he or she were an HDC. A person who does not qualify as an HDC but who received title through an HDC may have the rights and privileges of an HDC. This is called the **shelter principle**. Thus, an ordinary holder can succeed to HDC status if any prior holder was an HDC.

Anyone, no matter how far removed from an HDC, comes within the shelter principle. Normally, a person who acquires an instrument from an HDC receives HDC rights under the principle that the transferee of an instrument receives at least the rights of the transferor.

◆ **shelter principle**
The principle that the holder of a negotiable instrument who cannot qualify as an HDC, but who gets his or her title through an HDC, acquires the rights of an HDC.

◆ LEGAL FOCUS ~ PROBLEM

Barry and Sheila convince Helen to write a check payable to the order of Barry in exchange for an autographed baseball rookie card of Will Clark. Helen is not aware that the autograph is really Sheila's, made five minutes before the sale. Barry indorses the check to Joseph for value. Barry and Sheila split the proceeds. Joseph is not aware of the circumstances surrounding the forged baseball card. Is Joseph an HDC?

Yes. Joseph paid value and was unaware of the fraudulent circumstances surrounding the drafting of the check. Helen must honor the check and pay Joseph. She, of course, has contract and tort rights against Barry and Sheila.

There are limitations on the shelter principle. Persons who formerly held instruments cannot improve their positions by later reacquiring the instruments from HDCs. Thus, a holder who is a party to some fraud or illegality that affects the instrument cannot improve his or her status by re-purchasing it from a later HDC. No person can "launder" an instrument by passing it into the hands of an HDC and then buying it back.

LEGAL BACKGROUND

A person who does not qualify as a holder in due course but who derives his or her title through a holder in due course can achieve the rights of a holder in due course. According to UCC 3-201(1), "Transfer of an instrument vests in the transferee such rights as the transferor has therein, except that a transferee who has himself been a party to any fraud or illegality affecting the instrument or who as a prior holder had notice of defense or claim against it cannot improve his position by taking from a later holder in due course."

Reteaching Activity

Ask a volunteer to define for the class the limitations on the shelter principle.

Have a student read this Legal Focus Example aloud to the class. Ask the class whether or not they think Barry is now a holder in due course. Make sure the students understand that Barry does not have holder-in-due-course status and that neither Barry nor Sheila can ever acquire a holder-in-due-course status. According to the UCC, neither can improve his or her position by taking from a later holder in due course.

Remind the students that they learned of breach of contract in Chapter 12, where it was defined as failure to perform part or all of the required duties under a contract.

420

Have a student volunteer read aloud this Legal Focus Example. Make sure the students understand that if the note is presented by Livingston, Rhodes is within his rights to use the personal defense and not honor the note; however, if the note has been negotiated and is presented for payment by a holder in due course, Rhodes must pay. Rhodes then, of course, can sue Livingston for breach of contract.

---

420   Commercial and Consumer Law

 LEGAL FOCUS – PROBLEM

In the example just given, suppose Joseph, the HDC, transfers the check, properly indorsed, to Paul as a gift. Paul then negotiates the check for value to Barry. Is Paul an HDC? Is Barry an HDC?

Paul has the status of an HDC. Although he did not pay value, he got the check from an HDC and is thus a holder through a holder in due course. Barry, however, does not have HDC status. Though Barry got the note through an HDC, he is not a holder through an HDC, because he was a participant in the fraud. Neither Barry nor Sheila can ever acquire HDC rights in this instrument.

DEFENSES TO PAYMENT

The key to liability on a negotiable instrument is a *signature*. The general UCC rule is this: "No person is liable on an instrument unless his [or her] signature appears on the instrument." Certain defenses can, however, prevent collection on even a properly signed instrument. What defenses will be effective depends on whether a holder or an HDC (or a holder through an HDC) makes a demand for payment. As mentioned earlier, there are two general categories of defenses—personal and real defenses.

PERSONAL DEFENSES

Personal defenses allow a person to avoid payment to an ordinary holder of a negotiable instrument but not a holder in due course. Personal defenses include breach of contract, fraud in the inducement, and mental incapacity, among others.

Breach of Contract   Breach of contract can be claimed as a defense to liability on an instrument. It is only a defense against ordinary holders.

 LEGAL FOCUS – EXAMPLE

Rhodes purchases several sets of imported china from Livingston. The china is to be delivered in four weeks. Rhodes gives Livingston a promissory note for $1,000, the price of the china. The china arrives, with many of the pieces broken, chipped, or cracked. Rhodes refuses to pay the note on the basis of breach of contract and breach of warranty. (Under sales law, a seller impliedly promises that the goods are at least merchantable, as discussed in Chapter 15.) If the note is presented by Livingston, the payee, Rhodes is within his rights to use the personal defense and not honor the note. If the note has been negotiated and is presented for payment by an HDC, however, Rhodes must pay. Breach of contract is not a defense against an HDC.

Reteaching Activity

To refresh the students' memories of ordinary duress, voidable contracts, and undue influence, have a student volunteer read aloud the Chapter 10 Summary, in which these concepts are discussed.

Vocabulary Activity

Have a student volunteer look up the word *forgery* in a dictionary and share the dictionary definition with the class. Have the student then relate this definition to the discussion of forgery found here.

Commercial Paper: Holder in Due Course, Defenses, and Checks   421

Fraud in the Inducement   A person who issues a negotiable instrument because of false statements by the other party can avoid payment on the instrument, unless the holder is an HDC.

> ### ◆ LEGAL FOCUS ~ EXAMPLE
>
> Jerry agrees to purchase Howard's used tractor for $24,500. Howard lies and tells Jerry that the tractor is in good working order and has been used for only one harvest. Jerry pays Howard $4,500 in cash and issues a negotiable promissory note for the balance. Then he finds out that the tractor is three years old and has been used in three harvests. Jerry can refuse to pay the note if it is held by an ordinary holder. However, if Howard has negotiated the note to an HDC, Jerry is legally required to pay the HDC. Of course, Jerry can then sue Howard.

Mental Incapacity   Ordinarily, mental incapacity is a personal defense. However, if a maker or drawer is held incapable by a court, the transaction is void. In that case, the defense is real, and it is good against an HDC as well as an ordinary holder.

Other Personal Defenses   Several other personal defenses can be used to avoid payment to an ordinary holder of a negotiable instrument, including the following:

1. Discharge of the instrument by payment or cancellation.
2. Unauthorized completion of an incomplete instrument.
3. Non-delivery of the instrument.
4. Ordinary duress, that duress which renders a contract voidable rather than void.
5. Undue influence.

REAL DEFENSES

Real, or universal, defenses are valid against all holders, including HDCs or holders through an HDC. These defenses include forgery, fraud in the execution or inception, material alteration, discharge in bankruptcy, minority, illegality, mental incapacity, and extreme duress.

Forgery   Forgery of a maker's or drawer's signature is a crime. When a person forges an instrument, the person whose name is forged has no liability. There are two exceptions:

1. The person whose unauthorized signature was used is liable if he or she ratifies the signature. To *ratify* the signature is to accept it after finding out about the forgery. Suppose Joe finds out his son forged his signature to buy a new stereo. If he agrees to pay the instrument or keeps the stereo for family use, he is ratifying the signature.

LEGAL BACKGROUND

To forge (a metaphorical expression, borrowed from the occupation of the smith who forges metal and iron) means, properly speaking, simply "to make or form," but in legal parlance it is always taken in a criminal sense.

Have a student volunteer read the first Legal Focus Example aloud to the class. Ask the class if they can think of any other examples of fraud in relationship to negotiable instruments that could also fit here. Allow volunteers to share their examples with the class.

Have a student read aloud to the class the second Legal Focus Example dealing with material alterations. Remind the students that they can use the Legal Focus features as review tools when studying for tests.

Critical Thinking Activity

Have the students write a paragraph explaining the similarities and differences between material alteration and forgery. Students should understand that forgery, in this case, deals solely with the signature, while material alteration deals with altering other aspects of a negotiable instrument.

---

2. A person's actions may in some way preclude him or her from denying the signature. Because of these actions, a court will not allow the person to say that the signature is not his or hers. For example, suppose Bill Jenkins watches as his brother Walt forges Bill's signature. He cannot not deny that the signature is his, unless he complained at the time of creation.

An unauthorized signature operates as the signature of the forger. The instrument can be enforced against the forger. Jill Walker forges Sean Astine's name. Sean is not liable on the instrument. Jill Walker is liable, even though she did not use her own name.

Fraud in the Execution or Inception   If a person is tricked into signing a negotiable instrument, fraud in the execution exists. This type of fraud is a real defense, which is good against even an HDC.

 LEGAL FOCUS – EXAMPLE

A consumer unfamiliar with the English language signs a paper presented by a salesperson as an estimate. Actually, it happens to be a promissory note. Even if the note is negotiated to an HDC, the consumer has a valid defense against payment.

As the example suggests, the signer's age, experience, and intelligence are important. These factors frequently determine whether the signer was really tricked or should have understood the transaction before signing.

Material Alteration   An alteration is *material* if it changes the contract terms between any two parties. Examples of material alterations include the following:

1. Completing an instrument in an unauthorized manner.
2. Adding to the writing as signed or removing any part of it.

 LEGAL FOCUS – EXAMPLE

Cutting off part of the paper of a negotiable instrument, adding clauses, or making any change in the amount, the date, or the rate of interest—even if the change is only one penny, one day, or 1 percent—is a material alteration.

It is not a material alteration to correct the maker's address. Nor is it material to correct the total final payment due when a mathematical error is discovered in the original computation. If the alteration is not material, any holder may enforce the instrument according to its original terms.

Divide the class into small groups. Read aloud to the groups the following sentences from the student text: "A material alteration is a *complete defense* against an ordinary holder but is sometimes only a *partial defense* against an HDC. If an original term—such as the monetary amount payable—has been altered, the HDC can enforce the instrument against the maker or drawer only according to the original terms." Have the students discuss this provision amongst themselves, and then have each group collaborate in writing a Legal Focus Example for this discussion of a material alteration as a partial defense against an HDC.

A material alteration is a *complete defense* against an ordinary holder but is sometimes only a *partial defense* against an HDC. If an original term—such as the monetary amount payable—has been altered, the HDC can enforce the instrument against the maker or drawer only according to the original terms. If the instrument was incomplete and was later completed in an unauthorized manner, however, the alteration is not a defense against an HDC. The HDC can enforce the instrument as completed. If an alteration is readily apparent, then obviously the holder has notice of some defect or defense and therefore cannot be an HDC.

Discharge in Bankruptcy A discharge in bankruptcy is an absolute defense on any instrument regardless of the status of the holder. The purpose of bankruptcy is to settle all of the insolvent party's debts. (This is discussed in Chapter 19.) The holder of the instrument is usually paid a percentage of the amount owed. Often, if there are few or no assets, the holder receives nothing.

Minority An instrument created or indorsed by a minor raises the defense of minority. Minority is a real defense when state law recognizes it as such, and state law does vary in this issue. Minority will provide a real defense, even though the instrument is only voidable rather than void.

Illegality When a transaction is void because of illegal conduct, then a real defense exists. Gambling contracts, for example, are void in many states. Thus, a negotiable instrument based on a gambling contract is not enforceable. If illegality merely makes a transaction voidable, then there is a defense against a holder but not against an HDC. Fraud in the inducement is often criminal, but an instrument obtained because of fraud in the inducement is voidable rather than void.

Mental Incapacity As mentioned earlier, mental incapacity is ordinarily a personal defense. If a person is judged mentally incompetent by state proceedings, however, then any instrument issued by that person afterwards is null and void. In that case, mental incapacity is a real defense.

Extreme Duress When a person signs and issues a negotiable instrument under extreme duress, the instrument is void. A void instrument is unenforceable by any holder, including an HDC. An example of extreme duress is an immediate threat of force or violence. Ordinary duress is a personal, not a real, defense.

FTC RULE LIMITING THE RIGHTS OF AN HDC

There is a special rule limiting the rights of an HDC when the debtor–buyer executes a negotiable promissory note as part of a consumer transaction. The rule, created by the Federal Trade Commission, provides that any personal defenses the buyer could assert against the seller can also be asserted against an HDC who has purchased the buyer's note from the seller. The seller must disclose this rule clearly on the sales agreement.

Ethical Concern

Only *real defenses* will prevent a holder in due course from receiving payment on an instrument. Stimulate a class discussion of this topic by asking the following questions: How do you think the drafters of the UCC decided which defenses were real and which were personal? Should there be a difference between defenses? In each case one party will bear the loss. Are the risks allocated fairly?

Teaching Note

As the students discuss **Discharge in Bankruptcy,** explain to them that the concept and practice of bankruptcy will be discussed in detail in Chapter 19.

1. A person becomes a holder of a negotiable instrument when he or she possesses an instrument that is "drawn, issued, or indorsed to him or his order or to bearer or in blank."

2. An executory promise is a promise to do something in the future that is valid consideration in a contract; however, the consideration must be performed in order for it to be considered value in a negotiation, making the holder a holder in due course.

3. A check drawn and payable in the United States is presumed to be overdue after 30 days.

4. Personal defenses are good against ordinary holders. Holders in due course can claim on the instrument even if a personal defense exists.

5. A person's age, experience, or intelligence frequently determine whether the signer was really tricked or should have understood the transaction before signing.

◆ CHECKING YOUR PROGRESS

1. How does a person become a holder of a negotiable instrument?

2. An executory promise is valid consideration in a contract, but it is not value for holder in due course status. Explain why.

3. When is a demand instrument such as a check drawn and payable in the United States presumed overdue?

4. What rights do a holder and a holder in due course have when there is a personal defense against an instrument?

5. Why are the age, experience and intelligence important when deciding if fraud in the execution exists as a real defense against a holder in due course?

◆ DISCHARGE

Discharge from liability on an instrument can occur in several ways, including payment and cancellation. The liability of all parties to an instrument is discharged when the party who is primarily liable on it pays to a holder the full amount. Payment by any other party discharges only the liability of that party and subsequent parties.

Cancellation of an instrument discharges the liability of all parties. If a holder writes "Paid" across the face of the instrument, it is canceled. If the holder tears it up, it is canceled. If a holder crosses out a party's signature, that party's liability and the liability of all later indorsers of the instrument are discharged.

◆ CHECKS

As checks are the most common type of commercial paper, they warrant additional study. Most exchanges of money today are made by checks, credit cards, and charge accounts. These means of payment are rapidly replacing currency in most transactions for goods and services.

Checks are the most common form of commercial paper regulated by the Uniform Commercial Code. More than 60 billion personal and commercial checks are written each year in the United States. These checks are more than a daily convenience; checkbook money is an essential part of the American economic system.

A check, as you learned in Chapter 17, is a special type of draft that is drawn on a bank, ordering it to pay a sum of money on demand. A drawee bank is not, however, liable to a payee or holder who presents the check for payment. This is true even though the drawer has sufficient funds to pay the check. It is the drawer who is liable to the payee or holder.

Stimulate a class discussion on the topic of *cashier's checks* by asking the following questions: What is a cashier's check? What makes a cashier's check different from a personal check? What are some examples of situations in which one would be compelled to pay by cashier's check? What are the advantages and disadvantages of using this type of check?

Have the students work with partners to explain this sentence from the student text: "Checks are usually three-party instruments involving a drawer, a drawee, and a payee." Allow student volunteers to share their explanations with the class.

Enrichment

Read aloud to the class the following sentence from the student text: "To protect the purchaser he or she must sign the (traveler's) check at the time it is bought and the time it is used." Ask the students how this protects the purchaser. Students should be made to understand that signing at the time of purchase places an example of the purchaser's signature on the traveler's check. When he or she uses or cashes the traveler's check, he or she signs it again. The person who cashes the traveler's check then can verify this signature against the existing signature on the check.

CASHIER'S CHECKS

Checks are usually three-party instruments involving a drawer, a drawee, and a payee. On certain types of checks, however, the bank can serve as both the drawer and the drawee. For example, when a bank draws a check on itself, the check is called a **cashier's check** (see Exhibit 18-1). A cashier's check is a negotiable instrument upon issue. In effect, with a cashier's check, the bank lends its credit to the purchaser of the check. Cashier's checks are provided by banks for a charge to the purchaser. They are often used by people who do not have their own checking accounts.

◆ **cashier's check**
A draft drawn by a bank on itself.

TRAVELER'S CHECKS

A **traveler's check** is like a cashier's check. It is an instrument on which a financial institution is both the drawer and the drawee. The institution is directly obligated to accept and pay its traveler's check according to the check's terms. A traveler's check is offered in pre-determined denominations, and is a benefit to travelers in another city or country. A person who is offered a traveler's check for payment is likely to accept the check because it is drawn on the financial institution's funds. The traveler benefits because he or she does not have to carry large amounts of cash, and if the checks are lost the issuing financial institution will replace them. To protect the purchaser, he or she must sign the check at the time it is bought and again at the time it is used. Exhibit 18-2 shows an example of a traveler's check.

◆ **traveler's check**
An instrument purchased from a financial institution that can be used as cash upon a second signature by the purchaser; comes in predetermined denominations.

EXHIBIT 18-1
CASHIER'S CHECK

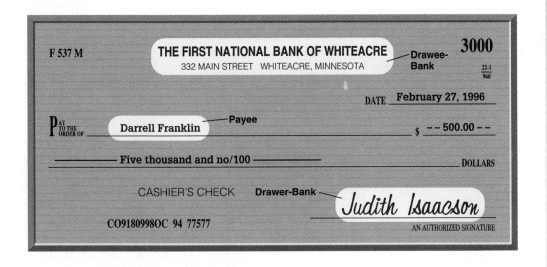

F 537 M	**THE FIRST NATIONAL BANK OF WHITEACRE** — Drawee-Bank	**3000**
	332 MAIN STREET WHITEACRE, MINNESOTA	22-1/960

DATE **February 27, 1996**

PAY TO THE ORDER OF ___ **Darrell Franklin** — Payee ___ $ -- 500.00 --

——— Five thousand and no/100 ——————————— DOLLARS

CASHIER'S CHECK   Drawer-Bank — *Judith Isaacson*

CO9180998OC 94 77577   AN AUTHORIZED SIGNATURE

In the past, banks often made customers wait for weeks to use their money when they deposited checks drawn on banks in other parts of the country. This was changed when Congress passed the Expedited Funds Availability Act. Under the act, banks were required to allow customers to use their money based on the following schedule (note that some states require even shorter waiting periods than are shown below): If the deposit is cash, the funds must be made available the next business day after the day of deposit. (Note: The first $100 of any deposit of checks must also be made available the next business day after the day of deposit.)

If the deposit is government, cashier's, certified, teller's checks, checks written on another account in the same institution, direct deposits, and/or other electronic transfers, the funds must be made available the next business day after the day of deposit.

Critical Thinking Activity

Have your students compare the differences among cashier's checks, traveler's checks, certified checks, and personal checks. Have students list at least two examples of situations in which each check could be used.

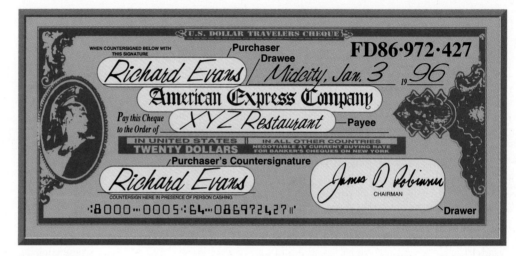

EXHIBIT 18-2
TRAVELER'S CHECK

CERTIFIED CHECKS

When a person writes a check, it is assumed that sufficient money is on deposit to cover that check. To protect against a bank's refusal to pay because of insufficient funds, a check may be certified by the drawee bank. A **certified check** is one recognized and accepted by a bank officer who thereupon promises the bank will honor it. The customer must pay the bank for the certification. The bank sets aside the specified amount drawn against the customer's funds held by the bank. Certification prevents the bank from denying liability. It is a promise that sufficient funds are on deposit and *have been set aside* to cover the check.

Sometimes certified checks are the required form of payment under state law. Purchases at a sheriff's sale, for example, must be made either by cash, cashier's check, or certified check. A sheriff's sale is an auction conducted by a sheriff or other court officer to sell property at the order of the court.

♦ **certified check**
A check drawn by an individual on his or her own account but bearing a guarantee by a bank.

◆ THE BANK–CUSTOMER RELATIONSHIP

The bank–customer relationship begins when the customer opens a checking account and deposits money. A creditor–debtor relationship is created between a customer and a bank. For example, when the customer makes cash deposits into a checking account the bank is a debtor to the customer for the deposit amount.

The rights and duties of the bank and the customer are based on contract and depend on the nature of the transaction. The bank promises to honor its customer's checks as long as there are sufficient funds in the account, the checks are timely, and the checks are properly drawn.

HONORING CHECKS

When a bank provides checking services, it agrees to honor the checks written by its customers. Of course, there must be sufficient funds in the account to pay each check. When a drawee bank *wrongfully* fails to honor a proper check, it is liable to its customer for damages resulting from its refusal to pay.

A bank need not refuse to honor a check when there are insufficient funds to cover the check. The bank may pay the check and charge the customer's account. If a bank has agreed with its customer to extend the customer credit, if he or she writes a check for more money than exists in the account, the payor bank is liable to its customer for damages caused by not honoring the check. This type of agreement is called *overdraft protection*.

The customer's agreement with the bank includes a general obligation to keep sufficient money on deposit to cover all checks written. The customer is liable to the payee or to the holder of a check in a civil suit if a check is not honored. If it can be proved that the customer intended to defraud, the customer can also be subject to criminal prosecution for writing a bad check.

Stale Checks   The bank's responsibility to honor its customers' checks is not absolute. A bank is not obliged to pay an uncertified check presented more than six months from its date. Commercial banking practice regards a check outstanding for longer than six months as a **stale check**. The bank has the option of paying or not paying on such a check without liability.

Missing Indorsements   The bank where a check is cashed is generally allowed to supply any necessary indorsements of a customer. The bank places a statement on the item that it was deposited by a customer or credited to that customer's account.

◆ **stale check**   A check, other than a certified check, that is presented for payment more than six months after its date.

◄ LEGAL FOCUS ~ EXAMPLE

Marisa Harper deposits her paycheck from Sam's Delicatessen in the night deposit box outside the First Southeastern Bank. She includes a deposit slip, properly completed, but she forgets to indorse her check. First Southeastern Bank can add a notation to the check that it was deposited by Marisa, and put the funds in Marisa's bank account.

Encourage students to discuss checking accounts and checking practices with their parents. Students might wish to ask their parents about both good and bad experiences involving their use of checking accounts. Students should also ask their parents if they have ever used a stop-payment order. What were the circumstances? Did they issue the stop-payment order orally? In the bank itself or by telephone? Did the bank charge a fee for a stop-payment order? How much? You may find that students acquire a wide variety of interesting and amusing anecdotes from talking with their parents about banking. Allow volunteers to share some of what they have learned with the class.

428

428   Commercial and Consumer Law

◆ **stop-payment order** An order by the drawer of a draft or check directing the drawer's bank not to pay the draft or check.

Stop-Payment Orders A **stop-payment order** directs the drawee bank not to pay a check. Only a customer can order payment stopped on a check. This right does not extend to holders—that is, payees or indorsees. The drawee bank's contract is not with them but with its drawers. A customer has no right to stop payment on a check that has been certified or accepted by a bank, however. Also, a stop-payment order must be received within a reasonable time and in a reasonable manner to permit the bank to act on it.

A stop-payment order can be given orally, usually by phone. An oral order is binding on the bank for fourteen calendar days. A written stop-payment order or an oral order confirmed in writing is effective for six months. At that time, it must be renewed in writing.

If the drawee bank pays the check over the customer's properly instituted stop-payment order, the bank must re-credit the account of the drawer–customer. The bank, however, is liable for no more than the actual loss suffered by the drawer because of the wrongful payment.

> ◆ **LEGAL FOCUS ~ EXAMPLE**
>
> Arlene Drury orders six bamboo palms from Waverly's Nursery at $25 each. Drury pays in advance for the trees with her check for $150. Later that day, Waverly's Nursery tells Drury that it will not deliver the palms as arranged. Drury immediately calls her bank and stops payment on the check. Two days later, in spite of the stop-payment order, the bank accidentally honors Drury's check to Waverly's Nursery. The bank is liable to Drury for the full $150.

The result would be different if Waverly's had delivered five of the six palms. Since Drury would have owed Waverly's $125 for the goods delivered, she could have established actual losses of only $25 resulting from the bank's payment. Consequently, the bank would have been liable to Drury for only $25.

A stop-payment order has its risks for a customer. The customer–drawer must have a *valid legal ground* for issuing such an order. Otherwise, the holder can sue the customer–drawer for payment. Moreover, defenses sufficient to refuse payment against a payee may not be valid grounds to prevent payment to a holder in due course.

A person who wrongfully stops payment on a check is liable to the payee for the amount of the check. The drawer might also be liable for special damages resulting from a wrongful stop-payment.

Overdrafts What happens when the bank receives an item properly payable from its customer's checking account, but there are insufficient

Read
Have a student recall the situations in which one might need to use a stop-payment order, as discussed on the previous page. Then ask a student volunteer to read this *Law in Action* feature aloud to the class.

Discuss
Stimulate a class discussion about this *Law in Action* feature by asking the following questions: What reasons can you give for thinking carefully before issuing a stop-payment order? Why might it be unwise to issue a stop-payment order on a check written for $5 or less? Why is it important to have a legal reason for issuing a stop-payment order? In what situations can you safely issue a stop-payment order?

Analyze and Apply
Divide the class into small groups to reread and discuss this *Law in Action* feature. Each group should then script two situations, one in which a customer wrongly or unwisely issues a stop-payment order, and one in which a customer is proper in issuing a stop-payment order and the manner in which he or she issues it. The script should include parts for all members of the group (such as bank customers, bank employees, and the payee for each of the checks in question). Allow the groups to perform their vignettes before the class.

Law in Action

LAW IN YOUR LIFE: CHECK STOP-PAYMENT ORDERS

As a bank customer, you should think carefully before issuing stop-payment orders. One reason is that bank charges for stop-payment orders are expensive compared with checks written for small amounts. (Charges range between $7 and $10.) Another reason is the risk that the stop-payment order may be issued too late. The bank has a reasonable amount of time to enforce your stop order before it is liable for improper payment. It is possible that the payee or another holder can cash the check despite your stop order if he or she acts quickly. Indeed, you could be writing out a stop order in the bank lobby while the payee or holder cashes the check next door.

Furthermore, you must not misuse the stop-payment order. Remember that a drawer must have a legal reason for issuing a stop-payment order. You cannot stop payment on a check simply because you have had a change of heart about the wisdom of your purchase. You can safely stop payment if you clearly did not get what you paid for

or were fraudulently induced to buy. You can also stop payment if a "cooling-off" law governs the transaction. (A cooling-off period, a few days to change your mind about a purchase, sometimes exists in consumer transactions.) Any wrongful stop-payment order subjects the drawer to liability to the payee or a holder, and this liability may include special damages that resulted from the order. When all is considered, it may be unwise to stop payment on a check because of a minor dispute with the payee.

CHECKLIST FOR STOP PAYMENTS

1. Compare the stop-payment fee with the disputed sum. Make sure it is worthwhile to issue a stop-payment order.
2. Make sure that your stop-payment order is made before the check has been honored by the bank.
3. Make sure you have a legal reason for issuing the stop-payment order.

funds in the account? The bank can either dishonor the item, or it can pay the item and charge the customer's account, creating an overdraft. The bank can subtract the difference from the customer's next deposit, because the check carries with it an enforceable implied promise to reimburse the bank.

When a check "bounces," a holder can resubmit the check, hoping that, later, sufficient funds will be available to pay it. The holder must notify any indorser on the check when the check is first dishonored. If indorsers are not notified, they are discharged from their signature liability. Unless the customer has an agreement with the bank by which the bank will loan money to cover the overdraft, the bank will charge the customer a fee every time a check bounces.

PAYMENT ON FORGED SIGNATURE OF DRAWER

A forged signature on a check has no legal effect as the signature of a drawer. Banks require a signature card from each customer who opens a checking account. The bank is responsible for determining whether the signature on a customer's check is genuine. The general rule is that the bank must re-credit the customer's account when it pays on a forged signature. There are exceptions to this rule, however.

Customer Negligence   When the customer's negligence substantially contributes to the forgery, the bank is not normally obliged to re-credit the customer's account for the amount of the check.

◆ LEGAL FOCUS - EXAMPLE

Gemco Corporation uses a mechanical check-writing machine to write its payroll and business checks. Gemco discovers that one of its employees used the machine to write himself a check for $10,000 and that the bank later honored it. Gemco requests that the bank re-credit $10,000 to its account for incorrectly paying on a forged check. If the bank can show that Gemco did not take reasonable care in controlling access to the check-writing equipment, Gemco cannot require the bank to re-credit its account for the amount of the forged check.

Timely Examination Required   A customer should examine monthly statements and canceled checks promptly with reasonable care and report any forged signatures immediately. This includes forged signatures of indorsers. Failure to examine and report, or any carelessness by the customer that results in a loss to the bank, makes the customer liable for the loss.

PAYMENT ON FORGED INDORSEMENT

A bank that pays a customer's check bearing a forged indorsement must re-credit the customer's account.

◆ LEGAL FOCUS - EXAMPLE

Brian issues a $50 check "to the order of Antonio." Jimmy steals the check, forges Antonio's indorsement, and cashes the check. When the check reaches Brian's bank, the bank pays it and debits Brian's account. The forgery is then brought to the bank's attention. The bank must re-credit Brian's account by $50, because it did not carry out Brian's order to pay "to the order of Antonio." Brian's bank will be able to recover from any bank that cashed the check. The bank that cashed the check has a claim against the wrongdoer, Jimmy.

Have a student volunteer read this Legal Focus Example aloud to the class. Make sure that students understand that Amy is solely responsible for the amount she ordered the bank to pay, in this case $11. The bank is normally responsible for the $100. Students should also understand, however, that the bank can seek damages from Ryan, who materially altered the check.

PAYMENT ON ALTERED CHECK

The customer's instruction to the bank is to pay the exact amount on the face of the check to the holder. The bank must examine each check before making final payment. If it fails to detect an alteration, it is liable to its customer for the loss because it did not pay as the drawer–customer ordered. The loss is the difference between the original amount of the check and the amount actually paid.

◀ LEGAL FOCUS ~ EXAMPLE

Amy writes a check for $11 and Ryan raises the figure to $111. The bank pays the $111. Amy's account is responsible for $11 (the amount Amy ordered the bank to pay). The bank is normally responsible for the $100.

The bank is entitled to recover the amount of loss from the transferor, because the transferor, by presenting the check for payment, warrants that the check has not been materially altered.

A customer's negligence can shift the risk of loss from the bank to the customer. A common example occurs when a person carelessly writes a check, leaving large gaps around the numbers and words so that additional numbers and words can be inserted. Exhibit 18-3 shows a carelessly written check.

EXHIBIT 18-3
POORLY FILLED-OUT CHECK

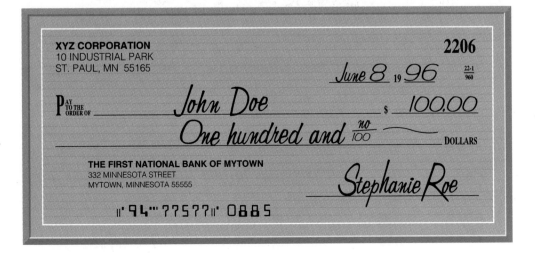

Enrichment

Obtain copies of a mock blank check, and distribute a few copies to each student. On the board, demonstrate the proper way to fill out a check. Have students write several checks on their own.

Make sure that students understand the words "For deposit into Account #4012 Only," restrict how this check can be deposited; therefore, this is a restrictive indorsement.

Similarly, a person who signs a check and leaves the dollar amount for someone else to fill in cannot protest when the bank unknowingly and in good faith pays that amount. The law governing the customer's duty to examine monthly statements and canceled checks, and to discover and report alterations to the drawee bank, is the same as that applied to forged customer signatures.

BANK'S LIABILITY FOR RESTRICTIVE INDORSEMENTS

Only the first bank to which the item is presented for collection must pay in a manner consistent with any restrictive indorsement.

◀ LEGAL FOCUS – EXAMPLE

Charles writes a check on his San Francisco bank account and sends it to Leota. Leota endorses the check with a restrictive indorsement that reads, "For deposit into Account #4012 only." A Dallas bank is the first bank to which this check is presented for payment. This bank must act consistently with the terms of the restrictive indorsement. Therefore, it must credit account #4012 with the money or be liable to Leota for conversion.

◆ CHECKING YOUR PROGRESS

1. Why is a discharge in bankruptcy an absolute defense on any instrument?
2. How can a party be discharged from liability on an instrument?
3. Why are checks covered by the Uniform Commercial Code?
4. What is the bank's liability on a "stale check?"
5. What parties to a check can order a stop-payment? How long is the order effective?
6. If a bank pays an altered check, what party is liable for payment of the incorrect amount?

Teaching A Case In Point

Read

Before the students read this *A Case In Point* feature, make sure that they understand the meaning of the term *post-dated check*. Explain to the students that to post-date a check is to write a date later than the execution. Say: "In other words, if I write a check to you today but put tomorrow's date on that check, it is a post-dated check and is not valid until tomorrow. In this way, post-dated checks are similar to time drafts or notes." Once you are sure that students understand the meaning of the term *post-dated check*, allow a student volunteer to read this *A Case In Point* feature aloud to the class.

Discuss

Stimulate a class discussion regarding this *A Case In Point* feature by asking the following questions: On what date did Thomas give the check for $2,500 to Ralph Gallo? What date was on the check? What date did Thomas decide to have a stop-payment order placed on the check? What discrepancy existed in the stop-payment order? When was the check presented for payment at the bank? What action did the bank take at this time? Why did Thomas bring an action against the bank? What decision did the Civil Court of the City of New York reach in this case? What reasons did the court give for its decision?

◆ A CASE IN POINT ◆

THOMAS v. MARINE MIDLAND TINKERS NATIONAL BANK

Civil Court of the City of New York, 1976.
86 Misc.2d 284,
381 N.Y.S.2d 797.

This case confirms the bank's duty to honor in a timely fashion a customer's stop-payment order. Note that postdated checks are generally legal. They are like time drafts or notes. The bank should not follow the order until the date on the check.

FACTS On December 8, 1973, the plaintiff (Thomas) gave Ralph Gallo a check for $2,500 as a down payment on two rugs Thomas was purchasing from Gallo. The check was postdated to December 10 and drawn on the Marine Midland Tinkers National Bank. On the morning of December 10, having changed his mind about the purchase, Thomas went to the Marine Midland bank and arranged with a bank officer whom he knew to have a stop-payment order placed on the check. Thomas gave the bank officer all the required information, but the check was described as #22 instead of #221, the correct number. On the afternoon of the following day, the check was presented for payment at the same bank, and the bank cashed it and debited the plaintiff's account in the amount of the $2,500. When Thomas called Gallo, de-manding the return of the $2,500, Gallo refused to pay and threatened to enforce the purchase agreement. Thomas then brought an action against the bank for wrongful payment. The bank moved for dismissal of the charge on the basis of the incorrect information (the erroneous check number) given by Thomas on the stop-payment order.

ISSUE Can Thomas recover the $2,500 from the bank?

DECISION Yes. The bank was held responsible for its act of improperly making payment on the check.

REASON The court held that "[a] day and a half is more than reasonable notice to enforce a stop order on a check presented at the very same branch, and payment of the item by the bank thereafter constitutes a breach of its obligations to honor the stop order. The normal problem of reasonable computer lag when dealing with a great number of other branches of a large bank has no relevancy to the facts at bar [this case], where all transactions occurred in a single branch." As to the error regarding the check number, the court stated, "The single digital mistake in describing the check in the stop order is deemed trivial, and insignificant. Enough information was supplied to the bank to reasonably provide it with sufficient information to comply with the stop-payment order. The bank is therefore held responsible for its act of improperly making payment upon the check."

Teaching Note

This case is included in the *West's Business and Personal Law Handbook of Selected Court Cases.*

In order to help students review what they have learned in Chapter 18, you might wish to:

1. Have a student volunteer, or volunteers, read aloud the Chapter Summary.
2. Allow the students to work with partners to complete the *Using Legal Language* activity.
3. Assign the *Checking for Comprehension* exercise as homework.
4. Allow the students to work in small groups to complete the *Applying Legal Concepts* activities.
5. As a class, complete the *Applying the Law* activities. (Please note that you may have to help students with vocabulary so that they adequately understand all of the *Applying the Law* material.)

In order to check student mastery of chapter concepts, you may wish to use the Chapter 18 test that is found in your *Teacher's Resource Binder* or use WESTEST computerized testing for Chapter 18.

CHAPTER 18 REVIEW

◆ SUMMARY

REQUIREMENTS FOR HOLDER-IN-DUE-COURSE STATUS

Must Be a Holder
A holder is a person who is in possession of an instrument "drawn, issued, or indorsed to him or his order or to bearer or in blank."

Must Take for Value
Value is given in three ways:

1. A holder gives value to the extent that agreed-upon consideration has been paid or a security interest or lien acquired.

2. A holder gives value by taking an instrument in payment of or as security for a past debt.

3. A holder gives value by giving a negotiable instrument or an irrevocable commitment as payment.

Must Take in Good Faith
Good faith is defined as "honesty in fact in the conduct or transaction concerned."

Must Take without Notice
1. *That the instrument is overdue:*
   a. Time instruments are overdue the moment after the due date for payment.
   b. Demand instruments are overdue after demand has been made or a reasonable time has passed from issue.
   c. Domestic checks are *presumed* to be overdue after thirty days from issue.
2. *That the instrument has been previously dishonored.*
3. *That a claim or a defense exists.*

The Shelter Principle (Holder through a Holder in Due Course)
A holder has the rights of a holder in due course if he or she gets title through a holder in due course.

VALID DEFENSES AGAINST HOLDERS OF NEGOTIABLE INSTRUMENTS

No person is liable on an instrument unless his or her signature appears on the instrument.

Personal Defenses (valid against mere holders; not valid against HDCs or holders with rights of HDCs)

1. Breach of contract.
2. Fraud in the inducement.
3. Mental incapacity—if the contract is voidable.
4. Discharge by payment or cancellation, unauthorized completion, nondelivery of the instrument, ordinary duress, or undue influence.

Real Defenses (valid against all holders, including HDCs and holders with the rights of HDCs)

1. Forgery.
2. Fraud in the execution or inception.
3. Material alteration.
4. Discharge in bankruptcy.
5. Minority—if the contract is voidable.
6. Illegality, mental incapacity, or extreme duress—if the contract is void.

DISCHARGE

A negotiable instrument can be discharged in several ways, including payment and cancellation of the instrument.

CHECKS—DEFINITIONS

Check—A special type of draft that is drawn on a bank, ordering the bank to pay a sum of money on demand.

Cashier's check—A draft drawn by a bank on itself.

Traveler's check—An instrument on which a financial institution is both the drawer and the drawee. The purchaser must provide his or her signature in order for a traveler's check to become a negotiable instrument.

Certified check—A check for which the drawee bank, for a fee, certifies that it will set aside funds in the drawer's account to ensure payment of the check upon presentation.

BANK–CUSTOMER RELATIONSHIPS

Honoring Checks

A bank agrees to honor the checks written by its customers who have sufficient funds in their accounts.

1. *Stale Checks*   A bank is not obligated to pay an uncertified check presented six months after it is drawn, but it may do so in good faith.

2. *Missing Indorsements*   A bank can supply any necessary indorsements of a customer.

3. *Stop-Payment Orders*   A customer can order a bank to stop payment on a check.

4. *Overdrafts*   A bank can refuse to honor a check written on an account which has insufficient funds to cover the check amount.

5. *Forged checks*   A bank is responsible for determining whether the signature on a customer's check is genuine. A customer is required to examine his or her bank statements and report apparent forgeries to the bank.

6. *Altered Checks*   A bank is expected to pay the exact amount on the face of the check to the holder. A customer is required to examine his or her bank statements and report apparent altered checks to the bank.

◆ USING LEGAL LANGUAGE

Directions: Match each term with the statement that best defines that term.

1. cashier's check
2. certified check
3. holder
4. holder in due course (HDC)
5. personal defense
6. real defense
7. shelter principle
8. stale check
9. stop-payment order
10. traveler's check

A. A _____ is given by the drawer of a draft or check to direct the drawer's bank not to pay the check.

B. Any holder who acquires a negotiable instrument for value, in good faith, and without notice that the instrument is overdue or that it has been dishonored, or that any defense or claim exists, becomes a _____.

C. When a check is drawn by an individual on his or her own account, it becomes a _____ if it bears a guarantee by a bank.

D. When a defense can be used to avoid payment to an ordinary holder of a negotiable instrument, it is a _____ if it is not a defense to an HDC.

E. A check is known as a _____ if it is presented for payment more than six months after its date.

Checking for Comprehension (Answers)

1. A holder of a negotiable instrument has the rights of an assignee of a contract right and cannot collect payment if there is a superior claim or defense to the instrument. A holder in due course acquires a higher level of immunity to payment defenses or claim of ownership to the instrument by other parties.
2. A holder of a negotiable instrument is not a holder in due course if he or she knows the instrument is overdue, has been dishonored, has a defense against it, or there is another claim to it.
3. Students may describe any two personal defenses: breach of contract, fraud in the inducement, mental incapacity, discharge by payment or cancellation, unauthorized completion of an incomplete instrument, nondelivery, and ordinary duress or undue influence. Personal defenses are not good against a holder in due course. Mental incapacity becomes a real defense and voids a transaction if a court holds the maker or drawer incapable of contracting.
4. When a negotiable instrument is issued under extreme duress, the instrument is void, therefore unenforceable by any holder or holder in due course. However, ordinary duress is a personal defense and can be used against an ordinary holder, not against a holder in due course.
5. Sherry can recover the $1,500 from Alfred if she is a holder in due course. She will be an HDC only if she,

as a holder, took the check a–for value, b–in good faith, and c–without notice that the check was overdue or dishonored or that a claim or defense against it exists. In this instance, Sherry qualifies for HDC status. First, she is a holder, as the check was properly negotiated to her (by indorsement). Second, the facts indicate that she gave value. Third, there is nothing to indicate that she took the instrument in bad faith. Fourth, she was unaware of Jules's fraud (claim or defense), and she took the check before it was overdue (within 30 days of issue). Thus, Sherry is a holder in due course and can hold Alfred liable.

6. Clemson was correct in examining his bank statement in a timely manner and notifying the bank of a forged check. Ordinarily, a forged signature on a check has no legal effect as the signature of the drawer. However, when the customer's negligence substantially contributes to the forgery, the bank is not normally obliged to recredit the customer's account for the amount of the check. Since the bank was accustomed to paying checks on which Clemson's signature was stamped, it had no way of knowing the signature was forged. If the bank can show that Clemson did not take reasonable care in controlling access to the signature stamp, Clemson cannot require the bank to recredit his account for the amount of the forged check.

Applying the Law . . .
You Be the Judge (Answers)

1. No. Epicycle failed in its defense against payment on the check. UCC 3-302(1) provides that a holder in due course is a holder who takes an instrument for value, in good faith, and without notice that it is overdue, or has been dishonored, or that any defense or claim exists against it. That Money Mart took the check for value and in good faith was not disputed, as Money Mart gave cash to the employee and was unaware that Epicycle had ordered that payment of the check be stopped. The central issue was whether Money Mart had taken the check without notice. In evaluating Epicycle's claim that Money Mart should have inquired into the validity of the check before cashing it, the court concluded that when an instrument is regular on its face, there is no duty to inquire as to possible defenses unless the holder has reason to feel such inquiry is necessary. In this case, there was nothing about Epicycle's

F. A holder of a negotiable instrument who cannot qualify as a holder in due course, but who gets his or her title through an HDC, under the _____ acquires the rights of an HDC.

G. A _____ is a draft drawn by a bank on itself.

H. Defenses that can be used to avoid payment to all holders of a negotiable instrument are _____, they can be used against an HDC.

I. The person who is in possession of a document of title or an instrument drawn, issued, or indorsed to him or to his order, or to bearer or in blank is a _____.

J. An instrument purchased from a financial institution that can be used as cash upon a second signature is a _____, it comes in pre-determined denominations.

◆ CHECKING FOR COMPREHENSION

1. How do the rights of a holder of a negotiable instrument differ from those of a holder in due course?

2. A person is not a holder in due course if he or she acquires an instrument knowing that it is defective. List four ways a negotiable instrument could be defective.

3. Describe two personal defenses to an instrument. Are either of these defenses good against a holder in due course?

4. What is the effect of duress on ordinary holders and on holders in due course?

5. Jules sold Alfred a small motorboat for $1,500, maintaining to Alfred that the boat was in excellent condition. Alfred gave Jules a check for $1,500, which Jules gave to Sherry for value with indorsement. When Alfred took the boat for a trial run, he discovered that the boat leaked, needed to be painted, and needed a new motor. Alfred stopped payment on his check, which had not yet been cashed. Jules has disappeared. Can Sherry recover from Alfred as holder in due course?

6. Clemson had a rubber stamp made with which he signed his checks. One day, Clemson's daughter used the stamp to sign a check she had written on her father's account. The check was for $300 and payable to a friend to whom she owed money. First Federal, Clemson's bank, honored the check. When Clemson's bank statement arrived and he noticed the check, he promptly notified the bank that the check was a forgery and requested that the bank return the funds to his account. Must the bank restore the funds to Clemson's account? Explain.

check that would have raised any suspicion that something would be wrong with it. Money Mart was, thus, held to be a holder in due course.

2. The court held that "a holder in due course of a negotiable instrument is one who takes the instrument for value, in good faith, without notice that it is overdue or has been dishonored or of any defense against it or claim to it on the part of any person" [UCC 3-302]. The only issue is whether First National Bank gave value. UCC 3-303(b) states that a holder takes for value if the instrument is given "in payment of or as security for an antecedent claim." Since the bank took the notes from the Dolly Cam Corp. as security for antecedent debt, the bank qualifies as a holder in due course.

3. The trial court entered a summary judgment in favor of Barnett, and this judgment was sustained by the appellate court. Ossip was thereby precluded from recovering the amounts paid out of its accounts by Barnett. A bank customer is required under the UCC to "exercise reasonable care and promptness" in examining its bank statements. If this duty is not met, UCC 4-406(2)(b) prevents recovery from the bank on a series of checks by the same wrongdoer containing unauthorized signatures that were paid by the bank at least 14 days after the first item and statements were made available to the customer. An exception to this rule exists, however, where the "customer establishes the lack of ordinary care on the part of the bank paying the item(s)." Here the court found that Ossip did not exercise reasonable care in examining the bank statements. In fact, Harris admitted that he did not actually review the signature on all of the company's canceled checks—actually, he did not even pay attention to the signatures—but rather was more concerned with the amounts and whether it was the "kind of check [Ossip] would pay." Furthermore, Ossip did not establish a lack of ordinary care on the part of Barnett. Barnett's internal procedures, including examining each check against the signature to determine the validity of the signature and referring any problems to supervisor-level employees, was not contradicted or shown to fall below accepted standards in the industry. The court held that Ossip's argument "that the bank was negligent in not detecting the forgery, is particularly unavailing in light of the fact that Edward Harris failed to detect the forgery of his own signature." As a result, Barnett was entitled to summary judgment.

APPLYING LEGAL CONCEPTS

1. Design a table in which the rights of holders and the rights of holders in due course are compared and contrasted.

2. Assume a friend of yours wrote a check to pay for some tapes from a mail-order music company. The record company has not shipped the tapes, and your friend realizes the check was written for twice the amount needed. Compose and key a letter to your friend explaining his or her options and the liability involved with all parties.

APPLYING THE LAW . . . YOU BE THE JUDGE

1. An employee of Epicycle Corp. cashed a payroll check at Money Mart Check Cashing Center. Money Mart deposited the check, with others, into its bank account. When the check was returned marked "payment stopped," Money Mart sought to recover from Epicycle for the value of the check. Money Mart claimed that it was a holder in due course on the instrument because it had accepted the check for value, in good faith, and without notice that a stop-payment order had been made. Epicycle argued that Money Mart was not a holder in due course because it had failed to verify that the check was good before it cashed the check. Did Money Mart's failure to inquire into the validity of the check preclude it from being a holder in due course? Explain. [*Money Mart Check Cashing Center, Inc. v. Epicycle Corp.*, 667 P.2d 1372 (Colo. 1983)]

2. On September 9, 1976, Rob-Glen Enterprises, Inc., executed and delivered promissory notes payable to the Dolly Cam Corp. in return for a loan of $46,000. In addition, to secure the loan a number of individuals of Rob-Glen Enterprises executed identical guarantees of payment for the notes. Shortly thereafter, prior to the notes' maturity, Dolly Cam indorsed the notes in blank and delivered them to the First National Bank of Long Island pursuant to an existing general loan and security agreement for past and future debts. Rob-Glen, at the date of maturity, refused to pay the notes held by the bank. The bank claimed it was entitled to payment as a holder in due course. Rob-Glen claimed that the bank was not a holder in due course because it had given no value. Discuss whether the bank was a holder in due course. [*First National Bank of Long Island v. Rob-Glen Enterprises, Inc.*, 101 A.D.2d 848, 476 N.Y.S.2d (1984)]

3. Ossip-Harris Insurance, Inc. (Ossip) maintained a checking account with Barnett Bank of South Florida, N.A. (Barnett). From May 1980 through June 1981, Ossip's bookkeeper used a facsimile signature stamp to forge the name of Ossip's president, Harris, to ninety-nine checks totaling $19,711.90. When the canceled checks came back to Ossip, the bookkeeper would replace the payee name with one of a legitimate Ossip business expense. Although Harris periodically reviewed the monthly statement and canceled checks, he did not detect the forgeries until June of 1981. At that time, Harris notified Barnett, and Barnett paid no further forged checks. Ossip alleged that Barnett wrongfully paid the forged checks drawn on Ossip's account. Discuss fully to what extent, if any, Barnett can be held liable for its payment of the forged checks. [*Ossip-Harris Insurance, Inc. v. Barnett Bank of South Florida, N.A.*, 428 So.2d 363 (Fla.App. 1983)]

Prereading Activity

Introduce this Legal Perspective by explaining to students that electronic fund transfers (EFTs) are conducted in a number of ways, including with the use of automated teller machines (ATMs), sometimes called cash machines, bank machines, etc. Ask a student volunteer who is familiar with ATMs to describe to the class how a consumer initiates a transaction on an ATM. If no students are sufficiently familiar with the process to discuss this, explain to the students that to initiate a transaction on an automated teller machine, a consumer generally uses a card that provides access to the system. Each card has an accompanying personal identification number (PIN) that is given only to the account holder. The number is meant to be kept secret so as to inhibit unauthorized use of the card. Consumers can then access the ATM and make deposits, withdrawals, and other transactions dealing with their accounts.

LEGAL BACKGROUND

Here are some rules to remember when using EFTs.

1. Be cognizant of your surroundings when using an ATM. Throughout the country there has been an increase in robberies of ATM customers. Use of ATMs should be limited to safe locations and safe times.

2. Always wait for an ATM's record of your transaction, and check it before you leave. Such records will tell you the date, location, and amount, as well as the type of transaction. The record will help you verify the bank's monthly statement when you receive it.

3. Keep all records. Put them in your wallet or purse.

LEGAL PERSPECTIVE

ELECTRONIC FUND TRANSFER SYSTEMS (EFTS)

Banks are finding it increasingly difficult to cope with the trillions of checks that are written. Recently, new systems of automatic payment and direct deposit, known as electronic fund transfer systems (EFTS), have become very common. These systems promise to rid banks of the burden of moving mountains of paper to transfer money.

The benefits of EFTS are obvious. Transferring funds electronically reduces the task of handling masses of information. Not surprisingly, it also poses difficulties on occasion, including the following:

1. It is difficult to issue stop-payment orders.
2. Fewer records are available.
3. The possibilities for tampering (with a resulting decrease in privacy) are increased.
4. The time between the writing of a check and its deduction from an account (*float* time) is lost.

TYPES OF EFTS

Funds can be transferred electronically by (1) automated teller machines, (2) point-of-sale systems, (3) systems handling direct deposits and withdrawals, and (4) pay-by-telephone systems.

AUTOMATED TELLER MACHINES

Automated teller machines (ATMs) are also called *customer bank communications terminals* or *remote service units*. ATMs are located on the bank's premises and at locations such as convenience and retail stores, supermarkets, drugstores, and shopping centers. Automated teller machines receive deposits,

dispense funds from checking or savings accounts, make credit card advances, and receive payments. The devices are connected on-line to the bank's computers. Customers usually have *debit cards* or *access cards*. These plastic cards allow the customers to use the computer banking system.

To make a withdrawal from an ATM, the customer uses an access card in addition to punching in a **personal identification number (PIN)**. The PIN protects the customer whose access card is lost or stolen. No one else can use the card without knowing the PIN.

POINT-OF-SALE SYSTEMS

Point-of-sale systems allow the consumer to transfer funds to merchants when making purchases. On-line terminals are located at checkout counters in the merchant's store. When a purchase is made, the customer's card is inserted into the terminal, which reads the data encoded on it. The computer at the customer's bank verifies that the card and identification code are valid. The computer also verifies that there is enough money in the customer's account. After the purchase is made, the customer's account is debited for the amount of the purchase.

DIRECT DEPOSITS AND WITHDRAWALS

A direct deposit may be made to a customer's account through an electronic terminal when authorized by the customer. The federal government often uses this EFTS to deposit Social Security payments directly into beneficiaries' accounts. Similarly, an employer may agree to make payroll and pension payments directly into an employee's account.

4. Transfer your records to a checkbook, and keep a running balance.

5. When you make a mistake that cannot be corrected at the ATM, call the bank's customer service line as soon as possible.

6. Do not share your PIN or debit card with anyone.

7. If you are using an ATM, have any person with you step aside so that the transaction can't be observed.

8. If your debit card is lost or stolen, notify your bank immediately.

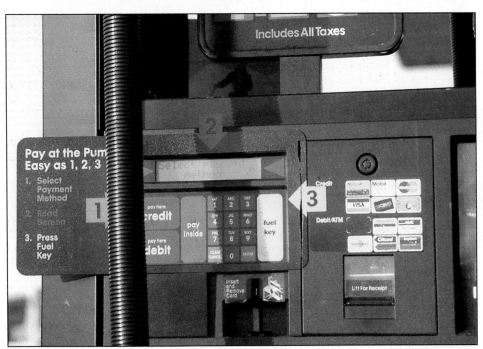

Is this an automated teller machine or a point-of-sale machine?

A customer may also authorize the bank (or other financial institution at which the customer's funds are on deposit) to make automatic payments to a third party. For example, insurance premiums, utility bills, home mortgage payments, and automobile installment loan payments may be made automatically.

Pay-by-Telephone Systems

Sometimes it is undesirable to arrange in advance for an automatic payment—for example, when the amount of a regular payment varies. Some financial institutions permit their customers to pay bills through a pay-by-telephone system. The customer can access the institution's computer system by telephone and direct a transfer of funds. Utility bills frequently are paid directly by customers using pay-by-telephone systems. Customers may also be permitted to transfer funds between accounts. For example, a customer can withdraw funds from a savings account and make a deposit in a checking account. Many consumers use personal computers and telephones to transact their banking business at home.

◆ The Electronic Fund Transfer Act of 1978 (EFTA)

In 1978, Congress passed the Electronic Fund Transfer Act (EFTA) "to provide a (continued on page 440)

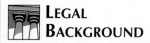

LEGAL BACKGROUND

Congress stated in 1978 that the use of electronic systems to transfer funds promised to provide substantial benefits for consumers, but Congress also concluded that given the unique characteristics of EFTs, existing consumer protection legislation governing the rights and obligations of consumers, financial institutions, and intermediaries was inadequate with respect to the types of fund transfers occurring by means of EFTs. In 1978 Congress passed the Electronic Funds Transfer Act (EFTA) "to provide a basic framework establishing the rights, liabilities, and responsibilities of participants in electronic fund transfers." The EFTA is essentially

LEGAL PERSPECTIVE (CONTINUED)

basic framework establishing the rights, liabilities, and responsibilities of participants in electronic fund transfers." The EFTA is a disclosure law benefiting consumers. It requires financial institutions to inform consumers about their rights in regard to EFTS. The EFTA is not concerned with commercial electronic fund transfers—transfers between businesses or between businesses and financial institutions.

REGULATION E—ELECTRONIC FUNDS TRANSFERS

The Federal Reserve Board has passed regulations called "Regulation E—Electronic Funds Transfers" to implement the act. Some of the major rules applying to the use of EFTS are as follows.

1. If a customer's debit card is lost or stolen and used without his or her permission, the customer's liability is generally limited to $50. The customer, however, must notify the bank of the loss or theft within two days of learning about it, or liability increases to $500. The customer may be liable for more than $500 if the unauthorized use is not reported within sixty days after it appears on the customer's statement. Furthermore, the $50 liability limit does not protect the customer if the customer gave the card to someone who then used it improperly.

2. Any error on the monthly statement must be discovered by the customer within sixty days, and the bank must be notified. The bank then has ten days to investigate and report its conclusions to the customer in writing. The bank must return the disputed amount of money to the customer's account if it takes longer than ten days to investigate the error. If there is no error, the customer has to give the money back to the bank.

3. The bank must furnish receipts for transactions made through computer terminals. It is not required that receipts be issued for telephone transfers.

4. A monthly statement must be made for every month in which there is an electronic transfer of funds. Otherwise, statements must be made every quarter. The statement must show the amount and date of the transfer, the names of any retailers involved, the identification of the terminal, and the fees. The statement must include an address and phone number for inquiries and error notices.

5. Any authorized prepayment (for example, for utility bills and insurance premiums) can be stopped three days before the scheduled transfer.

6. All of this information must be given to the customer who opens an EFTS account.

UNAUTHORIZED TRANSFERS

Unauthorized transfers of funds through EFT systems are a hazard of electronic banking. A check leaves highly visible evidence of a transaction. A customer can easily detect a forgery or an altered check with ordinary vigilance. With an electronic transfer, only a computer printout of debits and credits made to an account during a specified period (for example, a month) is available.

The Electronic Fund Transfer Act (EFTA) of 1978 defines an unauthorized transfer. A transfer is unauthorized if (1) it is initiated by a person other than the customer and without actual authority to initiate such transfer; (2) the customer receives

440

a disclosure law designed to benefit consumers; it requires financial institutions to inform consumers of their rights with respect to EFTs. The EFTA is not concerned with commercial electronic fund transfers—transfers between businesses and financial institutions.

Under the EFTA, the Federal Reserve System's Board of Governors is authorized to administer the Act and to promulgate regulations to carry out the purposes of the Act. The Board of Governors has issued a set of rules, called Regulation E, to protect users of EFTs; this regulation should be consulted for a complete understanding of the EFTA. The Board has also drafted model clauses for financial institutions to use in disclosing information about their electronic systems.

Extension Activity

Have a volunteer or group of volunteers research new banking technology. You might refer students to the *Reader's Guide to Periodical Literature,* in which they can look up "electronic fund transfer systems" or "technology and banking" to find sources for information regarding the influx of technology into modern banking. Have students present their findings to the class in the form of an oral report.

no benefit from it; and (3) the customer did not furnish such person "with the card, code, or other means of access" to his or her account.

ERROR RESOLUTION AND DAMAGES

The procedures prescribed by the EFTA must be followed strictly by a bank. If the bank does not investigate an error reported to it by a customer and report its conclusion promptly to the customer, it violates the act and is subject to civil liability. The bank is liable for actual damages experienced by a customer. The bank is also liable for the costs of a successful lawsuit brought against the bank by a customer, including attorneys' fees. The bank may also be liable for punitive damages ranging from $100 to $1,000.

COMMERCIAL TRANSFERS

Commercial parties also transfer funds electronically. The dollar volume of payments by electronic transfer is more than $1 trillion a day. This amount far exceeds the dollar volume of payments made by other means. The two major electronic payment systems are the Federal Reserve wire transfer network (Fedwire) and the New York Clearing House Interbank Payments Systems (CHIPS).

Unauthorized electronic transfers are possible and are a problem. If an imposter, for example, succeeds in having funds wired from another party's account, that party bears the loss (unless he or she can recover from the imposter). Disputes arising as a result of unauthorized or incorrectly made transfers are settled by the courts under the common law principles of tort law or contract law. In the future, however, these and other types of transfers (including payments by mail) may be subject to Article 4A of the UCC—when the provisions of that article are adopted by the states. Article 4A has recently been drafted to deal specifically with fund transfers that are not covered by the EFTA or other federal or state statutes.

  TERMS TO REMEMBER

♦ **automated teller machine (ATM)**
Machine that allows bank customers to transact business without the direct help of bank employees. ATMs receive deposits, dispense funds from checking or savings accounts, make credit card advances, and receive payments.

♦ **personal identification number (PIN)**
Secret number that allows a customer to get remote access to his or her bank account.

Mastery Objectives

By the end of this chapter, students will be able to:
- Explain remedies available to creditors
- Distinguish among mechanic's, artisan's and innkeeper's liens
- Differentiate writ of execution, attachment, and garnishment
- Establish liability in a suretyship and guaranty
- Identify laws assisting debtors
- Characterize exemption laws pertaining to real and personal property
- Compare Chapters 7, 11, 12, and 13 of the Bankruptcy Act

Prereading Activity

Bring to class advertisements for legal firms that handle bankruptcy cases. Pass the ads around the class. Discuss students' opinions about the advertising.

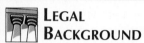

LEGAL BACKGROUND

Creditors have a right to be paid money they are owed, and state law outlines the legal methods to be followed when collecting debts. Many states give priority to claims by laborers and contractors. The debtor, however, is protected by homestead laws, and certain assets are exempt from seizure by most creditors. The law tries to strike a balance between the rights of creditors and protection of debtors.

Federal bankruptcy law is an available form of help for debtors who are in need of legal relief from people to whom they owe money. Provided for in the United States Constitution, bankruptcy law is designed to accomplish two main goals: to provide relief and protection to debtors who have "gotten in over their heads," and to provide a fair means of distributing a debtor's assets among creditors.

Chapter
19
Creditors' Rights and Bankruptcy

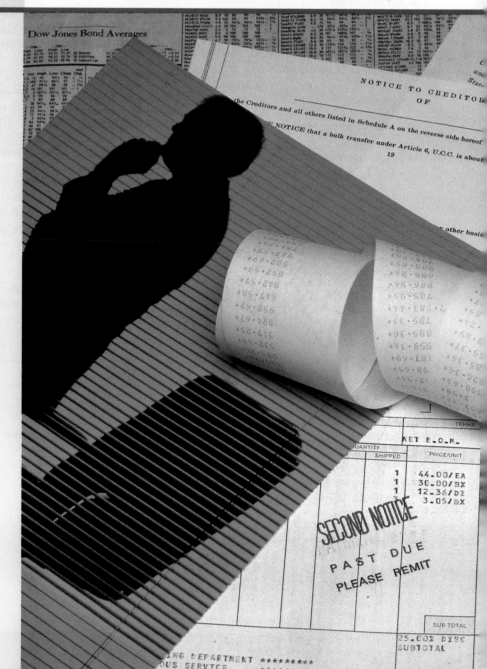

"Creditors are great observers of set days and times."
Benjamin Franklin, 1706–1790
American diplomat, author, and scientist

A **debtor** is a person or business that owes a debt to another. The person or business owed is a **creditor**. Normally, creditors can collect the debts owed them with few problems. Disputes with debtors do, however, arise. There are disputes over the amount owed, and disputes arise when a debtor *defaults*—when the debtor simply cannot or will not pay. What remedies are available to creditors when debtors default? What laws assist and protect debtors? The first part of this chapter provides some answers to these questions. The latter part of the chapter discusses bankruptcy as a last resort in resolving debtor–creditor problems.

◆ **debtor** A person or business that owes a debt to another.

◆ **creditor** A person or business owed money or property.

◆ LAWS ASSISTING CREDITORS

Numerous laws create rights and remedies for creditors. Here, we discuss liens, writs of execution, attachment, garnishment, creditors' composition agreements, and foreclosure.

LIENS

A **lien** is a right a creditor has against the property of the debtor. If a creditor has a lien against the debtor's property, the creditor may be able to sell or seize the property to pay an unpaid debt. Liens are usually (but not always) given voluntarily by the debtor to the creditor.

Many liens involve credit transactions.

◆ **lien** A right a creditor has against the property of the debtor.

◀ LEGAL FOCUS – EXAMPLE

Marsha wishes to purchase a new car. Although she has a steady job, she has only $2,000 in a savings account. The price of the car is $12,000. Marsha, like millions of other Americans, may buy the car by purchasing it on credit. She will make a down payment to the dealer and borrow the remainder of the selling price from a lender (the creditor). The lender will secure the loan by getting a lien on the car. To get the loan, Marsha must agree to let the lender seize the car and sell it if she does not pay her debt. If that happens, the lender will use the sale proceeds to pay off the debt.

Credit transactions of this kind allow buyers to purchase goods they otherwise would be unable to buy. Sellers benefit, too, by selling products they otherwise could not sell. Lenders benefit because they earn interest

---

Ask a student volunteer to read aloud to the class this Legal Focus Example dealing with a *mechanic's lien*. Ask the volunteer to answer the following questions: In this case, who is the debtor and who is the creditor? Why does the creditor place a lien on the debtor's property? In this case, has the lien been given voluntarily by the debtor to the creditor?

Vocabulary Activity

Have a student volunteer look up the word *encumbered* as it is used in the first Legal Focus Example on this page. Have the student read the dictionary definition to the class.

Legal Focus Example

Have a student volunteer read aloud to the class this Legal Focus Example dealing with an *artisan's lien*. Remind the students that they can use the Legal Focus features as review tools when studying for tests.

Vocabulary Activity

Have a student volunteer look up the word *artisan* in a dictionary and read the dictionary definition to the class.

Write the following on the board: "Timothy takes his automobile to a mechanic's shop to be repaired. When Timothy does not pay for the repairs, the mechanic has a lien on Timothy's automobile." Ask the students to read the scenario written on the board and then write a short paragraph stating whether this is a mechanic's lien, an artisan's lien, or an innkeeper's lien. Students' paragraphs should include the appropriate lien's definition.

---

444   Commercial and Consumer Law

◆ **mechanic's lien**
A lien on an owner's real property for labor, services, or materials furnished to or made on the property (for example, reroofing or adding a swimming pool to a house).

◆ **artisan's lien** A lien given to a person who has made improvements and added value to another person's personal property; acts as security for payment for services performed.

◆ **innkeeper's lien**
A lien allowing an innkeeper (the proprietor of a hotel or motel) to take personal property brought by a guest into the hotel (suitcases and contents) as security for a hotel bill the guest does not pay.

on the loans. The lenders protect themselves by getting liens. This type of lien is the subject of this chapter's Legal Perspective.

Other types of liens are provided to creditors without the express agreement of the debtor. For example, a creditor who is not immediately paid for improvements made to real property can place a **mechanic's lien** on the property. Improvements include labor, services, or material furnished for the real property. The real estate itself becomes security for the debt.

> ### ◀ LEGAL FOCUS ~ EXAMPLE
>
> A painter agrees to paint a house for a homeowner. The price covers labor and materials. If the homeowner cannot pay or pays only a portion of the charges, a mechanic's lien against the property can be created. The painter is the lienholder, and the real property is *encumbered* (burdened) with a mechanic's lien for the amount owed. If the homeowner does not pay the lien, the property can be sold to satisfy the debt.

State law governs mechanic's liens. The creditor must follow technical filing requirements to create a mechanic's lien. The creditor must file with a government official. The time to file is usually 60 to 120 days from the last date labor or materials were provided to a debtor.

Artisan's liens and **innkeeper's liens** are security devices for personal property that are similar to mechanic's liens. These liens secure payment for labor done, value added, or care of personal property.

> ### ◀ LEGAL FOCUS ~ EXAMPLE
>
> Cindy leaves her diamond ring at the jeweler's to be repaired and to have her initials engraved on the band. The jeweler can keep the ring until Cindy pays for the services provided. The jeweler has this right as a matter of law. The jeweler has an artisan's lien on Cindy's ring for the amount of the bill. The jeweler can sell the ring in satisfaction of the lien if Cindy does not pay. Any money in excess of the debt and the costs of sale should be returned to Cindy.

An innkeeper's lien is placed on the baggage of guests for unpaid hotel charges. If no express agreement has been made on what those charges are, then the lien is the reasonable value of the accommodations furnished.

WRIT OF EXECUTION

When a debt is past due, a creditor can begin legal action against a debtor. If the creditor wins the lawsuit, the creditor receives a judgment against the debtor. The judgment is usually for the amount of the debt plus any interest, as well as court costs spent in getting the judgment. Attorneys'

It is difficult to ensure the rights of debtors and creditors simultaneously, and laws governing debtor-creditor relationships are still sometimes seen as unfair to debtors. For example, when a creditor invokes a legal remedy, the creditor is often considered by the general public to be employing an unfair tactic. For many, the question of fairness revolves around the purpose for which a debt was incurred. If the debt was incurred for a needed item, common opinion seems to be that a debtor who fails to pay should be dealt with leniently. If a debt was incurred for a luxury, opinion is different.

Stimulate a class discussion about this topic by asking students the following questions: Do you feel that a debtor who went into debt to satisfy basic needs such as food, shelter, etc. should be dealt with in the same manner as a debtor who went into debt for a luxury item such as a power boat or a recreational vehicle? Why or why not?

fees are not usually part of the judgment unless provided for by statute or contract.

If the debtor does not pay the judgment, the creditor can go back to the court and get a **writ of execution**. The writ is an order directing the sheriff to seize and sell any of the debtor's nonexempt real or personal property. (Nonexempt property is property that is not protected by law from seizure. This subject is discussed later in this chapter.) The property must be within the court's geographic jurisdiction (usually the county in which the courthouse is located). The proceeds of the sale are used to pay off the judgment and the costs of the sale. Any excess is paid to the debtor. The debtor can pay the judgment and redeem the nonexempt property any time before the sale takes place.

ATTACHMENT

Attachment is a court-ordered seizure of property before a trial and judgment on a past-due debt. Attachment rights are created by state statutes. Numerous restrictions and requirements must be met before a creditor can attach property before a judgment. The due process clause of the Fourteenth Amendment to the Constitution limits the courts' power to authorize seizure of a debtor's property. Usually, a notice to the debtor and a hearing on the facts must take place before an attachment.

GARNISHMENT

Garnishment is the right to seize property of the debtor that is held by another. A garnishment is directed at a third party. The third person, the garnishee, is someone who owes a debt to the debtor or has property that belongs to the debtor. The most common garnishments are seizures of wages or bank accounts. Typically, a garnishment judgment is served on a person's employer, and some of the employee's paycheck is paid to the creditor.

Both federal laws and state laws limit the amount of money that can be garnished from a debtor's weekly take-home pay.[1] Federal law protects debtors from losing all their income to pay judgment debts. Under federal law, a debtor can retain 75 percent of his or her disposable earnings per week or the sum equivalent to thirty hours of work paid at federal minimum wage rates, whichever is greater. State laws also provide dollar exemptions. These amounts are often larger than those provided by federal law. Under federal law, garnishment of an employee's wages for any one indebtedness cannot be grounds for dismissal of the employee.

CREDITORS' COMPOSITION AGREEMENTS

Creditors may join together and contract with a debtor to release the debtor's debts upon payment of a sum less than that owed. These agreements are called *composition agreements* or **creditors' composition agreements**.

◆ **writ of execution** A court order directing the sheriff to seize and sell nonexempt property of the judgment debtor to satisfy an unpaid judgment.

◆ **attachment** A court-ordered seizure of property (generally prior to full resolution of the creditor's rights resulting in judgment). Attachment is available only in strict compliance with the applicable state statutes.

◆ **garnishment** A collection remedy that allows the creditor to attach a debtor's money or property (such as wages owed or bank accounts) that is in the hands of a third person.

◆ **creditors' composition agreement** An agreement formed by and among the creditors and the debtor. The creditors each agree to accept a lesser sum in payment, and the debtor is released after payment of the agreed sum.

Enrichment

Lead a class discussion about why property to be seized under a writ of execution must be within the court's geographic jurisdiction.

Critical Thinking Activity

Tell a student to read to the class the Fourteenth Amendment to the Constitution. Lead a class discussion about how and why the due process clause limits the court's power to authorize seizure of a debtor's property.

Collaborative Learning Activity

Under federal law, garnishment of an employee's wages for any one indebtedness cannot be grounds for dismissal of an employee. Debate the merits of this law. Divide the class into two groups. Have one group defend the law. Have the other group dispute the law.

---

1. Some states (for example, Texas) do not usually permit garnishment of wages by private parties except to enforce a child-support order.

Have student volunteer contact a local real estate agent to discuss foreclosure methods in your community. The student should ask the real estate agent what steps must be taken for a creditor who lends money against real estate to foreclose on the real estate. What type of legal notice must be given, etc.? Have the student report his or her findings to the class in an oral report. Encourage the student to use visual aids in the report.

The still frames listed below from the **West's Business Law and Legal Environment Videodisc** can be used with this chapter. To access this material, use the bar codes or the frame numbers included in the Videodisc Instructor's Manual found in the *TRB*.

Suretyship and Guaranty Parties
Defenses of Surety
Collection and Distribution of the Debtor's Estate

Legal Focus Example

Have a student volunteer read aloud to the class this Legal Focus Example. Stimulate a class discussion about this feature by asking the following questions: Did Van Cleave actually retain his home? In this case, how did the homestead exemption work for Van Cleave? (Students should understand that Van Cleave did not retain the family home but did retain its value to a specified dollar amount, in this case $25,000.)

Ethical Concern

Stimulate a class discussion by asking your students if they think the homestead exemption is fair. Does this mean that anyone can incur a large debt and have at least $25,000 protected from the debt owed?

FORECLOSURE

A creditor who lends money may secure a right against real property. The principal device to secure such a loan is a mortgage. Some states, such as California, secure an interest in real property through a deed of trust. In either case, the creditor has the right to foreclose on real property if a debtor defaults. In a **foreclosure**, the creditor sells the property to pay the debt. Methods of foreclosure vary from state to state. The usual method is by judicial sale of the property.

♦ **foreclosure** An action by a person who holds a mortgage to sell the property to pay off the mortgage debt.

PROTECTION FOR DEBTORS—EXEMPTIONS

In most states, certain types of real and personal property are exempt from writs of execution or attachment. Probably the most familiar of these exemptions is the **homestead exemption**. Each state permits the debtor to retain the family home, or at least its value to a specified dollar amount, free from the claims of unsecured creditors.[2] This allows the debtor some form of shelter.

♦ **homestead exemption** A law allowing an owner to designate his or her house and adjoining land as a homestead and thus exempt it from liability to creditors.

◁ LEGAL FOCUS ~ EXAMPLE

Van Cleave owes Goodwin $40,000. The debt is the subject of a lawsuit, and the court awards Goodwin a judgment of $40,000 against Van Cleave. The homestead of Van Cleave is valued at $50,000. There are no outstanding mortgages or other liens on his homestead. To satisfy the judgment debt, Van Cleave's family home is sold at public auction for $45,000. Assume the homestead exemption is $25,000. The proceeds of the sale are distributed as follows:

1. Van Cleave is given $25,000 as his homestead exemption.
2. Goodwin is paid $20,000 toward the judgment debt, leaving a $20,000 deficiency judgment (that is, "leftover debt") that can be paid from any other nonexempt property that Van Cleave may have, if allowed by state law.

Personal property may also be exempt from satisfaction of judgment debts. Most often, exempt personal property includes the following:

1. Household furniture up to a specified dollar amount.
2. Clothing and certain personal possessions, such as family pictures or a Bible.
3. A vehicle (or vehicles) for transportation (at least up to a specified dollar amount).

---

2. In Florida and Texas, a homeowner's equity in his or her personal residence is normally untouchable by creditors in a bankruptcy proceeding.

Have the students work in groups to create a poster that illustrates the type of personal property that may also be exempt from satisfaction of judgment debts, as described in the numbered list on these pages. Allow the groups to display their posters in your classroom. Then stimulate a class discussion regarding these exemptions by asking students these questions: Do you agree that all of these types of personal property should be exempt from satisfaction of judgment debts? Why or why not? Are there any other types of personal property that you feel should be exempt? Please explain.

To make sure that students understand the concept of secured creditors, have them write a Legal Focus Example of a debt in which the creditor is a secured creditor. Allow volunteers to share their examples with the class.

Critical Thinking Activity

Tell the students to list on a sheet of paper the property their family owns that should be exempt from satisfaction of judgment debts. Students should explain why each item on the list would (or should) be exempt.

Caption Answer

Livestock can be exempted from collection processes.

Creditors' Rights and Bankruptcy   447

Can livestock be exempted from collection processes?

4. Certain classified animals, usually livestock but also pets.
5. Equipment that the debtor uses in a business or trade, such as tools or professional instruments, up a specified dollar amount.

Exempt property is only protected from **unsecured creditors**—those who have no rights against any particular property of the debtor. **Secured creditors** do have an interest in specific property (for example, in an auto purchased on credit). These creditors can repossess the secured property.

LAWS PROVIDING SPECIAL PROTECTION FOR CONSUMER–DEBTORS

Numerous consumer protection statutes and rules apply to the debtor–creditor relationship. Many of these were discussed in Chapter 16, which described consumer protection.

◆ **unsecured creditor** A creditor that has no rights against any particular property of the debtor.

◆ **secured creditor** A creditor that secures payment of a debt by taking an interest in property. If the debt is not paid, the creditor can take or sell the property.

◆ SURETYSHIP AND GUARANTY

It is common for a third person to promise to pay the debt of another if the debtor does not pay it. A parent, for example, may make such a promise to a creditor who makes a loan to his or her child. These third-person promises create either a *suretyship* or a *guaranty* relationship. Exhibit 19-1 illustrates these relationships. The third person's credit becomes the security for the debt owed.

VIDEODISC NOTE
Much of the material and concepts that are conveyed in the exhibits of *West's Business and Personal Law* are also conveyed in the still-frames on the **West Business Law and Legal Environment Videodisc**. For more information and directions for use, please see the Index and Description of Contents for the **West Business Law and Legal Environment Videodisc** that is found in your *Teacher's Resource Binder*.

448   Commercial and Consumer Law

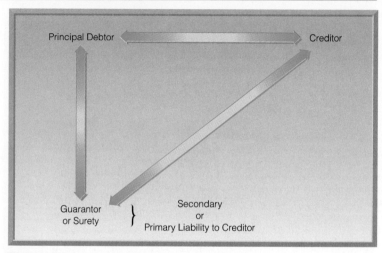

EXHIBIT 19-1
SURETYSHIP AND GUARANTY PARTIES

SURETYSHIP

◆ **suretyship** A contract promise made by a third person to be primarily responsible for another's debt. A surety is as responsible to the creditor as is the debtor.

A **suretyship** is a promise made by a third person, the *surety*, to be responsible for the debtor's obligation. The promise takes the form of an express contract between the surety and the creditor. The surety is *primarily* liable for the debt of the principal debtor. That means the creditor can demand payment from the surety at the moment the debt is due. The creditor need not exhaust all legal remedies against the principal debtor before holding the surety responsible for payment.

◀ LEGAL FOCUS - EXAMPLE

Robert Delmar (age eighteen) wants to borrow money from the bank to buy a used car. Because Robert is still in high school, the bank will not lend him the money unless his father, Joseph Delmar, cosigns the note. When Mr. Delmar cosigns the note, he becomes primarily liable to the bank. On the note's due date, the bank can seek payment from either Robert or Joseph Delmar, or both.

◆ **guaranty** A contract promise made by a third person to be secondarily liable for another's debt. The guarantor is liable only if the debtor has defaulted and the creditor has attempted to collect from the debtor.

GUARANTY

A **guaranty** contract is similar to a suretyship contract. However, the *guarantor*—the third person making the guaranty—is *secondarily* liable. That means the person is promising to pay the obligation only after the principal debtor has defaulted and the creditor has attempted to collect from that debtor.

Read

Introduce this feature by having a student volunteer find Bogotá, Colombia, on a map. You might point out to the students that Bogotá is the capital of Colombia and has a population in excess of 3.5 million people. If any of your students have been to Bogotá, Colombia, or are from Colombia, you might have them share what they know about this city. Then have a student volunteer read aloud this *Law*

in Action feature concerning debt collection methods employed in Bogotá, Colombia.

Discuss

Stimulate a class discussion about this *Law in Action* feature by asking students the following questions: What is a *chepito*? What do *chepitos* do? How do *chepitos* dress? How do you think a debtor feels about a *chepito* standing outside his or her home or business? What problems exist with using the court sys-

tem in Bogotá? Do you agree with the Colombian National Association of Litigation Lawyers that the use of *chepitos* is the equivalent of extortion? Why or why not? To what extent do the executives of collection agencies attribute ANDAL's outrage over the use of *chepitos*?

Legal Focus Example

Allow a student volunteer to read aloud to the class this Legal Focus Example. To make sure that the students understand this example, ask them the following questions: If BX Enterprises pays off its debt on time, will Dawson also have to pay anything to the bank? Why or why not?

 ## Law in Action

INTERNATIONAL PERSPECTIVES: HOW TO COLLECT DEBTS—IN BOGOTÁ

Creditors trying to collect unpaid bills in Bogotá, Colombia, do not always rely solely on attorneys or the court system. Certain collection agencies in Bogotá, such as *Universal de Cobranzas* and *Organizacion Juridica de Cobranzas*, send *chepitos* to the debtor's premises if standard form letters and telephone calls are ineffective. Loosely translated as "harassers," *chepitos* are men dressed in tuxedos and top hats, carrying canes and black briefcases. They stand in front of a debtor's home or business advertising (by the lettering on their briefcases) the fact that a *deudor moroso* (debtor in default) dwells there. No words are said, but the *chepitos* remain on the site until the debt is paid.

The use of *chepitos* has proved an extremely effective technique. For creditors trying to collect unpaid debts, it is an increasingly popular alternative to attorneys and court proceedings. Although the city's

population has nearly tripled in the last twenty years, the size of the court system has remained the same during that time. The result is that the courts are overcrowded. Lawsuits to collect debts usually take at least two years.

The Colombian National Association of Litigation Lawyers (ANDAL) maintains that using *chepitos* to collect debts is the equivalent of extortion, or debt collection by intimidation. ANDAL would like the *chepitos* outlawed. Indeed, it has referred to them as a "plague." ANDAL contends that the *chepitos* displace lawyers and take justice into their own hands. Executives of the collection agencies dismiss this criticism. They report that ANDAL's fury could result from the time the *chepitos* were sent to visit ANDAL offices when the lawyers' association would not pay one of its bills for an expensive banquet.

◆ **LEGAL FOCUS ~ EXAMPLE**

BX Enterprises needs to borrow money to meet its payroll. The bank is skeptical about the creditworthiness of BX. The bank decides to require Dawson, the BX president, to sign an agreement making himself personally liable for payment if BX does not pay off the loan. Dawson, a wealthy businessperson, owns 70 percent of BX Enterprises. Dawson agrees and specially signs as a guarantor. As a guarantor of the loan, Dawson is not liable until BX Enterprises is in default.

DEFENSES OF THE SURETY AND GUARANTOR

The defenses to payment for the surety and the guarantor are basically the same. One such defense involves changes in the contract. If the creditor makes a material change in the terms of the original contract with the

Have a student volunteer read aloud to the class the first Legal Focus Example. Make sure the students understand that in this example, the creditor makes a material change in the terms of the original contract with the debtor when allowing an extension of time to make payment.

Critical Thinking Activity

Have your students write a paragraph or two comparing the differences between a surety and a guaranty. Instruct them to include in their paragraphs which position is more secure for both the creditor and the debtor.

Legal Focus Example

Have a student volunteer read aloud to the class the second Legal Focus Example. Make sure that students understand that, under the *right of contribution,* the surety who paid the $10,000 has a right to recover a proportionate share from the co-surety. In this case, the proportionate share is $4,000 or 40 percent of the $10,000.

Read aloud the definition of *right of reimbursement* found here: "the legal right of a person to be repaid for costs, expenses, or losses incurred on behalf of another." Make sure that students understand that under the right of reimbursement the surety is entitled to receive from the debtor all payments made because of the suretyship contract. Then have the students work with partners to write an example of a surety invoking the right of reimbursement.

450

---

debtor, the surety is discharged completely or to the extent that he or she suffers a loss.

 LEGAL FOCUS ~ EXAMPLE

Allowing the debtor an extension of time to make payment is a material change. Unless the surety has agreed to the extension, the surety is released by it.

A release of the principal debtor without the surety's consent releases the surety unless the creditor expressly reserves his or her rights against the surety. If the debtor tries to pay, and the creditor rejects the payment, the surety is released from the debt obligation.

Any defense which would be available to a principal debtor can be used by the surety to avoid liability to the creditor. For example, if a creditor fails to deliver promised goods to the debtor, both the debtor and the surety would have a defense to payment. Defenses of the principal debtor that cannot be used are incapacity, bankruptcy, and the statute of limitations.

RIGHTS OF THE SURETY AND GUARANTOR

As with defenses, the rights of the surety and the guarantor are basically the same. When the surety pays the debt owed to the creditor, the surety has the legal **right of subrogation**. This means that any right the creditor had against the debtor is now the right of the surety. In short, the surety stands in the shoes of the creditor. He or she may pursue any remedies that were available to the creditor against the debtor.

The surety also has a **right of reimbursement** from the debtor. The surety is entitled to receive from the debtor all payments made because of the suretyship contract. Such outlays can include expenses as well as the actual amount of the debt paid to the creditor.

Co-sureties are two or more sureties to the same obligation. A co-surety who pays more than his or her proportionate share can recover from the other co-sureties any excess amount paid. This is called the **right of contribution**.

◆ **right of subrogation** A right of a person to stand in the place of another, giving the substituted party the same legal rights as the original party had.

◆ **right of reimbursement** The legal right of a person to be repaid for costs, expenses, or losses incurred on behalf of another.

◆ **co-sureties** Two or more sureties to the same obligation.

◆ **right of contribution** The right of a co-surety who pays more than his or her proportionate share upon a debtor's default to recover the excess paid from other co-sureties.

 LEGAL FOCUS ~ EXAMPLE

Two co-sureties are obligated under a suretyship contract to guarantee a debt. One surety's maximum liability is $15,000. The other's is $10,000. The debtor owes $10,000 and is in default. Assume the surety with the $15,000 maximum liability pays the creditor the entire $10,000. In the absence of a contrary agreement, the surety who paid has the right to recover $4,000 from the other surety ($10,000/$25,000 × $10,000 = $4,000).

1. Selling repaired property to secure payment for the work done is permissible through an artisan's lien. Any money in excess of the debt and the costs of sales should be returned to the customer.
2. If a debtor does not pay the judgment from a lawsuit, the creditor can collect by getting a writ of execution (having the sheriff seize and sell any of the debtor's nonexempt real or personal property).
3. A creditor may direct a garnishee (someone who owes a debt or has property of the debtor) to pay him or her rather than the debtor.
4. Some household furniture, clothing, personal possessions, a vehicle, animals, and business equipment may be exempt from satisfaction of judgment debts. Student answers as to why these items are exempt will vary.
5. A surety is primarily liable for the debt of the principal; a guarantor is secondarily liable.

CHECKING YOUR PROGRESS

1. If a customer does not pay for repairs on a personal item, the merchant doing the repairs may sell the repaired item to collect payment. What kind of lien is described? What happens to excess money if the item is sold for more than amount owed for repairs?

2. Why would a creditor ask for a writ of execution?

3. Explain the garnishment process.

4. What personal property might be exempt from satisfaction of judgment debts? Why?

5. What is the main difference between a suretyship and a guaranty contract?

◆ BANKRUPTCY

The U.S. Constitution, Article I, Section 8, states: "The Congress shall have the power . . . to establish . . . uniform laws on the subject of bankruptcies throughout the United States." The inclusion of this clause in the Constitution reflects the early conviction of our nation's leaders that debtors should be given a second chance. They should not have to spend months, and sometimes years, in debtors' prisons—which were a curse to the founding fathers.

Bankruptcy law in the United States has two goals. The first is to protect a debtor by giving him or her a fresh start, free from creditors' claims. The second is to give fair treatment to creditors competing for a debtor's assets.

Modern bankruptcy law was revised by the Bankruptcy Reform Act of 1978, as amended, which is part of the Bankruptcy Code. Bankruptcy proceedings are held in bankruptcy courts under the authority of U.S. district courts. There are several types of bankruptcies, which are named for chapters contained in the Bankruptcy Code: Chapter 7 liquidations, Chapter 11 reorganizations, Chapter 12 plans (for family farmers), and Chapter 13 plans (for individuals). Chapters 11, 12, and 13 are sometimes called *rehabilitation chapters*. Next, we look at each of these in more detail.

◆ CHAPTER 7 LIQUIDATIONS

Liquidation is the most familiar type of bankruptcy proceeding. It is often called an *ordinary* or *straight bankruptcy*. Put simply, debtors in straight bank-

LEGAL BACKGROUND

From a creditor's point of view, granting credit is a transfer of purchasing power from creditor to debtor, represented by a transfer of an asset for an asset. A debtor obtains money, goods, or services; a creditor obtains a legal obligation to pay. On a debtor's bankruptcy, the asset that the creditor owns most often has diminished value or sometimes no value. Bankruptcy law attempts to provide a fair means of distributing to creditors assets in a debtor's possession.

◆ **bankruptcy**
Proceeding under the Federal Bankruptcy Code whereby all assets of a debtor (excluding certain exempt property) are distributed to creditors. The debtor is then discharged or excused from the legal obligation to pay most of the debts.

Remind the students that as the student text explains, debtors in Chapter 7 bankruptcies state their debts and turn their assets over to trustees. The trustees then sell the assets and distribute the proceeds to creditors. Guide the students in going through the elements in the petition for voluntary bankruptcy found in the numbered list on this page. As you read each numbered element, ask a student how this applies to the functions of stating one's debts and turning over one's assets to trustees.

Extension Activity

Invite a local attorney who deals with bankruptcies to speak to your class. Ask the attorney to discuss the immediate, as well as the long-term, financial effects of bankruptcy on a debtor. Also ask the speaker to discuss the effects of bankruptcy on creditors and to compare the various types of bankruptcy—i.e., Chapters 7, 11, 12, and 13. You might want to have your students prepare questions in advance for your speaker to cover.

452

Ethical Concern

Bankruptcy filings have increased in recent years. Stimulate a class discussion regarding this fact by asking the following questions: Do you believe that debtors are abusing the protection of the laws? Do you think that the increase in bankruptcy filings is due solely to national economic conditions? Are there cases in which a bankruptcy should be denied? How should a court distinguish a justified case from an unjustified one?

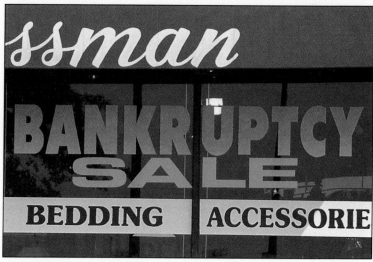

As part of a bankruptcy proceeding, a special company called a liquidator may be given the task of selling the bankrupt store's merchandise to raise cash to pay creditors.

ruptcies state their debts and turn their assets over to trustees. The trustees sell the assets and distribute the proceeds to creditors. With certain exceptions, the remaining debts are then discharged, and the debtors are relieved of their obligation to pay the debts. Individuals, partnerships, and corporations may use Chapter 7 bankruptcy. Railroads, insurance companies, banks, savings and loan associations, and credit unions cannot be Chapter 7 debtors, however. Other chapters of the Bankruptcy Act apply to them.

FILING THE PETITION

A straight bankruptcy may be begun by the filing of either a voluntary or an involuntary bankruptcy petition. A **voluntary bankruptcy** is brought by the debtor. The debtor does not have to be insolvent to file such a petition. (Persons are considered insolvent if they lack sufficient assets to pay their debts.)

The voluntary petition contains the following elements:

1. A list of both secured and unsecured creditors, their addresses, and the amount of debt owed to each.
2. A statement of the financial affairs of the debtor.
3. A list of all property owned by the debtor, including property claimed by the debtor to be exempt.
4. A listing of current income and expenses.

A debtor can also be the subject of an **involuntary bankruptcy**. This happens when the debtor's creditors force the debtor into bankruptcy proceedings. Under the code, an involuntary bankruptcy cannot be started

◆ **voluntary bankruptcy** A bankruptcy begun by the debtor.

◆ **involuntary bankruptcy** A bankruptcy begun by creditors against the will of the debtor.

against a farmer or a charitable institution. The following requirements must also be met:

1. If the debtor has twelve or more creditors, three or more of those having unsecured claims totaling at least $5,000 must join in the petition.
2. If a debtor has fewer than twelve creditors, one or more creditors having a claim of $5,000 may file.

A debtor can challenge an involuntary petition. The petition will be discharged if the debtor is found to be paying debts as they become due. The code provides penalties for the filing of frivolous petitions against debtors.

AUTOMATIC STAY

The filing of a petition, either voluntary or involuntary, operates as an *automatic stay* on (or suspension of) most litigation by creditors against the debtor. In other words, once a petition is filed, creditors cannot sue or enforce judgments against the debtor to recover claims.

PROPERTY OF THE ESTATE AND EXEMPTIONS

At the commencement of a Chapter 7 proceeding, an *estate in property* is created. The estate consists of all the debtor's interests in property.

Individual debtors are entitled to exempt certain property from the property of the estate. An individual debtor (or a husband and wife who file jointly) may choose either the exemptions provided under applicable state law or federal exemptions. A partial list of federal exemptions follows:

1. Up to $7,500 in equity in the debtor's residence.
2. Interest in a motor vehicle up to $1,200.
3. Interest, up to $200 for any particular item, in household goods and furnishings, wearing apparel, appliances, books, animals, crops, or musical instruments, totaling no more than $4,000.
4. Interest in jewelry up to $500.
5. Interest, up to $750, in any tools of the debtor's trade.
6. The right to receive Social Security and certain welfare benefits, alimony and support payments, and certain pension benefits.
7. The right to receive certain personal injury and other awards.

THE TRUSTEE

A trustee is appointed to preside over the distribution of the debtor's property. The basic duty of the trustee is to collect the debtor's available estate and reduce it to money for distribution to appropriate creditors. Proof of claims by creditors are filed with the trustee.

The code gives the trustee substantial powers to administer the debtor's property. For example, the trustee may use the power of the court to avoid fraudulent transfers or obligations on the part of the debtor.

Ask a student volunteer to read aloud this Legal Focus Example. Stimulate a class discussion regarding this example by asking the following questions: In what way did Carstairs and Mason commit a fraud? What steps can Breda Parsons now take? How are those steps in line with the basic duty of the trustee as defined on the previous page? ("The basic duty of the trustee is to collect the debtor's available estate and reduce it to money for distribution to appropriate creditors.")

As the student text points out, in bankruptcy, the secured party has priority over unsecured parties in claiming the proceeds from the disposition of the secured property. Make sure that students completely understand this decision. Have a student volunteer reread the definitions of unsecured creditor, and secured creditor as found on page 447 of this chapter.

454   Commercial and Consumer Law

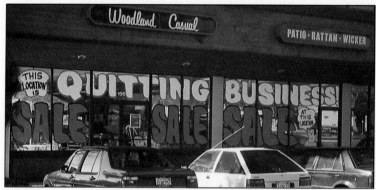

In hard economic times bankruptcy becomes all too common.

◆ LEGAL FOCUS ~ EXAMPLE

Mason Roberts, a hardware store owner, is in bankruptcy. His trustee, Brenda Parsons, finds out that just before the bankruptcy petition was filed, Mason paid a large sum of money to Carstairs Brooke for inventory at the hardware store, but few goods were actually purchased. Carstairs and Mason were actually using the transaction to hide money from Mason's creditors, a fraud. Brenda, through the court, can claim the money back for the benefit of creditors.

PROPERTY DISTRIBUTION

Creditors are either secured or unsecured. As mentioned earlier, a secured creditor has an interest in property that secures the debt. An unsecured creditor has no rights against any specific property of the debtor. The secured party has priority over unsecured parties to the proceeds from the disposition of the secured property.

Bankruptcy law establishes an order, or priority, for classes of debts owed to unsecured creditors. Each class must be fully paid before the next class can be paid. If insufficient funds exist to pay an entire class, money is distributed *proportionately* to each creditor in the class. All classes lower in priority than that class receive nothing. The general order of priority among classes of unsecured creditors is as follows:

1. All costs and expenses for preserving and administering the estate.
2. Claims for wages, salaries, and commissions up to an amount of $2,000 per claimant, if they were earned within ninety days of the filing of the petition in bankruptcy.
3. Unsecured claims for contributions to employee benefit plans arising under services rendered within 180 days before the filing of the petition.
4. Certain taxes and penalties legally due and owed to various government units.

As the text states, the primary purpose of Chapter 7 liquidation is to obtain a fresh start through the discharge of debts. There are, however, some exceptions to discharge. Guide the students in reading each of the exceptions to discharge found in the numbered list on this page. As you read each exception, ask the students to comment on whether they believe it is a fair exception. Is this exception fair to the debtor? Is this exception fair to creditors? Is this exception fair to society? Have the students explain their answers in each case.

Creditors' Rights and Bankruptcy   455

5. Claims of general creditors. These debts have the lowest priority and are paid only if funds remain after all the debts having priority are paid in full. If there are insufficient funds to pay general creditors in full, then each creditor is paid a percentage of the claim.
6. Any remaining balance is returned to the debtor.

DISCHARGE

From the debtor's point of view, the primary purpose of a Chapter 7 liquidation is to obtain a fresh start through the discharge of debts. However, there are circumstances under which a claim is not discharged.

Exceptions to Discharge   Exceptions to discharge include the following:

1. Claims for back taxes due within three years before bankruptcy.
2. Claims against property or money obtained by the debtor under false pretenses or by false representations.
3. Claims by creditors who were not notified of the bankruptcy.
4. Claims based on fraud or misuse of funds while the debtor was acting in a position of trust or claims involving the debtor's embezzlement or larceny.
5. Alimony and child support.
6. Claims based on willful or malicious injury by the debtor to another or to the property of another.
7. Certain fines and penalties payable to the government.
8. Certain student loans, unless payment of the loans imposes an undue hardship on the debtor and the debtor's dependents.
9. Consumer debts of more than $500 for luxury goods or services owed to a single creditor incurred within forty days of the beginning of the bankruptcy.
10. Cash advances totaling more than $1,000 as an extension of consumer credit obtained by the debtor within twenty days of the bankruptcy filing.
11. Judgments awarded against a debtor for liability incurred as a result of the debtor's operation of a motor vehicle while legally intoxicated.

Objections to Discharge   In addition to the exceptions listed above, several circumstances related to the debtor's conduct will cause a discharge to be denied.

> ### ◆ LEGAL FOCUS – EXAMPLE
>
> The debtor's concealment or destruction of records, or failure to keep adequate records, related to his or her financial condition is conduct that may cause a discharge to be denied. So is the debtor's concealment or destruction of property with the intent to hinder or delay or defraud a creditor.

After deregulation, the airline industry grew from 36 to over 150 airlines, and fare wars became common. Some companies were unsuccessful and ultimately declared bankruptcy. Have a student volunteer or group of volunteers look into airline bankruptcies. You might guide the students in their research by telling them to look under "Airlines" and "Bankruptcies" in the *Reader's Guide to Periodical Literature*. Have the students present their findings to the class in the form of oral reports.

Extension Activity

Select a group of students to research the Family Farmer Bankruptcy Act of 1986. Have them report their findings to the class, then lead a discussion about how Chapter 12 differs from Chapter 13.

Chapter 11
Reorganizations

In a Chapter 11 reorganization, the creditors and a debtor create a plan under which the debtor pays a portion of his or her debts and is discharged of the remainder. Then the debtor is allowed to continue in business. Although this type of bankruptcy is commonly a corporate reorganization, any debtor who is eligible for Chapter 7 relief is eligible for Chapter 11 relief.

A Chapter 11 plan must be "fair and equitable." It must also do the following:

1. Designate classes of claims and interests under the plan.
2. Specify the treatment to be afforded each class, and provide the same treatment for each claim in a particular class.
3. Provide a reasonable plan to make payments and continue the business.

Chapter 13 Plans

Chapter 13 of the Bankruptcy Code provides for "Adjustment of Debts of an Individual with Regular Income." Individuals (not partnerships or corporations) with regular incomes who owe unsecured debts of less than $100,000 or secured debts of $350,000 may take advantage of Chapter 13. Individual proprietors and individuals on welfare, Social Security, fixed pensions, or investment income are included. After a debtor has filed a Chapter 13 petition, creditors are prohibited from taking action against the debtor.

A Chapter 13 plan must do the following:

1. Provide that future earnings or income of the debtor be turned over to a trustee as is necessary to execute the plan.
2. Provide for full payment in deferred cash payments of all claims entitled to priority.
3. Provide for the same treatment of each claim within a particular class.

There are several advantages in filing a Chapter 13 plan when eligible. One of these advantages is that it is less expensive and less complicated than a Chapter 11 proceeding or a Chapter 7 liquidation.

Chapter 12 Plans

To help relieve economic pressure on small farmers, Congress created a new chapter in the Bankruptcy Code—Chapter 12. The new law defines a family farmer as one whose gross income is at least 50 percent farm dependent. The farmer's debts must be at least 80 percent farm related, and the total debt must not exceed $1,500,000. A Chapter 12 filing is very similar to a Chapter 13 filing. The content of the plan is basically the same as a Chapter 13 plan.

1. Under Chapter 7, a trustee sells the assets of the business and distributes the proceeds to creditors, but under Chapter 11, a plan is created to pay creditors a portion of the debt and discharge the remainder, thus allowing the debtor to continue in business.
2. Individuals (proprietorships) with regular income who owe unsecured debts of less than $100,000 or secured debts of $350,000 may file for Chapter 13 bankruptcy.
3. The first goal of federal bankruptcy law is to protect a debtor by giving him or her a fresh start; the second goal is to give fair treatment to creditors competing for a debtor's assets.

◆ CHECKING YOUR PROGRESS

1. What is the effect of Chapter 7 and Chapter 11 of the Bankruptcy Act on a debtor's business?
2. What type of business may file for Chapter 13 bankruptcy?
3. What are the two goals of bankruptcy law in the United States?

◆ A CASE IN POINT ◆

IN RE BAKER
United States Bankruptcy Court, Eastern District of Tennessee, 1981. 10 Bankr. 870.

In this case, the court considered the question of the discharge in bankruptcy of a student's college loan.

FACTS   Baker, while a student, received a number of educational loans. Some time after graduation, Baker filed for bankruptcy and sought a discharge of these loans in the bankruptcy decree. Baker's student loans were classified as generally not dischargeable under the code. Baker claimed that it would be an undue hardship on her to repay the loans. At the time of the bankruptcy filing, Baker claimed that her husband had deserted her, that she had been ill, and that two of her children had physical problems.

ISSUE   Would paying the debt pose an undue hardship for Baker?

DECISION   Yes. The debtor's student loans were discharged.

REASON   The purpose of the prohibition against discharge was "to remedy an abuse by students who, immediately upon graduation, would file bankruptcy to secure a discharge of educational loans." In this case, Baker did not file bankruptcy to secure a discharge only from her educational loans. The bankruptcy court found that Baker could reduce her expenses somewhat, but her expenses each month far exceeded her income. Given Baker's circumstances, the court found that forcing payment of Baker's debts would create an undue hardship and that the Bankruptcy Code was drafted to provide a fresh start for those such as Baker "who have truly fallen on hard times."

Teaching A Case In Point

Read
Before the students read this *A Case In Point* feature, remind them that bankruptcy law attempts to provide relief and protection to debtors who "get in over their heads." Ask the students to think about this as a volunteer reads aloud the *A Case In Point* feature.

Discuss
Stimulate a class discussion about this feature by asking the following questions: Why did Baker seek discharge of her student loans? How were these loans classified under the code? Why did Baker claim that it would be an undue hardship on her to repay the loans? What was the issue in this case? What was the decision of the United States bankruptcy court? What reasons did the court give for its decision?

In order to help students review what they have learned in Chapter 19, you might wish to:
1. Have a student volunteer, or volunteers, read the Chapter Summary aloud.
2. Allow the students to work with partners to complete the *Using Legal Language* activity.
3. Assign the *Checking for Comprehension* exercise as homework.
4. Allow the students to work in small groups to complete the *Applying Legal Concepts* activities.
5. As a class, complete the *Applying the Law* activities. (Please note that you may have to help students with vocabulary so that they adequately understand all of the *Applying the Law* material.)

In order to check student mastery of chapter concepts, you may wish to use the Chapter 19 test that is found in your *Teacher's Resource Binder* or use WESTEST computerized testing for Chapter 19.

458

---

458   Commercial and Consumer Law

CHAPTER REVIEW

 ## SUMMARY

LAWS ASSISTING CREDITORS

Mechanic's lien—A lien on an owner's real property for labor, services, or materials furnished to or made on the property.

Artisan's lien and innkeeper's lien—Liens on an owner's personal property for labor performed, value added, or care of personal property.

Writ of execution—A court order directing the sheriff to seize and sell nonexempt property of a debtor to satisfy an unpaid judgment.

Attachment—A court-ordered seizure of property before a trial and judgment on a past-due debt. Attachment is available only in strict compliance with the applicable state statutes.

Garnishment—A collection remedy that allows the creditor to attach a debtor's money or property (such as wages owed or bank accounts) that is held by a third person.

Creditors' Composition Agreement—An agreement between a debtor and his or her creditors whereby the debtor is discharged after paying a sum less than the amount of the original debt.

Foreclosure—An action by a person who holds a mortgage to sell the property to pay off the mortgage debt.

PROTECTION FOR DEBTORS—EXEMPTIONS

State laws exempt certain types of real and personal property from writs of execution or attachment.

1. *Real property*—Each state permits a debtor to retain some interest in the family home (the homestead exemption).

2. *Personal property*—Personal property most often exempt from satisfaction of judgment debts includes:

a. Household furniture up to a specified dollar amount.

b. Clothing and certain personal possessions.

c. Transportation vehicles up to a specified dollar amount.

d. Certain classified animals, such as livestock and pets.

SURETYSHIP OR GUARANTY

Under contract, a third person may agree to be primarily or secondarily liable for the debt owed by the principal debtor. Suretyship provides for primary liability and guaranty for secondary liability. A creditor can turn to this third person for satisfaction of the debt.

BANKRUPTCY

Bankruptcy law in the United States protects a debtor by giving him or her a fresh start, free from creditors' claims, while providing fair treatment to creditors competing for a debtor's assets. There are several types of bankruptcies:

Chapter 7 liquidations
Any person (including partnerships and corporations) except railroads, insurance companies, and certain financial institutions can declare a Chapter 7 bankruptcy. Nonexempt property is sold by a trustee with the proceeds distributed to creditors in certain priorities. Most debts are discharged after a distribution of the debtor's assets.

Chapter 11 reorganizations
Persons eligible for a Chapter 7 bankruptcy can seek a reorganization of their debts and business affairs. After filing the bankruptcy, the person seeking relief is protected from certain actions of creditors. Upon performance of a plan created under the program, the debtor's debts are discharged.

1. A mechanic's lien is placed on real property, but an artisan's lien and an innkeeper's lien apply to personal property.

2. A debtor must be able to live and earn a living, even if there is an execution or attachment to his or her property. Secured property cannot be exempt and can be repossessed by the creditor.

3. The first goal of federal bankruptcy law is to protect a debtor by giving him or her a fresh start, free from creditors' claim. The second is to give fair treatment to creditors competing for a debtor's assets.

4. Voluntary and involuntary bankruptcy differ in the way each is initiated. A voluntary bankruptcy is brought by the debtor, but creditors force the debtor into involuntary bankruptcy.

5. A trustee administers the debtor's property. The basic duty is to collect the debtor's available estate and reduce it to money for distribution to appropriate creditors.

6. Student answers may include back taxes, property or money obtained under false pretenses, creditors who were not notified of the bankruptcy, fraud, embezzlement, larceny, alimony, child support, fines payable to the government, student loans, certain luxury goods or cash obtained within a specific time period, or liability incurred as a result of operating a motor vehicle while intoxicated. Opinions will vary.

Chapter 13 (individuals) plans

A bankruptcy plan for individuals with a regular income which allows them to be protected from certain actions of creditors. Upon completion of the payment plan the debtor is discharged from further obligations. Plan provides for full payment for most debts.

Chapter 12 (family farmers)

A type of bankruptcy that provides family farmers a means to protect themselves from certain actions of creditors. Like Chapter 13, the plan expects the debtor to pay most debts under a scheduled plan, and upon successful completion the debtor is discharged from debts.

◆ USING LEGAL LANGUAGE

Directions: Match each term with the statement that best defines that term.

1. garnishment
2. homestead exemption
3. innkeeper's lien
4. lien
5. mechanic's lien
6. secured creditor
7. subrogation
8. surety
9. writ of attachment
10. writ of execution

A. a possessory or statutory lien allowing the hotel or motel to take the personal property brought into the hotel as security for an unpaid hotel bill

B. a contract promise made by a third person to be responsible for another's debt

C. a collection remedy that allows the creditor to attach a debtor's money and property

D. a right of a person to stand in the place of another, giving the substituted party the same legal rights that the original party had

E. a statutory lien on an owner's real estate for labor, services, or materials furnished to or made on the property

F. a court order directing the sheriff to seize and sell nonexempt property of the judgment debtor to satisfy an unpaid judgment

G. a creditor that secures payment of a debt by taking an interest in property

H. a law allowing an owner to designate his or her house and adjoining land as a homestead and thus exempt it from liability to creditors

I. a right a creditor has against the property of the debtor

J. a court order allowing seizure of property

◆ CHECKING FOR COMPREHENSION

1. What is the main difference between a mechanic's lien and an artisan's or innkeeper's lien?

2. Why are certain types of real and personal property exempt from execution or attachment? If the property is secured by

1. The court dismissed Busbin's petition. The court concluded that the primary purpose for the "substantial abuse" provision of Chapter 7 was to provide for the dismissal of cases of debtors who can pay their debts from their excess disposable income. The court discussed "a long line of cases which uniformly hold that a debtor's ability to pay his debts defines substantial abuse." The court noted that Busbin's "excess disposable income would allow him to pay off the entire remaining balance due to Bank South in less than 5 months. [He] could pay the entire debt of $1,450 in less than 12 months." The court pointed out, however, that "while courts have focused on the debtor's ability to pay as the principal factor in determining substantial abuse, the courts have by no means focused on ability to pay as the sole factor." As in non-bankruptcy cases, a court can "dismiss a petition . . . that is filed with a lack of good faith or as an abuse of process." The court explained that "[w]hile it does not appear [Busbin's] statement of his monthly expenses is excessive, it likewise does not appear to be understated. [He] has offered no evidence of any recent calamity which would affect his ability to pay. . . . Thus, it does not appear that [he] is inflicted with 'crushing debt burdens and severe financial problems' or even with debts he cannot pay. It is apparent

[he] filed his Chapter 7 petition for the sole purpose of discharging a single debt which he does not wish to pay."

2. Gull Air is correct. The only issue was whether the payments made by Gull Air within the 90 days prior to Gull's filing of the petition constitute a preference. The Bankruptcy Code permits the trustee to avoid preferences. The trustee may not avoid a payment made by the debtor in the ordinary course of business or financial affairs, however. The burden of proof is on the creditor receiving the pref-

erence. The code does not define what is meant by "ordinary course of business." The court held here that the transfers made were pursuant to the workout agreement and were in response to the civil action instituted by Beech. This created evidence of an unusual collection effort and not one ordinarily conducted between debtor and creditor. The court held that the payments were not made in the ordinary course of business and thus constituted a preference. Gull Air could recover these payments from Beech.

---

a creditor, can the property be exempt?

3. What are the two goals of bankruptcy law in the United States?

4. How do voluntary bankruptcy and involuntary bankruptcy differ?

5. What is the role of a trustee in bankruptcy proceedings?

6. From the debtor's point of view, the primary purpose of a Chapter 7 liquidation is to obtain a fresh start through the discharge of debts. However, there are certain circumstances where a claim is not discharged. Describe four exceptions to discharge and give your opinion as to why the exception exists.

APPLYING LEGAL CONCEPTS

1. Design a chart on which the characteristics of bankruptcy Chapter 7, Chapter 11, and Chapter 13 are listed and compared.

2. Write an essay discussing how bankruptcy

affects an individual. Include facts about creditors, property, and exemptions, as well as the effect on the individual and his or her family.

◆ APPLYING THE LAW . . . YOU BE THE JUDGE

1. In 1987, Bank South repossessed and sold Jamie Lee Busbin's 1979 Ford LTD automobile. The price that the automobile brought at the sale was $1,450 short of the amount Busbin owed Bank South. Bank South obtained a deficiency judgment for the $1,450 and garnished Busbin's wages, collecting $896.46. Busbin filed a voluntary petition for a Chapter 7 bankruptcy discharge, listing Bank South's claim for $1,450 as his sole debt. Busbin told the court that he intended to file a complaint to recover the $896.46 Bank South has already collected on the grounds that the sale had not been conducted so as to obtain the highest price for the car, but he offered no evidence to support his contention. Busbin showed that he had a monthly net income of $1,150, expenses of $970, and disposable income of $130 and that he expected an income tax refund of $500. A motion to dismiss Busbin's petition was filed, alleging that he had a present ability to pay his outstanding debts and that granting a discharge would be a

substantial abuse of the provisions of Chapter 7. Will the court dismiss Busbin's petition? [*In re Busbin*, 95 Bankr. 240 (Bankr.N.D.Ga 1989)]

2. In 1983, Beech Acceptance Corp. financed the sale of three airplanes to Gull Air, Inc. Approximately three years later, Gull Air defaulted on its obligations to Beech, and Beech filed suit. Before the trial, Gull Air and Beech negotiated a workout agreement that provided for large monthly payments over a certain period. Despite the workout agreement, Gull Air filed a Chapter 11 petition in bankruptcy. Gull Air claimed that the payments made under the workout agreement during the ninety days prior to the filing of the Chapter 11 petition amounted to a preference and must be returned to the debtor in possession (Gull Air). Beech claimed that the payments had been made in the ordinary course of business. Discuss who is correct. [*In re Gull Air, Inc.*, 892 Bankr. 1 (Bankr.D.Mass. 1988)]

LEGAL PERSPECTIVE

SECURED TRANSACTIONS

Often, purchasers—manufacturers, wholesalers, retailers, and consumers—lack the resources to pay cash for goods. Sellers still wish to sell the goods, though, and buyers still wish to buy. The answer, of course, is credit. Article 9 of the UCC provides a way to sell on credit with less than the usual risk. Through this method, payment is guaranteed, or *secured*, by personal property owned by the debtor. The transaction is known as a **secured transaction**. Any transaction, regardless of its form, that is intended to create a security interest in personal property is a secured transaction.

The importance of being a secured creditor cannot be overemphasized. Secured creditors are generally not hampered by state laws favorable to debtors. They have a favored position if the debtor becomes bankrupt. Business as we know it would not exist without secured transaction law.

The underlying philosophy of secured transaction law deals with two major concerns of the creditor:

1. Can the debt be satisfied from some specific property offered as security—that is, **collateral**—by the debtor?
2. Will satisfaction of that particular debt from that *collateral* be given priority over the claims of other creditors?

The answers to these two questions form the basis for the law of secured transactions.

ARTICLE 9 OF THE UCC

Article 9 applies to any transaction intended to create a security interest in personal property. Transactions excluded from Arti-

cle 9 include real estate mortgages, landlord's liens, mechanic's liens, and claims arising from judicial proceedings. Article 9 supplies certain definitions central to the formation of secured transactions. A brief summary of the definitions follows.

1. A *security interest* is every interest "in personal property or fixtures which secures payment or performance of an obligation."
2. A *secured party* is a lender, a seller, or any person in whose favor there is a security interest.
3. A *debtor* is the party who owes payment or performance of the secured obligation.
4. A *security agreement* is the agreement that creates or provides for a security interest between the debtor and a secured party.
5. *Collateral* is the personal property subject to a security interest.

These basic definitions form the concept under which a debtor-creditor relationship becomes a secured transaction relationship (see Exhibit LP 19-1).

CREATING A SECURITY INTEREST

As mentioned, the creditor's first concern is whether the debt can be satisfied from specific collateral. Three requirements must be met before a creditor can have an enforceable security interest in collateral. Once they are met, the creditor's rights are said to *attach* to the collateral.

1. There must generally be a written security agreement describing the collateral

More so than even commercial paper, this LP may present our most complex topic. In fact, much of the reason for its inclusion as an LP rather than a chapter is the detail and technical nature of this area. The more detail, the less understandable it may be to high school students. The secured transaction involves a loan, where the repayment is guaranteed by some property of the borrower or debtor. Again the concept of risk is important. By securing the loan, the lender has tried to reduce risk. The previous chapter on bankruptcy focused on unsecured creditors. A secured creditor can seize the secured property and often is unaffected by a bankruptcy, whereas the unsecured creditor is lucky to get back a small percentage of his or her money.

An example of a typical secured transaction is a car loan where the lender retains the right to repossess the car until the loan is paid. An unsecured loan, on the other hand, is not backed by specific property of the debtor; it may be called a "signature loan."

VIDEODISC NOTE
Much of the material that is conveyed in the exhibits of *West's Business and Personal Law* is also conveyed in the still frames on the **West Business Law and Legal Environment Videodisc**. For more information and directions for use, please see the Index and Description of Contents for the **West Business Law and Legal Environment Videodisc** that is found in your *Teacher's Resource Binder*.

Collaborative Learning Activity

Divide the class into small groups, and have them read the section of the LP under the title *Purchase-Money Security Interest*. Each group should work up its own example of a purchase-money security interest for the purchase of a major appliance. The group should then work together to draw up and complete a sample security agreement for this purchase. Have each group choose a leader to share its sample security agreement with the class.

LEGAL PERSPECTIVE (CONTINUED)

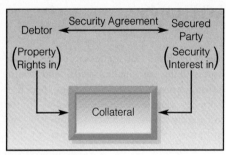

EXHIBIT LP 19-1
SECURED TRANSACTIONS—CONCEPT AND TERMINOLOGY

and signed by the debtor. If the creditor has possession of the collateral, however, no written agreement is required. See Exhibit LP 19-2 for a detailed sample security agreement.

2. The secured party must give *value*. Normally, the value given by a secured party is a direct loan or a promise to sell goods on credit.

3. The debtor must have *rights* in the collateral. The debtor's rights can represent either a current or a future legal interest in the collateral. For example, a retail seller–debtor can give a secured party a security interest in inventory owned by the retailer now and inventory to be acquired by the retailer later.

◆ PURCHASE-MONEY SECURITY INTEREST

Often, sellers of consumer durable goods, such as stereos and television sets, agree to sell goods on credit. Also, lenders who are not sellers of these goods often agree to lend

much of the purchase price. There is a special name for the security interest formed when credit is extended for the purchase of consumer goods. It is called a **purchase-money security interest**. Formally, such an interest exists when one of the following conditions occurs:

1. A security interest is retained in, or taken by the seller of, the collateral to secure part or all of its price.

2. A security interest is taken by a person who, by making advances or incurring an obligation, gives something of value that enables the debtor to get rights in the collateral.

In either case, a lender or seller has provided a buyer with the "purchase money" to buy the goods. Suppose Jamie wants to purchase a combination color television–stereo set from ABC Appliances. The purchase price is $900. He can't pay cash, so he signs

EXHIBIT LP 19-2
SAMPLE SECURITY AGREEMENT

Reteaching Activity

Have students define *perfecting a security* and list ways to perfect a security interest.

Critical Thinking Activity

Read aloud the following excerpt from the student text: "Possession by the secured party of collateral is often impractical, however. It denies the debtor the right to use, sell, or derive income from the property to pay off the debt." Ask the students to write a one-paragraph explanation of how possession by the secured party of collateral is impractical if the collateral is an automobile. Allow volunteers to share their explanations with the class.

a purchase agreement to pay $100 down. He agrees to pay $50 per month until the total amount, balance plus interest, is fully paid. ABC Appliances retains a security interest in the purchased set until full payment is made. Since the security interest was created as part of the purchase agreement, it is a purchase-money security interest.

◆ PERFECTING A SECURITY INTEREST

Again, a creditor has two main concerns if a debtor defaults: (1) whether the debt can be satisfied out of certain identified property and (2) whether priority over other creditors can be obtained. Attachment, which establishes the criteria for creating an enforceable security interest, deals with the former concern; **perfection** deals with the latter. Perfection represents the legal process by which a secured party gains protection against the claims of third parties who want their debts satisfied out of the same collateral.

METHODS OF PERFECTION

There are basically three methods of perfection, to which we now turn.

1. **Transfer of collateral**. The debtor can transfer possession of the collateral itself to the secured party. A debtor can, for example, give the lender stocks or bonds or even a piece of jewelry as collateral, thus securing the debt. Possession by the secured party of collateral is often impractical, however. It denies the debtor the right to use, sell, or derive income from the property to pay off the debt.

2. **Purchase-money security interest in consumer goods**. The security interest is perfected automatically at the time of a credit sale if the sale involves consumer goods and is covered by a written security agreement.

3. **Filing**. The third and most common method of perfection is filing a financing statement. Filing is done either centrally with the secretary of state or locally with the county clerk or other official.

The importance of perfecting a security interest cannot be overemphasized. A creditor that fails to perfect, or fails to perfect properly, may be treated the same as an unsecured creditor.

PRIORITIES

The consequences of perfection and nonperfection are important in determining priorities among parties with conflicting interests in the same collateral. An unperfected security interest is of little value when challenged by a third party. When two or more secured parties perfect security interests in the same collateral, usually the first to perfect—the first to file or to take possession of the collateral—has priority.

◆ DEFAULT BY THE DEBTOR

Article 9 defines the rights, duties, and remedies of a secured party and of the debtor when a debt is not paid. If a secured party does not exercise his or her rights properly, then the debtor is protected.

But what constitutes default? Parties can agree to what will constitute default. Any breach of the terms of a security agreement can constitute default. Most commonly, default occurs when the debtor fails to meet scheduled payments or when the debtor becomes bankrupt.

(continued on page 464)

Legal Focus Problem

Divide the class into small groups to read and discuss the Legal Focus Problem found here dealing with car repossession. Each group should choose a leader to explain his or her group's response to the question posed at the end of this problem.

LEGAL PERSPECTIVE (CONTINUED)

BASIC REMEDIES OF THE SECURED PARTY

After default, a secured creditor can sue on the debt, foreclose, or enforce a security interest by any available judicial process. The most common remedy is to enforce the security interest or, in other words, take back the collateral. The debtor may simply return the collateral at the request of the secured party, or the secured party may have to *seize or repossess* (take away from the debtor involuntarily) the collateral. When the secured party seizes the collateral care must be taken to assure that no *breach of the peace* (as determined by state law) occurs. The creditor or the creditor's agent cannot enter a debtor's home, garage, or place of business without the permission of the debtor.

◇ LEGAL FOCUS ~ PROBLEM

Max borrowed money from Acme Finance Company to purchase a car. Max gave Acme a security interest in the car to protect Acme from the possibility that Max would fail to pay his debt. After Max stopped making payments on the car, Acme sent Ben to seize it. Ben walked onto Max's property, and up his driveway where the car was parked. Ben entered the car and drove it off. Is this a lawful repossession?

It appears to be a lawful repossession as there was no confrontation with Max and no breach of the peace. And while Ben did go on Max's property, he did not enter any building. However, most car repossessions occur when the car is parked on a street or in a parking lot to avoid possible confrontations with the debtor.

The secured party can sometimes keep the goods in satisfaction of the debt by following strict notice requirements under the UCC. Alternatively, the secured party can resell the goods and apply the proceeds (money received from the sale) toward the debt.

Proceeds from Disposition Proceeds from a sale of retaken collateral must be applied in the following order:

1. Reasonable expenses stemming from the retaking, holding, or preparing for sale are covered first. When authorized by law and if provided for in the agreement, these can include reasonable attorneys' fees and legal expenses.
2. Satisfaction of the balance of the debt owed to the secured party.
3. Payment to owners of other security interests who have made a written demand received by the secured party before the proceeds have been distributed.
4. Return of any surplus amount received from the sale to the debtor.

Deficiency Judgment Often, after proper disposition of the collateral, the secured party has not collected all that is owed by the debtor. Unless otherwise agreed, the debtor is liable for any deficiency.

REDEMPTION RIGHTS OF THE DEBTOR

The debtor may be able to exercise the right of *redemption* of the collateral. The right of redemption is the right to have the collateral returned to the debtor. A redemption obviously must occur before the secured party disposes of the collateral. The debtor can exercise the right of redemption by paying the underlying debt. All expenses related to the enforcement of the security interest by the secured party must be paid.

Extension Activity

Have a student volunteer contact a local bank or savings and loan that grants car loans. The student should speak to a representative from this institution to find out how it disposes of repossessed cars. Is it through public auction? Is it through private sales? The student might also ask the representative of the institution whether the institution generally receives the full value of the defaulted agreement through this disposition.

 ## CHECKLIST FOR PERFECTING YOUR SECURITY INTEREST

1. File a financing statement promptly.
2. Describe the collateral well—it is better to give too much detail rather than to give too little detail.
3. Even with friends, relatives, or associates, be sure to perfect your security interest, perhaps by having the debtor transfer the collateral to your possession.

 ## TERMS TO REMEMBER

◆ **secured transaction** Any transaction, regardless of its form, that is intended to create a security interest in personal property.

◆ **collateral** Any property used as security for a loan.

◆ **purchase-money security interest** A security interest in property created at the time the property is sold to secure repayment of the debt incurred to make the purchase.

◆ **perfection** The method by which a secured party obtains priority over later creditors with regard to collateral.

Suggested Additional Resources

Bagley, Constance E. *Managers and the Legal Environment: Strategies for the 21st Century.* St. Paul, MN: West Publishing Co., 1991.

Cross, Frank B. and Miller, Roger LeRoy. *West's Legal Environment of Business.* St. Paul, MN: West Publishing Co., 1992.

The Guide to American Law. St. Paul, MN: West Publishing Co., 1983. - Annual updates are available.

Jentz, Miller, Cross. *West's Business Law Alternate Edition,* Fifth Edition. St. Paul, MN: West Publishing Co., 1993.

Leslie, Douglas L. *Leslie's Labor Law in a Nutshell,* 3d ed. St. Paul, MN: West Publishing Co., 1992.

Steffen, Roscoe T. *Steffen's Agency-Partnership in a Nutshell.* St. Paul, MN: West Publishing Co., 1977.

U.S. Department of Labor. *A Working Woman's Guide to Her Job Rights.* Washington, D.C.: Government Printing Office, 1988.

466

Unit

4 LEGAL PERSPECTIVE

UNIT 4

Agency and Employee Law

A single individual can rarely handle all the activities necessary to run a business. Thus, businesses rely on employees to carry out the many activities essential to success. These activities are actually performed by employees and agents of the business. Agency is a relationship between two persons in which one of them, the agent, is authorized to act on behalf of the other, called the principal. Within the scope of the agency agreement, the agent may negotiate contracts with third parties and bind principals to those contracts. If an agent is paid for his or her effort, he or she is also an employee.

In Chapter 20, we examine the agency relationship, its formation, and the rights and duties of agents and principals. We also examine issues involving employers, employees, and independent contractors. In Chapter 21, we look at unions and labor relations and other issues in employment contracts and relationships. In Chapter 22, we look at federal statutes regulating the work environment. Among these statutes are laws that restrict discrimination, regulate workplace safety, and provide workers' compensation.

LEGAL BACKGROUND

Up to this point, we have primarily discussed legal rules that make an individual responsible for his or her acts. This chapter introduces how one person's acts can create responsibility for another. This chapter applies some principles we learned in contracts and the tort chapter. One very important aspect of this chapter is its discussion of the concept of legal responsibility. Both an employer and an employee have a responsibility toward one another. This chapter discusses formation and termination of any agency, rights and duties of principal and agent, and the sources of the agent's authority. The relationships of principal/ agent, employer/employee, and independent contractor are also defined and distinguished.

In this chapter, students should be able to see how the principles relate to their experiences.

Mastery Objectives

By the end of this chapter, students will be able to:

- Characterize types of agency relationships
- Describe how an agency is formed
- Delineate duties of agents and principals
- Explain the nature of an agent's authority
- Determine liability for contracts
- List the ways an agency can be terminated

Prereading Activity

Ask students who work to describe their duties. Ask them if they have a contract. Ask students how they think the relationship may be terminated. Ask students what they think their liability is. Ask them what they think their employer's responsibility is to them as an employee. Ask other students in the class to provide responses to the questions also.

Chapter

Agency

<table>
<tr><td>

Chapter 20
Resources and Assignment Guide

Activity Sheets
Reviewing Legal Concepts 20 *TRB*
Enrichment Activity 20 *TRB*

Student Activity Workbook
Chapter 20 Activities

</td><td>

Tests
Chapter 20 Test *TRB*
Chapter 20 WESTEST Computerized Testing

Handbook of Selected Court Cases
Tarver v. *Landers*
Romero v. *Mervyn's*

West's Business Law and Legal Environment Videodisc
Still Frames and Motion Segments as shown

</td></tr>
</table>

"Success is simply a matter of luck. Ask any failure."
Earl Wilson, 1907–1987
Newspaper columnist and radio commentator

Buying a soda at the pizza parlor is not something you think about much. It is, however, a legal event. Your purchase is a contract; you have exchanged money for a soda. But when you buy that soft drink, do you give your money to the owner of the business? Not usually. You make the purchase from an employee, who may be one of your friends and who is selling sodas as part of her job. The boss hopes she sells lots of sodas. Your friend and her boss are in a common and important legal relationship called **agency**. A party called the **agent** agrees to represent or act for another party, the **principal**. An agency relationship requires the consent of both parties.

◆ THE NATURE OF AGENCY

If every business contract required that a customer deal directly with the owner, business as we know it would not exist. The legal doctrine of agency provides that an agent can contract on a principal's behalf with a third party, such as a customer. The contract that is created is viewed by the law as if the principal and customer had dealt with each other directly. The act of the agent is treated as if it were the act of the principal. Thus, an agency relationship allows a business owner to employ others to sell the business's goods and services.

The agency relationship is a **fiduciary relationship** and is at the heart of agency law. A fiduciary relationship is a relationship involving trust and confidence. Fiduciary relationships can be a special contract relationship, like an attorney and client or a doctor and patient, or can be based on social relationships, like parent and child or pastor and church member. Often the key to a successful business is finding and keeping competent and trustworthy agents.

◆ TYPES OF AGENCY RELATIONSHIPS

The first step in analyzing an agency relationship is to determine if one exists. There are three types of relationships usually discussed under the broad term of *agency*: (1) principal and agent, (2) employer and employee, and (3) principal or employer and independent contractor. These concepts overlap a great deal. For example, an employee can also be an agent. Still, though these categories are similar and do sometimes overlap, there are differences, and the following subsections look at each category separately.

◆ **agency** A relationship between two persons in which, by agreement, one (the principal) is bound by the words and acts of the other (the agent).

◆ **agent** A person authorized by another to represent or act for him or her.

◆ **principal** A person who authorizes another (an agent) to act on his or her behalf.

◆ **fiduciary relationship** A relationship involving trust and confidence between the parties involved.

Vocabulary Activity

Ask student volunteers to give some examples of agencies. Then have a student define, in his or her own words, the word *agency* as it is commonly used in relationship to such things as employment agencies, ticket agencies, etc. Explain that the use of the word *agency* usually refers to an administrative or professional division; however, in this chapter they will be learning a new definition of the word *agency* as it relates to law. Then have a student volunteer read aloud the definition for *agency* that appears in the margin in the student text.

Vocabulary Activity

Have a student look up the word *fiduciary* and read aloud the definition. Then have the student relate the dictionary definition of *fiduciary* to the definition of *fiduciary relationship* found here.

469

Legal Focus Example

Have a student read aloud this Legal Focus Example. Ask the class if they can think of any other examples of principal-agents that could also fit here. Allow volunteers to share their examples with the class.

Extension Activity

Sports agents and entertainment agents are examples of principal-agents. Have a student volunteer research sports agents or entertainment agents to find out what they do, how they are compensated, etc. Allow the volunteer to report his or her findings to the class in the form of an oral report. Encourage the student to use visual aids in the report.

Legal Focus Problem

Have a student volunteer read aloud this Legal Focus Problem. Allow the student to suggest a possible answer to the question posed at the end of this problem. (Students should understand that as Roxanne and Nita transact business with third parties in their role as salespeople, they are agents.)

Teaching with the Videodisc

The still frames listed below from the **West's Business Law and Legal Environment Videodisc** can be used with this chapter. To access this material, use the bar codes or the frame numbers included in the Videodisc Instructor's Manual found in the *TRB*.

Legal Relationships in
  Agency Law
Formation of Principal-
  Agent Relationship
Agent's Duties to Principal
Principal's Duties to Agent
Termination of an Agency
Termination of an Agency
  Notice Requirements
Contracts Liability of
  Disclosed Principal
Contract Liability of Partially
  Disclosed Principal
Contract Liability of
  Undisclosed Principal
Tort Liability of Principal
  and Agent

PRINCIPAL–AGENT

In a principal–agent relationship, the agent acts for the principal in negotiating and transacting business with third persons. An agent is given authority from the principal to carry out the principal's business.

An agent is authorized to perform legal acts that are binding on the principal, as the following example shows.

◀ LEGAL FOCUS – EXAMPLE

Bruce is hired as a booking agent for a rock group, The Crash. As the group's agent, Bruce can negotiate and sign contracts for the rock group to appear at concerts. The contracts are binding and legally enforceable on The Crash. If The Crash doesn't appear at a concert that Bruce has booked for the group, then the group may be liable for damages to the concert's producer.

EMPLOYER–EMPLOYEE

◆ **employee** A person who works for another: in agency law, one whose physical conduct is *controlled* by or is subject to control by the employer.

An **employee** is a person who is hired to perform services for another, the employer, and the employee's physical conduct is controlled by or is subject to control by the employer. The employment relationship is a contract relationship. Employees who transact business with third parties are often also agents.

◀ LEGAL FOCUS – PROBLEM

Donna owns a dress shop. She employs Myra, Roxanne, and Nita as salespeople and Kari as a janitor. Donna is the employer. Myra, Roxanne, Nita, and Kari are employees. Which of the employees, if any, are agents?

The key to an employer-employee relationship is the extent of the employer's right to control the employee's acts. The employees do not have *independent* business discretion. The dress shop salespeople are told how to sell the dresses. When they sell the dresses, however, they are agents as well as employees. They are given the authority by Donna to sell goods to customers. These sales are contracts between the customers and Donna. Kari, the janitor, does not have the authority to sell dresses or probably to enter into any contract for Donna. Kari is an employee but not an agent.

Many state and federal employment laws apply to those in employer-employee relationships. These laws cover such issues as social security, withholding of income taxes, workers' compensation, unemployment compensation, workplace safety laws, and the like. These laws, discussed in

Enrichment

Guide the students in looking at the list of questions on this page that are used in determining whether someone is an employee or an independent contractor. Tell the students to imagine that Robin, a lawyer, hires Jamal to build a greenhouse for her. Then have the students apply each of the questions in the numbered list to this example. Note that this activity can be completed orally as a class discussion or in writing as a homework assignment.

Legal Focus Example

Read this Legal Focus Example to the class. Ask the class if they can think of any other examples of independent contractors that could also fit here. Allow volunteers to share their responses with the class.

Critical Thinking Activity

Read aloud the following sentence from the student text: "Although an employer has little control over the way in which an independent contractor does his or her work, the independent contractor is still responsible for performing that work competently." Have a student volunteer relate this sentence to what the class has already learned regarding *breach of contract* and *performance*. Ask the students what possible results may occur if an independent contractor fails to perform his or her work competently.

Chapter 22, do not apply to the employer-independent contractor relationship, discussed below, in the same manner as they apply to the employer-employee relationship.

PRINCIPAL (EMPLOYER)–INDEPENDENT CONTRACTOR

Independent contractors are *not* employees because those who hire them have *little control* over the physical performance of the tasks they are hired to do. In determining whether someone is an employee or an independent contractor, the following questions are important:

1. What control does the employer exercise over the details of the work? Little or no control suggests an independent contractor.
2. Does the employed person work in an occupation or business distinct from that of the employer? A different business suggests an independent contractor.
3. Is the work usually done under the employer's direction or by a specialist without supervision? Little or no supervision suggests an independent contractor.
4. Does the employer supply the tools at the place of work? If the employer does not supply the tools, this suggests an independent contractor.
5. For how long is the person employed? The shorter the period, the more likely that the person is an independent contractor.
6. What is the method of payment—by time period or at the completion of the job? Payment at the completion of the job suggests an independent contractor.
7. What degree of skill is required of the person employed? A high degree of skill suggests an independent contractor.

♦ **independent contractor** A person who is hired to perform a particular task and performs the task largely how he or she chooses.

◇ LEGAL FOCUS ~ EXAMPLE

Building contractors and subcontractors are independent contractors. A property owner does not control the specific way in which either of these professionals performs his or her work. Truck drivers who own their equipment and hire out on a per delivery basis are independent contractors. However, truck drivers who drive company trucks are usually employees. Credit collection agents and real estate brokers are also usually independent contractors.

The relationship between a principal and an independent contractor also *may* or *may not* be an agency relationship. Attorneys are often both independent contractors and agents when they are hired to negotiate contracts for a client.

Although an employer has little control over the way in which an independent contractor does his or her work, the independent contractor is still responsible for performing that work competently.

Read to the class the Legal Focus Problem found here. Allow student volunteers to suggest possible answers to the question posed at the end of this problem.

Legal Focus Example

Allow a student volunteer to read aloud to the class this Legal Focus Example dealing with agency by agreement. Ask the students if they can think of any other examples of agency by agreement that could fit here. Allow volunteers to share their examples with the class.

Have a student volunteer contact a local real estate firm to obtain a copy of the written agreement form used to create an agency by agreement with home sellers.

472   Agency and Employee Law

 AGENCY FORMATION

Agency relationships are *consensual*; this means that they are formed by agreement of the parties. Most agency agreements can be oral, and consideration is not required. The principal must, however, have legal capacity to enter into contracts. A contract made with a third party by an agent is legally considered to be a contract between the third party and the principal. Thus, an agent's legal capacity to make a contract is not essential because the contract is with the principal. So any person can be an agent, regardless of whether he or she has the capacity to contract. Minors, for example, do not ordinarily have the legal capacity to contract, but they can be an agent for someone who does have that capacity.

An agency relationship can be created for any legal purpose. One created for an illegal purpose or contrary to public policy is unenforceable.

 LEGAL FOCUS – PROBLEM

Sharp (a principal) approaches Burke (an agent) to convince him to sell illegal narcotics for Sharp. Burke sells the narcotics to Franschet. Is this an enforceable agency relationship?

No, the agreement is not enforceable because selling narcotics is a crime. It is also illegal for medical doctors and other licensed professionals to employ unlicensed agents to perform professional services. For example, an attorney cannot employ someone who is not an attorney to appear in court in his or her place.

Generally, no special formalities are required to create an agency. An agency relationship can begin through one of three types of actions by the parties, discussed in the subsections that follow.

AGENCY BY AGREEMENT

An agency relationship can be created by an agreement of the principal and the agent. The agent must be willing to act for and at the principal's request. The principal must desire that the agent act on his or her behalf. The agreement can be either oral or in writing. Although a contract is not essential to create an agency, most agency agreements are contracts.

 LEGAL FOCUS – EXAMPLE

Ann enters into a written agreement with Troy, a real estate broker, for Troy to sell and transfer ownership to Ann's house. This agreement creates an agency relationship and a contract between Ann and Troy. The written agreement provides the details of that relationship.

Critical Thinking Activity

Ask a volunteer to answer the following question dealing with agency by ratification: What happens if the claimed principal does not ratify the contract? (Students should understand that if the claimed principal does not choose to ratify, he or she can avoid the obligation.)

Enrichment

Many of your students might hold jobs. Have students compile a list of the jobs held by class members. Then have the students discuss with each other the rights and responsibilities of each student's job to determine whether the student is an agent/employee, employee, or independent contractor. Allow a volunteer to list the student jobs and their classifications on the board.

Agency   473

AGENCY BY RATIFICATION

Sometimes a person who is not an agent enters into a contract claiming to represent another (the claimed principal). If the claimed principal later approves that contract by word or by action, an agency relationship is created after the fact by **ratification**. Ratification is the approval or validation of the activities of another after those activities have been performed. The actual requirements for ratification are discussed later in this chapter.

AGENCY BY ESTOPPEL

Estoppel is an equitable doctrine used by a court to stop a person from denying something that his or her previous statements or actions have claimed is true. The doctrine is every bit as complicated as this definition makes it seem. Estoppel is used when it is unfair that a person benefit from a situation in which he or she has misled someone. The *Stambovsky v. Ackley* case on pages 25–26 applied the doctrine of estoppel. In order for an agency to be formed by estoppel, several things must happen:

1. A person must claim to a third person that he or she is an agent when this is not true. The claimed principal has not given that person authority to act as his or her agent.
2. The third person must believe that the person who claims to be an agent is acting on behalf of the principal.
3. The claimed principal must have acted in some way that leaves the third party with the reasonable impression that the person claiming to be an agent actually has the authority to contract for the principal.

◆ **ratification** Accepting and giving legal force to an obligation that could have been avoided.

◆ **estoppel** An equitable judicial doctrine that keeps a person from denying something that his or her previous statements or actions have claimed or implied is true.

Reteaching Activity

Have students write a paragraph or two on agency formations. Instruct the students to include in their writing a description of the formation, characteristics of the formation, and at least one example of each formation.

Caption Answer

1. A person must claim to a third person that he or she is an agent when this is not true. The claimed principal has not given that person authority to act as his or her agent.
2. The third person must believe that the person who claims to be an agent is acting on behalf of the principal.
3. The claimed principal must have acted in some way that leaves the third party with the reasonable impression that the person claiming to be an agent actually has the authority to contract for the principal.

What are the requirements for agency by estoppel?

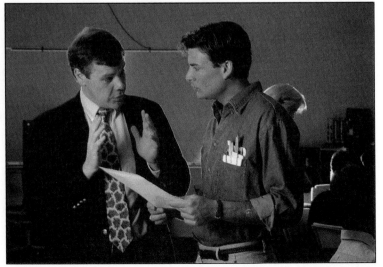

Have a student volunteer read aloud this Legal Focus Problem dealing with agency by estoppel and the case of Andrew, Longhorn Wholesale Feed, and Steve. Guide the students in discussing this feature by asking the following questions: Does Andrew claim to Steve that he is an agent when this is not true? Does Steve believe that Andrew is acting on behalf of Longhorn Wholesale Feed? Has Longhorn Wholesale Feed acted in some way that leaves Steve with the reasonable impression that Andrew actually has the authority to contract for Longhorn Wholesale Feed? After the students have discussed these questions, call on a student volunteer to provide the answer for the question posed at the end of this problem.

Ask a student volunteer to read aloud the second Legal Focus Problem. Then stimulate a class discussion regarding this problem by asking the following questions: Does Alice claim to Dru that she is an agent when this is not true? Does Dru believe that Alice is acting on behalf of Pierre Dumont? Has Pierre Dumont acted in some way that leaves Dru with the reasonable impression that Alice has the authority to contract for Dumont? After the students have discussed these questions, have a student volunteer provide the answer to the question posed at the end of this problem.

If these three events occur, then the claimed principal is not allowed to deny that an agency exists; in legal terms, the claimed principal is estopped from denying the agency. The most common situation where an agency by estoppel exists is when a person who used to be an agent has been dismissed, but third persons with whom the agent used to deal are not aware of the change in the former agent's employment status.

◆ LEGAL FOCUS – PROBLEM

For several years, Andrew sold seed for Longhorn Wholesale Feed and Seed to customers who included Steve. Andrew had authority to take orders and collect for the orders in cash. Because of work-related problems, Longhorn decided to fire Andrew. Angry about his firing, Andrew decided to collect a little extra cash and create some problems for Longhorn, so he visited Steve and took several orders for seed supplies. Steve paid Andrew for the supplies in cash. Steve was unaware that Andrew no longer worked for Longhorn. When the seed supplies did not arrive, Steve contacted Longhorn and found out that Longhorn did not know about the orders. Does Steve have legal rights against Longhorn?

Steve can effectively argue an agency by estoppel. Andrew claimed to be an agent of Longhorn but was not. When his job ended, his authority to create contracts on Longhorn's behalf ended as well. Steve, however, believed that Andrew was still an agent. This belief was reasonable; it had been created by Longhorn, who had accepted the orders made by Steve through Andrew over time. In this type of situation, a principal needs to protect himself or herself by letting the agent's customers know that the agent's authority no longer exists. In this case, Longhorn must fill Steve's orders. Longhorn, of course, has a right to be reimbursed by Andrew for any loss it suffers because of his wrongful action.

It should be noted that acts or statements of the principal are required to find an agency by estoppel, as the next problem illustrates.

◆ LEGAL FOCUS – PROBLEM

Alice walks into Dru's Dress Boutique and claims to be a sales agent for an exclusive Paris dress designer, Pierre Dumont. Dru has never had business relations with Pierre Dumont. Based on Alice's claim, however, Dru gives Alice an order and prepays 15 percent of the sales order. Alice is not an agent, and the dresses are never delivered. Can Dru hold Pierre Dumont liable?

No. Alice's acts and declarations, in and of themselves, do not create an agency by estoppel. Pierre did nothing to make Dru believe that Alice was his agent. Alice is, of course, responsible for her misrepresentations.

◆ AGENT'S DUTIES

Once the principal-agent relationship has been created, both parties have duties to each other. As we have said, the principal-agent relationship is a *fiduciary* one. In a fiduciary relationship, each party owes the other the duty to act with the utmost faith. Neither party may keep information from the other that is important to the agency relationship.

The duties that an agent owes to a principal are stated in the agency contract or are implied by law. Generally, the agent owes the principal five duties: performance, notification, loyalty, obedience, and accounting.

PERFORMANCE

An agent is expected to use reasonable effort and skill in performing the agreed-on tasks. When an agent fails to perform his or her tasks with ordinary skill and care, liability for breach of contract may result. An agent who is hired on the basis of special skills, such as those of an accountant or attorney, is expected to exercise the skills claimed.

Not all agency relationships are based on contract. In some situations, an agent acts gratuitously—that is, for free. If there is no contract, the gratuitous agent cannot be liable for breach of contract. Once a gratuitous agent has begun to act in an agency capacity, though, he or she has the duty to continue to perform in a reasonable manner. Liability for a breach of this duty is based on the tort of negligence. (See the discussion of negligence in Chapter 5.)

◆ LEGAL FOCUS ~ PROBLEM

Peterson's friend, Stendhof, is a real estate broker. Stendhof offers to sell Peterson's farm and to do so without being paid. What are Stendhof's duties to Peterson?

If Stendhof never attempts to sell the farm, Peterson cannot force Stendhof to do so. If Stendhof finds a buyer, however, he may well have duties. For instance, assume that Stendhof promises the buyer a sales contract but does not provide one within a reasonable time. After a time, the buyer becomes angry and buys another piece of property. In this situation, Peterson can file a lawsuit against Stendhof in tort for negligence.

Legal Focus Example

Have a student read aloud to the class the first Legal Focus Example. Remind the students that they can use the Legal Focus features as review tools when studying for tests.

Vocabulary Activity

Write the word *loyalty* on the board. Then go around the room asking students to give a synonym or definition for this word. Then ask the students why they think that loyalty would be described as a fundamental duty in a fiduciary relationship.

Legal Focus Example

Read aloud the second Legal Focus Example. Ask student volunteers why it would be important that both principals know of the dual representation.

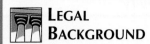

LEGAL BACKGROUND

An agent is required to notify a principal of all material matters that come to his or her attention concerning the subject matter of the agency. (For instance, an agent for the purchase of certain property who learns that the property is subject to another's right to subsurface minerals is required to notify the principal.) If the agent fails to notify the principal, the principal is nevertheless bound.

NOTIFICATION

Because the agent is the representative of the principal, third parties give information to the agent that is important to the principal. Once an agent is told or learns of a fact, the law expects that the principal also knows that fact. A common phrase describing this expectation is "notice to the agent is notice to the principal." Thus, it is expected that the agent will inform the principal of any important information.

 LEGAL FOCUS ~ EXAMPLE

Carly has an agreement with Food Tiger Stores to deliver strawberries every Friday during the growing season. When Carly makes her delivery, she is to put the produce on the loading dock and notify Food Tiger of the delivery. Carly delivers the strawberries and informs Arnold, the produce manager, of that fact. Arnold, in a hurry because he has an important social event to go to, forgets about the strawberries. By the next day, the strawberries are missing. By notifying Arnold, Carly has met her responsibility to the store. Arnold, however, has not met his responsibility as an agent of Food Tiger Stores. He should have either arranged to have the strawberries brought into the store or given the responsibility to another store official.

LOYALTY

Loyalty is a fundamental duty in a fiduciary relationship. The agent has the duty to act solely for the benefit of his or her principal. He or she may not act for his or her personal interests or for those of a third party.

 LEGAL FOCUS ~ EXAMPLE

An agent cannot represent two principals in the same transaction unless both principals know of the dual representation and consent to it. Thus, a real estate agent cannot represent both the seller and the buyer in the sale of a house unless both agree and know about the conflict of interest.

The duty of loyalty also means that important information or knowledge learned through the agency relationship is *confidential*. It is a breach of loyalty to disclose such information during the agency relationship and even after it ends. An example of confidential information would be a list of customers that belongs to the principal.

An agent hired to sell something cannot be the buyer unless the principal, after being made aware that the agent is the purchaser, specifically agrees to it. If an agent is selling a principal's product, he or she must report to the principal the true and accurate price obtained for the goods. If

Collaborative Learning Activity

Divide the class into small groups. Ask each group to read and discuss the information on these pages regarding the duty of loyalty in a principal-agent relationship. Ask each group to come up with a list of three to five examples of confidential information that a princi-

pal would not want an agent to disclose. Explain to the groups that one example is a retailer who would not want his or her salespeople to disclose the wholesale price he or she has paid.

an agent's job is to buy goods or services for the principal, he or she cannot falsely report what was paid or pay an excess amount and then receive a return of some of the excess payment from the seller. In short, the agent's loyalty must be absolute. The agent's actions must be strictly for the benefit of the principal. The actions must not result in any secret profit for the agent.

◇ LEGAL FOCUS – CASE EXAMPLE

Aztec Petroleum Corporation arranged to have Douglas buy oil and gas leases on the company's behalf. In return for his services, Douglas was paid $5,000 plus a royalty interest in the leases purchased. Douglas purchased several leases for Aztec. He told Aztec that he paid more for the leases than he actually did. Through various tricks, Douglas kept much of the money Aztec gave him to pay for the leases. Douglas used the money for personal purchases, including two new cars and a boat. When Aztec refused to grant Douglas the promised royalty interest in the leases, Douglas sued. Because Douglas had breached his fiduciary duty (specifically, the duty of loyalty) to Aztec, Aztec was not required to pay him any royalty.[1]

OBEDIENCE

When an agent is acting for a principal, the agent must follow all lawful and clearly stated instructions of the principal. Any deviation from these instructions violates the agent's fiduciary duty. Emergencies sometimes create exceptions. If a principal cannot be contacted, the agent may vary the instructions without violating this duty if circumstances require.

◇ LEGAL FOCUS – PROBLEM

Don has a small taco stand, and he employs Scott to sell food and drinks. Scott has been told that he can sell food and drinks, but he cannot buy any food supplies for the taco stand—or purchase anything else, for that matter. On Monday, Don is called away from the store. He leaves in a hurry, telling Scott he will return the next day but not telling Scott where he can be reached. A salesperson arrives and offers Scott an opportunity to buy lettuce at a 50 percent discount. Scott agrees and makes a $200 order. Later in the day, the store freezer, which holds all the frozen food supplies, breaks, and the food begins to thaw. Scott hires a repairperson who fixes the freezer. Is Scott responsible to Don for violating his responsibilities in either situation?

---

1. *Douglas v. Aztec Petroleum Corp.*, 695 S.W.2d 312 (Texas, 1985).

Legal Focus
Case Example

Have the class read aloud this Legal Focus Case Example dealing with the case of *Douglas* v. *Aztec Petroleum Corporation.* Guide the students in discussing this example by asking the following questions: In this example, who is the principal? Who is the agent? In what ways did the agent breach his fiduciary duty to Aztec? Explain to the students that in its decision, the Court of Appeals of Texas— Tyler stated that "Denial of the [royalty interest] to Douglas is a proper legal consequence of his established infidelity."

Legal Focus Problem

Have a student volunteer read aloud the second Legal Focus Problem. Ask the volunteer whether Scott was obedient to Don's instructions. Then have the volunteer suggest a possible answer for the question posed at the end of this problem. Make sure the students understand that even though Scott felt he was acting in Don's best interest by buying the lettuce, in this case he was acting without authority and is responsible to Don for the amount of the contract. However, the freezer repair is an emergency situation and, therefore, Scott's action would probably be deemed warranted.

Have a student read aloud to the class the first paragraph under the heading Principal's Duties. Point out to the class that a principal's duties do not include a duty of loyalty. Stimulate a class discussion about this fact by asking the following questions: Do you feel that it is appropriate that agents have a duty of loyalty to agents? Why or why not? Do you think this means that employers do not show loyalty to employees? Why or why not?

As a part of this discussion, you might ask students to list examples of employer loyalty to employees (i.e., not laying off senior employees when business is slow). Point out that although it is not a part of principal agent law, employer loyalty is based primarily on ethical considerations.

Teaching with Visuals

Have the students look at the photo of the bookkeeper shown here. Ask a student volunteer to describe what accounting duties an agent such as this bookkeeper has.

478   Agency and Employee Law

Scott did not have the authority to buy the lettuce. Even though it sounds like a good deal, this purchase was not an emergency, and Scott is responsible to Don for the amount of the contract. The freezer repair is another matter. Inaction by Scott would have destroyed much of Don's property. Although Scott did not follow Don's instructions when he contracted for the repair, it truly was an emergency, and Scott's actions were warranted.

ACCOUNTING

An agent has the duty to keep records of all property and money either received or distributed on the principal's behalf. The agent should maintain separate accounts for the principal's funds; in other words, the agent may not combine the principal's accounts with any of the agent's personal accounts. Mixing a principal's funds with the agent's funds is especially serious if done by a licensed professional. For example, if an attorney or accountant mixes funds, he or she may be subject to disciplinary proceedings and may lose his or her professional license.

◆ PRINCIPAL'S DUTIES

The principal also has certain duties to the agent. These duties include compensation, reimbursement, cooperation, and the provision of safe working conditions.

Keeping accurate records of spending and expenses is expected of an agent.

1. An agency relationship arises when a business owner hires a salesperson to sell the firm's products. It is a fiduciary relationship involving trust and confidence.
2. If an employee does not have the authority to act for the principal in transacting business with a third person, he or she is not an agent.
3. Estoppel is used when it is unfair that a person benefits from a situation in which he or she is responsible because someone was misled. This type of agency exists if: (1) a person claims to a third person that he or she is an agent, but is not, (2) the third person believes that the person claiming to be an agent is acting on behalf of a principal, and (3) the claimed principal has acted in some way that has left the reasonable impression with the third party that the person claiming to be an agent actually has authority to contract for the principal.
4. An agent owes the principal duties of performance, notification, loyalty, obedience, and accounting. The duties are stated in the agency contract or are implied by law.

COMPENSATION

Unless the agent is a volunteer, the principal must pay the agent the amount on which they have agreed. The principal has the duty to pay the compensation in a timely manner. If no amount has been agreed on, then the principal owes the agent the usual or reasonable pay for such services.

In general, when a principal requests certain services from an agent, the agent reasonably expects payment. For example, when an accountant or an attorney is asked to act as an agent, an agreement to pay for the service is implied, whether or not the fee is stated at the beginning.

REIMBURSEMENT

When an agent pays out money at the request of the principal, he or she has a right to be paid back, or *reimbursed*. This is also true whenever the agent pays money for necessary expenses involved in performing his or her tasks as an agent. Agents cannot, however, recover for expenses caused by their own misconduct or negligence.

COOPERATION

A principal has a duty to cooperate with and to assist an agent in performing the agency duties. The principal must do nothing to prevent such performance. For example, when a principal grants an agent the exclusive right to sell his or her product in Tulsa, Oklahoma, then the principal must not give the right to sell the product in that town to anyone else. If the principal visited Tulsa and began to sell the product himself, he would violate his promise and his duty of cooperation.

SAFE WORKING CONDITIONS

The principal must provide safe working premises, equipment, and conditions. The principal has a duty to inspect working areas and to warn agents and employees about any unsafe areas. If the agent is also an employee, the employer's liability is frequently covered by workers' compensation insurance. Workers' compensation, discussed in Chapter 22, is the primary remedy for an employee who is injured on the job.

◆ CHECKING YOUR PROGRESS

1. What legal and ethical relationship arises when a business owner hires a salesperson to sell the firm's products?

2. An employer-employee relationship is an agency relationship, but an employee is not always an agent. Explain.

3. Why and how is the doctrine of estoppel applied to principal-agency relationships?

4. What five duties does an agent owe to the principal?

Before the students read this material dealing with express authority, ask them to define the word *attorney*. (In general, your students will probably define *attorney at law* when asked to define *attorney*.) Then read aloud the following dictionary definition of the word *attorney*: "One who is legally appointed by another to transact business for him or her." Then have a volunteer read aloud the material under Express Authority, and ask him or her to relate the definition of *attorney* to the legal term *attorney-in-fact*.

Critical Thinking Activity

Ask the class to write a short paragraph discussing the practicality of the use of a durable power of attorney.

480

Divide the class into small groups. Read aloud the following sentences from the student text: "In general, for every duty of the principal, the agent has a corresponding right, and for every duty of the agent, the principal has a corresponding right. For example, it is the duty of the principal to provide a safe workplace and it is the right of an agent to have a safe place to work." Then ask the groups to look at the agent's duties of performance, notification, loyalty, obedience, and accounting as well as the principal's duties of compensation, reimbursement, and cooperation and for each of these duties list the corresponding right. Each group should choose a leader who will share the group's work with the class.

 ## RIGHTS AND REMEDIES IN AGENCY RELATIONSHIPS

In general, for every duty of the principal, the agent has a corresponding right, and for every duty of the agent, the principal has a corresponding right. For example, it is the duty of the principal to provide a safe workplace and it is the right of an agent to have a safe place to work. When one party to the agency relationship violates his or her duty to the other party, the remedies available for the innocent party arise out of contract law and tort law. These remedies include money damages, termination of the agency relationship, injunction, and an accounting.

 ## THE NATURE OF AN AGENT'S AUTHORITY

An agent's authority to complete the tasks he or she has been given can be either *actual* (express or implied) or *apparent*. If an agent enters into a contract that is not authorized by the principal, the principal is not usually liable on the contract. A principal can, however, become liable on an unauthorized contract by ratifying it.

EXPRESS AUTHORITY

Express authority is authority given orally or in writing to the agent by the principal. It can be as simple as a list of job responsibilities and duties that the principal gives to the agent. One example of express authority is a formal document called a **power of attorney**. An agent who holds the power of attorney is called an *attorney-in-fact*. An attorney-in-fact does not have to be an attorney-at-law.

The power of attorney is a written document. It is usually notarized, which means that it is signed by a notary public to verify the signature of the person—in this case, the principal—who completed the document. A power of attorney can authorize specific acts, or it can be general, permitting the agent to transact all business dealings for the principal. A sample power of attorney is shown in Exhibit 20-1.

An ordinary power of attorney ends with the *incapacity* of the person giving the power. Incapacity is the lack of legal capacity, and it can happen in several ways including a serious illness, an accident causing a coma, or even advanced age. In recent years, a special type of power of attorney, called a **durable power of attorney**, has become very popular. The durable power of attorney does not end when a person becomes incapacitated. The most common use of the durable power of attorney is to give a close relative or friend the power to make health care decisions for a person *if* they become seriously ill or the victim of an accident and become incapacitated.

◆ **power of attorney** A formal written document or instrument authorizing another to act as one's agent. Through the power of attorney, the agent becomes an attorney-in-fact.

◆ **durable power of attorney** A document authorizing a person to act and make decisions for another, including decisions about health care if the person becomes incapacitated.

POWER OF ATTORNEY
GENERAL

Know All Men by These Presents: That I, _____

_____

the undersigned (jointly and severally, if more than one) hereby make, constitute and appoint _____

_____

as a true and lawful Attorney for me and in my name, place and stead and for my use and benefit:

(a) To ask, demand, sue for, recover, collect and receive each and every sum of money, debt, account, legacy, bequest, interest, dividend, annuity and demand (which now is or hereafter shall become due, owing or payable) belonging to or claimed by me, and to use and take any lawful means for the recovery thereof by legal process or otherwise, and to execute and deliver a satisfaction or release therefor, together with the right and power to compromise or compound any claim or demand;

(b) To exercise any or all of the following powers as to real property, any interest therein and/or any building thereon: To contract for, purchase, receive and take possession thereof and of evidence of title thereto; to lease the same for any term or purpose, including leases for business, residence, and oil and/or mineral development; to sell, exchange, grant or convey the same with or without warranty; and to mortgage, transfer in trust, or otherwise encumber or hypothecate the same to secure payment of a negotiable or non-negotiable note or performance of any obligation or agreement;

(c) To exercise any or all of the following powers as to all kinds of personal property and goods, wares and merchandise, choses in action and other property in possession or in action: To contract for, buy, sell, exchange, transfer and in any legal manner deal in and with the same; and to mortgage, transfer in trust, or otherwise encumber or hypothecate the same to secure payment of a negotiable or non-negotiable note or performance of any obligation or agreement;

(d) To borrow money and to execute and deliver negotiable or non-negotiable notes therefor with or without security; and to loan money and receive negotiable or non-negotiable notes therefor with such security as he shall deem proper;

(e) To create, amend, supplement and terminate any trust and to instruct and advise the trustee of any trust wherein I am or may be trustor or beneficiary; to represent and vote stock, exercise stock rights, accept and deal with any dividend, distribution or bonus, join in any corporate financing, reorganization, merger, liquidation, consolidation or other action and the extension, compromise, conversion, adjustment, enforcement or foreclosure, singly or in conjunction with others of any corporate stock, bond, note, debenture or other security; to compound, compromise, adjust, settle and satisfy any obligation, secured or unsecured, owing by or to me and to give or accept any property and/or money whether or not equal to or less in value than the amount owing in payment, settlement or satisfaction thereof;

(f) To transact business of any kind or class and as my act and deed to sign, execute, acknowledge and deliver any deed, lease, assignment of lease, covenant, indenture, indemnity, agreement, mortgage, deed of trust, assignment of mortgage or of the beneficial interest under deed of trust, extension or renewal of any obligation, subordination or waiver of priority, hypothecation, bottomry, charter-party, bill of lading, bill of sale, bill, bond, note, whether negotiable or non-negotiable, receipt, evidence of debt, full or partial release or satisfaction of mortgage, judgment and other debt, request for partial or full reconveyance of deed of trust and such other instruments in writing of any kind or class as may be necessary or proper in the premises.

Giving and Granting unto my said Attorney full power and authority to do and perform all and every act and thing whatsoever requisite, necessary or appropriate to be done in and about the premises as fully to all intents and purposes as I might or could do if personally present, hereby ratifying all that my said Attorney shall lawfully do or cause to be done by virtue of these presents. The powers and authority hereby conferred upon my said Attorney shall be applicable to all real and personal property or interests therein now owned or hereafter acquired by me and wherever situate.

My said Attorney is empowered hereby to determine in his sole discretion the time when, purpose for and manner in which any power herein conferred upon him shall be exercised, and the conditions, provisions and covenants of any instrument or document which may be executed by him pursuant hereto; and in the acquisition or disposition of real or personal property, my said Attorney shall have exclusive power to fix the terms thereof for cash, credit and/or property, and if on credit with or without security.

The undersigned, if a married woman, hereby further authorizes and empowers my said Attorney, as my duly authorized agent, to join in my behalf, in the execution of any instrument by which any community real property or any interest therein, now owned or hereafter acquired by my spouse and myself, or either of us, is sold, leased, encumbered, or conveyed.

When the contest so requires, the masculine gender includes the feminine and/or neuter, and the singular number includes the plural.

WITNESS my hand this _____ day of _____, 19_____

_____   _____

_____   _____

State of California,   }
County of _____   } SS.

On _____, before me, the undersigned, a Notary Public in and for said

State, personally appeared _____

_____

known to me to be the person _____ whose name _____ subscribed

to the within instrument and acknowledged that _____ executed the same.

Witness my hand and official seal.   (Seal) _____

                                                              Notary Public in and for said State.

EXHIBIT 20-1
POWER OF ATTORNEY

Collaborative Learning Activity

Divide the class into small groups. Have the groups work together to read and discuss the sample power of attorney document found here. Ask the groups to note the purpose of the document, the rights and duties that are spelled out therein, and the signatures required.

Have a student volunteer read the first Legal Focus Problem aloud to the class. Have the volunteer suggest a possible answer for the question posed at the end of this problem. Make sure the students understand that a durable power of attorney could be drawn up to handle Mabel's property as well as to make decisions about Mabel's medical care if she became disabled or unable to manage her own affairs.

Guide the students in looking at the Legal Focus Problem dealing with implied authority. Ask the students what they think they would do if they were in Mueller's situation. Explain to students that the best way for Mueller to proceed would be to ask Al to specify his areas of authority.

Legal Focus Problem

Read to the class the Legal Focus Problem dealing with implied authority. Allow student volunteers to suggest possible answers to the question posed at the end of this problem.

◆ LEGAL FOCUS – PROBLEM

Mabel Bradshaw was elderly and concerned about being able to handle her affairs in the future. She wished to create a power of attorney for her daughter Ann. Mabel wanted Ann to have the power to handle her property. She also wanted Ann to be able to make decisions about Mabel's medical care if she became disabled or unable to manage her own affairs. Would you advise Mabel to create a power of attorney or a durable power of attorney?

Mabel's wishes suggest that a durable power of attorney is the more appropriate choice. This will allow Ann to handle Mabel's health care decisions, and it can also give Ann the power to make decisions about Mabel's property and investments should Mabel become unable to do so.

IMPLIED AUTHORITY

Implied authority is that authority customarily associated with the position of the agent or authority that is necessary to carry out expressly authorized tasks.

Authority can be implied by (1) custom, (2) the position the agent occupies, or (3) a reasonable necessity created by the need to carry out some express authority.

◆ LEGAL FOCUS – PROBLEM

Mueller is employed by Al's Grocery Chain to be the night manager at one of its stores. Al has not told Mueller whether he has the authority to contract with third persons. Would a manager have implied authority to enter into contracts for a store?

A position as manager of a business implies authority to do what is required, customary, and related to the manager's position to operate the business. These activities would include hiring employees, buying merchandise and equipment, and advertising the products sold in the store. All of these activities involve entering into contracts. Of course, a principal could specifically tell the manager that he or she does not have a certain authority, such as the authority to advertise.

APPARENT AUTHORITY

◆ **apparent authority** Exists when a principal does something that causes a third party reasonably to believe that someone is an agent when he or she is not.

Actual authority exists when the principal gives authority to the *agent*. **Apparent authority** may exist when actual authority is absent yet a principal does something that causes a *third party* reasonably to believe that someone is an agent when he or she is not. If the third party is harmed by

Vocabulary Activity

Have students use their own words to define the following terms referring to the nature of an agent's authority: *express authority, power of attorney, durable power of attorney, implied authority, apparent authority,* and *ratification.*

Legal Focus Problem

Ask a student volunteer to read aloud to the class this Legal Focus Problem dealing with apparent authority. Make sure the students understand that Carter had reason to believe that Erin had the authority to receive payments. As a followup question ask the students what course of action Rivercity can take to seek a remedy for this situation.

relying on that belief, the principal cannot deny that the agent had authority. As we discussed earlier in this chapter, this is called *estoppel*.

◆ LEGAL FOCUS – PROBLEM

Erin is a traveling saleswoman for Rivercity Company. Rivercity expressly told Erin that although she had the authority to take orders from customers, she did not have the authority to collect payments for the orders received. A customer, Carter, pays Erin for an order. Erin takes the payment to the principal's accounting department. The accountant accepts the payment and sends Carter a receipt. This procedure is followed for other orders. Later Erin solicits an order, and Carter pays her as before. This time, however, Erin runs away with the money. Can Carter claim that the payment to the saleswoman was authorized and thus, in effect, was a payment to the principal?

The answer is yes, because the principal's repeated acts of accepting Carter's payment led Carter to believe that Erin had the authority to receive payments. This is true even though Erin did not have that authority. The principal's conduct gave Carter the right to rely on Erin's *apparent* authority to collect.

RATIFICATION

As mentioned earlier in the chapter, ratification is the approval of a previously unauthorized contract or act. Ratification is not a concern if an agent had the authority to act.

Ratification can be either express or implied. The principal's ratification is binding only if the principal knows all the terms of the contract. The requirements for ratification are the following:

1. The person representing himself or herself as an agent must have acted for a principal.
2. That principal must later accept the benefits of the contract.
3. The principal must know of all the material facts involved in the transaction.

◆ LIABILITY FOR CONTRACTS

Whether the principal, the agent, or both are liable on a contract depends on the nature of the agency. In other words, the liability of the principal and the agent depends on whether the agency is disclosed, partially disclosed, or undisclosed.

A **disclosed principal** is a principal whose identity is known by the third party at the time the contract is made by the agent. Most agency relationships are disclosed.

◆ **disclosed principal** A principal whose identity and existence are known by a third party at the time the agent enters into a transaction.

Read to the class this first Legal Focus Example. Ask the class if they can think of any other examples of disclosed principal that could also fit here. Allow volunteers to share their examples with the class.

Legal Focus Example

Read aloud to the class this second Legal Focus Example. Make sure students understand that José is a partially disclosed principal because the seller is aware that John is acting as an agent but does not know for whom John is acting.

Legal Focus Example

Have a student volunteer read aloud to the class this Legal Focus Example dealing with an undisclosed principal. Remind the students that they can use the Legal Focus features as review tools when studying for tests.

Have a student volunteer or group of volunteers research the use of partially disclosed principals at art auctions. You might guide the students in their research by suggesting they look up "Art Auction" or "Art Sales" in *The Reader's Guide to Periodical Literature.* Allow the students to present their findings to the class in the form of an oral report. Encourage the students to incorporate visual aids into their presentation.

 LEGAL FOCUS ~ EXAMPLE

A purchasing agent for Ajax Corporation signs a contract for the purchase of office supplies. The agent signs her name and indicates that she is a purchasing agent for Ajax. The owner of the office supply store knows the purchasing agent and the principal company. A disclosed principal clearly exists.

◆ **partially disclosed principal** A principal whose identity is unknown by a third party, but the third party does know that an agency exists.

A **partially disclosed principal** is one whose identity is not known by the third party. However, the third party knows that the person with whom they are contracting is representing someone else.

 LEGAL FOCUS ~ EXAMPLE

José, a famous athlete, wishes to purchase some land for a possible business venture. He is concerned that any seller of land might overcharge if he or she knows that José is the purchaser. José hires John to buy the property. John makes it clear to the seller that he is buying the property for another person, but does not tell the seller who that person is. José is a partially disclosed principal because the seller knows that José is acting as an agent and is not buying the property for himself, but she does not know the identity of the principal.

◆ **undisclosed principal** A principal whose identity and existence are unknown by a third party.

An **undisclosed principal** is a principal whose existence and identity are both unknown by the third party. The third party does not know that the agent is acting in an agency capacity at the time the contract is made. An undisclosed agent has the same right to be reimbursed by the principal for any costs related to contracts he or she enters into on the principal's behalf as does an agent for a disclosed or partially disclosed principal.

 LEGAL FOCUS ~ EXAMPLE

Albright agrees to buy two truckloads of apples from Zimmer. Albright believes that he is buying the apples from Zimmer. Actually, Zimmer is the agent for Henderson, the owner of the apples. Henderson is an undisclosed principal. Albright is unaware of the agency and the identity of the true owner.

As the agency is undisclosed, the agent, Zimmer, is liable to Albright on the contract. If the apples are rotten or filled with insects, Albright could bring an action against Zimmer even though Zimmer is an agent. Zimmer

Vocabulary Activity

The legal doctrine of *respondeat superior* imposes vicarious liability on an employer for wrongful acts of an agent or employee that occur while the agent or employee is on the job. Lead a discussion of the meaning, "let the master respond." Ask a student to look up and read aloud the definition of the word *vicarious*. Ask students to create a sentence using the word in a situation other than *respondeat superior*.

has a right to reimbursement from the principal, Henderson, for any losses he might suffer because of this contract.

In the usual disclosed or partially disclosed agency contract, if an agent performs as agreed, the principal is liable to the third party for a contract made by the agent. The agent is not liable on the contract. If either the third party or the principal breaches the contract, they can only sue one another, not the agent.

If any agent exceeds his or her authority, the principal cannot be held liable in a contract by a third party, unless apparent authority exists. The agent is generally liable unless the third party knew of the agent's lack of authority.

When the principal is undisclosed, the agent is liable as a party to the contract. The rights to the contract can generally be transferred to the principal by assignment (see Chapter 12.) However, if the third party has already made it known that he or she does not want to deal with the principal, the contract cannot be assigned to the principal.

◆ LIABILITY FOR AN EMPLOYEE'S OR AGENT'S TORTS

The legal doctrine of **respondeat superior** imposes vicarious—that is, indirect—liability on an employer for the wrongful acts of an agent or employee that occur while the agent or employee is on the job. The Latin term *respondeat superior* means "let the master respond." Vicarious liability occurs even though the employer has not been careless. Because liability exists even without the fault of the employer, the doctrine is similar to the theory of strict liability discussed in Chapter 5.

The doctrine of *respondeat superior* has three supporting theories. The first concerns the issue of *control*. An employer or principal has the right to control the acts of the agent or employee and is thus responsible for injuries arising out of such service. The second theory is *economic* in nature. Since the employer or principal profits from the employee's or agent's service, he or she should also suffer the losses. The third reason is practical and is referred to as the *deep-pocket theory*. The principal or employer is more likely to be able to pay for the losses than the employee. In other words, the principal or employer usually has more money; this is where the saying "The employer has the deep pocket" comes from.

In the remainder of this section, we refer to employer and employee although the discussion generally applies to most principal and agent relationships as well.

SCOPE OF EMPLOYMENT

The employer is only responsible for the torts of the employee while the employee is on the job—or, in legal terms, is "acting within the scope of employment." There are several questions used to determine if the employee's act occurred within the scope of employment. The answers to all

◆ **respondeat superior**
[Latin: let the master respond.] A doctrine by which a principal or employer is held liable for the acts of the agent or employee that occur within the scope of his or her employment.

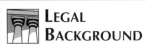

LEGAL BACKGROUND

Traditionally, the defense of assumption of risk prevented players from recovering damages for sports injuries. Recently, however, under the doctrine of *respondeat superior,* some players have recovered damages from team owners for intentional torts committed by other players. In one case, a Denver Bronco football player was injured so severely that he was forced to end his career. The court held that the Cincinnati Bengals player who inflicted the injury and the Bengals' owner could be liable under the doctrine.

The prevailing rationale for the doctrine of *respondeat superior* is that an employer is more likely to have the "deep pocket" and therefore be able to pay for relief to an injured party. This rationale weakens, however, in the area of professional sports where participants are among the highest paid employees in society. Another rationale for the doctrine is that employers who might be held liable will take greater precautions to deter their employees' wrongful acts.

For a complete discussion of this issue, see the *Law in Action* feature later in this chapter.

485

Teaching with the Videodisc

At this time you may wish to show the students the motion segment titled, *Agency and Respondeat Superior* from the **West's Business Law and Legal Environment Videodisc.** This fictional dramatization is a part of *West's Business Law's Drama of the Law Series.* Each of these dramatizations was written by award-winning writer John J. Osborne, Jr. (originator

Legal Focus Problem

Have a student volunteer read aloud to the class this Legal Focus Problem. Have the students discuss this problem by answering each of the questions in the numbered list above in the context of this particular instance. Then have a student volunteer answer the question posed at the end of this problem.

and author of *The Paper Chase).* Each of these was created by Osborne and West to bring points of law to life for your students.

The segment titled *Agency and Respondeat Superior* focuses on an employer's potential liability for a tort allegedly committed by an employee.

Each of the legal implications included in this motion segment is discussed in the *Drama*

of the Law Instructor's Manual, which is included in your *Teacher's Resource Binder.*

To access this motion segment, you can use the bar code provided here or punch in the frame number below.

Search Frame 35142

---

these questions assist a court in determining whether the employee was on the job for purposes of the doctrine of *respondeat superior.*

1. Was the act authorized by the employer? If the answer is yes, then the act is probably within the scope of employment.
2. What were the time, place, and purpose of the act? If it occurred on the work site, then the employee was probably on the job. If driving to or from work, then the employee is generally not acting within the scope of employment.
3. Was the act one commonly performed by employees for the employer? If yes, the employee was acting within the scope of employment.
4. To what extent was the employer's interest advanced by the act? If the act would ordinarily benefit the employer, then the employee was acting within the scope of employment.
5. To what extent were the private interests of the employee involved? If the act was primarily to benefit the employee, then perhaps the employee was not on the job. For example, an employee takes a break during the day and goes downtown to shoot a game of pool. An accident occurs while driving to the pool hall. The employee is probably not within the scope of employment.
6. Did the employer furnish the means or instrumentality (for example, a truck or a machine) by which the injury was inflicted? If the employee is using the employer's truck, he or she is more likely to be considered within the scope of employment.
7. Did the employer expect that the employee would do the act? Had the employee done the act before? If the answer is yes to both questions, the employee is more likely to be within the scope of employment.
8. Did the act involve the commission of a serious crime? If the act is a serious intentional wrong, the employee is not usually considered to be within the scope of employment, unless the employer requested that the employee perform that wrongful act.

◀ LEGAL FOCUS – PROBLEM

Walter Johnson was driving down Main Street on his way to deliver a package for Racehorse Delivery Service. Unfortunately, Walter was distracted for a second and ran into the rear of Felicia Ferguson's new Saturn automobile. Luckily, Felicia was not hurt, but the car suffered $3,000 in damages. Who is legally responsible for the harm to Felicia's car?

Johnson is, of course, liable for his own negligence. But because Johnson was an employee of Racehorse and because he injured another while driving the automobile on company business, Johnson was within the scope of his employment, and Racehorse Delivery is also liable under the

Legal Focus Problem

Allow a student volunteer to read aloud to the class this Legal Focus Problem. Ask the volunteer to suggest a possible answer to the question posed at the end of this problem. Remind students that they can use the Legal Focus features as review tools when studying for tests.

doctrine of *respondeat superior*. Although Felicia can sue both Johnson and Racehorse, she will collect her actual damages only once; she will not receive twice that amount.

MISREPRESENTATION

A principal is often responsible to third parties when an agent misrepresents important facts to those third parties. If the agent commits a fraud while acting for the principal, the principal can be held responsible.

◆ LEGAL FOCUS ~ PROBLEM

Pruitt is an automobile salesperson for Rivercity Motors. She tells a customer, Hawkins, that a used 1988 Ford pickup truck has 57,000 miles on the odometer. Hawkins, impressed with the pickup, buys it. Hawkins discovers later that the pickup had traveled 127,000 miles and that Pruitt had changed the odometer. What are Hawkins's rights against Pruitt and Rivercity Motors?

Pruitt has committed the tort of fraud and is responsible to Hawkins for her act. Even though Rivercity had no direct role in or knowledge of the fraudulent scheme, Rivercity is also responsible to Hawkins because Pruitt made the misrepresentation while selling cars for Rivercity.

◆ LIABILITY FOR THE TORTS OF AN INDEPENDENT CONTRACTOR

A principal is not usually liable for physical harm caused to a third person by the negligent act of an independent contractor. The reason that the doctrine of *respondeat superior* does not apply is because the employer does not have the *right to control* the details of an independent contractor's performance. Because an employer bargains with an independent contractor only for results and retains little control over the manner in which those results are achieved, the employer is generally not expected to bear the responsibility for torts committed by an independent contractor.

The exception is if the employer is engaged in especially hazardous activities. Examples of such hazardous activities include blasting operations, the transportation of highly volatile chemicals, and the use of poisonous gases. In these cases, a principal is not shielded from liability because he or she uses an independent contractor to help perform the task. Strict liability is imposed on the principal as a matter of law and, in some states, by statute.

Reteaching Activity

Have a student read aloud the two paragraphs on this page beneath the heading of Liability for the Torts of an Independent Contractor. Then point out that strict liability is discussed in this material. To refresh students' memories of the meaning of the term *strict liability,* have a volunteer look up the term in the glossary at the end of this book and read the definition aloud to the class. You might also remind students that strict liability was discussed in Chapter 5 and encourage them to reread the Chapter 5 Summary.

LAW AND THE BUSINESSPERSON: FAIRNESS AND *RESPONDEAT SUPERIOR*

The doctrine of *respondeat superior* raises an important ethical question. Why should innocent employers pay for the torts of their employees? This question is particularly relevant in the world of sports. Over the years, the doctrine of assumption of risk has prevented plaintiffs from recovering damages for their sports injuries. In other words, when players participated in a sport, knowing the risks involved, they were unable to recover damages for injuries. In the last several years, some courts have allowed plaintiffs to recover damages from sports team owners for intentional torts committed by professional sports players.

For example, in 1973 the Denver Broncos and the Cincinnati Bengals were playing a football game. Dale Hackbart was playing safety for the Broncos, and Charles Clark was playing fullback for the Bengals. When Hackbart attempted to block Clark after an intercepted pass, Clark hit Hackbart in the back of the head with his right forearm. The blow resulted in a severe neck injury, ending Hackbart's football career. The trial court dismissed the lawsuit, holding that Hackbart had assumed the risk of injury. The appellate court reversed the trial court holding. The court explained that participation in a football game does not mean that a

player is giving other players permission to injure them intentionally or recklessly. The court also ruled that as the harm occurred while Clark was on the job, the Cincinnati Bengals (as well as Clark) were liable under the doctrine of *respondeat superior*.[2]

As we have said, one reason for the doctrine of *respondeat superior* is the employer's assumed ability to pay. Thus, though an employer may be innocent, the employer has a "deeper pocket" and will be more likely to have the money necessary to pay the damages. Yet this rationale does not make as much sense in professional sports. The majority of professional athletes are among the highest-paid employees in our society. They frequently can afford to pay a substantial damage claim. In this context, does it seem right to apply the doctrine of *respondeat superior?*

Another reason for the doctrine of *respondeat superior* is the theory of deterrence. It is believed that employers will take precautions to discourage wrongful acts by their employees if they know that they may be liable for their employees' conduct.

_____
2. *Hackbart v. Cincinnati Bengals, Inc.*, 601 F.2d 516 (10th Cir. 1979).

 ## LIABILITY FOR AN AGENT'S CRIMES

There are other limits to the doctrine of *respondeat superior*. A principal or employer is generally not liable for an agent's or employee's *crime*, even if the employee is otherwise acting within the scope of authority or employment. To be held liable, the employer must have directed or encouraged the wrongful act or must have been careless in the supervision of the employee. Obviously, an agent is liable for his or her own crimes.

Some state and federal statutes specifically hold a principal liable for certain violations of public safety or health statutes. Examples of such laws include those governing food or workplace sanitation, weights of products bought or sold, and the sale of liquor.

 ## TERMINATION OF AN AGENCY RELATIONSHIP

An agency relationship can be terminated by an act of the parties or by operation of law. Once the relationship between the principal and the agent ends, the agent no longer has the right to bind the principal to a contract with a third party. Third persons may need to be notified, however, when the agency has been terminated in order to end an agent's apparent authority.

TERMINATION BY ACT OF THE PARTIES

An agency relationship may be terminated by an act of the parties in several ways, including lapse of time, purpose achieved, occurrence of a specific event, mutual agreement, and termination by one party.

Lapse of Time   An agency agreement may state the time period of the agency relationship. The agency ends when the time expires.

 ### LEGAL FOCUS – EXAMPLE

Allen signs an agency agreement with Proust "beginning January 1, 1992, and ending December 31, 1993." The agency automatically terminates on December 31, 1993.

If no definite time is stated, then the agency continues for a reasonable time, and the agency can be terminated at will by either party.

Purpose Achieved   An agent can be employed to accomplish a particular purpose. For example, an agent might be employed to purchase livestock for a cattle rancher. The agency would automatically end after the purchase of the cattle.

Occurrence of a Specific Event   An agency might be created and be expected to continue until a certain event occurs. For example, Proust appoints Allen to handle her business affairs while she is away. When Proust returns, the agency automatically terminates.

Mutual Agreement   Remember from the discussion of basic contract law that parties can cancel, or rescind, a contract by mutually agreeing to

Reteaching Activity

Have students list the five ways a termination of an agency by operation of law can take place.

Extension Activity

Have students look through magazines and newspapers to find examples of employees being released from employment before the end of their contracts. Tell the students to describe in writing why the employee was terminated and to give the outcome of termination for the employer and employee. (Sports figures are generally participants in highly visible breaches of contract.)

terminate the contract relationship. The same holds true in an agency relationship. Both parties can agree to end the relationship; at that time, responsibilities of both parties also end.

Termination by One Party   As a general rule, either party to an agency can terminate the agency relationship. When the agent ends the relationship, it is called a renunciation of authority. When the principal ends it, it is called a revocation of authority. But although both parties may have the *power* to terminate, they may not each possess the *right*. Wrongful termination can subject the canceling party to a suit for damages. A person is said to have the power to do something when the courts will not stop that person's act. A person has the right to do something when the act is consistent with the person's legal duties. In other words, courts will not make a principal and agent continue a relationship with one another if either of them does not wish the relationship to continue; thus, the *power* to terminate exists. If, however, the party terminating the relationship is violating the contract, he or she is responsible to the innocent party for damages for breach of contract.

◆ **LEGAL FOCUS ~ PROBLEM**

Allen has a four-year employment contract with Proust to act as a manager for her professional baseball team for $235,000 a year. Proust becomes dissatisfied with Allen's services when her team ends up in last place. Proust, however, has three years left on his contract, and he has performed all the duties expected of him. Can Proust discharge Allen before the contract period expires?

Yes, Proust has the *power* to terminate the employment contract, and she can fire Allen. However, Proust is liable to Allen for money damages for the remaining three years on the contract because Proust had no *right* to terminate Allen's services. She has breached the contract. As many of you know, this type of situation happens all the time.

TERMINATION BY OPERATION OF LAW

Termination of an agency by operation of law can take place when death or insanity, impossibility, changed circumstances, bankruptcy, or war occurs.

Death or Insanity   Death or mental incompetence of either the principal or the agent automatically and immediately terminates the ordinary agency relationship. Knowledge of the death is not required.

LEGAL FOCUS ~ EXAMPLE

Proust sends Allen to the Far East to purchase a rare book. Before Allen buys the book, Proust dies. Allen's agent status is terminated at the moment of death, even though Allen does not know that Proust has died.

Impossibility   When the subject matter of an agency is destroyed or lost, the agency terminates.

 LEGAL FOCUS ~ EXAMPLE

Proust employs Allen to sell Proust's house, but before the sale occurs, the house is destroyed by fire. Allen's agency and authority to sell Proust's house end. When it is impossible for the agent to perform the agency lawfully, the agency terminates.

Bankruptcy   Bankruptcy of the principal or the agent usually terminates the agency relationship.

War   When the principal's country and the agent's country are at war with each other, the agency is terminated or at least suspended.

NOTICE OF TERMINATION REQUIRED

When an agency terminates by operation of law, there is generally no duty to notify third persons.

If the principal and agent terminate the agency, however, the principal may be at risk. Third parties who have previously dealt with the agent may not know that the agency has ended. A third party can hold the principal to contracts made by the agent until the third party is notified that the agency has ended. The principal should inform third parties who have dealt with the agent that the agency has ended. This notice is necessary to stop the agent's apparent authority.

A principal can also be responsible for the acts of a former agent with third parties about whom the principal does not know. For example, a salesperson may have called on someone who did not place an order. That potential customer knows that the salesperson was an agent, but the principal may not know about the potential customer. The law allows the principal to protect himself or herself from liability to unknown third parties by giving all parties **constructive notice**. Constructive notice is often accomplished by publication of notice in a newspaper. After such notice is given, the law presumes that all third parties have received the notice, whether they actually have or not.

 Ethical Concern

Stimulate a class discussion by asking students to explain why no notice of termination is required for an agency terminated by an operation of law, but a notice is required if the principal and agent terminate the agency. Who is responsible in the latter situation? Who should notify the third party? Why? What is constructive notice?

◆   **constructive notice**   Notice to the general public given indirectly; after it is given, courts assume that everyone has been notified of the fact. Constructive notice is often accomplished by publication of an advertisement in a newspaper.

1. If either a principal or an agent violates his or her duty to the other, he or she can find remedy in contract or tort law.

2. The requirements for ratification are: (1) the person representing himself or herself as an agent must have acted for a principal, (2) the principal must later accept the benefits of the contract, and (3) the principal must know of all material facts involved in the transaction.

3. The reason why the doctrine of *respondeat superior* does not apply is because the employer does not have the right to control the details of an independent contractor's performance.

4. A principal is generally not liable for an agent's crime simply because the agent committed the crime, even if the employee is otherwise acting within the scope of authority. To be held liable, the employer must have directed or encouraged the wrongful act or have been careless in the supervision of the employee.

5. A principal-agency relationship can be terminated by an act of the parties or by operation of law.

6. No. Even though either party to an agency has the power to terminate the agency relationship, he or she may not possess the right. Wrongful termination can subject the canceling party to a suit for damages.

Legal Focus Example

Ask a student volunteer to read aloud to the class this Legal Focus Example. Remind students that they can use the Legal Focus features as review tools when studying for tests.

LEGAL FOCUS ~ EXAMPLE

Amy is a traveling salesperson, selling goods and accepting money for Tylke Computer Company. Her employment has ended, and Tylke would like to limit its responsibility. It is unlikely but possible that Amy could continue to act as though she is still Tylke's agent. Tylke should contact all known buyers and tell them that Amy is no longer servicing their accounts. This provides actual notice to the parties most likely to be misled by any wrongful behavior from Amy. Tylke should also publish an ad in newspapers in any areas in which Amy sold goods. The ad will provide constructive notice to the general public that Amy's authority has ended, and under the law, Tylke will be protected, whether anyone reads the ad or not.

◆ CHECKING YOUR PROGRESS

1. What kind of law applies if either a principal or an agent violates his or her duty to the other?

2. Name the three elements that must be present if a principal decides to ratify an unauthorized act of the agent.

3. Why does the doctrine of *respondeat superior* not usually apply to independent contractors?

4. Is a principal liable for an agent who commits a crime in the scope of the principal-agency relationship?

5. How can a principal-agency relationship be terminated?

6. Must both parties mutually agree to terminate an agency? Explain.

Read

Explain to the students that the *A Case In Point* feature for this chapter deals with a principal's duty of compensation to the agent. To fully understand this *A Case In Point* feature, students will need to have a firm grasp of the concepts of compensation and independent contractors. You might want to have a student volunteer reread the pertinent sections of this chapter. Then have him or her read aloud to the class this *A Case In Point* feature.

Discuss

Stimulate a class discussion regarding this *A Case In Point* feature by asking the following questions: What was Brenda Tarver's role within Diane Landers's real estate business? What role did Tarver play in the Smiths' purchase of the property listed by the agency? What role did Landers play in the Smiths' purchase of the property listed by the agency? Why did Tarver sue Landers? What was the decision of the trial court? What was the decision of the Court of Appeals of Louisiana, Third Circuit? What reasons did the court give for its decision?

◆ A CASE IN POINT ◆

TARVER v. LANDERS

Court of Appeals of Louisiana, Third Circuit, 1986.
486 So.2d 294.

In this case, the real estate agent sued her broker/employer to be paid what she believed was her rightful commission. Note the importance of usual employment practices and customs of the real estate agency.

FACTS Brenda Tarver worked as an independent contractor with Dianne Landers's real estate business. The agents in the firm were paid by a commission on each sale. Tarver's contract read that she would receive 30 percent of any sales commission for which she was "entitled as either listing and/or selling agent." In the spring of 1984, Charles Smith and his wife contacted the agency concerning some property listed by the agency and advertised in the local newspaper. The Smiths were referred to Tarver, who showed them the property. Tarver negotiated three offers and three counteroffers between the seller and the buyer, but none resulted in a contract. The Smiths returned to the office when Tarver was out of the office. Dianne Landers helped them modify the last counteroffer, and they finally reached an agreement with the seller and purchased the property. Landers would not pay Tarver a commission for the sale because Tarver did not negotiate the actual purchase. Tarver sued to recover her commission, arguing that it was customary in the real estate office that the initial selling agent be paid the commission. Landers argued that the office custom applied to the situation in which the initial agent was absent from the office and another agent handled negotiations. The assisting agent then would not receive the commission if a sale resulted. The trial court held for Tarver, and Landers appealed.

ISSUE Whether or not Landers had a duty to compensate Tarver rested on the issue of whether Tarver was the "selling agent" in this case. If so, by their contract terms, Tarver had a right to the commission.

DECISION The appellate court affirmed the trial court's holding that Tarver was the selling agent and was entitled to her commission.

REASON Lacking any written definition of "selling agent" in the sales conducted through the real estate business, the court based its decision on the customary practices followed in the office. Tarver was undoubtedly the selling agent in the court's eyes, because she had done all the negotiating with the Smiths and had written up the offers and counteroffers. When the Smiths paid their final visit to the office, they were apparently ready to buy but with minor modifications to the agreement. These modifications were penciled in by Landers. Landers therefore had a duty to compensate Tarver.

Teaching Note

This case is included in the *West's Business and Personal Law Handbook of Selected Court Cases.*

In order to help students review what they have learned in Chapter 20, you might wish to:

1. Have a student volunteer, or volunteers, read the Chapter Summary aloud.

2. Allow the students to work with partners to complete the *Using Legal Language* activity.

3. Assign the *Checking for Comprehension* exercise as homework.

4. Allow the students to work in small groups to complete the *Applying Legal Concepts* activities.

5. As a class, complete the *Applying the Law* activities. (Please note that you may have to help students with vocabulary so that they adequately understand all of the *Applying the Law* material.)

In order to check student mastery of chapter concepts, you may wish to use the Chapter 20 test that is found in your *Teacher's Resource Binder* or use WESTEST computerized testing for Chapter 20.

CHAPTER REVIEW

◆ SUMMARY

TYPES OF AGENCY RELATIONSHIPS

1. *Principal-agent*—An agent acts for and instead of the principal.

2. *Employer-employee*—An employee is a person whose physical conduct is controlled by or is subject to control by an employer. An employee may also be an agent.

3. *Principal (employer)-independent contractor*—The independent contractor is not an employee, and the employer or principal has little control over the details of the contractor's physical performance of his or her tasks.

AGENCY FORMATION

1. *By agreement*—Through express consent (oral or written) or implied by conduct.

2. *By ratification*—The principal, either by act or agreement, accepts the benefits of a contract to which he or she would otherwise not be bound.

3. *By estoppel*—Formed when the principal causes a third person to believe that another is his or her agent.

DUTIES OF AGENTS AND PRINCIPALS

1. *Duties of the agent:*

   a. Performance—The agent must use reasonable diligence and skill in performing his or her duties.

   b. Notification—The agent must notify the principal of all matters that come to his or her attention concerning the agency relationship.

   c. Loyalty—The agent has a duty to act solely for the benefit of the principal.

   d. Obedience—The agent must follow all lawful and clearly stated instructions of the principal.

   e. Accounting—The agent has a duty to make available to the principal records of all property and money received or paid for the principal.

2. *Duties of the principal:*

   a. Compensation—Except in a gratuitous agency relationship, the principal must pay for an agent's services.

   b. Reimbursement—The principal must reimburse the agent for money spent at the request of the principal and for money spent for necessary expenses during the performance of the agent's tasks.

   c. Cooperation—A principal must cooperate with and assist an agent in performing his or her duties.

   d. Safe working conditions—A principal must provide safe working conditions for the agent-employee.

NATURE OF AGENT'S AUTHORITY

1. *Express authority*—Can be oral or in writing.

2. *Implied authority*—Authority customarily associated with the position of the agent or authority that is necessary for the agent to carry out expressly authorized tasks.

3. *Apparent authority*—Exists when the principal, by word or action, causes a third party reasonably to believe that an agent has the authority to act.

4. *Ratification*—The approval by the principal of an agent's unauthorized action or promise.

1. The three categories of relationships under the broad term of agency are: (1) principal and agent, (2) employer and employee, and (3) principal or employer and independent contractor. Student examples will vary.

2. No. An agent's legal capacity to make a contract is not essential because the contract is with the principal.

3. Principals' duties to agents include compensation, reimbursement, cooperation, and the providing of safe working conditions.

4. If a principal or an agent does not perform his or her duties to the other, the breached party may seek money damages, termination of the agency relationship, injunction, or an accounting.

5. An ordinary power of attorney can authorize specific acts or can be general; however, it ends with the incapacity of the person giving the power. On the other hand, a durable power of attorney allows an agent very broad powers to act for the principal, and it does not end with the incapacity of the person giving the power.

LIABILITY FOR CONTRACTS

1. *Disclosed principals and partially disclosed principals*—Principal is liable to a third party for a contract made by the agent if the agent acted within the scope of his or her authority.

2. *Undisclosed principals*—Agent is liable to a third party for such contracts. If the agent acted within the scope of his or her authority, the principal is also bound by the contract. If the agent is forced to pay the third party damages and his or her actions were proper, the agent is entitled to repayment by the principal.

LIABILITY FOR AGENT'S TORTS

Under the doctrine of *respondeat superior*, the principal is liable for any harm caused to another through the agent's negligence if the agent was acting within the scope of his or her employment at the time that the harmful act occurred.

LIABILITY FOR INDEPENDENT CONTRACTOR'S TORTS

Generally, a principal is not liable for harm caused by an independent contractor's negligence.

LIABILITY FOR AGENT'S CRIMES

An agent is responsible for his or her own crimes, even if a crime is committed while acting within the scope of authority or employment. A principal is liable for an agent's crime only if the principal directed the action or was careless in his or her supervision.

TERMINATION OF AN AGENCY

1. *By act of the parties:*

   a. Lapse of time (when a definite time for the duration of the agency was agreed on when the agency was established).

   b. Purpose achieved.

   c. Occurrence of a specific event.

   d. Mutual agreement of principal and agent.

   e. Termination by act of either the principal (revocation) or the agent (renunciation).

2. *By operation of law:*

   a. Death or mental incompetence of either the principal or the agent.

   b. Impossibility (when the purpose of the agency cannot be achieved due to an event beyond the parties' control).

   c. Bankruptcy of the principal or the agent.

   d. War between the principal's and the agent's countries.

3. *Notification of termination:*

   a. When an agency relationship is terminated by an act of the parties, all third parties who have previously dealt with the agency must be notified directly. Constructive notice is sufficient for all other third parties.

   b. When an agency is terminated by operation of law, no notice to third parties is required.

◆ USING LEGAL LANGUAGE

Directions: Match each term with the statement that best defines that term.

1. agency

2. constructive notice

3. disclosed principal

4. durable power of attorney

A. The equitable judicial doctrine of _____ is used to keep a person from denying something even though it may be true.

B. An instrument called a _____ authorizes

6. If an employee was acting within the scope of employment, the principal is liable, under the doctrine of *respondeat superior*, for the agent's negligence. Since an independent contractor's actions cannot be controlled by the principal, however, the independent contractor carries the liability for torts. An exception exists if hazardous activities are involved, wherein the principal is strictly liable for any harm resulting from an independent contractor's negligence.

7. Legal termination of agency could be caused by: death or mental incompetence of either party, impossibility, bankruptcy, or war between the principal's and agent's countries.

8. Parker may very well be correct in his claim. Implied ratification by a principal of an agent's unauthorized action occurs when a principal accepts the benefits of the unauthorized transaction and/or does not object to the action within a reasonable time. It is essential, however, that the principal be aware of all material facts; otherwise, the ratification will not be effective. Maria knew that the banners had been ordered by her campaign workers without her authorization and in using the materials in spite of this knowledge; such use would constitute ratification of the unauthorized pur-

chase. In such a case, Parker could successfully sue to recover the purchase price of the banners. If Maria was unaware that the banners had been purchased without her authorization, the use of the banners would not constitute ratification. A good point for discussion is whether the campaign worker was impliedly authorized or had apparent authority to contract for the printing of the banners. There is no question that there was no express authorization. Maria's prohibition, unknown to Parker, may not relieve Maria of

liability, however. If the campaign worker is one who is placed in the position of a person who usually orders campaign printing, or if this campaign worker had previously ordered campaign materials from Parker, Parker can claim that the campaign worker had either implied authority to act or that previous conduct led Parker to believe that the worker had (apparent) authority to contract for the banners. If either is applicable, ratification is not necessary, as the worker's contract is authorized, and the principal, Maria, is liable.

5. estoppel
6. independent contractor
7. power of attorney
8. principal
9. ratification
10. *respondeat superior*

another person to act as one's agent.

C. An agency can be formed by _____ if the principal either by act or agreement validates the activities of another after they have been performed.

D. Presumed knowledge of a fact is _____ and is often accomplished by publication in a newspaper.

E. A person who authorizes another, an agent, to act on his or her behalf is called a _____.

F. _____ is a relationship between two persons in which, by agreement, the principal is bound by the words and acts of the other.

G. The doctrine of _____ holds an employer liable for the acts of the employee occurring within the scope of his or her employment.

H. The identity and existence of a _____ are known by a third party at the time a transaction is entered into by the agent.

I. An _____ is not an employee because those who do the hiring have little control over the details of the physical performance of the work.

J. A document called a _____ authorizes another person to make health care decisions for a person who becomes incapacitated.

◆ CHECKING FOR COMPREHENSION

1. List the three categories of relationships under the broad term of agency. Give an example of each.

2. Must an agent have the same legal capacity as a principal to be able to form valid contracts? Explain.

3. What duties does a principal have to the agent?

4. What kinds of remedy might a principal or an agent seek if the other does not perform his or her duties?

5. Explain the difference between an ordinary power of attorney and a durable power of attorney.

6. Compare agency liability for torts committed by employees and by independent contractors.

7. What events could cause an agency to be terminated by law?

8. Maria was running for president of the junior class at her school. She had volunteers helping her buy materials and pre-

1. Generally, whether a person is deemed an employee or independent contractor depends on the right of the employer to control the actions of that person and on how the employer holds that person out to the public. In this case, the hospital was liable because the hospital's acts, including providing emergency-room treatment, implied that the doctors were employee-agents and not indepen-

dent contractors. Thus, the doctors were treated as employee-agents despite the internal treatment of doctors as independent contractors for tax and accounting purposes.

2. The fact that an employee or agent is acting on behalf of someone else does not excuse the agent or employee from liability for torts committed by the agent or employee. Ralls was, therefore, liable for his negligence even though it occurred within the scope of his employment by the state.

3. Yes. Kademenos has breached his duty of

loyalty to Equitable Life. Under principal-agent law, an agent owes a duty of loyalty to the principal, and it is the agent's duty in all dealings affecting the subject matter of the agency to act with the utmost good faith, in loyalty, for furtherance and advancement of the principal's interests. Since Kademenos, as an agent of Equitable, had utilized Equitable's resources in advancing the interest of Equitable, he could not thereafter resign and sell a competitor's policy, since this would be detrimental to his principal. While an agent can normally terminate the relationship with the principal at will, he or she cannot immediately thereafter act contrary to the interests of the former principal by utilizing the principal's resources to the principal's detriment.

pare campaign posters. She did not have very much money to spend so she instructed her campaign staff not to purchase any campaign materials without her explicit authorization. In spite of these instructions, one of her campaign workers ordered Parker Printing Company to print some banners for Maria's campaign. When the banners were received, Maria did not return them but instead used them during her campaign.

When Parker failed to obtain payment from Maria for the materials, he sued for recovery of the price. Maria contended that she was not liable on the sales contract because she had not authorized her agent to purchase the printing services. Parker argued that Maria's use of the materials constituted ratification of her agent's unauthorized purchase. Is Parker correct? Explain.

APPLYING LEGAL CONCEPTS

1. Using a computer or typewriter, key a copy of the Power of Attorney in Exhibit 24-1. Make up the information necessary to prepare a completed form and fill in

missing information as you copy the form. Have classmates witness the document. Key or write the word, *SAMPLE*, at the top of the document.

APPLYING THE LAW . . . YOU BE THE JUDGE

1. Evan Smith experienced a heart attack in the emergency room of Baptist Memorial Hospital after being given a dose of penicillin for a sore throat. Smith sued the attending physician as well as the hospital. The hospital called itself a full-service hospital with emergency room facilities. Baptist Memorial considered the doctors to be independent contractors and not agents. For example for tax and accounting purposes, the doctors were not treated as employees of the hospital. Based on this information, discuss whether the doctors who treated patients in the emergency room were agents of the hospital. [*Smith v. Baptist Memorial Hospital System*, 720 S.W.2d 618 (Tex.App.—San Antonio 1986)]

2. Ralls was employed by the Arkansas State Highway Department. While he was working on a state highway, he negligently backed a state truck onto the highway. This caused an accident with a car driven

by Mittlesteadt, for which Mittlesteadt sued Ralls. Ralls raised the defense that he was not liable for his negligence because as an employee, he was acting on behalf of the state. What will the court decide? [*Ralls v. Mittlesteadt*, 268 Ark. 471, 596 S.W.2d 349 (1980)]

3. Sam Kademenos was about to sell a $1 million life insurance policy to a prospective customer when he resigned from this position with Equitable Life Assurance Society. Before resigning the company, he had expended substantial amounts of company money and had utilized Equitable's medical examiners to procure the $1 million sale. After resigning, Kademenos joined a competing insurance firm, Jefferson Life Insurance Co., and made the sale through it. Has he breached any duty to Equitable? [*Kademenos v. Equitable Life Assurance Society*, 513 F.2d 1073 (3d Cir. 1975)]

LEGAL BACKGROUND

The common law favored the position of management over workers. Employers discouraged employees' collective activities to improve conditions, but as labor gained political influence, legislators responded with minimum wage, maximum hour, and child labor laws. In the 1930s, Congress enacted a series of labor laws, which were designed to achieve some measure of equality between labor and management. In recent years, the issues of at-will employment and employee privacy have arisen. At-will employment involves the right of an employer to fire for any reason any employee without a long-term contract. New legal doctrines have begun and are developing that affect this long-held doctrine. Modern technology and social problems have combined to provide the reason and the means to monitor employee performance in ways that were only dreamed of by George Orwell. This chapter introduces these timely topics.

498

Prereading Activity

Have students watch a movie about labor unions. Commercially produced movies such as *Newsies* can be rented from video stores. Many documentaries are available for rental from school and college libraries. Discuss the reasons labor laws have been created.

Mastery Objectives

By the end of this chapter, students will be able to:
- List legislation pertaining to unions
- Describe legislation pertaining to employee rights
- Interpret the employment-at-will doctrine
- Evaluate privacy rights of employees

Chapter

21

Labor Law

Activity Sheets
Reviewing Legal Concepts 21 *TRB*
Enrichment Activity 21 *TRB*

Student Activity Workbook
Chapter 21 Activities

Tests
Chapter 21 Test *TRB*
Chapter 21 WESTEST Computerized Testing

Handbook of Selected Court Cases
Kenrich Petrochemicals Inc. v. *National Labor Relations Board*
O'Neill v. *Daniels*

West's Business Law and Legal Environment Videodisc
Still Frames and Motion Segments as shown

Discussion Starter

Stimulate a class discussion on labor laws. Ask the students what labor laws they are familiar with. What labor laws affect them?

 LEGAL BACKGROUND

Samuel Gompers, whose quote opens this chapter, founded the American Federation of Labor (AFL) in 1881, and by the 1890s, the AFL was the most important labor group in the country. Except for one year, Gompers, who was the guiding spirit of the union, served as president from its inception to his death in 1924. Gompers's tenure as leader of the AFL was marked by his pragmatic approach to labor's needs.

"I have my own philosophy and my own dreams," Gompers once said, "but first and foremost I want to increase the working man's welfare year by year."

Labor Law   499

Show me the country in which there are no strikes, and I'll show you the country in which there is no liberty.
Samuel Gompers, 1850–1924
American labor leader

Federal and state law do not allow the employment relationship to be defined solely by the employer and the employee. All American companies, from Rivercity Roller-Skate Rentals to General Motors, must pay close attention to laws regulating employment and labor relations in order to operate lawfully in the United States.

Until the early 1930s, federal and state law favored the interests of business owners over the interests of labor. Activities in which people banded together to work for change—unions are a prime example—were discouraged, sometimes forcibly, by employers. The employee usually had little or no bargaining power compared to the employer. And the law did little to interfere. In fact, legal rules often favored companies' intolerance of union activities.

Beginning in 1932, several federal laws were passed that changed employment law in the United States and expanded an employee's right to join unions. The heart of labor law is the right to organize unions and to bargain with management for improved working conditions, salaries, and benefits. The ultimate weapon of labor unions is the **strike**. A strike is the refusal by a group of workers to work for their employer. The strike's purpose is usually to gain some improvement in working conditions or benefits. The opening quotation from labor leader Samuel Gompers implies that without the right to strike, there is no liberty.

◆ UNIONS AND COLLECTIVE BARGAINING

Most early labor legislation focused on the right of workers to join unions and to engage in bargaining. These laws encouraged **collective bargaining**. Collective bargaining is the right given to a union to bargain with the employer over terms of employment, including wages, security, and benefits, covering all members of the worker group. Once a union is recognized as the bargaining agent for a group of workers, the union has the exclusive authority to bargain for all members of the group. An individual worker is no longer free to bargain with the company himself or herself after a union is recognized. Once a union is selected, it has not only the right but also the duty to bargain for all members of the group. It cannot refuse to represent a worker in the group even if the worker is not a member of the union. The specific federal laws that provide for recognition of unions and regulation of the relationship between management and unions are discussed in the subsections that follow.

◆ **strike** A refusal by a group of workers to work for their employer. Often the purpose of a strike is to force the employer to make improvements in salary, working conditions, or benefits.

◆ **collective bargaining** Bargaining between an employer and a union over wages and other terms of employment. When a union is duly elected by the employees, the employer must bargain with the union, and the union must represent all workers in the bargaining unit.

Discussion Starter

Ask the students to recall and discuss recent strikes and cases of picketing in or near their community. Who was on strike? What was the purpose of the strike? What effects did it appear to have? What other issues, if any, did the strike and any picketing involved in the strike raise? How were those issues resolved?

499

Have a student look up the Norris-LaGuardia Act of 1932. The student should research the following questions regarding the act: For whom was the Norris-LaGuardia Act of 1932 named? How was the Norris-LaGuardia Act of 1932 received by workers and by employers/management? Ask the student to present his or her findings to the class in the form of an oral report. Encourage the student to incorporate visual aids, such as relevant political cartoons, into his or her presentation.

Enrichment

Show a videotape in class on the organization and history of labor unions in the United States. Check your local library for free video rentals.

Teaching with the Videodisc

The still frames listed below from the **West's Business Law and Legal Environment Videodisc** can be used with this chapter. To access this material, use the bar codes or the frame numbers included in the Videodisc Instructor's Manual found in the *TRB*.

Evolution of Federal Labor Law
Unfair Labor Practices of Employers
Unfair Labor Practices of Unions

Divide the class into small groups. Have the students in each group work together to create a poster describing the unfair labor practices defined in the National Labor Relations Act of 1935, and the unfair practices defined in the Labor-Management Relations Act of 1947 (also called the Taft-Hartley Act). Students should then use their posters as visual aids in oral reports describing both the National Labor Relations Act of 1935 and the Labor-Management Relations Act of 1947. The reports should focus on how the Labor-Management Relations Act of 1947 built upon the foundation established by the National Labor Relations Act of 1935.

NORRIS-LAGUARDIA ACT OF 1932

◆ **injunction** An equitable remedy by which a court orders one party to refrain from certain conduct.

Congress provided protection for peaceful strikes, picketing, and boycotts by labor in 1932 with the Norris-LaGuardia Act. The act restricted the power of the federal courts to issue *injunctions* against unions engaged in peaceful strikes. Remember that an injunction is an order by a court not to do something. Before the Norris-LaGuardia Act, the typical labor-related injunction forbade a labor union strike. If someone violated an injunction, he or she could be charged with contempt of court, and that could lead to imprisonment. Thus, before the Norris-LaGuardia Act, injunctions had been used effectively by management to stop strikes. In effect, the Norris–LaGuardia Act declared a national policy permitting employees to organize into unions.

NATIONAL LABOR RELATIONS ACT OF 1935

The National Labor Relations Act of 1935 (called the Wagner Act) specially authorized the right of employees to engage in collective bargaining and to strike. The act created the National Labor Relations Board (NLRB), giving it the power to oversee elections held to determine whether employees wish to be represented by a labor union.

The NLRB was also given the power to prevent employers from engaging in specified unfair and illegal activities directed toward the union. These practices are referred to as unfair labor practices, and include:

1. Interference with the efforts of employees to form, join, or assist labor organizations or to engage in activities for their mutual aid or protection.
2. An employer's domination of a labor organization or contribution of financial or other support to it.
3. Discrimination in the hiring or retention of employees because of union membership.
4. Discrimination against employees for filing charges under the Wagner Act or giving testimony under the Wagner Act.
5. Refusal to bargain in good faith with the duly designated representative of the employees.

The NLRB has broad investigatory powers. It can issue and serve complaints against employers in response to employee charges of unfair labor practices. The board can also order an employer to cease and desist—that is, stop immediately—its activities when violations are found.

LABOR-MANAGEMENT RELATIONS ACT OF 1947

The Labor-Management Relations Act (also called the Taft-Hartley Act) of 1947 was passed to amend the Wagner Act. The act stated that certain practices by unions were also unfair labor practices. Among the acts that are unfair if committed by labor are the following:

1. Refusing to bargain with management in good faith.
2. Requiring members to pay excessive membership fees.

State Law

Both union shops and closed shops are illegal in right-to-work states. The following states are right-to-work states: Alabama, Arizona, Arkansas, Florida, Georgia, Idaho, Iowa, Kansas, Louisiana, Mississippi, Nebraska, Nevada, North Carolina, North Dakota, South Carolina, South Dakota, Tennessee, Texas, Utah, Virginia, and Wyoming.

3. Forcing employers to pay for work that was not performed.
4. Coercing employees to vote to be represented by a union.
5. Participating in **secondary boycotts**. A secondary boycott involves pressuring one company not to continue to do business with a second company, who is the employer with whom the union has the dispute. The goal is to cut off the second company's suppliers and customers.

Among other important parts of the act are the following:

1. The act included a *free-speech* provision that allows employers to propagandize (give one-sided favorable information) against unions before any National Labor Relations Board election.
2. The **closed shop** was made illegal. A closed shop is a company that makes all employees join a union before they can be hired. A company would not normally want this kind of arrangement. A strong employees' union, however, could bargain for this condition of employment in the union contract. The Taft-Hartley Act does allow a **union shop**. A union shop is one that requires all workers to join the union after a short time on the job. It does not require membership before employment.
3. The act allowed individual states to ban the union shop by passing **right-to-work laws**. A right-to-work law makes it illegal for union membership to be required for *continued* employment in any business. Thus, both union shops and closed shops are illegal in right-to-work states.[1]
4. The act provided for an eighty-day cooling-off period. The president of the United States is authorized to get a court injunction to stop a strike if the strike would create a national emergency. Such an injunction can last for up to eighty days. Presidents have not used this power very often.

LABOR-MANAGEMENT REPORTING AND DISCLOSURE ACT OF 1959

The Labor-Management Reporting and Disclosure Act (the Landrum-Griffin Act) regulates internal union activities. The act created an employee bill of rights. It also included reporting requirements for internal union business procedures and activities.

◆ secondary boycott
A situation in which other companies' employees refuse to deal with another company in order to get that company to stop doing business with the employer with whom the union has a dispute.

◆ closed shop
A company where employees must belong to a union before they can be hired. Made illegal by the Taft-Hartley Act.

◆ union shop
A company where employees are required to join a union after a short time on the job. Still a legal form of union security.

◆ right-to-work law
A state law that provides that an employee cannot be required to join a union to get or keep a job.

LEGAL FOCUS - EXAMPLE

Union elections are regulated by the Landrum-Griffin Act. The unions must schedule elections of officers at regular intervals, and the elections must use secret ballots. Ex-convicts and Communists cannot hold union office. Union officials are accountable for the use of union

---

1. Right-to-work states are Alabama, Arizona, Arkansas, Florida, Georgia, Idaho, Iowa, Kansas, Louisiana, Mississippi, Nebraska, Nevada, North Carolina, North Dakota, South Carolina, South Dakota, Tennessee, Texas, Utah, Virginia, and Wyoming.

Multicultural Perspectives

Since the early 1960s, Cesar Chavez has led the struggle for better conditions for migrant farm workers. In 1962 he organized farm workers into the organization called the United Farm Workers and started a five-year strike against California grape growers to force them to recognize the union. The UFW organized a nationwide boycott of table grapes. Sympathetic priests, civic groups, and students aided in Chavez's efforts. In 1965 he launched a strike that led to a nationwide boycott of produce not bearing the label of the United Farm Workers. In 1970 the strikers finally won, and the strike ended in a pact with the growers. By 1975, Chavez and the strikers had convinced the California legislature to pass a bill that gave farm workers the same rights held by union members elsewhere.

Legal Focus Example

Have a student volunteer read aloud to the class this legal rule. Remind students that they can use the Legal Focus features as review tools when studying for tests.

Ethical Concern

Ask the students if they think all workers should be allowed the right to strike. What about public employees, including teachers, and public safety employees such as fire fighters and police officers? Should they be allowed to strike? Why or why not? Note that during this discussion you may wish to discuss your own opinions regarding a teacher's right to strike.

502

Prior to the federal labor statutes, workers were often jailed for participating in what are today lawful strikes.

property and union money. Members have the right to attend and to participate in union meetings, to nominate officers, and to vote in most union proceedings.

◆ **hot-cargo contracts** An agreement in which an employer agrees with a union not to handle, use, or deal with the goods of other employers who do not use union workers. Outlawed by the Landrum-Griffin Act.

The Landrum-Griffin Act also outlawed **hot-cargo contracts** or agreements. A hot-cargo agreement existed when an employer agreed with a union not to handle, use, or deal with the goods of other employers who did not use union workers.

◆ LEGAL FOCUS – EXAMPLE

It shall be [an] unfair labor practice for any labor organization and any employer to enter into any contract or any agreement . . . whereby such employer . . . agrees to refrain from handling, using, selling, transporting or otherwise dealing in any of the products of any other employer, or to cease doing business with any other person.

◆ EMPLOYMENT AT WILL

The labor movement in the United States began and continues to exist for many reasons. Many nonunion people assume that higher wages and better benefits are the sole purpose of the union. While money is important, unions also provide an independent voice for the worker on important job-related issues. Job security is one of these important issues.

Historically in the United States, employment contracts have been *at will*. Under the **employment-at-will doctrine**, either party may terminate the employment contract at any time for any reason. Under the traditional at-will contract, an employer could fire a worker for a good, bad, or no reason.

In the last fifty years, major changes have occurred in the employment-at-will doctrine. Among the changes are those discussed in the subsections that follow: union contracts, federal and state statutes, public policy, implied contracts, and tort claims. Of course, contracts for a specified term (for example, five years) have always been an exception to the at-will doctrine. Specified-term contracts in business usually exist only for top leadership, such as corporate presidents. The at-will doctrine is still an important part of employment law. However, as the following subsections show, the firing of most employees can no longer be for just any reason.

◆ **employment-at-will doctrine**   A doctrine by which historically an employer was free to fire an employee at any time without notice. Today, the right to fire is subject to several federal and state restrictions.

UNION CONTRACTS

Most unions have successfully bargained for **just-cause** provisions in employment contracts. A just-cause clause in a contract means that the employer must have a legitimate provable reason to fire any employee. The just-cause provision thus limits the employer's ability to fire at will. Fired union employees often have a right to an independent arbitration that examines the employer's reason for the firing. The nature of arbitration is discussed in detail in the Legal Perspective in Chapter 5. The arbitrator hears evidence from the employer, the worker, and the union. The arbitrator then decides whether the firing was legitimate. All parties are then bound by the arbitrator's decision.

◆ **just cause**   A requirement that an employer have a legitimate provable reason before terminating an employee.

FEDERAL AND STATE STATUTES

Several federal statutes restrict an employer's ability to fire at will. Title VII of the Civil Rights Act of 1964, for example, prohibits discrimination on the basis of race, color, national origin, religion, and sex. An employee fired for discriminatory reasons has legal rights against the employer. Other federal statutes protect against discrimination on the basis of age, disability, or pregnancy. These statutes are discussed in more detail in Chapter 22.

Ask a student volunteer to read aloud to the class the Legal Focus Example found here. Remind students that they can use the Legal Focus features as review tools when studying for tests.

Checking Your Progress (Answers)

1. The Wagner Act benefits employees by authorizing their right to engage in collective bargaining and to strike. It also defines several employer practices as unfair to labor.
2. The National Labor Relations Board has the authority to oversee elections in which employees vote for or against the labor union representation. It also has the power to prevent employers from engaging in specified unfair and illegal activities directed toward the union. It can issue and serve complaints of unfair labor practices by employees against employers and order the employers to cease and desist when violations are found.
3. Unfair acts of labor, under the Taft-Hartley Act, include: (1) refusal to bargain with management in good faith, (2) requiring members to pay excessive membership fees, (3) forcing employers to pay for work that was not performed, (4) coercing employees to vote to be represented by a union, and (5) participating in secondary boycotts.
4. A *just-cause* clause in an employment contract limits the employer's ability to fire an employee at will.

Allow a student volunteer or group of volunteers to research the use of National Guard troops in the 1991 Persian Gulf War. Encourage students to look at articles that appeared in news magazines such as *Time* and *Newsweek* for anecdotal evidence regarding how active National Guard service affected the lives of the men and women of the National Guard. Allow the students to share their findings with the class in the form of oral reports.

There are also some state statutes that prohibit discrimination and that may provide additional remedies for employees. Sometimes these laws prohibit other types of discrimination, such as discrimination based on sexual preference, or they prohibit firings because employees are requested or required to perform public responsibilities.

◀ LEGAL FOCUS – EXAMPLE

Many states have laws that forbid an employer from firing an employee for participation in certain specified public activities. For example, an employer cannot fire an employee because he or she is called for jury service or grand jury service, is called as a witness at a court or legislative proceeding, or misses work due to participation in the National Guard.

Over half of the 15 million county, state, and federal public workers are protected by civil service statutes. Civil service statutes require just cause before an employee is fired, even though no union may be involved. Your classroom teacher, for example, probably has tenure, which is a form of just-cause protection.

◆ CHECKING YOUR PROGRESS

1. Does the Wagner Act benefit employers or employees? How?
2. Describe the authority of the National Labor Relations Board.
3. List five activities that the Taft-Hartley Act established as unfair if done by labor.
4. What is the effect of a *just-cause* clause in an employment contract?

PUBLIC POLICY

Sometimes the firing of an employee violates a clear public policy. The law of many states will not allow an employee to be fired because he or she performed an act encouraged by public need. An employee should also not be fired because he or she refused to perform an illegal or wrongful act. For example, employees who refuse to lie in court about their company practices and who are then fired have successfully challenged the firing.

What public policies are significant enough to warrant protection by the courts? This is a difficult question. The courts answer the question on a case-by-case basis. Employees fired because they file a workers' compensation claim have been protected. In states that lack specific laws protecting

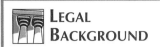

LEGAL BACKGROUND

Whistle blowers who sue their employers for wrongful discharge can also pose problems for courts. If there is no contract or statute covering the discharge, the case is subject to the common law employment-at-will doctrine. Courts decide, case by case, what policies are significant enough to warrant protection under the doctrine's public policy exception. In one case, in which an employee was discharged after expressing to his superiors his fears about the dangers of a new company product, the court held that the discharge was not a violation of public policy and that the employer had reasonable cause—the need to preserve administrative order—to discharge the employee.

 ## Law in Action

LAW AND THE BUSINESSPERSON: WHISTLEBLOWING AND PUBLIC POLICY

Employees are faced with a major dilemma when forced to choose between ignoring unethical, unsafe, or illegal activities in their workplace or "blowing the whistle" on their employer. If they do what the company asks, they may violate their own ethical standards or even the law. If the employee refuses to do what the company says or blows the whistle, the company may discipline or even fire the employee.

An employee who belongs to a labor union is likely to have clear rights. Most labor-management contracts contain just-cause clauses. These provisions give the employee some protection. If the employee is not a member of a union, her or his rights will probably be based on state public policy exceptions to the employer's right to fire at will.

In West Virginia, a bank was found to have fired an employee wrongfully who pressured the bank to comply with state and federal consumer credit laws.[2] In another case, a probationary police officer, who had only worked for the Globe, Arizona, police department for two months, was fired for seeking to prevent an injustice. The officer had discovered that a man had been arrested

for vagrancy under a local law that had been repealed. The man was sentenced to ten days in prison. Not only was he sentenced under a nonexistent law but he still remained in jail after twenty-one days. The police officer told a judicial officer of the situation, pointing out that the detention was illegal. The judicial officer informed the police chief. The chief fired the officer, saying, "he did not appreciate 'big-city cops' coming to Globe to tell him how to run his department." The officer sued the city for wrongful discharge.

The court held that the firing violated public policy, stating, "Whistleblowing activity that serves a public purpose should be protected. So long as employees' actions are not merely private or proprietary, but instead seek to further the public good, the decision to expose illegal or unsafe practices should be encouraged. . . . There is no public policy more important or fundamental than the one favoring the effective protection of the lives, liberty, and property of the people. The officer's successful attempt to free the arrestee from illegal confinement was a refreshing and laudable exercise that should be protected, not punished."[3]

2. *Harless v. First National Bank in Fairmont*, 162 W.Va. 116, 246 S.E.2d 270 (1978).

3. *Wagner v. City of Globe*, 150 Ariz. 82, 722 P.2d 250 (1986).

workers who serve on juries, courts have found such a firing to be a violation of public policy.

Perhaps the most interesting application of the public policy exception is the protection of workers who act as **whistleblowers**. A whistleblower is someone who tells the public about illegal or other wrongful activities in his or her organization. A discussion of whistleblowing is included in the above Law in Action feature.

♦ **whistleblower**
An employee who tells the public about illegal or other wrongful activities in his or her organization.

Have a student volunteer to read aloud to the class the Legal Focus Example found here. Point out to the students that the employer's handbook or bulletin acts as an implied contract regardless of whether the employee has taken the time to read it. Therefore, it is wise for anyone who is working to take the time to read any and all employer's handbooks and bulletins.

Ask volunteers to visit local businesses to ask if they have company handbooks in which the procedures for firing employees are described. Ask them to read the policies to the class and report their findings.

Read to the class the Legal Focus Problem found here. Allow student volunteers to suggest possible answers to the question posed at the end of this problem. As a followup, you might ask the students whether or not they felt the manager of the restaurant had acted ethically in his attempts to identify the thief.

---

506   Agency and Employee Law

IMPLIED CONTRACTS

A few courts have found that an implied contract may exist to protect employees from arbitrary firing. The court may find that the acts of the employer and employee have created the contract. An employee fired in breach of these implied terms can sue for breach of contract.

 LEGAL FOCUS – EXAMPLE

> An employer's handbook or personnel bulletin may state that as a matter of standard practice, workers will only be dismissed for good cause. If the employee is aware of this policy and works for the company relying on it, an implied contract may exist. The handbook or bulletin supplies the terms.

Oral statements, job evaluations, and other acts may also lead to an implied contract. This theory is most likely to be successful in cases involving long-term employees where the work relationship has existed for ten, fifteen, or even twenty years.

TORT CLAIMS

In a few unusual cases, employers who have fired an employee have been found to have committed a tort. If the firing is done in an abusive manner, the employer's act might be found to be either the tort of intentional infliction of emotional distress or the tort of defamation.

 LEGAL FOCUS – CASE PROBLEM

> A restaurant had suffered a theft of supplies. The manager gathered the employees together at a special meeting. At the meeting, he announced that he would start firing waitresses alphabetically until the thief was identified. The first waitress, Agis, was fired. She sued the restaurant, claiming she suffered emotional distress as a result of her firing. Do these facts support a tort claim?

The highest court of Massachusetts said the manager's acts were actionable as the tort of intentional infliction of emotional distress.[4]

4. *Agis v. Howard Johnson Co.*, 371 Mass. 140, 355 N.E.2d 315 (1976).

LEGAL BACKGROUND

The Privacy Act of 1974 was enacted after Congress specifically found that (1) the collection and use of personal information by federal agencies infringes on privacy; (2) the increasing use of computers and sophisticated technology enhances the possibility of harm to individual privacy; (3) the misuse of information can threaten employment, insurance, and credit opportunities; and (4) the right to privacy is a personal and fundamental right protected by the Constitution even though it is not expressly mentioned in the Constitution.

◆ PRIVACY RIGHTS OF EMPLOYEES

Sometimes new concerns arise after new technology develops. New technology can alter old habits and customs within a short time. For example, the addition of computers into our lives has aided business but has also created legal and ethical trade-offs. Many people find the trade-offs disturbing, particularly in relation to privacy rights.

Computers make it possible to accumulate, store, and retrieve vast amounts of information. Virtually all private institutions with which we deal, including insurance companies, mail-order houses, banks, and credit-card companies, gather information about us. They store that information in their computer files. Government agencies, like the U.S. Census Bureau, the Social Security Administration, and the Internal Revenue Service, also collect and store data.

These businesses and agencies collect information on income, expenses, marital status, and other aspects of personal history and habits. Frequently, this personal information finds its way to potential or present employers. We often do not give permission for—or even know about—the use of this information.

In recent years, the right to privacy has become a significant employment issue. Employers today must be careful to ensure that they do not abuse their employees' rights to privacy and personal security. Among these employee concerns are drug testing, the use of lie-detector tests, and electronic monitoring of employees.

THE RIGHT TO PRIVACY

The United States Supreme Court has recognized that each person has a general right to privacy under the U.S. Constitution. The court has found that this right deserves protection against government intrusion. As discussed in Chapter 5, an individual's right to privacy is also protected under the common law.

Congress has passed several laws to control the collection and circulation of information contained in computer files. The Privacy Act of 1974 may be the most important privacy law. It has been a model for many of the state laws regulating government records and recording practices. Privacy legislation regulates access to and the use of personal information kept in computer files. However, much of the use of such information is still unprotected by law.

DRUG TESTING IN THE WORKPLACE

Drug and alcohol abuse has been estimated to cost industry between $50 and $100 billion in absenteeism, impaired performance, and accidents each year. Employers are concerned about a decline in job performance and other harm resulting from the use of drugs. Some employers test employ-

Extension Activity

Discuss drug-testing policies of companies where students are employed. Have students research policies of large corporations and small businesses in your city. In a class discussion, compare the policies of large and small businesses.

Legal Focus
Case Problem

Divide the class into small groups to read and discuss this Legal Focus Problem. Each group should choose a leader to explain its response to the question posed at the end of this problem. Additionally, ask the groups to discuss whether they believe that drug testing of all employees, whether the employees are suspected of drug use or not, is ethical.

State Law

Have a group of volunteers research your state laws to determine what the law in your state says about permitting lie detector or drug testing of job applicants. Have the students report their findings to the class in the form of either a poster or an oral report.

508

Ethical Concern

Discuss the ethical implications of drug testing as a condition of employment. Ask students to write one or two paragraphs giving their opinions as to whether drug testing should be allowed before an employee is hired. Ask them to write additional paragraphs telling whether they think drug testing should be allowed during the course of employment.

Caption Answer

Most experts doubt the accuracy of polygraph test results.

ees to uncover drug use. Sometimes the tests are unreliable. Even when tests are accurate, a question exists: do drug tests violate the employee's right to privacy?

If the employer is a government agency, then testing is subject to the requirements of the U.S. Constitution. An employee has a Fourth Amendment right to be "secure in their persons . . . against unreasonable searches and seizures." The administration of drug tests is constitutional if there is a reasonable basis for suspecting the employee's use of drugs. Testing is also permitted when drug use in a particular government job could threaten public safety.

◆ LEGAL FOCUS – CASE PROBLEM

The Department of Transportation required employees working on oil and gas pipelines to submit to random drug testing. All employees were subject to the rule whether they were suspected of drug use or not. Does the drug-testing rule of the Department of Transportation violate the employees' constitutional rights?

In this case, the government's interest in promoting public safety was held to outweigh the employees' privacy interest.[5] To date, court decisions are often in conflict over whether and when drug testing is a violation of the employees' privacy rights.

Constitutional limitations do not usually restrict private employers from testing their employees for drugs. However, some state constitutions and statutes do restrict and regulate private drug testing. Also, some collective bargaining agreements regulate drug testing, stating when and how it is or is not permitted.

LIE-DETECTOR TESTS

At one time, many employers made employees or job applicants take lie-detector tests (called *polygraphs*). The purpose of the testing was to determine if an employee was answering honestly the questions asked by the employer. Many employees considered this test to be an invasion of their right to privacy and their privilege against self-incrimination. Other critics believe a lie-detector test creates a dangerous fantasy. Everyone wishes that a simple test existed to tell us when someone lies. However, most experts doubt the accuracy of the polygraph test results.

In 1988, Congress passed the Employee Polygraph Protection Act, which severely restricts the use of polygraphs. This act prohibits certain employers from (1) requiring, suggesting, requesting, or causing employees or job applicants to take lie-detector tests; (2) using, accepting, referring to, or asking about the results of lie-detector tests taken by employees or

Is the lie detector test considered to be accurate by all experts?

5. *Electrical Workers Local 1245 v. Skinner*, 913 F.2d 1454 (9th Cir. 1990).

applicants; and (3) taking or threatening negative employment-related action against employees or applicants based on results of lie-detector tests or because they refused to take the tests.

Some employers are excepted from these prohibitions against polygraph use. They include federal, state, and local government employers, certain security service firms, and companies manufacturing and distributing controlled substances. Other employers may use polygraph tests when investigating losses due to theft, including embezzlement and stealing of trade secrets. In all cases where lie-detector tests are still permitted, however, strict procedural requirements are imposed on employers.

MONITORING JOB PERFORMANCE

Another workplace privacy issue involves the monitoring of employees' performance by employers. Today, some employers electronically monitor employees' use of computer terminals or company telephones. Some employers use video cameras to evaluate employees' performance.

Current federal law recognizes the right of employers to listen in on telephone conversations in order to monitor employees' performance, but state laws vary. An employer may often be able to avoid state laws by informing employees who are subject to monitoring that the company may be listening. In an area such as this, there is very little case law, and an employer may wish to consider carefully whether its need to monitor employees' performance outweighs the employees' right to privacy. If the company's monitoring is called into question, a court will balance the purposes of the monitoring against its effect on the employees' privacy. Other methods of accomplishing an employer's goals will be considered important when balancing the interests.

◆ CHECKING YOUR PROGRESS

1. What is a whistleblower? Are the actions of a whistleblower protected by law?
2. Describe how the firing of an employee could be a tort on the part of the employer.
3. How has the increase in the use of computers affected an individual's right to privacy under the U.S. Constitution?
4. Does the Employee Polygraph Protection Act prohibit employers from administering lie-detector tests? Explain.

1. A whistleblower is someone who tells the public about illegal or other wrongful activities in his or her organization. A person who blows the whistle may be protected by state public policy exceptions to the employer's right to fire at will.
2. An employer could be guilty of committing a tort as a result of firing an employee if the firing is done in an abusive manner and the actions are an intentional infliction of emotional distress or defamation.
3. As businesses and agencies use computers to collect more and more information about individuals, information about individuals becomes available to more people, with the opportunity for misuse of the information.
4. The Employee Polygraph Protection Act does not specifically prohibit lie-detector tests, but it does prohibit certain employers from (1) requiring, suggesting, requesting, or causing employees or job applicants to take lie-detector tests; (2) using, accepting, referring to, or asking about the results of the tests taken by employees or applicants; and (3) taking or threatening negative employment-related action against employees or applicants based on the results or because they refused to take the tests.

Teaching Note

This case is included in the *West's
Business and Personal Law Handbook of
Selected Court Cases*.

Read

Explain to the students that
in this *A Case In Point* feature they will get a view of
just how acrimonious
union/management relationships can sometimes be.
This *A Case In Point* feature
also looks at how the
National Labor Relations
Board must sometimes step
in to ensure that fair practices are adhered to. Then
have a student volunteer
read aloud to the class this
A Case In Point feature.

Discuss

How long had Helen
Chizmar worked as office
manager for Kenrich
Petrochemicals? Was
Chizmar eligible for union
membership? Why not?
What happened in May of
1987, and how was
Chizmar involved in this?
How did Salvatore Monte
react to the news that staff
members were unionizing?
What reasons did Monte
give for firing Chizmar?
What was the NLRB's deci-
sion in the Chizmar case?
What was the decision of
the United States Court of
Appeals? What reasons did
the court give for its decision?

◆ A CASE IN POINT ◆

**KENRICH
PETROCHEM-
ICALS, INC. v.
NATIONAL
LABOR
RELATIONS
BOARD**

United States Court of Appeals,
Third Circuit, 1990.
907 F.2d 400.

The tension in union–management relationships is illustrated in this case. It involves
a small family-owned business and another
family of long-time employees.

FACTS Salvatore Monte was the president of Kenrich Petrochemicals, Inc., a
family-owned business. Helen Chizmar had
been Kenrich's office manager for 24 years.
Office managers are considered to be part of
company management and are not eligible
for union membership. Among the clerical
staff Chizmar supervised were her sister,
daughter, and daughter-in-law. In May
1987, Chizmar's three relatives and other
clerical staff members designated the Oil,
Chemical, and Atomic Workers International Union as their union. Chizmar was
not involved. Monte found out that the office was unionizing. Angry at the news, he
told Chizmar that someone else could do
her job for "$20,000" less and fired her.
Later, he told another employee that one of
his reasons for firing Chizmar was that he
"was not going to put up with any union
[expletive]." A few days later, he told the
clerical workers that if they voted for the
union they would have to "start from
scratch. No benefits, no salary, no vacations." Still later, during negotiations with
the union, Monte said that he planned to
"get rid of the whole family." Chizmar's
family complained to the National Labor
Relations Board that Chizmar's firing was
an unfair labor practice. The NLRB agreed
and ordered that Chizmar be reinstated with
back pay. Kenrich appealed.

ISSUE Can the NLRB order the reinstatement of a supervisor (or manager) who
although not a member of the union, was
fired in retaliation for her relatives' participation in a union organizational campaign?

DECISION The court upheld the
NLRB reinstatement and back-pay order.

REASON The NLRB was given broad
power under the National Labor Relations
Act to accomplish the goals of the act. As a
supervisor, Helen Chizmar was not an employee protected by the act. However,
Kenrich's acts were in retaliation for the
union activities of Helen's relatives. Thus,
they were an attempt to intimidate and interfere with the employees' lawful right to
unionize. "In our opinion, the net effect of
this conduct was to cause nonsupervisory
employees reasonably to fear that the [com-
pany] would take similar action against
them if they continued to support the
union. . . . The reinstatement and back-pay
order is reasonably calculated to dispel the
intimidation caused by her firing."

In order to help students review what they have learned in Chapter 21, you might wish to:

1. Have a student volunteer, or volunteers, read aloud the Chapter Summary.
2. Allow the students to work with partners to complete the *Using Legal Language* activity.
3. Assign the *Checking for Comprehension* exercise as homework.

4. Allow the students to work in small groups to complete the *Applying Legal Concepts* activities.
5. As a class, complete the *Applying the Law* activities. (Please note that you may have to help students with vocabulary so that they adequately understand all of the *Applying the Law* material.)

In order to check student mastery of chapter concepts, you may wish to use the Chapter 21 test that is found in your *Teacher's Resource Binder* or use WESTEST computerized testing for Chapter 21.

Labor Law   511

CHAPTER 21 REVIEW

 ## SUMMARY

UNIONS AND COLLECTIVE BARGAINING

1. *Norris-LaGuardia Act* (1932)—Permitted employees to organize into unions and to engage in peaceful strikes.

2. *National Labor Relations Act* (Wagner Act) (1935)—Established the right of employees to engage in collective bargaining; created the National Labor Relations Board to oversee elections of unions and to prevent employers from engaging in unfair and illegal union-labor activities and unfair labor practices.

3. *Labor-Management Relations Act* (Taft-Hartley Act) (1947)—Amended the Wagner Act; allowed for protection of employers as well as of employees by providing a list of unfair labor activities that both unions and management were forbidden to practice. Prohibited closed shops, allowed states to pass right-to-work laws, and provided for an eighty-day cooling-off period.

4. *Labor-Management Reporting and Disclosure Act* (Landrum-Griffin Act) (1959)—Regulated internal union elections and procedures and established reporting requirements for union activities.

EMPLOYMENT AT WILL

This is a type of employment contract in which either party may terminate the employment relationship at any time for any reason. Historically, this was the most common type of employment relationship. In recent years, the law has limited the application of the doctrine in several ways.

1. *Union contracts*—Unions bargain for a just-cause clause in employment contracts to limit an employer's right to fire at will.

2. *Federal and state statutes*—Several federal and state statutes limit the right of employers to terminate an employee for certain "wrong reasons."

3. *Public policy*—If a firing violates a clear public policy, it is unlawful. Firing an employee for filing a workers' compensation claim is an example.

4. *Implied contracts*—An implied contract may be created that limits the company's right to discharge an employee.

5. *Tort claims*—If an employer's act of firing is outrageous, it may be an intentional tort, such as intentional infliction of emotional distress or defamation.

PRIVACY RIGHTS OF EMPLOYEES

1. *Drug testing*—Rights based on the U.S. Constitution limit drug testing of government employees. For testing to be permitted, the employer must have a reasonable basis for suspecting that a government employee is using drugs, or the employee must work in a particular government job where drug use could threaten public safety. Private employers are often free to test for drugs unless they are restricted by state law or union contracts.

2. *Lie-detector tests*—The Employee Polygraph Protection Act severely restricts the use of polygraphs. Government employers, certain security service firms, and companies manufacturing and distributing controlled substances can still usually use these tests.

3. *Monitoring job performance*—Electronic monitoring of employees is largely unregulated. Claims of invasion of privacy of the employee can be made by employees for the acts of employers that are intrusive and unjustified.

USING LEGAL LANGUAGE

Directions: Match each term with the statement that best defines that term.

1. closed shop
2. collective bargaining
3. employment-at-will
4. hot-cargo contract
5. injunction
6. just cause
7. right-to-work
8. secondary boycott
9. strike
10. union shop

A. a type of state law that provides that an employee cannot be required to join a union to get or keep a job

B. a refusal by a group of workers to work for their employer

C. a company where employees must belong to a union before they can be hired

D. an agreement where an employer agrees with a union to not handle, use, or deal with the non-union-produced goods of other employers

E. an equitable remedy by which a court orders one party to refrain from certain conduct

F. negotiations between an employer and a union over wages and other terms of employment

G. a requirement that an employer have a legitimate provable reason before terminating an employee

H. a doctrine where historically an employer was free to fire an employee at any time without notice

I. a company where employees are required to join a union after a short time on the job

J. employees refuse to deal with a company for whom they do not work to get that company to stop doing business with the employer with whom the union has a dispute

CHECKING FOR COMPREHENSION

1. Why was the Labor-Management Relations Act passed? What benefits did employers gain from its passage?

2. Describe some changes that have occurred over the past fifty years in the at-will employment doctrine.

3. Describe an example of an action of an employee that would be encouraged by public need. Can an employee be fired for such an act?

4. Can a company personnel handbook be considered a contract? Explain.

5. Although Congress has passed several laws to control the collection and circulation

1. Phipps did win the appeal. The court stated that the common law doctrine of employment at will is subject to public policy exceptions. It rejected Clark Oil's contention that adoption of the public policy exception to the employment-at-will doctrine should be left to the legislature and not to the courts. The at-will doctrine is a creation of common law, and the judiciary may properly limit a judi-cially created doctrine. The Clean Air Act prohibits employees from selling leaded gasoline for a vehicle that is labeled "unleaded gasoline only." This act expresses a mandate of legislatively recognized public policy. An employee who is discharged because he refuses to violate this act may sue for wrongful termination under the public policy exception to the at-will doctrine.

2. Yes. The court refused to enforce that portion of the NLRB's order prohibiting the showing of the film. The court described the film as depicting what happens to union members when dominated by ruthless and unthinking union officials. Although the film "illustrated the management's anti-union attitude more graphically than did its speeches and pamphlets," the film could not reasonably be interpreted as threatening retaliation or force. The court noted that "[n]owhere in the film does the employer or his representative appear or make any representation." The court concluded that an employer's mere expression of anti-union sentiment is "an exercise of free speech protected by at least Section 8 (c) [of the National Labor Relations Act] and most likely by the First Amendment.

of information contained in computer files, why is the Privacy Act of 1974 considered the most important privacy law?

6. Which level of government controls drug testing in the workplace?

7. Describe current federal laws that give employers the right to electronically monitor employee's work performance.

8. Michael claims that he was discharged by his employer, Charity Clinic because he refused to throw away loose needles and blood samples in the local trash collection bins. Other employees had been routinely discarding all used medical supplies, including needles and blood samples, in the city trash. State law regulates the disposal of such waste and has very strict guidelines as to how it should be wrapped and prohibits disposal by public collection processes. Should Michael have obeyed his employer? Did the employer have a right to fire Michael for refusing to obey orders? Should Michael tell authorities? If he tells authorities, can the company punish him if he is rehired? Discuss.

APPLYING LEGAL CONCEPTS

1. Create a table listing the Federal Acts described in the chapter. Include the date, the title, and a brief description.

2. Create a database for the information described in activity 1. Print a hard copy. Save the database file to add additional Acts as you read about and discuss them in class.

APPLYING THE LAW . . . YOU BE THE JUDGE

1. Mark Phipps was employed at a Clark gas station. A customer asked Phipps to pump leaded gasoline into her 1976 Chevrolet (an automobile equipped to receive only unleaded gas). The station manager told Phipps to comply with the request, but he refused, believing that it was against the law to put leaded gas into an unleaded tank. Phipps stated that he was willing to pump unleaded gas into the tank, but the manager immediately fired him. Phipps sued Clark for wrongful termination. The trial court decided for Clark, stating the Minnesota law allowed Phipps, an employee at will, to be terminated for any reason or for no reason. Phipps appealed. Will he win the appeal? Explain. [*Phipps v. Clark Oil & Refining Corp.*, (Minn.App.) 396 N.W.2d 588 (1986)]

2. The management of Luxuray of New York's production facility in Fort Plain, New York, was trying to discourage employees who were attempting to form a union. To this end, the management sponsored various employee meetings. At one of these meetings the employees were shown a film that portrayed unions in a very unfavorable light. Employees in favor of the union filed a complaint with the National Labor Relations Board (NLRB), which, after finding that Luxuray had engaged in unfair labor practices, one of which was the showing of the film, ordered Luxuray to cease such practices. Luxuray appealed the NLRB's decision, claiming that its showing of the film was protected under the First Amendment right to freedom of speech. Did prohibiting the film's showing violate the employer's First Amendment rights? [*Luxuray of New York v. National Labor Relations Board*, 447 F.2d 112 (2d Cir. 1971)]

Critical Thinking Activity

Have the students write one paragraph stating their position on the following topic: The role of the referee in sports compared with the role of a judge in our legal system. Have students exchange their papers with partners to proofread each other's work. Then allow student volunteers to share their work with the class.

LEGAL BACKGROUND

This LP allows a discussion of contracts, torts, agency, and labor law in a broad topic of interest to students—sports. Actually, the discussion of the difference between rules and laws, and attitudes about rules may be the most interesting part of this chapter. What separates a rule from a law? The answer is, of course, who creates it and how it can be enforced—but it is an interesting discussion.

514

LEGAL PERSPECTIVE

LAW AND SPORTS

If people don't want to come out to the park, nobody's going to stop 'em.

Yogi Berra, 1925–
Hall of Fame baseball catcher for the New York Yankees

No one can quite turn a phrase like Yogi Berra, the Hall of Fame catcher for the New York Yankees. Yogi also gave us the saying, "It ain't over till it's over." Where do you find a colorful character like Yogi Berra? The obvious answer is in sports.

Most of us begin our association with sports while very young. Sports are a way for young people to have fun and learn social skills. Many lessons in life are learned from sports participation, including the relationship among effort, dedication, and performance. We learn the benefits and difficulty of working with others in team sports. Because there are winners and losers, we may learn how to win and to lose gracefully.

In any social activity that involves a large number of people, it is inevitable that legal issues will arise. In professional sports, the elements of glamour and money also exist, so legal problems are sure to follow. The sports issues discussed in this Legal Perspective are game rules, eligibility, recruitment, contracts, collective bargaining, torts, behavior of players, and equal opportunity.

◆ GAME RULES

Every sport has its game rules, whether the sport is horseshoes, basketball, darts, or football. The rules of the game are not the same as laws. Game rules are not enforced by the courts. Instead, they are enforced by

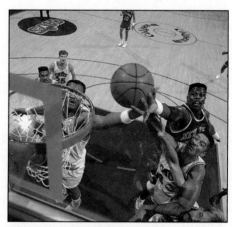

Add money to excitement and glamour and legal issues are sure to follow.

referees and umpires, and their decisions are not reviewed by courts.

In most sports activities, the referee acts as an impartial judge and jury for the game. Some sports allow for an appeal of a referee's decision, but it is rare that a referee's decision is reversed. Professional football, until recently, allowed instant-replay referees to overrule the on-field referee. The appeal took place while the game was in progress. In many sports, the performance of referees is reviewed after the game. Any errors that are identified may lead to the disciplining and even the firing of a referee, but very seldom is the result of the game changed.

Game rules are treated differently in different sports. Strictly following the rules is critical in one sport, while in another bending or using the rules is considered part of the game. Getting a jump on the gun in a track race leads to disqualification; if it is in-

Extension Activity

You might wish to ask a coach from one of your high school's athletic teams to speak to the class regarding eligibility rules. Ask the coach to describe the eligibility rules, the most common types of infractions, the penalties for the infractions, and any appeals process that is in place.

Discussion Starter

Stimulate a class discussion regarding eligibility rules for high school athletics by asking the following questions: What is the purpose of eligibility rules? Do you feel these rules work? Are the rules stringent enough? What changes, if any, would you make in eligibility rules for your high school?

tentional, it is considered cheating. In golf, not keeping track of your golf strokes can also lead to disqualification in a tournament. In modern professional basketball, fouling another player, which is contrary to the rules, is often considered a strategy of the game. Basketball announcers speak in terms of how many fouls each team has "to give." Each sport not only has its own rules but also its own value system and customs. Some rules define the purpose of the game while others ensure players' safety.

HIGH SCHOOL ATHLETICS ELIGIBILITY RULES

State education boards and local school districts set requirements that students must meet before they can participate in high school athletics. Since these standards are set by each state, they vary substantially. In general, the standards require a certain level of academic performance, such as minimum grades and number of units carried, before a student can participate in high school sports. Eligibility rules often consider the following:

1. Current course load (number of courses in which a student is currently enrolled).
2. Prior course load (number of courses a student took in the last grading period).
3. Overall grade average (whether the student has a C or 70% average in all course work in high school).
4. Minimum grade expectations for every class (for example, no single grade lower than a D).
5. Appropriate attendance at school; excessive absence leads to ineligibility.
6. Residence in high school enrollment area.
7. Age (for example, if you reach age nineteen by a certain time, you may be considered too old for high school sports).
8. Passage of an appropriate physical examination.
9. Good citizenship.
10. Maintenance of amateur status (not accepting money or gifts in return for participation in sports activities).

Your physical education staff should be able to provide a copy of eligibility rules for high school athletics at your school.

COLLEGE RECRUITMENT

In amateur college sports, private regulatory bodies set rules for the sports and the participants. The best known of these bodies is the National Collegiate Athletic Association (NCAA). The NCAA is a voluntary association of more than 800 U.S. colleges and universities. The participating colleges agree to be bound by NCAA rules governing athletic activities.

Several of the NCAA rules relate to the recruitment of high school athletes for college sports. NCAA rules regulate when and how a high school student may be contacted by a college. Financial rewards or gifts are strictly forbidden, although travel expenses and meals to visit prospective colleges are allowed. NCAA rules also relate to the academic eligibility that enables a student to participate in college athletics. For example, the NCAA requires that new freshman athletes have both a certain grade-point average and certain scores on standardized examinations before they are eligible for a scholarship or to participate in college competition.

As the student text points out, players' unions exist in most professional sports to bargain with the league or with owners' groups. Like other unions, professional sports unions also resort to the strike. For example, near the end of the 1991–92 season, the National Hockey League Players Association staged a ten-day strike. This was the first strike in the league's 75-year history. The strike ended when an agreement was reached that, among other things, did the following:

- Extended the regular season from 80 to 84 games beginning with the 1992–93 season (owners and players were to share the revenues from those final two games on a partnership basis). The players' play-off fund was increased from $7.5 million to $9 million.
- Minimum player's salary was increased to $100,000.
- The agency was made less restrictive and owners increased their contributions to the Players' Association Pension Fund.

Collaborative Learning Activity

Divide the class into five small groups. Each group should be assigned one of the following topics to research: free agency, pension plans, minimum salary, salary arbitration, and drug testing. Each group should then research that topic across professional baseball, professional football, and professional basketball in this country. How is that issue dealt with for each sport? In the groups' opinions, which sport has dealt with the issue in the most appropriate way, etc.? Allow the groups to present their findings to the class in the form of oral reports. Encourage the groups to incorporate visual aids into their presentations.

LEGAL PERSPECTIVE (CONTINUED)

 SELECTED CONTRACT ISSUES IN SPORTS

Most professional sports leagues use a standard form for their contracts. This form has been created by the team owners and modified by the league and by collective bargaining agreements between the league and the players' union. Certain provisions of the contract are standard for every player. Other terms and conditions are left to be negotiated separately by the athlete and the team.

Among the standard clauses in a sports agreement is a provision in which the athlete allows the team to assign its interest in the athlete's services to another team; in other words, this agreement allows the player to be traded. Other terms that these contracts cover include:

1. The length of the contract.
2. Salary per year or season.
3. Personal conduct requirements.
4. Bonus for signing the contract.
5. Performance or recognition bonuses.
6. Guarantees.
7. Injury and health protection.
8. Other special benefits such as life insurance, special equipment, or travel rights.

 UNIONS IN PROFESSIONAL SPORTS

Players' unions exist in most professional sports to bargain with the league or with owners' groups. Before the formation of players' unions, each athlete used to bargain individually with his or her team. As a result, team owners became very wealthy, and athletes were usually poorly paid. The legendary baseball player Willie Mays, considered by some to be the best baseball player ever to play the game, was paid only $105,000 in 1963 at the height of his career. Although this was the highest salary paid an athlete in 1963, it is very little compared to the million-dollar contracts paid today to ordinary professional athletes.

Some of the important issues bargained for in sports contracts include:

1. Free agency—The right of a player to terminate his or her team relationship and bargain to play for other teams.
2. Pension plans—The playing careers of most professional players are short, and their business skills may be limited. Pension plans provide money for the future to help ensure financial security after their playing days are over.
3. Minimum salary—The top players can command good salaries, but new and fringe players often cannot. The union bargains for minimum salaries.
4. Salary arbitration—If the team and player are unable to agree on a salary amount, then the dispute can be submitted to a neutral arbitrator.
5. Drug testing—Most players submit to different forms of drug testing in order to protect the integrity of the sport. What happens to a player who is found to be using an illegal substance? The union contract will often decide such an issue.

AGENTS IN PROFESSIONAL SPORTS

Professional athletes can hire agents to represent them in contract negotiations with team owners. Most do. Like many other professionals, sports agents are largely unregulated. This means that anyone who

Critical Thinking Activity

Have students write a paragraph or two on the differences and similarities of agents in sports and agents in a business such as real estate.

Extension Activity

Have students research current newspapers and magazines to find articles on illegal activities involving sports. Instruct your students to clip the articles and read them. Then have them share their information with the class.

Extension Activity

Invite a local sportswriter to speak to your class regarding such issues as professional sports salaries. Encourage your speaker to discuss all the factors involved with why salaries are going up or down for particular sports. He or she should also discuss the impact of television and ad revenues on sporting events. Have the students prepare questions in advance for your speaker.

wants to be a sports agent can become one simply by declaring it to be so. This doesn't mean, however, that after the declaration the self-appointed agent will have any clients. A few states, such as California, require that a sports agent be licensed. It is expected that licensing will be required by more states in the future.

Many sports agents are attorneys. An important part of an agent's job is negotiating contracts for the athlete, so legal training as an attorney is helpful. Some agents assist an athlete in his or her investments and budgeting. Because of the large amount of money involved, competition to represent athletes and the potential to abuse the relationship are great. Honesty and competence are among the critical traits that an athlete should seek in an agent.

◆ SELECTED TORT ISSUES IN SPORTS

Until recent years, most injuries occurring in sports activities were seen as a natural consequence of the sport. In football alone, there are estimated to be more than 1 million injuries per year in the United States, including high schools, colleges, and professional games and practices.

What contact in sports is allowed and appropriate? The type of behavior that can lead to liability for injury is obviously an important issue. Whether a sports activity is organized or casual, the usual defenses to tort activity make much of the contact that takes place in sports legal. For example, the tort defense of consent is important when considering what might otherwise be wrongful contact. In sports, consent is permission to others engaged in the activity to play the game. If the game is football, consent will include blocking and tackling and

other "ordinary and normal conduct" in the game. Before any behavior could be considered wrongful by a court, it would need to be significantly outside the normal expectations of the game.

Before a person can be considered wrongful when injuring another in sports, the wrongdoer must generally either intend to injure another or be grossly irresponsible in his or her actions. Sports participants do not assume these risks. Liability is more likely to be found in a recreational sport situation than in professional sports activities, where professional athletes are aware of the risks of the game.

Another area of tort law that is currently in the news as it relates to sports is product liability. Product liability was discussed in Chapter 15. Questions about whether equipment is designed to protect players and is thus deemed safe and effective can raise issues involving product liability. Football helmets, baseball batting machines, ice-hockey helmets, trampolines, and fencing protective masks are all examples of products which have been redesigned because of product liability suits.

◆ RESPONSIBILITY OF PLAYERS

Players who bet on sports activities have been a news item in the past few years. Pete Rose, who retired from baseball as the record holder for the most base hits in the sport, has been banned from participation in any major league baseball activity. His ban stemmed from his illegal gambling activities in baseball. His gambling led to a criminal conviction and time in prison. At the time charges were brought, Pete Rose was manager of the Cincinnati Reds. His ban also prohibits his selection into the baseball Hall

Have students research and report on the following incidents regarding professional sports: The Pete Rose gambling incident and his subsequent ban from baseball, the Marge Schott one-year suspension because of racial slurs and inappropriate comments, the death of basketball star Lyn Bias as a result of a drug overdose, and the death of former professional football player Lyle Alzado and its possible link to steroid abuse. Have the students present their findings to the class in the form of teaching posters. Each poster should talk about the event, the effects, and what it says about the effects of gambling, prejudice, cocaine abuse, and steroid abuse. Ask the students to explain their posters to the class.

Invite the coach from one of your female athletic teams to speak to your class regarding changes wrought by Title IX. What type of funding did girls' athletics receive prior to Title IX? What type of funding did the girls' programs receive after Title IX? What were the difficulties in implementing Title IX? What are the benefits? Have your students prepare questions in advance for your speaker.

LEGAL PERSPECTIVE (CONTINUED)

of Fame. Pete Rose is not the only sports figure to have lost a right to participate in his sport. Other sports figures have been banned for gambling, drug use, or other criminal activities.

Gambling is illegal in most states. However, even in states in which gambling is legal, betting on the sport in which you participate is a violation of the rules of the league or governing body. The potential for organized crime to "fix" games and the temptation of the betting athlete to be influenced by gambling make the activity wrong. The consequences of gambling for an athlete are designed to be severe enough to discourage the activity.

◆ EQUAL OPPORTUNITY IN SPORTS

Title IX of the Federal Educational Amendments Act of 1972 provides:

No person in the United States shall, on the basis of sex, be excluded from participation in, be denied the benefits of, or be subjected to discrimination under any educational program or activity receiving Federal financial assistance.

Legal guidelines have been provided by the government to assist educational institutions in complying with Title IX. These guidelines tell institutions that they must provide *similar* opportunities in sports rather than *identical* opportunities. In other words, the law has not been interpreted to require the creation of same-sport teams for both sexes. For example, a school does not have to offer both a football program for men and one for women. Similarly, a school need not have both men's and women's volleyball teams. The school is, however, expected to provide similar types of opportunities and treatment for student athletes. The impact of the law since its passage has been to increase the number of sports opportunities for women.

The equal protection clause of the Fourteenth Amendment to the United States Constitution also gives authority to those seeking equal opportunity for women in sports. The Fourteenth Amendment provides that no state shall "deny to any person within its jurisdiction the equal protection of the laws." The equal protection clause has been used to question different treatment of athletes based on sex. The equal protection clause does not require exact equality of treatment. It does require that a reasonable basis exist when people are treated differently. Several court cases have held that public schools must allow women to compete on men's teams when there are no comparable women's teams.

Mastery Objectives

By the end of this chapter, students will be able to:
- Interpret Title VII of the Civil Rights Act of 1964
- Delineate federal acts that prohibit discrimination
- Describe federal and state acts that protect workers
- Specify federal acts that provide for retirement
- Relate how unemployment compensation programs work

Chapter

Employment Law

22

LEGAL BACKGROUND

This chapter discusses federal employment laws that regulate the everyday workplace conditions for both union and nonunion workers. With the industrialization of the United States and the growth of corporate employers, federal laws have been passed to regulate the nature, conditions, and practices of the workplace. The Civil Rights Act of 1964 was a landmark in federal legislation that changed forever the nature of federal intervention in the workplace. Clearly since this law, hiring and retention policies have become matters of federal rather than state law.

The Americans with Disabilities Act is also introduced in this chapter. It is very much a modern social issue. Other worker issues include workplace safety, workers' compensation, health and retirement. The discussion of the vesting of workers' pension plans will, we hope, promote student awareness of the importance of workplace benefit plans.

519

Critical Thinking Activity

Have a student volunteer read aloud the quote from Thomas Jefferson that begins this chapter. Ask the student what is meant by this quote. What effect does hard work have on the appearance of luck? Then have the student compare this quote from Jefferson with the following two quotes from Thomas Alva Edison: "There is no substitute for hard work," and "Genius is 1 percent inspiration and 99 percent perspiration."

Extension Activity

Have a student volunteer or volunteers read about the Civil Rights Act of 1964. Encourage the students to use sources from 1964 in order to get a feeling of the times in which the act was passed and popular reaction to its passage. Have the students share their findings and impressions with the class in the form of short oral reports.

520

**Chapter 22
Resources and Assignment Guide**

Activity Sheets
Reviewing Legal Concepts 22 *TRB*
Enrichment Activity 22 *TRB*

Student Activity Workbook
Chapter 22 Activities

Tests
Chapter 22 Test *TRB*
Chapter 22 WESTEST Computerized Testing

Handbook of Selected Court Cases
Wise v. *Mead Corporation*
Smith v. *Smithway Motor Xpress, Inc.*

West's Business Law and Legal Environment Videodisc
Still Frames and Motion Segments as shown

"I'm a great believer in luck, and I find the harder I work the more I have of it.'
Thomas Jefferson, 1743–1826
Third president of the United States

Labor law, discussed in the previous chapter, protects the employee's right to participate in union activities. Other laws important to the employment relationship prohibit employer discrimination and address working conditions, compensation, retirement, and worker safety. As employment law varies significantly in each state, the focus in this chapter, except in the case of workers' compensation, is on federal law.

◆ **EMPLOYMENT DISCRIMINATION**

As discussed in Chapter 21, at common law, employment could be terminated *at will*. In recent years, as a result of judicial decisions, administrative agency actions, and legislation, the doctrine of employment at will has changed. The most important statute prohibiting **employment discrimination** and thus modifying the employment at will doctrine is Title VII of the Civil Rights Act of 1964.

TITLE VII OF THE CIVIL RIGHTS ACT OF 1964

Title VII of the Civil Rights Act of 1964, as amended by other laws that we will discuss, prohibits job discrimination *at any stage of employment* against employees, applicants, and union members on the basis of race, color, gender, national origin, or religion.

A group of persons defined by one or more of these criteria (race, color, gender, national origin, or religion) is referred to as a **protected class**. This act covers all employers and labor unions with fifteen or more workers and all employment agencies. It applies to all state and local governments. A special section of the law forbids discrimination in most federal government employment.

Discrimination on the basis of religion and the requirement that employers reasonably accommodate the religious needs of their employees have already been discussed in Chapters 2 and 6. We look here at other types of discrimination prohibited by Title VII.

Race, Color, and National-Origin Discrimination A company's standards or policies for selecting or promoting employees are illegal if they discriminate on the basis of race, color, or national origin. Discrimination in employment conditions and benefits based on these distinctions are also illegal. For example, an employer cannot grant higher holiday bonuses to whites than to blacks.

◆ **employment discrimination**
Treating employees or job applicants unequally on the basis of race, color, gender, national origin, or religion. Prohibited by Title VII of the Civil Rights Act of 1964, as amended.

◆ **protected class**
A group of persons specifically protected by the Civil Rights Act of 1964, as amended, from discriminatory treatment on the basis of race, color, gender, national origin, or religion.

As the student text makes clear, the Title VII protections against discrimination apply not only to employees but also to labor unions. Early labor unions often practiced discriminatory activities. For example, the AFL (which was founded by Samuel Gompers) did not expressly forbid African Americans from membership, but member unions made use of tactics such as high initiation fees, technical examinations, and other discriminatory means to discourage African-American membership.

As a part of the struggle to advance civil rights, Martin Luther King, Jr. appealed to labor unions. In his appeals, King said: "The Negro has the right to expect the resources of the American trade union movement to be used in assuring him—like all the rest of its members—of a proper place in American society. He has gained this right along with all the other workers whose mutual efforts have built this country's free and democratic trade unions."

Sex Discrimination The Equal Employment Opportunity Act (EEOA) of 1972, amending the Civil Rights Act of 1964, dramatically changed employment law relating to women. Before 1972, state law often prohibited the employment of women in certain jobs. For example, many state statutes barred women from working at night or working more than a certain number of hours per day or week. The EEOA struck down most of these limiting laws. Employers are forbidden to classify jobs as male or female, and they cannot have separate male and female seniority lists.

Sexual harassment in the workplace is another form of illegal sex discrimination. Sexual harassment occurs when job opportunities, promotions, and the like are given on the basis of sexual favors. Harassment also occurs when an employee encounters in the work environment sexual comments, jokes, or physical contact that is sexually offensive.

◇ LEGAL FOCUS - EXAMPLE

In a sexual harassment case, the employer may be liable when one employee harasses another employee. If the employee is a supervisor or manager, the employer will probably be liable. If a lower-level

Anita Hill's testimony during the confirmation hearings of Supreme Court Justice Clarence Thomas brought the issue of sexual harassment to the attention of the nation.

Extension Activity

Have students research current periodicals for cases of discrimination and write a one-page report on one, highlighting the important facts of the incident.

Extension Activity

Have students research the confirmation hearings of Justice Clarence Thomas of the Supreme Court and the charges of sexual harassment brought against Justice Thomas by Anita Hill. Students' reports should focus on the societal effects of these much publicized hearings. What effect did these hearings have on people's perceptions of sexual harassment? What effect did these hearings have on employers' policies regarding sexual harassment? You might guide the students in their research by referring them to weekly news magazines such as *Time* and *Newsweek* for articles that appeared in the weeks immediately following the Thomas-Hill hearings. Allow the students to present their findings to the class in the form of oral reports.

Legal Focus Example

Have a student volunteer read aloud the Legal Focus Example that begins on the previous page. Guide the students in discussing this example by pointing out that an employer may be liable when one employee harasses another employee if the employer knows, or should know, about the harassment and fails to take corrective action, or if the employee is in a supervisory position. Stimulate a class discussion regarding this Legal Focus Example by asking the following questions: What burden does possible employer liability place on employers? Do you feel that each individual employee should be held liable for his or her own conduct?

Critical Thinking Activity

Have the students write one or two paragraphs explaining their answers to the following question: Is pregnancy discrimination a form of discrimination against women or a form of discrimination against families?

Legal Focus Example

Have a student volunteer read aloud to the class this Legal Focus Example. Ask the class members to think of other situations in which a pregnant worker would need to be given lighter duty during her pregnancy. For example, what about female police officers or fire fighters? Allow volunteers to share their examples with the class.

522

Enrichment

If your school district has a policy regarding sexual harassment, either for employees or for students, obtain a copy of this policy and share it with the class. Encourage the students to discuss the policy by asking them the following questions: Do you feel this policy adequately protects individuals from sexual harassment? Does this policy go too far? What changes, if any, would you suggest for this policy?

---

employee is responsible for the harassment, liability will be based on the employer's knowledge. Did the employer know of the behavior? Should the employer have known of the behavior? If the answer to either question is yes, the employer should take steps to stop the harassment. If he or she doesn't take steps to stop the behavior, then it is likely that the employer will be liable.

Pregnancy Discrimination The Pregnancy Discrimination Act of 1978 also amended the Civil Rights Act. It prohibits discriminatory treatment of employees on the basis of pregnancy. Women affected by pregnancy, childbirth, or related medical conditions must be treated, for all employment-related purposes, in the same way as all other persons not so affected but similar in ability to work.

Pregnancy must be treated as a temporary disability and pregnant women should be treated just like as any other temporarily disabled employees. For example, the employer must change work assignments and grant paid disability leaves or leaves without pay if those are the ways the employer treats other temporarily disabled employees.

◆ LEGAL FOCUS - EXAMPLE

Rivercity Supply, Inc., hires several stock clerks to assist in maintaining the stock room, putting goods on the store shelves, and helping customers load purchased goods into their vehicles. If a clerk suffers a minor injury to his back or leg and is unable to lift, but can otherwise work, he or she is temporarily partially disabled. Rivercity's policy is to give the worker light duty until the condition heals. The worker may do inventory counting, watching goods in high theft areas, and act as a go-between for sales clerks and the stock clerks. The Pregnancy Discrimination Act would require that the store give a pregnant worker the same allowance for her condition during pregnancy.

Policies concerning an employee's return to work, seniority, pay increases, and so on must also result in equal treatment.

◆ **disparate-treatment discrimination** Employment practices that show intentional bias against a certain group of persons, such as African Americans or women.

Disparate-Treatment Discrimination Disparate-treatment discrimination is *intentional* discrimination against a certain group of persons, such as blacks or women. Any obvious discrimination qualifies as disparate-treatment discrimination.

◆ LEGAL FOCUS - PROBLEM

Carla is an honors graduate from a prestigious college with a degree in computer sciences. She is also an African American. Carla applies for an entry-level management position with a medium-sized computer software company. She passes a written test prepared by the company. At an oral interview, one of the interviewers tells her that "the company enjoys a harmonious work force" and she "probably would not fit in." The company has no black management employees. After the interview, the company does not hire her for the position but advertises again for new applicants. Is this disparate-treatment discrimination?

1. The plaintiff is a member of a protected class.
2. The plaintiff applied for and was qualified for the job.
3. The plaintiff was rejected by the employer.
4. The employer continued to seek applicants for the position.

If a plaintiff can prove these four conditions, she or he establishes a *prima facie* case—that is, she or he meets the necessary burden of proof. The employer is then required to establish a legal reason why the plaintiff was not hired.

Disparate-Impact Discrimination   Discrimination is not always blatant or obvious. Often it is not even intentional, but it exists anyway. Employers commonly use interviews, minimum educational requirements, and testing procedures to choose from many applicants for job openings. When such employer practices have a discriminatory effect on a class of people protected under Title VII, **disparate-impact discrimination** may result.

Disparate-impact discrimination happens when a screening method or other job requirement results in the employer's work force not reflecting the percentages of members of protected groups, such as nonwhites or women, in the local labor market. If the practices are not justified by legitimate business reasons and if they have a discriminatory effect, then even if the discrimination was not intentional, the practices are illegal.

♦ **disparate-impact discrimination** Discrimination that results from certain employer practices or procedures that although not obviously biased, have a discriminatory effect.

AFFIRMATIVE ACTION

Title VII and government regulations are designed to reduce or eliminate discriminatory practices that occur in hiring, retaining, and promoting employees. **Affirmative action** programs go a step further and attempt to "make up" for past patterns of discrimination. An affirmative action program gives qualified minorities and women preferential treatment when employees are hired or promoted. Affirmative action programs are controversial, particularly when they result in what is frequently called "reverse discrimination." *Reverse discrimination* is the term used to describe discrimination against a majority, such as white males.

The debate over affirmative action programs is an ethical one. How much should the current generation of white employees and other mem-

♦ **affirmative action**   Job hiring policies that give special consideration or compensatory treatment to protected groups in an effort to overcome the effects of past discrimination.

Legal Focus Example

Ask a student volunteer to read this Legal Focus Example aloud to the class. Guide the students in discussing this example by asking the following questions: How many men were hired as agents in California between 1970 and 1974? How many women? What anecdotal evidence of discrimination did Muriel Kraszewski offer?

Extension Activity

Two important test cases dealing with affirmative action are *Regents of the University of California* v. *Bakke* and *Kaiser Aluminum & Chemical Company* v. *Weber*. Have student volunteers research both these cases and then report their findings to the class, answering the following questions: What are the most important differences between the cases? Why do you think one case was decided in favor of affirmative action and the other against affirmative action? Would you have made the same decision in the two cases? Why or why not?

Collaborative Learning Activity

Divide the class into three groups. Tell each group that it is now an advertising agency assigned the task of creating a television commercial to promote awareness of a key discrimination issue. Have one group handle racial discrimination, one group discrimination based on gender, and one group age discrimination. Tell the groups that their commercials should accentuate the need for equal opportunities and should also mention the relevant statutes. Remind the groups that their commercials are for commercial television and should also be appropriate for your classroom. Provide each group with the opportunity to act out its commercial for the class.

---

bers of majority groups have to pay for past discriminatory practices of employers? To what extent and in what ways should the government regulate employment conditions to ensure equal opportunity?

The United States Supreme Court has generally held that affirmative action programs are legitimate under certain conditions: (1) if they are imposed to correct existing imbalances in the work force and (2) if race or gender is not the only factor considered by employers in making employment decisions. Generally, the Supreme Court looks at the special circumstances of each case in determining whether challenged affirmative action plans are legitimate. In a later Legal Focus, under the subheading Procedures and Remedies, we discuss the 1992 settlement of discrimination claims by 814 women plaintiffs against the defendant State Farm Insurance Company. This case involved an affirmative action program based on the following facts.

◆ LEGAL FOCUS – EXAMPLE

In 1985 the federal district court in San Francisco ruled that State Farm had engaged in discriminatory practices. In 1988, the court approved an agreement between State Farm and the injured employees in which State Farm agreed to hire 50 percent or more women for ten years in order to remedy past discriminatory practices in the hiring of sales agents. These discriminatory practices had occurred between 1970 and 1974, when State Farm hired 586 agents in California and only one of them was a woman. Many women had applied for positions and been turned down. One of the witnesses, Muriel Kraszewski, who worked for State Farm as an insurance agent's assistant, testified that she had applied for a sales agent job. When Muriel applied, she was told a college degree was a job requirement. State Farm was at that time hiring male agents without college degrees. Later Muriel was told that State Farm would not hire women agents.

PROCEDURES AND REMEDIES

The laws protecting employees from discriminatory activities give injured individuals the right to bring a lawsuit to enforce their rights and recover any damages they have suffered. However, a person who has been discriminated against cannot file a lawsuit immediately. The law requires that a complaint be filed first with the Equal Employment Opportunity Commission (EEOC). The EEOC is then expected to investigate the claim. If this agency finds that the claim has merit, it will seek a voluntary negotiated settlement to resolve the complaint. If a settlement is not achieved, the EEOC can sue the employer. The employee is allowed to sue the employer after the EEOC's investigation even if the EEOC takes no action, and whether or not the EEOC agrees that the complaint has merit.

Legal Focus Example

Explain to the students that this Legal Focus Example is a followup to the Legal Focus Example found on the previous page, which dealt with discriminatory practices by State Farm. Then have a student volunteer read this example aloud to the class. Ask the students whether they believe $157 million to be paid to 814 women plaintiffs was a fair settlement. Then have a volunteer divide $157 million by 814. What is the total? Remind students that out of this come lawyer fees, etc., which in this case were probably extensive. Does this settlement seem fair per person? Then remind the students that the discriminatory practices occurred between 1970 and 1974. How much money might each woman have made if she had been hired by State Farm during that period? How does this figure compare to the settlement figure per woman?

Employer liability under Title VII is extensive. Potential employee remedies include being reinstated and receiving back pay. A court may also grant an injunction prohibiting future violations.

 LEGAL FOCUS ~ EXAMPLE

The risk and complexity of Title VII lawsuits often lead defendants to settle cases out of court. In 1992 State Farm Insurance settled a class-action sex-discrimination lawsuit for $157 million to be paid to 814 women plaintiffs. The federal district court had ruled in 1985 that State Farm had engaged in discriminatory practices. As of 1992, this settlement was the largest settlement in the history of Title VII litigation for any type of discrimination.

AGE DISCRIMINATION

The Age Discrimination in Employment Act (ADEA) of 1967, as amended, prohibits employment discrimination against people forty years of age or older. Recent amendments to the act prohibit forced retirement for non-managerial workers. For the act to apply, the employer must have twenty or more employees, and the business must affect interstate commerce.

The Age Discrimination in Employment Act is similar to Title VII. It offers protection against both intentional (disparate-treatment) age discrimination and unintentional (disparate-impact) age discrimination.

Numerous complaints of age discrimination have been made against employers who try to cut costs by replacing older, higher salaried employees with younger, lower paid workers.

 LEGAL FOCUS ~ CASE PROBLEM

A fifty-four-year-old manager of a plant, who earned $15.75 an hour, was temporarily laid off when the company plant was closed for the winter. When spring came, the manager was replaced by a forty-three-year-old worker who earned $8.05 per hour. The older manager, who had worked for the company for twenty-seven years, was not given a chance to accept a lower wage rate. Was the action of the company permissible under the ADEA?

No. The court, which referred to the firm's dismissal of the manager as "industrial capital punishment," held that the manager's termination in these circumstances violated the ADEA.[1]

---

1. *Metz v. Transit Mix, Inc.*, 828 F.2d 1202 (7th Cir. 1987).

Legal Focus Case Problem

Have a student volunteer read aloud to the class this Legal Focus Case Problem dealing with age discrimination. Have the volunteer suggest a possible answer to the question posed at the end of this problem. Remind students that they can use the Legal Focus features as review tools when studying for tests.

 ## Ethical Concern

To reduce salary costs, many companies replace older workers with younger workers. Have a student lead a discussion about the legality and ethical considerations of this practice. Discuss whether there is a difference between the work performance of an older and that of a younger person. What does an older employee add to the company? What does a younger employee bring to the company?

LEGAL BACKGROUND

When the Americans with Disabilities Act was passed in 1990, its sponsor, Senator Tom Harkin (Democrat from Iowa), described the bill as "an emancipation proclamation for disabled Americans."

Teaching Note

Excerpts from the Americans with Disabilities Act of 1990 are included in the Resource Center at the back of this book.

Enrichment

Encourage the students to discuss the need for reasonable accommodations for disabled workers. Ask the students what reasonable accommodations could be made for wheelchair-bound workers, for hearing-impaired, or vision-impaired workers, etc. Then ask the students to make a list of the accommodations that have been made for disabled students at your school. Is there need for any further accommodations? Why or why not?

Caption Answer

Persons with disabilities are protected by the Americans with Disabilities Act of 1990.

Teaching with the Videodisc

The still frames listed below from the **West's Business Law and Legal Environment Videodisc** can be used with this chapter. To access this material, use the bar codes or the frame numbers included in the Videodisc Instructor's Manual found in the *TRB*.

Employment Discrimination–Proof in a Disparate Treatment Case
Employment Discrimination–Proof in a Disparate Impact Case

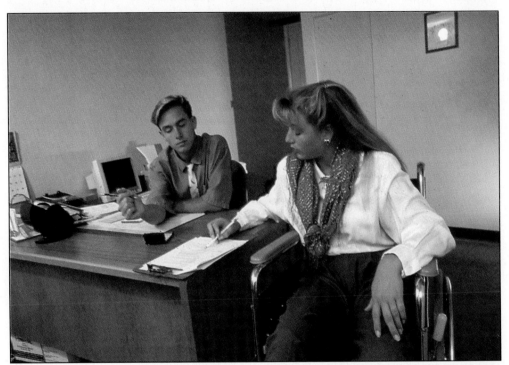

Are persons with disabilities protected against discrimination by federal law?

DISABILITY DISCRIMINATION

In 1990, the Americans with Disabilities Act (ADA) was passed. The act bars discrimination against persons with disabilities by most private employers, state and local governments, employment agencies, and labor unions. Disabilities include blindness, paralysis, heart disease, cancer, acquired immune deficiency syndrome (AIDS), emotional illness, and learning disabilities. The act generally prohibits discrimination in hiring, pay, promotions, and dismissal.

The law also requires employees to make reasonable accommodations for disabled workers unless such accommodations create an undue hardship for the employer. An undue hardship is an accommodation that is "significantly difficult or expensive." By July 1994, the ADA will apply to all businesses with fifteen or more employees. However, it will not affect all employers in the same way. The requirement that businesses make reasonable accommodations for disabled workers will vary depending on business size and the nature of the business activities. A large business with thousands of clerical employees will have a difficult time showing "undue hardship," and making such accommodations as installing wheelchair

Checking Your Progress (Answers)

1. Title VII of the Civil Rights Act of 1964 covers all employers and labor unions with 15 or more workers, as well as federal, state, and local governments.
2. The EEOA changed employment law relating to women.
3. Disparate-treatment discrimination is intentional, but disparate-impact discrimination may or may not be intentional.
4. Affirmative action programs go further than regulations against discrimination by attempting to "make up" for past patterns of discrimination. This is done by giving preferential treatment to qualified minorities and women when hiring and promoting employees.
5. Employers cannot discriminate against persons with disabilities in hiring, pay, promotions, and dismissal. They must make reasonable accommodations for disabled workers unless such accommodations create an undue hardship for them.

ramps and offering interpreters for the hearing impaired will be considered reasonable. For a small business, such accommodations might create economic hardships.

 ## CHECKING YOUR PROGRESS

1. What groups must follow the guidelines of Title VII of the Civil Rights Act of 1964?
2. What group was affected in the passage of the Equal Employment Opportunity Act of 1972 (EEOA)?
3. What is the difference between disparate-treatment and disparate-impact discrimination?
4. How do affirmative action programs extend the government regulations designed to eliminate discrimination?
5. What are the obligations of an employer under the Americans with Disabilities Act of 1990?

 ## INJURY, COMPENSATION, AND SAFETY

Numerous state and federal statutes are designed to protect employees and their families from the risk of accidental injury, death, or disease resulting from employment. Among these statutes are state workers' compensation laws, the Occupational Safety and Health Act of 1970, and fair employment laws (covered in this chapter's Legal Perspective). Unions frequently bargain for the safety and financial well-being of their member workers, but the following laws provide protection in addition to that provided in union contracts.

STATE WORKERS' COMPENSATION ACTS

Workers' compensation laws establish an administrative procedure for compensating workers who are injured on the job. Instead of suing, an injured worker files a claim with the local workers' compensation board, which has been established by state statute. Workers' compensation statutes are a form of *no-fault insurance*. No-fault insurance is a type of insurance where the insurance company pays benefits to the policy holder even if the injury to the policy holder was caused by his or her own actions. Every state has some form of workers' compensation law.

The right to recover for injuries under workers' compensation laws is usually based on two criteria being met: (1) an employment relationship must exist, and (2) the injury must be *accidental* and *arise out of and/or occur in*

 ## State Law

Problems with workers' compensation programs exist in virtually all states. As the costs of medical care and litigation, and the costs due to fraud soar, state workers' compensation programs suffer. Strategies for attacking these problems vary from state to state. In Texas, for example, problems with the workers' compensation system was the subject of two special legislative sessions in 1989 and of a third special session in 1991. As of 1992 in Texas, workers disabled on the job receive up to $428 per week in income replacement, as well as medical and death benefits. This represents a significant improvement over conditions in 1989, when the state was known for having the highest costs and lowest benefits of any U.S. state.

Extension Activity

Ask a volunteer to obtain a few workers' compensation insurance policies from a local insurance company. Pass the forms around to your students so that they may see what they consist of.

Stimulate a class discussion by asking students to share some experiences that they or a family member may have had with workers' compensation or some other labor law.

Critical Thinking Activity

Point out to students that as the text makes clear, recoveries under the workers' compensation plans are generally less than half what those in comparable tort suits would be. Ask the students whether they believe this is fair. Remind the students that the employer's insurance company basically is responsible under a system of strict liability, and the same would not be held true in a tort suit. In other words, while recoveries would be greater in tort suits, the worker would be less likely to recover anything at all than under the current system of workers' compensation.

Read aloud the following material from the student text:

"Employees can file complaints about health and safety violations. Under the act, an employer cannot discharge an employee who files a complaint. Employees who refuse in good faith to work in a high-risk area (where bodily harm or death might result) also cannot legally be fired. Good faith in these circumstances would mean that the employees' refusal was reasonable and made because of their belief that their safety is in jeopardy."

Have the students work with partners to write their own Legal Focus Example of a case in which a worker, or group of workers, refuse in good faith to work in a high-risk area.

---

528   Agency and Employee Law

the course of normal employment. If an injury is self-inflicted, for example, it is not accidental and is not covered under workers' compensation laws. In the past, heart attacks or other medical problems arising out of preexisting disease or physical conditions were not covered, but recently some states have allowed recovery.

Basically, the employer's insurance company is responsible under a system of strict liability. Few, if any, defenses (including the common law defenses of contributory negligence, assumption of risk, or injury caused by a fellow employee) exist to allow the employer to avoid having to pay. Therefore, the cost of treating workers' injuries is considered a cost of production and is passed on to consumers.

In exchange for compensation under these statutes, workers give up the right to sue in court for on-the-job injuries. Even if an injury is caused by an employer's negligence, the injured worker must accept workers' compensation as the sole remedy. Generally, recoveries under the workers' compensation plans are less than half what those in comparable tort suits would be.

HEALTH AND SAFETY PROTECTION

The primary federal legislation for employee health and safety protection is the Occupational Safety and Health Act of 1970. This act was passed to ensure safe and healthful working conditions for practically every employee in the country. The act requires that businesses be maintained free from recognized hazards. Virtually all employers are covered by the act.

Three federal agencies were created to develop and enforce the standards set by this act. The Occupational Safety and Health Administration (OSHA) has the authority to create standards, make inspections, and enforce the act. The National Institute for Occupational Safety and Health conducts research on safety and health problems and recommends standards for OSHA administrators to adopt. Finally, the Occupational Safety and Health Review Commission hears appeals from actions taken by OSHA administrators.

Employees can file complaints about health and safety violations. Under the act, an employer cannot discharge an employee who files a complaint. Employees who refuse in good faith to work in a high-risk area (where bodily harm or death might result) also cannot legally be fired. Good faith in these circumstances would mean that the employees' refusal is reasonable and made because of their belief that their safety is in jeopardy.

Employers with eleven or more employees must keep occupational injury and illness records for each employee. The records must be available for inspection when requested by an OSHA inspector. Employers must make reports to OSHA whenever a work-related injury or disease occurs. OSHA compliance officers may enter and inspect any establishment covered by the act if they follow the proper procedures.

Read

Remind the students that the Occupational Safety and Health Administration has the authority to create the standards, make inspections, and enforce the Occupational Safety and Health Act of 1970. Explain that in some cases, enforcing the Occupational Safety and Health Act of 1970 involves criminal penalties. Then have a student volunteer read this *Law in Action* feature aloud to the class.

Discuss

Stimulate a class discussion of this *Law in Action* feature by asking the following questions: What reasons does this feature give for oversight in safety areas by some managers? What criminal actions were the PYMN Thermometer executives guilty of? What action did the judge take in this case? Was this fair or unfair?

Enrich

Explain to students that the PYMN Thermometer case was appealed and that on appeal the appellate court held that the federal act does not preempt state prosecution of employers whose criminal activity is centered in the workplace or directed against employees.

Enrichment

Ask the students if they have heard people complain that, by the time they retire, there will be no money left in the social security system. Do they think this could be true? Then have the students research the functioning of the social security system and the predictions made for its future. Engage the students in a discussion of their findings and of the conclusions they draw from those findings.

 Law in Action

LAW AND THE BUSINESSPERSON: WORKER SAFETY—NOW IT'S A CRIMINAL ISSUE

Like most other business activities, the protection of worker safety involves a trade-off. An employer concerned about worker safety invests time and money to ensure that safety. In a competitive marketplace, these higher production costs are passed on to consumers (at least in part) through higher prices. But those who charge more than others for the same product or service end up losing customers and profits and may eventually go out of business. Not surprisingly, then, some aggressive managers may not be aggressive in ensuring safe working conditions.

Under the federal Occupational Safety and Health Act of 1970, there are specific safety regulations for the workplace, but the act limits criminal penalties for willful violations. Until recently, employers avoided serious criminal penalties even when they blatantly violated federal workplace guidelines.

For example, PYMM Thermometer Company of Brooklyn, New York, exposed its workers to poisonous mercury. One employee suffered permanent brain damage.

The public prosecutor was convinced that two PYMM Thermometer executives were guilty of assault and reckless endangerment for exposing their workers to the poisonous metal. The jury agreed. The judge, however, set aside the verdict, claiming that job safety could only be regulated by the federal Occupational Safety and Health Act. To many, this was an outrage.

In 1988, the Justice Department issued an opinion stating that the provisions about criminal penalties in the Occupational Safety and Health Act did not preempt state and local criminal laws. The federal Occupational Safety and Health Act does not shield employers from state criminal prosecution for willful disregard for worker safety. In 1989, in Elk Grove, Illinois, the Illinois Supreme Court upheld Cook County's criminal prosecution of five executives at Chicago Magnet Wire Company. The executives allegedly allowed workers to become ill from exposure to hazardous chemicals. Similar suits are pending in many states.

 ## RETIREMENT AND SECURITY INCOME

Federal and state governments participate in insurance programs designed to protect employees and their families by covering the financial impact of retirement, disability, death, hospitalization, and unemployment. The key federal law on this subject is the Social Security Act of 1935.

OLD AGE, SURVIVORS, AND DISABILITY INSURANCE (OASDI)

The Social Security Act provides for old age (retirement), survivors, and disability insurance. The name of the act uses the initials of these benefits: OASDI. Both employers and employees must "contribute" under the Federal Insurance Contributions Act (FICA) to this insurance fund. The employee's contribution is a percentage of his or her annual wage base. Benefits are fixed by statute but increase automatically as the cost of living increases.

MEDICARE

Medicare is a health insurance program administered by the Social Security Administration. Medicare provides health benefits for people sixty-five years of age and older and for people under sixty-five who are disabled. Medicare assists with both hospital costs and other medical costs, such as visits to the doctor. Recipients of Medicare can also get additional federal medical insurance by paying a small monthly premium.

PRIVATE RETIREMENT PLANS

There are several federal statutes regulating private employer retirement plans. The Employee Retirement Income Security Act of 1974 (ERISA)

When does a worker get ownership rights to his or her employment retirement plan?

Ethical Concern

Ask the students to write short one-paragraph descriptions of how the ERISA promotes ethical behavior among employers in terms of private retirement plans. Have the students trade papers with partners to proof and correct any misspellings or errors in grammar. Then allow student volunteers to share their work with the class.

---

allows regulation of individuals who operate private pension funds. A key provision of ERISA concerns **vesting**. Vesting gives an employee legal ownership of his or her pension funds before he or she reaches retirement age. A pension fund that has not been vested still belongs to the employer; if the employee is fired or quits before the fund has vested, the employee's right to the fund ends. Usually vesting occurs within five years of the beginning of employment.

◆ **vesting** The legal event signifying that a possible right to something has become an absolute right to something.

 LEGAL FOCUS ~ EXAMPLE

ERISA was passed to deal with common abuses of employee pension funds. Many times employees who had worked for a company for fifteen years were fired shortly before their scheduled retirement. Often, the fired employee would then have no right to retirement funds from the company because the company pension plans kept plan ownership with the employer until the employee reached retirement age. ERISA created early vesting of employee rights. Early vesting gives an employee rights in the retirement funds if the employee voluntarily changes jobs or even if he or she is fired.

UNEMPLOYMENT COMPENSATION

The Federal Unemployment Tax Act (FUTA) created a state system of unemployment insurance that provides compensation to eligible individuals when they are unemployed. Employers pay into a fund, and the proceeds are paid to qualified unemployed workers. Covered employers are taxed quarterly. These taxes are typically submitted to the states, which then deposit the money in the federal government's Unemployment Insurance Fund, in which each state has an account.

 CHECKING YOUR PROGRESS

1. If an employee is injured on the job and collects damages from a workers' compensation claim, what right does he or she give up?

2. What federal legislation protects the health and safety of employees?

3. Who is actually paying an employee who receives unemployment compensation?

Checking Your Progress (Answers)

1. In exchange for compensation from a workers' compensation claim, the employee gives up the right to sue in court for on-the-job injuries.
2. The Occupational Safety and Health Act of 1970 was passed to ensure the safe and healthful working conditions of employees.
3. Even though the unemployment compensation program is administered by federal and state governments, employers pay into the fund, which is used to pay unemployed workers. Thus, the employer is actually paying an employee who receives unemployment.

Teaching A Case In Point

Before the students read this *A Case In Point* feature, remind them that disparate treatment discrimination is illegal. Ask a student volunteer to recall for the class the definition of *disparate treatment discrimination* ("employment practices that show intentional bias against a certain group of persons such as African Americans or women"). Then have a volunteer read this *A Case In Point* feature aloud to the class.

Teaching Note

This case is included in the *West's Business and Personal Law Handbook of Selected Court Cases.*

Discuss

Stimulate a class discussion about the *A Case In Point* feature by asking the following questions: Wise was fired following what event? Does it seem fair to fire someone who is in a fight at work and who kicked, scratched, and used abusive and uncivil language? What did Wise allege in her suit against the Mead Corporation? What evidence was provided that Mead had engaged in sex discrimination in firing Wise? What was the decision of the United States District Court for the Middle District of Georgia? What reasons did the Court give for its decision?

◆ A CASE IN POINT ◆

WISE v. MEAD CORP.

United States District Court for the Middle District of Georgia, 1985. 614 F.Supp. 1131.

Ms. Wise claimed that she was fired from her job because she was a woman. She admitted that she had violated Mead Corporation rules by fighting with another employee, but she protested being fired. She argued that when men were disciplined for fighting, they had not been fired. Is Mead Corporation's otherwise justifiable firing of Ms. Wise sex discrimination because it had not fired men for similar offenses?

FACTS   A female employee of Mead Corporation, Ms. Wise, became involved in a dispute in the lunchroom of her place of employment with another employee, Pruitt. A fight began, and Wise kicked and scratched Pruitt. She also used "abusive and uncivil" language. Wise was fired. Wise brought suit, alleging sex discrimination on the part of Mead Corporation in violation of Title VII of the Civil Rights Act of 1964. She argued that at least four other fights at Mead had occurred under similar circumstances. In each of these cases, none of the participants was fired. None of these other fights had involved a female.

ISSUE   Was Wise's employment termination due to sex discrimination by Mead Corporation?

DECISION   Yes. Mead produced no convincing evidence that any other reason existed to terminate Wise's employment.

REASON   The court stated that a "plaintiff fired for misconduct makes out a *prima facie* case of discriminatory discharge if she shows (1) that she is a member of a protected class, (2) that she was qualified for the job from which she was fired, and (3) that the misconduct for which she was discharged was nearly identical to that engaged in by an employee outside the protected class whom the employer retained." Wise had established a *prima facie* case because Mead did not dispute that she was qualified for her job and because three male employees had engaged in conduct nearly identical to that of Wise, but the three men had kept their jobs. Even though Mead produced grounds for firing Wise (the fighting), the court concluded that discrimination made a difference in the decision. "In this case, a review of the facts proves beyond a doubt that it is more likely that Mead was motivated by discrimination. Therefore, plaintiff has proved that Mead's proffered reasons for firing plaintiff are in fact pretext for discrimination."

In order to help students review what they have learned in Chapter 22, you might wish to:

1. Have a student volunteer, or volunteers, read aloud the Chapter Summary.
2. Allow the students to work with partners to complete the *Using Legal Language* activity.
3. Assign the *Checking for Comprehension* exercise as homework.

4. Allow the students to work in small groups to complete the *Applying Legal Concepts* activities.
5. As a class, complete the *Applying the Law* activities. (Please note that you may have to help students with vocabulary so that they adequately understand all of the *Applying the Law* material.)

In order to check student mastery of chapter concepts, you may wish to use the Chapter 22 test that is found in your *Teacher's Resource Binder* or use WESTEST computerized testing for Chapter 22.

Employment Law 533

CHAPTER REVIEW

22

 ## SUMMARY

Using Legal Language (Answers)

1–E, 2–G, 3–D, 4–H, 5–F, 6–A, 7–B, 8–C, 9–J, 10–I

EMPLOYMENT DISCRIMINATION

Title VII of the Civil Rights Act of 1964 (amended in 1972)—Prohibits discrimination by most employers, labor unions, employment agencies, and state and local governments against employees, job applicants, and union members on the basis of race, color, national origin, religion, or sex.

Pregnancy Discrimination

The *Pregnancy Discrimination Act of 1978*—Prohibits discrimination of employees on the basis of pregnancy.

Age Discrimination

Age Discrimination in Employment Act (1967)—As amended, prohibits discrimination on the basis of age.

Disability Discrimination

Americans with Disabilities Act (1990)—Prohibits discrimination against workers with disabilities and requires that employers make workplace accommodations for disabled workers.

INJURY, COMPENSATION, AND SAFETY

1. *State workers' compensation acts*—Allow compensation to workers whose injuries arose out of and during the course of their employment. Regulated by state agency or board.

2. *Health and safety protection*—The Occupational Safety and Health Act (OSHA) of 1970 ensures safe and healthful working conditions for employees.

RETIREMENT AND SECURITY INCOME

1. *Social Security*—Old Age, Survivors, and Disability Insurance (OASDI) provides retired or disabled employees or their families with income created by mandatory employer and employee contributions. The Social Security Administration, created by the Social Security Act of 1935, also administers Medicare, a health insurance program for people sixty-five years of age and older and for some under age sixty-five who are disabled.

2. *Private retirement plans set up by employers*—These plans supplement Social Security income for retired individuals; most plans are regulated by the Employee Retirement Income Security Act (ERISA) of 1974.

3. *Unemployment compensation*—The Federal Unemployment Tax Act (FUTA) created a state system that provides unemployment compensation to eligible individuals; the money comes from taxes that employers pay.

◆ USING LEGAL LANGUAGE

Directions: Match each term with the statement that best defines the term.

1. affirmative action
2. disparate-impact discrimination
3. disparate-treatment discrimination
4. employment discrimination
5. Federal Insurance Contributions Act

A. Under the _____, employees cannot be discharged for refusing to work in high risk areas.

B. Persons of a _____ are specifically protected by the Civil Rights Act of 1964, as

1. No. Title VII of the Civil Rights Act, as amended, prohibits job discrimination against employees, applicants, and union members at any stage of employment.

2. Students may describe the Equal Employment Act of 1972, the Pregnancy Discrimination Act of 1978, the Age Discrimination in Employment Act of 1967, or the Americans with Disabilities Act of 1990.

3. Four requirements to support a claim of disparate-treatment discrimination are: (1) the plaintiff is a member of a protected class; (2) the plaintiff applied and was qualified for the job; (3) the plaintiff was rejected by the employer; and (4) the employer continued to seek applicants for the position.

4. Illegal discrimination may exist even if it is unintentional. If a screening method or other job requirement results in the employer's workforce not reflecting the general population of protected groups, a case of disparate-impact discrimination exists.

5. If employees think they have been discriminated against, they must first file a complaint with the Equal Employment Opportunity Commission. Once the EEOC has investigated and attempted to negotiate a settlement, employees may sue the employer.

6. The Social Security Act of 1935 affects the retirement

of employees by collecting FICA tax from employers and employees. The Employee Retirement Income Security Act of 1974 allows regulation of individuals who operate private pension funds.

7. a–Only employers with 15 or more employees who are engaged in an activity that affects interstate commerce come under the Civil Rights Act, Title VII. Tennington, Inc. has only ten employees; thus its employment of white males only is not a federal civil rights violation. Tennington could be in violation of

state law, however, depending on the requirements of the state statute.

b–Educational requirements can be legally imposed, providing the education requirement is directly related to, and necessary for, performance of the job. The requirement of a high school diploma is not a direct, job-related requirement in this case. Chinawa obviously comes under the 1964 Civil Rights Act, Title VII, as amended, and the educational requirement under the circumstances is definitely discriminatory against minorities.

6. Occupational Safety and Health
7. protected class
8. unemployment compensation
9. vesting
10. workers' compensation laws

amended, from discriminatory treatment on the basis of race, color, gender, national origin, and religion.

C. The Federal Unemployment Tax Act created a state system that provides _____ to eligible individuals, which is paid for by employer-paid taxes.

D. Employers are guilty of _____ if they show intentional bias against a certain group of persons.

E. Programs of _____ create job hiring policies that give special consideration or compensatory treatment to minority groups in an effort to overcome present affect of past discrimination.

F. Under the _____ both an employer and employee contribute toward the social security programs that provide for OASDI.

G. Discrimination that results from certain employer practices or procedures is _____ even if the practices are not intentional.

H. An employer who treats employees or job applicants unequally on the basis of race, color, gender, national origin, or religion is guilty of _____.

I. _____ establish procedures for compensating workers injured on the job.

J. _____ gives an employee legal ownership of pension funds before retirement age.

◆ CHECKING FOR COMPREHENSION

1. Does the Civil Rights Act prohibit discrimination only in the hiring practices of companies? Explain.

2. Describe two Acts that have amended the Civil Rights Act of 1964.

3. What are the four requirements that support a claim of disparate-treatment discrimination?

4. Must workplace discrimination be intentional to be considered illegal? Explain.

5. What is the procedure employees must follow to recover damages if they think

they have been discriminated against?

6. What government legislation affects the retirement of employees?

7. Discuss fully which of the following constitutes a violation of the 1964 Civil Rights Act, Title VII, as amended:

(A) Tennington, Inc., is a consulting firm and has ten employees. These employees travel on consulting jobs in seven states. Tennington has an employment record of hiring only white males.

1. Teal and the other employees were correct. The court emphasized the fact that the basic objectives of Congress in enacting Title VII of the Civil Right Act was "to achieve equality of employment opportunities and to remove barriers that have operated in the past to favor an identifiable group of white employees over other employees." At issue, in the court's eyes, was not how many black employees the Connecticut Department of Income Maintenance had promoted, relative to white employees, but whether the test was a non-job-related barrier that in effect denied an applicant an employment opportunity "because of race, color, religion, sex, or national origin." In this case, the court held that the test required for promotion effectively denied employment opportunities to blacks and presented a *prima facie* case of employment discrimination under Title VII legislation. The court rejected Connecticut's defense (that a greater percentage of black employees who took the test were promoted compared to white employees who took the test), stating that the "principal focus of the statute is the protection of the individual employee, rather than the protection of the minority group as a whole."

2. The Eleventh Circuit Court of Appeals held that the private school failed to establish a factual basis for believing that all or substantially all people of the age of 65 or over would be unable to perform safely the tasks of a bus driver or that it was impossible or highly impractical to deal with older employees on an individual basis. Thus, the school failed to establish a bona fide occupational qualification defense to Tullis's claim of age discrimination in employment.

(B) Chinawa, a major processor of cheese sold throughout the United States, employs 100 employees at its principal processing plant. The plant is located in Heartland Corners, whose population is 50 percent white, 25 percent black, and the balance Hispanic, Asian, and other minorities. Chinawa requires a high school diploma as a condition of employment for its clean-up crew. Three-fourths of the white population complete high school, as compared to only one-fourth of the minority groups. Chinawa has an all-white cleaning crew.

APPLYING LEGAL CONCEPTS

1. Retrieve the database about Federal Acts prepared for the APPLYING LEGAL CONCEPTS activity in Chapter 21. Add the Federal Acts presented in Chapter 22 to the database. Print a hard copy. Save the database file.

2. Write letters to large corporations in your state inquiring about the company's retirement plan. Specifically ask how many years an employee must work to be vested.

APPLYING THE LAW . . . YOU BE THE JUDGE

1. Several black employees of the Connecticut Department of Income Maintenance who sought promotion to supervisory position took the required written examination but failed to pass it. Of all who took the examination, 54 percent of the black employees passed it while nearly 80 percent of the white employees who took the test passed. Following the examination, the state of Connecticut promoted eleven black employees (representing 23 percent of all black employees) and thirty-five white employees (representing 14 percent of all white employees). Teal and three other black employees who failed the test sued the state of Connecticut and the Department of Income Maintenance. The employees asserted that the written test excluded a disproportionate number of black employees from promotion to supervisory positions and therefore violated Title VII of the Civil Rights Act. The state argued that since a greater percentage of black employees had been promoted, relative to white employees, the test was not discriminatory. Who was correct? [*Connecticut v. Teal*, 457 U.S. 440, 102 S.Ct. 2525, 73 L.Ed.2d 130 (1982)]

2. Tullis was hired as a bus driver by a private school in Dade County, Florida, in September, 1982. Tullis turned sixty-five on January 1, 1986. On January 3, 1986, because the insurance company would no longer insure drivers over the age of sixty-five, Tullis's employment was terminated. Tullis sued the school, alleging age discrimination in violation of the Age Discrimination in Employment Act (ADEA). Can the school successfully defend against the age discrimination charge by stating that an age of sixty-four years or younger was a bona fide occupational qualification? Is the increased cost of insurance a factor that would exempt the school from compliance with the ADEA? [*Tullis v. Lear School, Inc.*, 874 F.2d 1489 (11th Cir. 1989)]

Ask your students to raise their hands if they are currently employed. Ask each student where he or she works. What types of duties does he or she perform, and how many hours per week does he or she work? Explain to students that the types of duties one is allowed to perform and the number of hours one is allowed to work are limited by statute if one is a minor. Then have student volunteers take turns reading aloud to the class this Legal Perspective on minors and employment law.

LEGAL BACKGROUND

The Fair Labor Standards Act (FLSA) limits the use of child labor. These restrictions exist to combat abuses of child labor that took place before the law was passed in 1938. The federal law sets minimum standards but allows each state to provide additional protections. This LP closes with a general introduction to the wage and hour protection provided by the FLSA for most workers. Among the workers excluded from the wage and hour coverage of the act are professional workers such as yourself, as well as managers and other executives.

LEGAL PERSPECTIVE

MINORS AND EMPLOYMENT LAW

The golf links lie so near the mill
That almost every day
The laboring children can look out
And watch the men at play.

Sarah Norcliffe Cleghorn, 1876–1959
Poet

Working during childhood was a common condition for working-class children in the United States before and even during the early years of this century. The first mill in Pawtucket, New Jersey, which opened in 1790, hired seven boys and two girls, ages seven to eleven, to be part of its work force.

Among the pro-labor legislation passed during the Great Depression in the 1930s was the *Fair Labor Standards Act (FLSA)*. This law, also known as the "wage-hour law," was signed into law on June 25, 1938. Among its goals was the elimination of exploitative child labor practices. The act also dealt with other issues such as the maximum hours employers could require from employees and the minimum wages employers could pay.

States have also passed laws regulating the employment of minors. Both federal and state laws attempt to protect younger minors, prohibit dangerous working conditions and excess work, and reduce work conflicts with school. The FLSA sets minimum standards. Under the FLSA scheme, if a state law provides more protection for a minor's working conditions, it usually takes precedence over the federal law.

◆ EMPLOYMENT AGE

The FLSA defines the age at which minors can work. It also defines the conditions under which they can work. State law often provides additional restrictions on when and how much a minor can work.

UNDER THE AGE OF FOURTEEN

The types of employment permitted for children under the age of fourteen are very limited. Even when minors are allowed to work, the work cannot interfere with school or with the well-being of the child. A child under the age of fourteen:

1. Can be employed in work by parents or guardians, except in mining, manufacturing, or hazardous occupations.
2. Can work as actors.
3. Can work in certain agricultural activities. The nature and amount of work permitted depends on the minor's age, the hours of work, and whether he or she is working for his or her parents.
4. Can work in newspaper delivery and baby-sitting.

UNDER THE AGE OF SIXTEEN

Work for minors under age sixteen is also restricted. Minors under the age of sixteen cannot work in manufacturing, mining, public messenger services, jobs requiring power-driven machinery, warehouse work, and many other jobs considered "oppressive child labor." The work cannot interfere with schooling or with the health and well-being of the minor. The FLSA primarily covers what employers cannot do, rather than what they can. Work that is specifically authorized by the FLSA includes:

1. Office and clerical work, including the operation of office machines.

Critical Thinking Activity

Ask the students to answer orally the following questions: Why do you think minors under the age of 16 are not allowed to work in manufacturing, mining, public messenger services, jobs requiring power-driven machinery, and warehouse work, as well as many other jobs? Why do you think these jobs have been termed "oppressive child labor"?

Collaborative Learning Activity

Divide the class into small groups. Have each group prepare a poster illustrating the types of work that are prohibited for minors under the age of 16 and the types of work that are allowed for minors under the age of 16. Students may cull images from newspapers or magazines or may choose to use original artwork to illustrate their posters. Allow the groups to display their posters in the classroom.

2. Cashiering, selling, modeling, artwork, work in advertising departments, window trimming, and comparative shopping.
3. Price marking and tagging by hand or by machine, assembling orders, packing and shelving.
4. Bagging and carrying out customers' orders.
5. Errand and delivery work by foot, bicycle, and public transportation.
6. Clean-up work, if it does not involve the use of power-driven mowers or cutters.
7. Kitchen work.
8. Certain work around cars and trucks, such as dispensing gasoline or cleaning cars.

Individual states prohibit types of work that might otherwise be legal under the FLSA. California, for example, prohibits work in a bowling alley or pool hall. Minors between ages fourteen and sixteen can, of course, work at the occupations open to younger minors. They also can often work at other jobs, although both the hours and the conditions of work are strictly limited by the FLSA.

Minors under the age of sixteen are generally required to have either a work permit or a certificate of age before being employed. Because of penalties for violations of FLSA laws, many employers are reluctant to hire anyone under the age of sixteen.

UNDER THE AGE OF EIGHTEEN

There are far fewer restrictions for workers under age eighteen, but the nature of work and the hours are still regulated for such workers. For example, those under eighteen years old cannot be employed in hazardous jobs or in jobs detrimental to their health and well-being. Many states require minors under eighteen years of age to get work permits.

Certain jobs are specifically prohibited for minors under eighteen. These prohibitions include, but are not limited to, work in dangerous occupations. Those occupations determined to be hazardous by the U.S. secretary of labor include:

1. Coal and other mining.
2. Employment in plants that manufacture explosives, bricks, or tile.
3. Operation of power-driven hoisting equipment.
4. Employment in logging and sawmill operations.
5. Public road motor-vehicle driver or outside helper except where driving is occasional and incidental to employment. Applies to certain private property driving as well. Exception for driving a school-bus under limited circumstances.
6. Occupations where the employee is exposed to radioactive substances.
7. Operation of power-driven woodworking, metal-forming, punching, shearing, bakery, or paper-products machines.
8. Employment in slaughterhouses and meat-packing plants.
9. Operation and maintenance of circular saws, band saws, and guillotine shears.
10. Shipbreaking (tearing down ships for scrap) and wrecking or demolishing buildings.
11. Roofing operations.
12. Excavation.

(continued on page 538)

Most states require a minor to get a work permit before taking any employment. If your state requires a work permit, obtain a copy of the paperwork required to obtain a work permit, and with the class go through the steps required for completing this paperwork. You might also allow volunteers to describe any experiences they have had in applying for and obtaining work permits.

Guide the students in looking at the hour limitations for minors in the state of California, as spelled out here. Then ask the students to write short paragraphs explaining how these hour limitations have been designed to incorporate a minor's educational needs. Allow student volunteers to share their work with the class.

LEGAL PERSPECTIVE (CONTINUED)

WORK PERMITS

Most states require a minor to get a work permit before taking any employment. Depending on the state, work permits are granted by either a state agency or a local school district. In Idaho, Mississippi, South Carolina, and Texas, federal certificates of age are issued instead of state work permits.

Work permits protect the employer from unintentionally violating the FLSA by employing an underage minor for a particular job. Work permits are often not necessary for certain jobs, such as taking a newspaper route, baby-sitting, mowing lawns, doing odd jobs, or working for a parent or guardian. A sample work permit is found in Exhibit LP22-1.

HOUR LIMITATIONS

The hours a minor may work are limited depending on the age of the minor and the nature of the job. Many state limitations are more restrictive than the FLSA. It is difficult to specify exact hour limitations since they vary from state to state. Because California has both a manufacturing and an agricultural work force, it can serve as a representative state. California hour limitations (with a few exceptions) are the following:

1. On school days, a minor under age fourteen cannot work.
2. On school days, a minor older than fourteen can work up to four hours after school.
3. During vacations (including summer vacations), a minor older than fourteen

---

Permit to Employ and Work

California State Department of Education
Form No. B1-4 (Rev. 4-89)

Expires on: _____

Maximum number of hours of employment when school is in session:

Monday through Thursday _____ Friday* _____

*And any other school days immediately preceding school holidays and other nonschool days.

For weekly maximums and maximum hours of employment on holidays and other nonschool days, see reverse.

Type of Employee

Regular ☐   Vacation ☐

Work Experience ☐   Exempt ☐

Valid only at: _____

Name of minor (last name first) _____   Social Security Number ____   Age at issuance ____   Date of birth ____

Street address _____   City ____   ZIP code ____   Home phone ____

School name _____   Street address ____   City ____   ZIP code ____   School phone ____

Signature of minor _____   Signature of issuing authority ____   Date ____

Hours of compulsory school attendance (required for "regular" employees only): _____

Remarks: _____

Valid only if employer has filed Form B1-1, "Request for Work Permit and Statement of Intent to Employ Minor," with issuing school authority (except vacation employees).

CVUSD 96-0-0064   12/89   Copy–To be retained by issuing authority

Extension Activity

Have a student, or a group of students, research child-labor practices prior to the passage of the Fair Labor Standards Act in 1938. Students' reports should answer the following questions: What age limitations were there on child labor? Under what conditions were children allowed to work? How would you generally describe the treatment of children in the workplace? What economic necessities forced children into the workplace? What accommodations, if any, were made for schooling? Have the students present their findings to the class in the form of oral reports. Encourage students to cite original source documents in their reports.

can work up to forty-eight hours a week. But these minors cannot work more than eight hours a day. Work must be completed between 5 A.M. and 10 P.M. on any day preceding a school day. On nonschool days that precede another nonschool day, the minor can work until 12:30 A.M.

4. Minors who have graduated from high school can generally work full time. Other exceptions exist for minors who are supporting a family or who have legally left school.

◆ Provisions of the Fair Labor Standards Act That Apply to All Workers (Minors and Adults)

Maximum Hours

Under this act, any employee who agrees to work more than forty hours per week must be paid no less than one-and-a-half times his or her regular pay for all the hours worked over forty. Exceptions are made for employees working under the terms of a collective-bargaining agreement and in a few other circumstances.

Minimum Wage

The Fair Labor Standards Act provides that a minimum wage of a specified amount must be paid to employees in covered industries. Congress periodically revises such minimum wages. The term *wages* is meant to include the reasonable cost to the employer of furnishing employees with board, lodging, and other facilities if they are customarily furnished by that employer. In 1993, the minimum wage was $4.25 an hour. There are a few exceptional situations in which minors can be paid less than the minimum wage—for example, in some training programs.

Complaints About Violations of FLSA or State Minor Labor Laws

Complaints about violations of the FLSA should be made to the United States Department of Labor. Complaints about violations of state labor laws should be made to the appropriate state agency, which is often called the Department of Labor, the Commissioner of Labor, or the Department of Industry. Violations of labor laws can lead to civil lawsuits; in some cases, an employee can recover double his or her unpaid wages. Violators can also be subject to criminal prosecution.

Suggested Additional Resources

Bagley, Constance E. *Managers and the Legal Environment: Strategies for the 21st Century.* St. Paul, MN: West Publishing Co., 1991.

Bryan, Cynthia and Wasserman, Paul. *Small Business Information Source Book.* Phoenix, AZ: Onyx Press, 1987.

The Guide to American Law. St. Paul, MN: West Publishing Co., 1983. - Annual updates are available.

Halbert, Terry and Ingulli, Elaine. *Law and Ethics in the Business Environment.* St. Paul, MN: West Publishing Co., 1990.

Henn, Harry G., and Alexander, John R. *Henn and Alexander's Hornbook on Laws of Corporations,* 3d ed. St. Paul, MN: West Publishing Co., 1983/1986 pocket parts.

Kempin, Wiesen, and Bagby. *Legal Aspects of the Management Process: Cases and Material,* 4d ed. St. Paul, MN: West Publishing Co., 1990.

Moye, John. *The Law of Business Organizations,* 3d ed. St. Paul, MN: West Publishing Co., 1989.

United States Government Manual. Washington, D.C.: U.S. Government Printing Office - Published annually. The publication lists all federal departments and administrative agencies with information about their activities and personnel.

Chapter 23
Forms of Business Organization

Chapter 24
Corporations

Chapter 25
Government Regulation of Business

Unit
5 LEGAL PERSPECTIVE

Chapter 23—Entrepreneurs
Chapter 25—Environmental Law

UNIT 5

Doing Business

Every business activity involves a form of business organization. Such forms include sole proprietorships, partnerships, and corporations. Each type of organization provides businesspeople with a different amount of flexibility and different rights and liabilities.

Chapter 23 introduces the three major forms of business organization and describes the legal requirements of sole proprietorships and partnerships. Chapter 24 looks at corporation law. The modern corporation is perhaps the most important form of business organization in the history of the world. Some economists argue that without it, the economic growth of the Western World would never have happened.

A hundred years ago, the topic of governmental regulation of business would barely have appeared in a text like this one. Today, understanding the relationship between government and business is of critical importance. Chapter 25 introduces the general topic of governmental regulation of business.

CHAPTER 23

LEGAL BACKGROUND

The three major business forms: sole proprietorships, partnerships, and corporations are each defined in this chapter. Partnerships are discussed in the greatest detail because sole proprietorships are not complicated business forms, and corporations are featured in the next chapter. Partnerships are easy to create, as they can exist even without a formal agreement if parties join together in a business activity for a profit. However, the legal solutions to common partnership problems make clear the need for a well-considered partnership agreement. Applied agency law is discussed when considering the duties that partners owe to one another. The limited partnership is introduced as a statutory form of partnership that allows an investor to have an ownership position in a partnership and still protect his or her personal assets. We distinguish between a joint venture and a partnership at the close of this chapter.

542

Prereading Activity

Ask students to name businesses in your city or state. Encourage students to think about small local businesses. Write the names of the companies on the board. Tell the students to write a paragraph telling what kind of business they would start if they had the opportunity.

Mastery Objectives

By the end of this chapter, students will be able to:
- Describe a sole proprietorship
- Compare general and limited partnerships
- List the essential characteristics of a corporation
- Explain a joint venture

Chapter
23

Forms of Business Organization

*"It is a socialist idea that making profits is a vice. I consider the real vice is
making losses."*
Sir Winston Churchill, 1874–1965
British prime minister, 1940–1945, 1951–1955

In this chapter, we briefly examine the basic features of the three
major forms of business organization: sole proprietorships, partnerships, and corporations.

◆ SOLE PROPRIETORSHIPS

The simplest form of business organization is a **sole proprietorship**.
Here, the business is owned by one person. Anyone who does business
without taking the legal steps necessary to create another type of organization has, by default, a sole proprietorship. Sole proprietorships are common; they constitute more than two-thirds of all American businesses.
They are also usually small; less than 1 percent of the sole proprietorships
existing in the United States earn more than $1 million a year. Sole propri-
etors can own and manage any type of business, from writing books out of
an office at home to running a huge restaurant or a construction firm.

A sole proprietorship is the easiest and least costly type of business to
create. It requires no agreement or charter from the state to begin. Like
the owners of other businesses, a sole proprietor must be concerned about
obtaining certain business licenses from the government, but the detailed
planning that is required for more complicated business organizations is
not necessary. A sole proprietor's personal, as well as business, assets, are at
risk in the running of the business. An **asset** is an accounting term for anything of value, including cash, furniture, and buildings. This potential liability is called *unlimited liability for business losses*. If the sole proprietor goes
into debt, the sole proprietor may have to repay that money out of his or
her personal savings or property. On the other hand, the sole proprietor
doesn't have to share with anyone else any of the profits the business earns.

Owners of sole proprietorships are free to make all business decisions as
they wish without consulting others. Thus, the owner is his or her own
boss. For example, a sole proprietor can decide how hard to work and
when to take vacations. In fact, however, sole proprietors usually work
very hard and take shorter and fewer vacations than do their employees.

The sole proprietorship does not pay federal income tax. Instead, the
owner includes income from the business as part of his or her individual
tax filing with the Internal Revenue Service.

The major difficulty for most sole proprietors is finding sufficient resources to fund the business. When an owner is starting a business or wishes to expand an existing one, he or she must have cash and property
available. A sole proprietor also needs funds in order to pay the bills when
business slows down or economic times are hard.

◆ **sole
proprietorship** A
business owned by one
person. Anyone who
does business without
creating another type of
business organization is
a sole proprietor. The
owner is the business.

◆ **asset** An
accounting term for
anything of value; for
example, cash,
furniture, real property,
and automobiles.

Discussion Starter

On the board, write the
quote from Sir Winston
Churchill that begins this
chapter. Ask students what
the quote means to them
and how a socialist economy differs from the United
States' capitalistic economy
concerning business ownership.

Enrichment

You might point out to the
students that there are more
than 10 million sole proprietorships in the United
States and that one out of
eight people is self-
employed.

Critical Thinking
Activity

Ask your students to think
about the fact that sole proprietors usually work very
hard and take shorter and
fewer vacations than do
their employees. Ask your
students the following questions about this fact: Does it
make sense to you that a
sole proprietor would take
shorter and fewer vacations
than his or her employees?
Why or why not? How does
the sole proprietor have
more at stake in the business's success than his or
her employees?

Extension Activity

Invite a sole proprietor to
your classroom to discuss
the advantages and disad-
vantages of owning one's
own business. Instruct students to formulate a list of
questions to ask before the
business owner arrives.

Legal Focus Example

Have a student volunteer read aloud the Legal Focus Example found at the bottom of this page. Remind students that they can use the Legal Focus features as review tools when studying for tests.

To a great extent, partnership law is based on agency law. Because each partner is considered to be an agent of the partnership, certain agency concepts apply, including the imputation of knowledge of, and responsibility for, acts done within the scope of the partnership relationship. Partners are bound to one another by the fiduciary ties that bind an agent and principal under agency law.

A partnership is based on a voluntary agreement between two or more competent persons who agree to place some or all of their money, effects, labor, and skill in a business with the understanding that profits and losses will be proportionately shared. In a nonpartnership agency relationship, the agent usually does not have an ownership interest in the business, nor is the agent obligated to bear a portion of the ordinary business losses.

* **partnership** An association of two or more persons to carry on as co-owners of a business for profit.

* **capital** An accounting term for money or other assets invested in a business.

 ## PARTNERSHIPS

The Uniform Partnership Act (UPA) defines a **partnership** as "an association of two or more persons to carry on as co-owners of a business for profit." To meet the requirements for this form of business organization, the individuals involved should agree to create a partnership to contribute capital, to share profits and losses, and to participate in the management of the business. **Capital** is an accounting term for money or other assets invested in the business.

The *intent* to associate is a key element in a partnership. No one can join a partnership unless all the partners consent. Each partner is considered to be an agent (representative) for the other partners.

Partnerships can be either general partnerships or limited partnerships. The two forms have different legal requirements and provide different rights and responsibilities for the partners. The following subsections look at the characteristics and operation of a general partnership.

CHARACTERISTICS OF A GENERAL PARTNERSHIP

A partnership exists because of an agreement. The agreement can be express or implied. Partners are co-owners of the business. They have joint control over its operation and the right to share in its profits. No particular form of partnership agreement must be used. It is, however, very desirable that the partnership agreement be in writing.

Both general partnerships and sole proprietorships are creatures of common law rather than of statute. Partners can agree to almost any terms when establishing a partnership so long as the terms are legal and consistent with public policy. The Uniform Partnership Act governs the operation of the partnership and fills in the gaps if the partners do not have a written agreement or if they neglect to include a necessary term in their agreement. The UPA has been adopted in all states except Louisiana.

Most states allow a partnership to sue or be sued, collect judgments, and have all accounting procedures in the partnership name. Property may be held in the name of the partnership rather than in the names of the individual partners. For most other purposes, the partnership is a combination of the individual partners.

LEGAL FOCUS – EXAMPLE

A partnership itself does not pay federal income tax. The business income or losses are "passed through" the partnership to the partners. The partnership files an informational return stating how the income or losses were distributed among the partners. Each partner then reports his or her profit or loss from the business on an individual tax return.

Ethical Concern

Ask students to suppose that they started a partnership with a friend. Say: "Since you contributed more capital to the startup of the business, you both agreed orally that you would receive three-fifths of the profit, and your partner would receive two-fifths of the profit. What problems could occur because of this oral contract? What will go into effect if no one can prove the agreement? How could possible problems be avoided?" Have students discuss these questions and the ethics involved in a partnership.

GENERAL PARTNERSHIP FORMATION

General partnership agreements can be oral, written, or implied by conduct. Practically speaking, a partnership agreement should always be in writing because the terms of an oral agreement are difficult to prove. In addition, the process of drafting a written agreement often ensures that partners will discuss potential problems ahead of time; these problems might go unnoticed in an oral agreement.

 LEGAL FOCUS ~ PROBLEM

Terrence and Frank plan to form a partnership to sell tires. Among the contract provisions discussed is the agreement that Terrence is to provide two-thirds of the money to start the business, and in return he is to get two-thirds of the profits. Terrence and Frank never get around to drafting a written agreement, although they begin to sell tires. Does Terrence have a right to two-thirds of the profits?

If Terrence and Frank agreed orally on Terrence's two-thirds, then that is what he should receive. However, without putting the agreement in writing, Terrence will have a hard time proving his rights. If he cannot prove this agreement, the UPA provides that each partner will share profits and losses equally.

A partnership agreement, called the **articles of partnership**, usually states what each partner's share of the profits will be. The agreement is binding no matter how uneven a distribution appears. A sample partnership agreement is shown in Exhibit 23-1.

Partnership Duration If the partnership agreement states how long the partnership will exist, then it is called a *partnership for a term*. Dissolving, or ending, the partnership without the consent of all the partners before the agreed term is a breach of the agreement. The partner responsible for ending the partnership early can be liable for any losses that result.

If an expiration time for the partnership is not stated, then it is called a *partnership at will*. A partnership at will can be dissolved at any time. Normally, each partner must be given notice before the partnership comes to an end.

Indications of Partnership Parties may disagree about whether or not their business enterprise is a partnership, especially if there is no formal written contract. But in the eyes of the law, a partnership exists if the essential elements of partnership status are present: (1) a common ownership interest in a business, (2) the sharing of the profits and losses of the business, and (3) the right to manage the operations of the partnership. When these elements exist, parties cannot avoid partnership debt by claiming that they have formed another type of business. Also, joint ownership of property alone does not create a partnership.

◆ **articles of partnership** A written agreement that states each partner's rights in, and duties to, the partnership.

Legal Focus Problem

Ask a student volunteer to read aloud this Legal Focus Problem. Then call on volunteers to suggest possible answers to the question posed at the end of this problem. Make sure that the students understand that in the absence of a written agreement, Terrence may be forced to go to court to prove that he is due two-thirds of the profits.

Critical Thinking Activity

Call on a student volunteer to compare the employment-at-will doctrine to the explanation in the student text of a partnership at will.

545

Extension Activity

Ask your students if any of their parents are involved in partnerships for business purposes. If so, you might ask that parent, or those parents, to speak to your class regarding their partnerships. Parents should be encouraged to discuss the following questions: Why was the partnership formed? Is this a general or a limited partnership? Does your partnership have a written agreement? What are the advantages for you as a partner in this partnership? What are the disadvantages?

Legal Focus Problem

Have a student volunteer read aloud to the class this Legal Focus Problem. Ask a student volunteer to suggest a possible answer to the question posed at the end of this problem. Then have the volunteer read the paragraph immediately following this Legal Focus Problem to reveal the answer. Have a student volunteer suggest what changes would have to be made in an agreement between Allen, Burke, and Brenda in order to form a partnership among the three.

Enrichment

Guide the students in looking at Exhibit 23-1 by having a student volunteer read the partnership agreement aloud to the class.

Collaborative Learning Activity

Divide the class into groups of three. Have each group draw up a partnership agreement for a small business of its choice that includes each group member as a partner.

PARTNERSHIP AGREEMENT

This agreement, made and entered into as of the _____, by and among _____
_____ (hereinafter collectively sometimes referred to as "Partners").

WITNESSETH:

Whereas, the Parties hereto desire to form a General Partnership (hereinafter referred to as the "Partnership"), for the term and upon the conditions hereinafter set forth;

Now, therefore, in consideration of the mutual covenants hereinafter contained, it is agreed by and among the Parties hereto as follows:

Article I
BASIC STRUCTURE

Form. The Parties hereby form a General Partnership pursuant to the Laws of _____
_____.

Name. The business of the Partnership shall be conducted under the name of _____
_____.

Place of Business. The principal office and place of business of the Partnership shall be located at _____, or such other place as the Partners may from time to time designate.

Term. The Partnership shall commence on _____, and shall continue for _____years, unless earlier terminated in the following manner: (a) By the completion of the purpose intended, or (b) Pursuant to this Agreement, or (c) By applicable _____law, or (d) By death, insanity, bankruptcy, retirement, withdrawal, resignation, expulsion, or disability of all of the then Partners.

Purpose—General. The purpose for which the Partnership is organized is _____

Article II
FINANCIAL ARRANGEMENTS

Each Partner has contributed to the initial capital of the Partnership property in the amount and form indicated on Schedule A attached hereto and made a part hereof. Capital contributions to the Partnership shall not earn interest. An individual capital account shall be maintained for each Partner. If at any time during the existence of the Partnership it shall become necessary to increase the capital with which the said Partnership is doing business, then (upon the vote of the Managing Partner(s)): each party to this Agreement shall contribute to the capital of this Partnership within _ days notice of such need in an amount according to his then Percentage Share of Capital as called for by the Managing Partner(s).

The Percentage Share of Profits and Capital of each Partner shall be (unless otherwise modified by the terms of this Agreement) as follows:

Names	Initial Percentage Share of Profits and Capital

No interest shall be paid on any contribution to the capital of the Partnership. No Partner shall have the right to demand the return of his capital contributions except as herein provided. Except as herein provided, the individual Partners shall have no right to any priority over each other as to the return of capital contributions except as herein provided.

Distributions to the Partners of net operating profits of the Partnership, as hereinafter defined, shall be made at _____. Such distributions shall be made to the Partners simultaneously.

For the purpose of this Agreement, net operating profit for any accounting period shall mean the gross receipts of the Partnership for such period, less the sum of all cash expenses of operation of the Partnership, and such sums as may be necessary to establish a reserve for operating expenses. In determining net operating profit, deductions for depreciation, amortization, or other similar charges not requiring actual current expenditures of cash shall *not* be taken into account in accordance with generally accepted accounting principles.

Exhibit 23-1
Partnership Agreement

◆ LEGAL FOCUS ～ PROBLEM

Allen and Burke jointly own a piece of country property. They lease the property to a farmer, Brenda. Rather than receive set rental payments, all agree to share the profits from the farming operation. Is this a partnership?

Collaborative Learning Activity

Get permission from your school administrators to start a small business with your class. Have your students each contribute a small amount of money to purchase school supplies (or bring in food items) to sell to other students in the school. Have the students set up a booth before and after school to sell the products and have them manage the booth. After a week or two, divide the profits or have a class outing.

Extension Activity

Have students bring in articles from current news publications (newspapers, magazines) on businesses operated as partnerships. It is particularly interesting to discuss lawsuits involving partnerships. Discuss with students how they knew the businesses were partnerships and the reason that the articles were written.

No Partner shall be entitled to receive any compensation from the Partnership, nor shall any Partner receive any drawing account from the Partnership.

Article III
MANAGEMENT

The Managing Partner(s) shall be _____.
The Managing Partner(s) shall have the right to vote as to the management and conduct of the business of the Partnership as follows:

Names   **Vote**

Article IV
DISSOLUTION

In the event that the Partnership shall hereafter be dissolved for any reason whatsoever, a full and general account of its assets, liabilities and transactions shall at once be taken. Such assets may be sold and turned into cash as soon as possible and all debts and other amounts due the Partnership collected. The proceeds thereof shall thereupon be applied as follows:

(a) To discharge the debts and liabilities of the Partnership and the expenses of liquidation.

(b) To pay each Partner or his legal representative any unpaid salary, drawing account, interest or profits to which he shall then be entitled and in addition, to repay to any Partner his capital contributions in excess of his original capital contribution.

(c) To divide the surplus, if any, among the Partners or their representatives as follows: (1) First (to the extent of each Partner's then capital account) in proportion to their then capital accounts. (2) Then according to each Partner's then Percentage Share of [*Capital/Income*].

No Partner shall have the right to demand and receive property in kind for his distribution.

Article V
MISCELLANEOUS

The Partnership's fiscal year shall commence on January 1st of each year and shall end on December 31st of each year. Full and accurate books of account shall be kept at such place as the Managing Partner(s) may from time to time designate, showing the condition of the business and finances of the Partnership; and each Partner shall have access to such books of account and shall be entitled to examine them at any time during ordinary business hours. At the end of each year, the Managing Partner(s) shall cause the Partnership's accountant to prepare a balance sheet setting forth the financial position of the Partnership as of the end of that year and a statement of operations (income and expenses) for that year. A copy of the balance sheet and statement of operations shall be delivered to each Partner as soon as it is available.

Each Partner shall be deemed to have waived all objections to any transaction or other facts about the operation of the Partnership disclosed in such balance sheet and/or statement of operations unless he shall have notified the Managing Partner(s) in writing of his objectives within thirty (30) days of the date on which such statement is mailed.

The Partnership shall maintain a bank account or bank accounts in the Partnership's name in a national or state bank in the State of _____. Checks and drafts shall be drawn on the Partnership's bank account for Partnership purposes only and shall be signed by the Managing Partner(s) or their designated agent.

Any controversy or claim arising out of or relating to this Agreement shall only be settled by arbitration in accordance with the rules of the American Arbitration Association, one Arbitrator, and shall be enforceable in any court having competent jurisdiction.

Witnesses   **Partners**

_____   _____

_____   _____

Dated: _____

EXHIBIT 23-1(CONTINUED)
PARTNERSHIP AGREEMENT

This agreement alone does not make Allen, Burke, and Brenda partners. Sharing of profits alone does not prove the existence of a partnership, but sharing *both* profits and losses would.

RIGHTS AMONG PARTNERS

The rights and duties of partners are governed by the partnership agreement. If the agreement doesn't specify these rights and duties, then the UPA fills in the gaps as described in the subsections that follow. Of course, each partnership business is different from others, and the nature of the

LEGAL BACKGROUND

At common law, a partnership was never treated as a separate legal entity. A common law suit could not be brought by or against the firm in its own name; each individual partner had to sue or be sued.

Many states today provide specifically that the partnership can be treated as an entity for certain purposes, including filing and defending suits, collecting judgments, and conducting accounting procedures in the name of the partnership. In addition, the UPA recognizes that partnership property may be held in the name of the partnership rather than in the names of the individual partners. Finally, federal procedural laws frequently permit the partnership to be treated as an entity in such matters as suits in federal courts, bankruptcy proceedings, and filing of informational federal tax returns.

Enrichment

Guide the students in looking at the six actions in the numbered list that can significantly affect the nature of a partnership. For each action in the numbered list, call on a student volunteer to explain how this action would significantly affect the nature of a partnership.

Enrichment

Have the students read the section here on compensation from the partnership. Then have the students look again at Exhibit 23-1 and read the first paragraph on the top of the second page of this partnership agreement, where it says, "No Partner shall be entitled to receive any compensation from the Partnership, nor shall any Partner receive any drawing account from the Partnership."

Legal Focus Example

Have a student volunteer read aloud to the class this Legal Focus Example. Ask the class why they think compensation may be warranted in the case of a managing partner of an accounting firm. Remind students that they can use the Legal Focus features as review tools when studying for tests.

LEGAL BACKGROUND

Compensation for members of a partnership is generally not provided. Devoting time, skill, and energy to a partnership business is a partner's duty and generally not a compensable service. Partners can, of course, agree otherwise. The managing partner of a law firm, for example, often receives a salary in addition to his or her share of profits for performing special administrative duties in office and personnel management. The UPA also provides that on the death of a partner, a surviving partner is entitled to compensation for services winding up partnership affairs (and reimbursement for expenses incurred in the process) above and beyond his or her share in the partnership profits.

548

---

548   Doing Business

business influences how these rights and duties are applied.

Partnership rights relate to the following areas: management, interest in the partnership, compensation, inspection of books, accounting, and property rights.

Management of the Partnership   Under the Uniform Partnership Act, all partners have equal rights to manage the partnership. This means that in the usual partnership, each partner has one vote in management matters. This is the case even if his or her interest in the firm is larger than some of the others'. Often, in a large partnership, partners agree to delegate daily management responsibilities to a single manager or to a management committee that consists of some of the partners.

A majority vote controls ordinary partnership decisions unless otherwise specified in the agreement. However, the partners must vote unanimously in order to commit the firm to taking any of the following actions, because each of these significantly affects the nature of the partnership:

1. Altering the nature of the firm's business as expressed in the partnership agreement, or altering the ownership interests of the partnership.
2. Admitting any new partners or entering a new area of business.
3. Transferring partnership property into a trust for the benefit of creditors.
4. Disposing of the partnership's goodwill. *Goodwill* is an accounting term for any value of the business that exceeds its asset value. The value of ongoing relationships with customers or the name familiarity with the public are examples of goodwill.
5. Admitting responsibility in a lawsuit or submitting partnership legal matters to arbitration.
6. Performing any act that would make further conduct of partnership business impossible. For example, selling the only delivery truck owned by a pizza delivery business.

Ownership in the Partnership   If the partnership agreement does not allocate profits or losses, the UPA provides that profits and losses are shared equally. As discussed earlier, a partnership agreement can provide for profits to be shared in another way, such as according to how much capital each partner has contributed.

Compensation from the Partnership   A partner does not ordinarily receive a salary from the partnership. A partner's effort is seen as a duty rather than as a service for which he or she should be paid. Partners can, of course, agree otherwise.

LEGAL FOCUS – EXAMPLE

The managing partner of an accounting firm often receives a salary for performing the management duties. This payment is in addition to his or her share in the partnership profits.

Lead a discussion about partnership rights as they relate to management, interest in the partnership, compensation, inspection of books, accounting, and property rights. Ask students to talk about what kinds of problems might arise if a partner were denied any of these rights.

You might ask a student volunteer to research the business life of Richard Sears, who started as a sole proprietor in the Midwest, later entered into a partnership with Roebuck, and then started their corporation. Have the student report his or her findings to the class.

Ask a student volunteer to read aloud this Legal Focus Example dealing with tenants in partnership. Remind students that they can use the Legal Focus features as review tools when studying for tests.

Inspection of Partnership Books   The books and records of the business must be available for all partners to inspect. Each partner has the right to receive information concerning all facets of partnership business.

Accounting of Partnership Assets   An accounting of partnership assets or profits determines the value of each partner's interest in the partnership. An accounting can be performed voluntarily, or it can be compelled by the order of a court. If a legal dispute between partners occurs and the parties cannot agree on the value of each partner's share, an accounting will determine the value.

Property Rights in Partnership   A partner has two property rights:

1. *An interest in the partnership.* A partner's interest in the firm is a personal asset. It consists of a share of the profits and, after the partnership ends, a return of the capital invested.
2. *A right in specific partnership property.* All property purchased by or for the partnership is partnership property. Partners are **tenants in partnership** of all such property. This means that every partner is a co-owner with all the other partners of specific partnership property, such as office equipment, paper supplies, and vehicles. Each partner has an equal right to use the partnership property for business purposes. Partners do not have the right to use the property for personal reasons without the consent of all other partners.

Tenancy in partnership has several important effects. If a partner dies, the surviving partners have the right to the specific partnership property. The surviving partners have a duty to pay the dead partner's estate the *value* of the property. The partner's heirs do not, however, have a right or claim against any specific partnership property. A partner has no right to sell, assign, or in any way use partnership property as an exclusive owner.

◆ **tenants in partnership** A form of joint ownership of property by partners. Each partner is a co-owner with all other partners of specific partnership property. Each partner has equal rights to use the partnership property for business purposes.

◇ LEGAL FOCUS ~ EXAMPLE

The ABC partnership consists of Amos, Betty, and Carin. The business owns several items of property, including a bicycle used by the company's messenger service. The bicycle is partnership property. All three partners own it together and each is free to use and even sell the bicycle for the partnership's benefit. However, neither Amos, Betty, or Carin has the right to take the bicycle home for personal use without the permission of all three partners. If Carin were to die, her heirs would not have any specific interest in the bicycle; it remains partnership property. Carin's heirs have the right to receive a distribution of Carin's partnership interest, rather than any specific property.

LEGAL BACKGROUND

Partnership books and records must be kept accessible to all partners. Each partner has the right to receive (and the corresponding duty to produce) full and complete information concerning the conduct of all aspects of partnership business. Each firm retains books in which to record and secure such information. Partners contribute the information, and a bookkeeper typically has the duty to preserve it.

The books must be kept at the firm's principal business office unless the partners agree otherwise. Each partner, whether active or inactive, is entitled to inspect all books and records upon demand and can make copies of the materials. The personal representative of a deceased partner's estate has the same right of access to partnership books and records that the decedent would have had.

Reteaching Activity

The student text points out that partners have a fiduciary relationship to one another. The concept of fiduciary relationship was introduced as a part of the discussion of the agency-principal relationship in Chapter 20. In order to refresh students' memories on the concept of a fiduciary relationship, have a student volunteer turn to Chapter 20 or to the glossary at the end of this book to read aloud the definition of *fiduciary relationship*.

Caption Answer

Student answers may vary but should reflect an understanding of the fact that partners have a fiduciary relationship to one another.

Ethical Concern

Have students write an essay comparing a partnership to a marriage. What ethical principles and obligations do the two have in common?

DUTIES AND POWERS OF PARTNERS

The duties and powers of partners consist of a fiduciary duty of each partner to the other and general agency powers.

Fiduciary Duty   Partners have a fiduciary relationship to one another. The relationship mirrors the principal and agent relationship described in Chapter 20. It is a relationship of extraordinary trust and loyalty. The fiduciary duty requires that each partner act in good faith for the benefit of the partnership. It requires that each partner defer his or her personal interests if they conflict with the mutual welfare of the partners.

General Agency Powers   Each partner is an *agent* of every other partner. Each partner may act as both a principal and an agent in any business transaction within the scope of the partnership agreement. Each partner is a general agent of the partnership in carrying out the usual business of the firm. Thus, every contract concerning partnership business that a partner signs in the partnership name binds the firm.

What are the duties owed by one partner to another? What terms and conditions should each party seek to include in a partnership agreement?

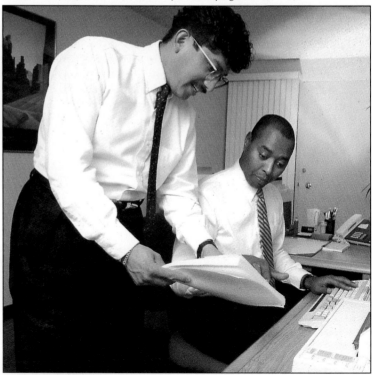

Legal Focus Example

Have a student volunteer read aloud the first Legal Focus Example found here. Ask the student to explain how this is an example of how the relationship among partners mirrors the principal and agent relationship.

Critical Thinking Activity

Have students suppose that a partner in their business applied for a loan without their consent. Ask: "If your partner received the loan, would you be liable too? What is this called? Why do you think that this law was made?" Have students discuss these questions and this issue.

> ### ◆ LEGAL FOCUS – EXAMPLE
>
> Paula, a partner in Rivercity Video Rentals, applies for a loan for the partnership. The bank manager knows that Paula is a partner and that she thus has partnership authority to apply for loans. If the bank manager grants her the loan, the partnership is responsible for paying it back.

Joint Liability   In most states, partners are subject to **joint liability** on partnership debts and contracts. Joint liability means that any person claiming payment must make a claim against all partners. For example, if a third person sued a partner to collect a debt, the partner could require the creditor to sue all the partners. If a third party is successful in a lawsuit, each partner is liable and may have to pay the entire amount of any partnership debt. When one partner pays a partnership debt, the partnership must indemnify (pay back) that partner. If the partnership cannot do so, the other partners must pay that partner back.

Joint and Several Liability   In some states,[1] partners are jointly and severally liable for partnership debts and contracts. Joint liability was defined in the previous paragraph. **Several liability** is separate and complete liability on an entire obligation even if others are also responsible. **Joint and several liability** means that a third party may sue any one or more of the partners without suing all of them or the partnership itself. If the lawsuit is successful, the creditor may collect from only the partners named as defendants.

In all states, partners are jointly and severally liable for torts and breaches of trust. Any partner who commits a tort is required to indemnify, or pay back, the partnership for any damages the partnership pays as a result of the tort.

◆ **joint liability**
Shared responsibility for debts or obligations. A third party must generally sue all liable parties together.

◆ **several liability**
Separate and complete responsibility for an entire obligation, even if others are also responsible.

◆ **joint and several liability**   A type of responsibility in which a third party may sue any one or more parties without suing all of them.

> ### ◆ LEGAL FOCUS – EXAMPLE
>
> Amos is a partner in the ABC partnership consisting of Amos, Betty, and Carin. While making a delivery on a bicycle, he carelessly and tortiously injures Madie Fricket. Madie could sue the partnership and/or any of the partners for her injuries. For example, if she sued and collected from Betty, Betty would have a right to be reimbursed by Amos. Amos as the wrongdoing party is liable to Madie, to the partnership, and to any partner who is required to pay Madie damages for his act.

Liability of Incoming Partner   A new partner to an existing partnership has limited liability for debts existing at the time he or she joins the partnership. The new partner has no personal liability for prior debts, but his

Legal Focus Example

Have a student volunteer read aloud this Legal Focus Example dealing with joint and several liability. Ask the students whether joint and several liability in this case would be applicable in all states or just in the seven states mentioned in the footnote on this page. (Students should understand that this is a tortious act and, as the student book points out, in all states, partners are jointly and severally liable for torts and breaches of trust.)

---

1.   Alabama, Arizona, Colorado, Missouri, North Carolina, Tennessee, and Texas.

Have a student volunteer read the first Legal Focus Example aloud to the class. Ask the students why any partner in a partnership that operates a retail tire store has implied authority to transfer title and make the usual warranties in selling a tire but does not have the implied authority to sell office equipment. Students should understand that the key words in this example are *products* and *property*. While a partner does have the authority to sell partnership products, he or she does not have the right to sell those partnership properties in which the partners are tenants in partnership.

Legal Focus Example

Ask a student volunteer to read the second Legal Focus Example aloud to the class. Remind students that they can use the Legal Focus features as review tools when studying for tests.

Divide the class into small groups. Have each group work together to compare the differences in the typical agency and partnership relationships. Although the law of partnerships includes many concepts of agency, the two areas do have significant differences, such as the fact that all partners have rights to partnership profits, while an agent generally has no proprietary rights in matters in which he or she acts on behalf of the principal. Have each group choose a leader to explain to the class his or her group's findings.

---

or her capital contribution to the partnership can be used to pay existing debts.

Authority of Partners   The agency concepts of apparent authority, actual authority, and ratification that were discussed in Chapter 20 apply to partnerships. The extent of *implied authority* is usually broader for partners than for ordinary agents. The character and scope of the partnership business and the customary nature of the particular business operation determine the implied powers.

In an ordinary partnership, partners can exercise all implied powers reasonably necessary and customary to carry on that particular business. If a partner acts within the scope of authority, the partnership is bound to any third parties who become involved because of the partner's action.

LEGAL FOCUS – EXAMPLE

A partner's authority to sell partnership products carries with it the implied authority to transfer title and to make the usual warranties. Hence, in a partnership that operates a retail tire store, any partner negotiating a contract with a customer for the sale of a set of tires can guarantee that "each tire will be warranted for normal wear for 40,000 miles." This same partner, however, would not have the authority to sell office equipment or the partnership office building without the agreement of all partners.

The fiduciary relationship implies that each partner will fully disclose to every other partner all important information about the partnership business.

PARTNERSHIP TERMINATION

The termination of a partnership has two stages: dissolution and winding up. Both must take place before termination is complete. *Dissolution* occurs when one or more partners indicate an intention to quit the partnership. *Winding up* is the actual process of collecting and distributing the partnership assets. Dissolution of a partnership can occur by acts of the partners, by operation of law, or by judicial decree.

Dissolution by Acts of the Partners   A partnership can be dissolved as provided in the partnership agreement or by an act of a partner.

LEGAL FOCUS – EXAMPLE

When a partnership agreement expresses a fixed term or a particular business objective to be accomplished, the passing of the date or the accomplishment of the objective dissolves the partnership.

Legal Focus Problem

Read to the class the Legal Focus Problem found here. Ask a student volunteer to suggest a possible answer to the question posed at the end of this problem. As followup questions you might ask the students whether or not River City Rafters can continue as a business. Why or why not?

Also, since a partnership is a voluntary association, a partner can quit the partnership at any time, and this will dissolve the partnership. If the partner quits before the partnership agreement allows, the act of quitting is a breach of contract. Courts will not make a partner remain in a partnership if he or she does not wish to, but the remaining partners can sue the quitting partner for damages.

Any change in the partnership, whether it is the withdrawal of a current partner or the admission of a new partner, results in dissolution. In practice, the remaining or new partners may agree to continue the firm's business. Nonetheless, a new partnership arises. Creditors of the prior partnership become creditors of the new partnership.

Dissolution by Operation of Law   If a partner dies, the partnership is dissolved by operation of law. Even if the partnership agreement provides that the business is to continue, it technically will dissolve. Remember: any change in partners results in a new partnership.

◀ LEGAL FOCUS ~ PROBLEM

Carl, Max, and Erin formed Rivercity Rafters, a small business in Coloma, California. They have a written partnership agreement. One clause of that agreement provides that if any partner should die, the other partners can continue the business. The clause requires the remaining partners to pay the deceased partner's heirs his or her interest in the partnership over a five-year period. If Max dies, does the partnership dissolve?

A partnership always dissolves when any partner dies. The agreement here, however, provides a way for Carl and Erin to form a new partnership that will continue the business. Carl and Erin need to pay Max's heirs the value of his interest over a five-year period. At Max's death, the partnership dissolves, and there should be accounting of Max's interest in Rivercity Rafters.

The bankruptcy of a partner or of the partnership dissolves a partnership by operation of law. Also, any event that makes it unlawful for the partnership to continue its business results in dissolution. For example, if one member of a law firm lost his or her license to practice law, the law firm would dissolve. A new firm without the disbarred lawyer would probably reform.

Dissolution by Judicial Decree   A partnership may be dissolved by judicial decree. This might happen when a partner becomes incapable of performing his or her duties under the partnership agreement.

Notice of Dissolution   A partner's intent to dissolve the partnership or to withdraw from a firm must be communicated clearly to each partner. This notice of intent can come from either a partner's actions or words.

LEGAL BACKGROUND

Dissatisfaction with the ambiguity surrounding the concept of partnership dissolution and its treatment in the UPA prompted the drafters of the Revised Uniform Partnership Act (RUPA) to attempt to identify the events that will cause the dissolution of a partnership. In particular, the RUPA distinguishes between those events that should result in the termination of a partnership and those events that are not so critical and should not affect the continued operation of the business. The sale by a single partner of his or her partnership interest is one event that should not typically affect the continued operation of the partnership.

Although RUPA 31 identifies certain departures that will automatically result in the dissolution of a partnership, RUPA 32 provides that any other types of departures will amount to a buyout of the departing partner that will not dissolve the partnership. In the event the partnership is dissolved and the partnership business must be concluded, RUPA 31Z requires that the assets of the partnership be applied first to the satisfaction of creditors' claims and that any remainder be distributed to the partners.

Read

You might want to introduce this *Law in Action* feature by asking students what happens when a married couple feels they can no longer stay married. Point out that ending a marriage involves a great many legal technicalities (which will be discussed in Chapter 27). Explain that ending a partnership also involves many legal technicalities, and that in this feature you will be reading about technicalities involved when one or more partners choose to buy out a partner.

Discuss

Stimulate a class discussion of this *Law in Action* feature by asking the following questions: What is a *buy-and-sell agreement,* as described in this feature? Why is it important that the partnership agreement provide ways for a business to continue to operate smoothly during a period when the partners disagree? What might happen if this was not provided for in the partnership agreement? In the absence of a buy-and-sell agreements the text advises that one group should decide the value of the business while the other group decides whether to buy or to sell. Do you believe this is a fair arrangement? Why or why not?

554   Doing Business

◆ Law in Action

LAW AND THE BUSINESSPERSON: PARTNERSHIP BUYOUTS

Most partnerships are created when the partners are getting along with each other. What happens if the situation changes and they can no longer work together? Who buys out whom, and at what price? Arrangements to handle such situations are usually called *buy-and-sell agreements*, and they should be made during the formation of the partnership. It is much easier to agree on such matters then than when the partners are at each other's throats.

A partnership agreement should provide ways for a business to continue to operate smoothly during a period when the partners disagree. Even if the partnership must be dissolved, the business itself should be able to continue. Agreements for small partnerships usually require the unanimous consent of all partners in order to do just about anything. But this is a problem when the partners disagree. Hence, it is wise for the partnership agreement to give one partner the principal management authority. That partner can then write the employees' paychecks, order new supplies, and, in general, run the business on a day-to-day basis, even during times of dispute.

If the partnership has to be dissolved and no buy-and-sell agreements have been established, it may be difficult to get partners to agree on who buys and who sells and at what price. One solution is to divide the disputing factions into two groups. One group decides the value of the business. The other group decides whether to buy or to sell. In other words, one group tells the other, "The business is worth $36,000. Do you want to buy us out, or shall we buy you out?" One group gets the business, and the other gets the cash.

CHECKLIST FOR A PARTNERSHIP BUYOUT

1. Include a buy-and-sell clause in the original partnership agreement.
2. Each partner should use a separate attorney to read and approve the buyout agreement. If each party is represented by his or her own counsel, then neither can later claim that the agreement was unfair to one party.

Dissolution of a partnership requires giving notice to all affected third persons as well.

The way in which notice is given to a third party depends on his or her relationship to the firm. Any third party who has extended credit to the firm must receive *actual notice*—that is, notice must be given to the party directly. All others should receive *constructive notice*, such as a newspaper announcement or other public notice.

Winding Up and Distribution of Assets   Once partners have been notified and dissolution occurs, the partners no longer have the authority to create new obligations for the partnership. Their only authority is to complete ongoing partnership business. Winding up includes collecting

LEGAL BACKGROUND

Until 1976, the law governing limited partnerships in all states except Louisiana was the Uniform Limited Partnership Act (ULPA).

Compared with the informal, private, and voluntary agreement that usually suffices for a general partnership, the formation of a limited partnership is a public and formal proceeding that must follow statutory requirements.

and preserving partnership assets, paying debts, and accounting to each partner for the value of his or her interest in the partnership.

Both creditors of the partnership and creditors of the individual partners can make claims on the partnership. Creditors of the partnership usually have priority over creditors of individual partners in the distribution of partnership assets.

Partners continue in their fiduciary relationship to one another until the winding-up process has been completed. After third-party debts have been paid, the partnership assets are distributed in the following order:

1. A partner who has made loans to the firm is paid back.
2. Partners are paid back their capital contributions.
3. What's left is divided among the partners according to their respective shares in the profits.

◆ CHECKING YOUR PROGRESS

1. Describe one advantage and one disadvantage to the sole proprietorship form of business.
2. In the absence of a written partnership agreement, how is the division of profits determined?
3. If a partner dies, what rights do the heirs have?
4. What fiduciary duty is required by partners?
5. If a new partner joins an existing firm, what is his or her obligation to existing debts?

◆ LIMITED PARTNERSHIPS

A **limited partnership** is a special type of partnership. It consists of at least one general partner and one or more limited partners. The liability of the limited partners is only equal to the amount of their investment. The **general partners** assume the management of the partnership and full liability for all debts of the partnership. The **limited partners** contribute cash or other property and own an interest in the firm.

Unlike a general partnership, a limited partnership is authorized and controlled by state statute. A limited partnership requires a formal written agreement. It does not begin to exist until a certificate of partnership is filed in the appropriate state office. If the rules of organizing a limited partnership are not followed, the courts may hold that a general partnership exists instead of a limited one. Investors who believe that their liability is limited can then find that they are liable to the full extent of their personal net worth, which means their assets minus their debts.

◆ **limited partnership** A special type of statutory partnership. Requires at least one general partner and one or more limited partners. The major benefit of a limited partnership is limited liability for limited partners.

◆ **general partner** In a limited partnership, a partner who assumes responsibility for the management of the partnership and liability for all partnership debts.

◆ **limited partner** In a limited partnership, a partner who contributes capital to the partnership but has a limited right to participate in the management and operation of the business. The limited partner has no liability for partnership debts beyond his or her investment in the business.

Obtain copies of general and limited partnership agreement forms, and ask students to discuss the significant differences between the two types of agreements. What sorts of concerns are addressed in each agreement? How might these agreements be improved?

Collaborative Learning Activity

Divide the class into small groups. Have each group work together to discuss the structure and contents of limited and general partnership agreements. Then ask each group to draft a brief limited or general partnership agreement. After the groups have finished, allow each group an opportunity to share with the class its drafted agreement. Groups should be encouraged to explain key points in their agreements.

Ethical Concern

In a limited partnership the limited partner's liability is limited to the amount of his investment, with no personal assets at stake. In exchange, the limited partner must refrain from taking on a management role in the business. Management is completely in the hands of the general partners. In light of these facts, is it fair that the limited partners have so few management rights at all? Should a certain amount of involvement be permitted to assure the limited partner that his investment is protected/managed properly? Why or why not?

It is not uncommon for wife and husband to also be business partners.

All states permit limited partnerships. Most states and the District of Columbia have adopted a uniform statute called the Revised Uniform Limited Partnership Act (RULPA). A comparison of the basic characteristics of general partnerships and limited partnerships appears in Exhibit 23-2.

FORMATION OF A LIMITED PARTNERSHIP

The formation of a limited partnership must follow statutory requirements. A limited partnership must have at least one general partner and one limited partner. The partners must sign a *certificate of limited partnership*. The certificate must be filed with the designated state official, often the secretary of state.

RIGHTS AND LIABILITIES OF LIMITED PARTNERS

General partners, unlike limited partners, are personally liable to the partnership's creditors. Thus, at least one general partner is necessary in a limited partnership.

Rights of Limited Partners   Limited partners have many of the same rights as general partners. They have the right to inspect partnership books and the right to an accounting of partnership business. When the limited partnership is dissolved, they are entitled to a return of their contributions as specified in the partnership certificate. They do not have the right of management and control of the business.

Liabilities of Limited Partners   A limited partner is only liable to creditors to the extent of any actual or promised capital partnership contribution. By contrast, the liability of a general partner for partnership debts is unlimited.

Limited Partners and Management   To retain limited liability, a limited partner cannot participate actively in the management of the business. A limited partner's name cannot be part of the partnership name. Participation in the day-to-day management of the business makes the limited partner as liable as a general partner to any creditor unaware that he or she is a limited partner.

DISSOLUTION OF A LIMITED PARTNERSHIP

The dissolution of a limited partnership is similar to that of a general partnership. The retirement, death, or mental incompetence of a general partner can dissolve the partnership. The limited partnership can, however, provide for another general partner to take over and continue the business. A limited partner's leaving does not generally dissolve the limited partnership.

Illegal business activities and bankruptcy of the general partners dissolve a limited partnership. A limited partnership can also be dissolved by court decree. Just as with the dissolution of a general partnership, creditors take first priority in the distribution of limited partnership assets.

EXHIBIT 23-2
A BASIC COMPARISON OF TYPES OF PARTNERSHIPS

Characteristic	General Partnership (UPA)	Limited Partnership (RULPA)
Creation	By agreement of two or more persons to carry on a business as co-owners for profit.	By agreement of two or more persons to carry on a business as co-owners for profit. Must include one or more general partners and one or more limited partners. Filing of certificate with secretary of state is required.
Sharing of Profits and Losses	By agreement, or in the absence thereof, profits are shared equally by partners, and losses are shared in the same ratio as profits.	Profits and losses are shared as required in the certificate agreement, up to their capital contribution. In the absence of provision in certificate agreement, profits and losses are shared on the basis of percentages of capital contributions.
Liability	Unlimited personal liability of all partners.	Unlimited personal liability of all general partners; limited partners only to extent of capital contributions.
Capital Contribution	No minimal or mandatory amount; set by agreement.	Set by agreement; may be cash, property, services or any obligation.
Management	By agreement, or in the absence thereof, all partners have an equal voice.	General partners by agreement, or else each has an equal voice. Limited partners have no voice, or else are subject to liability as a general partner. Limited partner may vote on amending certificate or sale or dissolution of the partnership.
Duration	By agreement, or can be dissolved by action of partner (withdrawal), operation of law (death or bankruptcy), or court decree.	By agreement in certification, or by withdrawal, death, or mental incompetence of general partner in absence of right of other general partners to continue the partnership.
Assignment	Interest can be assigned, although assignee does not have rights of substituted partner without consent of other partners.	Same as general partnership; if partners consent to assignee's becoming a partner, certificate must be amended. Upon assignment of all interest, the partner ceases to be a partner.
Priorities (order) upon Liquidation	1. Outside creditors. 2. Partner creditors. 3. Partners, according to capital contribution. 4. Partners, according to profits.	1. Outside creditors and partner creditors. 2. Partners and former partners entitled to distributions before withdrawal under the agreement or RULPA. 3. Partners, according to capital contributions. 4. Partners, according to profits.

Enrichment

Point out to the students that studies have shown that partnerships seem to fall apart at an alarming rate because of the physical and psychological demands that arise on a day-to-day basis within the partnership context. Ask the students to consider this fact; then stimulate a class discussion by asking the following questions: What are some of the stresses that would appear to exist in working as a partner in a general partnership? What are some of the stresses that would appear to exist in working as a partner in a limited partnership? How can these be minimized? Is one type of personality better suited to work as a general partner? What characteristics would you expect of an individual who could work successfully within a partnership?

Critical Thinking Activity

Have students write an essay comparing the characteristics of a general partnership with those of a limited partnership.

Reteaching Activity

Ask a student volunteer to explain the key difference between a joint venture and a partnership. Students should understand that a joint venture is treated much like a partnership, but it is created for a limited project or a single activity.

Legal Focus Problem

Have a student volunteer read this Legal Focus Problem aloud to the class. Ask the volunteer to suggest a possible answer to the question posed at the end of this problem. Remind students that they can use the Legal Focus features as review tools when studying for tests.

Multicultural

Perspectives

Ask volunteers to research partnership business relationships in other countries. Have them find out how partnerships between individuals in the United States and another country are treated. Have the volunteers report their findings to the class in the form of oral reports.

◆ CORPORATIONS

Corporations, which we will discuss in detail in Chapter 24, did not exist at common law and are considered an artificial legal entity. In contrast to sole proprietorships and partnerships, corporations have a separate and complete existence apart from their owners. All aspects of the corporation are controlled by statutory law. All states allow the corporate form of business, and most states have adopted a uniform statute called the Model Business Corporations Act (MBCA).

One of the key features of a corporation is that the liability of its owners is limited to their investment. The owners' personal assets are usually not liable for the debts of the corporation. Corporations, unlike other forms of business, do not die when their owners do. They are said to have perpetual existence.

Corporations' owners are called shareholders. A board of directors, elected by the shareholders, sets business policy. The board of directors normally employs officers to manage the day-to-day operations.

◆ OTHER ORGANIZATIONAL FORMS

A business venture does not have to be organized as a sole proprietorship, a partnership, or a corporation. Other organizational forms exist. Most are combination organizations—that is, they have characteristics similar to those of partnerships or corporations, or they combine features of both. One example of an alternate form of business is the joint venture.

JOINT VENTURE

◆ joint venture
Two or more persons or businesses combine their interests in a one-time business effort. The parties agree to share in losses or profits equally or according to their contributions.

When two or more persons or businesses combine their interests in a one-time business effort, it is probably a **joint venture**. The parties agree to share in the losses or profits jointly or in proportion to their contributions. A joint venture is treated much like a partnership, but it is created for a limited project or a single activity.

◀ LEGAL FOCUS ~ PROBLEM

Abe and Candie are old friends who have never done business together. Abe is a tennis pro, and Candie works as a stockbroker. They agree to pool their money to buy an old boat, remodel it, and sell it, dividing the profits. Is this a joint venture or a partnership?

It is a joint venture—a one-time business activity. Members of a joint venture usually have limited powers to bind their co-venturers. Joint ventures range in size from very small activities to huge, multimillion-dollar joint actions engaged in by some of the world's largest corporations.

1. The major difference between a general partnership and a limited partnership is that a limited partner's liability is limited to his or her investment. Also, limited partnerships are authorized and controlled by statute—mostly under the Revised Uniform Limited Partnership Act (RULPA).
2. Limited partners do not have the right of management and control of the business.

Their liability is limited to the extent of any actual or promised capital partnership contribution.
3. In a joint venture, two or more persons combine their interests and agree to share in losses or profits jointly or in proportion to their contributions, as is done in a partnership; however, it is created for a limited or single activity.

◆ CHECKING YOUR PROGRESS

1. What is the major difference between a general partnership and a limited partnership?

2. How do limited partner's rights and liabilities differ from those of a general partner?

3. How does a joint venture differ from a partnership, how is it the same?

◆ A CASE IN POINT ◆

HOFNER v. GLENN INGRAM & CO.

Appellate Court of Illinois, First District, Fourth Division, 1985.
140 Ill.App.3d 874,
489 N.E.2d 311.

Does a promise made by a partner in an accounting firm to a company employee, who is also a partner, bind the partnership? This case answers this question.

FACTS Glenn Ingram & Company is an accounting firm organized as a partnership. James Hofner, a certified public accountant, signed a partnership agreement with Ingram on May 4, 1978. The agreement provided for salaries for each partner. The salaries were not fixed, but instead were based on a percentage of the future year's earnings by the firm. After signing the agreement, Hofner told William Gifford, a senior managing partner, that he would leave the firm unless he (Hofner) made at least $40,000 that year in salary. Gifford told Hofner that he would make that amount. He orally guaranteed the salary. When Hofner did not make the $40,000 as promised, he left the

firm. He sued the firm for the difference between his actual salary and $40,000. The trial court dismissed Hofner's case for failure to state a cause of action. Hofner appealed.

ISSUE Is Hofner entitled to bring suit against the partnership to recover the balance of the promised salary?

DECISION The appellate court judged that Hofner had a cause of action—in other words, he could sue. The case was sent to the trial court.

REASON At the heart of the case is the question of whether the whole accounting firm is bound by Gifford's promise. The answer turns on whether Gifford had the authority to change the signed partnership agreement. Also, would a reasonable person in Hofner's position have assumed that Gifford had the authority to make promises concerning salary? If Gifford did not have the authority to change the express written agreement between Ingram and Hofner, a further question arises as to whether the firm knew of Gifford's promise and ratified it by its conduct. The appellate court believed the trial court should decide these questions.

Read
Remind the students that partners within a partnership have many of the same rights and duties as agents and principals in the agent-principal relationship. Remind the students that this case focuses on one aspect of the partnership relationship. Then have a student volunteer read this *A Case In Point* feature aloud to the class.

Discuss
Stimulate a class discussion of this *A Case In Point* feature by asking the following questions: What was James Hofner's relationship with Glenn Ingram & Company? Was he an employee or a partner or both? What promise did Gifford make to Hofner? Was this promise made in writing? Why did Hofner sue Glenn Ingram & Company? What was the issue before the Appellate Court of Illinois's First District's Fourth Division? What decision did the court reach? What reasons did the court give for its decision?

Teaching Note

This case is included in the *West's Business and Personal Law Handbook of Selected Court Cases.*

In order to help students review what they have learned in Chapter 23, you might wish to:
1. Have a student volunteer, or volunteers, read aloud the Chapter Summary.
2. Allow the students to work with partners to complete the *Using Legal Language* activity.
3. Assign the *Checking for Comprehension* exercise as homework.
4. Allow the students to work in small groups to complete the *Applying Legal Concepts* activities.
5. As a class, complete the *Applying the Law* activities. (Please note that you may have to help students with vocabulary so that they adequately understand all of the *Applying the Law* material.)

In order to check student mastery of chapter concepts, you may wish to use the Chapter 23 test that is found in your *Teacher's Resource Binder* or use WESTEST computerized testing for Chapter 23.

CHAPTER REVIEW

 ## SUMMARY

SOLE PROPRIETORSHIP ESSENTIAL CHARACTERISTICS

1. This is the simplest form of business organization. It is used by anyone who does business without creating a separate business form. The owner is the business.

2. The owner pays personal income taxes on all profits.

3. The owner is personally liable for all business debts.

GENERAL PARTNERSHIP ESSENTIAL CHARACTERISTICS

1. The partnership is created by agreement of the parties.

2. The company is not treated as a legal entity separate from the partners except for limited purposes.

3. Partners have unlimited liability for partnership debts.

4. Each partner has an equal voice in company management, unless the partnership agreement specifies otherwise.

5. How much money each partner contributes to the running of the company is determined by agreement.

6. Each partner pays a share of income taxes on the net profits of the partnership. The partnership files an informational tax return only.

7. The partnership is terminated by agreement or can be dissolved by an action of a partner, such as withdrawal, by operation of law (when a partner dies or goes bankrupt), or by court decree.

LIMITED PARTNERSHIP ESSENTIAL CHARACTERISTICS

1. Limited partnerships must be formed in compliance with statutory requirements.

2. There must be one or more general partners and one or more limited partners.

3. Only general partners can participate in management. Limited partners have a limited voice in management; if they do participate in management activities, they risk having the same liability as a general partner.

4. General partners have unlimited liability for partnership losses; limited partners are liable only to the extent of their investments.

CORPORATION ESSENTIAL CHARACTERISTICS

1. A corporation is created by state-issued charter.

2. It is a legal entity separate and distinct from its owners.

3. Owners have limited liability. They are not personally liable for the debts of the corporation.

4. Shareholders elect directors who set corporate policy and appoint officers to manage corporate affairs.

5. A corporation can have perpetual existence.

JOINT VENTURE

When two or more persons join together to conduct a limited business activity or a single transaction, they have engaged in a joint venture. The organization of a joint venture is similar to that of a partnership.

Checking for Comprehension
(Answers)

1. Both sole proprietorships and general partnerships are guided by common law. Partners can agree to almost any terms so long as the terms are legal and consistent with public policy. However, the Uniform Partnership Act guides this form of business if the partners do not have a partnership agreement or neglect to include necessary terms in the agreement.

Limited partnerships are authorized and controlled by statute.
2. A partnership for a term is part of the agreement that states how long the partnership will exist. A dissolution without the consent of all the partners before the agreed term expires is a breach of the agreement. On the other hand, a partnership at will can be dissolved at any time.
3. Unanimous consent is required to bind a partnership in (1) actions that alter the essential nature of the firm's business as agreed upon or that alter the capital structure of the partnership, (2) admitting new partners or entering a new business, (3) transferring partnership property into a trust for the benefit of creditors, (4) disposing of the partnership's good will, (5) admitting responsibility in a lawsuit or submitting partnership legal matters to arbitration, or (6) performing any act that would make further conduct of partnership business impossible. The higher level of unanimous consent is required because these actions would significantly affect the nature of the partnership.
4. Dissolution and winding up are the two stages in termination of a partnership. Dissolution occurs when any partner indicates an intention to quit the partnership. Winding up is the actual process of collecting and distributing the partnership assets. Dissolution of a partnership can occur by acts of the partners, by the operation of the law, and by judicial decree.
5. Dissolution of a partnership by the act of a partner requires notice to all affect-

◆ USING LEGAL LANGUAGE

Directions: Match each term with the statement that best defines that term.

1. constructive notice
2. corporation
3. dissolution
4. joint liability
5. joint venture
6. joint and several liability
7. limited partnership
8. partnership
9. sole proprietorship
10. tenants in partnership

A. When two or more persons enter into a _____ when they combine their interests in a one-time business effort.

B. In a _____ the owner is the business and does business without creating another type of organization.

C. The business format called a _____ is a legal entity separate and distinct from its owners.

D. _____ occurs when any partner indicates an intention to quit the partnership.

E. People form a _____ when they associate with others to carry on as co-owners of a business for profit.

F. Liability upon which a third party may sue any one or more parties or partners without suing all of them or the partnership itself is called _____.

G. A newspaper announcement may serve as _____ which is a requirement for dissolution of a partnership.

H. Under _____ all partners share liability for obligations.

I. When each partner is a co-owner with all other partners of specific partnership property, they are called _____.

J. _____ is a special type of statutory partnership requiring at least one general partner and one or more limited partners.

◆ CHECKING FOR COMPREHENSION

1. Are sole proprietorships and partnerships guided by common law or statute?

2. Explain the difference between a partnership for a term and a partnership at will.

3. Although a majority vote usually controls ordinary partnership decisions, unanimous consent of the partners is required to bind the firm to some actions. What are those

actions? Why is the higher level of unanimous consent required?

4. What two stages are involved in terminating a partnership? What occurs in each stage? How can dissolution be initiated?

5. What is the difference between actual notice and constructive notice of the dis-

ed third persons. Any third person who has extended credit to the firm must be given notice directly (actual notice). Public announcement (constructive notice) is sufficient for all other third parties.

6. A business owner who is a sole proprietor or a general partner is fully liable to all creditors of the business. His or her personal assets could be used to pay debts of the business. One who is a limited partner or a shareholder is only liable for the amount invested in the business.

7. No. As a partner, Byerly owned a one-third interest in the firm but could not claim ownership of one-third of specific partnership assets or property. The computers, as partnership property, were jointly owned by the partners, who held title as tenants in partnership. Byerly had no "right" to the personal use of the computer. He could "borrow" the computer from the firm for his personal use, but only with the consent of the other partners. Absent the other partners' consent, Byerly could not rightfully retain the computer for his personal use.

Applying the Law . . . You Be the Judge (Answers)

1. Yes. Carola's actions of removing various items of furniture, books, and files were effective to give notice of dissolution of the partnership. It is the date that a partner "manifests an unequivocal election" to dissolve the partnership that is the correct date of dissolution. Therefore, Carola's conduct on September 6,

1976, was an effective notice of dissolution to Grogan.

2. The court reviewed the evidence as to whether the limited partner's (Blinder's) actions were such as to control the business of the limited partnership and thus create liability as a general partner. The court held that "no one from Blinder had any control over or access to the limited partnership's . . . funds or checking account. None of its personnel engaged in any activities concerning the hiring or firing of anyone, arranging for the print-

ing, sale (other than as an outlet), or tally of tickets for the match, renting the stadium, negotiating for other fighters to precede the key match . . . obtaining police protection, or any other day-to-day control and management of the limited partnership's affairs." Since the statute "does not impose silence on a limited partner who has a material interest in the success" of the enterprise, the activities of the limited partner's president did not constitute active management. The limited partner could not be held liable as a general partner.

---

solution of a partnership?

6. Compare a business owner's liability if he or she is a sole proprietor, a partner, or a shareholder in a corporation.

7. Byerly, Samms, and Berg were partners in a business firm. The firm's business equipment included several expensive computers. One day Byerly borrowed one of the computers for use in his home but never bothered to return it. When the other partners asked him about it, Byerly claimed that since the computer represented less than one-third of the computers owned by the partnership, he had a right to keep the equipment. "After all, I own one-third of the business." Was he right? Explain.

APPLYING LEGAL CONCEPTS

1. Work with another student to develop a partnership agreement. Decide what type of business you will begin. Determine what each partner will bring to the business, what responsibilities each partner will have in running the business, and what ratio of profits each will take from the business. Print or key a PARTNERSHIP AGREEMENT.

2. Work with another pair of students to combine your two partnerships. Determine what each partner will bring to the business, what responsibilities each partner will have in running the business, and what ratio of profits each will take from the business. Print or key a new partnership agreement.

APPLYING THE LAW . . . YOU BE THE JUDGE

1. Carola and Grogan were partners in a law firm. The partnership began business in 1974 and was created by an oral agreement. On September 6, 1976, Carola withdrew from the partnership some of its files, furniture, books, and various other items of office equipment. The next day, Carola informed Grogan that he had withdrawn from the partnership. Were Carola's actions on September 6, 1976, effective notice of dissolution to Grogan? [*Carola v. Grogan*, 102 A.D.2d 934, 477 N.Y.S.2d 525 1984)]

2. Combat Associates was formed as a limited partnership to promote an exhibition boxing match between Lyle Alzado (a professional football player) and Muhammad Ali. Alzado and others had formed Combat Promotions; and this organization was to be a general partner, and Blinder, Robinson & Co. (Blinder) the limited partner, in Com-

bat Associates. The general partner's contribution consisted of assigning all contracts pertaining to the match, and the limited partner's contribution was a $250,000 letter of credit to ensure Ali's compensation. Alzado personally guaranteed to repay Blinder for any amount of loss if the proceeds of the match were less than $250,000. In preparation for the match, at Alzado's request, Blinder's president participated in interviews and promotional rally, and the company sponsored parties and allowed its local office to be used as a ticket sales outlet. The proceeds of the match were insufficient, and Blinder sued Alzado on his guaranty. Alzado counterclaimed that Blinder took an active role in the control and management of Combat Associates and thus should be held liable as a general partner. How did the court rule on Alzado's counterclaim? [*Blinder, Robinson & Co. v. Alzado*, 713 P.2d 1314 (Colo.App. 1985)]

You might want to point out to students that many of the most successful businesses in the United States started as small businesses. Ray Kroc started McDonald's as a small hamburger stand in San Diego. Federal Express was started by Fred Smith in 1973 as a result of a business project that he had done for a class while attending college. Initially, such huge corporations as General Motors, J. C. Penney, and H. J. Heinz all started out as small partnerships.

Ask students to identify entrepreneurs that have started their own businesses in the local community. Are these businesses successful?

LEGAL PERSPECTIVE

ENTREPRENEURS

An **entrepreneur** is a person who organizes, manages, and assumes all the *financial risk* of beginning a new business. In starting the business, the entrepreneur must choose a form of business organization for the enterprise. Entrepreneurs usually prefer the sole proprietorship form of business.

Most entrepreneurs start as sole proprietors. However, they often need to share ownership with others in order to attract the capital necessary for the business to grow. Capital is an accounting term for money or other assets that people invest in a business.

The following discussion considers some of the advantages and disadvantages to an entrepreneur of sole proprietorships, partnerships, and corporations. We conclude by introducing the franchise form of organization. A franchise sometimes gives the entrepreneur some of the advantages of a larger business without requiring him or her to sacrifice too much independence.

◆ ADVANTAGES OF THE MAJOR FORMS OF BUSINESS ORGANIZATION

SOLE PROPRIETORSHIPS

A major advantage of the sole proprietorship is that the owner receives all the profits (because he or she takes all the risk). It is usually easier and less costly to start a sole proprietorship than to start any other kind of business. There are fewer legal formalities. The sole proprietorship allows the owner more flexibility than does a partner-

ship or a corporation, since the sole proprietor is free to make any decision desired concerning the business. The owner pays income tax on the business's profits as part of his or her individual tax return. Thus, business profits are only taxed once because the business is not taxed separately.

PARTNERSHIPS

The primary advantage of both partnerships and corporations is that these organizations can attract more capital for starting or expanding a business than can a single person who owns a business alone. As new partners join a partnership, they bring in capital that allows the business to grow.

Partnership profits are only taxed once. Partnerships file tax returns, informing the government what profits are distributed to which partners. These profits are taxed on each partner's individual income tax return.

CORPORATIONS

The single greatest advantage of a corporation is that it provides limited liability to its owners. An investor can gain from the growth of a company without risking any more of his or her personal wealth than has been put into the corporation. A corporation has an unlimited life. In both sole proprietorships and partnerships, the death of an owner terminates the legal status of the business.

Corporations can often attract capital more easily than can other forms of business, through the sale of stock. A corporation has all the advantages of a larger organization, such as being able to pay for more advertising and to bargain for cost

(continued on page 564)

LEGAL BACKGROUND

This LP is about the fundamental choice that an entrepreneur makes as to business form. Why should an entrepreneur choose the sole proprietorship over a partnership form or vice versa to engage in business? We address some advantages and disadvantages of each major type of business form. We also introduce the private franchise and discuss some of that form's strengths and weaknesses.

Divide the class into small groups. Have each group create four charts, one listing the advantages and disadvantages of sole proprietorship, one listing the advantages and disadvantages of partnership, one listing the advantages and disadvantages of corporations, and one listing the advantages and disadvantages of private franchises. Explain to the groups that they are not limited to those advantages and disadvantages listed in the student text, and encourage the groups to add any original thoughts to their charts. Have each group choose a leader to share its work with the class. As a class, go over these charts and compare the advantages and disadvantages of each form of business ownership with the other three forms. Note: You might wish to leave the groups intact to complete the next Collaborative Learning Activity, found on the opposite page.

564

LEGAL PERSPECTIVE (CONTINUED)

breaks based on volume purchases. A large business can also hire specialists to perform different tasks. In a sole proprietorship or a small partnership, the few owners have to perform a wide variety of tasks. Finally, the costs of government regulation can be borne more easily by a large business.

If an investor wishes to get his or her investment out of the business, it is usually easy to sell his or her ownership interest. Getting your money back out of another type of business is far more difficult.

◆ DISADVANTAGES OF THE MAJOR FORMS OF BUSINESS ORGANIZATION

SOLE PROPRIETORSHIPS

The major disadvantage of the sole proprietorship is that the proprietor alone is liable for the business. This means that the owner may be the sole source of business ideas, and no one can know it all. It also means that the sole proprietor has unlimited liability for all debts or obligations resulting from the business.

Another disadvantage is that it is difficult to raise money. Usually the owner's personal funds, along with money from friends who are willing to make loans, are the extent of available capital.

PARTNERSHIPS

All partners can participate in business profits; on the other hand, their personal assets can be used to make up for business losses. It is not just the amount of money the partners invested that is at risk. Limited partnerships, however, do provide a way to be a partner and have limited liability.

In forming a partnership, an entrepreneur gives up the right to make sole management decisions; the other partners now participate. The entrepreneur also has to share profits rather than get them all. If other partners do not work hard or if there are personality conflicts, the work experience can be unsatisfying and unprofitable. Partnership conflicts can ruin a business, and the breakup of a partnership can be very much like a divorce.

If a partner dies, the partnership automatically dissolves. The remaining partners must pay the deceased partner's estate or heirs the value of that partner's investment. Also, when a partner wishes to leave the business, it is often difficult to get back his or her investment. The investment is not easily converted to cash.

CORPORATIONS

Corporations are the most legally complicated type of organization. They have to meet specific requirements for their formation and continued existence. The start-up costs for a corporation are usually higher than for other forms of business.

A corporation does not always guarantee its owners or investors limited liability. Often if a corporation has only a few shareholders (owners), each must personally sign for loans made to the corporation. The shareholder is then personally liable for the loan if the corporation cannot meet its debts. The corporate form of business does not prevent personal liability if a shareholder assumes the liability voluntarily.

Corporations pay taxes on corporate profits. When a corporation declares a dividend—that is, when it distributes profits to shareholders—the shareholders pay personal taxes on that income. Thus, the same money is taxed twice; this is called double taxation.

Collaborative Learning Activity

Have the students return to the groups that were formed for the last Collaborative Learning Activity. Or, if you did not choose to use the last Collaborative Learning Activity, divide the class into small groups. Explain to each group that its responsibility is to come up with a plan for a new business. The group will be responsible for deciding what product or service to market, a name for the business, advertising strategy and/or company slogan, and must choose which form of business ownership to employ. (Note that the choices will be limited to partnerships, corporations, or franchises.) After the groups have had time to complete the assignment, allow each group to present its work to the class. Be sure that each group explains why the particular form of business was chosen.

Enrichment

Ask the students to name some well-known franchises that are operating within your community. Have a volunteer list the franchises on the board.

EXHIBIT **LP23-1**
MAJOR BUSINESS FORMS COMPARED

Characteristic	Sole Proprietorship	Partnership	Corporation
1. Method of Creation	Created at will by owner.	Created by agreement of the parties.	Charter issued by state—created by statutory authorization.
2. Legal Position	Not a separate entity; owner is the business.	Not a separate legal entity in many states.	Legal entity separate from its owners—a legal fiction for the purposes of owning property and being a party to litigation.
3. Liability	Unlimited liability.	Unlimited liability (except for limited partners in a limited partnership).	Limited liability of shareholders—shareholders are not liable for the debts of the corporation.
4. Duration	Determined by owner; automatically dissolved on owner's death.	Terminated by agreement of the partners, by the death a partner, by withdrawal of a partner, by bankruptcy, etc.	Can have perpetual existence.
5. Transferability of interest	Interest can be transferred, but individual's proprietorship then ends.	Although partnership interest can be assigned, assignee does not have full rights of a partner.	Share of stock can be transferred.
6. Management	Completely at owner's discretion.	Each general partner has equal voice in management unless specified in the partnership agreement.	Shareholders elect directors who set policy and appoint officers.
7. Taxation	Owner pays personal taxes on business income.	Each partner pays pro rata share of income taxes on net profits, whether or not they are distributed.	Double taxation—corporation pays income tax on net profits, and shareholders pay income tax on disbursed dividends they receive.
8. Organizational Fees, Annual License Fees, and Annual Reports	None.	None.	All required.
9. Transaction of Business in Other States	Generally no limitation.	Generally no limitation.[a]	Normally must qualify to do business and obtain certificate of authority.

[a]A few states have enacted statutes requiring that foreign partnerships qualify to do business there—for example, 3 N.H.Rev.Stat.Ann. Chapter 305-A in New Hampshire.

Large organizations lack the flexibility of smaller companies. In a corporation, management decisions are shared with others. The entrepreneur loses much of his or her independence and flexibility with the addition of investors.

Exhibit LP23-1 lists the essential advantages and disadvantages of the three major forms of business organization.

 ### PRIVATE FRANCHISES

Today, over a third of all retail sales are generated by private franchises. A **franchise** is an arrangement where the owner of a business name, or trade name, licenses others to use the name in selling goods or services. A **franchisee** is the purchaser of a franchise, and he or she operates as an independent businessperson. The **franchisor** (the seller of the franchise) provides the business system, giving the franchisee the advantages of a large organization.

ADVANTAGES

A franchise arrangement appeals to many prospective businesspersons who want independence. Other advantages include having an established product or service. The franchise provides a management network that is regional or national in scope. Franchises also have a high survival rate (90 percent), compared to only 20 percent of small businesses that survive.

By operating a franchise, a businessperson can have many of the benefits of a large corporate operation, such as volume buying, mass advertising, training, and assistance in site selection. Sometimes the franchisor will assist with raising capital or with establishing credit.

DISADVANTAGES

Franchise agreements and operations may, nonetheless, lead to difficulties and financial losses for the franchisee. The proprietor must pay a franchise fee that is often a considerable sum of money. Often there are other fees to the franchisor that the proprietor did not expect. For example, sometimes the franchisee must purchase services or products from the franchisor that are not needed or that could be purchased for less elsewhere.

If the franchise company has serious financial problems, an individual franchise's ability to get supplies and the product's good name can suffer through no fault of a franchise holder. Sometimes disagreements between the franchisor and franchisee lead to a revocation of the franchise. A carefully drafted contract can provide protection against arbitrary treatment because revocation of a franchise puts a person out of business.

 ### TERMS TO REMEMBER

- **entrepreneur** A person who organizes, manages, and assumes all the financial risks of beginning a business.

- **franchise** An arrangement where the owner of a trade name licenses others to use the trade name in selling goods or services.

- **franchisee** A purchaser of a franchise.

- **franchisor** The seller of the franchise.

566

Mastery Objectives

By the end of this chapter, students will be able to:

- Describe the legal characteristics of corporations
- Classify corporations
- List the steps to form a corporation

- Identify corporate powers
- Differentiate management and shareholder rights
- Summarize corporate management responsibilities
- Outline shareholders' responsibilities

Corporations

Chapter

24

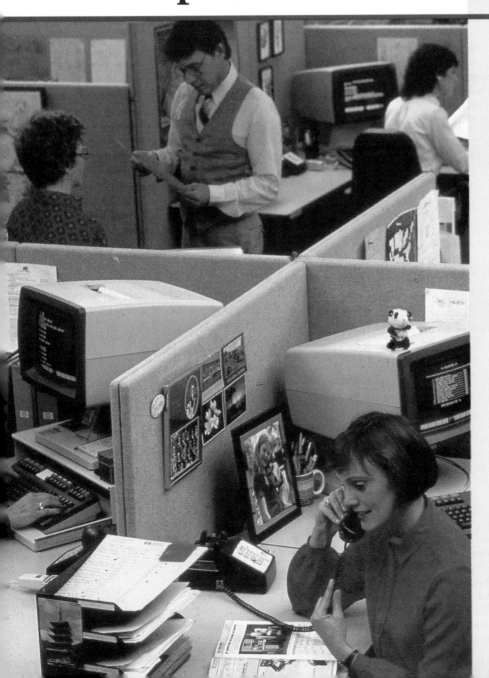

LEGAL BACKGROUND

Corporations are interesting creatures. In the case of corporations, the law beat science to the creation of artificial life forms. As a corporation is a creature of law, form becomes very important. Meeting the requirements to create the corporation, electing a board of directors, and holding annual meetings are all part of what is expected of a corporation. This chapter introduces some classifications of corporations, explains how to create a corporation, and enumerates the rights and duties of directors, officers, and shareholders.

In this chapter we also provide a mix of accounting and law by introducing types of stocks and their major attributes. Lastly, corporations, even though artificial life, can die; and we discuss the legal rules regarding how that might happen.

567

Discussion Starter

Have students refer to the quote that begins this chapter. Ask them why a corporation is referred to as an artificial being. What does this term mean? Discuss these questions with the class.

Critical Thinking Activity

Tell students to write a paragraph in which they interpret the statement, "A corporation is a creature of modern statute."

Extension Activity

You might ask a local stockbroker to speak to your class regarding stock ownership. He or she should explain how one acquires stock, what stock represents, why individuals choose to purchase stock rather than other possible investments, etc. Have students prepare questions in advance for the speaker.

568

Chapter 24
Resources and Assignment Guide

Activity Sheets
Reviewing Legal Concepts 24 *TRB*
Enrichment Activity 24 *TRB*

Student Activity Workbook
Chapter 24 Activities

Tests
Chapter 24 Test *TRB*
Chapter 24 WESTEST Computerized Testing

Handbook of Selected Court Cases
Morad v. *Coupounas*
Shlensky v. *Wrigley*

West's Business Law and Legal Environment Videodisc
Still Frames and Motion Segments as shown

> *"A corporation is an artificial being, invisible, intangible, and existing only in contemplation of law."*
> **John Marshall, 1755–1835**
> **Chief justice of the United States Supreme Court, 1801–1835**

◆ **corporation** A legal entity created under the authority of the laws of a state or the federal government. The entity is distinct from its owners, the shareholders.

A corporation is a creature of modern statute, created under the authority of the laws of a state or the federal government. The entity is distinct from its owners, the shareholders. The corporation as a business form did not exist at common law. Justice Marshall's quotation defining a corporation is expressed in legal terms, but there simply isn't any other way to define a corporation. You cannot see or touch a corporation; it exists as a being or "artificial person" only in the eyes of the law. This form of organization has been created as a way to do business efficiently.

Each state is free to create its own corporation law. In order to encourage the states to pass similar or even identical laws, two uniform statutes, the Model Business Corporation Act (MBCA) and the Revised Model Business Corporation Act (RMBCA) have been created. Although state governments have not usually adopted these statutes in total, these models have influenced corporation law in virtually every state.

The corporation is the most important form of business organization in the United States and has been for over one hundred years. In Chapter 23, we compared the corporation to a sole proprietorship and a partnership. In this chapter, we examine the nature, classification, and formation of corporations.

 NATURE OF THE CORPORATION

The corporation as an artificial person enjoys many but not all of the same rights and privileges that natural persons enjoy. The Bill of Rights guarantees a person, as a citizen, certain protections, and corporations are considered persons in most situations. For example, just like any other citizen, a corporation has the right under the Fourteenth Amendment to equal protection of the laws and to due process before a denial of life, liberty, or property. A corporation can also use the courts; it can sue or be sued.

 CHARACTERISTICS OF THE CORPORATE ENTITY

◆ **shareholder or stockholder** The owner of one or more shares of stock in a corporation.

A corporation, as an artificial person, has its own corporate name and is owned by individual shareholders. A **shareholder**, also called a stockholder, purchases stock in a corporation. The stock represents an ownership interest, so owning stock makes the shareholder a part owner of the corporation. Unlike members of a partnership, the body of shareholders can change constantly without affecting the continued existence of the corporation.

A corporation is a legal entity with rights and responsibilities. The corporation substitutes itself for its shareholders when it conducts corporate business. Its authority to act and the liability for its actions are generally separate from the individuals who own the corporation.

The management of the corporation is handled by a board of directors elected by the shareholders. Corporate officers and other employees are hired by the board of directors to run the daily business operations of the corporation.

Since a corporation is a separate legal entity, corporate profits are taxed by state and federal governments. Corporations have two choices for the use of their profits. The profits can be kept and invested back into the business. Or the profits can be distributed to shareholders in the form of dividends. The corporation pays taxes on its income and the individual shareholder pays income tax on the dividends he or she receives. This double-taxation feature of the corporation form of business organization is one of its major disadvantages.

◆ **stock** An ownership interest in a corporation measured in units of shares.

TORTS AND CRIMINAL ACTS

A corporation is liable for the torts committed by its agents or officers within the course and scope of their employment. Obviously, since a corporation is "invisible" and "intangible," it can act only through its agents and employees. The principle of *respondeat superior* applies to a corporation exactly as it applies to other agency relationships, discussed in Chapter 20.

Liability of a Corporation   Modern criminal law often holds a corporation liable for the criminal acts of its agents and employees. The punishment must be one that can be applied to a corporation, such as a fine. Obviously, corporations cannot be put in jail.

Liability of Officers and Directors   Corporate officers who could have prevented the crime may be held personally liable for the criminal act. It must be shown that the crimes were committed at the officer's direction or with her or his permission. The officer is not personally liable for the crimes of a corporation merely because he or she is an officer. When an employee under an officer's supervision commits a crime, the officer may be criminally liable for a negligent failure to supervise.

◆ **LEGAL FOCUS** - CASE EXAMPLE

The chief executive officer of a national supermarket chain was held personally liable for sanitation violations in corporate warehouses where food was exposed to contamination by rodents. The officer admitted that as president, he was responsible for the entire operation

LEGAL BACKGROUND

A foreign corporation does not have an automatic right to do business in a state other than its state of incorporation. It must obtain a certificate of authority in the states in which it plans to do business. Once the certificate has been issued, the powers conferred upon a corporation by its home state generally can be exercised in the other state. Should a foreign corporation do business without obtaining a certificate, the state can fine it, deny it the privilege of using state courts, and even hold its officers, directors, or agents personally responsible for corporate obligations incurred in that state.

570

Multicultural Perspectives

Divide the class into groups of three or five. Tell them to research how the Free Trade Agreement with Canada and Mexico has affected the legal applications of conducting business as alien corporations. Have them collaborate to write one paper (two- to three-pages) describing the effects.

◆ **domestic corporation** A corporation that does business in its home state where it was created.

◆ **foreign corporation** In a given state, a corporation that does business in that state but was incorporated in another state.

◆ **alien corporation** A corporation that was formed in another country but does business in the United States.

◆ **public corporation** A corporation formed by government to meet some political or governmental purpose.

◆ **private corporation** A corporation created either wholly or in part for private benefit.

◆ **publicly held corporation** A *large private corporation* whose stock is widely available for purchase by the general public.

Reteaching Activity

Hold up a copy of the stock market listings for a major stock exchange such as the New York or American Stock Exchange. Ask the students which of those companies listed with this stock exchange are publicly held corporations. Students should understand that any company listed on a major stock exchange is a publicly held corporation.

of the company, including sanitary conditions. He testified that he had to delegate duties, such as ensuring sanitation, to subordinates. He stated he did not suspect that these subordinates were violating the law. He claimed he did everything possible, again through subordinates, to correct the violations when they came to light. The prosecution, on the other hand, provided evidence of earlier violations at another warehouse. This evidence showed that the officer knew that he could not rely on his subordinates to prevent or correct unsanitary conditions. The court concluded that he was not justified in relying on his subordinates to handle sanitation matters and was thus personally responsible.[1]

◆ CLASSIFICATION OF CORPORATIONS

The classification of a corporation depends on its purpose, ownership characteristics, and location.

DOMESTIC, FOREIGN, AND ALIEN CORPORATIONS

A corporation is a **domestic corporation** in its home state, the state in which it was created. A corporation formed in one state but doing business in another is referred to in that other state as a **foreign corporation**. A corporation formed in another country—say, Mexico—but doing business in the United States is called an **alien corporation**.

A foreign corporation cannot automatically do business in a state other than its state of incorporation. It must get a *certificate of authority* in states where it plans to do business.

PUBLIC, PRIVATE, AND PUBLICLY HELD CORPORATIONS

A **public corporation** is formed by government to meet some political or governmental purpose. Cities and towns that incorporate are examples. Many federal government organizations, such as the U.S. Postal Service, the Tennessee Valley Authority, and Amtrak, are public corporations.

Private corporations are created either wholly or in part for private benefit. Most corporations are private. Many private corporations serve a public purpose, such as a public utility. They are still private corporations if they are owned by private persons rather than by the government.

Publicly held corporations are *large private corporations* whose stock is widely available for purchase by the general public. Any company listed on a major stock exchange, such as the New York or American Stock Exchange, is a publicly held corporation.

1. *United States v. Park*, 421 U.S. 658, 95 S.Ct. 1903, 44 L.Ed.2d 489 (1975).

Have the students use the newspaper listings for a major stock exchange, such as the New York or American Stock Exchange, to choose a publicly held corporation to track as they read and discuss this chapter. Students should list the opening price and keep a daily accounting of any changes in that stock's price. Additionally, students should scan the business section of the local newspaper on a daily basis to determine if the corporation they are following is in the news. Have each student report on his or her company's activity at the end of this chapter.

Ask the students to write short answers to the following question: Why is the nonprofit corporation a convenient form of organization? Students should understand it allows a nonprofit group to own property and to enter into contracts while protecting individual members from personal liability for the acts of the organization. Additionally, nonprofit corporations pay no income taxes.

NONPROFIT CORPORATIONS

Corporations that are formed without a profit-making purpose are called **nonprofit**, or not-for-profit, **corporations**. Private hospitals, educational institutions, charities, and religious organizations are frequently organized as nonprofit corporations. The nonprofit corporation is a convenient form of organization. It allows a group to own property and to enter into contracts, but individual members are protected from personal liability for the acts of the organization. As the corporation is nonprofit, the business pays no income taxes.

◆ **nonprofit corporation** A corporation formed without a profit-making purpose.

CLOSE CORPORATIONS

A **close corporation** is one whose shares are held by members of a family or by a few persons. Close corporations are also called *closely held, family,* or *privately held* corporations. Usually, shareholders in a close corporation are personally known to each other. In practice, a close corporation is often operated like a partnership. Some states recognize the special circumstances of close corporations and have specific statutes that apply to them. These laws allow a less formal operation than is normally required for a publicly held corporation.

◆ **close corporation** A corporation owned by a family or a few individuals. The transfer of shares in the corporation is usually restricted.

PROFESSIONAL CORPORATIONS

In the past, professional persons such as physicians, lawyers, dentists, and accountants could not incorporate. Today they can, and their corporations are typically called **professional corporations** or *professional service associations.* The laws governing the formation of professional corporations are

◆ **professional corporation** A corporation formed by professionals, such as doctors or lawyers.

Ethical Concern

Stimulate a discussion by asking students whether or not they think it is ethical for a nonprofit corporation to escape paying income taxes.

Critical Thinking Activity

Have students write an essay comparing the characteristics of a public corporation, a private corporation, and a publicly held corporation.

Caption Answer

No, doctors can still be held personally liable for malpractice.

Does professional corporation status protect a physician's personal wealth from a malpractice claim?

The professional corporation equalized the tax burden on professionals who, due to occupational ethics codes, could not incorporate their businesses. By 1981, however, this form of enterprise had come to be widely viewed as permitting unacceptable tax avoidance through many tax-deductible investments, including certain kinds of pension plans. Since 1981, stringent limitations enacted by Congress have helped stop the growth of professional corporations and eliminate the tax loopholes available through them.

Enrichment

Read aloud the definition of *promoter* found in the student text: "A person who takes the preliminary steps in organizing a corporation." Then have each student write a Legal Focus Example of an entrepreneur who acts as a promoter. Allow student volunteers to share their examples with the class.

572

Reteaching Activity

Ask a student to explain why many corporations have chosen to incorporate in Delaware. (Students should understand that corporations often choose Delaware because Delaware has historically had the most flexible corporation laws.)

---

similar to those governing the formation of other types of corporations. In most professional corporations, the doctrine of limited liability will not protect the individual shareholder from personal liability for professional negligence. For example, a doctor who has formed a professional corporation with other doctors can still be held personally liable for the business's malpractice.

FORMATION OF CORPORATIONS

◆ **promoter** A person who takes the preliminary steps in organizing a corporation.

Promoters are those who, for themselves or others, take the preliminary steps to organize a corporation. A promoter may contract with attorneys, accountants, or other professionals whose services are necessary in planning the proposed corporation. A promoter may convince people to purchase stock in the corporation. It is not unusual for a promoter to purchase or lease property that he or she will then sell to the corporation after the corporation is formed.

Promoters' activities create some interesting legal questions. The most important is whether a promoter is personally liable for contracts made for a corporation that does not yet exist. Agreements made before the corporation is formed are called preincorporation contracts. Once the corporation exists, does it assume liability on these contracts, or is the promoter still personally liable?

A promoter is usually personally liable on preincorporation contracts. Courts hold that a promoter cannot be an agent for a principal that does not yet exist. The promoter remains personally liable on the contract after the corporation is formed. Incorporation does not make a corporation liable for preincorporation contracts. The newly formed corporation must adopt the contract before a third party can expect the corporation to fulfill the promoter's agreement.

A promoter can protect himself or herself from personal liability. The promoter can request that the contracting party only hold the corporation (not the promoter) liable on the contract.

PROCEDURES AND REQUIREMENTS OF INCORPORATION

Exact procedures for incorporation, formally creating a corporation, differ among the states, but the basic requirements are similar.

State Chartering Since state incorporation laws differ, promoters often try to form a corporation in states with the most advantageous tax or incorporation laws. Delaware has historically had the most flexible laws, and as a result, many corporations, including several of the largest, have incorporated there. Closely held and professional corporations usually incorporate in the state in which their principal stockholders live and work.

Articles of Incorporation   The **articles of incorporation** are the primary document used to begin the incorporation process (see Exhibit 24-1). The articles include basic information about the corporation. They serve as a primary source of authority for its future organization and business functions. The person or persons who complete the articles are called *incorporators*. Generally, the articles of incorporation should include the following:

1. **Corporate name:** The choice of the corporate name is subject to state approval in order to ensure that names are not duplicated or deceitful. All states require the corporation name to include a form of the word *Corporation*, *Incorporated*, or *Limited*.
2. **Nature and purpose:** The intended business activities of the corporation must be stated in the articles. A general statement of corporate purpose is usually sufficient to give the organization all the necessary powers.

♦ **articles of incorporation**
The primary document used to begin the incorporation process.

EXHIBIT 24-1
ARTICLES OF INCORPORATION

ARTICLE ONE
The name of the corporation is _____ .

ARTICLE TWO
The period of its duration is perpetual (may be a number of years or until a certain date).

ARTICLE THREE
The purpose (or purposes) for which the corporation is organized is (are) _____ .

ARTICLE FOUR
The aggregate number of shares that the corporation shall have authority to issue is _____ of the par value of _____ dollar(s) each (or without par value).

ARTICLE FIVE
The corporation will not commence business until it has received for the issuance of its shares consideration of the value of $1,000 (can be any sum not less than $1,000).

ARTICLE SIX
The address of the corporation's registered office is _____ ,
New Pacum, and the name of its registered agent at such address is _____
(Use the street or building or rural route address of the registered office, not a post office box number.)

ARTICLE SEVEN
The number of initial directors is _____ , and the names and addresses of the directors are
_____
_____

ARTICLE EIGHT
The name and address of the incorporator is _____ .

(signed) _____
                                    Incorporator

Sworn to on _____ by the above-named incorporator.
              (date)

_____
Notary Public _____ County, New Pacum
(Notary Seal)

Have a student volunteer read aloud this Legal Focus Example dealing with the nature and purpose requirement of articles of incorporation. Remind students that they can use the Legal Focus features as review tools when studying for tests.

Divide the class into small groups. Tell each group that it is about to form a corporation. Each group should first choose a group leader, who will be the promoter for this particular corporation. Then each group should draw up its own articles of incorporation using Exhibit 24-1 as a guide. In order to complete the articles of incorporation, each group will need to decide on a corporate name, the nature and purpose of its corporation, the duration of the corporation, its capital structure, its internal organization, the location of a registered office, and the name of an agent, as well as a listing of the incorporators. Allow each group's promoter to share his or her group's work with the class.

Teaching with the Videodisc

The still frames listed below from the **West's Business Law and Legal Environment Videodisc** can be used with this chapter. To access this material, use the bar codes or the frame numbers included in the Videodisc Instructor's Manual found in the *TRB*.

Promoters' Pre-
*   Incorporation Contracts*
Contents of Articles of
*   Incorporation*
Sample Articles of
*   Incorporation*
Corporate Status:
*   Corporation de Jure*
Corporate Status:
*   Corporation de Facto*
Corporate Status:
*   Corporation by Estoppel*
Corporate Status: Defective
*   Corporation*
Management Structure of
*   Corporations*
Management Structure of a
*   Typical Closely Held*
*   Corporation*
Fiduciary Duties of
*   Directors and Officers*
Rights of Directors
Rights of Shareholders
Results of Cumulative
*   Voting*
Sources of Dividends
Fundamental Changes
Example of a Merger
Example of Consolidation

 LEGAL FOCUS – EXAMPLE

The corporate charter can say, for example, that the corporation is organized "to engage in the production and sale of agricultural products." There is a trend now to allow corporate charters to state that the corporation is organized for "any legal business," with no mention of specifics at all.

3. **Duration:** A corporation can have perpetual existence under most state corporate statutes. A few states prescribe a maximum duration, after which the corporation must formally renew its existence.

4. **Capital structure:** The capital structure of the corporation is usually included in the articles. Information concerning equity, capital, and credit must be outlined in the articles.

5. **Internal organization:** The internal management structure of the corporation may be described in the articles. Sometimes this information is included in bylaws adopted after the corporation is formed. The articles of incorporation start the corporation. The bylaws are created afterward by the board of directors. Bylaws must be consistent with the state's incorporation statute and the corporation's charter.

6. **Registered office and agent:** The corporation must state the location and address of its registered office within the state. Usually, the registered office is also the principal office, or headquarters, of the corporation. The corporation must give the name and address of a specific person who is designated as the corporation's agent and who can receive legal documents for the corporation.

7. **Incorporators:** Each incorporator must be listed by name and address. An incorporator is a person who applies to the state for the corporate charter. Incorporators are not required to be shareholders. The number of incorporators required can vary from as few as one to as many as three.

Certificate of Incorporation   The articles of incorporation are prepared and signed by the incorporators. The articles are then sent to the appropriate state official with the required filing fee. In many states, it is the secretary of state who then issues a *certificate of incorporation* representing the state's authorization for the corporation to conduct business. This certificate is called the *corporate charter*. The certificate and a copy of the articles are returned to the incorporators. The incorporators then hold an organizational meeting to elect directors and complete the details of the incorporation process.

CORPORATE STATUS

In some unusual situations, owners of a corporation use the business to perpetuate a fraud or get around the law. In these cases, courts will ignore

The procedures for incorporation are very specific. If they are not followed precisely, others may be able to challenge the existence of the corporation. Errors in the incorporation procedures can become important when, for example, a third person who is attempting to enforce a contract or bring suit for a tort injury learns of them. On the basis of improper incorporation, the plaintiff could seek to make the would-be shareholders personally liable.

If the defaulting party learns of a defect in the incorporation procedure when the corporation seeks to enforce a contract against a defending party, he or she may be able to avoid liability on that ground.

the corporate structure and "pierce the corporate veil," exposing the shareholders to personal liability.

Some factors that cause the courts to pierce the corporate veil include the following:

1. Parties are tricked or misled into dealing with the corporation when they believe they are dealing with an individual.
2. The corporation is set up to be unprofitable, or it is too "thinly capitalized"—that is, not enough money or property is invested in the business for it to have any chance at success. In such cases, the corporation has been created solely to shield the owner from liability.
3. The corporate formalities required by law, such as calling corporation meetings, are not followed.
4. Personal and corporate interests are commingled—that is, mixed together—and the corporation has no separate identity.

◇ LEGAL FOCUS - PROBLEM

Eagle Corporation, a close corporation, is formed by a few family members. The family shareholders keep corporate and personal funds in the same bank account. They fail to hold meetings of the board of directors. The shareholders often make personal use of corporate automobiles. Do they risk a piercing of the corporate veil?

The most dominant form of business in the world is the corporation.

GM Buick Motor Division Administration Building

Ask a student volunteer to explain the meaning of the phrase "pierce the corporate veil," as used here. (Students should understand that piercing the corporate veil occurs when courts ignore the corporate structure and expose shareholders to personal liability.) To illustrate this concept, you might draw a large circle on the board and within that circle write *Acme Corp.* and *Shareholder A, B, and C.* Explain to the students that if Acme Corp. were established to perpetuate a fraud and the courts chose to pierce the corporate veil, they would ignore the corporate structure (at this point you should erase *Acme Corp.* from inside your circle) and hold Shareholders A, B, and C personally liable.

Legal Focus Problem

Have a student volunteer read aloud this Legal Focus Problem. Ask the volunteer to suggest a possible answer to the question posed at the end of this problem.

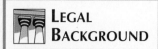

LEGAL BACKGROUND

The express powers of a corporation are found in its articles of incorporation, in the law of the state of incorporation, and in the state and federal constitutions. The following order of priority is used when conflicts arise among the documents involving corporations: (1) the U.S. Constitution, (2) state constitutions, (3) state statutes, (4) the certificate of incorporation (charter), (5) corporate bylaws, and (6) resolutions of the board of directors.

Legal Focus Example

Have a student read aloud this Legal Focus Example dealing with the need for a quorum of shareholders. Remind students that they can use the Legal Focus features as review tools when studying for tests.

Enrichment

You might wish to preface the discussion of corporate management—shareholders by pointing out to students that the acquisition of a share of stock makes a person an owner and shareholder in a corporation. As a shareholder, that person acquires certain powers in the corporation. These powers are discussed here, along with the relationship of the shareholders to the corporation.

Yes. When the corporate privilege is abused for personal benefit and the business is treated in such a careless manner, the corporation and shareholders are no longer separate. In such a case, a court may require an owner to assume personal liability for the corporation's debts.

◆ CORPORATE POWERS

Corporations have both express and implied powers. The express powers of a corporation come from the state laws, articles of incorporation, and the bylaws. The corporation has the implied power to perform all legal acts appropriate and necessary to accomplish its corporate purposes.

◆ CORPORATE MANAGEMENT— SHAREHOLDERS

Shareholders have the responsibility to elect the members of the board of directors of the corporation. The first board of directors is usually named in the articles of incorporation, and that board serves only until an election at the first shareholders' meeting. Although board members are elected to serve for a term, the shareholders can remove a director from office *for cause*, such as a breach of duty or misconduct.

Shareholders also have the power to approve fundamental changes affecting the corporation. Hence, shareholders can amend the articles of incorporation and bylaws, approve a merger or dissolution of the corporation, and approve the sale of the corporation. Some of these powers require approval by the board of directors before they are submitted for shareholder votes.

Shareholders must meet at least once a year. Additional meetings can be called to take care of urgent matters. Owners of small amounts of stock in publicly traded corporations usually do not attend shareholders' meetings. They issue or give a written authorization to a third person to vote their shares at the meeting. This authorization is called a **proxy**.

Shareholders must act together; they cannot bind the corporation by individual action. For shareholders to act, a minimum number of them (based on the number of shares they own) must be present at a meeting. This minimum number, called a *quorum*, is usually more than 50 percent. If a quorum is present, then a majority vote of the shares at the meeting is usually required to decide business matters.

◆ **proxy** A written authorization allowing another person to vote a shareholder's shares at a corporation meeting.

LEGAL FOCUS - EXAMPLE

Novo Pictures, Inc., has 10,000 outstanding shares of voting stock. The articles of incorporation set the quorum at 50 percent of outstanding shares. The articles also provided that a majority vote of

Ethical Concern

A proxy is a written authorization to a third person to vote a shareholder's shares at a stockholders' meeting. Proxies are often solicited by management. Have a student lead a discussion about why management solicits proxies. Discuss the reason why management would want the proxies and why shareholders would give proxies. What ethical considerations arise from this action?

the shares present decide ordinary matters. At the shareholders' meeting, a quorum of stockholders representing 5,000 outstanding shares must be present to conduct business. If 5,000 shares are present, a vote of at least 2,501 is needed to pass ordinary resolutions.

◆ CHECKING YOUR PROGRESS

1. Who manages a corporation?
2. What can corporations do with profits earned?
3. Can a corporation be held responsible for criminal actions of its employees? Explain.
4. What is the difference between a foreign corporation and an alien corporation?
5. How could a shareholder's liability be affected if corporate privilege is abused for personal benefit?

◆ CORPORATE MANAGEMENT— DIRECTORS

Every corporation is governed by directors. Subject to statutory limitations, the number of directors is stated in the corporation's articles or by-laws. Historically, the minimum number of directors has been three, but today many states allow fewer.

The term of office for a director is usually one year—from one annual meeting to the next. Longer and staggered terms are allowed in most states. A common practice is to elect one-third of the board members each year for a three-year term. In this way, there is greater management continuity.

DIRECTORS' MANAGEMENT RESPONSIBILITIES

Directors are responsible for all policy decisions necessary for the management of the corporation. Just as shareholders cannot act individually to bind the corporation, the directors must act as a body in carrying out routine corporate business. Each director has one vote, and generally the majority rules.

The general areas of responsibility for the board of directors include the following:

1. Declaration and payment of corporate dividends to shareholders.
2. Major corporate policy decisions—for example, determining which new products to develop and overseeing major contract negotiations, as well as negotiations between management and labor.

---

3. Appointment, supervision, and removal of corporate officers and other managerial employees, including setting management pay.

BOARD OF DIRECTORS' FORUM

The board of directors conducts business by holding formal meetings and recording the minutes. The date of regular meetings is usually established in the articles of incorporation, the bylaws, or by board resolution. Special meetings can be called if notice is sent to all directors.

Corporate Officers   The officers and other executive employees are hired by the board of directors. These employees act as agents of the corporation, and the ordinary rules of agency apply. In most states, a person can hold more than one office and can be both an officer and a director of the corporation. Corporate officers can be removed by the board of directors at any time. If the removal is without cause, the corporation may be liable for breach of contract.

 Law in Action

LAW AND THE BUSINESSPERSON: HOW TO INCORPORATE

Incorporation generally involves a modest investment in legal fees and filing fees. Just about anybody can form a corporation for any lawful purpose. The requirements differ in each state. You do not have to form a corporation in the state in which you live or the state in which you are doing business. Many individuals form their corporations, or obtain a corporate charter, from the state of Delaware. Delaware is believed to have the fewest restrictions on corporate formation and operation. Delaware also provides for limitations on the liability for directors for poor business judgment, a very attractive feature for many large companies.

Delaware is also the state most often chosen by the "mail-order incorporation" type of company. Perhaps you have even seen the ad—"You, too, can incorporate"—in various national and regional magazines. These ads are usually generated by organizations that have preprinted incorporation forms to be filled out and sent back with a small fee. These mail-order organizations send or take your forms to the appropriate state office in Delaware to get your certificate of incorporation. "Do-it-yourself" incorporating may be sufficient for a small business that does not expect to grow. However, promoters of a business with growth potential should contact a local lawyer to assist them in incorporating the business.

Checklist of Factors to Consider Concerning Incorporation

1. Tax considerations.
2. The initial cost of incorporation and any continuing costs.
3. Necessary formalities.
4. The amount of required record keeping.
5. What should be included in the bylaws.

Ethical Concern

Read aloud the following sentences from the student book concerning the duty of care: "Due care requires that directors carry out their responsibilities in an informed, business-like manner. Directors are expected to attend board of directors' meetings. Their votes should be entered into the minutes of those meetings. Unless a dissent is entered into the minutes, the director is presumed to have agreed. Directors are expected to be knowledgeable about corporate matters and to understand legal and other professional advice given to the board."

Stimulate a class discussion regarding the duty of care, by asking students the following questions: Can you think of other examples of due care that directors should be expected to adhere to? Do you agree that the standard of due care that is expected of directors and officers should be defined in state corporation laws? Why or why not? What penalties, if any, should be imposed upon a director who is guilty of not exercising due care? Who suffers damage when a director fails to exercise his or her duty of care? Please explain.

RIGHTS AND DUTIES OF DIRECTORS, MANAGERS, AND SHAREHOLDERS

DUTIES OF OFFICERS AND DIRECTORS

Directors and officers are fiduciaries of the corporation—that is, their relationship with the corporation and its shareholders is one of trust and confidence. Their duties include the duty of care and the duty of loyalty.

Duty of Care Directors must be honest and use careful business judgment in the conduct of corporate affairs. They must exercise the same degree of care that reasonably prudent people use in the conduct of their own personal business affairs.

Directors can be held answerable to the corporation and to the shareholders for breach of this duty of care. When directors delegate work to corporate officers and employees, they are expected to supervise the corporate officers. Otherwise, they can be held liable for negligence or mismanagement by them.

The standard of *due care* that is expected of directors and officers is defined in many state corporation laws and discussed in judicial decisions. Due care requires that directors carry out their responsibilities in an informed, businesslike manner. Directors are expected to attend board of directors' meetings. Their votes should be entered into the minutes of those meetings. Unless a dissent is entered into the minutes, the director is presumed to have agreed. Directors are expected to be knowledgeable about corporate matters and to understand legal and other professional advice given to the board.

Legal Focus Example

Have a student read aloud to the class this Legal Focus Example concerning the duty of care. Ask the student to outline specific examples of a breach of the duty of care in this example.

 LEGAL FOCUS ~ EXAMPLE

A corporate bank director did not attend any board of directors' meetings for five and a half years. He did not inspect any of the corporate books or records. Meanwhile, the bank president made several improper loans and permitted large overdrafts. The corporate director was held liable to the corporation for losses of nearly $20,000 resulting from the unsupervised actions of the bank president and the loan committee.

Duty of Loyalty One can define *loyalty* as being faithful to one's obligations and duties. Fiduciary duty requires that directors and officers place their own self-interests second to the interests of the corporation. It presumes constant loyalty to the corporation on the part of the directors and officers. The duty of loyalty prohibits directors from using corporate funds

Read aloud to the class the Legal Focus Problem found here. Ask a student volunteer to suggest a possible answer to the question posed at the end of this problem. Then ask the volunteer to describe the steps Alden took to avoid conflict of interest in this particular case.

Remind the students that, as the text points out, officers and directors must disclose to the corporation any corporate opportunity. Ask the students to compare this aspect of the duty of loyalty to the duty of notification in the agent and principal relationship, which was discussed in Chapter 20.

580   Doing Business

or confidential corporate information for their personal advantage. Officers and directors must disclose to the corporation fully any corporate opportunity. Any possible conflict of interest in a transaction must be avoided or disclosed.

When an officer or director is taken to court for breach of fiduciary duty, the case typically involves one or more of the following:

1. Competing with the corporation.
2. Taking a corporate opportunity.
3. Having an interest that conflicts with the interest of the corporation.
4. Using information that is not public to make a profit by trading shares or stock (called *insider trading*).
5. Authorizing a corporate transaction that is detrimental to minority shareholders.

Conflicts of Interest   Corporate directors often have many business affiliations, and they can even sit on the board of more than one corporation. Of course, they are precluded from entering into or supporting any business that operates in direct competition with the corporation. The fiduciary duty requires them to make a full disclosure of any potential conflicts of interest that might arise in any corporate transaction.

Sometimes a corporation enters into a contract or engages in a transaction in which an officer or director has a material interest. The director or officer must make a *full disclosure* of that interest and must not vote on the proposed transaction.

◆ LEGAL FOCUS – PROBLEM

Sunwood Corporation needs office space. Lambert Alden, one of its five directors, owns the building adjoining the corporation's offices. He negotiates a lease with Sunwood for the space. He fully discloses his interest to Sunwood and the other four directors. The lease arrangement is fair and reasonable. Alden does not vote on the contract. It is unanimously approved by the corporation's other four directors. Is this a violation by Alden of the conflict-of-interest rule?

No, the contract is valid. Alden disclosed his interest, provided a fair bargain, and refrained from voting on the contract. The conflict-of-interest rule is based on the standard of reasonableness. As long as directors use reasonable care, they can enter into business contracts with the corporation. Otherwise, directors would be prevented from ever giving financial assistance to the corporations they serve.

The Business Judgment Rule   Directors are expected to use their best judgment in guiding corporate management, but they are not expected to

In some cases the courts are very reluctant to resolve for corporations questions of policy and business management because that is the role played by the directors, and their judgment should be accepted as final unless shown to be tainted with fraud.

Other courts, however, will not accept the judgment of directors as final, even though it is not tainted with fraud. These courts maintain that the business judgment rule, in some circumstances, can be used as a defensive tool by directors to avoid

their responsibilities to stockholders. Those who share this attitude feel that there are times when directors' decisions should be closely scrutinized according to the benefit or detriment they cause to stockholders and the specific conflict of interest involved.

guarantee business success. Honest mistakes of judgment and poor business decisions on their part do not make them liable to the corporation for any losses that result. This is called the **business judgment rule**. The rule protects directors and officers from liability as long as the decisions they make are within their managerial authority, comply with their fiduciary duties, and are within the powers of the corporation.

To benefit from the rule, directors and officers must act in good faith. They must believe that the actions they take or decisions they make are in the best interests of the corporation. The director must exercise the care that an ordinarily prudent person would take under similar circumstances. In other words, the director must make an informed decision, with good reasons to back it up, and with no conflict between the director's personal interest and the interest of the corporation.

◆ **business judgment rule** A rule that protects corporate management from liability for actions taken in good faith.

RIGHTS OF DIRECTORS

A director of a corporation has several rights, including those of inspection and indemnification.

Inspection A director has the right to inspect all corporate books and records in order to make decisions and to supervise properly. This right of inspection cannot be restricted.

Indemnification It is not unusual for corporate directors to be sued because of their positions and their actions as directors. Most states allow a corporation to pay back, or *indemnify*, a director for legal costs, fees, and judgments involved in defending corporation-related suits. Many states permit a corporation to purchase liability insurance for the directors and officers in case they are sued and found responsible.

RIGHTS AND DUTIES OF MANAGEMENT EMPLOYEES

Corporate managers have the same fiduciary duties of care and loyalty in their conduct of corporate affairs as directors have. They have the same duties concerning corporate opportunities and conflicts of interest as directors. The rights of corporate managers are established by their employment contracts.

RIGHTS OF SHAREHOLDERS

As we have said, the purchase of a share of stock makes a person an owner and shareholder in a corporation. Although shareholders have no legal title to corporate property, such as buildings and equipment, they do have an *equitable* interest in the corporation. The rights of shareholders are established in the articles of incorporation and under the state's general incorporation law.

Shares of Stock When a shareholder purchases stock in a corporation, he or she receives a stock certificate as proof of ownership. Shareholders

Critical Thinking Activity

Ask the students to write one-paragraph explanations of how the right of inspection is necessary in order for a director to fulfill appropriately his or her duties of care and loyalty. Allow student volunteers to share their papers with the class.

Assign each student the responsibility of writing to a major publicly held corporation, asking for a copy of that corporation's annual report to stockholders. Have students prepare and present two-minute oral reports to the class based on the information in the annual reports they receive.

Vocabulary Activity

Have a student volunteer look up the word *residual* in a dictionary. Have him or her relate an appropriate dictionary definition of *residual* to the following sentence from the student book: "Holders of common stock have a *residual* position in the overall financial structure of a business."

Ethical Concern

Ask the class to discuss the extent to which ethical considerations guide the conduct of corporations. Must a corporation that is operating in a lawful manner concern itself with nonlegal ethical considerations? If the corporate officers attempt to operate the company so that it conforms to ethical standards that impose costs far in excess of those required to operate the corporation in a lawful manner, would such conduct constitute a breach of duty to the corporation's shareholders, who might ultimately suffer from reduced share values?

---

582   Doing Business

have the right to demand that the corporation issue a certificate and record their names and addresses in the corporate record books. But stock is *intangible* personal property—the ownership right exists independently of the certificate itself. A stock certificate may be lost or destroyed, but ownership still exists.

Notice of shareholders' meetings, dividends, and operational and financial reports are all distributed according to the stock ownership listed in the corporation's books. Exhibit 24–2 offers a summary of the types of stock issued by corporations. The two major types are common stock and preferred stock.

Common Stock   **Common stock** represents true ownership of a corporation. A shareholder's interest is usually in proportion to the number of shares owned out of the total number of shares issued. Each share usually represents one vote.

Holders of common stock have a *residual* position in the overall financial structure of a business. This means that if the company is liquidated, the common stockholder is the last to get back his or her investment. The receipt of dividends also depends on all the other groups—suppliers, employees, managers, bankers, governments, bondholders, and holders of

◆ **common stock**
The usual stock of voting ownership in a corporation. If other types of shares exist, common stockholders usually are the last to receive dividends.

EXHIBIT 24-2
STOCKS

Types	Definitions
Common Stock	Voting shares that represent ownership interests in a corporation with lowest priorities with respect to payment of dividends and distribution of assets upon the corporation's dissolution.
Preferred Stock	Shares of stock that have priority over common stock shares as to payment of dividends and distribution of assets upon corporate dissolution. Dividend payments are usually a fixed percentage of the face value of the share.
Cumulative Preferred Stock	Required dividends not paid in a given year must be paid in a subsequent year before any common stock dividends are paid.
Participating Preferred Stock	The owner is entitled to receive the preferred stock dividend and additional dividends after payment of dividends on common stock.
Authorized Shares	Shares allowed to be issued by the articles of incorporation.
Issued Shares	Shares that are actually transferred to shareholders.

Divide the class into small groups. Tell each group that it has been given $1,000 to invest in stocks. Each group should then decide how much of each type of stock (common or preferred) they will purchase with the $1,000. Explain to students that they can purchase 100 percent of common stock, 100 percent of preferred stock, or any combination of both types of stock, but they must invest all $1,000. Allow the groups some time to discuss their decisions; then have each group report to the class how it allocated its money and why its members made the choice they made.

Ask a student volunteer to explain why holders of common stock are willing to occupy the riskiest position among all shareholders.

Legal Focus Example

Have a student volunteer read aloud the Legal Focus Example that begins at the bottom of this page. Guide the students in discussing this example to ensure that all students understand the concept of preemptive rights. Remind students that they can use the Legal Focus features as review tools when studying for tests.

preferred stock—being paid what they are owed. Once those groups are paid, however, the owners of common stock are usually entitled to *all* the remaining earnings.

This is the central feature of ownership in any corporation. Whether it is a corner grocery, a retail store, an architectural firm, or a giant international oil corporation, the owners of common stock occupy the riskiest position. But they also have a right to the largest return on their investment.

Preferred Stock **Preferred stock** is stock that offers its owners a *preference*. Usually, this means that holders of preferred stock will be paid dividends first and will have their investment paid back, on dissolution of the corporation, before holders of common stock. Preferred-stock shareholders may or may not have the right to vote.

Preferred-stock shareholders receive periodic dividend payments in an amount that is usually a fixed percentage of the face value of each preferred share. In other words, if the rate is set at 9 percent, then preferred stock with a face value of $100 per share would pay its owner a $9 dividend per share each year. The corporation is not legally obliged to pay these dividends, but if any dividends are paid to any shareholder, preferred shareholders must be paid first.

Holders of preferred stock are investors with a *cautious* position in the corporation. A preferred stockholder receives fixed dividends periodically. As a result, they often do not share in the full prosperity of the firm if it grows over time. The fixed dividend is often the maximum return a preferred stockholder can expect. A common stockholder is less certain to receive a dividend but is not limited to receiving only a certain amount when a dividend is actually issued.

Dividends A **dividend** is the distribution of corporate profits or income ordered by the directors. Dividends are paid to the shareholders based on the number of shares in the corporation they own. Dividends can be paid in cash, property, or stock. State laws vary, but every state determines the general circumstances and legal requirements under which dividends are paid.

Preemptive Rights A **preemptive right** is a right given to a shareholder over all other purchasers to purchase a proportional amount of any new issue of stock. This allows the shareholder to maintain his or her same control, voting power, or financial interest in the corporation. Most states either (1) assume preemptive rights, but allow them to be canceled in the corporation's articles or (2) deny preemptive rights, except when they are granted in the articles.

◆ **preferred stock** A stock with a preference over common stock. Usually, this means that holders of preferred stock have priority over holders of common stock when dividends are issued and when investments are repaid.

◆ **dividend** A distribution of corporate profits or income ordered by the directors and paid to the shareholders of record.

◆ **preemptive rights** A preference a shareholder has over all other purchasers to subscribe to or purchase a new issue of stock. It allows the shareholder to maintain his or her proportionate control of the corporation.

◆ **LEGAL FOCUS – EXAMPLE**

Detering Corporation authorized and issued 1,000 shares of stock. Pat Southern purchased 100 shares, making her the owner of 10 percent of the company's stock. Later, Detering Corporation, by vote of its

All states have statutes authorizing mergers and consolidations for domestic corporations, and most states allow the combination of domestic (in-state) and foreign (out-of-state) corporations. Although the procedures vary somewhat among jurisdictions, the basic requirements tend to be fairly uniform: (1) the board of directors of each corporation involved must approve a merger or consolidation plan, (2) the shareholders of each corporation must vote approval of the plan at a shareholders' meeting (by simple majority, two-thirds, or four-fifths of the outstanding stock, depending on the state of incorporation), (3) after being approved by all the directors and the shareholders, the plan (articles of merger or articles of consolidation) is filed, usually with the secretary of state, and (4) when the state formalities are satisfied, the state issues a certificate of merger to the surviving corporation or a certificate of consolidation to the newly consolidated corporation.

Allow student volunteers to research recent mergers and consolidations. You might guide the students in their research by referring them to business newspapers such as the *Wall Street Journal*, business new magazines such as *Business Week*, or mainstream news magazines such as *Time* and *Newsweek*. Have each student present an oral report on his or her findings.

shareholders, amended the articles of incorporation and authorized the issuance of another 1,000 shares. This increased its stock to a total of 2,000 shares. If preemptive rights are provided, Pat Southern can purchase one additional share of the new stock for each share currently owned—100 additional shares. Thus, she would own 200 of the 2,000 shares outstanding. Her relative position as a shareholder would be maintained. If preemptive rights are not reserved, her proportionate control and voting power will be diluted. It would change from that of a 10 percent shareholder to that of a 5 percent shareholder, when the additional 1,000 shares were sold to others.

Preemptive rights are far more important in a close corporation than in a large one because of the small number of shares and the substantial interest held by each shareholder.

 MERGERS, CONSOLIDATION, AND TERMINATION OF THE CORPORATION

A corporation can expand its operations by combining with another corporation. This can be accomplished through either a merger or a consolidation. Dissolution and liquidation are the processes by which a corporation ends, or terminates, its existence. The following subsections look briefly at these processes.

MERGER AND CONSOLIDATION

The terms *merger* and *consolidation* are often used interchangeably, but they actually refer to two legally distinct proceedings. The rights and liabilities of the corporation, its shareholders, and its creditors are the same for both.

A **merger** is the combination of two or more corporations so that only one of the corporations continues to exist. For example, Corporation A and Corporation B decide to merge. The respective boards of directors agree that A will absorb B. When the merger occurs, B ceases to exist as a separate corporation. Corporation A continues as the *surviving corporation*. After the merger, A is the only corporation that remains, and it now possesses all the rights, privileges, and powers of itself and of B. This process is illustrated in Exhibit 24-3.

In a **consolidation**, two or more corporations combine so that each corporation ceases to exist and a new one emerges. For example, Corporation A and Corporation B consolidate to form an entirely new organization, Corporation C. In the process, A and B both terminate, and a new organization, C, comes into existence. Corporation C has the rights, privileges, and powers of both A and B. This process is illustrated in Exhibit 24-4.

◆ **merger** The legal combination of two or more corporations, the result of which is that the surviving corporation acquires all the assets and obligations of the other corporation, which then ceases to exist.

◆ **consolidation** The legal combination of two or more corporations, the result of which is that each corporation ceases to exist and a new one emerges. The new corporation assumes all the assets and obligations of the former corporations.

Checking Your Progress (Answers)

1. Directors, as a board, are responsible for all policy decisions necessary to the management of the corporation. General areas of responsibility include declaration and payment of dividends, major corporate policy decisions, appointment, supervision, removal of corporate officers and managers, and major financial decisions.

2. If the corporation enters into a contract in which an officer or director has a material interest, he or she must make a full disclosure of that interest and must not vote on the proposed transaction.

3. Most states allow a corporation to indemnify a director for costs incurred in defending corporation-related suits. Many states permit a corporation to purchase liability insurance for corporate directors.

4. Student opinions will vary. Common stockholders having a residual position in the overall financial structure of a business will be the last to get back their investment. However, they are entitled to all the earnings remaining after all other groups are paid.

5. Preemptive rights are important because they allow a shareholder to maintain his or her portion of interest in the company if new shares are issued. Students may discuss legal and ethical attempts to diminish a shareholder's rights.

6. A merger is a combination of two or more corporations so that only one of the corporations continues to exist, with the other becoming a part of it. In a consolidation neither corporation continues to exist. When they are combined, a completely new organization is formed.

EXHIBIT 24-3
MERGER

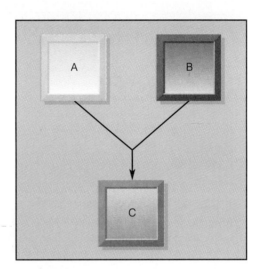

EXHIBIT 24-4
CONSOLIDATION

TERMINATION

Termination of a corporate life has two phases. **Dissolution** is the legal death of the "artificial person" of the corporation. **Liquidation** is the selling of corporate assets and the distribution of the cash to creditors and shareholders according to legal rules of preference. When dissolution takes place by voluntary action, the members of the board of directors act as trustees of the corporate assets. As trustees, they are responsible for winding up the affairs of the corporation so that corporate creditors and shareholders benefit as much as possible.

◆ **dissolution** The legal death of a corporation.

◆ **liquidation** The process by which corporate assets are converted into cash, which is then distributed to creditors and shareholders according to specified rules of preference.

◆ CHECKING YOUR PROGRESS

1. What are the responsibilities of directors of corporations?

2. What must a corporate officer or director do if the corporation enters into a contract in which the officer or director has a material interest?

3. What can be done to protect corporate directors from lawsuits against them because of their position and actions as directors?

4. Holders of common stock have a residual position in the overall financial structure of a business. Is this a good position to be in? Explain.

5. Discuss the reason preemptive rights are important.

6. What is the difference between a merger and a consolidation?

Read

Introduce this *A Case In Point* feature by reminding students that directors and officers of a corporation owe a duty of loyalty to the corporation. Explain to the students that this *A Case In Point* feature deals with an instance where the defendants were officers, directors, and shareholders of a corporation and were accused of usurping a corporate opportunity for personal gain. Then ask a student volunteer to read this *A Case In Point* feature aloud to the class.

Discuss

Stimulate a class discussion of this feature by asking the following questions: What were the roles of the defendants within the corporation? What was the role of Coupounas within the corporation? What was the relationship between Bio-Lab, Inc. and Med-Lab, Inc.? Why did Coupounas sue the defendants? What was the issue in this case? What was the decision of the Supreme Court of Alabama in this case? What reasons did the court give for its decision?

Teaching Note

This case is included in the *West's Business and Personal Law Handbook of Selected Court Cases.*

◆ A CASE IN POINT ◆

MORAD v. COUPOUNAS

Supreme Court of Alabama, 1978.
361 So.2d 6.

In this case, the Alabama Supreme Court reviewed a situation in which officers, directors, and shareholders attempted to gain profit for themselves at the expense of the corporation.

FACTS Dr. Morad, his wife Pamela Morad, and Thomson were officers, directors, and shareholders of Bio-Lab, Inc. Coupounas was a shareholder. While serving as officers and directors of Bio-Lab, Morad, Thomson, and Morad's wife incorporated and operated a competing business, Med-Lab, Inc. Med-Lab sold products to the same customers as Bio-Lab. Sometimes when orders were sent to Bio-Lab, the directors ensured that they were filled by Med-Lab. Coupounas sued on behalf of Bio-Lab. (This type of suit is called a *stockholder's derivative suit*). The suit claimed that the directors of Bio-Lab had breached their fiduciary duty. Coupounas claimed that the directors had taken advantage of a corporate opportunity by opening the competing business. The trial court held for Coupounas, and the defendants appealed.

ISSUE Did the directors of Bio-Lab breach their fiduciary duty to the corporation by opening a competing business? Was this a "taking of a corporate opportunity"?

DECISION The Bio-Lab directors were guilty of taking advantage of a corporate opportunity for their own personal gain.

REASON Officers and directors of a corporation may only take advantage of a corporate opportunity if the opportunity is first made known to the corporation, and the corporation refuses it. A director may not hide opportunities from the corporation and then exploit them. Ample evidence was presented that Bio-Lab expected to grow and was interested in new business opportunities. The court concluded that "[i]t is well settled that directors are subject to the rules which forbid such persons to secure an advantage for themselves." The Alabama Supreme Court determined that the appropriate remedy for the defendants' breach of their duty of loyalty was for the court to impose a "constructive trust," requiring all profits of Med-Lab to be paid to Bio-Lab.

In order to help students review what they have learned in Chapter 24, you might wish to:

1. Have a student volunteer, or volunteers, read the Chapter Summary aloud to the class.
2. Allow the students to work with partners to complete the *Using Legal Language* activity.
3. Assign the *Checking for Comprehension* exercise as homework.

4. Allow the students to work in small groups to complete the *Applying Legal Concepts* activities.
5. As a class, complete the *Applying the Law* activities. (Please note that you may have to help students with vocabulary so that they adequately understand all of the *Applying the Law* material.)

In order to check student mastery of chapter concepts, you may wish to use the Chapter 24 test that is found in your *Teacher's Resource Binder* or use WESTEST computerized testing for Chapter 24.

CHAPTER REVIEW 24

 ## SUMMARY

LEGAL CHARACTERISTICS OF CORPORATIONS

1. State law varies from state to state, and must be followed to form a corporation. The Model Business Corporation Act and the Revised Model Business Corporation Act have been adopted to some degree in every state.

2. The corporation is a legal entity distinct from its owners.

3. The shareholders own the corporation. They elect a board of directors to govern the corporation. The board of directors hires corporate officers and other employees to run the daily business of the firm.

4. The corporation pays income tax on net profits; shareholders pay income tax on dividends they receive from the corporation. This is called double-taxation.

5. The corporation can have perpetual existence or be chartered for a specific period of time.

6. The corporation is liable for the torts committed by its agents or officers. A corporation can fined for the criminal acts of its agents and employees.

CLASSIFICATION OF CORPORATIONS

1. Domestic, foreign, and alien corporations
2. Public, private, and publicly held corporations
3. Nonprofit corporations
4. Close corporations
5. Professional corporations

FORMATION OF THE CORPORATION

1. *Promoter*—One who takes the preliminary steps in organizing a corporation.

2. *Incorporation—basic requirements*:
   a. Preparation and filing of the articles of incorporation.
   b. Receipt of the certificate of incorporation or corporate charter.
   c. Holding the first organizational meeting.

CORPORATE STATUS

When fairness demands it, courts may "pierce the corporate veil" and hold a shareholder or shareholders personally liable for a judgment against the corporation.

CORPORATE MANAGEMENT— SHAREHOLDERS

1. Shareholder powers include: (a) Election of the board of directors. (b) Approval of all fundamental changes affecting the corporation, such as amendments to the charter or bylaws.

2. Shareholders' meetings must occur at least annually. A minimum number of shareholders (a quorum—usually 50 percent of shares held) must be present at a meeting. A shareholder may appoint a proxy, or substitute, to vote his or her shares.

CORPORATE MANAGEMENT— DIRECTORS

1. *Election and term of office:* Directors are elected by shareholders, and usually serve a one-year term.

2. *Management responsibilities include:*

Answers will vary.

1. The law treats corporations as people. Therefore, all constitutional rights guaranteed to citizens are also guaranteed to corporations. For example, a corporation has the right under the Fourteenth Amendment to equal protection under the laws and due process, etc.

2. The principle of *respondeat superior* holds a principal responsible for the actions of his or her agent. Since a corporation can act as an individual, it can act as a principal; thus it can be held accountable for the actions of its agent.

3. No. A corporation cannot go to jail, but officers of the corporation can. If a crime is committed at the officer's direction or with his or her permission, or if he or she is negligent in supervising employees, the officer may be held responsible and penalized by a jail sentence.

4. A public corporation is formed by the government to meet some political or governmental purpose. A private corporation is formed by private persons for private benefit or to serve a public purpose. A publicly held corporation is a private corporation formed by selling stock held to the general public, with the benefits going to the shareholders.

5. Corporate officers and directors breach their fiduciary duty if they compete with the corporation, take a corporate opportunity, have interests that conflict with the interests of the corporation, use information that is not public to make a profit trading shares or stocks, or authorize a corporate transaction that is detrimental to minority shareholders.

---

588   Doing Business

  a. Making all policy decisions necessary to the management of corporate affairs.

  b. Appointing, supervising, and removing corporate officers and other managerial employees.

  c. Declaring and paying corporate dividends to shareholders; issuing authorized shares or borrowing money.

Duties of Directors

Duty of Care: If a director fails to be honest and to use prudent business judgment in the conduct of corporate affairs, he or she can be answerable to the corporation and to the shareholders for the breach. The *business judgment rule* immunizes a director from liability in a corporate transaction if the director has acted in good faith.

Duty of Loyalty: Directors have a fiduciary duty to subordinate their own interests to those of the corporation in matters relating to the corporation.

Rights of Directors

Inspection: Directors have an absolute right to have access to corporate books and records.

Indemnification: Directors who have acted in good faith may be indemnified (paid back) by the corporation for court costs, legal fees, and judgments involved in defending corporation-related suits.

Rights of Shareholders

Voting Rights: Shareholders have the right to vote their shares, one vote per share. The articles of incorporation can exclude or limit voting rights for certain classes of shares.

Dividends: A dividend is a distribution of corporate profits or income ordered by the directors.

Preemptive Rights: Preemptive rights give preference to a shareholder over all other purchasers to subscribe to or purchase a new issue of stock.

MERGER AND CONSOLIDATION

1. *Merger*—Combination of two or more corporations, in which the surviving corporation acquires the other corporation, which then ceases to exist.

2. *Consolidation*—Combination of corporations, in which each corporation ceases to exist and a new one emerges.

Termination

The termination of a corporation involves the following two phases:

1. *Dissolution*—The legal death of the "artificial person" of the corporation.

2. *Liquidation*—The process by which assets are converted into cash, which is then distributed to creditors and shareholders according to specified rules of preference.

 ## USING LEGAL LANGUAGE

Directions: Write at least one sentence to explain the meaning of each term as it applies to law.

1. articles of incorporation
2. business judgment rule
3. close corporation
4. common stock
5. dividends

6. domestic corporation
7. merger
8. preferred stock
9. proxy
10. public corporation

1. When a corporate privilege is abused for personal shareholder profit or use, a court will look behind the corporate structure (pierce the corporate veil) and hold the shareholder(s) personally liable. To justify disregarding the corporate entity, it needs to be shown that there was a commingling of assets or that the shareholders converted the assets of the corporation to their own personal use, and that failure to disregard the corporate entity would result in fraud or injustice. Here, the shareholders are converting the funds to prevent Flynt from obtaining damages from the corporation, and the court would, most likely, pierce the corporate veil.

2. Yes. Fox, as the promoter of the corporation, is liable for the contract made on behalf of the future corporation. There was no agreement releasing him from liability. The fact that there is no express contract binding the promoter to pay is immaterial. The promoter has the burden of proving the existence of a release from such liability. Fox did not do so; therefore, he is liable to Cooper for the fee.

CHECKING FOR COMPREHENSION

1. How does the Constitution provide rights to corporations?

2. Does the principle of *respondeat superior* apply to corporations? Explain.

3. Can a jail sentence be imposed if a crime is committed by a corporation? Explain.

4. Explain the difference between public, private, and publicly-held corporations.

5. What types of activities could be considered a breach of fiduciary duty by officers and directors of a corporation?

APPLYING LEGAL CONCEPTS

1. Write and send a letter to your state inquiring about requirements for incorporating a business in your state. Use a typewriter or computer if possible. Design a flow chart showing the steps for incorporating a new business in your state. If you do not have specific state requirements, design a flow chart for the basic requirement described in the text.

APPLYING THE LAW . . . YOU BE THE JUDGE

1. Harvey's is a group of New York corporations. Five of these corporations entered into an agreement with Flynt Distributing Co. for Flynt to distribute their magazines. Following this agreement, Harvey's failed to pay Flynt or to ship the magazines to Flynt, causing Flynt injury. Two of Harvey's shareholders converted the assets of the five corporations to their own use, which left the corporations undercapitalized. Discuss whether this conduct amounted to an abuse of corporate business, allowing Flynt to pierce the corporate veil to obtain recovery. [*Flynt Distributing Co. v. Harvey*, 734 F.2d 1389 (9th Cir. 1984)]

2. Coopers and Lybrand (Coopers) performed accounting work for Garry Fox on behalf of a corporation that he was in the process of forming called G. Fox and Partners, Inc. Coopers took the job knowing that the corporation was not yet formed. Coopers performed the accounting work, and Fox's company was incorporated. When Coopers was not paid for its accounting work, it sued Garry Fox for $10,827, the value of the work done. Coopers was holding Garry Fox liable individually based on promoter liability. Fox defended the suit on the ground that he had not made any agreement as individual to pay the fee. Can Coopers collect from Garry Fox individually? [*Coopers & Lybrand v. Fox*, (Colo.App.) 758 P.2d 683 (1988)]

590

Prereading Activity

Ask students why they think businesses have to follow administrative rules. Explain that administrative rules are rules made by agencies that Congress establishes to handle many kinds of activities and problems. Brainstorm names of agencies and the kinds of activities or problems they handle. Ask students to give opinions about whether the government should have more or less control over individuals or over businesses.

Mastery Objectives

By the end of this chapter, students will be able to:
- Depict historical background of administrative law
- Describe creation of regulatory agencies
- Distinguish among administrative agencies
- Delineate the administrative process
- List administrative acts
- Explain legal sufficiency of consideration

Chapter

25

Government Regulation of Business

Activity Sheets
Reviewing Legal Concepts 25 *TRB*
Enrichment Activity 25 *TRB*

Student Activity Workbook
Chapter 25 Activities

Tests
Chapter 25 Test *TRB*
Chapter 25 WESTEST Computerized Testing

Handbook of Selected Court Cases
United States v. *Danube Carpet Mills, Inc.*
Goldberg v. *Kelly*

**West's Business Law and Legal
Environment Videodisc**
Still Frames and Motion Segments as shown

*"The rise of administrative bodies probably has been the most significant
legal trend of the last century, and perhaps more values are affected by
their decisions than by those of all the courts."*
**Robert Jackson, 1892–1954
U.S. Supreme Court Justice 1941–1954**

Because modern life is so complex, Congress cannot provide all the necessary laws. Many technical matters requiring regulation are beyond the knowledge and experience of most legislators without putting in hours of study. But members of Congress have limited time and many issues to consider. Laws under consideration may cover such diverse matters as maximum speed and minimum altitude limitations for commercial aircraft; limitations on the chemical composition of fertilizers and insecticides; salary requirements and job standards for thousands of civil service employees; limitations on bullfrog hunting; and proper safety equipment standards for two-wheel and three-wheel recreational vehicles. How can any one person be expected to cast informed votes on the thousands of laws proposed in each legislative session?

Obviously, the legislative branch must delegate power in order to cope with the volume and specialization of problems requiring legal solutions. Most delegations of congressional powers are made to **administrative agencies**. Administrative agencies are sub-branches of the executive branch of government set up to carry out laws. Sometimes these agencies are called the *bureaucracy*. Federal agencies include the National Labor Relations Board, Federal Maritime Commission, and the Internal Revenue Service.

To establish an agency, Congress passes a broad statute that delegates to the agency the authority to regulate a particular area of business. Agencies have issued tens of thousands of rules that regulate business activities. A company that violates these rules can end up paying millions of dollars in fines. In some cases, the company's officers may face criminal penalties. Federal regulations cover most aspects of a business operation—from creating and financing the business to its hiring and firing of employees. These detailed federal regulations are just part of the governmental control over business. State and county governments also issue administrative regulations. Since state and local rules vary widely, this chapter focuses on federal administrative law.

The amount of power possessed by administrative agencies has led some to call them the "headless fourth branch" of government. Most agencies are considered to be part of the executive branch, but the president's control over them is often limited. In addition, some agencies exist as **independent regulatory agencies**.

Independent agencies are led by officials who cannot be dismissed by the president except for cause, such as theft. These officials are

◆ **administrative
agency** A sub-branch
of the executive branch
of government set up to
carry out laws.

◆ **independent
regulatory agency**
An administrative body
that has the power to
regulate some policy
area and that is led by
officials who cannot be
dismissed by the
president except for
cause.

Enrichment

Ask the students to raise their hands if they ate breakfast this morning. Explain that if they did, bureaucrats—individuals who work in the offices of government—had a great deal to do with their breakfast. For example, if they had bacon, the meat was inspected by federal agents. If they drank milk, the price was affected by rules and regulations of the Department of Agriculture. If they looked at a cereal box, they saw fine print about minerals and vitamins, which was the result of the regulations instituted by several other federal agencies.

Enrichment

Federal regulations that come from administrative agencies are just a part of governmental control over business. Brainstorm additional ways in which the federal government exercises control over businesses.

Teaching Note

The concept of administrative law was introduced to your students in Chapter 1.

Extension Activity

Have a student volunteer or group of volunteers research President Franklin D. Roosevelt's New Deal policies. Encourage the students to focus their research on the growth of the federal bureaucracy as a result of New Deal legislation and policies. Have the students report their findings to the class in the form of an oral report.

Legal Focus Example

Have a student volunteer read aloud this Legal Focus Example. Remind students that they can use the Legal Focus features as review tools when studying for tests. As a followup to this Legal Focus Example, you might have a student volunteer relate this brief discussion of the SEC to what the students learned about corporations in the previous chapter.

592

Enrichment

Any discussion of the federal bureaucracy may become confusing because of the incredible number of acronyms that are tossed around. Your students may find it difficult to keep track of which agency is which in this alphabet soup. Encourage your students to keep their own glossary of bureaucratic agencies for handy reference. Students can set up their glossaries alphabetically or as they encounter each agency. For easy reference, each agency should be listed by its acronym first, followed by its full name.

---

592 Doing Business

less likely to be influenced by the president than executives in dependent agencies. Executives in dependent agencies can be fired by the president at will.

Virtually all administrative agencies have a broad range of authority called **administrative law**. Administrative law consists of rules, regulations, orders, and decisions of administrative agencies. The nature of administrative law and authority is legislative and judicial, as well as executive. Much of the discussion in this chapter will focus on the power of administrative agencies and the nature of administrative law.

◆ **administrative law** The body of law concerned with the power and actions of administrative agencies. It consists of the rules, regulations, orders, and decisions of the agencies.

HISTORICAL BACKGROUND OF ADMINISTRATIVE LAW

Administrative law was largely unknown in the early years of our nation. At that time, the United States had a relatively simple, agricultural economy. It required little regulation. As business grew, demand for regulation developed. The first true independent regulatory agency was the Interstate Commerce Commission (ICC). The ICC was created in 1887 to end abuses common in the railroad industry at that time. For example, certain shippers and geographical areas received better rates than others; there was cutthroat competition and exploitative rate structures. The ICC ensured order and uniformity of service at reasonable rates. It also controlled competition within the industry and between railroads and other transporters.

The amount of regulation increased dramatically during the Great Depression of the 1930s. President Franklin D. Roosevelt established regulatory programs in the hope of increasing employment and bringing relief from the depression. In 1934, the Securities and Exchange Commission (SEC) and the National Labor Relations Board (NLRB) were created. The SEC regulated the corporate securities market and the NLRB regulated the employment-union relationship. Most of these programs involved regulations designed to encourage free competition.

 LEGAL FOCUS - EXAMPLE

Securities law and regulations were established to provide those who wanted to buy stock with enough information so they could make informed judgments about their purchases. The SEC then and now requires that corporations provide information to potential purchasers of stock, such as how money invested in the corporation is to be used. If information is not provided or if the information provided is misleading or incorrect, the corporation, officers, or its promoters are legally responsible.

The greatest growth in regulation took place in the 1960s and 1970s.

Signs requiring protective headgear are a product of federal regulation.

Congress created the Environmental Protection Agency (EPA) and the Occupational Safety and Health Administration (OSHA) in 1970 and the Consumer Product Safety Commission (CPSC) in 1972. More than one-third of all the current federal agencies were created between 1970 and 1979. These agencies attempt to protect the public from the potentially harmful consequences of the free market.

◄ LEGAL FOCUS ~ EXAMPLE

Factories are necessary in order to produce the goods and jobs we need and want. However, many large industries also produce air pollution, which endangers the public health. Some of the goods, such as automobiles, produce even more pollution. The Environmental Protection Agency has passed regulations designed to protect the environment from air pollution and other environmental hazards. These regulations determine, for example, how many chemicals a factory can send out into the air and how often automobiles must pass a smog check.

In recent years there has been a backlash against the bureaucracy and especially against economic regulation. Some businesspeople have felt that agency rules create an unreasonable burden on businesses, as it is often costly to change business operations in order to meet the standards that agencies have set. But some efforts at *deregulation* have been overturned by the courts, and it is clear that regulation is here to stay.

THE CREATION OF ADMINISTRATIVE AGENCIES

To create an administrative agency, Congress passes legislation establishing the agency and broadly defining its powers. This is called *enabling legislation*. The enabling legislation specifies the name, number of board members, and powers of the agency being created.

 ### LEGAL FOCUS ‑ EXAMPLE

The Federal Trade Commission (FTC) was created by the Federal Trade Commission Act of 1914. The act prohibits unfair and deceptive trade practices; allows the FTC to define what an unfair and deceptive trade practice is; and gives the agency the power to investigate and make rules and regulations. It describes the procedures the agency must follow in order to charge violators. It also provides for court review of agency actions.

The administrative agency is often staffed by officials and employees selected for their knowledge and experience in the field to be regulated.

 ## THE OPERATION OF ADMINISTRATIVE AGENCIES

Most administrative agencies serve four basic legally related functions. These are investigation, enforcement, rulemaking, and adjudication. Together these functions are called *administrative process*. These functions give the agency enough power and flexibility to accomplish its objectives. Exhibit 25-1 shows the scope of administrative law.

Agency power is balanced by three external controls. First, the judiciary has the power to review agency actions. Judicial review is discussed later in the chapter. Second, the executive and legislative branches have political control over administrative agencies.

 ### LEGAL FOCUS ‑ EXAMPLE

Congress can change the statute that defines the agency, taking away certain powers. In addition, Congress controls the amount of money provided an agency in the yearly budget process, and this directly affects how much the agency can do.

The third external control is the **Administrative Procedure Act of 1946 (APA)**, which provides mandatory guidelines for an administrative

♦ **Administrative Procedure Act of 1946 (APA)** A federal law that sets mandatory procedures for an administrative agency to follow.

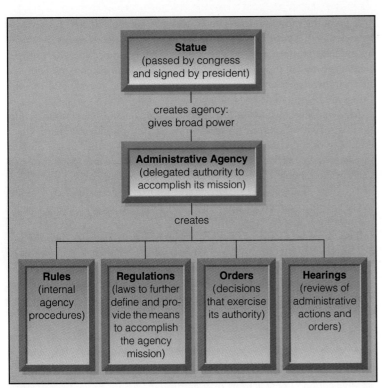

EXHIBIT 25-1
ADMINISTRATIVE LAW

VIDEODISC NOTE
Much of the material that is conveyed in the exhibits of *West's Business and Personal Law* is also conveyed in the still frames on the **West Business Law and Legal Environment Videodisc**. For more information and directions for use, please see the Index and Description of Contents for the **West Business Law and Legal Environment Videodisc** that is found in your *Teacher's Resource Binder*.

Legal Focus Example

Read aloud the Legal Focus Example dealing with the FDA that is found at the bottom of this page. Then have a student volunteer or group of volunteers search current newspapers and news magazines to locate articles regarding recent actions of the FDA. Allow the volunteers to present their findings to the class in the form of a short oral report.

agency to follow in carrying out its mission. The APA provides the requirements for how agencies make rules and adjudicate cases.

INVESTIGATION

To oversee an area or a type of business, an agency must know about the activities and organizations involved. Agencies use their *investigative* powers to get this information.

◆ LEGAL FOCUS – EXAMPLE

Before approving a new drug for sale in the United States, the Food and Drug Administration must determine its safety and effectiveness. The FDA will require that the company proposing the drug conduct research, and it may conduct studies itself as part of its investigative function. Sometimes the necessary information is provided voluntarily by businesses or groups.

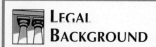

♦ **subpoena** An order to produce a witness or a thing, such as a document.

Two of the most important investigative tools available to administrative agencies are the **subpoena** and the ability to *search and seize*. A subpoena is an order to produce a witness or a thing. Using a subpoena, the administrative agency can order testimony to be given. It can also order a company or an individual to produce documents, papers, and records. All of these things are helpful in determining policy or completing an investigation.

Many agencies gather information through on-site inspections. Sometimes a search of a home, an office, or a factory provides evidence that a company or individual has violated a regulation. At other times, physical inspections are used instead of a formal hearing in order to correct or prevent an undesirable condition. Inspections and testing cover a wide range of activities. They include safety inspections of underground coal mines, safety tests of commercial equipment and automobiles, and environmental monitoring of factory emissions.

The Supreme Court has held that administrative agencies, like the police, must obey the Fourth Amendment, which requires that a warrant be obtained before a search is conducted. The requirements for obtaining an administrative warrant are less demanding than those for criminal warrants. There are even some exceptions to the requirement that an agency get a warrant, such as inspections of nuclear reactors at utility plants.

ENFORCEMENT

Once an investigation has been conducted, an agency may start an administrative action. These actions may be brought against individuals or organizations. Registering a complaint is the first step in an administrative action. Complaints may also be registered by private citizens and organizations, but they are always prosecuted by the agency.

An agency acts as prosecutor, judge, and jury. There are procedural safeguards against the abuse of this power by the agency. These safeguards are discussed in this chapter's "Law in Action."

A majority of actions brought by administrative agencies are resolved without formal adjudication, because regulated businesses often wish to avoid the appearance of being uncooperative with the agency. Settlements preserve the resources of both the agency and the business. Agencies also work hard to prevent violations and to negotiate with violators in order to avoid formal actions.

◀ LEGAL FOCUS – EXAMPLE

Between 1982 and 1992 over 2,500 savings and loan associations and banks in the United States failed. These failures occurred in part because of the poor business practices of many of these financial institutions. In the wake of the failures, legal actions were brought by government agencies against individuals and businesses accused of negligent practices. In December of 1992, three federal agencies announced a settlement of charges of wrongdoing with the

Ethical Concern

Guide your students in discussing the rule-making function of administrative agencies by asking the following questions: In our democratic system of government, we elect representatives to Congress to enact legislation; however, as you have learned, administrative agencies also create rules that are treated the same as statutes. Do you feel that this is appropriate, given our system of government? Why or why not?

accounting firm of Ernst and Young. The firm agreed to pay $400 million dollars in exchange for the government's dropping of its legal actions. Ernst and Young did not admit or deny the charges brought, but explained that the settlement was necessary to stop an endless stream of lawsuits that were expensive to defend.

RULEMAKING

The third major function of an administrative agency is rulemaking, the formulation of new regulations. Congress gives the agency the power to make rules in the agency's enabling legislation.

There are three types of rules that an agency may create: (1) regulations or legislative rules, (2) interpretative rules, and (3) procedural rules.

Regulations   These rules are treated the same as statutes. Their validity, though, depends on certain strict requirements being met. First, a regulation must be consistent with the U.S. Constitution (for example, it must

Can you think of some ways that prescription drugs are regulated?

Reteaching Activity

Have students work with partners to make charts of the four basic functions of most administrative agencies. Instruct students to use the following headings: Name of Function, Definition, and Example.

Enrichment

Guide the students in looking at the photo of the pharmacist found on this page. Ask student volunteers to detail some ways in which administrative agencies might affect the life and work of this pharmacist.

Caption Answer

Student answers will vary.

Have a student volunteer read aloud the first Legal Focus Example of a regulation from the IRS. Ask the volunteer to explain the regulation to the class as best he or she can. You might then point out that regulations such as this are part of the reason why so many people hire outside experts to prepare their income tax returns.

Legal Focus Example

Read aloud the second Legal Focus Example found here. Ask a student volunteer to explain why he or she thinks interpretive rules are needed.

Divide the class into groups of four, and have each group form its own regulatory agency. Instruct students to devise regulations for the school concerning safety, detentions, suspensions, lunches, or any other issues they desire. They must include in a written report the proposed methods of investigation (interviews with administrators, students, etc.), proposed methods of enforcement, a specific rule, and the proposed adjudication process for their agencies. Each group member should be primarily responsible for explaining to the class a particular function of the agency.

---

598   Doing Business

meet due process requirements). Second, the rule must not exceed the power given to the agency by Congress. Third, the enabling statute must provide reasonable standards to guide the agency in carrying out its administrative tasks. Finally, regulations usually must be consistent with the procedural rules in the APA.

◆ LEGAL FOCUS - EXAMPLE

If you travel away from home primarily to obtain education, the expenses of which are deductible, you may deduct your expenditures for travel, meals, and lodging while away from home. However, if you engage in incidental personal activities, such as sightseeing, social visiting, or entertaining, the portion of your expenses attributable to those personal activities are nondeductible. I.R.S. Regulation § 1.162-5(e).

This regulation created by the Internal Revenue Service helps define, in part, what travel expenses can be deducted from income for federal income tax purposes.

The process for establishing new regulations is complicated. The agency is required to give notice of the proposed rule. Notice usually involves the publication of the proposed regulation or of the intent to regulate in the *Federal Register*. The *Federal Register* is the official publication of the federal government for all agency regulations.

◆ *Federal Register*
The official publication of the federal government for all agency regulations.

Next, the agency must give any interested parties an opportunity to participate in formulating the regulation. To provide this opportunity, the agency may conduct an open hearing, or it may invite interested parties to send written comments to the agency.

Finally, all parties affected by the proposed regulation must have access to it. The final version of a regulation is published in the *Federal Register*, which can be found in any law library.

Interpretative Rules   These are statements and opinions issued by an agency explaining how the agency intends to apply the law it enforces.

◆ LEGAL FOCUS - EXAMPLE

The Internal Revenue Service has an interpretative rule about whether it allows tax deductions for charitable gifts. These rules also identify the information a taxpayer must submit to justify the charitable deduction.

Interpretative rules do not have the force of a regulation or a law. They are not automatically binding on private individuals or organizations. They also do not carry the same weight in court as do statutes and regulations. If someone believes the agency's interpretative rule is incorrect, it can be challenged in court. In practice, however, the courts often do turn to interpretative rules to help them decide cases involving agency regulations.

Procedural Rules   These rules describe an agency's method of operation and establish procedures for dealing with the agency. They cover hearings, negotiations, settlements, presentations of evidence, and other activities.

◈ LEGAL FOCUS ~ EXAMPLE

The Internal Revenue Service routinely audits taxpayers. An audit requires the taxpayer to produce the records (such as pay stubs and receipts for deducted expenses) that he or she used to fill out the tax forms. Procedural rules are used to determine who will be audited. For example, a procedural rule might say that every 1,000th taxpayer will be audited.

ADJUDICATION

Enforcement of agency rules may involve the fourth function of administrative agencies: adjudication, or the prosecution of accused offenders. These prosecutions take place in trial-like proceedings before an administrative law judge (ALJ). Sometimes the appointed heads of the agency hear the cases instead of the ALJ or they hear a case as an appeal of an ALJ decision.

An adjudication may also question the denial by the agency staff of government benefits. For example, a denied benefit might be the termination of social security benefits or of a government license.

Administrative Law Judges   An **administrative law judge** is a government employee appointed to hear administrative cases. ALJs are usually attorneys. Many times they are also employees of the very agency prosecuting the case. Certain safeguards exist to promote fairness in the proceedings. The ALJ is kept separate in the agency's organization from the investigative and prosecutorial staff. Private communication between the ALJ and anyone who is a party to an agency proceeding is forbidden.

The Process of Adjudication   After investigating a suspected rule violation, an agency may decide to file an administrative complaint against a party. This agency action may originally have been prompted by complaints from private individuals or interest groups. For example, FTC actions on alleged false advertising are often based on a series of complaints

◆ **administrative law judge (ALJ)**   A government employee appointed to hear and decide administrative agency hearings.

1. Congress gives administrative agencies authority to
act by passing broad statutes
that delegate to the agencies
the authority to regulate a
wide range of activities.
2. Regulations and laws
were established under the
direction of the Securities
and Exchange Commission
in an attempt to make the
free market work better.
They were established to
provide purchasers of stock
with enough information to
make informed judgments
about stock purchases.
3. Congress passes legislation establishing an administrative agency and broadly
defining its powers. The
enabling law specifies the
name, composition, and
powers of the agency being
created.
4. The four basic legally
related functions of administrative agencies are investigation, enforcement, rule
making, and adjudication.
5. Two of the most impor-
tant investigative tools available to administrative agencies are the subpoena (an
order to produce a witness
or thing) and the ability to
search and seize, provided a
warrant is issued before the
search is conducted (in most
instances).
6. An agency may create:
(1) regulations or legislative
rules, (2) interpretive rules,
and (3) procedural rules.
7. The *Federal Register* is
the official publication of
the federal government for
all agency regulations.

Stimulate a class discussion by asking students why it is important that the ALJ not be
allowed to have communication with anyone
who is a party to an agency proceeding.

from consumers. The procedures used in an administrative hearing vary
among the agencies.

♦ **administrative
hearing** An
adjudication held by an
administrative agency to
hear and decide some
factual question related
to agency action.

The Administrative Hearing   An **administrative hearing** is somewhat
similar to a trial. The charged party may be represented by a lawyer. The
lawyer may cross-examine agency witnesses and present his or her own evidence to counter that of the agency's. There are, however, significant differences between an administrative hearing and a court trial. The ALJ
decides both questions of law and facts, as there is no jury. The rules of evidence are also usually relaxed in an administrative hearing because no jury
is used. For example, the hearsay rule does not apply to an administrative
hearing.

After the case is concluded, the ALJ gives an initial order. Either side
may appeal the ALJ's initial order. Often the appeal is made to the board or
commission that governs the agency. Some boards consider all aspects of
the case anew, as though no ALJ decision existed. Sometimes an appeal
may be taken to a federal court.

If the appeal is unsuccessful or if no appeal is made, the ALJ's initial
order becomes the final order of the agency. If it is successfully appealed,
the final order may come from the commission or from a reviewing court.

A final order may compel a party to pay damages. A special type of
order, called a cease-and-desist order, may forbid some specified activity. A
cease-and-desist order is like a court injunction. An ALJ may also order an
agency to reinstate benefits that the agency previously denied.

◆ CHECKING YOUR PROGRESS

1. How does Congress give authority to act to administrative
   agencies?
2. Why were securities law and regulations established under the
   direction of the Securities and Exchange Commission?
3. How is a regulatory agency created?
4. What are the four basic legally related functions of most
   administrative agencies?
5. Describe two important investigative tools available to
   administrative agencies.
6. What three types of rules may an administrative agency create?
7. What is the *Federal Register*?

◆ CONTROL OVER ADMINISTRATIVE AGENCIES

Agency authority is held in check in several ways. We have discussed some
of these already: the U.S. Constitution provides limits on agency authority,

Enrichment

Call on student volunteers to explain each of the reasons included in the numbered list, which a plaintiff can present in a judicial review as a defense against an agency action. Ask each volunteer to read one of the numbered items and then repeat the description in his or her own words. For example, the volunteer for no. 1 would say, "One. The agency exceeded the authority conferred by the agency's enabling legislation. In other words. . . ."

the APA has a significant effect on the formal administrative process, and the source of agency authority, the enabling statute, is also a limitation. Both the executive and legislative branches of government have some control over administrative agencies. Judicial control is exercised when the federal courts conduct an independent review of agency action. This is called *judicial review.*

JUDICIAL REVIEW

The courts provide a direct avenue for the review of agency action. However, not all agency action is subject to judicial review, nor does every individual have a right to challenge an agency's actions.

The Scope of Judicial Review   The APA allows judicial review of most agency actions. In addition, a court may force an agency to take an action that the court decides has been unlawfully withheld. A court may also prevent any action by the agency that goes beyond the agency's authority. As we have said, the courts are reluctant to review questions of fact; usually, the courts defer to the facts found in agency proceedings. This is partly based on the attitude of the courts that those who hear and see the evidence firsthand are best suited to decide. Also, the agency is considered to be an expert in the area that it regulates and thus is usually more knowledgeable about the facts of a case than the judge would be.

A court will grant *de novo* review (new hearing) in a few unusual situations such as when a review is required by statute, or the agency's factfinding proceeding was inadequate.

Defense to Agency Enforcement   The following are the reasons that a plaintiff can present in a judicial review as a defense against an agency action:

1. The agency exceeded the authority conferred by the agency's enabling legislation.
2. The agency improperly interpreted the laws that apply to the agency action under review.
3. The agency violated a constitutional provision.
4. The agency did not follow the procedures required by law.
5. The agency acted in a manner that was arbitrary or was an abuse of discretion.
6. The conclusion drawn by the agency was not supported by substantial evidence.

Parties seeking to have action reviewed must satisfy several preliminary requirements. Some are discussed in the paragraphs that follow.

Reviewability   The challenger, or plaintiff, must show that the action is reviewable. The Administrative Procedure Act provides that the action of each authority of the government of the United States is subject to judicial review except where there is a clear statutory prohibition of review.

LEGAL BACKGROUND

In addition to judicial review, administrative agency authorities are held in check by executive control and legislative control. **Executive control** generally rests with the President, who may exercise veto power over any enabling legislation or legislative modifications to agency authority. The President may appoint and remove agency officers. Even in independent agencies whose officers serve for fixed terms and cannot be removed without just cause, terms of employment are staggered, and many do not serve a full term. Also, the President generally has the power to designate which of the commissioners will serve as chairman.

Legislative Control Congress can abolish an agency or take away agency power (for instance, Congress may pass a law prohibiting an agency from issuing a specific regulation). Congress's taxing and spending powers also give it power to influence agency policy because there must be authorization for appropriation of funds for an agency. Additionally, Congress can investigate the implementation of its laws and the agencies that it creates.

Read

You might introduce this *Law in Action* feature by having a student volunteer turn to the U.S. Constitution printed in the Resource Center at the back of this text and read aloud to the class the Fifth and Fourteenth Amendments. Then ask the class what these amendments say about due process. After the students have discussed due process as enumerated in the U.S. Constitution, explain to them that this *Law in Action* feature deals with due process in an administrative hearing. Then allow student volunteers to take turns reading this *Law in Action* feature aloud to the class.

Discuss

Stimulate a class discussion of this *Law in Action* feature by asking the students the following questions: What is the importance of the *Goldberg* v. *Kelly* case? What did the U.S. Supreme Court rule in the *Goldberg* v. *Kelly* case regarding due process of law? What is meant by the phrase "an unbiased tribunal"?

Why is an unbiased tribunal important? Why is notification important? Is a person always allowed to hear all the evidence against him or her in administrative hearings? Why or why not? Why is the making of a record important? Do you think it is important that the public be allowed to attend? Why or why not?

Teaching Note

This case is included in the *West's Business and Personal Law Handbook of Selected Court Cases*.

---

602   Doing Business

Law in Action

LAW IN YOUR LIFE: DUE PROCESS IN AN ADMINISTRATIVE HEARING

When do parties have a right to an administrative hearing? What government actions can be questioned in an administrative hearing? If you have a right to a hearing, what form does it take?

These and other questions were considered by the United States Supreme Court in the landmark case of *Goldberg v. Kelly*.[1] Kelly was a New York City resident receiving welfare aid under the federal program, Aid to Families with Dependent Children (AFDC). The New York City Social Service Agency stopped her benefits. The agency told Goldberg that she could request a formal hearing after her benefits were stopped. She sued, claiming she had a right to a hearing *before* her AFDC benefits were stopped.

The U.S. Supreme Court agreed. The court held that the importance of the benefits to the recipient must be weighed against the state's interest in efficient and fast processes. Since welfare benefits provide such important things as food, clothing, and shelter, Kelly had a right to a hearing before the benefits ceased. The state could not "deprive any person of life, liberty, or property without due process of law." The court held that a termination of benefits without a hearing before the termination denied Kelly due process.

Since the *Goldberg v. Kelly* case, the courts have attempted to balance the individual's interests and the interests of government. The question in every case is similar. If a government action adversely affects someone, does that person have a right to have it independently reviewed? Agencies now normally provide hearings when the agency's action would deny a person some license, right, or privilege.

Closely related to the question of whether a person can expect a hearing is the question as to what type of hearing it must be. Government takes millions of actions every day. How can citizens be protected from arbitrary treatment without paralyzing the government's ability to make decisions and act effectively?

Judge Henry Friendly[2] identified eleven attributes of a fair hearing. Not all of these attributes are constitutionally required. However, many of them define what American citizens expect as fair treatment not only from the government but from any large organization. With some editorial license, we have reproduced Judge Friendly's list here with a brief discussion of each item:

1. *An unbiased tribunal.* In a court proceeding, an unbiased tribunal would be a neutral court with a judge and/or jury deciding the case. In the usual administrative hearing, an agency employee who was not a party to the original decision is considered sufficiently unbiased.

2. *Notice of the proposed action and the grounds for the action.* In a judicial process, the complaint notifies the sued party of the nature of the claim against him or her. In an administrative action, some statement is expected of what governmental action is proposed and why.

---

1. 397 U.S. 254, 90 S.Ct. 1011, 25 L.Ed. 287 (1970).

2. Friendly, *Some Kind of Hearing,* 123 University of Pennsylvania Law Review 1289 (1975).

Allow a group of interested volunteers to stage a mock administrative hearing in which your class can participate. In order to prepare the group to complete this task, distribute to each member of the group copies of the mock trial package found in your *Teachers Resource Binder*. Instruct the group to use this mock trial package as an example of the types of materials to prepare; then have them stage a mock administrative hearing that adheres to each of the 11 elements of a fair hearing listed in this *Law in Action* feature.

 ## Law in Action (Continued)

3. *An opportunity to present reasons why the proposed action should not be taken.* Fundamental to all fair processes is an opportunity to tell and prove your view of the facts.

4. *The right to call witnesses.* In a court trial, you have the right to subpoena witnesses. You can usually force a witness to attend a trial. While parties to an administrative hearing can call witnesses, they do not always have the right to force the witnesses' attendance.

5. *The right to know the evidence against you.* A person subject to a government action should be aware of all the evidence that was used to make the decision. Any information that a hearing officer receives should be shared with the affected party. In administrative hearings, however, there are some situations where parties are not allowed to know all the evidence against them. A hearing to discipline a prisoner, for example, is an administrative hearing. If the prisoner hears testimony used against him or her, there might be an attempt to take revenge on the witness; this could even cost a person's life.

6. *To have a decision based on evidence presented at the hearing.* If the decision is based on information presented at the hearing, then an opportunity to counter or contradict that information exists. If a decision is made on facts learned outside the hearing, the claimant cannot challenge the information.

7. *Counsel.* The right to legal or other qualified representation is important.

Most administrative hearings allow counsel. If the person cannot afford representation, however, the agency will not usually provide it.

8. *Making of a record.* If a record is not available, how can an unfair hearing be contested? Trial courts provide records, and so do some (but not all) administrative hearings.

9. *Statement of reasons for the decision.* If reasons for a decision are given, faulty reasoning can be appealed. If reasons are not given, how can a decision be appealed? A statement of reasons, even though it might be brief, is usually expected as part of the administrative hearing process.

10. *Public attendance.* Open attendance in court trials is based on the general belief that the activities of the court should be open to the public to protect individuals from possible abuse of government power. In an administrative hearing, sometimes open attendance is allowed; many times it is not.

11. *Judicial review.* Court decisions can be appealed. In administrative hearings, an appeal is also allowed. Experience has shown, however, that courts seldom overturn administrative rulings or actions. Usually, the best chance for a successful appeal is one within the agency. The best basis for a court appeal is that the procedure was unfair, rather than that an incorrect result was reached. Courts are the experts on procedure, but they usually defer to agency experts on the application of the facts.

Ask a student volunteer to read aloud to the class this Legal Focus Example. Ask the students if they can think of any examples in which a challenging party has standing to sue an administrative agency. Allow volunteers to share their examples with the class.

An injury to an economic interest or even, in some cases, to an emotional, environmental, or aesthetic interest is sufficient to show standing to sue.

Legal Focus Problem

Have a volunteer read aloud to the class this Legal Focus Problem. Ask the volunteer to suggest a possible answer for the question posed at the end of this problem.

If a private citizen objects to log-stacking procedures, would he or she have standing to sue the lumber company?

Standing The challenging party must have *standing to sue*. To have standing to sue, the challenger must have a direct stake in the outcome of the judicial proceeding. This direct interest can be shown if the challenger has been substantially affected by the agency's action. An injury to an economic interest or even in some cases to an emotional, environmental, or aesthetic interest is sufficient to show standing to sue.

◆ LEGAL FOCUS ~ EXAMPLE

One reason for the requirement of standing to sue is to discourage petty lawsuits. The courts will require that a plaintiff show an actual injury by or because of an agency action. Protest lawsuits or lawsuits from taxpayers that are simply angry about some government action are often dismissed because of lack of standing.

Exhaustion of Available Remedies Courts are reluctant to interfere with regulatory agencies. They hope agencies will correct their own mistakes. Courts, therefore, will not usually review an action until the challenging party has gone through all the other possible alternatives for resolving the problem within the agency.

Although this chapter discusses federal agencies, most of this discussion, including the requirements regarding judicial review, applies to state administrative actions as well. For an example of the requirement that one must exhaust administrative remedies before filing a court action, a state agency action seems relevant.

◆ LEGAL FOCUS ~ PROBLEM

Joy had received five speeding tickets within one year. She was notified by her state's Department of Motor Vehicles that her license was suspended for six months but that she could appeal the suspension before a department hearing officer. Joy immediately filed a lawsuit claiming the suspension of her license violated her rights. Will her lawsuit be allowed?

Her lawsuit will be dismissed because Joy did not appeal her suspension with the Department of Motor Vehicles. She did not exhaust her administrative remedies.

◆ PUBLIC ACCOUNTABILITY

Congress has passed several laws to make agencies answerable to the public. The most significant of these public scrutiny laws are the Freedom of

Information Act, the Government-in-the-Sunshine Act, and the Regulatory Flexibility Act.

FREEDOM OF INFORMATION ACT

The Freedom of Information Act (FOIA) requires that the federal government disclose most records to any person on request. The person need not tell why he or she is asking for the information. Certain records, such as information related to security risks or ongoing criminal investigations, cannot be requested. The most frequent requests under the FOIA are from the news media and businesses. If a government agency refuses to provide the requested information, this action can be challenged in court.

GOVERNMENT-IN-THE-SUNSHINE ACT

This law requires that most meetings of federal agencies be open for public observation. It also requires that advance notice be given of agency meetings and that the expected topics of discussion be announced.

REGULATORY FLEXIBILITY ACT

Whenever a new regulation will have a significant impact upon a substantial number of small businesses, an agency must conduct a flexibility analysis. The agency must measure how much complying with the rule will cost small businesses. It must also consider any less costly alternatives.

◆ CHECKING YOUR PROGRESS

1. Why do the courts generally defer the facts found in agency proceedings?
2. Explain "standing to sue."

Enrichment

Ask a volunteer to find out the details of the Freedom of Information Act and share them with the class in an oral presentation. Brainstorm the kinds of information the government would have about individuals. Discuss the ethical considerations in disclosing records to any person on request.

Checking Your Progress (Answers)

1. The courts generally defer to the facts found in agency proceedings because of the judicial attitude that those who hear and see a case firsthand are best suited to decide. Also, the agency is considered an expert in the topic it hears and, as such, is usually more knowledgeable about the topic than the judge.
2. A party who challenges an administrative action must have a direct stake in the outcome of the judicial proceeding. This "standing to sue" may be caused by an injury to an economic, emotional, environmental, or aesthetic interest.

Teaching A Case In Point

Read

Introduce this *A Case In Point* feature by asking a student volunteer to suggest possible functions of the Consumer Product Safety Commission. You might also have volunteers cite any examples of Consumer Product Safety Commission actions of which they are aware. Then explain to the class that this *A Case In Point* feature deals with a challenge to the enforcement powers of the Consumer Product Safety Commission. Have a volunteer read this *A Case In Point* feature aloud to the class.

Teaching Note

This case is included in the *West's Business and Personal Law Handbook of Selected Court Cases.*

Discuss

Stimulate a class discussion of the *A Case In Point* feature by asking the following questions: How does the Flammable Fabrics Act affect Danube Carpet Mills? Who has the authority to enforce the Flammable Fabrics Act? What is a consent decree? What did Danube do in 1973 that made the fabric more flammable? How did the CPSC react to this change in the fabrics? What was the decision of the district court in this case? What was the issue before the United States Court of Appeals? How did the court decide in this case? What reasons did the court give for its decision?

◆ A CASE IN POINT ◆

UNITED STATES v. DANUBE CARPET MILLS, INC.
United States Court of Appeals, Eleventh Circuit, 1984.
737 F.2d 988.

The enforcement powers of the Consumer Product Safety Commission were challenged in this case by a company subject to the regulations.

FACTS Danube Carpet Mills, Inc., prepares carpet yarn for the production of carpeting. Finished carpets are manufactured by other firms who contract with Danube to buy its yarn. Because carpeting can catch fire and because it is a fabric, it must meet the minimum safety requirements set by the Flammable Fabrics Act (FFA). The authority to enforce this act currently rests in the Consumer Product Safety Commission (CPSC). In 1972 Danube's carpet material did not comply with the FFA minimum flammability standards, but at that time, no fines were imposed. Rather, Danube entered into a consent decree, which meant that it promised to comply with FFA requirements. During 1973 Danube made a minor change in its yarn-coloring process that made the fabric more flammable. This was detected by the CPSC between November 1974 and March 1975 when it conducted tests on the carpet. Seven rolls of carpet failed to meet FFA requirements.

The CPSC ordered Danube to pay a penalty of $24,500 ($3,500 per roll of carpet). Danube argued that the penalty was inappropriate because no one had been harmed by the more flammable fabric. The district court granted the CPSC's motion for summary judgment, and Danube appealed.

ISSUE Was the imposition of fines by the CPSC appropriate in this case?

DECISION Yes. The appellate court affirmed the ruling of the trial court. Danube had to pay the $24,500.

REASON The court noted that it is the CPSC's responsibility to ensure that the public is safe from unnecessarily flammable fabric. Under the Flammable Fabrics Act, fines may be imposed when the act's requirements are not met. Had Danube made a good faith effort to conduct testing according to the requirements of the FFA, the damages the agency imposed might have been inappropriate. But Danube had never done more than random testing of any of its fabric, and it had never once tested the fabric after it started using the new coloring process. Also, even though no harm had been caused to consumers by the more flammable carpet fabric, Danube had failed to comply with the flammability standards required by the FFA. Failing to comply with the standards was enough to make Danube pay penalties. Danube was required to pay the $24,500 fine.

In order to help students review what they have learned in Chapter 25, you might wish to:
1. Have a student volunteer, or volunteers, read aloud the Chapter Summary.
2. Allow the students to work with partners to complete the *Using Legal Language* activity.
3. Assign the *Checking for Comprehension* exercise as homework.

4. Allow the students to work in small groups to complete the *Applying Legal Concepts* activities.
5. As a class, complete the *Applying the Law* activities. (Please note that you may have to help students with vocabulary so that they adequately understand all of the *Applying the Law* material.)

Assessment Strategies

In order to check student mastery of chapter concepts, you may wish to use the Chapter 25 test that is found in your *Teacher's Resource Binder* or use WESTEST computerized testing for Chapter 25.

Government Regulation of Business   607

CHAPTER 25 REVIEW

 ## SUMMARY

ADMINISTRATIVE AGENCIES

Government bodies with power to regulate, monitor, or control government interests and programs. Independent regulatory agencies are those led by officials who hold office without being under the direct control of the president.

CREATION OF REGULATORY AGENCIES

Statutes called enabling legislation establish each administrative agency and define its powers.

THE OPERATION OF ADMINISTRATIVE AGENCIES

The functions of administrative agencies include investigation, enforcement, rulemaking, and adjudication. The Administrative Procedure Act of 1946 (APA) provides mandatory guidelines for administrative action.

1. *Investigation*—The ability of an agency to get information. Agencies usually have the power of **subpoena** and the ability to **search and seize**.
2. *Enforcement*—Complaints may be brought by and through administrative agencies.
3. *Rulemaking*—Agencies have the power to pass regulations and rules. There are three types of rules:
   a. Regulations or legislative rules are treated the same as statutes or laws. Regulations must be published in the *Federal Register*.
   b. Interpretative rules are statements and opinions explaining how an agency interprets and intends to apply the law it enforces.
   c. Procedural rules describe an agency's methods of operation, and they establish procedures for how the agency will deal with the public.

4. *Adjudication*—Trial-like proceedings before an administrative law judge (ALJ) or appointed heads of the agency.
   a. *Administrative law judge*—A government employee appointed to hear administrative cases.
   b. *Administrative hearing*—Like a court trial. Parties have minimum rights of due process such as notice, and the right to present evidence.

CONTROL OVER ADMINISTRATIVE AGENCIES

Agency authority is controlled by Congress through the statutory law that defines agency power, by the president through the budget process, and by the courts.

Judicial Review
Courts have the power to review agency action.

PUBLIC ACCOUNTABILITY

Congress has passed several laws to make agencies accountable to the public.

1. *Freedom of Information Act*—Requires disclosure of most government records on request.
2. *Government-in-the-Sunshine Act*—Most federal agency meetings must be open to the public.
3. *Regulatory Flexibility Act*—Requires an investigation of the effects of new regulations on small businesses.

Using Legal Language (Answers)

1–B, 2–F, 3–E, 4–G, 5–H, 6–J, 7–C, 8–A, 9–I, 10–D

Checking for Comprehension (Answers)

1. The greatest growth in regulation took place in the 1960s and 1970s. Student answers as to why will vary. They may discuss the public's change in attitudes toward protection of the environment and the rights of individuals that were diminishing.
2. Judicial, executive, and legislative branches of government all have political control over administrative agencies. For example, Congress can change the agency's authority and financial resources. Additionally, the Administrative Procedure Act of 1946 provides mandatory guidelines for an administrative agency to follow and carry out its mission.
3. The administrative process begins with an investigation because an agency must be able to get information to oversee an area of business. At the conclusion of the investigation, an agency brings an action against individuals or organizations in the form of a complaint. The agency acts as the prosecutor, judge, and jury.
4. The major functions of an administrative agency are investigation of violations, enforcement of regulations, and formation of new regulations.
5. An administrative law judge (ALJ) is a government employee who is appointed to hear administrative cases. He or she presides over a trial-like proceeding. An ALJ may work at the agency prosecuting the case, but is separated in the agency's organization from the investigative and prosecutorial staff.
6. An administrative hearing is like a trial in that the charged party may be represented by a lawyer, who may cross examine agency

---

USING LEGAL LANGUAGE

Directions: Match each term with the statement that best defines that term.

1. judicial review
2. Administrative Law Judge
3. administrative hearing
4. Administrative Procedure Act of 1946
5. administrative law
6. administrative agency
7. *Federal Register*
8. Freedom of Information Act
9. independent regulatory agency
10. subpoena

A. The _____ requires the federal government to disclose most records to any person on request.

B. The courts provide for an oversight of administrative action through the power of _____.

C. The final version of a regulation is published in the _____ which can be found in any law library.

D. The two most important investigative tools available to administrative agencies are the _____ and the ability to search and seize.

E. An _____ is an adjudication given by an administrative agency to hear and decide some factual question related to agency action.

F. A government employee, an _____, is appointed to hear administrative cases.

G. The _____ provides mandatory guidelines for an administrative agency to follow to carry out its mission.

H. The body of law concerned with the power of administrative agencies is known as _____.

I. An _____ is an administrative body empowered to regulate some policy area led by officials who cannot be dismissed by the President except for cause.

J. A government body which exercises power delegated to by the executive or legislative branch is an _____.

CHECKING FOR COMPREHENSION

1. At what time in history did the greatest growth in federal regulation take place?

2. What external controls ensure the power of federal agencies is balanced?

3. Describe the administrative process followed for a violation of administrative law.

4. What are the major functions of an administrative agency?

5. Describe the role of an ALJ.

witnesses and present evidence to counter that of the agency's. The differences lie in the fact that the administrative law judge decides both questions of law and facts, and there is no jury. After the case is concluded, the ALJ gives an initial order.

7. Agency authority is controlled by constitutional limits, by the Administrative Procedures Act, by the enabling statute, and by political control from the executive, legislative, and judicial branches of government.

6. How is an administrative hearing like a trial, how is it different?

7. How is the authority of agencies controlled?

◆ APPLYING LEGAL CONCEPTS

1. Assume your class has decided to produce and sell a new breakfast cereal. Compose a one-minute commercial to advertise your cereal on the radio. You must be certain that you do not make any statements that the Federal Trade Commission (FTC) would consider to be "unfair or deceptive" to consumers.

2. Under the Freedom of Information Act, you have a right to obtain information from federal government agencies. Compose a letter to a specific agency requesting information. For example, you may request information about yourself from the Internal Revenue Service (IRS) or the Federal Bureau of Investigation (FBI).

◆ APPLYING THE LAW . . . YOU BE THE JUDGE

1. The Federal Home Loan Bank Board (FHLBB) is an independent federal agency that operated the Federal Savings and Loan Insurance Corporation (FSLIC). The agency's regulatory duties included examining all FSLIC-insured institutions to determine whether they were being operated properly under applicable laws and regulations. As part of an investigation of Texas-based Vision Banc Savings and Loan, the FHLBB became suspicious of several large loans made by Vision Banc, including one made to Sandsend Financial Consultants, Ltd. Hoping to trace the proceeds of the loans, the FHLBB subpoenaed Sandsend's financial records from a second bank, West Belt. Sandsend requested that the federal district court invalidate the subpoena. The district court judge did invalidate the subpoena. The FHLBB appealed the decision. Although the government has a right to subpoena bank records, the question to be answered was how much authority the FHLBB has. Will the appellate court agree or disagree with the district court? [*Sandsend Financial Consultants, Ltd. v. Federal Home Loan Bank Board*, (5th Cir. 1989) 878 F.2d 875]

2. In 1977, the Department of Transportation (DOT) adopted a passive-restraint standard (known as Standard 208) that required new cars to have either air bags or automatic seat belts. By 1981, it became clear that all the major auto manufacturers would install automatic seat belts to comply with this rule. The DOT determined that most purchasers of cars would detach their automatic seat belts, thus making them ineffective. Consequently, the department repealed the regulation. State Farm Mutual Automobile Insurance Co., and other insurance companies sued in the District of Columbia Circuit Court of Appeals for a review of the DOT's repeal of the regulation. That court held that the repeal was arbitrary and capricious because the DOT has reversed its rule without sufficient support. The motor vehicle manufacturers then appealed this decision to the United States Supreme Court. What will result? Discuss. [*Motor Vehicle Manufacturer's Association v. State Farm Mutual Automobile Insurance Co.*, 463 U.S. 29, 103 S.Ct. 2856, 77 L.Ed.2d 443 (1983)]

Applying the Law . . . You Be the Judge (Answers)

1. The appellate court reversed the district court's decision and directed the district court to enforce the FHLBB's subpoena. The court examined the language and legislative history of 12 U.S.C. Section 1730(m)(1), (2) and compared it to the statutory authority conferred on the Federal Deposit Insurance Corporation and that of federal bank examiners. They found no basis in the request to invalidate the subpoena. "First, it is undisputed that the FHLBB's examination of Vision Ban is a legitimate law enforcement inquiry. Second, Sandsend's records are relevant to the FHLBB's inquiry. For purposes of an administrative subpoena, the notion of relevancy is a broad one. An agency can investigate merely on the suspicion that the law is being violated, or even just because it wants assurance that it is not." So long as the material requested "touches a matter under investigation," an administrative subpoena will survive a challenge that the material is not relevant.

2. The United States Supreme Court held that the rescission of the standard was arbitrary and capricious. The Court remanded the case to the court of appeals, with directions to remand to the Department of Transportation for further consideration of the airbag rule. A major reason for finding the rescission arbitrary and capricious was that the NHTSA apparently did not consider modifying the standard to require that airbag technology be used. "Standard 208 sought to achieve automatic crash protection by requiring automobile manufacturers to install either of two passive restraint devices: airbags or automatic seatbelts. There was no suggestion in the long rule-making process that led to Standard 208 that, if only one of these options were feasible, no passive restraint standard should be promulgated."

LEGAL BACKGROUND

Although only in an early stage of development, environmental law has become an area of vast federal regulation. Thirty years ago, there were only a handful of statutes and regulations, plus old common law concepts, governing the area. A century ago and beyond, when the population was relatively small and industry was limited, environmental degradation was not a significant problem. People assumed that the environment would absorb whatever was put into it. As the world became more populated, urbanized, and industrialized, however, concerns about the environment increased. In this century, urban industrial society appears to have stained the environment's capacity to handle pollution. Only in the last 25 years has the law attempted to control waste and its effects.

Initially, regulation was aimed at curing damage that had occurred. At the end of the 1970s, there was a shift toward preventive regulation, on the theory that preventing injury to the environment is less expensive than curing it. Controlling waste is not without a price. For many businesses, the costs are high.

610

Introduce this Legal Perspective on environmental law by using the following questions to stimulate a class discussion on the topic of environmental law: Do you think there is a need for environmental laws? Why or why not? Are the current environmental laws adequate? Do you think the current environmental laws go too far? What additional environmental laws, if any, would you recommend? What environmental laws, if any, do you think should be abolished? After the students have discussed their feelings toward environmental laws in general, have student volunteers take turns reading this Legal Perspective aloud to the class.

LEGAL PERSPECTIVE

ENVIRONMENTAL LAW

In the twentieth century, the world has become more heavily populated, urbanized, and industrialized. The earth's capacity to handle the pollution being discharged into the air and water is being challenged. The waste produced by industrial society has threatened and continues to threaten the existence of human life. For many businesses, the costs of controlling this waste are high, and for some they are too high. There is a constant tension between business's goals of increasing profits and productivity and the need to restore quality in the environment. In the last two decades, statutory and administrative laws that try to balance business goals with the need to protect the environment have become known as **environmental law**. Environmental law is an important type of government regulation.

◆ COMMON LAW AND THE ENVIRONMENT

Common law remedies against environmental pollution originated centuries ago in England, but remedies that worked historically are very limited in their ability to deal with modern environmental problems. The law of *nuisance* protected property owners who could identify a harm that specifically affected them and not just the general public. Thus, if a factory polluted the air and killed a farmer's crops, the farmer could seek an injunction and damages from the factory.

Under the common law, citizens lacked *standing*—that is, they couldn't bring a case

to court—unless a specific harm could be shown. For example, a group of citizens wishing to stop a new development because of a water pollution threat could not sue. They lacked standing because the harm was to the public, not to the individual plaintiffs. The government, however, could sue for public nuisance.

An injured party could—and still can—sue a business polluter for negligence. The basis of such a suit is the failure of the business to use reasonable care toward the plaintiff. For example, employees might sue an employer who did not use proper pollution controls and contaminated the air, causing the employees to suffer respiratory illnesses. Injured parties might also recover under a theory of strict liability. In other words, businesses engaging in ultrahazardous activities—such as blasting operations or the transportation of radioactive materials—are liable for whatever injuries the activities cause.

Under the common law, it was difficult to obtain relief from pollution if the harm was caused by two or more independent sources. For example, if several businesses were polluting the air, a harmed individual could sue any one firm. However, until recently, the plaintiff could not sue all of the polluters in the same lawsuit. Consequently, it was often impossible to prove that one firm had caused the damages. These difficulties in seeking relief in pollution cases, along with the fact that pollution has increased so dramatically, have led to statutory regulation of environmental quality.

Ask students to name any local regulations that control aspects of the environment. Remind students that the laws might include carpooling regulations, water rationing, zoning, recycling programs, etc. Have a volunteer list on the board appropriate examples of local regulations.

Let an interested volunteer research the 1969 explosion of Union Oil's well near Santa Barbara, California. What were the results? How did the media cover the incident? How did the public respond? Have the volunteer write a short report on his or her findings and distribute copies of the report to the other students.

Have a small group of students research the Clean Air Act of 1990, especially as it applies to your state and community. Have them determine what programs have been instituted locally, what procedures have been altered or eliminated, and why. Ask these students to plan and make a bulletin board display showing how this act has affected local businesses and individuals.

Teaching with the Videodisc

The still frame listed below from the **West's Business Law and Legal Environment Videodisc** can be used with this Legal Perspective. To access this material, use the bar codes or the frame numbers included in the Videodisc Instructor's Manual found in the *TRB*.

Federal Environmental Statutes

◆ LOCAL REGULATION

City, county, and other local governments control many aspects of the environment. For instance, local zoning laws control land use. Local laws may be designed to slow down or to direct the growth of cities and suburbs or aimed directly at protecting the natural environment. Methods of removing and disposing of waste and garbage, for example, can have an important impact on a community.

◆ STATE REGULATION

Many states regulate land use through regional or statewide zoning laws that are part of a master plan. States also often regulate the degree to which the environment may be polluted. For example, a business's proposed development may have to be changed if the development's impact on the environment is negative. State laws may restrict a business's discharge of chemicals into the air or water or regulate its disposal of toxic wastes. States may also regulate the disposal or recycling of other wastes, including glass, metal, and plastic containers and paper. States may also restrict the emissions from motor vehicles.

◆ FEDERAL REGULATION

Congress has passed numerous laws to control the impact of human activities on the environment. Statutes cover the maintenance of air and water quality and the regulation of toxic chemicals—such as pesticides and herbicides—and other hazardous wastes.

The National Environmental Policy Act (NEPA) of 1969 requires that all federal agencies consider the environment when making important decisions. For every major federal action that significantly affects the quality of the environment, an **environmental impact statement (EIS)** must be prepared. For example, building a new nuclear reactor involves federal action because a federal license is required.

An EIS must analyze (1) the impact on the environment that the action will have, (2) any adverse effects on the environment and alternative actions that might be taken, and (3) irreversible effects the action might generate. Environmental impact statements have been used by private citizens, consumer interest groups, businesses, and others to challenge federal agency actions.

In 1970 the Environmental Protection Agency (EPA) was created to coordinate federal regulation of environmental issues. The EPA administers most federal environmental policies and statutes.

AIR POLLUTION

Federal laws provide the basis for regulations issued by the EPA that control air pollution coming primarily from factories and motor vehicles. The EPA sets air quality standards for major pollutants. General guidelines set out requirements for protecting vegetation, climate, visibility, and certain economic conditions. Regulations governing air pollution from automobiles specify pollution standards.

WATER POLLUTION

The major sources of water pollution are business, government, and agriculture. Pollutants entering streams, lakes, and oceans include natural wastes, heated water, soil

(continued on page 612)

612

LEGAL PERSPECTIVE (CONTINUED)

runoff, nutrients (such as detergents, fertilizers, and human and animal wastes), and toxic chemicals and other hazardous substances.

Certain types of fish cannot live in waters in which natural wastes decompose, turning the water dark and smelly. Heated water speeds the growth of algae and disrupts fish reproduction. Soil runoff and nutrients speed the dying of lakes, an otherwise natural process that turns lakes into land. Toxic chemicals and hazardous substances make water and fish, even after treatment, unsafe for human consumption.

Federal regulations require a permit for dumping refuse into navigable waterways. The Clean Water Act establishes these goals and standards: (1) make waters safe for swimming, (2) protect fish and wildlife, and (3) eliminate the discharge of pollutants into the water. Regulations usually require that parties needing to dump refuse use the best available technology available to reduce the harmful effects of the refuse.

TOXIC CHEMICALS

Chemicals released into the environment in small amounts may pose a considerable threat to human life and health. Control of these toxic chemicals has become an important part of environmental law.

Pesticides and Herbicides The first toxic chemical problem to receive widespread public attention was that posed by pesticides and herbicides. Using these chemicals to kill insects and weeds has increased agricultural productivity. However, the residue of these poisons remains in the environment. In some instances, this residue has killed animals. Scientists have also identified potential long-term effects that are harmful to people.

The Federal Insecticide, Fungicide, and Rodenticide Act (FIFRA) requires that pesticides and herbicides must be (1) registered before they can be sold, (2) certified and used only for approved applications, and (3) used in limited quantities when applied to food crops. If a substance is identified as harmful, the EPA can cancel its registration after a hearing. If the harm is immediate, the EPA can suspend registration pending the hearing. The EPA may also inspect factories in which these chemicals are manufactured.

Toxic Substances The Toxic Substances Control Act regulates chemicals and chemical compounds known to be poisonous. The Environmental Protection Agency can require that manufacturers, processors, and other organizations planning to use chemicals first determine the chemicals' effect on human health and the environment. The EPA can regulate substances that might pose an immediate hazard or an unreasonable risk of injury to health or the environment.

Hazardous Wastes Some industrial, agricultural, and household wastes pose serious threats. If not properly disposed of, these toxic chemicals may present a substantial danger to human health and the environment. If released into the environment, they may contaminate public drinking water resources.

The Resource Conservation and Recovery Act (RCRA) provides the EPA with the authority to monitor and control hazardous waste disposal. Regulations require all producers of hazardous waste materials to label and package properly any hazardous waste to be transported.

The Comprehensive Environmental Response, Compensation, and Liability Act (CERCLA), commonly known as Superfund, regulates the clean-up of leaking hazardous waste disposal sites. It created a special federal fund to clean up the hazardous sites. The EPA can recover the cost of the clean-up from (1) the person who generated the wastes disposed of at the site,

(2) the person who transported the wastes to the site, (3) the person who owned or operated the site at the time of the disposal, or (4) the current owner or operator.

◆ Conclusion

Uncontrolled pollution is eventually paid for by everyone. If the costs of pollution are not paid by the party producing the pollution, eventually the taxpayer will bear the cost. It is possible to combine profit-making activities *and* environmental protection programs. Dow Chemical is one example of a company that has done it. Dow Chemical devised and implemented a massive program of pollution control directed toward waste reduction and the conservation of raw materials. Manufacturing processes were closely examined to find ways to increase operating efficiency, to recycle raw materials formerly vented into the air or dumped in the sewer, and to use waste products. The company has profited by these programs. Pollution control has meant savings that have led to higher company profits.

 Terms to Remember

◆ **environmental law**   Statutory and administrative laws which protect the environment.

◆ **environmental impact statement (EIS)**   A report required by law before any major federal action can be taken that might affect the environment. The report analyzes the proposed action's impact on the environment and possible alternative actions.

Suggested Additional Resources

Bernhardt, Roger. *Bernhardt's Real Property in a Nutshell*, 2d ed. St. Paul, MN: West Publishing Co., 1981.

Burke Jr., Barlow. *Burke's Personal Property in a Nutshell*, 2d ed. St. Paul, MN: West Publishing Co., 1993.

Clifford, Denis. *The Power of Attorney Book*, 2d ed. Berkeley, CA: Nolo Press, 1987.

Dobbyn, John F. *Dobbyn's Insurance Law in a Nutshell*, 2d ed. St. Paul, MN: West Publishing Co., 1989.

Krause, Harry A. *Krause's Family Law in a Nutshell*, 2d ed. St. Paul, MN: West Publishing Co., 1986.

You & the Law. Pleasantville, NY: The Reader's Digest Association, 1984.

UNIT 6

Personal Law

We use the title personal law to introduce very different areas of law that have two things in common. The first is they relate to the personal life of most people. The second is that most of us will benefit from knowing more about the law in these areas. These topics relate both to everyday life and to current social conditions.

This unit covers topics as diverse as the legal status of minors and juvenile justice to the requirements to prepare a valid will. Other topics include marriage, child custody, ownership rights in different types of property, renting an apartment, and varieties of insurance. Legal Perspectives in this unit cover high interest areas of mediation and legal issues involving motor vehicles. Much of the material in these chapters will apply concepts which were introduced in earlier chapters. While your understanding of this new material does not require mastery of the earlier material, you should benefit from seeing how these legal rules apply in everyday real-life situations.

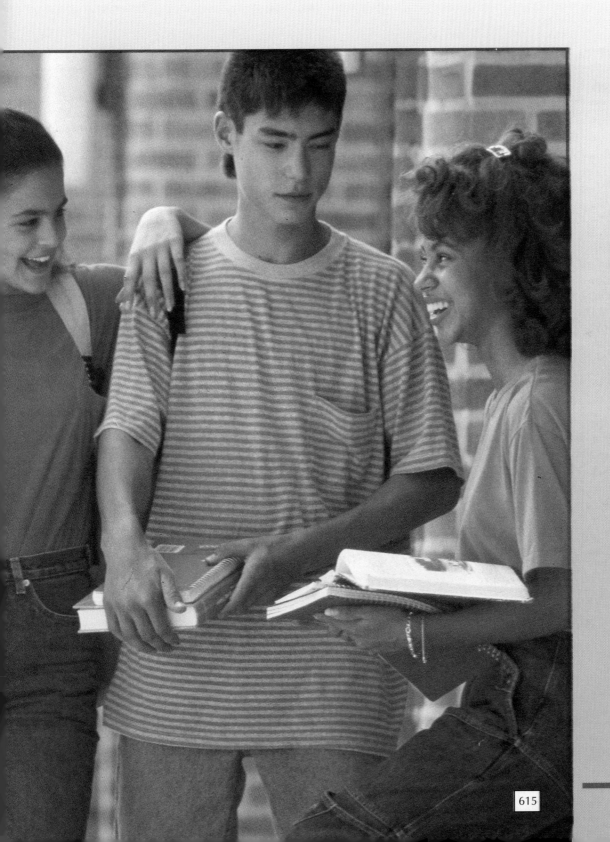

Mastery Objectives

By the end of this chapter, students will be able to:

- Know the age of majority
- Describe an emancipated minor
- Explain the relationship between schools and minors

- Discuss the question of equality in schools
- Identify a minor's responsibility and liability for torts
- Determine responsibility for crimes under the juvenile justice system

LEGAL BACKGROUND

A special chapter for high schools students begins our unit on personal law. The legal background of the student-school relationship is introduced by a discussion of the duty to attend school, student discipline, search and seizure in school, corporal punishment, privacy, and equality of opportunity. The law of the family relationship from the child's viewpoint is introduced. Tort law is revisited in this chapter when we discuss a minor's responsibility for her or his tortious acts.

A significant portion of the chapter is devoted to the unique way the American criminal justice system deals with juvenile offenders.

Chapter

26

Minors and the Law

"My mother loved children—she would have given anything if I had been one."

(Julius) Groucho Marx, 1895–1977
Comedian/actor

Whether or not Groucho Marx felt that he had ever been a child would not have mattered under the law. In every state, as long as you are under a certain age, you are considered a **minor**, and if you are a minor, there are lots of things you can and cannot do. There are also certain responsibilities that your parents are required by law to carry out. If your parents decide tomorrow that you are "just too much of a bother," for example, they can't throw you out in the street with a suitcase and $25 and tell you to get lost.

As a minor, you also have certain limitations on the agreements you can legally sign and to which you can be bound. Both now when you are a minor and later when you enter the world of business, you need to know about the law as it relates to minors.

♦ **minor** Any individual under the legal age of majority, when one is considered an adult.

 REACHING THE AGE OF MAJORITY

Until you are a certain age, common law says that you have not reached the age of **majority**. You are still a minor. The age of majority in most states is eighteen.[1] What does it mean to reach the age of majority, to become an adult? It means that you have all of the rights, privileges, and duties of an adult. Normally, these rights include the capacity to enter into legally binding and enforceable contracts (see the Legal Perspective feature in Chapter 9).

As of 1971, with the passage of the Twenty-sixth Amendment to the United States Constitution, everyone who is eighteen has the right to vote:

The right of citizens in the United States, who are 18 years or older, to vote shall not be denied or abridged by the United States or by any State on account of age.

♦ **majority** The legal age when each individual can acquire all the rights and responsibilities of an adult.

LIMITS REGARDING ALCOHOL

There is one activity that is prohibited to everyone below the age of twenty-one. Today you cannot legally purchase alcoholic beverages in any state in the union until you are twenty-one years old. At age twenty-one, you are considered an adult for all purposes in every state.

---

1. States with a later age of majority are Alabama, 19; Nebraska, 19; Pennsylvania, 21; and Wyoming, 19. Even in these states, older minors do have some rights of majority. For example, in Pennsylvania where the age of majority is 21, the age of capacity to contract or to make a will is 18.

EMANCIPATED MINORS

In your study of American history, you may have come across a famous document issued during the Civil War on September 17, 1862, by President Abraham Lincoln. It is called the Emancipation Proclamation. It was Lincoln's formal declaration that all slaves residing in the states still in rebellion against the United States on January 1, 1863, would be free once those states had come under the military control of the Union army.

The term *emancipation* means setting free. Therefore, an **emancipated minor** is "set free" from his or her parents. This means that the parents no longer have control over their child. But the law also sets the *parents* free, so to speak. Once a minor becomes emancipated, the parents no longer have a legal duty to support or care for that minor. Emancipated minors take on all of the rights and responsibilities of adults except for certain ones such as being able to legally purchase alcoholic beverages.

The normal way in which a minor becomes emancipated is for him or her to reach the age of majority. A number of states, though, allow for the emancipation of a minor before the age of majority. If you get married or join the military, usually you are considered emancipated. (Note that to join the military and to get married prior to the age of majority, you normally have to have the written approval of your parents.) Also, if you become financially self-supporting, you might be eligible to become an emancipated minor. To do so, you normally have to reach an agreement with your parents. In some states, even after you have reached this agreement, you must petition the state for approval.

◆ **emancipation**
The act by which a minor child becomes free of parental control and custody.

◆ **emancipated minor** An individual who has not yet reached the age of majority, but who has been set free of the control and custody of his or her parents either by voluntary agreement or otherwise.

◆ THE RELATIONSHIP BETWEEN SCHOOLS AND MINORS

Because every state in the union provides free public education to any minor, there is a whole body of law that has developed around the rights and responsibilities of students. There is also a body of law that has grown up around the rights and responsibilities of schools and their administrators.

Most people take for granted the fact that free education is available to all residents of the United States through the twelfth grade. But not everybody in all parts of the world can claim this right. In truth, free education is a remarkable opportunity for citizens of this country. In most states, this free education also extends past high school and into at least junior college and sometimes college.

You also have the right to and possibility of attending private schools, beginning with preschools and going all the way through universities offering postgraduate degrees in law, medicine, music, and so on. These private institutions charge what is called **tuition**. But many of them offer scholarships and other forms of financial help for those individuals who cannot afford the tuition.

◆ **tuition** The fees that are paid in order to receive instruction at any institution of learning; sometimes called tuition and fees.

State Law

As the student text makes clear, compulsory attendance laws vary from state to state. Here are some data regarding compulsory attendance laws in selected states.

State	Enactment	Age limits	State	Enactment	Age limits
Arkansas	1909	5–17	Minnesota	1885	7–16
California	1874	6–16	Ohio	1877	6–18
Florida	1915	6–16	Texas*	1915	7–17
Illinois	1883	7–16			
Indiana	1897	7–16			
Michigan	1871	6–16			

* Must complete academic year in which 16th birthday occurs. Source: Dept. of Education, National Center for Educational Statistics

While the types and goals of various public and private schools throughout the United States are different, there are basic rules and regulations that govern their behavior and the behavior of their students. Let's look at some of them now.

HOW LONG DO YOU HAVE TO STAY IN SCHOOL?

"I don't want to go to school." What small child hasn't uttered this statement at least once? Can you, at some point, legally tell your teachers good-bye? The answer is yes, but normally not before the age of sixteen. Every state has a **compulsory attendance law** for minor students. If you do not attend school between the legally required ages of six and sixteen years (in most states), you are considered truant—you have engaged in **truancy**. A truant officer can locate you and take you before a juvenile court for being truant.

Your parents have a responsibility, too. They must allow you and assist you to attend school. If they don't, they may be charged with child neglect. After the age of sixteen, most states allow parents and children to do what they want about school. So far, most states do not have laws that prevent high school students from "dropping out" after the age of sixteen, even though high school dropouts are a serious problem in our society. High school dropouts are typically unable to find jobs with a future. High school dropouts normally have higher levels of unemployment, higher rates of poverty, and tend to be involved in crime more often than high school and college graduates.

Exemptions for minors under age sixteen do exist under certain circumstances. These exemptions allow a minor student to avoid compulsory attendance in a public school:

- If the student is attending an approved private full-time school.
- If the student has a mental or physical condition that prevents school attendance or makes such attendance not advisable.
- If the student is being taught by a private tutor at home and that private tutor has valid state-accepted credentials.
- If the minor student is lawfully married and is emancipated.
- If the student is from a family whose religion does not allow the student to attend public school. Note that under these circumstances, the parents or the organized religion must provide an appropriate alternative to educate this minor student, as you can read about in the following case.

◆ **compulsory attendance law** A state law that specifies the ages between which each minor must attend a public or private school.

◆ **truancy** The willful and unjustified failure to attend school by anyone who is required to attend under compulsory attendance laws.

LEGAL FOCUS - CASE EXAMPLE

The Yoder family belonged to the Amish Mennonite Church. Some members of this church believed that sending their children to public high schools went against their religious teachings. Jonas Yoder was one of three parents who refused to allow his child to continue in the Wisconsin public school system. Yoder was convicted of violating state compulsory attendance laws. He challenged the conviction,

Extension Activity

You might ask a guidance counselor from your school to speak to the class regarding your school's dropout rate, as well as the career and life prospects for most dropouts. Your speaker might also address the steps taken in your community to enforce the compulsory attendance laws. Have students prepare questions in advance for your speaker.

Critical Thinking Activity

Have a student volunteer read aloud the list of exemptions (found on this page) that allow a minor student to avoid compulsory attendance in public school. For each item in the bulleted list, ask the students the following questions: What provisions, if any, are made to ensure that despite the exemption, the child is still receiving a proper education? Is this exemption in the best interests of the child? Why or why not?

Have students read aloud the Legal Focus Case Example that begins on the previous page. Then guide the students in discussing this example. Why did Jonas Yoder refuse to allow his child to continue in the Wisconsin public school system? What law was Yoder convicted of violating? On what grounds did he challenge this conviction? What reasons did the court give for finding for Yoder in this case?

Discussion Starter

Stimulate a class discussion of school discipline by asking students the following questions: What methods of discipline are used at our school? What is the purpose of these methods of discipline? Do you believe that the methods of discipline employed in our school are fair? Why or why not? What changes, if any, would you make in our school's discipline policy? What would the effects of these changes be? Do these changes serve the best interests of the students? How do these changes serve the best interests of the school?

Multicultural
Perspectives

Have a student volunteer or group of volunteers research the Amish. Students should prepare an oral report for the class that addresses the following topics: Who are the Amish? What are their basic beliefs? What is unique about the way in which they live?

Where do most Amish live? What difficulties do the Amish face in preserving their way of life in our increasingly technological society? Encourage the students to quote from original source material in their oral report.

---

using the argument that such laws violate the free exercise clause of the First Amendment to the Constitution, which states that "Congress shall make no law . . . prohibiting the free exercise [of religion]."

Yoder had not objected to his children attending school in the earlier grades. His church's doctrine allowed learning "the three R's—readin', ritin', and 'rithmetic." After that, he believed that the compulsory attendance law required him to disobey church law.

When the case was appealed, the reviewing court reversed Yoder's conviction. The court held that the state's compelling interest in educating its citizens was more important than religious doctrine except in one situation. If the goals of the state to educate its citizens are met, then religious doctrine can prevail. In this case, the court felt that the way the Amish trained its members to lead useful, productive lives satisfied the state's goals. The compelling interest of the state did not require depriving the Amish of their religious freedom when the children's interests were met in other ways.[2]

In this example, the Amish tradition and life-style apparently assured the state that the Amish youth would be prepared to lead useful lives even without the additional years of mandatory education. The factors important in deciding this case included the Amish religion's long-standing beliefs, the alternative benefits provided for the children by Amish training, and the children's completion of school prior to high school. You should understand, though, that most other attempts to exempt children from compulsory education for religious reasons have failed.

THE SCHOOL'S RIGHT TO DISCIPLINE

What is the best kind of situation in which to learn? Opinions may vary, but everyone is in agreement on one thing: a noisy, chaotic, undisciplined school setting does not lead to very much learning. Therefore, all school officials need to be able to control student behavior.

The right to regulate school behavior, however, does not give school officials the right to make and enforce just any rule at any time. The behavior of school officials in setting rules is governed by both school boards and state law. No state would allow your school's vice-principal to lock you up in a closet overnight as punishment for some alleged violation of school behavior rules. No state would allow your school vice-principal to suspend you from school for two months because you were chewing gum while reciting your homework assignment in English class. Every school official's actions must be reasonable and cannot violate state or federal constitutions.

In other words, there are limits to the right to discipline and the methods that can be used. These limits are identified by balancing the need to control student behavior against an individual student's right to fair treat-

2. *Wisconsin v. Yoder*, 406 U.S. 205, 92 S.Ct. 1526, 32 L.Ed. 2d 15 (1972).

Divide the class into small groups. Each group should select one of your school's rules and discuss whether or not they believe this rule to be "reasonable and proper." Each group should then prepare a list of five to ten reasons why they believe the rule they have discussed is reasonable and proper, or five to ten reasons why the rule they have discussed is not reasonable and proper. Have each group select a leader to explain to the class it's findings.

Have a student volunteer read aloud to the class this Legal Focus Example. Ask the students whether they think it is appropriate for this decision, which was handed down in 1888, to be applied to school situations in Wisconsin today. Why or why not? (You might want to point out to students that the wording of this decision is not overly specific and, therefore, it is still flexible enough to apply today.)

ment. In recent years, this balancing act has become even more difficult. Increased violence in our schools has made it more difficult for school administrators to maintain a good learning environment for all students.

TYPE OF RULES

All school disciplinary rules cannot violate the laws of the individual states. Typically, individual school districts and even individual schools can adopt their own disciplinary rules, as long as they are consistent with state law.

◀ LEGAL FOCUS ~ EXAMPLE

In 1888, the Wisconsin Supreme Court had the following ideas about how far school disciplinary rules could go:

The rules and regulations made must be reasonable and proper . . . for the government, good order, and efficiency of the schools, such as will best advance the pupils in their studies, tend to their educational and mental improvement, and promote their interest and welfare. But the rules and regulations must relate to these objects.

To this day, any school disciplinary rule that is not consistent with this statement has usually been thrown out by a state or a federal court.

If you were a teacher, what rules of conduct would you make to keep order and enhance learning? Be serious and thoughtful; it is easier to criticize than develop ideas.

Read aloud to the class the following excerpt from the student text: "Every day in every school in America, some students break minor disciplinary rules. Teachers and school administrators impose minor discipline when the rule broken is minor. The work of many schools would come to a grinding halt if every time minor discipline was used, there had to be a full-scale investigation by outside parties and a full-scale defense by the student."

Point out to the students that in effect, a student's due process rights are often ignored in instances where minor discipline is used. Stimulate a class discussion of this fact by asking the following questions: Is it fair that students' due process rights are often ignored when minor discipline is used? Why or why not? Who suffers when students' due process rights are ignored in instances of minor discipline? How significant is that suffering? Who would suffer if a full-scale investigation by outside parties and a full-scale defense by the student were employed in each case of minor discipline? How significant would that suffering be?

Have a student volunteer talk with a guidance counselor or dean from your school to learn about procedures that are used for suspension and expulsion. What steps does your school take to ensure that the students' due process rights are not abridged? Is the procedure a school policy or a district policy?

Many schools have a code of conduct explaining students' rights and responsibilities. Have a student lead a class discussion of your school's document. Discuss the benefits to students, teachers, administrators, parents, and society as a whole for following the procedures. If your school does not have a code, work together as a class to develop a fair, workable plan.

Students' Procedural Safeguards   When a student violates one of the rules in school, the school can take disciplinary action, such as suspending the student. But before this action can be taken, the school official must follow the proper procedure. Just because students are minors does not mean that school officials can ignore students' due process rights, as the United States Supreme Court case of *Goss v. Lopez*[3] showed. As you learned in Chapter 25, there are minimum requirements of due process in student discipline cases. This includes the following:

1. An existing rule must have been broken.
2. The student must be notified that he or she breached the rule.
3. The student must be given an opportunity to present a defense.

Students can take this due process requirement to an extreme, however. Every day in every school in America, some students break minor disciplinary rules. Teachers and school administrators impose minor discipline when the rule broken is minor. The work of many schools would come to a grinding halt if every time minor discipline was used, there had to be a full-scale investigation by outside parties and a full-scale defense by the student.

Certainly, balancing the due process rights of students with the many decisions that must be made in schools daily is a challenge. Consequently, the courts have held that the due process requirements are not fixed. Rather, they are flexible and related to the time, place, and circumstance of the rule violation. In other words, school administrators do have some discretion; that is, they can decide on their own what to do.

School administrators are not required to have a formal hearing before action can be taken for minor breaches of the rules. Moreover, if the presence of a student presents a danger to persons or property at the school, a school official has the legal right to remove that student from school without a hearing. Students who are disruptive to teaching and learning can be removed or dismissed under most circumstances. If a school administrator decides that a student should be suspended for a long time or kicked out completely (this is called *expulsion*), then full due process often must be given to the student. Before a student is formally suspended for a long time or expelled, due process normally requires that she or he be given some opportunity to challenge the charges.

Here are some guidelines for rules and processes that would meet the minimum due process requirements:

1. Rules should be related to the educational mission of the school. (Rules should not change on a whim.)
2. Rules should be spelled out in some detail. Behavior that is appropriate and inappropriate should be presented. The penalties for violations of these rules should also be clearly stated. (A rule should not be vague.)
3. Rules should be made available to students and parents before they attend the school. (It would be unfair if the rules were not made public.)

---

3.   419 U.S. 656, 95 S.Ct. 729, 42 L.Ed. 2d 725 (1975).

Allow a group of interested volunteers to stage a mock disciplinary hearing in which your class can participate. In order to prepare the group to complete this task, distribute copies of the mock trial package, found in your *Teachers Resource Binder*, to each member of the group. Instruct the group to use this mock trial package as an example of the types of materials to prepare. Then have them stage a mock disciplinary hearing that adheres to the guidelines for due process discussed in this chapter.

If students choose to act out the disciplinary infraction for which the disciplinary hearing is to be held, you may wish to counsel them to ensure that the infraction is appropriate for your classroom. You might also wish to explain to the students that they are not to use this as an opportunity to caricature individual students or faculty members.

4. Rules should not conflict with protected rights unless an overriding public interest requires it. (Free speech and free expression are basic rights in this country, protected by the Constitution. School rules should not improperly or unfairly restrict free speech.)

5. Rules should not be changed to apply to situations after they have occurred. (Rules changed after the fact are not right. If a certain activity did not break any existing rules, then school administrators cannot punish that behavior.)

6. When rules are violated, the rule violations should be made known and explained to the accused student as soon as possible. (Administrators should never wait very long to tell students what they did wrong.)

7. Procedural safeguards should be provided that are consistent with the rule violations and possible punishments. Each accused student should be allowed to tell his or her story to an individual who can be fair and impartial. The accusing administrator may allow the disciplinary action to be appealed to another administrator. The more significant the possible punishment, the more formal the hearing process required. (School administrators cannot simply ignore students' attempts to tell their sides of the story.)

8. Punishment should be consistent with the age, gender, mental condition, and past disciplinary history of the student. The factual basis for the discipline should be explained to the student. (School administrators cannot ignore individual circumstances when applying discipline.)

The Disciplinary Hearing You have already learned about court procedure in previous chapters. You know that most court procedure is relatively formal. There are rules that have to be followed during any presentation of an actual case in court. A school disciplinary hearing, in contrast, does not require a formal court proceeding, even when it is to expel or suspend a student. The major requirement of such a disciplinary hearing is that it be fair. The student must be aware of the charges made and the rule that he or she supposedly violated. The student has to have time to prepare for the hearing. At the hearing, the accused student should be allowed to present and examine witnesses. Typically, disciplinary hearings are held in the principal's or vice-principal's office. Present are the student, his or her parents, witnesses, and the school administrator who will decide the appropriate disciplinary action.

SEARCHES AND SEIZURES ON THE SCHOOL GROUNDS

If two members of your local police department decide to see what they can "dig up" in your house, they can't simply barge in while you are studying, rummage through your drawers, and then leave. Why? Because you and everybody else are protected by the Fourth Amendment to the United States Constitution. It reads:

The right of the people to be secure in their persons, houses, papers, and effects, against unreasonable searches and seizures, shall not be violated.

If your school has a stated or published policy regarding locker searches, obtain a copy of this policy and share it with the class. Ask the students to discuss this policy, explaining its purpose and debating its fairness.

Furthermore, the Fourteenth Amendment does not allow any state to deprive any person of property without due process of law or to deny any person the equal protection of the laws.

Do the Fourth and Fourteenth Amendments apply to students when they are at school? If so, does this mean that school officials must obtain a warrant that shows probable cause before they search a locker, for example? These are complex questions that are not easily answered.

The courts have determined that public schools are part of the government. Therefore, they are subject to the same restrictions that apply to governmental conduct. Further, students are individuals protected by the Constitution. They do not "shed their constitutional rights at the schoolhouse gate."[4] There is, though, a standard of reasonableness that applies to any governmental search. Even certain searches by police can be conducted without a warrant when, for example, they are fearful that a suspect's access to a hidden firearm may endanger their lives. Consequently, searches that are conducted by school officials are valid even when they follow a less formal procedure than that expected from other government officials.

There are two standards of reasonableness when carrying out a search of a student's person, property, or locker while at school. First, there has to be a justifiable reason for the search. It cannot be random or just because school officials want to see "what's going on." The school official has to believe that the student in question is violating some school rule or state law. Second, the scope of the search must be reasonable under the circumstances. What is reasonable is based on, among other things, the age and gender of the student, the circumstances of the event, and the seriousness of the suspected violation. At the end of this chapter, "A Case in Point" deals with this very question of when a search is reasonable.

◄ LEGAL FOCUS ~ PROBLEM

In most schools, students are assigned lockers. Most students have to provide their own combination or key-operated locks. This means that no school official has a master key that can open all the locks. In principle, what you keep in your locker is your own affair. Most students do not abuse this privilege. Their lockers contain only lawful items. But others do abuse this privilege and keep illegal drugs or firearms in their lockers. Can school officials require students to unlock their lockers for searches?

The answer to this problem has been settled in many courts. In general, courts have found that students have little cause to expect privacy in student lockers. Searches that were conducted under the belief that the inspected locker contained items that violated school rules have usually been

---

4.   *Hazelwood School District v. Cathy Kuhlmeier*, 484 U.S. 260 108 S.Ct. 562, 98 L.Ed.2d. 592 (1988).

upheld. If, however, the search is conducted at the request of the police, a search warrant should normally be issued. Some states have actually passed laws allowing the inspection of school lockers without a search warrant.

CORPORAL PUNISHMENT

Many adults today know from personal experience what corporal punishment at school means. The definition of **corporal punishment** is the use of physical force to punish a student. Many of us have unpleasant memories of at least one occasion in junior high when we were swatted with a large paddle by a teacher or the vice-principal for some violation of school rules. Indeed, some teachers had their special paddles hanging behind their desks at all times in order to remind students of what was in store if the rules were violated.

In some states, it is now specifically against the law to use corporal punishment in school. Other states specifically authorize its use "when appropriate." Still other states require parental approval before corporal punishment can be given to a student. Often this parental approval is obtained at the beginning of the school year by the parents signing a form and handing it back to the school.

Just because corporal punishment is authorized does not mean that it is allowed to be excessive. If it leaves a permanent or lasting injury, the school official who administered the punishment and the school district will have clearly exceeded their authority. They then become legally responsible. A general rule of thumb is that the amount of force used should be no more than necessary under the circumstances.

Some parents do not agree with the use of corporal punishment and have taken their cases into the courts, arguing that corporal punishment is the equivalent of "cruel and unusual punishment" and therefore is in violation of the Eighth Amendment to the United States Constitution. To date, none of these parents have been successful in their challenges.

◆ **corporal punishment** The use of physical pain to punish a student. Examples of physical force include paddling, swatting, or spanking.

◆ LEGAL FOCUS ~ CASE EXAMPLE

In a Louisiana high school, the physical education teacher set up a basketball drill. One of his students was unable to complete it either because he could not understand it or did not want to. After the teacher became frustrated with the student's conduct, the 5'11" 230-pound teacher picked up the 4'11" 101-pound student. In the ensuing struggle, the student was dropped (or thrown) to the ground. He suffered a broken arm. The student's parents sued for the civil tort of battery. The Louisiana court held that the force used under the circumstances was excessive. The student and his family were awarded $11,000.[5]

5. *Frank v. Orleans Parish School Board*, 195 So.2d 451 (1967).

Enrichment

You might point out to students that schools are not the only institutions in which corporal punishment might still occur. In modern times corporal punishment is permissible to maintain the order and safety of prisons. This is true, however, only where less drastic alternatives have been unsuccessful.

Collaborative Learning Activity

Divide the class into two groups to participate in a debate. Prepare and debate the topic, "Corporal punishment should/should not be allowed in school."

Legal Focus Case Example

Have a student volunteer read this Legal Focus Case Example aloud to the class. Ask the class whether they believe the court's decision was justified. Have students explain their reasoning.

Discussion Starter

The Buckley Amendment provides access to student records. If a discrepancy is found but not changed, a parent may place a statement in the file indicating his or her objections to the information. Brainstorm what effects inaccurate information in school records could have on a student's future.

Legal Focus Problem

Have a student volunteer read aloud this Legal Focus Problem dealing with the Family Educational Rights and Privacy Act of 1974. Ask the volunteer to suggest a possible answer to the question posed at the end of this problem.

SCHOOL RECORD PRIVACY

Ever since you were a little kid, somebody has been keeping records on you at school. There are records about your attendance, your days absent and why, your grades, and your teachers' comments. The question of who can have access to your school records is an important one and involves your privacy. But this question also involves whether or not your parents or guardian can have free access to your school records. In 1974, the Family Educational Rights and Privacy Act was passed. (It is commonly known as the Buckley amendment.) This act provides that parents of minors can have access to most of their children's educational records. These records definitely include all grades, conduct evaluations, and teachers' comments. In contrast, the law severely restricts who has access to this information without parental consent. Under the act, when the child reaches age eighteen, he or she assumes the rights of the parents.

◆ LEGAL FOCUS ~ PROBLEM

Your mother goes to school one day and asks to see your records. In examining them, she comes across a note about your numerous days absent last year. A school official has written into the record that he believes you were faking an illness. Your mother knows that you were actually in the hospital with a serious illness. Is there anything she can do?

The answer is certainly yes. Under the Family Educational Rights and Privacy Act, your mother can make a request to modify the information in the file that is clearly inaccurate. If your school administrators will not modify the records, then your parents have a right to a hearing. The hearing officer can be an employee of the school district, but he or she cannot be the person who refused to modify the report in the first place. If the hearing officer also refuses to modify the report, your parents have an absolute right to place a statement in the file indicating their objections to the information.

◆ THE QUESTION OF EQUALITY IN SCHOOLS

Sarah loves school. She gets to use computers, interactive videodiscs, and CDs when she learns about geometry and calculus. Her teachers always have the latest textbooks with up-to-date information.

Kim's teachers in another school district have books that are fifteen years old, and the school has no computers. Kim's teachers do not have access to any of the latest technological marvels that help students learn. The reason

State Law

One of the more important recent cases dealing with the question of equality in the schools focused on disparate state financing for the poorest and richest districts in the state of Texas. This case, *Edgewood* v. *Kirby*, is included in the *Handbook of Selected Court Cases to Accompany West's*

Business and Personal Law. At this time, you might wish to reproduce this case from the *Handbook of Selected Court Cases* and distribute it to your students. Have the students read the case. Then stimulate a class discussion regarding this case.

Do all children have access to the same educational opportunities? Should they?

Extension Activity

Have students find out where the money comes from to run your school district. Have students compare the amount your school district receives with other districts in your area. If there are differences, tell why.

Extension Activity

Invite your principal or vice principal to speak to your class on your school's budget so that students can have a better understanding of where the money goes.

Teaching Note

Brown v. *Board of Education of Topeka* is included in the *Handbook of Selected Court Cases to Accompany West's Business and Personal Law.* This landmark case was also discussed in a *Law in Action* feature in Chapter 1.

Caption Answer

The amount of money available per pupil in different school districts is often quite different.

for this difference is that the amount of money available per student in Sarah's school district is twice what is available in Kim's school district.

This situation exists in many places in the United States. The amount of money available per pupil in different school districts is often quite different, even within the same state. Is such a situation against the law? This question, like many others with respect to education, is not easily answered. After all, there is nothing in the Constitution that gives minors a right to free public education. It is clear, though, that once government undertakes to provide a public education, it must do so for all children in the state. This requirement derives from the Fourteenth Amendment, which prohibits states from denying "to any person within its jurisdiction equal protection of the laws." At least in part, this constitutional doctrine led to the desegregation of American schools in the landmark case of *Brown v. Board of Education of Topeka*[6] in 1954. The *Brown* decision held that separate school systems on the basis of race were unequal.

EQUAL OPPORTUNITY

But what about equal opportunity? This concept is difficult to put into practice. Should all male members of the senior class be allowed on the varsity basketball team? Should all students, no matter what their grades and abilities, be in advanced placement courses?

The United States Supreme Court has developed three tests to determine whether equality of treatment is legal. The first is the *rational-basis test.* This test allows the government to treat individuals differently as long

6.   347 U.S. 483, 74 S.Ct. 686, 98 L.Ed. 873 (1954).

Reteaching Activity

In order to refresh students' memories on the basics of tort law, you might have a student volunteer read the Chapter Summary for Chapter 5 before students begin the section titled Minors' Responsibility for Torts.

Checking Your Progress (Answers)

1. In most states, reaching the age of majority means that someone is no longer a minor and has all the rights, privileges, and duties of an adult. The age of majority is 21.

2. A juvenile who is between the ages of 6 and 16 is truant if he or she does not attend school. A truancy officer can take the juvenile before a juvenile court. The parents could be charged with child neglect.

3. Yes, schools can usually develop their own rules; however, they must be consistent with the policies of the school district and with the laws of the state.

4. Corporal punishment is legal in some states. In approving states, it may be used "when appropriate" or with parental approval. If the punishment is excessive, the official who administered it and the school district become legally responsible.

5. The Supreme Court tests to determine legal equality of treatment are the rational-basis test, the means test, and the test for a compelling reason for unequal treatment.

as the reasons for different treatment are related to a legitimate governmental goal. The second test is the *means test*. This test requires that the methods or means that are selected by the government and that involve unequal treatment must be substantially related to accomplishing the stated goals. The third test requires that if a distinction is a "suspect one" relating to some basic interest, the government reason for that unequal treatment must be compelling. Suspect classifications include those made on the basis of race, sex, alienage, and national origin. It is virtually impossible for governmental programs (such as those related to schooling) to provide different opportunities on the basis of these classifications and still be legal.

What classifications generating unequal treatment are legal in school? Certainly those based on ability or achievement are usually considered legal. Therefore, it is legal for schools to keep only the best players on basketball teams and the best students in advanced placement courses.

◆ CHECKING YOUR PROGRESS

1. What does it mean to reach the age of majority? What age is the age of majority?

2. If a juvenile is between the ages of 6 and 16 and does not attend school, what legal consequences might the juvenile face? What consequences could the parents face?

3. Can individual schools develop their own disciplinary rules?

4. Is corporal punishment in schools legal? Explain.

5. What tests has the Supreme Court developed to determine whether equality of treatment is legal?

◆ MINORS' RESPONSIBILITY FOR TORTS

Remember that a tort is a civil, rather than a criminal, wrong. Common torts are trespassing, assault, and battery. In general, a minor is personally liable for any torts he or she commits. Nonetheless, courts weigh the factors of age, mental capacity, and maturity before determining a minor's responsibility for torts. For example, there are states in which a minor under the age of seven is legally incapable of the tort of negligence. In most states, some torts, such as fraud or battery, require a certain state of mind which normally includes *willful* intent. The age of the minor obviously is related to the ability of the minor to have a particular state of mind.

The courts also consider the question of reasonableness. In negligence actions, appropriate behavior is measured against what is reasonable under the circumstances. A certain behavior might be unreasonable if performed by a seventeen-year-old but not if it is performed by an eight-year-old. For example, an eight-year-old playing with a gun might not be held

Legal Focus Problem

Have a student volunteer read this Legal Focus Problem aloud to the class. Then stimulate a class discussion of this problem by asking students the following questions: What torts does Michael commit? Why is Michael's contract with Rivercity voidable? Why is it likely that Michael would be found liable to Natasha for the damages to her boat that resulted from his negligence?

Extension Activity

Ask a volunteer to research parental responsibility for the contracts and torts of minors in your state. Have the volunteer report his or her findings to the class, along with the procedure he or she went through to find the information. Tell students to write a one-page essay telling whether they agree that parents should be held responsible. If the students agree with the premise, they should give two examples of instances in which parents should be held responsible.

responsible for its going off and harming another child. A seventeen-year-old, however, would probably be held responsible. In short, age and mental capacity are very much factors in determining ultimate responsibility for torts.

Sometimes minors will breach a contract when they commit a tort, as the problem that follows shows. But minors, simply because they are minors, typically cannot be held to most contracts. Therefore, even if a minor is found to be legally responsible for the tort he or she committed, he or she may not be held to the contract because of his or her lack of majority. The following problem will help make this situation clear.

◀ LEGAL FOCUS – PROBLEM

Michael, age sixteen, rents a boat from Rivercity Rentals. The rental agreement provides that the renter will use due care to prevent damage to the boat. Michael uses the boat in a careless way. He damages both Rivercity's boat and the boat of a third party owned by Natasha. Is Michael responsible to Rivercity Rentals for his negligence? In other words, would a court decide that he has to pay Rivercity Rentals for the damages to the boat he rented? And what about Michael's responsibility to Natasha? Would a court order that he pay for the damages to her boat?

Michael's contract with Rivercity is **voidable** because he is a minor. He lacks contractual capacity. Consequently, many courts would not find Michael liable for the damages to Rivercity's boat, although a small number of courts would find him liable. Almost all courts would find Michael liable to Natasha for the damages to her boat that resulted from his negligence.

In reality, even when a minor is found financially responsible for his or her negligence, he or she usually does not have the resources to pay the injured victim. Then it becomes a matter of trying to make the minor's parents pay. What are the parents' responsibilities?

PARENTAL RESPONSIBILITY FOR THE CONTRACTS AND TORTS OF A MINOR

In the problem just discussed, some might argue that Michael's parents should pay for Michael's negligence. After all, they are his parents. The general rule, though, is that parents are not held liable for the torts of their minor children simply because of the parent-child relationship. There are special circumstances under which they can be held liable, however. For example, if the minor commits the tort under the direction of, or while performing an act requested by, either parent, the injured party can hold the parent liable. In addition, parents are liable in many states up to an amount set by law for willful misconduct by a minor living in the home of the parent.

◆ **voidable** That which can be avoided or declared void. Contracts that are voidable are ones that can be gotten out of by one party but not the other. When a minor makes most contracts, that minor can get out of the contract, but the party with whom the minor made the contract normally cannot.

Law in Action

INTERNATIONAL PERSPECTIVES: LIABILITY OF OTHERS FOR THE ACTS OF MINORS

In the United States a parent is usually not liable for the acts of his or her minor children. As discussed in the Chapter, some exceptions commonly exist by statute for malicious mischief or when the minor is driving an automobile. This rule of non-liability applies, without exceptions, for teachers and other persons who are supervising children. If a child commits a tort, the teacher, or the supervisor, is not responsible unless it can be proved they are negligent in some way themselves.

Like many other legal rules and principles, other countries provide different solutions to the same issues. There are three main ways in which the liability of others for the acts of children are classified. The first classification is the common law rule followed in the United States and most other common law countries, such as United Kingdom, Canada, India, South Africa, and Australia. The rule is also followed in many Scandinavian countries, such as Denmark, Norway, and Sweden. Muslim or Islamic law holds that in the case of the minor "there is no claim whatever on the person who exercises the authority of the father."[7]

The second solution is that the parents, and in some countries even a supervisor, is presumed liable for the harm caused by a minor. If the minor is found responsible, then the liability is joint, with both the supervisor and the child liable. If the minor lacks capacity to commit the tort, then the adult is solely responsible. The French extend this liability only to parents, "The father and the mother, to the extent they exercise the right of guardianship, are jointly liable for the damage caused by their minor children living with them.[8]" Some other countries, such as Germany extend this rule to persons supervising the minor. Versions of this rule exist in most Western European countries, such as Germany, France, Belgium, and Spain. It also has been accepted in countries where either French or German law has been influential, such as Turkey, Ethiopia, Chile, and Colombia.

A third solution is that a parent, teacher, or supervisor is presumed to be responsible *if the minor is not liable*—based on lack of capacity—or if that person is actually negligent themselves in their supervision. If the minor is older, say sixteen, the supervisor would probably not be responsible. If the minor is younger, say twelve, the supervisor would probably be responsible. In Japan, which generally follows this solution, minors become responsible for their tortious acts after the age of twelve years. This rule has been commonly followed in Eastern European countries, such as Russia, as well as Japan.

This discussion of legal rules should be understood with two cautions. First, although theoretical liability exists in many countries, the social reality is that the likelihood that a person will actually sue or enforce a right varies dramatically in different countries. In others words, the fact a legal right exists does not mean people commonly take advantage of it. Second, the presumption of liability that exists in most of the world is very easy to rebut in many of these countries by proof of minimal supervision.

---

7. Madjalla art. 916 par. 2.

8. French Civil Code art. 1384 par. 4.

Legal Focus Example

Have a student volunteer read aloud this Legal Focus Example dealing with the California Civil Code. Remind the students that they can use the Legal Focus features as review tools when studying for tests.

Ethical Concern

Guide the students in discussing the ethical implications of the California civil statutes described in the Legal Focus Example on this page by asking the following questions: Do you think it is fair that parents should be held liable for a minor's willful misconduct? Do you think it is fair that a parent should be liable for the defacing of property (graffiti)? Why or why not? What legal obligations are created by these statutes? What ethical obligations are created by these statutes?

Extension Activity

You might invite a representative from a local social service agency that deals with child abuse to speak to your class. He or she should concentrate on discussing the following issues: What steps are taken to protect the child from further abuse? What steps are taken to protect the child's privacy rights, and what reporting laws, if any, exist within your state? Have your students prepare questions in advance for the speaker.

◇ LEGAL FOCUS - EXAMPLE

In California, if a minor goes on a window-breaking rampage in the local neighborhood, his or her parents would be liable for replacing the broken windows because California has a law to that effect. This statute provides that parents are jointly liable with the minor for the minor's *willful* (voluntary) misconduct. The liability of the parent is limited to $10,000 for each tort. This statute also provides that parents are liable for the defacing of property (commonly called graffiti), again up to $10,000. If the harm is caused by the discharge of a firearm, liability can climb up to $30,000. (See California Civil Code, Sections 1714.1 and 1714.3.)

In many states, parents are also liable for a minor's torts while that minor is driving a motor vehicle. But even in those states where statutes create parental liability, the minor is usually jointly liable. What if you are sixteen and go out and buy a car from a used-car lot? Are your parents liable for the payments you must make on that car? As a general rule, the answer is no. Usually, parents are not liable for the contracts made by their minor children except under limited circumstances, as you learned in the Legal Perspective feature in Chapter 9. Normally, businesses try to avoid any problems that might arise in a contract with a minor by making both the parents and the minor sign the contract.

◆ ABUSE OF CHILDREN

Child abuse is a serious crime that is difficult to detect. It often occurs in complete privacy. Child abuse includes physical, sexual, emotional, and verbal abuse of a child. It can also include the neglect of a child, such as failing to feed and clothe the child.

Sexual abuse is a serious felony in which an adult or older child uses a child for his or her sexual gratification. The victimized child may be the only witness and may be reluctant or unable to testify adequately. Forced testimony in open court may result in the child suffering serious emotional distress. The child may be hurt by this experience, and the usefulness of the information given may be questioned.

Most states have laws to protect child witnesses. Protective procedures include using closed-circuit testimony from a private room and videotaping out-of-court testimony. Some of these protective laws clash with a defendant's Sixth Amendment right to confront witnesses. Challenges by defendants to many of these laws are under way.

Many states have statutes requiring certain persons who may have insight into the physical condition of a child to report their suspicions of child abuse. Physicians, other medical personnel, social workers, and teachers are among those who may often have this duty by law.

Extension Activity

Have a student research the McMartin case. Guide the student by referring him or her to news magazines such as *Time* or *Newsweek* for articles regarding this well-publicized Los Angeles child abuse case. Tell the student to report to the class on the following issues related to this case: Why was the case so expensive? What steps were taken to protect the privacy rights of the children? What specific lessons were learned from the McMartin case? Allow the student to report his or her findings to the class in the form of an oral report.

Legal Focus Example

Read aloud to the class this Legal Focus Example. Remind students that they can use the Legal Focus features as review tools when studying for tests.

Caption Answer

Yes, but the usefulness of the information given may be questioned.

632

Extension Activity

Ask a volunteer to research a case in which a child has sued his or her parents. Ask them to outline the events and orally present the case to the class.

 LEGAL FOCUS - EXAMPLE

The McMartin case is the longest case in American legal history. From start to jury verdict, it took 2½ years. It was also one of the costliest cases, running in excess of $15 million in expenses for lawyers and the use of the courts. The case alleged fifty-two counts of sexual molestation by two defendants at McMartin's Day Care Center in Los Angeles. One of the defendants was found not guilty. The jury was unable to reach a verdict on several counts for the other defendant, Raymond Buckey. A new trial jury was also unable to reach a verdict. The district attorney finally declined to retry Raymond Buckey a third time. Because of the expensive lessons learned in the McMartin case, interview, investigation, and prosecution techniques for child molestation cases have been radically changed.

LAWSUITS AGAINST PARENTS

At common law, children were unable to sue their parents for personal injuries caused by parental negligence. This doctrine was called *family immunity*, where "immunity" means protection from prosecution. Its purpose was to promote and preserve family harmony. Parents were not ordinarily immune, however, when they committed intentional torts, such as a se-

Are minors allowed to testify in a trial?

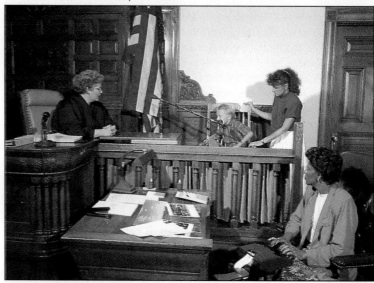

vere battery. Most states now permit negligence actions by children against their parents. In these cases, the parents' insurance company may be expected to pay any judgment in favor of the child against the parent.

Occasionally a child sues a parent for being an unfit or unsatisfactory parent. These "child divorce court" cases make national headlines when they occur. Although these so-called poor-parenting suits make the television news, they do not represent a significant number of the lawsuits involving minors.

◆ RESPONSIBILITY FOR CRIMES—THE JUVENILE JUSTICE SYSTEM

"I've been struck by the upside-down priorities of the juvenile system. We are willing to spend the least amount of money to keep a kid at home, more to put him in a foster home, and the most to institutionalize him."
Marian Wright Edelman
American lawyer

Perhaps because the word *minor* combined with the word *justice* to make the phrase *minor justice* sounds funny, an alternative phrase is used to describe the legal system that applies to those who have not reached the age of majority. It is called the *juvenile justice system*, and it defines the way in which minors are treated by the courts. The juvenile justice system is separate from the adult legal system. The juvenile justice system is based on the legal doctrine of *parens patriae*; these Latin words mean that the state has the power to stand in the place of the parent.

The juvenile courts usually have jurisdiction over four types of situations that involve individuals under the age of eighteen (or, depending on the state's age of majority, under the age of sixteen or seventeen):

1. When they have violated criminal laws.
2. When their conduct is out of control, such as being continuously absent from school or running away from home.
3. When they are abandoned or abused by their parents.
4. When their parents are unable to provide for them.

You may have heard the term *juvenile delinquent*; it typically only applies to a minor who has engaged in the first situation listed here. The definition of **delinquent** is usually a minor who has committed an act that is a crime for adults under federal, state, or local law. Sometimes those minors who are absent from school are called delinquents, too, because they have violated a state law requiring compulsory schooling. In any event, the foundation for the juvenile justice system is the belief that a delinquent child can

Ethical Concern

be rehabilitated with the appropriate guidance. The state should guide this process, as would a parent, during the period of a child's life before she or he is expected to have mature judgment.

Age is an important factor in determining whether a child can be charged with a crime. Under the common law, children under the age of seven were considered incapable of committing a crime because they did not have the moral sense to understand that they were doing wrong. Children between the ages of seven and fourteen were presumed also to be incapable of committing a crime unless it could be demonstrated that they understood the wrongful nature of their acts. (See Exhibit 4-1 in Chapter 4.)

This "defense of infancy" that prevents minors from being held responsible for their criminal acts varies from state to state. Today, the common law approach has been retained, but the age limits have been changed, probably due to the increasing number of violent acts by very young minors in some cities. At any rate, all states have juvenile court systems that handle children below the age of criminal responsibility who commit delinquent acts. The aim of these court systems is to reform, rather than to punish. Once a juvenile court has jurisdiction, it can retain supervision over the individual even after the age of eighteen. Some states go so far as to allow juvenile court jurisdiction to stay in place until the individual is twenty-three years old.

More and more, the courts are proclaiming that minors who have committed horrible crimes should be tried as adults. The criteria used by juvenile courts to determine whether a minor should be tried as an adult include:

1. The type of offense with which the youth is charged—The more serious the criminal act, the more likely a trial in an adult court.
2. The juvenile's prior record—A juvenile delinquent with a prior record of violent or serious criminal acts is more likely to be tried in an adult court.
3. The nature of past treatment efforts—Previous unsuccessful attempts at reform suggest that new ones will be useless; when this is the case, the minor is more likely to be tried as an adult.
4. Availability of rehabilitative services—If a jurisdiction finds that it has virtually no resources available to rehabilitate the minor, the minor may be more likely to be tried as an adult for his or her crime.
5. The reasonable likelihood of the child being rehabilitated in the juvenile court system—If there is no reasonable likelihood, then the minor is more likely to be tried as an adult.

Whenever the minor is tried in an adult court, the normal criminal procedures afforded every adult are given to the minor. And sentencing in the adult court will follow the normal sentencing guidelines of criminal law.

The rise of more violent juvenile acts and the increase in gang activity have led to a major questioning of the juvenile justice system. It would not be surprising to see major modifications, which are already under way, completely reshape the system before the year 2000.

Invite guest speakers such as a police officer, a judge, or a probation officer to talk to the class about the juvenile justice system in your city.

Have a student volunteer read aloud the Legal Focus Problem dealing with a minor's ability to waive his or her Miranda rights. Ask the volunteer to suggest a possible answer to the question posed at the end of this problem.

CONSTITUTIONAL RIGHTS OF A JUVENILE

Because minors who commit crimes and are tried in juvenile court may be put in jail, they are entitled to many of the normal constitutional protections. For example, a minor in juvenile court has the right to representation by an attorney (without charge, if the minor is very poor) and cannot be forced to be a witness against himself or herself.

If a juvenile is taken into custody by the police, he or she has generally the same rights as an adult. The juvenile has the right to Miranda warnings: "In order to be able to use statements obtained during custodial interrogation of the accused, the State must warn the accused prior to such questioning of his right to remain silent and of his right to have counsel, retained or appointed, present during interrogation." In other words, a juvenile has the right to an attorney and the right to remain silent.[9]

LEGAL FOCUS ~ PROBLEM

After the Miranda warnings are given, adults can waive their Miranda rights. That is, they can decide to talk with police without an attorney present, and they can voluntarily give incriminating information. It happens all the time. Can a minor waive his or her Miranda rights?

The U.S. Supreme Court has held that minors can waive their Miranda rights if they make a knowing, intelligent, and voluntary waiver. A few states, under their state constitutions or by statute, require that the waiver be made in the presence of the juvenile's parents or attorney. Courts in these states have concluded that a youth is not mature enough, without benefit of adult advice, to appreciate the importance of the right to remain silent.

The Fourth Amendment protection against unreasonable searches and seizures protects minors from warrantless illegal searches just as it does an adult. Evidence that is illegally seized can be prevented from being used in a juvenile proceeding. This is called *suppression of evidence*.

There is no constitutional right to bail for a minor. A prehearing release, however, is common in juvenile matters. Many state statutes require release of the juvenile to the parents unless the nature of the accused crime or the youth's family situation makes release not advisable.

TRIAL COURTS AND JUVENILES

At the hearing, the juvenile has many but not all of the same constitutional rights as adults who are on trial. The juvenile has the right to counsel, the right to notice of the charges, the right to confront and cross-examine hostile witnesses, and the right to avoid self-incrimination. The burden of proof for juvenile matters is generally the same as in criminal cases—"beyond a reasonable doubt."

---

9. *Fare v. Michael C.*, 442 U.S. 707, 99 S.Ct. 2560, 61 L.Ed.2d 197 (1979).

Ethical Concern

Guide the students in discussing the concept of punishment as it relates to juvenile justice. Point out to students that under the law, juveniles technically are not punished; rather, as the text makes clear, arrangements are made to influence the behavior of the juvenile in a positive way. Stimulate a class discussion regarding this issue by asking students the following questions: What kinds of "sentences" are given to juveniles? Do these seem to be punishments? Why or why not? Do you feel that punishment is called for in dealing with juvenile offenses? Why or why not?

Critical Thinking Activity

Ask a student volunteer to explain why juvenile court hearings are generally not open to the public. Why is this in the best interest of the juvenile?

Critical Thinking Activity

Have your students write a few paragraphs discussing the differences between the arrest, trial, and punishment procedures for adults and those for minors.

Ordinarily, juvenile court hearings are not open to the public, and the names of offenders are kept private. Also, no right to trial by jury exists in juvenile court. The matter is heard by a single judge.

PUNISHMENT

Technically, juveniles are not punished; instead, arrangements are made to influence the behavior of the child in a positive way. Factors to be considered are the best interests of the child, of his or her family, and of the community. The determination of how to treat the juvenile is made by the juvenile judge, who has a lot of choice in this situation.

If the accused person is found to have committed the offense that he or she is charged with, the court will declare the minor a ward of the court. Juvenile courts can make various orders, such as issuing a suspended judgment, putting the juvenile on probation, sending him or her to a training program, fining the juvenile, and committing him or her to a juvenile home, ranch, camp, or to a special jail for youthful offenders.

Probation involves assigning the juvenile offender to a probation officer for counseling and supervision for a specific period of time. The offender must meet with the probation officer at specified times for a period determined by the court. If the minor commits a crime during the probation period, probation can be revoked, and institutionalization on the former charge can take place.

When juveniles are institutionalized, they are often given **indeterminate sentences.** An indeterminate sentence is one where the length of time is not specified. Release is based, at least in part, on an evaluation of the juvenile's rehabilitation. But even with indeterminate sentences, a maximum amount of time is set; once that time has been served, the juvenile must be released. Most states have **determinate sentences** for adult criminal behavior. Determinate sentences set specific times to be served for a criminal act.

CRIMINAL RECORD

Under specified conditions (usually the passage of several years), many juvenile courts will officially seal all records related to a minor's case. The minor then officially has no criminal record and will not be handicapped in the future when seeking employment. In recent years, several states have modified this treatment. These states allow prior juvenile records to be opened by court order, by law enforcement agencies, by the military, and by other public agencies. The records may be used to influence later sentencing in adult court or perhaps to show a history of prior criminal behavior.

STATUS OFFENDERS

Juveniles who cut school, run away from home, repetitively violate curfew laws, or engage in other behavior that is not a crime but is forbidden to a minor are often classified as *status offenders* rather than as juvenile delin-

◆ **indeterminate sentence** A sentence of confinement for the maximum period defined by law subject to termination by the parole board or other agency at any time after the minimum period has been served.

◆ **determinate sentence** A sentence of confinement for a fixed period as specified by law.

1. In some states, parents are responsible up to a statutory amount for willful misconduct, such as vandalism, for damages caused when the minor drives a motor vehicle or when the parent directs the minor's action, under the general rule of *respondeat superior*.

2. The doctrine of family immunity protects family members from being legally responsible to other family members. Its purpose is to promote and preserve family harmony. You might ask students whether they believe the doctrine promotes that purpose.

3. (1) When minors have violated criminal laws, (2) when their conduct is out of control, (3) when they are abandoned or abused by their parents, and (4) when their parents are unable to provide for them.

4. No. The case is heard by a juvenile court judge. Although a minor has most of the same protections as an adult, because the juvenile court is a court of equity, this right has not been found to be constitutionally required. You might discuss how your students feel about the lack of the right to trial by jury for minors.

quents. Phrases such as PINS (persons in need of supervision), MINS (minors in need of supervision), and CHIPS (children in need of protective services) are used to identify these juveniles.

If a minor is accused of a status offense, his or her constitutional rights are relaxed. For instance, the burden of proof required to find that an offense was committed is reduced from "beyond a reasonable doubt." Evidence that is not acceptable in a criminal charge may well be allowable in a hearing on a status offense. Although status offenders can be institutionalized, most states require they be housed in different places than are criminal delinquents.

◆ CHECKING YOUR PROGRESS

1. Name two situations where a parent may be liable for the torts of his or her child.

2. What is the doctrine of family immunity? What is its purpose?

3. When do juvenile courts have jurisdiction over minors?

4. Does a minor have the right to a jury trial in juvenile court?

◆ A CASE IN POINT ◆

NEW JERSEY v. T. L. O.

United States Supreme Court, 1985.
469 U.S. 325.
83 L.Ed.2d 720.
105 S.Ct. 733.

A minor is protected by the Fourth Amendment from a warrantless search and seizure by the police, but do the same rules apply to searches by school officials?

FACTS A teacher at Piscataway High School in Middlesex County, New Jersey, walked in on two girls smoking in the rest room. As you might expect, this violated a high school disciplinary rule. One of the students was fourteen-year-old T. L. O. (initials are used because the student is a minor). When questioned later by Mr. Choplick, the assistant vice-principal, T. L. O. denied she had been smoking or that she smoked at all.

Choplick, suspecting he had been lied to, demanded to inspect T. L. O.'s purse. He opened the purse and found a pack of cigarettes and cigarette rolling paper. Aware that rolling paper was often used to smoke marijuana, he thoroughly searched the purse. He found a small amount of marijuana, a pipe, several empty plastic bags, forty $1 bills, an index card that appeared to be a list of students that owed T. L. O. money, and two letters that implicated T. L. O. in marijuana dealing.

Teaching A Case In Point

Read
Introduce this *A Case In Point* feature by reminding students that search and seizure laws are not as clearly defined for minors on school property as they are for adults in private homes. Explain to the students that this *A Case In Point* feature discusses a New Jersey case dealing with whether the Fourth Amendment, which prohibits unreasonable searches and seizures, applies to searches conducted by school officials.

Teaching Note

This case is included in the *West's
Business and Personal Law Handbook of
Selected Court Cases.*

Discuss
Stimulate a class discussion
of this *A Case In Point* feature by asking the following
questions: Who is TLO?
Why are initials used in this
case? Why did Choplick
demand to inspect TLO's
purse? What did Choplick
find? What did the trial
court rule in this case? What
did the New Jersey Supreme
Court rule in this case? Who
appealed this case to the
United States Supreme
Court? What was the issue
before the United States
Supreme Court in dealing
with this case? What was
the decision of the United
States Supreme Court? What
reasons did the Supreme
Court give for its decision?

◆ A CASE IN POINT (CONTINUED) ◆

Choplick notified the local police and
turned over the evidence to them. Later at
police headquarters with her mother present, T. L. O. confessed to selling marijuana
at her school.

At a juvenile court proceeding, T. L. O.
moved to suppress the evidence of the
search. She argued that her confession
should also be suppressed as it was tainted
by the unlawful search. The trial court denied the motion and found T. L. O. to be a
delinquent. The New Jersey supreme court
reversed the trial court holding. The court
held that the Fourth Amendment protection against warrantless searches applies to
searches by school officials and that evidence from an illegal search should be suppressed. The state of New Jersey appealed to
the United States Supreme Court.

ISSUE Does the Fourth Amendment
prohibition against unreasonable searches
and seizures apply to searches conducted
by school officials? Should evidence from
the search be excluded in the juvenile
proceeding?

DECISION The Fourth Amendment
does apply to searches conducted by school
officials. The U.S. Supreme Court, however, held that the search in this case was reasonable. The decision of the supreme court
of New Jersey was reversed, and the evi-

dence was held to be admissible in the juvenile court proceeding.

REASON The Fourth Amendment has
long been interpreted as a restraint against
police searches but not necessarily other
searches by government. The "basic purpose of this Amendment . . . is to safeguard
the privacy and security of individuals
against arbitrary invasions by governmental
officials."

Despite a few contrary state court decisions, the U.S. Supreme Court held that
school officials are subject to search and
seizure controls.

The Fourth Amendment commands that
searches be *reasonable.* The determination of
what is reasonable in a school requires a balancing of interests. The student has a right
to expect privacy as to his or her personal
belongings. However, a school has the right
and duty to maintain discipline on the
school grounds. The court noted, "Maintaining order in the classroom has never
been easy, but in recent years . . . drug use
and violent crime in the schools have become major social problems."

Because of the charge of smoking against
T. L. O. and her denial, the search of her
purse for cigarettes seemed logical and reasonable. If the search is reasonable at the beginning, it does not become unreasonable
just because evidence of a more serious
crime is found.

Reviewing Chapter 26

In order to help students review what they have learned in Chapter 26, you might wish to:
1. Have a student volunteer, or volunteers, read aloud the Chapter Summary.
2. Allow the students to work with partners to complete the *Using Legal Language* activity.
3. Assign the *Checking for Comprehension* exercise as homework.

4. Allow the students to work in small groups to complete the *Applying Legal Concepts* activities.
5. As a class, complete the *Applying the Law* activities. (Please note that you may have to help students with vocabulary so that they adequately understand all of the *Applying the Law* material.)

Assessment Strategies

In order to check student mastery of chapter concepts, you may wish to use the Chapter 26 test that is found in your *Teacher's Resource Binder* or use WESTEST computerized testing for Chapter 26.

CHAPTER 26 REVIEW

 ## SUMMARY

AGE OF MAJORITY

The age of majority in most states is eighteen. The Twenty-sixth Amendment to the Constitution allows eighteen-year-olds to vote.

Emancipated Minors

Many states allow a minor to become emancipated before reaching the age of majority.

SCHOOLS

1. The federal constitution does not guarantee children the right to an education.
2. All fifty states have compulsory attendance laws for minor students. Generally, minors between the ages of six and sixteen years must attend school unless exempted.
3. Schools have the right to regulate behavior and enforce violations of school rules.
4. The equal protection clause of the Constitution requires that schools provide similar opportunities to all students unless different treatment is related to a legitimate government goal.
5. Although the U.S. Constitution does not require the same amount of money to be spent on each pupil, several state constitutions require uniform funding.
6. The Family Educational Rights and Privacy Act (1974) provides that parents of minors can have access to most of their children's educational records, and it restricts the availability of this information to other parties.

LIABILITY FOR TORTS

A minor is usually held liable for the torts he or she commits. The age and mental capacity of the minor are generally taken into consideration in determining responsibility.

Parental Responsibility for Contracts and Torts of a Minor

1. Usually parents are not liable for contracts made or torts committed by their minor children.
2. Exceptions include where the minor commits the tort under the direction of the parent, the minor commits vandalism, or is involved in a car accident.

ABUSE OF CHILDREN

Child abuse includes neglect and physical, sexual, emotional, and verbal abuse of a child.

LAWSUITS AGAINST PARENTS

Historically, the doctrine of family immunity made lawsuits for negligence by a minor child against an adult impossible. Today, many states allow lawsuits against parents for negligence.

JUVENILE JUSTICE SYSTEM

1. The system is based on the concept of *parens patriae*, the power of the state to stand in the place of the parent. The system is designed to protect and rehabilitate a juvenile offender.
2. Under the common law, children up to seven years of age were considered incapable of committing a crime. Children between the ages of seven and fourteen were also presumed to be incapable of committing a crime unless it could be shown that they understood that their behavior was wrong.
3. All states have juvenile court systems that handle children below the age of criminal responsibility who commit delinquent acts.
4. Juvenile offenders can be turned over to adult courts if a juvenile court determines that they should be treated as adults.

Checking for Comprehension
(Answers)

1. A citizen becomes an emancipated minor when his or her parents no longer have control. This can occur when a juvenile reaches the age of majority or, possibly, by marriage or joining the military. In some states, a juvenile must petition the state for approval. An emancipated minor acquires all the rights of an adult.

2. The courts have held that due process requirements are flexible and related to the time, place, and circumstance of the rule violation. School administrators have some discretion as to how to handle minor breaches of the rules.

3. A student's person, property, or locker can be searched while he or she is at school if there is a justifiable reason for the search, and the scope of the search must be reasonable under the circumstances. Since schools are

640   Personal Law

Constitutional Rights of a Juvenile

A minor charged with committing a crime has the right to Miranda warnings and the right to representation by an attorney. The juvenile has the right to notice of charges, the right to confront and cross-examine hostile witnesses, and cannot be forced to engage in self-incrimination. The Fourth Amendment protection against unreasonable searches and seizures protects minors against warrantless illegal searches. The minor does not have the right to bail or to an open or jury trial.

Punishment

Technically, juveniles are not punished. Alternatives include suspended judgment, probation, training programs, fines, and commitment to juvenile homes, ranches, camps, or to special jails for youthful offenders.

Criminal Record

Some states allow juvenile records to be sealed after the passage of several years.

Status Offenders

Juveniles who cut school, run away from home, repetitively violate curfew laws, or engage in other behavior forbidden to a minor are often classified as status offenders.

 ## USING LEGAL LANGUAGE

Directions: Match each term with the statement that best defines that term.

1. age of majority
2. compulsory attendance
3. corporal punishment
4. disciplinary hearing
5. emancipated minor
6. Family Educational Rights and Privacy Act
7. juvenile criminal justice system
8. means test
9. *parens patriae*
10. rational-basis test

A. test for equality of treatment that allows the government to treat individuals differently as long as the reason for the different treatment is related to a legitimate government goal

B. an underage person who is "set free" from his or her parents

C. use of physical pain to punish a student

D. provides that parents of minors should have access to most of the child's educational records

E. the power of the state to stand in the place of the parent

F. the age at which one ceases to be a minor

G. requirement that minor students attend school

H. involves the way in which minors are treated in the courts

I. procedure in which a decision is made about a student's guilt in breaking a school rule

J. test for equality of treatment that requires that the methods selected by government that involve unequal treatment must be substantially related to accomplishing the stated goal part of the government, they are subject to restrictions on governmental conduct. However, if the search is conducted at the request of the police, a search warrant should normally be issued.

4. The Family Educational Rights and Privacy Act provides that parents of minors should have access to most of the child's educational records, especially grades, conduct evaluations, and teachers' comments. The child acquires this right when he or she reaches 18.

5. The four types of situations under the jurisdiction of juvenile courts are: (1) those who have violated criminal laws, (2) those whose conduct is out of control, (3) those who are abandoned or abused by their parents, and (4) those whose parents are unable to provide for their children.

6. Minors are legally responsible for their torts if their age and mental capacity are considered to be reasonable for their actions. However, contracts made by minors are void-

able, so a minor who breaches a contract cannot be held liable for the contract.

Applying the Law . . . You Be the Judge (Answers)

1. Both the district court and the appeals court concluded that the only thing done improperly was the strip-search of Diane. The court of appeals said, "It does not require a constitutional scholar to conclude that a nude search of a 13-year-old child is an invasion of constitutional rights of some magnitude. More than that: It is a violation of any known principle of human decency." Sniffing of student lockers and cars was not considered a search because it occurred when the lockers and cars were unattended and in public view.

2. The justices determined that the intent of the Eighth Amendment was to protect those convicted of crimes. For this reason, the Eighth Amendment was deemed inapplicable to corporal punishment of school-children. As to due process, the court said, "We conclude that the Due Process clause does not require notice and a hearing prior to the imposition of corporal punishment in the public schools, as that practice is authorized and limited by common law." In a later case, (Miera v. Garcia, 56 USLW 3390 [1987]), the Tenth Circuit Court of Appeals ruled that "grossly excessive" corporal punishment may indeed constitute a violation of substantive due process rights.

◆ CHECKING FOR COMPREHENSION

1. How does a citizen become an emancipated minor and what rights does he or she acquire as a result of emancipation?

2. Are due process requirements fixed in instances where students violate school discipline rules? Explain.

3. Can a student's person, property, or locker be searched while at school? Explain.

4. What are the provisions of the Family Educational Rights and Privacy Act?

5. What four types of situations relating to minors are under the jurisdiction of juvenile courts?

6. A minor is personally responsible for torts he or she commits, unless there is a question of reasonableness. Explain.

◆ APPLYING LEGAL CONCEPTS

1. Write a set of disciplinary rules, along with consequences, for your class. Write one or two sentences explaining why, in your opinion, each rule is important.

2. Acquire records from your school district about the number of students who have been suspended in the last year. Design a line graph showing how many students were suspended each month.

◆ APPLYING THE LAW . . . YOU BE THE JUDGE

1. For two and one-half hours junior and senior high-school students in Highland, Indiana, waited in their seats while six officials using trained dogs searched the 2,780 students for drugs. A school official, police officer, dog handler, and German shepherd entered the classroom where Diane Doe, thirteen, was a student. The dog went up and down the aisles sniffing students. The dog reached Diane, sniffed her body, and repeatedly pushed its nose on her and between her legs. The officer understood this behavior to be an "alert" signaling the presence of drugs. Diane emptied her pockets as requested, but no drugs were found. Still the dog kept sniffing her. Finally, Diane was taken to the nurse's office and strip-searched. No drugs were found. Diane had played with her own dog before school. Her dog was in heat and this smell remaining on her body

had alerted the police dog. Did the school officials have a right to use a dog to search the school? Did they have a right to search Diane? [*Doe v. Renfrow*, 635 F. 2d 582 (7th Cir. 1980), cert denied, 101 U.S. 3015 (1981)]

2. James Ingraham and Roosevelt Andrews were junior high school students in Florida. Because Ingraham had been slow to respond to the teacher's instructions, he received twenty paddle swats administered in the principal's office. As a consequence, he needed medical treatment and missed a few days of school. Andrews was paddled also, but less severely. Is the use of corporal punishment a violation of the Eighth Amendment barring cruel and unusual punishment? Is prior notice and some form of due process required before administering punishment? [*Ingraham v. Wright*, 430 U.S. 651 (1977)]

Mastery Objectives

By the end of this chapter, students will be able to:
* Describe the marriage contract
* Delineate the legal rights and obligations of marriage
* Explain the legal processes involved in dissolution of a marriage
* Discuss the legal questions involved with property distribution, spousal support, and child custody and support as it relates to dissolution of a marriage
* Describe agreements that modify the marriage contract

LEGAL BACKGROUND

The law begins its relationship with families at the marriage ceremony, which is a legal, as well as social, event. The law is in this instance part of a joyous occasion. Unfortunately, except for adoption, most other situations involving the family and law are not celebrations. The law is in the background for this most important of social relationships. When called to the forefront, it's usually because something challenging family harmony has occurred. In other words, family law is about divorce, annulment, custody of children, spousal support, prenuptial agreements, parental rights and duties, cohabitation, spousal abuse, and other topics. These are tough topics, but very important ones. You might also note that these discussions all arrive with a considerable amount of differing social opinion.

642

Chapter

Family Law

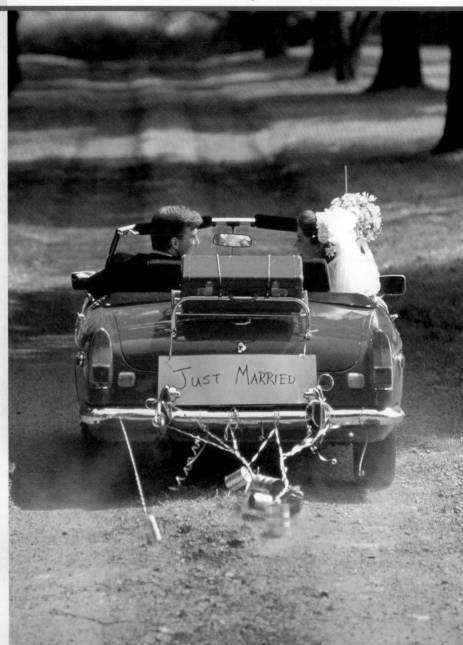

Activity Sheets
Reviewing Legal Concepts 27 *TRB*
Enrichment Activity 27 *TRB*

Student Activity Workbook
Chapter 27 Activities

Tests
Chapter 27 Test *TRB*
Chapter 27 WESTEST Computerized Testing

Handbook of Selected Court Cases
*In re Marriage of McElwee, Doris McElwee
v. Charles McElwee*

**West's Business Law and Legal
Environment Videodisc**
Still Frames and Motion Segments as shown

Enrichment

Brainstorm ideas about why some researchers believe that a strong family structure is critically important for determining economic well-being. Write the ideas on the board; then divide the class into groups of five, and tell each group to analyze the ideas and discuss their implications.

Enrichment

Encourage students to speak with their parents, their friends, and others and ask them for a definition of marriage. Allow students to share the responses with the class. Compare these definitions of marriage with the rather legalistic definition used here. What does this say about our views of marriage? Are these views more shaped by social and religious customs than by legalities?

Legal Focus Problem

Have a student volunteer read this Legal Focus Problem aloud to the class. Ask the volunteer to share a possible answer to the question posed at the end of this problem.

Family Law 643

"In this country today, family structure is the most important determinant of economic standing—more important than race, geography, anything else."

**Karl Zinsmeister,
Scholar from the American Enterprise Institute**

The desire to be happy is universal. The ways in which every individual discovers happiness are limitless. Throughout time and across all nations, though, most individuals find a tremendous amount of joy and happiness within their families. The family, the smallest of our social units, is for most countries the most important. Some researchers, such as Professor Zinsmeister in the above quote, even believe that a strong family structure is critically important for determining economic well-being. Although modern ideas about the family evolve, most Americans will marry and raise children. Unless you are in the statistical minority, you will someday get married. You will someday be a parent and provide a role model for your children. While the law defines many of the rights and duties among husbands and wives, as well as among parents and their children, much of what goes on in the family is not touched by the law. In fact, a well-functioning family never has to think about the legal aspects of what is called domestic law. Sometimes families don't stay together, and that is when knowledge of the law, as it concerns family relations, is important. A good place to start a study of this type of law is with the marriage contract.

◆ THE MARRIAGE CONTRACT

The U.S. Bureau of the Census reports that more than ninety percent of Americans marry at some time in their lives. For most, marriage is a relationship based on faith, custom, and religion. For all, it is a relationship that is also based on law; it is a type of contract. One definition of **marriage** is the legal union of husband and wife. This legal relationship is based on state rather than federal law. Each state has its own legal requirements for marriage. Once two people are married, the law provides certain rights and protections to each party based on marital status. For example, marital partners gain rights in property acquired during the marriage.

◆ **marriage** The legal union of husband and wife.

◆ LEGAL FOCUS – PROBLEM

Naomi Naice and Martin Neiderhasen were in the middle of completing their wedding vows at their church before their families and close friends. During the exchange of the vows, Martin collapsed. He died on the way to the hospital without regaining consciousness. What legal difference will it make whether the vows had been completed before Martin's death?

Critical Thinking Activity

Tell students to write one or two paragraphs explaining why marriage is a relationship that is based on law. Explain the contractual relationship.

Discussion Starter

Stimulate a class discussion by asking the following questions: At what age do you feel the law should allow two people to marry? At what age do you think most people are socially and psychologically ready to marry? Why?

Critical Thinking Activity

Point out to the students that many states allow 16-year-old individuals to marry if they have parental consent. Tell the students to write one paragraph explaining how, based on what they know about minors and contract law, a 16-year-old married couple might face greater obstacles than an 18-year-old married couple. Allow volunteers to share their papers with the class.

Legal Focus Example

Have a student volunteer read this Legal Focus Example aloud to the class. Ask the volunteer how this example of the form and documentation required for a marriage compares to the writing and form requirements for many contracts.

644

Ethical Concern

Guide the students in examining the Legal Focus Problem from the previous page and the first paragraph on this page, where students discover that the Legal Focus Problem is based on an actual dispute between an alleged spouse and the surviving parents. Do you think that in this case, Naice should be accorded the same rights that she would have been accorded had the vows been completed? Why or why not? Do you think the parents were correct in trying to deny Naice those rights? Do you think the court would be fair in denying Naice those rights?

Whether the vows were completed can be very important if Martin owned property. Obviously, there was no time for Naomi and Martin to have acquired any property as a married couple. However, Martin may well have had ample separate property at the time of the marriage. Naomi's right to Martin's separate property is affected by whether the marriage took place. A surviving spouse has significant rights in the property of a deceased spouse. This is particularly true if the deceased spouse leaves no will. Whether or not the marriage was of short duration is irrelevant. If the vows were not complete and there was no marriage, Martin's parents will probably inherit, and Naomi will get nothing. Thus, ten seconds can make a big difference. This seemingly absurd example is based on an actual dispute between an alleged spouse and the surviving parents.

LEGAL AGE TO MARRY

In every state, a person must meet a minimum age requirement in order to marry. The typical minimum age for marriage is eighteen. Many states, however, allow a sixteen-year-old to marry if he or she has parental consent. If the parents are divorced or separated, the parent who has custody of the child usually can grant consent. If the child has a guardian, the guardian is the party authorized to give permission. Some states allow even younger minors to marry once they have shown good cause, received parental consent, and been granted approval by the court. See the Resource Center for a table of the laws of marriage in each state.

OTHER LEGAL REQUIREMENTS OF MARRIAGE

 LEGAL FOCUS ~ EXAMPLE

Marriage is a personal relation arising out of a civil contract, to which the consent of the parties capable of making that contract is necessary. Consent alone will not constitute marriage; it must be followed by the issuance of a license and solemnized as authorized. (California Civil Code §4100.)

As we have said, the legal requirements for marriage vary from state to state. The legal requirements of the state of Pennsylvania are typical. Both parties must be age eighteen unless permission is granted by the parents or the court. The parties must be examined by a physician. The physician must certify that neither of the parties has syphilis, a sexually transmitted disease. Applicants must apply for a marriage license with the clerk of the family court and pay the required fee. The applicants must then wait three days before they can be married. The waiting period is designed to discourage parties who decide to marry on a whim. The marriage must be solemnized, which is the reciting of an oath of marriage before a mayor, judge, alderman (local politician), minister, rabbi, or priest.

Multicultural

Perspectives

Ask a volunteer to research marriage age requirements in other countries and compare those findings to U.S. requirements. Have the student report his or her findings to the class in the form of an oral report.

All states prohibit marriage between persons of the same sex. Also prohibited are marriages between members of an immediate family, such as brothers and sisters or parents and children. Many states also prohibit marriage between other close relatives, such as an uncle and niece or an aunt and nephew.

 LEGAL FOCUS ~ PROBLEM

Fern Hall is planning to marry Jack Hanna at the end of next month. She is curious about whether she is legally required to take Jack's last name (which is called his *surname*). Is a wife legally required to take her husband's name?

Many attributes of marriage are based on custom rather than law; in the United States, the taking of the husband's name by the wife has been the usual custom. Fern is not legally required to take Jack's name. She can keep her own name or use his name in combination with hers (Fern Hall-Hanna) if she wishes.

Common Law Marriage   Fifteen states, listed in Exhibit 27-1, and the District of Columbia recognize a type of marriage that exists without meeting the requirement of a license or a formal ceremony. This is known as a **common law marriage**. Texas is typical of those states that recognize a common law marriage. Texas requires that the parties have the legal capacity to marry, give the impression in the community that they are married, and agree to be married. The longer the relationship, the more likely it will be recognized as a common law marriage.

Article IV, Section 1, of the U.S. Constitution provides: "Full faith and credit shall be given in each state to the public acts, records, and judicial proceedings of every other state." The effect of the "full faith and credit" provision is that a marriage valid in one state must be recognized in the other states.

◆ **common law marriage** An informal marriage occurring without a marriage license when persons agree to be married, live together as husband and wife, and hold themselves out to the community as married. This type of marriage is recognized in fifteen states.

LEGAL FOCUS ~ PROBLEM

Bill Farney and Tina Willis lived together in Galveston, Texas, for eleven years as husband and wife. Everyone thought they were legally married, but they had neglected to purchase a license and have a marriage ceremony. Tina was transferred to a new job in California, and the family followed. Tina was killed in an automobile accident and died without leaving a will. Bill's right to the property of the relationship depends on whether they were married. California law does not recognize a common law marriage. Were Bill and Tina married?

Legal Focus Problem

Have a student volunteer read the first Legal Focus Problem aloud to the class. Ask the volunteer to suggest a possible answer to the question posed at the end of this problem. As a followup you might ask the volunteer whether or not he or she feels that a wife should take her husband's surname as her own. Why or why not?

Discussion Starter

Ask the students if they have ever heard the term *common law marriage* before. How was it used? Are common law marriages accepted in the same way as traditional marriages by society? Why or why not?

Legal Focus Problem

Have a student volunteer read aloud the Legal Focus Problem found at the bottom on this page. Make sure students understand that the question posed at the end of this problem, "Were Bill and Tina married?", refers to a legalistic argument rather than a religious and/or social argument.

Multicultural Perspectives

Anthropologists have defined two sets of rules that govern marriages among the many different cultures of our world. The first set of rules is termed *exogamous* rules. Exogamy means "outmarriage." Exogamous rules are those rules that prohibit an individual from marrying within his or her own family or other kin group. In some cases exogamous rules also prohibit marriage within the same village or settlement. Exogamous rules are related to the incest taboo. It is interesting to know that exogamous rules often apply to large kin groups with hundreds of members—i.e., no one in the kin group can marry any other member, although many of these individuals are not biologically related. Another kind of marriage rules are *endogamous* rules. Endogamous means "inmarriage." In cultures with endogamous rules, an individual *must* marry someone in his or her own social group. The caste society of traditional Hindu India is a classic example of a culture in which endogamous rules applied. Endogamous rules were instituted to maintain social barriers between groups of people of different social rank.

646

Extension Activity

Ask volunteers to find articles in periodicals about palimony suits and report the circumstances and outcomes to the class.

Teaching Note

The complete text of the U.S. Constitution, including Article IV, Section 1, in which the "full faith and credit" clause can be found, is included in the Resource Center at the back of this text. You might ask students if they can think of any other ways in which the full faith and credit provision of Article IV, Section 1 might apply.

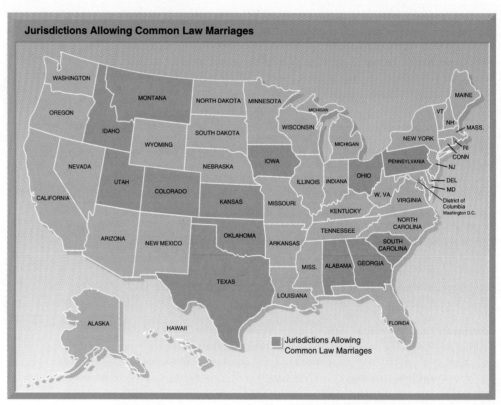

EXHIBIT 27-1
JURISDICTIONS ALLOWING COMMON LAW MARRIAGES

Although California does not recognize a common law marriage, the marriage between Tina and Bill appears valid. Tina and Bill had met the requirements of a common law marriage in the state of Texas before they moved to California. California is bound by the U.S. Constitution to recognize the Texas marriage.

LIVING TOGETHER OUTSIDE OF MARRIAGE

Living together outside of marriage is called *cohabitation*. Until the latter part of the 1970's, such conduct was considered criminal in most states. Today there are still many states that consider cohabitation illegal. Sexual relations between unmarried persons are also a crime in many states. These laws are seldom enforced, but if they are, they often carry stiff fines and jail sentences.

Some states have recognized that property rights exist in some nonmarital living arrangements. Parties may create an agreement regarding the di-

You might wish to call on a female volunteer to read the first paragraph under Property Rights and Obligations of a Spouse. Ask your volunteer to discuss the ethics of this legal condition, which existed until recently. You might also ask your volunteer whether or not this fact surprises her.

Read aloud the following sentence from the student text: "From a legal point of view, marriage creates a continuing and mutual obligation of support for each spouse for the other." Stimulate a class discussion of this point by asking the following questions: Does marriage create a continuing and mutual obligation of support from a social point of view? Does marriage create a continuing and mutual obligation of support from a religious point of view?

Reteaching Activity

Have the students work with partners to read and discuss the definitions of separate property and marital property found here. Each pair of students should then write one Legal Focus Example for separate property and one Legal Focus Example for marital property. Allow volunteers to share their examples with the class.

vision of property if the relationship should end. Some courts will honor these agreements. The term *palimony* was created by journalists to describe financial support of a partner or other property arrangements honored by the courts after the termination of a living arrangement. The majority of states still do not recognize property rights based on parties living together without being married.

LEGAL RIGHTS AND OBLIGATIONS OF MARRIAGE

In most marriages, there is never any question of each spouse providing for the other. That is to say, in most marriages there is a definite understanding that the husband and wife work together for the benefit of each other and for the benefit of the family. Indeed, much of the joy of a marriage is making one's partner happy. From a legal point of view, marriage creates a continuing and mutual obligation of support for each spouse for the other. This support includes providing food, shelter, clothing, medicine, and nonessential items, all in a way that is consistent with family wealth and the family's established standard of living. Courts seldom become involved in issues of support unless the marriage is ending or one spouse has left the other. Married couples also have mutual rights and obligations in marital property and raising children.

PROPERTY RIGHTS AND OBLIGATIONS OF A SPOUSE

Common Law States   Until recently, in common law states, all property owned by a woman automatically became her husband's property when they married. During the marriage, the wife owned no property.

Forty-one states now recognize a modernized version of the common law concept of marital property. These states have adopted parts of the Uniform Marriage and Divorce Act, which distinguishes between separate and marital property. **Separate property** is all property owned by one of the spouses before the marriage or received by a spouse during the marriage by gift or inheritance. Separate property usually remains the property of the owning spouse during the marriage. **Marital property** is property acquired during the marriage. The law views the modern marriage as a partnership with regard to marital property. How this property is treated if a marriage ends is discussed later in this chapter.

Community Property States   Nine states[1] have adopted the concept of **community property**. Community property is a form of property ownership that evolved in Spain. In community property states, all property acquired during a marriage by the husband or wife, other than by gift or

---

◆ **separate property**
Property individually owned by one spouse. Separate property usually remains separate even after marriage.

◆ **marital property**
Property owned by a wife and husband jointly. Usually this property is acquired during, not before, the marriage.

◆ **community property** All property acquired (in a community property state) by the husband or wife during a marriage other than property acquired by gift or inheritance.

---

1. Arizona, California, Idaho, Louisiana, Nevada, New Mexico, Texas, Washington, and Wisconsin; also Puerto Rico.

Legal Focus Problem

Allow a volunteer to read aloud this Legal Focus Problem dealing with marital debts. Ask the volunteer to suggest a possible answer to the questions posed at the end of this problem. Ask the volunteer whether he or she feels this is fair. Why or why not?

inheritance, is community property. The earnings of either spouse are owned equally when they are received. Spouses generally have equal rights to control and manage the community property. Neither spouse has the right to give away community property without the agreement of the other spouse. Separate property can be given by one spouse to the other. When a spouse commingles separate property with community property, the separate property is often considered to be a gift to the other spouse.

◆ LEGAL FOCUS – EXAMPLE

Commingling happens when separate property is mixed with community property. For example, the wife has a bank account before the marriage. After the marriage, the account is used to pay community bills, and the couple's earnings are also deposited in the account. The property will become mixed. A court would conclude that the wife intended to give the husband half her separate property. The moral is that separate property must be kept physically separate if a spouse wants it to remain legally separate.

In general, in either community or common law states, the property of the marriage can be used to pay the debts of the marriage.

◆ LEGAL FOCUS – PROBLEM

Fred and Mary are married, and both of them work. Mary is paid $5,000 a month, and Fred is paid $2,000. Mary is seriously injured; she cannot work, but she has medical bills of several thousand dollars. They are now both living on Fred's salary. Can the creditors owed because of Mary's medical bills seek payment out of Fred's earnings?

Yes. The medical bills are a marital debt, and Fred's income is marital income. It should not matter whether this is a common law or community property state; the answer should be the same.

◆ LEGAL RIGHTS AND OBLIGATIONS OF PARENTHOOD

State laws impose the obligation on parents to support their children until the children are adults. The duty to support a child may also end if the child becomes emancipated while he or she is still a minor.

In most states, child support is a joint obligation. It may, however, be divided between the parents according to their respective financial circumstances.

Extension Activity

You might wish to ask a health teacher or a biology teacher from your school to speak to your class regarding surrogate mothers and test-tube babies. When were these processes invented? With what type of reaction were these processes met? How did society react? How did the medical community react? Have your students prepare questions for your speaker in advance.

Teaching Note

Like many topics dealing with families, adoption can be a sensitive issue in the classroom. This is especially true if any of your students were adopted themselves.

Extension Activity

In early 1993, a number of adoption cases were disputed based on racial compatibility questions. Ask volunteers to use periodical accounts to research the disputes and discover the circumstances surrounding the disputes. Tell them to write the facts and to report on developments and/or results.

Checking Your Progress (Answers)

1. Eighteen. States do have different age requirements, sometimes based on gender. A minor can often marry at an earlier age with parental permission.
2. No, only 15 states allow a common law marriage. However, all states must recognize a marriage that has been validly created in another state.
3. There are no differences. Once a child is adopted, he or she has exactly the same rights as a child born to a parent.

Parents have the right to custody of their children, and both parents have the right to an equal say in decisions about their children.

RECENT DEVELOPMENTS IN PARENTHOOD

Legal rules typically develop after decades, if not centuries, of experience with social conditions and relationships. Laws are usually consistent with the dominant social customs. When science dramatically changes the nature of the human condition, those changes place difficult tests on legal theory. For example, it is now medically possible to create life without sexual contact and to conceive a child in a test tube. This means that the issues of who is the mother and who is the father of such a child become more complex. The laws of most states are changing in an attempt to deal with parenthood issues raised by these new techniques of creating life.

ADOPTION

Adoption is a legal process that creates a parent–child relationship. After adoption, a child has the same rights and duties as a child who is born to the parent or parents. The parent, likewise, has identical rights and duties to the adoptive child as he or she would to a child born of that parent.

The adoption process is regulated by the state, and parents who wish to adopt must comply with state laws. Children are made available for adoption through public agencies and licensed private agencies. A child can be adopted if its parents are unknown, if they are both dead, or if parental rights are renounced.

Many states require that a child over the age of twelve must consent to the adoption before it can take place. The factors considered by the courts to approve an adoption include:

- The jobs, earnings, and stability of the prospective parents.
- The medical, emotional, and physical needs of the child.
- The "clean" record of adoptive parents (that is, neither parent has a criminal record or record of child abuse).
- The age of the child.
- Whether adoption is by a married couple.
- Religious and racial compatibility and the social problems the child may face if adopted by a person of a different race or faith.

◆ **adoption** A legal process through which a person assumes the responsibility of parenthood for a child.

◆ CHECKING YOUR PROGRESS

1. What is the typical minimum legal age to marry in the United States?
2. Do all states allow common law marriages?
3. How are the rights of adoptive children different from children born to a married couple?

Read

Introduce this *Law in Action* feature by reminding the students that basically the discussion of marriage in this chapter has related to the legal aspects of marriage. Marriages, however, are also bound by social and cultural factors. Explain to students that in this *Law in Action* feature they will be looking at marriage in other cultures.

Discuss

Stimulate a class discussion of this *Law in Action* feature by asking the students the following questions: How do customs, traditions, and social practices affect marriage? Do you feel that marriages arranged by families are fair to the married couple? Why or why not? Why do Japanese couples generally marry late? What other marriage customs from other countries are you familiar with?

Law in Action

INTERNATIONAL PERSPECTIVES: MARRIAGE IN OTHER CULTURES

Rachael, looking lovingly at Ryan, finished her oath, " I take you, Ryan, to be my lawful wedded husband." Ryan, barely restraining his joy, said "And I take you, Rachel, to be my lawful wedded wife." They sealed their vows with a tender kiss. This scene sounds familiar to each of us, but it would be strange indeed to people in other parts of the world. This is because marriage customs vary dramatically from country to country in the world. Many of us accept without question, basic beliefs in social institutions, like marriage, only to be surprised to find very different attitudes in other places. Usually, views on marriage are based on the beliefs of that country's dominant religion. However, not only religion, but age-old customs and traditions affect the law, and the social practices in each country. The importance of age and love in marriage in some other countries are the subject of this *Law in Action*.

The age of eighteen is the common age for adulthood in much of the world. Not only does an eighteen-year-old generally gain the capacity to contract, but the right to marry, as well. Given the age differences allowed in states, it should not be surprising that, although eighteen is the common age, some countries have different age requirements. For example, in Argentina, a person cannot marry until twenty-one without parental consent. With parental consent, a female can marry at sixteen and a male can marry at eighteen. In Turkey, a female of fifteen and a male of seventeen can marry

without parental consent. China expects couples to be older, the legal age for marriage is twenty-two for a male and twenty for a female. In Pakistan, a male must be eighteen and a female sixteen in order to marry. However, if a couple marries before the legal age, the parents of the minor children, and the officials conducting the marriage ceremony, are subject to legal penalties, but the marriage is valid.

The reasons why a mate is selected and the method of that selection also differ dramatically in different parts of the world. In the United States, and in most western European nations, marriages are usually based on romantic love. The American public has an enormous appetite for songs, books, and movies about romantic love. However, a large percentage of the world's people believes love before marriage is a lousy basis for a decision to marry. In many countries, marriages are based on factors other than love. Indeed often, couples do not even know one another before the engagement or, in some cases, even the marriage.

For example, in Hindu societies, a marriage by mutual choice between Hindu couples is seen as improper. Instead, marriages are arranged by families. Hinduism is a complex religion, dominant in the country of India, with over 80 percent of India's inhabitants practicing it. It is also a common religion in Sri Lanka, Malaysia, Singapore, Pakistan, and parts of east Africa. The main concern in arranging a Hindu marriage is finding a suitable *bahus*, a daughter-in-law, who is compatible with the husband's family. Most marriages are very durable, perhaps in part, because remarriage is not common

Law in Action (Continued)

in a Hindu society. The requirement of a dowry is common in most Hindu societies, although the practice is often technically illegal. A dowry is a payment of money, or property, by one family to the other family in consideration of marriage. In Hindu society, the payment is from the family of the bride to the family of the groom.

In Japan, men and women are legally able to marry at the age of twenty without parental permission. However, in Japan, ritual and custom are often more important than law. Generally, Japanese couples marry late. For example, the woman is expected to reach *tekireiki*, a suitable age for marriage, which is more likely to be around twenty-five years old. *Tekireiki* for the male is usually three years older than the female, or around twenty-eight. The Japanese also put little store in romance as part of courtship. Instead, family background and standing, intelligence, and education are a more important part of match making than love. Advertising for potential mates and the use of marriage bureaus is commonplace and

socially accepted. The idea of marriage without parental approval and acceptance of the mate is generally socially unthinkable. It is also common that families hire detectives to investigate the background of potential in-laws.

In Muslim societies, religious rules of marriage are often made part of the legal rules of marriage in the country. Arranged marriages are common and dowries are generally legal. However, in the Muslim society, the groom pays the dowry to the father of the bride. Modesty is expected of Muslim women. A woman at puberty is expected to become veiled and wear very conservative clothing covering her entire body (to the neck, the ankle, and below the elbow). Marriages are arranged by the family, often with little or no contact between the bride and groom before the marriage. In many Muslim societies, polygamy is legal, with the husband allowed four wives if he gives to each wife equal material goods and companionship.

 ## TERMINATION OF A MARRIAGE

Alarming statistics about the frequency of marital breakups are well known. At the turn of the century, there was one divorce for every twelve marriages. In recent years, the rate has been one divorce for every two marriages. There are many reasons for the increased rate of divorce, including the fact that people are living longer. Even though the divorce rate is much higher today than it was, say 200 years ago, the average marriage today lasts for twenty-five years. The average marriage several hundred years ago, when divorce was virtually unheard of, lasted only fifteen years. Whatever the reasons, ending, or *dissolving*, a marriage is a legal process. All states provide a means of dissolving a marriage. The historic term for the termination of a marriage is **divorce**. Many states now refer to the termination of a marriage as a **dissolution**.

◆ **dissolution or divorce** A termination of a marriage by court order.

Critical Thinking Activity

Ask a student volunteer to recall where he or she has heard the term *dissolution* before. (Students should recall that *dissolution* was used in the discussion of termination of a partnership.) Explain how a business partnership is similar to a marriage. How is the breakup of a business partnership similar to the breakup of a marriage?

State Law

In Texas, the Texas Family Code recognizes the following grounds for divorce: insupportability, cruelty, adultery, felony conviction, abandonment, living apart, and confinement in a mental hospital. In the case of Texas, insupportability occurs when discord or conflict of personalities destroys the legitimate ends of a marital relationship and there is no reasonable expectation of reconciliation. Generally speaking, this insupportability ground for divorce acts as a no-fault ground for divorce in the state of Texas.

A high divorce rate creates many single parent families.

GROUNDS FOR DISSOLUTION

Most states provide for the end of a marriage with what are called *no-fault dissolution* laws. A no-fault law allows either spouse to dissolve a marriage without having to prove that the other party is a wrongdoer and without having to explain what went wrong with the marriage. In most states, the legal reason for a dissolution is "irreconcilable differences"—in other words, the parties can no longer get along.

Either the husband or the wife can file for the dissolution. It is granted after testimony that the marriage has broken down and that there is no chance to repair the relationship. The dissolution process requires that the spouse bringing the action be a resident of the state in which the dissolution is sought. After filing for a dissolution, the couple usually has to wait about six months before the dissolution is final.

Before no-fault divorce laws were common, a spouse seeking a dissolution had to prove some wrongful conduct by the other spouse. Grounds for divorce included adultery—where the accused spouse has participated in sexual relations with another party—or physical or mental cruelty, where the accused spouse's behavior makes continuation of the marriage impossible.

The fault system was abandoned because it was difficult to prove wrongful conduct. Many problems arose. For example, often parties who both wished for a divorce would fabricate grounds to get it. Sometimes one party would actually force the other party to give him or her major property or support advantages in exchange for going through with the divorce. Even in these situations, parties might lie about whether the legal

Critical Thinking Activity

Tell students to write a paragraph explaining the differences between a divorce and an annulment. Have them explain in a second paragraph why one would be chosen over the other.

Legal Focus Problem

Have a student volunteer read this Legal Focus Problem aloud to the class. Ask a volunteer to suggest a possible answer to the question posed at the end of this problem. Then have that volunteer read aloud the paragraph immediately following this Legal Focus Problem.

grounds for divorce actually existed. Before modern divorce laws, many wives or husbands traveled to foreign countries or states such as Nevada where the requirements for a divorce were easier to satisfy. Eventually, most lawmakers recognized that it did not make sense to require people to remain married if neither wished to be married.

ANNULMENT

If the marriage agreement is based on fraud, one of the parties can seek an **annulment**. An annulment is a declaration by a court that a previously recognized marriage is really void. As the marriage is void, it is usually treated as if it never existed. Besides fraud, other reasons for annulment include incest (marriage between close relatives), bigamy (one spouse is already married), mental incapacity or insanity, intoxication, or physical incapacity to consummate the marriage (inability to have sexual intercourse).

◆ **annulment** A court order canceling a marriage because some defect existed when the marriage was begun.

◆ LEGAL FOCUS ~ PROBLEM

Carl, aged twenty-one, and Mary, aged seventeen, met on the second day of Mardi Gras in New Orleans. They had a whirlwind courtship and fell madly in love. They discussed marriage, and each said that they wanted to have a family with up to six children. They took and passed a blood test and tried to get married immediately in Louisiana. Louisiana, however, required a three-day waiting period after getting the license, and they could not bear to wait. Instead, they drove to Texas where they were married. Several weeks later, both Mary and Carl were having second thoughts about the marriage. Mary had discovered that Carl hated children and had never really intended to have any. Mary, although of legal age in Louisiana, was too young to marry in Texas without her parents' consent. She had lied about her age on the Texas marriage license. Also, Carl had been married before to Sue, and although Sue had filed for divorce, the divorce was not yet final when he married Mary. Do grounds for an annulment exist?

Yes, several grounds exist for an annulment, and each of them alone is sufficient to dissolve the marriage. Carl's lie to Mary about the desire to have children is fraud. It is a misrepresentation of a fact that is material to the marriage decision. The misrepresentation of age by Mary is also fraud. In addition, Mary, without her parents' permission, lacked capacity to marry in Texas, where the marriage took place. Finally, as Carl's marriage to Mary occurred before his divorce to Sue was final, he committed the crime of bigamy. The second marriage is illegal and is thus void.

PROPERTY DISTRIBUTION

Often the husband and wife in a dissolution are able to agree to a property settlement. If the wife and husband agree to a division of property, the courts almost always approve the agreement.

Multicultural Perspectives MC

Have a few volunteers research other countries' views on marriage and marital property. Then have the volunteers share their findings with the rest of the class. Stimulate a discussion on the different countries' laws. Some suggested countries are: Great Britain, Italy, Japan, Mexico, and Saudi Arabia.

Read

Introduce this *Law in Action* feature by explaining to the class that the distribution of joint property is often a very difficult task. For the divorcing couple, it can be even more difficult, as decisions can be affected by the emotions that generally accompany a divorce. Explain to the students that this *Law in Action* feature deals with some court decisions regarding distribution of marital property.

Extension Activity

Have student volunteers research your state's divorce laws to determine whether or not you live in a community property state. Allow volunteers an opportunity to share their findings with the class in the form of oral reports.

Discuss

Stimulate a class discussion of this *Law in Action* feature by asking the following questions: How is property distributed in community property states? What property was in question in the *O'Brien* v. *O'Brien* case? What property was at stake in *McGowan* v. *McGowan?* Can you think of any other examples of "property" that might also be hard to distribute after the dissolution of a marriage?

654   Personal Law

Law in Action

LAW IN YOUR LIFE: JOINT PROPERTY—TO A DEGREE

Who owns what property is a serious question during a dissolution or divorce proceeding. Family law judges have to decide which spouse gets which assets after the dissolution of the marriage. In community property states, all property acquired after marriage is owned equally by each spouse. In virtually all other states, when a marriage ends, there is to be an "equitable" distribution of the household's property.

The term *equitable*, of course, has no objective definition. And even if it did, the decision would still have to be made as to what assets are subject to division during a divorce proceeding. Is the value of a professional license to practice psychotherapy, say, part of the marital property to be divided?

Yes, according to the New York Court of Appeals in *O'Brien v. O'Brien*.[2] What about a simple academic degree earned during the marriage by one party with the financial assistance of the other? Is such a degree to be considered distributable marital property? Yes again, said the New York Court of Appeals in *McGowan v. McGowan*.[3] On the other hand, a teaching certificate earned by a spouse *shortly after marriage* is not to be treated as marital property. Why? Because the certificate was the result of the person's educational efforts that took place before the marriage.

2. 66 N.Y.2d 576, 489 N.E.2d 712, 498 N.Y.S.2d 743 (1985).
3. 142 A.D.2d 355, 535 N.Y.S.2d 990 (1988).

If the parties cannot reach an agreement, the court hearing the dissolution has the power to divide the property. The nature of the division is dependent on many factors. The most important factor may be how the property of a marriage is treated in that particular state. In common law states, the court generally has the power to divide the property of a marriage based on the judge's notion of fairness. This is called an *equitable distribution*. In some common law states, a judge also has the power to give the separate property of one spouse to the other spouse when a marriage is dissolved to achieve an equitable distribution.

In a community property state, both husband and wife own fifty percent of the community property. A judge can only divide the property in a way that is consistent with that fifty-fifty ownership and must allow each spouse to retain his or her separate property. The issues in property settlement disputes in a community property state usually revolve around deciding what is community property, determining the value of assets, and deciding who will pay any debts.

◆ **alimony or spousal support** A continuing payment of money by one spouse for the living expenses of the other spouse.

ALIMONY OR SPOUSAL SUPPORT

Among the issues to be decided in a dissolution is whether one of the spouses needs and should be awarded **alimony**. Alimony is also referred to as maintenance and **spousal support**. Alimony payments may be awarded

Teaching Note

As with many family issues, the issue of child custody and support may be a very sensitive issue for your classroom.

Family Law   655

Critical Thinking Activity

Have the students write a short paper, one to two paragraphs in length, describing the differences between alimony and child support. Have volunteers share their work with the class.

by a court for a spouse after that spouse shows a genuine need. The majority of states do not consider marital fault important in determining whether or not alimony should be awarded. The factors that are considered include:

- The financial condition of the spouse seeking support payments.
- The length of the marriage.
- The age, health, education, and station in life of each spouse.
- The occupation, vocational skills, and employability of the requesting spouse.
- The contributions of each in acquiring or maintaining marital property.
- The need of the parent with whom the children will live to occupy the marital home.
- Tax considerations.

There are different types of alimony. *Permanent alimony* is an award of alimony without an ending date. *Limited-term alimony* ends after a specified period of time. Limited-term alimony may be rehabilitative—that is, it may allow one spouse to retrain or to gain new working skills. The modern trend is for courts to provide limited-term alimony, particularly when the marriage was of short duration or when the spouse has marketable working skills. All alimony awards are subject to reconsideration by the court if either person's circumstances change, such as through a new marriage or a new job. Most states allow alimony to be available to either spouse without reference to gender—in other words, either the husband or the wife can receive alimony.

CHILD CUSTODY AND SUPPORT

If the lives of a husband and wife are disrupted when they divorce, so, too, are the lives of their children. The existence of minor children brings up major issues in a dissolution, including the question of which parent should get custody. Other issues include what amount of support the non-custodial parent should pay to assist in the child's care. One serious reality in the United States is that a divorce often brings severe economic challenges and hardship. In the typical divorce, the man becomes single, and the woman becomes a single mother. Studies show that half the poor families in America are headed by single women.

Courts must decide issues of child custody along with the other issues of dissolution. If the parties can resolve the issue through agreement, the court will almost always approve. If the parties cannot resolve issues of custody or support, the court must take over. The standard used to decide child custody is what is "in the best interests of the child." Since these decisions are made by a family court, which is a court of equity, they are generally made by one judge. The judge may hear testimony from both spouses, witnesses for the parties, and court-appointed counselors. If the children are older, they are often allowed to express their wishes.

The custody standards provided in the Uniform Marriage and Divorce Act (adopted by forty-four states) are the following:

655

Invite a representative from the local family court to speak to your class on the issues of alimony, child custody, and child support. Ask the speaker to share any guidelines or rules the court uses in determining alimony, child custody, and child support. Have your students prepare questions for the speaker in advance.

You might ask a representative from the local district attorney or prosecuting attorney's office to speak to your class regarding the steps taken to enforce child support orders. The speaker should address the size of the issue, the laws that exist to help secure child support payments, and the amount of time and effort his or her office expends to enforce child support agreements. Have your students prepare questions for the speaker in advance.

Legal Focus Example

Have a student volunteer read aloud to the class this Legal Focus Example. Guide the students in discussing this example by asking the following questions: In this example, who has responsibility for the child Roger? How is Roger's schedule arranged? Does this arrangement seem fair to all of the parties involved? Why or why not?

---

656   Personal Law

- Wishes of the parents and the children.
- The child's adjustment to his or her home, school, and community.
- Mental and physical health of all individuals involved.

Courts have the power to appoint a **guardian ad litem** (*ad litem* is Latin, meaning "for the suit") to protect the interests of the child in a custody case. The *guardian ad litem*, who will usually be an attorney, will attempt to represent and protect the minor's interests when they are in need of special protection.

After custody is given to one parent, the noncustodial parent usually has visiting rights. In an unusual case, such as when one parent is viewed as violent or otherwise a danger to the child or spouse, visitation rights may not be allowed. Some states allow for joint custody in appropriate situations. With joint custody, both parents share decision-making power and usually split the housing arrangements. Joint custody makes the most sense in cases where spouses remain on good terms after the dissolution of the marriage and they still live close to one another.

♦ **guardian ad litem** (Latin: for the suit) A guardian appointed by the court to protect the interests of a minor in a lawsuit.

⬥ LEGAL FOCUS – EXAMPLE

Matt and Martie Karass have a joint custody arrangement for their only child, Roger, age twelve. Both parents have full responsibility for Roger and each have an equal say on important issues such as religion, school, and sports activities. Fortunately, Matt and Martie live within a few miles of one another, so as part of the arrangement, Roger lives with his mother on Monday, Tuesday and Wednesday and with his father on Thursday, Friday, and Saturday. Living arrangements for Sundays alternate each week with a different parent. The parents have agreed to be flexible as to these arrangements to accommodate Roger's needs and their own schedules.

Each parent retains a duty to support a minor child even if he or she does not have custody. The noncustodial parent usually is ordered by the court to pay child support to the custodial parent. The purpose of these funds is to help pay for the child's housing, food, clothes, and the other costs of raising a child.

The enforcement of orders to pay child support is a major problem in the U.S. legal system. Some noncustodial parents do not meet their child support obligations. Someone who fails to obey a child support order from a judge can also be charged with contempt of court. If the children are being provided public assistance, child support payments must often be paid to county officials. Failure to pay child support, when the parent is financially able, is a crime in many states.

If a parent moves, a law called the Uniform Reciprocal Enforcement of Support Act allows for enforcement of child support orders in the new state. Unpaid child support can be collected like any other debt. Unlike

Invite a social worker or other representative from a local social service agency dealing with foster care to speak to your class. He or she should address topics such as how foster parents are chosen, the role of the foster parent in caring for the child, and the role of his or her social service agency in monitoring foster care.

Explain to the class that some argue that prenuptial agreements are an example of planning for failure and seem to run contrary to the ideals most often expressed in marriage vows. Stimulate a class discussion on the pros and cons of prenuptial agreements by asking the following questions: Are prenuptial agreements a good idea? Why or why not? Do you believe prenuptial agreements run counter to the ideals expressed in marriage vows? Are prenuptial agreements a realistic way of addressing the fact that many marriages end in divorce or dissolution?

other debts, however, a child support debt cannot be discharged through a bankruptcy proceeding.

Some states provide support even after the child turns eighteen if it is ordered by a divorce court or provided by statute.[7] Even when postminority support is not required by law, most states will enforce marital agreements that call for such support. Usually postminority child support is intended to pay for a college education.

FOSTER CARE

Sometimes a child is temporarily taken away from his or her parents, or the parents are unable to care for or control the child. In such cases, a state agency or the court may provide that the child is cared for in a foster home. Foster parents provide housing, food, and care during this temporary arrangement. Foster parents are usually paid by the state for the care given to the child.

PARENTAL KIDNAPPING

Parental kidnapping is the taking of a child from the custodial parent without that parent's consent. Estimates are that more than 8,000 children were abducted by their noncustodial parents between 1984 and 1989. When the child is kidnapped, the authorities and custodial parent do not necessarily know who has taken the child. The kidnapping parent commits a serious crime and can be held liable in a civil suit for unlawful interference with custody rights. The Uniform Child Custody Act provides for enforcement of child custody decrees if the kidnapping parent can be found.

◆ AGREEMENTS THAT MODIFY THE MARRIAGE CONTRACT

PREMARITAL AGREEMENTS

A marital contract made before marriage is called a **prenuptial** or antenuptial **agreement**. These agreements often try to establish each spouse's property rights and understandings about support in case the marriage fails. Most states require that such agreements be in writing, and often they must be witnessed by other people. Such agreements usually make sense when someone wealthy marries someone who is not.

These agreements attempt to change the way a spouse would ordinarily be treated under the law. Before a court will enforce such an agreement, it will examine it to see if it is fair and to decide if it had the true consent of

◆ **prenuptial agreement** A contract made before a marriage that sets forth the property rights and support understandings of each spouse in case the marriage fails.

7. These states are California, Colorado, Iowa, Illinois, Indiana, Mississippi, Missouri, New Hampshire, New Jersey, New York, Oregon, Pennsylvania, and South Carolina.

Tell students to write a one-page paper telling why a couple should or should not sign a prenuptial agreement.

Legal Focus Example

Have a student volunteer read aloud the Legal Focus Example found at the bottom of this page. Then allow the class to discuss developments in the relationship between Prince Charles and Diana, Princess of Wales since December 1992. Have they reconciled? What legal steps, if any, have been taken to dissolve their marriage? What effect, if any, has their relationship had on the monarchy? Note that although this topic may prove to be somewhat "gossipy," it may also pique your students' interest in the area of family law.

Prenuptial agreements set forth the property rights and support understandings of each spouse in case the marriage fails.

---

658   Personal Law

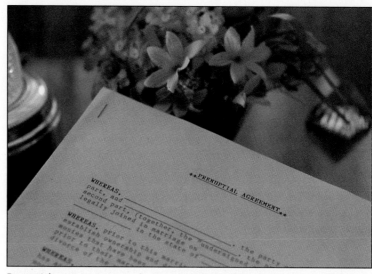

Prenuptial agreements serve what purpose? Do you think they are a good idea?

the signing parties. Courts will not enforce marital contracts of any kind that are unfair, unjust, or excessive. Contract provisions that involve the custody or care of children are subject to the approval and agreement of the court.

SEPARATION AGREEMENTS

Many states allow for a partial termination of a marriage. A legal separation allows a spouse to live apart without becoming a deserter. Couples may separate in order to live apart while they try to save the marriage. Or they may wish to live apart permanently but not divorce. Divorce may be unacceptable to the parties for religious reasons. Some separation agreements allow for support orders and division of property.

◆ LEGAL FOCUS ～ EXAMPLE

The United States is not the only country in the world that recognizes the concept of a legal separation in a marriage. The most publicized separation in years occurred in December 1992, when Queen Elizabeth of the United Kingdom announced the legal separation of Prince Charles, the heir to the throne, and his wife, Diana, Princess of Wales.

SPOUSE ABUSE

Approximately one-fourth of the murders occurring in the United States are family related; many are husband-wife killings. Criminologists believe that spouse abuse is one of the most underreported crimes in America. Like child abuse and rape, spouse abuse often occurs without other witnesses present.

Not many years ago, the doctrine of spousal immunity protected a spouse from being sued when he or she committed acts that would have been torts if they had been committed by someone unrelated to the victim. Thus, spousal immunity meant that one spouse could not sue another. Today, married persons can generally seek protection from the law from assault and the undesired sexual advances of the other spouse. Spouses can be held accountable civilly and criminally for such acts as assault, battery, and rape. Unfortunately, police officers must frequently respond to calls reporting violence between husband and wife.

CHECKING YOUR PROGRESS

1. What is a dowry? Who pays it? Is it legal in all societies?
2. What is the most common ground for a dissolution?
3. List some reasons why a court might allow an annulment.
4. What is alimony? Are there different types of alimony?
5. What is a *guardian ad litem*? Name a situation in which one might be used.
6. Why might a party seek a legal separation rather than a divorce?

Checking Your Progress (Answers)

1. A dowry is a payment of money from one betrothed to another. In some cultures (like India) the wife's parents pay it; in other cultures (like Saudi Arabia) the husband's family pays it. Not many countries consider it illegal, like India, but it is still a common practice, illegal or not.
2. The most common ground is irreconcilable differences; the couple does not want to stay married.
3. Grounds for annulment include fraud, incest, bigamy, mental incapacity, intoxication, and inability to consummate the marriage.
4. A continuing payment of money by one spouse for the living expenses of the other spouse. Permanent alimony means it is to be paid for the life of the collecting spouse. Limited alimony ends after a specified time.
5. A *guardian ad litem* is someone appointed by the court to protect the interests of a minor in a lawsuit. Student answers may vary as to when it might be used. Any lawsuit by the minor will require a *guardian ad litem*, including seeking to set aside a contract, suing another for a tort, and even representing the interests of a child in a child custody matter.
6. Student answers will vary. They could include situations where the couple has not decided whether to divorce and wishes to have some time to themselves, or when parties who cannot divorce for religious reasons seek a separation instead.

Teaching A Case In Point

Read

Before having a student volunteer read aloud this *A Case In Point* feature, remind the students that in most states the following factors are considered in determining the amount, if any, of spousal support.

- The financial condition of the spouse seeking support payments
- The length of the marriage
- The age, health, education, and station in life of each spouse
- The occupation, vocational skills, and employability of the requesting spouse
- The contributions of each in acquiring or maintaining marital property
- The need of the parent with whom the children will live to occupy the marital home
- Tax considerations

Explain to the students that this *A Case In Point* feature deals with two of these factors: the length of the marriage and the financial condition of the spouse seeking support payments. Then allow a volunteer to read this *A Case In Point* feature aloud to the class.

Discuss

Stimulate a class discussion of this *A Case In Point* feature by asking the following questions: How long were the McElwees married?

Teaching Note

This case is included in the *West's Business and Personal Law Handbook of Selected Court Cases.*

660

What was the dollar value of Doris's share of community property? What was the dollar value of Charles's child support payments per month? What was the dollar value of the spousal support payments Charles made per month? How long was Charles required to pay spousal support? What modification of the spousal support award did the court make in 1980? What modification of the spousal

support award did Doris request in 1983? What were the findings of the trial court? What was the amount of spousal support the trial court awarded Doris? For how long was this spousal support to continue? What was the issue before the Court of Appeal, Second District? What was the decision of the Court of Appeal? What reasons did the court give for its decision?

◆ A CASE IN POINT ◆

IN RE THE MARRIAGE OF McELWEE DORIS McELWEE v. CHARLES McELWEE

Court of Appeal, Second District, 1988.
197 Cal.App.3d 902,
243 Cal.Rptr. 179.

This case considers the length of a marriage and how well a spouse manages her affairs in deciding to end spousal support.

FACTS Charles and Doris McElwee separated after a fifteen-year marriage. Community property of approximately one million dollars was divided. Charles was ordered to provide child support of $2,000 per month for the couple's two children. Doris was awarded spousal support of $2,500 per month for three years beginning in 1977. The court retained jurisdiction to reexamine spousal support until April 5, 1983.

In November of 1980, the court modified the spousal support award to $1,800 per month to continue until April 5, 1983. In March 1983, Doris requested another modification of the spousal support award to increase it to $3,000 per month and to continue payment indefinitely. Charles asked the court to end his requirement to pay spousal support.

The trial court made several findings: (1) Doris held a bachelor's and a master's degree and was licensed as a marriage and family counselor; (2) Doris's share of the community property was substantial; (3) the origi-

nal support order was based on the court's belief that Doris would need assistance while she arranged for the management of her money, and time to establish her professional practice; the court found that instead of carefully investing her money, Doris had made high-risk investments, such as in gold mines, restaurants, cattle, and oil and gas exploration; (4) the couple's children were attending college with help from the father but without help from the mother.

The trial court awarded Doris $500 spousal support to continue until October 1986, at which time the spousal support would stop. Doris appealed the trial court order.

ISSUE Was the trial court wrong in its award for spousal support and its decision to end spousal support in October 1986?

DECISION The court of appeal affirmed the actions of the trial court.

REASON The court held that "just as lack of diligence in seeking employment may lead to a refusal to award spousal support, so too may improvident management of assets, which were sufficient to provide self-sufficiency in the accustomed life-style, justify termination of support and jurisdiction though such an order may result in an alteration in the supported spouse's lifestyle. To hold otherwise would encourage profligacy [wild extravagance] and discourage solid investment and prudent management to the detriment of all concerned." The trial court was within its discretion in its order as to both the amount of spousal support and the decision that the support should end.

In order to help students review what they have learned in Chapter 27, you might wish to:

1. Have a student volunteer, or volunteers, read the Chapter Summary aloud to the class.
2. Allow the students to work with partners to complete the *Using Legal Language* activity.
3. Assign the *Checking for Comprehension* exercise as homework.

4. Allow the students to work in small groups to complete the *Applying Legal Concepts* activities.
5. As a class, complete the Applying the Law activities. (Please note that you may have to help students with vocabulary so that they adequately understand all of the *Applying the Law* material.)

CHAPTER 27 REVIEW

 ## SUMMARY

THE MARRIAGE CONTRACT

Marriage is a special form of contract requiring:

1. Capacity.
2. A license, often with a waiting period of three days after the license is issued.
3. A medical examination.
4. A solemnization ceremony.

To marry, the parties cannot be closely related or of the same sex.

Fifteen states recognize common law marriages. A marriage that is valid in one state is valid in all other states.

LEGAL OBLIGATIONS OF MARRIAGE

1. Each spouse has a continuing and mutual obligation of support for the other.
2. Spousal property rights
   a. Common law states distinguish between separate property and marital property, which is acquired during the marriage.
   b. Community property states hold that all property acquired by the husband or wife during a marriage, other than by gift or inheritance, is community property.
   c. In either a community property or common law state, the property of the marriage can be used to pay the debts of the marriage.

LEGAL RIGHTS AND OBLIGATIONS OF PARENTHOOD

Parents are obligated to support their children until the children reach the age of majority or are emancipated.

Adoption

Adoption is a legal process regulated by the state that allows a child to be legally recognized as the child of the adopting parent.

TERMINATION OF A MARRIAGE

Divorce or dissolution is the termination of a marriage relationship. Modern state law allows the dissolution of a marriage because of irreconcilable differences.

Annulment

If the marriage contract was entered into under false pretenses or was otherwise illegal, it is void. A void marriage can be annulled.

Property Distribution

1. Property can be divided according to an agreement of the parties.
2. In common law property states, the court can generally divide the property based on notions of fairness and need.
3. In community property states, the court can determine the nature of the property, determine its value, and then divide it equally.

Alimony

Alimony, commonly called spousal support, is the continuing payment of money by one spouse for the living expenses of the other spouse. Awards are based on need, age and education of the spouse, and length of the marriage.

Child Custody and Support

A court can award custody of minor children to one or both spouses. The noncustodial spouse is usually required to provide child support until the child reaches the age of majority.

PREMARITAL AGREEMENTS

A contract made before marriage is called a *prenuptial agreement*. Such agreements often try

Assessment Strategies

In order to check student mastery of chapter concepts, you may wish to use the Chapter 27 test that is found in your *Teacher's Resource Binder* or use WESTEST computerized testing for Chapter 27.

Checking for Comprehension (Answers)

1. Marriage is a type of contract. Each state has its own legal requirements for marriage. Once two people are married, the law provides certain rights and protections to each party based on marital status. For example, marital partners gain rights in property acquired during the marriage.

2. A common law marriage is an informal marriage occurring without a marriage license when persons agree to be married, live together as husband and wife, and hold themselves out to the community as married.

3. Common law states have adopted parts of the Uniform Marriage and Divorce Act, which distinguishes between separate property and marital property. In common law states, separate property is property individually owned by one spouse. Separate property usually remains separate even after marriage. In common law states, marital property is property owned by a wife and husband jointly. Usually this property is acquired during, not before, the marriage. In community property states, all property acquired during a marriage by the husband or wife other than by gift or inheritance is community property.

---

to establish each spouse's property rights and support understandings if the marriage fails.

SEPARATION AGREEMENTS

A legal separation allows spouses to live apart but still be considered married.

SPOUSE ABUSE

A spouse can be held responsible under civil and criminal law for assault, battery, and rape of his or her spouse, among other acts.

USING LEGAL LANGUAGE

Directions: Match each term with the statement that best defines that term.

1. adoption
2. alimony
3. annulment
4. common law marriage
5. community property
6. dissolution
7. *guardian ad litem*
8. marital property
9. marriage
10. separate property

A. Spousal support called _____ is a continuing payment of money by one spouse for the living expenses of the other spouse.

B. When property is individually owned by one spouse, it is _____ and usually remains separate even after marriage.

C. A _____ occurs when a court order terminates a marriage.

D. One definition of _____ is the legal union of husband and wife.

E. In certain states, _____ is all property acquired by the husband or wife during a marriage other than property acquired by gift or inheritance.

F. A person who is appointed by the court to protect the interest of a minor in a lawsuit is a _____.

G. When two people live together as husband and wife, and hold themselves out to the community as married, but do not acquire a marriage license when they agree to live together, a _____ is formed and recognized in fifteen states.

H. Property owned by a wife and husband jointly, called _____, is usually acquired during, not before, the marriage.

I. After _____, a child has the same rights and duties as a child born to the parent or parents.

J. If the marriage agreement is based on fraud, one of the parties can seek an _____.

4. Any four of the following: the jobs; earnings and stability of the prospective parents; the medical, emotional, and physical needs of the child; the "clean" record of adoptive parents; the age of the child; whether adoption is by a married couple; religious and racial compatibility and the social problems the child may face if adopted by a person of a different race or faith.

5. Alimony (also called spousal support) is a continuing payment of money by one spouse for the living expenses of the other spouse. Permanent alimony is an award of alimony without an ending date. Limited-term alimony ends after a specified period of time. Additionally, limited-term alimony may be rehabilitative.

6. A prenuptial agreement is a contract made before marriage, the purpose of which is to set forth the property rights and support understandings of each spouse in case the marriage fails.

◆ CHECKING FOR COMPREHENSION

1. Explain the role of the law in marriages.

2. What is a common law marriage?

3. Explain how marital property is viewed in common law states, and in community property states.

4. Name four factors that are considered by the courts before approving an adoption?

5. Explain the difference between permanent alimony and limited term alimony.

6. What is a pre-nuptial agreement and what is its purpose?

◆ APPLYING LEGAL CONCEPTS

1. Using newspaper and magazine clippings as well as photographs and other images, put together a poster that shows both the social and legal aspects of marriage and divorce. Be sure to write captions for any photographs and/or artwork you include on your poster and use appropriate legal vocabulary wherever possible.

◆ APPLYING THE LAW . . . YOU BE THE JUDGE

1. Arnold and Donna Rinvelt were married on July 23, 1983. Three days before the marriage, the parties entered into a prenuptial agreement drafted by Arnold Rinvelt's attorney. The agreement provided that each party would ". . . separately retain all rights in his or her own property . . . [and] each of them shall have the absolute and unrestricted right to dispose of such property free from any such claims that may be made by the other by reason of their marriage . . ." The agreement also provided that "in the event that the marriage of the parties shall end in divorce . . . respective rights in and to the property of the other spouse shall be limited to:" ten percent (10%) of the net estate of the other spouse. The parties were divorced and Donna was awarded 10% of the Arnold's property in the amount of $228,585. Arnold argued the antenuptial agreement should not have been enforced. What arguments could Arnold make, and do you expect that he succeeded? [*Rinvelt v. Rinvelt*, 190 Mich.App. 372, 475 N.W.2d 478 (Mich. 1991)]

2. Jeanne Capen requested that her marriage to Tucker Capen be annulled. She testified in an uncontested action for annulment that Tucker had informed her he did not want children. The Court Referee recommended that the annulment not be granted because Jeanne and Tucker reconciled for six weeks after an initial separation which had occurred when Jeanne first became aware that Tucker did not want any children. New York law provides that when parties continue to live together "with full knowledge of facts constituting fraud" an annulment should not be allowed. Jeanne acknowledged that they had reconciled, but claimed she did so only after Tucker claimed he had changed his mind and really did want children. After six weeks, it became clear to her that he had continued to deceive her. Is a misrepresentation about the desire to have children grounds for annulment? Should the annulment be granted in this case? [*Capen v. Capen*, 137 N.Y.S.2d 223 (N.Y. 1954)]

Enrichment

Have the students brainstorm instances in which mediation might be used. Ask a volunteer to list each of the examples on the board. After the students have listed several examples, guide them in discussing each example by asking them how mediation might help in that particular instance.

LEGAL BACKGROUND

We continue the topic of alternatives to litigation (ADR) with a more in-depth discussion of mediation. It is not by accident that this topic accompanies a discussion of family law. Courts are used best as a last resort. Many other methods of dealing with social problems are preferable if parties can make them succeed. Mediation uses a third person knowledgeable about the topic of a dispute who is also skilled in helping parties see that a negotiated compromise may be more beneficial than an imposed judgment. Family disputes, and the related area of neighbor disputes, are both areas where mediation has shown tremendous success as a satisfactory alternative to the adversary process of our courts.

664

LEGAL PERSPECTIVE

MEDIATION

Scott Kinsey not only liked heavy metal music, he liked it loud and late. Occupying his first house, he really appreciated his freedom. He no longer had repeated orders from his parents that he "turn the darn thing down." Evan and Nita Russet lived next door in a house they had owned for forty years. After one week of 3:00 A.M. Guns 'n' Roses concerts, Evan was unable to hide his anger. Dressed in his robe, he stormed over to Scott's house and shouted, "Turn that awful noise off!" Scott was annoyed and shouted back, "I didn't move to get new parents. Anyway, it's a free country!" Then he turned the volume up. How do Evan and Nita get some sleep?

Evan and Nita have legal options. They can telephone the police, who will arrive and ask Scott to show more consideration for his neighbors. Scott is probably violating a criminal statute against disturbing the peace. The Russets could file a criminal complaint. The Russets can sue in civil court for damages for past harm and seek an injunction prohibiting the loud music as a continuing nuisance. These actions create a practical problem, however, since they cost time, money, and peace. They also ignore the reality that the parties will still live next door to each other after the legal actions are over.

Neighbor problems, like many other problems, require a mutual understanding that is not usually achieved through either the criminal or civil court process. The root of many problems referred to the courts is a problem in a human relationship. A poor relationship may only grow worse after a court case. The adversarial proceeding of a

trial usually makes the parties' existing anger worse. Neighbors living close to one another often find new reasons to argue and then find themselves in a new conflict. Similarly, when a marriage dissolves, arguments can occur over the division of property, spousal and child support, and child custody. These disagreements can create anger and animosity that may last for years.

A problem such as the neighbor dispute discussed here can often be solved without attorneys, courts, and complex procedures. The alternatives available can often be used at either no cost or at low cost. Parties may be able to solve their conflict in a way that improves long-term understanding and goodwill. The favored methods of resolution for problems where long-term relationships remain important are negotiation and mediation. We discussed the process of negotiation in the Legal Perspective at the end of Chapter 13. Mediation is the least formal and intrusive of any of the dispute resolution processes that use a third party.

Mediation is the use of a neutral third party to assist parties in voluntarily resolving their dispute. A mediator listens to all sides of a dispute, analyzes each party's arguments and suggestions, communicates with each party, and assists the parties to settle their own dispute. The mediator facilitates, or aids, communication between the contending parties. The mediator has no power to impose a resolution to a dispute.

◆ ADVANTAGES OF MEDIATION

Unlike litigation or arbitration, the use of mediation does not lead to a resolution that

Enrichment

Read aloud the following definition of *mediation,* found in the student text: "Mediation is the use of a neutral third party to assist parties in voluntarily resolving their dispute." Ask the students to write a short paragraph answering the following question: Why is it important that a mediator be neutral? Allow volunteers to share their answers with the class.

is imposed on the parties in a dispute. The parties control their own agreement. The difference between mediation and negotiation is that in mediation a neutral third party is used to assist parties in finding an acceptable solution. Because mediation involves an agreement, it can take place without the delays associated with litigation. The process is informal and private, while litigation is formal and public. Because mediation is less formal and can occur early in a dispute, it is usually far less expensive than litigation.

A mediator is selected by the parties to the dispute. They seek a person who is neutral and who is an experienced and skilled communicator. The mediator is an expert in the type of dispute in question. If the dispute is a family law problem, the mediator may be a social worker or family practice psychologist. If the dispute is about a breach of contract at a construction site, the mediator may be an architect, engineer, or construction law attorney. Besides expertise in the area, the mediator should be someone who listens well, is trustworthy, and can propose creative solutions.

While efficiency and the high cost of litigation are reasons enough to consider mediation, the most compelling reason is the opportunity for the parties to reach their own resolution. A mediation can reduce the bitterness of the disputing parties and preserve a relationship.

Even if the mediating parties are not able to resolve the dispute using this process, they can often agree to some of the facts in the dispute. With fewer issues to be resolved, either litigation or arbitration will be faster. Parties who mediate do not give up their right to litigate or arbitrate. Many mediation programs, however, claim success rates of more than 90 percent.

 ## DISADVANTAGES OF MEDIATION

Mediators often charge for their services. If the mediation is unsuccessful, then the cost and time spent may not seem worthwhile. The mediator may charge an hourly rate similar to what an attorney would charge. In these situations, parties normally split the cost of mediation. Sometimes mediators are available without charge, and low- or no-cost mediators are often available in family law and consumer disputes.

Some attorneys feel that the tactics they intend to use in trial might be disclosed to their disadvantage in a mediation. The mediation process also requires some compromise by each party. A belief by either party that no compromise is possible will lead to an unproductive mediation. The most difficult part of many mediations is getting the parties to agree to mediate.

 ## ANATOMY OF A MEDIATION

The parties to a dispute must first select a mediator. There are many types of mediators. There are labor, commercial, family, and construction mediators, among others. These mediators are considered experts in their areas, and they have a reputation for knowledge, leadership, fairness, and creativity. Some, but not all, mediators are lawyers. In consumer and neighborhood disputes, the mediator is often a volunteer from the community.

(continued on page 666)

You might invite a mediator to speak to your class. Mediators can be found through nonprofit groups such as the American Arbitration Association or through your Better Business Bureau. Ask the speaker to discuss the advantages and disadvantages of mediation and to share any particularly amusing anecdotes with your class. Have the students prepare questions for your speaker in advance.

LEGAL PERSPECTIVE (CONTINUED)

Mediators are found through nonprofit groups such as the American Arbitration Association or the Better Business Bureau. Family or neighborhood dispute mediators may be found through the courts or other government agencies. Private organizations offer mediators on a fee-for-hire basis.

Once the mediator is hired, the time and place for the mediation will be arranged. The mediation may take place in an attorney's office. Often in neighborhood conflicts, the mediation may occur in a community center, church, or neighbor's home.

Because the process does not lead to any findings or conclusions by the mediator, its form varies. However, appropriate behavior and techniques have been identified by professional organizations. The mediation begins when the mediator introduces himself or herself and discusses the process face to face with the parties. Usually the mediator allows each party to explain the disagreement in an informal atmosphere. There are few fixed procedural rules, and legal terminology is avoided. A mediator may meet with each party in private conferences to hear facts, opinions, and positions that a party might otherwise be reluctant to disclose.

All conversations with the mediator are private and confidential. The mediator can only share the information with the other side that a party allows. The mediator may act, with the approval of both parties, as a messenger to carry possible positions and resolutions between the parties. In this way, opposing parties can avoid face-to-face confrontation. To encourage the use of mediation, several states will not allow communications by the parties during mediation to be used in later court proceedings.

The dispute between the Russets and Kinsey is one that may be better solved through mediation than through the courts. **Neighborhood dispute centers**, common in major metropolitan areas, provide trained mediators to assist parties in resolving problems such as loud music at 3:00 A.M. Although any resolution is voluntary, the settlement success of neighborhood mediation has been remarkable and is more effective in resolving problems than court resolution.

◆ FAMILY MEDIATION

Mediation has gained popularity in family law proceedings since no-fault divorce laws have replaced adversarial methods. A professional and neutral third party can provide valuable assistance in resolving property division and spousal support disputes. A mediator can also help with issues of child custody, support, and visitation. Studies show that children of mediated divorces appear to adjust better and that their parents appear to be less hostile toward each other.

California is one of many states that has adopted mandatory mediation proceedings whenever child custody is part of a dissolution dispute. The mediator acts as a neutral adviser, an expert source of information suggesting options (including remaining married) for the couple. If the parties decide to divorce, then issues surrounding their divorce are considered. Agreements or settlements are made only with the full consent of the parties. A voluntary settlement, if reached, is presented to the court. Courts will usually incorporate the settlement into the court judgment.

Mastery Objectives

By the end of this chapter, students will be able to:

- Classify personal property
- Describe types of ownership of personal property
- Establish ways of acquiring personal property

- Differentiate between mislaid, lost, and abandoned property
- Specify elements of a bailment
- Distinguish ordinary and special bailments
- Identify duties and rights of bailors and bailees

Personal Property and Bailments

Chapter
28

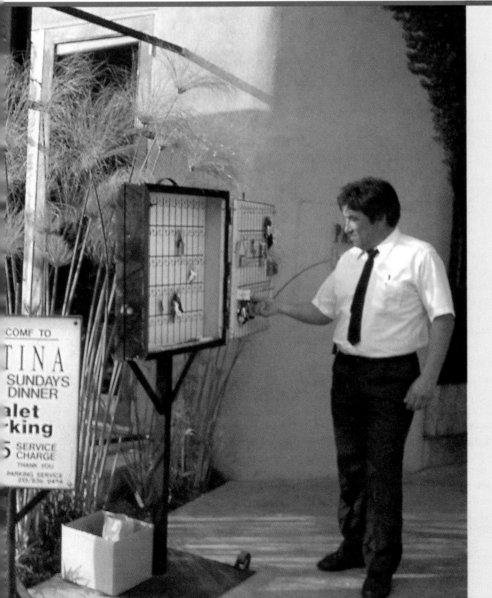

LEGAL BACKGROUND

Property consists of the legally protected rights and interests a person has in anything of value that is subject to ownership. Property would have little value if the law did not protect our rights to use it, to sell or dispose of it, and to prevent trespassing upon it.

In this chapter we examine ownership rights in personal property. We consider different types of joint ownership and how one initially acquires ownership rights, including a discussion of gifts.

We have already discussed sales in detail, but the topic of bailments remains. A bailment is formed by the delivery of personal property, without transfer of title, by one person (a bailor) to another (a bailee), usually under an agreement for a particular purpose—for example, to loan, store, repair, or transport property. Upon completion of the purpose, the bailee is obligated to return the bailed property in the same or better condition to the bailor or a third person, or to dispose of it as directed.

667

Allow a minute or two for students to write a list of things people can own. On the board, write the headings: real property, tangible personal property, and intangible personal property. Have them tell you some items on their lists as you write them on the board, placing them under the correct category heading.

Enrichment

Have a student read aloud the quote from John Locke that appears at the beginning of this chapter. Ask the student to explain the quote to the class.

You might want to explain to students that John Locke was an important English political philosopher, who in 1689 wrote *Two Treatises of Government,* in which he argued that neither custom nor tradition nor the fact of being born in a certain society were sufficient reasons to obey rulers. He stated that "no one could be subjected to the political power of another without his (or her) own consent." Locke further argued that all persons were born free, equal, and independent, and all persons had a natural right to life, liberty, and property—rights that everyone possessed even before government existed. Locke argued that the primary purpose of government was to protect those natural rights and believed that government was really a social contract between the people and their government.

668

Chapter 28
Resources and Assignment Guide

Activity Sheets
Reviewing Legal Concepts 28 *TRB*
Enrichment Activity 28 *TRB*

Student Activity Workbook
Chapter 28 Activities

Tests
Chapter 28 Test *TRB*
Chapter 28 WESTEST Computerized Testing

Handbook of Selected Court Cases
Augustine v. *Marriott Hotel*
Harris v. *Davis*

West's Business Law and Legal Environment Videodisc
Still Frames and Motion Segments as shown

> *"The great and chief end . . . of men united into commonwealths, and putting themselves under government, is the preservation of their property."*
> **John Locke, 1632–1704**
> **English political philosopher**

Property law protects the rights and interests that each person has in property. A property is something that is owned or possessed. Property law defines the right to use property, to sell or dispose of it, and to prevent interference with it. In the United States, the ownership of property has unique protection under the law. The Bill of Rights holds that "no person shall . . . be deprived of life, liberty, or property, without due process of law; nor shall private property be taken for public use, without just compensation."

At the beginning of this chapter, we will look at the nature of personal property and the legal rights involved in property ownership. In the second part of the chapter, we will consider bailment relationships. **Bailments** are created when personal property is temporarily delivered into the care of another person without transferring ownership. In a sale or a gift, ownership, called *title*, is transferred. In a bailment, possession is transferred but not the title to the property.

◆ **bailment** A temporary right to possess the personal property of another.

◆ **real property** Land and things permanently attached to the land.

◆ **personal property** Property that is movable; any property that is not real property.

◆ **tangible personal property** Personal property that has physical substance.

◆ **intangible personal property** Personal property that represents a set of rights and duties; it has no real physical existence.

THE NATURE OF PERSONAL PROPERTY

There are two categories of property, real and personal. **Real property** is land and everything permanently attached to the land. When a structure, such as a building, is built on land, everything permanently part of the structure and the structure itself are real property, or *realty*. Real property is discussed in Chapter 29. All property other than real property is **personal property**. Personal property is also called *personalty*.

Personal property, or personalty, can be either tangible or intangible. **Tangible personal property**, like a TV set or a car, has physical substance; you can touch it or hold it. **Intangible personal property** represents a set of rights and duties; its value is not its physical existence. Stocks, bonds, and copyrights are examples of intangible personal property.

Personal property includes newer types of ownership rights. For example, gas, water, and telephone services are now considered personal property. Federal and state statutes consider music compositions personal property and protect them against illegal copying. It is a crime to engage in the "bootlegging"—illegal copying for resale—of records and tapes. And the theft of computer software programs is now considered a theft of personal property.

Your students may not be familiar with the phrase *fee simple,* as used here. Ask the students if this phrase makes sense to them or seems old-fashioned. Then explain to the students that *fee simple* is a phrase that has been incorporated into our legal system from English common law, and that according to *Webster's Ninth New Collegiate Dictionary,* the earliest recorded use of *fee simple* occurred sometime during the 14th century.

PROPERTY OWNERSHIP

Property ownership can be viewed as a bundle of rights. This bundle of rights includes the right to possess the property. It also includes the right to transfer the property by sale, gift, rental, or lease.

FEE SIMPLE

Ownership of the entire bundle of rights is called **fee simple** ownership. The fee simple owner can use, possess, or dispose of the property during his or her lifetime. At his or her death, the fee simple ownership passes to the owner's heirs.

CONCURRENT OWNERSHIP

If only one person owns property, it is owned in **severalty**. If two or more persons share ownership rights in property, they are said to be *concurrent owners* or tenants. There are four principal types of **concurrent ownership**: tenancy in common, joint tenancy, tenancy by the entirety, and community property.

Each form of co-ownership has different characteristics and serves different purposes. A **tenancy in common** is the form of co-ownership most appropriate for unrelated owners. Tenants can own unequal shares in the property and acquire their ownership interests in the property at different times. The shares of ownership can be transferred easily. If any tenant dies, that tenant's interest passes to his or her heirs. Any tenant can transfer his or her interest to a third person.

LEGAL FOCUS ~ PROBLEM

Toshio wanted a jet ski more than almost anything else. He worked hard to save his money but could not raise enough to buy one. He discussed his frustration with Craig. Craig proposed a solution. "Let's pool our funds and buy the jet ski together." Toshio agreed. How should they own the property?

A tenancy in common is probably the most appropriate form of co-ownership for Toshio and Craig. They can own the property together in any way they wish, but when one of them dies, his interest in the jet ski goes to his family.

Another common form of joint ownership, called **joint tenancy**, provides for a very different result when a joint owner dies. Joint tenancy is co-ownership with the *right of survivorship*. If any joint tenant dies, his or her interest passes to the surviving joint tenants. The deceased tenant's interest expires at death and cannot pass to his or her heirs.

♦ **fee simple**
Ownership of the entire bundle of rights in property.

♦ **severalty** Only one person owns property.

♦ **concurrent ownership** Two or more persons own property together.

♦ **tenancy in common** A form of property co-ownership in which two or more persons own a fractional interest in the property; when one tenant dies, the property interest passes to his or her heirs.

♦ **joint tenancy** A form of property co-ownership with the right of survivorship. If any joint tenant dies, his or her interest passes to the surviving joint tenants.

Have a student volunteer read this Legal Focus Problem aloud to the class. Ask the volunteer to suggest a possible answer to the question posed at the end of this problem. Then ask the volunteer what problems, if any, might occur as a result of tenancy in common as it relates to this Legal Focus Problem. What happens if both Toschio and Craig wish to use the jet ski on the same day? Point out that these are issues that should be resolved before entering into any tenancy-in-common agreement.

Both joint tenancy and tenancy by the entirety require that certain pre-conditions exist before a valid tenancy can be said to exist. First, the owners of the estate must have both received their interest at the same time (unity of time). Second, the owners of the estate must both draw their title from the same deed or document (unity of title). Third, the owners of the estate must have equal interest in the land (unity of interest). Fourth, the owners must have an unrestricted right to use the entire property (unity of possession). These four preconditions are sometimes called the four unities. A tenancy in common may exist without any of these unities except the unit of possession because tenants in common, despite the unevenness of their respective interest in the property, still have the right to use the entire property.

Legal Focus Example

Have a student volunteer read aloud this Legal Focus Example dealing with joint tenancy. Make sure the students understand that under joint tenancy Craig's heirs receive absolutely no interest in the jet ski, while under tenancy in common Craig's heirs would receive all rights to his interest in the jet ski.

670   Personal Law

 LEGAL FOCUS - EXAMPLE

Assume that Toshio and Craig own their jet ski in a joint tenancy, rather than as tenants in common. If Craig dies before Toshio, the jet ski becomes the property of Toshio. Craig's heirs receive absolutely no interest in the jet ski.

A joint tenant does, however, have the right to transfer his or her ownership before death. The transfer will terminate the joint tenancy. Assume that Toshio transfers his interest to Rosalind, and Craig is still alive. Now Craig and Rosalind become owners of the jet ski as tenants in common.

A joint tenancy requires a written document and cannot be created casually or accidentally. Because of its survivorship feature, many states require the words *with right of survivorship* to be included in a document that creates the ownership.

There are two other forms of joint property ownership that can only exist for a husband and wife. The more common of the two forms of co-ownership between a husband and wife is **tenancy by the entirety**.[1] This type of joint ownership is similar to a joint tenancy—the surviving spouse automatically receives the ownership interest of the spouse who dies—but the ability of each spouse to transfer his or her individual interest in the property is limited. Specifically, a spouse cannot transfer his or her individual interest without the approval of the other spouse. In addition, creditors cannot make claims against this type of property unless both the husband and wife owe the creditor money.

Nine states allow marital property to be held as **community property**.[2] As described in Chapter 27, community property is all property acquired during the marriage except by gift or inheritance. Each spouse technically owns a one-half interest in the property acquired during the marriage. Unlike a joint tenancy, a spouse's community property interest may be transferred to another by will. Transfers during life must either be to benefit the marriage or with the approval of both spouses.

◆ **tenancy by the entirety** A form of property co-ownership between husband and wife. Similar to joint tenancy; when one spouse dies, his or her interest automatically transfers to the surviving spouse.

◆ **community property** All property acquired (in a community property state) by the husband or wife during a marriage other than property acquired by gift or inheritance. Each spouse technically owns a one-half interest.

◆ ACQUIRING OWNERSHIP OF PERSONAL PROPERTY

Ownership in personal property can be acquired in several ways: by possession, purchase, production, gift, will or inheritance, and accession. Each of these methods is discussed in the subsections that follow.

---

1. Some form of tenancy by the entirety is recognized in twenty-two states: Alaska, Arkansas, Florida, Hawaii, Indiana, Kentucky, Maryland, Massachusetts, Michigan, Mississippi, Missouri, New Jersey, New York, North Carolina, Oklahoma, Oregon, Pennsylvania, Rhode Island, Tennessee, Vermont, Virginia, and Wyoming.
2. Arizona, California, Idaho, Louisiana, Nevada, New Mexico, Texas, Washington, and Wisconsin. Also Puerto Rico.

Ask students if they have ever found any-thing. Ask them what they did with the item they found. Write on the board the names of different items. Ask students to think about what they would do if they found each of these items under various circumstances. (For example, an expensive-looking ring found in the restroom at your school or on a table in the employee break room at their job; the same ring found on the street in front of your school or under the cabinet in their kitchen at home; or a three-ring notebook or pencil found in the same locations, etc.)

POSSESSION

The person who finds abandoned property generally becomes the owner of it. A person who finds lost property may become the owner of that property if the true owner does not come forward. We will discuss lost and abandoned property later in this chapter.

The first person to take possession of a wild animal normally owns it.

PURCHASE OR PRODUCTION

Purchase is the most common means of acquiring and transferring owner-ship of personal property. The purchase or sale of personal property (called *goods*) is governed by the Uniform Commercial Code (see Chapter 14).

Production is another means of acquiring ownership of personal proper-ty. For example, writers, inventors, and manufacturers all produce personal property and get title to what they have produced.

GIFTS

 LEGAL FOCUS – PROBLEM

Mike's favorite aunt, Pauline, tells him that when he graduates from high school, she is going to give him a new Ford Mustang convertible. What right, if any, does Mike have to the new car upon his graduation?

When you purchase a CD, you have the right to use it only for personal use. If you play it for a public dance or broadcast, you owe royalty payments for your use.

Have a student read this Legal Focus Problem aloud to the class. Ask the volun-teer to suggest a possible answer to the question posed at the end of this problem. Then have the vol-unteer read the first para-graph at the top of the next page, which answers the question posed at the end of this Legal Focus Problem.

Teaching with the Videodisc

The still frames listed below from the **West's Business Law and Legal Environment Videodisc** can be used with this chapter. To access this material, use the bar codes or the frame numbers included in the Videodisc Instructor's Manual found in the *TRB*.

*Elements of a Bailment
Rights of a Bailee
Duties of a Bailee
Standard of Care Required
   of a Bailee
Personal Property—
   Ownership Title
Ways of Aquiring Owner-
   ship of Personal Property*

Legal Focus Problem

Have a student volunteer read aloud to the class this Legal Focus Problem dealing with gifts. Ask the volunteer to answer the following questions dealing with this problem: Who is the donor? Who is the donee? Then have the volunteer suggest an answer to the question posed at the end of this Legal Focus Problem.

Critical Thinking Activity

Have the students write a paragraph or two on the major differences between a tenancy in common and a joint tenancy. Allow volunteers to share their work with the class.

Collaborative Learning Activity

Divide the class into small groups. Have each group discuss the three requirements for an effective gift, listed here. Then have the students in each group work together to script an example of an effective gift. Each group should then act out its script before the class. As the groups act out their scripts, a narrator should describe how their examples meet each of the three requirements for an effective gift.

In the movie, *Field of Dreams*, a mysterious voice said to an Iowa farmer, "If you build it, he will come." The reference was to building a baseball field and the farmer believed the "he" was the ghost of the former baseball great, Shoeless Joe Jackson. Mike is in the same position as that Iowa farmer. If the farmer built the field and Joe didn't come, there would have been nothing he could do about it. In other words, "Mike will own it, if she gives it." Aunt Pauline has made a promise, but the Mustang does not become Mike's until and unless Pauline delivers it to him.

A **gift** is a voluntary transfer of property ownership. The very essence of a gift is that someone gives something without expecting anything in return. A promise to make a gift is not enforceable. The gift must actually be delivered in order to be an effective transfer of ownership. The person giving the gift is called a **donor**. The person receiving a gift is called a **donee**.

◆ **gift** A voluntary transfer of property without an expectation of receiving anything in return.

◆ **donor** A person giving a gift.

◆ **donee** A person receiving a gift.

◆ LEGAL FOCUS ~ PROBLEM

Linda wishes to make a gift to Patricia of some old rare coins stored in a safety deposit box at the Lone Star Savings and Loan. Linda is the donor. The intended recipient of Linda's generosity, Patricia, is the donee. How can Linda effectively transfer ownership of the rare coins to Patricia?

There are three requirements to an effective gift; they are "donative intent," delivery, and acceptance.

1. *Donative intent*—There must be evidence of the donor's intent to give the donee the gift. Donative intent is determined from the language of the donor and the surrounding circumstances. Linda can tell Patricia that she wishes to give her the coins, for example. Writing down her intention provides even better proof.

2. *Delivery*—Delivery is giving up *complete control and dominion* (that is, ownership rights) over the subject matter of the gift. Delivery is obvious in most gift situations. In the example of the rare coins, delivery could take place in several ways. Linda could get the coins out of the safety deposit box and deliver them to Patricia. Linda may, however, be reluctant to take the coins out of the bank. When a physical object cannot be delivered, then a symbolic, or *constructive*, delivery is sufficient.

   Constructive delivery is a term describing acts that the law holds to be the equivalent of an actual delivery of the property. In the rare-coin example, the delivery to Patricia of the key to the safety deposit box would be a constructive delivery of the contents of the box. The delivery of intangible property—such as stocks, bonds, insurance policies, contracts, and so on—is always accomplished by symbolic, or constructive, delivery.

3. *Acceptance*—The final requirement of a valid gift is acceptance by the donee. This rarely presents any problems since most donees readily ac-

Legal Focus Problem

Have a student volunteer read aloud to the class this Legal Focus Problem dealing with accession. Guide the students in discussing this problem by asking the following questions: Has the work of Juarez increased the value of the stone? Did Juarez complete his work on the stone in good faith? Who should get the statue of silver?

Vocabulary Activity

Tell students to read the section about confusion, commingling, and *fungible goods*. Ask them to list what items could fall into this category of property ownership transfer. Have the students discuss their lists.

---

cept their gifts. The courts generally assume acceptance unless shown otherwise.

WILL OR INHERITANCE

Ownership of personal property may be transferred by will or by inheritance under state statutes (see Chapter 32.) These transfers are called *bequests* (for personal property), *devises* (for real property), or *inheritances* (which include any or all property rights transferred at someone's death).

ACCESSION

Accession means "adding on" to something. This happens when someone adds value to a piece of personal property by either labor or materials. The installation of a stereo system in an automobile adds value to the automobile and becomes part of it.

If accession occurs without the permission of the owner of the personal property, the ownership rights in the improved property usually depend on the good faith of the improver. If the improver is a wrongdoer, most courts will not allow him or her to be reimbursed for the value added. For example, if a car thief puts new tires on a stolen car, he or she would not be paid for the value of the new tires.

◆ **accession** The adding of value to a piece of personal property by either labor or materials.

◆ LEGAL FOCUS – PROBLEM

Juarez is walking in a large country field. He discovers a huge stone shaped somewhat like a horse lying near a fence. Juarez works on the stone for twenty-seven weeks. He eventually transforms it into a replica of the Lone Ranger's horse, Silver. Juarez's artist friends are very impressed and convince him to move the stone horse to a gallery. The gallery appraises the art at $50,000. The owner of the field where Juarez found the stone now claims title to it. Who gets the statue of Silver?

Juarez should get title to the stone statue because the changes he made greatly increased its value and the accession was performed in good faith. Juarez is, however, responsible for paying the owner of the field the reasonable value of the unaltered stone.

If the increase in value is not significant, the original owner would keep title to the property. Many courts require the original owner to compensate an honest mistaken improver for the value he or she has added to the property.

CONFUSION

Confusion is the mixing of one person's personal property with another's, resulting in the goods becoming indistinguishable. This frequently occurs when the goods are **fungible**. "Fungible" means that each individual item

◆ **confusion** The mixing together of personal property belonging to two or more owners so that the independent goods cannot be identified.

◆ **fungible goods** Each item is identical to every other item, such as with grain or oil.

LEGAL BACKGROUND

A trespasser who finds an item of abandoned personal property does not acquire title to it. The owner of the real property on which it was found does acquire title. The same rule applies if the property was lost. Similarly, if a landowner employs a crew to install an underground septic tank and the crew digs up a cache of pioneer and covered wagon relics, the landowner has first claim to the relics because they were buried on his or her land. In contrast, if the crew had unearthed money, gold, silver, or bullion (instead of pewter dishes, tin cups, brass buttons, and old muskets), the find could be classified as treasure trove (treasure that is found), and the crew might be able to keep it. In the United States, in the absence of a statute, a finder has title to treasure trove against all but the true owner. In Great Britain, the Crown gets it. To constitute treasure trove, property need not have been buried—it could have been hidden in some other private place such as behind loose bricks in an old chimney—but its owner must be unknown, and its finders must not have been trespassing.

674

Have a student volunteer read aloud to the class this Legal Focus Problem dealing with mislaid property. Ask the student to suggest possible answers to the question posed at the end of this problem. Then have the student read the paragraph directly below this Legal Focus Problem to discover the answer.

Extension Activity

Have a student find out if your state has an estray statute and report the procedures one would follow to claim ownership to the property he or she found.

---

is identical to every other item; this is the case with grain and oil. For example, if two farmers put their Number 2–grade winter wheat into the same silo, confusion occurs.

If the confusion of goods was done to deceive or take advantage of another, the innocent party gets title to the whole. If the confusion occurs as a result of agreement, an honest mistake, or the act of some third party, the owners share ownership as *tenants in common*.

MISLAID, LOST, AND ABANDONED PROPERTY

If you find someone's property, it is important to learn whether the owner mislaid, lost, or simply abandoned the property because this affects who has what rights to the property. Each of these situations is discussed here.

Mislaid Property   Property that has been voluntarily placed somewhere by the owner and then forgotten is **mislaid property**.

◆ **mislaid property**
Property with which the owner has voluntarily parted and then cannot find or recover.

> ### ◀ LEGAL FOCUS – PROBLEM
>
> While at the movie theater, Dawn went to the concession stand to purchase some popcorn and a granola bar. She accidentally left her gloves at the concession stand. The next day she realized they were gone. What are Dawn's rights to a return of her gloves?

Dawn's gloves are mislaid property. Assuming the theater employees found the gloves, Dawn has a right to the return of them. The theater owner has the duty to care for the goods in a reasonable way. The finder does not get title to mislaid property. In the case of mislaid property, the true owner will probably return for the property.

◆ **lost property**
Property with which the owner has involuntarily parted and then cannot find or recover.

Lost Property   Property that is involuntarily left and forgotten is **lost property**. The finder of the property can claim title to the property against everyone but the true owner. If the true owner demands that the lost property be returned, the finder must return it.

If the finder knows who the true owner is, the property should be returned to him or her. Failure to return such property is the tort of *conversion* (see Chapter 5). Many states require the finder to make a diligent search in order to locate the true owner of lost property.

◆ **estray statute**
A state statute that requires the finder of lost property to report his or her discovery. After a specified time, if the true owner does not claim the property, the finder becomes the new owner.

Many states have **estray statutes** to encourage and aid the return of lost property. A common estray statute requires a finder to report a discovery; then the county clerk advertises the property that has been found in order to try to locate the owner. After a specified time, if the true owner does not claim the property, the finder becomes the new owner.

◆ **abandoned property**   Property with which the owner has voluntarily parted, with no intention of recovering it.

Abandoned Property   Property discarded by a true owner who has no intention of reclaiming the property is **abandoned property**. Generally, the person who finds the abandoned property gets title to it. This title is good against everyone, *including the original owner*. If the finder is trespassing

1. A fee simple owner can use, possess, or dispose of the property during his or her lifetime. At death, the fee simple ownership passes to the owner's heirs.
2. Persons who share ownership rights in property are concurrent owners or tenants.
3. Yes. A promise to make a gift is not enforceable. The gift must actually be delivered to the recipient before the recipient becomes the new owner.

4. If accession occurs without the permission of the owner, the ownership rights in the improved property usually depend on the good faith of the improver. Student examples will vary.
5. Ownership in personal property can be acquired by possession, purchase, production, gift, will or inheritance, confusion, and accession.

Enrichment

Tell students to write at least one example of a bailment in which they were the bailor or the bailee. Have them describe the circumstances and tell who was the bailee and who was the bailor and how the bailment ended.

Caption Answer

The auto repair facility is a bailor.

and finds abandoned property, then the title belongs to the owner of the land.

◆ CHECKING YOUR PROGRESS

1. What rights does a fee simple owner have in regard to property?
2. What are persons who share ownership rights in property called?
3. Must a gift be actually delivered for ownership to transfer? Explain.
4. Who would acquire ownership rights if accession occurs without the permission of the owner? Give an example.
5. In what ways can ownership in personal property be acquired?

◆ BAILMENTS

If you borrow your friend's clothes, books, or sports equipment, this is a bailment. All of us are affected by the law of bailments at some time. A *bailment*, as defined earlier in this chapter, is the temporary transfer to another person of possession of personal property. The title to the property is not transferred, just possession. The bailment occurs with the delivery of the personal property by the **bailor** (person transferring property) to another, called a **bailee**.

There is usually a purpose for the bailment—such as a loan, storage, repair, or transportation. When that purpose has been completed, the bailee must return the bailed property, usually to the bailor.

Most bailments are created by agreement but not necessarily by contract. For example, if you loan your bicycle to a friend, a bailment is created. However, as there is no payment, it is not a contract. Many bailments are, however, based on contract; one example is the delivery of your sleeping bag or of an item of clothing to the cleaners for dry cleaning.

◆ **bailor** A person who transfers possession of personal property to another.

◆ **bailee** A person to whom possession of personal property is transferred.

ELEMENTS OF A BAILMENT

For a transfer of property to be a bailment, the following three conditions must be met:

1. *Personal property*—Bailments involve only personal property. A bailment of your luggage is created when it is taken to an airline. But you, as an airline passenger, are not subject to a bailment. Real property also cannot be bailed; thus, renting a house is not a bailment.

2. *Delivery of possession*—The property must be transferred to the bailee. There are two requirements for effective delivery: (1) the bailee must be given both exclusive possession and control over the property, and (2) the bailee *must knowingly* accept the personal property.

Is the auto repair facility a bailee or bailor?

Extension Activity

Have student volunteers research modern salvage operations and/or treasure hunts. In each case, the students should list what is being sought, who is seeking it, and how they will acquire title to the treasure.

Read

Before reading this *Law in Action* feature, remind your students that under the law a finder may acquire good title to found personal property against everyone except the true owner. Ask the students whether they believe this to be fair. Then have a student volunteer read aloud this Law in Your Life feature about the law of finders.

Discuss

Stimulate a class discussion about this feature by asking the following questions: When the goldsmith kept the chimney sweep's jewel, did he maintain that he was its rightful owner? Why then did he believe he could keep the jewel rather than return it to the chimney sweep? Why did the court hold for the chimney sweep? Under what law did the United States try to claim title to the wreck of the *Atocha?* How did the court decide this case?

Law in Action

LAW IN YOUR LIFE: THE LAW OF FINDERS

The well-known children's adage, "finders keepers, losers weepers," is actually a legal principle as long as the rightful owner cannot be found. Several landmark cases have created the principle that a finder may acquire good title to found personal property *against everyone except the true owner.* An early English case involved Armory, a chimney sweep who found a jewel in its setting during his work. He took the jewel to a goldsmith to have it appraised. The goldsmith refused to return the jewel to Armory. The goldsmith claimed that Armory was not the rightful owner of the property. The court held that the finder, as prior possessor of the item, had rights to the jewel superior to all others except the rightful owner. The court said, "The finder of a jewel, though he does not by such finding acquire an absolute property of ownership, yet . . . has such a property as will enable him to keep it against all but the rightful owner."

The *Armory* case illustrates the doctrine of the *relativity of title.* Under this doctrine, if two competitors are before the court, neither of whom can claim absolute title to the property, the one who can claim prior possession is likely to win the case.

In an 1840 American case, a person found ten white pine logs floating in Delaware Bay after a sudden rise in the bay's water level. The finder tied the logs at the mouth of a creek, but the logs apparently broke free and floated up the creek. Another party then found the logs, and the first finder sued to recover possession. The court held that the first finder prevailed because he had not abandoned the property in dispute.

Several cases have pitted finders of shipwrecked treasure against either a state or the federal government. One case involved a Spanish galleon, one of a fleet of twenty-eight Spanish ships that had set sail from Cuba for Spain in the summer of 1622. In the Straits of Florida, the ships sailed into a hurricane, and several of them were ripped apart on the reefs. Among them was *Nuestra Señora de Atocha*, the richest ship of the fleet with more than forty-seven tons of gold and silver on board. Treasure Salvors, Inc., in 1971 found remnants of the *Atocha* forty-five miles off Key West, Florida. The wreckage was outside United States territorial waters. In 1975, Treasure Salvors discovered the bulk of the wreck. The search cost $2 million, and four members of the search party lost their lives. The discovery yielded gold, silver, and artifacts valued at more than $6 million.

When Treasure Salvors filed suit to confirm its title to the wreck of the *Atocha*, the United States government claimed title. The claim was made under the Antiquities Act (which primarily concerns the designation of historic landmarks and related activity) and the inherent right of a government to property found in its ocean waters. In rejecting the government's arguments, the court applied the law of finders. The court said the *Atocha* was not subject to U.S. control because it lay beyond U.S. territorial waters.

Today, the law of finders in relation to shipwrecks is as follows: if the find is outside U.S. territorial waters, then the finders can keep the property. If the find is within U.S. territorial waters, then the property belongs to the government.

After the students have worked through the Legal Focus Problem at the top of this page, ask volunteers to suggest other examples of bailments in which the bailee is given both exclusive possession and control over the property and the bailee knowingly accepts the property.

◆ LEGAL FOCUS – PROBLEM

Shannon Banks took Billie Saven out to dinner at an expensive restaurant. When they arrived at the restaurant, Shannon turned over her car to the parking attendant, who parked the car. Did a bailment of Shannon's car occur?

Yes, valet parking is usually a bailment. Self-parking is not. The difference lies in who controls the car keys. If Shannon had parked the car herself, locked it, and kept the keys, this would have been considered a lease of space. In such a case, the owner of the parking lot would be a *lessor* and Shannon a *lessee* of the space.

◆ LEGAL FOCUS – PROBLEM

When Millie entered the restaurant, she checked her coat. In the pocket of the coat was her mother's $5,000 diamond necklace. Was a bailment created? Did the bailment include the necklace?

A bailment of the coat exists as the restaurant has exclusive possession and control over the coat and has knowingly accepted it. No bailment of the necklace exists, however, because the restaurant did not knowingly accept it. They did not know nor could they reasonably expect that a valuable necklace would be in the coat pocket.

3. *Bailment agreement*—A bailment agreement can be *express* or *implied*. A written agreement is usually not required for a bailment. It is, however, a good idea to have one when valuable property is involved. Remember that not all bailment agreements are contracts. If you loan your next-door neighbor your hedge trimmer, it is an agreement and a bailment, but it is not a contract unless the neighbor pays for its use.

A bailment agreement expressly or implicitly expects the return of the property to the bailor. An agreement might also provide for the return of the property to a third person or for disposal by the bailee.

The bailee is also expected to return the identical goods given by the bailor. In certain types of bailments, such as a bailment of fungible goods, only equivalent property must be returned.

◆ LEGAL FOCUS – EXAMPLE

Holman stores his grain (*fungible goods*) in Joe's warehouse. At the end of the storage period, the warehouse does not have to return the exact same grain. The warehouse bailee must, however, return grain of the same *type*, *grade*, and *quantity*.

Legal Focus Problem

Read this Legal Focus Problem aloud to the class. Ask the class how this problem is different from the Legal Focus Problem above. Make sure the students understand that in this case the restaurant had not knowingly accepted possession of the diamond necklace.

Vocabulary Activity

Have a student volunteer define *express* and *implied*, as used in this sentence from the student book: "A bailment agreement can be *express* or *implied*."

Legal Focus Example

Have a student volunteer read aloud the Legal Focus Example dealing with fungible goods, found at the bottom of the page. Ask the class if they can think of any other examples that could also fit here. Allow volunteers to share their examples with the class.

Ask your students if renting your home to vacationers for a month is a bailment. Why or why not?

Divide the class into small groups. Have each group read and discuss the three types of ordinary bailments listed on this page. Then have the students in each group work together to create a Legal Focus Example for each of the three types of ordinary bailments. Have each group select a leader to share its examples with the class.

VIDEODISC NOTE
Much of the material that is conveyed in the exhibits of *West's Business and Personal Law* is also conveyed in the still frames on the **West Business Law and Legal Environment Videodisc**. For more information and directions for use, please see the Index and Description of Contents for the **West Business Law and Legal Environment Videodisc** that is found in your *Teacher's Resource Binder*.

678   Personal Law

ORDINARY BAILMENTS

The rights and duties of each party in a bailment relationship are often defined by an express contract. However, there are many rights and duties that are legally implied in different types of bailment relationships. These implied terms exist unless they are contradicted by an express agreement.

Two broad categories of bailment relationships are *ordinary* or *special (extraordinary) bailments*. There are three types of ordinary bailments. The distinguishing feature in these ordinary bailments is *which party receives a benefit from the bailment*. Which party receives the benefit also determines what the rights and liabilities of the parties are. See Exhibit 28-1.

The following are the three types of ordinary bailments:

◆ **mutual benefit bailment** A bailment where both the bailor and the bailee receive a contract benefit from the bailment.

1. **Mutual benefit bailment**—This is the most common type of bailment, where both the bailee and the bailor benefit. A mutual benefit bailment is also called a *contract bailment*. Examples of mutual benefit bailments include renting a car or paying for storage of property. Each party receives a contract benefit from the bailment.

2. *Bailment for the sole benefit of the bailor*—This is a gratuitous (free) bailment for the convenience and benefit of the bailor. For example, George agrees to store Mike's car in his garage for a week for free while Mike is on vacation. Mike, the bailor, benefits from the bailment while George, the bailee, does not.

3. *Bailment for the sole benefit of the bailee*—This is also a gratuitous (free) bailment; however, it is for the convenience and benefit of the bailee. For example, Shauna loans Katie a dress for the junior dance. Katie, the bailee, benefits from the bailment while Shauna, the bailor, does not.

Rights of the Bailee   The bailee has the *right to control and possess the property temporarily*. The bailee's right of possession allows him or her to sue

EXHIBIT 28-1
STANDARD OF CARE REQUIRED OF A BAILEE

Bailment for the sole benefit of the bailor	Mutual-benefit bailment	Benefit for the sole benefit of the bailee

SLIGHT   GREAT

REASONABLE
DEGREE OF CARE

Personal Property and Bailments   679

Critical Thinking Activity

third persons who damage the property. A bailee generally has the *right to use the bailed property.* For example, if you lease a baseball pitching machine, you, the bailee, expect to use the equipment to practice hitting baseballs. Sometimes, however, a bailee does not have the right to use the bailed property. For example, in a long-term storage of a car, the bailee is generally not allowed to use the car.

◆ LEGAL FOCUS ~ PROBLEM

Margo lost her pet dog, Mallet. Fortunately, Mallet was found by Judith, who took Margo's dog to her home and fed it. Though Judith took good care of Mallet, the dog became ill, and a veterinarian was called. Judith paid the veterinarian's bill and the cost of the medicine. Judith then placed an ad in the local paper describing Mallet. When Margo claimed Mallet, Judith requested that Margo pay her the costs of the services, medicine, and newspaper ad. What was the legal result?

In a mutual benefit bailment, a bailee has a *right to be paid.* Even in a gratuitous bailment, the bailee has a right to be reimbursed for his or her expenses. Judith should be paid by Margo for all reasonable costs incurred in the keeping of her dog and finding its owner.

To enforce a bailee's right of payment, the bailee has a right to place a claim, called a *possessory lien,* on the property until he or she has been fully paid. This type of lien, sometimes called an *artisan's* or *bailee's lien,* was discussed in Chapter 19.

Ordinary bailees can *limit their liability.* Such limitations should be in writing, and the bailor should know that they exist. Certain types of liability disclaimers, called *exculpatory clauses,* are held to violate public policy and to be illegal. The liability clauses most likely to be unenforceable are those that forgive a person for his or her own purposeful or negligent acts.

Duties of the Bailee   The bailee has two basic responsibilities in a bailment: (1) to take proper care of the property and (2) to surrender or dispose of the property at the end of the bailment.

A bailee's failure to exercise appropriate care in handling the bailor's property results in tort liability. The standard of care required of the bailee often depends on the type of bailment. In general, a bailment for the sole benefit of the bailee creates a high duty of care. A mutual benefit bailment creates an ordinary duty of care. A bailment for the sole benefit of the bailor creates a slight duty of care.

The duty to relinquish the property at the end of the bailment is based on principles of both contract and tort law. Failure to return the property constitutes a breach of contract or a tort of conversion. The bailee is then liable for damages. This obligation is excused if the property is destroyed, lost, or stolen through no fault of the bailee.

Proof of damage to the property usually raises a presumption that the bailee is guilty of negligence or conversion. The bailee must then prove that he or she was not negligent.

Duties of the Bailor   The *rights* of a bailor are similar to the *duties* of a bailee. If the bailment is a mutual benefit bailment or a bailment for the sole benefit of the bailor, the bailor has the duty to notify the bailee of any hidden defects that the bailor could have discovered with reasonable diligence and proper inspection.

LEGAL FOCUS ~ PROBLEM

Max leased farm equipment from Rivercity Equipment Rental Company. The equipment was defective, and the defect should have been discovered by Rivercity. It was not, however, readily discoverable by Max who was, to be kind, not mechanically inclined. Rivercity did not warn Max of the defect. Max was seriously injured by the use of the equipment. Is the fact that the equipment was leased rather than sold a defense that would protect Rivercity from product liability?

No, the law will treat the lease very much like a sale. The bailor has a duty to warn the bailee of defects that the bailor knew about or should have discovered. If the bailee is not warned, the bailor is liable to the bailee for the tort of negligence. Rivercity is liable. The bailor is also liable to any other person, besides the bailee, who might reasonably be expected to come into contact with the defective article.

LEGAL FOCUS ~ PROBLEM

Brenda asked to borrow Carl's car to pick up some job applications. While attempting to stop at a red light, the brakes on the car failed. Brenda was involved in a two-car collision. Is Carl liable to Brenda for injuries caused by the defective brakes?

The exception to the rule requiring a bailor to notify a bailee of defects is the case of a bailment that is for the sole benefit of the bailee. In such a case, the bailor is only responsible for informing the bailee of known defects. In this example, Carl loaned the car without any expectation of personal benefit. If Carl did not know of the defective brakes, he would not be held liable.

Termination of Bailments   Bailments for a specific time end when the stated period is over. When a period is not stated, the bailment can be ended at any time by (1) mutual agreement of the bailor and bailee, (2) a demand by either party, (3) the completion of the purpose of the bailment,

(4) an act by the bailee that is inconsistent with the terms of the bailment, or (5) operation of law.

SPECIAL BAILMENTS

Special bailments are those that require special attention. These include bailments where the bailee's duty of care is *extraordinary*. The bailee's liability for loss or damage to the property is absolute; this is generally true in cases involving common carriers and innkeepers. Warehouse companies have the same duty of care as ordinary bailees; however, like common carriers, they are subject to extensive federal and state laws.

Common Carriers   A *carrier* transports people and property. A **common carrier** is publicly licensed to provide transportation services to the public. A common carrier must arrange transportation for all who apply, within certain limitations. Private carriers operate transportation facilities for select customers. Private carriers are not required to provide service to everyone who makes a request.

The delivery of goods to a common carrier creates a bailment relationship. The common carrier is held to a much higher standard of care than an ordinary bailee. The common carrier is absolutely liable for losses or damage to goods, regardless of whether the common carrier is negligent. Under common law, there are five exceptions to this absolute liability: (1) an act of God (for example, a flood or earthquake), (2) an act of a public enemy (for example, damage caused by war), (3) an order of a public authority (for example, if the government confiscates the goods), (4) an act of

> ◆   **special bailment**
> A bailment that requires some special treatment, such as a shipment or warehouse bailment.

> ◆   **common carrier**
> A transportation carrier that is licensed to provide transportation services to the public.

Every time a truck transports property, a bailment exists.

Reteaching Activity

Ask a student volunteer to explain to the class what a warehouse receipt represents.

Legal Focus Problem

Have a student volunteer read aloud the Legal Focus Problem found at the bottom of this page. Ask the volunteer to suggest a possible answer to the question posed at the end of this problem.

the shipper (for example, the customer packs the goods carelessly), and (5) the inherent nature of the goods (for example, perishable goods become rotten).

In the shipment contract, common carriers cannot exclude their liability for damaged goods, but they can limit their maximum liability to an amount explicitly stated. State and federal laws, however, require common carriers to offer customers the opportunity to get higher dollar limits for losses by paying an additional fee.

Warehouse Companies   Warehousing is the business of providing storage of property for compensation. A warehouse company is a professional bailee whose responsibility differs from that of an ordinary bailee. For example, a warehouse company can issue documents of title—in particular, **warehouse receipts**. A warehouse receipt is a piece of paper that provides proof to a person that he or she has goods stored in a warehouse. It is a useful way for a person to provide evidence of ownership of goods that are not in his or her possession. Warehouse companies are also subject to many state and federal statutes that regulate how they do business.

Although considered an extraordinary bailee, a warehouse company's rights and duties are much like those of an ordinary bailee. The warehouse is liable for loss or damage to property and possessions resulting from *negligence*; thus, the warehouse does not have the same liability as a common carrier. Its duty is to offer reasonable care to protect and preserve the bailor's goods. A warehouse company is free to limit the dollar amount of the company's liability. The bailor, however, must be given the option of paying an increased storage rate in exchange for an increase in the liability limit.

When a warehouse company accepts goods for storage, it issues a warehouse receipt. The receipt describes the property and the terms of the bailment contract. A warehouse receipt can be negotiable or nonnegotiable, depending on how it is written. It is negotiable if its terms provide that the warehouse company will deliver the goods "to the bearer" of the receipt or "to the order of" a person named on the receipt. Exhibit 28-2 provides an example of a *non*negotiable warehouse receipt. Note that it is not made out to the bearer, nor do the words "to the order of" appear on this receipt.

◆ **warehouse receipt**   A receipt issued by a warehouser for goods stored in a warehouse.

◈ LEGAL FOCUS ~ PROBLEM

Ossip, a processor and canner of corn, delivered 6,000 cases of corn to Shaney, the owner of a warehouse. Shaney issued a negotiable warehouse receipt payable "to bearer." She gave it to Ossip. Ossip sold and delivered the warehouse receipt to a large supermarket chain, Better Foods, Inc. Does Better Foods have the right to claim the goods?

Warehouse Receipt—Not Negotiable

Agreement No. _____   Vault No. _____ _____ _____ _____

Service Order _____   _____ _____ _____ _____ _____

Receipt and
Lot Number _____   Date of Issue _____ 19 ____

Received for the account of and deliverable to * _____

whose latest known address is _____ SAMPLE _____

_____ the goods enumerated on the inside or attached schedule to be

stored in Company warehouse, located at _____
which goods are accepted only upon the following conditions set forth below:

READ CAREFULLY That the value of all goods stored, including the contents of any container, and all goods hereafter stored for Depositor's account to be not over $ _____ per pound † per article unless a higher value is noted in the schedule, for which an additional monthly storage charge of _____ ¢ on each $ _____ valuation in excess of $ _____ per pound † per article or fraction thereof will be made.

If there are any items enumerated in this receipt valued in excess of the above limitations per pound per article and not so noted in the schedule, return this receipt within 10 days with proper values so indicated in writing in order that the receipt may be re-issued and proper higher storage rates assessed.

OWNERSHIP. The Customer, Shipper, Depositor, or Agent represents and warrants that he is lawfully possessed of goods to be stored and/or has the authority to store or ship said goods. (If the goods are mortgaged, notify the Company the name and address of the mortgagee.)

PAYMENT OF CHARGES. Storage bills are payable monthly in advance for each month's storage or fraction thereof. Labor charges, cartage and other services rendered are payable upon completion of work. All charges shall be paid at the warehouse location shown hereon, and if delinquent, shall incur interest monthly at the rate of ____ per cent ( ) per year. The Depositor will pay reasonable attorney's fee incurred by The Company in collecting delinquent accounts.

LIABILITY OF COMPANY. The company shall be liable for any loss or injury to the goods caused by its failure to exercise such care as a reasonably careful man would exercise under like circumstances. The company will not be liable for loss or damage to fragile articles not packed, or articles packed or unpacked by other than employees of this company. Depositor specifically agrees that the warehouse will not be liable for contamination of or for insect damage to articles placed in drawers of furniture by the depositor. Periodic spraying of the warehouse premises shall constitute ordinary and proper care, unless the depositor requests in writing and pays for anti-infestation treatment of articles in drawers and compartments of stored furniture.

CHANGE OF ADDRESS. Notice of change of address must be given the Company in writing, and acknowledged in writing by the Company.

TRANSFER OR WITHDRAWAL OF GOODS. The warehouse receipt is not negotiable and shall be produced and all charges must be paid before delivery to the Depositor, or transfer of goods to another person; however, a written direction to the Company to transfer the goods to another person or deliver the goods may be accepted by the Company at its option without requiring tender of the warehouse receipt.

ACCESS TO STORAGE. PARTIAL WITHDRAWAL. A signed order from the person in whose name the receipt is issued is required to enable others to remove or have access to goods. A charge is made for stacking and unstacking, and for access to stored goods.

BUILDING—FIRE—WATCHMAN. The Company does not represent or warrant that its building cannot be destroyed by fire or that the contents of said buildings including the said property cannot be destroyed by fire. The Company shall not be required to maintain a watchman or sprinkler system and its failure to do so shall not constitute negligence.

CLAIMS OR ERRORS. All claims for non-delivery of any article or articles and for damage, breakage, etc., must be made in writing within ninety (90) days from delivery of goods stored or they are waived. Failure to return the warehouse receipt for correction within ( ) days after receipt thereof by the depositor will be conclusive that it is correct and delivery will be made only in accordance therewith.

FUTURE SERVICE. This Contract shall extend and apply to future services rendered to the Depositor by the Company and to any additional goods deposited with the Company by the Depositor.

WAREHOUSEMAN'S LIEN. The Company reserves the right to sell the goods stored, in accordance with the provisions of the Uniform Commercial Code (Business and Commerce Code if stored in Texas), for all lawful charges in arrears.

TERMINATION OF STORAGE. The Company reserves the right to terminate the storage of the goods at any time by giving to the Depositor thirty (30) days' written notice of its intention so to do, and, unless the Depositor removes such goods within that period, the Company is hereby empowered to have the same removed at the cost and expense of the Depositor, or the Company may sell them at auction in accordance with state law.

DEPOSITOR WILL PAY REASONABLE LEGAL FEES INCURRED BY WAREHOUSE IN COLLECTING DELINQUENT CHARGES.

THIS DOCUMENT CONTAINS THE WHOLE CONTRACT BETWEEN THE PARTIES AND THERE ARE NO OTHER TERMS, WARRANTIES, REPRESENTATIONS, OR AGREEMENTS OF EITHER DEPOSITOR OR COMPANY NOT HEREIN CONTAINED.

Storage per month or fraction thereof	$ _____
Warehouse labor	$ _____
Cartage	$ _____
Packing at residence . . .	$ _____
Wrapping and preparing for storage	$ _____
Charges advanced	$ _____
	$ _____
	$ _____

By _____

* Insert "Mr. and/or Mrs." or, if military personnel, appropriate rank or grade.
† Delete the words "per pound" if the declared value is per article.
For goods stored for military personnel under PL 245, the contractor's liability for care of goods is as provided in Basic Agreement with U.S. Government.

THIS PROPERTY HAS NOT BEEN INSURED BY THIS COMPANY FOR FIRE OR ANY OTHER CASUALTY
SCHEDULE OF GOODS ON FOLLOWING PAGE OR ATTACHED

Source: Reprinted with permission of Hart Graphics, Inc. of Austin, Texas. © 1985 Hart Graphics, Inc.

EXHIBIT 28-2
A SAMPLE NONNEGOTIABLE WAREHOUSE RECEIPT

Enrichment

Guide the students in looking at Exhibit 28-2, a sample nonnegotiable warehouse receipt. Ask a student volunteer to find the wording that specifically deals with negotiability. (Under transfer or withdrawal of goods, this warehouse receipt states the following, "The warehouse receipt is not negotiable and shall be produced and all charges must be paid before delivery to the depositor or transfer of goods to another person; however, a written direction to the company to transfer the goods to another person or deliver the goods may be accepted by the company at its option without requiring tender of the warehouse receipt.")

Have a student volunteer read this Legal Focus Problem aloud to the class. Ask the volunteer to suggest a possible answer to the question posed at the end of this problem. Remind students that they can use the Legal Focus features as review tools when studying for tests.

Checking Your Progress (Answers)

1. Although property is in the possession of a bailee during a bailment, the title remains with the bailor. Therefore, the bailee does not become the owner of the property, even temporarily.
2. No. A bailment could end if the agreement provides for return of the property to a third person or for disposal by the bailee.
3. The distinguishing feature in the three ordinary bailments is which party receives a benefit from the bailment—mutual benefit, benefit for the bailor, or bailment for the bailee.
4. The bailee has two basic responsibilities in a bailment: (1) to take proper care of the property and (2) to surrender or dispose of the property at the end of the bailment.
5. Bailments end when a stated period lapses or at any time (1) by mutual agreement, (2) by demand of either party, (3) on completion of the purpose of the bailment, (4) by an act by the bailee that is inconsistent with the terms of the bailment, and (5) by operation of law.

A warehouse receipt serves multiple functions. It is a receipt for the goods stored, and it is a contract of bailment. It also indicates title to the goods. It is useful in assisting commercial transactions. In this example, Better Foods is now the owner of the corn. It has the right to get the cases of corn from Shaney. Better Foods can present the warehouse receipt to Shaney, who will then release the corn to the grocery chain.

Innkeepers At common law, innkeepers, hotel owners, or similar operators were held to the same strict liability as common carriers. Property brought into the rooms of a hotel or inn by guests was considered bailed. Today, the rule applies only to those who are temporary guests, not lodgers who are permanent residents of the hotel or inn.

◆ LEGAL FOCUS ~ PROBLEM

Jiminez stayed the night at the Harbor Hotel. He ate breakfast in the hotel restaurant. When he returned to his room he discovered that his room door had been forced open and his suitcase stolen. Jiminez claimed that the hotel was liable for his loss. The hotel maintained that it was not negligent and thus was not liable. Who is correct?

At common law, innkeepers were held strictly liable for the loss of the property of their guests. Today, most states have statutes that allow innkeepers to avoid strict liability if they provide a safe in which guests may keep their valuables. Each guest must be notified that a safe is available. If notice is provided and the articles are not kept in the safe, these statutes often limit the liability of innkeepers.

State laws also often limit the amount of innkeeper responsibility. They may even provide that the innkeeper has no liability unless he or she is negligent. Many statutes require that these limitations be posted. The notice is frequently found on the back of the door of each room in a motel or hotel. Obviously, Jiminez's rights will depend on whether the hotel was in a state with such a statute and then on whether the hotel had posted such a notice.

◆ CHECKING YOUR PROGRESS

1. Does the bailee become the temporary owner of the property while it is in his or her possession? Explain.
2. Must the property transferred to a bailee be returned to the bailor to end the agreement?
3. What is the distinguishing feature in the three ordinary bailments?
4. What are the duties of a bailee?
5. When does a bailment end?

Teaching A Case In Point

Read

Introduce this *A Case In Point* feature by having a student volunteer read aloud to the class the elements of a bailment listed in the Chapter Summary on page 687. Explain to the students that, in this *A Case In Point* feature, they should try to determine if the elements of a bailment are present. Have a student volunteer read this *A Case In Point* feature aloud to the class.

Discuss

Stimulate a class discussion of this *A Case In Point* feature by asking the students the following questions: Where did Augustine hang his coat and why? What happened when Augustine went to find his coat at the noon recess? Whom did Augustine sue? What was the issue in this case? What was the decision of the Town Court of Amherst, New York? What reasons did the court give for its decision? Which elements of a bailment were missing in this case? What steps could Augustine have taken to protect his coat?

◆ A CASE IN POINT ◆

AUGUSTINE v. MARRIOTT HOTEL

Town Court, Amherst, New York, 1986.
132 Misc.2d 180,
503 N.Y.S.2d 498.

A hotel patron sued a Marriott Hotel when his cashmere coat, which he had placed on a rack outside a seminar room, disappeared. As you read this case, try to decide if the elements of a bailment are present.

FACTS The plaintiff, Augustine, attended a seminar for dentists held at a Marriott Hotel. The seminar sponsor had rented the hotel banquet room. The sponsor asked the hotel to place a movable coatrack outside the banquet room in the public lobby. Augustine placed his coat on the rack before entering the seminar. He tried to find the coat at the noon recess. The rack had been moved a distance down the lobby and around a corner, near an exit. To his alarm, his cashmere coat was missing. Claiming the hotel was liable for the loss, Augustine sued.

ISSUE Was the hotel a bailee of the coat and thus liable to its owner for the loss?

DECISION The court held that the hotel was not liable to Augustine for the loss of the coat and dismissed the claim.

REASON The court stated that the relationship of bailor-bailee never came into existence because Augustine had not transferred his coat to the hotel. There had been no delivery of the coat to the hotel, nor was the hotel, in the eyes of the court, ever in possession of the coat. Furthermore, Augustine was not even directly a guest of the hotel. The court compared Augustine's relationship to the hotel to that of a "wedding guest of individuals who rent banquet facilities from a hotel." The court concluded that "a reasonable man would have wondered about the safety of his coat which he hung on a rack in a public lobby of a hotel, without ascertaining if there were a guard." The court could find no evidence that users of the rack were led to expect that the rack would be guarded. The court concluded that users of the coatrack placed their coats there at their own risk.

Teaching Note

This case is included in the *West's Business and Personal Law Handbook of Selected Court Cases.*

Assessment Strategies

In order to check student mastery of chapter concepts, you may wish to use the Chapter 28 test that is found in your *Teacher's Resource Binder* or use WESTEST computerized testing for Chapter 28.

CHAPTER REVIEW

◆ SUMMARY

PERSONAL PROPERTY

Definition of Personal Property

Personal property (personalty) includes all property not classified as real property (realty). It can be tangible (such as a TV set or a car) or intangible (such as stocks or bonds).

Property Rights

Property owners have the right to possess and dispose of or transfer the property by sale, gift, will, and so on.

Common Types of Ownership of Personal Property

1. *Fee simple*: Exists when individuals have the right to possess, use, or dispose of the property as they choose.

2. *Concurrent ownership:*

   a. Tenancy in common—Co-ownership in which two or more persons own an interest in the property; when a tenant dies, his or her property interest passes to his or her heirs.

   b. Joint tenancy—Exists when two or more persons own an interest in property; when a joint tenant dies, his or her property interest transfers to the remaining tenants, not to the heirs of the deceased.

   c. Tenancy by the entirety—A form of co-ownership of property between husband and wife. Like joint tenancy, there is a right of survivorship.

   d. Community property—Exists in nine states. Includes all property acquired by the husband or wife during their marriage, other than property acquired by gift or inheritance.

Acquiring Ownership of Personal Property

1. *Possession*—Ownership may be acquired by possession of the property if no other person has ownership title.

2. *Purchase*—The most common means of acquiring and transferring ownership of personal property is to buy it.

3. *Production*—Products or items produced by an individual become the property of that individual.

4. *Gift*—An effective gift exists when:

   a. The gift is delivered (physically or constructively) to the donee.

   b. There is evidence of *intent* to make a gift of the property in question.

   c. The gift is accepted by the donee or the donee's agent.

5. *Will or inheritance*—When the owner dies, the property of the deceased passes to named beneficiaries if there is a valid will. If no valid will exists, property passes to heirs determined by state inheritance laws.

6. *Accession*—When someone adds value to a piece of property by labor or materials, the added value generally becomes the property of the owner of the original property.

7. *Confusion*—If a person wrongfully and willfully commingles goods with those of another to render them indistinguishable, the innocent party acquires title to the whole.

Mislaid, Lost, and Abandoned Property

1. *Mislaid property*—Property that is placed somewhere *voluntarily* by the owner and then forgotten.

2. *Lost property*—Property that is *involuntarily* left and forgotten. A finder of lost property can claim title to the property *unless the true owner returns to claim it.*

3. *Abandoned property*—Property that has

1. The main difference between tenants in common and joint tenants is how ownership passes upon a tenant's death. In a tenant in common relationship, ownership passes to the heirs, but in a joint tenancy, the deceased tenant's interest passes to the surviving joint tenant(s). Also, a joint tenancy requires a written document, whereas a tenancy in common does not.

2. Constructive delivery means that something is not physically delivered, but some act demonstrates the intent and represents real delivery. It can be accomplished in many ways, such as delivering documents showing ownership or delivering a key to the goods.

3. For transfer of property to be a bailment (1) the property must be personal property, (2) the bailee must knowingly accept and take control of the property, and (3) the bailment agreement can be express or implied.

4. Two broad categories of bailment relationships are ordinary and special (extraordinary) bailments. In an ordinary bailment, either the bailee, the bailor, or both benefit from the transfer of property. In a special bailment, the bailee may have the duty of extraordinary care, above that of an ordinary bailment situation.

5. A bailee can place a possessory lien on the property until fully paid. This type of lien is sometimes called an artisan's lien or a bailee's lien.

6. Although innkeepers were strictly liable under common law for the loss of property of their guests, today they can limit that liability if they are in a state that has statutes allowing innkeepers to avoid strict liability if they provide a safe place for guests to keep valuables. Guests must be notified that a safe is available. Additionally, state laws often limit the amount of innkeeper responsibility. Usually, notice of the limitation must be posted where a guest will readily see it.

been discarded by the true owner with no intention of claiming title to it in the future. A finder of abandoned property can claim title to it.

BAILMENTS

Elements of a Bailment

1. *Personal property*—Bailments involve only personal property.

2. *Delivery of possession*—The bailee (the one receiving the property) must be given exclusive possession and control over the property for an effective bailment to exist.

3. *Bailment agreement*—Expressly or implicitly provides for the return of the bailed property to the bailor or to a third party or provides for disposal of the property by the bailee.

Ordinary Bailments

1. *Mutual benefit (contractual) bailment*—Involves compensation between the bailee and bailor for the service provided. Reasonable care to preserve the bailed property is required of the bailee.

2. *Bailment for the sole benefit of the bailor*—A gratuitous bailment undertaken for the sole benefit of the bailor. Only slight care to preserve the bailed property is required of the bailee.

3. *Bailment for the sole benefit of the bailee*—A gratuitous loan of an article to a person solely for the bailee's benefit. Great care to preserve the bailed property is required of the bailee.

Rights of a Bailee (Duties of a Bailor)

1. *The right to be compensated and reimbursed for expenses*—In the event of nonpayment, the bailee has the right to place a bailee's lien on the bailed property.

2. *The right to limit liability*—An ordinary bailee can limit his or her liability provided proper notice is given and the limitation is consistent with public policy. In special bailments, only limitations on the amount of liability are permitted.

Duties of a Bailee (Rights of a Bailor)

1. A bailee must exercise reasonable care over property entrusted to him or her.

2. Bailed goods in a bailee's possession must be either returned to the bailor or disposed of according to the bailor's directions.

Special Bailments

1. *Common carriers*—Carriers that are publicly licensed to provide transportation services to the public. The common carrier is *strictly liable* (with limited exceptions).

2. *Warehouse companies*—Professional bailees that differ from ordinary bailees because they (1) can issue documents of title (warehouse receipts) and (2) are subject to state and federal statutes. They must exercise reasonable care over the bailed property and are liable for loss of or damage to the property due to negligence.

3. *Innkeepers* (hotel operators)—The common law strict-liability standard to which innkeepers were held is today often limited by state statute.

◆ USING LEGAL LANGUAGE

Directions: Match each term with the statement that best defines that term.

1. accession
2. community property
3. fee simple
4. intangible personal property
5. joint tenancy

A. a form of property co-ownership with the right of survivorship

B. personal property that represents a set of rights and duties with its value not in its physical existence

7. Probably. Personal property voluntarily placed on another's premises and then forgotten is classified as mislaid property. Since the owner of the mislaid property is expected to remember where he or she has left the property and to return to the premises to pick it up, the owner of the premises has both the right of possession and the duty of a caretaker (as in involuntary bailee) over the property. As a caretaker, the owner of the premises must exercise reasonable care over the property and is liable for failure to do so. Since Trina's purse had been voluntarily placed on the counter and forgotten, the purse is mislaid property. The store had a duty to exercise reasonable care over the purse until Trina returned. Pam's failure to put the purse in a safe place amounts to a probable failure of that duty of care, and Trina will probably win a judgment against Numans Department Store.

Applying the Law . . . You Be the Judge (Answers)

1. The Tunica Indian tribe should succeed in their claim for title to the artifacts. Abandoned property is any chattel that the true owner discarded with no intention of ever claiming title. Impliedly, intent to abandon must include intent to let the first person who comes along acquire the property. Property that is

buried with the dead is not abandoned because there is no intent by the owner to allow anyone else to take possession; indeed, all personal property that is buried with a deceased is intended to remain buried forever with the body. The Indian artifacts were specifically placed in the ground as part of religious ceremonies and were intended to remain in their place. Therefore, Charrier should fail in his claim of title to the artifacts based upon first possession because the artifacts were not abandoned property.

2. Viers and Garcia were both held liable to Freeman for the loss of the watch. When an individual deposits property with a depositary, the depositary has the duty to use the same diligence in preserving the deposit that he or she uses in preserving his or her own property. This duty is strictly enforced when the depositary receives money for his or her services, as in the case of both Garcia and Viers. It is also the law that when one depositary accepts the property of another, delivers that property to another for repair, and the

6. mutual benefit bailment
7. personal property
8. severalty
9. special bailment
10. tenancy by the entirety

C. the adding of value to a piece of personal property by either labor or materials

D. a bailment that warrants special consideration, such as a bailment for transportation

E. a form of property co-ownership between husband and wife in which a deceased spouse's interest automatically transfers to the surviving spouse at death

F. ownership of the entire bundle of rights in property

G. a contract bailment in which reasonable care to preserve the bailed property is required of the bailee

H. all property acquired by either a husband or wife during their marriage except by gift or inheritance

I. property that is movable; any property that is not real property

J. only one person owns property

◆ CHECKING FOR COMPREHENSION

1. What is the main difference between tenants in common and joint tenants?

2. How is constructive delivery accomplished?

3. What conditions must be met to effect a bailment?

4. Describe the two broad categories of bailment relationships?

5. What rights does a bailee have if he or she is not paid for the bailment services?

6. In the past, innkeepers were strictly liable for the loss of the property of their guests. How can innkeepers avoid strict liability today?

7. Trina went to Numans Department Store to do some shopping. She became engrossed in looking at some silk blouses and did not notice the time. Suddenly, she realized that she had to leave quickly to meet her date for dinner. She hastily departed from the store, inadvertently leaving her purse on the sales counter. Pam, a sales clerk, noticed the purse on the counter but left it there expecting Trina to return for it. Later, when Trina returned to retrieve the purse, it was gone. Trina filed an action against Numans Department Store for the loss of her purse. Will she be able to recover damages for her loss?

◆ APPLYING LEGAL CONCEPTS

1. Look through magazines and newspaper to find pictures of real property, tangible personal property, and symbols of intangi-

ble property. Cut out or copy the pictures. Design a poster displaying each kind of property.

property is lost while in the possession of the co-depositary, both parties are equally liable unless they can show that they were not negligent. Since Viers did not have burglar alarms or other safeguards to protect his property, he was negligent. Because Garcia failed to inquire as to whether Viers had a burglar alarm system, guards, or other safeguarding equipment and did not check to find out whether Viers was insured against loss of property kept on his premises, Garcia was also negligent.

3. Smith should succeed in his claim to ownership of the boat as a finder. When property is lost or abandoned, the first finder is generally considered to have a better claim to the property than any third person. Property that is not voluntarily left and forgotten is lost property, and a finder can claim title to the property against the entire world, except the true owner. Property that has been discarded by the true owner with no intention of claiming title to it is considered abandoned property, and a finder can assert title over the property against the entire world, including the true owner. Thus, Smith can definitely claim title to the boat against the sheriff regardless of whether the property is lost or abandoned because physically picking up a found item is not required to take legal possession. By discovering the boat (being able to remove or exert control over it) and stating that he was claiming the right to take it against any but the rightful owner, Smith took first possession of the property. The police, although they had the right to impound the boat temporarily, took possession subject to the rights of Smith.

4. Yes. The court held that Welton had made a gift of the bonds to Gallagher. The intent to make a gift was clearly evidenced by the following facts: a–Welton knew at the time of transfer, through his business experience, that the bearer bonds could be transferred without indorsement and that upon transfer of the bonds to anyone, he lost ownership; b–Welton told Gallagher that the bonds were hers with "no strings attached"; and c–he told Gallagher that she should put the bonds in her safe-deposit box, where obviously Welton could not have access to them. These factors indicated a donative intent, and since there was a physical delivery and acceptance of the bonds, Gallagher became owner of the bonds.

2. Visit local businesses to collect bailment agreements. Collect agreement documents from friends. Examples of agreements can include: common carrier tickets, storage call tickets, parking lot ticket stubs, hotel check-in slips, etc. Create a poster categorizing the documents as an ordinary bailment or a special (extraordinary) bailment.

◆ APPLYING THE LAW . . . YOU BE THE JUDGE

1. Leonard Charrier, an amateur archaeologist in Louisiana uncovered artifacts from a several-hundred-year-old Indian burial ground. The artifacts had been made by the ancestors of the present-day Tunica Indian tribe of Louisiana. The Tunica tribe asked the court to award it custody of the property, which included burial pots, ornaments, and pottery. Charrier claimed that the property had been abandoned and that he had the right to title because he had taken possession of the property. Discuss whether the Tunica tribe, as heirs to the former owners of the property, should succeed in their claim to the artifacts or whether the property was abandoned. [*Charrier v. Bell*, 496 So.2d 601 (La.App.1st Cir. 1986)]

2. Robert Freeman owned a broken Bulova watch. Its band was encrusted with gold nuggets and contained two jade stones. He took the watch to John Garcia's jewelry store for repairs. Garcia did not have the necessary equipment to make all the repairs, so he sent the watch to a watch repair shop owned by Douglas Viers. While it was at Vier's shop, the watch, along with several others, was stolen. Viers did not have insurance, nor did he have any burglar alarm or other safeguards on the premises. Freeman, claiming that the watch had been worth $25,000, sued both Garcia and Viers for the value of the watch. Discuss whether Garcia or Viers or both are liable for the loss of the watch. [*Freeman v. Garcia*, 495 So.2d 351 (La.App.2d Cir. 1986)]

3. Danny Smith and his brother discovered a sixteen-foot boat lying beside a roadway in Alabama. Danny Smith informed the police, who immediately impounded the boat and stored it in a city warehouse. Although Smith acquiesced to the police action, he told the police that if the true boat owner did not claim the boat, he wanted it. When the true owner did not come forward, the police refused to relinquish the boat to Smith and instead told Smith that they planned to auction it to the highest bidder on behalf of the city. Smith sued for custody of the boat. Since Smith never physically held the boat but rather allowed the police to take possession, should Smith succeed in his claim to title as finder? [*Smith v. Purvis*, 474 So.2d 1131 (Ala.Civ.App. 1985)]

4. Welton, an experienced businessperson, transferred to Gallagher bearer bonds, stating that the bonds were hers with "no strings attached" and that she should place the bonds in her safe-deposit box for safekeeping. Later, Welton wanted Gallagher to return the bonds to him, claiming that he was still the owner. Gallagher refused, claiming that Welton's transfer was a gift. Was it? Discuss fully? [*Welton v. Gallagher*, 2 Hawaii App. 242, 630 P.2d 1077 (1981)]

Have the students brainstorm a list of trademarks or trade names with which they are familiar. Ask a volunteer to list the trademarks or trade names on the board.

LEGAL BACKGROUND

Oliver Wendell Holmes, Jr., in his 1881 treatise *The Common Law*, referred to law as the response of lawmakers to the "felt necessities of the time." Currently, the American legal system, at state and federal levels, is responding to changes brought on by the computer age. Some of these changes concern computers directly; some involve other sorts of intangible property.

Wealth includes intellectual property, which consists of the products of intellectual and creative processes. Television series, computer programs, and movies are all forms of intellectual property.

Computers represent another form of wealth. Unfair trade practices issues arise constantly in this industry. The protection of intellectual property relating to computers has posed difficulties for lawmakers because computers were not envisioned by the legislators who drafted patent, trademark, and copyright laws.

LEGAL PERSPECTIVE
INTELLECTUAL PROPERTY AND COMPUTER LAW

Some of the most valuable of personal property is intangible. Its value lies in what it represents, not its physical existence. A filled-out check is only valuable because the bank will exchange money for it. A blank check has very little value. This Legal Perspective will discuss the infringement of rights to important types of intangible personal property called *intellectual property* such as trademarks, patents, and copyrights. The specific problem of infringement of rights to computer software (programs) is also discussed.

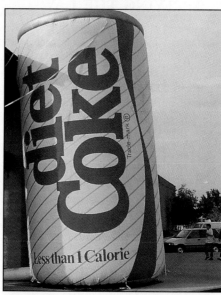

Does this art and packaging represent a property that the Coca Cola Company can protect?

◆ INTELLECTUAL PROPERTY

One important form of intangible property is **intellectual property**. This is property resulting from mental and creative processes. It is the product of an individual's mind. Intellectual property is vulnerable to a form of the tort of unfair competition called **passing off**. Passing off is falsely encouraging buyers to believe that one product is really another. It is usually done because the other product is well-known or has a reputation for quality. There are many examples—jeans, perfume, cameras, and a variety of other consumer goods are passed off through otherwise reputable merchants. Passing off is an infringement of a trademark, a trade name, a patent, or a copyright.

The tort requires that the ordinary customer, paying the usual amount of attention, be deceived. It is estimated that the unauthorized use of trademarks, trade names, patents, and copyrights costs American companies more than $60 billion a year.

TRADEMARKS OR TRADE NAMES

A **trademark** is a distinctive mark, motto, device, or implement that a manufacturer stamps or prints on its goods. Businesses hope that a customer can identify their products without confusion. If one business uses the trademark of another, consumers are misled as to who made the goods. The law seeks to avoid this kind of confusion.

Normally, personal names, words, or places that are descriptive of an article or its use cannot be trademarked. Anyone can use these names. Words that are used as part of a design or device, however, or words that are uncommon or fanciful may be trademarked. For example, the term *English*

Extension Activity

Have a student volunteer research the U.S. Patent Office. Guide the student in his or her research by asking the following questions: What is in the U.S. Patent Office? How does one secure a patent? When were the first patents issued? Have the student report his or her findings to the class in the form of a brief oral report.

leather may not be trademarked to describe leather processed in England. However, the term *English Leather* may be—and is—trademarked as the name of an after-shave lotion. The use of this phrase for an after-shave lotion is a *fanciful* use of the words. Even the common name of an individual may be trademarked if the name is accompanied by a picture or fanciful design that allows for easy identification of the product—for example, Smith Brothers' Cough Drops.

Once a trademark has been registered, a company is entitled to its exclusive use for business purposes. Whenever a trademark is copied by another, intentionally or unintentionally, the trademark has been infringed, and the wrongdoer may be stopped and sued for money damages.

A **trade name** is all or part of a business's name, whether the business is a sole proprietorship, a partnership, or a corporation. As with trademarks, the words in the name must be unusual or fanciful in order to be protected. The word *Safeway* has been found to be sufficiently fanciful for protection as a trade name for a food store chain. A trade name is a property interest that can be protected. Courts will allow businesses to seek both injunctions and money damages against defendants who use a company trade name without permission.

A company who fails to be attentive and protect its trade name can lose it. For example, *aspirin* and *thermos* were originally used only as trade names, but today they are used generically, which means that they are used to refer to a whole group of similar products. Other examples of lost trade names are *escalator*, *trampoline*, *nylon*, and *cornflakes*.

PATENTS

A **patent** is a grant from the government allowing an inventor the exclusive right to make, use, and sell an invention for seventeen years. Patents for a lesser period are given for designs, as opposed to inventions. A patent applicant must demonstrate to the patent office that the invention, discovery, or design is genuine, novel, and useful. It also cannot be obvious considering current technology.

A patent holder gives notice that an article or design is patented by placing on it the word *patent* or *pat.*, plus the patent number. If a firm makes, uses, or sells another's patented design, product, or process without the patent owner's permission, the tort of patent infringement exists. Patent infringement may exist even though not all features or parts of an invention are copied. Often, litigation for patent infringement is so costly that the patent holder will instead offer to sell the infringer a license to use the patented design, product, or process.

COPYRIGHT

A **copyright** is an intangible right given to the author or originator of certain literary or artistic productions. Works created after January 1, 1978, are automatically given statutory copyright protection for the life of the author plus fifty years. Copyrights owned by publishing houses expire seventy-five years after publication or 100 years from the date of creation, whichever comes first.

A copyright infringement occurs when someone copies another's copyrighted work. The reproduction does not have to be exactly the same as the original. Penalties can be imposed on those who infringe copyrights. These range from actual damages to statutory damages (ranging from $250 to $10,000) imposed at the court's discretion to criminal proceedings for willful violations, which may result in imprisonment.

(continued on page 692)

691

LEGAL PERSPECTIVE (CONTINUED)

An important exception to copyright infringement is the **fair use doctrine**. A person making a fair use can reproduce copyrighted material without paying royalties. The Copyright Act allows reproductions of copyrighted works for "purposes such as criticism, comment, news reporting, *teaching (including multiple copies for classroom use)*, scholarship, or research."

It is not possible to copyright an *idea*. The particular way in which an idea is expressed is what can be copyrighted, although it is not always easy to determine whether a work is an idea or an expression of an idea.

One does not need to place a © on the work to have the work protected against copyright infringement. Chances are that if somebody created it, somebody owns it.

◆ COMPUTER SOFTWARE

Computer software, because of its unique qualities, presents some particularly difficult legal challenges. What legal protection is available for computer software? How is the law evolving to deal with this relatively new form of personal property?

TRADEMARK, PATENT, AND COPYRIGHT PROTECTION

Computer software is a form of intellectual property and software manufacturers and developers can be protected under the trademark, patent, and copyright laws. Patent protection is difficult to get, however, since many of these products simply automate procedures that can be performed manually. Also, the basis for software is often a mathematical equation or formula, which is not patentable.

The time element is a particularly important consideration for someone seeking a patent on software. Since computer technology is changing and improving so rapidly, the delay between applying for and receiving a patent can undercut a product's success in the market. If a patent is infringed, the patent holder may sue to stop the infringement, for damages, for the destruction of all infringing copies, and for attorneys' fees and court costs.

The application of copyright law to computer software has also presented some difficult problems. Although the Computer Software Copyright Act of 1980 explicitly extends copyright protection to computer programs, the courts have been left to decide which elements of computer programs are copyrightable. Recent court cases have held that a program's source code is copyrightable. The structure, sequence, and organization of computer programs are also copyrightable.

Although a program may be protected under copyright law, this protection does not guarantee that it will not be copied illegally.

SOFTWARE PIRACY

For the average consumer, software is expensive. It can also be expensive to produce. Often, considerable sums are invested in the research and development necessary to create new, innovative software programs. Once marketed, new software requires that users be given support during its life on the market. It is not surprising that given the expense of software and the zealous competition in today's software market, many individuals and business firms have decoded and made unauthorized copies of software programs. This is known as *software piracy*. It has been estimated that the annual loss to developers from this practice is between $2 to $4 billion.

Extension Activity

Ask students to investigate what steps can be taken by vendors of intangible and easily duplicated property, such as computer software, to prevent unauthorized reproductions. Must vendors rely simply on the ethical scruples of users, or are there ways in which unauthorized duplications can be reduced?

Ethical Concern

Stimulate a class discussion centered on the problems with new forms of personal property. Point out to students that most of our laws were written to deal with traditional, tangible forms of property, such as a car or a book. In the modern economy, however, intangible personal property is increasingly important. The protection of rights in intangible property raises new difficulties.

A company may expend tremendous amounts of time and money in developing a new and improved software program, but a consumer, after buying one copy of the program, can duplicate the software innumerable times on new diskettes at very little expense. The company thus receives comparatively little economic benefit from developing the software. As a consequence, the incentives for innovation in software development are diminished.

The consumer who copies the software without permission is, in a sense, stealing the intangible personal property of the company. Yet, many individuals do not even consider the ethics in copying intangible personal property. Even if this copying is deemed a civil or criminal wrong, the legal system can do little about it. Such small-scale and frequent theft could not be practically prevented. We must depend largely upon the ethics of individuals in protecting property rights in many new forms of intangible personal property.

Manufacturers used to incorporate protective codes into their software to restrict its duplication. Breaking through these security codes became a game to some individuals, who then made illegal copies of the software. Consequently, many manufacturers have ceased attempting to protect their software. They now discourage software piracy by stressing the benefits—such as written instructions and user support—that come with authorized copies. Others are suing the users of unauthorized copies in tort for copyright or patent infringement.

Software piracy is illegal, but traditional tort law is difficult to apply because of the unique nature of computer programs. The application of criminal law statutes is also difficult. These statutes, designed to prohibit larceny, were passed to prohibit the theft of *tangible* property. Computer programs, however, are *intangible*, or intellectual, property.

Some states have expanded their definitions of property to bring the theft of computer programs under their larceny statutes. Software piracy is also fought internationally. However, copyright laws are not as clear in other countries as they are in the United States. Some countries do not even have copyright laws. For companies involved in research, development, and marketing of new computer software, legal protection for their products is very important.

 ## CONCLUSION

The law protecting intellectual property serves some understandable and desirable goals. Such law allows the most creative among us to profit from their artistry and inventiveness. Laws protecting those who create also inspire that creativity. Winning the lottery may be easier for many of us than thinking up a new idea, writing a song, or publishing a poem. The right to profit from these creative efforts should be protected just as your ownership in an automobile and other tangible property is protected. Intellectual property law has allowed such diverse enforcement as a lawsuit brought by the singer James Brown when his vocal style was imitated on commercials; rap artists who have sought out bootlegged copies of their records on the streets of New York; and multiple lawsuits by Levi Strauss Company brought against foreign manufacturers who make shoddy imitations of Levi's jeans and try to pass them off as the real thing.

  ## TERMS TO REMEMBER

♦ **intellectual property** Property resulting from intellectual or creative processes; the product of an individual's mind.

♦ **passing off** Falsely encouraging buyers to believe that one product is really another.

♦ **trademark** A distinctive mark, motto, device, or implement that a manufacturer stamps or prints on its goods.

♦ **trade name** A name used in a business activity to designate a business.

♦ **patent** A grant from the government allowing an inventor the exclusive right to make, use, and sell an invention for seventeen years.

♦ **copyright** An intangible right given to the author or originator of certain literary or artistic productions.

♦ **fair use doctrine** Allows a temporary, reasonable, and limited use of a copyrighted work without the need to get permission from the owner.

LEGAL BACKGROUND

In this chapter, we first look at the nature of ownership rights in real property. We then examine the legal requirements involved in the transfer of real property, including the types of rights that are transferred by various kinds of deeds; the property used in the sale of real estate; and a way in which real property can, under certain conditions, be transferred merely by possession.

We will also consider the limitations on real property rights, specifically the government's power of eminent domain, which permits it to take, in exchange for compensation, a private land for public use. The land sale transaction, with its players and unique features, is presented to close the chapter.

Chapter
29
Real Property

Activity Sheets
Reviewing Legal Concepts 29 *TRB*
Enrichment Activity 29 *TRB*

Student Activity Workbook
Chapter 29 Activities

Tests
Chapter 29 Test *TRB*
Chapter 29 WESTEST Computerized Testing

Handbook of Selected Court Cases
Metropolitan Life Insurance Co. v. *Reeves*
Klos v. *Molenda*

**West's Business Law and Legal
Environment Videodisc**
Still Frames and Motion Segments as shown

Enrichment

Have a student volunteer read aloud the quote found here from Jean Jacques Rousseau. Explain to the students that Rousseau, a French philosopher, believed that people had once lived in a state of nature and freedom but had many years ago entered into a contractual agreement with their government. He wrote that many governments in more recent times had come under the control of unjust rulers who ruled at the expense of their citizens' personal freedom. He argued that the people alone had the right to determine how they should be governed. In the *Social Contract,* published in 1762, he wrote that "Man is born free, yet everywhere he is found in chains." Rousseau was referring to the large number of people on the European continent living under oppressive governments. He proposed that because all human beings in a state of nature were born free, the main duty of government should be to maintain as much freedom as possible in a civilized society.

"[T]he right of property is the most sacred of all the rights of citizenship."
Jean Jacques Rousseau, 1712–1778
French writer and philosopher

From the earliest human history, property has provided a means of survival. Primitive people lived off the fruits of the land, eating the vegetation and wildlife. Later, as the wildlife was tamed and the vegetation cultivated, property provided pasturage and farmland. In the twelfth and thirteenth centuries, the power of the English lords was tied to the land. The more land, the more powerful they were. Land is still a symbol of family wealth and social position. In the Western world, the protection of an individual's right to property is one of the "most sacred of all the rights of citizenship."

In this chapter, we look at the nature of ownership rights in real property. We then examine the legal requirements involved in the transfer of real property and the way in which real property can, under certain conditions, be transferred by possession and the usual attributes of a real estate sales contract.

◆ THE NATURE OF REAL PROPERTY

Real property is the land and the buildings, plants, and trees on it. While personal property is movable, real property—also called *real estate* or *realty*—is immovable. Real property also includes air rights and subsurface (under-the-ground) rights, plant life and vegetation, and *fixtures,* things attached to realty. Fixtures are defined and discussed in more detail later in the chapter.

LAND

The soil on the surface of the earth and the natural or artificial structures that are attached to it are legally defined as land. Land also includes all the waters contained on or under the surface and the right to use much of the air space above it.

SUBSURFACE AND AIR RIGHTS

The owner of real property begins with rights to the air space above the land as well as to the soil and the minerals underneath it. An intrusion in this space can be the tort of trespass. Because of commercial airlines and high-rise office buildings and apartments, rights to air space have become important. Flights over private land do not normally violate the property owners' rights. The exception is when the flights are low, noisy, and frequent, causing a direct interference with the enjoyment and use of the land.

The distinction between real property and personal property is usually fairly easy to make. Real property consists of land and any vegetation or artificial structures such as houses and barns on the land. Personal property, by contrast, is property other than land that may be moved by the holder, such as jewelry, stocks, clothes, or automobiles.

Many contracts regarding the lease or sale of land use the terms *property, land,* and *premises* interchangeably, but these terms are distinguishable. *Property* refers to both the land and the premises. *Land,* by contrast, is generally used to refer to the land itself as well as any mineral deposits or vegetation on the land. *Premises,* however, is typically used to refer to the artificial structures on the land regardless of whether they are buildings, houses, or sheds. A lease or sale of developed property (land with permanent improvements, such as a farmhouse) should use the term *property* to refer to the land and building together because the use of the term *land* may suggest that the parties intend to exclude the farmhouse, while the use of the term *premises* may be regarded as a reference merely to the farmhouse itself.

Discussion Starter

Stimulate a class discussion on subsurface rights by asking the following questions: Why do you think subsurface rights are important? To whom are such rights important? Do you think subsurface rights are important to most homeowners? Why or why not?

Critical Thinking Activity

Tell students to write one or two paragraphs explaining why crops growing on land are real property, but when crops are sold by themselves, they are personal property. Read aloud some of the students' explanations and discuss.

Rights to subsurface property (below the ground) have been important for much longer than rights to air space. Mineral and water rights have been a source of value and contention for centuries. Subsurface rights include the ownership of coal, oil, natural gas, and water. In many states, the owner of the surface rights to land no longer owns the subsurface. Ownership rights in property, such as subsurface ownership, can be separated. Often when property is first improved—for example, when a house is built on it—the developer will specifically retain or sell the subsurface rights to the property.

PLANT LIFE AND VEGETATION

Plant life, both natural and cultivated, is also real property. Natural vegetation, such as trees, adds greatly to the value of the realty. When a parcel of land is sold with crops growing on it, the sale includes the crops unless otherwise stated in the sales contract. When crops are sold by themselves, however, they are considered to be personal property or goods, and the transaction is governed by the Uniform Commercial Code.

FIXTURES

◆ **fixture** Personal property attached to the land—a thing *affixed* to realty. The term *affixed* means attached to realty by roots, embedded in it, or permanently attached by cement, plaster, bolts, nails, or screws.

Structures, such as a house, are considered real property. Before the house is built, each part of it, such as plumbing pipe, lumber, and bricks, starts as personal property. At some point, this personal property becomes real property. Personal property attached to the land is known as a **fixture**—a thing *affixed* to realty. The term *affixed* means that the property is attached to realty by roots, is embedded in it, or is permanently attached by cement, plaster, bolts, nails, or screws.

Fixtures are included in the sale of land unless the sales contract specifically excludes them. The sale of a house includes the land and the house and the garage on it, as well as the cabinets, plumbing, and windows in the house. Since these are permanently affixed to the property, they are part of it. Curtains and throw rugs are examples of personal property that would not be fixtures. Items such as shutters and window-unit air conditioners are difficult to classify. A contract for the sale of a house or commercial realty should clarify how such items should be treated.

To determine whether or not a certain item is a fixture, the *intention* of the party who places the item on the property must be examined. If the facts indicate that the person intended the item to become a fixture, then it is one. When the intent of the party who placed the personal property on the realty is in dispute, the courts usually determine the intent based on either or both of the following factors:

1. If the property attached cannot be removed without causing substantial damage to the remaining realty, it is usually deemed a fixture. If your classroom has a blackboard, is it bolted and glued to the wall? If yes, it is a fixture. If it hangs on the wall loosely, then it is probably not a fixture.

Enrichment

Have students point to items placed in and around your classroom and tell whether each item is a fixture or an item of personal property. Have students explain each label.

Enrichment

Have a student volunteer read aloud the numbered list of items that a valid deed must contain. Ask the students what they think a legally sufficient description of the land would entail. Explain to students that a *metes and bounds legal description* involves the use of compass directions and distances from a specific point of beginning around the boundaries of the party. In earlier times, metes and bounds descriptions often used references to natural and artificial monuments such as boulders, the side of a road, etc., to describe the boundaries of a parcel of property. The disadvantage of describing a property line by reference to a stream, for example, became obvious when the stream dried up and the boundary line could no longer be ascertained. Modern metes and bounds descriptions typically avoid references to monuments, but instead use a succession of courses and distances that eventually return (if properly done) to the starting point.

Other types of legal descriptions of property may be used instead of metes and bounds descriptions. If a subdivision plat has been filed in the public records, for example, then it is not necessary for the deed to include a metes and bounds description because it can make a reference to a specified lot and block in that plat, which will suffice for the purpose of identifying the property being conveyed.

2. If the property attached is so adapted to the realty as to become a part of it, it is deemed to be a fixture. Custom drapes that are designed and made specifically to match the decor of a room are examples of this type of fixture.

 ## TRANSFER OF OWNERSHIP

Ownership of real property can pass from one person to another in several ways, including transfer by inheritance or will, by deed, by eminent domain, and by adverse possession.

TRANSFER BY INHERITANCE OR WILL

Property that is transferred on an owner's death is passed either by will or by state inheritance laws. If the owner of land dies leaving a will, his or her property passes to the person or people named in the will. If the owner dies without a will, state statutes tell how and to whom the property will pass.

CONVEYANCE BY DEED

The most common method of transferring title to land is by deed. A **deed** is a writing signed by the owner who is transferring title to his or her property to another person. **Conveyance** (the voluntary transfer of real property) by deed can be by sale or by gift.

Requirements of a Valid Deed   A deed is a requirement to change ownership in real property whether or not the property is being exchanged as part of a contract or being transferred because of a gift. Gifts of real property are common, and they require deeds even though there is no contract. A valid deed must contain the following:

1. The names of the buyer (grantee) and seller (grantor).
2. Words evidencing an intent to transfer (for example, "I hereby bargain, sell, grant, or give").
3. A legally sufficient description of the land.
4. The grantor's (and usually the grantor's spouse's) signature.

Finally, to be valid, a deed must be delivered.

Types of Deeds   Different types of deeds provide different degrees of protection for the buyer against potential problems affecting the title to the property. A **warranty deed** provides the greatest protection. In most states, a warranty deed requires special language. A warranty deed includes a promise to protect the buyer against all claims of ownership of the property by another. A sample warranty deed is shown in Exhibit 29-1.

A **quitclaim deed** offers the least protection against defects in the title. Basically, it conveys to the grantee whatever interest the grantor had. If the grantor has no interest, then the grantee receives no interest. A quitclaim deed seems strange to most people. After all, what value does a deed have when the person transferring it to you is not promising that he or she owns

◆ **deed** A document used to transfer ownership interest in real property.

◆ **conveyance** The voluntary transfer of real property from one person to another.

◆ **warranty deed** A deed under which the grantor makes several guarantees to the grantee. The grantor warrants that there are no claims against the property and that if claims are made, the grantor will defend against them.

◆ **quitclaim deed** A deed intended to pass any title or interest of the grantor in the property to another person. The deed does not include any warranties.

Enrichment

Guide the students in looking at Exhibit 29-1. Ask the students to point out where on this sample warranty deed they can find each of the following items that a valid deed must contain.
1. The names of the buyer (grantee) and seller (grantor)
2. Words evidencing an intent to transfer (for example, "I hereby bargain, sell, grant, or give")
3. A legally sufficient description of the land
4. The grantor's (and usually the grantor's spouse's) signature

Collaborative Learning Activity

Tell students to work in pairs to write a one-page paper explaining the difference between a warranty deed and a quitclaim deed. Students should include in the paper the advantages and disadvantages of each.

EXHIBIT 29-1 A SAMPLE WARRANTY DEED

Date: May 31, 1990

Grantor: GAYLORD A. JENTZ AND WIFE, JOANN H. JENTZ

Grantor's Mailing Address (including county):
        4106 North Loop Drive
        Austin, Travis County, Texas

Grantee: DAVID F. FRIEND AND WIFE, JOAN E. FRIEND AS JOINT TENANTS
          WITH RIGHT OF SURVIVORSHIP
Grantee's Mailing Address (including county):
        5929 Fuller Drive
        Austin, Travis County, Texas

Consideration:
For and in consideration of the sum of Ten and No/100 Dollars ($10.00) and other valuable consideration to the undersigned paid by the grantees herein named, the receipt of which is hereby acknowledged, and for which no lien is retained, either express or implied.

Property (including any improvements):
Lot 23, Block "A", Northwest Hills, Green Acres Addition, Phase 4, Travis County, Texas, according to the map or plat of record in volume 22, pages 331-336 of the Plat Records of Travis County, Texas.

Reservations from and Exceptions to Conveyance and Warranty:

This conveyance with its warranty is expressly made subject to the following:

Easements and restrictions of record in Volume 7863, Page 53, Volume 8430, Page 35, Volume 8133, Page 152 of the Real Property Records of Travis County, Texas, Volume 22, Pages 335-339, of the Plat Records of Travis County, Texas; and to any other restrictions and easements affecting said property which are of record in Travis County, Texas.

Grantor, for the consideration and subject to the reservations from and exceptions to conveyance and warranty, grants, sells, and conveys to Grantee the property, together with all and singular the rights and appurtenances thereto in any wise belonging, to have and hold it to Grantee, Grantee's heirs, executors, administrators, successors, or assigns forever. Grantor binds Grantor and Grantor's heirs, executors, administrators, and successors to warrant and forever defend all and singular the property to Grantee and Grantee's heirs, executors, administrators, successors, and assigns against every person whomsoever lawfully claiming or to claim the same or any part thereof, except as to the reservations from and exceptions to conveyance and warranty.

When the context requires, singular nouns and pronouns include the plural.

BY: _Gaylord A. Jentz_
    Gaylord A. Jentz

BY: _JoAnn H. Jentz_
    JoAnn H. Jentz

(Acknowledgment)

STATE OF TEXAS
COUNTY OF

This instrument was acknowledged before me on the   31st day of   May   , 1990
by Gaylord A. and JoAnn H. Jentz

Rosemary Potter
Notary Public, State of Texas
Notary's name (printed): Rosemary Potter

Notary Seal

Notary's commission expires: 1/31/1993

LEGAL BACKGROUND

There are three basic types of recording statutes, including (1) race statutes, which provide that the first purchaser to record a deed has superior rights to the property, regardless of whether he or she knew that someone else had already bought it but had failed to record the deed; (2) pure notice statutes, which provide that regardless of who files first, a person who knows that someone else has already bought the property cannot claim priority; and (3) race-notice statutes, which provide that a purchaser who does not know that someone else has already bought the property, and who records his or her deed first, can claim priority. Irrespective of the particular type of recording statute adopted by a state, recording a deed involves a fee. The grantee typically pays the fee because he or she is the one who will be protected by recording the deed.

Real Property   699

anything? A quitclaim deed says, in effect, "If I do have an ownership interest in this property, I hereby transfer that interest to you." Actually, quitclaim deeds are often used in situations where ownership rights are uncertain. The transfer of such a deed can help clarify ownership interests.

LEGAL FOCUS – PROBLEM

Lee and Patricia Caper own a house in California. The house was owned by Lee Caper as his separate property before his marriage to Patricia. Improvements were made to the house after the marriage and paid for with community property funds. Remember, California is a community property state, and most property acquired during a marriage is community property. Assume that Don Burgunder wishes to buy the property from Lee Caper. Don will want to be sure that all interests in the property are conveyed to him. Ownership records will show that Lee Caper is the sole owner. Don, however, should be concerned that Patricia may have some interest in the house because of the community property improvements to it. What types of deeds should Don expect from the Capers in order to protect his interests?

Don should obtain a warranty deed from Lee, which will include promises to protect Don from all claims of ownership made by others. However, he should also obtain a quitclaim deed from Patricia. She should be willing to convey this deed, for it only transfers what she has and does not guarantee that she owns anything. Quitclaim deeds are very useful for transferring an interest in cases such as this, when a person may have an ownership interest in a property but no formal records document its existence.

Recording Statutes **Recording statutes** exist in every state to give prospective buyers a way to check on whether there has been an earlier transaction concerning particular real property. The act of recording the interest gives notice to everyone of the interest, whether or not someone actually checks the records. Most deeds are recorded in the presence of a notary public in the county in which the property is located. A failure to record a deed creates an unnecessary risk for the purchaser.

In many states, if a deed is not recorded, a wrongful transfer by the former owner to a third party can cause the deed holder to lose his or her rights to the property. In such a case, the unrecorded deed holder usually has rights against the grantor of the deed, but he or she will still lose rights to the real property. The moral is simple: always record a deed.

EMINENT DOMAIN

Eminent domain is the power of the government to take land for public use. The government can exercise ownership rights over and acquire possession of real property owned by private parties. The United States Constitution and the laws of each state provide for eminent domain. Under the

◆ **recording statute**
A state law that allows a person owning an interest in real property to record that interest at a government office and thereby give notice to all of his or her interest.

◆ **eminent domain**
The power of the government to take private land for public use. The government is required to pay the owner just compensation for the property.

Legal Focus Example

Have a student volunteer read aloud to the class this Legal Focus Example dealing with *eminent domain.* Make sure that students understand that if an owner cannot reach agreement with the government, then the government will institute condemnation proceedings, in which the court determines whether the land is actually needed for public use and then determines what fair value is for the land.

Extension Activity

Have student volunteers research recent eminent domain actions taken in your community. For each case they find, they should report to the class on the following: How much land was seized through eminent domain, and for what public use was this land intended?

Caption Answer

Governments acquire land by reaching purchase agreements with existing owners or through eminent domain.

700

Ethical Concern

Stimulate a class discussion by asking students to define *eminent domain.* Why does the government have the power to take over real property owned by private citizens? Is this fair? What happens to the private citizen if the government exercises its right to take private property? What are some of the purposes for which the government would take land?

Fifth Amendment, the owners of private property taken for public use have a right to just compensation for land that is taken. Thus, if the government needs land for a public purpose, it usually makes an offer to buy the property. If the offer is refused, the government can take the property.

◆ LEGAL FOCUS – EXAMPLE

A new state highway is to be built. The government's Department of Transportation will decide where to build the highway and what land will be necessary for the highway's construction. The government will make an offer to buy this land from the owner. If the offer is refused, the Department of Transportation will begin a judicial proceeding (called a *condemnation proceeding*) seeking title to the land. Court proceedings will determine whether the land is needed for a public use and determine what is the *fair value* of the land. The fair value is usually the market value. Market value is usually established by what other similar properties have sold for in recent months.

ADVERSE POSSESSION

◆ **adverse possession** The acquisition of title to real property by occupying it openly without the consent of the owner, for a time specified by state statute.

Adverse possession provides a means of obtaining title to land without a voluntary transfer from the owner. Essentially, one person takes away the interest of another by possessing the other's property for a period of time determined by statute (from three to thirty years, with ten years being most common). The *adverse possessor* acquires title to the land and cannot

What are some of the ways that highway departments acquire land to build roadways?

Read

Introduce this *Law in Action* feature by pointing out to students that ownership of property has long been linked with liberty and democracy, and that our nation's founders were very interested in protecting private property, as is evidenced by the following quote from the Fifth Amendment: "No person shall . . . be deprived of life, liberty, or property, without due process of law; nor shall private property be taken for public use without just compensation." Even prior to the Bill of Rights, private property was also spelled out in the Virginia Bill of Rights, which was written in 1776 and is sometimes referred to as the parent of all American bills of rights. It states "That all men are by nature equally free and independent, and have certain inherent rights, of which, when they enter into a state of society, they cannot by a compact deprive or divest their posterity; namely the enjoyment of life and liberty, with the means of acquiring and possessing property, and pursuing and obtaining happiness and safety." Explain to students that this tradition of respecting private property rights can be seen throughout the development of American property laws. Then have a student volunteer read this *Law in Action* feature aloud to the class.

Discuss

Stimulate a class discussion of American property laws by asking the following questions: How were the needs of Americans different from those of the British with regard to property laws? Why was the simple, efficient transfer of land important in America? Why was the federal government so intent on facilitating the private ownership of the land acquired through the Louisiana purchase? How did Americans react to the English doctrine of *primo geniture?* How were American deeds different from English deeds? How did the ordinance of 1787 represent a major departure from British law dealing with wills?

Real Property   701

 Law in Action

LAW AND THE BUSINESSPERSON: HOW AMERICAN PROPERTY LAWS DEVELOPED

Much of American property law was inherited from English common law, but many of these English doctrines have been changed over the years because they clashed with the needs of the American economy. By the 1800s, the needs of Americans were far different from those of the British with regard to property laws. Specifically, Americans needed laws that allowed for the simple, efficient transfer of land.

To understand why, take yourself back to the late 1700s. The U.S. federal government claimed rights to millions and millions of acres of land. The Louisiana Purchase brought in millions more. American society faced an important question: how should it map, settle, and distribute this seemingly limitless treasure of land? The federal government decided that it was not in the business of managing land, so it wished to get rid of it in an orderly, productive way. Thus, a whole continent was sold or given away to veterans, settlers, squatters (one living on land without legal right), railroad companies, colleges, speculators, and land companies. The government's goal was to distribute public land to people who would develop it.

During the 1800s, the national territory no longer seemed limitless. The frontier moved west, and more and more public lands were purchased or homesteaded (a way pioneers were allowed to acquire ownership to public lands if they lived on and improved the land for a certain time) or otherwise acquired by private owners. Available land became scarcer. Entrepreneurs began to speculate in land, buying up as much as they could, clearing it, and selling it for a profit. City and state governments began to claim ownership of lands under their powers of eminent domain. They did this not only to expand the role of government but also to preserve the raw land and its natural beauty and to create public parks.

In short, both the abundance of land and the public policy promoting the purchase and sale of land in America contrasted sharply with the situation in England. British laws were complicated in regard to land transfers; they tended to discourage, rather than promote, the transfer of land. To accommodate American needs, legislators in the 1800s began to reform the land laws in this country. Listed are a few of the areas in which the laws were changed dramatically from the inherited English doctrines concerning real property:

1. **Primogeniture**—The doctrine of primogeniture gives the eldest son the right to succeed to his ancestor's estate to the exclusion of other sons, daughters, or relatives. This restriction on inheritance met with little success in America. The doctrine was abandoned in New England early on and vanished from the South by 1800.

2. **Deeds**—English law required elaborate forms for the conveyance of land. Americans found such elaborate forms unsuitable. Legal sophistication was scarce in this country. Furthermore, what was acceptable or tolerable to a small upper class of landlords became intolerable in the great American mass market. Land documents had to become simple and standard. Documents

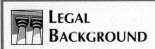

LEGAL BACKGROUND

There are a number of public policy reasons for permitting property to be acquired by adverse possession. One of these reasons is that such statutes aid in the resolution of boundary disputes and in quieting (determining) title when title to property is in question. More fundamentally, adverse possession statutes encourage the use of property. In the earlier days of this nation, for example, when uncultivated land was abundant, allowing those who possessed, cleared, and planted crops on land to acquire title to the land furthered the nation's goal of putting the land to productive use.

Extension Activity

Ask a volunteer to find information about adverse possession in your state, especially the time requirement for possession.

 Law in Action (Continued)

had to be mass produced at minimal cost. The reform here was clean and swift. Lawyers worked out two basic types of deeds. Although they were still beyond the grasp of most nonlawyers, they were understandable to lawyers and to crafty land dealers. These deeds became available in books of forms that became very popular. A businessperson or lawyer could use these books to make deeds of his or her own. They just copied the forms and filled in the blanks.

3. **Wills**—English law did not allow land to be transferred easily by will. In the United States, a major departure from

British law occurred with the passage of the Ordinance of 1787, which authorized the transfer of land in wills, provided that "such wills be duly proved." The process of "proving" a will, which is called *probate*, required more exact records, a greater standardization of land documents, and the development of objective, rational procedures. Eventually, the probate process led to the smooth, efficient transfer of land by will. The will, like the deed, became a fundamental instrument of land transfer. The requirements of wills are discussed in Chapter 32.

be removed from the land by the original owner. The adverse possessor has title just as if there had been a conveyance by deed.

Four elements must be satisfied for a person to acquire property by adverse possession:

1. Possession must be actual and exclusive—that is, the possessor must physically occupy the property and must be the only person doing so.
2. Possession must be open and visible, not secret. The possessor must occupy the land for all the world to see.
3. Possession must be continuous and peaceable for the required time. This means that the possession must not be interrupted by the true owner or by the courts.
4. Possession must be hostile and adverse. If one lives on the property with the permission of the owner, possession is not adverse. "Hostile" here does not mean that the adverse possessor has an evil intent or negative emotion against the true owner. Rather, it means that the adverse possessor claims his or her possession is superior to the claimed ownership of all others.

LEGAL FOCUS ~ CASE PROBLEM

In 1950, Michael and Albina Klos purchased a lot owned by John and Anne Molenda. The Kloses' lot was 50 feet wide and 135 feet deep and was next to the Molendas' house. Rather than surveying the property, the seller and buyer paced off the lot and placed stakes in the ground as boundary markers. In 1983, Mr. Molenda died, and his

1. The main difference between real property and personal property is that real property is immovable, while personal property is movable.

2. In addition to the land itself, real property also includes anything attached to it, such as buildings and trees. Both the air above and the land below the surface are legally defined as land also.

3. Laws differ between states.

4. A warranty deed includes a promise to protect the buyer against all claims of ownership by another. However, a quitclaim deed only transfers the interest the grantor may have in the property; the interest may not be sufficient to guarantee clear title.

widow hired a surveyor to determine the boundaries of the land. The survey found the rightful property line between the Molendas' and Kloses' land to be thirty inches closer to the Kloses' house than previously believed. On learning this, Mrs. Molenda dug up the grass strip alongside the Kloses' driveway and erected a fence marking the new property line. Did the Kloses own the disputed land by adverse possession?

Yes, the Kloses held title to the land by adverse possession. This Pennsylvania case held that if a person has actual, continuous, exclusive, visible, notorious, distinct, and hostile possession of land for a long period of time (in Pennsylvania, twenty-one years), that person gains title to the land. This means that the adverse possessor must use the land in a regular, normal, and obvious manner so that the original title owner would know, on inspection, of the possessor's use. If the original title owner does not evict the possessor or otherwise exercise his or her ownership rights, then the possessor will obtain title once the statutory time period has lapsed. Here the Kloses were certainly open, hostile, and notorious in their possession of the land in question, and they possessed the land for over thirty years, thereby passing the time limit. They therefore obtained title to the land by adverse possession.[1]

◆ CHECKING YOUR PROGRESS

1. What is the most significant difference between real property and personal property?

2. In addition to the land itself, what is included in real property?

3. If the owner of property dies without leaving a will, who receives the property?

4. How do a warranty deed and a quitclaim differ?

◆ NONPOSSESSORY INTERESTS

Some interests in land, called nonpossessory interests, do not include the right to possess the property. Nonpossessory interests include easements, profits, and licenses. Because easements and profits are similar, they are discussed together here.

1. *Klos v. Molenda*, 355 Pa.Super. 399, 513 A.2d 490 (1986).

**Legal Focus
Case Problem**

Have a student volunteer read aloud the Legal Focus Case Problem that begins on the previous page. Ask a student volunteer to suggest a possible answer to the question posed at the end of this problem. Note that the Kloses were found to have maintained hostile possession of the land even though both parties were mistaken as to the true location of the property line. A claim of right, adverse to all others, constitutes hostile possession. The fact that the Kloses had planted and maintained a hedge for 30 years and treated the land in question as their own satisfied the requirement of hostile possession.

Teaching Note

This case is included in the *West's Business and Personal Law Handbook of Selected Court Cases*.

Legal Focus Example

Have a student volunteer read aloud to the class this Legal Focus Example of a profit. Make sure that the students understand that by selling Alice the right to go on his land and remove the sand and gravel, Oliver has given Alice a profit.

Critical Thinking Activity

Have the students write a paragraph explaining the difference between an easement and a profit. Tell students that in their paragraphs they should include the definitions for both *easement* and *profit* and give an example of each.

Legal Focus Example

Have a student volunteer read aloud this Legal Focus Example of an *easement by implication*. Remind students that they can use the Legal Focus features as review tools when studying for tests.

Collaborative Learning Activity

Divide the class into groups of three or four. Tell them to brainstorm and write locations and/or descriptions of examples of easements in your neighborhood or city. Have them write who the property owner is and who might need to use the property and for what reason(s).

♦ **easement** The right of a person to make limited use of another person's property without taking anything from the property.

♦ **profit** The right of a person to go onto land in another's possession and remove some part of the land or products of the land.

EASEMENTS AND PROFITS

An **easement** is a right a person has to make limited use of another person's property. An easement, for example, can be the right to walk across another's property or to run a telephone line across it.

A **profit** is the right to take away some part of the land itself or some product of the land.

◄ LEGAL FOCUS ~ EXAMPLE

Oliver sells Alice the right to go into Blackwood Hills and remove all the sand and gravel that Alice needs for her cement business. Thus, Alice has a profit as to Oliver's land.

The difference between an easement and a profit is that an easement allows only the use of land while a profit allows a person to take something from the land.

Creation of Easements and Profits Easements and profits can be created by deed, will, implication, necessity, or prescription. If the easement or profit is created, the interest transferred should be clearly identified and the document must be delivered to the grantee (the person receiving the profit or easement). Creation by will simply requires inclusion of the described interest in a valid will.

Easements or profits may also be created by *implication*. This occurs when the circumstances surrounding the division of a piece of property implies the creation of an easement or profit.

◄ LEGAL FOCUS ~ EXAMPLE

Bailey divides a parcel of land, but only one well exists to supply drinking water for both parcels. She conveys the half without a well to David. A profit by implication arises, since David needs drinking water.

An easement may also be created by *necessity*. This does not require the division of property for its existence. A person who rents an apartment, for example, has an easement by necessity in the private road leading up to it.

Easements and profits by *prescription* arise when one person uses another person's land for a time equal to the applicable statute of limitations (this is usually the same as the time needed to acquire title by adverse possession). If the owner of the land does not object to the use of the land during this period, the person using the land has an easement or profit by prescription.

LICENSES

A **license** is the right that a person has to come onto another person's land. This is a personal privilege that arises from the consent of the owner of the land. The license can be revoked by the owner.

♦ **license** A revocable right to enter the land of another.

> ◀ **LEGAL FOCUS – EXAMPLE**
>
> A ticket to attend a movie at a theater is an example of a license. The theater owner issues a ticket that gives the holder the right to enter the movie theater, the property of the owner. If the ticket purchaser sells the ticket to someone else, the theater owner can refuse entry to the theater to the second purchaser. The ticket is a revocable license, not a conveyance of an interest in property.

◆ THE SALE OF REAL ESTATE

Transfers of ownership interests in real property are frequently accomplished by means of a sale. The sale of real estate is similar to the sale of goods because it involves a transfer of ownership, often with warranties. In

Identify the steps in the normal residential sales transaction.

Point out to students that most real estate firms charge sellers 6 to 7 percent commission to sell their property. As a result, the price that owners ask for their property tends to be higher when a real estate agent is used. Ask your students to identify and evaluate the benefits that home buyers may receive and the costs they may pay if they choose to buy directly from a property owner rather than using a real estate service. Do they believe that this is a choice that is more often wise or unwise? Ask them to explain the reasons for their answers. (They may get help in answering this question if they study the classified advertisements placed by private owners in the real estate section of their Sunday newspaper.)

Invite a local realtor to your classroom to speak to your students about some of the laws associated with buying and selling real property. Have your students prepare questions for the speaker.

the sale of real estate, however, certain formalities are observed that are not required in the sale of goods. For example, to meet the requirements of law, some type of deed must be signed and delivered.

Several steps ordinarily occur in any sale of real property. The first step is the formation of a land sales contract. Then a title search (to verify that the seller owns the property) follows, usually along with negotiations to obtain a loan to assist in the purchase. The final step is the closing, where money is exchanged for the deed to the property. In order for this process to begin, most sellers use the services of real estate agents or brokers to find a buyer for the real property.

REAL ESTATE AGENTS AND BROKERS

◆ **real estate agent or broker** A person licensed by the state to assist people in buying and selling real property.

A **real estate agent or broker** is a person licensed by the state to assist people in buying and selling real property. Many states require that brokers and agents meet continuing education or other requirements in order to retain their licenses. These professionals provide buyers and sellers of real estate with information and specialize in matching the wants of buyers with the property being offered for sale by sellers.

Normally, the broker is hired by the seller and acts as the seller's agent in the sale of the property. In compensation for his or her services, the broker usually receives a commission from the seller when and if a sale is concluded. A commission is a fee based on a percentage of the purchase price. A common commission for a real estate transaction is 6 or 7 percent of the selling price. Often, a broker will also act as an agent of the buyer, in which case a dual agency exists. Generally, a broker may not act as an agent for more than one party without the consent of all parties involved. Agency law is discussed in detail in Chapter 20.

A seller hires the services of a broker through a written *listing agreement*. In an *open listing*, the seller contracts for the services of more than one broker, and the first broker to produce a buyer receives the commission. This allows the seller's broker to find a buyer or to work with other real estate brokers or agents to assist him or her in selling the property. The first broker who produces an actual buyer is entitled to split the brokerage commission with the listing broker. In an *exclusive listing*, the seller contracts with just one broker, who receives the exclusive right to find a buyer and receive the commission from the seller. Under an exclusive listing agreement, the broker has the right to a commission even if another broker sells the property. Another type of agreement, an *exclusive agency agreement*, provides that the seller need not pay a commission if the property is sold without the assistance of the broker.

THE SALES CONTRACT

Once you find a buyer for your real estate, you must enter into a contract for the sale of the property. Generally, when someone decides to purchase real estate, he or she makes a written offer to purchase the property and puts a deposit or down payment on the property. If the offer is accepted and the offeror decides to withdraw his or her offer, the deposit is often

Enrichment

Obtain copies of a standard real estate sales contract, and ask students to discuss whether the apportionment of rights and duties between buyer and seller is fair and appropriate. Ask them for suggestions as to how these contracts could be improved and whether the buyer or seller should be better protected.

Reteaching Activity

Ask a student volunteer to explain why a title search is necessary. (Students should understand that a thorough title search reveals whether any other party has a valid claim to the property or a lien against the property. Without a title search, a buyer could lose part or all of the purchase price if another party has a lien against or a superior claim to the property.)

Extension Activity

Ask students to call local real estate brokers to find out all the costs that are involved in closing a residential real estate transaction, as well as those costs necessary for obtaining a home loan. How much money, in excess of the amount of the loan and down payment, is actually required to buy a house? Allow students to present their findings to the class in the form of brief oral reports. Encourage the students to incorporate visual aids into their presentations.

forfeited to the seller as liquidated damages. (See Chapter 13.) The essential elements of the sales contract include: (1) an identification of the parties, (2) a description of the property to be sold, (3) the purchase price, (4) whether the purchase is conditional on the buyer obtaining financing, (5) assurances required by the buyer as to the type of deed, and (6) the signatures of the buyer and seller.

ESCROW

The normal real estate transaction requires several sometimes complicated performances by both the buyer and seller. To assist the parties in assuring that both parties have performed as promised, parties to real estate sales transactions commonly use an **escrow**. An escrow is an arrangement whereby the buyer and seller designate one agent to act for both parties in carrying out specified instructions for gathering and distributing documents and funds necessary to the sales agreement. An **escrow agent** is the one who acts as this neutral party to facilitate the sale by monitoring the performance of both the buyer and seller. Each party meets the requirements of the contract by offering performance to the escrow agent. During escrow, several activities must take place, including a title search and having documents drafted and signed. Escrow allows the seller to place the property in the hands of a broker or escrow agent who delivers the property to the purchaser. After all conditions of performance are met, the escrow agent transfers the cash to the seller and the deed to the buyer.

Either the buyer's attorney or the escrow agent (or even a broker or a title insurance company) will begin a title search. This search of record title examines all past transfers and sales of the piece of property in question. This step is very important for the buyer. A thorough title search will reveal if another party has a valid claim to the property or a lien against the property. If a title search is not done, the buyer could stand to lose part or all of the purchase price if another party has a lien against or a superior claim to the property.

FINANCING REAL ESTATE

The buyer of real property typically will seek a mortgage—that is, the buyer will borrow money for much of the purchase price of the property. Usually, the property is put up as collateral (property to guarantee payment) for the mortgage. The mortgage is essentially a right against the real property. The mortgage allows the lender, such as a bank, to foreclose and to sell the real estate if the borrower fails to make timely payments.

THE REAL ESTATE CLOSING

The final stage of the sale of real estate is called the **real estate closing**. At the closing, the buyer normally pays the purchase price and the seller delivers the deed to the buyer. Legal title remains in the seller's name until

◆ **escrow** An arrangement whereby the buyer and seller designate an agent to act for both parties in carrying out specified instructions from the buyer and seller for gathering and distributing documents and funds necessary to a land sale agreement.

◆ **escrow agent** A neutral party in the sale of real estate who facilitates the sale by monitoring the performance of both the buyer and seller.

◆ **real estate closing** The point in a real estate sale where the buyer pays the purchase price and the seller delivers the deed to the buyer.

Collaborative Learning Activity

Divide the class into small groups. Ask each group to create a poster that incorporates the checklist for the sale of real estate found on this page. Explain to the students that this should be an informative/educational poster intended for home sellers. Additionally, each poster should be visually appealing. Allow the groups to display their posters in your classroom.

Checking Your Progress (Answers)

1. Yes. Adverse possession provides a means of obtaining title to land without a voluntary transfer from the owner. If one person possesses real property meeting the proper conditions for a statutory time, he or she acquires title to the land.
2. The difference between an easement and a profit is that an easement merely allows use of land only and a profit allows a person to take something from the land.
3. A title search is important for a buyer of real property because it will reveal if another party has a valid claim to the property or a lien against the property. The buyer could lose part or all of the purchase price if another party has a lien against or a superior claim to the property.

the escrow conditions are fully performed. An example of an escrow condition would be paying off the seller's mortgage. When the terms and conditions of the contract of sale are completed, the escrow is closed by the escrow agent. A closing statement is prepared that gives the details of the transaction, including the purchase price of the property, who pays what property taxes, the obligations chargeable to each party (such as a fee to record property title), the real estate broker's commission, and the title company charges.

CHECKLIST FOR THE SALE OF REAL ESTATE

1. For most real estate sales, it is useful to use an attorney who specializes in real estate law.
2. Both the seller and the buyer should understand all the terms and conditions of the sales contract.
3. If a seller doubts the potential buyer's ability to get financing for the purchase of real estate, the seller should be careful. If the transaction takes a long time to complete while the buyer seeks a mortgage, the seller may have been better off to keep the property on the market.

◆ CHECKING YOUR PROGRESS

1. Can land be transferred involuntarily? Explain.
2. What is the difference between an easement and profit regarding real property?
3. Why is a title search important for a buyer of real property?

◆ A CASE IN POINT ◆

METROPOLITAN LIFE INSURANCE CO. v. REEVES

Supreme Court of Nebraska, 1986.
223 Neb. 299,
389 N.W.2d 295.

This case gives the court's interpretation of whether a grain-storage silo became a fixture to a piece of real property or remained personal property.

FACTS Lawrence Reeves was a land-owning farmer whose land was being foreclosed (taken) by his mortgage holder, Metropolitan Life Insurance Company. Prior to the foreclosure, Mr. Reeves had contracted with Production Sale Company to build a grain-storage facility on the farm. Its total cost was $171,185.30. Prior to the foreclosure, Mr. Reeves had paid only $16,137.77 toward the silo's construction. When Metropolitan brought the foreclosure proceedings, the question arose as to whether the grain-storage facility was a fixture to the realty or was personal property. If it was considered to be a fixture, Metropolitan would benefit from the facility; if it was considered to be personal property, Production Sale Company could sell the storage facility separately. The trial court held that the facility was a fixture, and Production Sale Company appealed to the Supreme Court of Nebraska.

ISSUE Was the facility a fixture to the real property, or was it personal property?

DECISION The Supreme Court of Nebraska reversed the district court's ruling and deemed the storage facility to be personal property.

REASON The court cited three factors that determine whether an article or a combination of articles is a fixture: (1) whether the article was actually annexed to the realty, (2) whether the article had been appropriated to the use or purpose of that part of the realty with which it was connected, and (3) whether it was the intention of the parties making the contract to affix the article permanently to the land. The last factor was the most important in determining this case, and the court gave much weight to the circumstances of the purchase agreement between Reeves and Production Sales. The court concluded that under the provisions of that agreement, the parties had not intended the grain-storage facility to become a part of the real property until full payment had been made. Since full payment had not been made, the facility had not become a fixture.

In order to help students review what they have learned in Chapter 29, you might wish to:

1. Have a student volunteer, or volunteers, read aloud the Chapter Summary.

2. Allow the students to work with partners to complete the *Using Legal Language* activity.

3. Assign the *Checking for Comprehension* exercise as homework.

4. Allow the students to work in small groups to complete the *Applying Legal Concepts* activities.

5. As a class, complete the *Applying the Law* activities. (Please note that you may have to help students with vocabulary so that they adequately understand all of the *Applying the Law* material.)

In order to check student mastery of chapter concepts, you may wish to use the Chapter 29 test that is found in your *Teacher's Resource Binder* or use WESTEST computerized testing for Chapter 29.

CHAPTER REVIEW

 ## SUMMARY

NATURE OF REAL PROPERTY

Real property is immovable. It includes land, subsurface and air rights, plant life and vegetation, and fixtures.

FIXTURES

A fixture is an item of personal property that becomes part of real property. To determine whether something is a fixture, the courts consider the intent of the parties affixing the property, if the property can be removed without damage to the structure, or whether the property is adapted to the structure.

TRANSFER OF PROPERTY

1. *By inheritance or will*—If the owner dies without a will, the heirs inherit according to state laws. If the owner dies with a valid will, the land passes to the people named in the will.

2. *By deed*—The deed is the instrument of conveyance of real property. A deed must meet specific legal requirements. Among the types of deeds are *warranty deeds* and *quitclaim deeds*. Deeds should be recorded in the manner prescribed by *recording statutes* to give third parties notice of the owner's interest.

3. *By eminent domain*—The taking of private land by the government for public use. The government gives the owner just compensation for the land.

4. *By adverse possession*—When a person possesses the property of another for a stated period of time, that person acquires title to the property.

NONPOSSESSORY INTERESTS

1. *Easement*—The right of a person to make limited use of another person's property.

2. *Profit*—The right of a person to go onto land in another's possession and remove some part of the land or products of the land.

3. *License*—The revocable right of a person to come onto another person's land.

THE SALE OF REAL ESTATE

The sale of real estate involves a transfer of ownership by deed, often with warranties. The parties to a real estate sale typically use a real estate broker or agent.

1. *Real estate agent or broker*—A person licensed by the state to assist people in buying and selling real property.

2. *Listing agreements*—Types of contracts between sellers of property and real estate brokers.

THE SALES CONTRACT

1. *The contract*—When someone decides to purchase real estate, he or she makes a written offer to purchase the property and puts a deposit or down payment on the property.

2. *The escrow*—The use of a neutral party to facilitate the sale by monitoring the performance of both the buyer and seller.

3. *Financing the purchase*—The buyer of real property typically will seek a mortgage—that is, will borrow money to pay much of the purchase price of the property.

4. *Closing the deal*—When the terms and conditions of the contract of sale are completed, the deed is transferred to the buyer and the selling price is transferred to the seller.

Checking for Comprehension (Answers)

1. The courts usually determine that if removal of attached property would cause substantial damage, it is real property. Also, if the item is so adapted to the realty as to become part of it, it is real property. A contract for the sale of the house should clarify in writing whether a questionable item is real or personal property.

2. Ownership of real property can pass from one person to another by inheritance or will, deed, eminent domain, or adverse possession. Students should describe any two of these methods.

3. A valid deed must contain: (1) the names of the grantee and grantor, (2) words evidencing an intent to transfer, (3) a legally sufficient description of the land, and (4) the grantor's signature. A deed does not require legally sufficient consideration to be valid; however, a contract does.

4. To acquire property by adverse possession, the four elements that must be present are: (1) actual or exclusive possession, (2) open and visible possession, (3) continuous and peaceable possession for the required time, and (4) hostile and adverse possession.

5. Student examples will vary. They should explain circumstances that require one person to use another's property because of a division of the original property.

 # USING LEGAL LANGUAGE

Directions: Match each term with the statement that best defines that term.

1. adverse possession
2. conveyance
3. easement
4. eminent domain
5. fixture
6. license
7. quitclaim deed
8. real estate closing
9. recording statute
10. warranty deed

A. In a _____ the grantor warrants that there are no claims against the property and if claims are made they will defend them.

B. The government can use _____ to take private land for public use.

C. A person holding a _____ has a revocable right to enter the land of another.

D. If personal property is attached to the land it is considered a _____ and becomes part of the realty.

E. At a _____ the buyer pays the purchase price for real estate and the buyer delivers the deed.

F. _____ is the acquisition of title to real property by occupying it openly, without the consent of the owner, for a time specified by state statute.

G. When real property is transferred from one person to another, it is called a _____.

H. In a _____ the grantor intends to pass any title or interest he or she has in the property.

I. An _____ gives a person the right to make limited use of another person's property without taking anything from it.

J. A state law that allows a person owning an interest in real property to record that interest at a government office and thereby give notice to all of his or her interest is known as a _____.

CHECKING FOR COMPREHENSION

1. List some items that would be included as fixtures in the sale of a house. List some items that would be considered personal property in a house. What can be done to determine if an item that is difficult to classify as real or personal property is involved in the sale?

2. Describe two ways ownership of real property can pass from one person to another.

3. What elements must be present in a valid deed? How does a deed differ from a contract?

6. The essential elements of a sales contract for real property are: (1) identification of the parties, (2) description of the property to be sold, (3) purchase price, (4) whether the purchase is conditional on the buyer obtaining financing, (5) buyer assurances of the type of deed, and (6) signatures of buyer and seller.
7. Legal title passes to the buyer when the terms and conditions of the contract of sale are completed and the escrow is closed by the escrow agency.

Applying the Law . . . You Be the Judge (Answers)

1. Yes. The Naabs could claim title to the land in question because all of the elements required for adverse possession had been met. A portion of the Naab's garage was clearly situated on their neighbor's lot and had been for the required length of time under West Virginia law. Possession had thus been actual and adverse. Possession was also open and visible, continuous, and exclusive. The court held that the Naabs had thus acquired title to the land on which their garage was located by adverse possession.
2. O'Neill wins. The court held that Webster clearly intended that the easement across the land conveyed should benefit the land he retained. Otherwise, access to the water was cut off by the conveyance, appreciably diminishing the value of

the retained land. Therefore, an easement in which the owner of one parcel of land has the right to go onto an adjacent parcel of land owned by another was created by the language of the deed, and the property now owned by O'Neill carries the easement along with it.
3. Yes, The court declared that the term *public use* changes with changing conditions of society. The right of the public to receive and enjoy the benefit of the use determines whether the use is public or private. The city

was able to prove that new industrial development was needed to revitalize local industry because citizens were faced with severe economic conditions. It was determined that there was a lack of other adequate available sites for this GM plant. The court held that the power of eminent domain was to be used in this instance to accomplish the essential public purposes of alleviating unemployment and revitalizing the city's economic base. The benefit to a private corporation was merely incidental.

4. What elements must be present to acquire property by adverse possession?
5. Describe an example of an easement created by implication.
6. What elements are essential to form a valid sales contract for real property?
7. When does ownership of property pass during a real estate closing?

 ## APPLYING LEGAL CONCEPTS

1. Christina is a real estate broker hired by Allen to sell his house. Figure Christina's commission if she sells Allen's house at the following commission rates and sales prices.

Sales Price	Commission Rate
$ 90,000	5 percent
$ 83,000	6 percent
$175,000	8 percent

 ## APPLYING THE LAW . . . YOU BE THE JUDGE

1. As the result of a survey in 1976, the Nolans discovered that their neighbor's garage extended more than a foot onto their property. As a result, Nolan requested that his neighbor, Naab, tear down the garage. The Naabs refused to do this, stating that the garage had been built in 1952 and was on the property when the Naabs purchased it in 1973. In West Virginia, there is a ten-year statute of limitations covering adverse possession of property. Were the Naabs able to claim title to the land on which the garage was situated by adverse possession? [*Naab v. Nolan*, 327 S.E.2d 151 (W.Va. 1985)]

2. Moses Webster owned a parcel of land that extended down to the Atlantic Ocean. He conveyed the strip of the property fronting the ocean to another party. The deed included the following statement: "Reserve being had for said Moses Webster the right of way by land or water." The strip of property is now owned by Margaret Williams, and the portion retained by Webster now belongs to Thomas O'Neill. Williams is denying O'Neill access to the ocean. O'Neill has brought an action to establish his title to an easement over Williams's property. Who will win, and why? [*O'Neill v.*

Williams, 527 A.2d 322 (Me. 1987)]

3. The Detroit Economic Development Corporation (DEDC) was created by the city of Detroit to provide for the public's general health, safety, and welfare, by reducing unemployment, providing economic assistance to industry, and helping to rebuild rundown areas of the city by supporting urban redevelopment. Under its eminent domain powers, DEDC planned to purchase a large piece of land. The land was then to be conveyed to General Motors Corporation for a site for construction of an assembly plant. A neighborhood association and individuals filed suit to prevent this taking of private land. They argued that DEDC's action was for the ultimate benefit of the private corporation. Therefore, they claimed that the power of eminent domain was not available since the land being acquired was not for public use. Can a city use the power of eminent domain to condemn property for transfer to a private corporation to build a plant to promote industry and commerce, thereby adding jobs and taxes to the economic base of the city? [*Poletown Neighborhood Council v. City of Detroit*, 304 N.W.2d 455 (Mich.1981)]

Mastery Objectives

By the end of this chapter, students should be able to:

- Characterize the landlord-tenant relationship
- Describe tenants' rights and duties
- Describe landlords' rights and duties
- Delineate tenant remedies
- Delineate landlord remedies
- Differentiate four types of tenancy

Prereading Activity

To create interest in this chapter, discuss students' living-arrangement plans after graduation from high school. Most young people will enter a landlord-tenant arrangement at some time. Talk about what they expect from a landlord and what they think their responsibilities are as tenants.

Landlords and Tenants

Chapter

LEGAL BACKGROUND

In the past century—and particularly in the past two decades—landlord-tenant relations have become much more complex, as has the law governing them. The historic protections given landlords have been modified, adding protection to tenants. Contract law doctrines, such as implied warranties and unconscionability, have modified historic real property doctrines in landlord-tenant relationships. In recent years landlord-tenant relationships have also become more heavily regulated by specific state and local statutes and ordinances. Although uniform law has been proposed, most states have not yet accepted this approach. The result is widely differing rules from state to state. We have attempted to summarize some of the more common standard rules identifying the rights and responsibilities of both the landlord and the tenant.

Conventional topics, such as the types of leases and transferring a tenant's interests, are also discussed. To balance perspectives, we have included an article that appeared in the *Wall Street Journal* that presents some problems that confront landlords.

Have the students brainstorm a list of advantages and disadvantages of renting an apartment as opposed to owning a home. Ask a student volunteer to list each of the advantages and disadvantages on the board.

Enrichment

Give your students copies of part of the rental advertisements in your local newspaper's classified ads. Normally, the classified ads that appear in the Sunday newspaper are best for this purpose. Tell them to imagine that they are 20 years old, have graduated from high school, and have a job that pays them $350 a week. Ask them to identify an apartment they think would be a good choice for them to investigate further. Have them list the factors in the advertisement that attracted them and the additional types of information they would need in order to be able to make a final choice. Allow students to share their work with the class.

Critical Thinking Activity

Ask students to write essays stating their opinions why it is a good idea to put all leases in writing.

714

| Chapter 30 |
| Resources and Assignment Guide |

Activity Sheets
Reviewing Legal Concepts 30 *TRB*
Enrichment Activity 30 *TRB*

Student Activity Workbook
Chapter 30 Activities

Tests
Chapter 30 Test *TRB*
Chapter 30 WESTEST Computerized Testing

Handbook of Selected Court Cases
Detling v. *Edelbrock*
Wells v. *Citizens and Southern Trust Co.*

West's Business Law and Legal Environment Videodisc
Still Frames and Motion Segments as shown

---

714   Personal Law

"Live in a suburban atmosphere with all the convenience of downtown. Spacious 1, 2, & 3 bedroom apartments. Parking and close to shopping. Public transportation and easy access to freeway. Only 7 minutes from downtown. Remember to ask about our current specials and reasonable rates. Come see the Riverbank Apartments at 1244 Main Street."
Apartments for Rent section of any newspaper in any city on any day

A large and growing percentage of the population live in apartment houses. For example, 45 percent of all the people in California live in apartments. For many high school students, living away from their parents or guardians may be only months away. For most of those young men and women, living in an apartment is the only affordable option if they wish to be financially independent. Living in an apartment involves an important legal relationship covered by landlord-tenant law. A **landlord** is someone who rents property to another. A **tenant** is someone to whom property is rented; thus, he or she is also called a renter.

Landlord-tenant law combines notions of English property law, the law of contracts, and modern state statutes. Rental contracts or agreements create a special form of property interest, something more than with an ordinary contract. The rental agreement or contract is usually called a **lease**. The landlord grants the tenant an exclusive right to use and possess the land for a time in exchange for rent. The landlord is the **lessor**. The tenant is the **lessee**.

The temporary nature of the possession in a lease distinguishes a tenant from a purchaser. Although not a purchaser, a tenant has important rights to the property. In most states, leases for longer than one year (or three years in some states) must be in writing. It is a good idea to have a lease in writing no matter how long a period it covers.

◆ **landlord** One who rents property to another.

◆ **tenant** One to whom property is rented; also called a renter.

◆ **lease** A transfer by a landlord of the right to occupy or use land for a certain time to a tenant in exchange for rent.

◆ **lessor** A person who leases property to another.

◆ **lessee** A person who leases property from another.

◆ CREATION OF A LEASE

To create a landlord–tenant relationship, the document must:
1. Express an intent to establish the relationship.
2. Provide for transfer of the property's possession to the tenant at the beginning of the term.
3. Provide for the landlord to retake the property at the end of the lease.
4. Describe the property—for example, by giving the street address.
5. Provide for the length of the term, the amount of rent, and when rent is to be paid.

DISCRIMINATION

A property owner cannot legally discriminate against possible tenants because of race, color, religion, national origin, disabilities, or sex. In some

LEGAL BACKGROUND

A property owner cannot legally discriminate against prospective tenants on the basis of race, color, religion, national origin, or sex. Similarly, a tenant cannot legally promise to do something counter to laws prohibiting discrimination. A tenant, for example, cannot legally promise to do business only with members of a particular race. The public policy underlying these prohibitions is to treat all people equally.

states, it is illegal for a landlord to refuse to rent to families with children.

UNCONSCIONABILITY

The concept of unconscionability (gross unfairness) is an important contract doctrine that applies to leases. Many states will allow a court to declare the entire lease or any part of it unconscionable and illegal if it is grossly unfair.

> ### LEGAL FOCUS ~ EXAMPLE
>
> A clause claiming to release a landlord from responsibility for interruptions in essential services, such as central heating or air-conditioning, will not be enforced. The landlord will be responsible if a system breaks down.

RIGHTS AND DUTIES OF THE LANDLORD AND THE TENANT

At common law, the parties to a lease were free to agree to any terms they chose. As the landlord was generally the more powerful party, the lease often favored the landlord. In recent years, new laws have been enacted to protect the interests of tenants. Often these protective laws cannot be waived even by the lease agreement. In other words, any attempt to give up these rights is void. The landlord's and the tenant's rights and duties generally involve four broad areas: possession, use, maintenance, and rent. After we look at tenant and landlord rights and duties, we will discuss remedies for failure to perform duties under a rental agreement.

POSSESSION

The landlord has an obligation to deliver possession of the real property to the tenant at the beginning of the lease term. The tenant has the right to get and retain possession until the lease expires. Thus, every lease includes a **covenant of quiet enjoyment**. This is an implied promise by the landlord that during the lease term, the landlord will not disturb the tenant's use and enjoyment of the property. This implied promise is the essence of the landlord-tenant relationship. If the promise is breached, the tenant can terminate the lease and sue for damages.

It is considered an *eviction* if the landlord denies the tenant possession of the property or interferes with his or her use or enjoyment of it. An **eviction** is the process by which a landlord puts a tenant out of real property, either through direct action or through court action. For example, a landlord might change an apartment lock and refuse to give the tenant a

♦ **covenant of quiet enjoyment** An implied promise by the landlord that during the lease term, the landlord will not disturb the tenant's use and enjoyment of the property.

♦ **eviction** The process by which a landlord puts a tenant out of property, either through direct action or through court action.

 Ethical Concern

As the student text makes clear, in some states it is illegal for landlords to refuse to rent to families with children. Ask the students to consider this prohibition. Why might landlords seek to exclude families with children? What types of problems occur when one rents to families with children? Do you think it is fair to bar landlords from refusing to rent to families with children? Why or why not?

Legal Focus Example

Have a student volunteer read aloud this Legal Focus Example dealing with unconscionability. Ask the students how, in this example, the lease clause is grossly unfair.

715

new key. Such a direct act would violate the tenant's covenant of quiet enjoyment.

The tenant's right to quiet enjoyment can also be violated by a **constructive eviction**. The term *constructive* refers to a legal equivalent; thus, constructive eviction means doing something that is the legal equivalent of physically removing the tenant from the property. A constructive eviction occurs if the landlord wrongfully performs or fails to perform an important promise required by the lease. The breach must make the tenant's further use and enjoyment of the property exceedingly difficult or impossible.

♦ **constructive eviction** A wrongful breach by the landlord of the tenant's right to enjoy and use rental property that is so serious as to make reasonable use of the property difficult or impossible.

LEGAL FOCUS ~ EXAMPLE

Brenda and Julie lived at Shady Tree Apartments. The apartment complex was managed by Marta. After a disagreement with Julie about shoveling snow off apartment walkways, Marta turned off the electricity to Julie and Brenda's apartment. Turning off the electricity deprived Brenda and Julie of heat, light, and other essential utilities, and thus it was a constructive eviction.

USING THE PREMISES

Tenants may generally use the property in any reasonable way, subject to an agreement that limits the tenants' use. The tenants must always use the property in a legal way that is related to the purpose for which the property is suited or is ordinarily used. The use should not injure the landlord's interest.

The tenant cannot remove or otherwise damage leased property without the landlord's consent. The tenant also has a duty to refrain from **waste**. Waste is the abuse or destructive use of property by one in rightful possession.

♦ **waste** The abuse or destructive use of property by one in rightful possession.

LEGAL FOCUS ~ EXAMPLE

Carl, the tenant, knocks out an inside wall in a leased house to enlarge a living room. He also removes a fence and a grove of trees in the yard. All of these actions would be waste unless Carl first gets the landlord's permission to perform these acts.

The tenant is responsible for all damage that he or she causes intentionally or negligently. The tenant is liable for the expense of returning the property to the physical condition it was in at the lease's beginning. Unless the parties have agreed otherwise, the tenant is not responsible for *ordinary wear and tear*. Ordinary wear and tear is deterioration that occurs over time with reasonable use of the property.

Ask the students to write one paragraph comparing the implied warranty of habitability with the implied warranty of merchantability introduced in Chapter 15. (In Chapter 15, the implied warranty of merchantability was defined as "an implied promise by a merchant seller that goods are reasonably fit for the general purpose for which they are sold. This warranty exists in every sale by a merchant unless specifically disclaimed.") Have student volunteers share their work with the class.

MAINTAINING THE PREMISES

Usually, the landlord must follow state statutes and city ordinances that provide building construction and maintenance standards. Typically, these laws contain requirements about the construction, wiring, and plumbing of residential and commercial buildings. In some states, landlords of residential property are required by law to keep the apartment in good repair.

An **implied warranty of habitability** exists in most states. This warranty requires that a landlord leasing residential property keep it in a habitable condition. An apartment is habitable if the living conditions are safe and suitable during the term of the lease. Generally, this warranty applies to major—or *substantial*—physical defects in the property, such as a big hole in the roof. The landlord has a reasonable time to repair these major defects. An unattractive or annoying feature, such as a crack in the wall, will probably not violate the warranty. Unless the crack is a structural defect or affects the residence's heating capabilities, it is probably not serious enough to make the place uninhabitable. In deciding whether a defect violates the landlord's warranty, courts may consider the following:

1. Did the tenant cause the defect, or is the tenant responsible for it?
2. How long has the defect existed?
3. How old is the building? A newer building is expected to have fewer problems.
4. What is the impact—potential and real—of the defect on the tenant's health, safety, and activities such sleeping and eating?
5. Is the defect in violation of housing, building, or sanitation statutes?

The landlord is responsible for maintaining common areas, such as halls, stairways, and elevators. This duty requires repair of defects of which the landlord has actual knowledge and those about which the landlord should have known. For example, a landlord cannot avoid responsibility for a dangerous condition at the swimming pool by claiming that the area is not regularly inspected. The landlord must ensure that such inspections are made.

◆ **implied warranty of habitability** A warranty arising automatically in a lease that requires that a landlord leasing residential property keep it in a habitable condition (that is, keep it safe and suitable to live in).

RENT

The tenant's payment to the landlord for the tenant's use of the landlord's real property is called **rent**. A tenant must pay the rent even if the tenant decides not to live on the property or moves out, if this action is unjustified and the lease is in force. In some states, if an apartment is uninhabitable (for example, if electricity is denied during a cold winter), the tenant may be able to withhold rent until the premises are made habitable.

◆ **rent** The tenant's payment to the landlord for the use of the landlord's real property.

SECURITY DEPOSITS

At the beginning of a lease, the landlord usually requires a **security deposit** to protect his or her property. If the tenant fails to pay the rent or damages the property, the landlord may keep the deposit. Many states limit the amount that a tenant is expected to deposit to one month's rent. These states also require that the deposit be returned, less any amount owed for

◆ **security deposit** A sum of money paid to and held by the landlord to secure the tenant's obligations under the lease.

Have a student volunteer or group of volunteers contact local landlords (these can be found by using the rental advertisements in your local newspaper's classified ads) to determine the amount of money required for security deposits for the apartments that are for rent. Have the students report their findings to the class in the form of oral reports or in the form of bar graphs.

Invite a representative from a tenants' association to visit your class to explain tenants' and landlords' rights and responsibilities. Ask them to share anecdotes of situations where rights have been violated and to relate the outcome of the disputes.

You might want to point out to students that while this chapter deals with private housing, another important issue focuses on the need and availability of public housing. In 1988 there were 840,000 families, or almost 5 million people, who were on the government's waiting lists for public housing. It is estimated that by the year 2003, there will be 7.8 million people who will need low-income housing. Although the government is helping to pay for the construction of some new units, its efforts will fall far short of the need. To accomplish the task, private organizations and businesses will need to contribute to the effort.

Probably the most successful private, low-income housing program is the Enterprise Foundation, started by James W. Rouse in Washington, D.C. in 1973. By 1990, his organization had rebuilt 6,000 housing units and had another 5,700 in various stages of completion. Although he did not intend to earn a profit at this business, he nevertheless has. The equity that the Enterprise Foundation has in its buildings was estimated to be roughly $200 million in 1990.

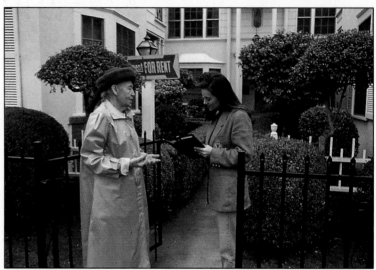

When first renting an apartment, inspect it with the landlord and agree on the condition of the property. Write down any damages existing in the apartment as part of the lease.

damages to the apartment or for unpaid rent, at the end of the lease term. Usually a deposit must be returned within fourteen days of the tenant's leaving the premises. If the landlord withholds any amount from the deposit to cover damages, the tenant must be given an itemized list of the damages. In some states, the landlord must pay interest on the deposit, minus a fee for the bookkeeping. If the landlord fails to meet these requirements, the tenant may recover at least the amount due. In some states, the tenant may recover triple the amount due and attorney's fees.

Many states will not allow a landlord to automatically keep any of the deposit. In these states, nonrefundable cleaning deposits are illegal. In order for the landlord to keep any of the deposit, the tenant must owe the landlord a sum of money. Security deposit disputes are among the types of cases frequently heard in small claims courts. These cases may involve the failure to return money to a tenant, to inform the tenant of the reason why damages were deducted, and to justify the amount charged for damages.

TENANT REMEDIES

A tenant has several remedies when a landlord does not maintain leased premises. These rights, however, depend on the circumstances and on the law of each state.

WITHHOLDING RENT

Rent withholding is a remedy that is associated with a landlord breaching the warranty of habitability. Sometimes rent withholding is authorized under a state law called a "rent strike" statute. The tenant must usually put the amount of rent withheld into an escrow account (a special bank account) pending resolution of the dispute. Generally, the tenant may withhold an amount equal to the amount that the defect reduces the property's rental value. The tenant who withholds more than is legally permissible is liable to the landlord for any excessive amount withheld.

REPAIRING AND DEDUCTING

Some states provide for the right to *repair and deduct*. This rule allows a tenant to pay for the repairs and deduct the costs from the rent owed. As in rent withholding, this remedy is associated with a landlord's breach of the warranty of habitability. Before a tenant can use this remedy, the problem must be the landlord's responsibility. Some states also require that the problem concern a basic service, such as heat or water. The landlord must be notified and must have failed to fix the problem within a reasonable time. Under some statutes, the amount deductible is restricted to one month's rent or some other amount. Often the repair-and-deduct remedy can only be used once a year.

CANCELING THE LEASE

The tenant may be able to terminate his or her lease when the landlord physically or constructively evicts the tenant. Recall that a physical eviction can involve the landlord's changing the locks on the apartment, and a constructive eviction can be a landlord's failure to repair something that violates the tenant's right of quiet enjoyment and breaches the warranty of habitability.

SUING FOR DAMAGES

A lawsuit for damages is always possible if the landlord acts in a way that is contrary to the lease or the law, but it is not always economical. The amount a tenant will win is usually either the cost of the repair of a defect or the difference between the value of the property with the defect and the rent.

◆ CHECKING YOUR PROGRESS

1. What must a lease include to create a landlord-tenant relationship?
2. Describe rights of tenants as to possession of property.
3. Compare (1) a direct action eviction of the tenant, (2) a constructive eviction of a tenant, and (3) a breach of the warranty of habitability.
4. What might courts consider in deciding whether a defect violates the landlord's warranty of habitability?

Checking Your Progress (Answers)

1. To create a landlord-tenant relationship, a lease must: (1) express an intent to establish a relationship; (2) provide for transfer of the property's possession to the tenant at the beginning of the term; (3) provide for the landlord to retake the property at the end of the lease; (4) describe the property; and (5) provide for the length of the term, amount of rent, and when rent is paid.
2. Tenants have the right to get and retain possession of the property until the lease expires.
3. When a landlord takes direct action such as changing locks and refusing to give a tenant notice, it is called a direct action eviction. A constructive eviction of a tenant is more subtle in that the landlord does something that is the legal counterpart to the physical removal of the tenant from the property. A breach of warranty of habitability protects the rights of the tenant, as he or she expects to have secure, safe possession of the property.
4. When deciding whether a defect violates the landlord's warrant of habitability, the courts may consider the following: (1) Did the tenant cause the defect, or is the tenant responsible for it? (2) How long has the defect existed? (3) How old is the building? (4) What is the defect's impact on the tenant's health, safety, and normal activities? (5) Is the defect in violation of housing, building, or sanitation statutes?

---

720   Personal Law

 Law in Action

LAW IN YOUR LIFE: LANDLORDS ARE PEOPLE, TOO

Tenants are often thought to be underdogs, and Americans love underdogs. Landlords are often portrayed in movies and the media in a very negative way. The law has historically favored wealth and power, so some of this negative image is deserved. However, as with most business relationships, there is another side to the story. An excerpt from a *Wall Street Journal* article provides some balance to the typical view of landlords. The title of the story is "Remember When the Landlord Was Your Bitter Enemy."[1] The reference in the story to an "accidental" landlord is to a landlord who begins renting property because of circumstance rather than choice. For example, a person moves from a house they cannot sell, and they rent it to help make payments.

> Last year, Barbara Aultman gave up trying to sell her Indianapolis home and rented it instead. "I wanted to be the best landlady on the face of the earth," recalls Ms. Aultman, a community development specialist. "All I wanted was my rent on time; I was willing to bend over backward to make them comfortable."
>
> For the first month, she did. When her tenants—two women recently out of the military—demanded to be let out of the lease because of a water stain on the floor, she says she removed the stain and offered to tear up the lease. When they complained the carpet smelled of cats, she had the carpet deodorized and offered to split the cost of new carpeting.
>
> But when they began refusing entry to brokers trying to sell the house and let the lawn

reach threshing height, her patience ran out. She ordered them out.

> They changed the locks.
>
> Like Ms. Aultman, many accidental landlords begin by vowing to become a new breed of landlord—understanding, rational, flexible.
>
> "They don't want to enforce the rules [in their leases]," says Mr. McCreary (an Atlanta property manager), "because they didn't like the rules when they were tenants. They will listen to all the sad stories about why tenants can't pay the rent. They become easy marks."
>
> Then they grow up.
>
> Ms. Aultman went to court for an eviction order, hired a locksmith to pick the new locks, and entered to find a broken washing machine and garbage disposal, contact paper melted on the stove, and giant mirrors glued to the wallpaper.
>
> "It stinks," she says of being a landlord. "Unless you want to go into it full time, you don't want to do it."
>
> Indeed, Jeffrey Taylor, a Norfolk, Virginia, publisher of a newsletter for landlords called Mr. Landlord, says the typical accidental landlord "doesn't survive more than three years."
>
> The first tenant to move into Daniel Pyne's San Francisco apartment was a professional con man who didn't pay a dime in rent, then changed the locks. Mr. Pyne spun his experience into the screenplay for Pacific Heights, a [movie] thriller about an extremely bad tenant.
>
> "If you're a normal person renting, you assume that landlords have a lot of power," says Mr. Pyne, who admits that he used to be terrified of his landlords. "What I discovered, as a kind of horror, is that tenants have all kinds of power."

---

1. Mitchell Pacelle, *Wall Street Journal*, April 10, 1992, pg. 1.

Extension Activity

You might wish to invite a local landlord to speak to your class regarding landlord/tenant relationships. He or she should be prepared to discuss how he or she handles the following: interviewing prospective tenants, security deposits, late charges, evictions, etc. Have the students prepare questions in advance for your speaker.

◆ Law in Action (Continued)

Some accidental landlords allow tenants to stay for months without paying rent. "We've got owners who come in begging us to save them from themselves," says Mr. McCreary. "They get way too personally involved in the tenant's woes."

"A lot of tenants will set a fire when they leave," says Janet Hair, an Indianapolis broker who mediates tenant-landlord disputes. "Or they'll turn the water on in the winter and leave all the doors open. We've even had a furnace stolen."

Reprinted by permission of *The Wall Street Journal*, ©1992 Dow Jones & Company, Inc. All rights reserved worldwide.

LANDLORD REMEDIES

LATE CHARGES

A landlord can charge a tenant a **late charge** if the tenant does not pay rent when due. The amount of a late charge cannot be excessive, and it should bear some logical connection to the amount of the rent or the lateness of the payment.

◆ **late charge** A charge by a landlord for late payment of rent.

SECURITY DEPOSIT

A landlord can keep all or part of a security deposit to cover money owed by the tenant. Any amount of the deposit in excess of that owed by the tenant must be returned to the tenant. The money may be kept for back rent or damage to the apartment. As we have already discussed, many states have strict requirements on how a landlord is to handle security deposits.

RECOVERY OF POSSESSION

A landlord can evict a tenant and recover possession of the property if the tenant breaches the lease. At common law, the eviction could take place—with force, if necessary—without legal proceedings. The tenant, with his or her belongings, could be thrown out on the street. Today, the landlord must use a legal process to evict a tenant. This is true even if the lease gives the landlord a right to entry and a right to retake possession peaceably.

The common court eviction procedure is called an **unlawful detainer**. This is a summary procedure that allows the landlord to retake possession rather quickly. Because eviction proceedings are so important—involving a person's shelter—most unlawful detainer actions have priority on crowded court calendars. These procedures usually (1) require the tenant to be given notice before the suit and allow the tenant an opportunity to correct his or her breach (for example, pay the rent) and (2) provide a jury to decide any factual dispute. To win the unlawful detainer action, the landlord must generally either prove that the tenant is in breach of the lease or that the lease has expired and the tenant still remains on the property. The

◆ **unlawful detainer** A summary court procedure that allows a landlord to retake possession of real property after a breach of the lease by the tenant.

Critical Thinking Activity

Have the students write one paragraph comparing the laws regarding retaliatory eviction with the laws dealing with whistleblowing and public policy (discussed in Chapter 21 in the *Law in Action* feature). You might remind the students that in one whistle-blowing court case the court held that "Whistle blowing activity that serves a public purpose should be protected. So long as employees' actions are not merely private or proprietary, but instead seek to further the public good, the decision to expose illegal or unsafe practices should be encouraged. . . ." Have student volunteers share their work with the class.

Collaborative Learning Activity

Divide the class into small groups. Have each group read and discuss the material under the heading Lien on this page. The students of each group should then work together to write their own Legal Focus Example illustrating a case in which a landlord would be acting properly in imposing a landlord's lien.

Ethical Concern

Divide the class into two groups. Debate the ethics of a landlord's lien. Have one group defend the landlord's right to this remedy, while the other group opposes it.

court makes a decision quickly, and if the landlord wins, orders a sheriff to remove the tenant.

If a landlord evicts a tenant for complaining to a government agency about the condition of the apartment, a **retaliatory eviction** occurs. Under some statutes, a retaliatory eviction is presumed if eviction proceedings are begun within a certain time after a tenant has complained. If a tenant can prove that a landlord's primary purpose in evicting or attempting to evict the tenant is in retaliation for reporting violations—of a housing or sanitation code, for example—regardless of the time elapsed, the tenant may be able to stop an eviction proceeding or collect damages.

♦ **retaliatory eviction** The eviction of a tenant for complaining to a government agency about the condition of an apartment.

SUING FOR DAMAGES

A landlord can sue a tenant for damaging leased property or to collect unpaid rent. As long as a tenancy exists, a landlord can collect rent in full, even if the tenant no longer occupies the property. Thus, when a tenant wrongfully abandons the premises, the landlord can bring a lawsuit to collect the rent as it comes due. In some states, the landlord must try to *mitigate* damages. This means that the landlord must try to reduce the amount the tenant must pay or must make a good faith attempt to rent the property to a new tenant. An unsuccessful attempt to rent the premises is necessary in some states (but not all) before a landlord can collect damages for the tenant's breach of the lease.

LIEN

Under the common law, when a tenant did not pay the rent, the landlord could take and keep or sell the defaulting tenant's personal property found on the leased premises. Today the landlord cannot do this unless the parties have agreed to it or it is permitted by state statute.

♦ **landlord's lien** A statutory right given a landlord on a tenant's personal property for the tenant's failure to pay rent.

States that still allow this remedy—known as a **landlord's lien**—give the landlord a lien on all of the tenant's personal property found in the apartment. The landlord is, however, required to begin court proceedings to exercise the lien. Typically, the court will authorize a sheriff to seize the tenant's property. Other states allow the landlord to seize specific items of the tenant's property and to hold them as security (that is, to ensure payment) for unpaid rent. The landlord must get a court order to sell the tenant's property.

 ## LANDLORD'S TORT LIABILITY

A landlord may be liable for injuries occurring on parts of the real property within the landlord's control, such as basements, hallways, and elevators. Also, when the landlord has an obligation to repair a defect, the landlord's liability may extend to injuries arising because of a failure to make repairs.

INJURIES CAUSED BY DEFECTS ON THE PREMISES

The landlord's liability extends to injuries resulting from a dangerous condition about which the landlord knew or should have known. For example, if the landlord fails to tell the tenant about a danger or conceals a danger, then the landlord is liable for any injuries that occur. For example, if a landlord knows that the mortar is loose in a brick wall but he or she fails to tell the tenant, and if a brick later falls and injures a tenant, then the landlord is liable.

In most states, the landlord is not required to inspect residential premises before leasing them unless there is reason to expect that a potential harmful defect exists. Also, the landlord is not under an obligation to tell the tenant about conditions that the tenant knows about when he or she signs the lease or that are obvious, such as a loose throw rug in the hall.

INJURIES CAUSED BY CRIMES OR THIRD PERSONS

The landlord is not normally required to set up an elaborate security system to protect tenants from criminals. But when crimes are reasonably foreseeable and the landlord fails to protect the tenants, he or she may be liable if an injury results. A reasonable attempt to protect the tenants can range from providing dead bolts on apartment doors to providing security guards.

Courts consider several factors to determine when a crime is foreseeable and preventable. Some prior criminal activity in the geographical area of the apartment is required before future crimes are considered reasonably predictable. The expectation of future crime is also based on how recently a prior crime occurred. Court decisions have varied as to what constitutes "recently" (possibly less than six months) and "area" (perhaps several blocks).

◆ LEGAL FOCUS – EXAMPLE

A series of automobile thefts from an apartment complex's parking garage may make a later apartment break-in foreseeable. A few assaults on tenants could indicate that steps should be taken before an assault escalates into rape or other serious bodily harm. When determining the landlord's duty, the court will consider the specific crime; automobile break-ins, for example, would not make murder a foreseeable risk.

Landlords have been held responsible when injuries have occurred to a tenant because of an act by another tenant. For example, if a landlord does not enforce a lease and does not evict an unruly tenant or a tenant who is otherwise violating the lease, and if another tenant is harmed because of this failure, the landlord can be held responsible.

Legal Focus Example

Have a student volunteer read aloud this Legal Focus Example dealing with injuries caused by the crime of a third person. Ask the students whether they feel it is fair to hold a landlord responsible in cases such as these. What steps might a landlord take in each of the cases outlined in this Legal Focus Example that would fulfill the requirement that a "reasonable" attempt to protect the tenants be made?

LEGAL BACKGROUND

Traditionally, when the landlord surrendered possession of his or her property to the tenant, the landlord also relinquished responsibility for injuries occurring on the property. This was true regardless of whether the injury was caused by a condition that existed at the time the property was leased or a condition that developed later. Today, however, in recognition of the policies underlying the warranty of habitability, the landlord bears greater responsibility for the condition of the premises and for injuries resulting from that condition.

Have a student volunteer read aloud to the class the Legal Focus Case Example found on this page that deals with the *Jendralski* v. *Black* case. Ask the students whether they feel it was fair in this case to hold the landlord liable for Angela's injuries. Do they feel that the tenant who owned the monkey should also be held liable? Why or why not? Point out to students that in this case, the landlord can seek to recover damages from the tenant who kept the monkey in violation of his or her lease.

Reteaching Activity

You might wish to remind students that exculpatory clauses were introduced in Chapter 10, where they were defined as "a contract provision that releases a party from liability for his or her wrongful acts."

Legal Focus
Case Example

Have a student volunteer read aloud to the class the Legal Focus Case Example that begins at the bottom of this page. Remind students that they can use the Legal Focus features as review tools when studying for tests.

724

Caption Answer

The landlord generally is responsible for the safety and condition of a parking lot.

---

724   Personal Law

Who is generally responsible for safety and condition of this parking lot, the landlord or the tenant?

◆ LEGAL FOCUS ~ CASE EXAMPLE

Angela brought an action against her landlord after she was bitten by a monkey that was being kept in another apartment. The lease did not allow tenants to keep animals, except small caged birds, in their apartments. The California court that heard the case held that a landlord is liable to an injured tenant if the landlord "knew or in the exercise of reasonable care should have known of the dangerous condition" (the monkey) and did not warn other tenants or evict the offending tenant.[2]

EXCULPATORY CLAUSES

A lease may contain a clause called an *exculpatory* (clear of guilt) *clause*, that attempts to protect the landlord from any liability for injuries or other damages, including injuries caused by the landlord's own negligence. When included in a residential lease, an exculpatory clause releasing a landlord from liability for his or her negligence is generally considered unenforceable, since it works against public policy because housing is considered essential for the public good.

◆ LEGAL FOCUS ~ CASE EXAMPLE

Lewis Crowell's father rented an apartment from the Dallas Housing Authority. The apartment contained a defective gas heater that leaked

---

2. *Jendralski v. Black*, 222 Cal.Rptr. 396 (1986).

carbon monoxide gas. The lease contained an exculpatory clause stating that the landlord would not be liable for any negligence. The father died of carbon monoxide poisoning, and the son sued. The court held that the exculpatory clause was against Texas public policy, and the court allowed the son to recover for the loss of his father.[3]

 ## TYPES OF TENANCIES

There are four types of tenancies: (1) a tenancy for years, (2) a periodic tenancy, (3) a tenancy at will, and (4) a tenancy at sufferance. All except a tenancy at sufferance involve the transfer of the right to possession for a specified time. The owner or lessor (landlord) conveys the property to the lessee (tenant) for a certain time. The tenant has a *qualified* right to exclusive possession. The tenant's right to exclusive possession is qualified by the landlord's right to inspect the premises in order to ensure that the tenant is properly caring for the property.

TENANCY FOR YEARS

A **tenancy for years** is created by express contract that leases the property for any specified time (even for less than a year). For example, signing a one-year lease to rent an apartment creates a tenancy for years. When the lease period has elapsed, the lease ends (without notice), and possession of the apartment returns to the lessor. If the tenant dies during the period of the lease, the lease passes to the tenant's heirs as personal property. Often, leases include provisions for their renewal or extension.

◆ **tenancy for years**
A tenancy created for a defined period stated by express agreement.

PERIODIC TENANCY

A **periodic tenancy** is created by a lease that may not specify a term but does specify that rent is to be paid at certain intervals. This type of tenancy is automatically renewed for another rental period unless properly terminated. For example, a periodic tenancy is created by a lease that states, "Rent is due on the tenth day of every month." This lease creates a tenancy from month to month. A periodic tenancy can be from week to week or from year to year. A periodic tenancy can also arise when a tenancy for years ends and the landlord allows the tenant to continue paying monthly or weekly rent.

At common law, to terminate a periodic tenancy, the landlord or tenant must give one period's notice to the other party. If the tenancy is month to month, one month's notice must be given. If the tenancy is week to week, one week's notice must be given. State law often determines what type of notice is required to end a periodic tenancy.

◆ **periodic tenancy**
A tenancy for a period determined by frequency of rent payments; automatically renewed unless proper notice is given.

3. *Crowell v. Housing Authority*, 495 S.W.2d 887 (Texas, 1973).

Discuss reasons why a tenant would want to assign his or her interest to a third person, and who carries the responsibility to the landlord. What are the advantages and disadvantages for each party involved?

Ask students to define the pros and cons of being a landlord and of being a tenant. Record their responses on the board, and stimulate a class discussion by asking students what possible conflicts could occur between a landlord and a tenant.

726   Personal Law

TENANCY AT WILL

- **tenancy at will** A tenancy for as long as both parties agree; no prior notice of termination is required.

If a landlord rents an apartment to a tenant "for as long as both agree," the tenant receives a **tenancy at will**. At common law, either party can terminate the tenancy without notice. This type of tenancy may come about when a tenant keeps possession after the termination of a tenancy for years with the landlord's consent. Before the tenancy is converted into a periodic tenancy (by the periodic payment of rent), it is a tenancy at will. The death of either party terminates a tenancy at will.

TENANCY AT SUFFERANCE

- **tenancy at sufferance** A possession of real property without legal right after the expiration of a lawful tenancy.

If a tenant remains in possession without the owner's permission after another form of tenancy ends, a **tenancy at sufferance** is created. A tenancy at sufferance is not a true tenancy, as it is created by a tenant *wrongfully* retaining possession of property. The tenant is, however, in a different position than a trespasser, who is someone with no right to be on the property. A trespasser can be summarily arrested; a tenant at sufferance must be evicted. The eviction process provides protection for the person accused of wrongfully possessing the property; this protection is not available for the trespasser.

 ## TRANSFERRING RIGHTS TO LEASED PROPERTY

Either the landlord or the tenant may wish to transfer his or her rights to the leased property during the term of the lease.

TRANSFERRING THE LANDLORD'S INTEREST

A landlord can transfer his or her interest in property. The new owner becomes the new landlord and may collect the rent but must follow the terms of the existing lease agreement.

TRANSFERRING THE TENANT'S INTEREST

The tenant's transfer of his or her entire interest in the leased property to a third person is an *assignment*. An assignment of a tenant's lease to another is an agreement to transfer all rights, title, and interest in the lease to the assignee. It is a complete transfer. Many leases require that the assignment have the landlord's written consent. Without the consent, the assignment is improper and the landlord can pursue his or her legal rights against the assignor and evict the assignee. A landlord who knowingly accepts rent from the assignee, however, waives the requirement for written consent.

A tenant does not end his or her lease responsibilities after the assignment. Even though an assignee may be required to pay rent, the original tenant still has a contractual obligation to the landlord. Whenever the assignee fails to pay, the landlord can expect the original tenant to pay the rent.

Have a student volunteer read aloud to the
class this Legal Focus Problem dealing with a
sublease situation. Then have the students
work with partners to diagram the relationships explained in this problem. Students'
diagrams should show who is actually
living in the apartment, who owes rent to
whom, etc.

When a tenant transfers all or part of the premises for a period shorter
than the lease term, it is called a **sublease**. The same restrictions that apply
to an assignment apply to a sublease. In a sublease, the tenant is the landlord
of the sublessee, so the sublessee should pay rent to the original tenant.

♦ **sublease** A
tenant leasing property
to another person, the
subtenant.

 LEGAL FOCUS - PROBLEM

Tami, a college student, leases an apartment for a two-year period.
Tami is offered a job in Europe for the summer months and accepts.
Since she does not wish to pay three months' rent for an unoccupied
apartment, she subleases the apartment to another student, Carl (the
sublessee). What are the liabilities of Tami and Carl?

Tami may have to get her landlord's permission to sublease the apartment. If the lease does not cover subleases, then subleases are allowed. The
sublessee, Carl, is bound by the same terms of the lease as the tenant, and if
Carl violates the lease, Tami can be held liable by the landlord. Unless Carl
and Tami have otherwise agreed, Carl will pay rent to Tami. Tami, of
course, must pay rent to the landlord. If the rent is unpaid, the landlord
can evict both Tami and Carl.

♦ RENT CONTROL

Many large cities have ordinances that provide for rent control. A **rent
control** law places limits on the amount of rent a landlord can charge for
an apartment once a tenant has moved in. Rent control laws vary widely,
but all of them limit the landlord's ability to raise rent, and such a landlord
will be diligent in enforcing the lease. Under most rent control statutes,
landlords can raise the rent for a new tenant. Thus, if an occupying tenant
does anything wrong, the landlord's interests are usually better served by
getting him or her out of the apartment. Then the landlord can rent to a
tenant who can be charged a higher rent.

♦ **rent control** A
law that places limits on
the amount of rent a
landlord can charge for
an apartment once a
tenant has moved in.

♦ CHECKING YOUR PROGRESS

1. What remedies does a landlord have if a tenant does not pay rent
   when due?

2. Is a landlord liable for injuries sustained by tenants on the
   landlord's property?

3. When does a tenancy at will occur?

4. Does a tenant's assignment of a lease relieve him or her of all
   lease responsibilities? Explain.

5. Who receives rent in a sublease?

Checking Your Progress (Answers)

1. A landlord can require
the tenant to pay a late
charge if rent is not paid
when due. The landlord can
keep all or part of a security
deposit to cover back rent.
2. The landlord's liability
extends to injuries resulting
from a dangerous condition
the landlord knew about or
should have known about.
The landlord may even be
liable for crimes of third
parties if crimes are reasonably foreseeable and he or
she fails to protect the tenants.
3. A tenancy at will exists if
a landlord rents an apartment to a tenant "for as long
as both agree." This may
occur when a tenant keeps
possession after the termination of a tenancy for years,
with the landlord's consent
and before the rent is paid,
at which time the tenancy is
converted into a periodic
tenancy.
4. No. Even though an
assignee may be required to
pay rent, the original tenant
still has a contractual obligation to the landlord.
5. In a sublease, the tenant
is the landlord of the sublease, and so the sublessee
should pay rent to the original tenant. The original tenant in turn pays the landlord.

Teaching A Case In Point

Read

Introduce this *A Case In Point* feature by explaining that this case deals with an implied warranty of habitability. You might remind students that the implied warranty of habitability is a warranty arising automatically in a lease that requires that a landlord leasing residential property keep it in habitable condition (that is, keep it safe and suitable to live in). Ask student volunteers to describe situations in which residential property would be unhabitable. Then allow a student volunteer to read this *A Case In Point* feature aloud to the class.

Teaching Note

This case is included in the *West's Business and Personal Law Handbook of Selected Court Cases*.

Discuss

Stimulate a class discussion of this *A Case In Point* feature by asking the students the following questions: Why did Dorothy Detling and several other tenants sue C. E. Edelbrock? In what ways did the tenants claim that the property they leased was unhabitable? Why did the lower court dismiss the petition? What was the issue in this case before the Supreme Court of Missouri? What decision did the court reach in this case? What reasons did the court give for its decision? What effects do you think this decision had on other implied warranty of habitability cases in the state of Missouri?

◆ A CASE IN POINT ◆

DETLING v. EDELBROCK
Supreme Court of Missouri, 1984.
671 S.W.2d 265.

In this case, the Supreme Court of Missouri departed from its former ruling based on the common law doctrine of *caveat emptor* ("let the buyer beware") to find an implied warranty of habitability in a lease.

FACTS Several tenants, including Dorothy Detling, sued their landlord, C. E. Edelbrock, for damages as a result of the landlord's breach of the implied warranty of habitability. The tenants claimed that the property they leased exhibited "material and substantial" violations of the local municipal housing code, including rodent and roach infestation, missing screens, exposed wiring, boiler malfunctions, rubbish strewn in passageways, water leakage, and unstable steps. The Missouri courts did not universally recognize an implied warranty of habitability. The lower court dismissed the petition for failure to state a cause of action (legal basis to sue), and the tenants appealed the dismissal to the Supreme Court of Missouri.

ISSUE Does a landlord owe the tenants an implied warranty of habitability? Do the alleged conditions violate such a warranty?

DECISION The Supreme Court of Missouri reversed the lower court's dismissal of the tenant's petition and remanded the case for a trial on the merits. They found that the landlord did owe the tenants an implied warranty of habitability and the conditions noted would be a breach of this warranty.

REASON Noting that many courts have abandoned the rule of *caveat emptor* ("let the buyer beware") for leased property, the court examined the basis for this warranty. "Several rationales have been advanced for replacing the common law with such a warranty, including: (1) doctrinal changes in the law, including recognition of the contractual nature of modern lease agreements and the trend against *caveat emptor* in favor of a warranty of fitness in consumer transactions; (2) the widespread enactment of state and local housing regulations establishing minimum community standards of habitability; (3) the tenant's reasonable expectation that property leased for the purpose of human habitation for a designated period of time will be fit for that use for the duration of the lease; and (4) the belief that tenants lack the means or abilities either to fully inspect (examine) modern dwelling units or maintain the premises during the term of the lease."

The court held that a landlord must keep residential property habitable and that "to constitute a breach of the warranty, a tenant must allege and prove conditions of such a nature as to render premises unsafe or unsanitary." The following elements must exist to find a breach: (1) a landlord-tenant relationship, (2) development of dangerous or unsanitary conditions at the dwelling that materially affect the life, health, and safety of the tenant, (3) reasonable notice of the defect to the landlord, and (4) failure of the landlord to remedy the defect.

In this case, the tenants' claims of unsanitary and dangerous conditions were told to the landlord, who should have made the apartment habitable.

In order to help students review what they have learned in Chapter 30, you might wish to:

1. Have a student volunteer, or volunteers, read aloud the Chapter Summary.
2. Allow the students to work with partners to complete the *Using Legal Language* activity.
3. Assign the *Checking for Comprehension* exercise as homework.

4. Allow the students to work in small groups to complete the *Applying Legal Concepts* activities.
5. As a class, complete the *Applying the Law* activities. (Please note that you may have to help students with vocabulary so that they adequately understand all of the *Applying the Law* material.)

In order to check student mastery of chapter concepts, you may wish to use the Chapter 30 test that is found in your *Teacher's Resource Binder* or use WESTEST computerized testing for Chapter 30.

Landlords and Tenants 729

CHAPTER 30 REVIEW

 ## SUMMARY

LANDLORD-TENANT RELATIONSHIP

The rental agreement is usually called a lease.

RIGHTS AND DUTIES OF LANDLORDS AND TENANTS

a. *Possession—*
   (1) The tenant has an exclusive right to possession of leased property.
   (2) Under the covenant of quiet enjoyment, the landlord promises that during the lease term, the landlord will not disturb the tenant's use and enjoyment of the property.

b. *Use*—Unless the parties agree otherwise, the tenant may make any legal use of the property. The tenant has a duty to refrain from waste. The tenant is responsible for any damages that she or he causes.

c. *Maintenance*—The landlord must comply with laws that set specific standards for the maintenance of real property. The implied warranty of habitability requires that a landlord furnish and maintain residential premises in a habitable condition.

d. *Rent*—The tenant must generally pay the rent while the lease is in force. A landlord may also require a security deposit.

TENANT REMEDIES

a. *Withholding rent*—In some states some rent may be withheld if the apartment is uninhabitable.

b. *Repairing and deducting*—Some states provide for the right to repair and deduct.

c. *Canceling the lease*—A tenant may be able to terminate his or her lease when the landlord evicts the tenant.

d. *Suing for damages*—A tenant can sue for damages if the landlord breaches the lease.

LANDLORD REMEDIES

a. *Late charges*—A landlord can charge a tenant a late charge if the tenant does not pay the rent when it is due.

b. *Security deposit*—A landlord can keep all or part of a security deposit to cover money owed by the tenant.

c. *Recovery of possession*—A landlord can recover possession of the property if the tenant breaches the lease. The usual court eviction procedure is called an *unlawful detainer.*

d. *Suing for damages*—A landlord can sue a tenant for damaging leased property or to collect unpaid rent.

LANDLORD'S TORT LIABILITY

A landlord is generally liable for injuries occurring on the part of the property within the landlord's control. The landlord is sometimes responsible for harm to a tenant caused by reasonably foreseeable criminal acts of third parties.

EXCULPATORY CLAUSES

Exculpatory clauses in leases are often not enforceable.

TYPES OF TENANCIES

There are four common types of leases:

a. *Tenancy for years*—Tenancy for a specified time period stated by express contract.

b. *Periodic tenancy*—Tenancy for a period determined by frequency of rent payments.

c. *Tenancy at will*—Tenancy for as long as both parties agree; no notice of termination required.

d. *Tenancy at sufferance*—Possession of land without legal right.

Using Legal Language
(Answers)

1–F, 2–C, 3–A, 4–E, 5–I,
6–B, 7–H, 8–G, 9–D, 10–J

Checking for
Comprehension
(Answers)

1. At common law, parties to a lease were free to agree to any terms they chose, usually favoring the landlord. However, laws have been enacted in recent years to protect the interest of tenants.
2. A covenant of quiet enjoyment is an implied promise by the landlord that during the lease term, the landlord will not disturb the tenant's use and enjoyment of the property. The tenant derives the most benefit from a covenant of quiet enjoyment and can terminate the lease and sue for damages if the landlord breaches.
3. Waste is the abuse or destructive use of property

by one in rightful possession. However, if the tenant has permission to do something such as cut down a tree, normally considered waste, the tenant would not be responsible for damages.
4. Landlords usually require a security deposit at the beginning of the lease to cover their losses if a tenant fails to pay the rent or damages the property. Many states limit the amount of the deposit to one month's rent.
5. Depending on the state, possible remedies available to a tenant for a landlord's failure to

maintain leased premises include withholding rent, repairing and deducting, canceling the lease, and suing for damages.
6. The common court eviction procedure is called an unlawful detainer. Procedures usually require that the tenant be given notice before the suit and provide for a jury to decide any factual disputes.
7. Tenancy for years, a periodic tenancy, and tenancy at will involve the transfer of the right to possession for a specified time. On the other hand, a tenancy at sufferance is not a

---

TRANSFERRING RIGHTS TO LEASED PROPERTY

a. If the landlord transfers complete title to the leased property, the new owner may then collect the rent but must abide by the existing lease.

b. Unless prohibited, tenants may *assign* their rights but not their duties under a lease contract to a third person.

c. Unless prohibited, tenants may *sublease* leased property to a third person, but the original tenant is not relieved of any obligations to the landlord under the lease.

 ## USING LEGAL LANGUAGE

Directions: Match each term with the statement that best defines that term.

1. constructive eviction
2. eviction
3. landlord
4. lease
5. periodic tenancy
6. rent
7. security deposit
8. sublease
9. tenancy at will
10. tenant

A. one who rents property to another

B. the tenant's payment to the landlord for the use of the landlord's real property

C. a landlord putting a tenant out of property either through direct action or through court action

D. a tenancy for as long as both parties agree; no notice of termination is required

E. a transfer by the possessor of property to another who has an exclusive right to use and possess property for a time in exchange for rent

F. a wrongful breach by the landlord of the tenant's right to enjoy and use rental property which is so serious as to make reasonable use of the property difficult or impossible

G. a tenant leasing property to another person

H. a sum of money paid to and held by the landlord to secure the tenant's obligations under the lease

I. a tenancy for a period determined by frequency of rent payments; automatically renewed unless proper notice is given

J. one to whom property is rented

 ## CHECKING FOR COMPREHENSION

1. How have laws pertaining to tenants and landlords changed over time?
2. What is a covenant of quiet enjoyment? Who benefits from this doctrine? What is

the recourse for breach?
3. A tenant *usually* has a duty to refrain from waste. Explain.
4. Why do landlords usually require a securi-

true tenancy because a tenant wrongfully retains possession of property.

8. Montford is a sublessee. A sublease exists if a tenant transfers all or part of the premises for a period shorter than the lease term, whereas an assignment is the transfer of a tenant's entire interest in leased property to a third person.

1. The court held that MCM's right to exercise the lease renewal option terminated when the lease term expired. As a general rule, a lessee must exercise an option to renew the lease on or before the expiration date of the original lease term. If the lessee fails to renew the lease within the required time, the option is forfeited. Once a lease term expires, if the tenant retains possession and continues paying rent, the tenancy becomes a month-to-month tenancy. Therefore, after December 31, 1988, MCM's tenancy was from month to month, which under state law could be terminated by the landlord on seven days' notice.

2. The court stated that a landlord of commercial property "impliedly represents that the premises are in fact suitable for that use and will remain in a suitable condition. The tenant's obligations to pay rent and the landlord's implied warrant . . . are therefore mutually dependent." In this case, Davidow had leased the office for use in his medical practice, and Inwood knew of that intended use. Because of Inwood's acts and omissions, the space was rendered unsuitable for use as a medical office. Davidow was thus justified in abandoning the premises and discontinuing his rent payments.

---

ty deposit at the beginning of a lease? How much can they charge?

5. Describe two remedies a tenant has when a landlord does not maintain leased premises.

6. A landlord can evict a tenant to recover possession of the property if a tenant breaches the lease. Describe the eviction process.

7. How does tenancy at sufferance differ from the three other types of tenancy?

◆ APPLYING LEGAL CONCEPTS

1. Assume you own a house that you want to rent to someone. Compose a classified ad to place in the newspaper. Create a lease agreement that tells your responsibilities as landlord and tells the tenant's responsibilities.

2. Look through the classified section of the newspaper. Calculate the average rental costs for apartments in your area. Based on the newspaper ads, what is the median cost to rent an apartment in your town?

◆ APPLYING THE LAW . . . YOU BE THE JUDGE

1. MCM Ventures, II Inc., leased premises from Rushing Construction Co. on which to operate a restaurant. The lease term was for two years, January 1, 1987, to December 31, 1988. The lease agreement stated in part that MCM "shall have a continuing option for a period of eight (8) consecutive years to renew this lease." Before the lease term expired on December 31, 1988, MCM did nothing to renew the lease and, after the lease expired, continued to make monthly rent payments in the same amount as before in January and February 1989. Then, on February 28, 1989, MCM notified Rushing by mail that it wanted to exercise its option to renew the lease. Rushing refused to renew the lease, contending that MCM had forfeited the option by not exercising it prior to the expiration of the lease agreement in which the option had been given. Discuss fully whether MCM still had a right to exercise the lease renewal option as late as February 28, 1989. [*Rushing Construction Co. v. MCM Ventures, II, Inc.*, 100 N.C.App. 259, 395 S.E.2d 130 (1990)]

2. Inwood North Professional Group—Phase I leased medical office space to Joseph Davidow, a physician. The terms of the five-year lease specified that Unwed would provide electricity, hot water, air-conditioning, janitorial and maintenance services, light fixtures, and security services. During his tenancy, Davidow encountered a number of problems. The roof leaked, and the air-conditioning did not function properly. The premises were not cleaned and maintained by Unwed as promised in the lease agreement, and as a consequence, rodents and pests infested the premises and trash littered the parking area. There was frequently no hot water, and at one point Davidow was without electricity for several days because Unwed had not paid the bill. About a year prior to the lease's expiration, Davidow moved to another office building and refused to pay the remaining rent due under the lease. Unwed sued for the unpaid rent. Must Davidow pay the remaining rent due under the lease? Discuss. [*Davidow v. Unwed North Professional Group—Phase I*, 747 S.W.2d 373 (Tex. (1988)]

Your students may view insurance as something that only parents have to worry about. This is a good example of a real-world topic that your students should know something about—now. Insurance is a precaution taken to protect against the hazards of life. Of course, no one can predict whether an accident or a fire will ever occur, but individuals and businesses must establish plans to protect their personal and financial interests should some event threaten to undermine their security. This concept is known as risk management. The most common method of risk management is the transfer of certain risks from the insured to the insurance company. Another method of risk management is reducing risk.

In this chapter we have presented the major types of insurance, identifying the protections offered, along with some standard rules relating to common insurance problems.

732

Prereading Activity

Bring samples of insurance policies to class. Pass the policies around for students to read. Ask students what they know about insurance. Ask students if they think individuals need insurance. Ask students to think about why statutes have been passed to regulate insurance companies.

Mastery Objectives

By the end of this chapter, students should be able to:
- Explain insurance concepts
- Apply insurance terminology
- Analyze an insurance contract
- Characterize types of insurance

Chapter

31

Insurance

"Insurance is part charity and part business, but all common sense."
Calvin Coolidge, 1872–1963
Thirtieth president of the United States

Insurance is a specific type of contract and, as Calvin Coolidge said, is "all common sense." Most people insure their real and personal property, their lives, and their health. Insurance protects us against loss. The insurance company (insurer) promises to pay another (either the insured or the beneficiary) if the insured is injured or experiences a loss as a result of certain events. Insurance is an arrangement for *transferring and allocating risk*. **Risk** can be described as a prediction of potential loss. In other words, when you own health insurance, you transfer the risk—the potential loss of money if you become sick and must be hospitalized, for instance—to your health insurance company. Insurance is, however, much more than a game of chance.

There are many ways to protect yourself against life's hazards. For example, you can wear a seat belt to protect yourself from injuries in an automobile accident. Installing smoke detectors can help protect you against the risk of fire.

No one can predict accurately whether or when an accident or a fire will happen. However, individuals and businesses need to plan to protect their personal and financial interests. Planning for risk is known as **risk management**. The most common method of risk management is to transfer some risks to an insurance company.

◆ **insurance** An arrangement for transferring and allocating risk.

◆ **risk** A prediction of potential loss.

◆ **risk management** Planning and managing risk, including transferring some risks to an insurance company.

◆ INSURANCE CONCEPTS AND TERMINOLOGY

As with other areas of law, the area of insurance has its own special concepts and terminology that you must understand in order to understand insurance law. The following subsections look at some of these terms and concepts.

RISK POOLING

All insurance companies use the principle of **risk pooling**. They spread the risk of loss among many people—the pool. Pooling allows people to pay small sums of money compared with the protection offered. Life insurance companies, for example, know that only a small proportion of the individuals in any particular age group will die in any one year. If a large percentage of this age group pays small sums of money to the company in exchange for a payment for an early death, there is enough money to pay the beneficiaries of a deceased person who purchased insurance (*policyholder*). Through analysis of information over time, insurers can estimate accu-

◆ **risk pooling** Spreading a risk among many people to keep the premiums charged policyholders small compared with the amount of insurance coverage offered.

Enrichment

Help the students focus on the topic of this chapter by asking them to brainstorm a list of different types of insurance or different things one can insure. Have a volunteer write the students' suggestions on the board. Then have a volunteer read aloud both the quote from Calvin Coolidge and the chapter introduction, which immediately follows that quote.

Critical Thinking Activity

The most common method of risk management is the transfer of some risks to an insurance company. Brainstorm some other ways risk can be managed. (Examples might include eating right, driving safely, etc.)

Critical Thinking Activity

Have the students write a one-paragraph explanation of the concept of risk pooling, using their own words. Allow students to exchange their papers with partners to proofread and correct each other's work. Allow volunteers to share their finished work with the class.

Extension Activity

You might ask an insurance agent or insurance broker to speak to your class regarding the types of insurance available to consumers and businesses, the advantages of each, and the relative costs. Have your students prepare questions in advance for the speaker.

Extension Activity

Have a volunteer or group of volunteers do a media search to find recent articles or news stories regarding the insurance industry. You might guide the students in their research by suggesting that they look under "Insurance" in the *Readers Guide to Periodical Literature*. Students should clip or copy any articles they find and present the articles to the class along with a brief oral summary.

Teaching with Visuals

Tell students to read the Insurance Classifications in Exhibit 31-1. Ask them if they currently have any of the kinds of insurance listed here. Ask them which they will need when they start working, when they graduate from high school, when they have their own family, when they buy a house, etc.

734   Personal Law

Type of Insurance	Coverage
Accident	Covers expenses, losses, and suffering incurred by the insured because of accidents causing physical injury and consequent disability; sometimes includes a specified payment to heirs of the insured if death results from an accident.
Automobile	May cover damage to automobiles resulting from specified hazards or occurrences (such as fire, vandalism, theft, or collision); normally provides protection against liability for personal injuries and property damage resulting from the operation of the vehicle.
Casualty	Protects against losses that may be incurred by the insured as a result of being held liable for personal injuries or property damage sustained by others.
Credit	Pays to a creditor the balance of a debt upon the disability, death, insolvency, or bankruptcy of the debtor; often offered by lending institutions.
Employer's liability	Insures employers against liability for injuries or losses sustained by employees during the course of their employment; covers claims not covered under workers' compensation insurance.
Fidelity or guaranty	Provides indemnity against losses in trade or losses caused by the dishonesty of employees, the insolvency of debtors, or breaches of contract.
Fire	Covers losses caused to the insured as a result of fire.
Floater	Covers movable property, as long as the property is within the territorial boundaries specified in the contract.

EXHIBIT 31-1
INSURANCE CLASSIFICATIONS

◆ **premium** The sum of money paid by a policyholder for insurance protection.

◆ **policy** An insurance contract.

◆ **insurer** The insurance company.

◆ **insured** The person covered by the insurance policy.

◆ **insurance agent** An employee of an insurance company.

◆ **insurance broker** An independent contractor who represents the buyer in purchasing insurance.

rately the total amount of loss they will pay. Then they can estimate the rates they need to charge each person to pay benefits and still make a profit. The payment made by the policyholder for insurance protection is called a **premium**.

CLASSIFICATIONS OF INSURANCE

Insurance is classified by the nature of the risk involved. For example, fire insurance, casualty insurance, life insurance, and title insurance apply to different types of risk. Policies of these types differ in the persons and interests that they protect. The potential losses vary with different activities. Exhibit 31-1 provides a comprehensive list of different insurance classifications.

INSURANCE TERMINOLOGY

An insurance contract is called a **policy**. The money paid to the insurance company is a *premium*. The insurance company is often called an *underwriter*. The parties to an insurance policy are the **insurer** (the insurance company) and the **insured** or *policyholder* (the person covered by the policy). Insurance contracts are purchased through either an **insurance agent** or an **insurance broker**. An *agent* ordinarily works for and is an agent of

Collaborative Learning Activity

Divide the class into small groups. Have the members of each group work together in reading and discussing the material found on these pages that deals with insurance terminology. Then have the students write short fictional accounts of a consumer purchasing automobile insurance, in which they use each of the following terms correctly: *premium, policy, insurer, insured, insurance agent, insurance broker.* Each group should select a leader to read its work to the class.

Type of Insurance	Coverage
Group	Provides individual life, medical, or disability insurance coverage but is obtainable through a group of persons, usually employees; the policy premium is paid either entirely by the employer or partially by the employer and partially by the employee.
Health	Covers expenses incurred by the insured resulting from physical injury or illness and other expenses relating to health and life maintenance.
Homeowners	Protects homeowners against some or all of the risks of loss to their residences and their contents or liability related to such property.
Key-person	Protects a business in the event of the death or disability of a key employee.
Liability	Protects against liability imposed on the insured resulting from injuries to the person or property of another.
Life	Covers the death of the policyholder. Upon the death of the insured, an amount specified in the policy is paid by the insurer to the insured's beneficiary.
Major medical	Protects the insured against major hospital, medical, or surgical expenses.
Malpractice	Protects professionals (doctors, lawyers, and others) against malpractice claims brought against them by their patients or clients; a form of liability insurance.
Mortgage	Covers a mortgage loan; the insurer pays the balance of the mortgage to the creditor upon the death or disability of the debtor.
No-fault auto	Covers personal injury and (sometimes) property damage resulting from automobile accidents. The insured submits his or her claims to his or her own insurance company, regardless of who was at fault. A person may sue the party at fault or that party's insurer only in cases involving serious medical injury and consequent high medical costs. Governed by state "no-fault" statutes.
Term	Provides life insurance for a specified period of time (term) with no cash surrender value; usually renewable.
Title	Protects against any defects in title to real property and any losses incurred as a result of existing claims against or liens on the property at the time of purchase.

Exhibit 31-1 (Continued)
Insurance Classifications

the insurance company. Usually, the insurance company is bound by the acts of its agents performed while they are acting within the agency relationship (see Chapter 20). A *broker* ordinarily is an independent contractor. When a broker deals with an applicant who wants insurance, the broker is the applicant's agent.

Insurable Interest

A person can insure anything in which he or she has an **insurable interest**. In property insurance, an insurable interest exists when the insured benefits from the continued existence of the property. In other words, you

◆ **insurable interest**
A real economic risk related to rights in property or a person's well-being.

Enrichment

You might wish to point out to the class that the insurance industry is often viewed in a negative light by many consumers, politicians, businesspeople, and others. As an example, noted American writer Ambrose Bierce described insurance as "an ingenious modern game of chance in which the player is permitted to enjoy the comfortable conviction that he is beating the man who keeps the table." Ask the students to share any complaints concerning the insurance industry that they might have heard. Why do they think the insurance industry consistently receives such negative comments?

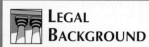
Critical Thinking Activity

Ask students to list on paper "things" in which they have an insurable interest as of today. Allow volunteers to share their lists with the class.

Legal Focus Problem

Have a student volunteer read this Legal Focus Problem aloud to the class. Remind the students that with life insurance, the insurable interest need only exist when the policy is purchased; however, with property insurance the insurable interest must exist at the time the loss occurs. Then have a student volunteer suggest a possible answer to the question posed at the end of this problem.

Key-person Insurance (sometimes referred to as business insurance) insures the life of a person who is important to an organization; premiums are paid by the organization. Because an organization expects to receive some pecuniary gain from the continuation of the key person's life or suffer some financial loss from the key person's death, the organization has an insurable interest. Typically, a partnership will insure the life of each because the death of any one partner will legally dissolve the firm and cause some degree of loss to the partnership. Similarly, a corporation has an insurable interest in the life expectancy of a key executive whose death would result in financial loss to the company.

The insurable interest in life insurance must exist at the time the policy is obtained. Because of this rule, under a key-person life insurance policy, it will not matter if the key person is no longer in the business's employ at the time of the loss—that is, the key person's death. Normally, however, a company will stop paying the premiums once the insured leaves its employ.

have an insurable interest in property if you would suffer a money loss from its destruction.

In life insurance, a person must have an expectation of benefit in the life of another to have an insurable interest in that person's life. Every person is presumed to have an insurable interest in his or her own life. The interest may be economic (such as with so-called *key-person insurance*, which insures the lives of important officers, usually in small companies). It may also be founded on a relationship between the parties (such as husband and wife or parent and child).

In life insurance, the insurable interest must exist when the policy is purchased. The opposite is true for property insurance, where the insurable interest must exist at the time the loss occurs. If there is no insurable interest, a contract is not enforceable. In such cases, the transaction to insure is treated as an illegal wager, and the insurance company is not required to pay the beneficiary.

◆ LEGAL FOCUS ~ PROBLEM

Wilma bought a life insurance policy on the life of her husband Jeff. She also purchased a fire insurance policy on the couple's home. Unfortunately, Wilma and Jeff got a divorce. In the property settlement between the couple, Jeff took sole ownership and responsibility for the house, and Wilma took other unrelated property. A fire occurred at the house and Jeff died from smoke inhalation. Will Wilma be able to collect on either insurance policy?

She can collect on the life insurance policy, but she cannot collect on the fire insurance policy. When Wilma bought the life insurance on Jeff, they were married and a real economic risk existed for her if he died. Because an insurable interest existed in his life at the time of the purchase, she can collect on the policy even though they are now divorced. The rule for property insurance is different, however; it requires that the risk exist at the time of the loss. When Wilma purchased the fire insurance she was part owner in the home. However, when the loss occurred, she no longer had an interest in the home, so she will be unable to collect on the fire insurance.

◆ THE INSURANCE CONTRACT

An insurance contract is governed by the general principles of contract law. The insurance industry is also regulated by each state. The filled-in application form for insurance is part of the insurance contract; it is usually attached to the policy. Thus, with a few exceptions, an insurance applicant is bound by any false statements in the application. The insurance company evaluates risk based on the information in the insurance application. Misstatements or misrepresentations can void a policy if the insurance company can show that it would not have issued insurance if it had known the true facts.

TIMING

When an insurance contract begins to protect the insured is obviously important. Sometimes, the insurance applicant is not protected until a formal written policy is issued by the insurance company. Other times, the applicant is protected between the time the applicant is received and the day it is accepted or rejected. The difference between a broker and an agent is often important in determining the effective date of an insurance policy. A broker is an independent contractor who acts as an agent of the applicant. An insurance agent is an employee of an insurance company, so he or she is an agent of that company. Four different situations that affect the timing of when an insurance policy takes effect are discussed here.

1. If the policy is purchased from a broker, the policy is not effective until and unless it is issued by the insurance company. If the company does not issue a policy, the applicant is not insured. If the broker negligently fails to submit the application, the broker is liable to the damaged applicant for the loss.

2. If the policy is purchased from an insurance company agent, the applicant is often protected from the time of the application. Some form of premium must have been paid if the policy is life insurance. Between the time the application is received and either rejected or accepted, the applicant is covered (possibly subject to medical examination). Usually, the agent will write a memorandum, or *binder*, stating that a policy is pending and describing its essential terms.

3. If the parties agree that the policy is to be issued and delivered at a later time, the contract is not effective until its terms are met. Thus, any loss that occurs between the time of application and the delivery of the policy is not covered.

4. Parties may agree that an insurance policy is binding at the time the applicant completes the application, pays the first premium, and meets some additional qualification, as the following example illustrates.

◆ LEGAL FOCUS ~ EXAMPLE

A common requirement for life insurance policies is that the applicant pay his or her premium, make his or her medical records available, and submit to a physical examination. Once the applicant has passed the physical examination, the policy coverage is considered effective from the time the premium was paid.

PROVISIONS AND CLAUSES

Some important clauses contained in insurance contracts are defined in this section. Judges know that most people do not understand the complicated

Two other important causes that are contained in some insurance contracts are co-insurance clauses and pro rata clauses.

A co-insurance clause provides that if the owner insures his or her property up to a specified percentage—usually 80 percent—of its value, he or she will recover any loss up to the face amount of the policy. These clauses are introduced to the students later in this chapter.

If an insured has multiple insurance coverage—that is, policies with several companies covering the same property—and the amount of the coverage exceeds the loss, the insured can collect from each insurer only the company's proportionate share of the liability to the total amount of the insurance. Many fire insurance policies include a pro rata clause, which requires any loss to be shared proportionately by all carriers. Pro rata clauses are not found in life insurance policies, for the obvious reason that a life cannot be subject to monetary valuation.

Critical Thinking Activity

Read aloud the definition of the incontestability clause. Then ask a student volunteer to explain whether incontestability clauses favor the insurance company or the insured. Have the volunteer explain his or her answer.

Legal Focus Example

Have a student volunteer read this Legal Focus Example aloud to the class. Ask the volunteer whether it is possible for the insured to avoid cancellation in each of the cases listed here. Students should understand that the insured can avoid cancellation by paying his or her premium; by dealing in good faith with the insurance company; and otherwise acting in a reasonable manner.

738   Personal Law

language used in insurance policies. Thus, the courts interpret the words used in an insurance contract by their ordinary meanings. When there is an ambiguity (that is, when terms can have more than one meaning) in the policy, the language is interpreted against the insurance company and in favor of the insured.

◆ **incontestability clause** A provision in an insurance contract that provides that after a policy has existed for a specified time—usually two or three years—the insurer cannot challenge statements made in the application.

Incontestability Clause An **incontestability clause** provides that after a policy has existed for a specified time—usually two or three years—the insurer cannot contest statements made in the application. Incontestability clauses are common in life insurance policies.

Appraisal Clause An appraisal clause provides a method to resolve disagreements between the insured and insurer over the value of lost or damaged property covered by a policy. An appraisal, which is an estimate of the value of something, by an impartial and qualified third party can be demanded. Appraisal clauses are common in property liability insurance policies.

Antilapse Clause An antilapse clause provides that the policy does not automatically lapse if no payment is made on the due date. Ordinarily, the insured has a *grace period* of thirty or thirty-one days to pay the premium before the policy is canceled. Antilapse clauses are common in many types of insurance policies.

Arbitration Clause Often insurance policies will provide for arbitration of disputes between the insurer and the insured concerning the settlement of claims. Arbitration clauses are most common in health insurance policies but are becoming more common in personal and property liability insurance.

Cancellation Clause Cancellation of an insurance policy can occur for several reasons, depending on the insurance type. Cancellation must take place before the effective date of an incontestability clause. State statutes usually require that an insurance company give advance written notice of its intent to cancel. An insurance company cannot cancel—or refuse to renew—a policy because of the national origin or race of an applicant. Companies also cannot cancel a policy because the insured has appeared as a witness in a case against the company.

◆ LEGAL FOCUS ~ EXAMPLE

Insurance policies can be canceled for many reasons. Among these is the failure to pay the premium—this is a reason to cancel any type of insurance policy. Automobile insurance can be canceled for a poor driving record or for suspension of the insured's driver's license. Property insurance can be canceled because of the insured's fraud or misrepresentation. Life and health policies can be canceled due to false statements made by the insured in the application.

Caption Answer

Driving under the influence is very expensive. A minor will probably lose his or her drivers license, spend time in juvenile hall, pay a fine, pay increased insurance premiums, or lose insurance altogether. Fines and increased driving costs associated with a single DUI for an adult are approaching $10,000.

Critical Thinking Activity

Tell students to read the Legal Focus Problem about Kirk Johnson. Ask them to write short papers telling whether they agree or disagree with the arguments and the ruling of the court. Discuss who acted illegally or unethically.

Legal Focus Case Problem

Have a student volunteer read aloud to the class this Legal Focus Case Problem and the paragraph at the top of page 740, in which the answer to the question posed at the end of this problem is found. You might then point out to the students that at another point in its opinion, the court sympathized with the plight of Kirk Johnson's father and other beneficiaries who were unable to receive life insurance proceeds because of the misrepresentations made on the application forms. But it also pointed to the public policy underlying its decision: "If the only consequence of a fraudulent misrepresentation in a life insurance application is to reduce the amount paid under the policy, there is every incentive for applicants to lie. If the lie is undetected during the two-year contestability period, the insured will have obtained excessive coverage for which he has not paid. If the lie is detected during the two-year period, the insured will still obtain what he could have had if he had told the truth. In essence, the applicant has everything to gain and nothing to lose by lying. Victims will be the honest applicants who tell the truth and whose premiums will rise over the long run to pay for the excessive insurance proceeds paid out as a result of undetected misrepresentations in fraudulent applications."

What will happen to a minor found responsible for driving under the influence of alcohol or another illegal substance?

DEFENSES AGAINST PAYMENT

An insurance company can raise the ordinary contract defenses discussed in the chapters on contracts. There are also defenses that are especially common to insurance claims. If the insurance company can show that the policy was purchased by fraud, misrepresentation, or failure to fulfill obligations, the company can refuse to pay the claim. Improper actions on the part of the insured—actions that are against public policy or otherwise illegal—can give an insurance company a defense to payment of a claim. The insurance company may also be able to rescind or revoke the entire insurance contract for the misrepresentation or illegal activity of the insured.

◆ LEGAL FOCUS – CASE PROBLEM

Kirk Johnson applied for a $50,000 life insurance policy with the New York Life Insurance Company. In completing the application, he claimed he had not smoked in the last twelve months and that he had never smoked cigarettes. In truth, he had smoked for thirteen years and had smoked ten cigarettes a day during the month preceding completing the application. Two years after the policy was issued, Kirk died due to reasons unrelated to smoking. New York Life refused to pay Kirk's father, his beneficiary, when it learned that Kirk had misrepresented his smoking on the application. Kirk's father sued, claiming that because the misrepresentation was unrelated to the cause of Kirk's death, the insurance company should pay. What was the result?

Checking Your Progress (Answers)

1. Since insurance companies collect small amounts from a large number of people, they are able to cover the costs of claims for the few who request payment.

2. Insurance is classified by the nature of the risk involved.

3. Someone has an insurable interest in property if he or she would suffer a monetary loss from destruction of the property.

4. In life insurance the interest must exist at the time the policy is purchased, but the interest must exist at the time of the loss of personal property in property insurance.

5. The courts generally interpret ambiguous language against the insurance company.

740

The court held for the insurance company, stating, "An insurance policy is void for misrepresentation when the insurer establishes three elements: (1) that the representation was false; (2) that the insured knew that the representation was false when made or made it in bad faith; (3) that the representation was material to the risk being insured."[1]

◆ Checking Your Progress

1. How does risk pooling lower the cost of insurance for individuals?

2. How is insurance classified?

3. What determines if someone has an insurable interest in property?

4. How does the time of insurable interest between property insurance and life insurance differ?

5. How is ambiguous language in an insurance policy treated by the courts?

◆ Types of Insurance

There are five general types of insurance coverage: life, health, fire and homeowners', automobile, and business liability. We will examine each briefly.

Life Insurance

◆ **life insurance**
Insurance to protect against financial loss to the beneficiaries because of the death of the insured.

◆ **whole life** Life insurance with a cash surrender value. Sometimes called straight life, ordinary life, or cash-value insurance.

Life insurance should probably be called death insurance, because that is what it is. But imagine how difficult it would be to sell it by that name. The purchaser of a life insurance policy pays a premium against the possibility of the insured's death. If the insured dies, the insurance company pays a designated beneficiary the value of the policy. There are several types of life insurance. Two common types are discussed here.

1. **Whole life** is sometimes called straight life, ordinary life, or cash-value insurance. This type of insurance provides both life insurance protection and a savings feature. The savings feature is called the cash surrender value. This amount can often be borrowed from the life insurance company during the policy life, and it is returned to the policyholder if he or she survives to a certain agreed-on age. Premiums are paid by the policyholder during his or her entire lifetime or to a specified age, and a fixed payment is made to the beneficiary on the death of the insured. Life insurance salespersons will usually try to sell whole life insurance because the commission paid the salesperson is high. Whole life insurance is very profitable for insurance companies.

---

1. *New York Life Insurance Co. v. Johnson*, 923 F.2d 279 (1991).

Read

Introduce this *Law in Action* feature by reminding the students that when individuals successfully perpetrate fraud on insurance companies, the costs of that fraud are eventually borne by the honest customers of that insurance company. Then have a student volunteer read this *Law in Action* feature aloud to the class.

Discuss

Stimulate a class discussion of this *Law in Action* feature by asking the following questions: When the *Aliakmon Runner* sank into the Indian Ocean on February 7, 1983, what cargo belonging to Frederick Knight was aboard? What was the 1981 appraised value of that cargo? What was the appraised value of that cargo in 1980? For what value was that cargo insured by the group of New York insurance companies? Why did these insurance companies cancel Knight's insurance policy of $30 million? What material information had Knight failed to disclose on his insurance application? What was significant about his prior cancellation?

Insurance   741

◆ Law in Action

LAW AND THE BUSINESSPERSON: MR. KNIGHT'S SUNKEN TREASURE

Economists have a term for costs that cannot be recovered. They are called "sunk costs"—costs that have, for all practical purposes, sunk to the bottom of the ocean. Frederick Knight faced *real* sunk costs. The *Aliakmon Runner* sank deep into the Indian Ocean on February 7, 1983. The ship was transporting his collection of antique bronze and stone statues of Buddhas and fable gods from Singapore to the Greek port of Piraeus. Knight's collection had been purchased in Bangkok, Thailand, in the late 1970s. The statues were appraised by a Bangkok appraiser in 1981 for $30,307,500. The same appraiser had valued the collection at $20,205,000 in 1980.

In late 1982, Knight made arrangements to ship the collection to a Greek buyer, George Papalios. On the basis of the Bangkok appraiser's evaluation and a letter of intent to purchase from the buyer, a group of New York insurance companies insured the shipment for $30,307,500. With this protection, Knight arranged for the collection to be shipped in January of 1983 on the *Aliakmon Runner.*

Knight ultimately lost both his collection and his insurance coverage. A New York district court held that the underwriters of Knight's insurance policy (of $30 million) were within their rights to cancel his policy.[2] The reason? Knight had not disclosed material information on his insurance application.

Knight did not disclose that a previous policy covering the statues had been canceled. Hogg Robinson, a London brokerage firm, had provided a policy in 1981 to cover a planned shipment of the statues from Singapore to a buyer in Marseilles. The policy had been for $20 million, based on the Bangkok appraiser's first valuation of the collection. After Knight got that policy, the London underwriters received two anonymous phone calls. The London group was told that Knight was attempting a fraud. They were also informed that Knight's collection was not worth anywhere near $20 million. Hogg Robinson arranged for an independent appraisal of the statues, which were in Singapore awaiting shipment. Shortly after the appraisal, Robinson sent a telex to Knight stating that the company had voided his policy because the statues were "grossly overvalued . . . and in some, if not all cases, replicas." The real value of the consignment was "possibly approximately 1 percent of the value declared."

Knight did not tell the New York underwriters of the cancellation of the earlier policy in his application. They learned about it during the investigation of the sinking of the *Aliakmon Runner.* Knight argued that the information was not relevant to his application. The insurance companies thought it highly relevant. The court agreed with the insurance companies.

---

2. *Knight v. United States Fire Insurance Co.,* 651 F.Supp. 477 (S.D.N.Y. 1986).

Divide the class into small groups. Have each group work together to create a poster comparing whole life and term insurance. Each group should select a spokesperson to display and explain its poster.

Health insurance is one aspect of our health care system. Have a student volunteer or group of volunteers research efforts to reform our health care system. What steps have been taken by government to reform our health care system? What obstacles to reform exist?

How will insurance providers be affected by this reform? Have the students present their findings to the class in the form of oral reports. Encourage the students to cite original source documents in their reports.

♦ **term insurance**
Life insurance with no savings element. Covers a specific time; then the policy expires unless renewed.

2. **Term insurance** is a type of policy for which premiums are paid for a specified term. Payment on the policy by the insurance company only happens if death occurs within the specified period. Premiums are less expensive than for whole life, as there is no cash surrender value. Frequently, this type of insurance can be converted to another type of life insurance. Term insurance is often called pure insurance because its only purpose is to insure against untimely death. In contrast, whole life policies are part insurance and part savings plan.

Selected Legal Issues in Life Insurance   The rights and liabilities of the parties in life insurance usually depend on the insurance contract. Most life insurance contracts exclude liability for deaths caused by suicide, military action during war, execution while imprisoned, or even death occurring while the insured is a passenger in a commercial vehicle such as an airplane.

Most life insurance policies permit the policyholder to change beneficiaries at any time. Some policies, however, do not allow for a change of beneficiaries. Death taxes are often reduced with policies in which the beneficiaries cannot be changed.

The policyholder can generally cancel and terminate the policy at any time, but the insurance company usually cannot. The company usually can only terminate the policy if one of the following happens:

1. The policyholder does not pay the policy premium.
2. The term of the policy expires.
3. The policyholder cancels the policy.

♦ **health insurance**
Broad term covering accident insurance, disability insurance, and medical expense insurance. Most often used when referring to medical expense insurance.

HEALTH AND DISABILITY INSURANCE

The term **health insurance** covers several different types of insurance policies. Among them are accident insurance, disability insurance, and medical expense insurance.

♦ **accident insurance**   Covers losses for certain injuries received through accidental means.

Accident insurance provides for the payment to the policyholder of a sum of money for certain injuries received by accidental means. For example, a specified amount is paid to a policyholder if he or she loses the use of an eye, arm, or leg. The more serious the injury, the greater the one-time dollar payment.

♦ **disability insurance**   Provides replacement income for a policyholder who becomes unable to work because of an injury or illness.

Disability insurance pays a policyholder if he or she becomes unable to work because of an injury or illness. Disability insurance provides a replacement income. Workers' compensation insurance, discussed in Chapter 22, is a form of disability insurance. Some states provide supplemental public disability insurance plans, and additional plans are available from private insurance companies. Often a person must be disabled for a specified time before becoming eligible to receive benefits under a policy. The definition of what qualifies as a disability is of major importance in these types of plans.

You might wish to ask a personnel manager from a local business or industry to speak to your class regarding the importance of health insurance as a benefit received by employees. The speaker should discuss the amount of coverage that is received, the dollar value of that coverage both to the employee and the employer, etc. Have your students prepare questions for the speaker in advance.

Ask a student volunteer to read this Legal Focus Example aloud to the class. Ask the students which of these definitions of disabilities seem the most fair to the injured worker. Which of these definitions of disabilities might insurance companies prefer?

Caption Answer

Her own policies such as health insurance, disability insurance (for time off work), accident insurance (if she has certain types of injuries), or automobile insurance may provide medical benefits. If another person caused her harm, that person's personal liability insurance, either automobile, homeowners', or renters', depending on where and how the accident occurred may provide benefits. If the accident was caused by car and she lives in a no-fault auto insurance state, then her own policy may pay for her injuries, or if her injuries are extensive then the other person may still be liable. If she was injured at a home or business, then either a homeowners' policy or a business liability policy may cover her injuries.

Insurance 743

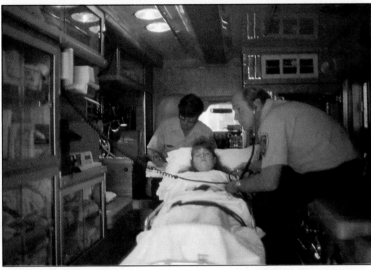

What are the types of insurance that may pay for her injuries?

◀ LEGAL FOCUS – EXAMPLE

One common definition of disability is "the inability of the insured to engage in any occupation." If a truck driver injured his foot, he would not qualify for benefits since there are still several jobs that he could perform. Another definition of disability is "the inability of the insured to engage in his or her own occupation." Under this definition, the truck driver would have a right to benefits.

Medical expense insurance is provided to cover doctor and hospital expenses when a person is ill. The reasons for the illness are usually not important to questions of coverage as long as the type of illness is covered in the policy. Most individuals who have health insurance are covered by group policies, which cover all employees (and sometimes families) at a workplace.

Some health insurance companies require policyholders to file claim forms after receiving benefits under the policy. In recent years, more and more health policies have been obtained from *health maintenance organizations* or HMOs. A health maintenance organization contracts with physicians and hospitals and other health care providers to prepay for a policyholder's health coverage. Usually if a person is a member of an HMO, they do not have to file claim forms. They are, however, required to seek health care from providers specified by the HMO.

The different types of health care companies and coverage are numerous and complicated. For example, some policies are limited to covering a

◆ **medical expense insurance** Covers doctor and hospital expenses when a person is ill.

Ask a student volunteer to read aloud the paragraph that begins with the heading Standard Fire Insurance Policies. Then ask the students to write a one-paragraph explanation of how a fire insurance policy can protect the homeowner against much more than simply damage or loss due to fire. Allow volunteers to share their work with the class.

Have a student volunteer contact local banks to research the availability and costs of safe deposit boxes. Ask the volunteer to report his or her findings to the class. Point out to students that by placing the records of personal property purchases in a safe deposit box, a homeowner is, in effect, ensuring against problems relating to the valuation of any personal property damaged in a fire, etc.

Legal Focus Example

Read aloud the Legal Focus Example found at the bottom of this page. Remind students that personal property was defined in Chapter 28 as "property that is movable; any property that is not real property."

---

744   Personal Law

specified type of illness, such as cancer. Other types of policies cover dental care or the care of a person's eyesight.

Issues regarding health care and health insurance coverage are among the major political issues currently being debated in the United States. With new expensive technology, with methods of sustaining life now available that were not anticipated even a few years ago, and with the prevalence of AIDS, questions of the availability of insurance, its cost, and the scope of its coverage will be important for the next several years.

FIRE AND HOMEOWNERS' INSURANCE

There are basically two types of insurance policies for a home—standard fire insurance policies and homeowners' policies. Policies also exist to protect the personal belongings of renters.

◆ **standard fire insurance** Policy that compensates the insured for losses caused by fire and lightning and by damage from smoke and water caused by the fire or the fire department.

Standard Fire Insurance Policies The **standard fire insurance** policy protects the homeowner against fire and lightning and against damage from smoke and water caused by the fire or the fire department. Paying a slightly higher amount will extend the coverage to damage caused by hail, windstorms, explosions, and so on. Personal theft insurance and a comprehensive liability policy can also be added to fire insurance. Liability insurance in fire policies protects a person from obligations that might arise because of the homeowner's torts. For example, if a neighbor slips and hurts himself or herself because of a toy left on the homeowner's entrance stairs, the homeowner's liability insurance will pay any damages that might result if the homeowner is found at fault.

As in all forms of insurance, the insurer's liability is determined by the terms of the policy. Most policies, however, limit recovery to losses resulting from a *hostile*, not a *friendly fire*. A *friendly fire* is one intentionally set and burning where it is supposed to burn—for example, in a fireplace. A *hostile fire* is one that was not intended.

Fire insurance policies require the insured to file a claim within a specified time. The claimant must prove loss within this time or risk that coverage will be revoked.

> ### ◄ LEGAL FOCUS ~ EXAMPLE
>
> When a house burns, proof of the fire is not difficult. The homeowner reports the loss, and an insurance company employee then inspects the house. Problems do occur, however, regarding personal property. Receipts that show the existence and the purchase price of the property can help establish what the homeowner owned. However, the receipts should not be kept in the house because they can be destroyed in the fire. Safe-deposit boxes at banks are usually the best place to keep such important records. In a safe-deposit box, the records are safe from fire and theft and can then be produced to prove the loss.

Have a student volunteer or group of volunteers research the aftermath of Hurricane Andrew, which struck south Florida in 1992. Guide the students in their research by telling them to focus on any news reports describing, criticizing, or evaluating the performance of insurance companies in responding to the needs of policy holders. Have the students present their findings to the class in the form of an oral report. Encourage the students to incorporate visual aids such as bar graphs, etc., into their presentation.

Have students create a chart showing the definition and characteristics of all the types of fire and homeowners' insurance discussed in this chapter.

Caption Answer

Standard fire insurance and homeowners' insurance protect against loss from fire.

Insurance   745

What types of insurance policies protect against loss from fire?

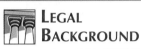

LEGAL BACKGROUND

A personal effects floater policy covers personal items that accompany the insured when he or she is travelling. In most cases, this coverage is not necessary because a regular homeowner's policy provides sufficient coverage. The personal effects floater covers articles only when they are taken off the insured's property. It does not cover theft from an attended automobile unless there is evidence of forced entry. Even then, the company's liability is generally limited to 10 percent of the amount of insurance, and no more than a specified amount, such as $250 or $500, for all property in any one loss. This restriction can be removed by payment of an additional premium, however.

Homeowners' Policies **Homeowners' insurance** provides protection against several risks under a single policy. This allows the policyholder to avoid the cost of buying each protection separately. There are two basic types of coverage in a homeowners' policy.

1. Property coverage includes the garage, house, and other private buildings on the policyholder's lot. This coverage also protects the personal possessions and property of the policyholder at home, while traveling, or at work. A claim can pay additional living expenses for living away from home because of a fire or some other covered danger. Some dangers, also called *perils*, are commonly excluded from coverage unless specifically requested and an additional premium paid. Among the types of perils that are sometimes excluded are war, earthquake, flood, and nuclear hazard.

2. Liability coverage protects for personal liability if someone is injured on the insured's property. This coverage also protects the insured who damages someone else's property or injures someone else. Two major exclusions from coverage are harm caused to others while in an automobile and liability for professional malpractice.

An insured can also pay a slightly higher premium to insure specific and expensive personal articles or to gain protection against certain events. Adding items to a policy is done with what is called a *floater*.

◆ **homeowners' insurance** Insurance policy that compensates the insured for several types of property damage and personal liability.

Have a student read aloud to the class the Legal Focus Example dealing with floaters, found here. Remind students that they can use the Legal Focus features as review tools when studying for tests.

Divide the class into small groups. Tell each group to imagine that they rent an apartment. Over the past five years, they have gradually purchased furniture that cost them a total of approximately $5,700. They have renter's insurance, for which they pay $189 a year. This renter's insurance policy insures the contents of their apartment for its market value.

Their insurance agent has tried to convince them that they should pay another $18 a year to insure the contents of their apartment for its replacement value instead of its market value. Ask the groups to decide what they would do in this situation and to write several paragraphs explaining their choice. In order to complete this activity, students will need to

---

LEGAL BACKGROUND

Another type of insurance is title insurance. Title insurance policies are issued by title insurance companies to insure title to real property against defects that might otherwise render title unmarketable. The amount of the policy is usually equal to the purchase price of the property being purchased. Title insurance policies are typically issued by title insurance companies after a title search of the property has been conducted, but before closing has occurred. A title insurance policy does not affect the quality of the title being purchased but simply provides a guarantee of accuracy regarding quality of title to the land itself. A property owner could file an action against the title insurance company if some defect that was not disclosed in the title insurance policy rendered title unmarketable.

LEGAL FOCUS – EXAMPLE

Any items of personal property with a higher than usual value, such as cameras, musical instruments, works of art, and jewelry, can be added by a floater to the homeowners' policy. The insured submits a list of what is to be covered along with affidavits giving the items' current market value.

It should also be remembered that the value of coverage is as important as the scope of coverage. If an insured has an extensive policy but low liability limits, he or she will have considerable risk. For example, if you are covered for most types of liability but only in the amount of $25,000, your coverage is still quite limited.

Coinsurance Clause   Both fire and homeowners' insurance usually have a **coinsurance clause** as standard language in the insurance contract. A coinsurance clause requires that the owner insure his or her property up to a specified percentage—usually 80 percent—of its value. If the owner insures for less than the required percentage, the owner will only be paid a proportionate share of his or her loss. It is important for homeowners to keep track of the current replacement value of their homes to be sure they have purchased sufficient insurance coverage.

RENTER'S INSURANCE

A renter can buy an insurance policy to cover losses to personal property. **Renter's insurance**, whose contract is called the "residence contents broad form," covers personal possessions against most perils and includes additional living expenses and liability coverage.

AUTOMOBILE INSURANCE

There are several types of automobile insurance. Automobile insurance includes liability, physical damage, medical payments, and uninsured motorist insurance. The typical family automobile insurance policy covers the policyholder or holders and residents of the same household. This includes children even when they are temporarily away from home, such as when they are attending a distant school. The policy covers other persons when they are using the vehicle with the permission of the policyholder.

When an insured person drives another person's car with permission, the driver's policy provides additional coverage if the owner's policy is insufficient to cover a claim or judgment. If persons other than the policyholder give permission to someone to use the family car, the automobile policy will not cover any loss.

Liability insurance covers losses from bodily injury (also called personal liability or PL insurance) and property damage (also called PD insurance) occurring as the result of the negligence of covered drivers. If your state requires insurance, this is the coverage required. Liability insurance

---

♦ **coinsurance clause** A standard clause in fire and homeowners' policies that requires that the homeowner insure his or her property up to a specified percentage—usually 80 percent—of its value.

♦ **renter's insurance** Insurance policy that compensates the insured renter for personal property losses and sometimes personal liability.

♦ **liability insurance** Automobile insurance that compensates the insured for losses for bodily injury (personal liability or PL insurance) and property damage (PD insurance) occurring as the result of the negligence of the insured or other covered drivers.

Enrichment Activity

understand the difference between replacement value and market value. Market value refers to the actual value of the item of personal property at the time the loss occurs, while replacement value refers to the value of a new or replacement item.

Many of your students may have first-hand experiences dealing with automobile insurance. Ask the students to share these experiences with the class. Ask them to discuss their feelings about the cost and availability of automobile insurance, whether they have had to file any claims with automobile insurance companies, etc.

compensates parties who are injured by the negligence of those insured. PL coverage pays claims against the insured for losses resulting from the injury or death of the victim or victims. PD coverage pays claims resulting from damage to the car or other property of the victim. This coverage is provided in most states with a single liability limit, such as $50,000. Some policies are written with "split limits," such as $20,000/$40,000/$10,000. In an accident, if the policyholder is liable, the company will pay up to $20,000 for injury or death to one person, or $40,000 to all persons injured, and $10,000 for any property damage. Higher liability limits can be purchased from the insurance companies. Many insurance companies offer liability coverage up to $500,000 or even higher.

Physical damage coverage is available to pay for damages to your own automobile. Two types of this coverage are available: collision and comprehensive. **Collision insurance** pays for damage to the insured's motor vehicle caused by a collision, no matter who is at fault. If the other party was at fault, your insurance company may pay the claim and then seek reimbursement from the wrongdoer by right of **subrogation**. The right of subrogation means that when an insurance company pay its policyholder's claim, it then has a right to pursue any claims the policyholder would have against the wrongdoer.

Comprehensive insurance, also called other-than-collision loss, protects against any losses to the insured's vehicle other than those caused by collision. Comprehensive applies if the vehicle is stolen, vandalized, or otherwise damaged (as by fire, earthquake, flood, or sandstorm). Most policies do not pay for losses caused by theft of personal belongings (such

Physical damage coverage is available to pay for damages to your own automobile.

- ◆ **physical damage coverage**
Automobile insurance that compensates the insured for damages to your own automobile.

- ◆ **collision insurance**
Automobile insurance that compensates the insured for damage to the insured's car in any type of collision, no matter who is at fault.

- ◆ **subrogation**
The right to succeed or substitute with reference to the claims against another. In insurance law, if the insurance company pays the claimant, it has the right to seek reimbursement from the wrongdoer (other than the insured).

- ◆ **comprehensive insurance**
Automobile insurance that compensates the insured for losses to his or her vehicle for reasons other than collision. Examples include vandalism, rock damage on highways, or theft of the vehicle.

Reteaching Activity

Have the students work with partners to create examples of insurance companies making use of their right of subrogation. Allow volunteers to share their completed examples with the class.

Many automobile owners drive without auto insurance because they have either allowed their original policies to lapse or neglected to acquire it altogether. Ask students to suggest ways in which automobile insurance laws might be changed so as to ensure that all car owners carry up-to-date insurance. If your state already has a law designed to achieve this goal, ask the students whether they feel this law is effective. What changes, if any, need to be made to this law?

Legal Focus Problem

Have a student volunteer read this Legal Focus Problem aloud to the class. Ask volunteers to suggest possible answers to the question posed at the end of this problem. Have the volunteer who read aloud the Legal Focus Problem list on the board each type of insurance that will protect Perez in this situation.

---

as clothing, cameras, or luggage) left in the vehicle or for the theft of radio or stereo equipment. To protect against these types of potential losses, the policyholder needs to purchase additional coverage.

Often, it is not advisable to purchase full collision or comprehensive coverage. If the cost of the insurance is high compared to the risk, then the purchaser should decide against full coverage. A common way in which people reduce the costs of comprehensive and collision insurance is by having a **deductible** on the policy. A deductible is a provision in the insurance contract through which the policyholder agrees to pay a certain amount of any loss—for example, the first $250 of a claim. Because processing claims is expensive for the insurance companies and small claims are frequent, the cost of collision and comprehensive is substantially reduced when a policyholder avoids making small claims by taking a deductible.

Uninsured motorist coverage insures the driver and passengers from injury caused by a driver without insurance or by a hit-and-run driver. Certain states require this coverage on all insurance policies.

> ### ◆ LEGAL FOCUS – PROBLEM
>
> Pedro Perez was at the wheel of his car, patiently waiting for the traffic light to turn green. Suddenly he heard and felt a horrendous crash from the rear. He was wearing a shoulder harness, but his head and chest were snapped in a violent whiplash. Although conscious, he was dazed and could not identify the hit-and-run driver. The car that rear-ended his car made a U-turn and sped off. What type of automobile insurance will protect Perez in this situation?

Perez can recover his medical expenses from his own insurance company if he has uninsured motorist insurance. In about half the states, uninsured motorist insurance will also cover his property damages. Collision insurance clearly would protect Perez from the property damage caused by the hit-and-run driver.

Medical payment coverage pays hospital and other medical bills and sometimes funeral expenses. This type of insurance protects all the persons in the policyholder's car when covered parties are driving. Payments are made without reference to fault. If the named insured or family members are injured by a motor vehicle while they are pedestrians or if they are injured while occupying another motor vehicle, they will still be protected by this coverage.

Other Types of Automobile Insurance

1. **Accidental death benefits** provide a payment to named beneficiaries if the policyholder dies in an automobile accident. This coverage usually is inexpensive but may not be necessary if the insured has a sufficient amount of life insurance.

Margin glossary:

◆ **deductible** A provision in the insurance contract through which the policyholder agrees to pay a certain amount of any loss—for example, the first $250 of a claim.

◆ **uninsured motorist coverage** Automobile insurance that compensates the insured for harm to the driver and passengers caused by a driver without insurance or by a hit-and-run driver.

◆ **medical payment coverage** Automobile insurance that pays hospital and other medical bills and sometimes funeral expenses of occupants of the insured's car.

◆ **accidental death benefits** Insurance that provides a payment to named beneficiaries if the policyholder dies in an automobile accident.

Guide the students in discussing no-fault insurance. Explain to the students that people who support this type of insurance believe it has two important advantages. It speeds up payments to injured people because there is no need to determine fault in a court of law. No-fault insurance is also expected to reduce legal costs and, therefore, premiums. In states that have no-fault insurance, a larger part of

each premium dollar goes to benefits. However, there is not much evidence that premiums have gone down. Premiums continue to remain high because many more people receive compensation now, even though the amount of each settlement tends to be smaller.

Opponents claim that the biggest problem with no-fault insurance is that it limits the

rights of people to sue for pain and suffering. In most cases, there is a limit on when people may sue and for how much. This may prevent people from receiving just compensation for their injuries.

2. **Other-driver coverage** protects the vehicle owner who has taken out the insurance and anyone who drives the vehicle with the owner's permission. It may also protect third parties driving the vehicle with the permission of the person to whom the owner gave permission.

3. **No-fault insurance** is a type of insurance requiring each driver to look to his or her own insurance carrier for reimbursement of losses after an accident. Under no-fault insurance, every driver is required to buy insurance. After an accident, each company pays the damages for physical injuries suffered by its insured up to some prescribed limit, regardless of fault. The label *no fault* means that covered parties will be paid even if they caused the accident. There are different versions of no-fault insurance, but in its purest form, neither party may sue the other nor may the insurance companies sue by right of subrogation after making a payment.

No-fault insurance replaces the typical method of establishing responsibility for wrongs related to automobile accidents. It replaces the tort fault system; thus, it is a system itself.

All the states that have adopted no-fault systems have implemented modified versions of the pure concept. For example, a modified plan may establish a *threshold for suit*. That threshold might be met when accidental death, permanent injury, or disfigurement results or when medical expenses exceed a specified minimum (such as $2,500 or $5,000 or ninety days of disability). When the threshold is met, the general prohibition against suits is waived. If it is then proved that the other party's negligence caused the accident, a larger sum may be recovered, including all special damages (for medical expenses, loss of wages, or destruction of property) and payment of general damages for pain, suffering, and disfigurement.

◆ **other-driver coverage** Insurance protection if the automobile is driven by someone who has the owner's permission.

◆ **no-fault insurance** A system of automobile insurance that provides benefits to the insured, regardless of who is at fault in an accident.

BUSINESS LIABILITY INSURANCE

A business is vulnerable to all sorts of risks. Comprehensive **business liability insurance** can cover virtually any risk. A business may insure against the ordinary expected risks of business or against unusual risks.

◆ **business liability insurance** Various types of insurance to cover risks in business. Types include comprehensive general liability insurance, key-employee insurance, product liability insurance, and professional malpractice insurance.

◆ **LEGAL FOCUS – EXAMPLE**

A business may wish to purchase insurance to cover liability from injuries occurring at company social functions. Ordinary business liability insurance will not usually cover such activities as a company picnic or employee Fourth of July party.

Because a key employee may die or become disabled and create severe loss for a business, a company can purchase key-employee insurance.

Critical Thinking Activity

Ask students why they think a company that loans money to an individual to purchase a car requires the individual to have collision and comprehensive insurance on the car.

Legal Focus Example

Have a student volunteer read this Legal Focus Example aloud to the class. Ask the student what types of injuries might occur at a company picnic or employee Fourth of July party.

1. A whole-life insurance policy provides both life insurance protection and a savings account. Premiums are paid by the policy holder during his or her entire lifetime or to a specified age. Term insurance policies, on the other hand, provide only life insurance, with premiums paid for a specified term—the term of coverage.

2. Health insurance policies include accident, disability, and medical expense.

3. A floater is an addition to an insurance policy that provides coverage for specific and expensive personal articles or events above the normal coverage in a standard policy.

4. The tenant's personal property is covered with a renter's insurance policy. Such policies sometimes also provide personal liability insurance.

5. States requiring drivers to have automobile insurance require liability insurance to protect parties that the driver may injure.

6. Malpractice insurance covers liability of professional people for serious mistakes they may make in the course of their business, thus creating a liability to their customers or clients.

Read this Legal Focus Example aloud to the class. Explain to students that partnerships are not the only type of business that employ key-employee (or key-person) insurance. For example, many corporations may take out key-employee insurance for their chief executive officer and other important company officials.

---

750   Personal Law

◀ LEGAL FOCUS – EXAMPLE

A partnership can suffer real economic problems if a partner dies. Often the remaining partners lack sufficient cash to pay off the deceased partner's estate. If they cannot pay off the partner's interest, the business must be liquidated. To avoid this, the business can purchase key-employee life insurance. If a partner dies, the life insurance payment is used to pay the deceased partner's heirs.

A customer may be injured when using a manufacturer's product. Product liability insurance can match the specific risks of a product. The coverage may also even include the expense of recalling and replacing a product that is defective.

A professional may overlook an important detail or make a serious mistake, causing liability for malpractice. Attorneys, physicians, architects, and engineers, for example, have increasingly become the targets of negligence suits. Professionals may purchase malpractice insurance to protect themselves against such claims. Large judgments in some highly publicized cases have led to what has been termed "the insurance crisis." The crisis consists of insurance companies becoming unwilling to insure certain risks or raising premiums to such a high level that they are not affordable. Malpractice insurance premiums have increased substantially in recent years.

◆ CHECKING YOUR PROGRESS

1. What is the difference between whole-life and term insurance policies?

2. What types of insurance policies fall under the broad term of health insurance?

3. What is a floater to an insurance policy?

4. What is covered in renter's insurance?

5. Most states require a driver to have automobile insurance to legally drive in the state. Of the many types of automobile coverage, which would be required in the states that require insurance?

6. What is malpractice insurance?

Teaching A Case In Point

Read

Introduce this *A Case In Point* feature by reminding students that judges know that most people do not understand the complicated language used in insurance policies. Therefore, as the student text pointed out, the courts interpret the words used in insurance contracts by their ordinary meanings, and when there is an ambiguity in the policy, the language is interpreted against the insurance company and in favor of the insured. Then have a student volunteer read this *A Case In Point* feature aloud to the class.

◆ A CASE IN POINT ◆

STANLEY v. SAFECO INSURANCE CO. OF AMERICA

Supreme Court of Washington, 1988.
109 Wash.2d 738,
747 P.2d 1091.

This case demonstrates how courts interpret technical language in insurance contracts.

FACTS Stanley was covered by an accidental death and dismemberment policy with Safeco Insurance Company of America. The policy provided for payment for the "loss of a foot if the loss was by actual severance at or above the ankle joint." Stanley was struck by an automobile while jogging, and as a result of his injury, the lower part of his body, up to the abdominal area, was permanently paralyzed. The insurance company denied coverage. They claimed that the policy only applied if Stanley's foot required amputation. The language in the caption at the top of the policy's coverage page was "Accidental Death and *Dismemberment* Insurance" (emphasis added). The lower court granted a summary judgment in favor of Safeco, and Stanley appealed. The court of appeals reversed the lower court's decision. Safeco appealed to the Supreme Court of Washington.

ISSUE Should the insurance policy be interpreted to cover Stanley's loss of the use of his foot even though it had not been amputated and no actual "dismemberment" had occurred?

DECISION Yes. The Supreme Court of Washington affirmed the decision of the court of appeals.

REASON The Washington Supreme Court stated "an insurance policy should be given a practical and reasonable rather than a literal interpretation"—an interpretation "such as would be given by the average person purchasing insurance. If the policy is ambiguous, a meaning and construction most favorable to the insured must be applied. Policy language is ambiguous when it is susceptible to two different interpretations, both of which are reasonable." The court noted that in this case "the language in the body of the policy provides what must occur (loss of foot) and how or where the loss is sustained (actual severance at or above the ankle joint)." Although the policy did not define "actual severance" or "loss of a foot," the court stated that its holding in a previous case established that a "loss" can occur as the result of a loss of use or function. The court concluded that "the language in the body of the policy is not ambiguous; it covers the plaintiff's loss." The court reasoned that Safeco's interpretation—taking from the caption the word *dismemberment* and inserting it in the coverage language—would make the language of the body of the policy ambiguous. Thus, the court held that even if the caption was taken to be a controlling part of the coverage language, the provision would be interpreted against Safeco.

Discuss

Stimulate a class discussion of this *A Case In Point* feature by asking the following questions: What type of insurance policy did Stanley have with Safeco Insurance Co. of America? How did Stanley receive his injury? What type of injury did Stanley receive? Why did Safeco deny coverage? What was the ruling of the lower court in this case? What was the issue before the Supreme Court of Washington? What decision did the Supreme Court of Washington make in this case? What reasons did the court give for its decision?

Teaching Note

This case is included in the *West's Business and Personal Law Handbook of Selected Court Cases.*

Assessment Strategies

In order to help students review what they have learned in Chapter 31, you might wish to:

1. Have a student volunteer, or volunteers, read aloud the Chapter Summary.

2. All the students to work with partners to complete the *Using Legal Language* activity.

3. Assign the *Checking for Comprehension* exercise as homework.

4. Allow the students to work in small groups to complete the *Applying Legal Concepts* activities.

5. As a class, complete the *Applying the Law* activities. (Please note that you may have to help students with vocabulary so that they adequately understand all of the *Applying the Law* material.)

In order to check student mastery of chapter concepts, you may wish to use the Chapter 31 test that is found in your *Teacher's Resource Binder* or use WESTEST computerized testing for Chapter 31.

---

752   Personal Law

CHAPTER REVIEW

◆ SUMMARY

INSURANCE

Risk Pooling

Insurance is based on the principle of pooling risks—spreading the risk among many people.

The Insurance Contract

1. *Laws*—The general principles of contract law are applied.

2. *Timing of coverage*—An insurance policy can begin when a *binder* is written, when the policy is issued, or after a certain time has elapsed.

3. *Provisions and clauses*—Words are given their ordinary meanings, and any ambiguity in the policy will be interpreted against the insurance company.

4. *Defenses against payment to the insured*—Include misrepresentation, fraud, or violation of the contract by the applicant.

Types of Insurance

1. *Life insurance*—insurance to protect against financial loss to the beneficiaries because of the death of the insured.

   a. *Whole life*—life insurance with a cash surrender value.

   b. *Term*—Pure insurance with no savings element. Covers a specific term.

2. *Health insurance*

   a. *Accident*—provides a sum of money for certain injuries received through accidental means.

   b. *Disability*—provides payments to a policyholder who is unable to work because of an injury or illness.

   c. *Health*—provides for medical expenses when a person is ill.

3. *Fire and homeowners' insurance*

   a. *Standard fire*—Protects the homeowner against damage from fire and lightning.

   b. *Homeowners'*—Protects against property damage and personal liability.

   c. *Renter's*—Covers a renter's personal property and sometimes personal liability.

4. *Automobile insurance*

   a. *Liability*—Protects against bodily injury and property damage occurring as the result of the negligence of the insured or other covered drivers.

   b. *Collision*—Protects against damage to the insured's car in any collision.

   c. *Comprehensive*—Protects against damage and destruction by fire, hurricane, hail, vandalism, and theft.

   d. *Uninsured motorist*—Protects against injury to the driver and passengers caused by a driver without insurance or by a hit-and-run driver.

   e. *Medical payment*—Pays hospital and other medical bills of occupants of the insured car.

   f. *Accidental death*—Pays a lump sum to named beneficiaries if the policyholder dies in an automobile accident.

   g. *Other-driver*—Provides protection if automobile is driven by anyone with the owner's permission.

   h. *No-fault*—A system in which all insurance payments for an accident are paid by the insured's insurance company no matter who is at fault.

5. *Business liability*—Covers risks in business. Includes general liability insurance, key-employee insurance, product liability insurance, and professional malpractice insurance.

◆ USING LEGAL LANGUAGE

Directions: Match each term with the statement that best defines that term.

1. coinsurance clause
2. incontestability clause
3. insurable interest
4. insurance
5. insurance broker
6. policy
7. premium
8. risk management
9. subrogation
10. term insurance

A. An insurance contract may contain an _____ which provides that after a policy has existed for a specified time, the insurer cannot challenge statements made in the application.

B. The insured pays a _____ which is the consideration paid to the insurer for an insurance policy.

C. Individuals practice _____ when they plan and manage risks and transfer some risks to an insurance company.

D. An independent contractor called a _____ represents the buyer of insurance in the purchase of insurance policies.

E. Life insurance with no savings element is _____; it covers a specific time, then the policy expires unless renewed.

F. _____ is an arrangement for transferring and allocating risk.

G. The insured receives a _____ when he or she enters an insurance contract.

H. In insurance law if the insurance company pays the claimant, they have a _____ right against the wrongdoer.

I. A standard clause, called a _____, requires a homeowner insure his or her property up to a specified percentage, usually 80 percent.

J. An _____ exists whenever an individual or entity benefits from the preservation of the health or life of the insured, or the property to be insured.

◆ CHECKING FOR COMPREHENSION

1. Describe the role of each party to an insurance contract.

2. How do the roles of an insurance agent and an insurance broker differ?

3. Describe clauses that may be included in an insurance policy and tell who would benefit from their inclusion.

4. How can an insured safeguard insurance policies? Why should policies such as fire insurance policies be kept in a safe deposit

1. The parties to an insurance contract are the insurer and the insured. The insurer is an insurance company that agrees to pay the insured or the beneficiary in the event the insured sustains a loss. The insured is the person who is covered by the policy.
2. An insurance agent is an agent of the insurance company, but an insurance broker is the applicant's agent. The difference between a broker and an agent is important in determining the effective date of an insurance policy.
3. (1) An incontestability clause provides that after a policy has existed for a specified time, the insurer cannot contest statements made, on the application. The insured would benefit from an incontestability clause. (2) An appraisal clause provides an estimate of value of the property made, by a third party. Both the insured and the insurer could benefit because disputes over the value would be avoided. (3) An antilapse clause provides that the policy does not automatically lapse if no payment is made on the due date. The insured benefits by having a grace period before the policy is canceled. (4) An arbitration clause provides for an outside party to settle disputes. Both parties to the insurance contract could benefit from a decision by an independent party. (5) A cancellation clause protects the insured against having a

policy canceled without notice or canceled as retaliation for prior activities.

4. Insurance policies can be safeguarded by being kept in secure fireproof files. A good place to store policies, such as those for fire insurance, is in a safe deposit box at a bank because they can be retrieved even if everything in the home is destroyed by the fire.

5. A coinsurance clause requires that the owner insure his or her property up to a specified percentage of its value.

6. Automobile insurance includes liability, physical damage, medical payments, and uninsured motorist insurance. The policy covers the insured and others to whom the policy holder has given permission to drive the car. It also covers the insured when he or she drives another person's car with permission.

Applying Legal Concepts (Activity)

In applying the above rules, Lorenzo will recover $120,000. Both Acme and Zocon must share in the $120,000 loss proportionately to the percentage of the total amount of insurance that each is responsible for. Because Acme insured up to $100,000 and Zocon $50,000, Acme is required to pay Lorenzo $80,000 ($100,000 ÷ $150,000 x $120,000 = $80,000) and Zocon $40,000 ($50,000 ÷ $150,000 x $120,000 = $40,000).

1. Yes. Federal was entitled to rescind the life insurance policy because Gurrentz had made a material misrepresentation by claiming that there had been no change in his health status between the time of the application and the time that he received the policies. Material misrepresentation allows for cancellation of the policy by the insurer with proper notice and an appropriate refund.

2. A partner or partnership has an insurable interest in the life of one of the partners. This interest continues even if the partnership is discontinued prior to the death of one of the partners. Thus Graves was entitled to the proceeds of the policy.

---

754   Personal Law

---

box at a bank?

5. What is a coinsurance clause in an insurance contract?

6. There are several types of automobile insurance. What are four areas covered in standard policies? Who is covered?

 ## APPLYING LEGAL CONCEPTS

A pro rata clause in insurance policies requires that when more than one insurer insures the property, the insurers will share the loss proportionately. Their proportionate share is determined by the percentage of the total amount of insurance each is responsible for. Lorenzo has two open fire insurance policies on his house: one with Acme Insurance Company for a maximum of $100,000 and one with Zocon Insurance Company for a maximum of $50,000. When Lorenzo's house burns down, it is valued at $120,000; he is entitled to this fair market value of his property. Figure the liability of Acme and Zocon to Lorenzo.

 ## APPLYING THE LAW . . . YOU BE THE JUDGE

1. Martin A. Gurrentz applied for life insurance from Federal Kemper Life Assurance Co. through an insurance agent named Alfrey. In September 1982, Gurrentz filled out an application but paid no premiums. Between the submission of the application and the delivery of the first two policies, Gurrentz sought medical advice from a physician relative to an ear problem. On examination, a throat lesion was noted. A biopsy was done, and Gurrentz was advised that he had a throat malignancy, for which he subsequently received radiation treatments. Upon delivery of the policies, Gurrentz signed a statement stating that there had been no changes in his health status and that he had not seen a doctor since filing the application for insurance. In April 1983, Federal learned of Gurrentz's throat problem when he filed a claim under a separate medical health policy. After an investigation, Federal notified Gurrentz in February 1984 that it was canceling the life insurance policies and refunding all premiums paid. Was Federal able to rescind Gurrentz's life insurance policies? [*Gurrentz v. Federal Kemper Life Assurance Co.*, 513 So.2d 241 (Fla.App. 4th Dist. 1987)]

2. James Norred and Clyde Graves were business partners for ten years. On May 7, 1979, Graves and Norred took out life insurance policies, with Graves being the beneficiary of Norred's policy, and Norred being the beneficiary of Graves's policy. They paid premiums with partnership funds. On February 28, 1983, Graves and Norred divided the partnership assets, but did not follow all the steps to dissolve the partnership. Graves became the sole owner of the business and continued to pay the premiums on both insurance policies, until James Norred died on December 5, 1983. Norred's wife, sued Graves claiming that she should receive the proceeds of the insurance policy. She claimed that Graves had no insurable interest in the life of James at the time of his death. The court awarded judgment to Mrs. Norred and Clyde Graves appealed. Who is entitled to the insurance claim? [*Graves v. Norred* (Ala.) 510 So.2d 816 (1987)]

Ask your students to demonstrate by a show of hands how many of them currently have their driver's license or learner's permit (if applicable). How many of them drive on a regular basis? How many of them own their own car? Stimulate a class discussion of auto-mobiles and driving by asking the following questions: How important is it to you to be able to drive? Why is driving so important? Do you consider driving a right or a privilege? Explain.

LEGAL PERSPECTIVE

LAW AND MOTOR VEHICLES

"Everything in life is somewhere else, and you get there in a car."

E. B. White, 1899–1985
Author of Charlotte's Web

Motor vehicles are the most valuable item of personal property owned by most Americans. Motor vehicles, especially automobiles, appeal to both the young and the old; however, they generate countless legal problems.

More than 180 million vehicles and 158 million drivers are licensed for the roadways in the United States. Comprehensive vehicle codes govern drivers. Administrative agencies regulate vehicle manufacturers, particularly in the areas of automobile emissions, safety, and fuel consumption.

There is no body of law called motor vehicle law. However, areas of law already discussed, such as contracts, torts, and crimes, apply to motor vehicles. The application of all these different areas of law to one type of personal property highlights the importance of motor vehicles.

 OWNING A MOTOR VEHICLE

The sale of a motor vehicle is an ordinary contract transaction. Because a motor vehicle is a good, the UCC governs its sale. The *statute of frauds* applies to any sale of a motor vehicle that exceeds $500. In order to comply with the statute, the purchaser must have a signed writing to enforce a contract.

Usually sellers of motor vehicles use standard form contracts. Buyers should realize that standard form contracts are written to protect the interests of the party who wrote

the contract. If important promises are made to a buyer, such as warranties or credit terms, the buyer should be sure that they are *included as part of the written contract.*

In motor vehicle sales transactions, there are also standard sales customs and techniques. An intelligent buyer will consult reliable references to help him or her select a vehicle and to find out how to negotiate the best deal.

 NEW AND USED-CAR WARRANTIES

The seller of a new motor vehicle transfers title to the goods with several *implied warranties.* In Chapter 15, we discussed implied warranties that occur, unless disclaimed, in most transactions. The most important of these implied warranties in the sale of a motor vehicle is the *warranty of title* and the *warranty of merchantability.* The warranty of title is a promise by the seller to the buyer that he or she has the right to transfer title to the motor vehicle. The warranty of merchantability concerns the quality of the vehicle. This warranty is a promise that the vehicle is of usual and ordinary quality and that it is fit for use. Given the value of a motor vehicle and its intended use, the implied warranty of merchantability is extensive.

All new motor vehicle manufacturers provide express warranties. These express warranties often limit the implied warranty of merchantability by a disclaimer included in the express warranty. The express warranties' scope and length of coverage are a

(continued on page 756)

Extension Activity

Have a student volunteer research recent automobile recalls. The student's research should focus on what product was recalled, the reason the product was recalled, and the cost of the recall for the manufacturer.

Extension Activity

Have a student volunteer obtain copies of all the paperwork required to register, or license, a vehicle in your state. Explain to the student that he or she should be prepared to explain how to complete these forms. Allow the student to present to the class his or her findings and an explanation of how to complete the necessary forms.

LEGAL PERSPECTIVE (CONTINUED)

very important part of any purchase of a new automobile.

Used cars purchased from dealers also carry implied warranties of merchantability because the dealers are merchants. Used cars purchased from private parties do not carry any warranty of quality unless it is made expressly. Remember that all warranties of quality can be disclaimed by the words *as is*.

Thirty states have **lemon laws** to protect consumers who are dissatisfied with extensive warranty work and would rather get a new car or their money back. A typical lemon law provides that if a car is a lemon, the dealer must refund to the customer the purchase price of the car, plus sales tax, registration, and license fees, minus a reasonable allowance for use. Lemon laws are discussed in greater detail in Chapter 15.

AUTOMOBILE RECALLS

After the sale of a motor vehicle, manufacturers have a continuing obligation to ensure vehicle safety. Under federal law, manufacturers must notify consumers and the National Highway Traffic Safety Administration (NHTSA) of safety defects and must describe how they propose to cure the defects.

MOTOR VEHICLE REGISTRATION

The government requires that ownership of motor vehicles be registered and that formal documents of ownership be properly completed. To be registered, the vehicle must comply with minimal safety and pollution standards governing brakes, lights, and exhaust emissions. Registration of ownership also ensures orderly transfer of title. Presentation of the signed certificate of ownership

gives the buyer confidence that he or she is receiving good title. The certificate of ownership and registration assists in, among other things, the identification of cars involved in an accident and the return of stolen cars to the owner.

LICENSING AND REGISTRATION PROCEDURES

Most states issue two certificates to the owners of motor vehicles. The first is a certificate of ownership, or title, showing who owns the vehicle. The second is a certificate of registration, permitting operation of the vehicle on the highways of the state. License plates, or annual renewal tags, are also issued to registered owners.

Most automobiles are bought on credit, and the lender retains a security interest in the vehicle. The purchaser-borrower is the registered owner (also called the equitable owner), with an ownership interest in the vehicle. The lender (or creditor) keeps a security interest in the vehicle and is the legal owner until the loan is paid.

REGISTERED OWNER LIABILITY FOR AN ACCIDENT

Some states hold a registered owner liable for damage caused by the negligence of any authorized user of the vehicle (the liability is usually limited). Because of this potential liability, it is very important to change registration when selling the vehicle. It is common to require a signed transfer of a certificate of ownership, or "pink slip." It is also necessary to notify the State Department of Motor Vehicles to change the registered owner of the vehicle.

Extension Activity

You might ask a driver's education teacher to speak to your class regarding your state's requirements for issuing a driver's license. Ask the speaker to explain to the class what paperwork is required, the age requirements, and the testing requirements. Have your students prepare questions for the speaker in advance.

◆ DRIVER'S LICENSES

Driving is a privilege, not a constitutionally protected right. As such, driving is regulated by state or local government. Prospective drivers must demonstrate an ability to drive in traffic and knowledge of the rules of the road. A license to drive may be suspended or revoked for violating traffic rules. Demerit points are assigned, and a person's license can be suspended or revoked if he or she accumulates too many points. An accident may count as one point; reckless or drunken driving, two points; causing property damage by hit-and-run, two points. A total of four points in one year may cause suspension of the license.

Auto insurance companies check government records for information about the driving record of people who apply for insurance or who have policies with the company. The insurance companies routinely charge higher premiums or cancel coverage after one or more moving violations. The individual must then purchase a minimum-coverage policy at a high price under an assigned-risk program. Most states have an assigned-risk program through which insurance companies are required to sell insurance to high-risk drivers on a rotating basis. They are allowed to charge higher premiums to cover their risk.

A minor may qualify (usually at age sixteen) to apply for a driver's license. See the Resource Center for the age requirements in your state. The usual requirements include:

1. Completing driver education and/or a driver training course.
2. Passing a written test.
3. Passing a driving test.
4. Passing a vision test.

Most states require that parents sign and verify the minor's application for a driver's license and consent to be responsible for harm caused by the minor while driving on a highway. Fortunately for most parents, this liability is usually limited. The amount of the parents' liability is often tied to the state's financial responsibility laws.

◆ NEGLIGENCE AND DRIVING AN AUTOMOBILE

The standard of care required when operating a motor vehicle is an example of the rules of negligence discussed in Chapter 5. Each driver has the duty to act as a reasonable person would on the highway and to refrain from injuring others. If someone is injured as a result of a driver's negligence, the driver is usually liable.

Any driver involved in an automobile accident who gets a traffic ticket because of the accident should be aware of the doctrine of **negligence** *per se*. Negligence *per se* means that proof of the act establishes the duty. In simpler terms, sometimes a certain behavior is so clearly negligent that if an injured party can show the defendant acted in that way, he or she can establish negligence on the other party's part. Often when an automobile accident occurs, it is because one party violated a motor vehicle law. The violation of that traffic law often is negligence *per se* if damage or an injury to another occurs. The violation of the traffic law raises a presumption or inference of negligence. The defendant is then required to prove that he or she was not negligent. Of course, the violation of the statute must bear some relationship to and be the proximate cause of the accident.

(continued on page 758)

Enrichment Activity

You might wish to point out to students that, as responsible citizens, they have a duty to obey all traffic laws in your community and those in other locations, wherever they are driving. If individuals didn't follow traffic laws, driving would be much more dangerous. Indeed, deaths on the highway remain a serious problem in this country, but there are many more deaths per passenger mile driven in countries in which the citizens do not obey traffic laws as well as we do.

LEGAL PERSPECTIVE (CONTINUED)

LIABILITY FOR THE NEGLIGENCE OF OTHER DRIVERS

An owner may be liable when someone else is the driver of the automobile under the principle of **vicarious liability** (liability for another). If the driver is an employee of the owner and if the driver is acting within the scope of his or her employment, the employer, as well as the employee, is liable for the accident. Many state statutes provide for liability when an owner permits others to use his or her vehicle.

Dramshop statutes are state laws that make it a crime for a tavern proprietor or employee to serve alcohol to an obviously drunk patron or to someone under the legal drinking age. Injured victims of accidents caused by these patrons have successfully sued the bars and restaurants when they can prove that a dramshop statute was violated. A few cases have found liability against social hosts of parties where intoxicating beverages or drugs were served and shortly afterward the guests were involved in automobile accidents.

GUEST STATUTES

A driver is also responsible to his or her vehicle passengers who are injured because of his or her negligence. Issues of comparative negligence and assumption of risk must be considered.

There are, however, nine states with **guest statutes**.[3] These statutes provide that a guest usually cannot sue a driver for ordinary negligence. The guest is a passenger as

3. Delaware, Georgia, Illinois, Indiana, Nebraska, Nevada, South Carolina, Texas, and Utah.

a result of his or her own voluntary choice and normally can get out of the vehicle at will. If the person is a paying passenger, the statute does not apply.

DRIVING UNDER THE INFLUENCE OF ALCOHOL OR OTHER DRUGS

People who drive under the influence (DUI) of mind-altering chemicals are a major social problem in the United States. Drinking of alcoholic beverages is the major cause of accidents on the highways and is an ingredient in most fatal accidents. Drunk drivers kill more than 25,000 people each year. DUIs have been identified as the crime most often committed by otherwise law-abiding persons.

Several organizations try to protect the rights of people who are victims of such criminal activity. These organizations include MADD (Mothers Against Drunk Driving). They have had a significant effect on public attitudes and laws concerning driving under the influence. In the past ten years, all states have established twenty-one as the age for legally drinking alcohol. The penalties for DUI have increased through longer sentences, license revocations, and larger fines. The percentage of drugs in the blood system necessary to classify a person as DUI has been lowered in most states.

Police officers are vigorous in enforcing DUI laws. When stopped for suspicion of intoxication, a driver must submit to a **field sobriety test**. The suspect may be asked to walk a straight line, to stand on one foot, or to perform some other similar act. If the person appears intoxicated, he or she may be taken to a police station and asked for a

Extension Activity

You might wish to invite a state trooper or local police officer to speak to your class regarding driver safety and traffic laws. Encourage the speaker to discuss the consequences of failing to take action on a traffic citation and of driving while under the influence of alcohol or drugs.

sample of breath, blood, or urine that will be analyzed for alcoholic content.

Refusal to take the test—by exercising your constitutional right against self-incrimination—may cause forfeiture of the driver's license. Every person who accepts a license to drive implies consent to sobriety tests on police suspicion, with probable cause, of the driver's intoxication. The driver has a right to a proper warning of the law's effect and an administrative hearing before the license is revoked.

Penalties for driving under the influence can be severe. In a representative state, a jail sentence of from two days to six months is imposed for persons convicted of drunk driving two or more times within five years. If the judge does not send the defendant to jail, a formal statement justifying the lack of a prison sentence must be written. A fine of from $500 to $2,000 is also charged. Under certain circumstances, the vehicle may be impounded.

In addition, the convicted offender's automobile insurance premiums will rise. A study of the effect of a single DUI on insurance costs found increases as high as $2,030 per year for three years in Baltimore, Maryland. DUIs often lead to a cancellation of insurance by the carrier, as well.

FINANCIAL RESPONSIBILITY LAWS

Most states have a **financial responsibility law**. About half the states demand certainty of financial responsibility and thus require **compulsory automobile insurance**. The other states do not absolutely require insurance. Instead, they require proof of financial responsibility from drivers after they are involved in an accident. Under financial responsibility statutes, after any accident that

causes more than a modest amount of property damage (such as $500) or in which someone is injured (no matter how slightly) or killed, each driver must report the accident within fifteen days. A driver without the minimum automobile insurance coverage must pay a cash deposit or post a bond. These procedures and requirements apply even if you are not at fault.

Failure to report a serious accident (one that involves $500 in damage, an injury, or a death) can mean suspension or revocation of the driver's license. Failure to prove financial responsibility can mean suspension until proof is presented. The minimum financial responsibility requirements vary among the states. A common required amount is $25,000 for injury to or death of any one person in any one accident, $50,000 for injury to or death of more than one person, and $10,000 for property damage. Many states have both financial responsibility requirements and compulsory insurance. All states have at least one or the other.

PROTECTING YOUR RIGHTS IF INVOLVED IN AN ACCIDENT

The following suggestions are made to help you protect your legal rights if you are in an accident while driving a car.

1. If your car is not stopped by the accident, park it in a safe place immediately ahead of the accident area and preferably off the highway. To hit and run is a serious crime and is morally wrong. Clear the other vehicle involved out of the way of oncoming traffic, if this is safe and practical. If possible, post someone to warn on-

(continued on page 760)

LEGAL PERSPECTIVE (CONTINUED)

coming vehicles, place warning flares, or do both. If you hit an unattended car or damage other property, leave your name, address, telephone number, and automobile license number on a note inside the car or under the windshield wiper.

2. Provide first aid to anyone injured if you are qualified to do so. Do not move anyone unless absolutely necessary.

3. Call or have someone else call for an ambulance, if necessary. As soon as practical, see a doctor if you have been injured. This is important because some serious injuries are not immediately obvious.

4. Call or have someone else call the highway patrol or local police when anyone is injured or killed or when there is serious property damage. Get the name or number of the officer who investigates the accident. Persons protecting your interests (such as your insurance company or your attorney) will want to begin their investigation of the accident immediately.

5. Even before the police arrive, write down (or have someone else write down) the vehicle license numbers, names, addresses, and phone numbers of all witnesses, since they might leave the scene after a few minutes. Get the same information from the driver and occupants of the other vehicle. Also ask the other driver for the name of his or her insurance company.

6. Do not admit responsibility for the accident. Any such admission of fault would be later held against you in court. Right after an accident is not the time to make dramatic conclu-

sions, especially since they may be wrong.

7. Notify your insurance company if the other party is injured or has suffered property damage.

8. As soon after the accident as possible, write down the full details of what happened immediately before, at the time of, and immediately after the accident. A map or sketch of the scene may help. Note the weather and road conditions, time, speed estimates, and skid marks. If you can, get pictures of the cars and any skid marks.

9. If the accident was serious, have your family contact an attorney as soon as possible. The attorney may have a professional photographer take pictures of the scene, including skid marks, aided by your notes of the event.

10. Notify the appropriate government agency, using its preprinted forms, to comply with the state's financial responsibility law.

11. If an insurance claims adjuster for the other driver contacts you or your family, refer them to your attorney. Be careful not to admit fault to the adjuster, who openly or with concealed equipment may be recording any conversation. Do not make any settlement until you know the extent of your damages. You cannot know this information until after you have been released by your doctor and have received legal advice. If you are an innocent victim of another driver's negligence, you may be entitled to damages sufficient to cover (a) medical and hospital expenses, present and future; (b) damage to property (car,

clothing); (c) loss of wages, actual and prospective; and (d) payment for pain, suffering, and disfigurement. When damages are high, you are well-advised to hire an attorney. Even after the attorney's fee, you will probably receive a sum larger than any direct offer from an insurance claims adjuster.

12. You will probably want to have your damaged car repaired. The insurance company may require two or more written estimates from reliable repair shops. The insurance company will pay you on the basis of the lower estimate. If it seems that a defect in your vehicle caused the accident, consult your attorney before you repair the car. The attorney may arrange to have an expert examine the suspect parts and then preserve them as evidence.

  ## TERMS TO REMEMBER

◆ **lemon laws**   State statutes designed to assist buyers of seriously defective goods in getting a replacement or full refund.

◆ **negligence** *per se* [Latin: of itself]   The proof of the act establishes the duty.

◆ **vicarious liability**   Legal responsibility of the acts of another person because of some relationship with that person; for example, the liability of an employer for an employee.

◆ **dramshop statute**   A state law that makes it a crime for a tavern proprietor or employee to serve intoxicants to an obviously drunk patron or to someone under the legal drinking age.

◆ **guest statute**   A state statute that forbids a guest passenger in an automobile from collecting damages for injuries from the driver for ordinary negligence.

◆ **field sobriety test**   A test given by a police officer to determine whether a driver of a vehicle is intoxicated. The test is given at the site where the person is detained.

◆ **financial responsibility law**   A state statute requiring that after an automobile accident, a driver prove either that he or she has insurance coverage or that he or she has the ability to pay for any harm caused by the accident.

◆ **compulsory accident insurance**   A state statute requiring that all drivers purchase automobile insurance.

LEGAL BACKGROUND

The law regarding the succession of property is a necessary part of private ownership of property. The law requires that when someone dies, title to the decedent's property must go somewhere. The decedent can direct the passage of property after death by will, subject to certain limitations imposed by the state. If no valid will has been executed, the decedent is said to have died intestate, and state law prescribes the distribution of the property among heirs or next of kin. If no heirs or kin can be found, the property goes to the state.

A person can also transfer property through a trust. The owner (settler) of the property transfers legal title to a trustee, who has a duty imposed by law to hold the property for the use and benefit of another (the beneficiary). This chapter will examine the laws of succession governing both wills and trusts, as well as the process by which estates are administered. Living wills and trusts are also introduced.

Prereading Activity

Tell students to write a list of real and personal property they will probably own ten years from today. Then ask the students to write what they would do to ensure that the property is given to the people they choose if they were to die. Read some of the papers aloud, applying appropriate terminology to the concepts the students have mentioned.

Mastery Objectives

By the end of this chapter, students will be able to:

- Discuss estate planning
- Describe types of wills
- Create a formal will
- Tell how wills are revoked
- Explain intestacy laws
- Define *trusts*
- Delineate types of trusts

Chapter

32

Wills and Trusts

Chapter 32
Resources and Assignment Guide

Tests
Chapter 32 Test *TRB*
Chapter 32 WESTEST Computerized Testing

Activity Sheets
Reviewing Legal Concepts 32 *TRB*
Enrichment Activity 32 *TRB*

Student Activity Workbook
Chapter 32 Activities

Handbook of Selected Court Cases
The Matter of Estate of Prigge
Payne v. *Payne*

**West's Business Law and Legal
Environment Videodisc**
Still Frames and Motion Segments as shown

Wills and Trusts   763

Discussion Starter

Stimulate a class discussion by asking your students why they should have a will. Ask them what would happen to their property if they didn't have a will.

Enrichment

Remind the students that there is an old saying," You can't take it with you." How does this relate to the subject of wills? Ask the students if they can think of other sayings or clichés that relate to wills and trusts.

Critical Thinking Activity

Have a student volunteer read aloud the four major objectives of estate planning listed here. Ask the volunteer which of these objectives is the most important to the person who is doing the estate planning. Why is this objective the most important? (Student answers should reflect an understanding of the idea that the first of the four major objectives provides for the needs of the planner while alive, which should be most important to the planner.)

"Nothing in life became him like leaving it."
William Shakespeare, 1564–1616
English dramatist and poet

How does property transfer to someone else when the property owner dies? The laws allowing property to transfer to another after a person's death are a necessary part of private ownership of property. United States law requires that title to the property of a decedent (one who has recently died) must go to someone. This chapter discusses how this transfer can be accomplished by will, through trusts, or through state laws establishing the method of property distribution to family.

A will implies a death, which is not the most pleasant topic. Because wills are related to death, the topic is more important to older people than to high school students. But if the truth be told, wills are fascinating. A person's ability to control how his or her property is distributed after that person's death is interesting. To whom do we give the property that is so important to us? This chapter discusses the relationship of wills and trusts to estate planning.

◆ ESTATE PLANNING

Estate planning is an analysis of what a person owns, expects to own, and what he or she owes—in other words, of that person's assets and liabilities—and it is a strategy for the use of these assets during that person's life and for their distribution at his or her death. Estate planning involves investment strategies, saving for the purchase of major assets, borrowing, and retirement planning. Estate plans usually include the following four major objectives:

1. To provide for the needs of the planner while alive. If married, the day-to-day needs of the spouse and other dependents are an important concern.
2. To reflect the desires of the planner in providing generously for those he or she wishes to give property to and to exclude those believed to be unworthy.
3. To minimize or avoid legitimately, income taxes payable both during life and also after the planner's death. Estate planning can also help to minimize estate and inheritance taxes (*death taxes*) that are placed on survivors after the planner's death.
4. To minimize or avoid the delays, costs, and publicity of probate (the process of proving the validity of a will in court, coupled with administering the decedent's estate).

DEATH TAXES

The federal government imposes an **estate tax** on the assets of a person at death. The estate tax is a tax on the privilege of giving your property to

◆ **estate planning**
An analysis of what a person owns, expects to own, and what he or she owes—in other words, a person's assets and liabilities; it is a strategy for the use of these assets during that person's life and for their distribution at his or her death.

◆ **estate tax**   A tax imposed by the federal government and some states on the property given to another after the death of the giver (donor).

Ethical Concern

Guide your students in a discussion of the ethics of death taxes by asking the following questions: Do you feel that death taxes are fair? Does it matter that the deceased already paid income taxes, etc. on the property that he or she has bequeathed? Do you feel that it is fair to place a tax on "the privilege of receiving property from the estate of a decedent"? Who pays the costs associated with death taxes? Who benefits from these taxes?

---

764   Personal Law

◆ inheritance tax
A tax imposed by some states on those who receive property from a person after he or she has died.

◆ death taxes
Estate and inheritance taxes. Taxes that arise because of one's death.

others when you die. Some state governments, in addition to the federal government, impose taxes on property transferred at death. States are, however, more likely to impose an **inheritance tax** than an estate tax. An inheritance tax is a tax on the privilege of receiving property from the estate of a decedent (person who died). The inheritance tax is paid by the individual who inherits the property. Inheritance and estate taxes together are called **death taxes**.

Inheritance tax rates vary widely from state to state, and they change often. Many states, including California and Washington, have no death taxes. The interested reader may wish to get a tax schedule from his or her state.

Federal estate taxes provide for a *unified estate and gift tax*. This tax system requires the taxpayer to keep track of larger gifts and combine the value of these lifetime gifts with the value of property transferred at death. Taxes are based on the total value of these gifts, after the deduction of a *unified credit* (exemption). The unified credit allows transfers totaling $600,000 in property value before the individual's estate is taxed. Once $600,000 is transferred by gift or will, the estate tax is imposed.

Most gifts are totally free of tax. An individual is allowed to make annual tax-free gifts of up to $10,000 to each of any number of *donees* (recipients of gifts). A husband and wife may give together $20,000 each year. If a gift amount exceeds $10,000, then a tax return should be filed, and the amount of the gift becomes part of the unified credit. If the gift is $10,000 or under, no tax return need be filed, and the gift amount has no tax consequences whatsoever.

Most modest estates are distributed free of federal tax. Large estates are heavily taxed, unless appropriate estate planning reduces this burden. The tax begins at 37 percent of the gift and increases to a maximum of 55 percent. The most effective ways to avoid taxes (both income and estate) legally are through exempt gifts, trusts, and wills. Wills and trusts are used to direct property where and how you want.

◆ will Legal expression of a person's wishes for the distribution of his or her property after death.

◆ testate When a person dies having left a will.

◆ WILLS

A **will** is the legal expression of a person's wishes for the distribution of his or her property after death. If a person dies with a will, he or she dies **testate**. If he or she dies without a will, that person dies **intestate**. If a person dies intestate without heirs, his or her property (after creditors of the deceased are paid) goes to the state. The term **decedent** is a more pleasant and less personal way of describing a person who is dead.

◆ intestate When a person dies without having left a will.

◆ decedent A deceased person.

The will is a conditional document. Although valid when properly created, it has no present or immediate legal effect. It becomes operative after a person dies if it has not been revoked before the testator's death. A **testator** is a person who makes a will. The will "speaks on the author's death"; if the testator destroys it or writes a later will, the earlier will loses legal authority. This conditional feature makes a will a unique document,

◆ testator A person who makes a will. A person who dies having left a will.

Divide the class into small groups. Have each group read and discuss the material under the heading Vocabulary of Wills. Have the students in each group work together to write a fictional account of a will in which the terms from this section are used correctly. Each group should choose a leader to read aloud its fictional account.

Have student volunteers research the many claims that were made on the estate of Howard Hughes upon his death. Student research might focus on the claim made by Melvin Dumars that he was in possession of a valid will written by Howard Hughes. Have the students report their findings to the class in the form of an oral report.

Legal Focus Example

Have a student volunteer read aloud this Legal Focus Example. Then ask the students to suggest other examples of specific bequests, general bequests, specific devices, and residuary gifts that could also fit here.

adding importance to proving its validity (a process called *authentication*) at the death of the testator.

The right to make a will and how to make one are determined by state law. To be valid, wills normally must follow state statutory requirements strictly. A will can serve other purposes besides the distribution of property. It can appoint a guardian for minor children or incapacitated adults, and it can appoint a personal representative to settle the affairs of the deceased.

VOCABULARY OF WILLS

Every area of law has its own special vocabulary, and the area of wills is no exception. The court responsible for administering any legal problems surrounding a will is a *probate court*. A gift of real estate by will is a **devise**, and a gift of personal property by will is a **bequest**, or **legacy**. When someone dies, a *personal representative* settles their affairs. An **executor** is a personal representative named in a will. An **administrator** is the personal representative appointed by the court for someone who dies without a will. An administrator may also be appointed if a person fails to name an executor in a will, names an executor who lacks the capacity to serve, or writes a will that the court refuses to admit to probate.

TYPES OF GIFTS BY WILL

Gifts by will can be specific, general, or residuary. A *specific* devise or bequest (legacy) describes particular property—for example, an inscribed gold watch or a specific collection of rare books. A *general* devise or bequest (legacy) usually specifies a sum of money but does not single out any particular item of property. Sometimes a will provides that any assets remaining after specific gifts are made and debts are paid are to be distributed through a **residuary** clause. A residuary clause disposes of all property not otherwise specifically given away. Such a clause is useful because the testator can never be exactly sure what property and debts will be left when he or she dies.

◆ **devise** A gift of real estate by will.

◆ **bequest or legacy** A gift of personal property by will.

◆ **executor** A personal representative named in a will. The person in charge of the deceased person's affairs after that person's death.

◆ **administrator** A personal representative who is appointed by the court for someone who dies without a will.

◆ **residuary clause** A clause in a will that disposes of all property not otherwise specifically given away.

◆ LEGAL FOCUS – EXAMPLE

Sample gift clauses in a will include:

1. A specific bequest: I give my grandfather's gold ring with the initials GSH to my son, Scott Bradshaw, of Mountain Oaks, Colorado.
2. A general bequest: I give the sum of ten thousand dollars ($10,000) from my account number ZX7865 in First Eastern Bank of Tahoe to the American Cancer Society.
3. A specific devise: I give my real property situated in Butte County, California, and commonly known as 1278 University Lane to my sister, Carolyn A. Hamilton.
4. A residuary gift: I give the residue of my estate both real and personal property to my wife, Patricia A. Jenkins.

LEGAL BACKGROUND

To probate ("prove") a will means to establish its validity and to carry the administration of the estate through a special court, which, as mentioned here, is called a probate court. Probate laws vary from state to state.

In 1969, the American Bar Association and the National Conference of Commissioners on Uniform State Laws approved the Uniform Probate Code (UPC). The UPC codifies general principles and procedures for the resolution of conflicts in settling estates and relaxes some of the requirements for a valid will contained in earlier state laws. Fifteen states have adopted some form of the UPC.

Legal Focus Example

Have a student volunteer read aloud this Legal Focus Example. Ask the volunteer why probate is essential in each of the cases listed here.

Reteaching Activity

Read aloud the following sentence from the student text: "Testamentary capacity means the testator must be of legal age and sound mind at the time the will is made." Ask a student volunteer to define the word *testator* as used in this sentence. (*Testator*, as defined on page 764, is "A person who makes a will. A person who dies having left a will.")

◆ **probate** The court process of proving the validity of a will and following the wishes of the testator. Includes distributing the property to appropriate beneficiaries.

◆ **family settlement agreements** Private agreements among beneficiaries to a will.

PROBATE VERSUS NONPROBATE

Probate is a court proceeding in which wills are proved to be either valid or invalid and estates of decedents are properly distributed. Probate serves several useful purposes. It provides an opportunity for creditors of the decedent to submit claims for payment. Probate also provides for death taxes to be paid. If the court finds a valid will, the net assets (after all debts are paid) and liabilities of the decedent are paid and distributed to the named beneficiaries. If there is no will, the probate court will accomplish similar tasks by complying with the state's law of succession (discussed later in this chapter). Probate laws vary from state to state. A Uniform Probate Code has been adopted by fifteen states.

Because the process of probate is time consuming and costly, many states have laws that allow for the distribution of assets without probate proceedings. Less formal methods of transferring title are used for estates with small property values. In some states, for example, the title to cars, savings and checking accounts, and certain other property can be passed merely by filling out forms. Summary proceedings are often available when there is only one heir, such as a spouse.

A majority of states provide for **family settlement agreements**. These are private agreements among the beneficiaries. Once a will is admitted to probate, the family members can agree to settle among themselves the distribution of the decedent's assets. A family settlement agreement speeds the settlement process. However, a court order is still needed to protect the estate from future creditors and to clear the title to estate assets.

The use of summary procedures in estate administration can save time and money. The expenses of a personal representative's commission, attorneys' fees, and appraisers' fees can be eliminated or at least minimized. But in some situations, probate cannot be avoided.

 LEGAL FOCUS ~ EXAMPLE

Probate is essential where a guardian for minor children or for an incompetent person must be appointed and a trust has been created to protect the minor or the incompetent person.

In the ordinary situation, a person can employ a substitute for a will to avoid the cost of probate. Among the substitutes are *inter vivos* trusts (discussed later), life insurance policies, or joint-tenancy arrangements. Not all of these methods are suitable for every estate, but they do exist as alternatives to probate administration.

TESTAMENTARY CAPACITY

Testamentary capacity means the testator must be of legal age and sound mind *at the time the will is made.* The legal age for executing a will varies, but in most states, the minimum age is eighteen. Thus, a will of a twenty-

Have a student volunteer or group of volunteers research the will of oil magnate J. Paul Getty, who died in 1976. Students' research should focus on the bequest in his will of more than $1 billion to the J. Paul Getty Museum in Malibu, California. What effect has this bequest had on the museum? What led to this bequest? Have the students share their findings with the class in the form of an oral report. Encourage the students to incorporate visual aids into their report.

one-year-old decedent that was written when she was sixteen is invalid.

The concept of "being of sound mind" refers to the testator's ability to formulate and to understand his or her plan to distribute property and the person's intent that the will put into effect the distribution plan.

FORMAL REQUIREMENTS OF WILLS

A will must comply with statutory formalities designed to show that the testator understood his or her actions at the time the will was made. These formalities are intended to help prevent fraud. If they are not followed, the will is void. The decedent's property is then distributed according to state laws of intestacy. Most states require the following to create a valid or **formal will**:

1. *The will must be in writing.* A written document is generally required. The writing itself can be informal as long as it complies with the statutory requirements. In some states, a will can be handwritten in crayon or ink. It can be written on a sheet or scrap of paper, on a paper bag, or on a piece of cloth. A will can also refer to a memorandum that, although not a will, contains information necessary to carry out the will.

> ◆ **formal will** A written will, signed by the testator, properly witnessed, and, where required, published; one that meets formal statutory requirements for a valid will.

◇ LEGAL FOCUS – EXAMPLE

Fran's will directed that a sum of money be divided among a group of charities named in a memorandum that Fran gave to Meehum on the

When oil magnate J. Paul Getty died in 1976, he left a bequest in his will of more than $1 billion to the J. Paul Getty Museum in Malibu, California. The bequest made the institution the richest art museum in the world.

Collaborative Learning Activity

Divide the class into small groups. Have each group read and discuss the requirements of a valid or formal will, which are listed here and on the previous page. Then have the students of each group work together to create a teaching poster that includes all the items in this list. Encourage students to incorporate visuals into their poster. Visuals may be clipped or copied from newspapers or magazines or may consist of original artwork. Allow each group to display its poster in your classroom.

Discussion Starter

Stimulate a brief discussion by asking students what qualifications a witness to a will must possess. How many witnesses must be present? Why do such strict qualifications for the witnessing of a will exist?

Vocabulary Activity

Ask a student volunteer to look up the word *holographic* in the dictionary. Have him or her compare the dictionary definition with the way *holographic* is used in the phrase "holographic will," defined here.

Enrichment

Bring a sample will to class. Have students look through the will to see if all the requirements of a formal will are present.

---

same day that the will was signed. The list of charities is "incorporated by reference" into the will only if it existed when the will was signed and is sufficiently described in the will.

Some states allow for an oral will called a *nuncupative will*. These states limit the property that can be disposed of in this manner to personal property of no more than a small sum (usually $1,000). Because of the limitations and special requirements, nuncupative wills are not common or very important.

2. *A will must be signed by the testator.* It is a fundamental requirement in almost all jurisdictions that the testator's signature appear, generally at the end of the will. Each jurisdiction dictates what is a sufficient signature. Initials, an "X" or other mark, and words like "Mom" have all been held valid when shown that the testator intended them to be a signature.

3. *A formal will must be witnessed.* A will must be witnessed by two and sometimes three witnesses. The number of witnesses, their qualifications, and how a will should be witnessed are set out in state statutes. Most states require a witness to be disinterested—that is, not a beneficiary under the will. There are no age requirements for witnesses, but they must be mentally competent.

The purpose of witnesses is to verify that the testator actually executed (signed) the will and had the required intent and capacity at that time. A witness does not have to read the contents of the will. Usually, the testator and witnesses must all sign in the sight or the presence of one another.

4. *Sometimes a will must be published.* A will is *published* by an oral declaration by the maker to the witnesses that the document they are about to sign is his or her "last will and testament." Publication is an unnecessary formality in most states.

In general, strict compliance with the preceding formalities is required before a formal document is accepted as the decedent's will.

HOLOGRAPHIC WILL

• **holographic will**
A self-prepared will written, signed, and dated entirely in the handwriting of the testator.

An exception to the formal witnessed will exists in some states. A **holographic will** is a type of self-prepared will. It is a will that is written, signed, and dated with a complete date, all entirely in the handwriting of the testator. Fewer than half the states recognize this type of will. In most states that allow a holographic will, certain requirements must be precisely followed. A major objection to the holographic will is the absence of witnesses. Without witnesses, there is little protection against forgery or undue influence. Many an attempted holographic will has been held invalid because it was partially typed (and thus was not entirely in the handwriting of the testator) or was not dated.

<table>
<tr><td>

Enrichment

You might point out to students that although the estate of actress Marilyn Monroe amounted to more than $500,000, the persons to whom she had left bequests in her will did not receive them. Federal and estate taxes, debts owed to creditors, and federal income tax on her estate, which consisted largely of deferred and future earnings, consumed virtually the entire estate.

</td><td>

Legal Focus Example

Have a student volunteer read aloud this Legal Focus Example. Ask the volunteer why he or she thinks the court might infer undue influence in cases where the testator ignores his or her blood relatives and names a non-relative as beneficiary.

</td><td>

Discussion Starter

Stimulate a class discussion on the practice of videotaping will signings by asking the following questions: How does the videotaping of will signings help to ensure that a will will be considered valid? How might beneficiaries react to viewing a videotaped will signing? How do you think you might react if you viewed a videotaped will signing?

</td></tr>
</table>

UNDUE INFLUENCE

A valid will represents the maker's intention to transfer and distribute his or her property. If it can be shown that the will was the result of improper pressure brought by another person, the will is void.

◆ LEGAL FOCUS - EXAMPLE

Undue influence may be inferred by the court if the testator ignores his or her blood relatives and instead names a nonrelative as a beneficiary. The likelihood of undue influence is greater if the beneficiary is a person who was in constant close contact with the deceased and able to influence the making of the will. The situation where a nurse or friend caring for the deceased near the time of death benefits from the will to the exclusion of family members will raise questions of undue influence.

Today many will signings are videotaped to provide proof that the ritual was correctly followed. The tape also provides evidence as to the demeanor (behavior) of the testator. These videotapes have been used effectively to defend challenges to the validity of a will (also called will contests).

REVOCATION OF WILLS

An executed will can be revoked by the maker at any time during the maker's lifetime. Revocation can be partial or complete, and it should follow certain strict formalities. A will can be revoked by a physical act. The physical acts by which a testator may revoke a will include intentionally burning, tearing, canceling, obliterating, or destroying it. Having someone else destroy the will at the maker's direction and in the maker's presence also revokes the will. The testator's intention to destroy the will is essential.

A will may also be revoked by another writing, a **codicil**. A codicil is a written instrument separate from the will that amends or revokes provisions in the will. A codicil eliminates the need to redraft an entire will if the creator only wants to change part of it. A codicil can also be used to revoke an entire will. The codicil must be created using the same formalities required for a will, and it must refer expressly to the will.

A *second*, or *new*, *will* can also be executed to revoke the first. The second will must use specific language like "This will hereby revokes all prior wills." If the first will is not revoked, then some courts will admit both wills into probate. The second will is treated like a codicil.

PROPERTY DISTRIBUTION CONTRARY TO THE TERMS OF A WILL

In most states, a failure to provide for a spouse or child can partially revoke a will. A **preterritted heir** is a child either unintentionally left out of a will or one born after the will is made. Most states have preterritted heir

◆ **codicil** A written instrument separate from the will that amends or revokes provisions in the will.

◆ **pretermitted heir** A child either unintentionally left out of a will or one born after the will is made. States often provide that unless a testator makes it clear that the omission was on purpose, such a child will get a share of the testator's property.

Legal Focus Example

Have a student volunteer read aloud this Legal Focus Example dealing with intestacy laws. Remind students that they can use the Legal Focus features as review tools when studying for tests.

Ethical Concern

Guide students in discussing the ethics of pretermitted heir statutes by asking the following questions: Whose rights are protected by a pretermitted child statute? Are such statutes more concerned with the letter of the will or its intent? Why?

770   Personal Law

statutes that give to a pretermitted child a statutory share of the testator's property. This statutory share overrides the will, unless the child receives a gift in the will or unless his or her exclusion is expressly and clearly made. A parent can give a child little or nothing, but he or she must do so expressly. If a child is not mentioned, the assumption is that the omission was a mistake.

Spouses sometimes have similar rights if they are not provided for in the will, unless the omission of the spouse is purposeful and mentioned in the will.

Because a will is a document subject to change whenever a person wishes, it has been the subject of much intrigue. A potential heir can be written out of a will anytime a person wishes. States have passed laws to protect individuals from anxious and evil beneficiaries. Anyone convicted of a crime that caused the death of a testator cannot receive benefits under the will.

PROPERTY DISTRIBUTION WHEN THERE IS NO WILL—INTESTACY LAWS

♦ **intestacy laws**
The rules that determine distribution of a deceased person's property if he or she dies without a will.

Each state can regulate how property shall be distributed when a person dies without a will. State laws attempt to carry out the likely intent and wishes of the decedent. These statutes are called **intestacy laws**, and they provide for the distribution of property to stated heirs.

The rules of distribution vary from state to state. There is, however, usually a special statutory provision for the rights of the surviving spouse and children. A surviving spouse usually receives a share of the estate—one-half if there is also a surviving child and one-third if there are two or or more children. Only where no children or grandchildren survive the decedent will a surviving spouse get the entire estate. In addition, the law provides that the debts of the decedent must be paid out of the estate first. The assets remaining after payment of debts then pass to the surviving spouse and to the children.

◀ LEGAL FOCUS ~ EXAMPLE

Allen dies intestate (without a will) and is survived by his wife, Della, and his children, Duane and Tara. Allen's property passes according to intestacy laws. After Allen's outstanding debts are paid, Della will ordinarily receive a one-third to one-half interest in the property, with Duane and Tara receiving equal shares in the remainder.

State distribution laws specify the order in which heirs of an intestate person share in the estate. When there is no surviving spouse or child, then grandchildren, brothers and sisters, and, in some states, parents of the decedent are the next in line to share.

Because state law differs so widely, few generalizations can be made about the laws of descent and distribution. It is extremely important to

Checking Your Progress (Answers)

1. Estate planning is an analysis of what a person owns, expects to own, and owes; the use of these assets during life; and their distribution at death.
2. Most gifts are tax-free. An individual may make annual tax-free gifts up to $10,000 ($20,000 from a husband and wife) to each of a number of donees.

3. A will becomes effective at the testator's death, provided it had not been revoked.
4. A devise is a gift of real property, but a bequest is a gift of personal property. Both are given by will.
5. Testamentary capacity means the testator must be of legal age and sound mind at the time the will is made.

Legal Focus Problem

Read aloud to the class this Legal Focus Problem. Ask the students to brainstorm a list of steps Joanna and Charles can take to keep their children from squandering their inheritance. Then have a student volunteer read aloud the paragraph immediately following this problem, in which trusts are introduced.

---

refer to the exact terms of the applicable state statutes in order to answer questions about intestate distribution.

STATUTORY WILLS

One type of formal will is a **statutory will**. A statutory will is a form will authorized by the legislature that contains blanks to be completed by the testator. Statutory wills have been in existence only since 1983 and are currently authorized in only four states.[1] Introduction of such wills has proven to be very popular. Statutory wills were designed to match the simple and usual circumstances of persons who might otherwise die intestate. States authorizing such wills commonly provide that no changes to the form will are permitted.

◆ **statutory will** A type of formal will authorized by a legislature with blanks to be completed by the testator.

 CHECKING YOUR PROGRESS

1. What is estate planning?
2. Are gifts taxed? Explain.
3. When does a will become effective?
4. What is the difference between a devise and a bequest?
5. Explain testamentary capacity.

 TRUSTS

 LEGAL FOCUS – PROBLEM

Johanna James and her husband, Charles, are concerned. They fear that when their children, Neil and Sue, inherit the family farm, they will sell it and squander the proceeds within a short time. The parents believe that their children "simply do not know the value of a dollar." What can Johanna and Charles do to keep their children from squandering their inheritance?

◆ **trust** Any arrangement through which property is transferred from one person to be administered by a trustee for a third party's benefit.

◆ **trustee** A person who holds property under a trust for the benefit of another.

One solution is the creation of a **trust**. A trust is a separate legal entity, governed by a **trustee**. The trustee is someone who holds property for the benefit of another, the **trust beneficiary**. The trust is created by a person

◆ **trust beneficiary** The person who has a beneficial interest in the property or income of a trust.

---

1. The first statutory will was adopted in California in 1983, Probate Code Section 6200. The other three states that have adopted such wills are Wisconsin, Michigan, and Maine.

Read

Ask a student volunteer to describe what is meant by the terms *baby boom* and *baby boomers*. Explain to the class that the group of Americans known as the baby boomers is aging, and this fact is having an impact

on business, government, and society. Then have a volunteer read aloud this *Law in Action* feature.

Discuss

Stimulate a class discussion of this *Law in Action* feature by asking the following questions: What technological factors are helping people to live longer? What is meant by the phrase "right to die"? What is a "living will"?

Why is "living will" an unfortunate choice of terminology for this type of document? How many states now provide for living wills? Which is more flexible, a living will or a durable power of attorney? Why? How do you think the laws regarding living wills and durable powers of attorney are likely to change? Why?

 Law in Action

LAW IN YOUR LIFE: LIVING WILLS

The population of the United States is aging. People born in recent years can expect to live longer than earlier generations. Miraculous advances in medicine are sustaining the lives of persons who in earlier decades would have died at a younger age. Increases in the number of aged persons influence social, political, and economic policy and related law. There is a growing acceptance of a document created by an individual that instructs his or her family and medical personnel about the medical procedures to follow under specified circumstances.

National attention focused on the "right-to-die" issue after an automobile accident put then 25-year-old Nancy Cruzan into a permanent coma in 1982. Five years after the accident, Nancy's parents sought a court order to remove a feeding tube from Nancy. Nancy had been existing in a "vegetative state" since the accident; without medical assistance, she would die. After several years of court battles, a Missouri circuit court granted the parents' wishes and the feeding tubes were removed. Twelve days after the court order on December 26, 1990, Nancy died. Among the reasons for the long court battle was the absence of any written evidence as to Nancy Cruzan's desires about life and death were she to be in a terminal medical circumstance.

A **living will** provides the written evidence that Nancy's parents lacked. The term *living will* is unfortunate—a living will has nothing to do with the transfer of property after a person's death. A less confusing term used in many states is **directive to physicians**. No matter what the name, this is a document directed to a physician that communicates a person's wishes regarding

the use of life support systems in the treatment of a terminal illness or permanent unconsciousness. All fifty states now provide for living wills, but requirements vary. A living will should not be confused with a living trust, which will be discussed later in the chapter.

Many living-will statutes require that the living will be created after a patient has learned of a terminal illness. This type of living will obviously would not have helped Nancy Cruzan, because her condition occurred without notice or time to plan. Also Nancy was not just permanently ill; she was brain dead in a permanent coma. Living wills must be witnessed by two or more disinterested persons and prepared using a specific format or form.

A *durable power of attorney* is a more flexible document than the living will. It authorizes another person to make health care decisions for a person who becomes incapacitated. Powers of attorney are common legal documents allowing the creator, a principal, to empower another to act on his or her behalf. The use of a power of attorney for life-and-death decisions involving health care is something new. The durable power of attorney allows an appointed person to decide whether to order the withdrawal of life support systems for another. Twenty states and the District of Columbia have statutes authorizing the durable power of attorney. This document also requires the signature of noninterested witnesses and must contain exact, approved statutory language.

The federal Patient Self-Determination Act requires that before a patient is admitted to certain health facilities, he or she must be given certain information. Patients must be

Extension Activity

Have a student volunteer research the aging of America. What effects will this demographic trend have on business? What effects will this trend have on government and social services? Have the student present his or her findings to the class in the form of an oral report. Encourage the student to cite original source documents in his or her report.

Enrichment

You might share with the class the following example of a trust. When newspaper publisher Joseph Pulitzer died in 1911, he left funds in trust to found a school of journalism at Columbia University and to establish the Pulitzer Prizes, which are given annually for achievements in journalism, letters, and music composition. Ask a volunteer to research the most recent Pulitzer Prize winners and report back to the class on their names and their work.

Extension Activity

Have a student volunteer research the trust established by James B. Duke, a North Carolina tobacco industrialist, in December 1924. Student research should focus on the amount of the Duke endowment and those institutions that benefit from that endowment today, such as Duke University and Furman University.

 Law in Action (Continued)

informed of their right to make health care decisions. They must be told about their right to execute a living will.

Laws dealing with these sensitive matters are in an early stage of development. More states will undoubtedly liberalize the living will and authorize the durable power of attorney in the next few years.

 TERMS TO REMEMBER

◆ **living will** or **directive to physician**   A document informing a physician of a person's wishes regarding the use of life-saving devices in the case of terminal illness.

◆ **durable power of attorney**   A document authorizing a person to act and make decisions for another including decisions about health care if the person becomes incapacitated.

---

called the **settlor**, or **trustor**. In the situation just described, Johanna and Charles would be the settlors, and Neil and Sue would be the trust beneficiaries. Johanna and Charles would need to select the trustee—the person or business to manage the trust. A trust can be created for any legal purpose consistent with public policy. Its essential elements include:

◆ **settlor** or **trustor**
Person who creates a trust.

1.   A designated beneficiary.
2.   A designated trustee.
3.   Money or property sufficiently identified to allow title to pass to the trustee.
4.   Delivery by the settlor with the intention of passing title of the money or property to the trustee.

If Johanna and Charles transfer the farm to the First Bank of Minnesota in trust for benefit of their children, the couple will have created a trust. This arrangement is illustrated in Exhibit 32–1.

EXPRESS TRUSTS

An *express* trust is created or declared in explicit terms, usually in writing. Two types of express trusts are *inter vivos* trusts and testamentary trusts.

An **inter vivos trust** is a trust executed by a grantor during his or her lifetime. *Inter vivos* means during life. The grantor executes a *trust deed*, and legal title to the trust property passes to the named trustee. The trustee has a duty to administer the property as directed by the grantor for the benefit of and in the interest of the beneficiaries. The trustee must preserve the trust property and make it productive. Usually the trust agreement requires the payment of income to the beneficiaries. Once the *inter vivos* trust is created, the grantor has given the property for the benefit of beneficiaries. Often, this type of trust has tax-related benefits.

◆ **inter vivos trust**
A trust created by a grantor during his or her lifetime.

VIDEODISC NOTE
Much of the material that is conveyed in the exhibits of *West's Business and Personal Law* is also conveyed in the still frames on the **West Business Law and Legal Environment Video-disc**. For more information and directions for use, please see the Index and Description of Contents for the **West Business Law and Legal Environment Video-disc** that is found in your *Teacher's Resource Binder*.

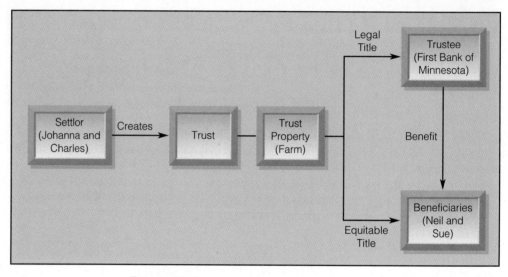

EXHIBIT 32-1
TRUST ARRANGEMENT

♦ **testamentary trust** A trust created by will and coming into existence on the death of the grantor.

A **testamentary trust** is a trust created in a will. Although it is created when the will is made, the trust does not begin until the settlor's death. If the will that sets up a testamentary trust is invalid, then the trust will also be invalid. The property that was supposed to be in the trust will then pass according to intestacy laws, not according to the terms of the trust.

DUTIES OF THE TRUSTEE

The trustee is a fiduciary to the beneficiary of the trust. This means that the trustee owes to the beneficiary a duty of highest care, honesty, and loyalty. The settlor may serve as trustee during his or her lifetime, or the settlor may select a relative or trusted friend. In addition, many commercial companies, such as banks, offer their services as commercial trustees. The legal responsibilities of trustees are the same in both *inter vivos* and testamentary trusts.

If it is not mentioned in the trust document, the trustee has a right to be paid for his or her services. The fees are determined consistent with state law or as allowed by the probate court. The settlor can provide how or even whether the trustee is paid in the trust. A person nominated as a trustee is free to decline to serve. If a successor or alternate is not named in the trust document, the court will usually name a trustee.

A trustee is duty bound to manage the assets of the trust properly. The trustee is accountable to the beneficiaries and must invest the property carefully. Because the trustee is a fiduciary (in a position of trust), it is a conflict of interest for the trustee to profit personally from the trust, other

Legal Focus Example

Have a student volunteer read aloud this first Legal Focus Example dealing with living trusts. Ask the student to explain to the class how Bill and Trish Carlton can use a living trust to avoid probate and its costs. Then ask the volunteer whether the Carltons can also avoid estate taxes through the use of this living trust. (Students should understand that a living trust will not by itself reduce death taxes.)

Reteaching Activity

Have a student volunteer turn to the Chapter Summary for Chapter 28 and read aloud the explanation of joint tenancy found there.

Legal Focus Example

Have a student volunteer read aloud to the class this second Legal Focus Example dealing with joint tenancy and probate. Ask a student volunteer how joint tenancy settles the question of ownership of this house if either Al or Beth dies.

than by the payment provided. The exact nature of trustee duties is specified in state statutes. These duties often are modified or further explained by the trust document.

LIVING TRUSTS

Living trust is a popular term for a type of *inter vivos* trust whose primary purpose is to avoid probate. A person may wish to avoid probate in order to reduce expenses and to maintain privacy in the settlement of family affairs. The living trust is usually less expensive than probate, and it is private. However, a living trust will not by itself reduce death taxes.

With the living trust, the settlor transfers all of his or her property into a trust before death. The settlor is the trustee and, during life, is one of the beneficiaries. Alternate beneficiaries are named, so at the death of the settlor, the benefits of the trust shift to another person or persons.

◆ **living trust** A popular term for an *inter vivos* trust whose primary purpose is to avoid the expenses and publicity of probate.

 LEGAL FOCUS ~ EXAMPLE

Bill and Trish Carlton wish to create a living trust. To do so, they should transfer all their property to the trust, which they create during their lives. They can name themselves as joint trustees and joint beneficiaries and thus retain full benefit of the property during their lives. However, they need to name an alternate beneficiary to receive the property on the death of the second spouse. As all property is transferred to the trust before death, there will be no property to probate.

 ## JOINT TENANCY AND PROBATE

Joint tenancy is a form of joint property ownership that allows two or more persons to have joint interests in both real and personal property. See Chapter 28 for a complete discussion of joint tenancy. An important feature of joint tenancy is its *right of survivorship*.

 LEGAL FOCUS ~ EXAMPLE

Al and Beth own a house in joint tenancy. If Beth dies, Al automatically becomes the sole owner of the house immediately and without probate. Full title passes to Al even if Beth has left a will that attempted to give her interest in the house to her mother, Sue. Surviving joint tenants automatically receive the interests of a deceased joint tenancy owner. As Al's interest is complete at the moment of Beth's death, there is no interest left to convey by will.

Read

Introduce this *A Case In Point* feature by reminding the students that undue influence may be inferred by the court if the testator ignores his or her blood relatives and instead names a nonrelative as a beneficiary. Furthermore, the likelihood of undue influence is greater if the beneficiary is a person who was in constant close contact with the deceased and was able to influence the making of the will. Then have a student volunteer read this *A Case In Point* feature aloud to the class.

Discuss

Stimulate a class discussion of this *A Case In Point* feature by asking the following questions: To whom did John Prigge leave his entire estate? What was his relationship with Marian? Who was excluded by Prigge's will? Who contested the will? On what grounds was the will contested? What was the ruling of the trial court in this case? What was the issue before the Court of Appeals of Minnesota? What was the decision of the Court of Appeals of Minnesota? What reasons did the court give for its decision?

Teaching Note

This case is included in the *West's Business and Personal Law Handbook of Selected Court Cases.*

---

1. An *inter vivos* trust is a trust executed by a grantor during his or her lifetime; a testamentary trust is executed after the settlor's death.
2. The main purpose of a living trust is to avoid probate; however, a person may also create a living trust to maintain privacy in the settlement of family affairs.

3. Since the ownership of property transfers automatically at the death of a joint tenant to the remaining tenant(s), joint tenancy property is not subject to probate.

Depending on the circumstances and desires of the co-owners, this feature is either a reason to or a reason not to own property in joint tenancy. Because the ownership transfers automatically at the death of a joint tenant to the remaining tenant or tenants, joint tenancy property is not subject to probate. It is thus an effective way to avoid probate. There are, however, disadvantages to holding title to property in joint tenancy. A joint tenant has a risk that the other joint tenant will transfer the property during life—for example, to pay a debt. Also, a creditor of the other joint tenant may be able to seize the joint property to pay the debts owed by that joint tenant.

 CHECKING YOUR PROGRESS

1. What is the difference between an *inter vivos* trust and a testamentary trust?
2. What is the main purpose of a living trust?
3. How does joint tenancy affect probate?

◆ A CASE IN POINT ◆

 THE MATTER OF ESTATE OF PRIGGE
Court of Appeals of Minnesota, 1984.
352 N.W.2d 443.

One of the charges in this will contest is that a sister exerted undue influence over her brother in the drafting of his will. Did John Prigge's sister exert undue influence?

FACTS John Prigge had never married and had spent his life farming. It was undisputed that he had often needed direction. His mother had often balanced his checkbook and taken care of his accounts. His memory was somewhat faulty, and he required constant reminding as to household chores and other duties. In 1980 he sold his farm and moved in with one of his sisters,

Marian. In 1981 Prigge executed a will in which he left his entire estate to Marian and her six children. He specifically excluded another sister, Jean, and a brother, Louis. When Prigge first drafted the will, he had asked Marian to help him by writing down his intentions for him. Prigge then took Marian's handwritten instructions to a lawyer. The lawyer drafted a will based on the document prepared by Marian. When Prigge died in 1982, Louis and Jean contested the will. They charged that John Prigge lacked testamentary capacity and that Marian had exerted undue influence over her brother. The trial court ruled that the will was valid. Jean and Louis appealed.

ISSUE (1) Did John Prigge have testamentary capacity? (2) Did Marian exert undue influence over her brother when the will was prepared?

In order to help students review what they have learned in Chapter 32, you might wish to:
1. Have a student volunteer, or volunteers, read the Chapter Summary aloud.
2. Allow the students to work with partners to complete the *Using Legal Language* activity.
3. Assign the *Checking for Comprehension* exercise as homework.

4. Allow the students to work in small groups to complete the *Applying Legal Concepts* activities.
5. As a class, complete the *Applying the Law* activities. (Please note that you may have to help students with vocabulary so that they adequately understand all of the *Applying the Law* material.)

In order to check student mastery of chapter concepts, you may wish to use the Chapter 32 test that is found in your *Teacher's Resource Binder* or use WESTEST computerized testing for Chapter 32.

Wills and Trusts   777

◆ A CASE IN POINT (CONTINUED) ◆

DECISION   Yes to the first issue; no to the second. The appellate court upheld the trial court's findings that the will was valid.

REASON   The court stated that a "testator will be found to have testamentary capacity if, when making the will, he understands the nature, situation, and extent of his property and the claims of others on his bounty or his remembrance, and he is able to hold these things in his mind long enough to form a rational judgment concerning them. Less mental capacity is required to make a will than to conduct regular business affairs." Evidence given by the lawyer who prepared the will and by others who had dealt with John Prigge at-

tested to Prigge's testamentary capacity. As to undue influence, the court concluded that the "relationship between John and his brothers and sisters negated undue influence. Whereas Marian and her husband had helped John on many occasions for at least eight years before he sold the family farm, John had an estranged relationship with Louis and Jean and had not associated with them except on a very limited basis." Based on the relationship between John and his brother and sisters and because the attorney testified that John had been quite clear about what his holdings were and how he wanted to dispose of them, the court found that no undue influence was present.

CHAPTER ◆32◆ REVIEW

 ## SUMMARY

ESTATE PLANNING

Goals:

1. To provide for the needs of the planner while alive.

2. To reflect the desires of the planner in providing for beneficiaries.

3. To minimize or avoid taxes.

4. To minimize or avoid problems of probate.

WILLS

Types of Wills

1. *Formal*—A written will, signed by the testator, properly witnessed, and, when required, published.

2. *Holographic*—A will completely in the

handwriting of the testator; valid where permitted by state statute.

3. *Statutory*—A type of form will authorized by the legislature with blanks to be completed by the testator.

4. *Living will*—Not really a will but a document that communicates the wishes of a person regarding the use of life support systems in the treatment of a terminal illness or permanent unconsciousness. Also called a *directive to physicians*.

Requirements of a Formal Will

1. A will must be in writing (except for nuncupative wills).

2. It must be signed by the testator.

---

3. It must be witnessed in the manner pre-scribed by state statute.

4. A will may be required to be *published*—that is, the testator may be required to announce to witnesses that this is his or her "last will and testament."

Methods of Revoking or Modifying a Will

1. Physical act—Tearing up, canceling, obliterating, or deliberately destroying part or all of a will.

2. Codicil—A formal separate document to amend or revoke an existing will.

3. Second or new will—A new, properly executed will, expressly revoking the existing will.

Gifts by Will

1. *Specific*—A devise or bequest of a particular piece of property in the testator's estate.

2. *General*—A devise or bequest that does not single out a particular item in the testator's estate; usually a sum of money.

3. *Residuary*—A devise or bequest of any properties left in the estate after all specific and general gifts have been made.

Intestacy Laws (Statutes of Descent and Distribution)

These vary widely from state to state. Usually,

the law provides that the surviving spouse and children inherit the property of the decedent.

TRUSTS

Definition

Any arrangement through which property is transferred from one person to be administered by a trustee for a third party's benefit. The essential elements of a trust include: (1) a designated beneficiary, (2) a designated trustee, (3) a fund sufficiently identified to enable title to pass to the trustee, and (4) actual delivery to the trustee with the intention of passing title.

Types of Trusts

Express trusts—Created by expressed terms, usually in writing.

a. Inter vivos *trust*—A trust executed by a grantor during his or her lifetime.

b. *Testamentary trust*—A trust created by will and coming into existence on the death of the grantor.

c. *Living trust*—A type of *inter vivos* trust whose primary purpose is to avoid probate.

Joint Tenancy

Holding property in joint tenancy is a method by which people transfer ownership of property at death as part of an estate plan.

◆ USING LEGAL LANGUAGE

Directions: Match each term with the statement that best defines that term.

1. estate tax
2. executor
3. inheritance tax
4. intestate
5. legacy
6. probate
7. settlor
8. testator
9. trust
10. will

A. a gift of personal property by will

B. the court process of proving the validity of a will and following the wishes of the testator

C. a tax imposed by the federal government and some states on the giving of property to another after the death of the giver

D. a person who makes a will

E. any arrangement whereby property is transferred from one person to be administered by a trustee for a third party's benefit

1. An estate tax is imposed on the assets of the person at death, but an inheritance tax is imposed on the person who inherits the property. The federal government and some states impose estate taxes; states usually impose inheritance taxes.

2. If a person dies intestate (without a will) and has no heirs, the property that remains after all creditors of the deceased are paid goes to the state.

3. Probate court is responsible for administering any legal problems surrounding wills and distribution of estates. Questions as to the validity of a will, claims of creditors, collection of taxes, and distribution of assets to beneficiaries are handled by this court.

4. To create a valid will, most states require the will to be in writing, signed by the testator, witnessed (nonholographic), and published (sometimes). The formalities are intended to help prevent fraud.

5. A codicil is a written instrument separate from the will that amends or revokes provisions in the will. A codicil eliminates the need to redraft an entire will.

6. If a child is born after the will is made or is unintentionally left out, the court will grant the child a statutory share of the testator's property. However, if the child received a gift in the will or if the child's exclusion is expressly and clearly made, a parent can give a child little or nothing.

7. Unless Robert made a codicil (changing Donna's inheritance to the 1989 Jaguar), Donna will not inherit the 1989 Jaguar under the terms of her father's will. The will specified that Donna was to inherit a 1986 Jaguar upon her father's death, and since her father did not own a 1986 Jaguar when he died, Donna receives nothing under this provision.

F. a personal representative named in a will who is the person in charge of the personal affairs of the deceased

G. legal expression of a person's wishes for the distribution of his or her property after death

H. person who creates a trust, also called a trustor

I. a tax imposed by some states on those who receive property from a deceased person's estate

J. when a person dies without having left a will

◆ CHECKING FOR COMPREHENSION

1. What is the difference between an estate tax and an inheritance tax?

2. If a person dies intestate and has no heirs, what happens to the estate?

3. Which court deals with wills and other questions about estates? What questions are usually answered in this court?

4. Describe the usual formal requirements of a will. Why are formalities required?

5. What is a codicil; why is a codicil prepared?

6. How does the court treat a will that fails to provide for a child of the testator?

7. Robert drew up a will in which he left his favorite car, a 1986 red Jaguar, to his daughter Donna. A year prior to his death, Robert sold the 1986 Jaguar and purchased a 1989 Jaguar. Discuss whether Donna will inherit the 1989 Jaguar under the terms of her father's will.

◆ APPLYING LEGAL CONCEPTS

1. Write a formal will using a typewriter or computer. Print a copy of the will. Have fellow students witness the will.

2. Write a holographic will.

3. Write a living trust naming you and your mother as beneficiaries.

◆ APPLYING THE LAW . . . YOU BE THE JUDGE

1. Tennie Joyner was eighty years old and about to be hospitalized for an illness. To provide for her son, Calvin, Joyner wrote a will and took it to her neighbors for them to type and witness. In the document, she stated that she was giving all her possessions to Calvin because he had taken care of her for years. The will was contested on the basis that Joyner had not met the formal requirement of publication, since she did not tell her neighbors explicitly that the document was her "last will and testament." Joyner had merely told her neighbors that she wanted "a piece of paper fixed up so I can sign it and Calvin will have a place to live." Joyner intended

Applying the Law . . . You Be the Judge (Answers)

1. No. The Supreme Court of Arkansas noted that the Arkansas statute, requiring that wills be published, did not state that a testator had to say specifically the words, "This is my last will and testament." Rather, the statute required that a testator "shall declare to the attesting witnesses that the instrument is his will." The court, citing an Arkansas

precedent from 1853, stated that the "statute says he shall declare it; but . . . no particular form of words is necessary, and . . . it would be unwise, if not unsafe, to speculate upon the precise mode of communication, as every case must depend upon its own peculiar circumstances." In this case, the court found that Mrs. Joyner "understood that she was making a testamentary disposition of her property," and it was undisputed that the understanding "was communicated to the witnesses and they understood."

2. The trial court—which struck the racial provision—held that the gift would go to the first educational institution named. On appeal, however, the court ruled that "where a gift or estate subject to a limitation is unlawful, in order to cure the defect the court must terminate the entire gift or estate." The "offending language"—the racial provisions—could not be stricken from the provision, according to the appellate court, without changing "the essential nature and quality of the estate." Since Adams had not placed any unconstitutional limitations upon the final beneficiary, Hermitage Methodist Homes, the court declared that Hermitage "has the only valid, remaining interest." Therefore, Hermitage would receive the entire trust.

3. Yes, the court held that Myrtle had revoked her will. In order to effectuate a revocation of a will, (1) there must be performance of one or more of the specified acts to a degree that materially and permanently destroys the efficacy of the document, and (2) the testator must intend for the act to revoke the will. One of the essential elements of a validly executed will is the signature of the testator. "The act of the testator in cutting out, erasing, or otherwise obliterating his signature on the instrument, or the removal of the signature page, is sufficient to revoke the entire will when performed with such intent." The fact that the signature page of the will was detached and missing created a rebuttable presumption of revocation. When the will is in the testator's possession and is not found at his or her death, the presumption arises that he or she destroyed it for the purpose of revocation. In the present case, the will was in Myrtle's possession and control; therefore, it is presumed that the missing signature page was removed and destroyed with the intention of revoking the will. The trustees failed to rebut the presumption of revocation, and Myrtle's will was held to be effectively revoked.

the document to dispose of her property, and the neighbors were fully aware of her intention. Does Joyner's failure to state "this is my last will and testament" invalidate the will? Explain. [*Faith v. Singleton,* 286 Ark. 403, 692 S.W.2d 239 (1985)]

2. In 1956, Jack Adams executed a will, the terms of which established a charitable trust. The trust income was to go to Prince Edward School Foundation as long as the foundation continued to operate and admitted to its school "only members of the White Race." If the foundation admitted nonwhites to its schools, the trust income was to go to the Miller School, under the same limitation, and so on to two other educational institutions. If all of the successively named educational beneficiaries violated the limitation, the income would go to Hermitage Methodist Homes of Virginia, Inc., without any limitation attending the bequest. In 1968, Adams dies. Subsequent to the execution of his will, all of the educational beneficiaries enrolled black students. The trustee, uncertain as to how to distribute the trust income under these circumstances, sought counsel from the court. Assuming that the racially discriminatory provisions are unconstitutional and void, which, if any, of the named beneficiaries should receive the trust income? [*Hermitage Methodist Homes of Virginia, Inc. v. Dominion Trust Co.,* 387 S.E.2d 740 (Va. 1990)]

3. Myrtle Courziel executed a valid will that provided for the establishment of a scholarship fund designed to encourage the study of corrosion as it affects metallurgical engineering. The recipients were to be students in the upper half of their class at the University of Alabama. Subsequently, Myrtle died. John Calhoun, the eventual administrator of her estate, obtained access to Myrtle's safe-deposit box to search for her will. He found the will intact, except that the last page of the will, which had contained Myrtle's signature and the signatures of the witnesses, had been removed from the document and was not in the safe-deposit box or anywhere else to be found. Since Myrtle had sole control over the will, should it have been presumed that her removal of the last page (or her having allowed it to be removed) effectively revoked the will? [*Board of Trustees of University of Alabama v. Calhoun,* 514 So.2d 895 (Ala. 1987)]

CONTENTS

Legal Source Documents

The Resource Center

Legal Source Documents

THE DECLARATION OF INDEPENDENCE

In Congress, July 4, 1776

A Declaration by the Representatives of the United States of America, in General Congress assembled. When in the Course of human Events, it becomes necessary for one People to dissolve the Political Bands which have connected them with another, and to assume among the Powers of the Earth, the separate and equal Station to which the Laws of Nature and of Nature's God entitle them, a decent Respect to the Opinions of Mankind requires that they should declare the causes which impel them to the Separation.

We hold these Truths to be self-evident, that all Men are created equal, that they are endowed by their Creator with certain unalienable Rights, that among these are Life, Liberty, and the Pursuit of Happiness—That to secure these Rights, Governments are instituted among Men, deriving their just Powers from the Consent of the Governed, that whenever any Form of Government becomes destructive of these Ends, it is the Right of the People to alter or to abolish it, and to institute new Government, laying its Foundation on such Principles, and organizing its Powers in such Forms, as to them shall seem most likely to effect their Safety and Happiness. Prudence, indeed, will dictate that Governments long established should not be changed for light and transient Causes; and accordingly all Experience hath shewn, that Mankind are more disposed to suffer, while Evils are sufferable, than to right themselves by abolishing the Forms to which they are accustomed. But when a long Train of Abuses and Usurpations, pursuing invariably the same Object, evinces a Design to reduce them under absolute Despotism, it is their Right, it is their Duty, to throw off such Government, and to provide new Guards for their future Security. Such has been the patient Sufferance of these Colonies; and such is now the Necessity which constrains them to alter their former Systems of Government. The History of the present King of Great-Britain is a History of repeated Injuries and Usurpations, all having in direct Object the Establishment of an absolute Tyranny over these States. To prove this, let Facts be submitted to a candid World.

He has refused his Assent to Laws, the most wholesome and necessary for the public Good.

He has forbidden his Governors to pass Laws of immediate and pressing Importance, unless suspended in their Operation till his Assent should be obtained; and when so suspended, he has utterly neglected to attend to them.

He has refused to pass other Laws for the Accommodation of large Districts of People, unless those People would relinquish the Right of Representation in the Legislature, a Right inestimable to them, and formidable to Tyrants only.

He has called together Legislative Bodies at Places unusual, uncomfortable, and distant from the Depository of their Public Records, for the sole Purpose of fatiguing them into Compliance with his Measures.

He has dissolved Representative Houses repeatedly, for opposing with manly Firmness his Invasions on the Rights of the People.

He has refused for a long Time, after such Dissolutions, to cause others to be elected; whereby the Legislative Powers, incapable of Annihilation, have returned to the People at large for their exercise; the State remaining in the mean time exposed to all the Dangers of Invasion from without, and Convulsions within.

He has endeavoured to prevent the Population of these States; for that Purpose obstructing the

Laws for Naturalization of Foreigners; refusing to pass others to encourage their Migrations hither, and raising the Conditions of new Appropriations of Lands.

He has obstructed the Administration of Justice, by refusing his Assent to Laws for establishing Judiciary Powers.

He has made Judges dependent on his Will alone, for the Tenure of their offices, and the Amount and payment of their Salaries.

He has erected a Multitude of new Offices, and sent hither Swarms of Officers to harrass our People, and eat out their Substance.

He has kept among us, in Times of Peace, Standing Armies, without the consent of our Legislatures.

He has affected to render the Military independent of, and superior to the Civil Power.

He has combined with others to subject us to a Jurisdiction foreign to our Constitution, and unacknowledged by our Laws; giving his Assent to their Acts of pretended Legislation:

For quartering large Bodies of Armed Troops among us:

For protecting them, by a mock Trial, from Punishment for any Murders which they should commit on the Inhabitants of these States:

For cutting off our Trade with all Parts of the World:

For imposing Taxes on us without our Consent:

For depriving us, in many cases, of the Benefits of Trial by Jury:

For transporting us beyond Seas to be tried for pretended Offences:

For abolishing the free System of English Laws in a neighbouring Province, establishing therein an arbitrary Government, and enlarging its Boundaries, so as to render it at once an Example and fit Instrument for introducing the same absolute Rule into these Colonies:

For taking away our Charters, abolishing our most valuable Laws, and altering fundamentally the Forms of our Governments:

For suspending our own Legislatures, and declaring themselves invested with Power to legislate for us in all Cases whatsoever.

He has abdicated Government here, by declaring us out of his Protection and waging War against us.

He has plundered our Seas, ravaged our Coasts, burnt our towns, and destroyed the Lives of our People.

He is, at this Time, transporting large Armies of foreign Mercenaries to compleat the works of Death, Desolation, and Tyranny, already begun with circumstances of Cruelty and Perfidy, scarcely paralleled in the most barbarous Ages, and totally unworthy the Head of a civilized Nation.

He has constrained our fellow Citizens taken Captive on the high Seas to bear Arms against their Country, to become the Executioners of their Friends and Brethren, or to fall themselves by their Hands.

He has excited domestic Insurrections amongst us, and has endeavoured to bring on the Inhabitants of our Frontiers, the merciless Indian Savages, whose known Rule of Warfare, is an undistinguished Destruction, of all Ages, Sexes and Conditions.

In every state of these Oppressions we have Petitioned for Redress in the most humble Terms: Our repeated Petitions have been answered only by repeated Injury. A Prince, whose Character is thus marked by every act which may define a Tyrant, is unfit to be the Ruler of a free People.

Nor have we been wanting in Attentions to our British Brethren. We have warned them from Time to Time of Attempts by their Legislature to extend an unwarrantable Jurisdiction over us. We have reminded them of the Circumstances of our Emigration and Settlement here. We have appealed to their native Justice and Magnanimity, and we have conjured them by the Ties of our common Kindred to disavow these Usurpations, which, would inevitably interrupt our Connections and Correspondence. They too have been deaf to the Voice of Justice and of Consanguinity. We must, therefore, acquiesce in the Necessity, which denounces our Separation, and hold them, as we hold the rest of Mankind, Enemies in War, in Peace, Friends.

We, therefore, the Representatives of the UNITED STATES OF AMERICA, in General Congress Assembled, appealing to the Supreme Judge of the World for the Rectitude of our Intentions, do, in the Name, and by the Authority of the good People of these Colonies, solemnly Publish and Declare, That these United Colonies are, and of Right ought to be, Free and Independent States; that they are absolved from all Allegiance to the British Crown, and that all political Connection between them and the State of Great-Britain, is and ought to be totally dissolved; and that as Free and

Independent States, they have full Power to levy War, conclude Peace, contract Alliances, establish Commerce, and to do all other Acts and Things which Independent States may of right do. And for the support of this declaration, with a firm Reliance on the Protection of divine Providence, we mutually pledge to each other our lives, our Fortunes, and our sacred Honor.

◆ THE CONSTITUTION OF THE UNITED STATES OF AMERICA*

The Preamble

We the People of the United States, in Order to form a more perfect Union, establish Justice, insure domestic Tranquility, provide for the common defence, promote the general Welfare, and secure the Blessings of Liberty to ourselves and our Posterity, do ordain and establish this Constitution for the United States of America.

The Preamble declares that "We the People" are the authority for the Constitution (unlike the Articles of Confederation, which derived their authority from the states). The Preamble also sets out the purposes of the Constitution.

Article I. (Legislative Branch)

The first part of the Constitution is called Article 1; it deals with the organization and powers of the lawmaking branch of the national government, the Congress.

Section 1. Legislative Powers

All legislative Powers herein granted shall be vested in a Congress of the United States, which shall consist of a Senate and House of Representatives.

Section 2. House of Representatives

Clause 1: Composition and Election of Members. The House of Representatives shall be composed of Members chosen every second Year by the People of the several States, and the Electors in each State shall have the Qualifications requisite for Electors of the most numerous Branch of the State Legislature.

Each state has the power to decide who may vote for members of Congress. Within each state, those who may vote for state legislators may also vote for members of the House of Representatives (and, under the Seventeenth Amendment, for U.S. senators). When the Constitution was written, nearly all states limited voting rights to white male property owners or taxpayers at least twenty-one years old. Subsequent amendments granted voting power to African-American men, all women, and eighteen-year-olds.

Clause 2: Qualifications. No Person shall be a Representative who shall not have attained to the Age of twenty five Years, and been seven Years a Citizen of the United States, and who shall not, when elected, be an Inhabitant of that State in which he shall be chosen.

Each member of the House must (1) be at least twenty-five years old, (2) have been a U.S. citizen for at least seven years, and (3) be a resident of the state in which she or he is elected.

Clause 3: Apportionment of Representatives and Direct Taxes. Representatives [and direct Taxes][1] shall be apportioned among the several States which may be included within this Union, according to their respective Numbers [which shall be determined by adding to the whole Number of free Persons, including those bound to Service for a Term of Years, and excluding Indians not taxed, three

---

*The spelling, capitalization, and punctuation of the original have been retained here. Brackets indicate passages that have been altered by amendments to the Constitution.
[1]Modified by the Sixteenth Amendment.

fifths of all other Persons].[2] The actual Enumeration shall be made within three Years after the first Meeting of the Congress of the United States, and within every subsequent Term of ten Years, in such Manner as they shall by Law direct. The Number of Representatives shall not exceed one for every thirty Thousand, but each State shall have at Least one Representative; and until such enumeration shall be made, the State of New Hampshire shall be entitled to chuse three, Massachusetts eight, Rhode Island and Providence Plantations one, Connecticut five, New York six, New Jersey four, Pennsylvania eight, Delaware one, Maryland six, Virginia ten, North Carolina five, South Carolina five, and Georgia three.

A state's representation in the House is based on the size of its population. Population is counted in each decade's census, after which Congress reapportions House seats. Since early in this century, the number of seats has been limited to 435.

Clause 4: Vacancies. When vacancies happen in the Representation from any State, the Executive Authority thereof shall issue Writs of Election to fill such Vacancies.

The "Executive Authority" is the state's governor. When a vacancy occurs in the House, the governor calls a special election to fill it.

Clause 5: Officers and Impeachment. The House of Representatives shall chuse their Speaker and other Officers; and shall have the sole Power of Impeachment.

The power to impeach is the power to accuse. In this case, it is the power to accuse members of the executive or judicial branch of wrongdoing or abuse of power. Once a bill of impeachment is issued, the Senate holds the trial.

Section 3. The Senate
Clause 1: Term and Number of Members. The Senate of the United States shall be composed of two Senators from each State [chosen by the Legislature thereof],[3] for six Years; and each Senator shall have one Vote.

Every state has two senators, each of whom serves for six years and has one vote in the upper chamber. Since the Seventeenth Amendment in 1913, all senators are elected directly by voters of the state during the regular election.

Clause 2: Classification of Senators. Immediately after they shall be assembled in Consequence of the first Election, they shall be divided as equally as may be into three Classes. The Seats of the Senators of the first Class shall be vacated at the Expiration of the second Year, of the second Class at the Expiration of the fourth Year, and of the third Class at the Expiration of the sixth Year, so that one third may be chosen every second Year; [and if Vacancies happen by Resignation, or otherwise, during the Recess of the Legislature of any State, the Executive thereof may make temporary Appointments until the next Meeting of the Legislature, which shall then fill such Vacancies].[4]

One-third of the Senate's seats are open to election every two years (unlike the House, all of whose members are elected simultaneously).

Clause 3: Qualifications. No Person shall be a Senator who shall not have attained to the Age of thirty Years, and been nine Years a Citizen of the United States, and who shall not, when elected, be an Inhabitant of that State for which he shall be chosen.

Every senator must be at least thirty years old, a citizen of the United States for a minimum of nine years, and a resident of the state in which he or she is elected.

Clause 4: The Role of the Vice President. The Vice President of the United States shall be President of the Senate, but shall have no Vote, unless they be equally divided.

The vice-president presides over meetings of the Senate but cannot vote unless there is a tie. The Constitution gives no other official duties to the vice-president.

Clause 5: Other Officers. The Senate shall chuse their other Officers, and also a President pro tempore, in the Absence of the Vice President, or

---

[2]Modified by the Fourteenth Amendment.
[3]Repealed by the Seventeenth Amendment.

[4]Modified by the Seventeenth Amendment.

when he shall exercise the Office of President of the United States.

The Senate votes for one of its members to preside when the vice-president is absent. This person is usually called the president pro tempore because of the temporary situation of the position.

Clause 6: Impeachment Trials.
The Senate shall have the sole Power to try all Impeachments. When sitting for that Purpose, they shall be on Oath or Affirmation. When the President of the United States is tried, the Chief Justice shall preside: And no Person shall be convicted without the Concurrence of two thirds of the Members present.

The Senate conducts trials of officials that the House impeaches. The Senate sits as a jury, with the vice-president presiding if the president is not on trial.

Clause 7: Penalties for Conviction.
Judgment in Cases of Impeachment shall not extend further than to removal from Office, and disqualification to hold and enjoy any Office of honor, Trust, or Profit under the United States: but the Party convicted shall nevertheless be liable and subject to Indictment, Trial, Judgment, and Punishment, according to Law.

On conviction on impeachment charges, the Senate can only force an official to leave office and prevent him or her from holding another office in the federal government. The individual, however, can still be tried in a regular court.

Section 4. Congressional Elections: Times, Manner, and Places
Clause 1: Elections.
The Times, Places and Manner of holding Elections for Senators and Representatives, shall be prescribed in each State by the Legislature thereof; but the Congress may at any time by Law make or alter such Regulations, except as to the Places of chusing Senators.

Congress set the Tuesday after the first Monday in November in even-numbered years as the date for congressional elections. In states with more than one seat in the House, Congress requires that representatives be elected from districts within each state. Under the Seventeenth Amendment, senators are elected at the same places as other officials.

Clause 2: Sessions of Congress.
[The Congress shall assemble at least once in every Year, and such Meeting shall be on the first Monday in December, unless they shall by Law appoint a different Day.][5]

Congress has to meet every year at least once. The regular session now begins at noon on January 3 of each year, subsequent to the Twentieth Amendment, unless Congress passes a law to fix a different date. Congress stays in session until its members vote to adjourn. Additionally, the president may call a special session.

Section 5. Powers and Duties of the Houses
Clause 1: Admitting Members and Quorum.
Each House shall be the Judge of the Elections, Returns, and Qualifications of its own Members, and a Majority of each shall constitute a Quorum to do Business; but a smaller Number may adjourn from day to day, and may be authorized to compel the Attendance of absent Members, in such Manner, and under such Penalties as each House may provide.

Each chamber may exclude or refuse to seat a member-elect.
  The quorum rule requires that 218 members of the House and 51 members of the Senate be present in order to conduct business. This rule is normally not enforced in the handling of routine matters.

Clause 2: Rules and Discipline of Members.
Each House may determine the Rules of its Proceedings, punish its Members for disorderly Behaviour, and, with the Concurrence of two thirds, expel a Member.

The House and the Senate may adopt their own rules to guide their proceedings. Each may also discipline its members for conduct that is deemed unacceptable. No member may be expelled without a two-thirds majority.

Clause 3: Keeping a Record.
Each House shall keep a Journal of its Proceedings, and from time to time publish the same, excepting such Parts as may in their Judgment require Secrecy; and the Yeas and Nays of the Members of either House on any question shall, at the Desire of one fifth of those Present, be entered on the Journal.

---

[5]Changed by the Twentieth Amendment.

The journals of the two houses are published at the end of each session of Congress.

Clause 4: Adjournment. Neither House, during the Session of Congress, shall, without the Consent of the other, adjourn for more than three days, nor to any other Place than that in which the two Houses shall be sitting.

Congress has the power to determine when and where to meet, provided, however, that both houses meet in the same city. Neither house may recess in excess of three days without the consent of the other.

Section 6. Rights of Members

Clause 1: Compensation and Privileges. The Senators and Representatives shall receive a Compensation for their services, to be ascertained by Law, and paid out of the Treasury of the United States. They shall in all Cases, except Treason, Felony and Breach of the Peace, be privileged from Arrest during their Attendance at the Session of their respective Houses, and in going to and returning from the same; and for any Speech or Debate in either House, they shall not be questioned in any other Place.

Congressional salaries are to be paid by the U.S. Treasury rather than by the members' respective states. The original salaries were $6 per day; in 1857 they were $3,000 per year. Both representatives and senators currently are paid $129,500 each year.

Members cannot be arrested for things they say during speeches and debates in Congress. This immunity applies to the Capitol Building itself and not to their private lives.

Treason is defined in Article III, Section 3. A felony is any serious crime. A breach of the peace is any indictable offense less than treason or a felony. Members cannot be arrested for anything they say in speeches or debates in Congress.

Clause 2: Restrictions. No Senator or Representative shall, during the Time for which he was elected, be appointed to any civil Office under the Authority of the United States, which shall have been created, or the Emoluments whereof shall have been encreased during such time; and no Person holding any Office under the United States,

shall be a Member of either House during his Continuance in Office.

During the term for which a member was elected, he or she cannot concurrently accept another federal government position.

Section 7. Legislative Powers: Bills and Resolutions

Clause 1: Revenue Bills. All Bills for raising Revenue shall originate in the House of Representatives; but the Senate may propose or concur with Amendments as on other Bills.

All tax and appropriation bills for raising money have to originate in the House of Representatives. The Senate, though, often amends such bills and may even substitute an entirely different bill.

Clause 2: The Presidential Veto. Every Bill which shall have passed the House of Representatives and the Senate, shall, before it becomes a Law, be presented to the President of the United States; If he approve he shall sign it, but if not he shall return it, with his Objections to the House in which it shall have originated, who shall enter the Objections at large on their Journal, and proceed to reconsider it. If after such Reconsideration two thirds of that House shall agree to pass the Bill, it shall be sent together with the Objections, to the other House, by which it shall likewise be reconsidered, and if approved by two thirds of that House, it shall become a Law. But in all such Cases the Votes of both Houses shall be determined by Yeas and Nays, and the Names of the Persons voting for and against the Bill shall be entered on the Journal of each House respectively. If any Bill shall not be returned by the President within ten Days (Sundays excepted) after it shall have been presented to him, the Same shall be a Law, in like Manner as if he had signed it, unless the Congress by their Adjournment prevent its Return in which Case it shall not be a Law.

When Congress sends the president a bill, he or she can sign it (in which case it becomes law) or send it back to the house in which it originated. If it is sent back, a two-thirds majority of each house must pass it again for it to become law. If the president neither signs it nor sends it back within ten days, it becomes law anyway, unless Congress adjourns in the meantime.

Clause 3: Actions on Other Matters. Every Order, Resolution, or Vote to which the Concurrence of the Senate and House of Representatives may be necessary (except on a question of Adjournment) shall be presented to the President of the United States; and before the Same shall take Effect, shall be approved by him, or being disapproved by him, shall be repassed by two thirds of the Senate and House of Representatives, according to the Rules and Limitations prescribed in the Case of a Bill.

The president must either sign or veto everything that Congress passes, except votes to adjourn and resolutions not having the force of law.

Section 8. The Powers of Congress

Clause 1: Taxing. The Congress shall have Power To lay and collect Taxes, Duties, Imposts and Excises, to pay the Debts and provide for the common Defence and general Welfare of the United States; but all Duties, Imposts and Excises shall be uniform throughout the United States;

Duties are taxes on imports and exports. Impost is a generic term for tax. Excises are taxes on the manufacture, sale, or use of goods.

Clause 2: Borrowing. To borrow Money on the credit of the United States;

Congress has the power to borrow money, which is normally carried out through the sale of U.S. treasury bonds on which interest is paid. Note that the Constitution places no limit on the amount of government borrowing.

Clause 3: Regulation of Commerce. To regulate Commerce with foreign Nations, and among the several States, and with the Indian Tribes;

This is the Commerce Clause, which gives to the Congress the power to regulate interstate and foreign trade. Much of the activity of Congress is based on this clause.

Clause 4: Naturalization and Bankruptcy. To establish a uniform Rule of Naturalization, and uniform Laws on the subject of Bankruptcies throughout the United States;

Only Congress may determine how aliens can become citizens of the United States. Congress may make laws with respect to bankruptcy.

Clause 5: Money and Standards. To coin Money, regulate the Value thereof, and of foreign Coin, and fix the Standard of Weights and Measures;

Congress mints coins and prints and circulates paper money. Congress can establish uniform measures of time, distance, weight, etc. In 1838 Congress adopted the English system of weights and measurements as our national standard.

Clause 6: Punishing Counterfeiters. To provide for the Punishment of counterfeiting the Securities and current Coin of the United States;

Congress has the power to punish those who copy American money and pass it off as real. Currently, the fine is up to $5,000 and/or imprisonment for up to fifteen years.

Clause 7: Roads and Post Offices. To establish Post Offices and post Roads;

Post roads include all routes over which mail is carried—highways, railways, waterways, and airways.

Clause 8: Patents and Copyrights. To promote the Progress of Science and useful Arts, by securing for limited Times to Authors and Inventors the exclusive Right to their respective Writings and Discoveries;

Authors' and composers' works are protected by copyrights established by copyright law. Copyrights are valid for the life of the author or composer plus fifty years. Inventors' works are protected by patents, which vary in length of protection from three and a half to seventeen years. A patent gives a person the exclusive right to control the manufacture or sale of her or his invention.

Clause 9: Lower Courts. To constitute Tribunals inferior to the supreme Court;

Congress has the authority to set up all federal courts, except the Supreme Court, and to decide what cases those courts will hear.

Clause 10: Punishment for Piracy. To define and punish Piracies and Felonies committed on the high Seas, and Offences against the Law of Nations;

Congress has the authority to prohibit the commission of certain acts outside U.S. territory and to punish certain violations of international law.

Clause 11: Declaration of War. To declare War, grant Letters of Marque and Reprisal, and make Rules concerning Captures on Land and Water;

Only Congress can declare war, although the president, as commander in chief, can make war without Congress's formal declaration. Letters of marque and reprisal authorized private parties to capture and destroy enemy ships in wartime. Since the mid-nineteenth century, international law has prohibited letters of marque and reprisal, and the United States has honored the ban.

Clause 12: The Army. To raise and support Armies, but no Appropriation of Money to that Use shall be for a longer Term than two Years;

Congress has the power to create an army; the money used to pay for it must be appropriated for no more than two-year intervals. This latter restriction gives ultimate control of the army to civilians.

Clause 13: Creation of a Navy. To provide and maintain a Navy;

This clause allows for the maintenance of a navy. In 1947 Congress created the air force.

Clause 14: Regulation of the Armed Forces. To make Rules for the Government and Regulation of the land and naval Forces;

Congress sets the rules for the military mainly by way of the Uniform Code of Military Justice, which was enacted in 1950 by Congress.

Clause 15: The Militia. To provide for calling forth the Militia to execute the Laws of the Union, suppress Insurrections and repel Invasions;

The militia is known today as the National Guard. Both Congress and the president have the authority to call the National Guard into federal service.

Clause 16: How the Militia is Organized. To provide for organizing, arming, and disciplining the Militia, and for governing such Part of them as may be employed in the Service of the United States, reserving to the States respectively, the Appointment of the Officers, and the Authority of training the Militia according to the discipline prescribed by Congress;

This clause gives Congress the power to "federalize" state militia (National Guard). When called into such service, the National Guard is subject to the same rules that Congress has set forth for the regular armed services.

Clause 17: Creation of the District of Columbia. To exercise exclusive Legislation in all Cases whatsoever, over such District (not exceeding ten Miles square) as may, by Cession of particular States, and the Acceptance of Congress, become the Seat of the Government of the United States, and to exercise like Authority over all Places purchased by the Consent of the Legislature of the State in which the Same shall be, for the Erection of Forts, Magazines, Arsenals, dock-Yards, and other needful Buildings;—And

Congress established the District of Columbia as the national capital in 1791. Virginia and Maryland had granted land for the District, but Virginia's grant was returned because it was believed it would not be needed. Today, the District is sixty-nine miles square.

Clause 18: The Elastic Clause. To make all Laws which shall be necessary and proper for carrying into Execution the foregoing Powers, and all other Powers vested by this Constitution in the Government of the United States, or in any Department or Officer thereof.

This clause—the Necessary and Proper Clause, or the Elastic Clause—grants no specific powers, and thus it can be stretched to fit different circumstances. It has allowed Congress to adapt the government to changing needs and times.

Section 9. The Powers Denied to Congress

Clause 1: Question of Slavery. The Migration or Importation of such Persons as any of the States now existing shall think proper to admit, shall not be prohibited by the Congress prior to the Year one thousand eight hundred and eight, but a Tax or duty may be imposed on such Importation, not exceeding ten dollars for each Person.

"Persons" referred to slaves. Congress outlawed the slave trade in 1808.

Clause 2: Habeas Corpus.   The privilege of the Writ of Habeas Corpus shall not be suspended, unless when in Cases of Rebellion or Invasion the public Safety may require it.

A writ of habeas corpus is a court order directing a sheriff or other public officer who is detaining another person to "produce the body" of the detainee so the court can assess the legality of the detention.

Clause 3: Special Bills.   No Bill of Attainder or ex post facto Law shall be passed.

A bill of attainder is a law that inflicts punishment without a trial. An ex post facto law is a law that inflicts punishment for an act that was not illegal when it was committed.

Clause 4: Direct Taxes.   [No Capitation, or other direct, Tax shall be laid, unless in Proportion to the Census or Enumeration herein before directed to be taken.][6]

A capitation is a tax on a person. A direct tax is a tax paid directly to the government, such as a property tax. This clause was intended to prevent Congress from levying a tax on slaves per person and thereby taxing slavery out of existence.

Clause 5: Export Taxes.   No Tax or Duty shall be laid on Articles exported from any State.

Congress may not tax any goods sold from one state to another or from one state to a foreign country. (Congress does have the power to tax goods that are bought from other countries, however.)

Clause 6: Interstate Commerce.   No Preference shall be given by any Regulation of Commerce or Revenue to the Ports of one State over those of another: nor shall Vessels bound to, or from, one

State, be obliged to enter, clear, or pay Duties in another.

Congress may not treat different ports within the United States differently in terms of taxing and commerce powers. Congress may not tax goods sent from one state to another. Finally, Congress may not give one state's port a legal advantage over those of another state.

Clause 7: Treasury Withdrawals.   No Money shall be drawn from the Treasury, but in Consequence of Appropriations made by Law; and a regular Statement and Account of the Receipts and Expenditures of all public Money shall be published from time to time.

Federal funds can be spent only as Congress authorizes. This is a significant check on the president's power.

Clause 8: Titles of Nobility.   No Title of Nobility shall be granted by the United States: And no Person holding any Office of Profit or Trust under them, shall, without the Consent of the Congress, accept of any present, Emolument, Office, or Title, of any kind whatever, from any King, Prince, or foreign State.

No person in the United States may be bestowed a title of nobility such as a duke or duchess. This clause also discourages bribery of American officials by foreign governments.

Section 10. Those Powers Denied to the States

Clause 1: Treaties and Coinage.   No State shall enter into any Treaty, Alliance, or Confederation; grant Letters of Marque and Reprisal; coin Money; emit Bills of Credit; make any Thing but gold and silver Coin a Tender in Payment of Debts; pass any Bill of Attainder, ex post facto Law, or Law impairing the Obligation of Contracts, or grant any Title of Nobility.

Prohibiting state laws "impairing the Obligation of Contracts" was intended to protect creditors. (Shays's Rebellion—an attempt to prevent courts from giving effect to creditors' legal actions against debtors—occurred only one year before the Constitution was written.)

Clause 2: Duties and Imposts.   No State shall, without the Consent of the Congress, lay any Im-

---

[6]Modified by the Sixteenth Amendment.

ports or Duties on Imports or Exports, except what may be absolutely necessary for executing its inspection Laws; and the net Produce of all Duties and Imposts, laid by any State on Imports or Exports, shall be for the Use of the Treasury of the United States; and all such Laws shall be subject to the Revision and Controul of the Congress.

Only Congress can tax imports. Further, the states cannot tax exports.

Clause 3: War. No State shall, without the Consent of Congress, lay any Duty of Tonnage, keep Troops, or Ships of War in time of Peace, enter into any Agreement or Compact with another State, or with a foreign Power or engage in War, unless actually invaded, or in such imminent Danger as will not admit of delay.

A duty of tonnage is a tax on ships according to their cargo capacity. No states may effectively tax ships according to their cargo unless Congress agrees. Additionally, this clause forbids any state to keep troops or warships during peacetime or to make a compact with another state or foreign nation unless Congress so agrees. States can, in contrast, maintain a militia, but its use has to be limited to internal disorders that occur within a state—unless, of course, the militia is called into federal service.

Article II. (Executive Branch)

Section 1. The Nature and Scope of Presidential Power

Clause 1: Four-Year Term. The executive Power shall be vested in a President of the United States of America. He shall hold his Office during the Term of four Years, and, together with the Vice President, chosen for the same Term, be elected, as follows.

The president has the power to carry out laws made by Congress, called the executive power. He or she serves in office for a four-year term after election. The Twenty-second Amendment limits the number of times a person may be elected president.

Clause 2: Choosing Electors From Each State. Each State shall appoint, in such Manner as the Legislature thereof may direct, a Number of Electors, equal to the whole Number of Senators and Representatives to which the State may be entitled in the Congress; but no Senator or Representative, or Person holding an Office of Trust or Profit under the United States, shall be appointed an Elector.

The "Electors" are more commonly known as the "electoral college." The president is elected by electors—that is, representatives chosen by the people—rather than by the people directly.

Clause 3: The Former System of Elections. [The Electors shall meet in their respective States, and vote by Ballot for two Persons, of whom one at least shall not be an Inhabitant of the same State with themselves. And they shall make a List of all the Persons voted for, and of the Number of Votes for each; which List they shall sign and certify, and transmit sealed to the Seat of the Government of the United States, directed to the President of the Senate. The President of the Senate shall, in the Presence of the Senate and House of Representatives, open all the Certificates, and the Votes shall then be counted. The Person having the greatest Number of Votes shall be the President, if such Number be a Majority of the whole Number of Electors appointed; and if there be more than one who have such Majority, and have an equal Number of Votes, then the House of Representatives shall immediately chuse by Ballot one of them for President; and if no Person have a Majority, then from the five highest on the List the said House shall in like Manner chuse the President. But in chusing the President, the Votes shall be taken by States, the Representation from each State having one Vote; A quorum for this Purpose shall consist of a Member or Members from two thirds of the States, and a Majority of all the States shall be necessary to a Choice. In every Case, after the Choice of the President, the Person having the greater Number of Votes of the Electors shall be the Vice President. But if there should remain two or more who have equal Votes, the Senate shall chuse from them by Ballot the Vice President.][7]

The original method of selecting the president and vice-president was replaced by the Twelfth Amendment. Ap-

---

[7]Changed by the Twelfth Amendment.

parently, the framers did not anticipate the rise of political parties and the development of primaries and conventions.

Clause 4: The Time of Elections. The Congress may determine the Time of chusing the Electors, and the Day on which they shall give their Votes; which Day shall be the same throughout the United States.

Congress set the Tuesday after the first Monday in November every fourth year as the date for choosing electors. The electors cast their votes on the Monday after the second Wednesday in December of that year.

Clause 5: Qualifications for President. No person except a natural born Citizen, or a Citizen of the United States, at the time of the Adoption of this Constitution, shall be eligible to the Office of President; neither shall any Person be eligible to that Office who shall not have attained to the Age of thirty five Years, and been fourteen Years a Resident within the United States.

The president must be a natural-born citizen, be at least thirty-five years of age when taking office, and have been a resident within the United States for at least fourteen years.

Clause 6: Succession of the Vice President. [In Case of the Removal of the President from Office, or of his Death, Resignation or Inability to discharge the Powers and Duties of the said Office, the same shall devolve on the Vice President, and the Congress may by Law provide for the Case of Removal, Death, Resignation or Inability, both of the President and Vice President, declaring what Officer shall then act as President, and such Officer shall act accordingly, until the Disability be removed, or a President shall be elected.][8]

This former section provided for the method by which the vice-president was to succeed to the presidency, but its wording is ambiguous. It was replaced by the Twenty-fifth Amendment.

Clause 7: The President's Salary. The President shall, at stated Times, receive for his Services, a Compensation, which shall neither be encreased

nor diminished during the Period for which he shall have been elected, and he shall not receive within that Period any other Emolument from the United States, or any of them.

The president maintains the same salary during each four-year term. Moreover, she or he may not receive additional cash payments from the government. Originally set at $25,000 per year, it is currently $200,000 a year plus a $50,000 taxable expense account.

Clause 8: The Oath of Office. Before he enter on the Execution of his Office, he shall take the following Oath or Affirmation: "I do solemnly swear (or affirm) that I will faithfully execute the Office of President of the United States, and will to the best of my Ability, preserve, protect and defend the Constitution of the United States."

The president is "sworn in" prior to beginning the duties of the office. Currently, the taking of the oath of office occurs on January 20, following the November election. The ceremony is called the inauguration. The oath of office is administered by the chief justice of the United States Supreme Court.

Section 2. Powers of the President

Clause 1: Commander in Chief. The President shall be Commander in Chief of the Army and Navy of the United States, and of the Militia of the several States, when called into the actual Service of the United States; he may require the Opinion, in writing, of the principal Officer in each of the executive Departments, upon any Subject relating to the Duties of their respective Offices, and he shall have Power to grant Reprieves and Pardons for Offences against the United States, except in Cases of Impeachment.

The armed forces are placed under civilian control because the president is a civilian, but still commander in chief of the military. The president may ask for the help of the heads of each of the executive departments (thereby creating the Cabinet). The Cabinet members are chosen by the president with the consent of the Senate, but they can be removed without Senate approval.

The president's clemency powers extend only to federal cases. In those cases, he or she may grant a full or conditional pardon, or reduce a prison term or fine.

---

[8]Modified by the Twenty-fifth Amendment.

Clause 2: Treaties and Appointment. He shall have Power, by and with the Advice and Consent of the Senate, to make Treaties, provided two thirds of the Senators present concur; and he shall nominate, and by and with the Advice and Consent of the Senate, shall appoint Ambassadors, other public Ministers and Consuls, Judges of the supreme Court, and all other Officers of the United States, whose Appointments are not herein otherwise provided for, and which shall be established by Law; but the Congress may by Law vest the Appointment of such inferior Officers, as they think proper, in the President alone, in the Courts of Law, or in the Heads of Departments.

Many of the major powers of the president are identified in this clause, including the power to make treaties with foreign governments (with the approval of the Senate by a two-thirds vote) and the power to appoint ambassadors, Supreme Court justices, and other government officials. Most such appointments require Senate approval.

Clause 3: Vacancies. The President shall have Power to fill up all Vacancies that may happen during the Recess of the Senate, by granting Commissions which shall expire at the end of their next Session.

The president has the power to appoint temporary officials to fill vacant federal offices without Senate approval if the Congress is not in session. Such appointments expire automatically at the end of Congress's next term.

Section 3. Duties of the President

He shall from time to time give to the Congress Information of the State of the Union, and recommend to their Consideration such Measures as he shall judge necessary and expedient; he may, on extraordinary Occasions, convene both Houses, or either of them, and in Case of Disagreement between them, with Respect to the Time of Adjournment, he may adjourn them to such Time as he shall think proper; he shall receive Ambassadors and other public Ministers; he shall take Care that the Laws be faithfully executed, and shall Commission all the Officers of the United States.

Annually, the president reports on the state of the union to Congress, recommends legislative measures, and proposes a federal budget. The State of the Union speech is

a statement not only to Congress but also to the American people. After it is given, the president proposes a federal budget and presents an economic report. At any time he or she so chooses, the president may send special messages to Congress while it is in session. The president has the power to call special sessions, to adjourn Congress when its two houses do not agree for that purpose, to receive diplomatic representatives of other governments, and to ensure the proper execution of all federal laws. The president further has the ability to empower federal officers to hold their positions and to perform their duties.

Section 4. Impeachment

The President, Vice President and all civil Officers of the United States, shall be removed from Office on Impeachment for, and Conviction of, Treason, Bribery, or other high Crimes and Misdemeanors.

Treason denotes giving aid to the nation's enemies. The definition of high crimes and misdemeanors is usually given as serious abuses of political power. In either case, the president or vice-president may be accused by the House (called an impeachment) and then removed from office if convicted by the Senate. (Note that impeachment does not mean removal, but rather the state of being accused of treason or high crimes and misdemeanors.)

Article III. (Judicial Branch)

Section 1. Judicial Powers, Courts, and Judges

The judicial Power of the United States, shall be vested in one supreme Court, and in such inferior Courts as the Congress may from time to time ordain and establish. The Judges, both of the supreme and inferior Courts, shall hold their Offices during good Behaviour, and shall, at stated Times, receive for their Services a Compensation, which shall not be diminished during their Continuance in Office.

The Supreme Court is vested with judicial power, as are the lower federal courts that Congress creates. Federal judges serve in their offices for life unless they are impeached and convicted by Congress. The payment of federal judges may not be reduced during their time in office.

Section 2. Jurisdiction

Clause 1: Cases Under Federal Jurisdiction. The judicial Power shall extend to all Cases, in Law and Equity, arising under this Constitution, the Laws of the United States, and Treaties made, or which shall be made, under their Authority;—to all Cases affecting Ambassadors, other public Ministers and Consuls;—to all Cases of admiralty and maritime Jurisdiction;—to Controversies to which the United States shall be a Party;—to Controversies between two or more States; [—between a State and Citizens of another State;—]⁹ between Citizens of different States;—between Citizens of the same State claiming Lands under Grants of different States, [and between a State, or the Citizens thereof, and foreign States, Citizens or Subjects.]¹⁰

The federal courts take on cases that concern the meaning of the U.S. Constitution, all federal laws, and treaties. They also can take on cases involving citizens of different states and citizens of foreign nations.

Clause 2: Cases for the Supreme Court.   In all Cases affecting Ambassadors, other public Ministers and Consuls, and those in which a State shall be a Party, the supreme Court shall have original Jurisdiction. In all the other Cases before mentioned, the supreme Court shall have appellate Jurisdiction, both as to Law and Fact, with such Exceptions, and under such Regulations as the Congress shall make.

In a limited number of situations, the Supreme Court acts as a trial court and has original jurisdiction. These cases involve a representative from another country or involve a state. In all other situations, the cases must first be tried in the lower courts and then can be appealed to the Supreme Court. Congress may, however, make exceptions. Today the Supreme Court acts as a trial court of first instance on rare occasions.

Clause 3: The Conduct of Trials.   The Trial of all Crimes, except in Cases of Impeachment, shall be by Jury; and such Trial shall be held in the State where the said Crimes shall have been committed; but when not committed within any State, the Trial shall be at such Place or Places as the Congress may by Law have directed.

Any person accused of a federal crime is granted the right to a trial by jury in a federal court in that state in which

---

⁹Modified by the Eleventh Amendment.
¹⁰Modified by the Eleventh Amendment.

the crime was committed. Trials of impeachment are an exception.

Section 3. Treason
Clause 1: The Definition of Treason.   Treason against the United States, shall consist only in levying War against them, or, in adhering to their Enemies, giving them Aid and Comfort. No Person shall be convicted of Treason unless on the Testimony of two Witnesses to the same overt Act, or on Confession in open Court.

Treason is the making of war against the United States or giving aid to its enemies.

Clause 2: Punishment.   The Congress shall have Power to declare the Punishment of Treason, but no Attainder of Treason shall work Corruption of Blood, or Forfeiture except during the Life of the Person attainted.

Congress has provided that the punishment for treason range from a minimum of five years in prison and/or a $10,000 fine to a maximum of death. "No Attainder of Treason shall work Corruption of Blood" prohibits punishment of the traitor's heirs.

Article IV. (Relations Among the States)

Section 1. Full Faith and Credit
Full Faith and Credit shall be given in each State to the public Acts, Records, and judicial Proceedings of every other State. And the Congress may by general Laws prescribe the Manner in which such Acts, Records and Proceedings shall be proved, and the Effect thereof.

All states are required to respect one another's laws, records, and lawful decisions. There are exceptions, however. A state does not have to enforce another state's criminal code. Nor does it have to recognize another state's grant of a divorce if the person obtaining the divorce did not establish legal residence in the state in which it was given.

Section 2. Treatment of Citizens
Clause 1: Privileges and Immunities.   The Citizens of each State shall be entitled to all Privileges and Immunities of Citizens in the several States.

A citizen of a state has the same rights and privileges as the citizens of another state in which he or she happens to be.

Clause 2: Extradition. A Person charged in any State with Treason, Felony, or other Crime, who shall flee from Justice, and be found in another State, shall on Demand of the executive Authority of the State from which he fled, be delivered up, to be removed to the State having Jurisdiction of the Crime.

Any person accused of a crime who flees to another state must be returned to the state in which the crime occurred.

Clause 3: Fugitive Slaves. [No Person held to Service or Labour in one State, under the Laws thereof, escaping into another, shall, in Consequence of any Law or Regulation therein, be discharged from such Service or Labour, but shall be delivered up on Claim of the Party to whom such Service or Labour may be due.][11]

This clause was struck down by the Thirteenth Amendment, which abolished slavery in 1865.

Section 3. Admission of States
Clause 1: The Process. New States may be admitted by the Congress into this Union; but no new State shall be formed or erected within the Jurisdiction of any other State; nor any State be formed by the Junction of two or more States, or Parts of States, without the Consent of the Legislatures of the States concerned as well as of the Congress.

Only Congress has the power to admit new states to the union. No state may be created by taking territory from an existing state unless the state's legislature so consents.

Clause 2: Public Land. The Congress shall have Power to dispose of and make all needful Rules and Regulations respecting the Territory or other Property belonging to the United States; and nothing in this Constitution shall be so construed as to Prejudice any Claims of the United States, or of any particular State.

---

[11]Repealed by the Thirteenth Amendment.

The federal government has the exclusive right to administer federal government public lands.

Section 4. Republican Form of Government
The United States shall guarantee to every State in this Union a Republican Form of Government, and shall protect each of them against Invasion; and on Application of the Legislature, or of the Executive (when the Legislature cannot be convened) against domestic Violence.

Each state is promised a form of government in which the people elect their representatives, called a republican form. The federal government is bound to protect states against any attack by foreigners or during times of trouble within a state.

Article V. (Methods of Amendment)
The Congress, whenever two thirds of both Houses shall deem it necessary, shall propose Amendments to this Constitution, or on the Application of the Legislatures of two thirds of the several States, shall call a Convention for proposing Amendments, which, in either Case, shall be valid to all Intents and Purposes, as Part of this Constitution, when ratified by the Legislatures of three fourths of the several States, or by Conventions in three fourths thereof, as the one or the other Mode of Ratification may be proposed by the Congress; Provided that no Amendment which may be made prior to the Year One thousand eight hundred and eight shall in any Manner affect the first and fourth Clauses in the Ninth Section of the First Article; and that no State, without its Consent, shall be deprived of its equal Suffrage in the Senate.

Articles may be proposed in either of two ways: a two-thirds vote of each house (Congress) or at the request of two-thirds of the states. Ratification of amendments may be carried out in two ways: by the legislatures of three-fourths of the states or by the voters in three-fourths of the states. No state may be denied equal representation in the Senate.

Article VI. (National Supremacy)
Clause 1: Existing Obligations. All Debts contracted and Engagements entered into, before the Adoption of this Constitution shall be as valid

against the United States under this Constitution, as under the Confederation.

During the Revolutionary War and the years of the Confederation, Congress borrowed large sums. This clause pledged that the new federal government would assume those financial obligations.

Clause 2: Supreme Law of the Land. This Constitution, and the Laws of the United States which shall be made in Pursuance thereof; and all Treaties made, or which shall be made, under the Authority of the United States, shall be the supreme Law of the Land; and the Judges in every State shall be bound thereby, any Thing in the Constitution or Laws of any State to the Contrary notwithstanding.

This is typically called the Supremacy Clause; it declares that federal law takes precedence over all forms of state law. No government, at the local or state level, may make or enforce any law that conflicts with any provision of the Constitution, acts of Congress, treaties, or other rules and regulations issued by the president and his or her subordinates in the executive branch of the federal government.

Clause 3: Oath of Office. The Senators and Representatives before mentioned, and the Members of the several State Legislatures, and all executive and judicial Officers, both of the United States and of the several States, shall be bound by Oath or Affirmation, to support this Constitution; but no religious Test shall ever be required as a Qualification to any Office or public Trust under the United States.

Every federal and state official must take an oath of office promising to support the U.S. Constitution. Religion may not be used as a qualification to serve in any federal office.

Article VII. (Ratification)

The Ratification of the Conventions of nine States shall, be sufficient for the Establishment of this Constitution between the States so ratifying the Same.

Nine states were required to ratify the Constitution. Delaware was the first and New Hampshire the ninth.

Done in Convention by the Unanimous Consent of the States present the Seventeenth Day of September in the Year of our Lord one thousand seven hundred and Eighty seven and of the Independence of the United States of America the Twelfth. In witness whereof we have hereunto subscribed our Names,

Go. WASHINGTON
Presid't. and deputy from Virginia

Attest
WILLIAM JACKSON
Secretary

DELAWARE
Geo. Read
Gunning Bedfordjun
John Dickinson
Richard Basset
Jaco. Broom

MASSACHUSETTS
Nathaniel Gorham
Rufus King

CONNECTICUT
Wm. Saml. Johnson
Roger Sherman

NEW YORK
Alexander Hamilton

NEW JERSEY
Wh. Livingston
David Brearley.
Wm. Paterson.
Jona. Dayton

PENNSYLVANIA
B. Franklin
Thomas Mifflin
Robt. Morris
Geo. Clymer
Thos. FitzSimons
Jared Ingersoll
James Wilson.
Gouv. Morris

NEW HAMPSHIRE
John Langdon
Nicholas Gilman

MARYLAND
James McHenry
Dan of St. Thos.
　Jenifer
Danl. Carroll.

VIRGINIA
John Blair
James Madison Jr.

NORTH CAROLINA
Wm. Blount
Richd. Dobbs Spaight.
Hu. Williamson

SOUTH CAROLINA
J. Rutledge
Charles Cotesworth
　Pinckney
Charles Pinckney
Pierce Butler.

GEORGIA
William Few
Abr. Baldwin

Articles in addition to, and amendment of the Constitution of the United States of America, proposed by Congress and ratified by the Legislatures of the several states, pursuant to the Fifth Article of the original Constitution.

Amendments to the Constitution of the United States

The Bill of Rights[12]

Amendment I.
Religion, Speech, Assembly, and Politics

Congress shall make no law respecting an establishment of religion, or prohibiting the free exercise thereof; or abridging the freedom of speech, or of the press; or the right of the people peaceably to assembly, and to petition the Government for a redress of grievances.

Congress may not create an official church or enact laws limiting the freedom of religion, speech, the press, assembly, and petition. These guarantees, like the others in the Bill of Rights (the first ten amendments), are not absolute—each may be exercised only with regard to the rights of other persons.

Amendment II.
Militia and the Right to Bear Arms

A well regulated Militia, being necessary to the security of a free State, the right of the people to keep and bear Arms, shall not be infringed.

To protect itself, each state has the right to maintain a volunteer armed force. States and the federal government regulate the possession and use of firearms by individuals.

Amendment III.
The Quartering of Soldiers

No Soldier shall, in time of peace be quartered in any house, without the consent of the Owner, nor in time of war, but in a manner to be prescribed by law.

---

[12]On September 25, 1789, Congress transmitted to the state legislatures twelve proposed amendments, two of which, having to do with Congressional representation and Congressional pay, were not adopted. The remaining ten amendments became the Bill of Rights.

Before the Revolutionary War, it had been common British practice to quarter soldiers in colonists' homes. Military troops do not have the power to take over private houses during peacetime.

Amendment IV.
Searches and Seizures

The right of the people to be secure in their persons, houses, papers, and effects, against unreasonable searches and seizures, shall not be violated, and no Warrants shall issue, but upon probable cause, supported by Oath or affirmation, and particularly describing the place to be searched, and the persons or things to be seized.

Here the word warrant *means "justification" and refers to a document issued by a magistrate or judge indicating the name, address, and possible offense committed. Anyone asking for the warrant, such as a police officer, must be able to convince the magistrate or judge that an offense probably has been committed.*

Amendment V.
Grand Juries, Self-incrimination, Double Jeopardy, Due Process, and Eminent Domain

No person shall be held to answer for a capital, or otherwise infamous crime, unless on a presentment or indictment of a Grand Jury, except in cases arising in the land or naval forces, or in the Militia, when in actual service in time of War or public danger; nor shall any person be subject for the same offence to be twice put in jeopardy of life or limb; nor shall be compelled in any criminal case to be a witness against himself, nor be deprived of life, liberty, or property, without due process of law; nor shall private property be taken for public use, without just compensation.

There are two types of juries. A grand jury considers physical evidence and the testimony of witnesses, and decides whether there is sufficient reason to bring a case to trial. A petit jury hears the case at trial and decides it. "For the same offence to be twice put in jeopardy of life or limb" means to be tried twice for the same crime. A person may not be tried for the same crime twice or forced to give evidence against herself or himself. No person's right to life, liberty, or property may be taken away except by lawful means, called the due process of law. Private property taken for use in public purposes must be paid for by the government.

Amendment VI.
Criminal Court Procedures

In all criminal prosecutions, the accused shall enjoy the right to a speedy and public trial, by an impartial jury of the State and district wherein the crime shall have been committed, which district shall have been previously ascertained by law, and to be informed of the nature and cause of the accusation; to be confronted with the witnesses against him; to have compulsory process for obtaining witnesses in his favor, and to have the assistance of counsel for his defence.

Any person accused of a crime has the right to a fair and public trial by a jury in the state in which the crime took place. The charges against that person must be so indicated. Any accused person has the right to a lawyer to defend him or her and to question those who testify against him or her, as well as the right to call people to speak in his or her favor at trial.

Amendment VII.
Trial by Jury in Civil Cases

In Suits at common law, where the value in controversy shall exceed twenty dollars, the right of trial by jury shall be preserved, and no fact tried by jury, shall be otherwise re-examined in any Court of the United States, than according to the rules of the common law.

A jury trial may be requested by either party in a dispute in any case involving more than $20. If both parties agree to a trial by a judge without a jury, the right to a jury trial may be put aside.

Amendment VIII.
Bail, Cruel and Unusual Punishment

Excessive bail shall not be required, nor excessive fines imposed, nor cruel and unusual punishments inflicted.

Bail is that amount of money that a person accused of a crime may be required to deposit with the court as a guarantee that she or he will appear in court when requested. The amount of bail required or the fine imposed as pun-

ishment for a crime must be reasonable compared with the seriousness of the crime involved. Any punishment judged to be too harsh or too severe for a crime shall be prohibited.

Amendment IX.
The Rights Retained by the People

The enumeration in the Constitution, of certain rights, shall not be construed to deny or disparage others retained by the people.

Many civil rights that are not explicitly enumerated in the Constitution are still hailed by the people.

Amendment X.
Reserved Powers of the States

The powers not delegated to the United States by the Constitution, nor prohibited by it to the States, are reserved to the States respectively, or to the people.

Those powers not delegated by the Constitution to the federal government or expressly denied to the states belong to the states and to the people. This clause in essence allows the states to pass laws under its "police powers."

Amendment XI
(Ratified on February 7, 1795).
Suits Against States

The Judicial power of the United States shall not be construed to extend to any suit in law or equity, commenced or prosecuted against one of the United States by Citizens of another State, or by Citizens or Subjects of any Foreign State.

This amendment has been interpreted to mean that a state cannot be sued in federal court by one of its citizens, by a citizen of another state, or by a foreign country.

Amendment XII
(Ratified on June 15, 1804).
Election of the President

The Electors shall meet in their respective states, and vote by ballot for President and Vice-President, one of whom, at least, shall not be an inhabitant of the same State with themselves; they shall name in their ballots the person voted for as President, and in distinct ballots the person voted for as Vice-

President, and they shall make distinct lists of all persons voted for as President, and of all persons voted for as Vice-President, and of the number of votes for each, which lists they shall sign and certify, and transmit sealed to the seat of the government of the United States, directed to the President of the Senate;—The President of the Senate shall, in the presence of the Senate and House of Representatives, open all the certificates and the votes shall then be counted;—The person having the greatest number of votes for President, shall be the President, if such number be a majority of the whole number of Electors appointed; and if no person have such majority, then from the persons having the highest numbers not exceeding three on the list of those voted for as President, the House of Representatives shall choose immediately, by ballot, the President. But in choosing the President, the votes shall be taken by States, the representation from each State having one vote; a quorum for this purpose shall consist of a member or members from two-thirds of the States, and a majority of all States shall be necessary to a choice. [And if the House of Representatives shall not choose a President whenever the right of choice shall devolve upon them, before the fourth day of March next following, then the Vice-President shall act as President, as in the case of the death or other constitutional disability of the President.][13]—The person having the greatest number of votes as Vice-President, shall be the Vice-President, if such number be a majority of the whole number of Electors appointed, and if no person have a majority, then from the two highest numbers on the list, the Senate shall choose the Vice President; a quorum for the purpose shall consist of two-thirds of the whole number of Senators, and a majority of the whole number shall be necessary to a choice. But no person constitutionally ineligible to the office of President shall be eligible to that of Vice-President of the United States.

The original procedure set out for the election of president and vice-president in Article II, Section 1, resulted in a tie in 1800 between Thomas Jefferson and Aaron Burr. It was not until the next year that the House of Representatives chose Jefferson to be president. This amendment changed the procedure by providing for separate ballots for president and vice-president.

---

[13]Changed by the Twentieth Amendment.

Amendment XIII
(Ratified on December 6, 1865).
Prohibition of Slavery

Section 1.
Neither slavery nor involuntary servitude, except as a punishment for crime whereof the party shall have been duly convicted, shall exist within the United States, or any place subject to their jurisdiction.

Some slaves had been freed during the Civil War. This amendment freed the others and abolished slavery.

Section 2.
Congress shall have power to enforce this article by appropriate legislation.

Amendment XIV
(Ratified on July 9, 1868).
Citizenship, Due Process, and Equal Protection of the Laws

Section 1.
All persons born or naturalized in the United States, and subject to the jurisdiction thereof, are citizens of the United States and of the State wherein they reside. No State shall make or enforce any law which shall abridge the privileges or immunities of citizens of the United States; nor shall any State deprive any person of life, liberty, or property, without due process of law; nor deny to any person within its jurisdiction the equal protection of the laws.

Under this provision, states cannot make or enforce laws that take away rights given to all citizens by the federal government. States cannot act unfairly or arbitrarily toward, or discriminate against, any person.

Section 2.
Representatives shall be apportioned among the several States according to their respective numbers, counting the whole number of persons in each State, excluding Indians not taxed. But when the right to vote at any election for the choice of electors for President and Vice President of the United States, Representatives in Congress, the Executive and Judicial officers of a State, or the members of the Legislature thereof, is denied to any of the male

inhabitants of such State, being [twenty-one][14] years of age, and citizens of the United States, or in any way abridged, except for participation in rebellion, or other crime, the basis of representation therein shall be reduced in the proportion which the number of such male citizens shall bear to the whole number of male citizens twenty-one years of age in such State.

Section 3.

No person shall be a Senator or Representative in Congress, or elector of President and Vice President, or hold any office, civil or military, under the United States, or under any State, who having previously taken an oath, as a member of Congress, or as an officer of the United States, or as a member of any State legislature, or as an executive or judicial officer of any State, to support the Constitution of the United States, shall have engaged in insurrection or rebellion against the same, or given aid or comfort to the enemies thereof. But Congress may by a vote of two-thirds of each House, remove such disability.

This provision forbade former state or federal government officials who had acted in support of the Confederacy during the Civil War to hold office again. It limited the president's power to pardon those persons. Congress removed this "disability" in 1898.

Section 4.

The validity of the public debt of the United States, authorized by law, including debts incurred for payment of pensions and bounties for services in suppressing insurrection or rebellion, shall not be questioned. But neither the United States nor any State shall assume or pay any debt or obligation incurred in aid of insurrection or rebellion against the United States, or any claim for the loss or emancipation of any slave, but all such debts, obligations and claims shall be held illegal and void.

Section 5.

The Congress shall have power to enforce, by appropriate legislation, the provisions of this article.

---

[14]Changed by the Twenty-sixth Amendment.

Amendment XV
(Ratified on February 3, 1870).
The Right to Vote

Section 1.

The right of citizens of the United States to vote shall not be denied or abridged by the United States or by any State on account of race, color, or previous condition of servitude.

No citizen can be refused the right to vote simply because of race or color or because that person was once a slave.

Section 2.

The Congress shall have power to enforce this article by appropriate legislation.

Amendment XVI
(Ratified on February 3, 1913).
Income Taxes

The Congress shall have power to lay and collect taxes on incomes, from whatever source derived, without apportionment among the several States, and without regard to any census or enumeration.

This amendment allows Congress to tax income without sharing the revenue so obtained with the states according to their population.

Amendment XVII
(Ratified on April 8, 1913).
The Popular Election of Senators

The Senate of the United States shall be composed of two Senators from each State, elected by the people thereof, for six years; and each Senator shall have one vote. The electors in each State shall have the qualifications requisite for electors of the most numerous branch of the State legislatures.

When vacancies happen in the representation of any State in the Senate, the executive authority of such State shall issue writs of election to fill such vacancies: *Provided,* That the legislature of any State may empower the executive thereof to make temporary appointments until the people fill the vacancies by election as the legislature may direct.

This amendment shall not be so construed as to affect the election or term of any Senator chosen before it becomes valid as part of the Constitution.

This amendment modified portions of Article I, Section 3, that related to election of senators. Senators are now elected by the voters in each state directly. When a vacancy occurs, either the state may fill the vacancy by a special election, or the governor of the state involved may appoint someone to fill the seat until the next election.

Amendment XVIII
(Ratified on January 16, 1919).
Prohibition.

Section 1.
After one year from the ratification of this article the manufacture, sale, or transportation of intoxicating liquors within, the importation thereof into, or the exportation thereof from the United States and all territory subject to the jurisdiction thereof for beverage purposes is hereby prohibited.

Section 2.
The Congress and the several States shall have concurrent power to enforce this article by appropriate legislation.

Section 3.
This article shall be inoperative unless it shall have been ratified as an amendment to the Constitution by the legislatures of the several States, as provided in the Constitution, within seven years from the date of the submission hereof to the States by the Congress.[15]

This amendment made it illegal to manufacture, sell, and transport alcoholic beverages in the United States. It was ended by the Twenty-first Amendment.

Amendment XIX
(Ratified on August 18, 1920).
Women's Right to Vote.

The right of citizens of the United States to vote shall not be denied or abridged by the United States or by any State on account of sex.

Congress shall have power to enforce this article by appropriate legislation.

Women were given the right to vote by this amendment, and Congress was given the power to enforce this right.

Amendment XX
(Ratified on January 23, 1933).
The Lame Duck Amendment

Section 1.
The terms of the President and Vice President shall end at noon on the 20th day of January, and the terms of Senators and Representatives at noon on the 3d day of January, of the years in which such terms would have ended if this article had not been ratified; and the terms of their successors shall then begin.

This amendment modified Article I, Section 4, Clause 2, and other provisions relating to the president in the Twelfth Amendment. The taking of the Oath of Office was moved from March 4 to January 20.

Section 2.
The Congress shall assemble at least once in every year, and such meeting shall begin at noon on the 3d day of January, unless they shall by law appoint a different day.

Congress changed the beginning of its term to January 3. The reason the Twentieth Amendment is called the Lame Duck Amendment is because it shortens the time between when a member of Congress is defeated for reelection and when he or she leaves office.

Section 3.
If, at the time fixed for the beginning of the term of the President, the President elect shall have died, the Vice President elect shall become President. If a President shall not have been chosen before the time fixed for the beginning of his term, or if the President elect shall have failed to qualify, then the

---

[15]The Eighteenth Amendment was repealed by the Twenty-first Amendment.

Vice President elect shall act as President until a President shall have qualified; and the Congress may by law provide for the case wherein neither a President elect nor a Vice President elect shall have qualified, declaring who shall then act as President, or the manner in which one who is to act shall be selected, and such person shall act accordingly until a President or Vice President shall have qualified.

This part of the amendment deals with problem areas left ambiguous by Article II and the Twelfth Amendment. If the president dies before January 20 or fails to qualify for office, the presidency is to be filled in the order given in this section.

Section 4.

The Congress may by law provide for the case of the death of any of the persons from whom the House of Representatives may choose a President whenever the rights of choice shall have devolved upon them, and for the case of the death of any of the persons from whom the Senate may choose a Vice President whenever the right of choice shall have devolved upon them.

Congress has never created legislation subsequent to this section.

Section 5.

Sections 1 and 2 shall take effect on the 15th day of October following the ratification of this article.

Section 6.

This article shall be inoperative unless it shall have been ratified as an amendment to the Constitution by the legislatures of three-fourths of the several States within seven years from the date of its submission.

Amendment XXI
(Ratified on December 5, 1933).
The Repeal of Prohibition.

Section 1.

The eighteenth article of amendment to the Constitution of the United States is hereby repealed.

Section 2.

The transportation or importation into any State, Territory, or possession of the United States for de-

livery or use therein of intoxicating liquors, in violation of the laws thereof, is hereby prohibited.

Section 3.

This article shall be inoperative unless it shall have been ratified as an amendment to the Constitution by conventions in the several States, as provided in the Constitution, within seven years from the date of the submission hereof to the States by the Congress.

The amendment repealed the Eighteenth Amendment but did not make alcoholic beverages legal everywhere. Rather, they remained illegal in any state that so designated them. Many such "dry" states existed for a number of years after 1933. Today, there are still "dry" counties within the United States, in which alcoholic beverages are illegal.

Amendment XXII
(Ratified on February 27, 1951).
Limitation of Presidential Terms.

Section 1.

No person shall be elected to the office of the President more than twice, and no person who has held the office of President, or acted as President, for more than two years of a term to which some other person was elected President shall be elected to the office of President more than once. But this Article shall not apply to any person holding the office of President when this Article was proposed by the Congress, and shall not prevent any person who may be holding the office of President, or acting as President, during the term within which this Article becomes operative from holding the office of President or acting as President during the remainder of such term.

Section 2.

This article shall be inoperative unless it shall have been ratified as an amendment to the Constitution by the legislatures of three-fourths of the several States within seven years from the date of its submission to the States by the Congress.

No president may serve more than two elected terms. If, however, a president has succeeded to the office after the halfway point of a term in which another president was originally elected, then that president may serve for more than eight years, but not to exceed ten years.

Amendment XXIII
(Ratified on March 29, 1961). Presidential Electors for the District of Columbia.

Section 1.

The District constituting the seat of Government of the United States shall appoint in such manner as the Congress may direct:

A number of electors of President and Vice President equal to the whole number of Senators and Representatives in Congress to which the District would be entitled if it were a State, but in no event more than the least populous State; they shall be in addition to those appointed by the States, but they shall be considered, for the purposes of the election of President and Vice President, to be electors appointed by a State; and they shall meet in the District and perform such duties as provided by the twelfth article of amendment.

Section 2.

The Congress shall have power to enforce this article by appropriate legislation.

Citizens living in the District of Columbia have the right to vote in elections for president and vice-president. The District of Columbia has three presidential electors, whereas before this amendment it had none.

Amendment XXIV
(Ratified on January 23, 1964). The Anti–Poll Tax Amendment.

Section 1.

The right of citizens of the United States to vote in any primary or other election for President or Vice President, for electors for President or Vice President, or for Senator or Representative in Congress, shall not be denied or abridged by the United States, or any State by reason of failure to pay any poll tax or other tax.

Section 2.

The Congress shall have power to enforce this article by appropriate legislation.

No government shall require a person to pay a poll tax in order to vote in any federal election.

Amendment XXV
(Ratified on February 10, 1967). Presidential Disability and Vice Presidential Vacancies.

Section 1.

In case of the removal of the President from office or of his death or resignation, the Vice President shall become President.

Whenever a president dies or resigns from office, the vice-president becomes president.

Section 2.

Whenever there is a vacancy in the office of the Vice President, the President shall nominate a Vice President who shall take office upon confirmation by a majority vote of both Houses of Congress.

Whenever the office of the vice-presidency becomes vacant, the president may appoint someone to fill this office, provided Congress consents.

Section 3.

Whenever the President transmits to the President pro tempore of the Senate and the Speaker of the House of Representatives his written declaration that he is unable to discharge the powers and duties of his office, and until he transmits to them a written declaration to the contrary, such powers and duties shall be discharged by the Vice President as Acting President.

Whenever the president believes she or he is unable to carry out the duties of the office, she or he shall so indicate to Congress in writing. The vice-president then acts as president until the president declares that she or he is again able to properly carry out the duties of the office.

Section 4.

Whenever the Vice President and a majority of either the principal officers of the executive departments or of such other body as Congress may by law provide, transmit to the President pro tempore of the Senate and the Speaker of the House of Representatives their written declaration that the President is unable to discharge the powers and duties of his office, the Vice President shall immediately assume the powers and duties of the office as Acting President.

Thereafter, when the President transmits to the President pro tempore of the Senate and the Speaker of the House of Representatives his written declaration that no inability exists, he shall resume the powers and duties of his office unless the Vice President and a majority of either the principal officers of the executive department or of such other body as Congress may by law provide, transmit within four days to the President pro tempore of the Senate and the Speaker of the House of Representatives their written declaration that the President is unable to discharge the powers and duties of his office. Thereupon Congress shall decide the issue, assembling within forty-eight hours for that purpose if not in session. If the Congress, within twenty-one days after receipt of the latter written declaration, or, if Congress is not in session, within twenty-one days after Congress is required to assemble, determines by two-thirds vote of both Houses that the President is unable to discharge the powers and duties of his office, the Vice President shall continue to discharge the same as Acting President; otherwise, the President shall resume the powers and duties of his office.

Whenever the vice-president and a majority of the members of the Cabinet believe that the president cannot carry out his or her duties, they shall so indicate in writing to Congress. The vice-president shall then act as president. When the president believes that she or he is able to carry out her or his duties again, she or he shall so indicate to the Congress. If, though, the vice-president and a majority

of the Cabinet do not agree, Congress must decide by a two-thirds vote within three weeks who shall act as president.

Amendment XXVI
(Ratified on July 1, 1971).
The Eighteen-Year-Old Vote.

Section 1.
The right of citizens of the United States, who are eighteen years of age or older, to vote shall not be denied or abridged by the United States or by any State on account of age.

No one over eighteen years of age can be denied the right to vote in federal or state elections by virtue of age.

Section 2.
The Congress shall have power to enforce this article by appropriate legislation.

Amendment XXVII
(Ratified on May 7, 1992).
Congressional Pay.
No law varying the compensation for the services of the Senators and Representatives shall take effect, until an election of representatives shall have intervened.

THE UNIFORM COMMERCIAL CODE (EXCERPTS)

Article 2
SALES

Part 1 **Short Title, General Construction and Subject Matter**

§ 2—102. **Scope; Certain Security and Other Transactions Excluded From This Article.**

Unless the context otherwise requires, this Article applies to transactions in goods; it does not apply to any transaction which although in the form of an unconditional contract to sell or present sale is intended to operate only as a security transaction nor does this Article impair or repeal any statute regulating sales to consumers, farmers or other specified classes of buyers.

§ 2—103. **Definitions and Index of Definitions.**

(1) In this Article unless the context otherwise requires

    (a) "Buyer" means a person who buys or contracts to buy goods.

    (b) "Good faith" in the case of a merchant means honesty in fact and the observance of reasonable commercial standards of fair dealing in the trade.

    (c) "Receipt" of goods means taking physical possession of them.

    (d) "Seller" means a person who sells or contracts to sell goods.

§ 2—106. **Definitions: "Contract"; "Agreement"; "Contract for Sale"; "Sale"; "Present Sale"; "Conforming" to Contract; "Termination"; "Cancellation".**

(1) In this Article unless the context otherwise requires "contract" and "agreement" are limited to those relating to the present or future sale of goods. "Contract for sale" includes both a present sale of goods and a contract to sell goods at a future time. A "sale" consists in the passing of title from the seller to the buyer for a price (Section 2—401). A "present sale" means a sale which is accomplished by the making of the contract.

(2) Goods or conduct including any part of a performance are "conforming" or conform to the contract when they are in accordance with the obligations under the contract.

(3) "Termination" occurs when either party pursuant to a power created by agreement or law puts an end to the contract otherwise than for its breach. On "termination" all obligations which are still executory on both sides are discharged but any right based on prior breach or performance survives.

(4) "Cancellation" occurs when either party puts an end to the contract for breach by the other and its effect is the same as that of "termination" except that the cancelling party also retains any remedy for breach of the whole contract or any unperformed balance.

§ 2—107. **Goods to Be Severed From Realty: Recording.**

(1) A contract for the sale of minerals or the like (including oil and gas) or a structure or its materials to be removed from realty is a contract for the sale of goods within this Article if they are to be severed by the seller but until severance a purported present sale thereof which is not effective as a transfer of an interest in land is effective only as a contract to sell.

(2) A contract for the sale apart from the land of growing crops or other things attached to realty and capable of severance without material harm thereto but not described in subsection (1) or of timber to be cut is a contract for the sale of goods within this Article whether the subject matter is to be severed by the buyer or by the seller even though it forms part of the realty at the time of contracting, and the parties can by identification effect a present sale before severance.

(3) The provisions of this section are subject to any third party rights provided by the law relating to realty records, and the contract for sale may be executed and recorded as a document transferring an interest in land and shall then constitute notice to third parties of the buyer's rights under the contract for sale.

Part 2 **Form, Formation and Readjustment of Contract**

§ 2—201. **Formal Requirements; Statute of Frauds.**

(1) Except as otherwise provided in this section a contract for the sale of goods for the price of $500 or more is not enforceable by way of action or defense unless there is some writing sufficient to indicate that a contract for sale has been made between the parties and signed by the party against whom enforcement is sought or by his authorized agent or broker. A writing is not insufficient because it omits or incorrectly states a term agreed upon but the contract is not enforceable under this paragraph beyond the quantity of goods shown in such writing.

(2) Between merchants if within a reasonable time a writing in confirmation of the contract and sufficient against the sender is received and the party receiving it has reason to know its contents, its sat-

isfies the requirements of subsection (1) against such party unless written notice of objection to its contents is given within ten days after it is received.

(3) A contract which does not satisfy the requirements of subsection (1) but which is valid in other respects is enforceable

   (a) if the goods are to be specially manufactured for the buyer and are not suitable for sale to others in the ordinary course of the seller's business and the seller, before notice of repudiation is received and under circumstances which reasonably indicate that the goods are for the buyer, has made either a substantial beginning of their manufacture or commitments for their procurement; or

   (b) if the party against whom enforcement is sought admits in his pleading, testimony or otherwise in court that a contract for sale was made, but the contract is not enforceable under this provision beyond the quantity of goods admitted; or

   (c) with respect to goods for which payment has been made and accepted or which have been received and accepted (Sec. 2—606).

§ 2—202. Final Written Expression: Parol or Extrinsic Evidence.

Terms with respect to which the confirmatory memoranda of the parties agree or which are otherwise set forth in a writing intended by the parties as a final expression of their agreement with respect to such terms as are included therein may not be contradicted by evidence of any prior agreement or of a contemporaneous oral agreement but may be explained or supplemented

(a) by course of dealing or usage of trade (Section 1—205) or by course of performance (Section 2—208); and

(b) by evidence of consistent additional terms unless the court finds the writing to have been intended also as a complete and exclusive statement of the terms of the agreement.

§ 2—204. Formation in General.

(1) A contract for sale of goods may be made in any manner sufficent to show agreement, including conduct by both parties which recognizes the existence of such a contract.

(2) An agreement sufficient to constitute a contract for sale may be found even though the moment of its making is undetermined.

(3) Even though one or more terms are left open a contract for sale does not fail for indefiniteness if the parties have intended to make a contract and there is a reasonably certain basis for giving an appropriate remedy.

§ 2—205. Firm Offers.

An offer by a merchant to buy or sell goods in a signed writing which by its terms gives assurance that it will be held open is not revocable, for lack of consideration, during the time stated or if no time is stated for a reasonable time, but in no event may such period of irrevocability exceed three months; but any such term of assurance on a form supplied by the offeree must be separately signed by the offeror.

§ 2—206. Offer and Acceptance in Formation of Contract.

(1) Unless other unambiguously indicated by the language or circumstances

   (a) an offer to make a contract shall be construed as inviting acceptance in any manner and by any medium reasonable in the circumstances;

   (b) an order or other offer to buy goods for prompt or current shipment shall be construed as inviting acceptance either by a prompt promise to ship or by the prompt or current shipment of conforming or non-conforming goods, but such a shipment of non-conforming goods does not constitute an acceptance if the seller seasonably notifies the buyer that the shipment is offered only as an accommodation to the buyer.

(2) Where the beginning of a requested performance is a reasonable mode of acceptance an offeror who is not notified of acceptance within a reasonable time may treat the offer as having lapsed before acceptance.

§ 2—207. Additional Terms in Acceptance or Confirmation.

(1) A definite and seasonable expression of acceptance or a written confirmation which is sent within a reasonable time operates as an acceptance even

though it states terms additional to or different from those offered or agreed upon, unless acceptance is expressly made conditional on assent to the additional or different terms.

(2) The additional terms are to be construed as proposals for addition to the contract. Between merchants such terms become part of the contract unless:

(a) the offer expressly limits acceptance to the terms of the offer;

(b) they materially alter it; or

(c) notification of objection to them has already been given or is given within a reasonable time after notice of them is received.

(3) Conduct by both parties which recognizes the existence of a contract is sufficient to establish a contract for sale although the writings of the parties do not otherwise establish a contract. In such case the terms of the particular contract consist of those terms on which the writings of the parties agree, together with any supplementary terms incorporated under any other provisions of this Act.

§ 2—208. Course of Performance or Practical Construction.

(1) Where the contract for sale involves repeated occasions for performance by either party with knowledge of the nature of the performance and opportunity for objection to it by the other, any course of performance accepted or acquiesced in without objection shall be relevant to determine the meaning of the agreement.

(2) The express terms of the agreement and any such course of performance, as well as any course of dealing and usage of trade, shall be construed whenever reasonable as consistent with each other; but when such construction is unreasonable, express terms shall control course of performance and course of performance shall control both course of dealing and usage of trade (Section 1—205).

(3) Subject to the provisions of the next section on modification and waiver, such course of performance shall be relevant to show a waiver or modification of any term inconsistent with such course of performance.

§ 2—209. Modification, Rescission and Waiver.

(1) An agreement modifying a contract within this Article needs no consideration to be binding.

(2) A signed agreement which excludes modification or rescission except by a signed writing cannot be otherwise modified or rescinded, but except as between merchants such a requirement on a form supplied by the merchant must be separately signed by the other party.

(3) The requirements of the statute of frauds section of this Article (Section 2—201) must be satisfied if the contract as modified is within its provisions.

(4) Although an attempt at modification or rescission does not satisfy the requirements of subsection (2) or (3) it can operate as a waiver.

(5) A party who has made a waiver affecting an executory portion of the contract may retract the waiver by reasonable notification received by the other party that strict performance will be required of any term waived, unless the retraction would be unjust in view of a material change of position in reliance on the waiver.

Part 3 General Obligation and Construction of Contract

§ 2—302. Unconscionable Contract or Clause.

(1) If the court as a matter of law finds the contract or any clause of the contract to have been unconscionable at the time it was made the court may refuse to enforce the contract, or it may enforce the remainder of the contract without the unconscionable clause, or it may so limit the application of any unconscionable clause as to avoid any unconscionable result.

(2) When it is claimed or appears to the court that the contract or any clause thereof may be unconscionable the parties shall be afforded a reasonable opportunity to present evidence as to its commercial setting, purpose and effect to aid the court in making the determination.

§ 2—312. Warranty of Title and Against Infringement; Buyer's Obligation Against Infringement.

(1) Subject to subsection (2) there is in a contract for sale a warranty by the seller that

(a) the title conveyed shall be good, and its transfer rightful; and

(b) the goods shall be delivered free from any security interest or other lien or encumbrance of which the buyer at the time of contracting has no knowledge.

(2) A warranty under subsection (1) will be excluded or modified only by specific language or by circumstances which give the buyer reason to know that the person selling does not claim title in himself or that he is purporting to sell only such right or title as he or a third person may have.

(3) Unless otherwise agreed a seller who is a merchant regularly dealing in goods of the kind warrants that the goods shall be delivered free of the rightful claim of any third person by way of infringement or the like but a buyer who furnishes specifications to the seller must hold the seller harmless against any such claim which arises out of compliance with the specifications.

§ 2—313. **Express Warranties by Affirmation, Promise, Description, Sample.**

(1) Express warranties by the seller are created as follows:

(a) Any affirmation of fact or promise made by the seller to the buyer which relates to the goods and becomes part of the basis of the bargain creates an express warranty that the goods shall conform to the affirmation or promise.

(b) Any description of the goods which is made part of the basis of the bargain creates an express warranty that the goods shall conform to the description.

(c) Any sample or model which is made part of the basis of the bargain creates an express warranty that the whole of the goods shall conform to the sample or model.

(2) It is not necessary to the creation of an express warranty that the seller use formal words such as "warrant" or "guarantee" or that he have a specific intention to make a warranty, but an affirmation merely of the value of the goods or a statement purporting to be merely the seller's opinion or commendation of the goods does not create a warranty.

§ 2—314. **Implied Warranty: Merchantability; Usage of Trade.**

(1) Unless excluded or modified (Section 2—316), a warranty that the goods shall be merchantable is implied in a contract for their sale if the seller is a merchant with respect to goods of that kind. Under this section the serving for value of food or drink to be consumed either on the premises or elsewhere is a sale.

(2) Goods to be merchantable must be at least such as

(a) pass without objection in the trade under the contract description; and

(b) in the case of fungible goods, are of fair average quality within the description; and

(c) are fit for the ordinary purposes for which such goods are used; and

(d) run, within the variations permitted by the agreement, of even kind, quality and quantity within each unit and among all units involved; and

(e) are adequately contained, packaged, and labeled as the agreement may require; and

(f) conform to the promises or affirmations of fact made on the container or label if any.

(3) Unless excluded or modified (Section 2—316) other implied warranties may arise from course of dealing or usage of trade.

§ 2—315. **Implied Warranty: Fitness for Particular Purpose.**

Where the seller at the time of contracting has reason to know any particular purpose for which the goods are required and that the buyer is relying on the seller's skill or judgment to select or furnish suitable goods, there is unless excluded or modified under the next section an implied warranty that the goods shall be fit for such purpose.

§ 2—316. **Exclusion or Modification of Warranties.**

(1) Words or conduct relevant to the creation of an express warranty and words or conduct tending to negate or limit warranty shall be construed wherever reasonable as consistent with each other; but subject to the provisions of this Article on parol or

extrinsic evidence (Section 2—202) negation or limitation is inoperative to the extent that such construction is unreasonable.

(2) Subject to subsection (3), to exclude or modify the implied warranty of merchantability or any part of it the language must mention merchantability and in case of a writing must be conspicuous, and to exclude or modify any implied warranty of fitness the exclusion must be by a writing and conspicuous. Language to exclude all implied warranties of fitness is sufficient if it states, for example, that "There are no warranties which extend beyond the description on the face hereof.

(3) Notwithstanding subsection (2)

(a) unless the circumstances indicate otherwise, all implied warranties are excluded by expressions like "as is", "with all faults" or other language which in common understanding calls the buyer's attention to the exclusion of warranties and makes plain that there is no implied warranty; and

(b) when the buyer before entering into the contract has examined the goods or the sample or model as fully as he desired or has refused to examine the goods there is no implied warranty with regard to defects which an examination ought in the circumstances to have revealed to him; and

(c) an implied warranty can also be excluded or modified by course of dealing or course of performance or usage of trade.

(4) Remedies for breach of warranty can be limited in accordance with the provisions of this Article on liquidation or limitation of damages and on contractual modification of remedy (Sections 2—718 and 2—719).

§ 2—317. Cumulation and Conflict of Warranties Express or Implied.

Warranties whether express or implied shall be construed as consistent with each other and as cumulative, but if such construction is unreasonable the intention of the parties shall determine which warranty is dominant. In ascertaining that intention the following rules apply:

(a) Exact or technical specifications displace an inconsistent sample or model or general language of description.

(b) A sample from an existing bulk displaces inconsistent general language of description.

(c) Express warranties displace inconsistent implied warranties other than an implied warranty of fitness for a particular purpose.

§ 2—318. Third Party Beneficiaries of Warranties Express or Implied.

Note: If this Act is introduced in the Congress of the United States this section should be omitted. (States to select one alternative.)

Alternative A

A seller's warranty whether express or implied extends to any natural person who is in the family or household of his buyer or who is a guest in his home if it is reasonable to expect that such person may use, consume or be affected by the goods and who is injured in person by breach of the warranty. A seller may not exclude or limit the operation of this section.

Alternative B

A seller's warranty whether express or implied extends to any natural person who may reasonably be expected to use, consume or be affected by the goods and who is injured in person by breach of the warranty. A seller may not exclude or limit the operation of this section.

Alternative C

A seller's warranty whether express or implied extends to any person who may reasonably be expected to use, consume or be affected by the goods and who is injured by breach of the warranty. A seller may not exclude or limit the operation of this section with respect to injury to the person of an individual to whom the warranty extends. As amended 1966.

§ 2—610. Anticipatory Repudiation.

When either party repudiates the contract with respect to a performance not yet due the loss of which will substantially impair the value of the contract to the other, the aggrieved party may

(a) for a commercially reasonable time await performance by the repudiating party; or

(b) resort to any remedy for breach (Section 2—703 or Section 2—711), even though he has notified the repudiating party that he would await the latter's performance and has urged retraction; and

(c) in either case suspend his own performance or proceed in accordance with the provisions of this Article on the seller's right to identify goods to the contract notwithstanding breach or to salvage unfinished goods (Section 2—704).

§ 2—611. Retraction of Anticipatory Repudiation.

(1) Until the repudiating party's next performance is due he can retract his repudiation unless the aggrieved party has since the repudiation cancelled or materially changed his position or otherwise indicated that he considers the repudiation final.

(2) Retraction may be by any method which clearly indicates to the aggrieved party that the repudiating party intends to perform, but must include any assurance justifiably demanded under the provisions of this Article (Section 2—609).

(3) Retraction reinstates the repudiating party's rights under the contract with due excuse and allowance to the aggrieved party for any delay occasioned by the repudiation.

§ 2—615. Excuse by Failure of Presupposed Conditions.

Except so far as a seller may have assumed a greater obligation and subject to the preceding section on substituted performance:

(a) Delay in delivery or non-delivery in whole or in part by a seller who complies with paragraphs (b) and (c) is not a breach of his duty under a contract for sale if performance as agreed has been made impracticable by the occurrence of a contingency the nonoccurrence of which was a basic assumption on which the contract was made or by compliance in good faith with any applicable foreign or domestic governmental regulation or order whether or not it later proves to be invalid.

(b) Where the causes mentioned in paragraph (a) affect only a part of the seller's capacity to perform, he must allocate production and deliveries among his customers but may at his option include regular customers not then under contract as well as his own requirements for further manufacture. He may so allocate in any manner which is fair and reasonable.

(c) The seller must notify the buyer seasonably that there will be delay or non-delivery and, when allocation is required under paragraph (b), of the estimated quota thus made available for the buyer.

◆ SHERMAN ANTITRUST ACT OF 1890 (EXCERPTS)

Section. 1 Every contract, combination in the form of trust or otherwise, or conspiracy, in restraint of trade or commerce among the several States, or with foreign nations, is hereby declared to be illegal. Every person who shall make any such contract or engage in any such combination or conspiracy shall be deemed guilty of a felony, and, on conviction thereof, shall be punished by fine not exceeding one million dollars if a corporation, or, if any other person, one hundred thousand dollars or by imprisonment not exceeding three years, or by both said punishments in the discretion of the court.

Section 2. Every person who shall monopolize, or attempt to monopolize, or conspire with any other person or persons, to monopolize any part of the trade or commerce among the several States, or with foreign nations, shall be deemed guilty of a felony, and, on conviction thereof, shall be punished by fine not exceeding one million dollars if a corporation, or, if any other person, one hundred thousand dollars or by imprisonment not exceeding three years, or by both said punishments, in the discretion of the court.

◆ FEDERAL TRADE COMMISSION ACT OF 1914 (EXCERPTS)

Section 5. (a)(1) Unfair methods of competition in or affecting commerce, and unfair or deceptive acts or practices in or affecting commerce, are hereby declared unlawful.

(2) The Commission is hereby empowered and directed to prevent persons, partnerships, or corporations from using unfair methods of competition in or affecting commerce and unfair or deceptive acts or practices in or affecting commerce.

(b) Any person, partnership, or corporation who violates an order of the Commission after it has become final, and while such order is in effect, shall forfeit and pay to the United States a civil penalty of not more than $10,000 for each violation, which shall accrue to the United States and may be recovered in a civil action brought by the Attorney General of the United States. Each separate violation of such an order shall be a separate offense, except that in the case of a violation through continuing failure to obey or neglect to obey a final order of the Commission, each day of continuance of such failure or neglect shall be deemed a separate offense. In such actions, the United States district courts are empowered to grant mandatory injunctions and such other and further equitable relief as they deem appropriate in the enforcement of such final orders of the Commission.

◆ TITLE VII OF THE CIVIL RIGHTS ACT OF 1964 (EXCERPTS)

Section 703. Unlawful Employment Practices.

(a) It shall be an unlawful employment practice for an employer—

(1) to fail or refuse to hire or to discharge any individual, or otherwise to discriminate against any individual with respect to his compensation, terms, conditions, or privileges of employment, because of such individual's race, color, religion, sex, or national origin; or

(2) to limit, segregate, or classify his employees or applicants for employment in any way which would deprive or tend to deprive any individual of employment opportunities or otherwise adversely affect his status as an employee, because of such individual's race, color, religion, sex, or national origin.

(b) It shall be an unlawful employment practice for an employment agency to fail or refuse to refer for employment, or otherwise to discriminate against, any individual because of his race, color, religion, sex, or national origin, or to classify or refer for employment any individual on the basis or his race, color, religion, sex, or national origin.

(c) It shall be an unlawful employment practice for a labor organization—

(1) to exclude or to expel from its membership, or otherwise to discriminate against, any individual because of his race, color, religion, sex, or national origin;

(2) to limit, segregate, or classify its membership or applicants for membership, or to classify or fail or refuse to refer for employment any individual, in any way which would deprive or tend to deprive any individual of employment opportunities, or would limit such employment opportunities or otherwise adversely affect his status as an employee or as an applicant for employment, because of such individual's race, color, religion, sex, or national origin; or

(3) to cause or attempt to cause an employer to discriminate against an individual in violation of this section.

(d) It shall be an unlawful employment practice for any employer, labor organization, or joint labor-management committee controlling apprenticeship or other training or retraining, including on-the-job training programs to discriminate against any individual because of his race, color, religion, sex, or national origin in admission to, or employment in, any program established to provide apprenticeship or other training.

(e) Notwithstanding any other provision of this subchapter—

(1) it shall not be an unlawful employment practice for an employer to hire and employ employees, for an employment agency to classify, or refer for employment any individual, for a labor organization to classify its membership or to classify or refer for employment any individual, or for an employer, labor organization, or joint labor-management committee controlling apprenticeship or other training or retraining programs to admit or employ any individual in any such program, on the basis of his religion, sex, or national origin in those certain instances where religion, sex, or national origin is a bona fide occupational qualification reasonably necessary to the normal operation of that particular business or enterprise, and

(2) it shall not be an unlawful employment practice for a school, college, university, or other educational institution or institution of learning to hire and employ employees of a particular religion if such school, college, university, or other educational institution or institution of learning is, in whole or in substantial part, owned, supported, controlled, or managed by a particular religion or by a particular religious corporation, association, or society, or if the curriculum of such school, college, university, or other educational institution or institution of learning is directed toward the propagation of a particular religion.

(f) As used in this subchapter, the phrase "unlawful employment practice" shall not be deemed to include any action or measure taken by an employer, labor organization, joint labor-management committee, or employment agency with respect to an individual who is a member of the Communist Party of the United States or of any other organization required to register as a Communist-action or Communist-front organization. * * *

(g) Notwithstanding any other provision of this subchapter, it shall not be an unlawful employment practice for an employer to fail or refuse to hire and employ any individual for any position, for an employer to discharge any individual from any position, or for an employment agency to fail or refuse to refer any individual for employment in any position, or for a labor organization to fail or refuse to refer any individual for employment in any position, if—

(1) the occupancy of such position, or access to the premises in or upon which any part of the duties of such position is performed or is to be performed, is subject to any requirement imposed in the interest of the national security of the United States * * * and

(2) such individual has not fulfilled or has ceased to fulfill that requirement.

(h) Notwithstanding any other provision of this subchapter, it shall not be an unlawful employment practice for an employer to apply different standards of compensation, or different terms, conditions, or privileges of employment pursuant to a bona fide seniority or merit system, or a system which measures earnings by quantity or quality of production or to employees who work in different locations, provided that such differences are not the result of an intention to discriminate because of race, color, religion, sex, or national origin, nor shall it be an unlawful employment practice for an employer to give and act upon the results of any professionally developed ability test provided that such test, its administration or action upon the results is not designed, intended or used to discriminate because of race, color, religion, sex, or national origin. * * *

(j) Nothing contained in this subchapter shall be interpreted to require any employer, employment agency, labor organization, or joint labor-management committee subject to this subchapter to grant preferential treatment to any individual or to any group because of the race, color, religion, sex, or national origin of such individual or group on account of an imbalance which may exist with respect to the total number or percentage of persons of any race, color, religion, sex, or national origin employed by any employer, referred or classified for employment by any employment agency or labor organization, or admitted to, or employed in, any apprenticeship or other training program, in comparison with the total number or percentage of persons of such race, color, religion, sex, or national origin in any community, State, section, or other area, or in the available work force in any community, State, section, or other area.

★   ★   ★   ★

Section 704. Other Unlawful Employment Practices. (a) It shall be an unlawful employment practice for an employer to discriminate against any of his employees or applicants for employment, for an employment agency, or joint labor-management committee controlling apprenticeship or other training or retraining, including on-the-job training programs, to discriminate against any individual, or for a labor organization to discriminate against any member thereof or applicant for membership, because he has opposed any practice made an unlawful employment practice by this subchapter, or because he has made a charge, testified, assisted, or participated in any manner in an investigation, proceeding, or hearing under this subchapter.

(b) It shall be an unlawful employment practice for an employer, labor organization, employment agency, or joint labor-management committee controlling apprenticeship or other training or retraining, including on-the-job training programs, to print or publish or cause to be printed or published any notice or advertisement relating to employment by such an employer or membership or any classification or referral for employment by such a labor organization, or relating to any classification or referral for employment by such an employment agency, or relating to admission to, or employment in, any program established to provide apprenticeship or other training by such a joint-labor-management committee, indicating any preference, limitation, specification, or discrimination, based on race, color, religion, sex, or national origin, except that such a notice or advertisement may indicate a preference, limitation, specification, or discrimination based on religion, sex or national origin when religion, sex, or national origin is a bona fide occupational qualification for employment.

◆ AMERICANS WITH DISABILITIES ACT OF 1990 (EXCERPTS)

TITLE I—EMPLOYMENT
Sec. 101. Definitions.

As used in this title: ★   ★   ★

(8) **Qualified individual with a disability.—** The term "qualified individual with a disability" means an individual with a disability who, with or without reasonable accommodation, can perform the essential functions of the employment position that such individual holds or desires. For the purposes of this title, consideration shall be given to the employer's judgment as to what functions of a job are essential, and if an employer has prepared a written description before advertising or interviewing applicants for the job, this description shall be considered evidence of the essential functions of the job.

(9) **Reasonable accommodation.—**The term "reasonable accommodation" may include—

(A) making existing facilities used by employees readily accessible to and usable by individuals with disabilities; and

(B) job restructuring, part-time or modified work schedules, reassignment to a vacant position, acquisition or modification of equipment or devices, appropriate adjustment or modifications of examinations, training materials or policies, the provision of qualified readers or interpreters, and other similar accommodations for individuals with disabilities.

(10) **Undue Hardship.—**

(A) **In general.—**The term "undue hardship" means an action requiring significant difficulty or expense, when considered in light of the factors set forth in subparagraph (B).

(B) **Factors to be considered.**—In determining whether an accommodation would impose an undue hardship on a covered entity, factors to be considered include—

(i) the nature and cost of accommodation needed under this Act;

(ii) the overall financial resources of the facility or facilities involved in the provision of the reasonable accommodation; the number of persons employed at such facility; the effect on expenses and resources, or the impact otherwise of such accommodation upon the operation of the facility;

(iii) the overall financial resources of the covered entity; the overall size of the business of a covered entity with respect to the number of its employees; the number, type, and location of its facilities; and

(iv) the type of operation or operations of the covered entity, including the composition, structure, and functions of the workforce of such entity; the geographic separateness, administrative, or fiscal relationship of the facility or facilities in question to the covered entity.

Sec. 102. Discrimination.

(a) **General Rule.**—No covered entity shall discriminate against a qualified individual with a disability because of the disability of such individual in regard to job application procedures, the hiring, advancement, or discharge of employees, employee compensation, job training, and other terms, conditions, and privileges of employment.

(b) **Construction.**—As used in subsection (a), the term "discriminate" includes—

(1) limiting, segregating, or classifying a job applicant or employee in a way that adversely affects the opportunities or status of such applicant or employee because of the disability of such applicant or employee;

(2) participating in a contractual or other arrangement or relationship that has the effect of subjecting a covered entity's qualified applicant or employee with a disability to the discrimination prohibited by this title (such relationship includes a relationship with an employment or referral agency, labor union, an organization providing fringe benefits to an employee of the covered entity, or an organization providing training and apprenticeship programs);

(3) utilizing standards, criteria, or methods of administration—

(A) that have the effect of discrimination on the basis of disability; or

(B) that perpetuate the discrimination of others who are subject to common administrative control;

(4) excluding or otherwise denying equal jobs or benefits to a qualified individual because of the known disability of an individual with whom the qualified individual is known to have a relationship or association;

(5)

(A) not making reasonable accommodations to the known physical or mental limitations of an otherwise qualified individual with a disability who is an applicant or employee, unless such covered entity can demonstrate that the accommodation would impose an undue hardship on the operation of the business of such covered entity; or

(B) denying employment opportunities to a job applicant or employee who is an otherwise qualified individual with a disability, if such denial is based on the need of such covered entity to make reasonable accommodation to the physical or mental impairments of the employee or applicant;

(6) using qualification standards, employment tests or other selection criteria that screen out or tend to screen out an individual with a disability or a class of individuals with disabilities unless the standard, test or other selection criteria, as used by the covered entity, is shown to be job-related for the position in question and is consistent with business necessity; and

(7) failing to select and administer tests concerning employment in the most effective manner to ensure that, when such test is administered to a job applicant or employee who has a disability that impairs sensory, manual, or speaking skills, such test results accurately reflect the skills, aptitude, or whatever other factor of such applicant or employee that such test purports to measure, rather than reflecting the impaired sensory, manual, or speaking skills of such employee or applicant (except where such skills are

the factors that the test purports to measure).

★ ★ ★

Sec. 104. Illegal Use of Drugs and Alcohol.

★ ★ ★

(b) **Rules of Construction.**—Nothing in subsection (a) shall be construed to exclude as a qualified individual with a disability an individual who—

(1) has successfully completed a supervised drug rehabilitation program and is no longer engaging in the illegal use of drugs, or has otherwise been rehabilitated successfully and is no longer engaging in such use;

(2) is participating in a supervised rehabilitation program and is no longer engaging in such use; or

(3) is erroneously regarded as engaging in such use, but is not engaging in such use; except that it shall not be a violation of this Act for a covered entity to adopt or administer reasonable policies or procedures, including but not limited to drug testing, designed to ensure that an individual described in paragraph (1) or (2) is no longer engaging in the illegal use of drugs. ★ ★ ★

Sec. 107. Enforcement.

(a) **Powers, Remedies, and Procedures.**—The powers, remedies, and procedures set forth in sections 705, 706, 707, 709, and 710 of the Civil Rights Act of 1964 (42 U.S.C. 2000e-4, 2000e-5, 2000e-6, 2000e-8, and 2000e-9) shall be the powers, remedies, and procedures this title provides to the Commission, to the Attorney General, or to any person alleging discrimination on the basis of disability in violation of any provision of this Act, or regulations promulgated under section 106, concerning employment.

(b) **Coordination.**—The agencies with enforcement authority for actions which allege employment discrimination under this title and under the Rehabilitation Act of 1973 shall develop procedures to ensure that administrative complaints filed under this title and under the Rehabilitation Act of 1973 are dealt with in a manner that avoids duplication of effort and prevents imposition of inconsistent or conflicting standards for the same requirements under this title and the Rehabilitation Act of 1973. The Commission, the Attorney General, and the Office of Federal Contract Compliance Programs shall establish such coordinating mechanisms (similar to provisions contained in the joint regulations promulgated by the Commission and the Attorney General at part 42 of title 28 and part 1691 of title 29, Code of Federal Regulations, and the Memorandum of Understanding between the Commission and the Office of Federal Contract Compliance Programs dated January 16, 1981 (46 Fed. Reg. 7435, January 23, 1981)) in regulations implementing this title and Rehabilitation Act of 1973 not later than 18 months after the date of enactment of this Act.

Sec. 108. Effective Date.

This title shall become effective 24 months after the date of enactment.

◆ CIVIL RIGHTS ACT OF 1991 (EXCERPTS)

Section 3. Purposes.

The purposes of this Act are—

(1) to provide appropriate remedies for intentional discrimination and unlawful harassment in the workplace;

(2) to codify the concepts of "business necessity" and "job related" enunciated by the Supreme Court in *Griggs v. Duke Power Co.*, 401 U.S. 424 (1971), and in the other Supreme Court decisions prior to *Wards Cove Packing Co. v. Atonio*, 490 U.S. 642 (1989);

(3) to confirm statutory authority and provide statutory guidelines for the adjudication of disparate impact suits under title VII of the Civil Rights Act of 1964 (42 U.S.C. 2000e *et seq.*); and

(4) to respond to recent decisions of the Supreme Court by expanding the scope of relevant civil rights statutes in order to provide adequate protection to victims of discrimination.

Section 101. Prohibition against All Racial Discrimination in the Making and Enforcement of Contracts.

Section 1977 of the Revised Statutes (42 U.S.C. 1981) is amended ★ ★ ★ by adding at the end the following new subsections:

(b) For purposes of this section, the term "make and enforce contracts" includes the making, performance, modification, and termination of contracts, and the enjoyment of all benefits, privileges, terms, and conditions of the contractual relationship.

(c) The rights protected by this section are protected against impairment by nongovernmental discrimination and impairment under color of State law.

Section 102. Damages in Cases of Intentional Discrimination.

The Revised Statutes are amended by inserting after section 1977 (42 U.S.C.1981) the following new section:

Section 1977A. Damages in Cases of Intentional Discrimination in Employment.

(a) Right of Recovery.—

(1) Civil Rights.—In an action brought by a complaining party under section 706 or 717 of the Civil Rights Act of 1964 (42 U.S.C. 2000e-5) against a respondent who engaged in unlawful intentional discrimination (not an employment practice that is unlawful because of its disparate impact) prohibited under section 703, 704, or 717 of the Act (42 U.S.C. 2000e-2 or 2000e-3), and provided that the complaining party cannot recover under section 1977 of the Revised Statutes (42 U.S.C.1981), the complaining party may recover compensatory and punitive damages as allowed in subsection (b), in addition to any relief authorized by section 706(g) of the Civil Rights Act of 1964, from the respondent.

★   ★   ★   ★

(b) Compensatory and Punitive Damages.—

(1) Determination of Punitive Damages.—A complaining party may recover punitive damages under this section against a respondent (other than a government, government agency or political subdivision) if the complaining party demonstrates that the respondent engaged in a discriminatory practice or discriminatory practices with malice or with reckless indifference to the federally protected rights of an aggrieved individual.

(2) Exclusions from Compensatory Damages.—Compensatory damages awarded under this section shall not include backpay, interest on backpay, or any other type of relief authorized under section 706(g) of the Civil Rights Act of 1964.

(3) Limitations.—The sum of the amount of compensatory damages awarded under this section for future pecuniary losses, emotional pain, suffering, inconvenience, mental anguish, loss of enjoyment of life, and other nonpecuniary losses, and the amount of punitive damages awarded under this section, shall not exceed, for each complaining party—

(A) in the case of a respondent who has more than 14 and fewer than 101 employees in each of 20 or more calendar weeks in the current or preceding calendar year, $50,000;

(B) in the case of a respondent who has more than 100 and fewer than 201 employees in each of 20 or more calendar weeks in the current or preceding calendar year, $100,000; and

(C) in the case of a respondent who has more than 200 and fewer than 501 employees in each of 20 or more calendar weeks in the current or preceding calendar year, $200,000; and

(D) in the case of a respondent who has more than 500 employees in each of 20 or more calendar weeks in the current or preceding calendar year, $300,000.

★   ★   ★   ★

Section 105. Burden of Proof in Disparate Impact Cases.

(a) Section 703 of the Civil Rights Act of 1964 (42 U.S.C. 2000e-2) is amended by adding at the end the following new [subsections to 703(k)(1)]—

(A) An unlawful employment practice based on disparate impact is established under this title only if—

(i) a complaining party demonstrates that a respondent uses a particular employment practice that causes a disparate impact on the basis of race, color, religion, sex, or national origin and the respondent fails to demonstrate that the challenged practice is job related for the position in question and consistent with business necessity; or

(ii) the complaining party makes the demonstration described in subparagraph (C) with respect to an alternative employment practice and the respondent refuses to adopt such alternative employment practice.

★   ★   ★   ★

(C) The demonstration referred to by subparagraph (A)(ii) shall be in accordance with the law as it existed on June 4, 1989, with respect to the concept of "alternative employment practice."

★   ★   ★   ★

Section 107. Clarifying Prohibition against Impermissible Consideration of Race, Color, Religion, Sex, or National Origin in Employment Practices.

(a) In General.—Section 703 of the Civil Rights Act of 1964 (42 U.S.C. 2000e-2) (as amended by sections 105 and 106) is further amended by adding at the end the following new subsection:

(m) Except as otherwise provided in this title, an unlawful employment practice is established when the complaining party demonstrates that race, color, religion, sex, or national origin was a motivating factor for any employment practice, even though other factors also motivated the practice.

★   ★   ★   ★

Section 109. Protection of Extraterritorial Employment.

(a) Definition of Employee.—Section 701(f) of the Civil Rights Act of 1964 (42 U.S.C. 2000e(f)) and section 101(4) of the Americans with Disabilities Act of 1990 (42 U.S.C. 12111(4)) are each amended by adding at the end the following: "With respect to employment in a foreign country, such term includes an individual who is a citizen of the United States."

Spanish Equivalents for Important Legal Terms in English

Abandoned property: bienes abandonados

Acceptance: aceptación; consentimiento; acuerdo

Acceptor: aceptante

Accession: toma de posesión; aumento; accesión

Accommodation indorser: avalista de favor

Accommodation party: firmante de favor

Accord: acuerdo; convenio; arregio

Accord and satisfaction: transacción ejecutada

Act of state doctrine: doctrina de acto de gobierno

Administrative law: derecho administrativo

Administrative process: procedimiento o metódo administrativo

Administrator: administrador (-a)

Adverse possession: posesión de hecho susceptible de proscripción adquisitiva

Affirmative action: acción afirmativa

Affirmative defense: defensa afirmativa

After-acquired property: bienes adquiridos con posterioridad a un hecho dado

Agency: mandato; agencia

Agent: mandatorio; agente; representante

Agreement: convenio; acuerdo; contrato

Alien corporation: empresa extranjera

Allonge: hojas adicionales de endosos

Answer: contestación de la demande; alegato

Anticipatory breach: anuncio previo de las partes de su imposibilidad de cumplir con el contrato

Appeal: apelación; recurso de apelación

Appellate jurisdiction: jurisdicción de apelaciones

Appraisal right: derecho de valuación

Arbitration: arbitraje

Arson: incendio intencional

Articles of partnership: contrato social

Artisian's lien: derecho de retención que ejerce al artesano

Assault: asalto; ataque; agresión

Assignment of rights: transmisión; transferencia; cesión

Assumption of risk: no resarcimiento por exposición voluntaria al peligro

Attachment: auto judicial que autoriza el embargo; embargo

Bailee: depositario

Bailment: depósito; constitución en depósito

Bailor: depositante

Bankruptcy trustee: síndico de la quiebra

Battery: agresión; física

Bearer: portador; tenedor

Bearer instrument: documento al portador

Bequest or legacy: legado (de bienes muebles)

Bilateral contract: contrato bilateral

Bill of lading: conocimiento de embarque; carta de porte

Bill of Rights: declaración de derechos

Binder: póliza de seguro provisoria; recibo de pago a cuenta del precio

Blank indorsement: endoso en blanco

Blue sky laws: leyes reguladoras del comercio bursátil

Bond: título de crédito; garantía; caución

Breach of contract: incumplimiento de contrato

Brief: escrito; resumen; informe

Burglary: violación de domicilio

Business judgment rule: regla de juicio comercial

Business tort: agravio comercial

Case law: ley de casos; derecho casuístico

Cashier's check: cheque de caja

Causation in fact: causalidad en realidad

Cease-and-desist order: orden para cesar y desistir

Certificate of deposit: certificado de depósito

Certified check: cheque certificado

Charitable trust: fideicomiso para fines benéficos

Chattel: bien mueble

Check: cheque

Chose in action: derecho inmaterial; derecho de acción

Civil law: derecho civil

Close corporation: sociedad de un solo accionista o de un grupo restringido de accionistas

Closed shop: taller agremiado (emplea solamente a miembros de un gremio)

Closing argument: argumento al final

Codicil: codicilo

Collateral: garantía; bien objeto de la garantía real

Comity: cortesía; cortesía entre naciones

Commercial paper: instrumentos negociables; documentos a valores commerciales

Common law: derecho consuetudinario; derecho común; ley común

Common stock: acción ordinaria

Comparative negligence: negligencia comparada

Compensatory damages: daños y perjuicios reales o compensatorios

Concurrent conditions: condiciones concurrentes

Concurrent jurisdiction: competencia concurrente de varios tribunales para entender en una misma causa

Concurring opinion: opinión concurrente

Condition: condición

Condition precedent: condición suspensiva

Condition subsequent: condición resolutoria

Confiscation: confiscación

Confusion: confusión; fusión

Conglomerate merger: fusión de firmas que operan en distintos mercados

Consequential damages: daños y perjuicios indirectos

Consideration: consideración; motivo; contraprestación

Consolidation: consolidación

Constructive delivery: entrega simbólica

Constructive trust: fideicomiso creado por aplicación de la ley

Consumer-protection law: ley para proteger el consumidor

Contract: contrato

Contract under seal: contrato formal o sellado

Contributory negligence: negligencia de la parte actora

Conversion: usurpación; conversión de valores

Copyright: derecho de autor

Corporation: sociedad anómina; corporación; persona juridica

Co-sureties: cogarantes

Counterclaim: reconvención; contrademanda

Counteroffer: contraoferta

Course of dealing: curso de transacciones

Course of performance: curso de cumplimiento

Covenant: pacto; garantía; contrato

Covenant not to sue: pacto or contrato a no demandar

Covenant of quiet enjoyment: garantía del uso y goce pacífico del inmueble

Creditors' composition agreement: concordato preventivo

Crime: crimen; delito; contravención

Criminal law: derecho penal

Cross-examination: contrainterrogatorio

Cure: cura; cuidado; derecho de remediar un vicio contractual

Customs receipts: recibos de derechos aduaneros

Damages: daños; indemnización por daños y perjuicios

Debtor: deudor

Debt securities: seguridades de deuda

Deceptive advertising: publicidad engañosa

Deed: escritura; título; acta translativa de domino

Defamation: difamación

Delegation of duties: delegación de obligaciones

Demand deposit: depósito a la vista

Depositions: declaración de un testigo fuera del tribunal

Devise: legado; deposición testamentaria (bienes inmuebles)

Directed verdict: veredicto según orden del juez y sin participación activa del jurado

Direct examination: interrogatorio directo; primer interrogatorio

Disaffirmance: repudiación; renuncia; anulación

Discharge: descargo; liberación; cumplimiento

Disclosed principal: mandante revelado

Discovery: descubrimiento; producción de la prueba

Dissenting opinion: opinión disidente

Dissolution: disolución; terminación

Diversity of citizenship: competencia de los tribunales federales para entender en causas cuyas partes intervinientes son cuidadanos de distintos estados

Divestiture: extinción prematura de derechos reales

Dividend: dividendo

Docket: orden del día; lista de causas pendientes

Domestic corporation: sociedad local

Draft: orden de pago; letrade cambio

Drawee: girado; beneficiario

Drawer: librador

Duress: coacción; violencia

Easement: servidumbre

Embezzlement: desfalco; malversación

Eminent domain: poder de expropiación

Employment discrimination: discriminación en el empleo

Entrepreneur: empresario

Environmental law: ley ambiental

Equal dignity rule: regla de dignidad egual

Equity security: tipo de participación en una sociedad

Estate: propiedad; patrimonio; derecho

Estop: impedir; prevenir

Ethical issue: cuestión ética

Exclusive jurisdiction: competencia exclusiva

Exculpatory clause: cláusula eximente

Executed contract: contrato ejecutado

Execution: ejecución; cumplimiento

Executor: albacea

Executory contract: contrato aún no completamente consumado

Executory interest: derecho futuro

Express contract: contrato expreso

Expropriation: expropriación

Federal question: caso federal

Fee simple: pleno dominio; dominio absoluto

Fee simple absolute: dominio absoluto

Fee simple defeasible: dominio sujeta a una condición resolutoria

Felony: crimen; delito grave

Fictitious payee: beneficiario ficticio

Fiduciary: fiduciaro

Firm offer: oferta en firme

Fixture: inmueble por destino, incorporación a anexación

Floating lien: gravamen continuado

Foreign corporation: sociedad extranjera; U.S. sociedad constituída en otro estado

Forgery: falso; falsificación

Formal contract: contrato formal

Franchise: privilegio; franquicia; concesión

Franchisee: persona que recibe una concesión

Franchisor: persona que vende una concesión

Fraud: fraude; dolo; engaño

Future interest: bien futuro

Garnishment: embargo de derechos

General partner: socio comanditario

General warranty deed: escritura translativa de domino con garantía de título

Gift: donación

Gift *causa mortis:* donación por causa de muerte

Gift *inter vivos:* donación entre vivos

Good faith: buena fe

Good-faith purchaser: comprador de buena fe

Holder: tenedor por contraprestación

Holder in due course: tenedor legítimo

Holographic will: testamento ológrafico

Homestead exemption laws: leyes que exceptúan las casas de familia de ejecución por duedas generales

Horizontal merger: fusión horizontal

Identification: identificación

Implied-in-fact contract: contrato implícito en realidad

Implied warranty: guarantía implícita

Implied warranty of merchantability: garantía implícita de vendibilidad

Impossibility of performance: imposibilidad de cumplir un contrato

Imposter: imposter

Incidental beneficiary: beneficiario incidental; beneficiario secundario

Incidental damages: daños incidentales

Indictment: auto de acusación; acusación

Indorsee: endorsatario

Indorsement: endoso

Indorser: endosante

Informal contract: contrato no formal; contrato verbal

Information: acusación hecha por el ministerio público

Injunction: mandamiento; orden de no innovar

Innkeeper's lien: derecho de retención que ejerce el posadero

Installment contract: contrato de pago en cuotas

Insurable interest: interés asegurable

Intended beneficiary: beneficiario destinado

Intentional tort: agravio; cuasidelito intenciónal

International law: derecho internaciónal

Interrogatories: preguntas escritas sometidas por una parte a la otra o a un testigo

***Inter vivos* trust:** fideicomiso entre vivos

Intestacy laws: leyes de la condición de morir intestado

Intestate: intestado

Investment company: compañia de inversiones

Issue: emisión

Joint tenancy: derechos conjuntos en un bien inmueble

Joint tenancy: derechos conjuntos en un bien inmueble en favor del beneficiario sobreviviente

Judgment *n.o.v.:* juicio no obstante veredicto

Judgment rate of interest: interés de juicio

Judicial process: acto de procedimiento; proceso jurídico

Judicial review: revisión judicial

Jurisdiction: jurisdicción

Larceny: robo; hurto

Law: derecho; ley; jurisprudencia

Lease: contrato de locación; contrato de alquiler

Leasehold estate: bienes forales

Legal rate of interest: interés legal

Legatee: legatario

Letter of credit: carta de crédito

Levy: embargo; comiso

Libel: libelo; difamación escrita

Life estate: usufructo

Limited partner: comanditario

Limited partnership: sociedad en comandita

Liquidation: liquidación; realización

Lost property: objetos perdidos

Majority opinion: opinión de la mayoría

Maker: persona que realiza u ordena; librador

Mechanic's lien: gravamen de constructor

Mediation: mediación; intervención

Merger: fusión

Mirror image rule: fallo de reflejo

Misdemeanor: infracción; contravención

Mislaid property: bienes extraviados

Mitigation of damages: reducción de daños

Mortgage: hypoteca

Motion to dismiss: excepción parentoria

Mutual fund: fondo mutual

Negotiable instrument: instrumento negociable

Negotiation: negociación

Nominal damages: daños y perjuicios nominales

Novation: novación

Nuncupative will: testamento nuncupativo

Objective theory of contracts: teoria objetiva de contratos

Offer: oferta

Offeree: persona que recibe una oferta

Offeror: oferente

Order instrument: instrumento o documento a la orden

Original jurisdiction: jurisdicción de primera instancia

Output contract: contrato de producción

Parol evidence rule: regla relativa a la prueba oral

Partially disclosed principal: mandante revelado en parte

Partnership: sociedad colectiva; asociación; asociación de participación

Past consideration: causa o contraprestación anterior

Patent: patente; privilegio

Pattern or practice: muestra o práctica

Payee: beneficiario de un pago

Penalty: pena; penalidad

Per capita: por cabeza

Perfection: perfeción

Performance: cumplimiento; ejecución

Personal defenses: excepciones personales

Personal property: bienes muebles

Per stirpes: por estirpe

Plea bargaining: regateo por un alegato

Pleadings: alegatos

Pledge: prenda

Police powers: poderes de policia y de prevención del crimen

Policy: póliza

Positive law: derecho positivo; ley positiva

Possibility of reverter: posibilidad de reversión

Precedent: precedente

Preemptive right: derecho de prelación

Preferred stock: acciones preferidas

Premium: recompensa; prima

Presentment warranty: garantía de presentación

Price discrimination: discriminación en los precios

Principal: mandante; principal

Privity: nexo jurídico

Privity of contract: relación contractual

Probable cause: causa probable

Probate: verificación; verificación del testamento

Probate court: tribunal de sucesiones y tutelas

Proceeds: resultados; ingresos

Profit: beneficio; utilidad; lucro

Promise: promesa

Promisee: beneficiario de una promesa

Promisor: promtente

Promissory estoppel: impedimento promisorio

Promissory note: pagaré; nota de pago

Promoter: promotor; fundador

Proximate cause: causa inmediata o próxima

Proxy: apoderado; poder

Punitive, or exemplary, damages: daños y perjuicios punitivos o ejemplares

Qualified indorsement: endoso con reservas

Quasi contract: contrato tácito o implícito

Quitclaim deed: acto de transferencia de una propiedad por finiquito, pero sin ninguna garantía sobre la validez del título transferido

Ratification: ratificación

Real property: bienes inmuebles

Reasonable doubt: duda razonable

Rebuttal: refutación

Recognizance: promesa; compromiso; reconocimiento

Recording statutes: leyes estatales sobre registros oficiales

Reformation: rectificación; reforma; corrección

Rejoinder: dúplica; contrarréplica

Release: liberación; renuncia a un derecho

Remainder: substitución; reversión

Remedy: recurso; remedio; reparación

Replevin: acción reivindicatoria; reivindicación

Reply: réplica

Requirements contract: contrato de suministro

Rescission: rescisión

Respondeat superior: responsabilidad del mandante o del maestro

Restitution: restitución

Restrictive indorsement: endoso restrictivo

Resulting trust: fideicomiso implícito

Reversion: reversión; sustitución

Revocation: revocación; derogación

Right of contribution: derecho de contribución

Right of reimbursement: derecho de reembolso

Right of subrogation: derecho de subrogación

Right-to-work law: ley de libertad de trabajo

Robbery: robo

Rule 10b-5: Regla 10b-5

Sale: venta; contrato de compreventa

Sale on approval: venta a ensayo; venta sujeta a la aprobación del comprador

Sale or return: venta con derecho de devolución

Sales contract: contrato de compraventa; boleto de compraventa

Satisfaction: satisfacción; pago

Scienter: a sabiendas

S corporation: S corporación
Secured party: acreedor garantizado
Secured transaction: transacción garantizada
Securities: volares; titulos; seguridades
Security agreement: convenio de seguridad
Security interest: interés en un bien dado en garantía que permite a quien lo detenta venderlo en caso de incumplimiento
Service mark: marca de identificación de servicios
Shareholder's derivative suit: acción judicial entablada por un accionista en nombre de la sociedad
Signature: firma; rúbrica
Slander: difamación oral; calumnia
Sovereign immunity: immunidad soberana
Special indorsement: endoso especial; endoso a la orden de una person en particular
Specific performance: ejecución precisa, según los términos del contrato
Spendthrift trust: fideicomiso para pródigos
Stale check: cheque vencido
Stare decisis: acatar las decisiones, observar los precedentes
Statutory law: derecho estatutario; derecho legislado; derecho escrito
Stock: acciones
Stock warrant: certificado para la compra de acciones
Stop-payment order: orden de suspensión del pago de un cheque dada por el librador del mismo
Strict liability: responsabilidad uncondicional
Summary judgment: fallo sumario

Tangible property: bienes corpóreos
Tenancy at will: inguilino por tiempo indeterminado (según la voluntad del propietario)
Tenancy by sufferance: posesión por tolerancia
Tenancy by the entirety: locación conyugal conjunta
Tenancy for years: inguilino por un término fijo
Tenancy in common: specie de copropiedad indivisa
Tender: oferta de pago; oferta de ejecución
Testamentary trust: fideicomiso testamentario
Testator: testador (-a)
Third party beneficiary contract: contrato para el beneficio del tercero-beneficiario
Tort: agravio; cuasi-delito
Totten trust: fideicomiso creado por un depósito bancario
Trade acceptance: letra de cambio aceptada
Trade name: nombre comercial; razón social
Trademark: marca registrada
Traveler's check: cheque del viajero
Trespass to land: ingreso no authorizado a las tierras de otro
Trespass to personal property: violación de los derechos posesorios de un tercero con respecto a bienes muebles
Trust: fideicomiso; trust

Ultra vires: ultra vires; fuera de la facultad (de una sociedad anónima)
Unanimous opinion: opinión unámine
Unconscionable contract or clause: contrato leonino; cláusula leonino
Underwriter: subscriptor; asegurador

Unenforceable contract: contrato que no se puede hacer cumplir
Unilateral contract: contrato unilateral
Union shop: taller agremiado; empresa en la que todos los empleados son miembros del gremio o sindicato
Universal defenses: defensas legitimas o legales
Usage of trade: uso comercial
Usury: usura

Valid contract: contrato válido
Venue: lugar; sede del proceso
Vertical merger: fusión vertical de empresas
Void contract: contrato nulo; contrato inválido, sin fuerza legal
Voidable contract: contrato anulable
Voir dire: examen preliminar de un testigo a jurado por el tribunal para determinar su competencia
Voting trust: fideicomiso para ejercer el derecho de voto

Waiver: renuncia; abandono
Warranty of habitability: garantía de habitabilidad
Watered stock: acciones diluídos; capital inflado
White-collar crime: crimen administrativo
Writ of attachment: mandamiento de ejecución; mandamiento de embargo
Writ of *certiorari*: auto de avocación; auto de certiorari
Writ of execution: auto ejecutivo; mandamiento de ejecutión
Writ of mandamus: auto de mandamus; mandamiento; orden judicial

Careers in Law

If the law interests you as a career, there is good news. There are many career opportunities available. Working with the law is fascinating. It is also a contribution to the community while providing the worker a good living.

Many law-related jobs, such as process server, require no more than a high school education. Many jobs, such as legal secretary and paralegal work, expect or require specialized training after high school. Some positions, such as claims adjuster and police officer, expect or require a college degree. To be a lawyer requires not only four years of college but a law degree afterwards. Judges are usually lawyers who are appointed or elected as judges after several years of practicing law.

After police and private investigators, the next most portrayed occupation in television and movies is probably the attorney-at-law. Attorneys are indispensable in a society honoring the rule of law. Attorneys assist individuals with legal problems. Lawyers advise people about the law and assist them in making legal choices. They do everything from writing wills, helping with adoptions, creating businesses and defending persons accused of criminal charges.

As an introduction to possible careers in law, we discuss attorneys-at-law.

Attorney-at-Law

A defendant in Superior Court decided to be his own lawyer, which some say was mistake number one. His second mistake was the first question he asked the victim: "Did you see my face clearly when I took your purse?" The sentence: Two to ten years.
Sacramento Bee, February 9, 1977

An attorney-at-law (also called a lawyer) is a person authorized by law to represent persons (clients) in legal matters. People involved in serious legal matters should be represented by skilled attorneys. If they are not, the result may be similar to that of the criminal defendant in the above story. Knowing which questions to ask in court is one of the things skilled attorneys do well. Attorneys, however, also draft documents involving legal rights and duties and give expert advice on legal questions. Countless businesses and public organizations routinely look to attorneys for such help.

It has been estimated that more than two-thirds of the adults in the United States will consult attorneys for assistance with personal legal problems. Most of these problems involve the preparation of wills, the purchase or sale of real property, divorce, or serious personal injuries caused by other persons. People also seek legal assistance when dealing with difficulties with governmental agencies and consumer problems (e.g., disputes with landlords or with lenders).

Only licensed attorneys may perform most legal services for clients. A person who provides legal services without a license may be guilty of a crime. State statutes provide for the regulation of lawyers and the practice of law. Each state sets its own qualifications for admission to practice law within its borders. To practice in more than one state, an attorney must get a separate license from each state.

To get a license to practice law a person must satisfy four requirements. These requirements are: 1) Possession of good moral character 2) Completion of certain minimum educational requirements. In most states an undergraduate degree from a college and a law degree from a law school. Usually a minimum of 7 years of college is required. Most law schools do not demand any particular major for an undergraduate degree. 3) Passage of an examination (the bar examination). In many states the examination takes two to three days to complete. 4) Taking an oath to support the law and the rules of professional conduct in the state.

A law license permits an attorney to practice all types of law. In reality most attorneys specialize in one or a few areas. Examples include divorce law, tax law, criminal law, personal injury law, business law, and consumer law. All attorneys are allowed to represent clients in court. However, trial work is considered a specialty by most attorneys. A majority of lawyers do not go to court.

Most attorneys make a very good living. However, the type of law practice, the size of the law firm, the nature of a lawyer's specialty, and whether the practice is in a city or the country are among the factors that determine a lawyer's salary. It is not unusual for lawyers in a big city law firm to work more than 60–70 hours a week and be very well paid. Some lawyers representing indigent (needy) clients work the same long hours and make far less money.

Some additional law-related careers include:

Claims Adjustor	Police Officer
Court Reporter	Private Investigator
Credit Counselor	Property or apartment
Escrow Agent	manager
Law Office Manager	Receptionist
Legal Secretary	Runner/Process Server
Paralegal or Legal	Video Technician
Assistant	

Claims Adjustor

America's transportation is primarily provided by the automobile. A secondary result of this fact is the traffic accident. Legal theories addressing automobile accidents have changed with increased dependence on the automobile. Most drivers buy automobile insurance to protect themselves from losses after an automobile accident. When you buy insurance, you meet the salesperson. When you make a claim on insurance, you may meet the claims adjustor.

An insurance claims adjustor examines the circumstances of an accident. The adjustor makes judgments as to who caused the accident. This requires that physical evidence be examined, witnesses be interviewed and experts be consulted. Accidents involving several cars, treacherous conditions or no eyewitnesses can make the adjustor's job difficult.

Typically adjustors work for insurance companies. Often smaller insurance companies will hire claims adjustors from independent agencies. Some adjustors will, at some point in their careers, "hop the fence" and go to work as private investigators for personal injury attorneys. Both occupations re-

quire an eye for detail and a thorough understanding of laws which govern the type of accidents under investigation.

In addition to automobile accidents, the claims adjustor may estimate damages caused by theft, looting or natural disasters. While the stakes may be higher, similar investigative techniques are used. Adjustors estimate the liability of the insurance company and seek settlements with the claimants soon after the harm. Adjustors often work with unresolved claims after a legal action is filed against or by the party whom the company insures.

Some companies hire employees with only a high school education. However, either a two-year degree or bachelor degree is very helpful in getting a job and later promotions. Companies either train in-house or arrange outside training for newly hired adjustors. Basic math skills are essential. Some mechanical ability and people skills are also important. Most states require adjustors to be licensed. Preparation for the license may involve some course work in insurance and a written examination.

Court Reporter

The court reporter uses a stenography machine to take down every word during court proceedings. Stenography machines record communications in shorthand. Shorthand is a language that uses symbols for phrases, words and letters. Commonly used words are signified by one symbol in shorthand. Court Reporters must take special classes to read and write proficiently in this language.

It is easy to spot court reporters. They normally sit with their machines directly in front of the judge in the middle of the courtroom. They are sometimes asked to read back something that was said earlier in the proceedings. When this happens, they must decipher the shorthand created by the stenography machine.

Many court reporters work for private attorneys as well as the courts. Private attorneys hire court reporters to record witness testimony at depositions. The recorded testimony from depositions can then be used against the same witness during a trial. Recently, however, some attorneys have begun to videotape testimony to capture the sights and sounds of the deposition. Some day, the videotaping of depositions and courtroom proceedings could make the court reporter's job as it now exists obsolete. A person considering this position should also acquire skills in word processing, computer graphics, and video operation.

A high school degree plus a specialized training program is the usual preparation for a court stenographer. These training programs are usually available at community colleges and business and trade schools. English skills, ability to memorize, and careful personal habits are among the necessary traits for this career.

Credit Counselor

Many of us living in the United States borrow so much money that our debts exceed our assets. College students, for example, often have large student loan obligations, and very few personal belongings. Others get into debt by charging too many purchases on their credit cards. Most adults have a regular income and can pay debts as they come due. However, an unexpected financial setback, such as the loss of a job, can make it difficult to pay every bill on time. People having a hard time meeting their financial obligations often seek advice from a credit counselor. Credit counselors help people establish budgets to better manage their finances.

A college degree in finance and economics is excellent preparation for this career. Many entrants to the field have prior experience working with banks or other lenders. Credit counselors need to understand bankruptcy laws. They should know when to recommend bankruptcy, and when to avoid it. Creditors of a person who declares bankruptcy often receive little or no repayment of their loan. Due to this, creditors will usually encourage debtors to seek credit counselors to help the debtor to avoid bankruptcy. Most people wish to avoid bankruptcy because it destroys their credit rating, making it difficult to obtain a new credit card or loan.

Escrow Agents

Can I trust you? The answer must be yes if you are an escrow agent. Escrow agents serve as intermediaries, holding important legal documents for other parties.

Typically the services of an escrow agent are an important part of the sale of real estate. In most of these sales, the buyer does not have enough cash to complete the purchase outright. A lending institution loans money to the buyer in exchange for a mortgage on the land. Mortgages allow banks to force a foreclosure sale of the land if payments on the loan are not made. The escrow agent holds technical legal title to the land until the loan is completely paid off. This prevents the buyer from reselling the land as though he owned it free and clear.

Simply holding documents in a fireproof safe sounds easy doesn't it? However the escrow agent does much more. Before the sale, escrow agents are often involved with clearing title to the land. This requires research to determine all previous owners of the property. Such research can be extremely complicated for property which passes through the hands of many people in a short time. And mistakes are quite costly. Imagine the new buyer's alarm when a stranger arrives claiming an ownership interest in the land.

Escrow agents may also be confronted by individuals hoping to learn about the specifics of certain real property sales. For one reason or another, some people do not wish their involvement in some transactions known. The escrow agent is actually hired by both the buyer and the seller. Agents are obliged to follow both parties' instructions as to privacy, financing terms and other matters (assuming no laws are violated). Now you know why this is a job for trustworthy people.

Law Office Manager

The law office manager supervises the law office staff personnel. The manager must also continually monitor court deadlines. Often the manager will keep a master calendar, with all important dates clearly marked, so the attorneys have ample advanced notice of impending deadlines.

The law officer manager needs good organizational skills, since attorneys rely heavily on them to handle the detail work. Judges typically have little sympathy for careless litigators. In fact deadlines are made explicit in laws called "statutes of limitation." The failure to meet these time limits are the most common form of attorney malpractice.

The law office manager may also maintain the office computer system and legal forms. This work involves purchasing equipment and supplies, implementing office standards and even developing new computer applications. As technology advances, so do the opportunities for law office managers in the area of computer applications.

Very few accredited schools teach law office management. The person filling this position may have a background in personnel, administration or secretarial work. Anyone interested in this field should be ready to face a variety of challenges, ranging from understanding office politics to dealing with pushy salespeople. After all, that is what management is all about.

In large law firms office managers usually have at least an undergraduate college degree. In smaller firms a community college degree and experience are the usual minimum requirements.

Legal Secretary

The backbone of the law firm is the legal secretary. Legal secretary work blends secretarial work with more specialized activities. Like a regular secretary, the legal secretary must receive phone calls, take dictation and keep files in order. The legal secretary must produce legal documents which are filed with the court. If the legal documents do not meet the standards required by the Rules of Court, then the court will not accept them. Therefore, the legal secretary should have a working knowledge of the local Rules of Court and other laws about the format and appearance of legal documents.

Some legal documents must be filed within strict time limits. The court will demand a formal explanation for missing the time limits and may assess a monetary penalty. Judges can even dismiss cases when certain documents are not filed on time. When this happens, the law firm will be sued for legal malpractice. For these reasons, the legal secretary keeps a calendar of important dates and follows it closely. Although attorneys are ultimately responsible for the timing and organization of documents filed with the court, they often rely heavily on their legal secretaries.

A high school degree is the minimum job requirement, although additional training at a community college or business or technical school is common. Good technical skills in grammar and spelling are critical. The ability to deal with distractions and emergency multiple tasks all due yesterday is essential. Many legal secretaries go on to law school. Because they have had previous exposure to the legal field, former legal secretaries often perform quite well as attorneys.

Paralegal or Legal Assistants

Paralegals engage in many of the same activities as attorneys. The difference is that paralegals do not have three years of law school training or a license to practice law.

The paralegal usually works under the supervision of an attorney. They often become expert in limited areas of the law through repetitive assignments in a particular area. Paralegals are especially helpful in probate work, family law, wills and trusts, real leases, among others. Paralegals may draft documents, interview witnesses or analyze depositions. Paralegals also often work for government, performing specialized legal research or tasks with an attorney supervisor.

You may see advertisements offering certain legal services, such as help with probate matters, bankruptcy and family law for a reduced price. These services are offered by independent paralegals. In many states these types of activities are legal unless the service gives specific legal advice. Offering legal advice without a license is, of course, illegal. A few states have relaxed the rules regarding the unauthorized practice of law to allow independent paralegals to perform different types of legal services.

With the proliferation of new attorneys, quality paralegals are currently in high demand, and usually enjoy excellent job security.

Many community colleges offer paralegal training. Some business and technical schools also provide paralegal training, as do even a few law schools. The programs may range from one year to four. English, written communication skills, and knowledge of the law are among the important knowledge requirements.

Sometimes the best training comes from work in a law firm. The key is finding a firm with the patience for an inexperienced but eager new employee. Many paralegals soon find themselves completing legal forms, interviewing clients, and even providing courtroom assistance.

Police Officer

It is impossible to watch television and not have some idea about police work. In recent years we not only have dramas but "real life" programs that follow officers about. Like many jobs, the work of the police officer varies depending on where they work. A police officers job in an urban area is very different from that of an officer in a less populated rural area.

The police officer's work is heavily influenced by criminal procedure law. Criminal procedure law limits the tactics which police officers may use to locate and arrest criminal suspects. These laws also describe how to collect the evidence needed to convict the suspects. Normally when an officer removes evidence such as a weapon from the scene of a crime, it goes directly to a police locker for safekeeping. No one touches the weapon except police lab technicians until the date of trial. At that time, the police officer produces the weapon for the jury to examine. The police officer knows everything that happened to the weapon since the day it was taken into custody. This helps to prove the evidence was not tampered with.

Police officers work closely with the district attorney's office. Police officers must gather the evidence which the district attorney uses to convict criminals. The district attorney advises the police officers about the type of evidence needed in each particular case.

Police officers must also understand search and seizure laws. Search and seizure laws protect the privacy of citizens by preventing the police from coming into people's homes without justification. Generally, officers may not enter and search private property without permission or a search warrant. If they do search private property without permission or a warrant, any evidence obtained may not be used to convict the occupant of the property. A different set of rules applies to automobiles. Police officers may search cars if they have probable cause to believe a crime has been committed in or around the vehicle.

Police officers need an arrest warrant before forcibly taking a suspect into custody unless they have witnessed the suspect committing a crime. When the police do arrest someone, they must tell the person their constitutional rights. An individual who has been arrested has the right to remain silent, and the right to an attorney. As with improper searches, when police officers fail to explain these rights, any confessions or other statements made by the suspect cannot be used in court.

Usual entry requirements for police officers are a high school diploma, certain age (usually 21), physical standards, and passing a competitive written examination. College degrees are required for some police forces and a degree usually helps with promotions.

Honesty, good observation skills, ability to work with people and deal with emotion and stress are necessary personal skills.

Private Investigator

When the term "private investigator" is mentioned, most people think of a life full of fast cars, danger and intrigue. However, unlike the Hollywood stereotype, most private investigators have little contact with the world of glamour. In fact, much of the private investigator's work is downright dull. When someone dies, the investigator is often called upon by the family attorney to locate missing heirs. Missing heirs are people who have inherited money or property, but for one reason or another have lost contact with their deceased relative. Locating these people can take months, or even years of painstaking research through telephone directories, yearbooks and historical documents. Rest assured, you will never find "TV P.I.s" spending the entire day in the basement of the public library.

Other P.I.s investigate traffic accidents for personal injury attorneys. Their counterparts are claims adjustors for insurance companies. Both will attempt to find the underlying cause of accidents. They take photographs and measurements, and also interview witnesses. Since skid marks and the memory of witnesses fade quickly, the private investigator may be called upon at a moment's notice, even during the middle of the night!

Many private investigators are former police officers. Some investigative companies hire and train their own staff. A high school education is essential to beginning employment. Most P.I.s have college degrees. P.I.s often must be licensed, but education requirements are not usually a prerequisite to the license.

Property or Apartment Manager

Most people in this country cannot afford to own their own home. Many individuals live in apartment complexes, owned by someone hoping to make a profit from the rentals. Professional residential property managers often administer large apartment complexes. Smaller apartment complexes usually have one or more individuals who live on the premises and manage the property. The landlord is a term often reserved for the owner of the property. The property manager is not the owner, but is the person with whom the tenant has contact.

The manager of an apartment complex is governed by landlord/tenant laws. These laws require the landlord to follow specific guidelines in dealing with tenants. For example, to evict a tenant for nonpayment of rent, most states require the landlord to serve a notice of eviction on the tenant. After the notice is served, the landlord must go to court for permission to remove the tenant. The landlord files a forcible entry and detainer action. These actions are often heard within ten days after the date they are filed. This prevents the freeloading tenant from using the courts to postpone eviction.

Renters must pay a certain amount of money as a security deposit before moving into most apartments. Landlords use the deposit to pay for any property damage caused by the tenant. Landlord/tenant laws set the maximum amount which property managers can collect as a security deposit. These laws also say how and when security deposits shall be returned. In most states, apartment managers who withhold the security deposit of departing tenants must provide a written accounting of how the money was spent.

Landlords must also warn tenants of any hidden dangers on the property, and must provide safe and habitable premises. The courts will close down unsafe apartment complexes. Apartment complexes can be unsafe for a variety of reasons, such as insect infestation, insufficient ventilation, fire hazards, a lack of hot water, or inadequate heating.

In rural areas, rental contracts often have fewer restrictions because fewer people are affected by loud or obnoxious activities. City tenants may never jeopardize the health and safety of other tenants by keeping ultrahazardous substances or performing other dangerous nonresidential activities on the premises. Apartment managers must identify such dangerous activities. The apartment manager is often the first person people turn to in an emergency.

Most apartment managers of medium or large complexes have college degrees in business or real estate. Small apartment managers may require less education but their job still requires an ability to work with people and keep business records.

Receptionist

Receptionists sit in the front of a law office and welcome clients. The receptionist also greets telephone callers.

In many ways the receptionists work is similar to a retail sales job. Fifteen people may come in at 10 AM, and then no one will show up from 10:15 to 12 Noon. The receptionist should enjoy working with people and helping several individuals all at the same time.

In a large firm, the receptionist may be connected to fifty or more attorneys and secretaries. The receptionist directs incoming calls, takes messages and makes announcements over the intercom.

Receptionists must have a professional appearance and demeanor, since they are usually the first person clients see when they enter the office. People make judgments about the quality of a firm based partly on the receptionist's level of professionalism.

By referring to a list of daily appointments, the receptionist can know whom to expect and at what time. Others will come into the office without an appointment. How such people are received depends on who they are and the nature of their business with the firm.

In smaller offices, the receptionist may also set appointments or perform other secretarial duties. Some people double as secretary and receptionist. This situation usually arises when there is not enough work for a full time receptionist.

Other law firms hire part time employees as receptionists. Many young people work as receptionists as a way to help pay for college. Full-time receptionists usually take several breaks during the day. A part-time receptionist can fill in during the lunch hour without having to spend the rest of the day at the office.

There are no special qualifications for a receptionist, but the person should be pleasant, courteous and resourceful.

Runner/Process Server

Good with a cellular phone and a bicycle? If so, you may be qualified to work as a runner. In many large metropolitan areas, thousands of practicing attorneys work within a few miles of the county and/or federal courthouse. Those with active court cases have strict deadlines within which they must file pleadings. These firms have found it quicker and cheaper to travel by bike rather than car. Often young people are hired to make daily trips to the courts to file pleadings, to pick up documents, copies and other materials available at the courthouse.

Runners also pick up and deliver documents to other firms in the area. Many runners keep in touch with the office by cellular phone. This allows for last-minute schedule changes. Some runners work for only one law firm, while others act as independent agents, serving several firms.

If you prefer a bit more excitement in your life, consider working as a process server. The process server must deliver a summons to people who have had a lawsuit filed against them. As you can imagine, most people react poorly to the news that they are being sued. Some people take out their frustration on the person delivering the news. Process servers have been verbally abused, punched, run down and even shot after delivering a summons.

Simply locating the person to be served can be difficult and treacherous. Many process servers double as private investigators.

There are no special qualifications for runners or process servers, but patience and resourcefulness are important.

Video Technician

The video camera has begun to find its place in the courtroom. People who testify at trials have usually been questioned previously at a deposition. During the deposition every word said is recorded for use at trial. Today many attorneys videotape depositions to preserve the facial expressions of witnesses along with the words. In response to this demand, several new companies specializing in the videotaping of depositions have started up within the past two decades.

Videotapes are used during trials to help demonstrate a variety of events which occur outside the courtroom. For example, a news broadcast tape showing the scene of an automobile accident may be used to prove who was at fault for the collision. Another videotape may have recorded a person making certain comments which damage the reputation of an innocent slander victim. The video technician will undoubtedly become more important to the judicial process as people continue to use their video cameras in business and to record important events.

Specialties in Law Practice

Although the license to practice law authorizes attorneys to work in any area of the law, they often specialize. To be knowledgeable and to keep current in theory and practice in all the fields of the law is impossible.

Many states (including Texas, New Mexico, Florida, and California) allow specially educated and experienced attorneys to identify and advertise themselves as certified specialists. To do so they must meet the standards of education and experience set by the state bar. In California, for example, specialties now include: criminal law; family law; immigration and nationality law; tax law; workers' compensation law; and probate, estate planning, and trust law.

Table of Cases

Glossary

A

abandoned property Property with which the owner has voluntarily parted, with no intention of recovering it.

acceptance An act or promise given in response to an offer and showing a desire to contract.

accession The adding of value to a piece of personal property by either labor or materials.

accident insurance Covers losses for certain injuries received through accidental means.

accidental death benefits Insurance that provides a payment to named beneficiaries if the policyholder dies in an automobile accident.

accord An agreement to perform an act to satisfy an existing contractual duty.

accusation Formal charge accusing a person of the commission of a specific crime; made before a trial.

act of state doctrine Doctrine that provides that the courts of one country will not question the public acts of a recognized foreign government within the foreign government's own territory.

actual malice Intent to harm someone. Ill will.

adhesion contract A standard "form" contract drafted by a dominant party and then presented to the other party—the adhering party—on a "take it or leave it" basis.

Administrative Procedure Act of 1946 (APA) A federal law that sets mandatory procedures for an administrative agency to follow.

administrative agency A sub-branch of the executive branch of government set up to carry out laws.

administrative hearing An adjudication held by an administrative agency to hear and decide some factual question related to agency action.

administrative law judge (ALJ) A government employee appointed to hear and decide administrative agency hearings.

administrative law The branch of public law concerned with the powers and actions of administrative agencies. It consists of the rules, regulations, orders, and decisions of the agencies.

administrator A personal representative who is appointed by the court for someone who dies without a will.

adoption A legal process through which a person assumes the responsibility of parenthood for a child.

adversary system A legal system in which parties to a legal action are opponents and are responsible for bringing the facts and law related to their case before the court.

adverse possession The acquisition of title to real property by occupying it openly without the consent of the owner, for a time specified by state statute.

affirmative action Job hiring policies that give special consideration or compensatory treatment to protected groups in an effort to overcome the effects of past discrimination.

agency A relationship between two persons in which, by agreement, one (the principal) is bound by the words and acts of the other (the agent).

agent A person authorized by another to represent or act for him or her.

agreement An understanding of two or more minds. An enforceable agreement is a contract.

alibi A declaration that the accused was someplace else at the time of the crime.

alien corporation A corporation that was formed in another country but does business in the United States.

alimony or spousal support A continuing payment of money by one spouse for the living expenses of the other spouse.

alternative dispute resolution (ADR) Methods of resolving disputes through means other than the courts.

American Arbitration Association (AAA) A nonprofit association that encourages and provides assistance in the use of alternative dispute resolution.

annulment A court order canceling a marriage because some defect existed when the marriage was begun.

answer Defendant's response to a complaint.

anticipatory breach Some act by one party to a contract that tells the other party that the first party will not perform when it comes time to do so (also called anticipatory repudiation).

apparent authority Exists when a principal does something that causes a third party reasonably to believe that someone is an agent when he or she is not.

appellant A party who appeals a case to another court.

appellate court Court that reviews the actions of trial courts.

G-1

appellee A party against whom an appeal is taken.

arbitration A method of resolving disputes in which the parties to a dispute select a neutral third person to hear and decide the dispute. The arbitrator's decision is binding.

arraignment Hearing at which an accused is brought before a court to hear the charges against him or her and to enter a plea to the charges.

arrest Official taking of a person into custody to charge him or her with a crime.

arson The willful and malicious burning of a building owned by another.

articles of incorporation The primary document used to begin the incorporation process.

articles of partnership A written agreement that states each partner's rights in, and duties to, the partnership.

artisan's lien A lien given to a person who has made improvements and added value to another person's personal property; acts as security for payment for services performed.

assault (civil) An intentional, unexcused act that creates in another a reasonable apprehension or fear of an immediate harmful or offensive contact.

assault (criminal) The wrongful threatened use of immediate force against another.

asset An accounting term for anything of value; for example, cash, furniture, real property, and automobiles.

assignment of rights The act of transferring to another all or part of one's rights arising under a contract.

assumption of risk A doctrine under which a plaintiff who voluntarily puts himself or herself in a risky situation, knowing the risk involved, is not allowed to recover. The defense of assumption of risk requires (1) knowledge of the risk and (2) voluntary assumption of the risk.

attachment A court-ordered seizure of property (generally prior to full resolution of the creditor's rights resulting in judgment). Attachment is available only in strict compliance with the applicable state statutes.

attorney-at-law or **lawyer** A person licensed by government to assist parties in resolving legal concerns.

automated teller machine (ATM) Machine that allows bank customers to transact business without the direct help of bank employees. ATMs receive deposits, dispense funds from checking or savings accounts, make credit card advances, and receive payments.

B

bail A sum of money or property given to the court by an accused in exchange for his or her release from jail before trial.

bail bond A promise by another to pay the bail if the defendant fails to appear at trial.

bailee A person to whom possession of personal property is transferred.

bailment A temporary right to possess the personal property of another.

bailor A person who transfers possession of personal property to another.

bait-and-switch advertising Advertising a product at a very attractive price (the "bait") and then informing the consumer, once he or she is in the door, that the advertised product is either not available or is of poor quality. The customer is then urged to purchase ("switched to") a more expensive item.

bankruptcy Proceeding under the Federal Bankruptcy Code whereby all assets of a debtor (excluding certain exempt property) are distributed to creditors. The debtor is then discharged or excused from the legal obligation to pay most of the debts.

battery (civil) Harmful or offensive physical contact that is intentional and unexcused.

battery (criminal) Unlawful harmful or offensive physical contact by one person against another.

bearer A person in possession of an instrument payable to bearer or indorsed in blank.

bearer instrument An instrument that does not designate a specific payee and is payable to anyone who has possession. Examples include an instrument made out to cash or to bearer.

bench trial Trial held before a judge, with no jury.

beneficiary A person who receives benefits from a contract.

bequest or legacy A gift of personal property by will.

bias A prior opinion or belief; a prejudice. A biased person may be unable to make a fair decision.

bilateral contract A contract that includes a promise in exchange for a promise.

bilateral mistake A mistake made by both parties to a contract about the same material fact.

Bill of Rights The first ten amendments to the Constitution; protects the individual from various types of interference by the federal government.

bill of lading A receipt for goods signed by a carrier, such as a trucker, that serves as a contract for the transportation of goods.

blank indorsement An indorsement made by the mere writing of the indorser's name on the back of the instrument.

blue laws Laws restricting business activities on Sunday.

booking Police term referring to searching, fingerprinting, and photographing the person being arrested.

breach of contract Failure to perform part or all of the required duties under a contract.

bribery The offering, requesting, or receiving of anything of value with the aim of influencing a public official.

burden of proof The requirement a party must meet to win the case.

burglary Unlawful entry into a building with the intent to commit a felony.

business ethics Ethical principles used in business decisions such as good faith, honesty, and reasonableness.

business judgment rule A rule that protects corporate management from liability for actions taken in good faith.

business liability insurance Various types of insurance to cover risks in business. Types include, comprehensive general liability insurance, key-employee insurance, product liability insurance, and professional malpractice insurance.

C

capital An accounting term for money or other assets invested in a business.

case law Rules of law announced in court decisions.

cashier's check A draft drawn by a bank on itself.

causation in fact An act or omission without which an injury would not have occurred.

cause of action Legal basis for a lawsuit.

caveat emptor "Let the buyer beware"; a doctrine under which the buyer took the risk as to the quality of goods purchased.

caveat venditor "Let the seller beware."

certificate of deposit (CD) An instrument created by a bank acknowledging the receipt of money with a promise to repay it.

certified check A check drawn by an individual on his or her own account but bearing a guarantee by a bank.

challenge for cause Challenge to a prospective juror based on possible bias in the dispute before the court.

check A draft drawn on a bank (the drawee) and payable to the payee on demand.

citation Information identifying legal research materials. For example, the citation for a court case gives the reporter's volume number, name, and page number.

civil law Law related to the duties that exist generally between persons or between persons and the government, except the duty not to commit crimes.

close corporation A corporation owned by a family or a few individuals. The transfer of shares in the corporation is usually restricted.

closed shop A company where employees must belong to a union before they can be hired. Made illegal by the Taft-Hartley Act.

closing arguments Arguments at the end of a trial by the opposing attorneys.

co-sureties Two or more sureties to the same obligation.

code A collection of statutes or rules on a particular subject.

codicil A written instrument separate from the will that amends or revokes provisions in the will.

coinsurance clause A standard clause in fire and homeowners' policies that requires that the homeowner insure his or her property up to a specified percentage—usually 80 percent—of its value.

collateral Any property used as security for a loan.

collective bargaining Bargaining between an employer and a union over wages and other terms of employment. When a union is duly elected by the employees, the employer must bargain with the union, and the union must represent all workers in the bargaining unit.

collision insurance Automobile insurance that compensates the insured for damage to the insured's car in any type of collision, no matter who is at fault.

comity The voluntary deference by one nation to the laws of another nation.

commerce clause Part of Article I, Section 8, of the U.S. Constitution; gives the federal government the right to regulate commerce.

commercial paper Signed writing that contains an unconditional promise or order to pay an exact sum of money, either when demanded or at an exact future time. Includes drafts, checks, promissory notes, and certificates of deposit.

common carrier A transportation carrier that is licensed to provide transportation services to the public.

common law marriage An informal marriage occurring without a marriage license when persons agree to be married, live together as husband and wife, and hold themselves out to the community as married. This type of marriage is recognized in fifteen states.

common law The body of judge-made law. The common law system originally developed under the English court system.

common stock The usual stock of voting ownership in a corporation. If other types of shares exist, common stockholders usually are the last to receive dividends.

community property All property acquired (in a community property state) by the husband or wife during a marriage other than property acquired by gift or inheritance. Each spouse technically owns a one-half interest.

comparative negligence A concept whereby liability for injury is shared by all persons whose carelessness led to the injury. Liability is shared on the basis of proportionate fault.

complaint The pleading used to begin a lawsuit. It contains (1) facts necessary for the court to take jurisdiction, (2) facts necessary to show the plaintiff's right to a remedy, and (3) remedy the plaintiff seeks (usually a request for money for injuries and damages).

comprehensive insurance Automobile insurance that compensates the insured for losses to his or her vehicle for reasons other than collision. Examples include vandalism, rock damage on highways, or theft of the vehicle.

compulsory accident insurance A state statute requiring that all drivers purchase automobile insurance.

compulsory attendance law A state law that specifies the ages between which each minor must attend a public or private school.

computer crime An act directed against computers or computer parts or a crime using computers as instruments of criminal conduct.

concurrent jurisdiction Jurisdiction that exists when more than one court has the power to hear a case.

concurrent ownership Two or more persons own property together.

concurring opinion A written opinion of a judge who agrees with the unanimous or majority opinion but feels strongly about making or emphasizing a point that was not made or emphasized in that opinion.

confusion The mixing together of personal property belonging to two or more owners so that the independent goods cannot be identified.

consent Voluntary agreement to a proposition or act of another.

consequential damages Indirect but foreseeable damages resulting from a party's breach of contract.

consideration Value given in return for a promise. Consideration consists of two parts: (1) something of *legal value* must be given in exchange for the promise, and (2) it must be part of a *bargained-for* exchange.

consignment A transaction in which the owner of goods delivers them to another who has the authority to sell them.

consolidation The legal combination of two or more corporations, the result of which is that each corporation ceases to exist and a new one emerges. The new corporation assumes all the assets and obligations of the former corporations.

conspiracy A plan by two or more persons to commit an illegal act. The conspiracy is complete once an act in furtherance of the crime is performed.

constitution A written document that spells out the powers and limits of a government.

constitutional law A fundamental law that spells out the general organization, powers, and limits of a government.

constructive eviction A wrongful breach by the landlord of the tenant's right to enjoy and use rental property that is so serious as to make reasonable use of the property difficult or impossible.

constructive notice Notice to the general public given indirectly; after it is given, courts assume that everyone has been notified of the fact. Constructive notice is often accomplished by publication of an advertisement in a newspaper.

consumer protection law All statutes, agency rules, and common law judicial rulings that protect the interests of consumers.

contempt of court Willful refusal to obey a legitimate order of a court; punishable by a fine and/or imprisonment.

contract A legally enforceable agreement to do or not do a specified thing.

contract under seal A formal contract with a special seal attached.

contractual capacity The legal right to contract.

contributory negligence A concept whereby a complaining party's own negligence contributed to his or her harm. Usually a complete defense to a negligence action.

conversion The unauthorized *taking* of the personal property of another and the wrongful exercise of the rights of ownership.

conveyance The voluntary transfer of real property from one person to another.

cooling-off statute FTC regulation that gives consumers three days to cancel any door-to-door sale.

copyright An intangible right given to the author or originator of certain literary or artistic productions.

corporal punishment The use of physical pain to punish a student. Examples of physical force include paddling, swatting, or spanking.

corporate social responsibility The duty of corporations to act in a manner consistent with what is best for society.

corporation A legal entity created under the authority of the laws of a state or the federal government. The entity is distinct from its owners, the shareholders.

cost-benefit analysis A way to reach a decision in which the costs of a given action are compared with the benefits of the action.

counteradvertising New advertising undertaken because of an FTC order to correct earlier false claims made about a product.

counterclaim Claim against the plaintiff by a defendant in a lawsuit; in effect the counterclaim sues the plaintiff.

counteroffer A rejection of the original offer together with a new offer.

course of dealing Prior conduct between contracting parties that establishes a common basis for their understanding.

course of performance The way the parties conduct themselves toward each other after the contract is created.

court A place provided by government where people may go to resolve legal disputes. There are different types of courts for different types of disputes.

covenant of quiet enjoyment An implied promise by the landlord that during the lease term, the landlord will not disturb the tenant's use and enjoyment of the property.

creditor A person or business owed money or property.

creditors' composition agreement An agreement formed by and among the creditors and the debtor. The creditors each agree to accept a lesser sum in payment, and the debtor is released after payment of the agreed sum.

crime A wrong against society, defined in a statute and punishable by society.

criminal intent A wrongful mental state in which a person knowingly and purposely intends to commit a criminal act.

criminal law Law related to wrongs committed against the public, punishable by fines, imprisonment, or both.

criminal solicitation An act requesting or encouraging another to commit a crime.

cross-examination The questioning of an opposing witness during the trial.

D

damages Money sought as a remedy for a wrong, such as a tortious act (tort).

deadly force Force likely to result in death or serious bodily harm.

death taxes Estate and inheritance taxes. Taxes that arise because of one's death.

debtor A person or business that owes a debt to another.

decedent A deceased person.

deceptive advertising Advertising that misleads consumers, either by making unjustified or misleading claims or by omitting important facts concerning a product's performance or a service.

deductible A provision in the insurance contract through which the policyholder agrees to pay a certain amount of any loss—for example, the first $250 of a claim.

deed A document used to transfer ownership interest in real property.

defamation Any unprivileged communication that is published or spoken and that causes injury to another's good name, reputation, or character.

default judgment Judgment entered against a defendant who fails to respond to a complaint.

defendant The person against whom an action in court is brought.

defense The counter-argument made by a defendant as to why he or she should not be held responsible in a legal proceeding.

delegation of duties The act of transferring to another all or part of one's duties arising under a contract.

deposition The taking of sworn testimony of witnesses before trial; a form of discovery.

destination contract A term in a sales contract where the seller is responsible for delivering the goods to a specific destination.

determinate sentence A sentence of confinement for a fixed period as specified by law.

determinate sentencing Sentencing that provides set penalties for specific types of crimes.

devise A gift of real estate by will.

direct examination In a trial, the first questioning of a witness by the side that called that witness.

disability insurance Provides replacement income for a policyholder who becomes unable to work because of an injury or illness.

disaffirmance Legal avoidance, or setting aside, of a contractual duty.

discharge The termination of one's contract obligation.

disclaimer A denial of a warranty that might otherwise exist.

disclosed principal A principal whose identity and existence are known by a third party at the time the agent enters into a transaction.

discovery The gathering of information from the opposing party or from witnesses before a trial.

disparate-impact discrimination Discrimination that results from certain employer practices or procedures that, although not obviously biased, have a discriminatory effect.

disparate-treatment discrimination Employment practices that show intentional bias against a certain group of persons, such as African Americans or women.

dissenting opinion A written opinion of a judge who does not agree with the majority opinion.

dissolution (1) The legal death of a corporation. (2) A termination of a marriage by court order.

diversity of citizenship A basis for federal court jurisdiction over a lawsuit when the parties are citizens of different states and the amount in controversy exceeds $50,000.

dividend A distribution of corporate profits or income ordered by the directors and paid to the shareholders of record.

divorce A termination of a marriage by court order.

document of title A paper, such as a bill of lading or warehouse receipt, exchanged in the regular course of business to show the right to possession of goods.

domestic corporation A corporation that does business in its home state where it was created.

donee A person receiving a gift.

donor A person giving a gift.

draft Any instrument drawn on another (drawee) that orders the drawee to pay a certain sum of money.

dramshop statute A state law that makes it a crime for a tavern proprietor or employee to serve intoxicants to an obviously drunk patron or to someone under the legal drinking age.

drawee The person who is ordered to pay money to another (the payee).

drawer A person who creates a draft (including a check).

due process clause Part of the Fourteenth Amendment to the U.S. Constitution; limits the government's power to deprive any person of life, liberty, or property without due process of law.

durable power of attorney A document authorizing a person to act and make decisions for another, including decisions about health care if the person becomes incapacitated.

duress (civil) Threat of or actual physical harm that deprives a person of the freedom of will to choose and decide.

duress A wrongful threat causing another person to perform an act that he or she would not otherwise perform.

duty of care The requirement that each of us behave reasonably in our conduct toward others.

duty-based ethics Ethical theory holding that proper behavior is measured by the performance of duties based on a set of deeply held values. Religious principles are an example of duty-based ethics.

E

easement The right of a person to make limited use of another person's property without taking anything from the property.

emancipated minor An individual who has not yet reached the age of majority, but who has been set free of the control and custody of his or her parents either by voluntary agreement or otherwise.

emancipation The act by which a minor child becomes free of parental control and custody.

embezzlement The fraudulent taking of another person's property or money by a person who was entrusted with it; often involves an employee who steals money from an employer.

eminent domain The power of the government to take private land for public use. The government is required to pay the owner just compensation for the property.

employee A person who works for another: in agency law, one whose physical conduct is *controlled* by or is subject to control by the employer.

employment discrimination Treating employees or job applicants unequally on the basis of race, color, gender, national origin, or religion. Prohibited by Title VII of the Civil Rights Act of 1964, as amended.

employment-at-will doctrine A doctrine by which historically an employer was free to fire an employee at any time without notice. Today, the right to fire is subject to several federal and state restrictions.

entrapment A defense that can be offered when a police officer or other government agent has suggested commission of a crime and has induced, or encouraged, an individual to commit it.

entrepreneur A person who organizes, manages, and assumes all the financial risks of beginning a business.

environmental impact statement (EIS) A report required by law before any major federal action can be taken that might affect the environment. The report analyzes the proposed action's impact on the environment and possible alternative actions.

environmental law Statutory and administrative laws which protect the environment.

equity A branch of law supplying special rules and procedures when legal rules are inadequate to promote justice and fairness.

escrow agent A neutral party in the sale of real estate who facilitates the sale by monitoring the performance of both the buyer and seller.

escrow An arrangement whereby the buyer and seller designate an agent to act for both parties in carrying out specified instructions from the buyer and seller for gathering and distributing documents and funds necessary to a land sale agreement.

establishment clause Part of the First Amendment to the U.S. Constitution; prohibits the government from establishing a state religion.

estate planning An analysis of what a person owns, expects to own, and what he or she owes—in other words, a person's assets and liabilities; it is a strategy for the use of these assets during that person's life and for their distribution at his or her death.

estate tax A tax imposed by the federal government and some states on the property given to another after the death of the giver (donor).

estoppel An equitable judicial doctrine that keeps a person from denying something that his or her previous statements or actions have claimed or implied is true.

estray statute A state statute that requires the finder of lost property to report his or her discovery. After a specified time, if the true owner does not claim the property, the finder becomes the new owner.

ethics Standards of fair and honest conduct applied to social behavior.

eviction The process by which a landlord puts a tenant out of property, either through direct action or through court action.

evidence Information presented at the trial by the parties and accepted by the court. Examples of evidence include testimony of witnesses, photographs, documents, handwriting samples, dented fenders, and the like.

exclusionary rule Rule that excludes evidence obtained as a result of unreasonable search and seizure from being used to convict the accused.

exclusive jurisdiction Jurisdiction that exists when a case can only be heard in a particular court.

exculpatory clause A contract provision that releases a party from liability for his or her wrongful acts.

executed contract A contract that has been fully performed by all parties.

executor A personal representative named in a will. The person in charge of the deceased person's affairs after that person's death.

executory contract A contract that has not been completely performed.

expert fact-finding A nonbinding process in which an appointed third-party expert investigates or hears facts on selected issues.

express contract A contract whose terms are stated in oral and/or written form (rather than being implied from the circumstances).

express warranty A statement, part of a sales contract, in which the seller assures the quality, condition, description, or performance potential of the goods.

expropriation Government seizure of a privately owned business or privately owned goods for a proper public purpose and with just compensation.

F

fair use doctrine Allows a temporary reasonable and limited use of a copyrighted work without the need to get permission from the owner.

false imprisonment The intentional confinement or restraint of another person's movements without justification.

family settlement agreements Private agreements among beneficiaries to a will.

Federal Register The official publication of the federal government for all agency regulations.

federal law Law consisting of the U.S. Constitution, statutes originated by Congress, treaties and presidential orders, regulations created by federal administrative agencies, and decisions of the federal courts.

federalism A system in which two or more levels of government direct the affairs of the same people in the same location.

fee simple Ownership of the entire bundle of rights in property.

felony A serious crime punishable by death or imprisonment in a federal or state penitentiary for more than a year. Murder, rape, robbery, burglary, selling illegal drugs, and kidnapping are felonies.

fiduciary relationship A relationship involving trust and confidence between the parties involved.

field sobriety test A test given by a police officer to determine whether a driver of a vehicle is intoxicated. The test is given at the site where the person is detained.

financial responsibility law A state statute requiring that after an automobile accident, a driver prove either that he or she has insurance coverage or that he or she has the ability to pay for any harm caused by the accident.

firm offer An offer for the sale of goods made in writing and signed by a merchant. The UCC provides that a firm offer is binding for the time stated, up to three months.

fixture Personal property attached to the land—a thing *affixed* to realty. The term *affixed* means attached to realty by roots, embedded in it, or permanently attached by cement, plaster, bolts, nails, or screws.

forbearance Refraining from, or promising to refrain from, doing something one has a legal right to do.

foreclosure An action by a person who holds a mortgage to sell the property to pay off the mortgage debt.

foreign corporation In a given state, a corporation that does business in that state but was incorporated in another state.

forgery The false or unauthorized signing of a document, or the false making of a document, with the intent to defraud.

formal contract A contract that by law requires a special form or method of creation (formation) to be enforceable.

formal will A written will, signed by the testator, properly witnessed, and, where required, published: one that meets formal statutory requirements for a valid will.

franchise An arrangement by which the owner of a trade name licenses others to use the trade name in selling goods or services.

franchisee A purchaser of a franchise.

franchisor The seller of the franchise.

fraud A misrepresentation of a material fact made knowingly with the intent to deceive another, who is then deceived to his or her detriment, or harm.

free exercise clause Part of the First Amendment to the U.S. Constitution; prohibits the government from interfering in people's free exercise of their religious beliefs.

fungible goods Each item is identical to every other item, such as with grain or oil.

G

gambling Any scheme that involves distribution of property by chance among persons who have paid something of value for the opportunity to receive the property.

garnishment A collection remedy that allows the creditor to attach a debtor's money or property (such as wages owed or bank accounts) that is in the hands of a third person.

general damages Compensation to the injured party for the actual loss of the bargain caused by the breach of contract.

general jurisdiction Court that is authorized to hear and decide virtually any type of case.

general partner In a limited partnership, a partner who assumes responsibility for the management of the partnership and liability for all partnership debts.

genuine assent A true objective "meeting of the minds."

gift A voluntary transfer of property without an expectation of receiving anything in return.

good faith Honesty in fact and the observance of reasonable commercial standards of fair dealing in the trade.

good faith purchaser A purchaser of goods who buys without knowledge of any circumstance that would cause her or him to have a reasonable doubt about the seller's title to the goods being sold.

goods Items of tangible, movable personal property.

gratuitous promise A promise given without expectation of receiving something in return.

guaranty A contract promise made by a third person to be secondarily liable for another's debt. The guarantor is liable only if the debtor has defaulted and the creditor has attempted to collect from the debtor.

guardian ad litem (Latin: for the suit) A guardian appointed by the court to protect the interests of a minor in a lawsuit.

guest statute A state statute that forbids a guest passenger in an automobile from collecting damages for injuries from the driver for ordinary negligence.

H

health insurance Broad term covering accident insurance, disability insurance, and medical expense insurance. Most often used when referring to medical expense insurance.

holder A person in possession of a negotiable instrument who is either the payee, a bearer, or one to whom the instrument is properly indorsed.

holder in due course (HDC) Any holder who acquires a negotiable instrument for value, in good faith, and without notice that the instrument is overdue, that it has been dishonored, or that any defense or claim to it exists on the part of any person.

holographic will A self-prepared will written, signed, and dated entirely in the handwriting of the testator.

homeowners' insurance Insurance policy that compensates the insured for several types of property damage and personal liability.

homestead exemption A law allowing an owner to designate his or her house and adjoining land as a homestead and thus exempt it from liability to creditors.

hot-cargo contracts An agreement in which an employer agrees with a union not to handle, use, or deal with the goods of other employers who do not use union workers. Outlawed by the Landrum-Griffin Act.

I

identification Designation of goods as the subject matter of sales contract.

immunity Exemption from prosecution.

implied warranty A warranty that the law implies through either the situation of the parties or the nature of the transaction.

implied warranty of fitness for a particular purpose A warranty that arises when a buyer, having stated the intended use of the goods to be purchased, relies on the expertise of the seller of the goods.

implied warranty of habitability A warranty arising automatically in a lease that requires that a landlord leasing residential property keep it in a habitable condition (that is, keep it safe and suitable to live in).

implied warranty of merchantability An implied promise by a merchant seller that goods are reasonably fit for the general purpose for which they are sold. This warranty exists in every sale by a merchant unless specifically disclaimed.

implied-in-fact contract A contract implied from the conduct of the parties (not an express contract).

impossibility of performance A doctrine by which a party to a contract is relieved of his or her duty to perform because performance becomes impossible.

incidental beneficiary A party who benefits from a contract but whose benefit was not the reason the contract was formed.

incontestability clause A provision in an insurance contract that provides that after a policy has existed for a specified time—usually two or three years—the insurer cannot challenge statements made in the application.

independent contractor A person who is hired to perform a particular task and performs the task largely how he or she chooses.

independent regulatory agency An administrative body that has the power to regulate some policy area and that is led by officials who cannot be dismissed by the president except for cause.

indeterminate sentence A sentence of confinement for the maximum period defined by law subject to termination by the parole board or other agency at any time after the minimum period has been served.

indeterminate sentencing Sentencing that provides a wide range of prison terms for a specific type of crime; the term to be served is decided by a state board.

indorsee The one to whom a negotiable instrument is transferred by indorsement.

indorsement A signature placed on an instrument for the purpose of transferring one's ownership in the instrument.

indorser A person, either the payee or the holder of an instrument, who signs her or his name on the back of the instrument.

infancy The state or period before the legal age of adulthood.

infliction of mental distress Extreme and outrageous intentional behavior that causes severe emotional distress to another.

informal contract A contract that does not require any special form to be valid. Most contracts are informal contracts.

inheritance tax A tax imposed by some states on those who receive property from a person after he or she has died.

injunction An equitable remedy by which a court orders one party to refrain from certain conduct.

innkeeper's lien A lien allowing an innkeeper (the proprietor of a hotel or motel) to take personal property brought by a guest into the hotel (suitcases and contents) as security for a hotel bill the guest does not pay.

inquisitorial system A legal system that allows the judge to investigate, question witnesses, and seek out evidence.

insanity The state in which mental illness or disease makes a person incapable of forming criminal intent.

installment loan A loan that requires payment of a debt over time, usually with monthly payments.

insurable interest A real economic risk related to rights in property or a person's well-being. A person with an insurable interest can purchase insurance coverage.

insurance agent An employee of an insurance company.

insurance An arrangement for transferring and allocating risk.

insurance broker An independent contractor who represents the buyer in purchasing insurance.

insured The person covered by the insurance policy.

insurer The insurance company.

intangible personal property Personal property that represents a set of rights and duties; it has no real physical existence.

intangible property Property right created by law whose value is not in its physical existence. Ownership in a business or of a contract is an intangible property.

intellectual property Property resulting from intellectual or creative processes; the product of an individual's mind.

intended beneficiary A third party beneficiary for whose benefit a contract is formed. Intended beneficiaries can sue the promisor to enforce the contract.

intentional tort A wrongful act knowingly committed.

inter vivos **trust** A trust created by a grantor during his or her lifetime.

international law The body of written and unwritten laws governing relations between independent nations.

interrogation Questioning of a suspect in a criminal investigation.

interrogatories Series of written questions for parties or witnesses, who prepare written answers and then sign under oath; a form of discovery.

intestacy laws The rules that determine distribution of a deceased person's property if he or she dies without a will.

intestate When a person dies without having left a will.

intoxication The state of being under the influence of either drugs or alcohol.

invasion of privacy Publishing or otherwise making known or using information relating to the private life and affairs of a person without that person's permission or approval.

involuntary bankruptcy A bankruptcy begun by creditors against the will of the debtor.

J

joint and several liability A type of responsibility in which a third party may sue any one or more parties without suing all of them.

joint liability Shared responsibility for debts or obligations. A third party must generally sue all liable parties together.

joint tenancy A form of property co-ownership with the right of survivorship. If any joint tenant dies, his or her interest passes to the surviving joint tenants.

joint venture Two or more persons or businesses combine their interests in a one-time business effort. The parties agree to share in losses or profits equally or according to their contributions.

judge or justice The person who presides over the court.

judgment rate of interest A rate of interest fixed by statute added to an unpaid money judgment until it is paid.

judgment The concluding pronouncement of the court.

judicial circuit The geographical limits of the jurisdiction of a federal circuit court of appeals.

judicial review The power of the federal courts to determine whether a particular law violates the Constitution.

jurisdiction The power of a court to hear and decide a specific case.

jury A group of persons chosen to decide questions of fact in legal actions.

just cause A requirement that an employer have a legitimate provable reason before terminating an employee.

L

landlord One who rents property to another.

landlord's lien A statutory right given a landlord on a tenant's personal property for the tenant's failure to pay rent.

larceny The wrongful taking of another's personal property.

late charge A charge by a landlord for late payment of rent.

law Enforceable rules that govern how individuals deal with each other and how each individual interacts with society as a whole.

lawsuit, or **litigation** Civil court proceeding brought to enforce a right between persons.

lease A transfer by a landlord of the right to occupy or use land for a certain time to a tenant in exchange for rent.

legal detriment Legal cost; for example, doing something one is not already required to do or refraining from doing something one has a right to do.

legal rate of interest A rate fixed by statute to be used when contracting parties forget to fix a rate of interest in a loan.

lemon laws State statutes designed to assist buyers of seriously defective goods in getting a replacement or full refund.

lessee A person who leases property from another.

lessor A person who leases property to another.

liability insurance Automobile insurance that compensates the insured for losses for bodily injury (personal liability or PL insurance) and property damage (PD insurance) occurring as the result of the negligence of the insured or other covered drivers.

libel Written defamation.

license A revocable right to enter the land of another.

lien A right a creditor has against the property of the debtor.

life insurance Insurance to protect against financial loss to the beneficiaries because of the death of the insured.

limited jurisdiction Court that is limited in the types of cases it can hear and decide.

limited partner In a limited partnership, a partner who contributes capital to the partnership but has a limited right to participate in the management and operation of the business. The limited partner has no liability for partnership debts beyond his or her investment in the business.

limited partnership A special type of statutory partnership. Requires at least one general partner and one or more limited partners. The major benefit of a limited partnership is limited liability for limited partners.

liquidated damages Damages of a certain amount, specified in a contract, to be paid if there is a future default or breach of contract.

liquidation The process by which corporate assets are converted into cash, which is then distributed to creditors and shareholders according to specified rules of preference.

living trust A popular term for an *inter vivos* trust whose primary purpose is to avoid the expenses and publicity of probate.

living will or directive to physician A document informing a physician of a person's wishes regarding the use of life-saving devices in the case of terminal illness.

long-arm statute State law that authorizes a court to hear cases brought against nonresidents in certain circumstances.

lost property Property with which the owner has involuntarily parted and then cannot find or recover.

M

M'Naghten test A legal test for criminal insanity. It holds that a defendant is not responsible if, at the time of the offense, he or she did not understand the nature and quality of the act or did not know that the act was wrong.

Magnuson-Moss Warranty Act A federal law designed to prevent deception in warranties by making them easier to understand. The act is enforced by the Federal Trade Commission (FTC).

mailbox rule Rule providing that an acceptance is effective when it is sent by an authorized manner (for example, placed in a mailbox).

majority opinion A written court decision outlining the views of the majority of the judges deciding the case.

majority The legal age when each individual can acquire all the rights and responsibilities of an adult.

maker A person who creates and is obligated under a promissory note or a certificate of deposit.

marital property Property owned by a wife and husband jointly. Usually this property is acquired during, not before, the marriage.

marriage The legal union of husband and wife.

mechanic's lien A lien on an owner's real property for labor, services, or materials furnished to or made on the property (for example, reroofing or adding a swimming pool to a house).

mediation The use of a neutral third party to assist disputing parties in voluntarily resolving their dispute.

medical expense insurance Covers doctor and hospital expenses when a person is ill.

medical payment coverage Automobile insurance that pays hospital and other medical bills and sometimes funeral expenses of occupants of the insured's car.

merchant A businessperson who regularly *deals in goods* of the kind involved in the sales contract.

merger The legal combination of two or more corporations, the result of which is that the surviving corporation acquires all the assets and obligations of the other corporation, which then ceases to exist.

mini-trial An informal, non-binding, trial-like proceeding voluntarily engaged in by disputing parties, usually large business organizations.

minor Any individual under the legal age of majority when one is considered an adult.

Miranda warnings Warnings police must give persons detained or arrested as criminal suspects.

mirror-image rule Rule requiring that an offeree's attempted acceptance match the terms of an offer exactly in order for a contract to be formed. If it does not match the offer exactly, it is considered an implied rejection and a counteroffer.

misdemeanor A crime punishable by a fine or by confinement for up to a year. Disorderly conduct, shoplifting, and trespass are common misdemeanors.

mislaid property Property with which the owner has voluntarily parted and then cannot find or recover.

mitigation of damages Rule requiring the injured party to try to reduce (mitigate) the damages suffered as a result of a breach of contract.

mortgage A written instrument giving a creditor an interest in the debtor's property as security for a debt.

motion for a directed verdict Argument to a judge by a defendant that the plaintiff did not present sufficient believable evidence in a trial to support the plaintiff's legal claim; asks the judge to rule in the defendant's favor.

motion for a new trial Request to a judge for a new trial.

motion for judgment notwithstanding a verdict Request to a judge to reverse the jury verdict; argues that there is no reasonable way the jury should have reached the verdict, given the evidence presented at trial.

motion for judgment on the pleadings Request for a judgment based on the argument that the pleadings fail to state a cause of action.

motion for summary judgment Request for a judgment based on the argument that no issues of fact exist in the dispute.

motion Formal request to a court for an action.

motion to dismiss, or **demurrer** Pleading in which a defendant claims that the plaintiff has failed to state a legal basis on which to sue. It is sometimes called a "so what" motion.

motive The reason for a criminal act.

mutual benefit bailment A bailment where both the bailor and the bailee receive a contract benefit from the bailment.

mutual rescission An enforceable agreement to cancel a contract and return the parties to the positions they occupied before the contract's formation.

N

national law The law of a particular nation.

natural law Basic moral law that is consistent with nature, applies to all persons, does not change, and lasts for all time.

natural rights Rights that are beyond the power of government to grant or deny.

negligence *per se* [Latin: of itself] The proof of the act establishes the duty.

negligence The failure to exercise the standard of care that a reasonable person would exercise in similar circumstances.

negotiable instrument Commercial paper that meets the requirements under the UCC for negotiability.

negotiation Communication for the purpose of persuasion. In commercial paper law the transferring of a negotiable instrument to another in such a way that the transferee becomes a holder.

no-fault insurance A system of automobile insurance that provides benefits to the insured, regardless of who is at fault in an accident.

nominal damages A small money award (often one dollar) granted to a plaintiff who suffered a wrong but no actual loss.

nonprofit corporation A corporation formed without a profit-making purpose.

novation The substitution, by agreement, of a new contract for an old one, with the rights under the old one being terminated. A new party is substituted for an original party.

O

objective theory of contracts Theory by which the intent to contract is judged by what a reasonably objective party would believe was meant by a person's language and conduct.

offer A promise to do or not do something proposed as an exchange for a specified act or promise of another.

offeree A person to whom an offer is made.

offeror A person who makes an offer.

ombudsman A neutral third party who investigates and encourages

opening statements Statements made by the parties' attorneys at a trial before presentation of evidence. The purpose is to inform the court of what evidence they intend to offer and what they believe it will prove.

opinion The written decision of the court, containing the reason for the decision, the rules of law that apply, and the judgment.

option contract An agreement whose subject matter is the right to buy or sell something at a certain price at a certain time.

order instrument A negotiable instrument that is payable to a specific payee or to any person the payee by indorsement designates.

original jurisdiction The power of a court to take a case, try it, and decide it.

other-driver coverage Insurance protection if the automobile is driven by someone who has the owner's permission.

output contract A contract in which the seller agrees to sell to the buyer, and the buyer agrees to purchase from the seller, all of something the seller produces.

overruled A ruling by which the judge disagrees with an objection to offered evidence.

P

parol evidence rule A rule of evidence that says a written contract can be proved only by itself; evidence of prior negotiations or agreements that contradict or vary the terms of the contract will not be allowed.

parole The release from prison of a convict who has not yet served his or her full term. The release requires that the parolee follow certain conditions to remain out of prison.

partially disclosed principal A principal whose identity is unknown by a third person, but the third party does know that an agency exists.

partnership An association of two or more persons to carry on as co-owners of a business for profit.

passing off Falsely encouraging buyers to believe that one product is really another.

past consideration Promise to reward a person for actions or events that took place before the promise to reward.

patent A grant from the government allowing an inventor the exclusive right to make, use, and sell an invention for seventeen years.

payee The person to whom a negotiable instrument is payable.

penalty An amount specified in a contract to be paid upon default or breach of contract, that is *designed to penalize* the breaching party. Penalty clauses are not enforceable.

peremptory challenge Challenge to a prospective juror without cause; limited in number by statute.

perfection The method by which a secured party obtains priority over later creditors with regard to collateral.

performance The fulfillment of one's obligation under a contract.

periodic tenancy A tenancy for a period determined by frequency of rent payments; automatically renewed unless proper notice is given.

personal defense Defense that can be used to avoid payment to an ordinary holder of a negotiable instrument but not to an HDC.

personal identification number (PIN) Secret number that allows a customer to get remote access to his or her bank account.

personal property Property that is movable; any property that is not real property.

petitioner Often used interchangeably with *appellant*. Also refers to a party who initiates a proceeding in equity.

petty offense, or **infraction** A minor offense against the state. Traffic offenses and violations of building codes are examples.

physical damage coverage Automobile insurance that compensates the insured for damages to your own automobile.

plaintiff The person who brings an action in court against another person.

plea-bargain Agreement between prosecution and defendant providing that the defendant will plead guilty to a lesser or related crime.

pleading Formal written statement or form presented to a court by each side in a dispute.

police powers The inherent rights and powers of the states to protect and promote the public health, safety, and general welfare of their citizens.

policy An insurance contract.

power of attorney A formal written document or instrument authorizing another to act as one's agent. Through the power of attorney, the agent becomes an attorney-in-fact.

precedent A court decision that provides an example or authority for deciding later cases involving identical or similar facts. To serve as precedents, cases must have been decided in the same state and in the same or a higher court.

preemptive rights A preference a shareholder has over all other purchasers to subscribe to or purchase a new issue of stock. It allows the shareholder to maintain his or her proportionate control of the corporation.

preferred stock A stock with a preference over common stock. Usually, this means that holders of preferred stock have priority over holders of common stock when dividends are issued and when investments are repaid.

premium The sum of money paid by a policyholder for insurance protection.

prenuptial agreement A contract made before a marriage that sets forth the property rights and support understandings of each spouse in case the marriage fails.

preponderance of the evidence Greater part of the evidence; the burden of proof in the usual civil case. Proving one's case by the preponderance of the evidence involves proving that the facts one is arguing are more probable than not.

pretermitted heir A child either unintentionally left out of a will or one born after the will is made. States often provide that unless a testator makes it clear that the omission was on purpose, such a child will get a share of the testator's property.

pretrial hearing Informal discussion between a judge and the opposing attorneys before a trial. The purpose is to plan the course of the trial and encourage settlement.

principal A person who authorizes another (an agent) to act on his or her behalf.

private corporation A corporation created either wholly or in part for private benefit.

private judging A method of alternative dispute resolution that uses legally trained arbitrators who follow court procedures in hearing a case. Normal rights of court appeal are usually available.

privilege A legal right to do (or not do) something.

privilege against self-incrimination The constitutional privilege that protects a defendant from being compelled to testify against himself or herself in a criminal case.

privity of contract A relationship created between parties to a contract.

probable cause Strong likelihood that a person has committed or is about to commit a crime.

probate The court process of proving the validity of a will and following the wishes of the testator. Includes distributing the property to appropriate beneficiaries.

probation A sentence under which a convicted defendant may avoid prison by meeting certain conditions over a stated period of time.

procedural law Legal rules for processing civil and criminal cases through the court system.

process server Person who delivers a copy of the summons and complaint personally to the defendant.

product liability Responsibility for injury or damage caused by a defective product.

professional corporation A corporation formed by professionals, such as doctors, or lawyers.

profit The right of a person to go onto land in another's possession and remove some part of the land or products of the land.

promise A declaration that something either will or will not happen in the future.

promisee A person to whom a promise is made.

promisor A person who makes a promise.

promissory estoppel A doctrine allowing enforcement of a promise otherwise unsupported by consideration. The doctrine applies when a person makes an important promise upon which another reasonably relies to his or her detriment.

promissory note An unconditional written promise to pay a sum of money to another by a certain time.

promoter A person who takes the preliminary steps in organizing a corporation.

property taxes Taxes applied to real and personal property. The most important tax is the one applied to real estate.

property The legally protected rights and interests a person has in anything with an ascertainable value that is subject to ownership.

protected class A group of persons specifically protected by the Civil Rights Act of 1964, as amended, from discriminatory treatment on the basis of race, color, gender, national origin, or religion.

proximate cause Substantial cause of an injury. An act that could have been foreseen to cause the injury.

proxy A written authorization allowing another person to vote a shareholder's shares at a corporation meeting.

public corporation A corporation formed by government to meet some political or governmental purpose.

publicly held corporation A *large private corporation* whose stock is widely available for purchase by the general public.

puffery Seller's talk. Claims about the quality of goods, usually exaggerated. Not considered fraud.

punitive, or **exemplary damages** Damages that punish the defendant or set an example for similar wrongdoers.

purchase-money security interest A security interest in property created at the time the property is sold to secure repayment of the debt incurred to make the purchase.

Q

qualified indorsement An indorsement to disclaim or limit the indorser's contract liability. "Without recourse" is a qualified indorsement.

quasi contract An obligation created by law. Not a true contract. The purpose is to prevent one party from being unjustly enriched at the expense of another.

quitclaim deed A deed intended to pass any title or interest of the grantor in the property to another person. The deed does not include any warranties.

R

ratification Accepting and giving legal force to an obligation that could have been avoided.

real defense Defense that can be used to avoid payment to all holders of a negotiable instrument (including an HDC).

real estate agent or broker A person licensed by the state to assist people in buying and selling real property.

real estate closing The point in a real estate sale where the buyer pays the purchase price and the seller delivers the deed to the buyer.

real property Land and things permanently attached to the land.

reasonable-person standard The standard of fair behavior that a reasonably careful and thoughtful person would observe. The test to meet to avoid responsibility for negligence.

recognizance An acknowledgement by a person in court of a duty to pay a certain sum if a certain event occurs.

recording statute A state law that allows a person owning an interest in real property to record that interest at a government office and thereby give notice to all of his or her interest.

reformation An equitable remedy whereby the court rewrites a contract to reflect the parties' true intentions.

release Relinquishing of a claim or right.

relevant evidence Evidence likely to prove the facts in dispute.

remedy Relief given to a wronged party, by law or by contract, to enforce a right or prevent or compensate for the violation of a right.

rent control A law that places limits on the amount of rent a landlord can charge for an apartment once a tenant has moved in.

rent The tenant's payment to the landlord for the use of the landlord's real property.

renter's insurance Insurance policy that compensates the insured renter for personal property losses and sometimes personal liability.

reply Plaintiff's answer to a counterclaim.

requirements contract A contract in which the buyer agrees to purchase from the seller, and the seller agrees to sell to the buyer, all of some good the buyer requires.

res ipsa loquitur "The facts speak for themselves." A legal principle that applies when the event creating an injury is one that ordinarily does not occur without negligence.

rescission An equitable remedy to undo, or cancel, a contract. The unmaking of a contract.

reserved powers Powers reserved by the states, spelled out in the Tenth Amendment to the U.S. Constitution.

residuary clause A clause in a will that disposes of all property not otherwise specifically given away.

resolutions of disputes.

respondeat superior [Latin: let the master respond.] A doctrine by which a principal or employer is held liable for the acts of the agent or employee that occur within the scope of his or her employment.

respondent Often used interchangeably with **appellee**. Sometimes refers to a party who responds in a matter in equity.

restitution An equitable remedy to require each party to a contract to return goods, property, or money previously transferred to him or her.

restrictive indorsement An indorsement that places conditions on the further transfer of the instrument. "For deposit only" is a restrictive indorsement.

retaliatory eviction The eviction of a tenant for complaining to a government agency about the condition of an apartment.

revocation The withdrawal of an offer by the offeror.

right of contribution The right of a co-surety who pays more than his or her proportionate share upon a debtor's default to recover the excess paid from other co-sureties.

right of reimbursement The legal right of a person to be repaid for costs, expenses, or losses incurred on behalf of another.

right of subrogation A right of a person to stand in the place of another, giving the substituted party the same legal rights as the original party had.

right-to-work law A state law that provides that an employee cannot be required to join a union to get or keep a job.

risk A prediction of potential loss.

risk management Planning and managing risk, including transferring some risks to an insurance company.

risk pooling Spreading a risk among many people to keep the premiums charged policyholders small compared with the amount of insurance coverage offered.

robbery The forceful and unlawful taking of personal property from another.

S

sale A transfer of ownership for a price. The passing of title to property from the seller to the buyer for a price.

sale on approval A conditional sale of goods that becomes absolute when the buyer decides to buy or use the goods in a way consistent with intent to buy the goods.

sale or return A conditional sale in which the buyer can return all or a portion of the goods.

satisfaction The performance of an accord agreement.

secondary boycott A situation in which other companies' employees refuse to deal with another company in order to get that company to stop doing business with the employer with whom the union has a dispute.

secured creditor A creditor that secures payment of a debt by taking an interest in property. If the debt is not paid, the creditor can take or sell the property.

secured transaction Any transaction, regardless of its form, that is intended to create a security interest in personal property.

security deposit A sum of money paid to and held by the landlord to secure the tenant's obligations under the lease.

self-defense The right to protect oneself from the criminal conduct of others.

separate property Property individually owned by one spouse. Separate property usually remains separate even after marriage.

service of process Proper delivery of legal documents.

settlor or **trustor** Person who creates a trust.

several liability Separate and complete responsibility for an entire obligation, even if others are also responsible.

severalty Only one person owns property.

shareholder or **stockholder** The owner of one or more shares of stock in a corporation.

shelter principle The principle that the holder of a negotiable instrument who cannot qualify as an HDC, but who gets his or her title through an HDC, acquires the rights of an HDC.

shipment contract A sales contract by which the seller is responsible for delivering the goods to a carrier.

shopkeeper's privilege Privilege, established by statute, by which a seller of goods may detain a suspected shoplifter in certain situations.

shoplifting Taking property from a retail store without paying for it; a type of larceny, usually a misdemeanor.

slander Oral defamation.

small claims court State court of limited jurisdiction created to consider matters involving a small sum of money damages.

sole proprietorship A business owned by one person. Anyone who does business without creating another type of business organization is a sole proprietor. The owner is the business.

sovereign immunity Immunity of a nation from the jurisdiction of another nation's courts.

special bailment A bailment that requires some special treatment such as a shipment or warehouse bailment.

special indorsement An indorsement that specifies to whom or to whose order the instrument is payable.

specific performance An equitable remedy that calls for the performance of the act promised in the contract.

stale check A check, other than a certified check, that is presented for payment more than six months after its date.

standard fire insurance Policy that compensates the insured for losses caused by fire and lightning, and by damage from smoke and water caused by the fire or the fire department.

stare decisis ("to stand on decided cases") The practice of deciding new cases with reference to former decisions, or precedents.

state law Law consisting of state constitutions, statutes originated by the state legislatures, regulations created by state agencies, and decisions of state courts.

Statute of Frauds Statute under which certain types of contracts must be proved by a signed writing to be enforced in court.

statute A law originated by the U.S. Congress or a state legislative body, passed by that body and usually signed by the executive official, the president or governor.

statute of limitations Statute that requires anyone claiming a legal right against another to begin proceedings to enforce that right within a specific period of time.

statutory will A type of formal will authorized by a legislature with blanks to be completed by the testator.

stock An ownership interest in a corporation measured in units of shares.

stop-payment order An order by the drawer of a draft or check directing the drawer's bank not to pay the draft or check.

strict liability Liability regardless of fault. Usually, strict liability involves damages caused by abnormally dangerous activities.

strike A refusal by a group of workers to work for their employer. Often the purpose of a strike is to force the employer to make improvements in salary, working conditions, or benefits.

subject-matter jurisdiction The type of cases a court is authorized to hear. The difference between courts of general jurisdiction and courts of special, or limited, jurisdiction lies in the different subject matter of cases heard.

sublease A tenant leasing property to another person, the subtenant.

subpoena An order to produce a witness or a thing, such as a document.

subrogation The right to succeed to or substitute for the rights against another. In insurance law, if the insurance company pays the claimant, it has the right to seek reimbursement from the wrongdoer (other than the insured).

substantial performance Performance whereby a party to a contract honestly performs most, but not all, elements of the contract.

substantive law Law that defines duties, establishes rights, and prohibits wrongs.

summary jury trial A non-binding process in which parties present their cases to a private mock jury, which advises the parties as to the probable verdict in an actual trial.

summons Document served on a defendant with a complaint. It tells the defendant that he or she should respond to the complaint or risk losing the lawsuit.

suretyship A contract promise made by a third person to be primarily responsible for another's debt. A surety is as responsible to the creditor as is the debtor.

sustained A ruling by which the judge agrees with an objection to offered evidence.

T

tangible personal property Personal property that has physical substance.

tangible property Property that has physical existence and can be distinguished by the senses of touch and sight. A car is tangible property.

tenancy at sufferance A possession of real property without legal right after the expiration of a lawful tenancy.

tenancy at will A tenancy for as long as both parties agree; no prior notice of termination is required.

tenancy by the entirety A form of property co-ownership between husband and wife. Similar to joint tenancy; when one spouse dies, his or her interest automatically transfers to the surviving spouse.

tenancy for years A tenancy created for a defined period stated by express agreement.

tenancy in common A form of property co-ownership in which two or more persons own a fractional interest in the property; when one tenant dies, the property interest passes to his or her heirs.

tenant One to whom property is rented; also called a renter.

tenants in partnership A form of joint ownership of property by partners. Each partner is a co-owner with all other partners of specific partnership property. Each partner has equal rights to use the partnership property for business purposes.

tender An unconditional offer to perform by a person who is ready, willing, and able to do so.

term insurance Life insurance with no savings element. Covers a specific time; then the policy expires unless renewed.

testamentary trust A trust created by will and coming into existence on the death of the grantor.

testate When a person dies having left a will.

testator A person who makes a will. A person who dies having left a will.

theft The guilty act of taking another person's property.

third party beneficiary contract A contract created at least in part to benefit a third party. The third party has rights to enforce the contract.

title The formal right of ownership of property.

tort A wrongful act for which a court may award damages.

tortfeasor A person who commits a tort.

trade acceptance A draft drawn by and payable to the seller of goods by the purchaser of the goods.

trade name A name used in a business activity to designate a business.

trademark A distinctive mark, motto, device, or implement that a manufacturer stamps or prints on its goods.

traveler's check An instrument purchased from a financial institution that can be used as cash upon a second signature by the purchaser; comes in predetermined dominations.

trespass to land Wrongful entry onto the real property of another.

trespass to personal property A brief, temporary, intentional interference with the personal property of another.

trial court The court where the facts of a dispute are heard and decided.

truancy The willful and unjustified failure to attend school by anyone who is required to attend under compulsory attendance laws.

trust Any arrangement through which property is transferred from one person to be administered by a trustee for a third party's benefit.

trust beneficiary The person who has a beneficial interest in the property or income of a trust.

trustee A person who holds property under a trust for the benefit of another.

tuition The fees that are paid in order to receive instruction at any institution of learning; sometimes called tuition and fees.

U

unanimous opinion A written court decision on which the judges deciding the case unanimously agree.

unconscionable contract or clause A contract or clause that is grossly unfair because of its terms or circumstances or both.

undisclosed principal A principal whose identity and existence are unknown by a third party.

undue influence A situation in which one party greatly influences another party, overcoming the party's free will.

unenforceable contract A valid contract that cannot be enforced because of some legal defense.

Uniform Commercial Code (UCC) A uniform law enacted in part by all fifty states to create certainty in the area of commercial contracts and make the law consistent with common business practices.

unilateral contract A contract that includes a promise in exchange for an act.

unilateral mistake A mistake by one party to a contract about some material fact.

uninsured motorist coverage Automobile insurance that compensates the insured for harm to the driver and passengers caused by a driver without insurance or by a hit-and-run driver.

union shop A company where employees are required to join a union after a short time on the job. Still a legal form of union security.

unlawful detainer A summary court procedure that allows a landlord to retake possession of real property after a breach of the lease by the tenant.

unsecured creditor A creditor that has no rights against any particular property of the debtor.

usage of trade A common business practice in a place, vocation, or trade.

usury Charging an illegal interest rate.

utilitarianism Ethical theory, proposed by Jeremy Bentham, that focuses on the consequences of an action. Acting ethically means generating the greatest good for the greatest number of people.

V

valid contract An agreement which includes all the necessary elements to be an enforceable contract.

venue The proper place within a judicial district to bring a lawsuit.

verdict The expressed opinion of the jury.

vesting The legal event signifying that a possible right to something has become an absolute right to something.

vicarious liability Legal responsibility of the acts of another person because of some relationship with that person; for example, the liability of an employer for an employee.

void contract An agreement that cannot be enforced. Not really a contract at all.

voidable contract A contract giving one party the right to cancel the contract without legal penalty.

voidable That which can be avoided or declared void. Contracts that are voidable are ones that can be gotten out of by one party but not the other. When a minor makes most contracts, that minor can get out of the contract, but the party with whom the minor made the contract normally cannot.

voir dire The questioning of prospective jurors to expose possible bias.

voluntary bankruptcy A bankruptcy begun by the debtor.

W

waiver An intentional, knowing relinquishment of a legal right.

warehouse receipt A receipt issued by a warehouser for goods stored in the warehouse.

warrant A written authorization from a judge to arrest an accused.

warranty deed A deed under which the grantor makes several guarantees to the grantee. The grantor warrants that there are no claims against the property and that if claims are made, the grantor will defend against them.

warranty of title An implied assurance that the seller owns or has the right to sell goods.

waste The abuse or destructive use of property by one in rightful possession.

whistleblower An employee who tells the public about illegal or other wrongful activities in his or her organization.

white-collar crime Nonviolent illegal act committed by an individual or corporation in business.

whole life Life insurance with a cash surrender value. Sometimes called straight life, ordinary life, or cash-value insurance.

will Legal expression of a person's wishes for the distribution of his or her property after death.

writ of attachment A court-ordered seizure of property (prior to full resolution of the creditor's rights resulting in judgment). Attachment is available only in strict compliance with the applicable state statutes.

writ of execution A court order directing the sheriff to seize and sell nonexempt property of the judgment debtor to satisfy an unpaid judgment.

◆ Index